Mathematics for Economic Analysis

Knut Sydsæter
University of Oslo

Peter J. Hammond
Stanford University

PRENTICE HALL, Upper Saddle River, New Jersey 07458

Library of Congress Cataloging-in-Publication Data

Sydsæter, Knut.
    Mathematics for economic analysis / Knut Sydsæter, Peter J.
Hammond.
        p.   cm.
    Includes bibliographical references and index.
    ISBN 0-13-583600-X
    1. Economics, Mathematical.   2. Economics–Mathematical models.
  I. Hammond, Peter J.   II. Title.
  HB135.S888   1995
  330'.01'51–dc20
                                            94-4225
                                              CIP

Production Editor: Lisa Kinne
Acquisitions Editor: J. Stephen Dietrich
Copy Editor: Peter Zurita
Cover Designer: Maureen Eide
Manufacturing Buyers: Patrice Fraccio and Marie McNamara
Editorial Assistant: Elizabeth Becker

Printed in the United States of America
10 9 8 7 6 5 4 3

ISBN 0-13-583600-X

Prentice-Hall International (UK) Limited, London
Prentice-Hall of Australia Pty. Limited, Sydney
Prentice-Hall Canada Inc., Toronto
Prentice-Hall Hispanoamericana, S.A., Mexico
Prentice-Hall of India Private Limited, New Delhi
Prentice-Hall of Japan, Inc., Tokyo
Pearson Education Asia Pte. Ltd., Singapore
Editoria Prentice-Hall do Brasil, Ltda., Rio De Janeiro

To our international spouses, Gull-Maj and Mrudula, whose ready laughter helps us so much.

Contents

——3——

Polynomials, Powers, and Exponentials 73

——4——

Single-Variable Differentiation 105

——5——

More on Differentiation 144

9

Single-Variable Optimization 282

10

Integration 320

11

Further Topics in Integration 348

12

Linear Algebra: Vectors and Matrices   374

13

Determinants and Matrix Inversion   420

14

Further Topics in Linear Algebra   460

⎓15⎓

Functions of Several Variables   489

⎓16⎓

Tools for Comparative Statics   537

▬17▬

Multivariable Optimization   595

▬18▬

Constrained Optimization   650

19

Linear Programming 704

20

Difference Equations 729

21

Differential Equations 759

Appendix A

Elementary Algebra   803

Appendix B

Sums, Products, and Induction   846

Appendix C

Trigonometric Functions   865

Appendix D

Geometry   884

Appendix E

Answers to Odd-Numbered Problems   887

References   963

Index   965

Preface

Purpose

Modern students of economics need several important mathematical tools. These include calculus for functions of one and several variables, as well as a basic understanding of multivariable optimization problems with or without constraints. Linear algebra is also used to some extent in economic theory, and even more in econometrics. Such tools are helpful, even essential, in upper-level undergraduate courses in many branches of economics, including labor economics, industrial organization, and public finance. Students in other areas of economics, such as development and environmental economics, in which the evolution of an economic system over time needs to be considered, can benefit enormously from knowing some of the theory of difference and differential equations.

Experience suggests that teachers in these different areas of economics would like to assign students recently published articles to read. They find, however, that the mathematical preparation of the students is inadequate for even some of the less technical "applied" literature. Students who may well have completed courses in intermediate micro- and macroeconomics quite successfully will often not have seen the use of much or even any calculus in economic analysis. If the students do know some calculus, it was learned before college or university, or in the mathematics department of their college or university. Moreover, their knowledge of calculus may barely extend beyond functions of a single variable, and they are often unused to seeing calculus applied to economic problems

The purpose of *Mathematics for Economic Analysis* is, therefore, to help students acquire the mathematical skills they need in order to read the less technical literature, at least, and so to function properly as economists or as business analysts in the contemporary world. As the title suggests, it is a mathematics book, with the material arranged to allow progressive learning of mathematical topics. If the student acquires some economic insights and intuitions at the same time, so much the better. At times, we do emphasize economics not only to motivate a mathematical topic, but also to help acquire mathematical intuition. Obviously, understanding our economic discussions will be easier with a certain very rudimentary understanding of economics and of what economics should be about. It should be possible, nevertheless, to study the material even before embarking on a course in elementary economics.

In particular, this is not a book about economics or even about mathematical economics. We expect students to learn economic theory systematically in other courses, based on other books. We will have succeeded if they can concentrate on the economics in these courses, having mastered beforehand the relevant mathematical tools we present.

Special Features

This is by no means the first textbook written with the foregoing aims in mind. But it benefits, we believe, from the way it has been put together. One author (Sydsæter) has a rather rare position as a Professor of Mathematics in a Department of Economics. He has many years experience in teaching material of this kind to students in Norway, and much of the material in this book is actually adapted and translated from textbooks originally in Norwegian that have been widely used throughout Scandinavia. The other author (Hammond) has taught and done research in economic theory on both sides of the Atlantic, and has long experience in seeing the different ways in which mathematical tools are used in actual economic analysis. For several years, he has also taught courses in mathematics for economists, primarily in the Department of Economics at Stanford University.

Over the course of these years of teaching, we have accumulated numerous worked examples as well as problems for the student to solve. A large selection of these is included in the book. We are well aware that we ourselves learned much of the material we want to teach here from numerous problems and examples. Such a large number of problems is standard in mathematics textbooks at this level, though apparently not in books on mathematics for economists. Answers to odd numbered problems are provided at the end of the book. The remaining answers are available in a separate *Instructor's Manual*.

One more feature of the problems is worth discussing. This concerns the apparent excess notation that appears in some of them—that is, where an expression such as $An_0^{\alpha}a^b$ could be replaced by a single constant. The whole point of such problems is to help the student learn to see when such replacements are possible and useful. (Often, the notation in these problems are taken directly from published economic research.)

Topics Covered

It will be apparent that we have included a lot of rather elementary material in the earlier chapters of this book, as well as in the appendices. In fact, experience suggests that it is quite difficult to start a book like this at a level that is really too elementary. These days, students who enter college or university and specialize in economics have an enormous range of mathematical backgrounds and aptitudes, from a shaky command of elementary algebra up to ready facility with the calculus of functions of one variable. Often, it is some years since economics students took their last formal mathematics course. As we move toward a situation where mathematics is often a requirement for specialist studies in economics, we felt the need to provide as much elementary material as possible in order to give those with weaker mathematical backgrounds the chance to get started.

In the accompanying *Instructor's Manual*, we have provided some diagnostic test material that teachers may wish to use so that they and the students can assess together what has already been mastered at the start of the course. Although the teacher will want to adust the starting point and pace of a course to the students' abilities, it is more important that the individual student appreciates his or her own strengths and weaknesses, and receive some help and guidance in overcoming the latter. Thus, it is likely that weaker students will appreciate the opportunity to work through the early more elementary chapters. And ample economic examples, such as the quadratic optimization problems of Chapter 3, are intended to help motivate students who may have found such material too tedious to master in the past.

After the introductory material in Chapters 1 to 3, a fairly leisurely treatment of single-variable calculus is contained in Chapters 4 to 11. This may be as far as some elementary courses will go. However, we have already suggested the importance for budding economists of linear algebra (Chapters 12 to 14), multivariable calculus (Chapters 15 and 16), optimization theory (Chapters 17 to 19), and difference or differential equations (Chapters 20 and 21). In some sense, Chapters 12 to 21, starting with linear algebra, represent the heart of the book. Students with a thorough grounding in single variable calculus can probably afford to concentrate on these chapters. From the first 11 chapters of the book, they may only need to go fairly quickly over some special topics that are often not thoroughly covered in standard calculus courses. Indeed, at Stanford University, where economics students typically take a one-quarter course in mathematics for economists soon after doing a one-quarter calculus course in the mathematics department, this is close to the syllabus in current use.

The ordering of the chapters is fairly logical, we believe. The main way in which another order could have been possible concerns Chapter 19, on linear programming. It could easily be moved forward to follow Chapter 14 or even Chapter 13 on linear algebra. Of course, if it were taught at this earlier stage, the cross-references to the Kuhn-Tucker theorem of Chapter 18 would not make sense until after that chapter had also been covered. It is also possible that some teachers will want to spend less time on integration, especially Chapter 11, and that pressure of time will prevent coverage of some of the later chapters.

Key Concepts and Techniques

The less ambitious student can concentrate on learning the key concepts and techniques of each chapter. Often, these appeared boxed, in order to emphasize their importance. Problems are essential to the learning process, and the easier ones should definitely be attempted. Those who are more ambitious, or are led on by more demanding teachers, can try the more difficult problems. They can also study optional sections and the material in smaller print. The latter often provides an explanation of why certain techniques are appropriate, or offers proofs of results. Indeed, wherever possible, we encourage students to ask why results are true, and why problems should be tackled in certain ways, and so we have tried to offer explanations at an appropriate level. We admit that whereas only a minority of students can be expected to understand this material fully, the others may also be interested in gaining at least a little additional insight into the mathematics they are studying.

Another reason for including such material is that the book may thereby become more suitable for teachers in mathematics departments who would like to arrange special courses, or sections of courses, for students who definitely intend to apply mathematics to economics rather than to the engineering or physical sciences. In fact, in comparison with many contemporary calculus textbooks used for courses in mathematics departments, it seems that we actually provide somewhat more explanation and proofs.

Acknowledgments

Nancy Halbin has read carefully through a preliminary version, and had a number of very valuable suggestions. She has also helped us avoid some embarrassing errors.

Arne Strøm has helped us in numerous ways with TEX macros, with figures, and with substantive comments on the material.

Anders Høyer Berg has checked the answers to most of the problems, and also suggested a number of corrections to the text.

Anders Fyhn has prepared most of the figures using MG (Mathematical Graphics System by Israel and Adams).

For helpful suggestions arising from their experience in teaching courses at Stanford and in Germany based on early drafts of the book, we are grateful to Thorsten Hens, Uday Rajan, Mario Epelbaum, Susan Snyder, and Reinhard John.

The Institute of Economics at the University of Oslo, and the Departments of Economics at both the European University Institute in Florence and Stanford University, have all been welcoming hosts to a co-author from another institution on several occasions. Our work has been facilitated by financial support from the Institute of Economics at the University of Oslo, as well as the European University Institute and the Alexander von Humboldt Foundation.

We express our appreciation to all these persons and institutions who have helped us in making this text possible.

Peter Hammond and Knut Sydsæter

Kiel and Oslo, February 1994

=1=

Introduction

The economic world is a misty region. The first explorers used unaided vision. Mathematics is the lantern by which what was before dimly visible now looms up in firm, bold outlines. The old phantasmagoria[1] disappear. We see better. We also see further.
—Irving Fisher (1892)

1.1 Why Economists Use Mathematics

Economic activity has been part of human life for thousands of years. The word "economics" itself originates from a classical Greek word meaning "household management." Even before the Greeks there were merchants and traders who exhibited an understanding of some economic phenomena; they knew, for instance, that a poor harvest would increase the price of corn, but that a shortage of gold might result in a decrease in the price of corn. For many centuries, the most basic economic concepts were expressed in simple terms requiring only the use of rudimentary mathematics. Concepts like integers and fractions, together with the operations of addition, subtraction, multiplication, and division, were sufficient to allow traders, merchants, farmers and other economic agents to discuss and debate the economic activities and events that affected their daily lives. These tools were enough to enable merchants to keep accounts and to work out what prices to charge.

[1] "Phantasmagoria" is a term invented in 1802 to describe an exhibition of optical illusions produced by means of a magic lantern.

1

Even calculations of interest on loans were not very complicated. Arithmetic could perform the tasks that merchants required of it even without the concept of zero and the decimal system of notation. Where a calculating device was required, the abacus was powerful enough.

The science of economics reached a turning point in the eighteenth century with the publication of works such as David Hume's *Political Discourses* (1752), François Quesnay's *Tableau Economique* (1758–1759), and Adam Smith's *The Wealth of Nations* (1776). Economic arguments began to be formalized and developed into theories. This created the need to express increasingly complex ideas and interrelationships in a straightforward manner. By the mid-1800s, some writers were beginning to use mathematics to communicate their theories. Some of the first to do this were economists such as Antoine Cournot (the first writer to define and draw an explicit demand curve, and to use calculus in solving a maximization problem in economics) and Léon Walras (who distinguished himself by writing down and solving the first multiequation model of general equilibrium of supply and demand in all markets simultaneously). They found that many of their ideas could be formulated most effectively by means of mathematical language, including algebraic symbols, simple diagrams, and graphs. Indeed, much more sophisticated economic concepts and increasingly complex economic theories have become possible as mathematical language has been used to express them.

Today, a firm understanding of mathematics is essential for any serious student of economics. Although simple economic arguments relying on only two or three variables can sometimes be made in a clear and convincing fashion without mathematics, if we want to consider many variables and the way they interact, it becomes essential to resort to a mathematical model.

As an example, suppose that some government agency is planning to allow a large amount of new housing to be constructed on some land it controls. What consequences will this have for employment? Initially, new jobs will be created in the construction sector as laborers are hired for the project. Moreover, the construction of new houses requires bricks, cement, reinforcing steel, timber, glass, and other building materials. Employment must also grow in firms that manufacture these materials. These producers in turn require materials from other producers, and so on. In addition to all these production effects, increased employment leads to increased incomes. If these income gains are not entirely neutralized by taxes, then a greater demand for consumer goods results. This in turn leads to an increased need for employment among producers of consumer goods, and again the flow of input requirements expands. At the same time, there are feedbacks in the system; for example, increased incomes also generate more demand for housing. In this manner, both positive and negative changes in one sector are transmitted to other sectors of the economy.

The point of this example is that the economic system is so complex that the final effects are difficult to determine without resorting to more formal mathematical devices such as a "circular-flow model" of the entire economy. An example will be the input–output model presented in Section 12.1.

Mathematical Analysis

The principal topic of this book is an important branch of mathematics called **mathematical analysis**. This includes differential and integral calculus and their extensions. Calculus was developed at the end of the seventeenth century by Newton and Leibniz. Their discoveries completely transformed mathematics, physics, and the engineering sciences, giving them all new life. In similar fashion, the introduction of calculus into economics has radically changed the way in which economists analyze the world around them. Calculus is now employed in many different areas of economics: for example, it is used to study the effects of relative price changes on demand, the effects of a change in the price or availability of an essential input such as oil on the production process, the consequences of population growth for the economy, and the extent to which a tax on energy use might reduce carbon dioxide emissions.

The following episode illustrates how economists can use mathematical analysis to solve practical problems. In February 1953, the Netherlands was struck by a catastrophic flood far more extensive than any previously recorded. The dikes protecting the country were washed away and over 1800 people died. Total damages were estimated at about 7% of national income for that year. A commission was established to determine how to prevent similar disasters in the future. Rebuilding the dikes to ensure 100% security would have cost an astronomical amount, even if it were possible at all. The real problem therefore involved a trade-off between cost and security: higher dikes would obviously cost more, but would reduce both the probability and likely severity of future flooding. So the commission had to try to select the optimal height for the dikes. Some economists on the commission applied *cost-benefit analysis*, a branch of economics that involves the use of mathematical analysis, in order to weigh the relative costs and benefits of different alternatives for rebuilding the dikes. This problem is discussed in more detail in Problem 7 in Section 8.4.

Such trade-offs are central to economics. They lead to optimization problems of a type that is naturally handled by mathematical analysis.

1.2 Scientific Method in the Empirical Sciences

Economics is now generally considered to be one of the *empirical sciences*. These sciences share a common methodology that includes the following as its most important elements:

1. Qualitative and quantitative observations of phenomena, either directly or by carefully designed experiment.
2. Numerical and statistical processing of the observed data.
3. Constructing theoretical models that describe the observed phenomena and explain the relationships between them.

4. Using these theoretical models in order to derive predictions.

5. Correcting and improving models so that they predict better.

Empirical sciences thus rely on processes of *observation, modeling,* and *verification.* If an activity is to qualify fully as an empirical science, each of the foregoing points is important. Observations without theory can only give purely descriptive pictures of reality that lack explanatory power. But theory without observation risks losing contact with the reality that it is trying to explain.

Many episodes in the history of science show the danger of error when "pure theory" lacks any foundation in reality. For example, around 350 B.C., Aristotle developed a theory that concluded that a freely falling object travels at a constant speed, and that a heavier object falls more quickly than a lighter one. This was convincingly refuted by Galileo Galilei in the sixteenth century when he demonstrated (partly by dropping objects from the Leaning Tower of Pisa) that, excluding the effects of air friction, the speed at which any object falls is proportional to the time it has fallen, and that the constant of proportionality is the same for all objects, regardless of their weight. Thus, Aristotle's theory was eventually disproved by empirical observation.

A second example comes from the science of astronomy. In the year 1800, Hegel advanced a philosophical argument to show that there could only be seven planets in the solar system. Hegel notwithstanding, an eighth planetary body, the asteroid Ceres, was discovered in January 1801. The eighth principal planet, Neptune, was discovered in 1846, and by 1930 the existence of Pluto was known.[2]

With hindsight, the falseness of these assertions by Aristotle and Hegel appears elementary. In all sciences, however, false assertions are being put forth repeatedly, only to be refuted later. Correcting inaccurate theories is an important part of scientific activity, and the previous examples demonstrate the need to ensure that theoretical models are supported by empirical evidence.

In economics, hypotheses are usually less precise than in the physical sciences, and so less obviously wrong than Aristotle's and Hegel's assertions just discussed. But there are a few old theories that have since become so discredited that few economists now take them seriously. One example is the "Phillips curve," that purported to show how an economy could trade off unemployment against inflation. The idea was that employment might be created through tax cuts and/or increased public expenditure, but at the cost of increased inflation. Conversely, inflation could be reduced by tax increases or expenditure cuts, but at the cost of higher unemployment.

---

[2]The process of discovery relied on looking at how the motion of other known planets deviated from the orbits predicted by Newton's theory of gravitation. These deviations even suggested where to look for an additional planet that could, according to Newton's theory, account for them. Until recently, scientists were still using Newton's theory to search for a tenth planetary body whose existence they suspected. However, more accurate estimates of the masses of the outer planets now suggest that there are no further planets to find after all.

Unlike Hegel, who could never hope to count all the planets, or Aristotle, who presumably never watched with any care the fall of an object that was dropped from rest, the Phillips curve was in fact based on rather careful empirical observation. In an article published in 1958, A. W. Phillips examined the average yearly rates of wage increases and unemployment for the economy of the United Kingdom over the long period from 1861 to 1957. The plot of those observations formed the Phillips curve, and the inflation–unemployment trade-off was part of conventional economic thinking until the 1970s. Then, however, the decade of simultaneous high inflation and high unemployment (stagnation and inflation, generally abbreviated "stagflation") that many Western economies experienced during the period 1973–1982 produced observations that obviously lay well above the usual Phillips curve. The alleged trade-off became hard to discern.

Just as Aristotle's and Hegel's assertions were revised in the light of suitable evidence, this stagflationary episode caused the theory behind the Phillips curve to be modified. It was suggested that as people learn to live with inflation, they adjust wage and loan contracts to reflect expected rates of inflation. Then the trade-off between unemployment and inflation that seemed to be described by the Phillips curve becomes replaced by a new trade-off between unemployment and the deviation in inflation from its expected rate. Moreover, this expected rate increases as the current rate of inflation rises. So lowering unemployment was thought to lead not simply to increased inflation, but to accelerating inflation that increased each period by more than was expected previously. On the other hand, when high inflation came to be expected, combating it with policies leading to painfully high unemployment would lead only to gradual decreases in inflation, as people's expectations of inflation fall rather slowly. Thus, the original Phillips curve theory has been significantly revised and extended in the light of more recent evidence.

Models and Reality

In the eighteenth century, the philosopher Immanuel Kant considered Euclidean geometry to be an absolutely true description of the physical space we observe through our senses. This conception seemed self-evident and was shared by all those who had reflected upon it. The reason for this agreement was undoubtedly that all the results of this geometry could be derived by way of irrefutable logic from only a few axioms, and that these axioms were regarded as self-evident truths about physical space. The first person to question this point of view was the German mathematician Gauss at the beginning of the 1800s. He insisted that the relationship between physical space and Euclid's model could only be made clear by empirical methods. During the 1820s, the first non-Euclidean geometry was developed—that is, a geometry built upon axioms other than Euclid's. Since that time it has been accepted that only observations can decide which geometric model gives the best description of physical space.

This shows how there can be an important difference between a mathematical model and its possible interpretations in reality. Moreover, it may happen that more than one model is capable of describing a certain phenomenon, such as the relationship between money supply and inflation in the United States or Germany. Indeed, this often seems to be the case in economics. As long as all the models to be considered are internally consistent, the best way to select among competing explanations is usually to see which one gives the best description of reality. But this is often surprisingly difficult, especially in economics.

In addition, we must recognize that a model intended to explain a phenomenon like inflation can never be considered as absolutely true; it is at best only an approximate representation of reality. We can never consider all the factors that influence such a complex phenomenon. If we tried to do so, we would obtain a hopelessly complicated theory. This is true not only for models of physical phenomena, but for all models within the empirical sciences.

These comments are particularly relevant for economic research. Consider once again the effects of allowing new housing to be built. In order to understand the full implications of this, an economist would require an incredible amount of data on millions of consumers, businesses, goods and services, etc. Even if it were available in this kind of detail, the amount of data would swamp the capacities of even the most modern computers. In their attempts to understand the underlying relationships in the economy, economists are therefore forced to use various kinds of aggregate data, among other simplifications. Thus, we must always remember that a model is only able to give an approximate description of reality; the goal of empirical researchers should be to make their models reflect reality as closely and accurately as possible.

1.3 The Use of Symbols in Mathematics

Before beginning to study any subject, it is important that everyone agrees on a common "language" in which to discuss it. Similarly, in the study of mathematics, which is in a sense a "language" of its own, it is important to ensure that we all understand exactly the same thing when we see a given symbol. Some symbols in mathematics nearly always signify the same definite mathematical object. Examples are 3, $\sqrt{2}$, π, and [0, 1], which respectively signify three special numbers and a closed interval. Symbols of this type are called *logical constants*. We also frequently need symbols that can represent **variables**. The objects that a variable is meant to represent are said to make up the **domain of variation**. For example, we use the letter x as a symbol for an arbitrary number when we write

$$x^2 - 16 = (x + 4)(x - 4)$$

In words the expression reads as follows:

> The difference between the square of the number (hereby called x) and 16 is always equal to the product of the two numbers obtained by adding 4 to the number and subtracting 4 from the number x.

The equality $x^2 - 16 = (x + 4)(x - 4)$ is called an *identity* because it is valid identically for all x. In such cases, we sometimes write $x^2 - 16 \equiv (x + 4)(x - 4)$, where $\equiv$ is the symbol for an identity.

The equality sign $(=)$ is also used in other ways. For example, we write $A = \pi r^2$ as the formula for the area A of a circle with radius r. In addition, the equality sign is used in equations such as

$$x^2 + x - 12 = 0$$

where x stands as a symbol for the unknown number. If we substitute various numbers for x, we discover that the equality sign is often invalid. In fact, the equation is only true for $x = 3$ and for $x = -4$, and these numbers are therefore called its *solutions*.

Example 1.1

A farmer has 1000 meters of fence wire with which to enclose a rectangle. If one side of the rectangle is x (measured in meters), find the area enclosed when x is chosen to be 150, 250, 350, and for general x. Which value of x do you believe gives the greatest possible area?

Solution   If the other side of the rectangle is y, then $2x + 2y = 1000$. Hence, $x + y = 500$, so that $y = 500 - x$. (See Fig. 1.1.) The area A (in m²) of this rectangle is, therefore,

$$A = x(500 - x) = 500x - x^2$$

Because both sides must be positive, x must be positive and $500 - x$ must be positive. This means that x must be between 0 and 500 m. The areas when $x = 150, 250,$ and 350 are $150 \cdot 350 = 52,500$, $250 \cdot 250 = 62,500$, and $350 \cdot 150 = 52,500$, respectively. Of these, $x = 250$ gives the greatest value. In Problem 7 of Section 3.1 you will be asked to show that $x = 250$ really does give the greatest possible area.

When studying problems requiring several (but not too many) variables, we usually denote these with different letters such as a, b, c, x, y, z, A, B, and so on. Often, we supplement the letters of the Latin alphabet with lowercase and capital

FIGURE 1.1

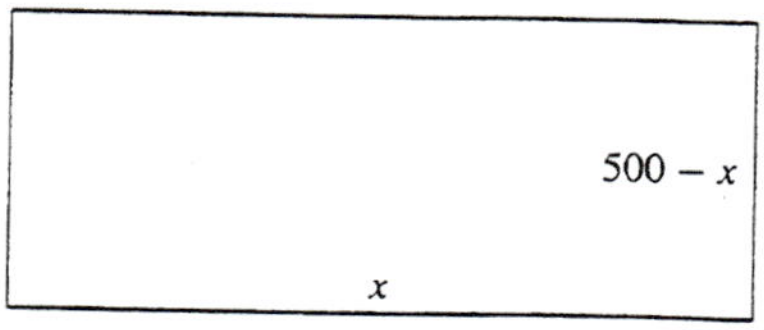

Greek letters such as α, β, γ, Γ, and Ω. If the number of variables becomes large, we can use subscripts or superscripts to distinguish variables from each other. For example, suppose that we are studying employment in a country that is divided into 100 regions, numbered from 1 to 100. We can then denote employment in region 1 by N_1, employment in region 2 by N_2, and so on. In general, we can define

$$N_i = \text{total employment in region } i, \qquad i = 1, 2, \ldots, 100$$

The suffixes $i = 1, 2, \ldots, 100$ suggest that the index i can be an arbitrary number in the range from 1 to 100. If $N_{59} = 2690$, this means that 2690 people are employed in region 59. If we want to go further and divide the employed into men and women, we could denote the number of women (men) employed in region i by $N_i^{(W)}$ ($N_i^{(M)}$). Then, we would have $N_i^{(W)} + N_i^{(M)} = N_i$, for $i = 1, 2, \ldots, 100$. Note that this notation is actually much clearer than if we were to use 100 different letters to represent the variables N_i—even if we could find 100 different letters from some combination of the Latin, Greek, Cyrillic, and Sanskrit alphabets!

Many students who are used to dealing with algebraic expressions involving only *one* variable (usually x) have difficulties at first in handling expressions involving several variables. For economists, however, the previous example shows how important it is to be able to handle algebraic expressions and equations with many different variables. Here is another example.

Example 1.2

Consider the simple macroeconomic model

$$Y = C + \bar{I}, \qquad C = a + bY \tag{1}$$

where Y is the net national product, C is consumption, and $\bar{I}$ is the total investment, which is treated as fixed.[3] The three letters, $\bar{I}$, a, and b, denote positive numerical constants—for example, $\bar{I} = 100$, $a = 500$, and $b = 0.8$ are possible values of these constants. Rather than thinking of the two models with $\bar{I} = 100$, $C = 500 + 0.8Y$ and with $\bar{I} = 150$, $C = 600 + 0.9Y$ as entirely different, however, it is often more sensible to regard them as two particular instances of the general model [1], where $\bar{I}$, a, and b are unknown, and can vary; they are often called **parameters**. But they should be distinguished from the **variables** C and Y of the model.

After this discussion of constants as parameters of the model, solve [1] for Y.

Solution Substituting $C = a + bY$ from the second equation of [1] for C into the first equation gives

$$Y = a + bY + \bar{I}$$

---

[3] In economics, we often use a bar over a symbol to indicate that it is fixed.

Now rearrange this equation so that all the terms containing Y are on the left-hand side. This can be done by adding $-bY$ to both sides, thus canceling the bY term on the right-hand side to give

$$Y - bY = a + \bar{I}$$

Notice that the left-hand side is equal to $(1 - b)Y$, so $(1 - b)Y = a + \bar{I}$. Dividing both sides by $1 - b$, so that the coefficient of Y becomes 1, then gives the answer, which is

$$Y = \frac{a}{1 - b} + \frac{1}{1 - b}\bar{I}$$

This solution is a formula expressing Y in terms of the three parameters $\bar{I}$, a, and b. The formula can be applied to particular values of the constants, such as $\bar{I} = 100$, $a = 500$, $b = 0.8$, to give the right answer in every case. Note the power of this approach: The model is solved only once, and then numerical answers are found simply by substituting appropriate numerical values for the parameters of the model.

Problems

1. **a.** A person buys x_1, x_2, and x_3 units of three goods whose prices per unit are, respectively, p_1, p_2, and p_3. What is the total expenditure?
   b. A rental car costs F dollars per day in fixed charges and b dollars per kilometer. How much must a customer pay to drive x kilometers in 1 day?
   c. A company has fixed costs of F dollars per year and variable costs of c dollars per unit produced. Find an expression for the total cost per unit (total average cost) incurred by the company if it produces x units in one year.
   d. A person has an annual salary of $\$L$ and then receives a raise of $p\%$ followed by a further increase of $q\%$. What is the person's new yearly salary?
   e. A square tin plate 18 cm wide is to be made into an open box by cutting out equally sized squares of width x in each corner and then folding over the edges. Find the volume of the resulting box. (Draw a figure.)

2. **a.** Prove that

$$a + \frac{a \cdot p}{100} - \frac{\left(a + \dfrac{a \cdot p}{100}\right) \cdot p}{100}$$

   can be written as

$$a\left[1 - \left(\frac{p}{100}\right)^2\right]$$

b. An item initially costs $2000 and then its price is increased by 5%. Afterwards the price is lowered by 5%. What is the final price?

c. An item initially costs a dollars and then its price is increased by $p\%$. Afterwards the (new) price is lowered by $p\%$. What is the final price of the item? (After considering this problem, look at the expression in part (a).)

d. What is the result if one first *lowers* a price by $p\%$ and then *increases* it by $p\%$?

3. Solve the following equations for the variables specified:

a. $x = \frac{2}{3}(y - 3) + y$ for y **b.** $ax - b = cx + d$ for x

c. $AK\sqrt{L} = Y_0$ for L **d.** $px + qy = m$ for y

e. $\dfrac{\dfrac{1}{1+r} - a}{\dfrac{1}{1+r} + b} = c$ for r **f.** $Y = a(Y - tY - k) + b + I_p + G$ for Y

4. The relationship between a temperature measured in degrees Celsius (or Centigrade) (C) and in Fahrenheit (F) is given by $C = \frac{5}{9}(F - 32)$.

a. Find C when F is 32; find F when $C = 100$.

b. Find a general expression for F in terms of C.

c. One day the temperature in Oslo was $40° F$, while in Los Angeles it was $80° F$. How would you respond to the assertion that it was twice as warm in Los Angeles as in Oslo? (*Hint:* Find the two temperatures in degrees Celsius.)

5. If a rope could be wrapped around the earth's surface at the equator, it would be approximately circular and about 40 million meters long. Suppose we wanted to extend the rope to make it 1 meter above the equator at every point. How many more meters of rope would be needed? (Guess first, and then find the answer by precise calculation. For the formula for the circumference of the circle, see Appendix D.)

Harder Problems

6. Solve the following pair of simultaneous equations for x and y:

$$px + (1 - q)y = R \quad \text{and} \quad qx + (1 - p)y = S$$

7. Consider an equilateral triangle, and let P be an arbitrary point within the triangle. Let h_1, h_2, and h_3 be the shortest distances from P to each of the three sides. Show that the sum $h_1 + h_2 + h_3$ is independent of where point P is placed in the triangle. (*Hint:* Compute the area of the triangle as the sum of three triangles.)

1.4 The Real Number System

God created the integers;
everything else is the work of man.
—L. Kronecker

Real numbers were originally developed in order to measure physical characteristics such as length, temperature, and time. Economists also use real numbers to measure prices, quantities, incomes, tax rates, interest rates, and average costs, among other things. We assume that you have some knowledge of the real number system, but because of its fundamental role, we shall restate its basic properties.

Natural Numbers, Integers, and Rational Numbers

The everyday numbers we use for counting are 1, 2, 3, ... These are called **natural numbers.** Though familiar, such numbers are in reality rather abstract and advanced concepts. Civilization crossed a significant threshold when it grasped the idea that a flock of four sheep and a collection of four stones have something in common, namely "fourness." This idea came to be represented by symbols such as the primitive :: (still used on dominoes or playing cards), the modern 4, and the Roman numeral IV. This notion is grasped again and again as young children develop their mathematical skills.

During the early stages of many cultures, day-to-day problems motivated the four basic arithmetic operations of addition, subtraction, multiplication, and division. If we add or multiply two natural numbers, we always obtain another natural number. Moreover, the operations of subtraction and division suggest the desirability of having a number zero $(4 - 4 = 0)$, negative numbers $(3 - 5 = -2)$, and fractions $(3 \div 5 = 3/5)$. The numbers $0, \pm 1, \pm 2, \pm 3, \ldots$ are called the **integers.** They can be represented on a **number line** like the one shown in Fig. 1.2.

The **rational numbers** are those like 3/5, that can be written in the form a/b, where a and b are both integers. An integer n is also a rational number, because $n = n/1$. Examples of rational numbers are

$$\frac{1}{2}, \qquad \frac{11}{70}, \qquad \frac{125}{7}, \qquad -\frac{10}{11}, \qquad 0 = \frac{0}{1}, \qquad -19, \qquad -1.26 = -\frac{126}{100}$$

The rational numbers can also be represented on the number line. Imagine that we first mark 1/2 and all the multiples of 1/2. Then we mark 1/3 and all the

FIGURE 1.2   The number line.

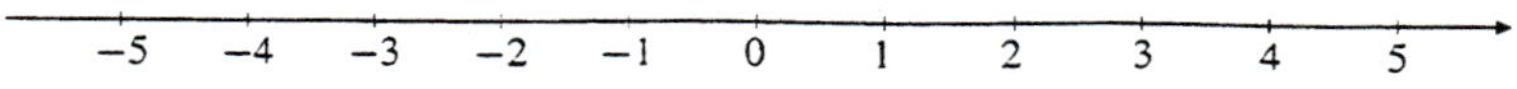

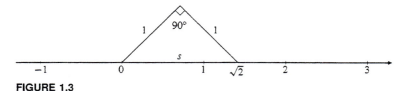

FIGURE 1.3

multiples of 1/3, and so forth. You can be excused for thinking that "finally" there will be no more places left for putting more points on the line. But in fact this is quite wrong. The ancient Greeks already understood that "holes" would remain in the number line even after all the rational numbers had been marked off. This is demonstrated in the construction in Fig. 1.3.

Pythagoras' theorem tells us that $s^2 = 1^2 + 1^2 = 2$, so $s = \sqrt{2}$. It can be shown, however, that there are no integers p and q such that $\sqrt{2} = p/q$. Hence, $\sqrt{2}$ is not a rational number. (Euclid proved this fact in about 300 B.C. See Problem 3 in Section 1.6.)

The rational numbers are therefore insufficient for measuring all possible lengths, let alone areas and volumes. This deficiency can be remedied by extending the concept of numbers to allow for the so-called **irrational numbers**. This extension can be carried out rather naturally by using decimal notation for numbers.

The Decimal System

The way most people write numbers today is called the **decimal system**, or the **base 10 system**. It is a positional system with 10 as the base number. Every natural number can be written using only the symbols, 0, 1, 2, ..., 9, that are called **digits**. You will note that "digit" also means "finger," or "thumb," and that most humans have 10 digits. The positional system defines each combination of digits as a sum of exponents of 10. For example,

$$1984 = 1 \cdot 10^3 + 9 \cdot 10^2 + 8 \cdot 10^1 + 4 \cdot 10^0$$

Each natural number can be uniquely expressed in this manner. With the use of the signs $+$ and $-$, all integers, positive or negative, can be written in the same way. Decimal points also enable us to express rational numbers other than natural numbers. For example,

$$3.1415 = 3 + 1/10^1 + 4/10^2 + 1/10^3 + 5/10^4$$

Rational numbers that can be written exactly using only a finite number of decimal places are called **finite decimal fractions**.

Each finite decimal fraction is a rational number, but not every rational number can be written as a finite decimal fraction. We also need to allow for **infinite**

decimal fractions such as

$$100/3 = 33.333\ldots$$

where the three dots indicate that the decimal 3 recurs indefinitely.

If the decimal fraction is a rational number, then it will always be **periodic**—that is, after a certain place in the decimal expansion, it either stops or continues to repeat a finite sequence of digits. For example, $11/70 = 0.1\,\underbrace{571428}\,\underbrace{571428}\,5\ldots$.

Real Numbers

The definition of a real number follows from the previous discussion. We define a **real number** as an arbitrary infinite decimal fraction. Hence, a real number is of the form $x = \pm m.\alpha_1\alpha_2\alpha_3\ldots$, where m is an integer, and α_n ($n = 1, 2\ldots$) is an infinite series of digits, each in the range 0 to 9. We have already identified the periodic decimal fractions with the rational numbers. In addition, there are infinitely many new numbers given by the nonperiodic decimal fractions. These are called **irrational numbers.** Examples include $\sqrt{2}$, $-\sqrt{5}$, π, $2^{\sqrt{2}}$, and $0.12112111211112\ldots$.

It turns out that, in general, it is very difficult to decide whether a given number is rational or irrational. It has been known since the year 1776 that π is irrational and since 1927 that $2^{\sqrt{2}}$ is irrational. However, we still do not know as of 1993 whether $2^{\sqrt{2}} + 3^{\sqrt{3}}$ is irrational or not. One might gain the impression that there are relatively few irrational numbers. In fact, there are (in a certain precise sense) infinitely more irrational numbers than there are rational numbers.

We mentioned earlier that each rational number can be represented by a point on the number line. But not all points on the number line represent rational numbers. It is as if the irrational numbers "close up" the remaining holes on the number line after all the rational numbers have been positioned. Hence, an unbroken and endless straight line with an origin and a positive unit of length is a satisfactory model for the real numbers. We frequently state that there is a *one-to-one correspondence* between the real numbers and the points on a number line.

The rational and irrational numbers are said to be "dense" on the number line. This means that between any two different real numbers, irrespective of how close they are to each other, we can always find both a rational and an irrational number—in fact, we can always find infinitely many of each.

When applied to the real numbers, the four basic arithmetic operations always result in a real number. The only exception is that we cannot divide by 0.

$$\frac{a}{0} \text{ is not defined for any real number } a$$

This is very important and should not be confused with $0/a = 0$, for all $a \neq 0$. Notice especially that $0/0$ is not defined as any real number. For example, if a car requires 60 liters of fuel to go 600 kilometers, then its fuel consumption is $60/600 = 10$ liters per 100 kilometers. However, if told that a car uses 0 liters of fuel to go 0 kilometers, we know nothing about its fuel consumption; $0/0$ is completely undefined.

Inequalities

In mathematics and especially in economics, inequalities are encountered almost as often as equalities. It is important, therefore, to know and understand the rules for carring out calculations involving inequalities. These are presented in Section A.7 in Appendix A. The following example is of interest in statistics.

Example 1.3

Show that if $a \geq 0$ and $b \geq 0$, then

$$\sqrt{ab} \leq \frac{a+b}{2} \qquad\qquad [1.1]$$

Solution   (You should first test this inequality by choosing some specific numbers, using a calculator if you wish.) To show the given inequality, it is enough to verify that $ab \leq (a+b)^2/4$ because then the square root of the left-hand side cannot exceed the square root of the right-hand side—that is, $\sqrt{ab} \leq \frac{1}{2}(a+b)$. To verify this, it is enough to check that the right-hand side minus the left-hand side is nonnegative. But indeed

$$\frac{(a+b)^2}{4} - ab = \frac{a^2 + 2ab + b^2 - 4ab}{4} = \frac{a^2 - 2ab + b^2}{4} = \frac{(a-b)^2}{4} \geq 0$$

In fact, essentially the same proof can be used to show that $\sqrt{ab} < \frac{1}{2}(a+b)$ unless $a = b$.

The number $\frac{1}{2}(a + b)$ is called the **arithmetic mean** of a and b, and $\sqrt{ab}$ is called the **geometric mean**. What does the inequality in [1.1] state about the different means?

Intervals

If a and b are two numbers on the number line, then we call the set of all numbers that lie between a and b an **interval**. In many situations, it is important to distinguish between the intervals that include their endpoints and the intervals that do not. When $a < b$, there are four different intervals that all have a and b as endpoints, as shown in Table 1.1. Note that the names in the table do not distinguish $[a, b)$ from $(a, b]$. To do so, one could speak of "closed on the left," "open on the right," and so on. Note, too, that an open interval includes neither of its endpoints, but a closed interval includes both of its endpoints. All four intervals, however, have the same length, $b - a$.

We usually illustrate intervals on the number line as in Fig. 1.4, with included endpoints represented by dots, and excluded endpoints at the tips of arrows. The intervals mentioned so far are all *bounded intervals*. We also use the word "interval" to signify certain unbounded sets of numbers. For example, we have

$$[a, \infty) = \text{all numbers } x, \text{ with } x \geq a$$

$$(-\infty, b) = \text{all numbers } x, \text{ with } x < b$$

with ∞ as the common symbol for infinity. Note that the symbol ∞ is not a number at all, and therefore the usual arithmetic rules do not apply to it. In $[a, \infty)$, the symbol ∞ is only a handy notation indicating that we are are considering the collection of *all* numbers larger than or equal to a, without any upper limit to the size of the number. From the preceding, it should be readily apparent what we mean

TABLE 1.1

Notation	Name	The interval consists of all x satisfying:
(a,b)	The **open** interval from a to b.	$a < x < b$
$[a,b]$	The **closed** interval from a to b.	$a \leq x \leq b$
$(a,b]$	The **half-open** interval from a to b.	$a < x \leq b$
$[a,b)$	The **half-open** interval from a to b.	$a \leq x < b$

FIGURE 1.4 $A = [-4, -2]$, $B = [0, 1)$, and $C = (2, 5)$.

by (a, ∞) and $(-\infty, b]$. The collection of all real numbers is sometimes denoted by the symbol $(-\infty, \infty)$.

Absolute Value

Let a be a real number and imagine its position on the number line. The distance between a and 0 is called the **absolute value** of a. If a is positive or 0, then the absolute value is the number a itself; if a is negative, then because distance must be positive, the absolute value is equal to the positive number $-a$.

The **absolute value** of a is denoted by $|a|$, and

$$|a| = \begin{cases} a, & \text{if } a \geq 0 \\ -a, & \text{if } a < 0 \end{cases}$$

[1.2]

For example, $|13| = 13$, $|-5| = -(-5) = 5$, $|-1/2| = 1/2$, and $|0| = 0$.

Note: It is a common fallacy to assume that a must denote a positive number, even if this is not explicitly stated. Similarly, on seeing $-a$, many students are led to believe that this expression is always negative. Observe, however, that the number $-a$ is positive when a itself is negative. For example, if $a = -5$, then $-a = -(-5) = 5$. Nevertheless, it is often a useful convention in economics to define variables so that, as far as possible, their values are positive rather than negative. Where a variable has a definite sign, we shall try to follow this convention.

Example 1.4

    (a) Compute $|x - 2|$ for $x = -3$, $x = 0$, and $x = 4$.
    (b) Rewrite $|x - 2|$ using (1.2).

    Solution

    (a) For $x = -3$,

$$|x - 2| = |-3 - 2| = |-5| = 5$$

    For $x = 0$,

$$|x - 2| = |0 - 2| = |-2| = 2$$

    For $x = 4$,

$$|x - 2| = |4 - 2| = |2| = 2$$

    (b) According to [1.2], $|x - 2| = x - 2$ if $x - 2 \geq 0$, that is, $x \geq 2$. However, $|x - 2| = -(x - 2) = 2 - x$ if $x - 2 < 0$, that is, $x < 2$.

Hence,

$$|x - 2| = \begin{cases} x - 2, & \text{if } x \geq 2 \\ 2 - x, & \text{if } x < 2 \end{cases}$$

(Check this answer by trying the values of x tested in part (a).)

Let x_1 and x_2 be two arbitrary numbers. The **distance** between x_1 and x_2 on the number line is equal to $x_1 - x_2$ if $x_1 \geq x_2$, and equal to $-(x_1 - x_2)$ if $x_1 < x_2$. Therefore, we have

$$|x_1 - x_2| = \text{distance between } x_1 \text{ and } x_2 \text{ on the number line} \qquad \text{[1.3]}$$

In Fig. 1.5, we have indicated geometrically that the distance between 7 and 2 is 5, whereas the distance between -3 and -5 is equal to 2, because $|-3 - (-5)| = |-3 + 5| = |2| = 2$.

Suppose $|x| = 5$. What values can x have? There are only two possibilities: either $x = 5$ or $x = -5$, because no other numbers have absolute values equal to 5. Generally, if a is greater than or equal to 0, then $|x| = a$ means that $x = a$ or $x = -a$. Because $|x| \geq 0$ for all x, the equation $|x| = a$ has no solution when $a < 0$.

If a is a positive number and $|x| < a$, then the distance from x to 0 is less than a, and so

$$|x| < a \text{ means that } -a < x < a \qquad \text{[1.4]}$$

Furthermore, when a is nonnegative, it is clear that

$$|x| \leq a \text{ means that } -a \leq x \leq a \qquad \text{[1.5]}$$

Example 1.5

Find all the x such that $|3x - 2| \leq 5$. Check first to see if this inequality is fulfilled for $x = -3$, $x = 0$, $x = 7/3$, and $x = 10$.

FIGURE 1.5   The distance between 7 and 2, and between -3 and -5.

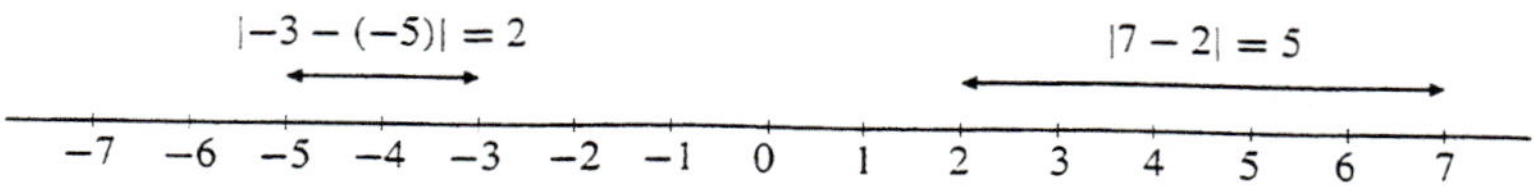

$|-3 - (-5)| = 2$ $|7 - 2| = 5$

$-7 \quad -6 \quad -5 \quad -4 \quad -3 \quad -2 \quad -1 \quad 0 \quad 1 \quad 2 \quad 3 \quad 4 \quad 5 \quad 6 \quad 7$

Solution   For $x = -3$, $|3x - 2| = |-9 - 2| = 11$; for $x = 0$, we have $|3x - 2| = |-2| = 2$; for $x = 7/3$, $|3x - 2| = |7 - 2| = 5$; and for $x = 10$, $|3x - 2| = |30 - 2| = 28$. Hence, we see that the given inequality is satisfied for $x = 0$ and $x = 7/3$, but not for $x = -3$ or $x = 10$.

From [1.5] we see that $|3x - 2| \leq 5$ means $-5 \leq 3x - 2 \leq 5$. Adding 2 to all three expressions gives $-5 + 2 \leq 3x - 2 + 2 \leq 5 + 2$, or $-3 \leq 3x \leq 7$. Dividing by 3 gives $-1 \leq x \leq 7/3$.

Problems

1. Which of the following numbers is a natural number, an integer, or a rational number?

   a. 3.1415926   **b.** $\sqrt{\frac{9}{2} - \frac{1}{2}}$ **c.** $(\sqrt{3} + \sqrt{2})(\sqrt{3} - \sqrt{2})$ **d.** $3\pi - \frac{1}{4}$

2. Which of the following statements are correct?
   a. 1984 is a natural number.
   b. -5 is to the right of -3 on the number line.
   c. -13 is a natural number.
   d. There is no natural number that is not rational.
   e. 3.1415 is not rational.
   f. The sum of two irrational numbers is irrational.

3. For what real numbers x is each of the following expressions defined?

   a. $\dfrac{3}{x - 4}$ **b.** $\dfrac{x - 1}{x(x + 2)}$ **c.** $\dfrac{3x}{x^2 + 4x - 5}$ **d.** $\dfrac{1/4}{x^2 + 4x + 4}$

4. Solve the following inequalities for y in terms of the other variables:

   a. $3x + 4y \leq 12$ **b.** $-x + 3y - z > y - (x - y) + \frac{1}{2}z$

   c. $px + qy \leq m$ $(q > 0)$

5. Consider Problem 1(c) in Section 1.3. Set up an inequality that determines how many units x the company must produce before the average cost falls below $\$q$. Solve the inequality for x. Put $F = 100,000$, $c = 120$, $q = 160$, and solve the problem for this case.

6. Calculate $|2x - 3|$, for $x = 0$, 1/2, and 7/2.

7. **a.** Calculate $|5 - 3x|$, for $x = -1$, 2, and 4.
   b. Solve the equation $|5 - 3x| = 0$.
   c. Rewrite $|5 - 3x|$ by using [1.2].

8. Determine x such that

   a. $|3 - 2x| = 5$ **b.** $|x| \leq 2$ **c.** $|x - 2| \leq 1$

   d. $|3 - 8x| \leq 5$ **e.** $|x| > \sqrt{2}$ **f.** $|x^2 - 2| \leq 1$

9. A 5-meter iron bar is to be produced. It is necessary that the length does not deviate more than 1 mm from its stated size. Write a specification for the

rod's length x in meters: (a) by using a double inequality and (b) with the aid of an absolute-value sign.

1.5 A Few Aspects of Logic

An astronomer, a physicist, and a mathematician were travelling on a train in Scotland. Through the window they saw a flock of sheep grazing in a meadow. The astronomer remarked, "In Scotland all sheep are black." The physicist protested, "Some Scottish sheep are black." The mathematician declared, "In Scotland there exists a flock of sheep all of which are black on at least one side."

So far we have emphasized the role of mathematical models in the empirical sciences, especially in economics. The more complicated the phenomena to be described, the more important it is to be exact. Errors in models applied to practical situations can have catastrophic consequences. For example, in the early stages of the U.S. space program, a rocket costing millions of dollars to develop and build had to be destroyed only seconds after launch because a semicolon had been left out of the computer program intended to control the guidance system.

Although the consequences may be less dramatic, errors in mathematical reasoning also occur rather easily. In what follows, we offer a typical example of how a student (or professor) might use faulty logic and thus end up with an incorrect answer to a problem.

Example 1.6

Find a possible solution for the equation $x + 2 = \sqrt{4 - x}$.

"Solution"   Squaring each side of the equation gives $(x + 2)^2 = (\sqrt{4 - x})^2$, and thus $x^2 + 4x + 4 = 4 - x$. Rearranging this last equation gives $x^2 + 5x = 0$. Canceling x results in $x + 5 = 0$, and therefore $x = -5$.

According to this reasoning, the answer should be $x = -5$. Let us check this. For $x = -5$, we have $x + 2 = -3$. Yet $\sqrt{4 - x} = \sqrt{9} = 3$, so this answer is incorrect. In Example 1.9, we explain how the error arose. (Note the wisdom of checking your answer whenever you think you have solved an equation.)

This example highlights the dangers of routine calculation without adequate thought. It may be easier to avoid similar mistakes after studying more closely the structure of logical reasoning.

Propositions

Assertions that are either true or false are called statements, or **propositions.** Most of the propositions in this book are mathematical ones, but others may arise in daily life. "All individuals who breathe are alive" is an example of a true proposition, whereas the assertion "all individuals who breathe are healthy" is an example of a false proposition. It should be noted that if the words used to express such assertions lack a precise meaning, it will often be difficult to distinguish between a true and a false proposition.

Suppose an assertion such as "$x^2 - 1 = 0$" includes one or more variables. By substituting various real numbers for the variable x, we can generate many different propositions, some true and some false. For this reason we say that the assertion is an **open proposition.** In fact, the proposition $x^2 - 1 = 0$ happens to be true if $x = 1$ or -1, but not otherwise. Thus, an open proposition is not simply true or false. It is neither true nor false until we choose a particular value for the variable. In practice we are somewhat careless about this distinction between propositions and open propositions; instead, we simply call both types propositions.

Implications

In order to keep track of each step in a chain of logical reasoning, it often helps to use implication arrows.

Suppose P and Q are two propositions such that whenever P is true, then Q is necessarily true. In this case, we usually write

$$P \implies Q \qquad\qquad [*]$$

This is read as "P implies Q," or "if P, then Q," or "Q is a consequence of P." The symbol $\implies$ is an **implication arrow,** and it points in the direction of the logical implication. Here are some examples of correct implications.

Example 1.7

      (a) $x > 2 \implies x^2 > 4$.
      (b) $xy = 0 \implies x = 0$ or $y = 0$.
      (c) x is a square $\implies x$ is a rectangle.
      (d) x is a healthy person $\implies x$ is breathing.

Notice that the word "or" in mathematics means the "inclusive or," signifying that "P or Q" means "either P or Q or both."

All the propositions in Example 1.7 are open propositions, just as are most propositions encountered in mathematics. An implication $P \implies Q$ means that for each value of some variable for which P is true, Q is also true.

In certain cases where the implication $[*]$ is valid, it may also be possible to draw a logical conclusion in the other direction:

$$Q \implies P$$

In such cases, we can write both implications together in a single **logical equivalence**:

$$P \iff Q$$

We then say that "P is equivalent to Q," or "P if and only if Q," or just "P iff Q." Note that the statement "P only if Q" expresses the implication $P \implies Q$, whereas "P if Q" expresses the implication $Q \implies P$.

The symbol $\iff$ is an **equivalence arrow**. In previous Example 1.7, we see that the implication arrow in (b) could be replaced with the equivalence arrow, because it is also true that $x = 0$ or $y = 0$ implies $xy = 0$. Note, however, that no other implication in Example 1.7 can be replaced by the equivalence arrow. For even if x^2 is larger than 4, it is not necessarily true that x is larger than 2 (for instance, x might be -3); also, a rectangle is not necessarily a square; and, finally, just because person x is breathing does not mean that he or she is healthy.

Necessary and Sufficient Conditions

There are other commonly used ways of expressing that proposition P implies proposition Q, or that P is equivalent to Q. Thus, if proposition P implies proposition Q, we state that P is a "sufficient condition" for Q. After all, for Q to be true, it is sufficient that P is true. Accordingly, we know that if P is satisfied, then it is certain that Q is also satisfied. In this case, we say that Q is a "necessary condition" for P. For Q must necessarily be true if P is true. Hence,

---

P is a **sufficient condition** for Q means: $P \implies Q$

Q is a **necessary condition** for P means: $P \implies Q$

For example, if we formulate the implication in Example 1.7(c) in this way, it would read:

> A necessary condition for x to be a square is that x be a rectangle.

or

> A sufficient condition for x to be a rectangle is that x be a square.

The corresponding verbal expression for $P \iff Q$ is simply: *P is a necessary and sufficient condition for Q, or P if and only if Q, or P iff Q.* It is evident from this that it is very important to distinguish between the propositions "P is a necessary condition for Q" (meaning $Q \implies P$) and "P is a sufficient condition for Q" (meaning $P \implies Q$). To emphasize the point, consider two propositions:

1. Breathing is a necessary condition for a person to be healthy.
2. Breathing is a sufficient condition for a person to be healthy.

Evidently proposition 1 is true. But proposition 2 is false, because sick (living) people are still breathing. In the following pages, we shall repeatedly refer to necessary and sufficient conditions. Understanding them and the difference between them is a necessary condition for understanding much economic analysis. It is not a sufficient condition, alas!

Solving Equations

We shall now give examples showing how using implication and equivalence arrows can help avoid mistakes in solving equations like that in Example 1.6.

Example 1.8

Find all x such that $(2x - 1)^2 - 3x^2 = 2\left(\frac{1}{2} - 4x\right)$.

Solution   By expanding $(2x - 1)^2$ and also multiplying out the right-hand side, we obtain a new equation that obviously has the same solutions as the original one:

$$(2x - 1)^2 - 3x^2 = 2\left(\tfrac{1}{2} - 4x\right) \iff 4x^2 - 4x + 1 - 3x^2 = 1 - 8x$$

Adding $8x - 1$ to each side of the second equality and then gathering terms gives the equivalent expression

$$4x^2 - 4x + 1 - 3x^2 = 1 - 8x \iff x^2 + 4x = 0$$

Now $x^2 + 4x = x(x + 4)$, and the latter expression is 0 if and only if $x = 0$ or $x + 4 = 0$. That is,

$$x^2 + 4x = 0 \iff x(x + 4) = 0 \iff x = 0 \quad \text{or} \quad x + 4 = 0$$
$$\iff x = 0 \quad \text{or} \quad x = -4$$

Putting everything together, we have derived a chain of equivalence arrows showing that the given equation is fulfilled for the two values $x = 0$ and $x = -4$, and for no other values of x. That is,

$$(2x - 1)^2 - 3x^2 = 2(\tfrac{1}{2} - 4x) \iff x = 0 \quad \text{or} \quad x = -4$$

Example 1.9

Find all x such that $x + 2 = \sqrt{4 - x}$. (Recall Example 1.6.)

Solution   Squaring both sides of the given equation yields

$$(x + 2)^2 = \left(\sqrt{4 - x}\right)^2$$

Consequently, $x^2 + 4x + 4 = 4 - x$, that is, $x^2 + 5x = 0$. From the latter equation it follows that

$$x(x + 5) = 0$$

which implies $x = 0$ or $x = -5$. Thus, a necessary condition for x to solve $x + 2 = \sqrt{4 - x}$ is that $x = 0$ or $x = -5$. Inserting these two possible values of x into the original equation shows that only $x = 0$ satisfies the equation. The unique solution to the equation is, therefore, $x = 0$.

In finding the solution to Example 1.9, why was it necessary to test whether the values we found were actually solutions, whereas this step was unnecessary in Example 1.8? To answer this, we must analyze the logical structure of our solution to Example 1.9. With the aid of numbered implication and equivalence arrows, we can express the previous solution as

$$x + 2 = \sqrt{4 - x} \overset{(1)}{\implies} (x + 2)^2 = 4 - x \overset{(2)}{\implies} x^2 + 4x + 4 = 4 - x$$

$$\overset{(3)}{\implies} x^2 + 5x = 0 \overset{(4)}{\implies} x(x + 5) = 0 \overset{(5)}{\implies} x = 0 \text{ or } x = -5$$

Implication (1) is true (because $a = b \implies a^2 = b^2$ and $\left(\sqrt{a}\right)^2 = a$). *It is important to note, however, that the implication cannot be replaced by an equivalence.* If $a^2 = b^2$, then either $a = b$ or $a = -b$; it need not be true that $a = b$. Implications (2), (3), (4), and (5) are also all true; moreover, all could have been written as equivalences, though this is not necessary in order to find the solution. Therefore, a chain of implications has been obtained that leads from the equation $x + 2 = \sqrt{4 - x}$ to the proposition "$x = 0$ or $x = -5$." Because the implication (1) cannot be reversed, there is no corresponding chain of implications going in the opposite direction. We have verified that if the number x satisfies $x + 2 = \sqrt{4 - x}$, then x must be either 0 or -5; no other value can satisfy the given equation. However, we have not yet shown that either 0 or -5 really satisfies the equation. Until we try inserting 0 and -5 into the equation, we cannot see that only $x = 0$ is a solution. *Note that in this case, the test we have suggested not only serves to check our calculations, but is also a logical necessity.*

Looking back at Example 1.6, we now realize that two errors were committed. Firstly, the implication $x^2 + 5x = 0 \implies x + 5 = 0$ is wrong, because $x = 0$ is also a solution of $x^2 + 5x = 0$. Secondly, it is logically necessary to check if 0 or -5 really satisfies the equation.

The method used to solve Example 1.9 is the most common. It involves setting up a chain of implications that starts from the given equation and ends with a set of its possible solutions. By testing each of these trial solutions in turn, we find which of them really do satisfy the equation. Even if the chain of implications is also a chain of equivalences (as it was in Example 1.8), such a test is always a useful check of both logic and calculations.

Problems

1. Implications and equivalences can be expressed in ways that differ from those already mentioned. Use the implication or equivalence arrows to mark in which direction you believe the logical conclusions proceed in the following propositions:
   a. The equation $2x - 4 = 2$ is fulfilled only when $x = 3$.
   b. If $x = 3$, then $2x - 4 = 2$.
   c. The equation $x^2 - 2x + 1 = 0$ is satisfied if $x = 1$.
   d. If $x^2 > 4$, then $x > 2$ or $x < -2$, and conversely.

2. Consider the following six implications and decide in each case: (i) if the implication is true, and (ii) if the converse implication is true. (x, y, and z are real numbers.)
   a. $x = 2$ and $y = 5 \implies x + y = 7$
   b. $(x - 1)(x - 2)(x - 3) = 0 \implies x = 1$
   c. $x^2 + y^2 = 0 \implies x = 0$ or $y = 0$
   d. $x = 0$ and $y = 0 \implies x^2 + y^2 = 0$
   e. $xy = xz \implies y = z$
   f. $x > y^2 \implies x > 0$

3. Consider the proposition $2x + 5 \geq 13$.
   a. Is the condition $x \geq 0$ necessary, sufficient, or both necessary and sufficient for the proposition to be satisfied?
   b. Answer the same question when $x \geq 0$ is replaced by $x \geq 50$.
   c. Answer the same question when $x \geq 0$ is replaced by $x \geq 4$.

4. Solve the equation

$$\frac{(x + 1)^2}{x(x - 1)} + \frac{(x - 1)^2}{x(x + 1)} - 2\frac{3x + 1}{x^2 - 1} = 0$$

5. Solve the following equations:
   a. $x + 2 = \sqrt{4x + 13}$ **b.** $|x + 2| = \sqrt{4 - x}$ **c.** $x^2 - 2|x| - 3 = 0$

6. Solve the following equations:
   a. $\sqrt{x - 4} = \sqrt{x + 5} - 9$ **b.** $\sqrt{x - 4} = 9 - \sqrt{x + 5}$

7. Fill in the blank rectangles with "iff" (if and only if) when this results in a true statement, or alternatively with "if" or "only if."
   a. $x = \sqrt{4}$ ☐ $x = 2$

b. $x^2 > 0$ ☐ $\quad x > 0$

c. $x^2 < 9$ ☐ $\quad x < 3$

d. $x(x^2 + 1) = 0$ ☐ $\quad x = 0$

e. $x(x + 3) < 0$ ☐ $\quad x > -3$

8. Consider the following attempt to solve the equation $x + \sqrt{x + 4} = 2$: "From the given equation, it follows that $\sqrt{x + 4} = 2 - x$. Squaring both sides gives $x + 4 = 4 - 4x + x^2$. After rearranging the terms, it is seen that this equation implies $x^2 - 5x = 0$. Canceling x, we obtain $x - 5 = 0$ and this equation is satisfied when $x = 5$."

    a. Mark with arrows the implications or equivalences expressed in the text. Which ones are correct?

    b. Give a correct solution to the equation.

9. For each of the following 6 propositions, state the negation as simply as possible.

    a. $x \geq 0$ and $y \geq 0$.

    b. All x satisfy $x \geq a$.

    c. Neither x nor y is less than 5.

    d. For each $\varepsilon > 0$, there exists a $\delta > 0$ such that B is satisfied.

    e. No one can avoid liking cats.

    f. Everyone loves someone at certain times.

10. "Supreme Court refuses to hear challenge to lower court's decision approving a trial judge's refusal to allow a defendant to refuse to speak." Has the defendant the right not to speak?

1.6 Mathematical Proof

In science, what can be proved should not be believed without proof.[4]
—R. Dedekind (1887)

In every branch of mathematics, the most important results are called **theorems.** Constructing logically valid proofs for these results often can be rather complicated. For example, the "four-color theorem" states that any map in the plane needs at most four colors in order that all contiguous regions should have different colors. Proving this involved checking hundreds of thousands of different cases, a task that was impossible without a sophisticated computer program.

    In this book, we often omit formal proofs of theorems. Instead, the emphasis is on providing a good intuitive grasp of what the theorems tell us. However,

---

[4]Here is the German original: "Was beweisbar ist, soll in der Wissenschaft nicht ohne Beweis geglaubt werden."

although proofs do not form a major part of this book, it is still useful to understand something about the different types of proof that are used in mathematics. In fact, a proof that is actually readable is likely to some extent to rely on the reader's intuition. Although many mathematical logicians do take care to present every step and every argument, and this may indeed be a necessary step in enabling computers to check a proof, the overall result is usually unreadable by most people.

Every mathematical theorem can be formulated as an implication

$$P \implies Q \qquad\qquad [*]$$

where P represents a proposition or a series of propositions called *premises* ("what we know"), and Q represents a proposition or a series of propositions that are called the *conclusions* ("what we want to know"). A statement of the form $P \iff Q$ can be regarded as two theorems.

Usually, it is most natural to prove a result of the type [*] by starting with the premises P and successively working forward to the conclusion Q; we call this a **direct proof**. Sometimes, however, it is more convenient to prove the implication $P \implies Q$ by an **indirect proof**. In this case, we begin by supposing that Q is not true, and on that basis demonstrate that neither can P be true. This is completely legitimate, because we have the following equivalence:

$$P \implies Q \quad \text{is equivalent to} \quad not\ Q \implies not\ P \qquad\qquad [1.6]$$

It is helpful to consider how this rule of logic applies to some concrete examples:

If it is raining, the grass is getting wet

asserts precisely the same thing as

If the grass is not getting wet, then it is not raining.

If T denotes a triangle, then

The base angles of T are equal implies that T is isosceles asserts the same as *If T is not isosceles, then its base angles are not equal.*

There is a third method of proof that is also sometimes useful. It is called **proof by contradiction**. The method is based upon a fundamental logical principle: that it is impossible for a chain of valid inferences to proceed from a true proposition to a false one. Therefore, if we have a proposition R and we can derive a contradiction on the basis of supposing that R is false, then it follows that R must be true.

Example 1.10

Use three different methods to prove that

$$-x^2 + 5x - 4 > 0 \Longrightarrow x > 0$$

Solution

(a) *Direct proof:* Suppose $-x^2 + 5x - 4 > 0$. Adding $x^2 + 4$ to each side of the inequality gives $5x > x^2 + 4$. Because $x^2 + 4 \geq 4$, for all x, we have $5x > 4$, and so $x > 4/5$. In particular, $x > 0$.

(b) *Indirect proof:* Suppose $x \leq 0$. Then $5x \leq 0$ and so $-x^2 + 5x - 4$, as a sum of three nonpositive terms, is ≤ 0.

(c) *Proof by contradiction:* Suppose that the statement is not true. Then there has to exist an x such that $-x^2 + 5x - 4 > 0$ and $x \leq 0$. But if $x \leq 0$, then $-x^2 + 5x - 4 \leq -x^2 - 4 \leq -4$, and we have arrived at a contradiction.

Deductive vs. Inductive Reasoning

The three methods of proof just outlined are all examples of *deductive reasoning*, that is, reasoning based on consistent rules of logic. In contrast, many branches of science use *inductive reasoning*. This process draws general conclusions based only on a few (or even many) observations. For example, the statement that "the price level has increased every year for the last n years; therefore, it will surely increase next year too," demonstrates inductive reasoning. Owners of houses in California know how dangerous such reasoning can be in economics. This inductive approach is nevertheless of fundamental importance in the experimental and empirical sciences, despite the fact that conclusions based upon it never can be absolutely certain.

In mathematics, inductive reasoning is not recognized as a form of proof. Suppose, for instance, that the students taking a course in geometry are asked to show that the sum of the angles of a triangle is always 180 degrees. If they painstakingly measure as accurately as possible 1000 or even 1 million different triangles, demonstrating that in each case the sum of the angles is 180, would this not serve as proof for the assertion? No; although it would represent a very good indication that the proposition is true, it is not a mathematical proof. Similarly, in business economics, the fact that a particular company's profits have risen for each of the past 20 years is no guarantee that they will rise once again this year.

Nevertheless, there is a *mathematical* form of induction that is much used in valid proofs. This is discussed in Section B.5 in Appendix B.

Problems

1. Consider the following (dubious) statement: "If inflation increases, then unemployment decreases." Which of the following statements are equivalent?

> **a.** For unemployment to decrease, inflation must increase.
> **b.** A sufficient condition for unemployment to decrease is that inflation increases.
> **c.** Unemployment can only decrease if inflation increases.
> **d.** If unemployment does not decrease, then inflation does not increase.
> **e.** A necessary condition for inflation to increase is that unemployment decreases.

2. Analyze the following epitaph: (a) using logic and (b) from a poetic viewpoint.

> Those who knew him, loved him.
> Those who loved him not, knew him not.

3. Fill in the details of the following proof that $\sqrt{2}$ is irrational. Suppose it were true that $\sqrt{2} = p/q$, where p and q are integers with no common factor. Then $p^2 = 2q^2$, which would mean that p^2, and hence p, would have 2 as a factor. Therefore, $p = 2s$ for some integer s, and so $4s^2 = 2q^2$. Thus, $q^2 = 2s^2$. It follows that q would also have 2 as a factor, a contradiction of the hypothesis that p and q have no common factor.

1.7 Set Theory

If you know set theory up to the hilt, and no other mathematics, you would be of no use to anybody. If you knew a lot of mathematics, but no set theory, you might achieve a great deal. But if you knew just some set theory, you would have a far better understanding of the language of mathematics.
—I. Stewart (1975)

In daily life, we constantly group together objects of the same kind. For instance, we refer to the university faculty to signify all the members of the academic staff at the university. A garden refers to all the plants that are growing in it. We talk about all firms with more than 1000 employees, all taxpayers in Los Angeles who earned between $50,000 and $100,000 in 1992, and so on. In all these cases, we have a collection of objects viewed as a whole. In mathematics, such a collection is called a **set**, and the objects are called the **elements** of, or the **members** of, the set.

How is a set specified? The simplest way is to list its members, in any order, between the two braces { and }. An example is the set

$$S = \{a, b, c\}$$

whose members are the first three letters in the alphabet of most languages of European origin, including English. Or it might be a set consisting of three members represented by the letters a, b, and c. For example, if $a = 0$, $b = 1$, and $c = 2$, then $S = \{0, 1, 2\}$. Also S denotes the set of roots of the cubic equation

$$(x - a)(x - b)(x - c) = 0$$

in the unknown x, where a, b, and c are any three real numbers.

Alternatively, suppose that you are to eat a meal at a restaurant that offers a choice of several main dishes. Four choices might be feasible—fish, pasta, omelette, and chicken. Then the *feasible set* F has these four members, and is fully specified as

$$F = \{\text{fish, pasta, omelette, chicken}\}$$

Notice that the order in which the dishes are listed does not matter. The feasible set remains the same even if the order of the items on the menu is changed.

Two sets A and B are considered **equal** if each element of A is an element of B and each element of B is an element of A. In this case, we write $A = B$. This means that the two sets consist of exactly the same elements. Consequently, $\{1, 2, 3\} = \{3, 2, 1\}$, because the order in which the elements are listed has no significance; and $\{1, 1, 2, 3\} = \{1, 2, 3\}$, because a set is not changed if some elements are listed more than once.

Specifying a Property

Not every set can be defined by listing all its members, however. Some sets can be infinite, that is, they contain an infinite number of members.

Actually, such infinite sets are rather common in economics. Take, for instance, the *budget set* that arises in consumer theory. Suppose there are two goods with quantities denoted by x and y that can be bought at prices p and q, respectively. A consumption bundle (x, y) is a pair of quantities of the two goods. Its value at prices p and q is $px + qy$. Suppose that a consumer has an amount m to spend on the two goods. Then the *budget constraint* is $px + qy \leq m$ (assuming that the consumer is free to underspend). If one also accepts that the quantity consumed of each good must be nonnegative, then the *budget set*, that will be denoted by B, consists of those consumption bundles (x, y) satisfying the three inequalities $px + qy \leq m$, $x \geq 0$, and $y \geq 0$. (The set B is shown in Fig. 2.41.) Standard notation for such a set is

$$B = \{(x, y) : px + qy \leq m, \ x \geq 0, \ y \geq 0\} \qquad [1.7]$$

The braces { } are still used to denote "the set consisting of." However, instead of listing all the members, which is impossible for the infinite set of points in the triangular budget set B, the set is specified in two parts. To the left of the colon, (x, y) is used to denote the form of the typical member of B, here a consumption bundle that is specified by listing the respective quantities of the two goods. To the right of the colon, the three properties that these typical members must satisfy are all listed, and the set thereby specified. This is an example of the general specification:

$$S = \{\text{typical member : defining properties}\}$$

Note that it is not just infinite sets that can be specified by properties—finite sets can also be specified in this way. Indeed, even some finite sets almost *have* to be specified in this way, such as the set of all human beings currently alive, or even (we hope!), the set of all readers of this book.

Mathematics makes frequent use of infinite sets. For example, in Section 1.4, we studied the set of positive integers, which is often denoted by N, as well as the set of rational numbers, denoted by Q, and the set of real numbers, denoted by R. All these sets are infinite.

Set Membership

As we stated earlier, sets contain members or elements. There is some convenient standard notation that denotes the relation between a set and its members. First,

$$x \in S$$

indicates that *x is an element of* S. Note the special symbol $\in$ (which is a variant of the Greek letter ϵ, or "epsilon"). Occasionally, one sees $S \ni x$ being used to express exactly the same relationship as $x \in S$. The symbol "$\ni$" is generally read as "owns," but is not used very often. To express the fact that x is *not* a member of S, we write $x \notin S$. For example, $d \notin \{a, b, c\}$ says that d is not an element of the set $\{a, b, c\}$.

For additional illustrations of set membership notation, let us return to our earlier examples. Given the budget set B in [1.7], let (x^*, y^*) denote the consumer's actual purchases. Then it must be true that $(x^*, y^*) \in B$. Confronted with the choice from the set of feasible main courses $F = \{\text{fish, pasta, omelette, chicken}\}$, let s denote your actual selection. Then, of course, $s \in F$. This is what we mean by "feasible set"—it is possible only to choose some member of that set but nothing outside it.

In the example of choice from four main courses, it may be argued that if none is to the customer's liking, then she cannot be prevented from ordering nothing at all from the menu. She can eat somewhere else instead, or simply go hungry. If that is what she does, she is not really choosing outside her feasible set. Rather, our previous description of the feasible set should be expanded to include the option of ordering none of the four available dishes. Thus, the customer's true feasible set is

$$F_5 = \{\text{fish, pasta, omelette, chicken, none of the previous four}\}$$

In the end, she can only avoid choosing something from this by choosing more than one item. If this is not allowed, then F_5 is her true feasible set.

Subsets

Let A and B be any two sets. Then A is a **subset** of B if it is true that every member of A is also a member of B. So A is smaller than B in some sense, even though A and B could actually be equal. This relationship is expressed symbolically by $A \subset B$:

$$A \subset B \iff [x \in A \Rightarrow x \in B]$$

A special case of a subset is when A is a *proper subset* of B, meaning that $A \subset B$ and $A \neq B$.[5]

Set Operations

Sets can be combined in many different ways. Especially important are three operations: union, intersection, and the difference of sets, as shown in Table 1.2.

TABLE 1.2

Notation	Name	The set consists of
$A \cup B$	A **union** B	The elements that belong to at least one of the sets A and B.
$A \cap B$	A **intersection** B	The elements that belong to both A and B.
$A \setminus B$	A **minus** B	The elements that belong to A, but not to B.

Thus,

$$A \cup B = \{x : x \in A \text{ or } x \in B\}$$

$$A \cap B = \{x : x \in A \text{ and } x \in B\}$$

$$A \setminus B = \{x : x \in A \text{ and } x \notin B\}$$

Example 1.11

Let $A = \{1, 2, 3, 4, 5\}$ and $B = \{3, 6\}$. Find $A \cup B$, $A \cap B$, $A \setminus B$, and $B \setminus A$.

Solution $A \cup B = \{1, 2, 3, 4, 5, 6\}$, $A \cap B = \{3\}$, $A \setminus B = \{1, 2, 4, 5\}$, $B \setminus A = \{6\}$.

---

[5]Sometimes the notation $A \subset B$ is reserved for the case when A is a subset of B satisfying $A \neq B$, just as $a < b$ is reserved for when $a \leq b$ and $a \neq b$. Then $A \subseteq B$ is used to denote that A is a subset of B. However, there is rarely any need to specify that A is a proper subset of B, and when there is, this can easily be done verbally.

An economic example can be obtained by considering particular sets of taxpayers in 1990. Let A be the set of all those taxpayers who had an income of at least \$15,000 and let B be the set of all who had a net worth of at least \$150,000. Then $A \cup B$ would be those taxpayers who earned at least \$15,000 or who had a net worth of at least \$150,000, whereas $A \cap B$ are those taxpayers who earned at least \$15,000 and who also had a net worth of at least \$150,000. Finally, $A \setminus B$ would be those who earned at least \$15,000 but who had less than \$150,000 in net worth.

If two sets A and B have no elements in common, they are said to be **disjoint**. The symbol "$\emptyset$" denotes the set that has no elements. It is called the **empty set**. Thus, sets A and B are disjoint if and only if $A \cap B = \emptyset$.

A collection of sets is often referred to as a family of sets. When considering a certain family of sets, it is usually natural to think of each set in the family as a subset of one particular fixed set Ω, hereafter called the **universal set**. In the previous example, the set of all taxpayers in 1990 would be an obvious choice for a universal set.

If A is a subset of the universal set Ω, then according to the definition of difference, $\Omega \setminus A$ is the set of elements of Ω that are not in A. This set is called the **complement** of A in Ω and is sometimes denoted by CA, so that $CA = \Omega \setminus A$. Other ways of denoting the complement of A include A^c and $\bar{A}$.

When using the notation CA, it is important to be clear about which universal set Ω is used to construct the complement.

Example 1.12

Let the universal set Ω be the set of all students at a particular university. Moreover, let F denote the set of female students, M the set of all mathematics students, C the set of students in the university choir, B the set of all biology students, and T the set of all tennis players. Describe the members of the following sets: $\Omega \setminus M$, $M \cup C$, $F \cap T$, $M \setminus (B \cap T)$, and $(M \setminus B) \cup (M \setminus T)$.

Solution $\Omega \setminus M$ consists of those students who are not studying mathematics, $M \cup C$ of those students who study mathematics and/or are in the university choir. The set $F \cap T$ consists of those female students who play tennis. The set $M \setminus (B \cap T)$ has those mathematics students who do not both study biology and play tennis. Finally, the last set $(M \setminus B) \cup (M \setminus T)$ has those students who either are mathematics students not studying biology or mathematics students who do not play tennis. Do you see that the last two sets are equal? (For arbitrary sets M, B, and T, it is true that $(M \setminus B) \cup (M \setminus T) = M \setminus (B \cap T)$. It will be easier to verify this equality after you have read the following discussion of Venn diagrams.)

Venn Diagrams

When considering the relationships between several sets, it is instructive and extremely helpful to represent each set by a region in a plane. The region is drawn so that all the elements belonging to a certain set are contained within some closed re-

gion of the plane. Diagrams constructed in this manner are called **Venn diagrams.**
The definitions discussed in the previous section can be illustrated as in Fig. 1.6.

By using the definitions directly, or by illustrating sets with Venn diagrams, one can derive formulas that are universally valid regardless of which sets are being considered. For example, the formula $A \cap B = B \cap A$ follows immediately from the definition of the intersection between two sets. It is somewhat more difficult to verify directly from the definitions that the following relationship is valid for all sets A, B, and C:

$$A \cap (B \cup C) = (A \cap B) \cup (A \cap C) \qquad [*]$$

With the use of a Venn diagram, however, we easily see that the sets on the right- and left-hand sides of the equality sign both represent the shaded set in Fig. 1.7. The equality in [*] is therefore valid.

It is important that the three sets A, B, and C in a Venn diagram be drawn in such a way that all possible relations between an element and each of the three sets are represented. In other words, the following eight different sets all should be nonempty: (1): $(A \cap B) \setminus C$; (2): $(B \cap C) \setminus A$; (3): $(C \cap A) \setminus B$; (4): $A \setminus (B \cup C)$; (5): $B \setminus (C \cup A)$; (6): $C \setminus (A \cup B)$; (7): $A \cap B \cap C$; and (8): $\mathcal{C}(A \cup B \cup C)$. (See Fig. 1.8.) Notice, however, that this way of representing sets in the plane easily becomes unmanageable if four or more sets are involved, because then there would have to be at least $16 (= 2^4)$ regions in any such Venn diagram.

From the definition of intersection and union (or by the use of Venn diagrams), it easily follows that $A \cup (B \cup C) = (A \cup B) \cup C$ and that $A \cap (B \cap C) = (A \cap B) \cap C$.

FIGURE 1.6 Venn diagrams.

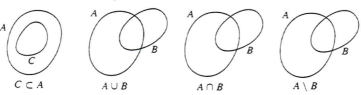

$$C \subset A \qquad\qquad A \cup B \qquad\qquad A \cap B \qquad\qquad A \setminus B$$

FIGURE 1.7

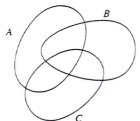

FIGURE 1.8

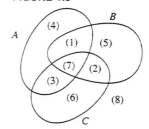

Consequently, it does not matter where the parentheses are placed. In such cases, the parentheses can be dropped and the expressions written as $A \cup B \cup C$ and $A \cap B \cap C$. Note, however, that the parentheses cannot generally be moved in the expression $A \cap (B \cup C)$, because this set is not always equal to $(A \cap B) \cup C$. Prove this fact by considering the case where $A = \{1, 2, 3\}$, $B = \{2, 3\}$, and $C = \{4, 5\}$, or by using a Venn diagram.

Problems

1. Let $A = \{2, 3, 4\}$, $B = \{2, 5, 6\}$, $C = \{5, 6, 2\}$, and $D = \{6\}$.
   a. Determine if the following statements are true: $4 \in C$; $5 \in C$; $A \subset B$; $D \subset \dot{C}$; $B = C$; and $A = B$.
   b. Find $A \cap B$; $A \cup B$; $A \setminus B$; $B \setminus A$; $(A \cup B) \setminus (A \cap B)$; $A \cup B \cup C \cup D$; $A \cap B \cap C$; and $A \cap B \cap C \cap D$.

2. a. Are the greatest painter among the poets and the greatest poet among the painters one and the same person?
   b. Are the oldest painter among the poets and the oldest poet among the painters one and the same person?

3. With reference to Example 1.12, write the following statements in set terminology:
   a. All biology students are mathematics students.
   b. There are female biology students in the university choir.
   c. Those female students who neither play tennis nor belong to the university choir all study biology.

4. Let F, M, C, B, and T be the sets in Example 1.12. Describe the following sets: $F \cap B \cap C$; $M \cap F$; and $((M \cap B) \setminus C) \setminus T$.

5. Justify the following formulas by either using the definitions or by using Venn diagrams:
   a. $A \cup B = B \cup A$ b. $A \cup A = A$
   c. $A \cap A = A$ d. $A \cap \emptyset = \emptyset$
   e. $A \cup \emptyset = A$ f. $A \cup (B \cap C) = (A \cup B) \cap (A \cup C)$

6. Determine which of the following formulas are true. If any formula is false, find a counterexample to demonstrate this, using a Venn diagram if you find it helpful.
   a. $A \setminus B = B \setminus A$ b. $A \subset B \iff A \cup B = B$
   c. $A \subset B \iff A \cap B = A$ d. $A \cap B = A \cap C \implies B = C$
   e. $A \cup B = A \cup C \implies B = C$ f. $A \setminus (B \setminus C) = (A \setminus B) \setminus C$

7. Make a complete list of all the different subsets of the set $\{a, b, c\}$. How many are there if the empty set and the set itself are included? Do the same for the set $\{a, b, c, d\}$.

8. A survey revealed that 50 people liked coffee, 40 liked tea, 35 liked both coffee and tea, and 10 did not like either coffee or tea. How many persons in all responded to the survey?

9. If A is a set with a finite number of elements, let $n(A)$ denote the number of elements in A. If A and B are arbitrary finite sets, prove the following:
   a. $n(A \cup B) = n(A) + n(B) - n(A \cap B)$
   b. $n(A \setminus B) = n(A) - n(A \cap B)$

10. If A and B are two arbitrary sets, define the **symmetric difference** between A and B as

$$A \triangle B = (A \setminus B) \cup (B \setminus A)$$

Obviously, $A \triangle B = B \triangle A$, whereas $A \setminus B \neq B \setminus A$ (in general). Prove by using a Venn diagram, or in some other way, the following:
   a. $A \triangle B = (A \cup B) \setminus (A \cap B)$
   b. $(A \triangle B) \triangle C$ consists of those elements that occur in just one of the sets A, B, and C, or else in all three.

11. One of the following identities is not generally valid. Which one?
   a. $(A \triangle B) \triangle C = A \triangle (B \triangle C)$
   b. $(A \cap C) \triangle B = (A \triangle B) \cap (C \triangle B)$
   c. $A \triangle A = \emptyset$

12. **a.** A thousand people took part in a survey to reveal which newspaper, A, B, or C, they had read on a certain day. The responses showed that 420 had read A, 316 had read B, and 160 had read C. Of these responses, 116 had read both A and B, 100 had read A and C, 30 had read B and C, and 16 had read all three papers.
   (i)   How many had read A, but not B?
   (ii) How many had read C, but neither A nor B?
   (iii) How many had read neither A, B, nor C?

   b. Denote the complete set of all 1000 persons in the survey by Ω (the universal set). Applying the notation in Problem 9, we have $n(A) = 420$ and $n(A \cap B \cap C) = 16$, for example. Describe the numbers given in part (a) in a similar manner. Why is the following equation valid?

$$n(\Omega \setminus (A \cup B \cup C)) = n(\Omega) - n(A \cup B \cup C)$$

   c. Prove that if A, B, and C are arbitrary finite sets, then

$$n(A \cup B \cup C) = n(A) + n(B) + n(C) - n(A \cap B) - n(A \cap C)$$
$$-n(B \cap C) + n(A \cap B \cap C)$$

2

Functions of One Variable: Introduction

... mathematics is not so much a subject as a way of studying any subject, not so much a science as a way of life.
—G. Temple (1981)

Functions are of fundamental importance in practically every area of pure and applied mathematics, including mathematics applied to economics. The language of mathematical economics is full of terms like supply and demand functions, cost functions, production functions, consumption functions, and so on. Here and in the next chapter, we present a general discussion of functions of one real variable, illustrated by some very important examples.

2.1 Introduction

One variable is a function of another if the first variable *depends* upon the second. For instance, the area of a circle is a function of its radius. If the radius r is given, then the area A is determined. In fact $A = \pi r^2$, where π is the numerical constant $3.14159\ldots$.

The measurement of temperature provides another example of a function. If C denotes the temperature expressed in degrees Centigrade (or Celsius), this is a function of F, the same temperature measured in degrees Fahrenheit, because $C = \frac{5}{9}(F - 32)$.

In ordinary conversation, we sometimes use the word "function" in a similar way. For example, we might say that the infant mortality rate of a country is a function of the quality of its health care, or that a country's national product is

TABLE 2.1 *Personal consumption expenditure in the United States, 1985–1991*

Year	1985	1986	1987	1988	1989	1990	1991
Personal consumption[1]	2,667.4	2,850.6	3,052.2	3,296.2	3,523.1	3,748.4	3,887.7

[1] In billions of dollars.

a function of the level of investment. In both these cases, it would be a major research task to obtain a formula that represents the function precisely.

One does not need a mathematical formula to convey the idea that one variable is a function of another: A table can also show the relationship. For instance, Table 2.1 shows the growth of annual total personal consumption expenditures, measured in current dollars, in the United States for the period 1985–1991. It is taken from figures in the *Economic Report of the President* dated January 1993. This table defines consumption expenditures as a function of the year. No allowance is made for inflation.

The dependence between two variables can also be illustrated by means of a graph or chart. Consider the following two examples.

In Fig. 2.1, we have drawn a curve that allegedly played an important role some years ago in the discussion of "supply side economics." It shows the presumed relationship between a country's income tax rate and its total income tax revenue. Obviously, if the income tax rate is 0%, then tax revenue is 0. However, if the tax rate is 100%, then tax revenue will also be (about) 0, because virtually no one is willing to work if his or her entire income is going to be confiscated. These ideas are obvious to virtually all competent economists (in cases like Problem 1 of Section 3.2). Nevertheless, a controversy was created by the American economist Arthur Laffer, who claimed to have drawn this curve on a restaurant napkin, and then later popularized its message with the public. Economists have hotly disputed what is the percentage rate a at which the government collects the maximum tax revenue.

FIGURE 2.1   The "Laffer curve," which relates tax revenue to tax rates.

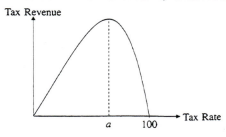

Figure 2.2 reproduces a postage stamp showing how Norway's gross national product grew during the first 100 years of the lifetime of its Central Bureau of Statistics.

FIGURE 2.2   The national product of Norway (*volume index*) 1876–1976.

All of the relationships just discussed have one characteristic in common: A definite rule relates each value of one variable to a definite value of another variable.

Notice that in all of the examples, it is implicitly assumed that the variables are subject to certain constraints. For instance, in the temperature example, F cannot be less than -459.67, the absolute zero point (which corresponds to -273.15 degrees Centigrade). In Table 2.1, only the years between 1985 and 1991 are relevant.

2.2 Functions of One Real Variable

The examples we studied in the preceding section lead to the following general definition of a real valued function of one real variable:

A **function** of a real variable x with **domain** D is a rule that assigns a unique real number to each number x in D.   [2.1]

The word "rule" is used in a very broad sense. *Every* rule with the properties described in [2.1] is called a function, whether that rule is given by a formula, described in words, defined by a table, illustrated by a curve, or expressed by any other means.

Functions are often given letter names, such as f, g, F, or ϕ. If f is a function and x is a number in its domain D, then $f(x)$ denotes the number that the function f assigns to x. The symbol $f(x)$ is pronounced "f of x." It is important to note the difference between f, which is a symbol for the function (the rule), and $f(x)$, which denotes the value of f at x.

If f is a function, we sometimes let y denote the value of f at x, so

$$y = f(x) \qquad [*]$$

Then we call x the **independent variable**, or the **argument** of f, whereas y is called the **dependent variable**, because the value y (in general) depends on the value of x. In economics, x is often called the *exogenous* variable, whereas y is the *endogenous* variable.

A function is often defined by a particular formula of the type [*], such as $y = 8x^2 + 3x + 2$. The function is then the rule that assigns the number $8x^2 + 3x + 2$ to x.

Functional Notation

To become familiar with the relevant notation, it helps to look at some examples of functions that are defined by formulas.

Example 2.1

A function is defined for all numbers by the following rule:

$$\text{Assign to any number the third power of that number.} \qquad [1]$$

This function will assign $0^3 = 0$ to 0, $3^3 = 27$ to 3, $(-2)^3 = -8$ to -2, and $(1/4)^3 = 1/64$ to 1/4. In general, it assigns the number x^3 to the number x. If we denote the function by f, then

$$f(x) = x^3 \qquad [2]$$

So $f(0) = 0^3 = 0$, $f(3) = 3^3 = 27$, $f(-2) = (-2)^3 = -8$, $f(1/4) = (1/4)^3 = 1/64$.

Substituting a for x in the formula for f gives $f(a) = a^3$, whereas

$$f(a + 1) = (a + 1)^3 = (a + 1)(a + 1)(a + 1) = a^3 + 3a^2 + 3a + 1 \qquad [3]$$

Note: A common error is to presume that $f(a) = a^3$ implies $f(a + 1) = a^3 + 1$. The error can be illustrated by looking at a simple interpretation of f. If a is the edge of a cube measured in meters, then $f(a) = a^3$ is the volume of the cube measured in cubic meters. Suppose that each edge of the cube has its length increased by 1 m. Then the volume of the new cube is $f(a + 1) = (a + 1)^3$ cubic meters. The number $a^3 + 1$ can be interpreted as the number obtained when the volume of a cube with edge a is increased by 1 m^3. In fact,

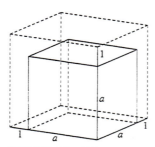

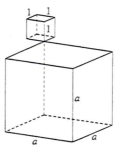

FIGURE 2.3   Volume
$f(a + 1) = (a + 1)^3$.

FIGURE 2.4   Volume
$a^3 + 1$.

$f(a + 1) = (a + 1)^3$ is quite different from $a^3 + 1$, as illustrated in Figs. 2.3 and 2.4.

Example 2.2

The total dollar cost of producing x units of a product is given by

$$C(x) = 100x\sqrt{x} + 500$$

Find the cost of producing 16, 100, and a units. Suppose the firm produces a units; find the *increase* in the cost from producing one additional unit.[1]

Solution   The cost of producing 16 units is found by substituting 16 for x in the formula for $C(x)$:

$$C(16) = 100 \cdot 16\sqrt{16} + 500 = 100 \cdot 16 \cdot 4 + 500 = 6900$$

Similarly,

$$C(100) = 100 \cdot 100 \cdot \sqrt{100} + 500 = 100{,}500$$

$$C(a) = 100a\sqrt{a} + 500$$

The cost of producing $a + 1$ units is $C(a + 1)$, so that the increase in cost is

$$C(a + 1) - C(a) = 100(a + 1)\sqrt{a + 1} + 500 - 100a\sqrt{a} - 500$$
$$= 100\left[(a + 1)\sqrt{a + 1} - a\sqrt{a}\right]$$

---

[1] This is the concept that economists often call **marginal cost.** However, they should really call it **incremental cost.** In Section 4.3, we will explain the difference between the two.

So far we have used x to denote the independent variable, but we could just as well have used almost any other symbol. For example, all of the following formulas define exactly the same function (and hence we can set $f = g = \phi$):

$$f(x) = \frac{x^2 - 3}{x^4 + 1}, \qquad g(t) = \frac{t^2 - 3}{t^4 + 1}, \qquad \phi(\xi) = \frac{\xi^2 - 3}{\xi^4 + 1} \qquad [*]$$

For that matter, we could also express the function in [*] as follows:

$$f(\cdot) = \frac{(\cdot)^2 - 3}{(\cdot)^4 + 1}$$

Here it is understood that the dot between the parentheses can be replaced by an arbitrary number or an arbitrary letter or even another function (like $1/y$). Thus,

$$f(1) = \frac{(1)^2 - 3}{(1)^4 + 1} = -1, \qquad f(k) = \frac{k^2 - 3}{k^4 + 1}, \qquad \text{and} \qquad f(1/y) = \frac{(1/y)^2 - 3}{(1/y)^4 + 1}$$

In economic theory, we often study functions that depend on a number of parameters in addition to the independent variable. A typical example follows.

Example 2.3

Suppose that the cost of producing x units of a commodity is

$$C(x) = Ax\sqrt{x} + B \qquad (A \text{ and } B \text{ are positive constants}) \qquad [1]$$

Find the cost of producing 0, 10, and $x + h$ units.

Solution   The cost of producing 0 units is

$$C(0) = A \cdot 0 \cdot \sqrt{0} + B = 0 + B = B$$

(Parameter B simply represents fixed costs. These are the costs that must be paid whether or not anything is actually produced, such as a taxi driver's annual license fee.) Similarly,

$$C(10) = A \cdot 10\sqrt{10} + B$$

Finally, substituting $x + h$ for x in (1) gives

$$C(x + h) = A(x + h)\sqrt{x + h} + B$$

The Domain and the Range

The definition of a function is incomplete unless its domain has been specified. The domain of the function f defined by $f(x) = x^3$ (see Example 2.1) is the set of all real numbers. In Example 2.2, where $C(x) = 100x\sqrt{x} + 500$ denotes the cost of producing x units of a product, the domain was not specified, but the natural domain is the set of numbers 0, 1, 2, ..., x_0, where x_0 is the maximum number of items the firm can produce. If output x is a continuous variable, the natural domain is the closed interval $[0, x_0]$.

If a function is defined using an algebraic formula, we adopt the convention that the domain consists of all values of the independent variable for which the formula gives a meaningful value (unless another domain is explicitly mentioned).

Example 2.4

Find the domains of

(a)
$$f(x) = \frac{1}{x + 3}$$

(b)
$$g(x) = \sqrt{2x + 4}$$

Solution

(a) For $x = -3$, the formula reduces to the meaningless expression "$1/0$." For all other values of x, the formula makes $f(x)$ a well-defined number. Thus, the domain consists of all numbers $x \neq -3$.

(b) The expression $\sqrt{2x + 4}$ is defined for all x such that $2x + 4$ is nonnegative. Solving the inequality $2x + 4 \geq 0$ for x gives $x \geq -2$. Hence, the domain of g is the interval $[-2, \infty)$.

Let f be a function with domain D. The set of all values $f(x)$ that the function assumes is called the **range** of f. Often, we denote the domain of f by D_f, and the range by R_f. These concepts are illustrated in Fig. 2.5, using the idea of the graph of a function. (Graphs are discussed in the next section, but you probably have been exposed to them before.)

Alternatively, we can think of any function f as an engine operating so that if the number x in the domain is an input, the output is the number $f(x)$. (See Fig. 2.6.) The range of f is then all the numbers we get as output using all numbers x in the domain as inputs. If we try to use as an input a number not in the domain, the engine does not work, and there is no output.

Example 2.5

Show that the number 4 belongs to the range of the function defined by $g(x) = \sqrt{2x + 4}$. Find the entire range of g. (Remember that $\sqrt{u}$ denotes the nonnegative square root of u.)

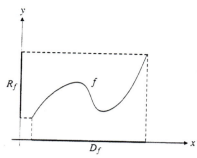

FIGURE 2.5   The domain and the range of f.

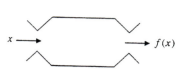

FIGURE 2.6   Function engine.

Solution   To show that a number such as 4 is in the range of g, we must find a number x such that $g(x) = 4$. That is, we must solve the equation $\sqrt{2x + 4} = 4$ for x. By squaring both sides of the equation, we get $2x + 4 = 4^2 = 16$, that is, $x = 6$. Because $g(6) = 4$, the number 4 does belong to the range R_g.

In order to determine the whole range of g, we must answer the question: As x runs through the whole of the interval $[-2, \infty)$, what are all the possible values of $\sqrt{2x + 4}$? For $x = -2$, $\sqrt{2x + 4} = 0$, and $\sqrt{2x + 4}$ can never be negative. We claim that whatever number $y_0 \geq 0$ is chosen, there exists a number x_0 such that $\sqrt{2x_0 + 4} = y_0$. Squaring each side of this last equation gives $2x_0 + 4 = y_0^2$. Hence, $2x_0 = y_0^2 - 4$, which implies that $x_0 = \frac{1}{2}(y_0^2 - 4)$. Because $y_0^2 \geq 0$, we have $x_0 = \frac{1}{2}(y_0^2 - 4) \geq \frac{1}{2}(-4) = -2$. Hence, for every number $y_0 \geq 0$, there is a number $x_0 \geq -2$ such that $g(x_0) = y_0$. The range of g is, therefore, $[0, \infty)$.

Even if we have a function that is completely specified by a formula, including a specific domain, it is not always easy to find the range of the function. For example, without using the methods of differential calculus, it is not at all simple to find R_f when $f(x) = 3x^3 - 2x^2 - 12x - 3$ and $D_f = [-2, 3]$.

Many pocket calculators have some special functions built into them. For example, many have the $\sqrt{\ }$ function that, given a number x, assigns the square root of the number, $\sqrt{x}$. If we enter a nonnegative number such as 25, and press the square-root key, then the number 5 appears. If we enter -3, then the word "Error" is shown, which is the way the calculator tells us that $\sqrt{-3}$ is not defined.

The concept of a function is entirely abstract. In Example 2.2, we studied a function that finds the production cost $C(x)$ in dollars associated with the number of units x of a commodity. Here x and $C(x)$ are concrete, measurable quantities. On the other hand, the letter C, which is the name of the function, does not represent a physical quantity; rather, it represents the dependence of cost upon the number of units produced, a purely abstract concept.

Problems

1. Let $f(x) = x^2 + 1$.
   a. Compute $f(0)$, $f(-1)$, $f(1/2)$, and $f(\sqrt{2})$.
   b. For what x is it true that (i) $f(x) = f(-x)$? (ii) $f(x+1) = f(x)+f(1)$? (iii) $f(2x) = 2f(x)$?

2. Suppose $F(x) = 10$, for all x. Find $F(0)$, $F(-3)$, and $F(a+h) - F(a)$.

3. Let $f(t) = a^2 - (t-a)^2$ (a is a constant).
   a. Compute $f(0)$, $f(a)$, $f(-a)$, and $f(2a)$.
   b. Compute $3f(a) + f(-2a)$.

4. Let f be defined for all x by

$$f(x) = \frac{x}{1+x^2}$$

   a. Compute $f(-1/10)$, $f(0)$, $f(1/\sqrt{2})$, $f(\sqrt{\pi})$, and $f(2)$.
   b. Show that $f(x) = -f(-x)$ for all x, and that $f(1/x) = f(x)$, for $x \neq 0$.

5. The cost of producing x units of a commodity is given by

$$C(x) = 1000 + 300x + x^2$$

   a. Compute $C(0)$, $C(100)$, and $C(101) - C(100)$.
   b. Compute $C(x+1) - C(x)$, and explain in words the meaning of the difference.

6. Let $F(t) = \sqrt{t^2 - 2t + 4}$. Compute $F(0)$, $F(-3)$, and $F(t+1)$.

7. H. Schultz has estimated the demand for cotton in the United States for the period 1915–1919 to be $D(P) = 6.4 - 0.3P$ [with appropriate units for the price P and the quantity $D(P)$].
   a. Find the demand if the price is 8, 10, and 10.22.
   b. If the demand is 3.13, what is the price?

8. The cost of removing $p\%$ of the impurities in a lake is given by

$$b(p) = \frac{10p}{105 - p}$$

   a. Find $b(0)$, $b(50)$, and $b(100)$.
   b. What does $b(50 + h) - b(50)$ mean?   ($h \geq 0$.)

9. a. If $f(x) = 100x^2$, show that for all t, $f(tx) = t^2 f(x)$.
   b. If $P(x) = x^{1/2}$, show that for all $t \geq 0$, $P(tx) = t^{1/2}P(x)$.

10. Only for special "additive" functions is it true that $f(a+b) = f(a) + f(b)$ for all a and b. Determine whether $f(2+1) = f(2) + f(1)$ for the

following:

   a. $f(x) = 2x^2$ **b.** $f(x) = -3x$ **c.** $f(x) = \sqrt{x}$

11. **a.** If $f(x) = Ax$, show that $f(a + b) = f(a) + f(b)$, for all a and b.
     b. If $f(x) = 10^x$, show that $f(a + b) = f(a) \cdot f(b)$, for all natural numbers a and b.

12. A student claims that $(x + 1)^2 = x^2 + 1$. Can you use a geometric argument to show that this is wrong?

13. Find the domains of the functions defined by the following equations:

   a. $y = \sqrt{5 - x}$ **b.** $y = \dfrac{2x - 1}{x^2 - x}$

   c. $y = \sqrt{\dfrac{x - 1}{(x - 2)(x + 3)}}$ **d.** $y = (x + 1)^{1/2} + 1/(x - 1)^{1/2}$

14. Consider the function f defined by the formula

$$f(x) = \frac{3x + 6}{x - 2}$$

   a. Find the domain of f.
   b. Show that the number 5 is in the range of f by finding a number x such that $(3x + 6)/(x - 2) = 5$.
   c. Show that the number 3 is not in the range of f.

15. Find the domain and the range $g(x) = 1 - \sqrt{x + 2}$.

16. Let $f(x) = |x|$. Which of the the following rules are valid for all possible pairs of numbers x and y?

   a. $f(x + y) = f(x) + f(y)$ **b.** $f(x + y) \le f(x) + f(y)$
   c. $f(xy) = f(x) \cdot f(y)$ **d.** $f(2x) = 2f(x)$
   e. $f(-2x) = -2f(x)$ **f.** $f(x) = \sqrt{x^2}$
   g. $f(-2x) = 2f(x)$ **h.** $|f(x) - f(y)| \le |x - y|$

17. Let

$$f(x) = \frac{ax + b}{cx - a}$$

where a, b, and c are constants, and $c \ne 0$. Assuming that $x \ne a/c$, show that

$$f\left(\frac{ax + b}{cx - a}\right) = x$$

2.3 Graphs

Three examples of equations in two variables x and y are

$$y = 2x - 1, \qquad x^2 + y^2 = 16, \qquad x\sqrt{y} = 2 \qquad\qquad [*]$$

In this section, we shall explain how *any* equation in two variables can be represented by a curve (a graph) in a coordinate system. In particular, any function given by an equation $y = f(x)$ has such a representation, that helps us to visualize the equation or the function. This is because the shape of the graph reflects the properties of the equation or the function.

A Coordinate System in the Plane

In Section 1.4, we claimed that real numbers can be represented by a number line. Analogously, every *pair* of real numbers can be represented by a point in a plane. Draw two perpendicular lines, called respectively the *x-axis* (or the *horizontal axis*) and the *y-axis* (or the *vertical axis*). The intersection point O is called the *origin*. We measure the real numbers along each of these lines, as shown in Fig. 2.7. Often, we measure the numbers on the two axes so that the length on the x-axis that represents the distance between x and $x+1$ is the same length as that along the y-axis that represents the distance between y and $y + 1$. But this does not have to be the case.

Figure 2.7 illustrates a **rectangular**, or a **Cartesian, coordinate system**, that we call the **xy-plane**. The coordinate axes separate the plane into four quadrants, which can be numbered as in Fig. 2.7. Any point P in the plane can be represented by a pair (a, b) of real numbers. These can be found by dropping perpendiculars onto the axes. The point represented by (a, b) lies at the intersection of the vertical straight line $x = a$ with the horizontal straight line $y = b$. Conversely, any pair of real numbers represents a unique point in the plane. For example, in Fig. 2.8, the ordered pair $(3, 4)$ corresponds to the point P that lies at the intersection of $x = 3$

FIGURE 2.7   A coordinate system.

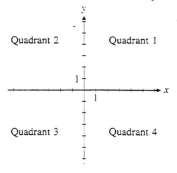

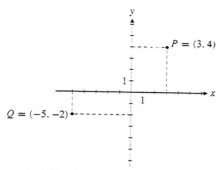

FIGURE 2.8   The points (3, 4) and (−5, −2).

with $y = 4$. Thus, P lies 3 units to the right of the y-axis and 4 units above the x-axis. We call $(3, 4)$ the **coordinates** of P. Similarly, Q lies 5 units to the left of the y-axis and 2 units below the x-axis, so the coordinates of Q are $(−5, −2)$.

Note that we call (a, b) an **ordered pair**, because the order of the two numbers in the pair is important. For instance, $(3, 4)$ and $(4, 3)$ represent two different points.

Example 2.6

Draw coordinate systems and indicate the coordinates (x, y) that satisfy each of the following three conditions:

(a) $x = 3$

(b) $x \geq 0$ and $y \geq 0$

(c) $-2 \leq x \leq 1$ and $-2 \leq y \leq 3$

Solution

(a) See Fig. 2.9, which represents a straight line.

(b) See Fig. 2.10, which represents the first quadrant.

(c) See Fig. 2.11, which represents a rectangle.

FIGURE 2.9 A straight line.

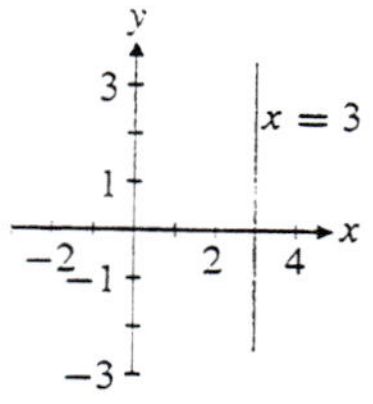

$x = 3$

FIGURE 2.10   The first quadrant.

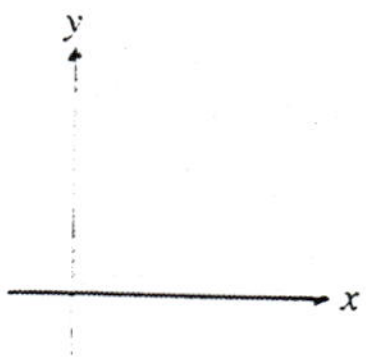

FIGURE 2.11 A rectangle.

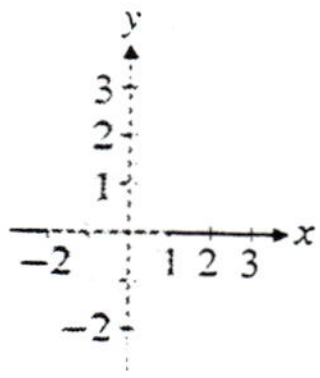

Graphs of Equations in Two Variables

A solution of an equation in two variables x and y is a pair (a, b) that satisfies the equation when we substitute a for x and b for y. The **solution set** of the equation is the set of all possible solutions. If we plot all the ordered pairs of the solution set in a coordinate system, we obtain a curve that is called the **graph** of the equation.

Example 2.7

Find some numerical solutions for each of the equations $y = 2x - 1$, $x^2 + y^2 = 16$, and $x\sqrt{y} = 2$, and try to sketch the graphs.

Solution   For $y = 2x - 1$, point $(0, -1)$ is a solution, because if $x = 0$, then $y = 2 \cdot 0 - 1 = -1$. Other solutions are $(1, 1)$, $(3, 5)$, and $(-1, -3)$. In Fig. 2.12, we have plotted the four solutions, and they all appear to lie on a straight line. There exist infinitely many other solutions, so we can never write them all down.

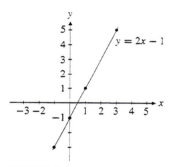

FIGURE 2.12 $y = 2x - 1$.

For $x^2 + y^2 = 16$, point $(4, 0)$ is a solution. Some other solutions are shown in Table 2.2.

TABLE 2.2   *Solutions of $x^2 + y^2 = 16$*

x	-4	-3	-1	0	1	3	4
y	0	$\pm\sqrt{7}$	$\pm\sqrt{15}$	±4	$\pm\sqrt{15}$	$\pm\sqrt{7}$	0

Figure 2.13 shows the plot of the points in the table, and the graph appears to be a circle.

From $x\sqrt{y} = 2$, we obtain $y = 4/x^2$, and it is easy to fill in Table 2.3. The graph is shown in Fig. 2.14.

Note: When plotting the graph of an equation such as $x^2 + y^2 = 16$, we must try to find a sufficient number of solution pairs (x, y), otherwise we might miss some

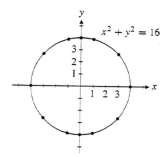

FIGURE 2.13 $x^2 + y^2 = 16.$

TABLE 2.3   *Solutions of* $x\sqrt{y} = 2$

x	1	2	4	6
y	4	1	1/4	1/9

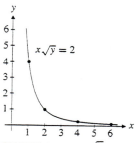

FIGURE 2.14 $x\sqrt{y} = 2.$

important features of the graph. Actually, by merely plotting a finite set of points, we can never be entirely sure that there are no wiggles or bumps we have missed. We shall see in what follows that the graph of the equation $x^2 + y^2 = 16$ really is a circle. For more complicated equations, we have to use differential calculus to decide how many bumps and wiggles there are.

The Distance Between Two Points in the Plane

Let $P_1 = (x_1, y_1)$ and $P_2 = (x_2, y_2)$ be the two points shown in Fig. 2.15. By Pythagoras' theorem, the distance d between these points satisfies the equation

$d^2 = (x_2 - x_1)^2 + (y_2 - y_1)^2$. Therefore, note that because $(x_1 - x_2)^2 = (x_2 - x_1)^2$ and $(y_1 - y_2)^2 = (y_2 - y_1)^2$, it does not make any difference which point is P_1 and which is P_2.

The Distance Formula

The distance between points (x_1, y_1) and (x_2, y_2) is

$$d = \sqrt{(x_1 - x_2)^2 + (y_1 - y_2)^2}$$

[2.2]

To prove the distance formula, we considered two points in the first quadrant. It turns out that the same formula is valid regardless of where the two points, P_1 and P_2, lie.

Example 2.8

Find the distance d between points $P_1 = (-4, 3)$ and $P_2 = (5, -1)$. (See Fig. 2.16.)

Solution   Using [2.2] with $x_1 = -4$, $y_1 = 3$, and $x_2 = 5$, $y_2 = -1$, we have

$$d = \sqrt{(-4 - 5)^2 + (3 - (-1))^2}$$
$$= \sqrt{(-9)^2 + 4^2} = \sqrt{81 + 16} = \sqrt{97} \approx 9.85$$

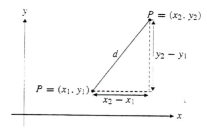

FIGURE 2.15

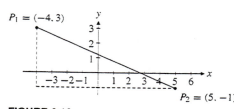

FIGURE 2.16

Circles

Let (a, b) be a point in the plane. *The circle with radius r and center at (a, b) is the set of all points (x, y) whose distance from (a, b) is equal to r.* Considering Fig. 2.17 and using the distance formula gives $\sqrt{(x - a)^2 + (y - b)^2} = r$. Squaring each side yields

---

The Equation of a Circle

The equation of a circle with center at (a, b) and radius r is

$$(x - a)^2 + (y - b)^2 = r^2$$

[2.3]

Note that if we let $a = b = 0$ and $r = 4$, then [2.3] reduces to $x^2 + y^2 = 16$. This is the equation of a circle with center at $(0, 0)$ and radius 4, as shown in Fig. 2.13.

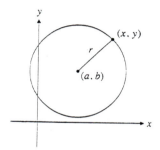

FIGURE 2.17   Circle with center (a, b) and radius r.

Example 2.9

Find the equation of the circle with center $(-4, 1)$ and radius 3.

Solution   Here $a = -4$, $b = 1$, and $r = 3$ (see Fig. 2.18). So the general formula in [2.3] becomes the specific equation

$$(x + 4)^2 + (y - 1)^2 = 9$$

[1]

FIGURE 2.18   Circle with center (-4, 1) and radius 3.

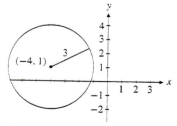

Expanding the squares in [1] gives

$$x^2 + 8x + 16 + y^2 - 2y + 1 = 9 \qquad [2]$$

This can be written as

$$x^2 + y^2 + 8x - 2y + 8 = 0 \qquad [3]$$

Note: The equation of the circle given in [3] has the disadvantage that we cannot immediately read off its center and radius. If we are given equation [3], we can "argue backwards" in order to deduce [1] via [2]. We then say that we have "completed the squares," which is actually one of the oldest tricks in mathematics. (See Section A.8, Appendix A.) The method is illustrated in Problem 9.

Problems

1. Draw a Cartesian coordinate system and plot the points $(2, 3)$, $(-3, 2)$, $(-3/2, 1/4)$, $(4, 0)$, and $(0, 4)$.

2. Sketch the six sets of points (x, y) satisfying the following conditions:
   a. $y = 4$ **b.** $x < 0$ **c.** $x \geq 1$ and $y \geq 2$
   d. $|x| = 2$ **e.** $y = x$ **f.** $y \geq x$

3. Sketch the graphs of each of the following equations:
   a. $y = 4x - 3$ **b.** $xy = 1$ **c.** $y^2 = x$

4. Try to sketch the graphs of each of the following equations:
   a. $x^2 + 2y^2 = 6$ **b.** $y + \sqrt{x - 1} = 0$ **c.** $y^2 - x^2 = 1$

5. Find the distance between each pair of points:
   a. $(1, 3)$ and $(2, 4)$ **b.** $(-1, 2)$ and $(-3, -3)$
   c. $(3/2, -2)$ and $(-5, 1)$ **d.** (x, y) and $(2x, y + 3)$
   e. (a, b) and $(-a, b)$ **f.** $(a, 3)$ and $(2 + a, 5)$

6. The distance between $(2, 4)$ and $(5, y)$ is $\sqrt{13}$. Find y. (Explain geometrically why there must be two values of y. What would happen if the distance were 2?)

7. Find the approximate distance between each pair of points:
   a. $(3.998, 2.114)$ and $(1.130, -2.416)$ **b.** $(\pi, 2\pi)$ and $(-\pi, 1)$

8. Find the equations of the following circles:
   a. Center at $(2, 3)$ and radius 4.
   b. Center at $(2, 5)$ and passes through $(-1, 3)$.

9. We can show that the graph of $x^2 + y^2 + 8x - 2y + 8 = 0$ is a circle by arguing like this: First, rearrange the equation to read $(x^2 + 8x \ldots) +$

$(y^2 - 2y ...) = -8$. Completing the two squares gives $(x^2 + 8x + 4^2) + (y^2 - 2y + (-1)^2) = -8 + 4^2 + (-1)^2 = 9$. Thus, the equation becomes $(x + 4)^2 + (y - 1)^2 = 9$, whose graph is a circle with center $(-4, 1)$ and radius $\sqrt{9} = 3$. Use this method to find the center and the radius of the two circles with equations:

    a. $x^2 + y^2 + 10x - 6y + 30 = 0$ **b.** $3x^2 + 3y^2 + 18x - 24y = -39$

10. Point P moves in the plane so that it is always equidistant from each of the points $A = (3, 2)$ and $B = (5, -4)$. Find a simple equation that the coordinates (x, y) of P must satisfy. Illustrate the problem and its solution geometrically. (*Hint:* Compute the square of the distance from P to A and to B, respectively.)

11. Prove that if the distance from a point (x, y) to the point $(-2, 0)$ is twice the distance from (x, y) to $(4, 0)$, then (x, y) must lie on the circle with center $(6, 0)$ and radius 4.

Harder Problems

12. Try to sketch the graph of the equation $\sqrt{x} + \sqrt{y} = 1$.

13. A firm has two plants A and B located 60 kilometers apart at the two points $(0, 0)$ and $(60, 0)$. See Fig. 2.19. It supplies one identical product priced at $\$p$ per unit. Shipping costs per kilometer per unit are $\$10$ from A and $\$5$ from B. An arbitrary purchaser is located at point (x, y).

    a. Give economic interpretations for the expressions:

$$p + 10\sqrt{x^2 + y^2} \qquad \text{and} \qquad p + 5\sqrt{(x - 60)^2 + y^2}$$

    b. Find the equation for the curve that separates the markets of the two firms, assuming that customers buy from the firm for which total costs are lower.

14. Generalize Problem 13 to the case where $A = (0, 0)$ and $B = (a, 0)$, and assume that shipping costs per kilometer are r and s dollars, respectively. Show that the curve separating the markets is a circle, and find its center and radius.

FIGURE 2.19

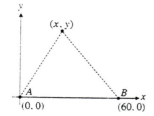

15. Show that the graph of

$$x^2 + y^2 + Ax + By + C = 0 \qquad (A, B, \text{ and } C \text{ are constants})$$

is a circle if $A^2 + B^2 > 4C$. Find its center and radius. (See Problem 9.) What happens if $A^2 + B^2 \leq 4C$?

2.4 Graphs of Functions

The **graph** of a function f is the set of all points $(x, f(x))$, where x belongs to the domain of f. This is simply the graph of the equation $y = f(x)$. Typical examples of graphs of functions are given in Figs. 2.20 and 2.21.

In Fig. 2.20, we show the graph of $f(x) = x^2 - 3x$. It is found by computing points $(x, f(x))$ on the graph and then drawing a smooth curve through the points.

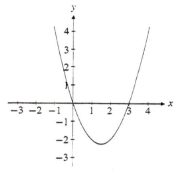

FIGURE 2.20 The graph of $f(x) = x^2 - 3x$.

The function whose graph is shown in Fig. 2.21 is of a type often encountered in economics. It is defined by different formulas on different intervals.

Example 2.10   (U.S. Federal Income Tax (1991) for Single Persons)
In Fig. 2.21, we show the graph of this income tax function. Income up to

FIGURE 2.21   U.S. federal income tax.

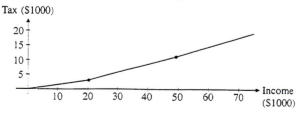

$20,250 was taxed at 15%, income between $20,251 and $49,300 was taxed at 28%, and income above $49,300 was taxed at 31%.

Graphs of different functions can have innumerable different shapes. However, not all curves in the plane are graphs of functions. A function assigns to each point x in the domain only one y-value. *The graph of a function therefore has the property that a vertical line through any point on the x-axis has at most one point of intersection with the graph.* This simple *vertical line test* is illustrated in Figs. 2.22 and 2.23.

The graph of the circle $x^2 + y^2 = 16$, as shown in Fig. 2.13, is a typical example of a graph that does *not* represent a function, because it does not pass the vertical line test. The vertical line $x = a$ for any a with $-4 < a < 4$ intersects the circle at *two* points. When we solve the equation $x^2 + y^2 = 16$ for y, we obtain $y = \pm\sqrt{16 - x^2}$. Note that the upper semicircle alone is the graph of the function $y = \sqrt{16 - x^2}$ and the lower semicircle is the graph of the function $y = -\sqrt{16 - x^2}$. Both these functions are defined on the interval $[-4, 4]$.

Choice of Units

A function of one variable is a rule assigning numbers in its range to numbers in its domain. When we describe an empirical relationship by means of a function, we must first choose the units of measurement. For instance, we might measure

FIGURE 2.22 This graph represents a function.

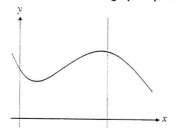

FIGURE 2.23 This graph does not represent a function.

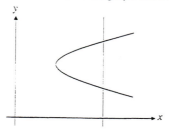

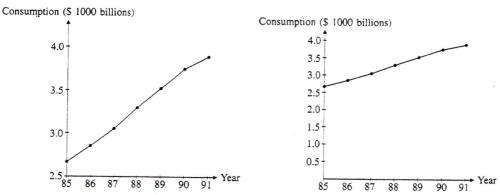

FIGURE 2.24 **Graphical representations of the function defined in Table 2.1 with different units of measurement.**

time in years, days, or weeks. We might measure money in dollars, yen, or francs. The choice we make may influence the visual impression conveyed by the graph of the function.

Figure 2.24 illustrates a standard trick that is often used to influence people's impressions of empirical relationships. In both diagrams, time is measured in years and consumption in billions of dollars. They both graph the same function. (Which graph would you think the Republicans in the United States might prefer for their advertising, and which is more to the liking of the Democrats?)

Shifting Graphs

Given the graph of a function f, it is sometimes useful to know how to find the graphs of the related functions:

$$f(x) + c, \qquad f(x + c), \qquad -f(x), \qquad \text{and} \qquad f(-x) \qquad [2.4]$$

Problem 3 of this section asks you to study these graphs in general. Here we consider a simple economic example.

Example 2.11

Suppose a person earning y (dollars) in a given year pays $f(y)$ (dollars) in income tax. It is decided to reduce taxes. One proposal is to allow all individuals to deduct d dollars from their taxable income before tax is calculated. An alternative proposal involves calculating income tax on the full amount of taxable income and then allowing each person a "tax credit" that deducts d dollars from the total tax due. Illustrate graphically the two proposals for a "normal" tax function f, and mark off the the income y^*, where the two proposals give the same tax.

Solution Figure 2.25 illustrates the solution. First, draw the graph of the original tax function, $T = f(y)$. If taxable income is y and the deduction is

Tax (T)

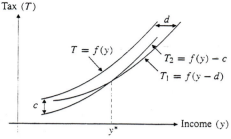

FIGURE 2.25 The graphs of $T_1 = f(y - c)$ and $T_2 = f(y) - d$.

d, then $y-d$ is the reduced taxable income, and so the tax liability is $f(y-d)$. By shifting the graph of the original tax function d units to the right, we obtain the graph of $T_1 = f(y-d)$.[2] The graph of $T_2 = f(y)-c$ is obtained by lowering the graph of $T = f(y)$ by c units. The income y^* that gives the same tax under the two different schemes is the value of y satisfying the equation

$$f(y - d) = f(y) - c$$

This value of y is marked y^* in the figure.

Problems

1. Determine the domain on which each of the following equations defines y as a function of x:

   a. $y = x + 2$ **b.** $y = \pm\sqrt{x}$ **c.** $y = x^4$ **d.** $y^4 = x$

   e. $x^2 - y^2 = 1$ **f.** $y = \dfrac{x}{x - 3}$ **g.** $y^3 = x$ **h.** $x^3 + y^3 = 1$

2. The graph of the function f is given in Fig. 2.26.

FIGURE 2.26

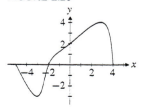

[2]As an example: $y = x^2$ is a parabola. whereas $y = (x - 1)^2$ is a parabola obtained by shifting the first parabola 1 unit to the right.

a. Find $f(-5)$, $f(-3)$, $f(-2)$, $f(0)$, $f(3)$, and $f(4)$ by examining the graph.

b. Find the domain and the range of f.

3. Explain how to get the graphs of the four functions defined by [2.4] based on the graph of $y = f(x)$.

4. Use the rules obtained in Problem 3 to sketch the graphs of the following:

a. $y = x^2 + 1$ **b.** $y = (x + 3)^2$

c. $y = 3 - (x + 1)^2$ **d.** $y = 2 - (x + 2)^{-2}$

2.5 Linear Functions

A *linear relationship* between the variables x and y takes the form

$$y = ax + b \qquad (a \text{ and } b \text{ are constants})$$

The graph of the equation is a straight line. If we let f denote the function that assigns y to x, then $f(x) = ax + b$, and f is called a **linear** function.[3] The number a is called the **slope** of the function and of the line. Take an arbitrary value of x. Then $f(x+1) - f(x) = a(x+1) + b - ax - b = a$. This shows that the slope a measures the change in the value of the function when x increases by 1 unit.

If the slope a is positive, the line slants upward to the right, and the larger the value of a, the steeper is the line. On the other hand, if a is negative, then the line slants downward to the right, and the absolute value of a measures the steepness of the line. For example, when $a = -3$, the steepness is 3. In the special case when $a = 0$, then $y = ax + b = b$ for all x, and the line is parallel to the x-axis. The three cases are illustrated in Figs. 2.27 to 2.29. If $x = 0$, then $y = ax + b = b$, and b is called the y-**intercept** (or often just the intercept).

FIGURE 2.27

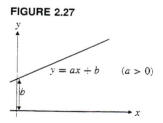

$y = ax + b \qquad (a > 0)$

FIGURE 2.28

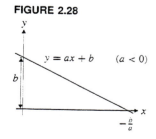

$y = ax + b \qquad (a < 0)$

[3] Actually, mathematicians usually reserve the term "linear" for the functions defined by $y = ax$ (with the y-intercept $b = 0$). They call $y = ax + b$ with $b \neq 0$ an "affine" function. Most economists call $f(x) = ax + b$ a linear function.

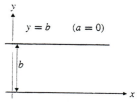

FIGURE 2.29

Example 2.12

Find and interpret the slopes of the following straight lines:

(a)
$$C = 55.73x + 182,100,000$$

which is the estimated cost function for the U.S. Steel Corp. over the period 1917–1938 (C is the total cost in dollars per year, and x is the production of steel in tons per year).

(b)
$$q = -0.15p + 0.14$$

which is the estimated annual demand function for rice in India for the period 1949–1964 (p is the price, and q is consumption per person).

Solution

(a) The slope is 55.73, which means that if production increases by 1 ton, then the cost *increases* by $55.73.
(b) The slope is -0.15, which tells us that if the price increases by 1 unit, then the quantity demanded *decreases* by 0.15 unit.

Finding the Slope

Consider an arbitrary, nonvertical (straight) line in the plane. Pick two distinct points on the line, $P = (x_1, y_1)$ and $Q = (x_2, y_2)$, as shown in Fig. 2.30. Because the line is not vertical and because P and Q are distinct, $x_1 \neq x_2$. The slope of the line is the ratio $(y_2 - y_1)/(x_2 - x_1)$. If we denote the slope by a, then the following holds.

The **slope of a straight line** l is

$$a = \frac{y_2 - y_1}{x_2 - x_1}, \qquad x_1 \neq x_2 \qquad\qquad [2.5]$$

where (x_1, y_1) and (x_2, y_2) are any two distinct points on l.

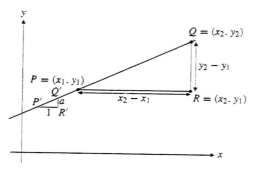

FIGURE 2.30   Slope $a = (y_2 - y_1)/(x_2 - x_1)$.

Multiplying both the numerator and the denominator of the fraction in [2.5] by -1, we obtain the fraction $(y_1 - y_2)/(x_1 - x_2)$. This shows that it does not make any difference which point is P and which is Q. Moreover, using the properties of similar triangles, we see by studying the two triangles PQR and $P'Q'R'$ in Fig. 2.30 that the number a in [2.5] is equal to the change in the value of y when x increases by 1 unit.

Example 2.13

Determine the slopes of the three straight lines l, m, and n in Figs. 2.31–2.33 using [2.5].

Solution   The lines l, m, and n all pass through $P = (2, 2)$. In Fig. 2.31, Q is $(4, 3)$. In Fig. 2.32, Q is $(1, -2)$. And in Fig. 2.33, Q is $(5, -1)$. Therefore, the respective slopes of the lines l, m, and n are

$$a_l = \frac{3-2}{4-2} = \frac{1}{2}, \qquad a_m = \frac{-2-2}{1-2} = 4, \qquad a_n = \frac{-1-2}{5-2} = -1$$

The following example illustrates a problem that is important in differential calculus, as will be seen in Chapter 4.

FIGURE 2.31   The line l.

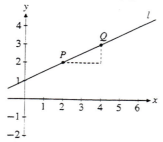

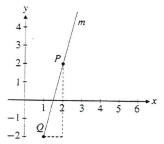

FIGURE 2.32   The line *m*.

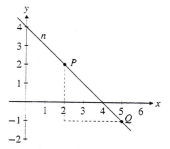

FIGURE 2.33   The line *n*.

Example 2.14

Find an expression for the slope of the line through the two points (x_0, x_0^2) and $\left(x_0 + h, (x_0 + h)^2\right)$, where $h \neq 0$.

Solution   Apply formula [2.5] with $(x_1, y_1) = (x_0, x_0^2)$ and $(x_2, y_2) = \left(x_0 + h, (x_0 + h)^2\right)$ to obtain

$$a = \frac{(x_0 + h)^2 - x_0^2}{x_0 + h - x_0} = \frac{x_0^2 + 2x_0 h + h^2 - x_0^2}{h} = \frac{2x_0 h + h^2}{h} = 2x_0 + h$$

The Point–Slope and Point–Point Formulas

Let us find the equation of a straight line l passing through point $P = (x_1, y_1)$ with slope a. If (x, y) is any other point on the line, the slope a is given by formula [2.5]:

$$\frac{y - y_1}{x - x_1} = a$$

Multiplying each side by $x - x_1$, we obtain $y - y_1 = a(x - x_1)$. Hence:

Point–Slope Formula of a Straight Line

The equation of the straight line passing through (x_1, y_1) with slope a is

$$y - y_1 = a(x - x_1) \qquad\qquad [2.6]$$

Note that when using equation [2.6], x_1 and y_1 are fixed numbers giving the coordinates of the fixed point. On the other hand, x and y are variables denoting an arbitrary point on the line.

Example 2.15

Find the equation of the line through $(-2, 3)$ with slope -4. Then find the point at which this line intersects the x-axis.

Solution   The point–slope formula with $(x_1, y_1) = (-2, 3)$ and $a = -4$
gives

$$y - 3 = (-4)[x - (-2)] \quad \text{or} \quad y - 3 = -4(x + 2) \tag{1}$$

The line intersects the x-axis at the point where $y = 0$, that is, where $0 - 3 = -4(x + 2)$ or $-3 = -4x - 8$. Solving for x, we get $x = -5/4$, so the point of intersection with the x-axis is $(-5/4, 0)$.

Often we need to find the equation of a straight line that passes through two given points. Combining [2.5] with [2.6], we obtain the following formula:

Point–Point Formula of a Straight Line

The equation of the straight line passing through (x_1, y_1) and (x_2, y_2), where $x_1 \neq x_2$, is obtained as follows:

1. Compute the slope of the line:

$$a = \frac{y_2 - y_1}{x_2 - x_1}$$

2. Substitute the expression for a into the point–slope formula $y - y_1 = a(x - x_1)$. The result is

$$y - y_1 = \frac{y_2 - y_1}{x_2 - x_1}(x - x_1) \tag{2.7}$$

Example 2.16
Find the equation of the line passing through $(-1, 3)$ and $(5, -2)$.

Solution   Let $(x_1, y_1) = (-1, 3)$ and $(x_2, y_2) = (5, -2)$. Then the point–point formula gives

$$y - 3 = \frac{-2 - 3}{5 - (-1)}[x - (-1)] \quad \text{or} \quad y - 3 = -\frac{5}{6}(x + 1)$$

$$\text{or} \quad 5x + 6y = 13$$

Linear Models

Linear relations occur frequently in applied models. The relationship between the Celsius and Fahrenheit temperature scales is an example of an exact linear relation between two variables. Most of the linear models in economics are approximations to more complicated models. Two typical relations are those shown in Example 2.12. Statistical methods have been devised to construct linear functions that approximate the actual data as closely as possible. Let us consider a very naïve attempt to construct a linear model based on some data.

Example 2.17

In a United Nations report, the European population in 1960 was estimated as 641 million, and in 1970 the estimate was 705 million. Use these estimates to construct a linear function of t that approximates the population in Europe (in millions), where t is the number of years from 1960 ($t = 0$ is 1960, $t = 1$ is 1961, and so on). Make use of the equation to estimate the population in 1975 and in 2000. How do you estimate the population in 1930 on the basis of this linear relationship?

Solution If P denotes the population in millions, we construct an equation of the form $P = at + b$. We know that the graph must pass through the points $(t_1, P_1) = (0, 641)$ and $(t_2, P_2) = (10, 705)$. Using the formula in [2.7], replacing x and y with t and P, respectively, we obtain

$$P - 641 = \frac{705 - 641}{10 - 0}(t - 0) = \frac{64}{10}t$$

or

$$P = 6.4t + 641 \qquad [1]$$

In Table 2.4, we have compared our estimates with UN forecasts. Note that because $t = 0$ corresponds to 1960, $t = -30$ will correspond to 1930.

Note that the slope of line [1] is 6.4. This means that if the European population had developed according to [1], then the annual increase in the population would have been constant and equal to 6.4 million.

Actually, Europe's population grew unusually fast during the 1960s. Of course, it grew unusually slowly when millions died during the war years 1939–1945. We see that formula [1] does not give very good results compared to the UN estimates. (For a better way to model population growth, see Example 3.12 in Section 3.5.)

Example 2.18 (The Consumption Function)

In Keynesian macroeconomic theory, total consumption expenditure on goods and services, C, is assumed to be a function of national income

TABLE 2.4 *Population estimates for Europe*

Year	1930	1975	2000
t	−30	15	40
UN estimates	573	728	854
Formula [1] gives	449	737	897

Y, with

$$C = f(Y) \qquad\qquad [2.8]$$

In many models, the consumption function is assumed to be linear, so that

$$C = a + bY$$

The slope b is called the **marginal propensity to consume.** If C and Y are measured in millions of dollars, the number b tells us by how many millions of dollars consumption increases if the national income increases by 1 million dollars. The number b will usually lie between 0 and 1.

In a study of the U.S. economy for the period 1929–1941, T. Haavelmo found the following consumption function:

$$C = 95.05 + 0.712\,Y$$

Here, the marginal propensity to consume is equal to 0.712.

Example 2.19

Some other economic examples of linear functions are the following demand and supply schedules:

$$D = a - bP$$
$$S = \alpha + \beta P$$

Here a and b (both positive) are parameters of the demand function D, while α and β (both positive) are parameters of the supply function. Such functions play an important role in quantitative economics. It is often the case that the market for a particular commodity, such as a specific brand of $3\frac{1}{2}$-inch computer diskettes, can be represented approximately by linear demand and supply functions. The equilibrium price P^e must equate demand and supply, so that $D = S$ at $P = P^e$. Thus,

$$a - bP^e = \alpha + \beta P^e$$

Adding $bP^e - \alpha$ to each side gives

$$a - bP^e + bP^e - \alpha = \alpha + \beta P^e + bP^e - \alpha$$

Thus, $a - \alpha = (\beta + b)P^e$. The corresponding equilibrium quantity is $Q^e = a - bP^e$. Hence, equilibrium occurs when

$$P^e = \frac{a - \alpha}{\beta + b}, \qquad Q^e = a - b\frac{a - \alpha}{\beta + b} = \frac{a\beta + \alpha b}{\beta + b}$$

If the four parameters, a, b, α, and β, were all known, then the model would be complete and the equilibrium price and quantity could be predicted. Suppose that there is a later shift in the supply or demand function—for instance, suppose supply increases so that S becomes $\tilde{\alpha} + \beta P$, where $\tilde{\alpha} > \alpha$. Then we could predict that the new equilibrium price and quantity would be

$$\tilde{P}^e = \frac{a - \tilde{\alpha}}{\beta + b}, \qquad \tilde{Q}^e = \frac{a\beta + \tilde{\alpha}b}{\beta + b}$$

Here $\tilde{P}^e$ is less than P^e, whereas $\tilde{Q}^e$ is greater than Q^e. In fact,

$$\tilde{P}^e - P^e = \frac{\alpha - \tilde{\alpha}}{\beta + b} \qquad \text{and} \qquad \tilde{Q}^e - Q^e = \frac{(\tilde{\alpha} - \alpha)b}{\beta + b} = -b(\tilde{P}^e - P^e)$$

This is in accord with Fig. 2.34. The rightward shift in the supply curve from S to $\tilde{S}$ moves the equilibrium down and to the right along the unchanged demand curve.

A peculiarity of Fig. 2.34 is that, although quantity is a function of price, here we measure price on the vertical axis and quantity on the horizontal axis. This has been standard practice in elementary price theory since the work of Alfred Marshall late in the nineteenth century.

The trouble with this method of analysis comes when the parameters are not known, so the supply and demand curves cannot be drawn with any certainty. Indeed, if all an economist observes is a decrease in price and an increase in quantity from (P^e, Q^e) to $(\tilde{P}^e, \tilde{Q}^e)$, there is no way of knowing (without more information) whether this results from just a rightward shift in the supply curve, as illustrated in Fig. 2.34, or from some combination of a shift to the right (or left) in demand *and* a shift to

FIGURE 2.34

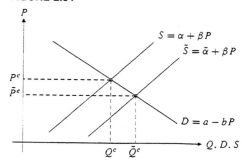

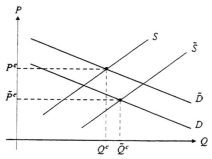

FIGURE 2.35

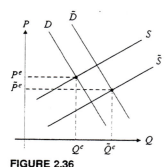

FIGURE 2.36

the right in supply, as illustrated in Figs. 2.35 and 2.36. All that can be said is that, because the equilibrium price falls and the quantity increases, there must have been some rightward shift in supply—but demand could have fallen, risen, or stayed the same. Moreover, there is also the possibility that the demand and supply curves could have changed their slopes—that is, the parameters b and β could also have changed.

The General Equation for a Straight Line

Any nonvertical line in the plane has the equation $y = ax + b$. A vertical line, that is parallel to the y-axis, will intersect the x-axis at some point $(c, 0)$. Every point on the line has the same x-coordinate c, so the line must be

$$x = c$$

This is the equation for a straight line through $(c, 0)$ parallel to the y-axis.
The equations $y = ax + b$ and $x = c$ can both be written as

$$Ax + By + C = 0 \qquad\qquad [2.9]$$

for suitable values of the constants A, B, and C. Specifically, $y = ax + b$ corresponds to $A = a$, $B = -1$, and $C = b$, whereas $x = c$ corresponds to $A = 1$, $B = 0$. and $C = -c$. Conversely, every equation of the form [2.9] represents a straight line in the plane, disregarding the uninteresting case when $A = B = 0$. If $B = 0$. it follows from [2.9] that $Ax = -C$, or $x = -C/A$. This is the equation for a straight line parallel to the y-axis. On the other hand, if $B \neq 0$, solving [2.9] for y yields

$$y = -\frac{A}{B}x - \frac{C}{B}$$

This is the equation for a straight line with slope $-A/B$. Equation [2.9] thus deserves to be called the *general equation for a straight line in the plane*.

Graphical Solutions of Linear Equations

Section A.9 of Appendix A deals with algebraic methods for solving a system of linear equations in two unknowns. The equations are linear, so their graphs are straight lines. The coordinates of any point on a line satisfy the equation of that line. Thus, the coordinates of any point of intersection of these lines will satisfy both equations. This means that a point of intersection solves the system.

Example 2.20

Solve each of the following three pairs of equations graphically:

(a) $x + y = 5$ and $x - y = -1$
(b) $3x + y = -7$ and $x - 4y = 2$
(c) $3x + 4y = 2$ and $6x + 8y = 24$

Solution

(a) Figure 2.37 shows the graphs of the straight lines $x + y = 5$ and $x - y = -1$. There is only one point of intersection $(2, 3)$. The solution of the system is, therefore. $x = 2$, $y = 3$.

FIGURE 2.37

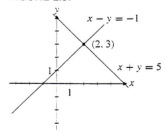

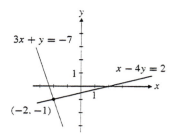

$3x + y = -7$

$x - 4y = 2$

$(-2, -1)$

FIGURE 2.38

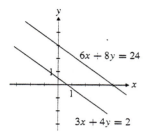

$6x + 8y = 24$

$3x + 4y = 2$

FIGURE 2.39

(b) Figure 2.38 shows the graphs of the straight lines $3x + y = -7$ and $x - 4y = 2$. There is only one point of intersection $(-2, -1)$. The solution of the system is, therefore, $x = -2$, $y = -1$.

(c) Figure 2.39 shows the graphs of the straight lines $3x + 4y = 2$ and $6x + 8y = 24$. These lines are parallel and have no point of intersection. The system has no solutions.

Linear Inequalities

This chapter concludes by discussing how to represent linear inequalities geometrically. Consider two examples.

Example 2.21

Sketch in the xy-plane the set of all pairs of numbers (x, y) that satisfy the inequality $2x + y \leq 4$. (Using set notation, this is $\{(x, y) : 2x + y \leq 4\}$.)

Solution   The inequality can be written as $y \leq -2x + 4$. The set of points (x, y) that satisfy the equation $y = -2x + 4$ is a straight line. Therefore, the set of points (x, y) that satisfy the inequality $y \leq -2x + 4$ must have y-values below those of points on the line $y = -2x + 4$. So it must consist of all points that lie on or below this straight line. See Fig. 2.40.

Example 2.22

A person has $\$m$ to spend on the purchase of two commodities. The prices of the two commodities are $\$p$ and $\$q$ per unit. Suppose x units of the first

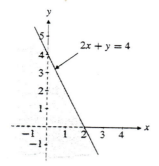

FIGURE 2.40 $\{(x, y) : 2x + y \leq 4\}$.

commodity and y units of the second commodity are bought. Assuming one cannot purchase negative units of x and y, the *budget set* is

$$B = \{(x, y) : \ px + qy \leq m, \ x \geq 0, \ y \geq 0\}$$

as in (1.7) in Section 1.7. Sketch the budget set B in the xy-plane. Find the slope of the budget line $px + qy = m$, and its points of intersection with the two coordinate axes.

Solution   The set of points (x, y) that satisfy $x \geq 0$ and $y \geq 0$ was sketched in Fig. 2.10. It is the first (nonnegative) quadrant. If we impose the additional requirement that $px + qy \leq m$, we obtain the triangular domain B shown in Fig. 2.41.

If we solve $px + qy = m$ for y, we get $y = (-p/q)x + m/q$, so the slope is $-p/q$. The budget line intersects the x-axis when $y = 0$. Then $px = m$, so $x = m/p$. The budget line intersects the y-axis when $x = 0$. Then $qy = m$, so $y = m/q$. So the two points of intersection are $(m/p, 0)$ and $(0, m/q)$, as shown in Fig. 2.41.

FIGURE 2.41   Budget set: $px + qy \leq m$, $x \geq 0$, and $y \geq 0$.

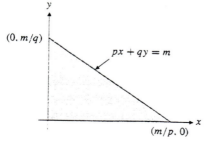

Problems

1. Find the slopes of the lines passing through the following points by using the formula in [2.5].

   a. $(2, 3)$ and $(5, 8)$ **b.** $(-1, -3)$ and $(2, -5)$ **c.** $\left(\frac{1}{2}, \frac{3}{2}\right)$ and $\left(\frac{1}{3}, -\frac{1}{5}\right)$

2. The consumption function $C = 4141 + 0.78\,Y$ for the UK was estimated for the period 1949–1975. What is the marginal propensity to consume?

3. Find the slopes of the five lines L_1 to L_5 shown in Fig. 2.42, and give equations describing them. (L_3 is horizontal.)

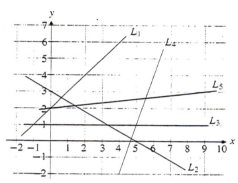

FIGURE 2.42

4. Draw graphs for the following equations:

   a. $3x + 4y = 12$ **b.** $\dfrac{x}{10} - \dfrac{y}{5} = 1$ **c.** $x = 3$

5. Decide which of the following relationships are linear:

   a. $5y + 2x = 2$ **b.** $P = 10(1 - 0.3t)$ **c.** $C = (0.5x + 2)(x - 3)$

   d. $p_1 x_1 + p_2 x_2 = R$ (p_1, p_2, and R constants)

6. **a.** Determine the relationship between Centigrade and Fahrenheit temperature scales when you know that (i) the relation is linear; (ii) water freezes at $0°C$ and $32°F$; and (iii) water boils at $100°C$ and $212°F$.

   b. Which temperature is measured by the same number in both Centigrade and Fahrenheit scales?

7. Determine the equations and draw graphs for the following straight lines:

   a. L_1 passes through $(1, 3)$ and has a slope of 2.

   b. L_2 passes through $(-2, 2)$ and $(3, 3)$.

   c. L_3 passes through the origin and has a slope of $-1/2$.

   d. L_4 passes through $(a, 0)$ and $(0, b)$ (suppose $a \neq 0$).

8. A line L passes through the point $(1, 1)$ and has a slope of 3. A second line M passes through $(-1, 2)$ and $(3, -1)$. Find the equations for L and M

and their point of intersection, P. Also determine the equation for the line N that passes through $(-1, -1)$ and is parallel to M. Draw the figure.

9. The total cost y of producing x units of some commodity is a linear function. Records show that on one occasion, 100 units were made at a total cost of \$200, and on another occasion, 150 units were made at a total cost of \$275. Express the linear equation for total cost in terms of the number of units x produced.

10. Find the equilibrium price in the model in Example 2.19 for the following.
    a. $D = 75 - 3P$, $S = 20 + 2P$ **b.** $D = 100 - 0.5P$, $S = 10 + 0.5P$

11. According to 20th report of the International Commission on Whaling, the number N of fin whales in the Antarctic for the period 1958–1963 was given by

$$N = -17,400t + 151,000, \qquad 0 \le t \le 5$$

   where $t = 0$ corresponds to January 1958, $t = 1$ corresponds to January 1959, and so on.
    a. According to this equation, how many fin whales would there be left in April 1960?
    b. If the decrease continued at the same rate, when would there be no fin whales left? (Actually, the 1993 estimate was approximately 21,000.)

12. The expenditure of a household on consumer goods, C, is related to the household's income, y, in the following way: When the household's income is \$1000, the expenditure on consumer goods is \$900, and whenever income is increased by \$100, the expenditure on consumer goods is increased by \$80. Express the expenditure on consumer goods as a function of income, assuming a linear relationship.

13. Solve the following three systems of equations graphically:
    a. $x - y = 5$ and $x + y = 1$
    b. $x + y = 2$, $x - 2y = 2$ and $x - y = 2$
    c. $3x + 4y = 1$ and $6x + 8y = 6$

14. Show that $-1/[x_0(x_0 + h)]$ is the slope of the line passing through P and Q in Fig. 2.43.

15. The following table shows the total consumption and net national income in some country for the period from 1955–1960, measured in millions of dollars. Plot the points from the table in the YC-plane. Draw the straight line through the "extreme points" (21.3, 17.4) and (24.7, 20.4). Find the equation for this line. What is the interpretation of its slope?

Year	1955	1956	1957	1958	1959	1960
Total consumption (C)	17.4	18.0	18.4	18.6	19.3	20.4
Net national product (Y)	21.3	22.4	23.0	22.6	23.4	24.7

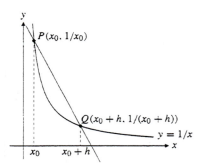

FIGURE 2.43

16. Sketch in the xy-plane the set of all pairs of numbers (x, y) that satisfy the following inequalities:

   a. $2x + 4y \geq 5$ **b.** $x - 3y + 2 \leq 0$ **c.** $100x + 200y \leq 300$

17. Sketch in the xy-plane the set of all pairs of numbers (x, y) that satisfy all the following three inequalities: $3x + 4y \leq 12$; $x - y \leq 1$; and $3x + y \geq 3$.

3

Polynomials, Powers, and Exponentials

The paradox is now fully established that the utmost abstractions are the true weapons with which to control our thought of concrete facts.
—A. N. Whitehead

The linear functions and associated linear models that were studied in some detail in the previous chapter are particularly simple. Not surprisingly, most economic applications require much more accuracy than is possible with only linear functions, and so economists most often use more complicated functions.

3.1 Quadratic Functions

Many economic models involve functions that either decrease down to some minimum value and then increase, or else increase up to some maximum value and then decrease. Simple functions with this property are the general **quadratic** functions

$$f(x) = ax^2 + bx + c \qquad (a, b, \text{ and are } c \text{ constants, } a \neq 0) \qquad [3.1]$$

(If $a = 0$, the function is linear, hence, the restriction $a \neq 0$.) Figure 2.20 of Section 2.4 shows the graph of $f(x) = x^2 - 3x$, which is obtained from [3.1] by choosing $a = 1$, $b = -3$, and $c = 0$. In general, the graph of $f(x) = ax^2 + bx + c$ is called a **parabola**. The shape of this parabola roughly

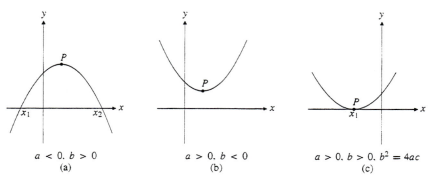

$$a < 0, b > 0 \qquad\qquad a > 0, b < 0 \qquad\qquad a > 0, b > 0, b^2 = 4ac$$
$$\text{(a)} \qquad\qquad\qquad \text{(b)} \qquad\qquad\qquad \text{(c)}$$

FIGURE 3.1   Graphs of the parabola $y = ax^2 + bx + c$.

resembles ∩ when $a < 0$ and ∪ when $a > 0$. Three typical cases are illustrated in Fig. 3.1.

In order to understand the function $f(x) = ax^2 + bx + c$ in more detail, we are interested in the answers to the following questions:

1. For what values of x (if any) is $ax^2 + bx + c = 0$?
2. What are the coordinates of the maximum/minimum point P?

In the case of question 1, we have to find solutions to the equation $f(x) = 0$. Geometrically, this involves determining points of intersection of the parabola with the x-axis. These points are called the **zeros** of the quadratic function. In Fig. 3.1(a), the zeros are given by x_1 and x_2, in Fig. 3.1(b) there are no zeros, whereas the graph in Fig. 3.1(c) has x_1 as its only point of intersection with the x-axis. In Section A.8 of Appendix A it is proved that, in the case when $b^2 \geq 4ac$ and $a \neq 0$, then

$$ax^2 + bx + c = 0 \iff x = \frac{-b \pm \sqrt{b^2 - 4ac}}{2a} \qquad\qquad [3.2]$$

To derive this formula, we used the method known as "completing the square." This technique will also help us answer question 2. In fact, when $a \neq 0$, the function defined by [3.1] can be expressed as

$$f(x) = a\left[x^2 + 2\left(\frac{b}{2a}\right)x + \left(\frac{b}{2a}\right)^2\right] - a\left(\frac{b}{2a}\right)^2 + c = a\left(x + \frac{b}{2a}\right)^2 - \frac{b^2 - 4ac}{4a}$$
$$[3.3]$$

Consider the expression after the second equality sign of [3.3]. When x varies, only the value of $a(x + b/2a)^2$ changes. This term is equal to 0 when $x = -b/2a$, and if $a > 0$, it is never less than 0. This means that when $a > 0$, then the function $f(x)$ attains its minimum when $x = -b/2a$, and the value of $f(x)$ is then equal to $f(-b/2a) = -(b^2 - 4ac)/4a = c - b^2/4a$. If $a < 0$ on the other hand, then $a(x + b/2a)^2 \leq 0$ for all x, and the squared term is equal to 0 when $x = -b/2a$. Hence, $f(x)$ attains its maximum when $x = -b/2a$ in this second case. To summarize, we have shown the following:

If $a > 0$, then $f(x) = ax^2 + bx + c$ has a **minimum** at

$$\left(-\frac{b}{2a}, \ c - \frac{b^2}{4a}\right)$$

If $a < 0$, then $f(x) = ax^2 + bx + c$ has a **maximum** at

$$\left(-\frac{b}{2a}, \ c - \frac{b^2}{4a}\right)$$

[3.4]

If you find it difficult to follow the argument leading up to [3.4], you should study the following special examples very carefully.

Example 3.1

Complete the square as in [3.3] for the following functions and then find the maximum/minimum point of each:

(a) $f(x) = x^2 - 4x + 3$
(b) $f(x) = -2x^2 + 40x - 600$
(c) $f(x) = \frac{1}{3}x^2 + \frac{2}{3}x - \frac{8}{3}$

Solution

(a) $x^2 - 4x + 3 = (x^2 - 4x) + 3 = (x^2 - 4x + 4) - 4 + 3 = (x - 2)^2 - 1$

The expression $(x - 2)^2 - 1$ attains its smallest value, which is -1, at $x = 2$.

(b) $-2x^2 + 40x - 600 = -2(x^2 - 20x) - 600$
$$= -2(x^2 - 20x + 100) + 200 - 600$$
$$= -2(x - 10)^2 - 400$$

The expression $-2(x - 10)^2 - 400$ attains its largest value, which is -400, at $x = 10$.

$$\textbf{(c)} \quad \tfrac{1}{3}x^2 + \tfrac{2}{3}x - \tfrac{8}{3} = \tfrac{1}{3}(x^2 + 2x) - \tfrac{8}{3}$$
$$= \tfrac{1}{3}(x^2 + 2x + 1) - \tfrac{1}{3} - \tfrac{8}{3}$$
$$= \tfrac{1}{3}(x + 1)^2 - 3$$

The expression $\tfrac{1}{3}(x + 1)^2 - 3$ attains its smallest value, which is -3, at $x = -1$.

A useful exercise is to solve the three cases in Example 3.1 by using the expressions set out in [3.4] directly, substituting appropriate values for the three parameters a, b, and c. You should then check that the same results are obtained.

Problems

1. **a.** Let $f(x) = x^2 - 4x$. Complete the following table:

x	-1	0	1	2	3	4	5
$f(x)$							

   b. Using the table in part (a), sketch the graph of f.
   c. Using [3.3], determine the minimum point.
   d. Solve the equation $f(x) = 0$.

2. **a.** Let $f(x) = -\tfrac{1}{2}x^2 - x + \tfrac{3}{2}$. Complete the following table:

x	-4	-3	-2	-1	0	1	2
$f(x)$							

   b. Use the information in part (a) to sketch the graph of f.
   c. Using [3.3], determine the maximum point.
   d. Solve the equation $-\tfrac{1}{2}x^2 - x + \tfrac{3}{2} = 0$ for x.
   e. Show that $f(x) = -\tfrac{1}{2}(x - 1)(x + 3)$, and use this to study how the sign of f varies with x. Compare the result with the graph.

3. Complete the squares as in [3.3] for the following quadratic functions, and then determine the maximum/minimum points:

   a. $x^2 + 4x$ **b.** $x^2 + 6x + 18$ **c.** $-3x^2 + 30x - 30$
   d. $9x^2 - 6x - 44$ **e.** $-x^2 - 200x + 30{,}000$ **f.** $x^2 + 100x - 20{,}000$

4. Find the zeros of each quadratic function in Problem 3, and write each function in the form $a(x - x_1)(x - x_2)$ (if possible).

5. Use the formula in [3.2] to find solutions to the following equations, where p and q are positive parameters.

   a. $x^2 - 3px + 2p^2 = 0$ b. $x^2 - (p+q)x + pq = 0$

   c. $x^2 + px + q = 0$

6. A person is given a rope of length L with which to enclose a rectangular area.

   a. If one of the sides is x, show that the area of the enclosure is $A(x) = Lx/2 - x^2$, where $0 \le x \le L/2$. Find x such that the area of the rectangle is maximized.

   b. Will a circle of circumference L enclose an area that is larger than the one we found in part (a)? (It is reported that certain surveyors in antiquity wrote contracts with farmers to sell them rectangular pieces of land in which only the circumference was specified. As a result, the lots were long narrow rectangles.)

7. Consider the function given by the formula $A = 500x - x^2$ in Example 1.1 of Section 1.3. What choice of x gives the largest value for the area A?

8. a. Solve $x^4 - 5x^2 + 4 = 0$. (*Hint:* Put $x^2 = u$ and form a quadratic equation in u.)

   b. Solve the equations (i) $x^4 - 8x^2 - 9 = 0$ and (ii) $x^6 - 9x^3 + 8 = 0$.

9. A model occurring in the theory of efficient loan markets involves the function

$$U(x) = 72 - (4+x)^2 - (4 - rx)^2$$

where r is a constant. Find the value of x for which $U(x)$ attains its largest value.

10. Find the equation for the parabola $y = ax^2 + bx + c$ that passes through the three points $(1, -3)$, $(0, -6)$, and $(3, 15)$. (*Hint:* Determine a, b, and c.)

Harder Problems

11. The graph of a function f is said to be *symmetric* about the line $x = p$ if

$$f(p - t) = f(p + t) \qquad \text{(for all } t)$$

Show that the parabola $f(x) = ax^2 + bx + c$ is symmetric about the line $x = -b/2a$. (*Hint:* Use [3.3].)

12. Let $a_1, a_2, \ldots, a_n$ and $b_1, b_2, \ldots, b_n$ be arbitrary real numbers. We claim that the following inequality (called the **Cauchy–Schwarz inequality**) is always valid:

$$(a_1 b_1 + a_2 b_2 + \cdots + a_n b_n)^2 \le (a_1^2 + a_2^2 + \cdots + a_n^2)(b_1^2 + b_2^2 + \cdots + b_n^2) \qquad [3.5]$$

a. Check the inequality for (i) $a_1 = 1$, $a_2 = 3$, $b_1 = 2$, and $b_2 = 5$; and for (ii) $a_1 = -3$, $a_2 = 2$, $b_1 = 5$, and $b_2 = -2$. (In both cases, $n = 2$.)

b. Prove [3.5] by means of the following trick: first, define f for all x by

$$f(x) = (a_1 x + b_1)^2 + \cdots + (a_n x + b_n)^2$$

We see that $f(x) \geq 0$ for all x. Write $f(x)$ as $Ax^2 + Bx + C$, where the expressions for A, B, and C are related to the terms in [3.5]. Because $Ax^2 + Bx + C \geq 0$ for all x, we must have $B^2 - 4AC \leq 0$. Why? The conclusion follows.

3.2 Examples of Quadratic Optimization Problems

Much of mathematical economics is concerned with optimization problems. Economics, after all, is the science of choice, and optimization problems are the form in which choice is usually expressed mathematically.

A general discussion of such problems must be postponed until we have developed the necessary tools from calculus. Here we show how the simple results from the previous section on maximizing quadratic functions can be used to illustrate some basic economic ideas.

Example 3.2   (A Monopoly Problem)

Consider a firm that is the only seller of the commodity it produces, possibly a patented medicine, and so enjoys a monopoly. The total costs of the monopolist are assumed to be given by the quadratic function

$$C = \alpha Q + \beta Q^2, \qquad Q \geq 0 \tag{1}$$

of its output level Q, where α and β are positive constants. For each Q, the price P at which it can sell its output is assumed to be determined from the linear "inverse" demand function

$$P = a - bQ, \qquad Q \geq 0 \tag{2}$$

where a and b are constants with $a > 0$ and $b \geq 0$. So for any nonnegative Q, the total revenue R is given by the quadratic function

$$R = PQ = (a - bQ)Q$$

and profit by the quadratic function[1]

$$\pi(Q) = R - C = (a - bQ)Q - \alpha Q - \beta Q^2$$
$$= (a - \alpha)Q - (b + \beta)Q^2 \qquad [3]$$

The monopolist's objective is to maximize $\pi = \pi(Q)$. By using [3.4], we see that there is a maximum of π (for the monopolist M) at

$$Q^M = \frac{a - \alpha}{2(b + \beta)} \qquad \text{with} \qquad \pi^M = \frac{(a - \alpha)^2}{4(b + \beta)} \qquad [4]$$

This is valid if $a > \alpha$; if $a \leq \alpha$, the firm will not produce, but will have $Q^M = 0$ and $\pi^M = 0$. The two cases are illustrated in Figs. 3.2 and 3.3. The associated price and cost can be found by routine algebra.

If we put $b = 0$ in [2], then $P = a$ for all Q. In this case, the firm's choice of quantity does not influence the price at all and so the firm is said to be *perfectly competitive*. By replacing a by P in [3] and putting $b = 0$, we see that profit is maximized for a perfectly competitive firm at

$$Q^* = \frac{P - \alpha}{2\beta} \qquad \text{with} \qquad \pi^* = \frac{(P - \alpha)^2}{4\beta} \qquad [5]$$

provided that $P > \alpha$. If $P \leq \alpha$, then $Q^* = 0$ and $\pi^* = 0$.

FIGURE 3.2   The profit function, $a > \alpha$.

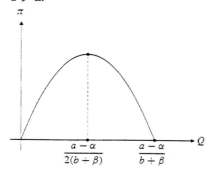

FIGURE 3.3   The profit function, $a \leq \alpha$.

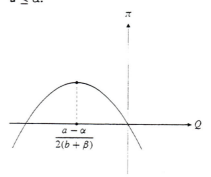

[1]Previously, π has been used to denote the constant ratio $3.14159\ldots$ between the circumference of a circle and its diameter. In economics, this constant is not used very often, so π has come to denote profit, or probability.

Solving the first equation in [5] for P yields $P = \alpha + 2\beta Q^*$. Thus,

$$P = \alpha + 2\beta Q \qquad [6]$$

represents the supply curve of this perfectly competitive firm for $P > \alpha$ when $Q^* > 0$, whereas for $P \leq \alpha$, the profit maximizing output Q^* is 0. The supply curve relating the price on the market to the firm's choice of output quantity is shown in Fig. 3.4; it includes points between the origin and $(0, x)$.

Let us return to the monopoly firm (which has no supply curve). If it could somehow be made to act like a competitive firm, taking price as given, it would be on the supply curve [6]. Given the demand curve $P = a - bQ$, equilibrium between supply and demand occurs when [6] is also satisfied, and so $P = a - bQ = \alpha + 2\beta Q$. Solving the second equation for Q, and then substituting for P and π in turn, we see that the equilibrium level of output, the corresponding price, and the profit would be

$$Q^e = \frac{a - \alpha}{b + 2\beta}, \qquad P^e = \frac{2a\beta + \alpha b}{b + 2\beta}, \qquad \pi^e = \frac{\beta(a - \alpha)^2}{(b + 2\beta)^2} \qquad [7]$$

In order to have the monopolist mimic a competitive firm by choosing to be at (Q^e, P^e), it may be desirable to tax (or subsidize) the output of the monopolist. Suppose that the monopolist is required to pay a specific tax of t per unit of output. Because the tax payment tQ is added to the firm's costs, the new total cost function is

$$C = \alpha Q + \beta Q^2 + tQ$$
$$= (\alpha + t)Q + \beta Q^2 \qquad [8]$$

Carrying out the same calculations as before, but with α replaced by $\alpha + t$,

FIGURE 3.4   The supply curve of a perfectly competitive firm.

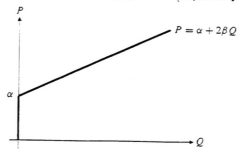

$P = \alpha + 2\beta Q$

gives the monopolist's choice of output as

$$Q_t^M = \begin{cases} \dfrac{a - \alpha - t}{2(b + \beta)}, & \text{if } a \geq \alpha + t \\ 0, & \text{otherwise} \end{cases} \qquad [9]$$

So $Q_t^M = Q^e$ when $(a - \alpha - t)/2(b + \beta) = (a - \alpha)/(b + 2\beta)$. Solving this equation for t yields $t = -(a - \alpha)b/(b + 2\beta)$. Note that t is actually negative, indicating the desirability of *subsidizing* the output of the monopolist in order to encourage additional production. (Of course, subsidizing monopolists is usually felt to be unjust, and many additional complications need to be considered carefully before formulating a desirable policy for dealing with monopolists. Still the previous analysis suggests that if justice requires lowering a monopolist's price or profit, this is much better done directly than by taxing output.)

Problem

1. If a cocoa shipping firm sells Q tons of cocoa in England, the price received is given by $P = \alpha_1 - \frac{1}{3}Q$. On the other hand, if it buys Q tons from its only source in Ghana, the price it has to pay is given by $P = \alpha_2 + \frac{1}{6}Q$. In addition, it costs γ per ton to ship cocoa from its supplier in Ghana to its customers in England (its only market). The numbers α_1, α_2, and γ are all positive.
   a. Express the cocoa shipper's profit as a function of Q, the number of tons shipped.
   b. Assuming that $\alpha_1 - \alpha_2 - \gamma > 0$, find the profit maximizing shipment of cocoa. What happens if $\alpha_1 - \alpha_2 - \gamma \leq 0$?
   c. Suppose the government of Ghana imposes an export tax on cocoa of t per ton. Find the new expression for the shipper's profits and the new quantity shipped.
   d. Calculate the government's export tax revenue as a function of t, and advise it on how to obtain as much tax revenue as possible.

3.3 Polynomials

After considering linear and quadratic functions, the logical next step is to examine **cubic functions** of the form

$$f(x) = ax^3 + bx^2 + cx + d \qquad (a, b, c, \text{ and } d \text{ are constants; } a \neq 0) \qquad [3.6]$$

It is relatively easy to understand the behavior of linear and quadratic functions from their graphs. Cubic functions are considerably more complicated, because

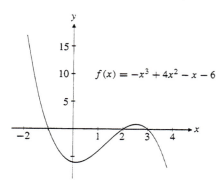

FIGURE 3.5   A cubic function.

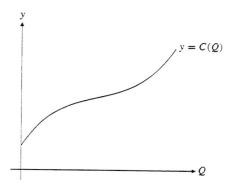

FIGURE 3.6   A cubic cost function.

the shape of their graphs changes drastically as the coefficients a, b, c, and d vary. Two examples are given in Figs. 3.5 and 3.6.

Cubic functions do occasionally appear in economic models. Let us look at a typical example.

Example 3.3

Consider a firm producing a single commodity. The total cost of producing Q units of the commodity is $C(Q)$. Cost functions often have the following properties: First, $C(0)$ is positive, because an initial fixed expenditure is involved. When production increases, costs also increase. In the beginning, costs increase rapidly, but the rate of increase slows down as production equipment is used for a higher proportion of each working week. However, at high levels of production, costs again increase at a fast rate, because of technical bottlenecks and overtime payments to workers, for example. The cubic cost function $C(Q) = aQ^3 + bQ^2 + cQ + d$ exhibits this type of behavior provided that $a > 0$, $b < 0$, $c > 0$, and $d > 0$ with $3ac > b^2$. Such a function is sketched in Fig. 3.6.

General Polynomials

Linear, quadratic, and cubic functions are all examples of **polynomials**. The function P defined for all x by

$$P(x) = a_n x^n + a_{n-1} x^{n-1} + \cdots + a_1 x + a_0 \qquad (a\text{'s are constants; } a_n \neq 0) \quad [3.7]$$

is called the **general polynomial of degree** n. When $n = 4$, we obtain $P(x) = a_4 x^4 + a_3 x^3 + a_2 x^2 + a_1 x + a_0$, which is the general polynomial of degree 4.

Numerous problems in mathematics and its applications involve polynomials. Often, one is particularly interested in finding the number and location of the zeros of $P(x)$—that is, the values of x such that $P(x) = 0$. The equation

$$a_n x^n + a_{n-1} x^{n-1} + \cdots + a_1 x + a_0 = 0 \qquad [3.8]$$

is called the **general nth-order equation**. It will soon be shown that this equation has *at most* n (real) solutions, also called **roots**, but it need not have any.

According to the **fundamental theorem of algebra**, every polynomial of the form [3.7] can be written as a product of polynomials of first or second degree. Here is a somewhat complicated case:

$$x^5 - x^4 + x - 1 = (x - 1)(x^4 + 1) = (x - 1)\left(x^2 - \sqrt{2}x + 1\right)\left(x^2 + \sqrt{2}x + 1\right)$$

Integer Roots

Suppose that x_0 is an integer that satifies the cubic equation $-x^3 + 4x^2 - x - 6 = 0$, or, equivalently, $-x^3 + 4x^2 - x = 6$. Then x_0 must also satisfy the equation

$$x_0(-x_0^2 + 4x_0 - 1) = 6 \qquad [*]$$

Because x_0 is an integer, it follows that x_0^2, $4x_0$, and $-x_0^2 + 4x_0 - 1$ must also be integers. But because x_0 multiplied by the integer $-x_0^2 + 4x_0 - 1$ is equal to 6, the number x_0 must be a factor of 6—that is, 6 must be divisible by x_0. Now, the only integers by which 6 is divisible are ± 1, ± 2, ± 3, and ± 6. Direct substitution into the left-hand side (LHS) of equation [*] reveals that of these eight possibilities, -1, 2, and 3 are roots of the equation. A third degree equation has at most three roots, so we have found all of them. In general, we can state the following result:

Suppose that a_n, a_{n-1}, ..., a_1, a_0 are all integers. Then all possible integer roots of the equation

$$a_n x^n + a_{n-1} x^{n-1} + \cdots + a_1 x + a_0 = 0 \qquad [3.9]$$

must be factors of the constant term a_0.

Proof   If x_0 is an integer root, then x_0 must satisfy the equation

$$x_0(a_n x_0^{n-1} + a_{n-1} x_0^{n-2} + \cdots + a_1) = -a_0$$

Both factors on the left are integers, so $-a_0$ must be divisible by each of them, and in particular by x_0. So must a_0.

Example 3.4

Find all possible integer roots to the equation $\frac{1}{2}x^3 - x^2 + \frac{1}{2}x - 1 = 0$.

Solution   We multiply both sides of the equation by 2 to obtain an equation whose coefficients are all integers:

$$x^3 - 2x^2 + x - 2 = 0$$

According to [3.9], all integer solutions of the equation must be factors of -2. So only ± 1 and ± 2 can be integer solutions. A check shows that $x = 2$ is the only integer solution. In fact, because $x^3 - 2x^2 + x - 2 = (x-2)(x^2+1)$, there is only one real root.

The Remainder Theorem

Let $P(x)$ and $Q(x)$ be two polynomials for which the degree of $P(x)$ is greater than or equal to the degree of $Q(x)$. Then there always exist unique polynomials $q(x)$ and $r(x)$ such that

$$P(x) = q(x)Q(x) + r(x) \qquad [3.10]$$

where the degree of $r(x)$ is less than the degree of $Q(x)$. This fact is called the **remainder theorem**. When x is such that $Q(x) \neq 0$, then [3.10] can be written in the form

$$\frac{P(x)}{Q(x)} = q(x) + \frac{r(x)}{Q(x)} \qquad [3.11]$$

If $r(x) = 0$ in [3.10] and [3.11], we say that $Q(x)$ *is a factor of* $P(x)$, or that $P(x)$ *is divisible by* $Q(x)$. Then $P(x) = q(x)Q(x)$ or $P(x)/Q(x) = q(x)$, which is the *quotient*. When $r(x) \neq 0$, it is the *remainder*.

An important special case is when $Q(x) = x - a$. Then $Q(x)$ is of degree 1, so the remainder $r(x)$ must have degree 0, and is therefore a constant. In this special case, for all x,

$$P(x) = q(x)(x - a) + r$$

For $x = a$ in particular, we get $P(a) = r$. Hence, $x - a$ divides $P(x)$ if and only if $P(a) = 0$. This is an important observation that can be formulated as follows:

Polynomial $P(x)$ has the factor $x - a \iff P(a) = 0$ [3.12]

It follows from [3.12] that an nth-degree polynomial $P(x)$ can have *at most n* different zeros. To see this, note that each zero $x = a_1, x = a_2, \ldots, x = a_k$ gives rise to a different factor of the form $x - a$. From this it follows that $P(x)$ can be expressed as $P(x) = A(x)(x - a_1) \ldots (x - a_k)$ for some polynomial $A(x)$. Thus, $P(x)$ has degree $\geq k$, and so k cannot exceed n.

Example 3.5

Prove that the polynomial $f(x) = -2x^3 + 2x^2 + 10x + 6$ has a zero at $x = 3$, and factorize the polynomial.

Solution   Inserting $x = 3$ into the polynomial yields

$$f(3) = -2 \cdot 3^3 + 2 \cdot 3^2 + 10 \cdot 3 + 6 = -54 + 18 + 30 + 6 = 0$$

So $x - 3$ is a factor. It follows that the cubic function $f(x)$ can be expressed as the product of $(x - 3)$ with a second degree polynomial. In fact,

$$f(x) = -2x^3 + 2x^2 + 10x + 6 = -2(x - 3)(x^2 + ax + b)$$

We must determine a and b. Expanding the last expression yields

$$f(x) = -2x^3 + (6 - 2a)x^2 + (6a - 2b)x + 6b$$

If this polynomial $f(x)$ is to equal $-2x^3 + 2x^2 + 10x + 6$ for all x, then the coefficients of like powers of x must be equal; thus, $6 - 2a = 2$, $6a - 2b = 10$, and $6b = 6$. Hence, $b = 1$ and $a = 2$. Because $x^2 + 2x + 1 = (x + 1)^2$, we conclude that

$$f(x) = -2x^3 + 2x^2 + 10x + 6 = -2(x - 3)(x^2 + 2x + 1)$$
$$= -2(x - 3)(x + 1)^2$$

The factorization procedure used in this example is called the *method of undetermined coefficients*. (Here a and b were the undetermined coefficients.) The alternative "long-division" method for factorizing polynomials will be considered next.

Polynomial Division

One can divide polynomials in much the same way as one divides numbers. Consider first a simple numerical example:

$$2735 \div 5 = 500 + 40 + 7$$
$$\underline{2500}$$
$$235$$
$$\underline{200}$$
$$35$$
$$\underline{35}$$
$$0 \qquad \text{remainder}$$

Hence, $2735 \div 5 = 547$. Note that the horizontal lines instruct you to subtract the numbers above the lines. (You might be more accustomed to a different way of arranging the numbers, but the idea is the same.)

Consider next

$$(-x^3 + 4x^2 - x - 6) \div (x - 2)$$

We write the following:

$$
\begin{array}{l}
(-x^3 + 4x^2 - x - 6) \div (x - 2) \qquad = -x^2 \qquad\quad + 2x + 3 \\
\underline{-x^3 + 2x^2} \qquad\qquad\qquad\qquad\quad \boxed{-x^2(x-2)} \\
\qquad 2x^2 - x - 6 \\
\qquad \underline{2x^2 - 4x} \qquad\qquad\qquad\qquad \boxed{2x(x-2)} \\
\qquad\qquad 3x - 6 \\
\qquad\qquad \underline{3x - 6} \qquad\qquad\qquad\qquad \boxed{3(x-2)} \\
\qquad\qquad\quad 0 \qquad \text{remainder}
\end{array}
$$

(You can omit the boxes, but they should help you to see what is going on.) We conclude that $(-x^3 + 4x^2 - x - 6) \div (x - 2) = -x^2 + 2x + 3$. Because it is easy to see that $-x^2 + 2x + 3 = -(x + 1)(x - 3)$, we have

$$-x^3 + 4x^2 - x - 6 = -(x + 1)(x - 3)(x - 2)$$

Polynomial Division with a Remainder

The division $2734 \div 5$ gives 546 and leaves the remainder 4. So $2734/5 = 546 + 4/5$. We consider a similar form of division for polynomials.

Example 3.6
$$(x^4 + 3x^2 - 4) \div (x^2 + 2x)$$

Solution

$$
\begin{array}{l}
(x^4 \qquad + 3x^2 \qquad\quad - 4) \div (x^2 + 2x) = x^2 - 2x + 7 \\
\underline{x^4 + 2x^3} \\
\quad\ -2x^3 + 3x^2 \qquad - 4 \\
\quad\ \underline{-2x^3 - 4x^2} \\
\qquad\qquad 7x^2 \qquad - 4 \\
\qquad\qquad \underline{7x^2 + 14x} \\
\qquad\qquad\qquad - 14x - 4 \qquad \text{remainder}
\end{array}
$$

(The polynomial $x^4 + 3x^2 - 4$ has no terms in x^3 and x, so we inserted some extra space between the powers of x to make room for the terms in x^3 and x that arise in the course of the calculations.) We conclude that

$$ x^4 + 3x^2 - 4 = (x^2 - 2x + 7)(x^2 + 2x) + (-14x - 4) $$

Hence,

$$ \frac{x^4 + 3x^2 - 4}{x^2 + 2x} = x^2 - 2x + 7 - \frac{14x + 4}{x^2 + 2x} \qquad [*] $$

Rational Functions

A **rational function** is a function $R(x) = P(x)/Q(x)$ that can be expressed as the ratio of two polynomials $P(x)$ and $Q(x)$. This function is defined for all x where $Q(x) \neq 0$. The rational function $R(x)$ is called **proper** if the degree of $P(x)$ is less than the degree of $Q(x)$. When the degree of $P(x)$ is greater than or equal to that of $Q(x)$, then $R(x)$ is called an **improper** rational function. By using polynomial division, any improper rational function can be written as a polynomial plus a proper rational function, as in [3.11] and Example 3.6.

Problems

1. By making use of [3.9], find all integer roots of the following equations:
   a. $x^2 + x - 2 = 0$ **b.** $x^3 - x^2 - 25x + 25 = 0$ **c.** $x^5 - 4x^3 - 3 = 0$
2. Find all integer roots of the following equations:
   a. $x^4 - x^3 - 7x^2 + x + 6 = 0$ **b.** $2x^3 + 11x^2 - 7x - 6 = 0$
   c. $x^4 + x^3 + 2x^2 + x + 1 = 0$ **d.** $\frac{1}{4}x^3 - \frac{1}{4}x^2 - x + 1 = 0$
3. Perform the following divisions:
   a. $(x^2 - x - 20) \div (x - 5)$ **b.** $(x^3 - 1) \div (x - 1)$
   c. $(-3x^3 + 48x) \div (x - 4)$

4. Perform the following divisions:

    a. $(2x^3 + 2x - 1) \div (x - 1)$ **b.** $(x^4 + x^3 + x^2 + x) \div (x^2 + x)$

    c. $(3x^8 + x^2 + 1) \div (x^3 - 2x + 1)$ **d.** $(x^5 - 3x^4 + 1) \div (x^2 + x + 1)$

5. Which of the following divisions leave no remainder? (*a* and *b* are constants; *n* is a natural number.)

    a. $(x^3 - x - 1)/(x - 1)$ **b.** $(2x^3 - x - 1)/(x - 1)$

    c. $(x^3 - ax^2 + bx - ab)/(x - a)$ **d.** $(x^{2n} - 1)/(x + 1)$

6. Write the following polynomials as products of linear factors:

    a. $p(x) = x^3 + x^2 - 12x$ **b.** $q(x) = 2x^3 + 3x^2 - 18x + 8$

7. Find possible formulas for each of the three polynomials with graphs in Fig. 3.7.

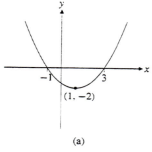
(a)

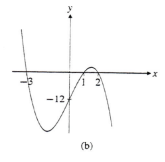
(b)

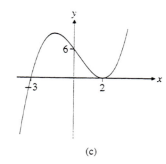
(c)

FIGURE 3.7

3.4 Power Functions

Consider the power function f defined by the formula

$$f(x) = x^r \qquad [3.13]$$

We know the meaning of x^r if r is any integer—that is, $r = 0, \pm 1, \pm 2, \ldots$. In fact, if r is a natural number, x^r is the product of r x's. Also if $r = 0$, then $x^r = x^0 = 1$ for all $x \neq 0$, and if $r = -n$, then $x^r = 1/x^n$ for $x \neq 0$. In addition, for $r = 1/2$, $x^r = x^{1/2} = \sqrt{x}$, defined for all $x \geq 0$. (See Section A.2 of Appendix A.) This section extends the definition of x^r so that it has meaning for any rational number r.

Here are some examples of why powers with rational exponents are needed:

1. The flow of blood (in liters per second) through the heart of an individual is approximately proportional to $x^{0.7}$, where x is the body weight.

2. The formula $S \approx 4.84V^{2/3}$ gives the approximate surface S of a ball as a function of its volume V. (See Example 3.10, which follows.)

3. The formula $Y = 2.262 K^{0.203} L^{0.763} (1.02)^t$ appears in a study of the growth of national output, and shows how powers with fractional exponents can arise in economics. (Here Y is the net national product, K is capital stock, L is labor, and t is time.)

These examples illustrate the need to define x^r for $r = 0.7 = 7/10$, $r = 2/3$, $r = 0.203$, and $r = 0.763 = 763/1000$. In general, we want to define x^r for $x > 0$ when r is an arbitrary rational number.

The following basic power rules (discussed in Section A.1, Appendix A) are valid for all integers r and s:

$$\text{(i) } a^r a^s = a^{r+s} \qquad \text{(ii) } (a^r)^s = a^{rs} \qquad\qquad [3.14]$$

When extending the definition of x^r so that it also applies to rational exponents r, it is natural to require that these rules retain their validity.

Let us first examine the meaning of $a^{1/n}$, where n is a natural number, and a is positive. For example, what does $5^{1/3}$ mean? If rule [3.14](ii) is still to apply in this case, we must have $(5^{1/3})^3 = 5$. This implies that $5^{1/3}$ must be a solution of the equation $x^3 = 5$. This equation can be shown to have a unique positive solution, denoted by $\sqrt[3]{5}$, the *cube root of 5*. (See Example 7.2 in Section 7.1.) Therefore, we must define $5^{1/3}$ as $\sqrt[3]{5}$. In general, $(a^{1/n})^n = a$. Thus, $a^{1/n}$ is a solution of the equation $x^n = a$. This equation can be shown to have a unique positive solution denoted by $\sqrt[n]{a}$, the *nth root of a*:

$$a^{1/n} = \sqrt[n]{a} \qquad\qquad [3.15]$$

In words: *if a is positive and n is a natural number, then $a^{1/n}$ is the unique positive number that, raised to the nth power, gives a—that is, $(a^{1/n})^n = a^1 = a$.* For example,

$$27^{1/3} = \sqrt[3]{27} = 3 \qquad \text{because} \qquad 3^3 = (27^{1/3})^3 = 27$$

$$\left(\tfrac{1}{625}\right)^{1/4} = \sqrt[4]{\tfrac{1}{625}} = \tfrac{1}{5} \qquad \text{because} \qquad \left(\tfrac{1}{5}\right)^4 = \left[\left(\tfrac{1}{625}\right)^{1/4}\right]^4 = \tfrac{1}{625}$$

Usually, we write $a^{1/2}$ as $\sqrt{a}$ rather than $\sqrt[2]{a}$ (see Section A.2 of Appendix A).

We proceed to define $a^{p/q}$ whenever p is an integer, q is a natural number, and $a > 0$. Consider $5^{2/3}$, for example. We have already defined $5^{1/3}$. For rule [3.14](ii) to apply, we must have $5^{2/3} = (5^{1/3})^2$. So we must define $5^{2/3}$ as $\left(\sqrt[3]{5}\right)^2$. In general, for $a > 0$, we define

$$a^{p/q} = \left(a^{1/q}\right)^p = \left(\sqrt[q]{a}\right)^p, \qquad p \text{ an integer, } q \text{ a natural number} \qquad\qquad [3.16]$$

Note: If q is an odd number and p is an integer, $a^{p/q}$ can be defined even when $a < 0$. For example, $(-8)^{1/3} = \sqrt[3]{-8} = -2$, because $(-2)^3 = -8$. However, in defining $a^{p/q}$ when $a < 0$, the fraction p/q must be reduced to lowest terms. If not, we would get contradictions such as "$-2 = (-8)^{1/3} = (-8)^{2/6} = \sqrt[6]{(-8)^2} = \sqrt[6]{64} = 2$."

Example 3.7

Compute $625^{0.75}$ and $32^{-3/5}$.

Solution $625^{0.75} = 625^{3/4} = (625^{1/4})^3 = 5^3 = 125$

$$32^{-3/5} = \left(32^{1/5}\right)^{-3} = 2^{-3} = 1/8$$

Many scientific calculators have a power key, often denoted by $\boxed{y^x}$. For instance, suppose we let $y = 625$ and $x = 0.75$, then instruct the calculator to compute y^x (the way this is done varies from calculator to calculator). The display may show the number 125.000—or possibly, if 7 decimals are shown, 125.0000001. This shows that the key $\boxed{y^x}$ does not always give an exact answer, even in simple cases. Try it with 2^3, and check the value for $32^{-3/5}$. Simple pocket calculators are usually exact enough for practical purposes, however.

With this definition of $a^{p/q}$, we can show that rules [3.14] are still valid when r and s are rational numbers. In particular,

$$a^{p/q} = \left(a^{1/q}\right)^p = \left(a^p\right)^{1/q} = \sqrt[q]{a^p}$$

Thus, to compute $a^{p/q}$, we could either first take the qth root of a and raise the result to p, or first raise a to the power p and then take the qth root of the result. We obtain the same answer either way. For example,

$$625^{0.75} = 625^{3/4} = \left(625^3\right)^{1/4} = (244140625)^{1/4} = \sqrt[4]{244140625} = 125$$

Note that this procedure involves more difficult computations than the one used in Example 3.7.

Example 3.8

If z denotes demand for coffee in tons per year and p denotes its price per ton, the approximate relationship between them over a specific time period is

$$z = 694{,}500p^{-0.3}$$

(a) Write the formula using roots.

(b) Use a calculator to compute demand when $p = 35{,}000$ and when $p = 55{,}000$.

Solution

(a) $p^{-0.3} = \dfrac{1}{p^{0.3}} = \dfrac{1}{p^{3/10}} = \dfrac{1}{\sqrt[10]{p^3}}$.

so we obtain

$$z = \frac{694,500}{\sqrt[10]{p^3}}$$

(b) $p = 35,000$ gives $z = 694,500 \cdot (35,000)^{-0.3} \approx 30,092$ (tons)

 $p = 55,000$ gives $z = 694,500 \cdot (55,000)^{-0.3} \approx 26,276$ (tons)

Note that when price increases, demand decreases.

Using the Power Rules

Powers with rational exponents often occur in economic applications, so you must learn to use them correctly. Before we consider some more examples, note that the power rules can easily be extended to more factors. For instance, we have

$$(abcd)^p = (ab)^p (cd)^p = a^p b^p c^p d^p$$

Example 3.9

Simplify the following expression so that the answer contains only a single exponent for each variable x and y:

$$\left(\frac{5x^{-2}y^{2/3}}{625x^4 y^{-4/3}} \right)^{-1/3}$$

Solution   One method begins by simplifying the expression inside the parentheses:

$$\left(\frac{5x^{-2}y^{2/3}}{625x^4 y^{-4/3}} \right)^{-1/3} = \left(\frac{1}{125} \cdot \frac{x^{-2}}{x^4} \cdot \frac{y^{2/3}}{y^{-4/3}} \right)^{-1/3} = \left(\frac{1}{125} \cdot x^{-6} \cdot y^2 \right)^{-1/3}$$

$$= \left(\frac{1}{125} \right)^{-1/3} \left(x^{-6} \right)^{-1/3} \left(y^2 \right)^{-1/3} = (125)^{1/3} x^2 y^{-2/3} = \frac{5x^2}{y^{2/3}}$$

Alternatively, we can also raise all the factors to the power $-1/3$ and use the relation $625 = 5^4$ to obtain

$$\left(\frac{5x^{-2}y^{2/3}}{625x^4 y^{-4/3}} \right)^{-1/3} = \frac{5^{-1/3} x^{2/3} y^{-2/9}}{(5^4)^{-1/3} x^{-4/3} y^{4/9}} = 5^{-1/3-(-4/3)} \cdot x^{2/3-(-4/3)} \cdot y^{-2/9-4/9}$$

$$= 5^1 x^2 y^{-2/3} = \frac{5x^2}{y^{2/3}}$$

Example 3.10

The formulas for the surface S and the volume V of a ball with radius r are $S = 4\pi r^2$ and $V = (4/3)\pi r^3$. Express S in terms of V.

Solution   We must eliminate r. From $V = (4/3)\pi r^3$ we obtain $r^3 = 3V/4\pi$. By raising each side of this equation to the power $1/3$ and using $(r^3)^{1/3} = r$, we obtain $r = (3V/4\pi)^{1/3}$. Hence,

$$S = 4\pi r^2 = 4\pi \left[\left(\frac{3V}{4\pi} \right)^{1/3} \right]^2 = 4\pi \frac{(3V)^{2/3}}{(4\pi)^{2/3}}$$

$$= (4\pi)^{1-(2/3)} 3^{2/3} V^{2/3} = (4\pi)^{1/3} (3^2)^{1/3} V^{2/3} = \sqrt[3]{36\pi}\, V^{2/3}$$

We have thus shown that

$$S = \sqrt[3]{36\pi}\, V^{2/3} \approx 4.84\, V^{2/3} \qquad [1]$$

Note: Perhaps the most commonly committed error in elementary algebra is to replace $(x + y)^2$ by $x^2 + y^2$ and hence lose the term $2xy$. If we replace $(x + y)^3$ by $x^3 + y^3$, then we lose the terms $3x^2 y + 3xy^2$. What error do we commit if we replace $(x - y)^3$ by $x^3 - y^3$? Tests also reveal that students who are able to handle these simple power expressions often make mistakes when dealing with more complicated powers. A surprisingly common error is replacing $\left(25 - \frac{1}{2}x \right)^{1/2}$ by $25^{1/2} - \left(\frac{1}{2}x \right)^{1/2}$, for example. In general:

$(x + y)^\alpha$ is usually NOT equal to $x^\alpha + y^\alpha$

$(x - y - z)^{1/\alpha}$ is usually NOT equal to $x^{1/\alpha} - y^{1/\alpha} - z^{1/\alpha}$

The *only* exception, for general values of x, y, and z, occurs when $\alpha = 1$.

Graphs of Power Functions

We return to the power function $f(x) = x^r$ in [3.13], which is now defined for all rational numbers r provided that $x > 0$. We always have $f(1) = 1^r = 1$, so the graph of the function passes through the point $(1, 1)$ in the xy-plane. The behavior of the graph depends crucially on whether r is positive or negative.

Example 3.11

Sketch the graphs $y = x^{0.3}$ and $y = x^{-1.3}$.

Solution   Using a pocket calculator allows us to complete the following table:

x	0	1/3	2/3	1	2	3	4
$y = x^{0.3}$	0	0.72	0.89	1	1.23	1.39	1.52
$y = x^{-1.3}$	*	4.17	1.69	1	0.41	0.24	0.16

*Not defined.

The graphs are shown in Figs. 3.8 and 3.9.

Figure 3.10 illustrates how the graph of $y = x^r$ changes with changing values of the exponent. Try to draw the graphs of $y = x^{-3}$, $y = x^{-1}$, $y = x^{-1/2}$, and $y = x^{-1/3}$.

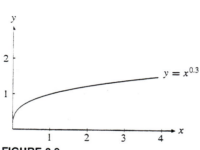

FIGURE 3.8

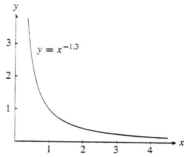

FIGURE 3.9

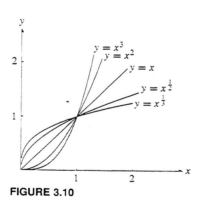

FIGURE 3.10

Problems

1. Compute the following:

    a. $16^{1/4}$ **b.** $243^{-1/5}$ **c.** $5^{1/7} \cdot 5^{6/7}$ **d.** $(4^8)^{-3/16}$

2. Using a pocket calculator or computer, find approximate values for the following:

    a. $100^{1/5}$ **b.** $16^{-3.33}$ **c.** $5.23^{1.02} \cdot 2.11^{-3.11}$

3. Compute the following:

    a. $\dfrac{4 \cdot 3^{-1/3}}{\sqrt[6]{81}}$ **b.** $(0.064)^{-1/3}$ **c.** $(3^2 + 4^2)^{-1/2}$

4. How can the number $50^{0.16}$ be expressed as a root?

5. Simplify the following expressions so that each contains only a single exponent of a.

    a. $\{[(a^{1/2})^{2/3}]^{3/4}\}^{4/5}$ **b.** $a^{1/2}a^{2/3}a^{3/4}a^{4/5}$

    c. $\{[(3a)^{-1}]^{-2}(2a^{-2})^{-1}\}/a^{-3}$ **d.** $\dfrac{\sqrt[3]{a}\,a^{1/12}\sqrt[4]{a^3}}{a^{5/12}\sqrt{a}}$

6. Solve the following equations for x:

    a. $2^{2x} = 8$ **b.** $3^{3x+1} = 1/81$ **c.** $10^{x^2-2x+2} = 100$

7. Which of the following equations are valid for all x and y?

    a. $(2^x)^2 = 2^{x^2}$ **b.** $3^{x-3y} = \dfrac{3^x}{3^{3y}}$

    c. $3^{-1/x} = \dfrac{1}{3^{1/x}}$ $(x \neq 0)$ **d.** $5^{1/x} = \dfrac{1}{5^x}$ $(x \neq 0)$

    e. $a^{x+y} = a^x + a^y$ **f.** $2^{\sqrt{x}} \cdot 2^{\sqrt{y}} = 2^{\sqrt{xy}}$ $(x$ and y positive$)$

8. Solve the following equations for the variables indicated:

    a. $3K^{-1/2}L^{1/3} = 1/5$ for K

    b. $p - abx_0^{b-1} = 0$ for x_0

    c. $ax(ax + b)^{-2/3} + (ax + b)^{1/3} = 0$ for x

    d. $\left[(1 - \lambda)a^{-\rho} + \lambda b^{-\rho}\right]^{-1/\rho} = c$ for b

9. A sphere of capacity 100 m³ is to have its outside surface painted. One liter of paint covers 5 m². How many liters of paint are needed? (*Hint:* Use formula [1] in Example 3.10.)

10. Show by using a pocket calculator (or a computer) that the equation

$$Y = 2.262K^{0.203}L^{0.763}(1.02)^t$$

has an approximate solution for K given by $K \approx 0.018Y^{4.926}L^{-3.759}(0.907)^t$. Then determine K numerically when $Y = 100$, $L = 6$, and $t = 10$.

11. Simplify the following expressions:

    a. $(a^{1/3} - b^{1/3})(a^{2/3} + a^{1/3}b^{1/3} + b^{2/3})$

    b. $\dfrac{bx^{1/2} - (x - a)b\frac{1}{2}x^{-1/2}}{(bx^{1/2})^2}$ $(x > 0)$

3.5 Exponential Functions

A quantity that increases (or decreases) by a fixed factor per unit of time is said to *increase* (or decrease) *exponentially*. If this fixed factor is a, this leads to the study of the exponential function f defined by

$$f(t) = Aa^t \qquad \text{similar to} \quad \boxed{1} \qquad [3.17]$$

where a and A are positive constants. Note that if $f(t) = Aa^t$, then $f(t+1) = Aa^{t+1} = Aa^t \cdot a^1 = af(t)$, so the value of f at time $t+1$ is a times the value of f at time t. If $a > 1$, then f is increasing; if $0 < a < 1$, then f is decreasing. Because $f(0) = Aa^0 = A$, we can write $f(t) = f(0)a^t$.

Exponential functions appear in many important economic, social, and physical models. For instance, economic growth, population growth, continuously accumulated interest, radioactive decay, and decreasing illiteracy have all been described by exponential functions. In addition, the exponential function is one of the most important in statistics.

Example 3.12   (Population Growth)

Consider a growing population like that of Europe. In Example 2.13, we constructed a linear function

$$P = 6.4t + 641$$

where P denotes the population in millions, $t = 0$ corresponds to the year 1960 when the population was 641 million, and $t = 10$ corresponds to the year 1970 when the population estimate was 705 million. According to this formula, the annual increase in population would be constant and equal to 6.4 million. This is a very unreasonable assumption. After all, populations tend to grow faster as they get bigger because there are more people to have babies, and the death rate usually decreases or stays the same. In fact, according to UN estimates, the European population was expected to grow by approximately 0.72% annually during the period 1960 to 2000. With a population of 641 million in 1960, the population in 1961 would then be

$$641 + \frac{641 \cdot 0.72}{100} = 641 \cdot \left(1 + \frac{0.72}{100}\right) = 641 \cdot 1.0072$$

which is approximately 645 million. Next year, in 1962, it would have grown to

$$641 \cdot 1.0072 + \frac{641 \cdot 1.0072 \cdot 0.72}{100} = 641 \cdot 1.0072 \cdot (1 + 0.0072)$$

$$= 641 \cdot 1.0072^2$$

which is approximately 650 million. Note how the population figure grows by the factor 1.0072 each year. If the growth rate were to continue at 0.72% annually, then t years after 1960 the population would be given by

$$P(t) = 641 \cdot 1.0072^t \qquad \text{or} \qquad A \cdot a^t \qquad [3.17]$$

Thus, $P(t)$ is an exponential function of the form [3.17]. For the year 2000, corresponding to $t = 40$, the formula yields the estimate $P(40) \approx 854$ million.

Many countries, particularly in Africa and Latin America, have recently had far faster population growth than Europe. For instance, during the 1970s and 1980s, the growth rate of Zimbabwe's population was close to 3.5% annually. If we let $t = 0$ correspond to the census year 1969 when the population was 5.1 million, the population t years after 1969 is given by

$$P(t) = 5.1 \cdot 1.035^t$$

If we calculate $P(20)$, $P(40)$, and $P(60)$ using this formula, we get roughly 10, 20, and 40. Thus, the population of Zimbabwe roughly doubles after 20 years; during the next 20 years, it doubles again, and so on. We say that the *doubling time* of the population is approximately 20 years. Of course, extrapolating so far into the future is quite dubious, because exponential growth of population cannot go on forever. (If the growth rate continued at 3.5% annually, and the Zimbabwean territory did not expand, in the year 2697, each Zimbabwean would on average have only 1 square meter of land. See Problem 7.)

If $a > 1$ and $A > 0$, the exponential function $f(t) = Aa^t$ is increasing. Its **doubling time** is the time it takes for it to double. Its value at $t = 0$ is A, so the doubling time t^* is given by the equation $f(t^*) = Aa^{t^*} = 2A$, or after cancelling A, by $a^{t^*} = 2$. Thus the doubling time of the exponential function $f(t) = Aa^t$ is the power to which a must be raised in order to get 2.[2] (In Problem 8 you will be asked to show that the doubling time is independent of which year you take as the base.)

Example 3.13

Use your calculator to find the doubling time of

(a) a population (like that of Zimbabwe) increasing at 3.5% annually (thus confirming the earlier calculations)

(b) the population of Kenya in the 1980s (which had the world's highest annual growth rate of 4.2%).

Solution

(a) The doubling time t^* is given by the equation $1.035^{t^*} = 2$. Using a calculator shows that $1.035^{15} \approx 1.68$, whereas $1.035^{25} \approx 2.36$. Thus,

[2] By using natural logarithms as explained in Section 8.2, we find that $t^* = \ln 2 / \ln a$.

t^* must lie between 15 and 25. Because $1.035^{20} \approx 1.99$, t^* is close to 20. In fact, $t^* \approx 20.15$.

(b) The doubling time t^* is given by the equation $1.042^{t^*} = 2$. Using a calculator, we find that $t^* \approx 16.85$. Thus, with a growth rate of 4.2%, Kenya's population would double in less than 17 years.

Example 3.14 (Compound Interest)

A savings account of K that increases by $p\%$ interest each year will have increased after t years to

$$K \left(1 + p/100\right)^t \tag{1}$$

(see Section A.1 of Appendix A). According to this formula, $1 ($K = 1$) earning interest at 8% per annum ($p = 8$) will have increased after t years to

$$\left(1 + 8/100\right)^t = 1.08^t \tag{2}$$

Table 3.1 indicates how this dollar grows over time:

TABLE 3.1 *How $1 of savings increases with time*

t	1	2	5	10	20	30	50	100	200
$(1.08)^t$	1.08	1.17	1.47	2.16	4.66	10.06	46.90	2,199.76	4,838,949.60

After 30 years, $1 of savings has increased to more than $10, and after 200 years, it has grown to more than $4.8 million! This growth is illustrated in Fig. 3.11. Observe that the expression 1.08^t defines an exponential function of the type [3.17] with $a = 1.08$. Even if a is only slightly larger than 1, $f(t)$ will increase very quickly when t is large.

Example 3.15 (Radioactive Decay)

Measurements indicate that radioactive materials decay by a fixed percentage per unit of time. Plutonium 239, which is a waste product of certain nuclear power plants and is used in the production of nuclear weapons, decays by 50% every 24,400 years. We say, therefore, that the *half-life* of plutonium 239 is 24,400 years. If there are I_0 units of plutonium 239 at time $t = 0$, then after t years, there will be

$$I(t) = I_0 \cdot \left(\tfrac{1}{2}\right)^{t/24,400} = I_0 \cdot 0.9999716^t$$

units remaining. (Observe that this is consistent with $I(24,400) = \tfrac{1}{2} I_0$.)

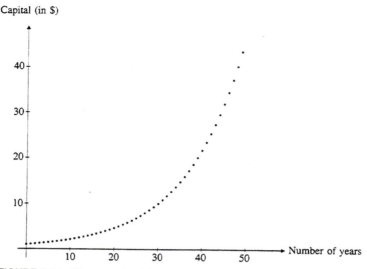

Capital (in $)

Number of years

FIGURE 3.11   The growth of $1 of savings after *t* years when the interest rate is 8% per year.

Chapter 8 discusses the exponential function in much greater detail. Observe the fundamental difference between the two functions

$$f(x) = a^x \qquad \text{and} \qquad g(x) = x^a$$

The second of these two is the **power function** discussed in Section 3.4. For the exponential function a^x, it is the exponent that varies, while the base is constant. For the power function x^a, on the other hand, the exponent is constant, while the base varies.

The most important properties of the exponential function are summed up by the following:

The **general exponential function** with base $a > 0$ is

$$f(x) = Aa^x$$

where $f(0) = A$, and a is the factor by which $f(x)$ changes when x increases by 1.

If $a = 1 + p/100$, where $p > 0$ and $A > 0$, then $f(x)$ will increase by $p\%$ for each unit increase in x.

If $a = 1 - p/100$, where $p > 0$ and $A > 0$, then $f(x)$ will decrease by $p\%$ for each unit increase in x.

Problems

1. If the population of Europe grew at the rate of 0.72% annually, what would be the doubling time?

2. The population of Botswana was estimated to be 1.22 million in 1989, and to be growing at the rate of 3.4% annually.
   a. If $t = 0$ denotes 1989, find a formula for the population at date t.
   b. What is the doubling time?

3. A savings account with an initial deposit of $100 earns 12% interest per year.
   a. What is the amount of savings after t years?
   b. Make a table similar to Table 3.1. (Stop at 50 years.)

4. Suppose that you are promised $2 on the first day, $4 on the second day, $8 on the third day, $16 on the fourth day, and so on (so that every day you get twice as much as the day before).
   a. How much will you receive on the tenth day?
   b. Find a function $f(t)$ that indicates how much you will obtain on the tth day.
   c. Explain why $f(20)$ is more than $1 million. (*Hint:* 2^{10} is a little larger than 10^3.)

5. Fill in the following table and then make a rough sketch of the graphs of $y = 2^x$ and $y = 2^{-x}$.

x	-3	-2	-1	0	1	2	3
2^x							
2^{-x}							

6. Fill in the following table and then sketch the graph of $y = 2^{x^2}$.

x	-2	-1	0	1	2
2^{x^2}					

7. The area of Zimbabwe is approximately $3.91 \cdot 10^{11}$ square meters. Referring to the text following Example 3.12 and using a calculator, solve the equation $5.1 \cdot 1.035^t = 3.91 \cdot 10^{11}$ for t, and interpret your answer. (Recall that $t = 0$ corresponds to 1969.)

8. With $f(t) = Aa^t$, if $f(t + t^*) = 2f(t)$, prove that $a^{t^*} = 2$. Explain why this shows that the doubling time of the general exponential function is independent of the initial time.

9. In 1964 a five-year plan was introduced in Tanzania. One objective was to double the real per capita income over the next 15 years. What is the average annual rate of growth of real income per capita required to achieve this objective?

10. Consider the function f defined for all x by $f(x) = 1 - 2^{-x}$.
   a. Make a table of function values for $x = 0, \pm1, \pm2$, and ±3. Then sketch the graph of f.
   b. What happens to $f(x)$ as x becomes very large and very small?

11. Which of the following equations do *not* define exponential functions of x?
   a. $y = 3^x$ **b.** $y = x^{\sqrt{2}}$ **c.** $y = (\sqrt{2})^x$
   d. $y = x^x$.   **e.** $y = (2.7)^x$ **f.** $y = 1/2^x$

12. Fill in the following table and then sketch the graph of $y = x^2 2^x$.

x	-10	-5	-4	-3	-2	-1	0	1	2
$x^2 2^x$									

13. Find possible exponential functions for the graphs of Fig. 3.12.

14. The radioactive isotope iodine 131, which has a half-life of 8 days, is often used to diagnose disease in the thyroid gland. If there are I_0 units of the material at time $t = 0$, how much remains after t days?

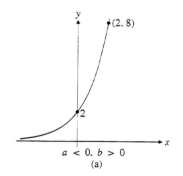

$a < 0, b > 0$
(a)

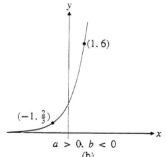

$a > 0, b < 0$
(b)

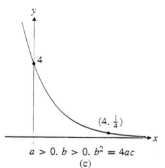

$a > 0, b > 0, b^2 = 4ac$
(c)

FIGURE 3.12

3.6 The General Concept of a Function

So far we have studied functions of one variable. These are functions whose domain is a set of real numbers, and whose range is also a set of real numbers. Yet a realistic description of many economic phenomena requires considering a large number of variables simultaneously. For example, the demand for a good like butter is a function of several variables such as the price of the good, the prices of complements and substitutes, consumers' incomes, and so on.

Actually, we have already seen many special functions of several variables. For instance, the formula $V = \pi r^2 h$ for the volume V of a cylinder with base radius r and height h involves a function of two variables. (Of course, in this case $\pi \approx 3.14159$ is a mathematical constant.) A change in one of these variables will not affect the value of the other variable. For each pair of positive numbers (r, h), there is a definite value for the volume V. To emphasize that V depends on the values of both r and h, we write

$$V(r, h) = \pi r^2 h$$

For $r = 2$ and $h = 3$, we obtain $V(2, 3) = 12\pi$, whereas $r = 3$ and $h = 2$ give $V(3, 2) = 18\pi$. Also, $r = 1$ and $h = 1/\pi$ give $V(1, 1/\pi) = 1$. Note in particular that $V(2, 3) \neq V(3, 2)$.

In some abstract economic models, it may be enough to know that there is some functional relationship between variables, without specifying the dependence more closely. For instance, suppose a market sells three commodities whose prices per unit are respectively p, q, and r. Then economists generally assume that the demand for one of the commodities by an individual with income m is given by a function $f(p, q, r, m)$ of four variables, without specifying the precise form of that function.

An extensive discussion of functions of several variables begins in Chapter 15. This section introduces an even more general type of function. In fact, general functions of the kind presented here are of fundamental importance in practically every area of pure and applied mathematics, including mathematics applied to economics.

Example 3.16

The following examples indicate how very wide is the concept of a function.

(a) The function that assigns to each triangle in a plane the area of that triangle (measured, say, in cm^2).

(b) The function that determines the social security number, or other identification number, of each taxpayer.

(c) The function that for each point P in a plane determines the point lying 3 units above P.

(d) Let A be the set of possible actions that a person can choose in a certain situation. Suppose that every action $a \in A$ produces a certain result (say, a certain profit $\varphi(a)$). In this way, we have defined a function φ with domain A.

Here is a general definition:

A **function** from A to B is a rule that assigns to each element of the set A one and only one element of the set B.

[3.18]

If we denote the function by f, the set A is called the **domain** of f, and B is called the **target**. The two sets A and B need not consist of numbers, but can be sets of quite arbitrary elements.

The definition of a function requires three objects to be specified:

1. A domain A
2. A target B
3. A rule that assigns a *unique* element in B to *each* element in A.

Nevertheless, in many cases, we refrain from specifying the sets A and/or B explicitly when it obvious from the context what these sets are.

An important requirement in the definition of a function is that to each element in domain A, there corresponds a *unique* element in target B. While it is meaningful to talk about the function that assigns the natural mother to every child, the rule that assigns the aunt to any child does not, in general, define a function, because many children have several aunts. Explain why the following rule, as opposed to the one in Example 3.16(c), does not define a function: "to a point P in a horizontal plane, assign a point that lies 3 units from P."

If f is a function with domain A and target B, we often say that f is a **function from** A **to** B, and write $f : A \rightarrow B$. The functional relationship is often represented as in Fig. 3.13. Other words that are sometimes used instead of "function" include **transformation** and **map** or **mapping**. The particular value $f(x)$ is often called the **image** of the element x by the function f. The set of elements in B that are images of at least one element in A is called

FIGURE 3.13 A function from *A* to *B*.

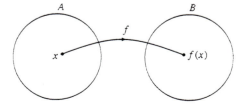

the **range** of the function. Thus, the range is a subset of the target. If we denote the range of f by R_f, then $R_f = \{f(x) : x \in A\}$. This is also written as $f(A)$. The range of the function in Example 3.16(a) is the set of all positive numbers. Explain why the range of the function in (c) must be the entire plane.

The definition of a function requires that only *one* element in B be assigned to each element in A. However, different elements in A might be mapped to the same element in B. In Example 3.16(a), for instance, many different triangles have the same area. If each element of B is the image of at most one element in A, function f is called **one-to-one**. Otherwise, if one or more elements of B are the images of more than one element in A, the function is many-to-one.

The social security function in Example 3.16(b) is intended to be one-to-one, because two different taxpayers should always have different numbers. (In very rare instances, errors cause this function to be many-to-one. These always create a great deal of confusion when they are noticed!) Can you explain why the function defined in Example 3.16(c) is also one-to-one, whereas the function that assigns to each child his or her mother is not?

Suppose f is a one-to-one function from a set A to a set B, and assume that the range of f is all of B. Thus:

1. f maps each element of A into an element of B (so f is a function).
2. Two different elements of A are always mapped into different elements of B (so f is one-to-one).
3. For each element v in B, there is an element u in A such that $f(u) = v$ (so the range of f is the whole of B).

We can then define a function g from B to A by the following obvious rule: Assign to each element v of B the element $u = g(v)$ of A that f maps to v— that is, the u satisfying $v = f(u)$. Because of rule 2, there can be only one u in A such that $v = f(u)$, so g is a function. Its domain is B and its target and range are both equal to A. The function g is called the **inverse function** of f. For instance, the inverse of the social security function mentioned earlier is the function that, to each social security number, assigns the person carrying that number. Section 7.6 provides more detail about inverse functions and their properties.

Problems

1. Decide which of the following rules defines a function:
   a. The rule that assigns to each person in a classroom his or her height.
   b. The rule that assigns to a mother her youngest child.
   c. The rule that assigns the circumference of a rectangle to its area.
   d. The rule that assigns the surface area of a spherical ball to its volume.

     e. The rule that assigns the pair of numbers $(x+3, y)$ to the pair of numbers (x, y).

2. Decide which of the functions defined in Problem 1 is one-to-one, and which then have an inverse. Determine the inverse when it exists.

3. Each person has red blood cells that belong to one and only one of four blood groups denoted A, B, AB, and O. Consider the function that assigns each person in a team to his or her blood group. Can this function be one-to-one if the team consists of at least five persons?

4

Single-Variable Differentiation

To think of it [differential calculus] merely as a more advanced technique is to miss its real content. In it, mathematics becomes a dynamic mode of thought, and that is a major mental step in the ascent of man.
—*J. Bronowski* (1973)

An important topic in scientific disciplines including economics is the study of how quickly quantities change over time. In order to compute the future position of a planet, to predict the growth in population of a biological species, or to estimate the future demand for a commodity, we need information about rates of change.

The mathematical concept used to describe the rate of change of a function is the derivative, which is *the* central concept in mathematical analysis. This chapter defines the derivative of a function and presents some of the simpler rules for calculating it. The next chapter develops some further rules allowing derivatives of quite complicated functions to be computed.

Isaac Newton (1642–1727) and Gottfried Leibniz (1646–1716) discovered most of these general rules independently of each other. This initiated the development of differential and integral calculus.

4.1 Slopes of Curves

Even though in economics we are usually interested in the derivative as a rate of change, we begin this chapter with a geometrical motivation for the concept.

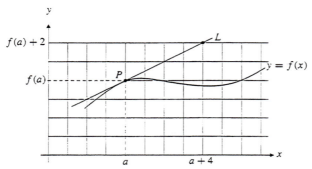

FIGURE 4.1 $f'(a) \approx 1/2$.

When we study the graph of a function, we would like to have a precise measure of the steepness of a graph at a point. We know that for the line $y = ax+b$, the number a denotes its slope. If a is large and positive, then the line rises steeply from left to right; if a is large and negative, the line falls steeply. But for an arbitrary function f, what is the steepness of its graph? A natural answer is to define the steepness of a curve at a particular point as the slope of the tangent to the curve at that point—that is, as the slope of the straight line that just touches the curve at that point. For the curve in Fig. 4.1 the steepness at point P is therefore $1/2$, because the tangent passes through the pair of points $(a, f(a))$ and $(a + 4, f(a) + 2)$, for instance. In Fig. 4.1, point P has coordinates $\left(a, f(a)\right)$. The slope of the tangent to the graph at P is called the **derivative** of f at point a and we denote this number by $f'(a)$ (read as "f prime a"). In general, we have

$$f'(a) = \text{the slope of the tangent to the curve } y = f(x) \text{ at the point } \left(a, f(a)\right) \qquad [4.1]$$

Thus, in Fig. 4.1, we have $f'(a) = [f(a) + 2 - f(a)]/(a + 4 - a) = 2/4 = 1/2$.

Example 4.1

Use definition [4.1] to determine $f'(1)$, $f'(4)$, and $f'(7)$ for the function whose graph is shown in Fig. 4.2.

Solution   At $P = (1, 2)$, the tangent goes through $(0, 1)$, and so has slope 1. At $Q = (4, 3)$ the tangent is horizontal, and so has slope 0. At $R = (7, 2\frac{1}{2})$, the tangent goes through $(8, 2)$, and so has slope $-\frac{1}{2}$. Therefore, we obtain: $f'(1) = 1$, $f'(4) = 0$, and $f'(7) = -1/2$.

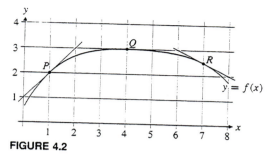

FIGURE 4.2

4.2 The Slope of the Tangent and the Derivative

The previous section gave a rather vague definition of the tangent to a curve at a point, because we said that it is a straight line that just touches the curve at that point. We now give a more formal definition of the same concept.

The geometrical idea behind the definition is easy to understand. Consider a point P on a curve in the xy-plane (see Fig. 4.3). Take another point Q on the curve. The entire straight line through P and Q is called a *secant* (from a Latin word meaning "cutting"). If we keep P fixed, but let Q move along the curve toward P, then the secant will rotate around P, as indicated in Fig. 4.4. The limiting straight line PT toward which the secant tends is called the **tangent (line)** to the curve at P. Suppose that P is a point on the graph of the function f. We shall see how the preceding considerations enable us to find the slope of the tangent at P. This is shown in Fig. 4.5.

Point P has the coordinates $\left(a, f(a)\right)$. Point Q lies close to P and is also on the graph of f. Suppose that the x-coordinate of Q is $a + h$, where h is a small number $\neq 0$. Then the x-coordinate of Q is not a (because $Q \neq P$), but a

FIGURE 4.3

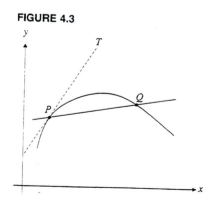

FIGURE 4.4

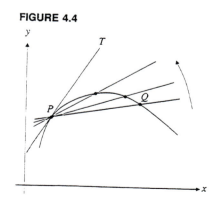

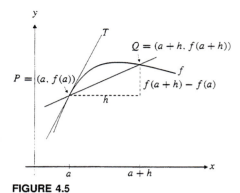

FIGURE 4.5

number close to a. Because Q lies on the graph of f, the y-coordinate of Q is equal to $f(a + h)$. Hence, the coordinates of the points are $P = (a, f(a))$ and $Q = (a + h, f(a + h))$. The slope m_{PQ} of the secant PQ is

$$m_{PQ} = \frac{f(a + h) - f(a)}{h} \qquad [4.2]$$

In mathematics, this fraction is often called a **Newton** (or **differential**) **quotient of** f. Note that when $h = 0$, the fraction in [4.2] becomes 0/0 and so is undefined. But choosing $h = 0$ corresponds to letting $Q = P$. When Q moves toward P (Q tends to P) along the graph of f, the x-coordinate of Q, which is $a + h$, must tend to a, and so h tends to 0. Simultaneously, the secant PQ tends to the tangent to the graph at P. This suggests that we ought to *define* the slope of the tangent at P as the number that m_{PQ} in [4.2] approaches as h tends to 0. In [4.1], we called this value the slope $f'(a)$. So we propose the following definition of $f'(a)$:

$$f'(a) = \left\{ \begin{array}{l} \text{the limit as } h \\ \text{tends to 0 of} \end{array} \right\} \quad \frac{f(a + h) - f(a)}{h}$$

In mathematics, it is common to use the abbreviated notation $\lim_{h \to 0}$ for "the limit as h tends to zero" of an expression involving h. We therefore have the following definition:

The **derivative** $f'(a)$ of the function f at point a of its domain is given by the formula

$$f'(a) = \lim_{h \to 0} \frac{f(a + h) - f(a)}{h} \qquad [4.3]$$

As in [4.1], the number $f'(a)$ gives the slope of the tangent to the curve $y = f(x)$ at the point $(a, f(a))$. The equation for a straight line passing through (x_1, y_1) and having a slope b is given by $y - y_1 = b(x - x_1)$. Hence, we obtain:

The equation for the **tangent** to the graph of $y = f(x)$ at the point $(a, f(a))$ is

$$y - f(a) = f'(a)(x - a) \qquad\qquad [4.4]$$

So far the concept of a limit in the definition of $f'(a)$ is not quite clear. Section 6.7 gives a precise definition. Because it is relatively complicated, we rely on intuition for the time being. Consider a simple example.

Example 4.2

Use [4.3] to compute $f'(a)$ when $f(x) = x^2$. Find in particular $f'(1/2)$, $f'(0)$, and $f'(-1)$. Give geometric interpretations, and find the equation for the tangent at the point $(1/2, 1/4)$.

Solution For $f(x) = x^2$, we have $f(a+h) = (a+h)^2 = a^2 + 2ah + h^2$, and so $f(a+h) - f(a) = (a^2 + 2ah + h^2) - a^2 = 2ah + h^2$. Hence, for all $h \neq 0$, we obtain

$$\frac{f(a+h) - f(a)}{h} = \frac{2ah + h^2}{h} = \frac{h(2a+h)}{h} = 2a + h \qquad\qquad [1]$$

because we can cancel h whenever $h \neq 0$. But as h tends to 0, so $2a + h$ obviously tends to $2a$. Thus, we can write

$$f'(a) = \lim_{h \to 0} \frac{f(a+h) - f(a)}{h} = \lim_{h \to 0} (2a + h) = 2a \qquad\qquad [2]$$

This shows that when $f(x) = x^2$, then $f'(a) = 2a$. For $a = 1/2$, we obtain $f'(1/2) = 2 \cdot 1/2 = 1$. Similarly, $f'(0) = 2 \cdot 0 = 0$ and $f'(-1) = 2 \cdot (-1) = -2$.

In Fig. 4.6, we provide the geometric interpretation of [1]. In Fig. 4.7, we have drawn the tangents to the curve $y = x^2$ corresponding to $a = 1/2$ and $a = -1$. At $a = 1/2$, we have $f(a) = (1/2)^2 = 1/4$ and $f'(1/2) = 1$. According to [4.4], the equation of the tangent is $y - 1/4 = 1 \cdot (x - 1/2)$ or $y = x - 1/4$. (Show that the other tangent drawn in Fig. 4.7 has the equation $y = -2x - 1$.) Note that the formula $f'(a) = 2a$ shows that $f'(a) < 0$ when $a < 0$, and $f'(a) > 0$ when $a > 0$. Does this agree with the graph?

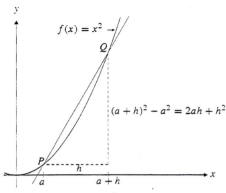

FIGURE 4.6 *f(x) = x²*.

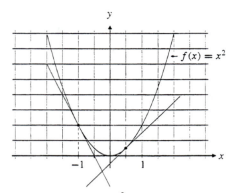

FIGURE 4.7 *f(x) = x²*.

If f is a relatively simple function, we can find $f'(a)$ as follows:

Recipe for computing $f'(a)$:

1. Add h to a ($h \neq 0$) and compute $f(a + h)$.
2. Compute the corresponding change in the function value:
   $f(a + h) - f(a)$.
3. For $h \neq 0$, form the Newton quotient

$$\frac{f(a + h) - f(a)}{h}$$

   [4.5]

4. Simplify the fraction in step 3 as much as possible. Wherever possible, cancel h from both numerator and denominator.
5. Then $f'(a)$ is the number that

$$\frac{f(a + h) - f(a)}{h}$$

approaches as h tends to 0. ·

Let us apply this recipe to another example.

Example 4.3

Compute $f'(a)$ when $f(x) = x^3$.

Solution   We follow the recipe in [4.5].

1. $f(a + h) = (a + h)^3 = a^3 + 3a^2h + 3ah^2 + h^3$

2. $f(a+h) - f(a) = (a^3 + 3a^2h + 3ah^2 + h^3) - a^3$
$$= 3a^2h + 3ah^2 + h^3$$

3–4. $\dfrac{f(a+h) - f(a)}{h} = \dfrac{3a^2h + 3ah^2 + h^3}{h} = 3a^2 + 3ah + h^2$

5. As h tends to 0, so $3ah + h^2$ will also tend to 0; hence, the entire expression $3a^2 + 3ah + h^2$ tends to $3a^2$. Therefore, $f'(a) = 3a^2$.

We have thus shown that the graph of the function $f(x) = x^3$ at the point $x = a$ has a tangent with slope $3a^2$. Note that $f'(a) = 3a^2 > 0$ when $a \neq 0$, and $f'(0) = 0$. The tangent points upwards to the right for all $a \neq 0$, and is horizontal at the origin. You should draw the graph of $f(x) = x^3$ to confirm this behavior.

It is easy to use the recipe in [4.5] on simple functions. However, the recipe becomes difficult or even impossible if we try to use it on slightly more complicated functions such as $f(x) = \sqrt{3x^2 + x + 1}$. The next chapter develops rules for computing the derivative of quite complicated functions, without the need to use [4.5]. Before presenting such rules, however, we must examine the concept of a limit a little more carefully. This is done in Section 4.4.

On Notation

We showed in Example 4.2 that, if $f(x) = x^2$, then for every a, we have $f'(a) = 2a$. We frequently use x as the symbol for a quantity that can take any value, so we write $f'(x) = 2x$. If we use this new notation for the function in Example 4.3, we can briefly formulate our main results from the two last examples as follows:

$$f(x) = x^2 \implies f'(x) = 2x \qquad\qquad\qquad [4.6]$$

$$f(x) = x^3 \implies f'(x) = 3x^2 \qquad\qquad\qquad [4.7]$$

Equation [4.6] is a special case of the following rule, which you are asked to show in Problem 6.

$$f(x) = ax^2 + bx + c \implies f'(x) = 2ax + b \qquad (a,\ b,\ \text{and } c \text{ are constants})\ [4.8]$$

For $a = 1$, $b = c = 0$, this reduces to [4.6]. Here are some special cases of [4.8]:

$$f(x) = 3x^2 + 2x + 5 \implies f'(x) = 3 \cdot 2x + 2 = 6x + 2$$

$$f(x) = -16 + \tfrac{1}{2}x - \tfrac{1}{16}x^2 \implies f'(x) = -\tfrac{1}{8}x + \tfrac{1}{2}$$

$$f(x) = (x - p)^2 = x^2 - 2px + p^2 \implies f'(x) = 2x - 2p \qquad (p \text{ constant})$$

If we use y to denote the value of the function $y = f(x)$, we often denote the derivative by y'. We can then write $y = x^3 \Rightarrow y' = 3x^2$.

Several other forms of notation for the derivative are often used in mathematics and its applications. One of them, originally due to Leibniz, is called the **differential notation**. If $y = f(x)$, we write

$$\frac{dy}{dx} = dy/dx \;\; \text{or} \;\; \frac{df(x)}{dx} = df(x)/dx \;\; \text{or} \;\; \frac{d}{dx} f(x) \;\; \text{in place of} \;\; f'(x)$$

For instance, if $y = x^2$, then

$$\frac{dy}{dx} = 2x = \frac{d}{dx}(x^2) = 2x$$

At this point, we will only think of the symbol dy/dx as meaning $f'(x)$ and will not consider it as dy divided by dx. Later chapters discuss this notation in greater detail. In fact, d/dx really denotes an instruction to differentiate what follows with respect to x. Differentiation with respect to a variable occurs so often in mathematics that it has become standard to use **w.r.t.** as an abbreviation for "with respect to."

When we use letters other than f, x, and y, the notation for the derivative changes accordingly. For example: $P(t) = t^2 \Rightarrow P'(t) = 2t$; $Y = K^3 \Rightarrow Y' = 3K^2$; and $A = r^2 \Rightarrow dA/dr = 2r$.

Problems

1. Let $f(x) = 4x^2$. Show that $f(5 + h) - f(5) = 40h + 4h^2$. Hence,

$$\frac{f(5 + h) - f(5)}{h} = 40 + 4h$$

Using this result, find $f'(5)$. Compare the answer with [4.8].

2. Let $f(x) = 3x^2 + 2x - 1$. Show that for $h \neq 0$,

$$\frac{f(x + h) - f(x)}{h} = 6x + 2 + 3h$$

Use this result to find $f'(x)$. Find in particular $f'(0)$, $f'(-2)$, and $f'(3)$, and the equation for the tangent to the graph at the point $(0, -1)$.

3. Figure 4.8 shows the graph of a function f. Determine whether the following derivatives are > 0, $= 0$, or < 0: $f'(a)$, $f'(b)$, $f'(c)$, and $f'(d)$.

4. Show that

$$f(x) = \frac{1}{x} \implies f'(x) = -\frac{1}{x^2}$$

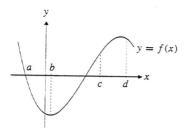

FIGURE 4.8

Hint: Show that $[f(x+h) - f(x)]/h = -1/x(x+h)$. (See Problem 14, Section 2.5.)

5. Find the slope for the tangent to the graph of the following functions at the specified points:

   a. $f(x) = 3x + 2$ at $(0, 2)$ **b.** $f(x) = x^2 - 1$ at $(1, 0)$

   c. $f(x) = \dfrac{3}{x} + 2$ at $(3, 3)$ **d.** $f(x) = x^3 - 2x$ at $(0, 0)$

   e. $f(x) = x + \dfrac{1}{x}$ at $(-1, -2)$ **f.** $f(x) = x^4$ at $(1, 1)$

6. **a.** If $f(x) = ax^2 + bx + c$, show that $[f(x+h) - f(x)]/h = 2ax + b + ah$. Use this to show that $f'(x) = 2ax + b$.

   b. For what value of x is $f'(x) = 0$? Explain this result in the light of [3.4] in Section 3.1.

7. **a.** The demand function for a commodity with price P is given by the formula $D(P) = a - bP$. Find $dD(P)/dP$.

   b. The cost of producing x units of a commodity is given by the formula $C(x) = p + qx^2$. Find $C'(x)$.

8. **a.** Show that $\left(\sqrt{x+h} - \sqrt{x}\right)\left(\sqrt{x+h} + \sqrt{x}\right) = h$.

   b. If $f(x) = \sqrt{x}$, show that $[f(x+h) - f(x)]/h = 1/\left(\sqrt{x+h} + \sqrt{x}\right)$.

   c. Use the result in part (b) to show that for $x > 0$,

   $$f(x) = \sqrt{x} \implies f'(x) = \frac{1}{2\sqrt{x}}$$

   d. Show that the result could also be written as

   $$\frac{d}{dx} x^{1/2} = \frac{1}{2} x^{-1/2}$$

9. **a.** If $f(x) = ax^3 + bx^2 + cx + d$, show that

   $$[f(x+h) - f(x)]/h = 3ax^2 + 2bx + c + 3axh + ah^2 + bh$$

   and hence that $f'(x) = 3ax^2 + 2bx + c$.

    b. Show that the result in part (a) generalizes the results in Example 4.3 and in Problem 6.

Harder Problems

  10. **a.** If $f(x) = x^{1/3}$, show that

$$\frac{f(x+h) - f(x)}{h} = \frac{1}{(x+h)^{2/3} + (x+h)^{1/3} \cdot x^{1/3} + x^{2/3}}$$

by using the result in Problem 11(a), Section 3.14, with $a = x + h$ and $b = x$.

    b. Use the result in part (a) to show that

$$\frac{d}{dx}(x^{1/3}) = \frac{1}{3}x^{-2/3}$$

4.3 Rates of Change and Their Economic Significance

We have so far interpreted the derivative of a function as the slope of the tangent to its graph at a particular point. In economics, other interpretations are more important. Let us first see how the derivative in general can be interpreted as a rate of change.

Suppose that a quantity y is related to a quantity x by $y = f(x)$. If x has a given value a, then the value of the function is given by $f(a)$. Suppose that a is changed to $a + h$. The new value of y is $f(a+h)$, and the change in the value of the function when x is changed from a to $a + h$ is $f(a+h) - f(a)$. The change in y per unit change in x has a particular name, the *average rate of change of f over the interval from a to $a + h$*. It is equal to

$$\frac{f(a+h) - f(a)}{h} \qquad [4.9]$$

Note that this fraction is precisely the Newton quotient of f. Taking the limit as h tends to 0 gives the derivative of f at a. Therefore:

The **instantaneous rate of change** of f at a is $f'(a)$ [4.10]

This very important concept appears whenever we study quantities that change. When time is the independent variable, we often use the "dot notation" for differentiation with respect to time. For example, if $x(t) = t^2$, we write $\dot{x}(t) = 2t$.

Sometimes we are interested in studying the proportion $f'(a)/f(a)$. We introduce a name for this:

> The **proportional rate of change** of f at a is $f'(a)/f(a)$ [4.11]

In economics, proportional rates of change are seen very often. Sometimes they are called **relative rates of change**. They are usually quoted in percentages—or when time is the independent variable, as percentages per year, or *per annum*. Often we will describe a variable as increasing at, say, 3% a year if there is a proportional rate of change of 3/100 each year.

Example 4.4

Let $N(t)$ be the number of individuals in a population (of humans, animals, or plants) at time t. If t increases to $t + h$, then the change in population is equal to $N(t + h) - N(t)$ individuals. Hence, $[N(t + h) - N(t)]/h$ is *the average rate of change*. Taking the limit as h tends to 0 gives $\dot{N}(t) = dN/dt$ for *the rate of change of population at time* t. (At the end of this section, we will discuss the problem that arises when $N(t)$ takes only integer values.)

Example 6 of Section 2.5 was based on the case when P denotes the number (in millions) of inhabitants of Europe, which was given by the formula

$$P = 6.4t + 641 \tag{1}$$

Here t is the number of years, as computed from 1960. In this case, the rate of change is the same for all t:

$$\frac{dP}{dt} = 6.4 \text{ million per year}$$

Economic Interpretations

Example 4.5

Consider a firm producing some commodity in a given period. Let

$C(x) = $ cost of producing x units

$R(x) = $ revenue from selling x units

$\pi(x) = R(x) - C(x) = $ profit from producing (and selling) x units

We call $C'(x)$ the **marginal cost** (at x), $R'(x)$ the **marginal revenue**, and $\pi'(x)$ the **marginal profit**. Economists often use the word **marginal** in this way in order to signify a derivative.

Other examples of the derivative in economics include the following. The **marginal propensity to consume** is the derivative of the consumption function with respect to income; similarly, the **marginal product** (or **productivity) of labor** is the derivative of the production function with respect to labor input.

According to the definition, marginal cost is equal to

$$C'(x) = \lim_{h \to 0} \frac{C(x+h) - C(x)}{h} \quad \text{(marginal cost)} \quad [4.12]$$

Usually, the firm will produce many units of x. Then $h = 1$ can be considered a number close to 0, and we obtain the approximation

$$C'(x) \approx \frac{C(x+1) - C(x)}{1} = C(x+1) - C(x)$$

Marginal cost is then approximately equal to the **incremental cost** $C(x+1) - C(x)$, that is, the *additional cost of producing one more unit of x*. In elementary economics courses, marginal cost is often defined as the difference $C(x+1) - C(x)$ because more appropriate concepts from differential calculus cannot be used.

Example 4.6

Let $K(t)$ be the capital stock in an economy at time t. The rate of change $\dot{K}(t)$ of $K(t)$ is called the **rate of investment** at time t. It is usually denoted by $I(t)$, so

$$\dot{K}(t) = I(t) \quad [4.13]$$

Differentiability and Empirical Functions

The very definition of derivative assumes that arbitrary small increments in the independent variable are possible. In practical problems, however, it is usually impossible to implement, or even measure, arbitrary small changes in the variable. For example, economic quantities that vary with time, such as the price of a commodity or the national income of a country, are usually measured at intervals of days, weeks, or years. Further, the cost functions of the type we discussed in Example 4.5 are often properly defined only for integer values of x. In all these cases, the variables only take discrete values. The graphs of such functions, therefore, will only consist of discrete points. For functions of this type in which time and numbers both change discretely, the concept of the derivative is not defined. To remedy this, the actual function is usually replaced by a differentiable function that is a "good approximation" to the original function. As an illustration, Fig. 4.9 graphs observations of the number of registered unemployed in Norway for each month of the years 1928–1929. In Fig. 4.10

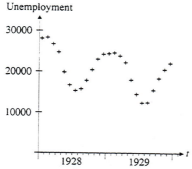

FIGURE 4.9   Unemployment in Norway (1928–1929).

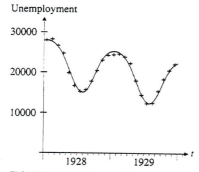

FIGURE 4.10   A smooth curve approximating the points in Fig. 4.9.

we show the graph of a differentiable function that is an approximation to the points plotted in Fig. 4.9. (The graph in Fig. 4.10 is drawn using a computer program.)

Problems

1. Let $C(x) = x^2 + 3x + 100$ be the cost function of a firm. Show that the average rate of change when x is changed from 100 to $100 + h$ is

$$\frac{C(100 + h) - C(100)}{h} = 203 + h \qquad (h \neq 0)$$

What is the marginal cost $C'(100)$? Use [4.8] to find $C'(x)$ and in particular $C'(100)$.

2. If the cost function of a firm is $C(x) = kx + I$, give economic interpretations of the parameters k and I.

3. If the total savings of a country is a function $S(Y)$ of the national product Y, then $S'(Y)$ is called the *marginal propensity to save* (MPS). Find the MPS

for the following functions:

a. $S(Y) = a + bY$ **b.** $S(Y) = 100 + 10Y + 2Y^2$

4. If the tax a family pays is a function of its income y given by $T(y)$, then $dT(y)/dy$ is called the *marginal tax rate*. Characterize the following tax function by determining its marginal rate:

$$T(y) = ty \qquad (t \text{ is a constant number} \in (0, 1))$$

5. Refer to the definitions given in Example 4.5. Compute the marginal revenue, marginal cost, and marginal profit in the following two cases (where p, a, b, a_1, b_1, and c_1 are all positive constants), and in each case find an expression for the value of x at which the marginal profit is equal to 0:

a. $R(x)$, $C(x) = a_1x^2 + b_1x + c_1$
b. $R(x) = ax^2 - bx^2$, $C(x) = a_1x + b_1$

4.4 A Dash of Limits

The previous section defined the derivative of a function based on the concept of a limit. The same concept is important for other reasons as well, so now we should take a closer look. Here we give a preliminary definition and formulate some important rules for limits. In Chapter 6, we discuss the limit concept more closely, as well as the related concept of continuity.

As an example, consider the formula

$$F(x) = \frac{x^2 - 16}{4\sqrt{x} - 8}$$

Note that if $x = 4$, then the fraction collapses to the absurd expression "0/0." Thus, the function F is not defined for $x = 4$, but one can still ask what happens to $F(x)$ when x is close to 4. Using a calculator (except when $x = 4$), we find the values shown in Table 4.1.

TABLE 4.1   *Values of $F(x) = (x^2 - 16)/(4\sqrt{x} - 8)$ when x is close to 4*

x	3.9	3.99	3.999	3.9999	4.0	4.0001	4.001	4.01	4.1
$F(x)$	7.850	7.985	7.998	8.000	*	8.000	8.002	8.015	8.150

*Not defined.

It seems obvious from the table that as x gets closer and closer to 4, so the fraction $F(x)$ gets closer and closer to 8. It therefore seems reasonable to say that

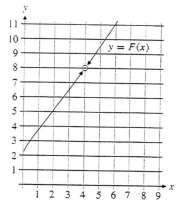

FIGURE 4.11 $y = F(x) = \dfrac{x^2 - 16}{4\sqrt{x} - 8}$

$F(x)$ tends to 8 in the limit as x tends to 4. We write

$$\lim_{x \to 4} \frac{x^2 - 16}{4\sqrt{x} - 8} = 8 \qquad \text{or} \qquad \frac{x^2 - 16}{4\sqrt{x} - 8} \to 8 \quad \text{as} \quad x \to 4$$

In Fig. 4.11 we have drawn a portion of the graph of F. The function F is defined for all $x \geq 0$, except at $x = 4$. Also $\lim_{x \to 4} F(x) = 8$. (A small circle is used to indicate that the corresponding point $(4, 8)$ is not in the graph of F.)

A Preliminary Definition of the Limit Concept

Suppose, in general, that a function f is defined for all x near a, but not necessarily at $x = a$. Then we say that *$f(x)$ has the number A as its limit as x tends to a, if $f(x)$ tends to A as x tends to (but is not equal to) a.* We write

$$\lim_{x \to a} f(x) = A \qquad \text{or} \qquad f(x) \to A \quad \text{as} \quad x \to a$$

It is possible, however, that the value of $f(x)$ does not tend to any fixed number as x tends to a. Then we say that $\lim_{x \to a} f(x)$ *does not exist*, or that *$f(x)$ does not have a limit as x tends to a.*

Example 4.7

Use a calculator to examine the following limits:

(a) $\lim_{x \to 3} (3x - 2)$

(b) $\lim_{h \to 0} \dfrac{\sqrt{h + 1} - 1}{h}$

(c) $\lim_{x \to -2} \dfrac{1}{(x + 2)^2}$

Solution

(a) We obtain Table 4.2 when x is a number close to 3. As $x \to 3$, it seems that $3x - 2$ tends to 7, so that $\lim_{x \to 3} (3x - 2) = 7$. (If x is precisely equal to 3, then $3x - 2$ is equal to 7. But the definition of $\lim_{x \to 3} (3x - 2)$ ignores the value of $3x - 2$ at $x = 3$.)

TABLE 4.2   *Values of $3x - 2$ when x is close to 3*

x	2.9	2.95	2.99	2.999	3.001	3.01	3.05	3.1
$3x - 2$	6.7	6.85	6.97	6.997	7.003	7.03	7.15	7.3

(b) Some values of h close to 0 give the values in Table 4.3. This suggests that

$$\lim_{h \to 0} \frac{\sqrt{h + 1} - 1}{h} = 0.5$$

TABLE 4.3   *Values of $(\sqrt{h + 1} - 1)/h$ when h is close to 0*

h	−0.5	−0.2	−0.1	−0.01	0.0	0.01	0.1	0.2	0.5
$\frac{\sqrt{h+1}-1}{h}$	0.586	0.528	0.513	0.501	*	0.499	0.488	0.477	0.449

*Not defined.

(c) We choose x values close to -2 and obtain the values in Table 4.4. As x gets closer and closer to -2, we see that the value of the fraction becomes larger and larger. By extending the values in the table, it is clear, for example, that for $x = -2.0001$ and $x = -1.9999$, the value of the fraction is 100 million. Hence, we conclude that $1/(x + 2)^2$ does not tend to any limit as x tends to -2. Because the fraction becomes larger and larger as x tends to -2, we say that it tends to infinity, and write $\lim_{x \to -2} 1/(x + 2)^2 = \infty$.

TABLE 4.4   *Values of $1/(x + 2)^2$ when x is close to -2*

x	−1.8	−1.9	−1.99	−1.999	−2.0	−2.001	−2.01	−2.1	−2.2
$\frac{1}{(x+2)^2}$	25	100	10,000	1,000,000	*	1,000,000	10,000	100	25

*Not defined.

The limits found previously were all based on shaky numerical foundations. For instance, in Example 4.7(b), can we really be certain that our guess is correct? Could it be that if we chose h values even closer to 0, the fraction would tend to a limit other than 0.5, or maybe not have any limit at all? Further numerical computations will support our belief that the initial guess is correct, but we can never make a table that has *all* the values of h close to 0, so numerical computation alone can never establish with certainty what the limit is. This illustrates the need to have a rigorous procedure for finding limits. First of all, however, a precise mathematical definition of the limit concept is required. One such definition is given in Section 6.7. Meanwhile, here is a preliminary definition.

> Writing $\lim_{x \to a} f(x) = A$ means that we can make $f(x)$ as close to A as we want for all x sufficiently close to (but not equal to) a.   [4.14]

We emphasize:

1. The number $\lim_{x \to a} f(x)$ depends on the value of $f(x)$ for x values close to a, but not on how f behaves at the precise value of $x = a$. When finding $\lim_{x \to a} f(x)$, we are simply not interested in the value $f(a)$, or even in whether f is actually defined at a.

2. When we compute $\lim_{x \to a} f(x)$, we must take into consideration x values on both sides of a.

The next example illustrates the limit concept geometrically.

Example 4.8

Figure 4.12 shows the graph of a particular function f, defined in the closed interval $[0, 9]$. Determine $\lim_{x \to a} f(x)$ for $a = 2, 3, 4,$ and 6. (The point at the end of each arrow is not part of the graph, but is the limit of points on the graph.)

Solution   We see that $\lim_{x \to 2} f(x) = 3$. Note that $f(2) = 2$. Also $\lim_{x \to 3} f(x) = 1$. Here $f(3) = 1$. The limit $\lim_{x \to 4} f(x)$ does not exist.

FIGURE 4.12

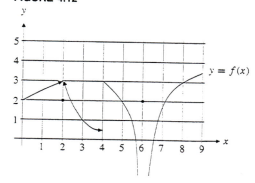

For x close to 4 and $x < 4$, $f(x)$ tends to 1/2, and for x close to 4 and $x > 4$, $f(x)$ tends to 3. Thus, $f(x)$ does not tend to *one* specific number as x tends to 4. Finally, $\lim_{x \to 6} f(x)$ does not exist. As x tends to 6, $f(x)$ will decrease without limit. We write $\lim_{x \to 6} f(x) = -\infty$.

Rules for Limits

Of course, one cannot really determine limits by means of numerical computations. Instead, we use some simple rules for finding limits whose validity can be shown once we have a precise definition of the limit concept. These rules are very straightforward and we have even used a few of them already in the previous section. Let us briefly discuss some of them.

Suppose that f and g are defined as functions in the neighborhood of a (but not necessarily at a). Then we have the following rules:

Rules for Limits

If $\lim_{x \to a} f(x) = A$ and $\lim_{x \to a} g(x) = B$, then

  i. $\lim_{x \to a} [f(x) + g(x)] = A + B$

  ii. $\lim_{x \to a} [f(x) - g(x)] = A - B$

  iii. $\lim_{x \to a} [f(x)g(x)] = A \cdot B$

  iv. $\lim_{x \to a}[f(x)/g(x)] = A/B$ (provided $B \neq 0$)

  v. $\lim_{x \to a} [f(x)]^{p/q} = A^{p/q}$ (if $A^{p/q}$ is defined)

[4.15]

It is easy to give intuitive explanations for these rules. If $\lim_{x \to a} f(x) = A$ and $\lim_{x \to a} g(x) = B$, then we know that, when x is close to a, then $f(x)$ is close to A and $g(x)$ is close to B. So presumably the sum $f(x) + g(x)$ is close to $A + B$, the product $f(x)g(x)$ is close to $A \cdot B$, and so on.

The rules in [4.15] can be used repeatedly to obtain new extended rules such as

$$\lim_{x \to a} [f_1(x) + f_2(x) + \cdots + f_n(x)] = \lim_{x \to a} f_1(x) + \lim_{x \to a} f_2(x) + \cdots$$
$$+ \lim_{x \to a} f_n(x) \qquad [4.16]$$

$$\lim_{x \to a} [f_1(x) \cdot f_2(x) \cdots f_n(x)] = \lim_{x \to a} f_1(x) \cdot \lim_{x \to a} f_2(x) \cdots \lim_{x \to a} f_n(x) \qquad [4.17]$$

In words, we can say that *the limit of a sum is the sum of the limits, and the limit of a product is equal to the product of the limits.*

Suppose the function $f(x)$ is equal to the same constant value c for every x. Then

$$\lim_{x \to a} c = c \qquad \text{(at every point } a\text{)} \qquad\qquad [4.18]$$

It is also evident that if $f(x) = x$, then

$$\lim_{x \to a} f(x) = \lim_{x \to a} x = a \qquad \text{(at every point } a\text{)} \qquad\qquad [4.19]$$

Combining these two simple limits with the general rules [4.15]–[4.17] allows easy computation of the limits for certain combinations of functions.

Example 4.9
Compute the following limits:

(a) $\lim_{x \to -2} (x^2 + 5x)$

(b) $\lim_{x \to 4} \dfrac{2x^{3/2} - \sqrt{x}}{x^2 - 15}$

(c) $\lim_{x \to a} Ax^n$

Solution   Using the rules in [4.15]–[4.17], we get

(a) $\displaystyle \lim_{x \to -2} (x^2 + 5x) = \lim_{x \to -2} (x \cdot x) + \lim_{x \to -2} (5 \cdot x)$

$$= \left(\lim_{x \to -2} x \right)\left(\lim_{x \to -2} x \right) + \left(\lim_{x \to -2} 5 \right)\left(\lim_{x \to -2} x \right)$$

$$= (-2)(-2) + 5 \cdot (-2) = -6$$

(b) $\displaystyle \lim_{x \to 4} \frac{2x^{3/2} - \sqrt{x}}{x^2 - 15} = \frac{2 \lim_{x \to 4} x^{3/2} - \lim_{x \to 4} \sqrt{x}}{\lim_{x \to 4} x^2 - 15} = \frac{2 \cdot 4^{3/2} - \sqrt{4}}{4^2 - 15} = 14$

(c) $\displaystyle \lim_{x \to a} Ax^n = \left(\lim_{x \to a} A \right)\left(\lim_{x \to a} x^n \right) = A \cdot \left(\lim_{x \to a} x \right)^n = A \cdot a^n$

It was easy to find the limits in this example by using rules [4.15]–[4.19]. The example that started this section and Example 4.7(b) both present more difficulties. They involve a fraction whose numerator and denominator both tend to 0. Rule [4.15](iv) cannot be applied directly in such cases. However, a simple observation can still help us find the limit (provided that it exists). Because $\lim_{x \to a} f(x)$ can only depend on the values of f when x is close to, but not equal to a, we have the following:

If the functions f and g are equal for all x close to a (but not necessarily at $x = a$), then $\lim_{x \to a} f(x) = \lim_{x \to a} g(x)$ whenever either limit exists.   [4.20]

Here are some examples of how this rule works.

Example 4.10

Compute the following limits:

(a) $\lim_{x \to 2} \dfrac{3x^2 + 3x - 18}{x - 2}$

(b) $\lim_{h \to 0} \dfrac{\sqrt{h + 1} - 1}{h}$

(c) $\lim_{x \to 4} \dfrac{x^2 - 16}{4\sqrt{x} - 8}$

Solution

(a) We see that both numerator and denominator tend to 0 when x tends
to 2. Because the numerator $3x^2 + 3x - 18$ is equal to 0 for $x = 2$, it
has $x - 2$ as a factor. In fact, $3x^2 + 3x - 18 = 3(x - 2)(x + 3)$. Hence,

$$f(x) = \frac{3x^2 + 3x - 18}{x - 2} = \frac{3(x - 2)(x + 3)}{x - 2}$$

For $x \neq 2$, we can cancel $x - 2$ from both numerator and denominator
to obtain $3(x + 3)$. So the functions $f(x)$ and $g(x) = 3(x + 3)$ are
equal for all $x \neq 2$. According to [4.20], this implies that

$$\lim_{x \to 2} \frac{3x^2 + 3x - 18}{x - 2} = \lim_{x \to 2} 3(x + 3) = 3(2 + 3) = 15$$

(b) Again both numerator and denominator tend to 0 as h tends to 0. Here
we must use a little trick. We multiply both numerator and denominator
by $\sqrt{h + 1} + 1$ to get

$$\frac{\sqrt{h + 1} - 1}{h} = \frac{\left(\sqrt{h + 1} - 1\right)\left(\sqrt{h + 1} + 1\right)}{h\left(\sqrt{h + 1} + 1\right)}$$

$$= \frac{h + 1 - 1}{h\left(\sqrt{h + 1} + 1\right)} = \frac{1}{\sqrt{h + 1} + 1}$$

where the common factor h has been canceled. For all $h \neq 0$ (and
$h \geq -1$), the given function is equal to $1/(\sqrt{h + 1} + 1)$, which tends
to $1/2$ as h tends to 0. We conclude that the limit of our function is
equal to $1/2$, which confirms the result in Example 4.7(b).

(c) We must try to simplify the fraction because $x = 4$ gives $0/0$. Again
we can use a trick to factorize the fraction as follows:

$$\frac{x^2 - 16}{4\sqrt{x} - 8} = \frac{(x + 4)(x - 4)}{4\left(\sqrt{x} - 2\right)} = \frac{(x + 4)\left(\sqrt{x} + 2\right)\left(\sqrt{x} - 2\right)}{4\left(\sqrt{x} - 2\right)} \qquad [*]$$

Here we have used the factorization $x-4 = \left(\sqrt{x}+2\right)\left(\sqrt{x}-2\right)$, which is correct for $x \geq 0$. In the last fraction of [*], we can cancel $\sqrt{x}-2$ when $\sqrt{x}-2 \neq 0$—that is, when $x \neq 4$. Using [4.20] again gives

$$\lim_{x \to 4} \frac{x^2 - 16}{4\sqrt{x} - 8} = \lim_{x \to 4} \frac{1}{4}(x+4)(\sqrt{x}+2) = \frac{1}{4}(4+4)(\sqrt{4}+2) = 8$$

This confirms the claim we made in the introduction to this section. Section 7.5 treats more systematically limits of fractions of the type studied in Example 4.10.

Problems

1. Determine the following by using the rules for limits:

   a. $\lim_{x \to 0} (3 + 2x^2)$ **b.** $\lim_{x \to -1} \dfrac{3 + 2x}{x - 1}$ **c.** $\lim_{x \to 2} (2x^2 + 5)^3$

   d. $\lim_{t \to 8} \left(5t + t^2 - \frac{1}{8}t^3\right)$ **e.** $\lim_{y \to 0} \dfrac{(y+1)^5 - y^5}{y + 1}$ **f.** $\lim_{z \to -2} \dfrac{1/z + 2}{z}$

2. Consider the following limit:

$$\lim_{x \to 1} \frac{x^2 + 7x - 8}{x - 1}$$

   a. Examine the limit numerically by making a table of values of the fraction when x is close to 1.

   b. Find the limit by using [4.20].

3. For the function h whose graph is given in Fig. 4.13, examine $\lim_{\to a} h(t)$ for $a = -1, 0, 2, 3,$ and 4.

4. Compute the following limits:

   a. $\lim_{x \to 2} (x^2 + 3x - 5)$ **b.** $\lim_{y \to -3} \dfrac{1}{y + 8}$

FIGURE 4.13

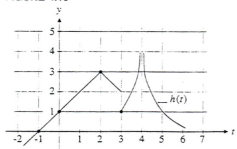

c. $\lim\limits_{x \to 0} \dfrac{x^3 - 2x - 1}{x^5 - x^2 - 1}$ **d.** $\lim\limits_{x \to 0} \dfrac{x^3 + 3x^2 - 2x}{x}$

e. $\lim\limits_{h \to 0} \dfrac{(x + h)^3 - x^3}{h}$ **f.** $\lim\limits_{x \to 0} \dfrac{(x + h)^3 - x^3}{h}$ $(h \neq 0)$

5. Compute the following limits:

a. $\lim\limits_{h \to 2} \dfrac{1/3 - 2/3h}{h - 2}$ **b.** $\lim\limits_{x \to 0} \dfrac{x^2 - 1}{x^2}$ **c.** $\lim\limits_{t \to 3} \sqrt[3]{\dfrac{32t - 96}{t^2 - 2t - 3}}$

d. $\lim\limits_{h \to 0} \dfrac{\sqrt{h + 3} - \sqrt{3}}{h}$ **e.** $\lim\limits_{t \to -2} \dfrac{t^2 - 4}{t^2 + 10t + 16}$ **f.** $\lim\limits_{x \to 4} \dfrac{2 - \sqrt{x}}{4 - x}$

6. If $f(x) = x^2 + 2x$, compute the following limits:

a. $\lim\limits_{x \to 1} \dfrac{f(x) - f(1)}{x - 1}$ **b.** $\lim\limits_{x \to 2} \dfrac{f(x) - f(1)}{x - 1}$

c. $\lim\limits_{h \to 0} \dfrac{f(2 + h) - f(2)}{h}$ **d.** $\lim\limits_{x \to a} \dfrac{f(x) - f(a)}{x - a}$

e. $\lim\limits_{h \to 0} \dfrac{f(a + h) - f(a)}{h}$ **f.** $\lim\limits_{h \to 0} \dfrac{f(a + h) - f(a - h)}{h}$

7. Compute the following limits numerically by using a calculator:

a. $\lim\limits_{h \to 0} \dfrac{2^h - 1}{h}$ **b.** $\lim\limits_{h \to 0} \dfrac{3^h - 1}{h}$ **c.** $\lim\limits_{h \to 0} (1 + h)^{1/h}$

Harder Problems

8. Compute the following limits. (*Hint:* For part (b), substitute $\sqrt[3]{27 + h} = u$.)

a. $\lim\limits_{x \to 2} \dfrac{x^2 - 2x}{x^3 - 8}$ **b.** $\lim\limits_{h \to 0} \dfrac{\sqrt[3]{27 + h} - 3}{h}$

c. $\lim\limits_{x \to 1} \dfrac{x^n - 1}{x - 1}$ (n is a natural number)

4.5 Simple Rules for Differentiation

In Section 4.2, we defined the derivative of a function f by the formula

$$f'(x) = \lim\limits_{h \to 0} \frac{f(x + h) - f(x)}{h} \qquad [*]$$

If this limit exists, we say that f is **differentiable** at x. The process of finding the derivative of a function is called **differentiation**. It is useful to think of this as an operation that transforms one function f into a new function f'. The function f' is then defined for the values of x where the limit in [*] exists. If $y = f(x)$, we can use the symbols y' and dy/dx as alternatives to $f'(x)$.

In the examples and problems in Section 4.2, we used formula [*] and the recipe in [4.5] in order to find the derivatives of some simple functions. However, it is often difficult to apply the definition directly. The next chapter uses the recipe in [4.5] systematically to devise rules that can be used to find the derivatives of quite complicated functions. Here we only consider some very simple rules.

If f is the constant function $f(x) = A$, then the derivative $f'(x)$ is equal to 0:

$$f(x) = A \implies f'(x) = 0$$

[4.21]

The result is easy to see geometrically. The graph of $f(x) = A$ is a straight line parallel to the x-axis. The tangent to the graph has slope 0 at each point (see Fig. 4.14). You should now use the definition of $f'(x)$ to get the same answer.

Additive constants disappear with differentiation:
$$y = A + f(x) \implies y' = f'(x)$$

[4.22]

Multiplicative constants are preserved by differentiation:
$$y = Af(x) \implies y' = Af'(x)$$

[4.23]

FIGURE 4.14   The derivative of a constant is 0.

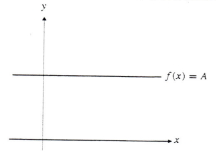

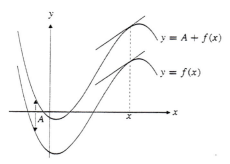

FIGURE 4.15 The graphs of the functions are parallel, and the functions have the same derivative at each point.

Rule [4.22] is illustrated in Fig. 4.15. The graph of $A + f(x)$ is that of $f(x)$ shifted upwards by A units in the direction of the y-axis. The graphs of $f(x)$ and $f(x) + A$ are thus parallel, and the tangents to the two curves at each x value must have the same slope. Again you should use the definition of $f'(x)$ to give a formal proof of this assertion.

We prove the rule in [4.23] by using the definition of a derivative. If $g(x) = Af(x)$, then $g(x+h) - g(x) = Af(x+h) - Af(x) = A[f(x+h) - f(x)]$, and so

$$g'(x) = \lim_{h \to 0} \frac{g(x+h) - g(x)}{h} = A \lim_{h \to 0} \frac{f(x+h) - f(x)}{h} = Af'(x)$$

In Leibniz's notation, the three results are as follows:

$$\frac{d}{dx} A = 0, \qquad \frac{d}{dx}[A + f(x)] = \frac{d}{dx} f(x), \qquad \frac{d}{dx}[Af(x)] = A\frac{d}{dx} f(x)$$

Example 4.11

Suppose we know $f'(x)$. Use rules [4.22] and [4.23] to find the derivatives of

(a) $5 + f(x)$

(b) $f(x) - 1/2$

(c) $3f(x)$

(d) $-\dfrac{f(x)}{5}$

(e) $\dfrac{Af(x) + B}{C}$

Solution   With a little mixed notation, we obtain the following:

(a) $\dfrac{d}{dx}[5 + f(x)] = f'(x)$

(b) $\dfrac{d}{dx}[f(x) - 1/2] = \dfrac{d}{dx}[(-1/2) + f(x)] = f'(x)$

(c) $\dfrac{d}{dx}[3f(x)] = 3f'(x)$

(d) $\dfrac{d}{dx}\left[-\dfrac{f(x)}{5}\right] = \dfrac{d}{dx}\left[-\dfrac{1}{5}f(x)\right] = -\dfrac{1}{5}f'(x)$

(e) $\dfrac{d}{dx}\left[\dfrac{Af(x) + B}{C}\right] = \dfrac{d}{dx}\left[\dfrac{A}{C}f(x) + \dfrac{B}{C}\right] = \dfrac{A}{C}f'(x)$

Power Rule

Few rules of differentiation are more useful than the following:

Power Rule

$$f(x) = x^a \Longrightarrow f'(x) = ax^{a-1} \quad (a \text{ is an arbitrary constant})$$

[4.24]

For the examples of $a = 2$ and $a = 3$, this rule was confirmed in Section 4.2. The method used for these two examples can be generalized, as the following proof shows.

Proof of [4.24] when a is a natural number n: We put $f(x) = x^n$ and form the Newton quotient

$$\frac{f(x + h) - f(x)}{h} = \frac{(x + h)^n - x^n}{h} \qquad [*]$$

Let us multiply out $(x + h)^n = (x + h)(x + h)\cdots(x + h)$. The resulting expression must contain the term x^n that results from choosing x from each of the n terms in parentheses. The expression will also contain terms of the type $x^{n-1}h$. There are n such terms obtained by choosing $n - 1$ of the x-only terms together with *one* h. All remaining terms must contain at least two h's, so

$$(x + h)^n = x^n + nx^{n-1}h + (\text{terms that contain } h^2 \text{ as a factor})$$

Hence,

$$(x + h)^n - x^n = nx^{n-1}h + (\text{terms that contain } h^2 \text{ as a factor})$$

So, whenever $h \neq 0$, we have

$$\frac{(x + h)^n - x^n}{h} = nx^{n-1} + (\text{terms that contain } h \text{ as a factor})$$

Now let h tend to 0. Then each term that contains h as a factor also tends to 0, and the sum of all these terms will tend to 0. Thus, the right-hand side tends to the expression $nx^{n-1} + 0 = nx^{n-1}$. Because the fraction in [*] tends to nx^{n-1} as h tends to 0, [4.24] *is* true when a is a natural number, according to the definition of $f'(x)$.

Example 4.12

Compute the derivative of the following:

(a) $y = x^5$

(b) $y = 3x^8$

(c) $y = \dfrac{x^{100}}{100}$

Solution

(a) $y = x^5 \implies y' = 5x^{5-1} = 5x^4$

(b) $y = 3x^8 \implies y' = 3 \cdot 8x^{8-1} = 24x^7$

(c) $y = \dfrac{x^{100}}{100} = \dfrac{1}{100}x^{100} \implies y' = \dfrac{1}{100}100x^{100-1} = x^{99}$

The previous proof covers only the case when a is a natural number. But the result in [4.24] is also valid if a is a negative integer, or even if a is a positive or negative rational number. Actually [4.24] is also correct even if a is an irrational number. All these cases will be considered later.

Example 4.13

Compute the following:

(a) $\dfrac{d}{dx}\left(x^{-0.33}\right)$

(b) $\dfrac{d}{dr}(-5r^{-3})$

(c) $\dfrac{d}{dp}(Ap^\alpha + B)$

(d) $\dfrac{d}{dx}\left(\dfrac{A}{\sqrt{x}}\right)$

Solution

(a) $\dfrac{d}{dx}\left(x^{-0.33}\right) = -0.33x^{-0.33-1} = -0.33x^{-1.33}$

(b) $\dfrac{d}{dr}(-5r^{-3}) = (-5)(-3)r^{-3-1} = 15r^{-4}$

(c) $\dfrac{d}{dp}(Ap^\alpha + B) = A\alpha p^{\alpha-1}$

(d) $\dfrac{d}{dx}\left(\dfrac{A}{\sqrt{x}}\right) = \dfrac{d}{dx}(Ax^{-1/2}) = A\left(-\dfrac{1}{2}\right)x^{-1/2-1} = -\dfrac{A}{2}x^{-3/2} = \dfrac{-A}{2x\sqrt{x}}$

Problems

1. Compute the derivative of the following:

    a. $y = 5$ **b.** $y = x^4$ **c.** $y = 9x^{10}$ **d.** $y = \pi^7$

2. Suppose we know $g'(x)$. Find an expression for the derivative of the following:

    a. $2g(x) + 3$ **b.** $-\frac{1}{6}g(x) + 8$ **c.** $\dfrac{g(x) - 5}{3}$

3. Find the derivative of the following:

    a. x^6 **b.** $3x^{11}$ **c.** x^{50} **d.** $-4x^{-7}$

    e. $\dfrac{x^{12}}{12}$ **f.** $-\dfrac{2}{x^2}$ **g.** $\dfrac{3}{\sqrt{x}}$ **h.** $-\dfrac{2}{x\sqrt{x}}$

4. Compute the following:

    a. $\dfrac{d}{dr}(4\pi r^2)$ **b.** $\dfrac{d}{dy}\left(Ay^{b+1}\right)$ **c.** $\dfrac{d}{dA}\left(\dfrac{1}{A^2\sqrt{A}}\right)$

5. Explain why

$$f'(a) = \lim_{x \to a} \frac{f(x) - f(a)}{x - a}$$

    Use this equation to find $f'(a)$ when $f(x) = x^2$.

6. For each of the following functions, find a function $F(x)$ that has $f(x)$ as its derivative. (Note that you are not asked to find $f'(x)$.)

    a. $f(x) = x^2$ **b.** $f(x) = 2x + 3$ **c.** $f(x) = x^a$ $(a \neq -1)$

Harder Problems

7. The following limits are all written in the form $\lim_{h \to 0}[f(a + h) - f(a)]/h$. Use your knowledge of derivatives to find the limits.

    a. $\lim_{h \to 0} \dfrac{(5 + h)^2 - 5^2}{h}$ **b.** $\lim_{s \to 0} \dfrac{(s + 1)^5 - 1}{s}$

    c. $\lim_{h \to 0} \dfrac{5(x + h)^2 + 10 - 5x^2 - 10}{h}$

4.6 Differentiation of Sums, Products, and Quotients

If we know $f'(x)$ and $g'(x)$, then what are the derivatives of $f(x) + g(x)$, $f(x) - g(x)$, $f(x) \cdot g(x)$, and $f(x)/g(x)$? You will probably guess the first two correctly, but are less likely to be right about the last two (unless you have already learned the answers).

Sums and Differences

Suppose that f and g are functions both defined on a set A of real numbers. The function F defined by the formula $F(x) = f(x) + g(x)$ is called the *sum* of f and g, written as $F = f + g$. The function G defined by $G(x) = f(x) - g(x)$ is called the *difference* between f and g, written as $G = f - g$. The following rules of differentiation are important.

Differentiation of Sums and Differences

If f and g are both differentiable at point x, then the sum $F = f + g$ and the difference $G = f - g$ are also differentiable at x, with

$$F(x) = f(x) + g(x) \implies F'(x) = f'(x) + g'(x) \qquad\qquad [4.25]$$

$$G(x) = f(x) - g(x) \implies G'(x) = f'(x) - g'(x) \qquad\qquad [4.26]$$

In Leibniz's notation:

$$\frac{d}{dx}[f(x) + g(x)] = \frac{d}{dx}f(x) + \frac{d}{dx}g(x)$$

$$\frac{d}{dx}[f(x) - g(x)] = \frac{d}{dx}f(x) - \frac{d}{dx}g(x)$$

Proof   In [4.25], the Newton quotient of F is

$$\frac{F(x+h) - F(x)}{h} = \frac{[f(x+h) + g(x+h)] - [f(x) + g(x)]}{h}$$

$$= \frac{f(x+h) - f(x)}{h} + \frac{g(x+h) - g(x)}{h}$$

When $h \to 0$, the last two fractions tend to $f'(x)$ and $g'(x)$, respectively, and thus the sum of the fractions tends to $f'(x) + g'(x)$. Hence,

$$F'(x) = \lim_{h \to 0} \frac{F(x+h) - F(x)}{h} = f'(x) + g'(x)$$

The proof of [4.26] is similar—only some of the signs change in the obvious way.

Example 4.14
Compute

$$\frac{d}{dx}\left(3x^8 + \frac{x^{100}}{100}\right) \qquad \text{and} \qquad \frac{d}{dx}\left(3x^8 - \frac{x^{100}}{100}\right)$$

Solution

$$\frac{d}{dx}\left(3x^8 + \frac{x^{100}}{100}\right) = \frac{d}{dx}(3x^8) + \frac{d}{dx}\left(\frac{x^{100}}{100}\right) = 24x^7 + x^{99}$$

where we used [4.25] and results from Example 4.12. Similarly,

$$\frac{d}{dx}\left(3x^8 - \frac{x^{100}}{100}\right) = 24x^7 - x^{99}$$

Example 4.15

In Example 4.5, we defined $\pi(x) = R(x) - C(x)$, and so [4.26] implies that $\pi'(x) = R'(x) - C'(x)$. In particular, $\pi'(x) = 0$ when $R'(x) = C'(x)$. In words: *Marginal profit is 0 when marginal revenue is equal to marginal cost.*

Rule [4.25] can be extended to the sum of an arbitrary number of terms:

The derivative of a sum is the sum of the derivatives:

$$\frac{d}{dx}[f_1(x) + \cdots + f_n(x)] = \frac{d}{dx}f_1(x) + \cdots + \frac{d}{dx}f_n(x)$$

The rules previously developed can now be used to differentiate any polynomial.

Example 4.16

Find the derivative of a general nth-degree polynomial.

Solution

$$\frac{d}{dx}\left(a_n x^n + a_{n-1}x^{n-1} + \cdots + a_2 x^2 + a_1 x + a_0\right)$$

$$= na_n x^{n-1} + (n-1)a_{n-1}x^{n-2} + \cdots + 2a_2 x + a_1$$

There is usually no reason to use so general a formula, because it is quite easy to apply the earlier rules to each specific case.

Products

If f and g are defined in a set A, then the function F defined by the formula $F(x) = f(x) \cdot g(x)$ is called the *product* of f and g, and we write $F = f \cdot g$ (or $F = fg$). For example, if $f(x) = x$ and $g(x) = x^2$, then $(f \cdot g)(x) = x^3$. Here $f'(x) = 1$, $g'(x) = 2x$ and $(f \cdot g)'(x) = 3x^2$. Hence, we see that the derivative of $(f \cdot g)(x)$ is *not* equal to $f'(x) \cdot g'(x) = 2x$. The correct rule for differentiating a product is a little more complicated.

The Derivative of a Product

If f and g are both differentiable at point x, then the function $F = f \cdot g$ is also differentiable at x, and   [4.27]

$$F(x) = f(x) \cdot g(x) \implies F'(x) = f'(x) \cdot g(x) + f(x) \cdot g'(x)$$

Briefly formulated in words: *The derivative of the product of two functions is equal to the derivative of the first times the second, plus the first times the derivative of the second.* The formula, however, is much easier to understand than these words. In Leibniz's notation, the product rule is expressed as:

$$\frac{d}{dx}[f(x) \cdot g(x)] = \frac{d}{dx}f(x) \cdot g(x) + f(x) \cdot \frac{d}{dx}g(x)$$

Before demonstrating why [4.27] is valid, here are two examples:

Example 4.17

Find $h'(x)$ when $h(x) = (x^3 - x) \cdot (5x^4 + x^2)$.

Solution   We see that $h(x) = f(x) \cdot g(x)$ with $f(x) = x^3 - x$ and $g(x) = 5x^4 + x^2$. Here $f'(x) = 3x^2 - 1$ and $g'(x) = 20x^3 + 2x$. Thus,

$$h'(x) = f'(x) \cdot g(x) + f(x) \cdot g'(x)$$
$$= (3x^2 - 1) \cdot (5x^4 + x^2) + (x^3 - x) \cdot (20x^3 + 2x)$$

Usually (but not always), we can simplify the answer by multiplying out to obtain just one polynomial. Simple computation gives

$$h'(x) = 35x^6 - 20x^4 - 3x^2$$

Alternatively, we can begin by multiplying out the expression for $h(x)$ to get

$$h(x) = (x^3 - x)(5x^4 + x^2) = 5x^7 - 4x^5 - x^3$$

Differentiating this polynomial gives the same expression for $h'(x)$ as before.

Example 4.18

We will illustrate the product rule for differentiation by considering the extraction of oil from a well. Suppose that both the amount of oil extracted per unit of time and the price per unit change with time t. We define

$$x(t) = \text{rate of extraction in barrels per day at time } t \qquad [1]$$

$$p(t) = \text{price in dollars per barrel at time } t \qquad [2]$$

Then we obtain

$$R(t) = p(t)x(t) \text{ as the revenue in dollars per day} \qquad [3]$$

and according to the product rule (recalling that we often use "dot notation" for differentiation with respect to time),

$$\dot{R}(t) = \dot{p}(t)x(t) + p(t)\dot{x}(t) \qquad [4]$$

The right-hand side of [4] can be interpreted as follows. Suppose that $p(t)$ and $x(t)$ both increase over time, because of inflation and because the oil company operating the well steadily expands the capacity of its extraction equipment. Then $R(t)$ increases for two reasons. First, $R(t)$ increases because of the price increase. This increase is proportional to the amount of extraction $x(t)$ and is equal to $\dot{p}(t)x(t)$. But $R(t)$ also rises because extraction increases. Its contribution to the rate of change of $R(t)$ must be proportional to the price, and is equal to $p(t)\dot{x}(t)$. Equation (4) merely expresses the simple fact that $\dot{R}(t)$, the total rate of change of $R(t)$, is the sum of these two parts.

Note too that the proportional rate of growth of revenue can be found by dividing [4] by [3] to obtain

$$\frac{\dot{R}}{R} = \frac{\dot{p}x + p\dot{x}}{px} = \frac{\dot{p}}{p} + \frac{\dot{x}}{x}$$

In words, the proportional rate of growth of revenue is the sum of the proportional rates at which the price and quantity are changing.

We have now seen how to differentiate products of two functions. What about products of more than two functions? For example, suppose that

$$y = f(x)g(x)h(x)$$

What is y'? We extend the same technique shown earlier and put $y = \left[f(x)g(x)\right]h(x)$. Then the product rule gives

$$
\begin{aligned}
y' &= [f(x)g(x)]'\, h(x) + [f(x)g(x)]\, h'(x) \\
&= \left[f'(x)g(x) + f(x)g'(x)\right] h(x) + f(x)g(x)h'(x) \\
&= f'(x)g(x)h(x) + f(x)g'(x)h(x) + f(x)g(x)h'(x)
\end{aligned}
$$

If none of the three functions is equal to 0, we can write the result in the following way:

$$\frac{(fgh)'}{fgh} = \frac{f'}{f} + \frac{g'}{g} + \frac{h'}{h}$$

By analogy, it is easy to write down the corresponding result for a product of n functions.

Proof of [4.27]   Suppose f and g are differentiable at x, so that the two Newton quotients

$$\frac{f(x+h) - f(x)}{h} \quad \text{and} \quad \frac{g(x+h) - g(x)}{h} \tag{1}$$

tend to the limits $f'(x)$ and $g'(x)$, respectively, as h tends to 0. We must show that the Newton quotient of F also tends to a limit, which is given by $f'(x)g(x) + f(x)g'(x)$. But the Newton quotient of F is

$$\frac{F(x+h) - F(x)}{h} = \frac{f(x+h)g(x+h) - f(x)g(x)}{h} \tag{2}$$

To proceed further we must somehow transform the right-hand side (RHS) to involve the Newton quotients of f and g. We use a trick: The numerator of the RHS of (2) is unchanged if we both subtract and add the number $f(x)g(x+h)$. Hence, with suitable regrouping of the terms, we have

$$\frac{F(x+h) - F(x)}{h}$$

$$= \frac{f(x+h)g(x+h) - f(x)g(x+h) + f(x)g(x+h) - f(x)g(x)}{h} \tag{3}$$

$$= \left[\frac{f(x+h) - f(x)}{h} \right] g(x+h) + f(x) \left[\frac{g(x+h) - g(x)}{h} \right]$$

As h tends to 0, the two Newton quotients in the square brackets tend to $f'(x)$ and $g'(x)$, respectively. Now we can write $g(x+h)$ for $h \neq 0$ as

$$g(x+h) = \left[\frac{g(x+h) - g(x)}{h} \right] h + g(x)$$

which tends to $g'(x) \cdot 0 + g(x) = g(x)$ as h tends to 0. It follows that the Newton quotient of F in (3) tends to $f'(x)g(x) + f(x)g'(x)$ as h tends to 0.

Quotients

Let f and g be functions which are differentiable at x, and define $F(x) = f(x)/g(x)$. We naturally assume that $g(x) \neq 0$, so that F is defined at x. We call F the *quotient* of f and g and write $F = f/g$. We would like to find a formula for $F'(x)$. Bearing in mind the complications in the formula for the derivative of a product, one should be somewhat reluctant to make a quick guess as to how the correct formula for $F'(x)$ will turn out.

In fact, it is quite easy to find the formula for $F'(x)$ if we *suppose* that $F(x)$ *is* differentiable, for $F(x) = f(x)/g(x)$ implies that $f(x) = F(x)g(x)$. Thus, the product rule gives

$$f'(x) = F'(x) \cdot g(x) + F(x) \cdot g'(x)$$

Solving for $F'(x)$ in terms of the other functions yields

$$F'(x) = \frac{f'(x) - F(x)g'(x)}{g(x)} = \frac{f'(x) - [f(x)/g(x)]g'(x)}{g(x)}$$

Multiplying both numerator and denominator of the last fraction by $g(x)$ gives

$$F'(x) = \frac{f'(x)g(x) - f(x)g'(x)}{[g(x)]^2}$$

Formally, the theorem can be stated as follows.

The Derivative of a Quotient

If f and g are differentiable at x and $g(x) \neq 0$, then $F = f/g$ is differentiable at x, and

[4.28]

$$F(x) = \frac{f(x)}{g(x)} \implies F'(x) = \frac{f'(x) \cdot g(x) - f(x) \cdot g'(x)}{[g(x)]^2}$$

In words: *The derivative of a quotient is equal to the derivative of the numerator times the denominator minus the numerator times the derivative of the denominator, this difference then being divided by the square of the denominator.* (To prove that F is differentiable in x, under the earlier assumptions, we must study the Newton quotient of F as we did for the product rule. See Problem 12.) In simpler notation, we have

$$\left(\frac{f}{g}\right)' = \frac{f'g - fg'}{g^2}$$

Note: In the product rule formula, the two functions appear symmetrically, so that it is easy to remember. In the formula for the derivative of a quotient, the expressions in the numerator must be in the right order. The following suggestion checks whether you have the order right. Write down the formula you believe is correct. Consider the case when $g \equiv 1$. Then $g' \equiv 0$, and your formula ought to reduce to f'. If you get $-f'$, then your signs are wrong.

Example 4.19

Compute $F'(x)$ and $F'(4)$ when $F(x) = (3x - 5)/(x - 2)$.

Solution   We apply [4.28] with $f(x) = 3x - 5$, $g(x) = x - 2$. Then $f'(x) = 3$ and $g'(x) = 1$. So we obtain, for $x \neq 2$:

$$F'(x) = \frac{3 \cdot (x - 2) - (3x - 5) \cdot 1}{(x - 2)^2}$$

$$= \frac{3x - 6 - 3x + 5}{(x - 2)^2} = -\frac{1}{(x - 2)^2}$$

To find $F'(4)$, we put $x = 4$ in the formula for $F'(x)$ to get $F'(4) = -1/(4 - 2)^2 = -1/4$.

Example 4.20 .

Let $C(Q)$ be the total cost of producing Q units of a commodity. (See Example 3.3.) The quantity $C(Q)/Q$ is called the *average cost* of producing Q units. Find an expression for

$$\frac{d}{dQ}\left[C(Q)/Q\right]$$

Solution

$$\frac{d}{dQ}\left[\frac{C(Q)}{Q}\right] = \frac{QC'(Q) - C(Q)}{Q^2} = \frac{1}{Q}\left[C'(Q) - \frac{C(Q)}{Q}\right]$$

Note that for positive output levels Q, the marginal cost $C'(Q)$ exceeds the average cost $C(Q)/Q$ if and only if the rate of change of the average cost as output increases is positive. (In a similar way, if a basketball team recruits a new player, the average height of the team increases if and only if the new player's height exceeds the old average height.)

The formula for the derivative of a quotient becomes easier to understand if we consider proportional rates of change. (See [4.11].) By using [4.28], simple computation shows that

$$F(x) = \frac{f(x)}{g(x)} \implies \frac{F'(x)}{F(x)} = \frac{f'(x)}{f(x)} - \frac{g'(x)}{g(x)} \qquad [4.29]$$

The proportional rate of change of a quotient is equal to the proportional rate of change of the numerator minus the proportional rate of change of the denominator.

An economic application of rule [4.29] is as follows. Let $W(t)$ be the nominal wage rate and $P(t)$ the price index at time t. Then $w(t) = W(t)/P(t)$ is called the **real wage rate**. According to [4.29],

$$\frac{\dot{w}(t)}{w(t)} = \frac{\dot{W}(t)}{W(t)} - \frac{\dot{P}(t)}{P(t)}$$

The proportional rate of change of the real wage is equal to the difference between the proportional rates of change of the nominal wage and the price index. Thus, if nominal wages increase at the rate of 5% per year but prices rise by 6%, then real wages fall by 1%. (Recall from Section 4.3 that these are proportional rates of change.)

Problems

In Problems 1–4, differentiate the functions defined by the various formulas.

1. a. $x + 1$ **b.** $x + x^2$ **c.** $3x^5 + 2x^4 + 5$

   d. $8x^4 + 2\sqrt{x}$ **e.** $\frac{1}{2}x - \frac{3}{2}x^2 + 5x^3$ **f.** $1 - 3x^7$

2. a. $\frac{3}{5}x^2 - 2x^7 + \frac{1}{8} - \sqrt{x}$ **b.** $(2x^2 - 1)(x^4 - 1)$ **c.** $\left(x^5 + \frac{1}{x}\right)(x^5 + 1)$

3. a. $\dfrac{1}{x^6}$ **b.** $x^{-1}(x^2 + 1)\sqrt{x}$ **c.** $\dfrac{1}{\sqrt{x^3}}$ **d.** $\dfrac{x + 1}{x - 1}$

   e. $\dfrac{x + 1}{x^5}$ **f.** $\dfrac{3x - 5}{2x + 8}$ **g.** $3x^{-11}$ **h.** $\dfrac{3x - 1}{x^2 + x + 1}$

4. a. $\dfrac{\sqrt{x} - 2}{\sqrt{x} + 1}$ **b.** $\dfrac{(x + 1)(x - 1)}{(x^2 + 2)(x + 3)}$ **c.** $(3x + 1)\left(\dfrac{1}{x^2} + \dfrac{1}{x}\right)$

   d. $\dfrac{x^2 - 1}{x^2 + 1}$ **e.** $\dfrac{x^2 + x + 1}{x^2 - x + 1}$ **f.** $\dfrac{1}{2} + \dfrac{1}{3}\left(\dfrac{x - 1}{x + 1}\right)(1 + x^{-2})$

5. If $D(P)$ denotes the demand for a product when the price per unit is P, then the revenue function $R(P)$ is given by $R(P) = PD(P)$. Find an expression for $R'(P)$.

6. For each of the following functions, determine the value(s) of x at which $f'(x) = 0$.

   a. $f(x) = 3x^2 - 12x + 13$ **b.** $f(x) = \frac{1}{4}(x^4 - 6x^2)$

   c. $f(x) = \dfrac{2x}{x^2 + 2}$ **d.** $f(x) = \dfrac{x^2 - x^3}{2(x + 1)}$

7. Find the equations for the tangents to the graphs of the following functions at the specified points:

   a. $y = 3 - x - x^2$ at $x = 1$ **b.** $y = \dfrac{x^2 - 1}{x^2 + 1}$ at $x = 1$

   c. $y = \left(\dfrac{1}{x^2} + 1\right)(x^2 - 1)$ at $x = 2$ **d.** $y = \dfrac{x^4 + 1}{(x^2 + 1)(x + 3)}$ at $x = 0$

8. Differentiate the following functions of t:

   a. $\dfrac{at + b}{ct + d}$ **b.** $t^n\left(a\sqrt{t} + b\right)$ **c.** $\dfrac{1}{at^2 + bt + c}$

9. Compute the following:

   a. $\dfrac{d}{dp}\left(\dfrac{Ap^2 + B}{Cp^2 + D}\right)$ **b.** $\dfrac{d}{dy}\left(\dfrac{y^2 + 2}{y^8}\right)$ **c.** $\dfrac{d}{dx}\left(\dfrac{1 - f(x)}{1 + f(x)}\right)$

10. If $f(x) = \sqrt{x}$, then $f(x) \cdot f(x) = x$. Use the product rule to find a formula for $f'(x)$. Compare this with the result in Problem 8 of Section 4.2.

11. Prove the power rule [4.24] for $a = -n$, where n is a natural number, by using the relation $f(x) = x^{-n} = 1/x^n$ and the quotient rule [4.28].

Harder Problems

12. Let $F(x) = f(x)/g(x)$. Write out the Newton quotient of F, and show that it tends to the expression for $F'(x)$ in [4.28]. *Hint:* The Newton quotient of F is equal to

$$\frac{1}{g(x)g(x+h)}\left[g(x)\frac{f(x+h) - f(x)}{h} - f(x)\frac{g(x+h) - g(x)}{h}\right]$$

Then use the same idea as in the proof of [4.27].

4.7 Second- and Higher-Order Derivatives

The derivative of a function f is often called the **first derivative** of f. If f' is also differentiable, then we can differentiate f' in turn. In fact, we call $(f')'$ the **second derivative** of f. We write f'' instead of $(f')'$, and let $f''(x)$ denote the second derivative of f evaluated at the particular point x.

Example 4.21
   Find $f'(x)$ and $f''(x)$ when $f(x) = 2x^5 - 3x^3 + 2x$.

   Solution   Using the rules for differentiating polynomials, we first differentiate $2x^5 - 3x^3 + 2x$ to get

$$f'(x) = 10x^4 - 9x^2 + 2$$

Then we differentiate $10x^4 - 9x^2 + 2$ to get

$$f''(x) = 40x^3 - 18x$$

The different forms of notation for the second derivative are analogous to those for the first derivative. For example, we write $y'' = f''(x)$ in order to denote the second derivative of $y = f(x)$. The Leibniz notation for the second derivative is also used. In the notation dy/dx or $df(x)/dx$ for the first derivative, we interpreted the symbol d/dx as an operator indicating that what follows is to be differentiated with respect to x. The second derivative is obtained by using the operator d/dx twice: $f''(x) = (d/dx)(d/dx)f(x)$. We usually think of this as $f''(x) = (d/dx)^2 f(x)$, and so write it as follows:

$$f''(x) = \frac{d^2 f(x)}{dx^2} = d^2 f(x)/dx^2 \quad \text{or} \quad y'' = \frac{d^2 y}{dx^2} = d^2 y/dx^2$$

Pay special attention to where the superscripts 2 are placed.

Of course, the notation for the second derivative must change if the variables have other names.

Example 4.22

(a) Find Y'' when $Y = AK^a$ is a function of K ($K > 0$), with A and a as constants.

(b) Find $d^2 L/dt^2$ when $L = t/t + 1$, and $t \geq 0$.

Solution

(a) Differentiating $Y = AK^a$ with respect to K gives

$$Y' = AaK^{a-1}$$

A second differentiation with respect to K yields

$$Y'' = Aa(a-1)K^{a-2}$$

(b) First, we use the quotient rule to find that

$$\frac{dL}{dt} = \frac{d}{dt}\left(\frac{t}{t+1}\right) = \frac{1 \cdot (t+1) - t \cdot 1}{(t+1)^2} = \frac{1}{t^2 + 2t + 1}$$

The quotient rule can be used again to yield

$$\frac{d^2 L}{dt^2} = \frac{0 \cdot (t^2 + 2t + 1) - 1 \cdot (2t + 2)}{(t^2 + 2t + 1)^2} = \frac{-2(t+1)}{(t+1)^4} = -2\frac{1}{(t+1)^3}$$

Later, both first and second derivatives will be given important geometric and economic interpretations. Corresponding simple interpretations are not available for derivatives of higher order, but they are used from time to time.

Higher-Order Derivatives

The derivative of $y'' = f''(x)$ is called the **third derivative**, and we use the notation $y''' = f'''(x)$ for this. It is notationally cumbersome to continue using primes to indicate differentiation, so the **fourth derivative** is usually denoted by $y^{(4)} = f^{(4)}(x)$. (We must put the number 4 in parentheses so that it will not get confused with y^4, the fourth power of y.) The same derivative can be expressed as d^4y/dx^4. In general, let

$$y^{(n)} = f^{(n)}(x) \quad \text{or} \quad d^n y/dx^n \quad \text{denote the } n\text{th derivative of } f \text{ at } x$$

The number n is called the **order** of the derivative. For example, $f^{(6)}(x_0)$ denotes the sixth derivative of f calculated at x_0, found by differentiating six times.

Example 4.23

Compute all the derivatives up to and including order 4 of

$$f(x) = 3x^{-1} + 6x^3 - x^2 \quad (x \neq 0)$$

Solution   Repeated differentiation gives

$$f'(x) = -3x^{-2} + 18x^2 - 2x$$

$$f''(x) = 6x^{-3} + 36x - 2$$

$$f'''(x) = -18x^{-4} + 36$$

$$f^{(4)}(x) = 72x^{-5}$$

In the same way that a function need not be differentiable at x_0, a higher-order derivative need not exist at x_0. If $f'(x_0), f''(x_0), \ldots, f^{(n)}(x_0)$ all exist, then we say that f is n *times differentiable* at x_0. If $f^{(n)}(x_0)$ is continuous, then f is said to be n *times continuously differentiable* at x_0—or more concisely, a C^n **function** at x_0.

Example 4.24

Differentiate $f(x) = 3x^{11/3}$ four times.

Solution $f'(x) = 11x^{8/3}$

$$f''(x) = (88/3)x^{5/3}$$

$$f'''(x) = (440/9)x^{2/3}$$

$$f^{(4)}(x) = (880/27)x^{-1/3}$$

Note that $f'(0) = f''(0) = f'''(0) = 0$, but $f^{(4)}(0)$ does not exist. Hence, f is three times differentiable everywhere, but it is not four times differentiable at 0.

Problems

1. Find the second derivative of the following:

   a. $y = x^5 - 3x^4 + 2$ **b.** $y = \sqrt{x}$ **c.** $y = \dfrac{x}{x + 1}$

2. Find d^2y/dx^2 when $y = x^a + x^{-a}$.

3. Compute the following:

   a. y'' for $y = 3x^3 + 2x - 1$ **b.** Y''' for $Y = 1 - 2x^2 + 6x^3$

   c. d^3z/dt^3 for $z = 120t - (1/3)t^3$ **d.** $f^{(4)}(1)$ for $f(z) = 100z^{-4}$

4. Find $g''(2)$ when $g(t) = t^2/(t-1)$.

5. Find formulas for y'' and y''' when $y = f(x)g(x)$.

6. If n is a natural number, let $n!$ (read as "n factorial") be defined as

$$n! = 1 \cdot 2 \cdot 3 \cdots (n-1) \cdot n$$

For example, $5! = 1 \cdot 2 \cdot 3 \cdot 4 \cdot 5 = 120$. Show (by using mathematical induction) that

$$y = x^n \implies y^{(n)} = n!$$

Harder Problems

7. Find a function that is five times differentiable, but not six times differentiable at $x = 0$. (*Hint:* See Example 4.24.)

5

More on Differentiation

Although this may seem a paradox, all science is dominated by the idea of approximation.
—*Bertrand Russell*

This chapter presents some extensively used techniques of differentiation. It begins with the generalized power rule and then proceeds to a discussion of the highly useful chain rule. In many economic models, functions are defined implicitly by one or more equations. In some simple but economically relevant cases, we show how to compute derivatives of such functions. Next we consider differentials and linear, quadratic, or higher-order approximations, all of which occur in many applications of mathematics to economics. A discussion of the important economic concept of elasticity ends the chapter.

5.1 The Generalized Power Rule

It is often necessary to differentiate expressions of the form

$$y = \left[g(x)\right]^a$$

where g is a differentiable function, and a is a constant. For $a = 1$, the derivative is just $g'(x)$. For $a = 2$, we can use the product rule as follows:

$$y = \left[g(x)\right]^2 = g(x) \cdot g(x) \implies y' = g'(x) \cdot g(x) + g(x) \cdot g'(x) = 2g(x) \cdot g'(x)$$

For $a = 3$, we can combine the previous result with the product rule as follows:

$$y = \left[g(x)\right]^3 = \left[g(x)\right]^2 \cdot g(x) \implies y' = \left[2g(x) \cdot g'(x)\right] \cdot g(x) + \left[g(x)\right]^2 \cdot g'(x)$$
$$= 3\left[g(x)\right]^2 \cdot g'(x)$$

See if you can discern a pattern here. In general, we have the following rule (where a is an arbitrary real number):

The Generalized Power Rule

$$y = \left[g(x)\right]^a \implies y' = a\left[g(x)\right]^{a-1} \cdot g'(x) \qquad\qquad [5.1]$$

Note this important formula. If we put $g(x) = x$, then $g'(x) = 1$ and [5.1] reduces to $y = x^a \implies y' = ax^{a-1}$, which is the power of Section 4.5. A generalization of [5.1] is proved in Section 5.2. In the meantime, ambitious students may want to try proving [5.1] by mathematical induction for the case when a is a natural number. (See Problem 10.)

Example 5.1

Differentiate the functions:

(a) $y = (x^3 + x^2)^{50}$

(b) $y = \left(\dfrac{x-1}{x+3}\right)^{1/3}$

(c) $y = \sqrt{x^2 + 1}$

Solution   The key to applying the generalized power rule is to determine how the given function can be expressed as a power. In the first problem, it is rather obvious:

(a) $y = (x^3 + x^2)^{50} = \left[g(x)\right]^{50}$ where $g(x) = x^3 + x^2$.
Differentiating this directly gives $g'(x) = 3x^2 + 2x$, and so formula [5.1] yields

$$y' = 50\left[g(x)\right]^{50-1} \cdot g'(x) = 50(x^3 + x^2)^{49}(3x^2 + 2x)$$

(b) Again it is obvious how to apply [5.1]:

$$y = \left(\frac{x-1}{x+3}\right)^{1/3} = \left[g(x)\right]^{1/3}$$

where $g(x) = (x-1)/(x+3)$. In this case, the quotient rule implies that

$$g'(x) = \frac{1 \cdot (x+3) - (x-1) \cdot 1}{(x+3)^2} = \frac{4}{(x+3)^2}$$

Hence, [5.1] gives

$$y' = \frac{1}{3}[g(x)]^{(1/3)-1} \cdot g'(x) = \frac{1}{3}\left(\frac{x-1}{x+3}\right)^{-2/3} \cdot \frac{4}{(x+3)^2}$$

$$= \frac{4}{3}(x+3)^{-4/3}(x-1)^{-2/3}$$

(c) Here we first notice that $y = \sqrt{x^2+1} = (x^2+1)^{1/2}$. So $y = [g(x)]^{1/2}$, where $g(x) = x^2 + 1$. Hence,

$$y' = \frac{1}{2}[g(x)]^{(1/2)-1} \cdot g'(x) = \frac{1}{2}(x^2+1)^{-1/2} \cdot 2x = \frac{x}{\sqrt{x^2+1}}$$

The generalized power rule can also be formulated in Leibniz's notation.

The Generalized Power Rule (Leibniz's Notation)

When $u = g(x)$ is a function of x, then

$$y = u^a \implies \frac{dy}{dx} = au^{a-1}\frac{du}{dx} \qquad\qquad [5.2]$$

Often we need to combine the generalized power rule with the other rules of differentiation shown earlier. Here is an example from economics.

Example 5.2

Suppose that the relationship between gross income Y and total income tax T is for taxpayers with incomes between 80,000 and 120,000. The following values for the constants in [*] were estimated, given by the equation

$$T = a(bY+c)^p + kY \qquad\qquad [*]$$

where a, b, c, p, and k are positive constants.

(a) Find an expression for the *marginal tax rate*, dT/dY.
(b) In an empirical study

$$a = 0.000338, \qquad b = 0.81, \qquad c = 6467, \qquad p = 1.61, \qquad k = 0.053$$

Use these numbers to find the values of T and dT/dY when $Y = 100{,}000$.

Solution

(a) Let $z = (bY + c)^p = u^p$ with $u = bY + c$. Then [5.2] gives

$$\frac{dz}{dY} = pu^{p-1}\frac{du}{dY} = p(bY + c)^{p-1}b$$

Because $T = az + kY$, differentiation of [*] gives

$$\frac{dT}{dY} = a\frac{dz}{dY} + k = apb(bY + c)^{p-1} + k$$

(b) We have

$$T = 0.000338(0.81 \cdot 100{,}000 + 6467)^{1.61} + 0.053 \cdot 100{,}000 \approx 35{,}869.33$$

and

$$\frac{dT}{dY} = 0.000338 \cdot 0.81 \cdot 1.61 \cdot (0.81 \cdot 100{,}000 + 6467)^{0.61} + 0.053 \approx 0.51$$

Thus, the marginal tax rate on an income of 100,000 is approximately 51%.

Problems

1. Compute $f'(x)$ when $f(x) = (3x^2 + 1)^2$ by (a) expanding the square and then differentiating; (b) using [5.1]. Compare the answers.

2. Find the derivatives of the functions defined by the following:

   a. $(2x + 1)^3$ **b.** $(1 - x)^5$ **c.** $(x^2 - 2x + 2)^2$

   d. $\dfrac{(x + 1)^5}{x}$ **e.** $(3x - 4)^{-7}$ **f.** $(2x^2 + 3x - 4)^{-2}$

3. Find the derivatives of the functions defined by the following:

   a. $(1 + x)^{1/2}$ **b.** $\sqrt{x^3 + 1}$ **c.** $\left(\dfrac{2x + 1}{x - 1}\right)^{1/2}$

   d. $(1 - x^2)^{33}$ **e.** $x^3\sqrt{1 - x}$ **f.** $\sqrt[3]{1 + x} \cdot \sqrt[5]{1 - x}$

4. Find the derivatives of the following functions of t (where a, b, and n are constants):

   a. $(at^2 + 1)^{-3}$ **b.** $(at + b)^n$ **c.** $\left(\dfrac{at + b}{nt}\right)^{a+1}$

5. If f is differentiable at x, find expressions for the derivatives of the following functions:

a. $x + f(x)$ **b.** $[f(x)]^2 - x$ **c.** $[f(x)]^4$

d. $x^2 f(x) + [f(x)]^3$ **e.** $xf(x)$ **f.** $\sqrt{f(x)}$

g. $\dfrac{x^2}{f(x)}$ **h.** $\dfrac{[f(x)]^2}{x^3}$ **i.** $\left\{ f(x) + [f(x)]^3 + x \right\}^{1/3}$

6. Let $x = (Ap + B)^r$ and $p = at^2 + bt + c$. Find an expression for dx/dt.

7. Compute dy/dv when $y = A(av^p + b)^q$.

Harder Problems

8. Suppose that [5.1] has already been proved when a is a natural number. Prove that [5.1] is then also valid when $a = -n$, where n is a natural number. (*Hint:* Put $y = [g(x)]^{-n} = 1/[g(x)]^n$, and then use the quotient rule.)

9. Let a, b, m, and n be fixed numbers, where $a < b$, and m and n are positive. Define the function f for all x by $f(x) = (x - a)^m \cdot (x - b)^n$. For the equation $f'(x) = 0$, find a solution x_0 that lies between a and b.

10. Prove by induction that [5.1] holds when a is a natural number.

11. Prove that

$$\frac{d}{dx} [f(x)]^m [g(x)]^n = \left[mf'(x)g(x) + nf(x)g'(x) \right] [f(x)]^{m-1} [g(x)]^{n-1}$$

What do you get if $m = n = 1$, and if $m = -n = 1$?

5.2 Composite Functions and the Chain Rule

If y is a function of u, and u is a function of x, then y is a function of x. In this case, we call y a **composite function** of x. (In the previous section, we considered the special case where y was given by u^a.) Suppose that x changes. This will lead to a change in u and hence a change in y. A change in x, therefore, causes a "chain reaction." If we know the rates of change du/dx and dy/du, then what is the rate of change dy/dx? It turns out that the relationship between these rates of change is simply:

The Chain Rule

$$\frac{dy}{dx} = \frac{dy}{du} \cdot \frac{du}{dx} \qquad\qquad [5.3]$$

A slightly more detailed formulation of the rule says that *if y is a differentiable* *function of u, and u is a differentiable function of x, then y is a differentiable function of x,* and [5.3] holds.

The chain rule is a further generalization of the generalized power rule from the previous section. In the special case where $y = u^a$, we have $dy/du = au^{a-1}$, and substituting this expression into [5.3] gives the formula in [5.2].

It is easy to remember the chain rule when using Leibniz's notation. The left-hand side of [5.3] is exactly what results if we "cancel" the du on the right side. Of course, because dy/du and du/dx are not fractions (but merely symbols for derivatives) and du is not a number, canceling is not defined.

When we interpret the derivatives involved in [5.3] as rates of change, the chain rule becomes rather intuitive, as the next example from economics will indicate.

Example 5.3

The demand x for a commodity depends on price p. Suppose that price p is not constant, but depends on time t. Then x is a composite function of t, and according to the chain rule,

$$\frac{dx}{dt} = \frac{dx}{dp} \cdot \frac{dp}{dt} \qquad [*]$$

Suppose, for instance, that the demand for butter decreases by 5000 pounds if the price goes up by \$1 per pound. So $dx/dp \approx -5000$. Suppose further that the price per pound increases by \$0.05 per week, so $dp/dt \approx 0.05$. What is the decrease in demand in pounds per week?

Solution: Because the price per pound increases by \$0.05 per week, and the demand decreases by 5000 pounds for every dollar increase in the price, the demand *decreases* by $5000 \cdot 0.05 \approx 250$ pounds per week. This means that $dx/dt \approx -250$ (measured in pounds per week). Note how this argument roughly confirms [*].

The chain rule is very powerful. Facility in applying it comes only from a lot of practice.

Example 5.4

(a) Find dy/dx when $y = u^5$ and $u = 1 - x^3$.

(b) Find dy/dx when

$$y = \frac{10}{(x^2 + 4x + 5)^7}$$

Solution

(a) We can use [5.3] directly. Because $dy/du = 5u^4$ and $du/dx = -3x^2$, we have

$$\frac{dy}{dx} = \frac{dy}{du} \cdot \frac{du}{dx} = 5u^4(-3x^2) = -15x^2u^4 = -15x^2(1 - x^3)^4$$

(b) In this case, it is not immediately obvious how to apply the chain rule. However, if we rewrite y as $y = 10(x^2 + 4x + 5)^{-7}$, then

$$y = 10u^{-7}$$

where $u = x^2 + 4x + 5$. Thus,

$$\frac{dy}{du} = 10(-7)u^{-7-1} = -70u^{-8} \quad \text{and} \quad \frac{du}{dx} = 2x + 4$$

So using [5.3] yields

$$\frac{dy}{dx} = \frac{dy}{du} \cdot \frac{du}{dx} = -70u^{-8} \cdot (2x + 4) = -140(x+2)/(x^2 + 4x + 5)^8$$

Note 1: After a little training, the intermediate steps become unnecessary. For example, to differentiate

$$y = (\underbrace{1 - x^3}_{u})^5$$

we can *think* of y as $y = u^5$, where $u = 1 - x^3$. We can then differentiate both u^5 and $1 - x^3$ in our heads, and immediately write down $y' = 5(1 - x^3)^4(-3x^2)$.

Note 2: Of course, one could differentiate $y = x^5/5$ using the quotient rule, rather than writing y as $y = (1/5)x^5$ to get $y' = (1/5)5x^4 = x^4$. But the latter method is much easier. In the same way, it is unnecessarily cumbersome to apply the quotient rule to the function given in Example 5.4(b). The chain rule is much more effective.

The next example uses the chain rule several times.

Example 5.5

Find $x'(t)$ when $x(t) = 5 \left(1 + \sqrt{t^3 + 1}\right)^{25}$.

Solution   The initial step is easy. Let $x(t) = 5u^{25}$, where $u = 1 + \sqrt{t^3 + 1}$, to obtain

$$x'(t) = 5 \cdot 25u^{24} \frac{du}{dt} = 125u^{24} \frac{du}{dt} \tag{1}$$

The new feature in this example is that we cannot write down du/dt at once. Finding du/dt requires using the chain rule a second time. Let $u = 1 + \sqrt{v} = 1 + v^{1/2}$, where $v = t^3 + 1$. Then

$$\frac{du}{dt} = \frac{1}{2}v^{1/2-1} \cdot \frac{dv}{dt} = \frac{1}{2}v^{-1/2} \cdot 3t^2 = \frac{1}{2}(t^3 + 1)^{-1/2} \cdot 3t^2 \tag{2}$$

From [1] and [2], we get

$$x'(t) = 125 \left(1 + \sqrt{t^3 + 1}\right)^{24} \cdot \tfrac{1}{2}(t^3 + 1)^{-1/2} \cdot 3t^2$$

Suppose, as in the last example, that x is a function of u, u is a function of v, and v is in turn a function of t. Then x is a composite function of t, and the chain rule can be used twice to obtain

$$\frac{dx}{dt} = \frac{dx}{du} \cdot \frac{du}{dv} \cdot \frac{dv}{dt}$$

This is precisely the formula used in the last example. Again the notation is suggestive because the left-hand side is exactly what results if we "cancel" both du and dv on the right-hand side.

An Alternative Formulation of the Chain Rule

Although Leibniz's notation makes it very easy to remember the chain rule, it suffers from the defect of not specifying where each derivative is evaluated. We remedy this by introducing names for the functions involved. So let $y = f(u)$ and $u = g(x)$. Then y can be written in the form

$$y = f\big(g(x)\big)$$

Note that when we compute $f\big(g(x)\big)$, we *first* compute $g(x)$, and then *second*, we apply f to the result. We say that we have a **composite function**, with $g(x)$ as the the **kernel**, and f as the **exterior function**.

Most scientific calculators have several built-in functions. When we punch a number x_0 and strike the key for the function f, we obtain $f(x_0)$. When we compute a composite function given f and g, and try to obtain the value of $f\big(g(x)\big)$, we proceed in a similar manner: punch the number x_0, then strike the g key to get $g(x_0)$, and again strike the f key to get $f\big(g(x_0)\big)$. Suppose the machine has the functions $\boxed{1/x}$ and $\boxed{\sqrt{x}}$. If we press the number 9, then strike the button $\boxed{1/x}$ followed by $\boxed{\sqrt{x}}$, we get $1/3 = 0.33 \ldots$. The computation we have performed can be illustrated as follows:

$$\boxed{1/x} \qquad\qquad \boxed{\sqrt{x}}$$

$$9 \quad\longrightarrow\quad 1/9 \quad\longrightarrow\quad 1/3$$

Using function notation, $f(x) = \sqrt{x}$ and $g(x) = 1/x$, so $f\big(g(x)\big) = f(1/x) = \sqrt{1/x} = 1/\sqrt{x}$. In particular, $f\big(g(9)\big) = 1/\sqrt{9} = 1/3$.

The Chain Rule

If g is differentiable at x_0 and f is differentiable at $u_0 = g(x_0)$, then $F(x) = f\big(g(x)\big)$ is differentiable at x_0 and

$$F'(x_0) = f'\big(g(x_0)\big)g'(x_0)$$

[5.4]

In words: *to differentiate a composite function, first differentiate the exterior function and substitute in the value of the kernel, then multiply by the derivative of the kernel.* It is important to notice that the derivatives f' and g' appearing in formula [5.4] are evaluated at *different* points; the derivative g' is evaluated at x_0, whereas f' is evaluated at $g(x_0)$.

Example 5.6

Find the derivative of $F(x) = f(g(x))$ at $x_0 = -3$ if $f(u) = u^3$ and $g(x) = 2 - x^2$.

Solution　　In this case, $f'(u) = 3u^2$ and $g'(x) = -2x$. So [5.4] gives

$$F'(-3) = f'(g(-3))\, g'(-3)$$

Now $g(-3) = 2 - (-3)^2 = 2 - 9 = -7$; $g'(-3) = 6$; and $f'(g(-3)) = f'(-7) = 3(-7)^2 = 3 \cdot 49 = 147$. So $F'(-3) = f'(g(-3))\, g'(-3) = 147 \cdot 6 = 882$.

Note: The function that maps x to $f\big(g(x)\big)$ is often denoted by $f \circ g$, and is read as "f of g" or "f compounded with g." Correspondingly, $g \circ f$ denotes the function that maps x to $g\big(f(x)\big)$. Thus, we have

$$(f \circ g)(x) = f\big(g(x)\big) \qquad \text{and} \qquad (g \circ f)(x) = g\big(f(x)\big)$$

Usually, $f \circ g$ and $g \circ f$ are quite different functions. For instance, the functions used in Example 5.6 give $(f \circ g)(x) = (2 - x^2)^3$, whereas $(g \circ f)(x) = 2 - (x^3)^2 = 2 - x^6$; the two resulting polynomials are not the same.

It is easy to confuse $f \circ g$ with $f \cdot g$, especially typographically. But these two functions are defined in entirely different ways. When we evaluate $f \circ g$ at x, we first compute $g(x)$ and then evaluate f at $g(x)$. On the other hand, the product $f \cdot g$ of f and g is the function whose value at a particular number x is simply the product of $f(x)$ and $g(x)$, so $(f \cdot g)(x) = f(x) \cdot g(x)$.

Proof of the chain rule　　To find the derivative of $F(x) = f\big(g(x)\big)$ at $x = x_0$, we must examine the limit of the following Newton quotient as h

tends to 0:

$$N = \frac{F(x_0 + h) - F(x_0)}{h} = \frac{f\big(g(x_0 + h)\big) - f\big(g(x_0)\big)}{h}$$

The change in x from x_0 to $x_0 + h$ causes the value of g to change by the amount $k = g(x_0 + h) - g(x_0)$. As h tends to 0, so $k = \big\{[g(x_0 + h) - g(x_0)]/h\big\} \cdot h$ tends to $g'(x_0) \cdot 0 = 0$. *Suppose that $k \neq 0$ whenever $h \neq 0$ is small enough.* Because $g(x_0 + h) = g(x_0) + k$, we can write the Newton quotient as

$$N = \frac{f\big(g(x_0) + k\big) - f\big(g(x_0)\big)}{k} \cdot \frac{k}{h}$$

$$= \frac{f\big(g(x_0) + k\big) - f\big(g(x_0)\big)}{k} \cdot \frac{g(x_0 + h) - g(x_0)}{h}$$

As $h \to 0$, so $k \to 0$, and the last two fractions tend to $f'\big(g(x_0)\big)$ and $g'(x_0)$, respectively. This yields the desired formula.

We cannot divide by 0, so the argument fails if $g(x_0 + h) = g(x_0)$ for arbitrary small values of h, because then $k = 0$. A more complicated proof takes care of this case as well.

Problems

1. Use the chain rule [5.3] to find dy/dx for the following:
   a. $y = 5u^4$ and $u = 1 + x^2$
   b. $y = u - u^6$ and $u = 1/x + 1$

2. Compute the following:
   a. dY/dt when $Y = -3(V + 1)^5$ and $V = \frac{1}{3}t^3$.
   b. dK/dt when $K = AL^a$ and $L = bt + c$ (A, a, b, and c are positive constants).

3. Find the derivatives of the following functions, where a, p, q, and b are constants:
   a. $y = \dfrac{1}{(x^2 + x + 1)^5}$ **b.** $y = \sqrt{x + \sqrt{x + \sqrt{x}}}$ **c.** $y = x^a(px + q)^b$

4. If Y is a function of K, and K is a function of t, find the formula for the derivative of Y with respect to t at $t = t_0$.

5. If $Y = F(K)$ and $K = h(t)$, find the formula for dY/dt.

6. Compute dx/dp for the demand function

$$x = b - \sqrt{ap - c} \qquad (a, b, \text{ and } c \text{ are positive constants})$$

where x is the number of units demanded, and p is the price per unit, with $p \geq c/a$.

7. If $h(x) = f(x^2)$, find a formula for $h'(x)$.

8. Let $s(t)$ be the distance in kilometers traveled by a car in t hours. Let $B(s)$ be the number of liters of fuel the car uses to go s kilometers.
    a. Provide an interpretation of the function $b(t) = B(s(t))$.
    b. Find and interpret the formula for $b'(t)$.

9. If $a(t)$ and $b(t)$ are positive-valued differentiable functions of t, and if A, α, and β are constants, find expressions for $\dot{x}/x$ where:

    a. $x = \left[a(t)\right]^2 b(t)$

    b. $x = \dfrac{\left[(a(t)\right]^5}{b(t)}$

    c. $x = A\left\{\left[a(t)\right]^\alpha + \left[b(t)\right]^\beta\right\}^{\alpha+\beta}$

    d. $x = A\left[a(t)\right]^\alpha \left[b(t)\right]^\beta$

10. Suppose that $f(x) = 3x + 7$. Compute $f(f(x))$. Find x such that $f(f(x)) = 100$.

11. Express (in at least one way) the following functions as composites of simpler functions, and find $h'(x)$ in each case:

    a. $h(x) = (1 + x + x^2)^{1/2}$

    b. $h(x) = 1/(x^{100} + 28)$

12. Suppose that $C = 20q - 4q\left(25 - \frac{1}{2}x\right)^{1/2}$, where q is a constant and $x < 50$. Find dC/dx.

13. Differentiate each of the following in two different ways:

    a. $y = (x^4)^5 = x^{20}$

    b. $y = (1 - x)^3 = 1 - 3x + 3x^2 - x^3$

14. If $p(x) = (x - a)^2 q(x)$ and q is differentiable at $x = a$, show that $p'(a) = 0$.

15. If $R = S^\alpha$, $S = 1 + \beta K^\gamma$, and $K = At^p + B$, find an expression for dR/dt.

16. If $F(x) = f(x^n g(x))$, find a formula for $F'(x)$.

5.3 Implicit Differentiation

We know how to differentiate functions given explicitly by certain formulas. Now we consider how to differentiate functions defined implicitly by an equation.

An Introductory Example

The following equation was studied in Example 2.7 of Section 2.3:

$$x\sqrt{y} = 2 \qquad (x > 0, \ y > 0) \qquad\qquad [*]$$

Note that $y = 4$ when $x = 1$, that $y = 1$ when $x = 2$, that $y = 1/4$ when $x = 4$, and $y = 1/9$ when $x = 6$. In general, for each positive number x, there is a unique number y such that the pair (x, y) satisfies the equation. We say that equation $[*]$ *defines y implicitly as a function of x.* The graph of equation $[*]$ shown in Fig. 5.1 is reproduced from Fig. 2.14.

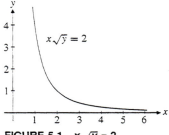

FIGURE 5.1 $x\sqrt{y} = 2$.

It is natural to ask what is the slope of the tangent at an arbitrary point on the graph. In other words, what is the derivative of y as function of x? The answer can be found by implicit differentiation of equation [∗]. Let f denote the function defined by equation [∗]. Substituting $f(x)$ for y gives

$$x\sqrt{f(x)} = 2 \qquad \text{(for all } x > 0)$$

The derivative of the left-hand side of this identity must be equal to the derivative of the right-hand side, for all $x > 0$. Now use the product rule to differentiate $x\sqrt{f(x)} = 2$ w.r.t. x. The implication is that

$$1 \cdot \sqrt{f(x)} + x\frac{d}{dx}\sqrt{f(x)} = 0 \qquad\qquad [∗∗]$$

But the chain rule yields

$$\frac{d}{dx}\sqrt{f(x)} = \frac{1}{2\sqrt{f(x)}} \cdot f'(x)$$

Inserting this into [∗∗] and rearranging gives

$$\frac{x}{2\sqrt{f(x)}}f'(x) = -\sqrt{f(x)}$$

When $x > 0$, solving for $f'(x)$ leads to

$$f'(x) = \frac{-2f(x)}{x}$$

For $x = 2$, we get $f(2) = 1$, and hence $f'(2) = -1$, which agrees with Fig. 5.1.

Usually, we do not introduce a name for y as a function of x. Instead, we differentiate directly, using the following reasoning. Differentiating [∗] with respect to x, while recalling that y is a differentiable function of x, gives

$$1 \cdot \sqrt{y} + x \cdot \frac{1}{2\sqrt{y}}y' = 0$$

Solving for y' gives

$$y' = -\frac{2y}{x} \qquad\qquad [***]$$

For this particular example, there is another way to find the answer. Squaring each side of equation [*] yields $x^2y = 4$, and so $y = 4/x^2 = 4x^{-2}$ for $x > 0$. Differentiating w.r.t. x yields $y' = 4(-2)x^{-3} = -8/x^3$. Note that substituting $4/x^2$ for y in [***] yields $y' = -8/x^3$ again.

The method used to derive [***] can be summarized as follows:

The Method of Implicit Differentiation

If two variables x and y are related by an equation, to find dy/dx:

1. Differentiate each side of the equation w.r.t. x, considering y as a function of x. (Usually, you will need the chain rule.)
2. Solve the resulting equation for dy/dx.

Further Examples

It is important for economists to master the technique of implicit differentiation, so here are some further examples.

Example 5.7

Suppose that y is a differentiable function of x given by

$$x + y^3 = y^5 - x^2 + 2y \qquad\qquad [1]$$

for all x in a given interval I. Find an expression for y'. The graph of Equation [1] passes through $(x, y) = (1, 1)$. Find y' at this point.

Solution   In this case, it is impossible to solve the equation explicitly for y. It is still possible, however, to find an explicit expression for y'. We suppose that an (unspecified) function of x is substituted for y. Then $x + y^3$ and $y^5 - x^2 + 2y$ are both functions of x, and these expressions must be equal for all x in I. This implies that their derivatives must be equal. According to the chain rule, the derivative of y^3 with respect to x is $3y^2y'$ and the derivative of y^5 is equal to $5y^4y'$. Thus,

$$1 + 3y^2y' = 5y^4y' - 2x + 2y'$$

To find y', collect all terms containing y' on the right-hand side and all others on the left. The result is

$$1 + 2x = (5y^4 + 2 - 3y^2)y'$$

Solving for y' gives

$$y' = \frac{2x + 1}{5y^4 - 3y^2 + 2}$$

Because we have no explicit expression for y as a function of x, we cannot express y' explicitly as a function of x. At $(x, y) = (1, 1)$, however, we get $y' = 3/4$.

Example 5.8

Consider the following standard macroeconomic model for determining national income in a closed economy:

$$[1] \quad Y = C + I$$

$$[2] \quad C = f(Y)$$

Here [2] is the consumption function discussed in Example 2.18 of Section 2.5, whereas [1] states that the national income Y goes either to consumption C or to investment I. We suppose that $f'(Y)$, *the marginal propensity to consume*, is between 0 and 1.

(a) Suppose first that $C = f(Y) = 95.05 + 0.712\,Y$ (see Example 2.18), and use equations [1] and [2] to find Y in terms of I. Find the change ΔY in Y if I is changed by ΔI units.

(b) Equations [1] and [2] define Y as a differentiable function of I. Find an expression for dY/dI.

Solution

(a) In this case, we find that $Y = 95.05 + 0.712\,Y + I$. Solving for Y yields

$$Y = (95.05 + I)/(1 - 0.712) \approx 3.47\,I + 330.03 \qquad [3]$$

Suppose now that I changes by ΔI. The corresponding change ΔY in Y satisfies

$$Y + \Delta Y \approx 3.47(I + \Delta I) + 330.03 \qquad [4]$$

Subtracting [3] from [4] gives

$$\Delta Y \approx 3.47\,\Delta I \qquad [5]$$

In particular, if I is changed by one unit (for example, $1 billion) so that $\Delta I = 1$, then the corresponding change in the national product is $\Delta Y \approx 3.47$ (billion).

(b) Inserting the expression for C from [2] into [1] gives

$$Y = f(Y) + I \tag{6}$$

Suppose that this equation defines Y as a differentiable function of I. Differentiating [6] with respect to I, and using the chain rule, we have

$$\frac{dY}{dI} = f'(Y)\frac{dY}{dI} + 1 \quad \text{or} \quad \frac{dY}{dI}\left[1 - f'(Y)\right] = 1$$

Solving for dY/dI yields

$$\frac{dY}{dI} = \frac{1}{1 - f'(Y)} \tag{7}$$

For example, if $f'(Y) = 1/2$, then $dY/dI = 2$. Also $f'(Y) = 0.712$ gives $dY/dI \approx 3.47$. In general, we see that because $f'(Y)$ lies between 0 and 1, so $1 - f'(Y)$ also lies between 0 and 1. Hence, $1/\left[1 - f'(Y)\right]$ is always larger than 1. In this model, therefore, a \$1 billion increase in investment will always lead to a more than \$1 billion increase in the national product. The larger is $f'(Y)$, the marginal propensity to consume, the larger is dY/dI.

Example 5.9

In the linear supply and demand model of Example 2.19, Section 2.5, suppose that a tax of t per unit is imposed on consumers. Then

$$D = a - b(P + t), \qquad S = \alpha + \beta P \tag{1}$$

Here a, b, α, and β are positive constants. The equilibrium price is determined by equating supply and demand, so that

$$a - b(P + t) = \alpha + \beta P \tag{2}$$

(a) Equation [2] implicitly defines the price P as a function of the unit tax t. Compute dP/dt by implicit differentiation. What is its sign? Check the result by first solving Equation [2] for P and then finding dP/dt explicitly.

(b) Compute tax revenue T as a function of t. For what value of t does the quadratic function T reach its maximum?

(c) Generalize the foregoing model by assuming that

$$D = f(P + t) \qquad \text{and} \qquad S = g(P)$$

where f and g are differentiable functions with $f' < 0$ and $g' > 0$. The equilibrium condition

$$f(P + t) = g(P) \qquad [3]$$

defines P implicitly as a differentiable function of t. Find an expression for dP/dt by implicit differentiation.

Solution

(a) Differentiating [2] w.r.t. t yields $-b(dP/dt + 1) = \beta\, dP/dt$. Solving for dP/dt gives

$$\frac{dP}{dt} = \frac{-b}{b + \beta}$$

We see that dP/dt is negative. Because P is the price received by the producer, this price will go down if the tax rate t increases. But $P + t$ is the price paid by the consumer. Because

$$\frac{d}{dt}(P + t) = \frac{dP}{dt} + 1 = \frac{-b}{b + \beta} + 1 = \frac{-b + b + \beta}{b + \beta} = \frac{\beta}{b + \beta} > 0$$

it follows that $0 < d(P + t)/dt < 1$. Thus, the consumer price increases, but by less than the increase in the tax.

If we solve [2] for P, we obtain

$$P = \frac{a - \alpha - bt}{b + \beta} = \frac{a - \alpha}{b + \beta} - \frac{b}{b + \beta}\, t$$

This equation shows that the equilibrium price is a linear function of the tax per unit with slope $-b/(b + \beta)$.

(b) The total tax revenue is $T = St = (\alpha + \beta P)t$, where P is the equilibrium price. Thus,

$$T = \left[\alpha + \beta \left(\frac{-bt}{b + \beta} + \frac{a - \alpha}{b + \beta} \right) \right] t = \frac{-b\beta t^2}{b + \beta} + \frac{(a\beta + \alpha b)t}{b + \beta}$$

This quadratic function has its maximum at $t = (\alpha b + \beta a)/2b\beta$.

(c) Differentiating [3] w.r.t. t yields $f'(P+t)\,(dP/dt + 1) = g'(P)\,dP/dt$. Solving for dP/dt gives

$$\frac{dP}{dt} = \frac{f'(P + t)}{g'(P) - f'(P + t)}$$

Because $f' < 0$ and $g' > 0$, we see that dP/dt is negative in this case as well. Moreover,

$$\frac{d}{dt}(P+t) = \frac{dP}{dt} + 1 = \frac{f'(P+t)}{g'(P) - f'(P+t)} + 1$$

$$= \frac{g'(P)}{g'(P) - f'(P+t)}$$

which implies that $0 < d(P+t)/dt < 1$ in this case also.

The Second Derivative of Functions Defined Implicitly

The following examples suggest how to compute the second derivative of a function that is defined implicitly by an equation.

Example 5.10

Compute y'' when y is given implicitly as function of x by

$$x\sqrt{y} = 2 \tag{1}$$

Solution   In the introductory example to this section, we found that $y' = -2y/x$ by implicit differentiation. Using the quotient rule to differentiate this equation implicitly w.r.t. x, while taking into account how y is a function of x, we obtain

$$y'' = -\frac{2y'x - 2y \cdot 1}{x^2}$$

Inserting the expression $-2y/x$ we already have for y' gives

$$y'' = -\frac{2(-2y/x)x - 2y}{x^2} = \frac{6y}{x^2} \tag{2}$$

In this case, we can check the answer directly. From [1], we have $y = 4/x^2$, which when inserted into [2] gives $y'' = 24/x^4$. On the other hand, because $y = 4/x^2 = 4x^{-2}$, direct differentiation gives $y' = -8x^{-3}$ and $y'' = 24x^{-4} = 24/x^4$.

Example 5.11

Find d^2Y/dI^2 when $Y = f(Y) + I$.

Solution   We found in Example 5.8 that $dY/dI = 1/[1 - f'(Y)] = [1 - f'(Y)]^{-1}$. Differentiation with respect to I using the chain rule yields

$$\frac{d^2Y}{dI^2} = (-1)\left[1 - f'(Y)\right]^{-2} \cdot \left[-f''(Y)\right]\frac{dY}{dI} = f''(Y)\left[1 - f'(Y)\right]^{-2}\frac{dY}{dI}$$

(We had to differentiate $1 - f'(Y)$ with respect to I. The result is $0 - f''(Y)(dY/dI)$.) Using the expression for dY/dI gives

$$\frac{d^2Y}{dI^2} = f''(Y)\left[1 - f'(Y)\right]^{-3}$$

$$= \frac{f''(Y)}{\left[1 - f'(Y)\right]^3}$$

Problems

1. For the following equations, find dy/dx by implicit differentiation:

    a. $xy = 1$ **b.** $x - y + 3xy = 2$ **c.** $y^6 = x^5$

    Check by solving each equation w.r.t. y and then differentiating.

2. Suppose that y is a differentiable function of x that satisfies the equation

$$2x^2 + 6xy + y^2 = 18$$

Find an expression for y' by implicit differentiation. The point $(x, y) = (1, 2)$ lies on the graph of the equation. Find y' at this particular point.

3. A curve in the uv-plane is given by

$$u^2 + uv - v^3 = 0$$

Compute dv/du by implicit differentiation. Find the point (u, v) on the curve where $dv/du = 0$ and $u \neq 0$.

4. For each of the following equations, answer the question: If $y = f(x)$ is a differentiable function that satifies the equation, what is y'? (a is a positive constant.).

    a. $x^2 + y^2 = a^2$ **b.** $\sqrt{x} + \sqrt{y} = \sqrt{a}$ **c.** $x^4 - y^4 = x^2y^3$

5. According to Wold, the demand Q for butter in Stockholm during the period 1925–1937 was related to the price P by the equation

$$Q \cdot P^{1/2} = 38$$

Find dQ/dP by implicit differentiation. Check the answer by using a different method to compute the derivative.

6. Suppose that f and g are two functions defined in an open interval I.

    a. If $f(x_0) = g(x_0)$ for some $x_0 \in I$, what can you conclude about $f'(x_0)$ and $g'(x_0)$?

    b. If $f(x) = g(x)$ for all $x \in I$, and if $x_0 \in I$, what can you conclude about $f'(x_0)$ and $g'(x_0)$?

7. A standard model for income determination in an open economy is

$$Y = C + I + \bar{X} - M \qquad [1]$$

$$C = f(Y) \qquad [2]$$

$$M = g(Y) \qquad [3]$$

where $0 < f'(Y) < 1$. Here $\bar{X}$ is an exogeneous constant that denotes exports, whereas M denotes the volume of imports. The function g in [3] is called an *import function*. By inserting [2] and [3] into [1], we obtain an equation that defines Y as a function of exogeneous investment I. Find a expression for dY/dI by implicit differentiation. What is the likely sign of $g'(Y)$? Discuss the sign of dY/dI.

8. If $a = m/n$, where m and n are integers, the power rule (4.24) gives

$$y = x^{m/n} \implies y' = (m/n)x^{(m/n)-1}$$

Verify this result (assuming that y *is* differentiable) by differentiating the equation $y^n = x^m$ implicitly with respect to x.

9. If f and g are differentiable and $g(f(x)) = x$ for all x, find an expression for $f'(x)$ in terms of the derivative of g.

5.4 Linear Approximations and Differentials

When a complicated function is difficult to work with, we sometimes try to find a simpler function that in some sense approximates the original one. Linear functions are very easy to manipulate. It is therefore natural first to try to find a "linear approximation" to a given function.

Consider a function $f(x)$ that is differentiable at $x = a$. The tangent to the graph at $(a, f(a))$ has the equation $y = f(a) + f'(a)(x - a)$ (see [4.4] of Section 4.2). If we approximate the graph of f by its tangent line at $x = a$, as shown in Fig. 5.2, the resulting approximation has a special name.

The **linear approximation** to f about a is

$$f(x) \approx f(a) + f'(a)(x - a) \qquad (x \text{ close to } a) \qquad [5.5]$$

Note that if $p(x)$ is the linear function $f(a) + f'(a)(x - a)$ of x, then f and p have both the same value and the same derivative at $x = a$.

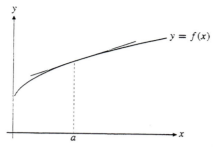

FIGURE 5.2   The approximation of a function by its tangent.

Example 5.12

Find the linear approximation to $f(x) = \sqrt[3]{x}$ about $a = 1$.

Solution   We have $f(x) = \sqrt[3]{x} = x^{1/3}$, so $f'(x) = \frac{1}{3}x^{-2/3}$ and $f'(1) = 1/3$. Because $f(1) = 1$, using [5.5] yields

$$\sqrt[3]{x} \approx 1 + \tfrac{1}{3}(x - 1) \qquad (x \text{ close to } 1)$$

For example, $\sqrt[3]{1.03} \approx 1 + \frac{1}{3}(1.03 - 1) = 1 + \frac{1}{3}(0.03) = 1.01$. The correct value to 4 decimals is 1.0099.

Example 5.13

In a paper by economists Samuelson and Swamy, the authors were concerned with the behavior of the following function about $\varepsilon = 0$:

$$f(\varepsilon) = \left(1 + \tfrac{3}{2}\varepsilon + \tfrac{1}{2}\varepsilon^2\right)^{1/2}$$

Find the linear approximation to $f(\varepsilon)$ about $\varepsilon = 0$.

Solution   Here $f'(\varepsilon) = \frac{1}{2}\left(1 + \frac{3}{2}\varepsilon + \frac{1}{2}\varepsilon^2\right)^{-1/2} \cdot \left(\frac{3}{2} + \varepsilon\right)$ and so $f'(0) = \frac{3}{4}$. Because $f(0) = 1$, using [5.5] yields

$$\left(1 + \tfrac{3}{2}\varepsilon + \tfrac{1}{2}\varepsilon^2\right)^{1/2} \approx 1 + \tfrac{3}{4}\varepsilon \qquad (\varepsilon \text{ close to } 0)$$

The Differential of a Function

Consider a differentiable function $f(x)$, and let dx denote an arbitrary change in the variable x. In this notation, "dx" is not a product of d and x. Rather, dx is a single symbol representing the change in the value of x. The expression $f'(x)\,dx$ is called the **differential** of $y = f(x)$, and it is denoted by dy (or df), so that

$$dy = f'(x)\,dx \qquad\qquad [5.6]$$

Note that dy is proportional to dx, with $f'(x)$ as the factor of proportionality.

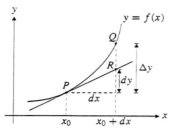

FIGURE 5.3 A geometric representation of the differential.

Now if x changes by dx, then the corresponding change in $y = f(x)$ is

$$\Delta y = f(x + dx) - f(x) \qquad [5.7]$$

By using the definitions of dy and Δy, replacing x by $x + dx$ and a by x, the approximation in [5.5] takes the form

$$\Delta y \approx dy = f'(x)\, dx$$

The differential dy is not the actual increment in y as x is changed to $x + dx$, but rather the change in y that would occur if y continued to change at the fixed rate $f'(x)$ as x changes to $x + dx$. Figure 5.3 illustrates the difference between Δy and dy. Consider, first, the movement from P to Q along the curve $y = f(x)$: as x changes by dx, the actual change in the vertical height of the point is Δy. Suppose instead that we are only allowed to move along the tangent to the graph at P. Thus, as we move from P to R along the tangent, the change in height that corresponds to dx is dy. Note that, as in Fig. 5.3, the approximation $\Delta y \approx dy$ is usually better if dx is smaller in absolute value, because the length of line segment RQ representing the difference between Δy and dy tends to 0 as dx tends to 0.

Rules for Differentials

The notation $(d/dx)(\ \ )$ calls for the expression in parentheses to be differentiated with respect to x. In the same way, we let $d(\ \ )$ denote the differential of whatever is inside the parentheses.

Example 5.14

Compute the following:

(a) $d\left(Ax^a + B\right)$ (A, B, and a are constants)

(b) $d\left(f(K)\right)$ (f a differentiable function of K)

Solution

(a) Putting $f(x) = Ax^a + B$, we get $f'(x) = Aax^{a-1}$, so $d(Ax^a + B) = Aax^{a-1} dx$.

(b) $d(f(K)) = f'(K) dK$.

All the usual rules for differentiation can be expressed in terms of differentials. If f and g are two differentiable functions of x, then the following holds.

Rules for Differentials

$$d(af + bg) = a\,df + b\,dg \qquad (a \text{ and } b \text{ are constants})$$

$$d(fg) = g\,df + f\,dg$$

$$d\left(\frac{f}{g}\right) = \frac{g\,df - f\,dg}{g^2} \, (g \neq 0)$$

[5.8]

Here is a proof of the second of these formulas:

$$d(fg) = (fg)'\,dx = (f'g + fg')\,dx = gf'\,dx + fg'\,dx = g\,df + f\,dg$$

You should now prove the other rules in the same way.

Suppose that $y = f(x)$ and $x = g(t)$ is a function of t. Then $y = h(t) = f(g(t))$ is a function of t. The differential of $y = h(t)$ is $dy = h'(t)\,dt$. According to the chain rule, $h'(t) = f'(g(t))\,g'(t)$, so that $dy = f'(g(t))g'(t)\,dt$. Because $x = g(t)$, the differential of x is equal to $dx = g'(t)\,dt$, hence

$$dy = f'(x)\,dx$$

This shows that if $y = f(x)$, then the differential of y is equal to $dy = f'(x)\,dx$, whether x depends on another variables or not.

Economists often use differentials in their models. A typical example follows.

Example 5.15

Consider again the model in Example 5.8 of Sec. 5.3:

$$[1] \; Y = C + I \qquad [2] \; C = f(Y)$$

Find the differential dY expressed in terms of dI. If in addition to [1] and [2] it is assumed that employment $N = g(Y)$ is a function of Y, find also the differential dN expressed in terms of dI.

Solution   Differentiating [1] and [2], we obtain

$$[3] \; dY = dC + dI \qquad [4] \; dC = f'(Y)\,dY$$

Substituting dC from [4] into [3] and solving for dY yields

$$dY = \frac{1}{1 - f'(Y)} \, dI \qquad [5]$$

which corresponds exactly to [7] in Example 5.8. From $N = g(Y)$, we get $dN = g'(Y) \, dY$, so

$$dN = \frac{g'(Y)}{1 - f'(Y)} \, dI \qquad [6]$$

Provided that $g'(Y) > 0$ and $f'(Y)$, the marginal propensity to consume, is between 0 and 1, we see from [6] that if investment increases, then employment increases.

Problems

1. Prove that $\sqrt{1 + x} \approx 1 + \frac{1}{2}x$, for x close to 0, and illustrate this approximation by drawing the graphs of $y = 1 + \frac{1}{2}x$ and $y = \sqrt{1 + x}$ in the same coordinate system.

2. Use [5.5] to find the linear approximation to $f(x) = (5x + 3)^{-2}$ about $x_0 = 0$.

3. Find the linear approximation to the following functions about $x_0 = 0$:
   a. $f(x) = (1 + x)^{-1}$ **b.** $f(x) = (1 + x)^5$ **c.** $f(x) = (1 - x)^{1/4}$

4. Find the linear approximation to $F(K) = AK^{\alpha}$ about $K_0 = 1$.

5. Prove that $(1 + x)^m \approx 1 + mx$, for x close to 0, and use this approximation to find approximations to the following numbers:

   a. $\sqrt[3]{1.1} = \left(1 + \frac{1}{10}\right)^{1/3}$ **b.** $\sqrt[5]{33} = 2\left(1 + \frac{1}{32}\right)^{1/5}$

   c. $\sqrt[3]{9} = \sqrt[3]{8 + 1}$ **d.** $(1.02)^{25}$

   e. $\sqrt{37} = \sqrt{36 + 1}$ **f.** $(26.95)^{1/3} = \left(27 - \frac{5}{100}\right)^{1/3}$

6. Compute $\Delta y = f(x + dx) - f(x)$ and the differential $dy = f'(x) \, dx$ for the following:
   a. $f(x) = x^2 + 2x - 3$ when (i) $x = 2$, $dx = 1/10$, and (ii) $x = 2$, $dx = 1/100$.
   b. $f(x) = 1/x$ when (i) $x = 3$, $dx = -1/10$, and (ii) $x = 3$, $dx = -1/100$.
   c. $f(x) = \sqrt{x}$ when (i) $x = 4$, $dx = 1/20$, and (ii) $x = 4$, $dx = 1/100$.

7. The radius of a ball increases from 2 to 2.03. Estimate the increase in volume of the ball by using a linear approximation. Compare with the actual increase in volume. (Hint: See Appendix D.)

Harder Problems

8. Find the linear approximation to the function

$$g(\mu) = A(1 + \mu)^{a/(1+b)} - 1 \qquad (A, a, \text{ and } b \text{ are positive constants})$$

about the the point $\mu = 0$.

5.5 Polynomial Approximations

The previous section discussed approximations of functions of one variable by linear functions. In particular, Example 5.12 established the approximation

$$\sqrt[3]{x} \approx 1 + \tfrac{1}{3}(x - 1) \qquad (x \text{ close to } 1) \tag{1}$$

In this case, at $x = 1$, the functions $y = \sqrt[3]{x}$ and $y = 1 + \tfrac{1}{3}(x - 1)$ have the same value, 1, and the same derivative, 1/3.

If approximation by linear functions is insufficiently accurate, it is natural to try quadratic approximations, or approximations by polynomials of higher order.

Quadratic Approximations

We begin by showing how a twice differentiable function $y = f(x)$ can be approximated near $x = a$ by a quadratic polynomial

$$f(x) \approx p(x) = A + B(x - a) + C(x - a)^2$$

There are three coefficients, A, B, and C, to be determined. So we are free to impose three conditions on the polynomial. We will assume that $f(x)$ and $p(x) = A + B(x - a) + C(x - a)^2$ have the same value, the same derivative, and the same second derivative at $x = a$. In symbols, we require that $f(a) = p(a)$, $f'(a) = p'(a)$, and $f''(a) = p''(a)$. Now

$$p'(x) = B + 2C(x - a), \qquad p''(x) = 2C$$

So, after inserting $x = a$ into our expressions for $p(x)$, $p'(x)$, and $p''(x)$, it follows that $A = p(a)$, $B = p'(a)$, and $C = \tfrac{1}{2}p''(a)$. Hence:

The **quadratic approximation** to $f(x)$ about $x = a$ is

$$f(x) \approx f(a) + f'(a)(x - a) + \tfrac{1}{2}f''(a)(x - a)^2 \qquad (x \text{ close to } a) \tag{5.9}$$

For $a = 0$, in particular, we obtain the following:

$$f(x) \approx f(0) + f'(0)x + \tfrac{1}{2}f''(0)x^2 \qquad (x \text{ close to } 0) \qquad\qquad [5.10]$$

Example 5.16

Find the quadratic approximation to $f(x) = \sqrt[3]{x}$ about $a = 1$.

Solution   Here $f'(x) = \tfrac{1}{3}x^{-2/3}$ and $f''(x) = \tfrac{1}{3}(-\tfrac{2}{3})x^{-5/3}$. It follows that $f'(1) = \tfrac{1}{3}$ and $f''(1) = -\tfrac{2}{9}$. Because $f(1) = 1$, using [5.9] yields

$$\sqrt[3]{x} \approx 1 + \tfrac{1}{3}(x-1) - \tfrac{1}{9}(x-1)^2 \qquad (x \text{ close to } 1)$$

For example, $\sqrt[3]{1.03} \approx 1 + \tfrac{1}{3}\cdot 0.03 - \tfrac{1}{9}(0.03)^2 = 1 + 0.01 - 0.0001 = 1.0099$, which is correct to 4 decimals.

Example 5.17

Find the quadratic approximation to $f(x) = (5x + 3)^{-2}$ about $x = 0$.

Solution   Here $f'(x) = -10(5x + 3)^{-3}$ and $f''(x) = 150(5x + 3)^{-4}$, so that $f(0) = 1/9$, $f'(0) = -10/27$, and $f''(0) = 50/27$. Hence, [5.10] gives

$$\frac{1}{(5x+3)^2} \approx \frac{1}{9} - \frac{10}{27}x + \frac{25}{27}x^2 \qquad\qquad [*]$$

Example 5.18

Find the quadratic approximation to $y = y(x)$ about $x = 0$ when y is defined implicitly as a function of x near $(x, y) = (0, 1)$ by

$$xy^3 + 1 = y \qquad\qquad [1]$$

Solution   Implicit differentiation of [1] with respect to x yields

$$y^3 + 3xy^2y' = y' \qquad\qquad [2]$$

Substituting $x = 0$ and $y = 1$ into [2] gives $y' = 1$. Differentiating [2] with respect to x now yields

$$3y^2y' + (3y^2 + 6xyy')y' + 3xy^2y'' = y''$$

Substituting $x = 0$, $y = 1$, and $y' = 1$, we obtain $y'' = 6$. Hence, according to [5.10],

$$y(x) \approx y(0) + y'(0)x + \tfrac{1}{2}y''(0)x^2 = 1 + x + 3x^2$$

Higher-Order Approximations

So far, we have considered linear and quadratic approximations. We can find better approximations near one point by using polynomials of a higher degree. Suppose we want to approximate a function $f(x)$ over an interval centered at $x = a$ with an nth-degree polynomial of the form

$$p(x) = A_0 + A_1(x - a) + A_2(x - a)^2 + A_3(x - a)^3 + \cdots + A_n(x - a)^n \quad [1]$$

Because $p(x)$ has $n+1$ coefficients, we can impose the following $n+1$ conditions on this polynomial:

$$f(a) = p(a), \qquad f'(a) = p'(a), \qquad \dots \qquad f^{(n)}(a) = p^{(n)}(a) \qquad [2]$$

These conditions require that $p(x)$ and its first n derivatives agree with the value of $f(x)$ and its first n derivatives at $x = a$. Let us see what these conditions become when $n = 3$. In this case,

$$p(x) = A_0 + A_1(x - a) + A_2(x - a)^2 + A_3(x - a)^3$$

and we find that

$$p'(x) = A_1 + 2A_2(x - a) + 3A_3(x - a)^2$$
$$p''(x) = 2A_2 + 2 \cdot 3A_3(x - a)$$
$$p'''(x) = 2 \cdot 3A_3$$

Thus, when $x = a$, we have[1]

$$p(a) = A_0, \qquad p'(a) = 1!\,A_1, \qquad p''(a) = 2!\,A_2, \qquad p'''(a) = 3!\,A_3$$

This implies the following approximation:

$$f(x) \approx f(a) + \frac{1}{1!}f'(a)(x - a) + \frac{1}{2!}f''(a)(x - a)^2 + \frac{1}{3!}f'''(a)(x - a)^3$$

The general case follows the same pattern. When $p(x)$ is given by [1], yields

---

[1] For the definition of $n!$, see Problem 6 of Section 4.7.

successive differentiation of $p(x)$

$$p'(x) = A_1 + 2A_2(x - a) + 3A_3(x - a)^2 + \cdots + nA_n(x - a)^{n-1}$$

$$p''(x) = 2A_2 + 3 \cdot 2A_3(x - a) + \cdots + n(n - 1)A_n(x - a)^{n-2}$$

$$p'''(x) = 3 \cdot 2A_3 + \cdots + n(n - 1)(n - 2)A_n(x - a)^{n-3}$$

$$p^{(4)}(x) = 4 \cdot 3 \cdot 2A_4 + \cdots + n(n - 1)(n - 2)(n - 3)A_n(x - a)^{n-4}$$

$$\cdots\cdots\cdots\cdots\cdots\cdots\cdots\cdots\cdots\cdots\cdots\cdots\cdots\cdots\cdots\cdots\cdots\cdots\cdots$$

$$p^{(n)}(x) = n(n - 1)(n - 2) \cdots 2 \cdot 1A_n$$

[3]

Substituting $x = a$ into [3] gives

$$p'(a) = 1! A_1, \quad p''(a) = 2! A_2, \quad \ldots, \quad p^{(n)}(a) = n! A_n \qquad [4]$$

This leads to the following approximation to $f(x)$ by an nth degree polynomial.

Approximation to $f(x)$ about $x = a$:

$$f(x) \approx f(a) + \frac{f'(a)}{1!}(x - a) + \frac{f''(a)}{2!}(x - a)^2 + \cdots + \frac{f^{(n)}(a)}{n!}(x - a)^n$$

[5.11]

The polynomial on the right-hand side of [5.11] is called the **nth-order Taylor polynomial** for f about $x = a$.

  The function f and its nth-order Taylor polynomial have such a high degree of contact at $x = a$ that it is reasonable to expect the approximation in [5.11] to be good over some (possibly small) interval centered about $x = a$. Section 7.4 analyses the error that results from using such polynomial approximations. In the case when f is itself a polynomial whose degree does not exceed n, the formula becomes exact, without any approximation error at any point.

Example 5.19

  Find the third-order Taylor approximation of $f(x) = \sqrt{1 + x}$ about $a = 0$.

  Solution   We write $f(x) = \sqrt{1 + x} = (1 + x)^{1/2}$. Then we have $f'(x) = (1/2)(1 + x)^{-1/2}$, $f''(x) = (1/2)(-1/2)(1 + x)^{-3/2}$, and $f'''(x) = (1/2)(-1/2)(-3/2)(1 + x)^{-5/2}$. Putting $x = 0$ gives $f(0) = 1$, $f'(0) = 1/2$, $f''(0) = (1/2)(-1/2) = -1/4$, and finally $f'''(0) = (1/2)(-1/2)(-3/2) = 3/8$. Hence, by [5.11] for the case $n = 3$, we have

$$f(x) \approx 1 + \frac{1}{1!}\frac{1}{2}x + \frac{1}{2!}\left(-\frac{1}{4}\right)x^2 + \frac{1}{3!}\frac{3}{8}x^3 = 1 + \frac{1}{2}x - \frac{1}{8}x^2 + \frac{1}{16}x^3$$

Problems

1. Find quadratic approximations to the following functions about the given points:

   a. $f(x) = (1 + x)^5$, $a = 0$

   b. $F(K) = AK^\alpha$, $K_0 = 1$

   c. $f(\varepsilon) = \left(1 + \frac{3}{2}\varepsilon + \frac{1}{2}\varepsilon^2\right)^{1/2}$, $\varepsilon_0 = 0$

   d. $H(x) = (1 - x)^{-1}$, $a = 0$

2. In connection with a study of attitudes to risk, the following approximation to a consumer's utility function is encountered. Explain how to derive this approximation.

$$U(y + M - s) \approx U(y) + U'(y)(M - s) + \tfrac{1}{2}U''(y)(M - s)^2$$

3. Find the quadratic approximation about $x = 0$, $y = 1$ for y when y is defined implicitly as a function of x by the equation $1 + x^3 y + x = y^{1/2}$.

4. Let the function $x(t)$ be given by the conditions $x(0) = 1$ and

$$\dot{x}(t) = tx(t) + 2\big[x(t)\big]^2$$

   Determine the second order Taylor polynomial for $x(t)$ about $t = 0$.

5. Establish the approximation

$$\left(1 + \frac{p}{100}\right)^n \approx 1 + n\frac{p}{100} + \frac{n(n-1)}{2}\left(\frac{p}{100}\right)^2$$

6. The function h is defined for all $x > 0$ by

$$h(x) = \frac{x^p - x^q}{x^p + x^q} \qquad (p > q > 0)$$

   Find the first-order Taylor polynomial about $x = 1$ for $h(x)$.

5.6 Elasticities

Why do economists so often use elasticities instead of derivatives? Suppose we study how demand for a certain commodity reacts to price changes. We can ask by how many units the quantity demanded will change when the price increases by $1. In this way, we obtain a concrete number, a certain number of units. There are, however, several unsatisfactory aspects of this way of measuring the sensitivity of demand to price changes. For instance, a $1 price increase per pound of coffee may be considerable, whereas a $1 increase in the price of a car is insignificant.

  This problem arises because the sensitivity of demand to price changes is being measured in the same arbitrary units as those used to measure both quantity demanded and price. The difficulties are eliminated if we use relative changes instead. We ask by what percentage the quantity demanded changes when the price increases by 1%. The number we obtain in this way will be independent of the units in which both quantities and prices are measured. It is called the **price elasticity of demand**, measured at a given price.

In 1960, the price elasticity of butter in a certain country was calculated to be approximately −1. This means that an increase of 1% in the price would lead to a decrease of 1% in the quantity of butter demanded, if all the other factors that influence the demand for butter remained constant. In the same year, the demand elasticity for potatoes was calculated to be −0.2. What does this mean? Why do you think the absolute value of this elasticity is so much less than that for butter?

Assume now that the demand for a commodity can be described by the function

$$x = D(p) \qquad\qquad [1]$$

When the price changes from p to $p+\Delta p$, the quantity demanded, x, also changes. The absolute change in x is $\Delta x = D(p + \Delta p) - D(p)$, and the *relative* (or proportional) change is

$$\frac{\Delta x}{x} = \frac{D(p + \Delta p) - D(p)}{D(p)}$$

The ratio between the relative change in the quantity demanded and the relative change in the price is

$$\frac{\Delta x}{x} \Big/ \frac{\Delta p}{p} = \frac{p}{x}\frac{\Delta x}{\Delta p} = \frac{p}{D(p)}\frac{D(p + \Delta p) - D(p)}{\Delta p} \qquad\qquad [2]$$

When $\Delta p = p/100$ so that p increases by 1%, then [2] becomes $(\Delta x / x) \cdot 100$, which is the percentage change in the quantity demanded. We call the proportion in [2] *the average elasticity of x in the interval* $[p, p + \Delta p]$. Observe that the number defined in [2] depends both on the price change Δp and on the price p, but is unit-free. Thus, it makes no difference whether quantities are measured in tons, kilograms, or pounds, or whether the prices are measured in dollars, pounds, or crowns.

We would like to define the elasticity of D at p so that it does not depend on the size of the increase in p. We can do this if D is a differentiable function of p. For then it is natural to define the elasticity of D in p as the limit of the ratio in [2] as Δp tends to 0. Because the Newton quotient $[D(p + \Delta p) - D(p)]/\Delta p$ tends to $D'(p)$ as Δp tends to 0, we obtain

the elasticity of $D(p)$ with respect to p is $\dfrac{p}{D(p)}\dfrac{d D(p)}{dp}$

Usually, we get a good approximation to the elasticity by letting $\Delta p / p = 1/100 = 1\%$ and computing $p\, \Delta x / x\, \Delta p$.

Example 5.20

Assume that the quantity demanded for a particular commodity is given by the formula

$$D(p) = 8000p^{-1.5}$$

Compute the elasticity of $D(p)$ and find the percentage change in quantity demanded when the price increases by 1% from $p = 4$.

Solution   We find that

$$\frac{dD(p)}{dp} = 8000 \cdot (-1.5)p^{-1.5-1} = -12,000p^{-2.5}$$

so that the elasticity of $D(p)$ with respect to p is

$$\frac{p}{D(p)} \cdot \frac{dD(p)}{dp} = \frac{p}{8000 \cdot p^{-1.5}} \cdot (-12,000)p^{-2.5}$$

$$= -\frac{12,000}{8000} \frac{p \cdot p^{-2.5}}{p^{-1.5}} = -1.5$$

The elasticity is a constant equal to -1.5, so that an increase in the price of 1% causes quantity demanded to decrease by about 1.5%.

In this case we, can compute the decrease in demand exactly. When the price is 4, the quantity demanded is $D(4) = 8000 \cdot 4^{-1.5} = 1000$. If the price $p = 4$ is increased by 1%, the new price will be $4 + 4/100 = 4.04$, so that the *change* in demand is

$$D(4.04) - D(4) = 8000 \cdot 4.04^{-1.5} - 1000 \approx -14.81$$

The percentage change in demand from $D(4) = 1000$ is approximately $-(14.81/1000) \cdot 100 = -1.481$.

The General Definition of Elasticity

Suppose function f is differentiable at x. If $f(x) \neq 0$, we define the following:

The **elasticity** of f with respect to x is

$$\text{El}_x f(x) = \frac{x}{f(x)} f'(x) \qquad [5.12]$$

Other notation used instead of $\text{El}_x f(x)$ for the elasticity when $y = f(x)$ includes $\text{El}_x y$ and ε_{yx}.

Example 5.21

Find the elasticity of $f(x) = ax^b$ (a and b are constants, and $a \neq 0$).

Solution   In this case, $f'(x) = abx^{b-1}$. Hence,

$$\text{El}_x\left(ax^b\right) = \frac{x}{ax^b} abx^{b-1} = b$$

Example 5.22

Let $D(p)$ denote the demand function for a product. By selling $D(p)$ units at price p, the producer earns revenue $R(p)$ given by

$$R(p) = pD(p)$$

By the product rule,

$$R'(p) = D(p) + pD'(p) = D(p)\left[1 + \frac{p}{D(p)}D'(p)\right]$$

so that

$$R'(p) = D(p)\left[1 + \text{El}_p D(p)\right]$$

and

$$\text{El}_p R(p) = \frac{pR'(p)}{R(p)} = \frac{R'(p)}{D(p)} = 1 + \text{El}_p D(p)$$

Observe that if $\text{El}_p D(p) = -1$, then $R'(p) = 0$. When the price elasticity of the demand at a point is equal to -1, a small price change will have (almost) no influence on the revenue. More generally, the marginal revenue generated by a price change is positive if the price elasticity of demand is greater than -1, and negative if the elasticity is less than -1. And the elasticity of revenue w.r.t. price is exactly one greater than the price elasticity of demand.

There are some rules for elasticities of sums, products, quotients, and composite functions that are occasionally useful. You are encouraged to derive these rules in Problem 7.

Problems

1. Find the elasticities of the functions given by the following formulas:

   a. $3x^{-3}$ **b.** $-100x^{100}$ **c.** $\sqrt{x}$ **d.** $\dfrac{A}{x\sqrt{x}}$ (A constant)

2. A study of transport economics uses the relation $T = 0.4K^{1.06}$, where K is expenditure on building roads, and T is a measure of traffic volume. Find the elasticity of T w.r.t. K. An increase in expenditure of 1% corresponds

in this model to an increase in the volume of traffic of approximately how many percent?

3. A study of Norway's State Railways reveals that, for rides up to 60 km, the price elasticity of the volume of traffic is approximately -0.4.

   a. According to this study, what is the consequence of a 10% increase in fares?

   b. The corresponding elasticity for journeys over 300 km is calculated to be approximately -0.9. Can you think of a reason why this elasticity is larger in absolute value than the previous one ?

4. Use the definition [5.12] to find $\text{El}_x f(x)$ for the following:

   a. $f(x) = A$ (A constant)   **b.** $f(x) = x + 1$ **c.** $f(x) = (1 - x^2)^{10}$

5. Prove that $\text{El}_x f(x)^p = p\, \text{El}_x f(x)$ (p constant).

6. Compute $\text{El}_x A f(x)$ and $\text{El}_x [A + f(x)]$ (A constant).

Harder Problems

7. Prove that if f and g are differentiable functions of x and A is a constant, then the following rules hold (where we write, for instance, $\text{El}_x f$ instead of $\text{El}_x f(x)$).

   a. $\text{El}_x A = 0$

   b. $\text{El}_x (fg) = \text{El}_x f + \text{El}_x g$

   c. $\text{El}_x (f/g) = \text{El}_x f - \text{El}_x g$

   d. $\text{El}_x (f + g) = \dfrac{f\, \text{El}_x f + g\, \text{El}_x g}{f + g}$

   e. $\text{El}_x (f - g) = \dfrac{f\, \text{El}_x f - g\, \text{El}_x g}{f - g}$

   f. $\text{El}_x f(g(x)) = \text{El}_u f(u)\, \text{El}_x u$ (where $u = g(x)$)

8. Use the rules in Problem 7 to calculate the following:

   a. $\text{El}_x 3x^{-3}$ **b.** $\text{El}_x (x + x^2)$ **c.** $\text{El}_x (x^3 + 1)^{10}$

   d. $\text{El}_x \text{El}_x 5x^2$ **e.** $\text{El}_x (1 + x^2)$ **f.** $\text{El}_x \left(\dfrac{x - 1}{x^5 + 1} \right)$

9. Assume that f is a differentiable function with $f(x) \neq 0$. Find expressions for the elasticity of the following:

   a. $x^5 f(x)$ **b.** $(f(x))^{3/2}$ **c.** $x + \sqrt{f(x)}$ **d.** $1/f(x)$

10. Find the elasticity of y with respect to x for the following:

    a. $y^6 = x^5$ **b.** $\dfrac{y}{x} = (x + 1)^a (y - 1)^b$ (a and b are constants)

6

Limits, Continuity, and Series

We could, of course, dismiss the rigorous proof as being superfluous: if a theorem is geometrically obvious why prove it? This was exactly the attitude taken in the eighteenth century. The result, in the nineteenth century, was chaos and confusion: for intuition, unsupported by logic, habitually assumes that everything is much nicer behaved than it really is.
—I. Stewart (1975)

This chapter is concerned with limits, continuity, and series—key ideas in mathematics, and also very important in the application of mathematics to economic problems. The preliminary discussion of limits in Section 4.4 was necessarily very sketchy. In this chapter, we take a closer look at this concept and extend it in several directions.

Without limits, the real number system would be seriously incomplete. We would essentially be confined to those numbers that can be calculated precisely in a finite number of steps—for example, integers and rational numbers. In order to assert that the equation $x^2 - 2 = 0$ has a positive solution $x = \sqrt{2}$, and (perhaps more important) to be able to give arbitrarily accurate approximations to $\sqrt{2}$, we really need to be able to define $\sqrt{2}$ as a limit. This is implicitly what we do when we write $\sqrt{2} \approx 1.41421\ldots$. We have in mind an infinite sequence of decimal expansions, starting with 1, 1.4, 1.41, 1.414, ..., which get closer and closer to the *limit* $\sqrt{2}$. In this way, $\sqrt{2}$ is effectively regarded as a limit of a sequence of rational numbers; the same is true for all irrational numbers. Thus, limits arise in the study of infinite series, another topic in this chapter.

Recall too that the derivative of a function, measuring its rate of change, was defined using limits. In fact, in Section 4.2 we defined the derivative of f at a as $f'(a) = \lim_{h \to 0}[f(a + h) - f(a)]/h$. There is in addition a close connection between the limit concept and the idea of *continuity*, which will also be discussed. An optional section giving a precise definition of limits ends this chapter.

6.1 Limits

Section 4.4 gave a preliminary discussion of limits. We now supplement this with some additional concepts and results, still keeping the discussion at an intuitive level. The reason for this gradual approach is that it is important and quite easy to acquire a working knowledge of limits. Experience suggests, however, that the precise definition is rather difficult to understand, as are proofs based on this definition.

Limits That Do Not Exist: One-Sided Limits

Suppose f is defined for all x close to a, but not necessarily at a. According to [4.14] of Section 4.4, the function $f(x)$ has the number A as its limit as x tends to a, provided that the number $f(x)$ can be made as close to A as one pleases for all x sufficiently close to (but not equal to) a. Then we write

$$\lim_{x \to a} f(x) = A \quad \text{or} \quad f(x) \to A \quad \text{as} \quad x \to a$$

In this case, we say that the limit exists. The graphs of Figs. 6.1 and 6.2 show two cases where $f(x)$ *does not* tend to any limit as x tends to a.

FIGURE 6.1 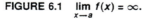 $\lim_{x \to a} f(x) = \infty$.

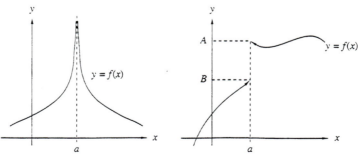

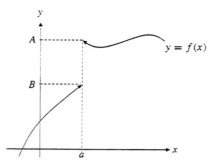

FIGURE 6.2 $\lim\limits_{x \to a} f(x)$ **does not exist.**

Figure 6.1 shows the graph of a function such as $f(x) = 1/|x - a|$ or $f(x) = 1/(x - a)^2$, which increases without bound as x tends to a (either from the right or from the left). We write $f(x) \to \infty$ as $x \to a$, or $\lim_{x \to a} f(x) = \infty$. Because $f(x)$ does not tend to a definite (finite) number as x tends to a, we say that the limit does not exist. (In a sense, there is an infinite limit, but we follow standard mathematical practice in insisting that limits be *finite* numbers.) The straight line $x = a$ is called a **vertical asymptote** for the graph of f.

The function whose graph is shown in Fig. 6.2 also fails to have a limit as x tends to a. However, it seems from the figure that if x tends to a from below, then $f(x)$ tends to the number B. We say, therefore, that the *limit of $f(x)$ as x tends to a from below is B*, and we write

$$\lim_{x \to a^-} f(x) = B \quad \text{or} \quad f(x) \to B \quad \text{as} \quad x \to a^-$$

Analogously, also referring to Fig. 6.2, we say that the *limit of $f(x)$ as x tends to a from above is A*, and we write

$$\lim_{x \to a^+} f(x) = A \quad \text{or} \quad f(x) \to A \quad \text{as} \quad x \to a^+$$

We call these *one-sided limits*, the first from below and the second from above. They can also be called *left limits* and *right limits*, respectively.

Necessary and sufficient conditions for the (ordinary) limit to exist are that the two one-sided limits of f at a exist and are equal:

$$\lim_{x \to a} f(x) = A \iff \lim_{x \to a^-} f(x) = A \quad \text{and} \quad \lim_{x \to a^-} f(x) = A \qquad [6.1]$$

It should now also be clear what is meant by

$$\lim_{x \to a^-} f(x) = \infty \ (\text{or} -\infty) \quad \text{and} \quad \lim_{x \to a^+} f(x) = \infty \ (\text{or} -\infty)$$

In these cases, despite the notation, we say that the limits do not exist.

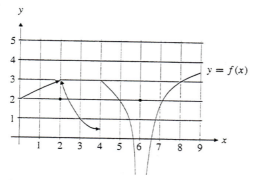

y = f(x)

FIGURE 6.3

Example 6.1

Figure 6.3 reproduces Fig. 4.12 of Section 4.4, and shows the graph of a function f defined on $[0, 9]$. Using the figure, verify (roughly) that the following limits are correct:

$$\lim_{x \to 4^-} f(x) = 1/2, \qquad \lim_{x \to 4^+} f(x) = 3, \qquad \lim_{x \to 9^-} f(x) = 3.5$$

Example 6.2

Explain the following limits:

$$\lim_{x \to 0^-} \frac{1}{x} = -\infty, \qquad \lim_{x \to 0^+} \frac{1}{x} = \infty,$$

$$\lim_{x \to 2^-} \frac{1}{\sqrt{2 - x}} = \infty, \qquad \lim_{x \to 2^+} \frac{-1}{\sqrt{x - 2}} = -\infty$$

Solution   If x is negative and close to 0, then $1/x$ is a large negative number. For example, $1/(-0.001) = -1000$. In fact, $1/x$ decreases without bound as x tends to zero from below, and it is reasonable to say that $1/x$ tends to minus infinity as x tends to 0 from below.

The second limit is very similar, except that $1/x$ is large and positive when x is positive and close to 0.

If x is slightly smaller than 2, then $2 - x$ is positive, so $\sqrt{2 - x}$ is close to 0, and $1/\sqrt{2 - x}$ is a large positive number. For example, $1/\sqrt{2 - 1.9999} = 1/\sqrt{0.0001} = 100$. As x tends to 2^-, so $1/\sqrt{2 - x}$ tends to ∞.

The fourth limit is similar, because when x is slightly larger than 2, then $\sqrt{x - 2}$ is positive and close to 0, so $-1/\sqrt{x - 2}$ is a large negative number.

Limits at Infinity

We can also use the language of limits to describe the behavior of a function as its argument becomes infinitely large through positive or negative values. Let f be defined for arbitrarily large positive numbers x. We say that $f(x)$ *has the limit A as x tends to infinity* if $f(x)$ can be made arbitrary close to A for all x sufficiently large. We write

$$\lim_{x \to \infty} f(x) = A \qquad \text{or} \qquad f(x) \to A \quad \text{as} \quad x \to \infty$$

In the same way,

$$\lim_{x \to -\infty} f(x) = B \qquad \text{or} \qquad f(x) \to B \quad \text{as} \quad x \to -\infty$$

indicates that $f(x)$ can be made arbitrary close to B for all x sufficiently large and negative. The two limits are illustrated in Fig. 6.4. The horizontal line $y = A$ is a (horizontal) **asymptote** for the graph of f as x tends to ∞, whereas $y = B$ is a (horizontal) asymptote for the graph as x tends to $-\infty$.

Example 6.3

Examine the behavior of the following functions, both as $x \to \infty$ and as $x \to -\infty$:

(a) $f(x) = \dfrac{3x^2 + x - 1}{x^2 + 1}$

(b) $g(x) = \dfrac{1 - x^5}{x^4 + x + 1}$

FIGURE 6.4 $y = A$ and $y = B$ are horizontal asymptotes.

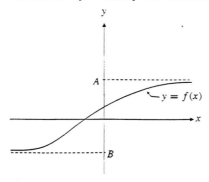

Solution

(a) A rough argument is as follows: If x is a large negative or a large positive number, then the term $3x^2$ "dominates" in the numerator, whereas x^2 dominates in the denominator. Thus, if $|x|$ is a large number, $f(x)$ behaves like the fraction $3x^2/x^2 = 3$. We conclude that $f(x)$ tends to 3 as $|x|$ tends to ∞.

More formally we argue as follows. First, divide each term in the numerator and the denominator by the highest power of x, which is x^2, to obtain

$$f(x) = \frac{3x^2 + x - 1}{x^2 + 1} = \frac{3 + (1/x) - (1/x^2)}{1 + (1/x^2)}$$

If x is large in absolute value, then both $1/x$ and $1/x^2$ will be close to 0. Thus, $f(x)$ is arbitrarily close to 3 if $|x|$ is sufficiently large, and

$$\lim_{x \to \infty} f(x) = \lim_{x \to -\infty} f(x) = 3$$

(b) A first rough argument is that if $|x|$ is a large number, then $g(x)$ behaves like the fraction $-x^5/x^4 = -x$. Therefore, $g(x) \to -\infty$ as $x \to \infty$, whereas $g(x) \to \infty$ as $x \to -\infty$. Alternatively,

$$g(x) = \frac{1 - x^5}{x^4 + x + 1} = \frac{(1/x^4) - x}{1 + (1/x^3) + 1/x^4}$$

You should now finish the argument yourself along the lines given in part (a).

Warnings

We have extended the original definition of a limit in several different directions. For these extended limit concepts, the previous limit rules set out in Section 4.4 still apply. For example, all the results in [4.15] on sums, products, and ratios of limits as $x \to a$ are valid if we consider only left limits with $x \to a^-$, or only right limits with $x \to a^+$. Also, if we replace $x \to a$ by $x \to \infty$ or $x \to -\infty$ in [4.15], then again the corresponding limit properties are valid.

When $f(x)$ and $g(x)$ both tend to ∞ as x tends to a (possibly with $x \to a$ replaced by $x \to a^-$ or $x \to a^+$), we must be much more careful. Because $f(x)$ and $g(x)$ each can be made arbitrarily large if x is sufficiently close to a, both $f(x) + g(x)$ and $f(x) \cdot g(x)$ also can be made arbitrarily large. But, in general, we cannot say what are the limits of $f(x) - g(x)$ and $f(x)/g(x)$. The limits of these expressions will depend on how "fast" $f(x)$ and $g(x)$, respectively, tend to

∞ as x tends to a. Briefly formulated:

$$\lim_{x \to a} f(x) = \infty \quad \text{and} \quad \lim_{x \to a} g(x) = \infty \implies \begin{cases} \lim_{x \to a} \left[f(x) + g(x) \right]) = \infty \\ \lim_{x \to a} \left[f(x) \cdot g(x) \right] = \infty \\ \lim_{x \to a} \left[f(x) - g(x) \right] = ? \\ \lim_{x \to a} \left[f(x)/g(x) \right] = ? \end{cases}$$

The two question marks mean that we cannot determine the limits of $f(x) - g(x)$ and $f(x)/g(x)$ without having more information about f and g. We do not even know if these limits exist or not. The following example illustrates some of the possibilities.

Example 6.4

Let $f(x) = 1/x^2$ and $g(x) = 1/x^4$. As $x \to 0$, then $f(x) \to \infty$ and $g(x) \to \infty$. Determine the limits as $x \to 0$ of the following:

(a) $f(x) - g(x)$
(b) $g(x) - f(x)$
(c) $f(x)/g(x)$
(d) $g(x)/f(x)$

Solution

(a) $\qquad f(x) - g(x) = \dfrac{x^2 - 1}{x^4} \to -\infty \quad \text{as} \quad x \to 0$

(b) $\qquad g(x) - f(x) = \dfrac{1 - x^2}{x^4} \to \infty \quad \text{as} \quad x \to 0$

(c) $\qquad f(x)/g(x) = x^2 \to 0 \quad \text{as} \quad x \to 0$

(d) $\qquad g(x)/f(x) = 1/x^2 \to \infty \quad \text{as} \quad x \to 0$

These examples serve to illustrate that infinite limits require extreme care. Let us consider some other tricky examples.

Suppose we study the product $f(x) \cdot g(x)$ of two functions, where $g(x)$ tends to 0 as x tends to a. Will $f(x) \cdot g(x)$ also tend to 0 as x tends to a? Not necessarily. If $f(x)$ tends to a limit A, then by rule [4.15](iii) of Sec. 4.4, $f(x) \cdot g(x)$ tends to $A \cdot 0 = 0$. On the other hand, if $f(x)$ tends to $\pm\infty$, then it is easy to construct examples in which the product $f(x) \cdot g(x)$ does not tend to 0 at all. (You should try to construct some examples of your own before turning to Problem 4.)

The rules for limits in [4.15] are fundamental. However, one must be careful not to read more into them than what they actually say. If $f(x)$ tends to the number A and $g(x)$ tends to the number B as x tends to a, then by [4.15](a) we see that $f(x) + g(x)$ tends to $A + B$ as x tends to a. But the sum $f(x) + g(x)$ might very well tend to a limit even though $f(x)$ and $g(x)$ do not tend to a limit. The same goes for the fraction $f(x)/g(x)$.

Example 6.5

Let $f(x) = 3 + 1/x$ and $g(x) = 5 - 1/x$. Examine the limits as $x \to 0$ of **(a)** $f(x) + g(x)$ and **(b)** $f(x)/g(x)$.

Solution   We find that

(a) $$f(x) + g(x) = 8 \to 8 \quad \text{as} \quad x \to 0$$

(b) $$\frac{f(x)}{g(x)} = \frac{3x + 1}{5x - 1} \to -1 \quad \text{as} \quad x \to 0$$

But in this case neither $f(x)$ nor $g(x)$ tends to a limit as x tends to 0. In fact, $f(x) \to \infty$ and $g(x) \to -\infty$ as $x \to 0^+$, whereas $f(x) \to -\infty$ and $g(x) \to \infty$ as $x \to 0^-$.

Problems

1. Evaluate the following limits:

   a. $\lim_{x \to 0^-} (x^2 + 3x - 4)$ **b.** $\lim_{x \to 0^-} \dfrac{x + |x|}{x}$ **c.** $\lim_{x \to 0^-} \dfrac{x + |x|}{x}$

   d. $\lim_{x \to 0^+} \dfrac{-1}{\sqrt{x}}$ **e.** $\lim_{x \to 3^+} \dfrac{x}{x - 3}$ **f.** $\lim_{x \to 3^-} \dfrac{x}{x - 3}$

2. Evaluate the following limits:

   a. $\lim_{x \to \infty} \dfrac{x - 3}{x^2 + 1}$ **b.** $\lim_{x \to -\infty} \sqrt{\dfrac{2 + 3x}{x - 1}}$ **c.** $\lim_{x \to \infty} \dfrac{(ax - b)^2}{(a - x)(b - x)}$

3. A function f defined for $x > b$ has a graph indicated by Fig. 6.5.
   a. Determine likely values of the following limits: (i) $\lim_{x \to b^+} f(x)$, (ii) $\lim_{x \to a^-} f(x)$, (iii) $\lim_{x \to a^-} f(x)$, (iv) $\lim_{x \to \infty} f(x)$.
   b. Only one of the following limits is defined. Which one?

   $$\lim_{x \to -\infty} f(x), \quad \lim_{x \to 0} f(x), \quad \lim_{x \to b^-} f(x)$$

FIGURE 6.5

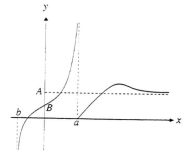

4. Let $f_1(x) = x$, $f_2(x) = x$, $f_3(x) = x^2$, and $f_4(x) = 1/x$. For $i = 1, 2, 3, 4$, determine $\lim_{x \to \infty} f_i(x)$. Then examine the limits of the following functions as $x \to \infty$:

   a. $f_1(x) + f_2(x)$ **b.** $f_1(x) - f_2(x)$ **c.** $f_1(x) - f_3(x)$

   d. $f_1(x)/f_2(x)$ **e.** $f_1(x)/f_3(x)$ **f.** $f_1(x) \cdot f_2(x)$

   g. $f_1(x) \cdot f_4(x)$ **h.** $f_3(x) \cdot f_4(x)$

5. The nonvertical line $y = ax + b$ is said to be an **asymptote** as $x \to \infty$ (or $x \to -\infty$) to the curve $y = f(x)$ if

$$f(x) - (ax + b) \to 0 \quad \text{as} \quad x \to \infty \ (\text{or } x \to -\infty)$$

   This condition means that the vertical distance between point $(x, f(x))$ on the curve and point $(x, ax + b)$ on the line tends to 0 as $x \to \pm\infty$. (See Figure 6.6.)

   If $f(x) = P(x)/Q(x)$ is a rational function where the degree of the polynomial $P(x)$ is *one greater* than that of the polynomial $Q(x)$, then $f(x)$ will have an asymptote that can be found by performing the long division $P(x) \div Q(x)$ and ignoring the remainder. Use this method to find asymptotes for the graph of each of the functions defined by the following formulas:

   a. $\dfrac{x^2}{x + 1}$ **b.** $\dfrac{2x^3 - 3x^2 + 3x - 6}{x^2 + 1}$ **c.** $\dfrac{3x^2 + 2x}{x - 1}$ **d.** $\dfrac{5x^4 - 3x^2 + 1}{x^3 - 1}$

6. Consider the following cost function defined for $x \geq 0$ by

$$C(x) = A\frac{x(x + b)}{x + c} + d$$

   Here A, b, c, and d are positive constants. Find the asymptotes.

FIGURE 6.6

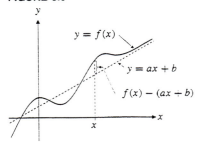

6.2 Continuity

The word *continuous* is rather common in everyday language. We use it, in particular, to characterize changes that are gradual rather than sudden. This usage is closely related to the idea of a continuous function. Roughly speaking, a function is continuous if small changes in the independent variable produce small changes in the function values. Geometrically, *a function is continuous if its graph is connected—that is, it has no breaks*. An example is indicated in Fig. 6.7.

It is often said that a function is continuous if its graph can be drawn without lifting one's pencil off the paper. On the other hand, if the graph makes one or more jumps, we say that f is *discontinuous*. Thus, the function whose graph is shown in Fig. 6.8 is discontinuous at $x = a$, but continuous at all other points of the interval that constitutes its domain.

Why are we interested in distinguishing between continuous and discontinuous functions? One important reason is that we must usually work with numerical approximations. For instance, if a function f is given by some formula and we wish to compute $f(\sqrt{2})$, we usually take it for granted that we can compute $f(1.4142)$

FIGURE 6.7   A continuous function.

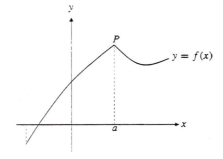

FIGURE 6.8   A discontinuous function.

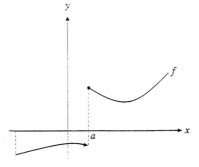

and obtain a good approximation to $f(\sqrt{2})$. In fact, this implicitly assumes that f is continuous. Then, because 1.4142 is close to $\sqrt{2}$, the value $f(1.4142)$ must be close to $f(\sqrt{2})$.

In applications of mathematics to natural sciences and economics, a function will often represent the change in some phenomenon over time. The continuity of the function will then reflect the continuity of the phenomenon, in the sense of a gradual development without sudden changes. We might, for example, think of a person's body temperature as a function of time. Here we may assume that it changes continuously and that it does not jump from one value to another without passing through the intermediate values. On the other hand, if we consider the price of a barrel of oil in a certain market, this function of time will be discontinuous. One reason is that the price (measured in dollars or some other currency) must always be a rational number. A second, more interesting, reason for occasional large jumps in the price is the sudden arrival of news or a rumor that significantly affects either the demand or supply function.

The concept of continuity just discussed must obviously be made more precise before we can operate with it as a mathematical concept. We must search for a definition of continuity not solely based on intuitive geometric ideas.

Continuous Functions

We suggested earlier that a function is continuous if its graph is a "connected" curve. In particular, we say that f is continuous at a point a if the graph of f has no break at a. How do we define this precisely? It is evident that we must consider the value of f at points x close to a. If the graph of f has no break at a, then $f(x)$ cannot differ much from $f(a)$ when x is close to a. Stated differently, if x is close to a, then $f(x)$ must be close to $f(a)$. This motivates the following definition:

Suppose f is defined on a domain that includes an open interval around a. Then f is **continuous** at $x = a$ provided that $f(x)$ tends to $f(a)$ in the limit as x tends to a:

$$f \text{ is continuous at } x = a \text{ if } \lim_{x \to a} f(x) = f(a) \qquad [6.2]$$

Hence, we see that in order for f to be continuous at $x = a$, the following three conditions must all be fulfilled:

1. the function f must be defined at $x = a$
2. the limit of $f(x)$ as x tends to a must exist
3. this limit must be exactly equal to $f(a)$

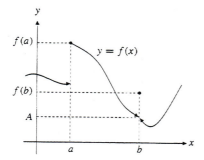

FIGURE 6.9 *f* **has two points of discontinuity.** *x = a* **is an irremovable discontinuity and** *x = b* **is a removable discontinuity.**

Unless all three of these conditions are satisfied, we say that f is **discontinuous** at a. Figure 6.9 indicates two important types of discontinuity that can occur. At $x = a$, the function is discontinuous because $f(x)$ clearly has no limit as x tends to a. Hence, condition 2 is not satisfied. This is an "irremovable" discontinuity. On the other hand, the limit of $f(x)$ as x tends to b exists and is equal to A. But because $A \neq f(b)$, condition 3 is not satisfied, so f is discontinuous at b. This is a "removable" discontinuity that would disappear if $f(b)$ were redefined as A.

Example 6.6

Let $f(x) = 3x - 2$. In Example 4.7(a) of Sec. 4.4, we argued that $f(x)$ tends to 7 as x tends to 3. Because $f(3) = 7$, this means that f is continuous at $a = 3$. Actually, this function is continuous at all points a, because $f(x) = 3x - 2$ always tends to $3a - 2 = f(a)$ as x tends to a.

Properties of Continuous Functions

Many of the central results of mathematical analysis are true only for continuous functions. It is therefore important to be able to decide whether or not a given function is continuous. The rules for limits given in Section 4.4 make it is easy to prove continuity of many types of functions. Note that because of [4.18] and [4.19],

$$f(x) = c \quad \text{and} \quad f(x) = x \text{ are continuous everywhere} \qquad [6.3]$$

This is as it should be, because the graphs of these functions are straight lines. Now, using definition [6.2] and the limit rules in [4.15], we have the following:

Results on Continuous Functions

If f and g are continuous at a, then

   (a) $f + g$ and $f - g$ are continuous at a [6.4]

   (b) $f \cdot g$ is continuous at a

   (c) f/g is continuous at a if $g(a) \neq 0$

   (d) $\left[f(x) \right]^{p/q}$ is continuous at a if $\left[f(a) \right]^{p/q}$ is defined

The proofs of these properties are straightforward if we use the limit laws from Section 4.4. For instance, to prove (b), if both f and g are continuous at a, then $\lim_{x \to a} f(x) = f(a)$ and $\lim_{x \to a} g(x) = g(a)$. According to [4.15](iii), therefore, $\lim_{x \to a} f(x)g(x) = f(a)g(a)$, which means that $f \cdot g$ is continuous at a.

    By combining [6.3] and [6.4], it follows that, say, $h(x) = x + 8$ and $k(x) = 3x^3 + x + 8$ are continuous. In general, because a polynomial $p(x) = a_n x^n + a_{n-1} x^{n-1} + \cdots + a_0$ is a sum of continuous functions, it is continuous everywhere. Moreover, a rational function

$$R(x) = \frac{P(x)}{Q(x)} \qquad (P(x) \text{ and } Q(x) \text{ are polynomials})$$

is continuous at all x where $Q(x) \neq 0$.

    Consider a composite function $f(g(x))$ where f and g are assumed to be continuous. If x is close to a, then by the continuity of g at a, $g(x)$ is close to $g(a)$. In turn, $f(g(x))$ becomes close to $f(g(a))$ because f is continuous at $g(a)$, and thus $f(g(x))$ is continuous at a. A more formal proof of this result requires the $\varepsilon\delta$-definition of limits (see Section 6.7). For future reference:

Composites of continuous functions are continuous:

If g is continuous at $x = a$, and f is continuous at $g(a)$, then $f\big(g(x)\big)$ is continuous at $x = a$.   [6.5]

By using the results just discussed, a mere glance at the formula defining a function will usually suffice to determine the points at which it is continuous.

In general:

Any function that can be constructed from continuous functions by combining one or more operations of addition, subtraction, multiplication, division (except by zero, of course), and composition is continuous at all points where it is defined.

[6.6]

Example 6.7

Determine at which values of x the functions given by the following formulas are continuous:

(a)
$$f(x) = \frac{x^4 + 3x^2 - 1}{(x - 1)(x + 2)}$$

(b)
$$g(x) = (x^2 + 2)(x^3 + 1/x)^4 + 1/\sqrt{x + 1}$$

Solution

(a) This is a rational function that is continuous at all x, except where the denominator $(x - 1)(x + 2) = 0$. Hence, f is continuous at all x different from 1 and -2.

(b) This function is defined when $x \neq 0$ and $x + 1 > 0$, or when $x \neq 0$ and $x > -1$. Hence, g is continuous in the domain $(-1, 0) \cup (0, \infty)$.

Knowing where a function is continuous simplifies the computation of many limits. For instance, using the rules for limits, Example 4.9(a) showed the result that $\lim_{x \to -2} (x^2 + 5x) = -6$. Because $f(x) = x^2 + 5x$ is a continuous function of x, we know that $\lim_{x \to -2} (x^2 + 5x)$ is simply $f(-2) = (-2)^2 + 5(-2) = 4 - 10 = -6$. Thus, we find the limit by just evaluating $f(x) = x^2 + 5x$ at $x = -2$.

Functions that are defined "piecewise" by different formulas applying to different intervals are frequently discontinuous at the junction points. For example, the amount of postage you pay for a letter is a discontinuous function of the weight. (As long as we use preprinted stamps, it would be extremely inconvenient to have the "postage function" be even approximately continuous.) On the other hand, the tax you pay as a function of your net income is (essentially) a continuous function (although many people seem to believe that it is not). An actual tax function for the U.S. is shown in Fig. 6.13 at the end of Sec. 6.3.

Example 6.8

For what values of a is the following function continuous everywhere?

$$f(x) = \begin{cases} ax^2 + 4x - 1, & \text{if } x \leq 1 \\ -x + 3, & \text{if } x > 1 \end{cases}$$

Solution   The function is obviously continuous at all $x \neq 1$. For $x = 1$, the function is given by the upper formula, so $f(1) = a + 3$. If x is slightly larger than 1, then $f(x) = -x + 3$ is close to 2, and $f(x) \to 2$ as $x \to 1^+$. In order to have f continuous at $x = 1$, we must have $f(1) = a + 3 = 2$, which requires $a = -1$. Thus, for $a = -1$ the function is continuous at all x, including at $x = 1$. If $a \neq -1$, the function is discontinuous at $x = 1$, but continuous at all other points. (Draw the graph of f for $a = 1$ and for $a = -1$.)

One-Sided Continuity

Section 6.1 introduced one-sided limits. These allow us to define one-sided continuity. Suppose f is defined on a domain including the half-open interval $(c, a]$. If $f(x)$ tends to $f(a)$ as x tends to a^-, we say that f is **left-continuous** at a. Similarly, if f is defined on a domain including $[a, d)$, we say that f is **right-continuous** at a if $f(x)$ tends to $f(a)$ as x tends to a^+. For example, the function f indicated earlier in Fig. 6.8 is right-continuous at a. Although f tends to a limit as x tends to a from the left, f is not left-continuous at a, because the limit is different from $f(a)$.

Making use of [6.1] in Section 6.1, we readily see that a function f is continuous at a if and only if f is both left- and right-continuous at a.

If a function f is defined on a closed, bounded interval $[a, b]$, we usually say that f is continuous in $[a, b]$ if it is continuous at each point of (a, b), and is in addition right-continuous at a and left-continuous at b. It should be obvious how to define continuity on half-open intervals. The continuity of a function at all points of an interval, including any endpoints it contains, is often a minimum requirement we impose when speaking about "well-behaved" functions.

Problems

1. Which of the following functions are likely to be continuous functions of time?
    a. The price in the Zürich gold market of an ounce of gold.
    b. The height of a growing child.
    c. The height of an aeroplane above the ground.
    d. The distance traveled by a car.

2. Consider the functions defined by the six graphs shown in Fig. 6.10.
    a. Are any of these functions continuous at a?
    b. For which of the functions will $f(x)$ tend to a limit as x tends to a?
    c. Determine the limits of $f(x)$ as $x \to a^-$ and $x \to a^+$ in each case.
    d. Which of the functions are left-continuous at a, and which of them are right-continuous at a?
    e. What seems to be the limit of $f(x)$ as $x \to \infty$ in graphs (v) and (vi) of the figure?

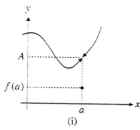
(i)

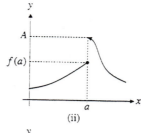
(ii)

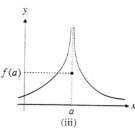
(iii)

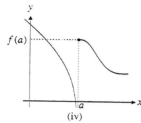
(iv)

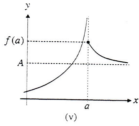
(v)

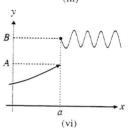
(vi)

FIGURE 6.10

3. Let f and g be defined for all x by

$$f(x) = \begin{cases} x^2 - 1, & \text{for } x \le 0 \\ -x^2, & \text{for } x > 0 \end{cases} \quad \text{and} \quad g(x) = \begin{cases} 3x - 2, & \text{for } x \le 2 \\ -x + 6, & \text{for } x > 2 \end{cases}$$

Draw a graph of each function. Is f continuous at $x = 0$? Is g continuous at $x = 2$?

4. Determine the values of x at which each of the following functions is continuous:

a. $f(x) = x^5 + 4x$

b. $f(x) = \dfrac{x}{1 - x}$

c. $f(x) = \dfrac{1}{\sqrt{2 - x}}$

d. $\dfrac{x}{x^2 + 1}$

e. $\dfrac{x^8 - 3x^2 + 1}{x^2 + 2x - 2}$

f. $\left(\dfrac{x + 1}{x - 1}\right)^{1/2}$

g. $\dfrac{\sqrt{x} + 1/x}{x^2 + 2x + 2}$

h. $|x| + \dfrac{1}{|x|}$

i. $\dfrac{1}{\sqrt{x}} + x^7(x + 2)^{-3/2}$

5. For what value of a is the following function continuous for all x?

$$f(x) = \begin{cases} ax - 1, & \text{for } x \le 1 \\ 3x^2 + 1, & \text{for } x > 1 \end{cases}$$

6. Draw the graph of y as a function of x if y depends on x as indicated in Fig. 6.11—that is, y is the height of the aeroplane above the point on the ground vertically below. Is y a continuous function of x? Suppose $d(x)$ is the distance from the aeroplane to the *nearest* point on the ground. Is d a continuous function of x?

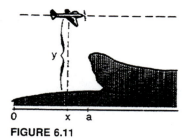

FIGURE 6.11

7. Functions f and g are discontinuous at $x = a$. Are $f + g$ and $f \cdot g$ necessarily discontinuous at a? If not, supply examples.

8. Let f be defined by $f(x) = x^2 - 2$ for $x < 0$, and $f(x) = -3x^2 + 15$ for $x > 2$. Can you define $f(x)$ as a linear function on $[0, 2]$ so that f is continuous for all x?

6.3 Continuity and Differentiability

Consider the function f graphed in Fig. 6.12. At point $(a, f(a))$, the graph does not have (a unique) tangent. Thus f has no derivative at $x = a$, but f is continuous at $x = a$. So a function can be continuous at a point without being differentiable at that point. (For a standard example, see Problem 2.) On the other hand, it is easy to see that differentiability implies continuity:

If f is differentiable at $x = a$, then f is continuous at $x = a$.   [6.7]

FIGURE 6.12   *f* **is continuous, but not differentiable at** *x = a.*

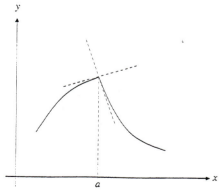

Proof   Function f is continuous at $x = a$ provided that $f(a + h) - f(a)$ tends to 0 as $h \to 0$. Now, for $h \neq 0$,

$$f(a + h) - f(a) = \frac{f(a + h) - f(a)}{h} \cdot h \qquad [*]$$

If f is differentiable at $x = a$, the Newton quotient $\left[f(a+h) - f(a)\right]/h$ tends to the number $f'(a)$ as $h \to 0$. So the right-hand side of $[*]$ tends to $f'(a) \cdot 0 = 0$ as $h \to 0$. Thus, f is continuous at $x = a$.

Suppose that f is some function whose Newton quotient $\left[f(a+h) - f(a)\right]/h$ tends to a limit as h tends to 0 through positive values. Then the limit is called the **right derivative** of f at a, and we use the notation

$$f'(a^+) = \lim_{h \to 0^-} \frac{f(a + h) - f(a)}{h} \qquad [6.8]$$

The **left derivative** of f at a is defined similarly:

$$f'(a^-) = \lim_{h \to 0^-} \frac{f(a + h) - f(a)}{h} \qquad [6.9]$$

if the one-sided limit exists.

If f is continuous at a, and if $f'(a^+) = \alpha$ and $f'(a^-) = \beta$ with $\alpha \neq \beta$, then we say that the graph of f has a **corner** (or **kink**) at $(a, f(a))$. Then f is not differentiable at a. Thus, the function in Fig. 6.12 has a corner at $(a, f(a))$. If f is continuous at a and $\alpha = \beta$, then the corner gets smoothed out and f is seen to be differentiable at a.

Example 6.9   (U.S. Federal Income Taxes (1991) for single persons)

This income tax function was discussed in Example 2.10 of Section 2.4. Figure 6.13 reproduces Fig. 2.21.[1] If $t(x)$ denotes the tax paid at income x,

FIGURE 6.13   U.S. Federal income taxes (1991) (for single persons).

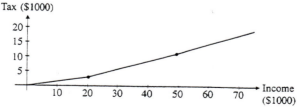

[1] Of course, Fig. 6.13 is an idealization. The true income tax function is defined only for integral numbers of dollars—or, more precisely, it is a discontinuous "step function" which jumps up slightly whenever income rises by another dollar.

its graph has corners at $x = 20,250$ and at $x = 49,300$. We see, for instance, that $t'(20,250^-) = 0.15$ because on the last dollar you earn before reaching $20,250, you pay 15 cents. Also $t'(20,250^+) = 0.28$ because on the first dollar you earn above $20,250, you pay 28 cents in tax. Because $t'(20,250^-) \neq t'(20,250^+)$, the tax function t is not differentiable at $x = 20,250$. Check that $t'(49,300^+) = 0.31$.

Problems

1. Graph the function f defined by $f(x) = 0$ for $x \leq 0$, and $f(x) = x$ for $x > 0$. Compute $f'(0^+)$ and $f'(0^-)$.

2. Function f is defined for all x by $f(x) = |x|$. Compute $f'(0^+)$ and $f'(0^-)$. Is f continuous and/or differentiable at $x = 0$? (The graph is shown in Fig. 9.31 of Section 9.6.)

3. The graph of a continuous function f is said to have a **cusp** at a if $f'(x) \to \infty$ as x tends to a from one side, whereas $f'(x) \to -\infty$ as x tends to a from the other side. Show that $f(x) = |\sqrt[3]{x}|$ has a cusp at $x = 0$, and draw its graph.

4. Give an algebraic definition of the tax function $t(x)$ in Example 6.9. (The function is called piecewise linear, since it is linear on each of the different income intervals.) Compute $t(22,000)$ and $t(50,000)$.

6.4 Infinite Sequences

Consider the function f defined for $n = 1, 2, 3, \ldots$ by the formula $f(n) = 1/n$. Then $f(1) = 1$, $f(2) = 1/2$, $f(3) = 1/3$, and so on. The list of numbers

$$1, \quad \frac{1}{2}, \quad \frac{1}{3}, \quad \frac{1}{4}, \quad \ldots, \quad \frac{1}{n}, \quad \ldots \qquad [*]$$

is called an **infinite sequence**. Its first *term* is 1, and its general (nth) term is $1/n$. In general, any function whose domain is the entire set of positive integers is called an **infinite sequence**. Similarly $s_n = 100 \cdot 1.08^{n-1} (n = 1, 2, \ldots)$ determines an infinite sequence whose first terms are

$$100, \quad 100 \cdot 1.08, \quad 100 \cdot 1.08^2, \quad 100 \cdot 1.08^3, \quad \ldots \qquad [**]$$

If s is an infinite sequence, its terms $s(1), s(2), s(3), \ldots, s(n), \ldots$ are usually denoted by using subscripts: $s_1, s_2, s_3, \ldots, s_n, \ldots$. We use the notation $\{s_n\}_{n=1}^{\infty}$, or simply $\{s_n\}$, for an arbitrary infinite sequence.

Consider the previous sequence [*]. If we choose n large enough, the terms can be made as small as we like. We say that the sequence *converges* to 0. In general, we introduce the following definition:

A sequence $\{s_n\}$ is said to **converge** to a number s if s_n is arbitrarily close to s for all n sufficiently large. We write

$$\lim_{n \to \infty} s_n = s \qquad \text{or} \qquad s_n \to s \quad \text{as} \quad n \to \infty$$

A sequence that does not converge to any real number is said to **diverge**. For example, the sequence in [**] earlier diverges because $100 \cdot 1.08^{n-1}$ tends to ∞ as n tends to ∞.

The definition of convergence for a sequence is a special case of the previous definition that $f(x) \to A$ as $x \to \infty$. All the ordinary limit rules in Section 4.4 apply to limits of sequences.

Example 6.10

Write down the first five terms of the following sequences:

(a) $\left\{(-1)^{n-1}\dfrac{1}{n}\right\}$

(b) $\left\{3 + \left(\dfrac{1}{10}\right)^n\right\}$

(c) $\left\{\dfrac{n^3 + 1}{n^2 + 2}\right\}$

Then decide whether or not each converges.

Solution

(a) $\left\{(-1)^{n-1}\dfrac{1}{n}\right\}$: $\quad 1, \ -\dfrac{1}{2}, \ \dfrac{1}{3}, \ -\dfrac{1}{4}, \ \dfrac{1}{5}, \ \dots$

(b) $\left\{3 + \left(\dfrac{1}{10}\right)^n\right\}$: $\quad 3.1, \ 3.01, \ 3.001, \ 3.0001, \ 3.00001, \ \dots$

(c) $\left\{\dfrac{n^3 + 1}{n^2 + 2}\right\}$: $\quad \dfrac{2}{3}, \ \dfrac{9}{6}, \ \dfrac{28}{11}, \ \dfrac{65}{18}, \ \dfrac{126}{27}, \ \dots$

The sequence in (a) converges to 0, because $1/n$ tends to 0 as n tends to ∞. The sequence in (b) converges to 3, because $(1/10)^n$ tends to 0 as n tends to ∞. The sequence in (c) is divergent. To see this note that

$$s_n = \frac{n^3 + 1}{n^2 + 2} = \frac{n + 1/n^2}{1 + 2/n^2}$$

Clearly, $s_n \to \infty$ as $n \to \infty$, so $\{s_n\}$ diverges.

Example 6.11

For $n \geq 3$ let A_n be the area of a regular n-polygon inscribed in a circle with radius 1. For $n = 3$, A_3 is the area of a triangle; for $n = 4$, A_4 is the area of a square; for $n = 5$, A_5 is the area of a pentagon; and so on (see Fig. 6.14).

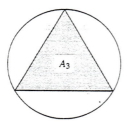 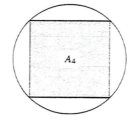 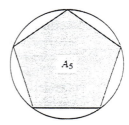

FIGURE 6.14

The larger n is, the larger is A_n, but each A_n is less than π, the area of a circle with radius 1. It seems intuitively evident that we can make the difference between A_n and π as small we wish if only n becomes sufficiently large, so that

$$A_n \to \pi \quad \text{as} \quad n \to \infty$$

In this example, A_1 and A_2 have no meaning, so the sequence starts with A_3.

The sequence $\{A_n\}$ in the previous example converges to the irrational number $\pi = 3.14159265\ldots$. Another sequence that converges to π starts this way: $s_1 = 3.1$, $s_2 = 3.14$, $s_3 = 3.141$, $s_4 = 3.1415$, etc. Each new number is obtained by including an additional digit in the decimal expansion for π. For this sequence, $s_n \to \pi$ as $n \to \infty$.

Consider an arbitrary irrational number r. Just as for π, the decimal expansion of r will define one particular sequence r_n of rational numbers that converges to r. Actually, each irrational number is the limit of infinitely many different sequences of rational numbers.

Example 6.12

It is often difficult to determine whether or not a sequence is convergent. For example, consider the sequence whose general term is $s_n = (1 + 1/n)^n$. Do you think that this converges? The values of s_n for some values of n are given by

n	1	2	3	5	10	100	10,000	100,000
$\left(1 + \frac{1}{n}\right)^n$	2	2.25	2.37	2.49	2.59	2.70	2.7181	2.7182

This table seems to suggest that s_n tends to a number close to 2.718. One can prove that $\{s_n\}$ *does* converge by relying on the general property. Any increasing sequence of real numbers that has an upper bound is convergent. The limit of $\{s_n\}$ is an irrational number denoted by e, which is one of the most important constants in mathematics. See Section 8.1.

Problems

1. Let

$$\alpha_n = \frac{3 - n}{2n - 1} \quad \text{and} \quad \beta_n = \frac{n^2 + 2n - 1}{3n^2 - 2} \quad (n = 1, 2, \ldots)$$

Find the following limits:

a. $\lim\limits_{n\to\infty} \alpha_n$ b. $\lim\limits_{n\to\infty} \beta_n$ c. $\lim\limits_{n\to\infty} (3\alpha_n + 4\beta_n)$

d. $\lim\limits_{n\to\infty} \alpha_n \beta_n$ e. $\lim\limits_{n\to\infty} \alpha_n / \beta_n$ f. $\lim\limits_{n\to\infty} \sqrt{\beta_n - \alpha_n}$

2. Examine the convergence of the sequences whose general terms are as follows:

a. $s_n = 5 - \dfrac{2}{n}$ b. $s_n = \dfrac{n^2 - 1}{n}$ c. $s_n = \dfrac{3n}{\sqrt{2n^2 - 1}}$

6.5 Series

This section primarily studies finite and infinite geometric series. These have many applications in economics such as in calculations concerning compound interest. Some other applications are studied more closely in the next section.

Finite Geometric Series

Let us begin with an example.

Example 6.13

This year a firm has a revenue of $100 million that it expects to increase by 16% per year throughout the next decade. How large is its expected revenue in the tenth year, and what is the total revenue expected over the whole period?

Solution   The second year's expected revenue is $100(1 + 16/100) = 100 \cdot 1.16$ (in millions), and in the third year, it is $100 \cdot (1.16)^2$. In the tenth year, the expected revenue is $100 \cdot (1.16)^9$. The total revenue expected during the decade is thus

$$100 + 100 \cdot 1.16 + 100 \cdot (1.16)^2 + \cdots + 100 \cdot (1.16)^9 \qquad [*]$$

With a calculator, we find that the sum is approximately $2,132 million.

We found the sum in [∗] by adding 10 numbers on the calculator. Especially in cases where there are many terms to add, this method is troublesome. There is an easier method to find such sums, as will be explained now.

Consider n numbers $a, ak, ak^2, \ldots, ak^{n-1}$. Each term is obtained by multiplying the previous one by a constant k. We wish to find the sum

$$s_n = a + ak + ak^2 + \cdots + ak^{n-2} + ak^{n-1} \tag{1}$$

of these numbers. We call this sum a (finite) **geometric series** with **quotient** k. The sum [∗] occurs in the special case when $a = 100$, $k = 1.16$, and $n = 10$.

To find the sum s_n of the series, first multiply both sides of [1] by k to obtain

$$ks_n = ak + ak^2 + ak^3 + \cdots + ak^{n-1} + ak^n \tag{2}$$

Subtracting [2] from [1] yields

$$s_n - ks_n = a - ak^n \tag{3}$$

because all the other terms, $(ak + ak^2 + \cdots + ak^{n-1}) - (ak + ak^2 + \cdots + ak^{n-1})$, cancel.

If $k = 1$, then all terms in [1] are equal to a, and the sum is equal to $s_n = an$. For $k \neq 1$, because $s_n - ks_n = (1 - k)s_n$, [3] implies that

$$s_n = \frac{a - ak^n}{1 - k} \tag{4}$$

In conclusion:

Summation Formula for a Finite Geometric Series

$$a + ak + ak^2 + \cdots + ak^{n-1} = a\,\frac{1 - k^n}{1 - k} \qquad (k \neq 1)$$

[6.10]

Example 6.14

For the sum [∗] in Example 6.13 we have $a = 100$, $k = 1.16$, and $n = 10$. Hence, [6.10] yields

$$100 + 100 \cdot 1.16 + \cdots + 100 \cdot (1.16)^9 = 100\,\frac{1 - (1.16)^{10}}{1 - 1.16}$$

It takes fewer operations on the calculator than in Example 6.13 to show that the sum is about 2,132.

Infinite Geometric Series

Consider the infinite sequence of numbers

$$1, \quad \frac{1}{2}, \quad \frac{1}{4}, \quad \frac{1}{8}, \quad \frac{1}{16}, \quad \frac{1}{32}, \quad \cdots$$

Each term in the sequence is formed by halving its predecessor, so that the nth term is $1/2^{n-1}$. The sum of the first n terms is a finite geometric series with quotient $k = 1/2$ and the first term $a = 1$. Hence, [6.10] gives

$$1 + \frac{1}{2} + \frac{1}{2^2} + \cdots + \frac{1}{2^{n-1}} = \frac{1 - (1/2)^n}{1 - 1/2} = 2 - \frac{1}{2^{n-1}} \qquad [*]$$

We ask now what is meant by the "infinite sum"

$$1 + \frac{1}{2} + \frac{1}{2^2} + \frac{1}{2^3} + \cdots + \frac{1}{2^{n-1}} + \cdots \qquad [**]$$

Because all the terms are positive, and there are infinitely many terms, you might be inclined to think that the sum must be infinitely large. However, if we look at formula [*], we see that the sum of the n first terms is equal to $2 - 1/2^{n-1}$, and this number is never larger than 2, irrespective of our choice of n. As n increases, $1/2^{n-1}$ comes closer and closer to 0, and the sum in [*] tends to 2 in the limit. This makes it natural to *define* the infinite sum in [**] as the number 2.

An Illustration: At a birthday party, there are two identical cakes. The person having the birthday takes all of one cake. From the second cake, the first guest is given one-half, the second guest is given one-quarter, and so on. Each successive guest is given half what is left. The sum in [*] shows how much has been taken after $n - 1$ guests have received their allocation. (The person having the birthday is not regarded as a guest.) Thus, we see that infinitely many guests can be invited to this party. (However, even if each cake were worth as much as \$100, the thirteenth guest would get only slightly more than 1 cent's worth of cake.)

In general, we ask what meaning can be given to the "infinite sum"

$$a + ak + ak^2 + \cdots + ak^{n-1} + \cdots \qquad [6.11]$$

We use the same idea as in [**], and consider the sum s_n of the n first terms in [6.11]. According to [6.10],

$$s_n = a \frac{1 - k^n}{1 - k} \qquad (k \neq 1)$$

What happens to this expression as n tends to infinity? The answer evidently depends on k^n, because only this term depends on n. In fact, k^n tends to 0 if

$-1 < k < 1$, whereas k^n does not tend to any limit if $k > 1$ or $k \leq -1$. (If you are not yet convinced that this claim is true, study the cases $k = -2$, $k = -1$, $k = -1/2$, $k = 1/2$, and $k = 2$.) Hence, it follows that if $|k| < 1$, then the sum s_n of the n first terms in [6.11] will tend to the limit $a/(1 - k)$ as n tends to infinity. We let this limit be the *definition* of the sum in [6.11], and we say that the infinite series [6.11] **converges** in this case. To summarize:

Summation Formula for an Infinite Geometric Series:

$$a + ak + ak^2 + \cdots + ak^{n-1} + \cdots = \frac{a}{1 - k} \qquad \text{(if } |k| < 1\text{)} \qquad \text{[6.12]}$$

Using summation notation as in Sec. B1 of Appendix B, [6.12] becomes:

$$\sum_{n=1}^{\infty} ak^{n-1} = \frac{a}{1 - k} \qquad \text{(if } |k| < 1\text{)} \qquad \text{[6.13]}$$

If $|k| \geq 1$, we say that the infinite series [6.11] **diverges**. A divergent series has no (finite) sum. Divergence is obvious if $|k| > 1$. When $k = 1$, then $s_n = na$, which tends to $+\infty$ if $a > 0$ or to $-\infty$ if $a < 0$. When $k = -1$, then s_n is a when n is odd, but 0 when a is even; again there is no limit as $n \to \infty$.

Geometric series appear in many economic applications. Let us look at a somewhat contrived example.

Example 6.15

A rough estimate of the total oil and gas reserves in the Norwegian continental shelf at the beginning of 1981 was 12 billion ($12 \cdot 10^9$) tons. Production that year was approximately 50 million ($50 \cdot 10^6$) tons.

(a) When will the reserves be exhausted if production is kept at the same level?

(b) Suppose that production is reduced each year by 1% per year beginning in 1982. How long will the reserves last in this case?

Solution

(a) The number of years the reserves will last is given by

$$\frac{12 \cdot 10^9}{5 \cdot 10^7} = 2.4 \cdot 10^2 = 240$$

The reserves will be exhausted around the year 2220.

(b) In 1981, production was $a = 5 \cdot 10^7$. In 1982, it becomes $a - a/100 = a \cdot 0.99$. In 1983, it becomes $a \cdot 0.99^2$, and so on. If this continues forever, the total amount extracted will be

$$a + a \cdot 0.99 + a \cdot (0.99)^2 + \cdots + a \cdot (0.99)^{n-1} + \cdots$$

This is a geometric series with quotient $k = 0.99$. According to [6.12], the sum is

$$s = \frac{a}{1 - 0.99} = 100a$$

Because $a = 5 \cdot 10^7$, we get $s = 5 \cdot 10^9$, which is less than $12 \cdot 10^9$. The extraction, therefore, may be continued indefinitely, and there will never be less than 7 billion tons left.

General Series (Optional)

The determination of $\sum 1/n$ occupied Leibniz all his life but the solution never came within his grasp.
—H. H. Goldstine (1977)

We briefly consider general infinite series that are not necessarily geometric,

$$a_1 + a_2 + a_3 + \cdots + a_n + \cdots \qquad [6.14]$$

What does it mean to say that this infinite series converges? By analogy with the definition for geometric series, we form the "partial" sum s_n of the n first terms:

$$s_n = a_1 + a_2 + \cdots + a_n \qquad [6.15]$$

In particular, $s_1 = a_1$, $s_2 = a_1 + a_2$, $s_3 = a_1 + a_2 + a_3$, and so on. As n increases, these partial sums include more and more terms of the series. Hence, if s_n tends toward a limit s as n tends to ∞, it is reasonable to consider s as the sum of *all* the terms in the series. Then we say that the infinite series is **convergent** with sum s. If s_n does not tend to a finite limit as n tends to infinity, we say that the series is **divergent**. The series then has no sum. (As with limits of functions, if $s_n \to \pm\infty$ as $n \to \infty$, this is not regarded as a limit.)

For geometric series, it was easy to determine when there is convergence because we found a simple expression for s_n. Usually, it will not be possible to find such a simple formula for the sum of the n first terms in a series, and the problem of determining whether a given series converges or diverges can be very difficult. No general method exists that will reveal whether or not any given series is convergent. However, there are a number of standard tests, so called *convergence* and *divergence criteria*, that will give the answer in many cases. These criteria are seldom used directly in economics.

Let us make a general observation: If the series [6.14] converges, then the nth term must tend to 0 as n tends to infinity. The argument is simple: If the series is convergent, then s_n in [6.15] will tend to a limit s as n tends to infinity. Now $a_n = s_n - s_{n-1}$, and by the definition of convergence, s_{n-1} will also tend to s as n tends to infinity. It follows that $a_n = s_n - s_{n-1}$ must tend to $s - s = 0$ as n tends to infinity. Expressed briefly,

$$a_1 + a_2 + \cdots + a_n + \cdots \text{ converges} \implies \lim_{n \to \infty} a_n = 0 \qquad [6.16]$$

The condition in [6.16] is necessary for convergence, but not sufficient. That is, a series may satisfy the condition $\lim_{n \to \infty} a_n = 0$ and yet diverge. This is shown by the following standard example (which gave Leibniz infinite trouble!).

Example 6.16
The series

$$1 + \tfrac{1}{2} + \tfrac{1}{3} + \tfrac{1}{4} + \cdots + \tfrac{1}{n} + \cdots \qquad [6.17]$$

is called the **harmonic series**. The nth term is $1/n$, which tends to 0. But the series is still divergent. To see this, we group the terms together in the following way:

$$1 + \tfrac{1}{2} + \left(\tfrac{1}{3} + \tfrac{1}{4}\right) + \left(\tfrac{1}{5} + \cdots + \tfrac{1}{8}\right) + \left(\tfrac{1}{9} + \cdots + \tfrac{1}{16}\right) + \left(\tfrac{1}{17} + \cdots + \tfrac{1}{32}\right) + \cdots \quad [*]$$

Between the first pair of parentheses there are two terms, one greater than $1/4$ and the other equal to $1/4$, so their sum is greater than $2/4 = 1/2$. Between the second pair of parentheses there are four terms, three greater than $1/8$ and the last equal to $1/8$, so their sum is greater than $4/8 = 1/2$. Between the third pair of parentheses there are eight terms, seven greater than $1/16$ and the last equal to $1/16$, so their sum is greater than $8/16 = 1/2$. Between the fourth pair of parentheses there are sixteen terms, fifteen greater than $1/32$ and the last equal to $1/32$, so their sum is greater than $16/32 = 1/2$. This pattern repeats itself infinitely often. Between the nth pair of parentheses there will be 2^n terms, of which $2^n - 1$ are greater than 2^{-n-1} whereas the last is equal to 2^{-n-1}, so their sum is greater than $2^n \cdot 2^{-n-1} = 1/2$. We conclude that the series in $[*]$ must diverge because its sum is larger than that of an infinite number of $1/2$'s.

An illustration: If you plan a birthday party with infinitely many guests where the person having the birthday takes 1 cake, the best friend is given half a cake, the next person a third, and so on, then you must bake infinitely many cakes!

One can prove in general (see Problem 11 in Section 11.3) that

$$\sum_{n=1}^{\infty} \frac{1}{n^p} \text{ is convergent} \iff p > 1 \qquad [6.18]$$

Problems

1. Find the sum s_n of the finite geometric series

$$1 + \frac{1}{3} + \frac{1}{3^2} + \cdots + \frac{1}{3^{n-1}}$$

What limit does s_n tend to as n tends to infinity? Evaluate

$$\sum_{n=1}^{\infty} \frac{1}{3^{n-1}}$$

2. Determine whether the following series are geometric, and find the sums of those geometric series that do converge:

   a. $8 + 1 + 1/8 + 1/64 + \cdots$ **b.** $-2 + 6 - 18 + 54 - \cdots$
   c. $2^{1/3} + 1 + 2^{-1/3} + 2^{-2/3} + \cdots$ **d.** $1 - 1/2 + 1/3 - 1/4 + \cdots$

3. Examine the convergence of the following geometric series and find the sums when they exist:

   a. $\dfrac{1}{p} + \dfrac{1}{p^2} + \dfrac{1}{p^3} + \cdots$ **b.** $x + \sqrt{x} + 1 + 1/\sqrt{x} + \cdots$

   c. $\displaystyle\sum_{n=1}^{\infty} x^{2n}$ **d.** $1 + \dfrac{1}{1+x} + \dfrac{1}{(1+x)^2} + \cdots$

4. Find the sum

$$\sum_{k=0}^{\infty} b\left(1 + \frac{p}{100}\right)^{-k} \qquad (p > 0)$$

5. Total world consumption of iron in 1971 was approximately 794 million tons. If consumption increases by 5% each year and the world's total resources of iron are 249 billion tons, how long will these resources last?

6. Show that the following series diverge:

   a. $\displaystyle\sum_{n=1}^{\infty} \frac{n}{1+n}$ **b.** $\displaystyle\sum_{n=1}^{\infty} (101/100)^n$ **c.** $\displaystyle\sum_{n=1}^{\infty} \frac{1}{(1 + 1/n)^n}$

7. Examine the convergence or divergence of the following series:

   a. $\displaystyle\sum_{n=1}^{\infty} (100/101)^n$ **b.** $\displaystyle\sum_{n=1}^{\infty} \frac{1}{\sqrt{n}}$ **c.** $\displaystyle\sum_{n=1}^{\infty} \frac{1}{n^{1.00000001}}$

   d. $\displaystyle\sum_{n=1}^{\infty} \frac{1+n}{4n-3}$ **e.** $\displaystyle\sum_{n=1}^{\infty} \left(-\frac{1}{2}\right)^n$ **f.** $\displaystyle\sum_{n=1}^{\infty} (\sqrt{3})^{1-n}$

8. Let

$$s_n = \sum_{k=1}^{n} \frac{1}{k(k+1)} = \frac{1}{1 \cdot 2} + \frac{1}{2 \cdot 3} + \frac{1}{3 \cdot 4} + \cdots + \frac{1}{n(n+1)}$$

By using the identity

$$\frac{1}{k(k+1)} = \frac{1}{k} - \frac{1}{k+1}$$

prove that $s_n = n/(n+1)$, and then find the sum of the infinite series

$$\sum_{k=1}^{\infty} \frac{1}{k(k+1)}$$

6.6 Present Discounted Values and Investment

The sum of $1000 in your hand today is worth more than $1000 received at some future date. One important reason is that you can invest the $1000.[2] If the interest rate is 11% per year, then after 6 years, the original $1000 will have grown to an amount $1000(1 + 11/100)^6 = 1000 \cdot (1.1)^6 \approx \$1870$. (See Section A.1 of Appendix A.) So if the amount $1870 is due for payment 6 years from now and the interest rate is 11% per year, then the *present value* of this amount is $1000. Because $1000 is less than $1870, we often speak of $1000 as the *present discounted value* (or PDV) of $1870. The ratio $1000/$1870 is called the *discount factor*. The interest rate, 11% per year in this case, is often called the *discount rate* as well.

Suppose three payments are to be made, with the amount $1000 being paid after 1 year, $1500 after 2 years, and $2000 after 3 years. How much must be deposited in an account today in order to have enough savings to cover these three payments, given that the interest rate is 11% per year? We call this total amount the *present value* of the three payments.

In order to have $1000 after 1 year, the amount x_1 we must deposit today is given by

$$x_1 \cdot \left(1 + \frac{11}{100}\right) = 1000, \qquad \text{that is,} \qquad x_1 = \frac{1000}{1 + 11/100} = \frac{1000}{1.11}$$

In order to have $1500 after 2 years, we must deposit an amount x_2 today, where

$$x_2 \cdot \left(1 + \frac{11}{100}\right)^2 = 1500, \qquad \text{that is,} \qquad x_2 = \frac{1500}{(1 + 11/100)^2} = \frac{1500}{(1.11)^2}$$

---

[2] If prices are expected to increase, another reason for preferring $1000 today is inflation, because $1000 to be paid at some future date will buy less then than $1000 does today.

Finally, to have $2000 after 3 years, we must deposit an amount x_3 today, where

$$x_3 \cdot \left(1 + \frac{11}{100}\right)^3 = 2000, \qquad \text{that is,} \qquad x_3 = \frac{2000}{(1 + 11/100)^3} = \frac{2000}{(1.11)^3}$$

So the total present value of the three payments, which is the total amount A that must be deposited today in order to cover all three payments, is given by

$$A = \frac{1000}{1.11} + \frac{1500}{(1.11)^2} + \frac{2000}{(1.11)^3}$$

The total is approximately $900.90 + 1217.43 + 1462.38 = 3580.71$.

Suppose now that n successive payments $a_1, \ldots, a_n$ are to be made, with a_1 being paid after 1 year, a_2 after 2 years, and so on. How much must be deposited into an account today in order to have enough savings to cover all these future payments, given that the interest rate is $p\%$ per year? In other words, what is the *present value* of all these payments? Let $r = p/100$ represent the *interest factor*.

In order to have a_1 after 1 year, we must deposit $a_1/(1+r)$ today, to have a_2 after 2 years we must deposit $a_2/(1+r)^2$ today, and so on. The total amount A_n that must be deposited today in order to cover all n payments is therefore

$$A_n = \frac{a_1}{1+r} + \frac{a_2}{(1+r)^2} + \cdots + \frac{a_n}{(1+r)^n} \qquad [6.19]$$

In other words:

The **present value** of the n installments $a_1, a_2, \ldots, a_n$, where the first amount a_1 has to be paid after 1 year and the remaining amounts at intervals of 1 year, and with the interest rate $p\%$ per year, is given by

$$A_n = \sum_{i=1}^{n} \frac{a_i}{(1+r)^i} \qquad \text{where } r = p/100 \qquad [6.20]$$

Often, the annual payments are equal, so that $a_1 = a_2 = \cdots = a_n = a$. Then [6.19] is a finite geometric series with n terms. The first term is $a/(1+r)$ and the quotient is $1/(1+r)$. According to formula [6.10] with $k = (1+r)^{-1}$, the sum is

$$A_n = \frac{a}{1+r} \frac{1 - (1+r)^{-n}}{1 - (1+r)^{-1}} = \frac{a}{r}\left[1 - \frac{1}{(1+r)^n}\right]$$

(where the second equality holds because the denominator of the middle expression reduces to r). Hence, we have the following:

> **The present value** of n installments of $\$a$ each, where the first amount has to be paid 1 year from now and the remaining amounts at intervals of 1 year, with the interest rate at $p\%$ per year, is given by
>
> $$A_n = \frac{a}{1+r} + \cdots + \frac{a}{(1+r)^n} = \frac{a}{r}\left[1 - \frac{1}{(1+r)^n}\right] \qquad [6.21]$$
>
> where $r = p/100$.

Example 6.17

What is the present value of 10 annual deposits of $1000 if the first payment occurs after 1 year and the interest rate is 14% per year?

Solution   Using [6.21] with $a = 1000$, $n = 10$, and $r = 14/100 = 0.14$ yields

$$A_{10} = \frac{1000}{0.14}\left[1 - \frac{1}{(1.14)^{10}}\right] \approx 5216.12$$

Example 6.18

A house loan valued at $50,000 today is to be repaid in equal annual amounts over 15 years, the first repayment starting 1 year from now. The interest rate is 8%. What are the annual amounts?

Solution   We can use [6.21] again. This time $A_{15} = 50,000$, $r = 0.08$, and $n = 15$. Hence, we obtain the following equation for determining the annual amount a:

$$50,000 = \frac{a}{0.08}\left[1 - \frac{1}{(1.08)^{15}}\right]$$

We find $50,000 = a \cdot 8.55948$, so that $a \approx 5841$.

If n tends to infinity in [6.21] and if $r > 0$, then $(1+r)^n$ will tend to infinity, and thus A_n will tend to $A = a/r$:

$$A = \frac{a}{1+r} + \frac{a}{(1+r)^2} + \cdots = \frac{a}{r} \qquad (r > 0) \qquad [6.22]$$

Thus, $a = rA$. This corresponds to the case where an investment of $\$A$ pays $\$a$ per year in perpetuity when the interest rate is r.

Investment Projects

Consider n numbers $a_0, a_1, \ldots, a_{n-1}$ that represent the returns in successive years to an investment project. Negative numbers represent losses, positive numbers represent profits, and we think of a_i as associated with year i, whereas a_0 is associated with the present period. In most investment projects, a_0 is a big negative number, because a large expense precedes any returns. If we consider an interest rate of $p\%$ per year and let $r = p/100$, then the net present value of the profits accruing from the project is given by

$$A = a_0 + \frac{a_1}{1+r} + \frac{a_2}{(1+r)^2} + \cdots + \frac{a_{n-1}}{(1+r)^{n-1}}$$

Several different criteria are used to compare alternative investment projects. One is simply this: Choose the project whose profit stream has the largest net present value A. The interest rate to use could be an accepted rate for capital investments. This rule is the natural extension to many periods of static profit maximization, with the discount factors $(1 + r)^{-1}$, $(1 + r)^{-2}$, $\ldots$ attached to future profits like the prices of future money (which is less valuable than present money).

A different criterion is based on the **internal rate of return**, defined as an interest rate that makes the present value of all payments equal to 0. For the investment project yielding returns $a_0, a_1, \ldots, a_{n-1}$, the internal rate of return is thus a number r such that

$$a_0 + \frac{a_1}{1+r} + \frac{a_2}{(1+r)^2} + \cdots + \frac{a_{n-1}}{(1+r)^{n-1}} = 0 \qquad [6.23]$$

If two investment projects both have a unique internal rate of return, then a criterion for choosing between them is to prefer the project that has the higher internal rate of return. Note that [6.23] is a polynomial equation of degree $n - 1$ in the discount factor $(1+r)^{-1}$. In general, this equation does not have a unique positive solution r. Nevertheless, Problem 7 asks you to show that there exists a unique positive internal rate of return in an important special case.

Problems

1. What is the present value of 15 annual deposits of $3500 each when the first deposit is 1 year from now and the interest rate is 12% per year?

2. An author is to be paid a royalty for a book. Two alternative offers are made:
   (a) The author can be paid $21,000 immediately,
   (b) There can be five equal annual payments of $4600, the first being paid at once.

   Which of these offers will be more valuable if the interest rate is 6% per annum?

3. A is obliged to pay B the amount $1000 yearly for 5 years, the first payment in 1 year's time. B sells this claim to C for $4340 in cash. Find an equation that determines the rate of return p that C obtains from this investment. Can you prove that it is a little less than 5%?

4. A construction firm wants to buy a building site and has the choice between three different payment schedules:
   (a) Pay $67,000 in cash.
   (b) Pay $12,000 per year for 8 years, where the first installment is to be paid at once.
   (c) Pay $22,000 in cash and thereafter $7000 per year for 12 years, where the first installment is to be paid after 1 year.
   Determine which schedule is least expensive if the interest rate is 11.5% and the firm has at least $67,000 available to spend in cash. What happens if the firm can only afford $22,000 as an immediate payment? Or if the interest rate is 12.5%?

5. Suppose that in [6.23] we have $a_0 < 0$ and $a_i = a$ for $i = 1, 2, \ldots$. If n is very large, find an approximate expression for the internal rate of return.

6. The present discounted value of a payment D growing at a constant rate g when the discount rate is r is given by

$$\frac{D}{1+r} + \frac{D(1+g)}{(1+r)^2} + \frac{D(1+g)^2}{(1+r)^3} + \cdots$$

where r and g are positive. What is the condition for convergence? Show that if the series converges with sum P_0, then $P_0 = D/(r-g)$.

7. Consider an investment project with an initial loss, so that $a_0 < 0$, and thereafter no losses. Suppose too that the sum of the later profits is larger than the initial loss. Prove that there exists a unique positive internal rate of return. (*Hint:* Define $f(r)$ as the expression on the left side of [6.23]. Then study $f(r)$ and $f'(r)$ on the interval $(0, \infty)$.)

6.7 A Rigorous Approach to Limits (Optional)

Our preliminary definition of the limit concept [4.14] of in Section 4.4 was this:

$\lim_{x \to a} f(x) = A$ means that $f(x)$ in as close to A as we want, for all x sufficiently close (but not equal) to a [1]

The closeness or, more generally, the distance between two numbers can be measured by the absolute value of the difference between them. Let us briefly consider some examples of the use of absolute values before proceeding further.

Example 6.19

Use both absolute values and double inequalities to answer the following questions:

(a) Which numbers x have a distance from 5 that is less than 0.1?

(b) Which numbers x have a distance from a that is less than δ?

Solution

(a) The distance between x and 5 is $|x - 5|$, so the requirement is that $|x - 5| < 0.1$. Using [1.4] in Section 1.4, we have alternatively $-0.1 < x - 5 < 0.1$. Adding 5 to each side gives $4.9 < x < 5.1$. (The result is obvious: The numbers x that differ from 5 by less than 0.1 are those lying between 4.9 and 5.1.)

(b) Here $|x - a| < \delta$ or $-\delta < x - a < \delta$. Adding a to each side yields $a - \delta < x < a + \delta$. We can also write $x \in (a - \delta, a + \delta)$.

Absolute values can be used to reformulate [1] as follows:

$\lim_{x \to a} f(x) = A$ means that $|f(x) - A|$ is as small as we want for all $x \neq a$ with $|x - a|$ sufficiently small.   [2]

Note that the condition $x \neq a$ is equivalent to $0 < |x - a|$.

The German mathematician Heine was the first to realize (in 1872) that this formulation could be made precise with the following $\varepsilon\delta$ definition:

We say that $f(x)$ tends to A in the limit as x tends to a, and write $\lim_{x \to a} f(x) = A$, provided that for each number $\varepsilon > 0$ there exists a number $\delta > 0$ such that   [6.24]

$$|f(x) - A| < \varepsilon \quad \text{whenever} \quad 0 < |x - a| < \delta$$

Definition [6.24] is illustrated in Fig. 6.15. Note that the tolerance for the deviation in $f(x)$, which is ε, is marked off along the y-axis, and the corresponding deviation in x, which

FIGURE 6.15   For every ε, there is a δ, so $\lim_{x \to a} f(x) = A$.

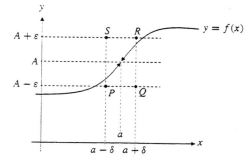

is δ, is marked off along the x-axis. Geometrically, $f(x)A$ as $x \to a$ means that the graph must not only intersect box $PQRS$, but also "come out of" its vertical sides. Note how $\delta > 0$ must be chosen so that if $x \neq a$ and $x \in (a - \delta, a + \delta)$, then $f(x)$ belongs to the interval $(A - \varepsilon, A + \varepsilon)$. If $\varepsilon > 0$ is chosen smaller, then δ usually has to be chosen smaller as well. Our choice of δ must therefore, in general, depend on the choice of ε. *This interplay between ε and δ is the whole point of the definition:* However small we choose $\varepsilon > 0$, it must be possible to find a $\delta > 0$ so small that whenever x is closer to a than δ (and $x \neq a$), then $f(x)$ is closer to A than ε.

It must be regarded as a part of one's general mathematical education *to have seen* this $\varepsilon\delta$ definition of a limit. However, if you have difficulties with this definition and with arguments based on it, you are in very good company indeed. Hundreds of thousands of mathematics students all over the world struggle with this definition every year. Furthermore, many of the world's best mathematicians in the nineteenth century were unable to solve some important problems for want of a precise definition of limits, so the concept did not come easily to them either.

Example 6.20

Use [6.24] to show that

$$\lim_{x \to 3} (3x - 2) = 7 \qquad [1]$$

Solution   In this case, $f(x) = 3x - 2$, $a = 3$, and $A = 7$. Hence,

$$|f(x) - A| = |(3x - 2) - 7|$$
$$= |3x - 9| = 3|x - 3| \qquad [2]$$

Let $\varepsilon > 0$ be given. We see from [2] that $|f(x) - A| = 3|x - 3| < \varepsilon$ provided that $0 < |x - 3| < \varepsilon/3$. So $|f(x) - A| < \varepsilon$ if $|x - 3| < \delta$, where $\delta = \varepsilon/3$. According to definition [6.24], we conclude that [1] is correct.

Note that the value of δ in definition [6.24] is not unique. Having found *one* value of δ, any smaller value of δ will work as well. In Example 6.20, we chose $\delta = \varepsilon/3$; we could also have chosen any $\delta \leq \varepsilon/3$, but not $\delta = \varepsilon/2$.

The proof in Example 6.20 is about as easy as a limit proof can get. Usually, a little more ingenuity is required. Let us consider a more typical example.

Example 6.21

Show by using the $\varepsilon\delta$ definition that if $a > 0$, then

$$\lim_{x \to a} \sqrt{x} = \sqrt{a} \qquad [1]$$

Solution   Here $f(x) = \sqrt{x}$ and $A = \sqrt{a}$. Given any $\varepsilon > 0$, we must find a $\delta > 0$ such that

$$|f(x) - A| = |\sqrt{x} - \sqrt{a}| < \varepsilon \qquad \text{whenever} \qquad 0 < |x - a| < \delta \qquad [2]$$

It seems a good idea to try to express $|\sqrt{x} - \sqrt{a}|$ in terms of $|x - a|$. We use a common algebraic trick:

$$|\sqrt{x} - \sqrt{a}| = \left| \frac{(\sqrt{x} - \sqrt{a})(\sqrt{x} + \sqrt{a})}{\sqrt{x} + \sqrt{a}} \right| = \frac{|x - a|}{\sqrt{x} + \sqrt{a}} \qquad [3]$$

Because $\sqrt{x} + \sqrt{a} \geq \sqrt{a}$ whatever the value of $x \geq 0$, we obtain from [3] that

$$|\sqrt{x} - \sqrt{a}| = \frac{|x - a|}{\sqrt{x} + \sqrt{a}} \leq \frac{1}{\sqrt{a}}|x - a|$$

Thus, we see that if $|x - a|$ is small, then $|\sqrt{x} - \sqrt{a}|$ is small as well. *More precisely:*

$$|\sqrt{x} - \sqrt{a}| \leq \frac{1}{\sqrt{a}} \cdot |x - a| < \varepsilon$$

provided that $0 < |x - a| < \delta = \varepsilon\sqrt{a}$.

So far we have concentrated on cases in which the limit exists. What does it mean to say that $f(x)$ does *not* tend to the number A as x tends to a? Negating statement [6.24], we have (compare Problem 9(d) in Section 1.5):

> $f(x)$ does not tend to A as a limit as x tends to a if we can find an $\varepsilon > 0$ such that, for all $\delta > 0$, there exists a number x satisfying $0 < |x - a| < \delta$ and   [6.25]
> $|f(x) - A| \geq \varepsilon$.

Definition [6.25] is illustrated in Fig. 6.16. If we choose ε as in the figure, we see that if x is slightly larger than a, then the distance $|f(x) - A|$ is larger than ε. For every $\delta > 0$, there exists a number x satisfying $0 < |x - a| < \delta$ and $|f(x) - A| \geq \varepsilon$. This shows that $f(x)$ does not tend to A as a limit as x tends to a.

FIGURE 6.16

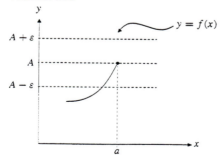

Extensions of the Limit Concept

In Section 6.1 we extended the limit concept heuristically in several different ways. All these definitions can be made precise in the same way as [6.24]. We include only the following definition:

$\lim_{x \to \infty} f(x) = A$ means that for each $\varepsilon > 0$, there exists
a number N such that $|f(x) - A| < \varepsilon$ for all $x > N$ [6.26]

Illustrate this definition in connection with Fig. 6.4 of Section 6.1.

The following "geometrically obvious" theorem is quite useful:

The Squeezing Rule for Limits

Suppose that $f(x) \le g(x) \le h(x)$ for all x in an interval around a, but not necessarily   [6.27]
at a. If there exists a number M such that $\lim_{x \to a} f(x) = \lim_{x \to a} h(x) = M$, then
$\lim_{x \to a} g(x) = M$.

The theorem is illustrated in Fig. 6.17. Because $g(x)$ is "squeezed" between two functions that both tend to M as $x \to a$, $g(x)$ must also tend to M as $x \to a$. One can prove this theorem by using definition [6.24], but we skip the proof. Ambitious readers may want to try it for themselves.

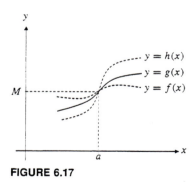

FIGURE 6.17

An $\varepsilon \delta$ Definition of Continuity

In [6.2] of Section 6.2 we defined continuity in terms of the limit concept. The precise definition [6.24], leads to the following $\varepsilon \delta$ definition of continuity:

---

f is **continuous** at $x = a$ if for every $\varepsilon > 0$, there is a $\delta > 0$ such that $|f(x) - f(a)| <$ [6.28]
ε whenever $|x - a| < \delta$.

Note that $0 < |x - a|$ is unnecessary because if $|x - a| = 0$, then $x = a$, and so $|f(x) - f(a)| = 0$.

Problems

1. Use [6.24] to show that $\lim_{x \to -1} (5x + 2) = -3$.

2. Prove that for $|x| \leq 1$, one has $|(x + 1)^3 - 1| \leq 7|x|$. Use this and the definition of limits to show that $\lim_{x \to 0} (x + 1)^3 = 1$. Is $f(x) = (x + 1)^3$ continuous at $x = 0$?

3. Let $f(x) = 2 - \frac{1}{2}x^2$ and $h(x) = 2 + x^2$. Suppose that the only thing we know about the function g is that $f(x) \leq g(x) \leq h(x)$ for all x. What is $\lim_{x \to 0} g(x)$?

4. Show by using the definition of limits that:

   a.
   $$\lim_{x \to 5} \frac{4x^2 - 100}{x - 5} = 40$$

   b.
   $$\lim_{x \to -\pi} \frac{x^2 - \pi^2}{x + \pi} = -2\pi$$

   Hint: Try to simplify the fractions.

7

Implications of Continuity and Differentiability

In fact the Mean Value Theorem is a
wolf in sheep's clothing and is THE
fundamental theorem of differential calculus.
—R. G. Bartle (1964)

The first three sections of this chapter deal with some theorems that are very important from a theoretical point of view. All these results are intuitively "rather obvious," but precise proofs (which we usually omit) rely on a careful study of continuity and of the real number system.

In Section 7.1, the most useful result is the intermediate-value theorem, and its corollary, Theorem 7.2, which you should know how to apply. The results in Section 7.2 form the theoretical base for the optimization theory discussed in Chapter 9, which is such a key topic in economics. Section 7.3 deals with the mean-value theorem and some of its implications. This theorem is a principal tool for a precise treatment of calculus. Actually, most of us find the result and its corollaries eminently reasonable. The problem is that most of us are only too willing to accept that, say, a function cannot be continuous at one point only— until we see an example of such a function like Problem 4 in Section 7.1. Still, we readily concede that understanding this section is not really required for reading the rest of this book.

The last part of the chapter presents several mathematical topics that frequently arise in economic analysis. Section 7.4 studies Taylor's formula, which makes it possible to analyze the resulting error when a function is approximated by a polynomial. Section 7.5 presents l'Hôpital's rule for indeterminate forms, which is sometimes useful for evaluating limits. Finally, in Section 7.6, we investigate in some detail inverse functions, already discussed briefly in Section 3.6.

7.1 The Intermediate-Value Theorem

An important reason for introducing the concept of a continuous function was to distinguish between functions whose graphs are "connected" and those that make one or more jumps. Can we rest assured that the $\varepsilon\delta$ definition of a continuous function is the right one in this respect? The following important theorem gives the answer.

Theorem 7.1   (The Intermediate-Value Theorem)   Let f be a function that is continuous for all x in the closed interval $[a, b]$, and assume that $f(a) \neq f(b)$. As x varies between a and b, so $f(x)$ takes on every value between $f(a)$ and $f(b)$.

The geometric content of the theorem is illustrated in Fig. 7.1. Here m is any number between $f(a)$ and $f(b)$. The theorem tells us that the graph of the continuous function f must intersect the line $y = m$ at at least one point (c, m), where $f(c) = m$. The theorem is by no means obvious. A proper proof requires the $\varepsilon\delta$ definition of continuity.

An immediate and useful consequence of the intermediate-value theorem is the following:

Theorem 7.2   Let f be a function continuous in $[a, b]$ and assume that $f(a)$ and $f(b)$ have different signs. Then there is at least one $c \in (a, b)$ such that $f(c) = 0$.

This theorem is important in assuring the existence of solutions to equations in cases where these solutions cannot be obtained exactly.

FIGURE 7.1

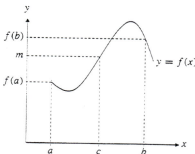

Example 7.1

Prove that the following equation has at least one solution between 0 and 1:

$$x^6 + 3x^2 - 2x - 1 = 0 \qquad [*]$$

Solution   Put $f(x) = x^6 + 3x^2 - 2x - 1$. Because it is a polynomial, f is continuous for all x—in particular, for all x in $[0, 1]$. Moreover, $f(0) = -1$ and $f(1) = 1$. We conclude from Theorem 7.2 that there exists at least one number $c \in (0, 1)$ such that $f(c) = 0$. So equation $[*]$ has at least one solution between 0 and 1. See Fig. 7.2.

If we were interested in locating a more accurate solution of equation $[*]$ in the interval $[0, 1]$, we might proceed as follows. Take the midpoint between 0 and 1, $x = \frac{1}{2}$. We find that $f(\frac{1}{2})$ is negative. Hence, there is a solution in the interval $(\frac{1}{2}, 1)$. By taking the midpoint of this interval, $x = \frac{3}{4}$, and computing $f(\frac{3}{4})$, again we get a negative number. Hence, there is a solution in $(\frac{3}{4}, 1)$. By proceeding in this way, we can determine the solution as accurately as we desire. However, much better methods for finding a solution numerically are available.

Example 7.2

Prove that for any positive number a, the equation

$$x^3 = a \qquad [*]$$

has a unique positive solution $x = c$. (This solution is denoted by $\sqrt[3]{a}$, the third root of a.)

Solution   Let $f(x) = x^3 - a$. Then f is continuous for all x and in particular in the interval $[0, a + 1]$. Here $f(0) = -a < 0$ whereas $f(a + 1) = (a + 1)^3 - a = a^3 + 3a^2 + 2a + 1 > 0$. So there exists a number $c \in (0, a + 1)$ such that $f(c) = c^3 - a = 0$, and thus $c^3 = a$.

FIGURE 7.2

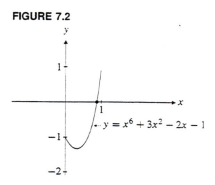

$y = x^6 + 3x^2 - 2x - 1$

To prove that c is unique, suppose that c_1 and c_2 are two positive solutions of the equation. Now

$$c_1^3 - c_2^3 = (c_1 - c_2)(c_1^2 + c_1 c_2 + c_2^2) \qquad [**]$$

as can be verified by simplifying the right-hand side. Because $c_1^2 + c_1 c_2 + c_2^2$ is positive, it follows from [**] that $c_1 \neq c_2 \Rightarrow c_1^3 \neq c_2^3$. We conclude that equation [*] has a unique solution $x = \sqrt[3]{a}$. (In fact, [*] has a unique solution also when a is negative.)

Note: Because of the intermediate-value theorem, the $\varepsilon\delta$ definition of continuity implies that when a function is continuous in an interval, it has a graph that deserves to be called "connected." However, you should be warned against interpreting the concept of a continuous function too intuitively. In fact, if you rely merely on intuition, it is difficult to understand the following facts:

1. There exist functions that are continuous at only one point (see Problem 4).
2. There exist functions that are discontinuous for all x (see Problem 4).
3. There exist continuous functions that are not differentiable anywhere.

The last fact may be the most surprising. It is impossible to draw an accurate graph of such a function. It is as if it oscillates so wildly that "corners" occur everywhere. Yet such functions have recently played an important role in the analysis of financial markets.

Problems

1. Prove that each of the following equations has at least one solution in the given interval.
   a. $x^7 - 5x^5 + x^3 - 1 = 0$ in $(-1, 1)$.
   b. $x^3 + 3x - 8 = 0$ in $(-2, 3)$.
   c. $\sqrt{x^2 + 1} = 3x$ in $(0,1)$.

2. Prove that for all choices of the coefficients, the equation

$$x^3 + ax^2 + bx + c = 0$$

has at least one real root. Generalize this result by considering

$$x^n + a_1 x^{n-1} + \cdots + a_{n-1}x + a_n = 0$$

where n is an odd number. What can go wrong if n is even?

3. "Prove" that you were once exactly 1 meter tall.

Harder Problems

4. Consider functions f and g defined for all x by

$$f(x) = \begin{cases} x, & x \text{ irrational} \\ 0, & x \text{ rational} \end{cases} \quad \text{and} \quad g(x) = \begin{cases} 1, & x \text{ rational} \\ 0, & x \text{ irrational} \end{cases}$$

Prove that f is continuous only at $x = 0$, and that g is discontinuous for all x.

5. Suppose $f(x)$ is a continuous function from $[a, b]$ to $[a, b]$. (Thus, f has the same set $[a, b]$ as both its domain and its target.)

    a. Graph such a function together with the line $y = x$.

    b. Prove that the equation $f(x) = x$ has at least one solution in $[a, b]$. (Any solution to $f(x) = x$ is called a *fixed point*. The theorem proved here is a simple instance of *Brouwer's fixed point theorem*, which is often used in economics.[1])

7.2 The Extreme-Value Theorem

Finding the points in the domain of a function at which it reaches its largest and its smallest values is one of the oldest and most important applications of calculus. The quadratic examples of Section 3.2, and the general discussions of later chapters, show how such problems play an especially important role in economic analysis. We usually refer to these points as maximum and minimum points—or, if we do not want to bother with the distinction between maxima and minima, as **extreme points**. Thus, if $f(x)$ has domain D, then

$$c \in D \text{ is a } \textbf{maximum point} \text{ for } f \iff f(x) \leq f(c) \text{ for all } x \in D \qquad [7.1]$$

$$d \in D \text{ is a } \textbf{minimum point} \text{ for } f \iff f(x) \geq f(d) \text{ for all } x \in D \qquad [7.2]$$

In [7.1], we call $f(c)$ the **maximum value**; in [7.2], we call $f(d)$ the **minimum value**.

    The following theorem gives important sufficient conditions for the existence of a maximum and a minimum.

Theorem 7.3 (The Extreme-Value Theorem) If a function f is continuous in a closed, bounded interval $[a, b]$, then f attains both a maximum value and a minimum value in $[a, b]$.

---

[1] See, for example, K. C. Border, *Fixed Point Theorems with Applications to Economics and Game Theory*, Cambridge University Press, New York, 1990.

The proof of this theorem is surprisingly difficult. Yet the result is not hard to believe. Imagine, for example, a cyclist going for a ride on hilly roads. The height of the road above sea level is a continuous function of the distance traveled, as illustrated in Fig. 7.3. During the trip, the cyclist has to pass through a highest point P and a lowest point Q, as shown in the figure.

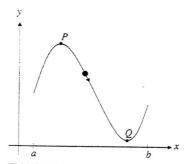

FIGURE 7.3

Note: One of the most common misunderstandings in connection with Theorem 7.3 is illustrated by the following statement from a student's exam paper: "The function is continuous, but since it is not defined on a closed bounded interval, the extreme value theorem shows that there is no maximum." The misunderstanding here is that although the conditions of the theorem are sufficient, they certainly are not *necessary* for the existence of an extreme point. In Problem 3, you are asked to study a function defined in an interval that is neither closed nor bounded, and moreover the function is not even continuous. Still it has a maximum.

If we drop any of the conditions in Theorem 7.3, the maximum or minimum value will not necessarily exist. This is illustrated in Figs. 7.4 to 7.6.

The extreme-value theorem does not tell you how to solve the problem of finding maximum and minimum values of a function. Here we give a formal proof of a result that is intuitively very reasonable: At any interior maximum or minimum

FIGURE 7.4 *f* **is defined in [a, b], but is discontinuous at x = c. No maximum exists.**

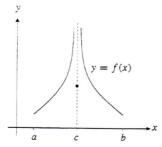

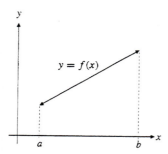

FIGURE 7.5 **f is defined in (a, b). f is continuous, but has neither a maximum nor a minimum.**

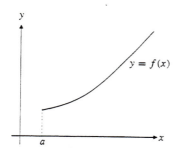

FIGURE 7.6 **f is defined in [a, ∞). f is continuous, but no maximum exists.**

of a differentiable function, the derivative must be zero. Geometrically, the tangent to the graph of the function is parallel to the x-axis at the corresponding point on the graph.

Theorem 7.4   Let f be defined in an interval I and let c be an interior point of I (that is, not an end point of I). If c is a maximum or a minimum point of f and if $f'(c)$ exists, then

$$f'(c) = 0$$

[7.3]

Proof   Suppose that f has a maximum at c (the proof in the case when c is a minimum point is similar). If the absolute value of h is sufficiently small, then $c + h \in I$ because c is an interior point of I. Because c is a maximum point, $f(c+h) - f(c) \leq 0$. If h is sufficiently small and positive, the Newton quotient $[f(c + h) - f(c)]/h \leq 0$. The limit of this quotient as $h \to 0^+$ is therefore ≤ 0 as well. But because $f'(c)$ exists, this limit is equal to $f'(c)$, so $f'(c) \leq 0$. For negative values of h, on the other hand, $[f(c + h) - f(c)]/h \geq 0$. The limit of this expression as $h \to 0^-$ is therefore ≥ 0. So, $f'(c) \geq 0$. We have now proved that $f'(c) \leq 0$ and $f'(c) \geq 0$. Hence, $f'(c) = 0$.

Points at which $f'(c) = 0$ are called **stationary points**. Chapter 9 discusses the essential role played by stationary points in the theory of optimization.

Problems

1. Explain why function f defined for all $x \in [0, 5]$ by

$$f(x) = \frac{x^6 + 5x^3 - 2x + 8}{x^4 + 10}$$

has both a maximum and a minimum value. (Do *not* try to find these values!)

2. Let f be defined for all $x \in [-1, 1]$ by

$$f(x) = \begin{cases} x, & \text{for } x \in (-1, 1) \\ 0, & \text{for } x = -1 \text{ and for } x = 1 \end{cases}$$

   a. Does f attain maximum and minimum values in $[-1, 1]$?
   b. Is f continuous for all $x \in [-1, 1]$?

3. Let f be defined for all x in $(0, \infty)$ by

$$f(x) = \begin{cases} x + 1, & \text{for } x \in (0, 1] \\ 1, & \text{for } x \in (1, \infty) \end{cases}$$

   Prove that f attains maximum and minimum values. Verify that nevertheless *none* of the conditions in the extreme-value theorem is satisfied.

7.3 The Mean-Value Theorem

Consider a function f defined on an interval $[a, b]$, and suppose that the graph of f is connected and without corners, as illustrated in Fig. 7.7. Because the graph of f joins A to B by a connected curve having a tangent at each point,

FIGURE 7.7

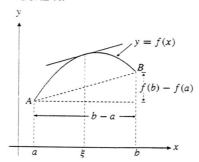

it is geometrically plausible that for at least one value of x between a and b, the tangent to the graph at x should be parallel to the line AB. In Fig. 7.7, ξ appears to be such a value of x. Line AB has slope $\left[f(b) - f(a)\right]/(b - a)$. So the condition for the tangent line at $(\xi, f(\xi))$ to be parallel to line AB is that $f'(\xi) = \left[f(b) - f(a)\right]/(b - a)$. In fact, ξ can be chosen so that the vertical distance between $(\xi, f(\xi))$ and AB is as large as possible. The proof that follows is based on this fact.

This result, made plausible by a geometric argument, is in fact a major theorem in mathematical analysis.

Theorem 7.5   (The Mean-Value Theorem)   If f is continuous in the closed bounded interval $[a, b]$ and differentiable in the open interval (a, b), then there exists at least one interior point ξ in (a, b) such that

$$f'(\xi) = \frac{f(b) - f(a)}{b - a}$$

[7.4]

Proof   Consider the function

$$g(x) = f(x) - f(a) - \alpha(x - a)$$

where

$$\alpha = \frac{f(b) - f(a)}{b - a}$$

Then $g(a) = g(b) = 0$. Function $g(x)$ obviously inherits from f the properties of being continuous in $[a, b]$ and differentiable in (a, b). By the extreme-value theorem, $g(x)$ has a maximum M over $[a, b]$ at some point x^* and a minimum m over $[a, b]$ at some point x_* of $[a, b]$. Because $g(a) = g(b) = 0$, these maximum and minimum values must satisfy $m \leq 0 \leq M$. Now there are three possible cases:

1. If $M > 0$, then x^* cannot be a or b, so $x^* \in (a, b)$. Hence, by Theorem 7.4, $g'(x^*) = 0$. Then take $\xi = x^*$.
2. If $m < 0$, then x_* cannot be a or b, so $x_* \in (a, b)$. Hence, by Theorem 7.4, $g'(x_*) = 0$. Then take $\xi = x_*$.
3. If $M = m = 0$, then $g(x) = 0$ for all x in (a, b), and so ξ can be chosen as any point in (a, b).

In each case, there exists $\xi \in (a, b)$ with $g'(\xi) = f'(\xi) - \alpha = 0$ and so $f'(\xi) = \alpha$.

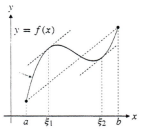

FIGURE 7.8

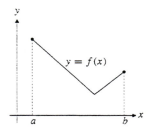

FIGURE 7.9

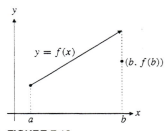

FIGURE 7.10

It is important to note carefully the conditions and the conclusion of the theorem. The geometric examples in Figs. 7.8 to 7.10 illustrate the following facts: (1) the point ξ is not necessarily unique; (2) the condition that f is differentiable everywhere in (a, b) cannot be dropped; and (3) the condition that f is continuous everywhere in $[a, b]$ cannot be dropped.

Example 7.3

Test the mean-value theorem on $f(x) = x^3 - x$ in $[0, 2]$.

Solution   We find that

$$\frac{f(2) - f(0)}{2 - 0} = 3 \quad \text{and} \quad f'(x) = 3x^2 - 1$$

The equation $f'(x) = 3$ has two solutions, $x = \pm 2\sqrt{3}/3$. Because the positive root $\xi = 2\sqrt{3}/3 \in (0, 2)$, we have

$$f'(\xi) = \frac{f(2) - f(0)}{2 - 0}$$

Thus, the mean-value theorem is confirmed in this case.

The terms *increasing* and *decreasing* functions have been used previously to describe the behavior of a function as we travel from *left to right* along its

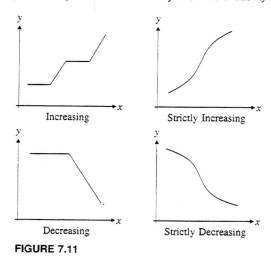

FIGURE 7.11

graph. See Fig. 7.11. In order to establish a definite terminology, we introduce the following definitions. We understand that f is defined in an interval and that x_1 and x_2 are numbers from that interval.

If $f(x_1) \le f(x_2)$ whenever $x_1 < x_2$, then f is **increasing**.

If $f(x_1) < f(x_2)$ whenever $x_1 < x_2$, then f is **strictly increasing**.

If $f(x_1) \ge f(x_2)$ whenever $x_1 < x_2$, then f is **decreasing**.   [7.5]

If $f(x_1) > f(x_2)$ whenever $x_1 < x_2$, then f is **strictly decreasing**.

Note that these definitions allow an increasing (or decreasing) function to have sections where the graph is horizontal. This does not quite agree with common language. Few people would say that their salary increases when it stays constant! Some authors therefore reserve the term increasing for functions that are really increasing in the sense of being strictly increasing in our terminology. (They would then refer to a function f where $f(x_1) \le f(x_2)$ whenever $x_1 < x_2$ as nondecreasing.) We shall remain with the terminology in [7.5], as do most mathematics textbooks.

To find out on which intervals a function is increasing or decreasing using the definitions in [7.5], we have to consider the sign of $f(x_1) - f(x_2)$ whenever $x_1 - x_2 < 0$. This is usually quite difficult to do directly by checking the values of $f(x)$ at different points x. So it is extremely convenient that the mean-value theorem gives us a good test of whether a function is (strictly) increasing or (strictly) decreasing.

Theorem 7.6   Let f be a function continuous in the interval I and differentiable in the interior of I (that is, at points other than end points).

(a) If $f'(x) > 0$ for all x in the interior of I, then f is strictly increasing in I.

(b) If $f'(x) < 0$ for all x in the interior of I, then f is strictly decreasing in I.

Proof   Let $x_1 < x_2$ be two arbitrary numbers in I. According to the mean-value theorem, there exists a number ξ in (x_1, x_2) such that $f'(\xi) = \left[f(x_2) - f(x_1)\right]/(x_2 - x_1)$. Hence,

$$f(x_2) - f(x_1) = f'(\xi)(x_2 - x_1) \qquad [*]$$

To prove (a), suppose $f'(x) > 0$ for all x in the interior of I. Then $f'(\xi) > 0$, and the product $f'(\xi)(x_2 - x_1)$ is > 0. So from [*] we conclude that $f(x_1) < f(x_2)$. This proves that f is strictly increasing. The proof of (b) is entirely similar—the only difference is that the last four inequality signs should all be reversed.

The implications in (a) and (b) give sufficient conditions for f to be increasing or decreasing. They cannot be reversed to give necessary conditions. For example, if $f(x) = x^3$, then $f'(0) = 0$. Yet f is strictly increasing because, if $x_1 < x_2$, then $x_1^3 - x_2^3 = (x_1 - x_2)(x_1^2 + x_1 x_2 + x_2^2) = (x_1 - x_2)\left[(x_1 + \frac{1}{2}x_2)^2 + \frac{3}{4}x_2^2\right] < 0$.

It is useful to note the following logical equivalences over any interval I:

$$f'(x) \geq 0 \text{ for all } x \text{ in the interior of } I \iff f \text{ is increasing in } I \qquad [7.6]$$

$$f'(x) \leq 0 \text{ for all } x \text{ in the interior of } I \iff f \text{ is decreasing in } I \qquad [7.7]$$

These follow directly from equation [*] in the previous proof.

Chapter 9 includes many examples in which conditions [7.6] and [7.7] are used to find the intervals over which functions increase and decrease.

Note: In student papers (and economics books), the following statement is often seen: "Suppose that f is strictly increasing—that is, $f'(x) > 0$." The example $f(x) = x^3$ shows that the statement is wrong. A function can be strictly increasing even though the derivative is 0 at certain points. In fact, suppose that $f'(x) \geq 0$ for all x in I and $f'(x) = 0$ at only a finite number of points in I. Then $f'(x) > 0$ in any subinterval between two zeros of $f'(x)$, and so f is strictly increasing on each such subinterval. It follows that f is strictly increasing on the whole interval. (One might want to call a function "differentiably increasing" if $f'(x) > 0$ everywhere in its domain.)

If $f(x)$ is a constant function, it is very easy to show that its derivative is zero everywhere (see (4.21) in Section 4.5). Using the mean-value theorem, we can prove the converse. This intuitively very reasonable result plays a major role in the theory of integration in Chapter 10.

Theorem 7.7   If $f'(x) = 0$ for all x in the interior of I, then f is constant on I.

Proof   Let x_1 and x_2 be two arbitrary real numbers in I. By the mean-value theorem, there is some ξ between x_1 and x_2 for which equation [∗] in the proof of Theorem 7.6 holds. Because ξ lies between x_1 and x_2, it is an interior point of I and so $f'(\xi) = 0$. From equation [∗], we conclude that $f(x_1) = f(x_2)$. This means that given any two points of the interval, the values of the function are equal, and hence the function is constant.

Problems

1. For the following functions, determine all numbers ξ in the specified intervals such that $f'(\xi) = \big[f(b) - f(a)\big]/(b - a)$:

   a. $f(x) = x^2$ in $[1, 2]$ **b.** $f(x) = \sqrt{1 - x^2}$ in $[0, 1]$

   c. $f(x) = 2/x$ in $[2, 6]$ **d.** $f(x) = \sqrt{9 + x^2}$ in $[0, 4]$

2. The mean-value theorem does not hold for the following functions in the indicated intervals. Explain why, and draw the graphs of these functions.

   a. $y = x^{2/3}$, $x \in [-1, 1]$ **b.** $y = |x - 3|$, $x \in [0, 5]$

   c. $y = 1/(x - 1)$, $x \in [0, 2]$

3. Draw the graph of $f(x) = 1 - x^{1/3}$, for $x \in [-1, 1]$. Is there a number ξ in $(-1, 1)$ such that $f'(\xi) = \big[f(1) - f(-1)\big]/(1 - (-1))$? Does the mean-value theorem apply?

4. You are supposed to sail from point A in a lake to point B. What does the mean-value theorem have to say about your trip?

7.4 Taylor's Formula

Section 5.5 presented polynomial approximations. According to [5.11], the **nth-order Taylor polynomial** approximation of $f(x)$ about $x = 0$ is

$$f(x) \approx f(0) + \frac{1}{1!}f'(0)x + \frac{1}{2!}f''(0)x^2 + \cdots + \frac{1}{n!}f^{(n)}(0)x^n \qquad [∗]$$

The usefulness of such polynomial approximations is limited unless something is known about the error that results. Taylor's formula remedies this deficiency. This formula is often used by economists, and is regarded as one of the main results in mathematical analysis. It can be proved by using the mean-value theorem.

Consider the approximation in [∗]. Except at $x = 0$, function $f(x)$ and the Taylor polynomial on the RHS of [∗] are usually different. The difference between the two will depend on x as well as on n, and is called the *remainder*. We denote it by $R_{n+1}(x)$. Hence,

$$f(x) = f(0) + \frac{1}{1!} f'(0)x + \cdots + \frac{1}{n!} f^{(n)}(0)x^n + R_{n+1}(x) \qquad [7.8]$$

The following theorem gives an important explicit formula for the remainder.[2] (The proof will be deferred until the end of this section.)

Lagrange's Form of the Remainder

Suppose f is $n + 1$ times differentiable in an interval including 0 and x. Then the remainder $R_{n+1}(x)$ given in [7.8] can be written as

$$R_{n+1}(x) = \frac{1}{(n + 1)!} f^{(n+1)}(c)x^{n+1} \qquad [7.9]$$

for some number c between 0 and x.

Using this formula for $R_{n+1}(x)$ in [7.8], we obtain

Taylor's Formula

$$f(x) = f(0) + \frac{1}{1!} f'(0)x + \cdots + \frac{1}{n!} f^{(n)}(0)x^n + \frac{1}{(n + 1)!} f^{(n+1)}(c)x^{n+1} \qquad [7.10]$$

for some number c between 0 and x

Note that the remainder resembles the preceding terms in the sum. The only difference is that in the formula for the remainder, $f^{(n+1)}$ is evaluated at a point c, where c is some unspecified number between 0 and x, whereas in all the other terms, the

---

[2] The English mathematician Taylor had already found polynomial approximations of the general form [∗] in 1715. Lagrange proved [7.9] approximately 50 years later.

derivatives are evaluated at 0. The number c is not fixed, because it depends on x as well as on n.

If we put $n = 1$ in formula [7.10], we obtain

$$f(x) = f(0) + f'(0)x + \tfrac{1}{2}f''(c)x^2 \qquad \text{for some } c \text{ between 0 and } x \qquad [7.11]$$

This formula tells us that $\tfrac{1}{2}f''(c)x^2$ is the error that results if we replace $f(x)$ with its linear approximation about $x = 0$.

How do we use the remainder formula? It suggests an upper limit for the error that results if we replace f with its nth Taylor polynomial. Suppose, for instance, that for all x in an interval I, the absolute value of $f^{(n+1)}(x)$ is at most M. Then we can conclude that in this interval

$$|R_{n+1}(x)| \leq \frac{M}{(n+1)!}|x|^{n+1} \qquad [7.12]$$

Note that if n is a large number and if x is close to 0, then $|R_{n+1}(x)|$ is small for two reasons: first, if n is large, the number $(n+1)!$ in the denominator in [7.12] is large; second, if $|x|$ is less than 1, then $|x|^{n+1}$ is also small when n is large.

Example 7.4

Find Taylor's formula for $f(x) = \sqrt{x+25} = (x+25)^{1/2}$ with $n = 1$, and use it to give an estimate of $\sqrt{25.01}$.

Solution   We use the approximation in [7.11]. Here $f(0) = 5$, and

$$f'(x) = \tfrac{1}{2}(x+25)^{-1/2}, \qquad f''(x) = \tfrac{1}{2}(-\tfrac{1}{2})(x+25)^{-3/2}$$

Thus, $f'(0) = 1/2 \cdot 1/5 = 1/10$ and $f''(c) = -(1/4)(c+25)^{-3/2}$. So by [7.11], for some c between 0 and x, one has

$$\sqrt{x+25} = 5 + \frac{1}{10}x + \frac{1}{2}\left(-\frac{1}{4}\right)(c+25)^{-3/2}x^2$$

$$= 5 + \frac{1}{10}x - \frac{1}{8}(c+25)^{-3/2}x^2 \qquad [*]$$

In order to estimate $\sqrt{25.01}$, we write $25.01 = 0.01 + 25$ and use [*]. If $x = 0.01$, then c lies between 0 and 0.01, so $c+25 > 25$. Then $(c+25)^{-3/2} <$

$(25)^{-3/2} = 1/125$, so the absolute value of the remainder is

$$|R(0.01)| = \left| -\frac{1}{8}(c + 25)^{-3/2} \left(\frac{1}{100}\right)^2 \right| \le \frac{1}{80,000} \cdot \frac{1}{125} = 10^{-7}$$

We conclude that $\sqrt{25.01} \approx 5 + 1/10 \cdot 1/100 = 5.001$, with an error less than 10^{-7}.

Note: If we consider the Taylor formula on an interval centered about $x = x_0$, the remainder is

$$R_{n+1}(x) = \frac{1}{(n+1)!} f^{(n+1)}(c)(x - x_0)^{n+1} \qquad (c \text{ is between } x \text{ and } x_0) \qquad [7.13]$$

This term must be added to the right-hand side of (5.11) in order to obtain equality.

Binomial Formulas

Applying Taylor's formula [7.10] to

$$f(x) = (1 + x)^m \qquad (m \text{ is an arbitrary real number}) \qquad [*]$$

gives interesting results. For $x > -1$, we find that

$$f'(x) = m(1 + x)^{m-1}, \qquad\qquad\qquad f'(0) = m$$

$$f''(x) = m(m - 1)(1 + x)^{m-2}, \qquad\qquad f''(0) = m(m - 1)$$

$$\cdots\cdots\cdots\cdots\cdots\cdots\cdots\cdots\cdots\cdots\cdots\cdots\cdots\cdots\cdots\cdots$$

$$f^{(n)}(x) = m(m - 1) \cdots [m - (n - 1)](1 + x)^{m-n}, \quad f^{(n)}(0) = m(m - 1) \cdots [m - (n - 1)]$$

Substitution into [7.10] gives

$$(1+x)^m = 1 + \frac{m}{1!}x + \frac{m(m-1)}{2!}x^2 + \cdots + \frac{m(m-1)\cdots[m-(n-1)]}{n!}x^n + R_{n+1}(x)$$

where

$$R_{n+1}(x) = \frac{m(m-1)\cdots(m-n)}{(n+1)!}x^{n+1}(1+c)^{m-n-1}$$

To simplify the notation, we introduce the definition

$$\binom{m}{k} = \frac{m(m-1)\cdots(m-k+1)}{k!} \qquad (m \text{ is real and } k \text{ is a positive integer})$$

$$[7.14]$$

For instance,

$$\binom{3}{2} = \frac{3 \cdot 2}{1 \cdot 2} = 3, \qquad \binom{1/2}{3} = \frac{(1/2)(1/2 - 1)(1/2 - 2)}{1 \cdot 2 \cdot 3} = \frac{1}{16}$$

In particular, we see that

$$\binom{m}{1} = m \qquad \text{and} \qquad \binom{m}{m} = 1$$

Using this notation, we obtain the following:

Newton's binomial formula (*m* is an arbitrary real number and *n* is a positive integer):

$$(1+x)^m = 1 + \binom{m}{1}x + \cdots + \binom{m}{n}x^n + \binom{m}{n+1}x^{n+1}(1+c)^{m-n-1} \qquad [7.15]$$

for some number *c* between 0 and *x* with $x > -1$.

One can show that for $|x| < 1$ the remainder approaches 0 as *n* approaches infinity. For example, formula [7.15] can be used to compute the *n*th root of different numbers.

Example 7.5

   Compute $\sqrt[3]{1.1}$ to three decimal places.

   Solution   We apply [7.15] with $x = 0.1$, $m = 1/3$, and $n = 2$. (The last choice is a result of trial and error.) We obtain

$$\sqrt[3]{1.1} = 1 + \binom{1/3}{1}(0.1) + \binom{1/3}{2}(0.1)^2 + \binom{1/3}{3}(0.1)^3(1+c)^{1/3-2-1}$$

$$= 1 + \frac{1}{30} - \frac{1}{900} + \frac{1}{16,200}\frac{1}{(1+c)^{8/3}}$$

for some number *c* between 0 and 0.1. The last term is the remainder $R_3(0.1)$, and

$$|R_3(0.1)| = \frac{1}{16,200}\frac{1}{(1+c)^{8/3}} < \frac{1}{16,200} \approx 0.000061728$$

because $(1+c)^{8/3} > 1$ when $c \in (0, 0.1)$. We conclude that $\sqrt[3]{1.1} \approx 1 + 1/30 - 1/900 \approx 1.032$ (to three decimal places).

Newton's Binomial Formula for Positive Integer Exponents

Formula [7.15] is often used in the case where m is a positive integer. From [7.14], we see that if $k > m$, then $m - m = 0$ is a factor in $\binom{m}{k}$. Hence, $\binom{m}{k}$ is 0 for all positive integers $k > m$. Then [7.15] with $n = m$ reduces to

$$(1 + x)^m = 1 + \binom{m}{1}x + \binom{m}{2}x^2 + \cdots + \binom{m}{m}x^m$$

Putting $x = b/a$ and multiplying by a^m yields the following:

Newton's binomial formula (m is a positive integer):

$$(a + b)^m = a^m + \binom{m}{1}a^{m-1}b + \binom{m}{2}a^{m-2}b^2 + \cdots + \binom{m}{m}b^m \qquad [7.16]$$

This formula is discussed further in Section B.2 of Appendix B.

Note: For most functions, Taylor's formula leads to polynomial approximations whose error terms are small provided the degree of the polynomial is sufficiently high. This does not hold true for all functions. An example is given in Problem 10, Section 8.3.

Proof of Lagrange's remainder formula [7.9] We start by proving that the formula is correct for $n = 1$. This means that we want to prove formula [7.11]. For $x \neq 0$, let us define the function $S(x)$ implicitly by the equation

$$f(x) = f(0) + f'(0)x + \tfrac{1}{2}S(x)x^2 \qquad [1]$$

If we can prove that there exists a number c between 0 and x such that $S(x) = f''(c)$, then [7.11] is established. Keep x fixed and define the function g for all t between 0 and x by

$$g(t) = f(x) - \left[f(t) + f'(t)(x - t) + \tfrac{1}{2}S(x)(x - t)^2\right] \qquad [2]$$

Then [1] and [2] imply that $g(0) = f(x) - \left[f(0) + f'(0)x + \tfrac{1}{2}S(x)x^2\right] = 0$ and that $g(x) = f(x) - \left[f(x) + 0 + 0\right] = 0$. So by the mean-value theorem (Theorem 7.5), there exists a number c strictly between 0 and x such that $g'(c) = 0$. Differentiating [2] with respect to t with x fixed, we get

$$g'(t) = -f'(t) + f'(t) - f''(t)(x - t) + S(x)(x - t)$$

Thus,

$$g'(c) = -f''(c)(x - c) + S(x)(x - c)$$

Because $g'(c) = 0$ and $c \neq x$, it follows that $S(x) = f''(c)$. Hence. we have proved [7.11].

The proof in the general case is based on precisely the same idea, with $S(x)$ and $g(t)$ defined by generalizing [1] and [2] in the obvious way. See Problems 4 and 5.

Problems

1. Write Taylor's formula [7.10] with $n = 2$ for $f(x) = 1/(1 + x)$.
2. Use the approximation $(1+x)^m \approx 1 + \binom{m}{1}x + \binom{m}{2}x^2$ to find values of (a) $\sqrt[3]{25}$ and (b) $\sqrt[5]{33}$. Check these approximations by using your calculator. (*Hint:* Note that $\sqrt[3]{25} = 3(1 - 2/27)^{1/3}$.)
3. Show that $\sqrt[3]{9} = 2(1 + 1/8)^{1/3}$. Use formula [7.15] (with $n = 2$) to compute $\sqrt[3]{9}$ to the third decimal.

Harder Problems

4. Prove [7.9] for $n = 2$ as follows. Define $S(x)$ implicitly for $x \neq 0$ by

$$f(x) = f(0) + \frac{x}{1!}f'(0) + \frac{x^2}{2!}f''(0) + \frac{x^3}{3!}S(x) \qquad [1]$$

Define further the function g for $t \in [0, x]$ by

$$g(t) = f(x) - \left[f(t) + \frac{x-t}{1!}f'(t) + \frac{(x-t)^2}{2!}f''(t) + \frac{(x-t)^3}{3!}S(x) \right] \qquad [2]$$

Show that $g(0) = g(x) = 0$, that g is differentiable in $(0, x)$, and moreover $g'(t) = -\frac{1}{2}(x-t)^2[f'''(t) - S(x)]$. Hence, there exists a number $c \in (0, x)$ such that $g'(c) = 0$. Show that the conclusion follows.

5. Generalize the proof of [7.9] given in Problem 4 so that it is valid for an arbitrary natural number n.

7.5 Indeterminate Forms and L'Hôpital's Rule

We often need to examine the limit as x tends to a of a quotient in which both numerator and denominator tend to 0. Then we write[3]

$$\lim_{x \to a} \frac{f(x)}{g(x)} = \frac{\text{``0''}}{0} \qquad [1]$$

---

[3]In this section. we permit ourselves to use the notation "0/0" (with quotes) to represent the particular kind of indeterminacy we are discussing.

We call such a limit an **indeterminate form of type 0/0**. Here a may be replaced by a^+, a^-, or $\pm\infty$. The words "indeterminate form" indicate that the limit cannot be found without further examination. We have already evaluated several such limits. For instance, in Example 4.10(c) in Section 4.4, we used an old trick and the laws for limits to determine that

$$\lim_{x \to 4} \frac{x^2 - 16}{4\sqrt{x} - 8} = 8$$

There is a standard method for the systematic treatment of such indeterminate forms that goes by the name of **l'Hôpital's rule**.

We start with the simple case in which we have an indeterminate form [1] where f and g are differentiable and $f(a) = g(a) = 0$. When $x \neq a$ and $g(x) \neq g(a)$, then some routine algebra shows that

$$\frac{f(x)}{g(x)} = \frac{[f(x) - f(a)]/(x - a)}{[g(x) - g(a)]/(x - a)}$$

As $x \to a$, we see that the numerator and denominator of the right-hand fraction tend to $f'(a)$ and $g'(a)$ respectively (see Problem 5 of Section 4.5). So provided that $g'(a) \neq 0$, the limit is $f'(a)/g'(a)$. Hence:

L'Hôpital's Rule (Simple Version)

If f and g are differentiable at a, with $f(a) = g(a) = 0$ and $g'(a) \neq 0$, then

$$\lim_{x \to a} \frac{f(x)}{g(x)} = \frac{f'(a)}{g'(a)}$$ [7.17]

According to [7.17], we can find the limit of an indeterminate form of type "0/0" by differentiating the numerator and the denominator separately.

Example 7.6
Use [7.17] to find

$$\lim_{x \to 4} \frac{x^2 - 16}{4\sqrt{x} - 8}$$

Solution   Here $f(x) = x^2 - 16$ and $g(x) = 4\sqrt{x} - 8$. So $f(4) = g(4) = 0$, $f'(x) = 2x$, and $g'(x) = 2/\sqrt{x}$. Hence, [7.17] gives

$$\lim_{x \to 4} \frac{x^2 - 16}{4\sqrt{x} - 8} = \frac{\text{``0''}}{0} = \frac{f'(4)}{g'(4)} = \frac{8}{1} = 8$$

Notice how much simpler it is to use [7.17] than to carry out the limit computation used to solve Example 4.10(c).

Example 7.7
Find

$$\lim_{x \to 7} \frac{\sqrt[3]{x+1} - \sqrt{x-3}}{x-7}$$

Solution

$$\lim_{x \to 7} \frac{\sqrt[3]{x+1} - \sqrt{x-3}}{x-7} = \frac{2-2}{7-7} = \frac{\text{``0''}}{0}$$

$$= \lim_{x \to 7} \frac{\frac{1}{3}(x+1)^{-2/3} - \frac{1}{2}(x-3)^{-1/2}}{1}$$

$$= \frac{1}{3}(8^{-2/3}) - \frac{1}{2}(4^{-1/2}) = \frac{1}{12} - \frac{1}{4} = -\frac{1}{6}$$

where the third equality is an implication of l'Hôpital's rule.

Suppose we have a "0/0" form as in [7.17], but that $f'(a)/g'(a)$ is also of the type "0/0". Because $g'(a) = 0$, the argument for [7.17] breaks down. What do we do then? The answer is to differentiate once more both numerator and denominator separately. If we still obtain an expression of the type "0/0", we go on differentiating numerator and denominator repeatedly until the limit is determined (if possible). Here is an example.

Example 7.8
Find

$$\lim_{x \to 2} \frac{x^4 - 4x^3 + 5x^2 - 4x + 4}{x^3 - 2x^2 - 4x + 8}$$

Solution   The numerator and denominator are both 0 at $x = 2$. Applying l'Hôpital's rule twice, we have

$$\lim_{x \to 2} \frac{x^4 - 4x^3 + 5x^2 - 4x + 4}{x^3 - 2x^2 - 4x + 8} = \frac{\text{``0''}}{0} = \lim_{x \to 2} \frac{4x^3 - 12x^2 + 10x - 4}{3x^2 - 4x - 4}$$

$$= \frac{\text{``0''}}{0} = \lim_{x \to 2} \frac{12x^2 - 24x + 10}{6x - 4} = \frac{5}{4}$$

Note: Here are some important warnings concerning the most common errors in applying l'Hôpital's rule:

1. Check that you really do have an indeterminate form; otherwise, the method usually gives an erroneous result (see Problem 3).
2. Do not differentiate f/g as a fraction, but compute f'/g' instead.

The method we have explained here and used to solve Example 7.8 is built on the following theorem. Note that the requirements on f and g are weaker than might have appeared from the examples presented so far. For instance, f and g need not even be differentiable at $x = a$. For a proof, see Bartle (1976), for example.

Theorem 7.8   (L'Hôpital's Rule for "0/0" Forms)   Suppose that f and g are differentiable in an interval (α, β) around a, except possibly at a, and suppose that $f(x)$ and $g(x)$ both tend to 0 as x tends to a. If $g'(x) \neq 0$ for all $x \neq a$ in (α, β), and if $\lim_{x \to a} f'(x)/g'(x) = L$ (L finite, $L = \infty$, or $L = -\infty$), then

$$\lim_{x \to a} \frac{f(x)}{g(x)} = \lim_{x \to a} \frac{f'(x)}{g'(x)} = L$$

[7.18]

Extensions of L'Hôpital's Rule

L'Hôpital's rule can be extended to some other cases. For instance, a can be an endpoint of the interval (α, β). Thus, $x \to a$ can be replaced by $x \to a^+$ or $x \to a^-$. Also it is easy to see that a may be replaced by ∞ or $-\infty$ (see Problem 6). The rule also applies to other indeterminate forms such as "$\pm\infty/\pm\infty$", although the proof is more complicated (see Problem 8 and Bartle (1976)). An easy example is this:

$$\lim_{x \to \infty} \frac{1 - 3x^2}{5x^2 + x - 1} = \frac{\text{``}-\infty\text{''}}{\infty} = \lim_{x \to \infty} \frac{-6x}{10x + 1} = \frac{\text{``}-\infty\text{''}}{\infty} = \lim_{x \to \infty} \frac{-6}{10} = -\frac{3}{5}$$

Indeed, a variety of other indeterminate forms can sometimes be transformed into expressions of the type we have already mentioned by means of algebraic manipulations or substitutions.

Example 7.9
   Find

$$L = \lim_{x \to \infty} (\sqrt[5]{x^5 - x^4} - x)$$

Solution   We reduce this "$\infty - \infty$" case to a "0/0" case by some algebraic manipulation. Note first that for $x \neq 0$,

$$\sqrt[5]{x^5 - x^4} - x = \left[x^5(1 - 1/x) \right]^{1/5} - x = x(1 - 1/x)^{1/5} - x$$

Thus,

$$\lim_{x \to \infty} (\sqrt[5]{x^5 - x^4} - x) = \lim_{x \to \infty} \frac{(1 - 1/x)^{1/5} - 1}{1/x} = \frac{\text{``}0\text{''}}{0}$$

Using l'Hôpital's rule, we have

$$L = \lim_{x\to\infty} \frac{(1/5)\,(1-1/x)^{-4/5}\,(1/x^2)}{-1/x^2} = \lim_{x\to\infty}\left[-\frac{1}{5}\left(1-\frac{1}{x}\right)^{-4/5}\right] = -\frac{1}{5}$$

We shall be able to study many more interesting examples of indeterminate forms after introducing exponential and logarithmic functions in Chapter 8.

Problems

1. Use l'Hôpital's rule to find the following limits:

   a. $\displaystyle\lim_{x\to 1}\frac{x-1}{x^2-1}$
   b. $\displaystyle\lim_{x\to a}\frac{x^2-a^2}{x-a}$
   c. $\displaystyle\lim_{x\to -2}\frac{x^3+3x^2-4}{x^3+5x^2+8x+4}$

2. Find the following limits:

   a. $\displaystyle\lim_{x\to 2}\frac{x^4-4x^3+6x^2-8x+8}{x^3-3x^2+4}$
   b. $\displaystyle\lim_{x\to 0}\frac{2\sqrt{1+x}-2-x}{2\sqrt{1+x+x^2}-2-x}$

3. Find the error in the following:

$$\lim_{x\to 1}\frac{x^2+3x-4}{2x^2-2x} = \lim_{x\to 1}\frac{2x+3}{4x-2} = \lim_{x\to 1}\frac{2}{4} = \frac{1}{2}$$

   What is the correct value of the first limit?

4. Let β and γ be positive constants. Find

$$\lim_{v\to 0^+}\frac{1-(1+v^\beta)^{-\gamma}}{v}$$

   (Consider the three cases $\beta = 1$, $\beta > 1$, and $\beta < 1$ separately.)

5. Examine the following limit for different values of the constants a, b, c, and d, assuming that b and d are positive:

$$\lim_{x\to 0}\frac{\sqrt{ax+b}-\sqrt{cx+d}}{x}$$

Harder Problems

6. Suppose that f and g are both differentiable for all large x, that $f(x)$ and $g(x)$ both tend to 0 as $x \to \infty$, and that $\lim_{x\to\infty} g'(x) \neq 0$. Show that

$$\lim_{x\to\infty}\frac{f(x)}{g(x)} = \text{``}\frac{0}{0}\text{''} = \lim_{x\to\infty}\frac{f'(x)}{g'(x)}$$

   by introducing $x = 1/t$ in the first fraction and then using l'Hôpital's rule as $t \to 0^+$.

7. Following the method used to solve Example 7.9, show that

$$\lim_{x \to \infty} \left(\sqrt[n]{x^n + a_1 x^{n-1} + \cdots + a_{n-1}x + a_n} - x \right) = \frac{a_1}{n}$$

8. Suppose that $\lim_{x \to a} f(x)/g(x) = $ "$\pm\infty/\pm\infty$" $= L$. By applying l'Hôpital's rule to the equivalent limit, $\lim_{x \to a} \left[1/g(x)\right]/\left[1/f(x)\right] = $ "$0/0$", show that $L = \lim_{x \to a}[f'(x)/g'(x)]$ provided this limit exists and is $\neq 0$.

7.6 Inverse Functions

This section takes a closer look at inverse functions of one variable. They were briefly discussed in Section 3.6. We start with an economic problem.

Example 7.10

Suppose that the demand quantity D for a commodity depends on the price per unit p according to

$$Dp^{1/3} = 30 \qquad (p > 0, \ D > 0) \qquad [1]$$

To most people, it seems natural to solve equation [1] for D. The result is

$$D = \frac{30}{p^{1/3}} = 30p^{-1/3} \qquad [2]$$

which tells us directly the demand D corresponding to a given price p. If, for example, $p = 27$, then $D = 30/27^{1/3} = 10$. So D is a function of p. That is, $D = f(p)$ with $f(p) = 30/p^{1/3}$.

If we look at the matter from a firm's point of view, however, it may be more natural to treat output as something it can choose and consider the resulting price. From equation [1], we obtain $p^{1/3} = 30/D$ and $(p^{1/3})^3 = (30/D)^3$, so that [1] is equivalent to

$$p = \frac{27,000}{D^3} = 27,000D^{-3} \qquad [3]$$

This equation gives us directly the price p corresponding to a given output D. For example, if $D = 10$, then $p = 27,000/10^3 = 27$. In this case, p is a function $g(D)$ of D, with $g(D) = 27,000/D^3$.

The two variables D and p in this example are related in a way that allows each of them to be considered as a function of the other. The two functions

$$f(p) = 30p^{-1/3} \qquad \text{and} \qquad g(D) = 27,000D^{-3} \qquad [4]$$

are called *inverses* of each other. We say also that f is the inverse of g, and that g is the inverse of f.

General Definition

Given a function f defined on a domain A of real numbers, we often need to find the inverse of f, assuming there is one. Recall that if f has domain A, then the range of f is the set $B = \{f(x) : x \in A\}$, which is also denoted by $f(A)$. The range B consists of all numbers $f(x)$ that one can obtain by letting x vary in A. Furthermore, f is **one-to-one** on A if f never has the same value at any two different points in A. In other words, f is one-to-one in A provided it has the property that, whenever x_1 and x_2 both lie in A and $x_1 \neq x_2$, then $f(x_1) \neq f(x_2)$. It is evident that if a function is strictly increasing in all of A, or strictly decreasing in all of A, then it is one-to-one. A particular one-to-one function f is illustrated in Fig. 7.12, and another function g that is not one-to-one is shown in Fig. 7.13.

FIGURE 7.12 f **is one-to-one with domain A and range B. f has an inverse.**

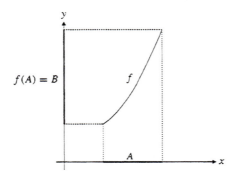

FIGURE 7.13 g **is *not* one-to-one and has therefore no inverse over A. Which value of x should be associated with y_1?**

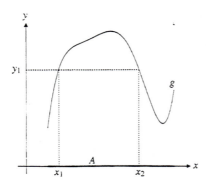

Definition of an Inverse Function

Let f be a function with domain A and range B. If f is one-to-one (and only then), it has an **inverse function** g with domain B and range A. The function g is given by the following rule: For each $y \in B$, the value $g(y)$ is the unique number x in A such that $f(x) = y$. Then

$$g(y) = x \iff y = f(x) \qquad (x \in A, \ y \in B) \qquad\qquad [7.19]$$

Replace y by $f(x)$ in the left-hand equation of [7.19] to get $g(f(x)) = x$. And replace x by $g(y)$ in the right-hand equation to get $f(g(y)) = y$. Thus, it is a direct consequence of [7.19] that

$$g(f(x)) = x \text{ for all } x \in A \qquad \text{and} \qquad f(g(y)) = y \text{ for all } y \in B \qquad [7.20]$$

The equation $g(f(x)) = x$ shows that if we first apply f to x and then g to $f(x)$, then we get x back: *g undoes what f did to x*. Let us check that this is valid for the particular pair of functions given by [4] in Example 7.10. In fact,

$$g(f(p)) = g\left(30p^{-1/3}\right) = \frac{27,000}{\left(30p^{-1/3}\right)^3} = \frac{27,000}{27,000p^{-1}} = p$$

(Prove for yourself that $f(g(D)) = D$ also.)

Note: If g is the inverse of f, one often uses the notation f^{-1} for g. This notation sometimes leads to excusable confusion. If a is a number, then a^{-1} means $1/a$. But $f^{-1}(x)$ does *not* mean $1/f(x)$. For example: *The functions defined by the equations $y = 1/(x^2 + 2x + 3)$ and $y = x^2 + 2x + 3$ are* **not** *inverses of each other, but reciprocals.* In fact, $1/f(x)$ is generally written as $[f(x)]^{-1}$.

In simple cases, we can use the same method as in Example 7.10 to find the inverse of a given function (and hence automatically verify that the inverse exists). Some more examples follow.

Example 7.11

Solve the following equations for x and find the corresponding inverse functions:

$$\textbf{(a)} \quad y = 4x - 3 \qquad \textbf{(b)} \quad y = \sqrt[5]{x+1} \qquad \textbf{(c)} \quad y = \frac{3x-1}{x+4}$$

Solution

(a) Solving the equation for x, we have the following equivalences for all x and all y:

$$y = 4x - 3 \iff 4x = y + 3 \iff x = \tfrac{1}{4}y + \tfrac{3}{4}$$

We conclude that $f(x) = 4x - 3$ and $g(y) = y/4 + 3/4$ are inverses of each other.

(b) Also in this case, we solve the equation for x. We begin by raising each side to the fifth power and so obtain the logical equivalences

$$y = \sqrt[5]{x+1} \iff y^5 = x+1 \iff x = y^5 - 1$$

These are valid for all x and all y. Hence, we have shown that $f(x) = \sqrt[5]{x+1}$ and $g(y) = y^5 - 1$ are inverses of each other.

(c) We solve the given equation for x by first multiplying both sides by $x + 4$:

$$y(x + 4) = 3x - 1$$

From this equation, we obtain

$$yx + 4y = 3x - 1 \quad \text{or} \quad x(3 - y) = 4y + 1$$

Hence,

$$x = \frac{4y + 1}{3 - y}$$

We conclude that $f(x) = (3x - 1)/(x + 4)$ and $g(y) = (4y + 1)/(3 - y)$ are inverses of each other. Observe that f is only defined for $x \neq -4$, and g is only defined for $y \neq 3$. So the equivalence in [7.19] is valid only with these restrictions.

In all the examples examined so far, the inverse could be expressed in terms of known formulas. It turns out that even if a function has an inverse, it may be impossible to express it in terms of a function we know. *Inverse functions are actually an important source of new functions.*

Suppose that a differentiable function f is defined on an interval I. How can we determine if f has an inverse in cases where we are unable to solve $y = f(x)$ for x? The following criterion is easy to use:

If f is differentiable, then f has an inverse on I provided that: either (a) $f'(x) > 0$ for all x in the interval I; or (b) $f'(x) < 0$ for all x in I.   [7.21]

The argument is simple: if $f'(x) > 0$ (< 0) for all x, then f is strictly increasing (decreasing), and hence one-to-one. Note that the conclusion in [7.21] is actually still valid if $f'(x) > 0$ except at a finite number of points (see the *Note* to

Theorem 7.6 of Sec. 7.3). Note too that [7.21] is sufficient but not necessary for f to have an inverse; in fact, $y = x^3$ has an inverse $x = \sqrt[3]{y}$ even though $dy/dx = 0$ at $x = 0$.

Example 7.12

Show that the function f defined for all x by

$$f(x) = 3x^9 + x^3 - 6x^2 + 12x - 8$$

has an inverse.

Solution   Differentiating $f(x)$ yields

$$f'(x) = 27x^8 + 3x^2 - 12x + 12 = 27x^8 + 3(x - 2)^2$$

We see that $f'(x) > 0$ for all x. So according to [7.21], f has an inverse. This means that the equation $y = 3x^9 + x^3 - 6x^2 + 12x - 8$ defines x as a function of y. In this case, however, it is impossible to find an explicit formula for x in terms of y; the inverse can be numerically approximated only.

A Geometric Characterization of Inverse Functions

In Example 7.10, we saw that $f(p) = 30p^{-1/3}$ and $g(D) = 27,000D^{-3}$ were inverse functions. Because of the concrete interpretation of symbols p and D, it was natural to describe the functions the way we did.

   In other circumstances, it may be convenient to use the same variable as argument in both f and g. In Example 7.11(a), we saw that $f(x) = 4x - 3$ and $g(y) = \frac{1}{4}y + \frac{3}{4}$ were inverses of each other. If also we use x instead of y as the variable of the function g, we find that

$$f(x) = 4x - 3 \quad \text{and} \quad g(x) = \tfrac{1}{4}x + \tfrac{3}{4} \quad \text{are inverses of each other} \quad [*]$$

In the same way, on the basis of Example 7.11(b) we can say that

$$f(x) = (x + 1)^{1/5} \quad \text{and} \quad g(x) = x^5 - 1 \quad \text{are inverses of each other} \ [**]$$

There is an interesting geometric property of the graphs of inverse functions. For the pairs of inverse functions in [*] and [**], the graphs of f and g are mirror images of each other with respect to the line $y = x$. This point is illustrated in Figs. 7.14 and 7.15.

   Suppose in general that f and g are inverses of each other. The fact that (a, b) lies on the graph f means that $b = f(a)$. According to [7.19], this implies that $g(b) = a$, so that (b, a) lies on the graph of g. Because (a, b) and (b, a)

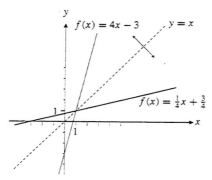

FIGURE 7.14

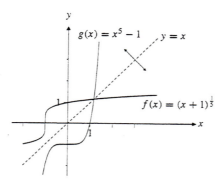

FIGURE 7.15

lie symmetrically about the line $y = x$ (see Problem 8), we have the following conclusion:

> When two functions f and g are inverses of each other, then the graphs of $y = f(x)$ and $y = g(x)$ are symmetric about the line $y = x$. (For this to be true the units on the coordinate axes must be same.) [7.22]

Note: When f and g are inverses of each other, then by definition [7.19], the equations $y = f(x)$ and $x = g(y)$ are equivalent. They represent exactly the same graph. On the other hand, the graphs of $y = f(x)$ and $y = g(x)$ are symmetric about the line $y = x$.

Suppose that f is a one-to-one function defined in an interval I. Then f has an inverse function g. What properties of f are "inherited" by g? If we rely on geometric intuition, the answers are simple: Because the graphs of f and g are symmetric about $y = x$, continuity and differentiability of f (except at points where $f'(x) = 0$) must be inherited by g.

What is the relation between the derivatives of f and g? *Assume* that both f and g are differentiable. The identity $g(f(x)) = x$ can be differentiated with respect to x, using the chain rule. The result is $g'(f(x))f'(x) = 1$. Solving for $g'(f(x))$ when $f'(x) \neq 0$, we obtain

$$g'(y) = \frac{1}{f'(x)} \qquad (y = f(x)) \tag{7.23}$$

If $f'(x) = 0$, then the graph of g has a vertical tangent line at (y, x), and g is *not* differentiable at y.

It follows from [7.23] that f' and g' have the same sign. Thus, either both the functions are strictly increasing, or both are strictly decreasing.

The previous results were built partly on intuitive geometric ideas. We formulate the most important facts in the following theorem:

Theorem 7.9 (Theorem on Inverse Functions) If f is continuous and strictly increasing (or strictly decreasing) in an interval I, then f has an inverse function g that is continuous and strictly increasing (strictly decreasing) in the interval $f(I)$. If x_0 is an interior point of I and f is differentiable at x_0 with $f'(x_0) \neq 0$, then g is differentiable at point $y_0 = f(x_0)$ (which is interior to $f(I)$) and

$$g'(y_0) = \frac{1}{f'(x_0)} \tag{7.24}$$

Note: Formula [7.24] is used as follows to find the derivative of g at a point y_0. First find, if possible, the point x_0 in I at which $f(x_0) = y_0$. Thereafter, compute $f'(x)$, and then find $f'(x_0)$. If $f'(x_0) \neq 0$, then g has a derivative at y_0 given by $g'(y_0) = (f'(x_0))^{-1}$.

Example 7.13
Use formula [7.24] to find $g'(-8)$ if g is the inverse of the function

$$f(x) = 3x^9 + x^3 - 6x^2 + 12x - 8$$

discussed in Example 7.12. (Note that $f(0) = -8$.)

Solution We use formula [7.24] with $x_0 = 0$ and $y_0 = -8$. Because $f'(0) = 12$, we obtain $g'(-8) = 1/f'(0) = 1/12$. Note that we have found $g'(-8)$ even though it is impossible to find a formula for the function g.

In the examples studied so far, it has been easy to find the domains and the ranges of the pairs of functions f and g. Sometimes we must be very careful to find the correct inverse. If we use x as the free variable for both functions, then we proceed as follows to find the inverse of a function f defined in an interval I:

How to find the inverse of $y = f(x)$:

1. Write the equation that defines the function

$$y = f(x)$$

2. Interchange x and y to obtain

$$x = f(y)$$

3. Solve the equation $x = f(y)$ for y in terms of x (if possible), with $x \in f(I)$ and $y \in I$. If the solution $y = g(x)$ is always unique, then the function g is the inverse function.

[7.25]

Let us look at a simple example.

Example 7.14

Find the inverse of $y = x^{p/q}$ (defined for $x > 0$), where p and q are integers.

Solution   The recipe in [7.25] yields

(1) $y = x^{p/q}$ (2) $x = y^{p/q}$ (3) $y = x^{q/p}$

The inverse of $y = x^{p/q}$ is therefore $y = x^{q/p}$.

Example 7.15

Prove that the function $f(x) = \sqrt{3x + 9}$ defined in the interval $[-3, \infty)$ has an inverse, and find a formula for the inverse. (See Fig. 7.16.)

Solution   We have $f'(x) = (3/2)\sqrt{3x + 9} > 0$ for all $x > -3$, so f is strictly increasing in the interval $[-3, \infty)$ (see Theorem 7.6). Note that the range of f is $[0, \infty)$. Thus, f has an inverse g defined in $[0, \infty)$. To find the formula for the inverse, we again use the recipe in [7.25]:

(1) $y = \sqrt{3x + 9}$ (2) $x = \sqrt{3y + 9}$
(3) $x^2 = 3y + 9$,   that is, $y = \frac{1}{3}x^2 - 3$

Thus, the inverse function is $g(x) = \frac{1}{3}x^2 - 3$ defined in $[0, \infty)$. The graphs of f and g are given in Fig. 7.16.

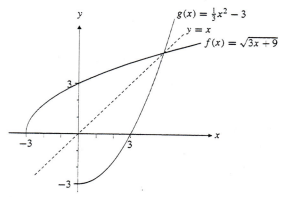

$g(x) = \frac{1}{3}x^2 - 3$

$y = x$

$f(x) = \sqrt{3x + 9}$

FIGURE 7.16

Problems

1. Demand D as a function of price p is given by

$$D = \frac{32}{5} - \frac{3}{10}p$$

Solve the equation for p and find the inverse function.

2. The demand D for sugar in the United States in the period 1915–1929, as a function of the price p, was estimated by H. Schultz as

$$D = f(p) = \frac{157.8}{p^{0.3}} \qquad (D \text{ and } p \text{ are measured in appropriate units})$$

Solve the equation for p and so find the inverse of f.

3. Find the inverses of the functions given by the formulas
  (a) $y = -3x$ (b) $y = 1/x$ (c) $y = x^3$
  Check that [7.20] is valid in each case.

4. Why does $f(x) = x^2$, for $x \in (-\infty, \infty)$, have no inverse function? Show that f restricted to $[0, \infty)$ has an inverse, and find that inverse.

5. Use the method in [7.25] to find the inverses of the following functions:
  (a) $f(x) = (x^3 - 1)^{1/3}$ (b) $f(x) = (x + 1)/(x - 2)$
  (c) $f(x) = (1 - x^3)^{1/5} + 2$

6. Show that the following function has an inverse function g:

$$f(x) = x^7 + 5x^5 + 2x - 2$$

Compute $g'(-2)$ using [7.24]. (*Hint:* $f(0) = -2$.)

7. Let f be defined on $[0, 1]$ by $f(x) = 2x^2 - x^4$.
   a. Find the range of f.
   b. Show that f has an inverse function g, and find a formula for g.

8. a. Draw a coordinate system in the plane. Show that points $(3, 1)$ and $(1, 3)$ are symmetric about the line $y = x$, and the same for $(5, 3)$ and $(3, 5)$.
   b. Use properties of congruent triangles to prove that points (a, b) and (b, a) in the plane are symmetric about the line $y = x$.

9. Formalize the following statements:
   a. Halving and doubling are inverse operations.
   b. The operation of multiplying a number by 3 and then subtracting 2 is the inverse of the operation of adding 2 to the number and then dividing by 3.
   c. The operation of subtracting 32 from a number and then multiplying the result by 5/9 is the inverse of the operation of multiplying a number by 9/5 and then adding 32. (See Problem 4 in Section 1.3.)

10. Draw the graph of a function f that is one-to-one, but neither strictly increasing nor strictly decreasing. (*Hint:* f cannot be continuous.)

11. If f is the function that tells you how many kilograms of meat you can buy for a specified amount of money, then what does f^{-1} tell you?

12. Suppose that f and g are twice differentiable functions that are inverses of each other, so that $f(g(x)) = x$ for all x. Express g'' in terms of f' and f''. Show that if $f' > 0$, then f'' and g'' have opposite signs. Show that if $f' < 0$, then f'' and g'' have the same sign.

13. Explain why the function f defined on $[0, \sqrt{3}]$ by

$$f(x) = \tfrac{1}{3}x^3\sqrt{4 - x^2}$$

has an inverse function g. Compute $g'(\tfrac{1}{3}\sqrt{3})$. (*Hint:* $f(1) = \tfrac{1}{3}\sqrt{3}$.)

Harder Problem

14. Find the inverse of $f(x) = \sqrt{x + 1} + \sqrt{x - 1} = (x + 1)^{1/2} + (x - 1)^{1/2}$ defined for $x \geq 1$.

=8=

Exponential and Logarithmic Functions

Exponential functions of the form a^x were briefly considered in Sections 3.5. They were shown to be well suited to describing certain economic phenomena such as growth and compound interest. This chapter shows how such functions can be differentiated. And it introduces logarithms, which are inverses of exponential functions. Logarithms also feature in an alternative definition of elasticity.

8.1 The Natural Exponential Function

Recall that an exponential function with base a is

$$f(x) = a^x$$

where a is the factor by which $f(x)$ changes when x increases by 1. Each base a gives a different exponential function. In mathematics, one particular value of a gives an exponential function that is far more important than the others. One might guess that $a = 2$ or $a = 10$ would be this special base. Strangely enough, it turns out that an irrational number a little larger than 2.7 is the most important base for an exponential function.

In order to explain why, we must study the derivative of $f(x) = a^x$. Earlier rules of differentiation cannot help here. So we rely on the definition of the

247

derivative and consider the Newton quotient of $f(x) = a^x$, which is

$$\frac{f(x+h) - f(x)}{h} = \frac{a^{x+h} - a^x}{h} \qquad [*]$$

If this fraction tends to a limit as h tends to 0, then $f(x) = a^x$ is differentiable and $f'(x)$ is precisely equal to this limit.

Substituting $x = 0$ in $[*]$ and letting $h \to 0$ yields in particular

$$f'(0) = \lim_{h \to 0} \frac{a^h - 1}{h} \qquad [8.1]$$

(provided the limit exists).

The fraction in $[*]$ can be simplified if we use the rule $a^{x+h} = a^x \cdot a^h$. Then we have $a^{x+h} - a^x = a^x(a^h - 1)$, so that

$$\frac{f(x+h) - f(x)}{h} = a^x \cdot \frac{a^h - 1}{h}$$

When taking the limit of this last expression as h tends to 0, the term a^x is a constant, whereas according to [8.1], the fraction $(a^h - 1)/h$ tends to $f'(0)$. Hence,

$$f(x) = a^x \implies f'(x) = a^x f'(0) \qquad [8.2]$$

We have thus shown that if $f(x) = a^x$ has a derivative at 0 (in the sense that the limit in [8.1] exists), then f is differentiable for every x, and $f'(x) = a^x f'(0)$. *Note:* Observe that $f'(0)$ is a function of a. For each $a > 0$, the number $f'(0)$ is defined as the limit of $(a^h - 1)/h$ as h tends to 0. One can prove that this limit exists for every $a > 0$. Later we shall see that $f'(0) = \ln a$, the natural logarithm of a.

Geometrically, $f'(0)$ may be interpreted as the slope of the tangent to the graph of $y = a^x$ at $(0, 1)$. In Figs. 8.1 and 8.2 we have measured these slopes for

FIGURE 8.1

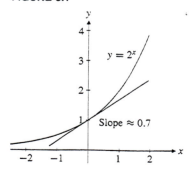

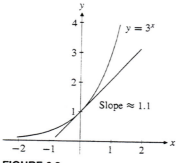

FIGURE 8.2

2^x and 3^x, and they are respectively ≈ 0.7 and ≈ 1.1. (Accordingly, [8.2] implies that $f(x) = 2^x \implies f'(x) \approx 0.7 \cdot 2^x$, and $f(x) = 3^x \implies f'(x) \approx 1.1 \cdot 3^x$.)

It is reasonable to assume that, as a increases from 2 to 3, so $f'(0)$ increases from ≈ 0.7 to ≈ 1.1 without skipping any intermediate values. For some value a between 2 and 3, we ought then to have $f'(0) = 1$ in particular. This value of a is a fundamental constant in mathematical analysis. It is an irrational number so distinguished that it is usually denoted by the single letter e, and is given by

$$e = 2.7\,1828\,1828\,4590\,45\ldots$$

Because $a = e$ is precisely the choice of a that gives $f'(0) = 1$ in [8.2], we obtain

$$f(x) = e^x \implies f'(x) = e^x \qquad [8.3]$$

The **natural exponential function** $f(x) = e^x$, *therefore has the remarkable property that its derivative is equal to the function itself.* This is the main reason why the function appears so often in mathematics and applications. Observe also that $f''(x) = e^x$. Because $e^x > 0$ for all x, both $f'(x)$ and $f''(x)$ are positive. Hence, both f and f' are strictly increasing. This confirms the shape of the graph in Fig. 8.3.

Powers with e as their base are difficult to compute by hand—even $e^1 = e$. A scientific calculator with an $\boxed{e^x}$ function key can do this immediately, however. For instance, one finds that $e^{0.5} \approx 1.6487$, $e^{-\pi} \approx 0.0432$.

By combining [8.3] with other rules of differentiation, we can differentiate complicated expressions involving the exponential function e^x. Before looking at some special examples, let us consider general functions of the form $y = e^{g(x)}$. To

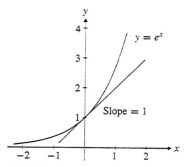

FIGURE 8.3 **The natural exponential function.**

differentiate these we apply the chain rule $dy/dx = dy/du \cdot du/dx$ with $y = e^u$ and $u = g(x)$. Thus, $y' = e^u u' = e^{g(x)} g'(x)$, and so

$$y = e^{g(x)} \quad \Longrightarrow \quad y' = e^{g(x)} g'(x) \qquad\qquad [8.4]$$

Example 8.1
Differentiate the following:

    (a) $y = e^{3x}$ **(b)** $y = e^x/x$ **(c)** $y = \sqrt{e^{2x} + x}$

Solution

    (a) Use [8.4] with $g(x) = 3x$. Then $g'(x) = 3$ so $y = e^{3x} \Longrightarrow y' = e^{3x} \cdot 3 = 3e^{3x}$.

    (b) Using the quotient rule yields

$$y = \frac{e^x}{x} \Longrightarrow y' = \frac{e^x x - e^x \cdot 1}{x^2} = \frac{e^x(x - 1)}{x^2}$$

    (c) Here $y = \sqrt{e^{2x} + x} = \sqrt{u}$, with $u = e^{2x} + x$, and so $u' = 2e^{2x} + 1$, where we used the chain rule. Using the chain rule again yields

$$y = \sqrt{e^{2x} + x} = \sqrt{u} \Longrightarrow y' = \frac{1}{2\sqrt{u}} \cdot u' = \frac{2e^{2x} + 1}{2\sqrt{e^{2x} + x}}$$

Example 8.2
Find the derivative of

$$f(x) = x^2 e^x$$

Where is $f(x)$ increasing? (Its graph is drawn in Fig. 9.23 of Sec. 9.5.)

Solution   Differentiating using the product rule yields

$$f'(x) = 2xe^x + x^2 e^x = xe^x(2+x)$$

We see that $f'(x) = 0$ for $x = 0$ and for $x = -2$. The accompanying sign diagram tells us that f is increasing in the intervals $(-\infty, -2]$ and $[0, \infty)$ (but decreasing in $[-2, 0]$).

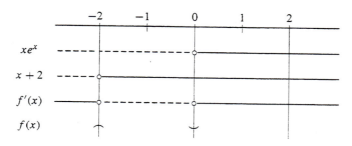

Note 1: A common error when differentiating exponential functions is to believe that the derivative of e^x is "xe^{x-1}". This is due to confusing the exponential function with a power function.

Note 2: Sometimes the notation $\exp(u)$ is used in place of e^u. If u is a complicated expression like $x^3 + x\sqrt{x - 1/x}$, it is easier (typographically) to read and write $\exp(x^3 + x\sqrt{x - 1/x})$ instead of $e^{x^3 + x\sqrt{x-1/x}}$.

A Survey of the Properties of e^x

The natural exponential function

$$f(x) = e^x \qquad (e = 2.71828\ldots)$$

is differentiable and strictly increasing for all real numbers x. In fact,   [8.5]

$$f(x) = e^x \implies f'(x) = f(x) = e^x$$

The following properties hold for all exponents s and t:

(a) $e^s e^t = e^{s+t}$ (b) $e^s/e^t = e^{s-t}$ (c) $(e^s)^t = e^{st}$

Problems

1. Differentiate the following functions, using the chain rule:

    a. $y = e^{-3x}$ **b.** $y = 2e^{x^3}$ **c.** $y = e^{1/x}$ **d.** $y = 5e^{2x^2 - 3x + 1}$

2. Find the following:

   a. $\dfrac{d}{dx}\left(e^{e^x}\right)$ **b.** $\dfrac{d}{dt}\left(e^{t/2} + e^{-t/2}\right)$

   c. $\dfrac{d}{dt}\left(\dfrac{1}{e^t + e^{-t}}\right)$ **d.** $\dfrac{d}{dz}\left(e^{z^3} - 1\right)^{1/3}$

3. Consider the function f defined for all x by $f(x) = xe^x$.
   a. Compute $f'(x)$ and $f''(x)$. Find the intervals on which f is increasing.
   b. Draw the graph of f.

4. In an economic model, the number of families with income $\leq x$ is given by

   $$p(x) = a + k(1 - e^{-cx}) \qquad (a, k, \text{ and } c \text{ are positive constants})$$

   Determine $p'(x)$ and $p''(x)$, and then draw the graph of p.

5. Let $f(x) = (x^2 - 2x - 3)e^x$. Draw the graph of f for $-4 \leq x \leq 3$.

Harder Problems

6. The expressions $\frac{1}{2}(e^x - e^{-x})$ and $\frac{1}{2}(e^x + e^{-x})$ occur so often that they have been given the special symbols

   $$\sinh x = \frac{e^x - e^{-x}}{2}, \qquad \cosh x = \frac{e^x + e^{-x}}{2}$$

   indicating the *hyperbolic sine* and *hyperbolic cosine* respectively. Draw the graphs of the two functions, and show that the following formulas hold for all x:
   a. $\cosh(x + y) = \cosh x \cosh y + \sinh x \sinh y$
   b. $\cosh 2x = (\cosh x)^2 + (\sinh x)^2$
   c. $\sinh(x + y) = \sinh x \cosh y + \cosh x \sinh y$
   d. $\sinh 2x = 2 \sinh x \cosh x$
   e. $(\cosh x)^2 - (\sinh x)^2 = 1$
   f. $\sinh^2 x = \frac{1}{2}(\cosh 2x - 1)$
   g. $\frac{d}{dx}(\sinh x) = \cosh x$
   h. $\frac{d}{dx}(\cosh x) = \sinh x$

7. Show by induction that the nth derivative of xe^x is $(x + n)e^x$.

8. Let $f(x) = a^x$. Show that

   $$f(z + x) = f(z)f(x) \qquad \text{(for all } x \text{ and } z) \qquad [*]$$

   Assume that f is differentiable. Differentiate [*] with respect to z (holding x fixed), and then put $z = 0$. Explain why this gives an alternative justification for [8.2].

8.2 The Natural Logarithmic Function

In Section 3.5, the doubling time of an exponential function $f(t) = a^t$, with $a > 1$, was defined as the time it takes for $f(t)$ to become twice as large. In order to find the doubling time t^*, we must solve the equation $a^{t^*} = 2$ for t^*. In economics, we often need to solve similar problems:

1. At the present rate of inflation, how long will it take the price level to triple?
2. If the national debt of the U.S. continues to grow at the present proportional rate, how long will it take to reach $10 trillion?
3. If $1000 is invested in a savings account bearing interest at the rate of 8% per annum, how long does it take for the account to reach $10,000?

All these questions involve solving equations of the form $a^x = b$ for x. For instance, problem 3 is to find which x solves the equation $1000(1.08)^x = 10,000$, or $(1.08)^x = 10$.

We begin with equations in which the base of the exponentials is e. Here are some examples:

$$e^x = 4 \tag{1}$$

$$5e^{-3x} = 16 \tag{2}$$

$$A\alpha e^{-\alpha x} = k \tag{3}$$

In all these equations, the unknown occurs as an exponent. We therefore introduce the following useful definition. If $e^u = a$, we call u the **natural logarithm** of a, and we write $u = \ln a$. Hence, we have the following definition of the symbol $\ln a$:

$$e^{\ln a} = a \qquad (a \text{ is any positive number}) \tag{8.6}$$

Thus, $\ln a$ is the power of e you need to get a.

Because e^u is a strictly increasing function of u, it follows that $\ln a$ is uniquely determined by the definition [8.6]. You should memorize this definition. It is the foundation for everything in this section, and for a good part of what comes later. In the following, we practice applying this definition.

Example 8.3
Find the following:

(a) $\ln 1$ (b) $\ln e$ (c) $\ln(1/e)$ (d) $\ln 4$ (e) $\ln(-6)$

Solution

(a) $\ln 1 = 0$, because $e^0 = 1$ and so 0 is the power of e that you need to get 1.

(b) $\ln e = 1$, because $e^1 = e$ and so 1 is the power of e that you need to get e.

(c) $\ln(1/e) = \ln e^{-1} = -1$, because -1 is the power of e that you need to get $1/e$.

(d) $\ln 4$ is the power of e you need to get 4. Because we have $e^1 \approx 2.7$ and $e^2 = e^1 \cdot e^1 \approx 7.3$, the number $\ln 4$ must lie between 1 and 2. By experimenting with the $\boxed{e^x}$ key on a scientific calculator, you should able to find a good approximation to $\ln 4$ by trial and error. However, it is easier to press 4 and the $\boxed{\ln x}$ key. Then you find that $\ln 4 \approx 1.386$. Thus, $e^{1.386} \approx 4$.

(e) $\ln(-6)$ would be the power of e you need to get -6. Because e^x is positive for all x, it is obvious that $\ln(-6)$ must be undefined.

Box [8.7] collects some useful rules for natural logarithms. All are simple implications of the rules for powers.

Useful Rules for ln

$$\ln(xy) = \ln x + \ln y \qquad (x \text{ and } y \text{ are positive}) \qquad \text{(a)}$$

(The logarithm of a product is equal to the *sum* of the logarithms of each of the factors.)

$$\ln \frac{x}{y} = \ln x - \ln y \qquad (x \text{ and } y \text{ are positive}) \qquad \text{(b)}$$

(The logarithm of a quotient is equal to the *difference* between the logarithms of its numerator and denominator.)

[8.7]

$$\ln x^p = p \ln x \qquad (x \text{ is positive}) \qquad \text{(c)}$$

(The logarithm of a power is equal to the exponent multiplied by the logarithm of the base.)

$$\ln 1 = 0, \qquad \ln e = 1, \qquad x = e^{\ln x} \qquad \text{and} \qquad \ln e^x = x \qquad \text{(d)}$$

To show (a), observe first that the definition of $\ln(xy)$ implies that $e^{\ln(xy)} = xy$. Furthermore, $x = e^{\ln x}$ and $y = e^{\ln y}$, so

$$e^{\ln(xy)} = xy = e^{\ln x} e^{\ln y} = e^{\ln x + \ln y} \qquad [*]$$

where we have used property [8.5](a). In general, $e^u = e^v$ implies $u = v$, so we conclude from [*] that $\ln(xy) = \ln x + \ln y$. The proofs of (b) and (c) are based on properties [8.5](b) and (c), respectively, and are left to the reader. Finally, [8.7](d) displays some important properties for convenient reference.

Warning: There are no simple rules for the logarithms of sums and differences. It *is* tempting to replace $\ln(x + y)$ by $\ln x + \ln y$, for instance, but this is quite wrong. In fact, $\ln x + \ln y$ is equal to $\ln(xy)$, not to $\ln(x + y)$.

There are no simple formulas for $\ln(x + y)$ and $\ln(x - y)$

Here are some examples that apply the previous rules.

Example 8.4

Express each of (a) $\ln 4$, (b) $\ln \sqrt[3]{2^5}$, and (c) $\ln(1/16)$ in terms of $\ln 2$.

Solution

(a) $\ln 4 = \ln(2 \cdot 2) = \ln 2 + \ln 2 = 2 \ln 2$. (Or $\ln 4 = \ln 2^2 = 2 \ln 2$.)

(b) We have $\sqrt[3]{2^5} = 2^{5/3}$. Therefore, $\ln \sqrt[3]{2^5} = \ln 2^{5/3} = (5/3) \ln 2$.

(c) $\ln(1/16) = \ln 1 - \ln 16 = 0 - \ln 2^4 = -4 \ln 2$. (Or $\ln(1/16) = \ln 2^{-4} = -4 \ln 2$.)

Example 8.5

Solve the following equations for x:

(a) $5e^{-3x} = 16$ (b) $A\alpha e^{-\alpha x} = k$

(c) $(1.08)^x = 10$ (d) $e^x + e^{-x} = 2$

Solution

(a) Take $\ln$ of each side of the equation to obtain $\ln(5e^{-3x}) = \ln 16$. The product rule gives $\ln(5e^{-3x}) = \ln 5 + \ln e^{-3x}$. Here $\ln e^{-3x} = -3x \ln e = -3x$, because $\ln e = 1$. Hence, $\ln 5 - 3x = \ln 16$, which gives

$$x = \tfrac{1}{3}(\ln 5 - \ln 16) = \tfrac{1}{3} \ln \tfrac{5}{16}$$

(b) We argue as in (a) and obtain $\ln(A\alpha e^{-\alpha x}) = \ln k$, or $\ln(A\alpha) + \ln e^{-\alpha x} = \ln k$, so $\ln(A\alpha) - \alpha x = \ln k$. Finally, therefore,

$$x = \frac{1}{\alpha}[\ln(A\alpha) - \ln k] = \frac{1}{\alpha} \ln \frac{A\alpha}{k}$$

(c) Again we take the $\ln$ of each side of the equation and obtain $x \ln 1.08 = \ln 10$. So the solution is $x = \ln 10 / \ln 1.08$, which is ≈ 29.9. Thus, it takes just short of 30 years for $1 to increase to $10 when the interest rate is 8%.

(d) It is very tempting to begin with $\ln(e^x + e^{-x}) = \ln 2$, but this leads nowhere, because $\ln(e^x + e^{-x})$ cannot be further evaluated. Instead, we argue like this: Putting $u = e^x$ gives $e^{-x} = 1/e^x = 1/u$, so the equation is $u + 1/u = 2$, or $u^2 + 1 = 2u$. Solving this quadratic equation for u yields $u = 1$ as the only solution. Hence, $e^x = 1$, and so $x = 0$. (Check this solution. Consider also the graph of $\cosh x$ in Problem 6 of Section 8.1.)

The Function $g(x) = \ln x$

For each positive number x, the number $\ln x$ is defined by $e^{\ln x} = x$. We call the function

$$g(x) = \ln x \qquad (x > 0) \qquad\qquad [8.8]$$

the **natural logarithmic function**. This definition is illustrated in Fig. 8.4. Think of x as a point moving upwards on the vertical axis from the origin. As x increases from values less than 1 to values greater than 1, so $g(x)$ increases from negative to positive values. In fact, because $f(u) = e^u$ is strictly increasing with range $(0, \infty)$, it follows from Theorem 7.9 of Section 7.6 that f *has* an inverse function g that is also strictly increasing with domain $(0, \infty)$. Because f has the domain $(-\infty, \infty)$, we know that g has the range $(-\infty, \infty)$. Thus, the exponential function $f(x) = e^x$ and the natural logarithm function $g(x) = \ln x$ are inverses of each other. In particular, we have (see (7.20)):

$$\ln e^x = x \qquad \text{for all } x$$

$$e^{\ln y} = y \qquad \text{for all } y > 0$$

FIGURE 8.4 Illustration of the definition of $g(x) = \ln x$.

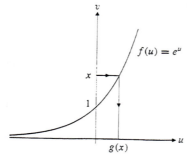

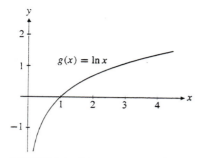

FIGURE 8.5   The graph of the natural logarithmic function $g(x) = \ln x$.

In Fig. 8.5 we have drawn the graph of $g(x) = \ln x$. The shape of this graph ought to be remembered. According to Example 8.3, we have $g(1/e) = -1$, $g(1) = 0$, and $g(e) = 1$. Observe that this corresponds well with the graph.

Differentiation of Logarithmic Functions

If we assume that $g(x) = \ln x$ has a derivative for all $x > 0$, then this derivative can be easily found. Differentiate implicitly the equation

$$e^{g(x)} = x \qquad\qquad [*]$$

with respect to x, using the result in [8.4]. This gives

$$e^{g(x)} g'(x) = 1$$

Because $e^{g(x)} = x$, so $x g'(x) = 1$. Hence:

$$g(x) = \ln x \quad\Longrightarrow\quad g'(x) = \frac{1}{x} \qquad\qquad [8.9]$$

Thus, the derivative of $\ln x$ at point x is simply the number $1/x$. For $x > 0$, we have $g'(x) > 0$, so that $g(x)$ is *strictly* increasing. Note moreover that $g''(x) = -1/x^2$, which is less than 0 for all $x > 0$, so that $g'(x)$ is *strictly* decreasing. This confirms the shape of the graph in Fig. 8.5. In fact, the growth of $\ln x$ is quite slow. For example, $\ln x$ first attains the value 10 when $x > 22,026$, because $\ln x = 10$ gives $x = e^{10} \approx 22,026.5$.

Note: We derived [8.9] *assuming* that $g(x) = \ln x$ was differentiable. In fact, by Theorem 7.9 in Section 7.6, the logarithmic function g *is* differentiable. Because the derivative of $f(x) = e^x$ is e^x, applying (7.24) to $y_0 = e^{x_0}$ tells us that $g'(y_0) = 1/e^{x_0} = 1/y_0$. This is the same as [8.9], except that the symbol y_0 has replaced x.

Often, we need to consider composite functions involving natural logarithms. Because $\ln u$ is defined only when $u > 0$, a composite function of the form $y = \ln h(x)$ will only be defined for values of x satisfying $h(x) > 0$.

Combining the rule for differentiating $\ln x$ with the chain rule allows us to differentiate many different types of function. Suppose, for instance, that $y = \ln h(x)$, where $h(x)$ is differentiable and positive. By the chain rule, $y = \ln u$ with $u = h(x)$ implies that $y' = (1/u)u' = \left[1/h(x)\right]h'(x)$, so:

$$y = \ln h(x) \quad \Longrightarrow \quad y' = \frac{h'(x)}{h(x)} \qquad\qquad [8.10]$$

Example 8.6

Find the domains of the following functions and compute their derivatives:

(a) $y = \ln(1 - x)$ (b) $y = \ln(4 - x^2)$

(c) $y = \ln\left[(x - 1)/(x + 1)\right] - \frac{1}{4}x$

Solution

(a) $\ln(1-x)$ is defined if $1 - x > 0$, that is, if $x < 1$. To find the derivative, we use [8.10] with $h(x) = 1 - x$. Then $h'(x) = -1$, so by [8.10],

$$y' = \frac{-1}{1 - x}$$

(b) $\ln(4 - x^2)$ is defined if $4 - x^2 > 0$, that is, if $(2 - x)(2 + x) > 0$. This is true if $-2 < x < 2$. Formula [8.10] yields

$$y' = \frac{-2x}{4 - x^2}$$

(c) We require that $(x - 1)/(x + 1) > 0$. A sign diagram shows this to be satisfied if $x < -1$ or $x > 1$. We have $y = \ln u - \frac{1}{4}x$, where $u = (x - 1)/(x + 1)$. Using [8.10], we find that

$$f'(x) = \frac{u'}{u} - \frac{1}{4}$$

where

$$u' = \frac{1 \cdot (x + 1) - 1 \cdot (x - 1)}{(x + 1)^2} = \frac{2}{(x + 1)^2}$$

Thus,

$$f'(x) = \frac{2(x+1)}{(x+1)^2(x-1)} - \frac{1}{4} = \frac{9 - x^2}{4x^2 - 4} = \frac{(3-x)(3+x)}{4(x-1)(x+1)}$$

Note: If we apply the quotient rule [8.7](b) for ln to the formula in (c) of Example 8.6, we obtain

$$f(x) = \ln(x-1) - \ln(x+1) - \tfrac{1}{4}x \qquad [*]$$

By differentiating this expression, it is easier to derive a correct formula for $f'(x)$. But note that the expression in [*] is only defined when $x > 1$, whereas the formula in (c) is also defined for $x < -1$. The point is that the formula $\ln(p/q) = \ln p - \ln q$ is correct only when p and q are both positive, whereas $\ln(p/q)$ also is meaningful when p and q are both negative. Then $\ln(p/q) = \ln(-p) - \ln(-q)$.

Logarithmic Differentiation

When differentiating an expression containing products, quotients, roots, powers, and combinations of these, it is often an advantage to use **logarithmic differentiation**. The method is illustrated by the following example:

Example 8.7

Find the derivative of

$$y = A\frac{x^p(ax+b)^q}{(cx+d)^r} \qquad [1]$$

Solution   First, take the natural logarithm of each side to obtain

$$\ln y = \ln A + p \ln x + q \ln(ax+b) - r \ln(cx+d)$$

Differentiation with respect to x yields

$$\frac{y'}{y} = p\frac{1}{x} + q\frac{1}{ax+b}a - r\frac{1}{cx+d}c$$

Multiplying by y, which is given by [1], yields

$$y' = A\frac{x^p(ax+b)^q}{(cx+d)^r} \cdot \left(\frac{p}{x} + \frac{aq}{ax+b} - \frac{cr}{cx+d} \right)$$

A Survey of the Properties of ln

The natural logarithmic function

$$g(x) = \ln x$$

is differentiable and strictly increasing for all $x > 0$. In fact,

$$g'(x) = 1/x$$

The following properties hold for all $x > 0$, $y > 0$:

   (a) $\ln(xy) = \ln x + \ln y$ (b) $\ln(x/y) = \ln x - \ln y$ (c) $\ln x^p = p \ln x$

Moreover, $\ln e^x = x$ for all real x, and

$$\ln x \to -\infty \text{ as } x \to 0^+, \qquad \ln x \to \infty \text{ as } x \to \infty$$

Problems

1. Express the following in terms of $\ln 3$:

   a. $\ln 9$ **b.** $\ln \sqrt{3}$ **c.** $\ln \sqrt[5]{3^2}$ **d.** $\ln \dfrac{1}{81}$

2. Solve the following equations for x:

   a. $3^x = 8$ **b.** $\ln x = 3$ **c.** $\ln(x^2 - 4x + 5) = 0$

   d. $\ln[x(x - 2)] = 0$ **e.** $\dfrac{x \ln(x + 3)}{x^2 + 1} = 0$ **f.** $\ln(\sqrt{x} - 5) = 0$

3. Solve the following equations for x:

   a. $3^x 4^{x+2} = 8$ **b.** $3 \ln x + 2 \ln x^2 = 6$ **c.** $4^x - 4^{x-1} = 3^{x+1} - 3^x$

4. Solve the following equations for t:

   a. $x = e^{at+b}$ **b.** $e^{-at} = 1/2$ **c.** $\dfrac{1}{\sqrt{2\pi}} e^{-t^2} = \dfrac{1}{8}$

5. Prove the following equalities (with appropriate restrictions on the variables):

   a. $\ln x - 2 = \ln(x/e^2)$
   b. $\ln x - \ln y + \ln z = \ln(xz/y)$
   c. $3 + 2 \ln x = \ln(e^3 x^2)$
   d. $\dfrac{1}{2} \ln x - \dfrac{3}{2} \ln \dfrac{1}{x} - \ln(x + 1) = \ln \dfrac{x^2}{x + 1}$
   e. $-p_1 \ln p_1 - p_2 \ln p_2 - \cdots - p_n \ln p_n = \displaystyle\sum_{i=1}^{n} p_i \ln(1/p_i)$

6. True or false: (a) $\pi^e < e^\pi$ and   (b) $\sqrt[e]{e} > \sqrt[\pi]{\pi}$?

7. Decide whether the following formulas are always correct or sometimes wrong (all variables are positive):

   a. $(\ln A)^4 = 4 \ln A$ **b.** $\ln B = 2 \ln \sqrt{B}$ **c.** $\ln A^{10} - \ln A^4 = 3 \ln A^2$

8. Decide whether the following formulas are always correct or sometimes wrong (all variables are positive):

a. $\ln \dfrac{A + B}{C} = \ln A + \ln B - \ln C$ **b.** $\ln \dfrac{A + B}{C} = \ln(A + B) - \ln C$

c. $\ln \dfrac{A}{B} + \ln \dfrac{B}{A} = 0$ **d.** $p \ln(\ln A) = \ln(\ln A^p)$

e. $p \ln(\ln A) = \ln(\ln A)^p$ **f.** $\dfrac{\ln A}{\ln B + \ln C} = \ln A(BC)^{-1}$

9. Determine the domains of the functions given by the following:

a. $y = \ln(x + 1)$ **b.** $y = \ln \dfrac{3x - 1}{1 - x}$ **c.** $y = \ln|x|$

d. $y = \ln(x^2 - 1)$ **e.** $y = \ln(\ln x)$ **f.** $y = \dfrac{1}{\ln(\ln x) - 1}$

10. Find the derivatives of the functions defined by the following:

a. $\ln(x + 1)$ **b.** $\ln x + 1$ **c.** $x \ln x$ **d.** $\dfrac{x}{\ln x}$

11. Find the derivatives of the functions defined by the following:

a. $\ln(\ln x)$ **b.** $\ln \sqrt{(1 - x^2)}$ **c.** $e^x \ln x$

d. $e^{x^3} \ln x^2$ **e.** $\ln(e^x + 1)$ **f.** $\ln(x^2 + 3x - 1)$

12. Find the equation of the tangent line for the following:
  a. $y = \ln x$ at the point with the x-coordinate: (i) 1; (ii) $\frac{1}{2}$; and (iii) e.
  b. $y = xe^x$ at the point with the x-coordinate: (i) 0; (ii) 1; and (iii) -2.

13. Use logarithmic differentiation to find the derivatives of the following:

a. $f(x) = \left(\dfrac{x + 1}{x - 1} \right)^{1/3}$ **b.** $f(x) = x^x$

c. $f(x) = \sqrt{x - 2}\,(x^2 + 1)(x^4 + 6)$

14. If $f(x) = e^x - 1 - x$, then $f(0) = 0$ and $f'(x) = e^x - 1 > 0$ for all $x > 0$. Hence, $f(x)$ is strictly increasing and $f(x) > 0$ for all $x > 0$, so $e^x > 1 + x$ for all $x > 0$. Prove the following inequalities using the same method.
  a. $e^x > 1 + x + x^2/2$ for $x > 0$
  b. $\frac{1}{2}x < \ln(1 + x) < x$ for $0 < x < 1$
  c. $\ln \left(\dfrac{1 + t}{1 - t} \right) > 2t$ for $0 < t < 1$

15. Consider the function f defined for all x by

$$f(x) = e^{x-1} - x$$

a. Show that $f(x) \geq 0$ for all x. (*Hint:* Study the sign of $f'(x)$. Draw the graph.)

b. Show that the equation $e^{x-1} - x = 1$ has precisely two solutions.

c. Define the function g by the formula

$$g(x) = \frac{1}{\ln(e^{x-1} - x)}$$

For which x is g defined? Examine $g(x)$ as $x \to \infty$ and $x \to -\infty$.
d. Draw the graph of g.

16. Simplify the following expressions:

    a. $\exp\left[\ln(x)\right] - \ln\left[\exp(x)\right]$ **b.** $\ln\left[x^4 \exp(-x)\right]$

    c. $\exp\left[\ln(x^2) - 2\ln y\right]$

17. The *extreme-value distribution* in statistics is given by

$$F(x) = \exp\left[-\exp(-x)\right]$$

    a. Write $F(x)$ in standard form.
    b. Compute $f(x) = F'(x)$, and write the result in two ways.
    c. Function f is called the *density function* associated with F. Compute $f'(x)$.

18. The elasticity of $y = f(x)$ with respect to x is defined in Section 5.6 as

$$\mathrm{El}_x y = \frac{x}{y} y'$$

Use this definition to find the elasticities of the following:

    a. $y = e^x$ **b.** $y = \ln x$ **c.** $y = a^x$

19. Compute the elasticities of the following functions (where a and δ are constants, $\delta \neq 0$):

    a. $y = e^{ax}$ **b.** $y = x^3 e^{2x}$ **c.** $y = x\ln(x+1)$ **d.** $y = (x^{-\delta} + 1)^{-1/\delta}$

20. Differentiate the following functions using logarithmic differentiation:

    a. $x^{\sqrt{x}}$ **b.** $\left(\sqrt{x}\right)^x$ **c.** $x^{(x^x)}$

21. Show by logarithmic differentiation that if u and v are differentiable functions of x, and if $u > 0$, then

$$y = u^v \implies y' = u^v \left(v'\ln u + \frac{vu'}{u}\right)$$

22. In an article on production theory, the function

$$F(\alpha) = a \left(\frac{N^\alpha K^\alpha}{N^\alpha + bK^\alpha}\right)^{v/\alpha} \qquad (a,\, b,\, v,\, N, \text{ and } K \text{ are positive constants})$$

was studied. Find an expression for $F'(\alpha)$.

23. Find the inverse of $y = \sinh x = \frac{1}{2}(e^x - e^{-x})$. (See Problem 6 in Section 8.1.) (*Hint:* You will have to solve a quadratic equation for $u = e^x$.)

8.3 Generalizations

Every positive number a can be written in the form $a = e^{\ln a}$, so using the general property $(e^r)^s = e^{rs}$, we have the formula

$$a^x = (e^{\ln a})^x = e^{x \ln a}$$

just replace a with $e^{\ln a}$ & you get $(e^{\ln a})^x$

In problems where function a^x occurs, we can just as easily work with the special exponential function e^{bx}, where b is a constant equal to $\ln a$. In particular, we can differentiate a^x by differentiating $e^{x \ln a}$. Letting $g(x) = x \ln a$ and applying the chain rule [8.4], we obtain the following:

$$\ast \qquad y = a^x \implies y' = a^x \ln a \qquad\qquad\qquad [8.11]$$

If $a = 10$, for example, then $y = 10^x \implies y' = 10^x \ln 10$. Whereas if $a = e$, we obtain $y = e^x \implies y' = e^x$, because $\ln e = 1$.

Note: Comparing [8.11] with [8.2] in Section 8.1, we see that $f'(0) = \ln a$. From the definition of $f'(0)$ in [8.1], it follows that $(a^h - 1)/h \to \ln a$ as $h \to 0$. Replacing a by x, we have

$$\lim_{h \to 0} \frac{x^h - 1}{h} = \ln x \qquad (x > 0)$$

Let us take a closer look at this limit. For any $h > 0$, define the function g_h by[1]

$$g_h(x) = \frac{x^h - 1}{h}$$

for all $x > 0$. Then

$$\lim_{h \to 0} g_h(x) = \lim_{h \to 0} \frac{x^h - 1}{h} = \ln x$$

In fact, $\ln x$ is bounded above by each of the functions $g_h(x)$ ($h > 0$). To see this, consider for each $h > 0$ the function $F_h(x) = g_h(x) - \ln x = (x^h - 1)/h - \ln x$

---

[1] Function g_h and its limit as h approaches 0 are related to the well known Box–Cox transformation in statistics.

$\ast \; a^x = x^{x \ln a} = e^{x \ln a} = e^{g(x)}$ let $g(x) = x \ln a$ $\implies \frac{da}{dx} = \frac{de^{x \ln a}}{dx} = \frac{de^{x \ln a}}{dx \ln a} \cdot \frac{dx \ln a}{dx} = e^{x \ln a} \cdot \ln a = a^x \ln a$

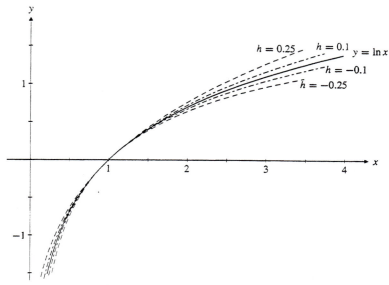

FIGURE 8.6 $y = (x^h - 1)/h$ $(h = \pm 0.25, \pm 0.1)$ and $y = \ln x$.

defined for $x > 0$. Then $F_h(1) = 0$ and

$$F_h'(x) = \frac{hx^{h-1}}{h} - \frac{1}{x} = \frac{x^h - 1}{x} \begin{cases} < 0, & \text{if } 0 < x < 1 \\ > 0, & \text{if } x > 1 \end{cases}$$

Thus, $F_h(x)$ decreases from positive values to 0 when $0 < x < 1$, but increases from 0 to positive values when $x > 1$. It follows that $F_h(x) > 0$ for all $x > 0$, except at $x = 1$, and so

$$g_h(x) = \frac{x^h - 1}{h} > \ln x \qquad \text{(for all } x > 0, \ x \neq 1)$$

Figure 8.6 illustrates how $g_h(x)$ tends to $\ln x$ as h tends to 0.

Logarithms with Bases Other Than e

Recall that we defined $\ln x$ as the exponent to which we must raise the base e in order to obtain x. From time to time, it is useful to have logarithms based on numbers other than e. For many years, until the use of mechanical and then electronic calculators became widespread, tables of logarithms to the base 10 were frequently used to simplify complicated calculations involving multiplication, division, square roots, and so on.

Suppose that a is a fixed positive number (usually chosen > 1). If $a^u = x$, then we call u the **logarithm of x to base a** and write $u = \log_a x$. The symbol $\log_a x$ is then defined for every positive number x by the following:

$$a^{\log_a x} = x \qquad\qquad [8.12]$$

For instance, $\log_2 32 = 5$, because $2^5 = 32$, whereas $\log_{10}(1/100) = -2$, because $10^{-2} = 1/100$. By taking the ln of each side of [8.12], we obtain

$$\log_a x \cdot \ln a = \ln x$$

so that

$$\log_a x = \frac{1}{\ln a} \ln x \qquad\qquad [8.13]$$

This reveals that the logarithm of x in the system with base a is proportional to $\ln x$, *with a proportionality factor* $1/\ln a$. It follows immediately that $\log_a$ obeys the same rules as ln (compare [8.7] of Section 8.2):

Rules for $\log_a$

$$\log_a(xy) = \log_a x + \log_a y \qquad\qquad (a)$$

$$\log_a \frac{x}{y} = \log_a x - \log_a y \qquad\qquad (b) \qquad [8.14]$$

$$\log_a x^p = p \log_a x \qquad\qquad (c)$$

$$\log_a 1 = 0 \quad \text{and} \quad \log_a a = 1 \qquad\qquad (d)$$

For example, 8.14(a) follows from the corresponding rule [8.7](a) for ln:

$$\log_a(xy) = \frac{1}{\ln a} \ln(xy) = \frac{1}{\ln a}(\ln x + \ln y)$$

$$= \frac{1}{\ln a} \ln x + \frac{1}{\ln a} \ln y = \log_a x + \log_a y$$

From [8.13] and [8.9], we obtain

$$y = \log_a x \quad \Longrightarrow \quad y' = \frac{1}{\ln a} \frac{1}{x} \qquad\qquad [8.15]$$

A Characterization of the Number e

In Section 8.2, we showed by implicit differentiation that if $g(x) = \ln x$ is differentiable, then $g'(x) = 1/x$. More specifically, $g'(1) = 1$. If we use the *definition* of $g'(1)$ and [8.7](c), together with the fact that $\ln 1 = 0$, we obtain

$$1 = g'(1) = \lim_{h \to 0} \frac{\ln(1+h) - \ln 1}{h} = \lim_{h \to 0} \frac{1}{h} \ln(1+h) = \lim_{h \to 0} \ln(1+h)^{1/h}$$

Because $\ln(1+h)^{1/h}$ tends to 1 as h tends to 0, it follows that $(1+h)^{1/h}$ itself must tend to e, and so

$$e = \lim_{h \to 0} (1+h)^{1/h} \qquad [8.16]$$

TABLE 8.1   *Values of* $(1+h)^{1/h}$

h	1	1/2	1/10	1/1000	1/100000	1/1000000
$(1+h)^{1/h}$	2.00	2.25	2.5937...	2.7169...	2.71825...	2.718281828...

Table 8.1 has been computed using a scientific calculator. The results seem to confirm that the decimal expansion we gave for e is correct. From the table, we can see that a closer and closer approximation to e is obtained by choosing h smaller and smaller. If we let $h = 1/n$, where the natural number n becomes larger and larger, we obtain the following:

$$e = \lim_{n \to \infty} (1 + 1/n)^n \qquad [8.17]$$

Another Important Limit

If a is an arbitrary number greater than 1, then $a^x \to \infty$ as $x \to \infty$. For example, $(1.0001)^x \to \infty$ as $x \to \infty$. Furthermore, if p is an arbitrary positive number, then $x^p \to \infty$ as $x \to \infty$. If we compare $(1.0001)^x$ and x^{1000}, it is clear that the former increases quite slowly at first, whereas the latter increases very quickly. Nevertheless, $(1.0001)^x$ eventually "overcomes" x^{1000}. In general, we claim the following:

$$\lim_{x \to \infty} \frac{x^p}{a^x} = 0 \qquad (a > 1, \ p \text{ is a fixed number}) \qquad [8.18]$$

For example x^2/e^x and $x^{10}/(1.1)^x$ will both tend to 0 as x tends to ∞. The result [8.18] is actually quite remarkable. It can be expressed briefly by saying that, for an arbitrary base greater than 1, *the exponential function increases faster than any power of x.* Even more succinctly: *"Exponentials drown powers."*

To prove [8.18], it suffices to prove that $\ln(x^p/a^x) \to -\infty$ as $x \to \infty$, for then $x^p/a^x \to 0$ as $x \to \infty$ (see Fig. 8.5). In fact,

$$\ln \frac{x^p}{a^x} = p \ln x - x \ln a = x \left(p \frac{\ln x}{x} - \ln a \right)$$

Because $a > 1$, we have $\ln a > 0$. If we could show that

$$\frac{\ln x}{x} \to 0 \qquad \text{as} \qquad x \to \infty \tag{8.19}$$

then we would be able to infer that $p(\ln x/x) - \ln a \to -\ln a$, and so the proof would be complete. But [8.19] is an easy consequence of l'Hôpital's rule for the "$\pm\infty/\pm\infty$" case. In fact,

$$\lim_{x \to \infty} \frac{\ln x}{x} = \frac{``\infty"}{\infty} = \lim_{x \to \infty} \frac{1/x}{1} = 0$$

The General Power Function

In Section 4.5 we claimed that, for all real numbers a,

$$f(x) = x^a \implies f'(x) = ax^{a-1} \tag{*}$$

Actually, however, we did not even define x^a for irrational values of a. Now we can give such a definition for all $x > 0$. Because $x = e^{\ln x}$, we can define

$$x^a = (e^{\ln x})^a = e^{a \ln x}$$

Using the chain rule, we obtain

$$\frac{d}{dx}(x^a) = \frac{d}{dx}(e^{a \ln x}) = e^{a \ln x} \cdot \frac{a}{x} = x^a \frac{a}{x} = ax^{a-1}$$

In this way, the differentiation rule [*] is proved also when a is an irrational number.

Taylor's Formula for e^x

If $f(x) = e^x$, then all the derivatives of f are equal to e^x, and so the kth derivative of f at $x = 0$ is 1—that is, $f^{(k)}(0) = 1$ for $k = 1, 2, \ldots, n$. Therefore, Taylor's theorem [7.10] in Section 7.4 says that, for some number c between 0 and x, one has

$$e^x = 1 + \frac{x}{1!} + \frac{x^2}{2!} + \cdots + \frac{x^n}{n!} + \frac{x^{n+1}}{(n+1)!}e^c \qquad [8.20]$$

One can show that for every fixed number x, the remainder in [8.20] approaches 0 as n approaches infinity. So [8.20] allows one to compute the value of e^x for any x to an arbitrary degree of accuracy. However, if $|x|$ is large, we must be prepared to use a large number of terms in order to obtain a good approximation, because the remainder in this case approaches 0 very slowly as n approaches infinity—indeed, the early terms will grow bigger quite fast before eventually starting to decline.

Let us see what estimate of $e^{0.1} = \sqrt[10]{e}$ emerges when $n = 3$. Putting $x = 0.1$ and $n = 3$ in [8.20] yields

$$e^{0.1} = 1 + \frac{1}{10} + \frac{1}{200} + \frac{1}{6000} + \frac{(0.1)^4}{24}e^c \qquad [*]$$

for some c in the interval $(0, 0.1)$. Because $c < 0.1$, so $e^c < e^{0.1} < 1.2$, where the last inequality holds because $(e^{0.1})^{10} = e < (1.2)^{10} \approx 6.2$. Hence,

$$0 < \frac{(0.1)^4}{24}e^c < \frac{1}{240000} 1.2 = 0.000005$$

So when we drop the remainder in [*], the error that results is less than 0.000005. The approximation $e^{0.1} \approx 1 + 0.1 + 0.005 + 0.00017 = 1.10517$ is accurate to five decimal places.

Problems

1. Compute the following:

   a. $\log_5 25$ **b.** $\log_5 \sqrt{125}$ **c.** $\log_5 1/25$ **d.** $\log_{10} 100^{-3}$

2. Find x for the following:

   a. $\log_2 x = 2$ **b.** $\log_x e^2 = 2$ **c.** $\log_3 x = -3$ **d.** $\log_{10} x^2 = 100$

3. Differentiate the functions given by the following:

   a. $y = 5 \cdot 3^x$ **b.** $y = 2^x \ln x$ **c.** $y = x \log_2 x$ **d.** $y = \log_2 \sqrt{1 + x^2}$

4. Solve for x:

   a. $\dfrac{e^{x+1}}{e^{4/x}} = e$ **b.** $\left[\ln(x + e)\right]^3 - \left[\ln(x + e)^2\right]^2 = \ln(x + e) - 4$

5. Solve the following inequalities:

   a. $\ln x \leq -1$ **b.** $\ln(x^2 - x - 1) \geq 0$ **c.** $\ln x + \ln(x - 3) \leq \ln 4$

6. By using l'Hôpital's rule (Theorem 7.8 in Section 7.5), or otherwise, determine the following limits:

   a. $\lim\limits_{x \to 0} \dfrac{e^x - 1}{x}$

   b. $\lim\limits_{t \to 0} \dfrac{e^{t+1} - e^{t-1}}{t^2}$

   c. $\lim\limits_{x \to 2} \dfrac{\ln(x - 1)}{\sqrt{2+x} - \sqrt{8 - x^2}}$

   d. $\lim\limits_{x \to \infty} x^{1/x}$

   e. $\lim\limits_{x \to 0^+} x \ln x$

   f. $\lim\limits_{x \to 0^+} x^x$

7. Evaluate the limit

$$\lim_{\lambda \to 0^+} \frac{x^\lambda - y^\lambda}{\lambda}$$

where x and y are positive constants.

8. For the following functions, find Taylor approximations of order 3 about $x = 0$ by using [5.11] in Section 5.5. (You can partly check the results by using [8.20].)

   a. xe^x

   b. e^{2x}

   c. $x^2 + e^{x/2}$

   d. $\sqrt{e^x + 1}$

9. Use Taylor polynomials of degree 3 to find approximate solutions of the equation

$$\tfrac{1}{3}x^3 + x(e^x + e^{-x}) - (e^x - e^{-x}) - x = 0$$

Harder Problems

10. For the function $f(x) = e^{-1/x^2}$ $(x \neq 0)$, $f(0) = 0$, verify that $f^{(k)}(x) = x^{-3k} p_k(x) e^{-1/x^2}$ $(x \neq 0)$, where $p_k(x)$ denotes some polynomial whose degree is $2k - 2$. Hence, show that $f^{(k)}(0) = 0$ for all positive integers k. (For this function, *all* Taylor polynomials at the origin are identically equal to 0, but the function itself is 0 only at the origin. The lesson of this example is that in order to be certain that the Taylor polynomials of a function give a good approximation to the function, one *must* estimate the size of the remainder.)

8.4 Applications of Exponentials and Logarithms

Suppose that $f(t)$ denotes the stock of some quantity at time t. The ratio $f'(t)/f(t)$ is the *relative* or *proportional rate of increase* of the stock at time t. In many applications, the relative rate of increase is a constant r. Then

$$f'(t) = rf(t) \qquad \text{(for all } t) \tag{8.21}$$

Which functions have a constant relative rate of increase? Functions of the type $f(t) = Ae^{rt}$ certainly have, because $f'(t) = Are^{rt} = rf(t)$. We claim that there are no other functions having this property. Suppose that g is *any* function satisfying $g'(t) = rg(t)$, for all t. Define a new function h by $h(t) = g(t)e^{-rt}$. Then $h'(t) = g'(t)e^{-rt} + g(t)(-r)e^{-rt} = e^{-rt}[g'(t) - rg(t)]$, which is 0 for all t. Thus, $h(t) = A$ for some constant A, so that $g(t) = Ae^{rt}$. Hence, we have proved that

$$f'(t) = rf(t) \quad \text{for all } t \iff f(t) = Ae^{rt} \quad \text{for a constant } A \qquad [8.22]$$

We now consider some applications where [8.22] is important.

Ecology

Suppose that $f(t)$ denotes the number of individuals in a population at time t. The population could be, for instance, a particular colony of bacteria, or the polar bears in the Arctic. We call $f'(t)/f(t)$ the *per capita rate of increase* of the population. If there is neither immigration nor emigration, then the per capita rate of increase of the population will be equal to the difference between the per capita birth and death rates. These rates will depend on many factors such as food supply, age distribution, available living space, predators, disease, and parasites, among other things.

Equation [8.21] specifies a very simple model of population increase. The result [8.22] implies that the population must grow exponentially. In reality, of course, exponential growth can go on only for a limited time. Instead of assuming that the relative rate of increase is constant, it is more realistic to assume that once the population is above a certain quantity K (called the population's *carrying capacity*), the per capita rate of increase is negative. A special form of this assumption is expressed by the equation

$$f'(t) = rf(t)\left(1 - \frac{f(t)}{K}\right) \qquad [8.23]$$

Observe that when the population $f(t)$ is small in proportion to K, so that $f(t)/K$ is small, then $f'(t) \approx rf(t)$, and $f(t)$ increases (approximately) exponentially. As $f(t)$ becomes larger, however, the factor $1 - f(t)/K$ increases in significance. In general, one can show (see Problem 8) that if $f(t)$ satisfies [8.23] (and is not identically equal to 0), then $f(t)$ must have the form

$$f(t) = \frac{K}{1 + Ae^{-rt}} \qquad \text{(for some constant } A) \qquad [8.24]$$

If there are N_0 individuals at time $t = 0$, then $f(0) = N_0$, and [8.24] gives $N_0 = K/(1 + A)$, so that $A = (K - N_0)/N_0$. Provided that $N_0 < K$, then $A > 0$. So it follows from [8.24] that $f(t)$ is strictly increasing, and $f(t) \to K$ as $t \to \infty$ (assuming that $r > 0$). The graph of $f(t)$ is shown in Fig. 8.7.

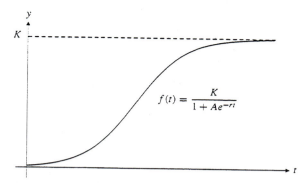

FIGURE 8.7   Logistic growth towards the level *K*.

Equations like [8.23] with solutions of the form [8.24] appear in numerous models—see, for instance, Problems 5 and 6. Function f defined by [8.24] is called a **logistic function.**

Log-Linear Relations

Suppose that two variables x and y are related by the equation

$$y = Ax^a \qquad (x, y, \text{ and } A \text{ are positive}) \qquad [1]$$

Let log denote the logarithm to any base. By taking the log of each side of [1] while applying the rules [8.14], we find that [1] is equivalent to the equation

$$\log y = \log A + a \log x \qquad [2]$$

From [2], we see that $\log y$ is a linear function of $\log x$, and so we say that [1] is a *log-linear* relation between x and y. The transformation from [1] to [2] is often seen in economic models, usually with natural logarithms. (See Problems 9 and 10, for example.)

Suppose that the relation between the two positive variables x and y is set out in a table. Make a new table for the relation between $\ln x$ and $\ln y$. Plot the results in a new coordinate system where $\ln x$ and $\ln y$ are measured along the two axes. If, to a good approximation, the resulting points are all on a straight line, then the relation between x and y will be approximately of the form $y = Ax^a$. (In Section 15.7 we show how to find a straight line that, in a certain precise sense, fits the data as well as possible.)

Example 8.8

Table 8.2 is from *Consumer Survey 1980–1982* (published by the Norwegian Central Bureau of Statistics, 1984). It gives the relationship between y, consumption expenditure on health care, and x, total consumption expenditure, for married couples without children whose total consumption expenditure was below 150,000 Norwegian crowns. For this purpose, the population has been divided into four different consumption expenditure groups.

TABLE 8.2   *From the Consumer Survey 1980–1982*

x	28,316	49,412	77,906	122,085
y	664	1028	1501	2010

(a) Make a table for the relation between $\ln x$ and $\ln y$, and plot this data in a coordinate system where $\ln x$ and $\ln y$ are measured along the two axes.

(b) Roughly fit a straight line through the point pairs in the resulting diagram, and construct an empirical formula for y as a function of x.

Solution

(a) We construct Table 8.3.

TABLE 8.3

$\ln x$	10.25	10.81	11.26	11.71
$\ln y$	6.50	6.94	7.31	7.61

(b) The straight line we have drawn through the two extreme points in Fig. 8.8 seems to give a good approximation to all the numbers in the table. The equation for the line is of the form $\ln y = \ln A + a \ln x$.

FIGURE 8.8

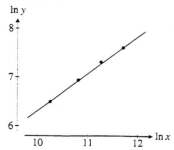

Using the extreme points $(10.25, 6.50)$ and $(11.71, 7.61)$, we find that the slope of the line is

$$a = \frac{7.61 - 6.5}{11.71 - 10.25} = \frac{1.11}{1.46} \approx 0.76$$

If we require the line to pass through $(11.71, 7.61)$, then $7.61 = \ln A + 0.76 \cdot 11.71$. Hence, $\ln A = 7.61 - 0.76 \cdot 11.71 = -1.2896$, so that $A = e^{-1.2896} \approx 0.275$. The relation between y and x is then

$$y = 0.275\, x^{0.76}$$

Suppose that y is an exponential function

$$y = Aa^x \qquad (a \text{ and } A \text{ are positive})$$

Taking the log of each side gives

$$\log y = \log A + x \log a \qquad\qquad [*]$$

We see that in this case $\log y$ becomes *a linear function of x*. In a coordinate system where there is an ordinary (linear) scale on the horizontal axis and a $\log y$ scale along the vertical axis, $[*]$ represents a straight line with slope $\log a$.

Elasticities and Logarithmic Differentiation

In Example 5.20 of Section 5.6, we considered the demand function $D(p) = 8000p^{-1.5}$ and showed that the elasticity $\text{El}_p D = (p/D)\,(dD/dp)$ is equal to the exponent -1.5. Taking natural logarithms of this demand relation gives

$$\ln D(p) = \ln 8000 - 1.5 \ln p$$

So $\text{El}_p D$ is also equal to the (double) logarithmic derivative $d \ln D(p)/d \ln p$, which is the constant slope of this *log-linear* relationship.

This example illustrates the general rule that elasticities are equal to such logarithmic derivatives. In fact, whenever x and y are both positive variables, with y a differentiable function of x, one has

$$\text{El}_x y = \frac{x}{y}\frac{dy}{dx} = \frac{d \ln y}{d \ln x} = \frac{d \log_a y}{d \log_a x} \qquad\qquad [8.25]$$

where a is any positive base for constructing logarithms. The first equality just repeats the definition of elasticity. To see why the second must hold, note that ln y is a differentiable function of y, whereas y is assumed to be a differentiable function of x, and $x = e^{\ln x}$ is a differentiable function of $\ln x$. So the chain rule can be applied twice to give

$$\frac{d \ln y}{d \ln x} = \frac{d \ln y}{dy} \cdot \frac{dy}{dx} \cdot \frac{dx}{d \ln x}$$

But

$$\frac{d \ln y}{dy} = \frac{1}{y}, \qquad \frac{dx}{d \ln x} = \frac{de^{\ln x}}{d \ln x} = e^{\ln x} = x$$

Substituting these values into the previous expression for $d \ln y / d \ln x$ implies that

$$\frac{d \ln y}{d \ln x} = \frac{1}{y} \cdot \frac{dy}{dx} \cdot x = \frac{x}{y} \frac{dy}{dx} = \mathrm{El}_x\, y$$

Finally, from [8.13], it follows that $\log_a z$ is proportional to $\ln z$, so the third equality in [8.25] is easy to verify.

Problems

1. Compute the relative rate of increase $\dot{x}/x$ for the following:

   a. $x = 5t + 10$ **b.** $x = \ln(t + 1)$ **c.** $x = 5e^t$

   d. $x = -3 \cdot 2^t$ **e.** $x = e^{t^2}$ **f.** $x = e^t + e^{-t}$

   Which of these functions have a constant relative rate of increase? Compare your findings with the result in [8.22].

2. In a stable market where no sales promotion is carried out, the decrease in $S(t)$, sales per unit of time of a commodity, has shown a tendency to be proportional to the quantity of sales, so that

   $$S'(t) = -a S(t)$$

   a. Find an expression for $S(t)$ when sales at time 0 are S_0. (*Hint:* Use [8.22].)

   b. Solve the equation $S_0 e^{-at} = \frac{1}{2} S_0$ for t. Interpret the answer.

3. The world's population in 1975 was almost 4 billion, and increasing by nearly 2% per year. If we assume that the population increases exponentially at this relative rate, then t years after the year 1975 the population in billions will be equal to

   $$P(t) = 4e^{0.02t}$$

   a. Estimate the world's population by the year 2000 ($t = 25$).

b. How long will it take before the world's population doubles, if its growth continues at the same rate?

4. Let $P(t)$ denote Europe's population in millions t years after 1960. According to Example 2.17 of Section 2.5, we have $P(0) = 641$ and $P(10) = 705$. Suppose that $P(t)$ grows exponentially, with $P(t) = 641e^{kt}$. Compute k and then find $P(15)$ and $P(40)$ (estimates of the population in 1975 and in 2000). Compare with the UN numbers in Table 2.4.

5. The number $N(t)$ of persons who develop influenza t days after a group of 1000 persons has been in contact with a carrier of infection is given by

$$N(t) = \frac{1000}{1 + 999e^{-0.39t}}$$

   a. How many develop influenza after 20 days?
   b. How many days does it take until 800 are sick?
   c. Will everyone eventually get influenza?

6. A study of tractors in British agriculture from 1950 onwards estimated that the number y in use (measured in 1000 tractors), as a function of t (measured in years, so that $t = 0$ corresponds to 1950), is given by

$$y = 250.9 + \frac{228.46}{1 + 8.11625e^{-0.340416t}}$$

   a. Find the number of tractors in 1950. How many tractors were added in the decade up to 1960?
   b. Find the limit for y as $t \to \infty$, and draw the graph.

7. After the big flood catastrophe in Holland in 1953, a research project was initiated to determine the optimal height of the dikes. One of the (simpler) models involved finding the value of x that minimizes the function

$$f(x) = I_0 + kx + Ae^{-\alpha x} \qquad (x \geq 0)$$

where x denotes the number of meters that should be added to the dikes, $I_0 + kx$ is the construction cost, and $Ae^{-\alpha x}$ is an estimate of the losses caused by flooding. I_0, k, A, and α are all positive constants.
   a. Suppose that $f(x)$ has minimum for some $x_0 > 0$. Find x_0.
   b. What condition must we put on α, A, and k for x_0 to be positive? Show that if the condition is satisfied, then x_0 solves the minimization problem.
   c. Constant A is given by the formula

$$A = \frac{100}{\delta} p_0 V \left(1 + \frac{\delta}{100}\right)$$

where p_0 is the probability that the dikes will be flooded if they are not rebuilt, V is an estimate of the cost of flood damage, and δ is an interest rate. Show that x_0 may be written in the form

$$x_0 = \frac{1}{\alpha} \ln \frac{100 \alpha p_0 V (1 + \delta/100)}{k\delta}$$

Examine what happens to x_0 when one of the variables p_0, V, δ, or k increases. Comment on the reasonableness of the results.[2]

8. Suppose that $f(t)$ is a function satisfying [8.23], and define a new function h by $h(t) = -1 + K/f(t)$. Prove that $h'(t) = -rh(t)$ for a constant A, so (using [8.22]) one has $h(t) = Ae^{-rt}$ for some constant A. Then what can be said about $f(t)$?

9. Voorhees and colleagues studied the transportation systems in 37 American cities and estimated the average travel time to work, m (in minutes), as a function of the number of inhabitants, N. They found that

$$m = e^{-0.02} N^{0.19}$$

Write the relation in ln-linear form. What is the value of m when $N = 480,000$?

10. The following data are taken from a survey of persons who in 1933 migrated to Tartu in Estonia from the surrounding countryside. Here y is the number of persons that moved per 100,000 rural inhabitants, and x is the distance moved (measured in kilometers and rounded to the nearest whole number divisible by 20).

x	20	40	60	80	100	120	140	160	180	200
y	1700	550	230	120	75	60	45	35	25	20

a. Construct a table of the relationship between $\ln x$ and $\ln y$, and plot the data in a coordinate system where $\ln x$ and $\ln y$ are plotted along the two axes.

b. Roughly fit a straight line to the pairs of points in the diagram plotted for part (a), and derive an empirical formula for y as a function of x.

11. Write the relation $z = 694,500p^{-0.3}$ in ln-linear form (see Example 3.8 in Section 3.4). In addition, find p expressed in terms of z.

12. a. Determine the constants A and a such that the graph of $y = Ax^a$ passes through the points $(x, y) = (2, 5)$ and $(3, 7)$. (*Hint:* Use the ln-linear form.)

---

[2]The problem is discussed in D. van Dantzig. "Economic Decision Problems for Flood Prevention." *Econometrica*. 24 (1956): 276–287.

b. Repeat part (a) when the graph goes through points (x_1, y_1) and (x_2, y_2), where $x_1 \neq x_2$.

13. The effect on chicken embryos of cooling the eggs has been studied. The following table shows results from an experiment where the pulse of a chicken embryo was measured at different temperatures.

Temperature T (°C)	36.3	35.0	33.9	32.4	24.7	24.2
Pulse n (heartbeats/minute)	154	133	110	94	38	36

a. Prepare a table showing the relationship between T and $\ln n$, and plot the pairs of numbers $(T, \ln n)$ in a coordinate system with $\ln n$ on the vertical axis and T on the horizontal axis. Fit a straight line to these points.

b. We want to find an empirical function $f(T) = ce^{aT}$ that approximates the pulse rate as a function of the temperature T. Using the line obtained in part (a), determine a and c.

c. By how many degrees does the temperature have to fall in order to halve the pulse rate?

Harder Problems

14. All organic material contains stable carbon 12 and some (very little) of the radioactive isotope carbon 14. The proportion between the quantities of carbon 14 and of stable carbon in living organisms is constant, and seems to have been constant for thousands of years. When an organism dies, carbon 14 decays according to the law

$$f(t) = f(t_0)e^{-1.25 \cdot 10^{-4}(t - t_0)}$$

where $f(t_0)$ is the quantity of carbon at the moment of death t_0, and $f(t)$ is the quantity that is left at time t. Show that t_0 is given by

$$t_0 = t + 8000 \ln \frac{f(t)}{f(t_0)}$$

(This formula is the basis for "radioactive dating." In 1960, the American W. F. Libby received the Nobel prize in chemistry for the discovery of radioactive dating.)

15. Helge and Anne Stine Ingstad found several Viking tools on old settlements in Newfoundland. The charcoal from the fireplaces was analyzed in 1972, and the percentage of carbon 14 in the charcoal (compared with the content of carbon 14 in fresh wood) was 88.6%. Use the result from Problem 14 to determine when the Viking settlers lived in Newfoundland.

8.5 Compound Interest and Present Discounted Values

Equation [8.21], $f'(t) = rf(t)$ for all t, has a particularly important application to economics. After t years, a deposit of $\$K$ earning interest at the rate $p\%$ per year will increase to

$$K(1 + r)^t \quad \text{(where} \quad r = p/100) \tag{1}$$

(see Section A.1, Appendix A). Each year the principal increases by the factor $1 + r$.

Formula [1] assumes that the interest is added to the principal at the end of each year. Suppose instead that payment of interest is offered each half year, but at an interest rate $p/2$. Then the principal after $1/2$ year will have increased to

$$K + K\frac{p/2}{100} = K\left(1 + \frac{r}{2}\right)$$

Therefore, the principal increases by the factor $1 + r/2$ each half year. After 1 year, the principal will have increased up to $K(1 + r/2)^2$, and after t years it will be

$$K\left(1 + \frac{r}{2}\right)^{2t} \tag{2}$$

It is clear that a biannual interest payment at the rate $\frac{1}{2}p\%$ is better for a lender than an annual interest payment at the rate $p\%$. This is easily seen also from the fact that $(1 + r/2)^2 = 1 + r + r^2/4 > 1 + r$.

More generally, suppose that interest at the rate $p/n\%$ is added to the principal at n different times distributed evenly over the year. Then the principal will be multiplied by a factor $(1 + r/n)^n$ each year. After t years, the principal is

$$K\left(1 + \frac{r}{n}\right)^{nt} \tag{3}$$

The greater is n, the more profitable is the investment for the lender. See Problem 3.

In practice, there is a limit to how frequently interest can be added to savings accounts. However, let us examine what happens to the expression in [3] as the annual frequency n tends to infinity. We put $r/n = 1/m$. Then $n = mr$ and so

$$K\left(1 + \frac{r}{n}\right)^{nt} = K\left(1 + \frac{1}{m}\right)^{mrt} = K\left[\left(1 + \frac{1}{m}\right)^m\right]^{rt} \tag{4}$$

As $n \to \infty$ (with r fixed), so $m = n/r \to \infty$, and according to [8.17], we have $(1 + 1/m)^m \to e$. Hence, the expression in [4] approaches Ke^{rt} as n tends to infinity. When we let n approach infinity, the accumulation of interest happens more and more frequently. In the limit, we talk about **continuous compounding** of interest. After t years, an initial amount $\$K$ will have increased to

$$K(t) = Ke^{rt} \qquad \textbf{(continuous compounding)} \qquad [8.26]$$

The number r is often referred to as the **rate of interest**. By differentiating [8.26], we have the following important fact.

With continuous compounding of interest at rate r, the principal increases at the constant relative rate r, so that $K'(t)/K(t) = r$.

From [8.26], we infer that $K(1) = Ke^r$, so that the principal increases by the factor e^r during the first year. In general, $K(t+1) = Ke^{r(t+1)} = Ke^{rt}e^r = K(t)e^r$, so that with continuous compounding of interest, the principal increases *each* year by the fixed factor e^r.

Comparing Different Forms of Interest

At an interest rate of $p\%$ ($= 100r$) per year, continuous compounding of interest is best for the lender. (See Problem 3.) For comparatively low interest rates, however, the difference between annual and continuous compounding of interest is quite small.

Example 8.9

Find the amount by which $\$1$ increases in the course of a year when the interest rate is 8% per year and interest is added:

(a) only at the end of the year
(b) at the end of each half year
(c) continuously

Solution In this case, $r = 8/100 = 0.08$, so we obtain the following:

(a) $K = (1 + 0.08) = 1.08$
(b) $K = (1 + 0.08/2)^2 = 1.0816$
(c) $K = e^{0.08} \approx 1.08329$

If we increase the interest rate or increase the number of years over which interest accumulates, then the difference between yearly and continuous compounding of interest increases.

Note: A consumer who wants to take out a loan may be faced with several offers from financial institutions. It is therefore of considerable importance to compare the various offers. The concept of **effective interest rate** is often used in making such comparisons. Imagine an offer that implies a yearly interest rate $p\%$ with interest p/n added n times during the year. A principal amount of K will then have increased after 1 year to $K(1 + r/n)^n$, where $r = p/100$. Define the *effective interest rate* P as the annual percentage interest rate that, when compounding is continuous, gives the same total interest over the year. If $R = P/100$, then after 1 year, the initial amount K increases to Ke^R. Hence, R is defined by the equation

$$Ke^R = K(1 + r/n)^n$$

Canceling K and then taking ln of both sides gives

$$R = n\ln(1 + r/n) \qquad [8.27]$$

If $r = 0.08$ and $n = 1$, for example, then $R = \ln(1 + 0.08) \approx 0.077$. Thus, a yearly interest rate of 8% corresponds to an effective interest rate (with continuous compounding) of about 7.7%.

The Present Value of a Future Claim

Suppose that an amount K is due for payment t years after the present date. What is the *present value* of this amount when the interest rate is $p\%$ per year? Equivalently, how much must be deposited today earning $p\%$ annual interest in order to have the amount K after t years?

If interest is paid annually, the amount A will have increased to $A(1 + p/100)^t$ after t years, so that we need $A(1 + p/100)^t = K$. Thus, $A = K(1 + p/100)^{-t} = K(1 + r)^{-t}$, where $r = p/100$. If interest is compounded continuously, however, then the amount A will have increased to Ae^{rt} after t years. Hence, $Ae^{rt} = K$, or $A = Ke^{-rt}$. Altogether, we have the following:

If the interest rate is $p\%$ per year and $r = p/100$, an amount K that is payable in t years has the present value:

$K(1 + r)^{-t}$, with yearly interest payments

Ke^{-rt}, with continuous compounding of interest

$\qquad [8.28]$

Problems

1. An amount \$1000 earns interest at 5% per year. What will this amount have grown to after (a) 10 years, and (b) 50 years, when interest is compounded (i) yearly, (ii) monthly, (iii) continuously?

2. Suppose that the price of a commodity after x years is given by $f(x) = Ae^{kx}$, where A and k are constants.

  a. Find A and k when $f(0) = 4$ and $f'(0) = 1$. In this case, what is the price after 5 years?

  b. We assume now that $A = 4$ and $k = 0.25$. When the price has increased to 18, it becomes controlled so that the annual price increase is limited to 10%. When are price controls first needed? What length of time is needed for the price to double before and after price controls are introduced?

Harder Problems

3. We showed (in the discussion following Equation [4]) that $(1 + r/n)^n \to e^r$ as $n \to \infty$. For each fixed $r > 0$, we claim that $(1 + r/n)^n$ is strictly increasing in n, so that

$$\left(1 + \frac{r}{n}\right)^n < \lim_{n \to \infty} \left(1 + \frac{r}{n}\right)^n = e^r \qquad \text{(for } n = 1, 2, \ldots) \qquad [*]$$

This shows that continuous interest at interest rate p% per year, with $r = p/100$, is more profitable for the lender than interest payments n times a year at interest rate $p/100n$.

To confirm this, define the function g for all $x > 0$ by

$$g(x) = \left(1 + \frac{r}{x}\right)^x \qquad (r \text{ is a positive constant})$$

Show that

$$g'(x) = g(x) \left[\ln\left(1 + \frac{r}{x}\right) - \frac{r/x}{1 + r/x}\right]$$

(Use logarithmic differentiation.) Put $h(u) = \ln(1 + u) - u/(1 + u)$. Then $h(0) = 0$. Show that $h'(u) > 0$ for $u > 0$, and hence that $g'(x) > 0$ for all $x > 0$. What conclusion can you draw?

9

Single-Variable Optimization

If you want literal realism, look at the world around
you; if you want understanding, look at theories.
—*R. Dorfman* (1964)

Looking for the best way of pursuing a certain goal involves what are called **optimization problems.** Examples can be drawn from almost all areas of human activity. A manager seeks those combinations of inputs (such as capital and labor) that maximize profits or minimize costs. A doctor might want to know when the concentration of a drug in the bloodstream is at its greatest. A farmer might want to know what amount of fertilizer per square yard will maximize profits. An oil company may wish to find the optimal rate of extraction from one of its wells.

Studying an optimization problem of this sort using mathematical methods requires us to construct a mathematical model for the problem. This is usually not easy, and only in simple cases will the model lead to the problem of maximizing or minimizing a function of a single variable—the main topic of this chapter.

In general, no mathematical methods have more important applications in economics than those designed to solve optimization problems. Though economic optimization problems usually involve several variables, the examples of quadratic optimization in Section 3.2 indicate how useful economic insights can be gained even from simple one-variable optimization.

9.1 Some Basic Definitions

Recall from Section 7.2 that, if $f(x)$ has domain D, then

$$c \in D \text{ is a \textbf{maximum point} for } f \iff f(x) \leq f(c), \text{ for all } x \in D \quad [9.1]$$

$$d \in D \text{ is a \textbf{minimum point} for } f \iff f(x) \geq f(d), \text{ for all } x \in D \quad [9.2]$$

In [9.1], we call $f(c)$ the **maximum value**, and in [9.2], we call $f(d)$ the **minimum value**. If the value of f at c is strictly larger than at any other point in D, then c is a **strict** maximum point. Similarly, d is a **strict** minimum point if $f(x) > f(d)$ for all $x \in D$, $x \neq d$. As collective names, we use **optimal points** and **values**, or **extreme points** and **values**.

If f is any function with domain D, then $-f$ is defined in D by $(-f)(x) = -f(x)$. Note that $f(x) \leq f(c)$ for all $x \in D$, if and only if $-f(x) \geq -f(c)$ for all $x \in D$. Thus, c maximizes f in D if and only if c minimizes $-f$ in D. This simple observation, which is illustrated in Fig. 9.1, can be used to convert maximization problems to minimization problems and vice versa.

Our main task in this chapter is to study how to determine the possible maximum and minimum points of a function. In this connection, the following definition is crucial:

$$x_0 \text{ is a \textbf{stationary} point for } f \text{ if } f'(x_0) = 0 \qquad [9.3]$$

Geometrically, stationary points occur where the tangent to the graph of the function is parallel to the x-axis.

Before starting to explore systematically the properties of maxima and minima, we provide some geometric examples based on the graph of the function. They will indicate for us the role played by the stationary points of a function in the theory of optimization.

FIGURE 9.1   Point c is a maximum point for $f(x)$ and a minimum point for $-f(x)$.

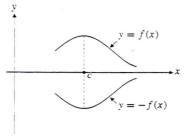

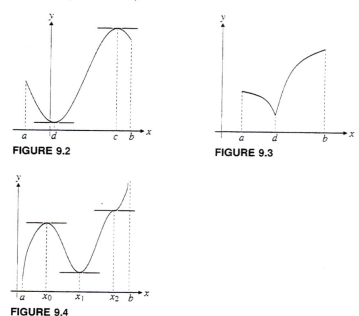

FIGURE 9.2

FIGURE 9.3

FIGURE 9.4

Figure 9.2 is the graph of a function f having two stationary points, c and d. At c, there is a maximum; at d, there is a minimum.

In Fig. 9.3, the function has no stationary points. There is a maximum at the end point b and a minimum at d. At d, the function is not differentiable. At b, the derivative (the left-hand derivative) is not 0.

Finally, the function f whose graph is shown in Fig. 9.4 has three stationary points, x_0, x_1, and x_2. At end point a, there is a minimum, whereas f does not have any maximum value because it approaches ∞ as x tends to b. At the critical point x_0, function f has a local maximum in the sense that its value at that point is higher than at all neighboring points. Similarly, at x_1, it has a local minimum, whereas at x_2 there is a stationary point that is neither a local maximum nor a local minimum. We call x_2 an *inflection point*.

The three figures represent the most important properties of single-variable optimization problems. Because the theory is so important in practical applications, we must not simply rely on geometric insights, but must rather develop a firmer analytical foundation for optimization theory.

9.2 A First-Derivative Test for Extreme Points

In many important cases, we can find maximum or minimum values for a function just by studying the sign of its first derivative. Suppose $f(x)$ is differentiable on an interval I and suppose $f(x)$ has only one stationary point, $x = c$. If

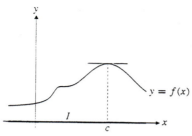

FIGURE 9.5 Point *x* = *c* is a
maximum point.

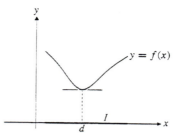

FIGURE 9.6 Point *x* = *d* is a
minimum point.

$f'(x) \geq 0$ for all $x \in I$ such that $x \leq c$, whereas $f'(x) \leq 0$ for all $x \in I$ such that $x \geq c$, then $f(x)$ is increasing to the left of c and decreasing to the right of c. It follows that $f(x) \leq f(c)$ for all $x \leq c$ and $f(c) \geq f(x)$ for all $x \geq c$. Hence, $x = c$ is a maximum point for f in I, as illustrated in Fig. 9.5.

With obvious modification, a similar result holds for minimum points, as illustrated in Fig. 9.6. Briefly stated:[1]

A First-Derivative Test for Max/Min

If $f'(x) \geq 0$ for $x \leq c$, and $f'(x) \leq 0$ for $x \geq c$, then $x = c$ is a maximum point for f.

If $f'(x) \leq 0$ for $x \leq c$, and $f'(x) \geq 0$ for $x \geq c$, then $x = c$ is a minimum point for f.

[9.4]

Example 9.1

Measured in milligrams per liter, the concentration of a drug in the bloodstream t hours after injection is given by the formula

$$c(t) = \frac{t}{t^2 + 4}$$

Find the time of maximum concentration.

Solution   Differentiation with respect to t yields

$$c'(t) = \frac{1 \cdot (t^2 + 4) - t \cdot 2t}{(t^2 + 4)^2} = \frac{4 - t^2}{(t^2 + 4)^2} = \frac{(2 + t)(2 - t)}{(t^2 + 4)^2}$$

---

[1]Many books in mathematics for economists instruct students always to check so-called second-order conditions, even in cases where the first-derivative test [9.4] is much easier to check.

For $t \geq 0$, the term $(2-t)$ alone determines the algebraic sign of the fraction, because the other terms are positive. In fact, if $t \leq 2$, then $c'(t) \geq 0$, whereas if $t \geq 2$, then $c'(t) \leq 0$. From [9.4], we conclude that $t = 2$ maximizes $c(t)$. Thus, the concentration of the drug is highest 2 hours after injection. Because $c(2) = 0.25$, the maximum concentration is 0.25 milligrams per liter.

Example 9.2

Suppose $Y(N)$ bushels of wheat are harvested per acre of land when N pounds of fertilizer per acre are used. If P is the dollar price per bushel of wheat and q is the dollar price per pound of fertilizer, then profits in dollars per acre are

$$\pi(N) = PY(N) - qN \qquad (N \geq 0) \qquad [1]$$

Suppose that for some N^*, $\pi'(N) \geq 0$ for $N \leq N^*$, and $\pi'(N) \leq 0$ for $N \geq N^*$. Then N^* maximizes profits, and $\pi'(N^*) = 0$, that is, $PY'(N^*) - q = 0$, so

$$PY'(N^*) = q \qquad [2]$$

Let us give an economic interpretation to this condition. Suppose N^* units of fertilizer are used and we contemplate increasing N^* by one unit. What do we gain? If N^* increases by one unit, then $Y(N^* + 1) - Y(N^*)$ more bushels are produced. Now $Y(N^*+1) - Y(N^*) \approx Y'(N^*)$. For each of these bushels, we get P dollars, so

by increasing N^* by one unit, we gain $\approx PY'(N^*)$ dollars

On the other hand,

by increasing N^* by one unit, we lose q dollars

because this is the cost of one unit of fertilizer. Hence, we can interpret [2] as follows: In order to maximize profits, you should increase the amount of fertilizer to the level N^* at which an additional pound of fertilizer equates your gains and losses.

In a certain study from Iowa in 1952, the yield function $Y(N)$ was estimated as

$$Y(N) = -13.62 + 0.984N - 0.05N^{3/2}$$

If the price of wheat is \$1.40 per bushel and the price of fertilizer is \$0.18 per pound, find the amount of fertilizer that maximizes profits.

Solution In this case,

$$\pi(N) = 1.4(-13.62 + 0.984N - 0.05N^{3/2}) - 0.18N,$$

so

$$\pi'(N) = 1.4 \left[0.984 - (3/2) \cdot 0.05 \cdot N^{1/2} \right] - 0.18 \qquad [3]$$

Thus, $\pi'(N^*) = 0$ provided that

$$1.4 \cdot (3/2) \cdot 0.05(N^*)^{1/2} = 1.4 \cdot 0.984 - 0.18$$

This implies that

$$(N^*)^{1/2} = \frac{1.4 \cdot 0.984 - 0.18}{1.4(3/2)0.05} = \frac{1.1976}{0.105} \approx 11.406$$

Hence,

$$N^* \approx (11.406)^2 \approx 130$$

Looking at [3], we see that $\pi'(N) \geq 0$ for $N \leq N^*$, and $\pi'(N) \leq 0$ for $N \geq N^*$. Hence, $N^* \approx 130$ maximizes profits.

Example 9.3 ("Neither a Borrower nor a Lender Be")[2]

A student has current income y_1 and expects future income y_2. She plans current consumption c_1 and future consumption c_2 in order to maximize the utility function

$$\ln c_1 + \frac{1}{1 + \delta} \ln c_2$$

where δ is her discount rate. If she borrows now, so that $c_1 > y_1$, then future consumption, after repaying the loan amount $c_1 - y_1$ with interest charged at rate r, will be

$$c_2 = y_2 - (1 + r)(c_1 - y_1)$$

Alternatively, if she saves now, so that $c_1 < y_1$, then future consumption will be

$$c_2 = y_2 + (1 + r)(y_1 - c_1)$$

after receiving interest at the same rate on her savings. Find the optimal borrowing or saving plan.

---

[2]According to Shakespeare. Polonius' advice to Hamlet was "Neither a borrower nor a lender be."

Solution   Whether the student borrows or saves, second period consumption will be given by

$$c_2 = y_2 - (1+r)(c_1 - y_1)$$

in either case. So the student will want to maximize

$$U = \ln c_1 + \frac{1}{1+\delta} \ln[y_2 - (1+r)(c_1 - y_1)]$$

Differentiating this function with respect to c_1 gives

$$\frac{dU}{dc_1} = \frac{1}{c_1} - \frac{1+r}{1+\delta} \cdot \frac{1}{y_2 - (1+r)(c_1 - y_1)}$$

Rewriting the fractions so that they have a common denominator yields

$$\frac{dU}{dc_1} = \frac{(1+\delta)[y_2 - (1+r)(c_1 - y_1)] - (1+r)c_1}{c_1(1+\delta)[y_2 - (1+r)(c_1 - y_1)]} \qquad [1]$$

Rearranging the numerator and equating the derivative to 0, we have

$$\frac{dU}{dc_1} = \frac{(1+\delta)[(1+r)y_1 + y_2] - (2+\delta)(1+r)c_1}{c_1(1+\delta)[y_2 - (1+r)(c_1 - y_1)]} = 0 \qquad [2]$$

The unique solution of this equation is

$$c_1^* = \frac{(1+\delta)[(1+r)y_1 + y_2]}{(2+\delta)(1+r)} = y_1 + \frac{(1+\delta)y_2 - (1+r)y_1}{(2+\delta)(1+r)} \qquad [3]$$

From [2], we see that for $c_1 > c_1^*$ one has $dU/dc_1 < 0$, whereas for $c_1 < c_1^*$ one has $dU/dc_1 > 0$. We conclude that c_1^* indeed maximizes U. Moreover, the student lends if and only if $(1+\delta)y_2 < (1+r)y_1$. In the more likely case when $(1+\delta)y_2 > (1+r)y_1$ because future income is considerably higher than present income, she will borrow. Only if by some chance $(1+\delta)y_2$ is exactly equal to $(1+r)y_1$ will she be neither a borrower nor a lender. However, this discussion has neglected the difference between borrowing and lending rates of interest that one always observes in reality.

Problems

1. Let y denote the total weekly weight of pigs slaughtered by the butcheries of Chicago during 1948 (in millions of pounds) and let x be total weekly work effort (in thousands of hours). Nichols estimated the relation

$$y = -2.05 + 1.06x - 0.04x^2$$

Determine the value of x that maximizes y by studying the sign variation of y'.

2. Find the derivative of the function h defined for all x by

$$h(x) = \frac{8x}{3x^2 + 4}$$

Use the sign variation of $h'(x)$ to find the maximum/minimum value of $h(x)$.

3. Consider the function V defined by

$$V(x) = 4x(9 - x)^2 = 4x^3 - 72x^2 + 324x \qquad (x \in [0, 9])$$

(See Problem 1(e) in Section 1.3 for an interpretation of V.)

  a. Compute $V'(x)$ and show that V is increasing in $(0, 3)$ and decreasing in $(3, 9)$. Find the maximum point of V in $[0, 9]$.

  b. Explain what the result in part (a) implies for Problem 1(e) in Section 1.3.

  c. Also solve the problem by logarithmic differentiation of $V(x)$, for $x \in (0, 9)$. Which method do you prefer?

4. **a.** Show that

$$f(x) = \frac{2x^2}{x^4 + 1} \implies f'(x) = \frac{4x(1 + x^2)(1 + x)(1 - x)}{(x^4 + 1)^2} \qquad [*]$$

  b. Use [*] to find the maximum value of f on $[0, \infty)$. Show that $f(-x) = f(x)$, for all x. What are the maximum points for f on $(-\infty, \infty)$?

5. Occasionally, one can find maximum/minimum points of a function just by studying the formula. For example, consider $f(x) = \sqrt{x - 5} - 100$, defined for $x \geq 5$. Because $\sqrt{x - 5}$ is ≥ 0 for all $x \geq 5$, so $f(x) \geq -100$ for all $x \geq 5$. Because $f(5) = -100$, we conclude that $x = 5$ is a minimum point. Use similar direct arguments to find maximum/or minimum points for the following:

  a. $f(x) = \dfrac{8}{3x^2 + 4}$ **b.** $g(x) = 3 - (x - 2)^2$

  c. $h(x) = 5(x + 2)^4 - 3$ **d.** $F(x) = \dfrac{-2}{2 + x^2}$

  e. $G(x) = 2 - \sqrt{1 - x}$ **f.** $H(x) = \dfrac{1}{1 + x^4}$ $(x \in [-1, 1])$

6. Study the sign variation of the derivative of each function in Problem 5 and confirm the conclusions obtained there.

Harder Problems

7. If the tax T a person pays on gross income Y is $T = a(bY + c)^p + kY$, where a, b, and c are positive constants, then the average tax rate is

$$\overline{T}(Y) = \frac{T}{Y} = a\frac{(bY + c)^p}{Y} + k \qquad (p > 1)$$

Find the value of Y that maximizes the average tax.

8. Given n numbers $a_1, a_2, \ldots, a_n$, find the number x that approximates these numbers best, in the sense that

$$d(x) = (x - a_1)^2 + (x - a_2)^2 + \cdots + (x - a_n)^2$$

is as small as possible. What do you call this x value?

9.3 Alternative Ways of Finding Extreme Points

Sometimes it is awkward or impossible to locate extreme points by considering how the sign of the first derivative varies. Other ways of characterizing extreme points are often more useful, as this section demonstrates.

We begin by examining precisely the role played by stationary points of a function in locating extreme points. Suppose we know that a function f has a maximum at a point c in an interval I. That maximum might very well occur at an end point of the interval, as is the case in Fig. 9.3. However, when c is not an end point, and if f is differentiable, it seems geometrically obvious that the tangent to the graph at c must be horizontal. In other words, c must be a stationary point. The same conclusion applies to a minimum point. A formal statement and a proof of this important result were given in Theorem 7.4 of Section 7.2. Thus, the condition $f'(c) = 0$ is a *necessary* condition for an interior point c at which f' exists to be an optimal point. The condition is not sufficient, however. In Fig. 9.4 of Section 9.1, points x_0, x_1, and x_2 are all stationary points, but none is an optimal point. (In fact, x_0 is a local maximum point, x_1 a local minimum point, and x_2 an inflection point.)

How to Search for Maxima/Minima

Suppose we know that a function f has a maximum and/or a minimum in a bounded interval I. The optimum must occur either at an interior point of I or at one of the end points. If it occurs at an interior point (inside the interval I) and f is differentiable, then by Theorem 7.4 in Section 7.2 the derivative f' is zero at that point. In addition, there is the possibility that the optimum occurs at a point where f is not differentiable. Hence, extreme points can be only one of the following three types:

---

1. interior points in I where $f'(x) = 0$
2. end points of I
3. points in I where f' does not exist

A typical example showing that a minimum can occur at a point of type 3 is suggested in Fig. 9.3 of Section 9.1. However, the functions economists study are usually differentiable everywhere. The following recipe, therefore, covers most problems of interest.

Problem:

Find the maximum and the minimum values of a differentiable function f defined on a closed, bounded interval $[a, b]$.

Solution

(a) Find all stationary points of f in (a, b)—that is, find all points $x \in (a, b)$ that satisfy the equation $f'(x) = 0$.   [9.5]
(b) Evaluate f at the end points a and b of the interval and at all stationary points found in (a).
(c) The largest function value in (b) is the maximum value of f in $[a, b]$.
(d) The smallest function value in (b) is the minimum value of f in $[a, b]$.

A differentiable function is continuous, so the extreme-value theorem (Theorem 7.3 of Section 7.2) assures us that maximum and minimum points do exist. Following the procedure just given, we can, in principle, find these extreme points. (In very special examples, there could be an infinite number of stationary points. Such "pathological" functions almost never appear in applied problems.)

Example 9.4

Find the maximum and minimum values of

$$f(x) = \tfrac{1}{9}x^3 - \tfrac{1}{6}x^2 - \tfrac{2}{3}x + 1, \qquad (x \in [-3, 3])$$

Solution   The function is differentiable everywhere, and

$$f'(x) = \tfrac{1}{3}x^2 - \tfrac{1}{3}x - \tfrac{2}{3} = \tfrac{1}{3}(x^2 - x - 2) = \tfrac{1}{3}(x + 1)(x - 2)$$

Thus, there are two points in the interval $(-3, 3)$ where $f'(x) = 0$, namely, $x = -1$ and $x = 2$. Evaluating f at these points and the end points, we have

$$f(-3) = -3/2, \qquad f(-1) = 25/18, \qquad f(2) = -1/9, \qquad f(3) = 1/2$$

The minimum value is $-3/2$ at $x = -3$, and the maximum value is $25/18$ at $x = -1$.

Example 9.5

A firm is producing some commodity and wants to maximize its profits. The total revenue generated in a certain period by producing and selling Q units is $R(Q)$ dollars, whereas $C(Q)$ denotes the associated total dollar cost. The profit obtained as a result of producing and selling Q units is then

$$\pi(Q) = R(Q) - C(Q) \tag{1}$$

Because of technical limitations, suppose there is a maximum quantity $\bar{Q}$ that can be produced by the firm in a given period. Assume that R and C are differentiable functions of Q in the interval $[0, \bar{Q}]$. The profit function π is then differentiable, so continuous, and consequently π *has* a maximum value. In special cases, that maximum might occur at $Q = 0$ or at $Q = \bar{Q}$. If not, the maximum production level Q^* satisfies $\pi'(Q^*) = 0$, and so

$$R'(Q^*) = C'(Q^*) \tag{2}$$

Hence, *production should be adjusted to a point where the marginal revenue is equal to the marginal cost*.

Let us assume that the firm gets a fixed price P per unit sold. Then $R(Q) = PQ$, and [2] takes the form

$$P = C'(Q^*) \tag{3}$$

Thus, in the case in which the firm has no control over the price, *production should be adjusted to a level at which the marginal cost is equal to the price per unit of the commodity* (assuming that π does not have a maximum at 0 or at $\bar{Q}$).

For special choices of $R(Q)$ and $C(Q)$, it might happen that [2] has several solutions. If so, the maximum profit occurs at that point among the solutions of [2] that gives the highest value to $\pi(Q)$.

An interpretation of [2] in line with that given for the corresponding optimality condition in the wheat example in Example 9.2 of Section 9.2 is as follows. Suppose we contemplate increasing production from the level Q^* by one unit. Revenue will increase by: $R(Q^* + 1) - R(Q^*) \approx R'(Q^*)$. We would lose the amount $C(Q^*+1) - C(Q^*) \approx C'(Q^*)$, because this is the cost increase by increasing production by one unit. Equation [2] equates $R'(Q^*)$ and $C'(Q^*)$, so that marginal revenue of selling an extra unit is exactly offset by the marginal cost of producing that unit.

Suppose a tax of t dollars per unit is imposed on the production of the commodity. Then the profit function becomes

$$\pi(Q) = R(Q) - C(Q) - tQ \qquad [4]$$

because selling Q units incurs a total additional cost of tQ. Assuming again that the maximum profit is not at $Q = 0$ or $Q = \bar{Q}$, it can only occur at a level Q^* where $\pi'(Q^*) = 0$. Now, $\pi'(Q) = R'(Q) - C'(Q) - t$, so the condition for maximum profit is

$$R'(Q^*) = C'(Q^*) + t \qquad [5]$$

What we gain by increasing production by one unit from the level Q^* is still (approximately) $R'(Q^*)$. What we lose is $C'(Q^*) + t$, because we have to pay t dollars in tax for the extra unit of output.

In the previous examples that involved explicit functions, we had no trouble in finding the solutions to the equation $f'(x) = 0$. However, in some cases, finding all the solutions to $f'(x) = 0$ might constitute a formidable problem. For instance, the continuous function

$$f(x) = x^{26} - 32x^{23} - 11x^5 - 2x^3 - x + 28 \qquad (x \in [-1, 5])$$

does have a maximum and a minimum in $[-1, 5]$, but it is impossible to find the exact solutions to the equation $f'(x) = 0$.

Difficulties of this kind are often encountered in practical optimization problems. In fact, only in very special cases can the equation $f'(x) = 0$ be solved exactly. Fortunately, there are standard numerical methods available for use on a computer that in most cases will find points arbitrarily close to the actual solutions of such equations.

Note: Suppose f is differentiable in an interval $[a, b]$ and let x_0 be a maximum point for f in $[a, b]$. If $x_0 = a$, then $f'(a)$ cannot be positive because then there would exist points x to the right of a where f had a higher value than at a. Arguing analogously, if $x_0 = b$ is a maximum point of f in $[a, b]$, then $f'(b)$ cannot be negative. If $x_0 \in (a, b)$, then $f'(x_0) = 0$. Figure 9.7 illustrates the three cases.

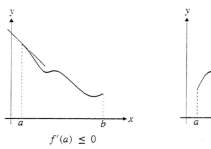

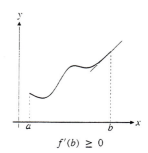

$f'(a) \leq 0$ $f'(x_0) = 0$ $f'(b) \geq 0$

FIGURE 9.7 Maximum at a, x₀, or b.

Problems

1. Find the maximum and minimum of

$$f(x) = 4x^2 - 40x + 80, \qquad x \in [0, 8]$$

Draw the graph of f over $[0, 8]$.

2. Find the maximum and minimum of each function over the indicated interval:

   a. $f(x) = -2x - 1,$ $[0, 3]$ **b.** $f(x) = x^3 - 3x + 8,$ $[-1, 2]$

   c. $f(x) = \dfrac{x^2 + 1}{x},$ $[\frac{1}{2}, 2]$ **d.** $f(x) = x^5 - 5x^3,$ $[-1, \sqrt{5}]$

   e. $f(x) = x^3 - 4500x^2 + 6 \cdot 10^6 x,$ $[0, 3000]$

3. Find two positive numbers whose sum is 16 and whose product is as large as possible.

4. A sports club plans to charter a plane. The charge for 60 passengers is $800 each. For each additional person above 60, all travelers get a discount of $10. The plane can take at most 80 passengers.

   a. What is the total cost when there are 61, 70, and 80 passengers?

   b. If $60 + x$ passengers fly, what is the total cost?

   c. Find the number of passengers that maximizes the total amount of airfares paid out by the sports club members.

5. Consider Example 9.5 and let $R(Q) = pQ$ and $C(Q) = \beta Q + \gamma Q^2$.

   a. Find the solution Q^* to Equation [2] in this case.

   b. Which value of Q maximizes profits in the following cases, assuming that $Q \in [0, 500]$?

      (i) $R(Q) = 1840Q$ and $C(Q) = 2Q^2 + 40Q + 5000$

      (ii) $R(Q) = 2240Q$ and $C(Q) = 2Q^2 + 40Q + 5000$

     (iii) $R(Q) = 1840Q$ and $C(Q) = 2Q^2 + 1940Q + 5000$

6. The height of a plant after t months is given by

$$h(t) = \sqrt{t} - \tfrac{1}{2}t \qquad (t \in [0, 3])$$

At what time is the plant at its highest?

7. Find the maximum of $y = x^2 e^{-x}$ on $[0, 4]$.

8. Let $C(Q)$ be the total cost function for a firm in producing Q units of some commodity. $A(Q) = C(Q)/Q$ is then called the *average cost function*. If $C(Q)$ is differentiable, prove that $A(Q)$ has a stationary point at $Q_0 > 0$ if and only if the marginal cost and the average cost are equal at Q_0. ($C'(Q_0) = A(Q_0)$.)

9. With reference to the previous problem, let $C(Q) = aQ^3 + bQ^2 + cQ + d$, where $a > 0$, $b \geq 0$, $c > 0$ and $d > 0$. Prove that $A(Q) = C(Q)/Q$ has a minimum in the interval $(0, \infty)$. Let $b = 0$ and find the minimum point in this case.

10. With reference to Problem 8, let $C(Q) = aQ^b + c$, for $a > 0$, $b > 1$, and $c \geq 0$. Prove that the average cost function has a minimum on $(0, \infty)$, and find it.

9.4 Local Maxima and Minima

So far in this chapter we have studied what are often referred to as *global* optimization problems. The reason for this terminology is that we have been seeking the absolutely largest or smallest values of a function, when we compare the function values at *all* points in the domain. In applied optimization problems, it is usually these global maxima and minima that are of interest. However, sometimes one is interested in the local maxima and minima of a function. In this case, we compare the function value at the point in question only with alternative function values at nearby points. For example, considering Fig. 9.8 and thinking of the graph as representing the profile of a landscape, mountain tops P_1 and P_2 represent local maxima, whereas valley bottoms Q_1 and Q_2 represent local minima.

FIGURE 9.8   Points c_1 and c_2 are local maxima; d_1 and d_2 are local minima.

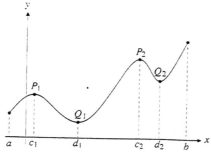

If $f(x)$ is defined on domain A, the precise definitions are as follows:

Function f has a **local maximum** at c if there is an interval (α, β) about c such that $f(x) \leq f(c)$ for all those x in A that also lie in (α, β). [9.6]

Function f has a **local minimum** at d if there is an interval (α, β) about d such that $f(x) \geq f(d)$ for all those x in A that also lie in (α, β). [9.7]

Note: These definitions imply that point a in Fig. 9.8 is a local minimum point and b is a local (and global) maximum point. Some authors restrict the definition of local maximum/minimum points only to *interior* points of the domain of the function. According to this definition, a global maximum that is not an interior point of the domain is not a local maximum point. We want a global maximum/minimum point always to be a local maximum/minimum point, so we stick to definitions [9.6] and [9.7].

It is obvious what we mean by local maximum/minimum values of a function, and the collective names are **local extreme points** and **values**.

In searching for maximum and minimum points, Theorem 7.4 of Section 7.2 is very useful. Actually, the same result is valid for local extreme points: *At a local extreme point in the interior of the domain of a differentiable function, the derivative must be zero.* This is clear if we recall that the proof of Theorem 7.4 was concerned only with the behavior of the function in a small interval about the optimal point. Consequently, in order to find possible local maxima and minima for a function f defined in an interval I, we can again search among the following types of points:

---

1. interior points in I where $f'(x) = 0$
2. end points of I
3. points in I where f' does not exist

We have thus established *necessary* conditions for a function f defined in an interval I to have a local extreme point. But how do we decide whether a point satisfying the necessary conditions is a local maximum, a local minimum, or neither? In contrast to global extreme points, it does not help to calculate the function value at the different points. To see why, consider again the function whose graph is given in Fig. 9.8. Point c_1 is a local maximum point and d_2 is a local minimum point, but the function value at c_1 is *smaller* than the function value at d_2.

The First-Derivative Test

There are two main ways of determining whether a given stationary point is a local maximum, a local minimum, or neither. One of them is based on studying the sign of the first derivative about the stationary point, and is an easy modification of [9.4] in Section 9.2.

Theorem 9.1 (The first-derivative test for local extrema)
Suppose c is a stationary point for $y = f(x)$.

(a) If $f'(x) \geq 0$ throughout some interval (a, c) to the left of c and $f'(x) \leq 0$ throughout some interval (c, b) to the right of c, then $x = c$ is a local maximum point for f.

(b) If $f'(x) \leq 0$ throughout some interval (a, c) to the left of c and $f'(x) \geq 0$ throughout some interval (c, b) to the right of c, then $x = c$ is a local minimum point for f.

(c) If $f'(x) > 0$ both throughout some interval (a, c) to the left of c and throughout some interval (c, b) to the right of c, then $x = c$ is not a local extreme point for f. The same conclusion holds if $f'(x) < 0$ on both sides of c.

Only case (c) is not already covered by [9.4] in Section 9.2. In fact, if $f'(x) > 0$ in (a, c) and in (c, b), then $f(x)$ is strictly increasing in $(a, c]$ as well as in $[c, b)$. Then $x = c$ cannot be a local extreme point.

Example 9.6

Classify the stationary points of $f(x) = \frac{1}{9}x^3 - \frac{1}{6}x^2 - \frac{2}{3}x + 1$.

Solution   In this case (see Example 9.4), we have $f'(x) = \frac{1}{3}(x+1)(x-2)$, so $x = -1$ and $x = 2$ are the stationary points. The sign diagram for $f'(x)$ is:

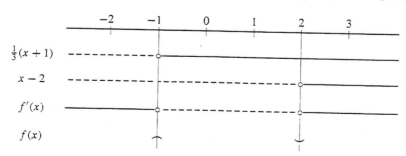

We conclude from this sign diagram that $x = -1$ is a local maximum point whereas $x = 2$ is a local minimum point.

Example 9.7

Classify the stationary points of

$$f(x) = \frac{6x^3}{x^4 + x^2 + 2}$$

Solution   Because $x^4 + x^2 + 2$ is ≥ 2 for all x, the denominator is never 0, so $f(x)$ is defined for all x. Differentiation of $f(x)$ yields

$$f'(x) = \frac{-6x^6 + 6x^4 + 36x^2}{(x^4 + x^2 + 2)^2} = \frac{-6x^2(x^4 - x^2 - 6)}{(x^4 + x^2 + 2)^2}$$

In order to study the sign variation of $f'(x)$, we must factorize $x^4 - x^2 - 6$. In fact, we have $x^4 - x^2 - 6 = (x^2)^2 - (x^2) - 6 = (x^2 - 3)(x^2 + 2) = (x - \sqrt{3})(x + \sqrt{3})(x^2 + 2)$. Hence,

$$f'(x) = \frac{-6x^2(x - \sqrt{3})(x + \sqrt{3})(x^2 + 2)}{(x^4 + x^2 + 2)^2}$$

Both the denominator and the factor $(x^2 + 2)$ in the numerator are always positive. Hence, the sign variation of $f'(x)$ is determined by the other factors in the numerator, as in the following sign diagram. Studying it we conclude from (a) in Theorem 9.1 that $x = \sqrt{3}$ is a local maximum point, and from (b) that $x = -\sqrt{3}$ is a local minimum point. According to (c), $x = 0$ is neither a local maximum, nor a local minimum point, because $f'(x) > 0$ in $(-\sqrt{3}, 0)$ and in $(0, \sqrt{3})$.

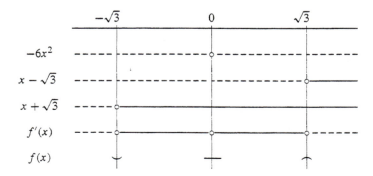

The graph is shown in Fig. 9.9. Note that $f(-x) = -f(x)$ for all x, so the graph of f is symmetric about the origin.

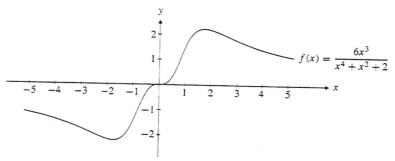

FIGURE 9.9

The Second-Derivative Test

For most problems of practical interest in which an explicit function is specified, Theorem 9.1 will determine whether a stationary point is a local maximum, a local minimum, or neither. Note that the theorem requires the knowledge of $f'(x)$ at points in a neighborhood of the given stationary point. In the next sufficiency theorem, we need only properties of the function at the stationary point.

Theorem 9.2 (The Second-Derivative Test)   Let f be a twice differentiable function in an interval I. Suppose c is an interior point of I. Then:

(a) $f'(c) = 0$ and $f''(c) < 0 \Longrightarrow c$ is a strict local maximum point.
(b) $f'(c) = 0$ and $f''(c) > 0 \Longrightarrow c$ is a strict local minimum point.
(c) $f'(c) = 0$ and $f''(c) = 0 \Longrightarrow$?

Proof   To prove part (a), assume $f'(c) = 0$ and $f''(c) < 0$. By definition of $f''(c)$ as the derivative of $f'(x)$ at c.

$$f''(c) = \lim_{h \to 0} \frac{f'(c+h) - f'(c)}{h} = \lim_{h \to 0} \frac{f'(c+h)}{h} \qquad [*]$$

Because $f''(c) < 0$, it follows from [*] that $f'(c+h)/h < 0$ if $|h|$ is sufficiently small. In particular, if h is a small positive number, then $f'(c+h) < 0$, so f' is negative in an interval to the right of c. In the same way, we see that f' is positive in some interval to the left of c. But then c is a strict local maximum point for f. Part (b) can be proved in the same way; for the inconclusive part (c), see the comments that follow.

Theorem 9.2 leaves unsettled case (c) when $f'(c) = f''(c) = 0$. Then "anything" can happen. Each of three functions $f(x) = x^4$, $f(x) = -x^4$, and $f(x) = x^3$ satisfies $f'(0) = f''(0) = 0$. At $x = 0$, they have, respectively, a (local)

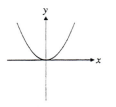

FIGURE 9.10
$f'(0) = f''(0) = 0$.
0 is a minimum
point.

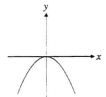

FIGURE 9.11
$f'(0) = f''(0) = 0$.
0 is a maximum
point.

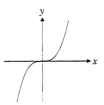

FIGURE 9.12
$f'(0) = f''(0) = 0$.
0 is an inflection
point.

minimum, a (local) maximum, and a point of inflection, as shown in Figs. 9.10 to 9.12. Usually (as here), Theorem 9.1 can be used to classify stationary points at which $f'(c) = f''(c) = 0$. (For the definition of an inflection point, see [9.11] in Section 9.5.)

Theorem 9.2 can be used to obtain a useful necessary condition for local extrema. Suppose f is differentiable in the interval I and suppose that c is an interior point of I that is a local maximum point. Then $f'(c) = 0$. Moreover, $f''(c) > 0$ is impossible, because by Theorem 9.2 (b) this inequality would imply that c is a strict local minimum. Hence, $f''(c)$ has to be ≤ 0. In the same way, we see that $f''(c) \geq 0$ is a necessary condition for local minimum. Briefly formulated:

$$c \text{ is a local maximum for } f \implies f''(c) \leq 0 \qquad [9.8]$$

$$c \text{ is a local minimum for } f \implies f''(c) \geq 0 \qquad [9.9]$$

The function studied in Example 9.7 is a typical example of when it is convenient to study the sign variation of the first derivative in order to classify the stationary points. (Using Theorem 9.2 requires finding $f''(x)$, which is a rather involved expression.)

In theoretical economic models, it is more common to restrict the signs of second derivatives than to postulate a certain behavior in the sign variation of first derivatives. We consider a typical example.

Example 9.8

If a firm producing some commodity has revenue function $R(Q)$, cost function $C(Q)$, and there is a sales tax of t dollars per unit, then $Q^* > 0$ can only maximize profits provided that

$$R'(Q^*) = C'(Q^*) + t \qquad [*]$$

(See Example 9.5 of Section 9.3, Equation [5].) Suppose $R''(Q^*) < 0$ and $C''(Q^*) > 0$. Equation [*] implicitly defines Q^* as a differentiable function of t. Find an expression for dQ^*/dt and discuss its sign. Also compute the derivative with respect to t of the optimal value $\pi(Q^*)$ of the profit function, and show that $d\pi(Q^*)/dt = -Q^*$.

Solution   Differentiating [∗] totally with respect to t yields

$$R''(Q^*)\frac{dQ^*}{dt} = C''(Q^*)\frac{dQ^*}{dt} + 1$$

Solving for dQ^*/dt gives

$$\frac{dQ^*}{dt} = \frac{1}{R''(Q^*) - C''(Q^*)} \qquad [\ast\ast]$$

The sign assumptions on R'' and C'' imply that $dQ^*/dt < 0$. Thus, the optimal number of units produced will decline if the tax rate t increases.

The optimal value of the profit is $\pi(Q^*) = R(Q^*) - C(Q^*) - tQ^*$. Taking into account the dependence of Q^* on t, we get

$$\frac{d\pi^*(Q^*)}{dt} = R'(Q^*)\frac{dQ^*}{dt} - C'(Q^*)\frac{dQ^*}{dt} - Q^* - t\frac{dQ^*}{dt}$$

$$= \left[R'(Q^*) - C'(Q^*)\right]\frac{dQ^*}{dt} - Q^* - t\frac{dQ^*}{dt} = -Q^*$$

where we used [∗]. Thus, we see that by increasing the tax rate by one unit, the optimal profit will decline by Q^* units. Note how the terms in dQ^*/dt disappear from this last expression because of the first-order condition [∗]. This is an instance of the "envelope theorem," which will be discussed in Section 18.7.

Example 9.9   (When to Harvest a Tree?)

Consider a tree that is planted at time $t = 0$, and let $P(t)$ be its current market value at time t, where $P(t)$ is differentiable. When should this tree be cut down in order to maximize its present discounted value? Assume that the interest rate is $100r\%$ per year, compounded continuously.

Solution   By using [8.28] in Section 8.5, the present value is

$$f(t) = P(t)e^{-rt} \qquad [1]$$

whose derivative is

$$f'(t) = P'(t)e^{-rt} + P(t)(-r)e^{-rt} = e^{-rt}\left[P'(t) - rP(t)\right] \qquad [2]$$

A necessary condition for $t^* > 0$ to maximize $f(t)$ is that $f'(t^*) = 0$. We see from [2] that this occurs when

$$P'(t^*) = rP(t^*) \qquad [3]$$

The tree, therefore, should be cut down precisely at time t^* when the increase in the value of the tree over time interval $(t^*, t^* + 1)$ ($\approx P'(t^*)$) is equal to the interest one would obtain over this time interval by investing amount $P(t^*)$ at interest rate r ($\approx r P(t^*)$).

Let us look at the second-order condition. From [2], we find that

$$f''(t) = -re^{-rt}\left[P'(t) - rP(t)\right] + e^{-rt}\left[P''(t) - rP'(t)\right]$$

Evaluating $f''(t)$ at t^* and using [3] yields

$$f''(t^*) = e^{-rt^*}\left[P''(t^*) - rP'(t^*)\right] \qquad\qquad [4]$$

Assuming $P(t^*) > 0$ and $P''(t^*) < 0$, from [3] we have $P'(t^*) > 0$. Then [4] gives $f''(t^*) < 0$, so t^* defined by [3] is a local maximum point. An example is given in Problem 4.

In this example, we did not consider how the ground the tree grows on may be used after cutting—for example, by planting a new tree. See Problem 5.

Note: In accepting maximization of present discounted value as a reasonable criterion for when a tree ought to be felled, one automatically dismisses the naïve solution to the problem: Cut down the tree at the time when its current market value is greatest. Instead, the tree is typically cut down a bit sooner, because of "impatience" associated with discounting.

Problems

1. Consider the function f defined for all x by

$$f(x) = x^3 - 12x$$

   Find the two stationary points of f and classify them both by using the first- and second-derivative tests.

2. Determine all local extreme points and corresponding extreme values for the functions given by the following formulas:

   a. $f(x) = -2x - 1$ **b.** $f(x) = x^3 - 3x + 8$

   c. $f(x) = x + 1/x$ **d.** $f(x) = x^5 - 5x^3$

   e. $f(x) = \frac{1}{2}x^2 - 3x + 5$ **f.** $f(x) = x^3 + 3x^2 - 2$

3. A function f is given by the formula

$$f(x) = (1 + 2/x)\sqrt{x + 6}$$

   a. Find the domain of f, the zeros of f, and the intervals where $f(x)$ is positive.

   b. Find possible local extreme points and values.

c. Examine $f(x)$ as $x \to 0^-$, $x \to 0^+$, and $x \to \infty$. Also determine the limit of $f'(x)$ as $x \to \infty$. Has f a maximum or a minimum in the domain?

4. With reference to the tree-cutting problem of Example 9.9, consider the case where

$$f(t) = (t^2 + 10t + 25)e^{-0.05t} \qquad (t \geq 0)$$

a. Find the value of t that maximizes $f(t)$. Prove that the maximum point has been found.

b. Find $\lim_{t \to \infty} f(t)$ and draw the graph of f.

5. Consider Example 9.9. Assume now that immediately after a tree is felled, a new tree of the same type is planted. If we assume that a new tree is planted at times t, $2t$, $3t$, etc., then the present value of all the trees will be

$$f(t) = P(t)e^{-rt} + P(t)e^{-2rt} + \cdots$$

a. Find the sum of this infinite geometric series.

b. Prove that if $f(t)$ has a maximum for some $t^* > 0$, then

$$P'(t^*) = r \frac{P(t^*)}{1 - e^{-rt^*}}$$

and compare this condition to condition [3] in Example 9.9.

6. What requirements must be imposed on constants a, b, and c in order that

$$f(x) = x^3 + ax^2 + bx + c$$

a. will have a local minimum at $x = 0$?

b. will have stationary points at $x = 1$ and $x = 3$?

7. Figure 9.13 graphs the *derivative* of a function f. Which of points a, b, c, d, and e are local maximum or minimum points for f?

8. Let function f be defined by

$$f(x) = \frac{x}{x^2 + 3x + 2}$$

FIGURE 9.13

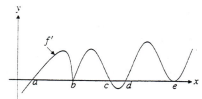

    a. Find $f'(x)$ and $f''(x)$, and find the local extreme points of f.
    b. Find the global extreme points, and draw the graph of f.
    c. Use the previous results to find global extreme points for the function g
       defined for all x by $g(x) = f(e^x)$.

  9. Consider the function

$$f(x) = \frac{3}{x^4 - x^2 + 1}$$

    a. Compute $f'(x)$ and find all local maximum and minimum points for f.
       Has f any global extreme points?
    b. Draw the graph of f.

Harder Problems

  10. Discuss local extreme points for the function $f(x) = x^3 + ax + b$. Use the
     result to show that the equation $f(x) = 0$ has three different real roots if and
     only if $4a^3 + 27b^2 < 0$.

  11. Let f be defined for all x by $f(x) = (x^2 - 1)^{2/3}$.
    a. Compute $f'(x)$ and $f''(x)$.
    b. Find the local extreme points of f, and draw the graph of f.

9.5 Convex and Concave Functions and Inflection Points

What can be learnt from the sign of the second derivative? Recall how the sign of
the first derivative determines whether a function is increasing or decreasing:

$$f'(x) \geq 0 \text{ on } (a, b) \iff f(x) \text{ is increasing on } (a, b) \qquad [1]$$

$$f'(x) \leq 0 \text{ on } (a, b) \iff f(x) \text{ is decreasing on } (a, b) \qquad [2]$$

The second derivative $f''(x)$ is the derivative of $f'(x)$. Hence:

$$f''(x) \geq 0 \text{ on } (a, b) \iff f'(x) \text{ is increasing on } (a, b) \qquad [3]$$

$$f''(x) \leq 0 \text{ on } (a, b) \iff f'(x) \text{ is decreasing on } (a, b) \qquad [4]$$

The equivalence in [3] is illustrated in Fig. 9.14. The slope of the tangent,
$f'(x)$, is increasing as x increases. On the other hand, the slope of the tangent to the graph in Fig. 9.15 is decreasing as x increases. (Place a ruler as
a tangent to the graph of the function. As the ruler slides along the curve
from left to right, the tangent rotates counterclockwise in Fig. 9.14, clockwise
in Fig. 9.15.)

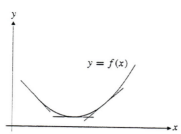

FIGURE 9.14 The slope of the tangent increases as *x* increases. *f'(x)* is increasing.

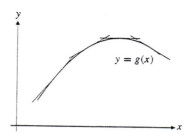

FIGURE 9.15 The slope of the tangent decreases as *x* increases. *g'(x)* is decreasing.

We introduce the following definitions, assuming that f is continuous in the interval I and twice differentiable in the interior of I, denoted by I^0:

f is **convex** on I $\iff$ $f''(x) \geq 0$ for all x in I^0

f is **concave** on I $\iff$ $f''(x) \leq 0$ for all x in I^0

[9.10]

The distinction between convexity and concavity of a function is absolutely crucial in many economic models. Study carefully the cases illustrated in Fig. 9.16.

Example 9.10

Check the convexity/concavity of the following:

(a) $f(x) = x^2 - 2x + 2$ and (b) $f(x) = ax^2 + bx + c$

Solution

(a) Here $f'(x) = 2x - 2$ so $f''(x) = 2$. Because $f''(x) > 0$ for all x, f is convex.

(b) Here $f'(x) = 2ax + b$, so $f''(x) = 2a$. If $a = 0$, then f is linear and f is convex as well as concave. If $a > 0$, then $f''(x) > 0$, so f is convex. If $a < 0$, then $f''(x) < 0$, so f is concave. Compare with the graphs in Fig. 3.1 in Section 3.1.

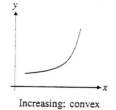

Increasing: convex

Increasing: concave

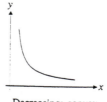

Decreasing: convex

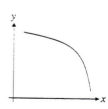

Decreasing: concave

FIGURE 9.16

Some Typical Examples

We consider two typical examples of convex and concave functions. In Fig. 9.17 we have drawn roughly the graph of function P, where

$$P(t) = \text{world population (in 1000 millions) in year } t$$

It appears from the figure that not only is $P(t)$ increasing, but the rate of increase increases. (Each year the *increase* becomes larger.) So $P(t)$ is convex.

The graph in Fig. 9.18 shows the crop of wheat $Y(N)$ when N pounds of fertilizer per acre are used, based on fertilizer experiments in Iowa during 1952 (see Example 9.2 in Section 9.2). The function has a maximum at $N = N_0 \approx 172$. Increasing the amount of fertilizer beyond N_0 will cause wheat production to decline. Moreover, $Y(N)$ is concave. If $N < N_0$, increasing N by one unit will lead to less *increase* in $Y(N)$ the larger is N. On the other hand, if $N > N_0$, increasing N by one unit will lead to a larger *decrease* in $Y(N)$ the larger is N.

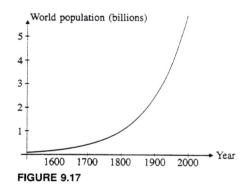

FIGURE 9.17

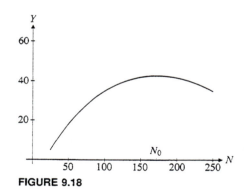

FIGURE 9.18

Example 9.11

Examine the concavity/convexity of the production function

$$Y = AK^a \qquad (A > 0, \quad 0 < a < 1)$$

defined for all $K > 0$.

Solution   Differentiating Y twice with respect to K yields

$$Y'' = Aa(a - 1)K^{a-2}$$

Because $a \in (0, 1)$, coefficient $Aa(a - 1) < 0$, so that $Y'' < 0$ for all $K > 0$. Hence, the function is concave. The graph of $Y = AK^a$, for $0 < a < 1$, is

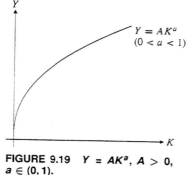

FIGURE 9.19 $Y = AK^a$, $A > 0$, $a \in (0, 1)$.

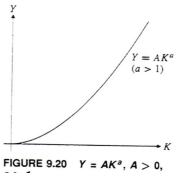

FIGURE 9.20 $Y = AK^a$, $A > 0$, $a > 1$.

shown in in Fig. 9.19. If $a > 1$, then $Y'' > 0$ and Y is a convex function of K, as shown in Fig. 9.20.

Example 9.12

Suppose that functions U and g are both increasing and concave, so that $U' \geq 0$, $U'' \leq 0$, $g' \geq 0$, and $g'' \leq 0$. Prove that the composite function

$$f(x) = g(U(x))$$

is also increasing and concave.

Solution Using the chain rule yields

$$f'(x) = g'(U(x)) \cdot U'(x) \qquad [*]$$

Because g' and U' are both ≥ 0, so $f'(x) \geq 0$. Hence, f is increasing. (*An increasing transformation of an increasing function is increasing.*)

In order to compute $f''(x)$, we must differentiate the product of the two functions $g'(U(x))$ and $U'(x)$. According to the chain rule, the derivative of $g'(U(x))$ is equal to $g''(U(x)) \cdot U'(x)$. Hence,

$$f''(x) = g''[U(x)] \cdot (U'(x))^2 + g'(U(x)) \cdot U''(x) \qquad [**]$$

Because $g'' \leq 0$, $g' \geq 0$, and $U'' \leq 0$, it follows that $f''(x) \leq 0$. (*An increasing concave transformation of a concave function is concave.*)

Inflection Points

Functions we study in economics are often convex in some parts of the domain but concave in others. Points at which a function changes from being convex to being concave, or vice versa, are called inflection points.

Inflection Points

Point c is an **inflection point** for a twice differentiable function f if there is an interval (a, b) containing c such that either of the following two conditions holds:

[9.11]

    (a) $f''(x) \geq 0$ if $a < x < c$ and $f''(x) \leq 0$ if $c < x < b$

or

    (b) $f''(x) \leq 0$ if $a < x < c$ and $f''(x) \geq 0$ if $c < x < b$

Briefly, $x = c$ is an inflection point if $f''(x)$ changes sign at c. We also refer to the point $(c, f(c))$ as an inflection point on the graph. An example is given in Fig. 9.21. Figure 9.22 shows the profile of a ski jump. Point P, where the hill is steepest, is an inflection point.

Theorem 9.3   (Test for Inflection Points)   Let f be a function with a continuous second derivative in an interval I, and suppose that c is an interior point of I.

(a) If c is an inflection point for f, then $f''(c) = 0$.
(b) If $f''(c) = 0$ and f'' changes sign at c, then c is an inflection point for f.

FIGURE 9.21   Point *P* is an inflection point on the graph (*x = c* is an inflection point for the function).

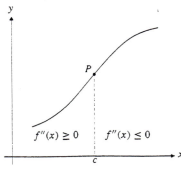

FIGURE 9.22   Point *P*, where the slope is steepest, is an inflection point.

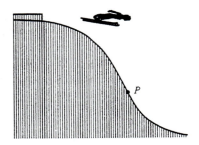

Proof

(a) Because $f''(x) \leq 0$ on one side of c and $f''(x) \geq 0$ on the other, $f''(c) = 0$.

(b) If f'' changes sign about point c, then c is an inflection point for f according to [9.11].

According to Theorem 9.3 (a), the condition $f''(c) = 0$ is a *necessary* condition for c to be an inflection point. It is not a sufficient condition, however, because $f''(c) = 0$ does not imply that f'' changes sign at $x = c$. A typical case is given in the next example.

Example 9.13

Show that $f(x) = x^4$ does not have an inflection point at $x = 0$, even though $f''(0) = 0$.

Solution   Here $f'(x) = 4x^3$ and $f''(x) = 12x^2$, so that $f''(0) = 0$. But $f''(x) > 0$ for all $x \neq 0$, and hence f'' does not change sign at $x = 0$. Hence, $x = 0$ is not an inflection point. (In fact, it is a global minimum, of course, as shown in Fig. 9.10 in Section 9.4.)

Example 9.14

Find possible inflection points for $f(x) = \frac{1}{9}x^3 - \frac{1}{6}x^2 - \frac{2}{3}x + 1$.

Solution   We find the first and second derivatives to be

$$f'(x) = \frac{1}{3}x^2 - \frac{1}{3}x - \frac{2}{3} \quad \text{and} \quad f''(x) = \frac{2}{3}x - \frac{1}{3} = \frac{2}{3}\left(x - \frac{1}{2}\right)$$

Hence, $f''(x) < 0$ for $x < 1/2$, whereas $f''(1/2) = 0$ and $f''(x) > 0$ for $x > 1/2$. According to Theorem 9.3(b), $x = 1/2$ is an inflection point for f.

Example 9.15

Find possible inflection points for $f(x) = x^2 e^x$. Draw its graph. (See Example 8.2, Section 8.1.)

Solution   The first derivative of f is $f'(x) = 2xe^x + x^2 e^x$, so the second derivative is

$$f''(x) = 2e^x + 2xe^x + 2xe^x + x^2 e^x = e^x(x^2 + 4x + 2) = e^x(x - x_1)(x - x_2)$$

where $x_1 = -2 - \sqrt{2} \approx -3.41$ and $x_2 = -2 + \sqrt{2} \approx -0.59$ are the two roots of the quadratic equation $x^2 + 4x + 2 = 0$. The sign diagram associated with $f''(x)$ is shown below. From this diagram we see that f has inflection points at $x = x_1$ and at $x = x_2$. The graph is convex in the intervals $(-\infty, x_1]$ and $[x_2, \infty)$, and it is concave in $[x_1, x_2]$. See

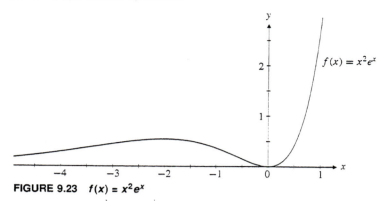

FIGURE 9.23 $f(x) = x^2 e^x$

Fig. 9.23 in which we have also taken advantage of the results of Example 8.2.

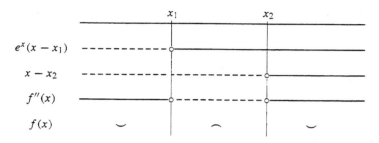

Example 9.16

A firm produces a commodity using only one input. Let $x = f(v)$, $v \geq 0$, be the maximum production obtainable when v units of the input are used. Then f is called a **production function**. It is often assumed that the marginal product $f'(v)$ is increasing up to a certain production level v_0, and then decreasing. Such a production function is indicated in Fig. 9.24. If f is

FIGURE 9.24 f is a production function. v_0 is an inflection point.

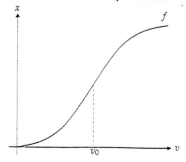

twice differentiable, then $f''(v)$ is ≥ 0 in $[0, v_0)$ and ≤ 0 in (v_0, ∞). Hence, f is first convex and then concave, with v_0 as an inflection point. An example of such a function is given in Problem 9.

A Useful Result

Suppose that $f''(x) \leq 0$ for all x in an interval I. Then $f'(x)$ is decreasing in I. So if $f'(c) = 0$ for an interior point c in I, then $f'(x)$ must be ≥ 0 to the left of c, whereas $f'(x) \leq 0$ to the right of c. This implies that the function itself is increasing to the left of c, and decreasing to the right of c. We conclude that $x = c$ is a maximum point for f in I. This important observation is illustrated in Fig. 9.25. We have a corresponding result for the minimum of a convex function.

Theorem 9.4   (Maximum/Minimum for Concave/Convex Functions)
Suppose f is a concave (convex) function in an interval I. If c is a stationary point for f in the interior of I, then c is a maximum point (minimum point) for f in I. Briefly stated, when c is an interior point of I, then

$$f''(x) \leq 0 \text{ for all } x \in I, \text{ and } f'(c) = 0 \Longrightarrow$$
$$x = c \text{ is a maximum point for } f \text{ in } I \qquad [9.12]$$

$$f''(x) \geq 0 \text{ for all } x \in I, \text{ and } f'(c) = 0 \Longrightarrow$$
$$x = c \text{ is a minimum point for } f \text{ in } I \qquad [9.13]$$

Example 9.17
Let the total cost of producing Q units of a commodity be

$$C(Q) = aQ^2 + bQ + c, \qquad (Q > 0)$$

FIGURE 9.25   *f* is concave, *f'(c)* = 0, and *c* is a maximum point.

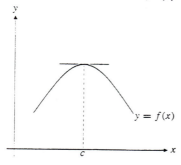

$y = f(x)$

where a, b, and c are positive constants. Prove that the average cost function $A(Q) = aQ + b + c/Q$ has a minimum at $Q^* = \sqrt{c/a}$. (See also Problem 8 in Section 9.3.)

Solution   The first-order derivative of $A(Q)$ is

$$A'(Q) = a - c/Q^2$$

and the only stationary point is $Q^* = \sqrt{c/a}$. Because $A''(Q) = 2c/Q^3 > 0$ for all $Q > 0$, $A(Q)$ is convex, and by Theorem 9.4, $Q^* = \sqrt{c/a}$ is the minimum point.

Problems

1. Determine the concavity/convexity of $f(x) = -\frac{1}{3}x^2 + 8x - 3$.

2. Let f be defined for all x by $f(x) = x^3 + \frac{3}{2}x^2 - 6x + 10$.
   a. Find $f'(x)$ and $f''(x)$.
   b. Find the stationary points of f and the intervals where f is increasing.
   c. Find the inflection points of f and the intervals of concavity/convexity.

3. A competitive firm receives a price p for each unit of its output, pays a price w for each unit of its only variable input, and incurs fixed costs of F. Its output from using x units of variable input is $f(x) = \sqrt{x}$.
   a. Write the firm's revenue, cost, and profit functions.
   b. Write the first-order condition for profit maximization, and give it an economic interpretation.
   c. Check whether profit really is maximized at a point satisfying the first-order condition.
   d. Explain how your answers would change if $f(x) = x^2$.

4. What are the extreme points and the inflection points of function f whose graph is given in Fig. 9.26?

5. Decide where the following functions are convex and determine possible inflection points:

   a. $f(x) = \dfrac{x}{1 + x^2}$ b. $g(x) = \dfrac{1 - x}{1 + x}$ c. $h(x) = xe^x$

FIGURE 9.26

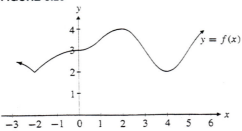

6. Find numbers a and b such that the graph of

$$f(x) = ax^3 + bx^2$$

passes through $(-1, 1)$ and has an inflection point at $x = 1/2$.

7. Find the intervals where the following cubic cost function is convex and where it is concave, and find the unique inflection point:

$$C(Q) = aQ^3 + bQ^2 + cQ + d, \qquad (a > 0, \quad b < 0, \quad c > 0, \quad d > 0)$$

8. With reference to Example 9.5, let $R(Q) = PQ$ and $C(Q) = aQ^b + c$, where P, a, b, and c are positive constants with $b > 1$. Find the value of Q that maximizes profits $\pi(Q) = PQ - (aQ^b + c)$. (Use Theorem 9.4.)

Harder Problems

9. With reference to Example 9.16, let $f(v) = (v - 1)^{1/3} + 1$ for $v \geq 0$.
   a. Show that f is an increasing function of v and that $f''(v) > 0$ in $[0, 1)$, $f''(v) < 0$ in $(1, \infty)$. Draw the graph of f.
   b. Suppose that the price per unit of the commodity is 1 and that the price the firm must pay per unit of the input is p. The profit is then $\pi(v) = f(v) - pv$. Suppose that $v_m > 0$ maximizes $\pi(v)$ for the given value of $p > 0$. Find v_m expressed in terms of p.
   c. Draw the graph of π for the case $p = 1$. Use the same diagram as in part (a).
   d. Find the nonnegative roots of the equation $\pi(v) = 0$. For which values of p are there three real roots?
   e. For all values of p, find the solution of the problem

$$\text{maximize } \pi(v) \text{ subject to } v \geq 0$$

9.6 More on Concave and Convex Functions

So far convexity and concavity have been defined only for functions that are twice differentiable. An alternative geometric characterization of convexity and concavity suggests a more general definition that is valid even for functions that are not differentiable. It is also easier to extend this new generalized definition to functions of several variables.

Function f is called **concave (convex)** if the line segment joining any two points on the graph is never above (below) the graph. [9.14]

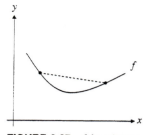

FIGURE 9.27 *f* is convex.

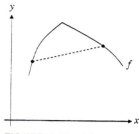

FIGURE 9.28 *f* is concave.

These definitions are illustrated in the Figs. 9.27 and 9.28. For twice differentiable functions, one can prove that the definition in [9.14] is equivalent to the definitions of convexity/concavity in terms of the sign of the second derivative.

In order to use [9.14] to examine convexity/concavity of a given function, we must have an algebraic formulation of this definition. To this end, note that an arbitrary point x in the interval $[a, b]$ (with $a < b$) can be written as

$$x = (1 - \lambda)a + \lambda b = a + \lambda(b - a) \qquad \text{(for some } \lambda \in [0, 1])$$

For if $b > a$ and $0 \le \lambda \le 1$, then $a \le a + \lambda(b - a) \le b$. Conversely, if $x \in [a, b]$ and we put $\lambda = (x - a)/(b - a)$, then $0 \le \lambda \le 1$ and

$$(1 - \lambda)a + \lambda b = \left(1 - \frac{x - a}{b - a}\right) a + \frac{x - a}{b - a} b = \frac{ba - a^2 - xa + a^2 + xb - ab}{b - a} = x$$

(Here $\lambda = (x - a)/(b - a)$ is the ratio between the distance from x to a and the total distance from a to b.)

Consider Fig. 9.29. We want to calculate the number s. According to the point–point formula (2.7) of Section 2.5, the line through $(a, f(a))$ and $(b, f(b))$ has the equation

$$y - f(a) = \frac{f(b) - f(a)}{b - a}(x - a)$$

Let $x = (1 - \lambda)a + \lambda b$. Then $y = s$, and so

$$s - f(a) = \frac{f(b) - f(a)}{b - a}\left[(1 - \lambda)a + \lambda b - a\right] = \lambda\left[f(b) - f(a)\right]$$

implying that $s = (1 - \lambda)f(a) + \lambda f(b)$. Now, as λ takes on all values in $[0, 1]$, so the number $(1 - \lambda)a + \lambda b$ will take on all values in $[a, b]$. The requirement that the line segment joining $(a, f(a))$ and $(b, f(b))$ always lies below (or on) the

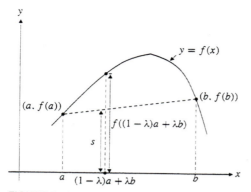

FIGURE 9.29

graph of f is therefore equivalent to the requirement that $s \leq f((1 - \lambda)a + \lambda b)$ for all $\lambda \in [0, 1]$. The following definitions should now be quite understandable.

Function f is **concave** in the interval I if for all $a, b \in I$ and all $\lambda \in (0, 1)$,

$$f((1 - \lambda)a + \lambda b) \geq (1 - \lambda)f(a) + \lambda f(b)$$

[9.15]

Function f is convex if $-f$ is concave (see Fig. 9.1). So the following holds:

Function f is **convex** in the interval I if for all $a, b \in I$ and all $\lambda \in (0, 1)$,

$$f((1 - \lambda)a + \lambda b) \leq (1 - \lambda)f(a) + \lambda f(b)$$

[9.16]

Note that these definitions can be applied to functions that are not even differentiable.

In definition [9.15], if we require that the inequality is strict for $a \neq b$, then f is called **strictly concave**; the graph of f will always be strictly above the line segment joining any two points on the graph. For instance, the function graphed in Fig. 9.29 is strictly concave. Fig. 9.30 shows a typical case in which the function is concave, but not strictly concave. Function f is **strictly convex** if $-f$ is strictly concave.

Example 9.18

Prove that $f(x) = |x|$ is convex in $(-\infty, \infty)$. (See the graph of f in Fig. 9.31.)

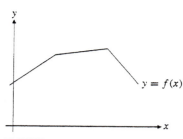

FIGURE 9.30 Concave; not
strictly concave.

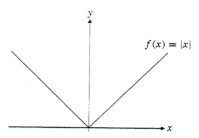

FIGURE 9.31 Convex; not
differentiable at $x = 0$.

Solution Let a and b be arbitrary numbers, and let $\lambda \in [0, 1]$. We have to show that the difference D between the left and the right side of the inequality in [9.16] is always ≤ 0. Because $|xy| = |x||y|$ and $|x + y| \leq |x| + |y|$ for all real x, y, it follows that

$$f((1 - \lambda)a + \lambda b) - [(1 - \lambda)f(a) + \lambda f(b)] = |(1 - \lambda)a + \lambda b| - (1 - \lambda)|a| - \lambda|b|$$
$$\leq (1 - \lambda)|a| + \lambda|b| - (1 - \lambda)|a| - \lambda|b|$$
$$= 0$$

Thus, $f(x) = |x|$ is convex.

For twice differentiable functions, it is usually much easier to decide concavity/convexity by checking the sign of the second derivative than by using definitions [9.15] and [9.16]. However, in theoretical arguments, the latter definitions are often very useful, and they generalize easily to functions of several variables.

Example 9.19

Suppose $U(x)$ is a concave function defined in an interval I. Let g be an increasing concave function defined in an interval containing the range of U, and define $f(x) = g(U(x))$. Prove that $f(x)$ is concave in I. (In Example 9.12 in Section 9.5 we proved this result with "unnecessary" differentiability assumptions.)

Solution Let a and b belong to I, with $a < b$, and let $\lambda \in [0, 1]$. By definition of f,

$$f((1 - \lambda)a + \lambda b) = g(U((1 - \lambda)a + \lambda b)) \tag{1}$$

Because U is concave,

$$U((1 - \lambda)a + \lambda b) \geq (1 - \lambda)U(a) + \lambda U(b) \tag{2}$$

Because g is increasing, $r \geq s$ implies $g(r) \geq g(s)$. Hence, applying g to each side of [2] yields

$$g(U((1 - \lambda)a + \lambda b)) \geq g((1 - \lambda)U(a) + \lambda U(b)) \qquad [3]$$

By the concavity of g,

$$g((1 - \lambda)U(a) + \lambda U(b)) \geq (1 - \lambda)g(U(a)) + \lambda g(U(b))$$
$$= (1 - \lambda)f(a) + \lambda f(b) \qquad [4]$$

From [1], [3], and [4], we see that $f((1 - \lambda)a + \lambda b) \geq (1 - \lambda)f(a) + \lambda f(b)$, so f *is* concave.

An easy test for strict concavity/convexity is the following, which we present without proof:

$$\boxed{\begin{aligned} &f''(x) < 0 \text{ for all } x \in (a, b) \implies f(x) \text{ is strictly concave in } (a, b) \\ &f''(x) > 0 \text{ for all } x \in (a, b) \implies f(x) \text{ is strictly convex in } (a, b) \end{aligned}} \qquad [9.17]$$

The reverse implications are not correct. For instance, one can prove that $f(x) = x^4$ is strictly convex in the interval $(-\infty, \infty)$, but $f''(x)$ is not > 0 everywhere, because $f''(0) = 0$.

Note: Here are some of the most commonly used functions that are concave (convex) in their domains:

Concave: $ax^2 + bx + c$ $(a \leq 0)$, x^a $(0 \leq a \leq 1, \ x > 0)$, $\ln x$ $(x > 0)$ [1]

Convex: $ax^2 + bx + c$ $(a \geq 0)$, x^a $(a \geq 1, \ x > 0)$, e^{ax}, $|x|$ [2]

It follows immediately from definitions [9.15 $f(x)$, $g(x)$] and [9.16] that nonnegative linear combinations $af(x) + bg(x)(a, b \geq a)$ of concave (convex) functions are concave (convex). Using these facts and [1] and [2], we can often quite easily decide concavity/convexity. In Sections 17.7 and 17.8, we shall prove many other properties that will help us decide concavity (convexity).

Jensen's Inequality

Looking at definition [9.15] of a concave function, suppose we put $a = x_1$, $b = x_2$, $1 - \lambda = \lambda_1$, and $\lambda = \lambda_2$. Then definition [9.15] would read: $f(x)$ is concave on I if for all x_1 and x_2 in I, and for all $\lambda_1 \geq 0$ and $\lambda_2 \geq 0$ with $\lambda_1 + \lambda_2 = 1$,

$$f(\lambda_1 x_1 + \lambda_2 x_2) \geq \lambda_1 f(x_1) + \lambda_2 f(x_2)$$

Jensen's inequality is a generalization of this inequality.

Jensen's Inequality

A function f is concave in the interval I if and only if the following inequality is satisfied for all $x_1, \ldots, x_n$ in I, and for all $\lambda_1 \geq 0, \ldots, \lambda_n \geq 0$ with $\lambda_1 + \cdots + \lambda_n = 1$:

$$f(\lambda_1 x_1 + \cdots + \lambda_n x_n) \geq \lambda_1 f(x_1) + \cdots + \lambda_n f(x_n) \qquad [9.18]$$

The corresponding result for the case where f is convex is obtained by reversing the inequality in [9.18]. The more general vector version of this result is given in Section 17.6.

Example 9.20 **(Production Smoothing)**
Consider a manufacturing firm producing a single commodity. The cost of maintaining an output level y per year for a fraction λ of a year is $\lambda C(y)$, where $C'(y) > 0$ and $C''(y) \geq 0$ for all $y \geq 0$. In fact, the firm's output level can fluctuate over the year. Show that, given the total output Y that the firm produces over the whole year, the firm's total cost per year is minimized by choosing a constant flow of output.

Solution Suppose the firm chooses different output levels $y_1, \ldots, y_n$ per year for fractions of the year $\lambda_1, \ldots, \lambda_n$, respectively. Then the total output is $\sum_{i=1}^{n} \lambda_i y_i = Y$ produced at total cost $\sum_{i=1}^{n} \lambda_i C(y_i)$. Applying Jensen's inequality to the convex function C gives

$$\sum_{i=1}^{n} \lambda_i C(y_i) \geq C\left(\sum_{i=1}^{n} \lambda_i y_i\right) = C(Y)$$

The right-hand side is the cost of maintaining the constant output level Y over the whole year, and this is the minimum cost.

Problems

1. Suppose $f(x) = 1 - x^2$.
   a. Show that $D = f((1 - \lambda)a + \lambda b) - (1 - \lambda)f(a) - \lambda f(b)$ can be written in the form

   $$D = \lambda(1 - \lambda)(a^2 - 2ab + b^2) = \lambda(1 - \lambda)(a - b)^2$$

   b. If $\lambda \in (0, 1)$, what is the sign of D? Is f concave, convex, or neither?
   c. Is f strictly concave/convex?
   d. Check the result in part (c) by using [9.17].

2. Suppose that a function f is concave. What restrictions on a and b will guarantee that $g(x) = af(x) + b$ is also concave?

3. Are the following functions concave/convex (assuming that $x > 0$ in parts (b) and (c))?

   a. $\frac{1}{2}e^x + \frac{1}{2}e^{-x}$ **b.** $2x - 3 + 4\ln x$ **c.** $5x^{0.5} - 10x^{1.5}$

   d. $3x^2 - 2x + 1 + e^{-x-3}$

Harder Problems

4. A consumer is planning to choose a lifetime consumption stream $c_1, \ldots, c_T$ to maximize $(1/T) \sum_{t=1}^{T} u(c_t)$ subject to the budget constraint $(1/T) \sum_{t=1}^{T} c_t \leq (1/T) \sum_{t=1}^{T} y_t$. Here y_t is the income stream, and the utility function satisfies $u'(c) > 0$ and $u''(c) < 0$.

   a. Use Jensen's inequality to show that the optimal consumption is constant and equal to the mean lifetime income.

   b. Replace $(1/T) \sum_{t=1}^{T} u(c_t)$ by $\sum_{t=1}^{T} (1+r)^{-t} u(c_t)$, with the new budget constraint

   $$\sum_{t=1}^{T} (1+r)^{-t}(c_t - y_t) \leq 0$$

   where $r > -1$ is the rate of interest. What is the new optimal consumption stream?

5. Prove that if f and g are both concave, then

   $$h(x) = \min\{f(x), g(x)\}$$

   is concave. Illustrate. (Note that for each given x, $h(x)$ is the smaller of the two numbers $f(x)$ and $g(x)$.)

10

Integration

Indeed, models basically play the same role in economics as in fashion. They provide an articulated frame on which to show off your material to advantage, ... a useful role, but fraught with the dangers that the designer may get carried away by his personal inclination for the model, while the customer may forget that the model is more streamlined than reality.
—*J. H. Drèze* (1984)

The geometric problem of finding the steepness of a curve at a point leads to the concept of the derivative of a function. The derivative turns out to have important interpretations apart from the geometric one. Particularly important in economics is the fact that the derivative represents the rate of change of a function.

The main concept to be discussed in this chapter can also be introduced geometrically. In fact, we begin with the problem of measuring the areas of certain plane regions that are bounded not only by straight lines. Solving this problem will involve the concept of the definite integral of a function over an interval. This concept also has a number of important interpretations in addition to the geometric one.

As early as about 360 B.C., the Greek mathematician Eudoxos developed a general method for determining the areas of plane regions, known as the *method of exhaustion*. The idea was to inscribe and circumscribe the region (say, a circular disk) by simpler geometric regions such as rectangles, triangles, or general polygonal regions—whose area we already know how to measure. Now, if the area of the inscribed region and the area of the circumscribed region tend to the same limit

320

as more and more refined polygons are chosen, this limit is defined as the *area* of the region.

The method of exhaustion was used by Eudoxos and Archimedes to determine the areas of a number of specific plane regions. Similar methods were developed to determine the lengths of curves and the volumes of solids. However, the method of exhaustion turned out to work only in a limited number of cases, partly because of the algebraic problems encountered. Nearly 1900 years passed after Archimedes before anyone else made significant progress in measuring areas of plane regions. In the seventeenth century, a new method of finding areas was devised, called integration, that is closely related to differential calculus. Demonstrating the precise relationship between differentiation and integration is one of the main achievements of mathematical analysis. It has even been argued that this discovery is the single most important in all of science. Barrow, who was Newton's teacher, and Newton and Leibniz in particular, are the mathematicians associated with this discovery.

After these introductory comments, we begin by solving the geometric problem of finding the areas of certain specific plane regions. We then develop the theory of integration based on this foundation.

10.1 Areas under Curves

The problem to be considered in this section is illustrated in Fig. 10.1. It can be formulated as follows: How do we compute the area A under the graph of f from a to b, assuming that $f(x)$ is positive and continuous?

To answer this question, we first introduce the function $A(x)$ that measures the area under the curve $y = f(x)$ over the interval $[a, x]$, as shown in Fig. 10.2. Clearly, $A(a) = 0$, because there is no area from a to a, and the area in Fig. 10.1 is $A = A(b)$.

It is obvious from Fig. 10.2 that because f is always positive, $A(x)$ increases as x increases. Suppose we increase x by a positive amount Δx. Then $A(x + \Delta x)$

FIGURE 10.1

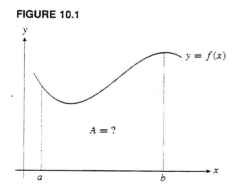

FIGURE 10.2

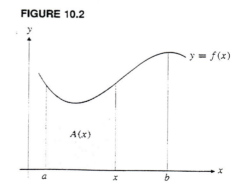

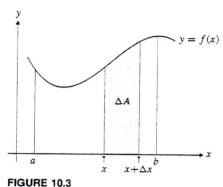

FIGURE 10.3

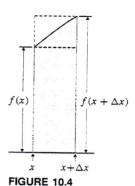

FIGURE 10.4

is the area under the curve $y = f(x)$ over the interval $[a, x + \Delta x]$. Hence, $A(x + \Delta x) - A(x)$ is the area ΔA under the curve over the interval $[x, x + \Delta x]$, as shown in Fig. 10.3.

In Fig. 10.4, area ΔA is magnified. It cannot be larger than the area of the rectangle with edges Δx and $f(x + \Delta x)$, nor smaller than the area of the rectangle with edges Δx and $f(x)$. Hence, for all $\Delta x > 0$,

$$f(x)\,\Delta x \le A(x + \Delta x) - A(x) \le f(x + \Delta x)\,\Delta x \qquad [*]$$

But then

$$f(x) \le \frac{A(x + \Delta x) - A(x)}{\Delta x} \le f(x + \Delta x) \qquad [**]$$

(If $\Delta x < 0$, the inequalities in $[*]$ are reversed, whereas the inequalities in $[**]$ are preserved. The following argument is equally valid when $\Delta x < 0$.) Let us consider what happens to $[**]$ as $\Delta x \to 0$. The interval $[x, x + \Delta x]$ shrinks to the single point x, and by continuity of f, the value $f(x + \Delta x)$ approaches $f(x)$. The Newton quotient $[A(x + \Delta x) - A(x)]/\Delta x$, squeezed between $f(x)$ and a quantity that approaches $f(x)$, must therefore approach $f(x)$ as $\Delta x \to 0$.[1] So we arrive at the remarkable conclusion that the function $A(x)$, which measures the area under the graph of f over the interval $[a, x]$, is differentiable, with derivative given by

$$A'(x) = f(x) \qquad \text{(for all } x \in (a, b))$$

This proves that *the derivative of the area function $A(x)$ is the curve's "height" function $f(x)$.*

---

[1] The function f in the figures is increasing in the interval $[x, x + \Delta x]$. It is easy to see that the same conclusion is obtained whatever the behavior of f in the interval $[x, x + \Delta x]$. On the left-hand side of $[*]$, just replace $f(x)$ by $f(c)$, where c is the minimum point of the continuous function f in the interval; and on the right-hand side, replace $f(x + \Delta x)$ by $f(d)$, where d is the maximum point of f in $[x, x + \Delta x]$.

Suppose that $F(x)$ is another continuous function with $f(x)$ as its derivative, so that $F'(x) = A'(x) = f(x)$ for all $x \in (a, b)$. Because $(d/dx)[A(x) - F(x)] = A'(x) - F'(x) = 0$, it must be true that $A(x) = F(x) + C$ for some constant C (see Theorem 7.7 of Section 7.3). Recall that $A(a) = 0$. Hence, $0 = A(a) = F(a) + C$, so $C = -F(a)$. Therefore,

$$A(x) = F(x) - F(a) \quad \text{when} \quad F'(x) = f(x) \qquad \text{[10.1]}$$

This leads to the following.

Method for finding the area below the curve $y = f(x)$ and above the x-axis from $x = a$ to $x = b$:

1. Find an arbitrary function F that is continuous on $[a, b]$ such that $F'(x) = f(x)$ for all $x \in (a, b)$.
2. The required area is then $F(b) - F(a)$.

[10.2]

A function F with the property that $F'(x) = f(x)$ for all x in some open interval, is often called an **antiderivative** of f. Note that there are always many such antiderivatives because $(d/dx)[F(x) + C] = F'(x) = f(x)$ whenever C is any real constant.

Example 10.1

Calculate the area under the parabola $f(x) = x^2$ over the interval $[0, 1]$.

Solution   The area in question is the shaded region A in Fig. 10.5. According to step 1 of [10.2], we must find a function having x^2 as its derivative. We look for a power function. Indeed $(d/dx)ax^n = anx^{n-1} = x^2$ when $n = 3$ and $a = 1/3$. So we put $F(x) = \frac{1}{3}x^3$ and then $F'(x) = x^2$. Thus, the

FIGURE 10.5

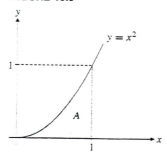

required area is

$$A = F(1) - F(0) = \tfrac{1}{3} \cdot 1^3 - \tfrac{1}{3} \cdot 0^3 = \tfrac{1}{3}$$

Figure 10.5 suggests that this answer is reasonable, because the shaded region appears to have roughly 1/3 the area of a square whose side is of length 1.

Note: If you tried seriously to use the method of exhaustion for determining the area in Fig. 10.5, you would appreciate the extreme simplicity of the method based on [10.2].

Example 10.2

Find the area A under the straight line $f(x) = cx + d$ over the interval $[a, b]$. (We assume that the constants c and d are chosen so that $f(x) \geq 0$ in $[a, b]$.)

Solution   The area is shown in Fig. 10.6. If we put $F(x) = \tfrac{1}{2}cx^2 + dx$, then $F'(x) = cx + d$, and so

$$A = F(b) - F(a) = (\tfrac{1}{2}cb^2 + db) - (\tfrac{1}{2}ca^2 + da)$$
$$= \tfrac{1}{2}c(b^2 - a^2) + d(b - a)$$

Compute the same area in another way and check that you get the same answer.

The argument leading to [10.2] was based on rather intuitive considerations. However, the concept of area that emerges agrees with the usual concept for regions bounded by straight lines. Example 10.2 is a case in point.

Formally, we choose to *define* the area under the graph of a continuous and nonnegative function f over the interval $[a, b]$ as the number $F(b) - F(a)$, where $F'(x) = f(x)$. Suppose $G(x)$ is any other function with $G'(x) = f(x)$ for $x \in (a, b)$. Then $G(x) = F(x) + C$, for some constant C. Hence,

$$G(b) - G(a) = F(b) + C - [F(a) + C] = F(b) - F(a)$$

FIGURE 10.6

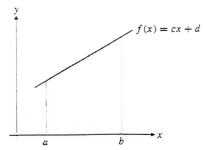

This argument tells us that the area we compute using [10.2] is independent of which antiderivative of f we choose. Moreover, according to Theorem 10.1 of Section 10.3, *any* continuous function f in $[a, b]$ has an antiderivative.

What Happens if $f(x)$ Has Negative Values in $[a, b]$?

We assumed before that f was continuous and positive-valued. Let us consider the case in which f is a function defined and continuous in $[a, b]$, with $f(x) \leq 0$ for all $x \in [a, b]$. The graph of f, the x-axis, and the lines $x = a$ and $x = b$ still enclose an area. If $F'(x) = f(x)$, we define the area to be $-[F(b) - F(a)]$. We choose this definition because we want the area of a region always to be positive.

Example 10.3

Compute the area shaded in Fig. 10.7. It is the area between the x-axis and the graph of $f(x) = e^{x/3} - 3$, over the interval $[0, 3 \ln 3]$.

Solution   We need to find a function $F(x)$ whose derivative is $e^{x/3} - 3$. Trial and error leads to the suggestion $F(x) = 3e^{x/3} - 3x$. (Check that $F'(x) = e^{x/3} - 3$.) The area is therefore equal to

$$-\left[F(3 \ln 3) - F(0)\right] = -(3e^{\ln 3} - 3 \cdot 3 \ln 3 - 3e^{0})$$

$$= -(9 - 9 \ln 3 - 3) = 9 \ln 3 - 6 \approx 3.89$$

Is the answer reasonable? (Yes, because the shaded set in Fig. 10.7 seems to be a little less than 4 units in area.)

Suppose f is defined and continuous in $[a, b]$, positive in some subintervals, and negative in others, as is the case in Fig. 10.8. The total area bounded

FIGURE 10.7

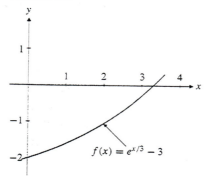

$f(x) = e^{x/3} - 3$

FIGURE 10.8

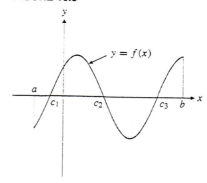

$y = f(x)$

by the graph of f, the x-axis, and the lines $x = a$ and $x = b$ is then calculated by computing the positive areas in each subinterval $[a, c_1]$, $[c_1, c_2]$, $[c_2, c_3]$, and $[c_3, b]$ in turn according to the previous definitions, and then adding these areas.

Problems

1. Compute the area under the graph of $f(x) = x^3$ over $[0, 1]$ by using [10.2].

2. For each of the following cases, draw a rough graph of f and indicate (by shading) the area of the set bounded by the x-axis, the lines $x = a$ and $x = b$, and the graph of f. Also calculate the area in question.

   a. $f(x) = 3x^2$ in $[0, 2]$ **b.** $f(x) = x^6$ in $[0, 1]$

   c. $f(x) = e^x$ in $[-1, 1]$ **d.** $f(x) = 1/x^2$ in $[1, 10]$

3. Compute the area A bounded by the graph of $f(x) = 1/x^3$, the x-axis, and the lines $x = -2$ and $x = -1$. (Make a drawing.)

4. Compute the area A bounded by the graph of $f(x) = \frac{1}{2}(e^x + e^{-x})$, the x-axis, and the lines $x = -1$ and $x = 1$.

10.2 Indefinite Integrals

The problem of computing areas under the graph of a function f leads to the problem of finding an *antiderivative* of f—that is, a function F whose derivative is f.

Although the name antiderivative is very appropriate, we shall follow the usual practice and call F an **indefinite integral** of f. As a symbol for an indefinite integral of f, we use $\int f(x)\, dx$. Two functions having the same derivative throughout an interval must differ by a constant, so we write

$$\int f(x)\, dx = F(x) + C \qquad \text{when} \qquad F'(x) = f(x) \qquad\qquad [10.3]$$

For instance,

$$\int x^3\, dx = \tfrac{1}{4}x^4 + C \qquad \text{because} \qquad \left(\tfrac{1}{4}x^4\right)' = x^3$$

where $(\ )'$ denotes differentiation. The symbol $\int$ is the **integral sign**, the function $f(x)$ appearing in [10.3] is the **integrand**, and C is the **constant of integration**. The dx part of the integral notation indicates that x is the **variable of integration**.

Let a be a fixed number $\neq -1$. Because the derivative of $x^{a+1}/(a+1)$ is x^a.

$$\int x^a \, dx = \frac{1}{a+1} x^{a+1} + C \qquad (a \neq -1)$$ [10.4]

This very important integration result states that the indefinite integral of any power of x (except x^{-1}) is obtained by increasing the exponent of x by 1, dividing by the new exponent, and then adding the constant of integration. Here are some examples:

(a) $\displaystyle \int x \, dx = \int x^1 \, dx = \frac{1}{1+1} x^{1+1} + C = \frac{1}{2} x^2 + C$

(b) $\displaystyle \int \frac{1}{x^3} \, dx = \int x^{-3} \, dx = \frac{1}{-3+1} x^{-3+1} + C = -\frac{1}{2x^2} + C$

(c) $\displaystyle \int \sqrt{x} \, dx = \int x^{1/2} \, dx = \frac{1}{1/2+1} x^{1/2+1} + C = \frac{2}{3} x^{3/2} + C$

When $a = -1$, the formula in [10.4] is not valid, because the right-hand side involves division by zero and so becomes meaningless. The integrand is then $1/x$, and the problem is thus to find a function having $1/x$ as its derivative. Now $\ln x$ has this property, but it is only defined for $x > 0$. Note, however, that $\ln(-x)$ is defined for $x < 0$, and according to the chain rule, its derivative is $[1/(-x)](-1) = 1/x$. Recall that $|x| = x$ when $x \geq 0$ and $|x| = -x$ when $x < 0$. Thus, whether we integrate over an interval where $x > 0$ or $x < 0$, we have

$$\int \frac{1}{x} \, dx = \ln |x| + C$$ [10.5]

Consider next the exponential function. The derivative of e^x is e^x. Thus, $\int e^x \, dx = e^x + C$. More generally,

$$\int e^{ax} \, dx = \frac{1}{a} e^{ax} + C \qquad (a \neq 0)$$ [10.6]

because the derivative of $(1/a)e^{ax}$ is e^{ax}.

For $a > 0$ we can write $a^x = e^{x \ln a}$. As an application of [10.6], for $\ln a \neq 0$ (that is, for $a \neq 1$), we have

$$\int a^x \, dx = \frac{1}{\ln a} a^x + C \qquad (a > 0 \text{ and } a \neq 1) \tag*{[10.7]}$$

Some General Rules

Two rules of differentiation are $(aF(x))' = aF'(x)$ and $(F(x) + G(x))' = F'(x) + G'(x)$. They immediately imply the following integration rules:

Constant Multiple Property

$$\int af(x) \, dx = a \int f(x) \, dx \qquad (a \text{ is a real constant}) \tag*{[10.8]}$$

The integral of a sum is the sum of the integrals

$$\int \left[f(x) + g(x) \right] dx = \int f(x) \, dx + \int g(x) \, dx \tag*{[10.9]}$$

Repeated use of these two properties yields the general rule

$$\int \left[a_1 f_1(x) + \cdots + a_n f_n(x) \right] dx = a_1 \int f_1(x) \, dx + \cdots + a_n \int f_n(x) \, dx \tag*{[10.10]}$$

for the indefinite integral of any linear combination of continuous functions.

Example 10.4

Find the integral $\int (3x^4 + 5x^2 - 2) \, dx$.

Solution

$$\int (3x^4 + 5x^2 - 2)\, dx = 3 \int x^4\, dx + 5 \int x^2\, dx - 2 \int 1\, dx$$

$$= 3\left(\tfrac{1}{5}x^5 + C_1\right) + 5\left(\tfrac{1}{3}x^3 + C_2\right) - 2\left(x + C_3\right)$$

$$= \tfrac{3}{5}x^5 + \tfrac{5}{3}x^3 - 2x + 3C_1 + 5C_2 - 2C_3$$

$$= \tfrac{3}{5}x^5 + \tfrac{5}{3}x^3 - 2x + C$$

Because C_1, C_2, and C_3 are arbitrary constants, $3C_1 + 5C_2 - 2C_3$ is also an arbitrary constant. So in the last line we have replaced it by C for simplicity.

It is not necessary to write all the intermediate steps when integrating in this way. More simply, we write

$$\int (3x^4 + 5x^2 - 2)\, dx = 3 \int x^4\, dx + 5 \int x^2\, dx - 2 \int 1\, dx$$

$$= \frac{3}{5}x^5 + \frac{5}{3}x^3 - 2x + C$$

By systematically using the proper rules, we can *differentiate* very complicated functions. On the other hand, finding the indefinite integral of even quite simple functions can be very difficult, or impossible. Note, however, that it is usually quite easy to check whether a proposed indefinite integral is correct. We simply differentiate the proposed function to see if its derivative is equal to the integrand.

Example 10.5

Verify that (in an interval where $ax + b > 0$)

$$\int \frac{x}{\sqrt{ax + b}}\, dx = \frac{2}{3a^2}(ax - 2b)\sqrt{ax + b} + C$$

Solution   We put $F(x) = (2/3a^2)(ax - 2b)\sqrt{ax + b} = (2/3a^2)u \cdot v$, where $u = ax - 2b$ and $v = \sqrt{ax + b}$. Now

$$F'(x) = \frac{2}{3a^2}(u'v + uv')$$

where, after introducing the new variable $w = ax + b$, one has

$$u' = a, \qquad v = \sqrt{ax + b} = \sqrt{w} \implies v' = \frac{1}{2\sqrt{w}}w' = \frac{a}{2\sqrt{ax + b}}$$

Hence,

$$F'(x) = \frac{2}{3a^2}\left[a\sqrt{ax+b} + (ax-2b)\frac{a}{2\sqrt{ax+b}}\right]$$

$$= \frac{2}{3a^2}\left[\frac{2a(ax+b)+(ax-2b)a}{2\sqrt{ax+b}}\right] = \frac{2}{3a^2}\frac{2a^2x+2ab+a^2x-2ab}{2\sqrt{ax+b}}$$

$$= \frac{2}{3a^2}\frac{3a^2x}{2\sqrt{ax+b}} = \frac{x}{\sqrt{ax+b}}$$

which shows that the integral formula is correct.

Initial-Value Problems

As was seen before, there are infinitely many "antiderivatives," or indefinite integral functions, having a given function as their common derivative. For instance, the derivative of $\frac{1}{5}x^5 + C$ is x^4 for all choices of the constant C. The graphs of these functions are all translates of each other in the direction of the y-axis. Given any point (x_0, y_0), there is one and only one of these curves that passes through (x_0, y_0).

Example 10.6
Find all functions $F(x)$ such that

$$F'(x) = -(x-1)^2 \tag{1}$$

and draw some of the graphs in the xy-plane. Find in particular the function whose graph passes through the point $(x_0, y_0) = (1, 1)$.

Solution   Equation [1] implies that

$$F(x) = \int -(x-1)^2\,dx = -\tfrac{1}{3}(x-1)^3 + C$$

All values of C are possible. Some of the associated graphs are drawn in Fig. 10.9. The curve that passes through $(1, 1)$ is found by solving the equation $F(1) = 1$, or

$$-\tfrac{1}{3}(1-1)^3 + C = 1$$

This gives $C = 1$, so the required function is

$$F(x) = 1 - \tfrac{1}{3}(x-1)^3$$

The last part of Example 10.6 can be formulated this way: Find the unique function $F(x)$ such that $F'(x) = -(x-1)^2$ and $F(1) = 1$. This is called an **initial-value problem** and the requirement that $F(1) = 1$ is called an **initial condition**.

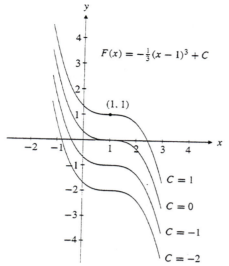

FIGURE 10.9 $F(x) = -\frac{1}{3}(x-1)^3 + C.$

Example 10.7

The marginal cost of producing x units of some commodity is $1 + x + 3x^2$ and fixed costs are 150. Find the total cost function.

Solution   Denoting the total cost function by $c(x)$, we have

$$[1] \quad c'(x) = 1 + x + 3x^2 \quad \text{and} \quad [2] \quad c(0) = 150$$

because $c(0)$ is the cost incurred even if nothing is produced. Integrating [1] yields

$$c(x) = x + \tfrac{1}{2}x^2 + x^3 + C \tag{3}$$

Substituting $x = 0$ in [3] gives $c(0) = C$, and so $C = 150$ because of [2]. Hence, the required total cost function is

$$c(x) = x + \tfrac{1}{2}x^2 + x^3 + 150$$

So far, we have always used x as the variable of integration. In economics, the variables often have other labels.

Example 10.8

Find the following:

(a) $\int \dfrac{B}{r^{2.5}} \, dr$

(b) $\int (a + bq + cq^2) \, dq$

Solution

(a) Writing $B/r^{2.5}$ as $Br^{-2.5}$, we see that formula [10.4] applies, and so

$$\int \frac{B}{r^{2.5}} \, dr = B \int r^{-2.5} \, dr = B\frac{1}{-2.5+1} r^{-2.5+1} + C = -\frac{B}{1.5} r^{-1.5} + C$$

(b) $\int (a + bq + cq^2) \, dq = aq + \frac{1}{2} bq^2 + \frac{1}{3} cq^3 + C$

Problems

1. Find the following integrals using [10.4]:

   a. $\int x^{13} \, dx$ **b.** $\int x\sqrt{x} \, dx$ **c.** $\int \frac{1}{\sqrt{x}} \, dx$ **d.** $\int \sqrt{x\sqrt{x\sqrt{x}}} \, dx$

2. Find the following integrals:

   a. $\int (t^3 + 2t - 3) \, dt$ **b.** $\int (x - 1)^2 \, dx$ **c.** $\int (x-1)(x+2) \, dx$

   d. $\int (x + 2)^3 \, dx$ **e.** $\int (e^{3x} - e^{2x} + e^x) \, dx$ **f.** $\int \frac{x^3 - 3x + 4}{x} \, dx$

3. Find the following integrals:

   a. $\int \frac{(y - 2)^2}{\sqrt{y}} \, dy$ **b.** $\int \frac{x^3}{x + 1} \, dx$ **c.** $\int x(1 + x^2)^{15} \, dx$

   (*Hint:* In part (a), first expand $(y - 2)^2$ and then divide each term by $\sqrt{y}$. In part (b), do long division. In part (c), what is the derivative of $(1 + x^2)^{16}$?)

4. **a.** Show that

   $$\int (ax + b)^p \, dx = \frac{1}{a(p + 1)} (ax + b)^{p+1} + C \qquad (a \neq 0, \ p \neq -1)$$

   b. Find the following:

   (i) $\int (2x + 1)^4 \, dx$ (ii) $\int \sqrt{x + 2} \, dx$ (iii) $\int \frac{1}{\sqrt{4 - x}} \, dx$

5. Show that

   $$\int x\sqrt{ax + b} \, dx = \frac{2}{15a^2} (3ax - 2b)(ax + b)^{3/2} + C$$

6. Solve the following initial-value problems:
   a. Find $F(x)$ if $F'(x) = \frac{1}{2} - 2x$ and $F(0) = 1/2$.
   b. Find $F(x)$ if $F'(x) = x(1 - x^2)$ and $F(1) = 5/12$.

7. In the manufacture of a product, the marginal cost of producing x units is $c'(x) = 3x + 4$. If fixed costs are 40, find the total cost function $c(x)$.

8. Find the general form of a function f whose second derivative is x^2. If we require in addition that $f(0) = 1$ and $f'(0) = -1$, what is $f(x)$?

9. **a.** Suppose that $f''(x) = 2$ for all x, and $f(0) = 2$, $f'(0) = 1$. First find $f'(x)$ and then $f(x)$.

   b. Similarly, suppose that $f''(x) = 1/x^2 + x^3 + 2$ for $x > 0$, and $f(1) = 0$, $f'(1) = 1/4$. Find $f(x)$.

10.3 The Definite Integral

Let f be a continuous function defined in the interval $[a, b]$. Suppose that the function F is continuous in $[a, b]$ and has a derivative satisfying $F'(x) = f(x)$ for every $x \in (a, b)$. Then the difference $F(b) - F(a)$ is called the **definite integral** of f over $[a, b]$. As observed in Section 10.1, this difference does not depend on which of the infinitely many indefinite integrals of f we choose as F. The definite integral of f over $[a, b]$ is therefore a number that depends only on the function f and the numbers a and b. We denote it by

$$\int_a^b f(x)\, dx \qquad\qquad [10.11]$$

This notation makes explicit the function $f(x)$ we integrate, which is called the **integrand**, and the interval of integration $[a, b]$. The numbers a and b are called, respectively, the **lower** and **upper limits of integration**. The letter x is a *dummy variable* in the sense that the integral is independent of its label. For instance,

$$\int_a^b f(x)\, dx = \int_a^b f(y)\, dy = \int_a^b f(\xi)\, d\xi$$

In many other mathematical writings, the difference $F(b) - F(a)$ is often denoted by $F(x) \Big|_a^b$, or by $[F(x)]_a^b$. But $\Big|_a^b F(x)$ is also common, and this is the notation we shall use. Thus:

Definition of the Definite Integral

$$\int_a^b f(x)\, dx = \Big|_a^b F(x) = F(b) - F(a) \qquad\qquad [10.12]$$

where $F'(x) = f(x)$ for all $x \in (a, b)$.

Definition [10.12] does not necessarily require $a < b$. However, if $a > b$ and $f(x)$ is positive throughout the interval $[b, a]$, then $\int_a^b f(x)\, dx$ is a negative number.

Note that we have defined the definite integral without necessarily giving it a geometric interpretation. In fact, depending on the context, it can have different interpretations. For instance, if $f(r)$ is an income density function, then $\int_a^b f(r)\,dr$ is the proportion of people with income between a and b. (See the next section.)

With the new notation, the results in Examples 10.1 and 10.2 can be written as

$$\int_0^1 x^2\,dx = \left.\tfrac{1}{3}x^3\right|_0^1 = \tfrac{1}{3}$$

$$\int_a^b (cx + d)\,dx = \left.\left(\tfrac{1}{2}cx^2 + dx\right)\right|_a^b$$

$$= (\tfrac{1}{2}cb^2 + db) - (\tfrac{1}{2}ca^2 + da) = \tfrac{1}{2}c(b^2 - a^2) + d(b - a)$$

Although the notations for definite and for indefinite integrals are similar, they are entirely different concepts. In fact, $\int_a^b f(x)\,dx$ denotes a single number, whereas $\int f(x)\,dx$ represents any one of the infinite set of functions all having $f(x)$ as their derivative. The relationship between the two is that $\int f(x)\,dx = F(x) + C$ over an interval I, if and only if $\int_a^b f(x)\,dx = F(b) - F(a)$ for all a and b in I.

Properties of the Definite Integral

From the definition of the definite integral in [10.12], a number of properties can be derived. If f is a continuous function in an interval that contains a, b, and c, then

$$\int_a^b f(x)\,dx = -\int_b^a f(x)\,dx \qquad\qquad [10.13]$$

$$\int_a^a f(x)\,dx = 0 \qquad\qquad [10.14]$$

$$\int_a^b \alpha f(x)\,dx = \alpha \int_a^b f(x)\,dx \qquad (\alpha \text{ is an arbitrary number}) \quad [10.15]$$

$$\int_a^b f(x)\,dx = \int_a^c f(x)\,dx + \int_c^b f(x)\,dx \qquad\qquad [10.16]$$

All these rules follow easily from [10.12]. For example, [10.16] can be proved as follows. Let F be continuous in $[a, b]$, and suppose that $F'(x) = f(x)$ for all x

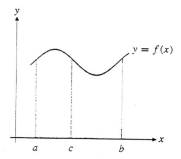

FIGURE 10.10 $\int_a^b f(x)\,dx = \int_a^c f(x)\,dx + \int_c^b f(x)\,dx.$

in the interior of an interval long enough to include a, b, and c. Then

$$\int_a^c f(x)\,dx + \int_c^b f(x)\,dx = \left[F(c) - F(a)\right] + \left[F(b) - F(c)\right]$$

$$= F(b) - F(a) = \int_a^b f(x)\,dx$$

When the definite integral is interpreted as an area, [10.16] is the additivity property of areas, as illustrated in Fig. 10.10. Of course, [10.16] easily generalizes to the case in which we partition the interval $[a, b]$ into an arbitrary finite number of subintervals.

The constant multiple property [10.8] and the summation property [10.9] are also valid for definite integrals. In fact, if f and g are continuous in $[a, b]$, and if α and β are real numbers, then

$$\int_a^b \left[\alpha f(x) + \beta g(x)\right] dx = \alpha \int_a^b f(x)\,dx + \beta \int_a^b g(x)\,dx \qquad [10.17]$$

The proof is simple. Let $F'(x) = f(x)$ and $G'(x) = g(x)$ for all $x \in (a, b)$. Then $[(\alpha F(x) + \beta G(x)]' = \alpha F'(x) + \beta G'(x) = \alpha f(x) + \beta g(x)$. Hence,

$$\int_a^b \left[\alpha f(x) + \beta g(x)\right] dx = \left. \left[\alpha F(x) + \beta G(x)\right] \right|_a^b$$

$$= \left[\alpha F(b) + \beta G(b)\right] - \left[\alpha F(a) + \beta G(a)\right]$$

$$= \alpha \left[F(b) - F(a)\right] + \beta \left[G(b) - G(a)\right]$$

$$= \alpha \int_a^b f(x)\,dx + \beta \int_a^b g(x)\,dx$$

The rule in [10.17] can obviously be extended to more than two functions.

Some Important Observations

It follows directly from the definition of the indefinite integral that the derivative of the integral is equal to the integrand:

$$\frac{d}{dx} \int f(x)\,dx = f(x) \qquad [10.18]$$

Also

$$\int F'(x)\,dx = F(x) + C \qquad [10.19]$$

Moreover,

$$\int_a^t f(x)\,dx = \Big|_a^t F(x) = F(t) - F(a)$$

So, differentiating w.r.t. t with a fixed, it follows that

$$\frac{d}{dt} \int_a^t f(x)\,dx = F'(t) = f(t) \qquad [10.20]$$

In other words: *The derivative of the definite integral w.r.t. the upper limit of integration is equal to the integrand as a function evaluated at that limit.*
    Correspondingly,

$$\int_t^a f(x)\,dx = \Big|_t^a F(x) = F(a) - F(t)$$

so that

$$\frac{d}{dt} \int_t^a f(x)\,dx = -F'(t) = -f(t) \qquad [10.21]$$

In other words: *The derivative of the definite integral w.r.t. the lower limit of integration is equal to minus the integrand as a function evaluated at that limit.*
    The results in [10.20] and [10.21] can be generalized. In fact, if $a(t)$ and $b(t)$ are differentiable and $f(x)$ is continuous, then

$$\frac{d}{dt} \int_{a(t)}^{b(t)} f(x)\,dx = f(b(t))\,b'(t) - f(a(t))\,a'(t) \qquad [10.22]$$

To prove this formula, let $F'(x) = f(x)$. Then $\int_u^v f(x)\,dx = F(v) - F(u)$, so in particular,

$$\int_{a(t)}^{b(t)} f(x)\,dx = F(b(t)) - F(a(t))$$

Using the chain rule to differentiate the right-hand side of this equation w.r.t. t, we obtain $F'(b(t))b'(t) - F'(a(t))a'(t)$. But $F'(b(t)) = f(b(t))$ and $F'(a(t)) = f(a(t))$, so [10.22] results. (Formula [10.22] is a special case of Leibniz's formula discussed in Section 16.2.)

Continuous Functions Are Integrable

Suppose $f(x)$ is a continuous function in $[a, b]$. Then we defined $\int_a^b f(x)\,dx$ as the number $F(b) - F(a)$, provided that $F(x)$ is some function whose derivative is $f(x)$. In some cases, we are able to find an explicit expression for $F(x)$. For instance, we can evaluate $\int_0^1 x^5\,dx$ as $1/6$ because $(1/6)x^6$ has x^5 as its derivative. On the other hand, for the integral

$$\int_0^2 e^{-x^2}\,dx$$

(closely related to the "normal distribution" in statistics), there is no standard function whose derivative is e^{-x^2}.[2] Still, the integrand function is continuous in $[0, 2]$ and there should be an area under the graph from 0 to 2.

In fact, one can prove that any continuous function has an antiderivative:

Theorem 10.1   If f is a continuous function in $[a, b]$, then there exists a continuous function $F(x)$ in $[a, b]$ such that $F'(x) = f(x)$, for all $x \in (a, b)$.

A sketch of a proof: Let $x \in (a, b)$. Subdivide the interval $[a, x]$ into n equal parts so that the points of subdivision are $a+(x-a)/n,\ a+2(x-a)/n,\ \dots,\ a+(n-1)(x-a)/n$. For each natural number n, define the new function F_n as an approximation to F using the formula

$$F_n(x) = \frac{x-a}{n}\left[f(a) + f\left(a + \frac{x-a}{n}\right) + f\left(a + 2\frac{x-a}{n}\right) \right.$$
$$\left. + \cdots + f\left(a + (n-1)\frac{x-a}{n}\right)\right]$$

(Try to illustrate this definition of $F_n(x)$.) Define $F(x) = \lim_{n \to \infty} F_n(x)$. It is possible (but not easy) to show that this limit exists for each $x \in [a, b]$, that F is continuous in $[a, b]$, and finally that $F(x)$ has $f(x)$ as its derivative in (a, b).

The Riemann Integral

The kind of integral discussed so far, which is based on the antiderivative, is called the *Newton–Leibniz* (N–L) *integral*. Several other kinds of integral are considered by mathematicians. For continuous functions, they all give the same result as the N–L integral.

---

[2]See (11.4) in Section 11.2 for other examples of "unsolvable integrals."

We briefly sketch the so-called *Riemann integral*. The idea behind the definition is closely related to the exhaustion method that was described in the introduction to this chapter.

Let f be a *bounded* function in the interval $[a, b]$, and let n be a natural number. Subdivide $[a, b]$ into n parts by choosing points $a = x_0 < x_1 < x_2 < \cdots < x_{n-1} < x_n = b$. Put $\Delta x_i = x_{i+1} - x_i$, $i = 0, 1, \ldots, n-1$, and choose an arbitrary number ξ_i in each interval $[x_i, x_{i+1}]$ (draw a figure). The sum

$$f(\xi_0)\Delta x_0 + f(\xi_1)\Delta x_1 + \cdots + f(\xi_{n-1})\Delta x_{n-1}$$

is called a *Riemann sum* associated with the function f. This sum will depend on f as well as on the subdivision and on the choice of the ξ_i's. Suppose that, when n approaches infinity and simultaneously the largest of the numbers $\Delta x_0, \Delta x_1, \ldots, \Delta x_{n-1}$ approaches 0, the limit of the sum exists. Then f is called *Riemann integrable* (R-integrable) in the interval $[a, b]$, and we put

$$\int_a^b f(x)\, dx = \lim \sum_{i=0}^{n-1} f(\xi_i)\, \Delta x_i$$

The value of the integral is independent of the choice of the ξ_i's. One can show that every continuous function is R-integrable, and that the R integral in this case can be evaluated using [10.12]. The N–L integral and the R integral thus coincide for continuous functions.

Problems

1. Evaluate the following integrals by using [10.12]:

   a. $\displaystyle\int_0^1 x\, dx$ **b.** $\displaystyle\int_1^2 (2x + x^2)\, dx$ **c.** $\displaystyle\int_{-2}^3 \left(\tfrac{1}{2}x^2 - \tfrac{1}{3}x^3\right) dx$

2. Evaluate the following integrals:

   a. $\displaystyle\int_0^2 (t^3 - t^4)\, dt$ **b.** $\displaystyle\int_1^2 \left(2t^5 - \frac{1}{t^2}\right) dt$ **c.** $\displaystyle\int_2^3 \left(\frac{1}{t-1} + t\right) dx$

3. The profit of a firm as a function of its output x $(x > 0)$ is

$$f(x) = 4000 - x - \frac{3000000}{x}$$

   a. Find the output that maximizes profit. Draw the graph of f.
   b. The actual output varies between 1000 and 3000 units. Compute the average profit

$$I = \frac{1}{2000} \int_{1000}^{3000} f(x)\, dx$$

4. Evaluate the integrals:

    a. $\displaystyle\int_1^3 \frac{3x}{10}\,dx$ **b.** $\displaystyle\int_{-3}^{-1} \xi^2\,d\xi$

    c. $\displaystyle\int_0^1 \alpha e^{\beta\tau}\,d\tau$ $(\beta \neq 0)$ **d.** $\displaystyle\int_{-2}^{-1} \frac{1}{y}\,dy$

5. By using [10.22] or otherwise, evaluate the following:

    a. $\displaystyle\frac{d}{dt}\int_0^t x^2\,dx$ **b.** $\displaystyle\frac{d}{dt}\int_t^3 e^{-x^2}\,dx$ **c.** $\displaystyle\frac{d}{dt}\int_{-t}^t e^{-x^2}\,dx$

    d. $\displaystyle\frac{d}{dt}\int_{\sqrt{t}}^t \ln x\,dx$ **e.** $\displaystyle\frac{d}{dt}\int_{t^{1/6}}^{t^{1/3}} x^6\,dx$ **f.** $\displaystyle\frac{d}{dt}\int_{-t}^t \frac{1}{\sqrt{x^4+1}}\,dx$

6. Compute $\int_0^2 2x^2(2-x)^2\,dx$. Give a rough check of the answer by drawing the graph of $f(x) = 2x^2(2-x)^2$ over $[0, 2]$.

7. Find the area between the two parabolas defined by the equations $y + 1 = (x-1)^2$ and $3x = y^2$. (The points of intersection have integer coordinates.)

8. Compute the following:

    a. $\displaystyle\int_0^1 (x + \sqrt{x} + \sqrt[4]{x})\,dx$ **b.** $\displaystyle\int_1^b \left(A\frac{x+b}{x+c} + \frac{d}{x}\right)dx$

    c. $\displaystyle\int_0^1 \frac{x^2 + x + \sqrt{x+1}}{x+1}\,dx$

Harder Problems

9. A theory of investment has used a function W defined for all $T > 0$ by

$$W(T) = \frac{K}{T}\int_0^T e^{-\varrho t}\,dt \qquad (K \text{ and } \varrho \text{ are positive constants})$$

Evaluate the integral, and prove that $W(T)$ takes values in the interval $(0, K)$ and is strictly decreasing.

10.   **a.** Show that if f is continuous in $[a, b]$, then there exists a number $x^* \in [a, b]$ such that

$$f(x^*) = \frac{1}{b-a}\int_a^b f(x)\,dx$$

    This is called the **mean-value theorem for integrals**, and $f(x^*)$ is called the *mean value* of f in $[a, b]$. (*Hint:* Put $F(x) = \int_a^x f(t)\,dt$, and use Theorem 7.5 of Section 7.3.)

  b. Find the mean value of $f(x) = \sqrt{x}$ in $[0, 4]$, and illustrate.

10.4 Economic Applications of Integration

We motivated the definite integral as a tool for computing the area under a curve. However, the integral has many other important interpretations. For instance, we are led to a definite integral when we want to find the volume of a solid of revolution or the length of a curve. Several of the most important concepts in statistics are also expressed by integrals of continuous probability distributions. This section presents some examples showing more directly the importance of integrals in economics.

Extraction from an Oil Well

Assume that at time $t = 0$ we start extracting oil from a well that contains K barrels of oil. Let us define

$$x(t) = \text{amount of oil in barrels that is left at time } t$$

In particular, $x(0) = K$. If we assume that we cannot pump oil back into the well, then $x(t)$ is a decreasing function of t. The amount of oil that is extracted in a time interval $[t, t + \Delta t]$ (where $\Delta t > 0$) is $x(t) - x(t + \Delta t)$. Extraction per unit of time is, therefore,

$$\frac{x(t) - x(t + \Delta t)}{\Delta t} = -\frac{x(t + \Delta t) - x(t)}{\Delta t} \qquad [*]$$

If we assume that $x(t)$ is differentiable, then the limit as Δt approaches zero of the fraction $[*]$ is equal to $-\dot{x}(t)$. Letting $u(t)$ denote the rate of extraction at time t, we have

$$\dot{x}(t) = -u(t) \qquad \text{with} \qquad x(0) = K \qquad [10.23]$$

The solution to the initial-value problem [10.23] is

$$x(t) = K - \int_0^t u(\tau)\, d\tau \qquad [10.24]$$

Indeed, we check [10.24] as follows. First, setting $t = 0$ gives $x(0) = K$. Moreover, differentiating [10.24] w.r.t. t according to rule [10.20] in Section 10.3 yields $\dot{x}(t) = -u(t)$. The result [10.24] may be interpreted as follows: The amount of oil left at time t is equal to the initial amount K, minus the total amount that has been extracted during the time span $[0, t]$, namely $\int_0^t u(\tau)\, d\tau$.

If the rate of extraction is constant, with $u(t) = \bar{u}$, then [10.24] yields

$$x(t) = K - \int_0^t \bar{u}\, d\tau = K - \Big|_0^t \bar{u}\tau = K - \bar{u}t$$

In particular, we see that the well will be empty when $K - \bar{u}t = 0$, or when

$t = K/\bar{u}$. (Of course, this particular answer could have been found more directly, without recourse to integration.)

The example illustrates two concepts that are important to distinguish in many economic arguments. The quantity $x(t)$ is a *stock*, measured in barrels. On the other hand, $u(t)$ is a *flow*, measured in barrels *per unit of time*.

A Country's Foreign Exchange Reserves

Let $F(t)$ denote a country's foreign exchange reserves at time t. Assuming that F is differentiable, the rate of change in the foreign exchange reserves per unit of time will be

$$f(t) = F'(t) \tag{10.25}$$

If $f(t) > 0$, this means that there is a net flow of foreign exchange into the country at time t, whereas $f(t) < 0$ means that foreign exchange is flowing out. From the definition of the definite integral, it follows that

$$F(t_1) - F(t_0) = \int_{t_0}^{t_1} f(t)\, dt \tag{10.26}$$

We see that this expression measures the change in the foreign exchange reserves over the time interval $[t_0, t_1]$. An example is illustrated in Fig. 10.11. Here there is a net flow of foreign exchange into the country from t_0 to t', then a net flow out of the country from t' to t'', and, finally, there is a net flow into the country from t'' to t_1. (Note that $\int_{t_0}^{t_1} f(t)\, dt$ does not denote the total area bounded by the graph, the x-axis, and the lines $t = t_0$ and $t = t_1$ in this case. See the end of Section 10.1.)

Income Distribution

In many countries, anonymous data from income tax authorities can be used to reveal some properties of the income distribution within a given year, as well as how the distribution changes from year to year.

FIGURE 10.11   The rate of change of foreign exchange.

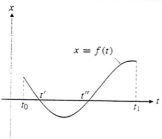

We measure income in dollars and let $F(r)$ denote the proportion of individuals who receive no more than r dollars. Thus, if there are n individuals in the population, $nF(r)$ is the number of individuals with income no greater than r. If r_0 is the lowest and r_1 is the highest (registered) income in the group, we are interested in the function F in the interval $[r_0, r_1]$. By definition, F is not continuous and therefore also not differentiable in $[r_0, r_1]$ because r has to be a multiple of $\$0.01$ and $F(r)$ has to be a multiple of $1/n$. However, if the population consists of a large number of individuals, then it is usually possible to find a "smooth" function that gives a good approximation to the true income distribution. Assume, therefore, that F is a function with a continuous derivative denoted by f, so that

$$f(r) = F'(r) \qquad \text{(for all } r \in (r_0, r_1))$$

According to the definition of the derivative, we have

$$f(r)\,\Delta r \approx F(r + \Delta r) - F(r)$$

for all small Δr. Thus, $f(r)\,\Delta r$ is approximately equal to the proportion of individuals who earn between r and $r + \Delta r$. The function f is called an **income density function**, and F is the associated **cumulative distribution function**.[3]

Suppose that f is a continuous income distribution for a certain population with incomes in the interval $[r_0, r_1]$. If $r_0 \leq a \leq b \leq r_1$, then the previous discussion and the definition of the definite integral imply that $\int_a^b f(r)\,dr$ is the proportion of individuals with incomes in $[a, b]$. Thus,

$$n \int_a^b f(r)\,dr = \begin{cases} \text{the } \textbf{number of individuals} \\ \text{with incomes in the interval } [a, b] \end{cases} \qquad [10.27]$$

We will now find an expression for the combined income of those who earn between a and b dollars. Let $M(r)$ denote the total income of those who earn no more than r dollars, and consider the income interval $[r, r + \Delta r]$. There are approximately $nf(r)\,\Delta r$ individuals with incomes in this interval. Each of them has an income approximately equal to r, so that the total income of these individuals, $M(r + \Delta r) - M(r)$, is approximately equal to $nrf(r)\,\Delta r$. So we have

$$\frac{M(r + \Delta r) - M(r)}{\Delta r} \approx nrf(r)$$

---

[3]Readers who know some elementary statistics will see the analogy with probability density functions and with cumulative (probability) distribution functions.

The approximation improves (in general) as Δr decreases, and by taking the limit as $\Delta r \to 0$, we obtain $M'(r) = nrf(r)$, so $n \int_a^b rf(r)\, dr = M(b) - M(a)$. Hence,

$$n \int_a^b rf(r)\, dr \;=\; \begin{cases} \text{the \textbf{total income} of individuals} \\ \text{with incomes in the interval } [a, b] \end{cases} \qquad [10.28]$$

The argument that leads to [10.28] can be made more exact: $M(r + \Delta r) - M(r)$ is the total income of those who have income in the interval $[r, r + \Delta r]$, when $\Delta r > 0$. In this income interval, there are $n[F(r + \Delta r) - F(r)]$ individuals each of whom earns at most $r + \Delta r$ and at least r. Thus,

$$nr\big[F(r + \Delta r) - F(r)\big] \leq M(r + \Delta r) - M(r) \leq n(r + \Delta r)\big[F(r + \Delta r) - F(r)\big] \qquad [1]$$

If $\Delta r > 0$, division by Δr yields

$$nr\, \frac{F(r + \Delta r) - F(r)}{\Delta r} \leq \frac{M(r + \Delta r) - M(r)}{\Delta r} \leq n(r + \Delta r)\frac{F(r + \Delta r) - F(r)}{\Delta r} \qquad [2]$$

(If $\Delta r < 0$, then the inequalities in [1] are left unchanged, whereas those in [2] are reversed.) Letting $\Delta r \to 0$ gives $nrF'(r) \leq M'(r) \leq nrF'(r)$, so that

$$M'(r) = nrF'(r) = nrf(r) \qquad [3]$$

The ratio between the total income and the number of individuals belonging to a certain income interval $[a, b]$, is called the mean income for the individuals in this income interval. We have, therefore,

$$\left.\begin{array}{l} \text{The \textbf{mean income} of individuals} \\ \text{with incomes in the interval } [a, b] \end{array}\right\} : \quad m = \frac{\int_a^b rf(r)\, dr}{\int_a^b f(r)\, dr} \qquad [10.29]$$

An income distribution function that approximates actual income distributions quite well, particularly for large incomes, is the **Pareto distribution**. In this case, the proportion of individuals who earn at most r dollars is given by

$$f(r) = Br^{-\beta} \qquad [10.30]$$

Here B and β are positive constants. Empirical estimates of β are usually in the range $2.4 < \beta < 2.6$. For values of r close to 0, the formula is of no use when $\beta \geq 1$, because $\int_a^b f(r)\, dr \to \infty$ as $r \to 0$ (See Section 11.3).

Example 10.9

In a population with incomes between a and b, suppose the income distribution is given by

$$f(r) = Br^{-2.5} \qquad (B \text{ a positive constant}) \qquad [1]$$

Determine the mean income in this group.

Solution   Here

$$\int_a^b f(r)\,dr = \int_a^b Br^{-2.5}\,dr = B \left. \left(-\tfrac{2}{3}r^{-1.5}\right) \right|_a^b = \tfrac{2}{3}B\left(a^{-1.5} - b^{-1.5}\right)$$

Also

$$\int_a^b rf(r)\,dr = \int_a^b rBr^{-2.5}\,dr = B \left. \int r^{-1.5}\,dr \right|_a^b$$

$$= -2B \left. r^{-0.5} \right|_a^b = 2B\left(a^{-0.5} - b^{-0.5}\right)$$

So the mean income of the group is

$$m = \frac{2B\left(a^{-0.5} - b^{-0.5}\right)}{(2/3)B\left(a^{-1.5} - b^{-1.5}\right)} = 3\frac{a^{-0.5} - b^{-0.5}}{a^{-1.5} - b^{-1.5}} \qquad [2]$$

Suppose that b is very large. Then $b^{-0.5}$ and $b^{-1.5}$ are both close to 0, and so [2] implies that $m \approx 3a$. The mean income of those who earn at least a is therefore approximately $3a$.

The Influence of Income Distribution on Demand

Assume that the individuals in a population are offered a commodity for which demand depends only on the price p and the income r of each individual. Let $D(p, r)$ be a continuous function that denotes the number of commodity units demanded by an individual with income r when the price per unit is p. If the incomes in the group vary between a and b, and the income distribution is $f(r)$, what is the total demand for the commodity when the price is p?

Let the price p be fixed, and denote by $T(r)$ the total demand for the commodity by all individuals who earn less than or equal to r. Consider the income interval $[r, r + \Delta r]$. There are approximately $nf(r)\,\Delta r$ individuals with incomes in this interval. Because each of them demands approximately $D(p, r)$ units of the commodity, the total demand of these individuals will be approximately $nD(p, r)f(r)\,\Delta r$. However, the actual total demand of individuals with incomes in the interval $[r, r + \Delta r]$ is given by $T(r + \Delta r) - T(r)$. So we must have $T(r + \Delta r) - T(r) \approx n D(p, r) f(r) \Delta r$, and thus

$$\frac{T(r + \Delta r) - T(r)}{\Delta r} \approx n D(p, r) f(r)$$

The approximation improves (in general) as Δr decreases, and by taking the limit as $\Delta r \to 0$, we obtain $T'(r) = n D(p, r) f(r)$. By definition of the definite integral, $T(b) - T(a) = n \int_a^b D(p, r) f(r) \, dr$. But $T(b) - T(a)$ is the desired measure of total demand for the commodity by all the individuals in the group. This will naturally depend on the price p. So we denote it by $x(p)$, and thus have

$$x(p) = \int_a^b n D(p, r) f(r) \, dr \qquad \textbf{(total demand)} \qquad [10.31]$$

Example 10.10

Let the income distribution function be that of Example 10.9, and let $D(p, r) = A p^{-1.5} r^{2.08}$. (This function describes the demand for milk in Norway during the period 1925–1935. See Example 15.2.) Compute the total demand.

Solution   Using [10.31] gives

$$x(p) = \int_a^b n A p^{-1.5} r^{2.08} B r^{-2.5} \, dr = n A B p^{-1.5} \int_a^b r^{-0.42} \, dr$$

Hence,

$$x(p) = n A B p^{-1.5} \left. \frac{1}{0.58} r^{0.58} \right|_a^b = \frac{n A B}{0.58} p^{-1.5} (b^{0.58} - a^{0.58})$$

Present Discounted Value of a Continuous Future Income Stream

Section 6.6 discussed the present value of a series of future payments made at specific discrete moments in time. It is often more natural to consider revenue as accruing continuously, such as the proceeds from a large growing forest.

Suppose that income is to be received continuously from time $t = 0$ to time $t = T$ at the rate of $f(t)$ dollars per year at time t. We assume that interest is compounded continuously at rate r. Let $P(t)$ denote the present discounted value of all payments made over the time interval $[0, t]$. This means that $P(t)$ represents the amount of money you would have to deposit at time $t = 0$ in order to match what results from (continuously) depositing the income stream $f(t)$ over the time interval $[0, T]$. If dt is any number, the present value of the income received in the interval $[t, t + dt]$ is $P(t + dt) - P(t)$. If dt is a small number, the income received in this interval is approximately $f(t) \, dt$, and the present discounted value (PDV) of this amount is approximately $f(t) e^{-rt} \, dt$. Thus, $P(t + dt) - P(t) \approx f(t) e^{-rt} \, dt$ and so

$$\frac{P(t + dt) - P(t)}{dt} \approx f(t) e^{-rt}$$

This approximation gets better the smaller is dt, and in the limit as $dt \to 0$, we have

$$P'(t) = f(t)e^{-rt}$$

By the definition of the definite integral, $P(T) - P(0) = \int_0^T f(t)e^{-rt}\,dt$. Because $P(0) = 0$, we have the following:

The **present discounted value** (at time 0) of a continuous income stream at the rate of $f(t)$ dollars per year over the time interval $[0, T]$, with continuously compounded interest at rate r, is given by

$$\text{PDV} = \int_0^T f(t)e^{-rt}\,dt \qquad\qquad [10.32]$$

Equation [10.32] gives the value at time 0 of income stream $f(t)$ received during time interval $[0, T]$. The value of this amount at time T, with continuously compounded interest at rate r, is $e^{rT}\int_0^T f(t)e^{-rt}\,dt$. Because the number e^{rT} is a constant, we can rewrite the integral as $\int_0^T f(t)e^{r(T-t)}\,dt$. This is called the future discounted value (FDV) of the income stream:

The **future discounted value** (at time T) of a continuous income stream at the rate of $f(t)$ dollars per year over the time interval $[0, T]$, with continuously compounded interest at rate r, is given by

$$\text{FDV} = \int_0^T f(t)e^{r(T-t)}\,dt \qquad\qquad [10.33]$$

An easy modification of [10.32] will give us the discounted value (DV) at time $s \in [0, T]$ of an income stream $f(t)$ received during time interval $[s, T]$. In fact, the DV at time s of income $f(t)$ received in the small time interval $[t, t+dt]$ is $f(t)e^{-r(t-s)}\,dt$. So we have the following:

The **discounted value** at time s of a continuous income stream at the rate of $f(t)$ dollars per year over the time interval $[s, T]$, with continuously compounded interest at rate r, is given by

$$\text{DV} = \int_{t=s}^T f(t)e^{-r(t-s)}\,dt \qquad\qquad [10.34]$$

Example 10.11

Find the PDV and the FDV of a constant income stream of $1000 per year over the next 10 years, assuming an interest rate of $r = 8\% = 0.08$ annually, compounded continuously.

Solution

$$\text{PDV} = \int_0^{10} 1000 e^{-0.08t}\, dt = \Big|_0^{10} 1000 \left(-\frac{e^{-0.08t}}{0.08} \right) = \frac{1000}{0.08}(1 - e^{-0.8}) \approx 6883.39$$

$$\text{FDV} = e^{0.08 \cdot 10}\text{PDV} \approx e^{0.8} \cdot 6883.39 \approx 15{,}319.27$$

Problems

1. Assume that the rate of extraction $u(t)$ from an oil well decreases exponentially over time, with $u(t) = \bar{u}e^{-at}$, where a is a positive constant. Given the initial stock $x(0) = x_0$, find an expression $x(t)$ for the remaining amount of oil at time t. Under what condition will the well never be exhausted?

2. **a.** Follow the pattern in Example 10.9 and find the mean income m over the interval $[b, 2b]$ when $f(r) = Br^{-2}$.
   b. Assume that the individual's demand function is $D(p, r) = Ap^{\gamma}r^{\delta}$, $A > 0$, $\gamma < 0$, $\delta > 0$, $\delta \neq 1$. Compute the total demand $x(p)$ by using formula [10.31], assuming that there are n individuals in the population.

3. Let $K(t)$ denote the capital stock of an economy at time t. Then **net investment** at time t, denoted by $I(t)$, is given by the rate of increase $\dot{K}(t)$ of $K(t)$.
   a. If $I(t) = 3t^2 + 2t + 5$ $(t \geq 0)$, what is the total increase in the capital stock during the interval from $t = 0$ to $t = 5$?
   b. If $K(t_0) = K_0$, find an expression for the total increase in the capital stock from time $t = t_0$ to $t = T$ when the investment function $I(t)$ is as in part (a).

4. Find the present and future values of a constant income stream of $500 per year over the next 15 years, assuming an interest rate of $r = 6\% = 0.06$ annually, compounded continuously.

5. **a.** Find the present discounted value (PDV) of a constant income stream of a dollars per year over the next T years, assuming an interest rate of r annually, compounded continuously.
   b. What is the limit of the PDV as $T \to \infty$? Compare this result with (6.22) in Section 6.6.

=11

Further Topics in Integration

The true mathematician is not a juggler of numbers, but of concepts.
—*I. Stewart* (1975)

This chapter continues the study of integration started in Chapter 10. In particular, it presents some methods of integration that are used quite often in economics and even more often in statistics. These include integration by parts and by substitution, integrals of discontinuous functions, and integrals over infinite intervals. The last part of this chapter considers Lorenz curves, which can be a useful way of visualizing income distributions and some of their properties.

11.1 Integration by Parts

We often need to evaluate integrals such as $\int x^2 e^{2x}\,dx$ whose integrand is a product of two functions. We know that $\frac{1}{3}x^3$ has x^2 as its derivative and that $\frac{1}{2}e^{2x}$ has e^{2x} as its derivative, but $(\frac{1}{3}x^3)(\frac{1}{2}e^{2x})$ certainly does not have $x^2 e^{2x}$ as its derivative. In general, because the derivative of a product is *not* the product of the derivatives, the integral of a product is not the product of the integrals.

The correct rule for differentiating a product allows us to derive an important and useful rule for intergrating products. In fact,

$$\bigl(f(x)g(x)\bigr)' = f'(x)g(x) + f(x)g'(x) \qquad [*]$$

Taking the indefinite integral of each side and using the rule for integrating a sum gives

$$f(x)g(x) = \int f'(x)g(x)\,dx + \int f(x)g'(x)\,dx$$

where the constants of integration are implicit in the indefinite integrals on the right-hand side of this equation. Rearranging this last equation yields:

Formula for Integration by Parts

$$\int f(x)g'(x)\,dx = f(x)g(x) - \int f'(x)g(x)\,dx \qquad\qquad [11.1]$$

At first sight, this formula does not look at all helpful. Yet the examples that follow show how this impression is quite wrong, once one has learned to use it properly.

Suppose we are asked to integrate a function $H(x)$ that can be written in the form $f(x)g'(x)$. By using [11.1], the problem can then be transformed into that of integrating $f'(x)g(x)$. Usually, a function $H(x)$ can be written as $f(x)g'(x)$ in several different ways. The point is, therefore, to choose f and g so that it is easier to find $\int f'(x)g(x)\,dx$ than it is to find $\int f(x)g'(x)\,dx$. Sometimes the method works not by producing a simpler integral, but one that is similar. See Example 11.2(a).

Example 11.1

Use integration by parts to evaluate $\int xe^x\,dx$.

Solution   In order to use [11.1], we must write the integrand in the form $f(x)g'(x)$. Let $f(x) = x$ and $g(x) = e^x$. Then $f(x)g'(x) = xe^x$, and so

$$\int \underset{\substack{\downarrow \;\;\;\; \downarrow \\ f(x)\;\; g'(x)}}{x \;\cdot\; e^x}\;dx = \underset{\substack{\downarrow \;\;\;\; \downarrow \\ f(x)\;\; g(x)}}{x \;\cdot\; e^x} - \int \underset{\substack{\downarrow \;\;\;\; \downarrow \\ f'(x)\;\; g(x)}}{1 \;\cdot\; e^x}\;dx = xe^x - \int e^x\,dx = xe^x - e^x + C$$

The derivative of $xe^x - e^x + C$ is $e^x + xe^x - e^x = xe^x$, so the integration has been carried out correctly.

The right choice of f and g enabled us to evaluate the integral. Let us see what happens if we try $f(x) = e^x$ and $g(x) = \frac{1}{2}x^2$ instead. Again $f(x)g'(x) = e^x x = xe^x$, and by [11.1]:

$$\int \underset{\substack{\downarrow \;\;\;\; \downarrow \\ f(x)\;\; g'(x)}}{e^x \;\cdot\; x}\;dx = \underset{\substack{\downarrow \;\;\;\; \downarrow \\ f(x)\;\; g(x)}}{e^x \;\cdot\; \tfrac{1}{2}x^2} - \int \underset{\substack{\downarrow \;\;\;\; \downarrow \\ f'(x)\;\; g(x)}}{e^x \;\cdot\; \tfrac{1}{2}x^2}\;dx$$

In this case, the integral on the right-hand side is more complicated than the original one. Thus, this second choice of f and g does not simplify the integral.

The example illustrates that we must be careful how we split the integrand. Insights into making a good choice, if any, will come only with practice. Often, even experienced "integrators" must resort to trial and error.

Example 11.2

Evaluate the following:

(a) $I = \displaystyle\int \frac{1}{x} \ln x \, dx$

(b) $J = \int e^{2x} x^3 \, dx$

Solution

(a) Choosing $f(x) = 1/x$ and $g'(x) = \ln x$ does not work well because it is difficult to find $g(x)$. Choosing $f(x) = \ln x$ and $g'(x) = 1/x$ works better:

$$I = \int \frac{1}{x} \ln x \, dx = \int \ln x \; \frac{1}{x} \, dx = \ln x \ln x - \int \frac{1}{x} \ln x \, dx$$

$$\underset{f(x)\,g'(x)}{\downarrow\;\downarrow} \qquad \underset{f(x)\,g(x)}{\downarrow\;\downarrow} \qquad \underset{f'(x)g(x)}{\downarrow\;\downarrow}$$

In this case, the last integral is exactly the one we started with, namely I. So it must be true that $I = (\ln x)^2 - I$, implying that $I = \frac{1}{2}(\ln x)^2$. Adding an arbitrary constant, we conclude that

$$\int \frac{1}{x} \ln x \, dx = \frac{1}{2}(\ln x)^2 + C$$

(b) We begin by arguing rather loosely as follows. Differentiation makes x^3 simpler by reducing the power in the derivative $3x^2$ from 3 to 2. On the other hand, e^{2x} is about equally simple whether we differentiate or integrate it. Therefore, we choose $f(x) = x^3$ and $g'(x) = e^{2x}$ so that we differentiate f and integrate g'. This yields $f'(x) = 3x^2$ and we can choose $g(x) = \frac{1}{2}e^{2x}$. Therefore,

$$J = \int x^3 e^{2x} \, dx = x^3 \left(\tfrac{1}{2}e^{2x}\right) - \int (3x^2)\left(\tfrac{1}{2}e^{2x}\right) dx$$

$$= \tfrac{1}{2}x^3 e^{2x} - \tfrac{3}{2}\int x^2 e^{2x} \, dx \qquad\qquad [1]$$

The last integral *is* somewhat simpler than the one we started with because the power of x has been reduced. Integrating by parts once more yields

$$\int x^2 e^{2x}\, dx = x^2\left(\tfrac{1}{2}e^{2x}\right) - \int (2x)\left(\tfrac{1}{2}e^{2x}\right) dx$$

$$= \tfrac{1}{2}x^2 e^{2x} - \int x e^{2x}\, dx \qquad\qquad [2]$$

Using integration by parts a third and final time gives

$$\int x e^{2x}\, dx = x\left(\tfrac{1}{2}e^{2x}\right) - \int \tfrac{1}{2}e^{2x}\, dx = \tfrac{1}{2}x e^{2x} - \tfrac{1}{4}e^{2x} + C \qquad [3]$$

Successively inserting the results of [3] and [2] into [1] yields (with $3C/2 = c$):

$$J = \tfrac{1}{2}x^3 e^{2x} - \tfrac{3}{4}x^2 e^{2x} + \tfrac{3}{4}x e^{2x} - \tfrac{3}{8}e^{2x} + c$$

It is a good idea to double-check your work by verifying that $dJ/dx = x^3 e^{2x}$.

There is a corresponding result for definite integrals. From the definition of the definite integral and [∗] (the product rule for differentiation), we have

$$\int_a^b \left[f'(x)g(x) + f(x)g'(x)\right] dx = \int_a^b \frac{d}{dx}\left[f(x)g(x)\right] dx = \left.f(x)g(x)\right|_a^b$$

implying that

$$\int_a^b f(x)g'(x)\, dx = \left.f(x)g(x)\right|_a^b - \int_a^b f'(x)g(x)\, dx \qquad\qquad [11.2]$$

Example 11.3
Evaluate $\int_0^3 x\sqrt{1+x}\, dx$.

Solution   We must write the integrand in the form $f(x)g'(x)$. If we let $f(x) = x$ and $g'(x) = \sqrt{1+x} = (1+x)^{1/2}$, then what is g? A certain amount of reflection should suggest choosing $g(x) = \tfrac{2}{3}(1+x)^{3/2}$. Using

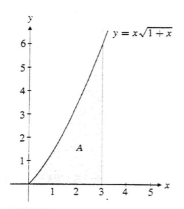

FIGURE 11.1

[11.2] then gives

$$\int_0^3 x\sqrt{1+x}\, dx = \left.x\cdot\tfrac{2}{3}(1+x)^{3/2}\right|_0^3 - \int_0^3 1\cdot\tfrac{2}{3}(1+x)^{3/2}\, dx$$

$$= 3\cdot\tfrac{2}{3}\cdot4^{3/2} - \tfrac{2}{3}\left.\tfrac{2}{5}(1+x)^{5/2}\right|_0^3$$

$$= 16 - \tfrac{4}{15}(4^{5/2} - 1) = 16 - \tfrac{4}{15}\cdot31 = 7\tfrac{11}{15}$$

Alternatively, we could have found the indefinite integral of $x\sqrt{1+x}$ first, and then evaluated the definite integral by using definition [10.12] of the definite integral. Figure 11.1 shows the area under the graph of $y = x\sqrt{1+x}$ over the interval $[0, 3]$, and you should ask yourself if $7\tfrac{11}{15}$ is a reasonable estimate of area A.

Problems

1. Use integration by parts to find the following:

   a. $\displaystyle\int xe^{-x}\, dx$ **b.** $\displaystyle\int 3xe^{4x}\, dx$ **c.** $\displaystyle\int (1+x^2)e^{-x}\, dx$ **d.** $\displaystyle\int x\ln x\, dx$

2. Evaluate the following: (a) $\int_{-1}^{1} x\ln(x+2)\, dx$ (b) $\int_0^2 x2^x\, dx$ (c) $\int_0^1 x^2 e^x\, dx$

3. Of course, $f(x) = 1 \cdot f(x)$ for any function $f(x)$. Use this fact to prove that

$$\int f(x)\, dx = xf(x) - \int xf'(x)\, dx$$

Apply this formula to the case when $f(x) = \ln x$.

4. Suppose $\mu(t_0) = \mu(t_1) = 0$. Show that, with appropriate requirements on F and μ,

$$\int_{t_0}^{t_1} F(t)\dot{\mu}(t)\, dt = -\int_{t_0}^{t_1} \dot{F}(t)\mu(t)\, dt$$

(Recall that the dot notation $\dot{\mu}(t)$ and $\dot{F}(t)$ means differentiation w.r.t. t.)

5. Show that

$$\int x^\rho \ln x\, dx = \frac{x^{\rho+1}}{\rho+1}\ln x - \frac{x^{\rho+1}}{(\rho+1)^2} + C \qquad (\rho \neq -1)$$

6. With appropriate requirements on the functions involved, show that if $U(C(0)) = 0$, then

$$\int_0^T U(C(t))e^{-rt}\, dt = \frac{1}{r}\left(\int_0^T U'(C(t))C'(t)e^{-rt}\, dt - U(C(T))e^{-rT} \right)$$

Harder Problems

7. Compute the following integral when $\gamma > c$:

$$T^* = k \int_0^{\bar{u}} u^2(\bar{u} - u)^{\gamma-1}\, du$$

11.2 Integration by Substitution

In this section, we shall see how the chain rule for differentiation leads to an important method for evaluating many complicated integrals. We start with a simple example,

$$\int (x^2 + 10)^{50} 2x\, dx \tag{1}$$

One way of integrating this would be to write out all 51 terms of $(x^2 + 10)^{50}$, and then integrate term by term. But this would be extremely cumbersome.[1] Instead, let us introduce $x^2 + 10$ as a new variable. We pretend that the symbol dx in [1] denotes the differential of x, and argue as follows: If we let $u = x^2 + 10$, then $du = 2x\, dx$, and using this in [1] yields

$$\int u^{50}\, du$$

---

[1] The expression $(x^2 + 10)^{50}$ can be evaluated using the Newton binomial formula (7.16) in Section 7.4.

This integral is easy, $\int u^{50}\,du = \frac{1}{51}u^{51} + C$. Because $u = x^2 + 10$, it appears that

$$\int (x^2 + 10)^{50} 2x\,dx = \frac{1}{51}(x^2 + 10)^{51} + C \qquad [2]$$

By the chain rule, the derivative of $\frac{1}{51}(x^2 + 10)^{51} + C$ is precisely $(x^2 + 10)^{50} 2x$, so the result in [2] *is* confirmed.

Let us try this method on another example, namely

$$\int \frac{e^x\,dx}{\sqrt[3]{1 + e^x}} \qquad [3]$$

This time we introduce $u = 1 + e^x$ as a new variable. Then $du = e^x\,dx$, and so the integral reduces to

$$\int \frac{du}{\sqrt[3]{u}} = \int u^{-1/3}\,du$$

This integral is equal to $\frac{3}{2}u^{2/3} + C$. Because $u = 1 + e^x$, it appears that

$$\int \frac{e^x\,dx}{\sqrt[3]{1 + e^x}} = \frac{3}{2}(1 + e^x)^{2/3} + C \qquad [4]$$

Again, using the chain rule, we can quickly confirm that [4] is correct, because the derivative of $\frac{3}{2}(1 + e^x)^{2/3}$ is $(1 + e^x)^{-1/3}e^x = e^x/\sqrt[3]{1 + e^x}$. (Actually, the substitution $u = \sqrt[3]{1 + e^x}$ works even better.)

In both of these examples, the integrand could be written in the form $f(u)u'$, where $u = g(x)$. (In [1], put $f(u) = u^{50}$ and $u = g(x) = x^2 + 10$. In [3], put $f(u) = 1/\sqrt[3]{u}$ and $u = g(x) = 1 + e^x$.)

Let us try the same method on the more general integral

$$\int f\big(g(x)\big)g'(x)\,dx \qquad [5]$$

If we put $u = g(x)$, then $du = g'(x)\,dx$, and so (5) reduces to

$$\int f(u)\,du$$

Suppose we could find an antiderivative function $F(u)$ such that $F'(u) = f(u)$. Then

$$\int f(u)\,du = F(u) + C$$

which implies that

$$\int f\big(g(x)\big)g'(x)\,dx = F\big(g(x)\big) + C \qquad [6]$$

Does this purely formal method always give the right result? To convince you that it does, we use the chain rule to differentiate $F\big(g(x)\big) + C$ w.r.t. x. The derivative is $F'\big(g(x)\big)g'(x)$, which is precisely equal to $f\big(g(x)\big)g'(x)$, thus confirming [6]. We frame this result for further reference:

Integration by Substitution

$$\int f\big(g(x)\big)g'(x)\,dx = \int f(u)\,du \qquad (u = g(x)) \qquad\qquad [11.3]$$

Note: Precise assumptions for this formula to be valid are as follows: g is continuously differentiable, and $f(u)$ is continuous whenever u belongs to the range of g.

It is quite easy to integrate by substitution when the integrand is directly of the form $f\big(g(x)\big)g'(x)$, as in the previous examples. Sometimes we need to make some preliminary adjustments.

Example 11.4

Integrate the following:

$$\int 8x^2(3x^3 - 1)^{16}\,dx$$

Solution   We substitute $u = 3x^3 - 1$. Then $du = 9x^2\,dx$ and so $8x^2\,dx = (8/9)9x^2\,dx = (8/9)\,du$. Thus,

$$\int 8x^2(3x^3 - 1)^{16}\,dx = (8/9)\int u^{16}\,du$$

$$= (8/9) \cdot (1/17)u^{17} + C$$

$$= (8/153)(3x^3 - 1)^{17} + C$$

Check your understanding of this method by doing Problems 1 and 2 right now.

More Complicated Cases

The examples of integration by substitution considered so far were rather simple. More challenging applications of this integration method are to cases where it is difficult to see how the integrand can be expressed in the form $f\big(g(x)\big)g'(x)$.

Example 11.5

Try to evaluate the integral

$$\int \frac{x - \sqrt{x}}{x + \sqrt{x}}\, dx \qquad (x > 0)$$

Solution   Because $\sqrt{x}$ occurs in the numerator as well as in the denominator, it might be a good idea to try to simplify the integral by substituting $u = \sqrt{x} = g(x)$. Then $du = g'(x)\, dx = dx/2\sqrt{x}$. This last expression does not occur in the given integral. However, we can remedy this problem by multiplying the integrand by $2\sqrt{x}/2\sqrt{x}$, obtaining

$$\int \frac{x - \sqrt{x}}{x + \sqrt{x}}\, dx = \int \frac{x - \sqrt{x}}{x + \sqrt{x}}\, 2\sqrt{x}\, \frac{1}{2\sqrt{x}}\, dx \qquad [*]$$

Now, if we replace $\sqrt{x}$ by u and hence x by u^2, and also replace $dx/2\sqrt{x}$ by du, then the integral becomes

$$\int \frac{u^2 - u}{u^2 + u}\, 2u\, du = 2 \int \frac{u^2 - u}{u + 1}\, du$$

$$= 2 \int \left(u - 2 + \frac{2}{u + 1} \right) du$$

$$= u^2 - 4u + 4 \ln |u + 1| + C$$

where we have performed the division $(u^2 - u) \div (u + 1)$ in order to derive the second equality. Replacing u by $\sqrt{x}$ yields the result

$$\int \frac{x - \sqrt{x}}{x + \sqrt{x}}\, dx = x - 4\sqrt{x} + 4 \ln \left(\sqrt{x} + 1 \right) + C$$

Actually, the trick used in $[*]$ is unnecessary. If $u = \sqrt{x}$, then $x = u^2$ and $dx = 2u\, du$, so we get immediately

$$\int \frac{x - \sqrt{x}}{x + \sqrt{x}}\, dx = \int \frac{u^2 - u}{u^2 + u}\, 2u\, du$$

$$= 2 \int \frac{u^2 - u}{u + 1}\, du$$

The last method in the previous example is the one used most frequently. We can summarize it as follows:

Method for Finding a Complicated Integral $\int G(x)\,dx$:

1. Pick out a "part" of $G(x)$ and introduce this "part" as a new variable, $u = g(x)$.
2. Compute $du = g'(x)\,dx$.
3. Using the substitution $u = g(x)$, $du = g'(x)\,dx$, transform (if possible) $\int G(x)\,dx$ to an integral of the form $\int f(u)\,du$.
4. Find (if possible) $\int f(u)\,du = F(u) + C$.
5. Replace u by $g(x)$. The final answer is then

$$\int G(x)\,dx = F\big(g(x)\big) + C$$

At step 3 of this procedure, it is crucial that after substituting you are integrating a function that only contains u (and du), without any x's. Probably the most common error when integrating by substitution is to replace dx by du, rather than use the correct formula $du = g'(x)\,dx$. If one particular substitution does not work, one can try another. *Note:* There is always the possibility (assumed much too quickly by some students) that no substitution works because the integral is "insoluble." Here are some quite common integrals that really are impossible to "solve," except by introducing special new functions:

$$\int e^{x^2}\,dx, \quad \int e^{-x^2}\,dx, \quad \int \frac{e^x}{x}\,dx, \quad \int \frac{1}{\ln x}\,dx, \quad \int \frac{dx}{\sqrt{x^4+1}}\,dx \qquad [11.4]$$

Example 11.6

Find the following:

(a) $\displaystyle\int x^3\sqrt{1+x^2}\,dx$

(b) $\displaystyle\int_0^1 x^3\sqrt{1+x^2}\,dx$

Solution

(a) We follow previous steps 1 to 5:
   1. We pick a "part" of $x^3\sqrt{1+x^2}$ as a new variable. Let us try $u = \sqrt{1+x^2}$.

2. When $u = \sqrt{1+x^2}$, then $u^2 = 1 + x^2$ and so $2u\,du = 2x\,dx$, implying that $u\,du = x\,dx$. (Note that this is easier than differentiating u directly.)

3. $\displaystyle \int x^3 \sqrt{1+x^2}\,dx = \int x^2 \sqrt{1+x^2} \cdot x\,dx = \int (u^2 - 1) u \cdot u\,du$

$$= \int (u^4 - u^2)\,du$$

4. $\displaystyle \int (u^4 - u^2)\,du = \tfrac{1}{5}u^5 - \tfrac{1}{3}u^3 + C$

5. $\displaystyle \int x^3 \sqrt{1+x^2}\,dx = \tfrac{1}{5}\left(\sqrt{1+x^2}\right)^5 - \tfrac{1}{3}\left(\sqrt{1+x^2}\right)^3 + C$

(b) Using the result in part (a),

$$\int_0^1 x^3 \sqrt{1+x^2}\,dx = \Big|_0^1 \left[\tfrac{1}{5}\left(\sqrt{1+x^2}\right)^5 - \tfrac{1}{3}\left(\sqrt{1+x^2}\right)^3 \right]$$

$$= \tfrac{2}{15}(\sqrt{2} + 1)$$

Note 1: In this example, show that the substitution $u = 1 + x^2$ also works.

Note 2: One is inclined to think that an integral like $\int x^2\sqrt{1+x^2}\,dx$ should be even easier to find than the one considered in Example 11.6. However, the substitution $u = \sqrt{1+x^2}$ leads to the integral $\int xu^2\,du = \int \pm\sqrt{u^2 - 1}\,u^2\,du$, which is *not* very encouraging. (Actually, one has to introduce a rather bizarre substitution in order to find this integral. The substitution suggested in Problem 11 works.)

The definite integral in the previous example can also be evaluated by "carrying over the limits of integration" as follows. We substituted $u = \sqrt{1+x^2}$. As x varies from 0 to 1, so u varies from 1 to $\sqrt{2}$, and the right answer is obtained as follows:

$$\int_0^1 x^3 \sqrt{1+x^2}\,dx = \int_1^{\sqrt{2}} (u^4 - u^2)\,du$$

$$= \Big|_1^{\sqrt{2}} \left(\tfrac{1}{5}u^5 - \tfrac{1}{3}u^3 \right) = \tfrac{2}{15}(\sqrt{2} + 1)$$

This method of carrying over the limits of integration works in general. Under the same assumptions as in the note to [11.3], we obtain

$$\int_a^b f\big(g(x)\big) g'(x)\,dx = \int_{g(a)}^{g(b)} f(u)\,du \qquad (u = g(x)) \qquad\qquad [11.5]$$

The reason is simple. If $F'(u) = f(u)$, then

$$\int_a^b f(g(x))g'(x)\,dx = \left.F(g(x))\right|_a^b = F(g(b)) - F(g(a)) = \int_{g(a)}^{g(b)} f(u)\,du$$

Problems

1. Find the following integrals by using [11.3]:

   a. $\displaystyle\int (x^2 + 1)^8 \, 2x \, dx$ **b.** $\displaystyle\int (x + 2)^{10} \, dx$ **c.** $\displaystyle\int \frac{2x - 1}{x^2 - x + 8} \, dx$

2. Find the following integrals by means of an appropriate substitution:

   a. $\displaystyle\int x(2x^2 + 3)^5 \, dx$ **b.** $\displaystyle\int x^2 e^{x^3 + 2} \, dx$ **c.** $\displaystyle\int \frac{\ln(x + 2)}{2x + 4} \, dx$

   d. $\displaystyle\int x\sqrt{1 + x} \, dx$ **e.** $\displaystyle\int \frac{x^3}{(1 + x^2)^3} \, dx$ **f.** $\displaystyle\int x^5 \sqrt{4 - x^3} \, dx$

3. Find the following integrals:

   a. $\displaystyle\int_0^1 x\sqrt{1 + x^2} \, dx$ **b.** $\displaystyle\int_1^e \frac{\ln y}{y} \, dy$ **c.** $\displaystyle\int_1^3 \frac{1}{x^2} e^{2/x} \, dx$

4. Solve the following equation for x:

   $$\int_3^x \frac{2t - 2}{t^2 - 2t} \, dt = \ln\left(\tfrac{2}{3}x - 1\right)$$

5. Find the following integrals:

   a. $\displaystyle\int_0^1 (x^4 - x^9)(x^5 - 1)^{12} \, dx$ **b.** $\displaystyle\int \frac{\ln x}{\sqrt{x}} \, dx$ **c.** $\displaystyle\int_0^4 \frac{dx}{\sqrt{1 + \sqrt{x}}}$

6. Show that

   $$\int_{t_0}^{t_1} S'(x(t))\dot{x}(t) \, dt = S(x(t_1)) - S(x(t_0))$$

7. **a.** Show that if $a \neq b$, then for all $x \neq a$ and $x \neq b$,

   $$\frac{cx + d}{(x - a)(x - b)} = \frac{1}{a - b}\left(\frac{ac + d}{x - a} - \frac{bc + d}{x - b}\right)$$

   b. Use the identity in part (a) to compute:

   (i) $\displaystyle\int_3^4 \frac{x \, dx}{x^2 - 3x + 2}$ (ii) $\displaystyle\int_4^5 \frac{2x + 3}{x^2 - 5x + 6} \, dx$

8. Show that if f is continuous in the interval $[a, b]$, and λ is a constant $\neq 0$, then

   a. $\int_a^b f(x) \, dx = \int_{a+\lambda}^{b+\lambda} f(x - \lambda) \, dx$

   b. $\int_a^b f(x) \, dx = \frac{1}{\lambda} \int_{\lambda a}^{\lambda b} f\left(\frac{x}{\lambda}\right) \, dx$

Harder Problems

9. In a model of optimal macroeconomic stabilization, A. J. Preston makes investment I a function of the time that is given by the integral

$$I = \int_0^t \frac{A(1 - De^{\beta\tau})}{1 + CDe^{\beta\tau}}\, d\tau$$

All constants are positive. Find I by using the substitution $x = CDe^{\beta\tau}$ and also the identity in Problem 7(a).

10. Find the following:

$$I = \int \frac{x^{1/2}}{1 - x^{1/3}}\, dx$$

(*Hint:* How can you eliminate the fractional exponents in $x^{1/2}$ and $x^{1/3}$ *simultaneously* using only one substitution?)

11. Sometimes the change of variable formula [11.3] is used the other way around in the following sense: To evaluate $\int f(x)\, dx$, we introduce $x = g(t)$, $dx = g'(t)\, dt$, and try to solve the new integral expressed in terms of t. Finally, we use $t = g^{-1}(x)$ to get the answer in terms of x. (This requires g to have an inverse.) Apply this method to

(a) $\displaystyle\int \frac{dx}{\sqrt{x^2 + 1}}$ (b) $\displaystyle\int \sqrt{x^2 + 1}\, dx$

(*Hint:* Introduce the substitution $x = \frac{1}{2}(e^t - e^{-t})$. This might strike you as rather odd, but it works. You will need the answers to Problem 6 of Section 8.1 and Problem 23 of Section 8.2.)

11.3 Extending the Concept of the Integral

In this section, we extend the concept of the integral in several directions. Again, each of these extensions is useful in economics and/or statistics.

Integrals of Certain Discontinuous Functions

So far we have only been integrating continuous functions. It is useful to extend the definition to certain discontinuous functions. A function f is called *piecewise continuous* over the interval from a to b if it has at most a finite number of discontinuity points in the interval, with one-sided limits on both sides at each discontinuity point.

A typical graph of a piecewise continuous function is shown in Fig. 11.2, where the discontinuity points are at $x = c$ and at $x = d$. Suppose we replace

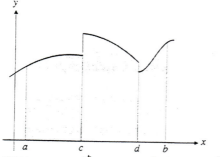

FIGURE 11.2 $\int_a^b f(x)\,dx = \int_a^c f(x)\,dx + \int_c^d f(x)\,dx + \int_d^b f(x)\,dx.$

$f(x)$ in $[a, c]$ by the continuous function $f_1(x)$ that is equal to $f(x)$ throughout $[a, c)$ and has the value $f_1(c) = \lim_{x \to c^-} f(x)$ at $x = c$. Then $\int_a^c f_1(x)\,dx$ is well defined and it is reasonable to define $\int_a^c f(x)\,dx = \int_a^c f_1(x)\,dx$. By a similar trick, we define $\int_c^d f(x)\,dx$ and $\int_d^b f(x)\,dx$ by considering continuous functions in the intervals $[c, d]$ and $[d, b]$, respectively, that are equal to f except at one or both of the end points. The only sensible definition now is

$$\int_a^b f(x)\,dx = \int_a^c f(x)\,dx + \int_c^d f(x)\,dx + \int_d^b f(x)\,dx$$

Then the interpretation of $\int_a^b f(x)\,dx$ is simply the sum of the three areas in Fig. 11.2. This should make clear how $\int_a^b f(x)\,dx$ can be defined for all functions $f(x)$ that are piecewise continuous on $[a, b]$.

Infinite Intervals of Integration

Suppose f is a function that is continuous for all $x \geq a$. Then $\int_a^b f(x)\,dx$ is defined for each $b \geq a$. If the limit of this integral as $b \to \infty$ exists (and is finite), then we say that f is *integrable over* $[a, \infty)$, and define

$$\int_a^\infty f(x)\,dx = \lim_{b \to \infty} \int_a^b f(x)\,dx \qquad [11.6]$$

The *improper integral* $\int_a^\infty f(x)\,dx$ is then said to *converge*. If the limit does *not* exist, the improper integral is said to *diverge*. If $f(x) \geq 0$ in $[a, \infty)$, we interpret the integral [11.6] as the *area* below the graph of f over the interval $[a, \infty)$.

Analogously, we define

$$\int_{-\infty}^b f(x)\,dx = \lim_{a \to -\infty} \int_a^b f(x)\,dx \qquad [11.7]$$

when f is continuous in $(-\infty, b]$. If this limit exists, the improper integral is said to converge. Otherwise, it diverges.

Example 11.7

The *exponential distribution* in statistics is defined by

$$f(x) = \lambda e^{-\lambda x} \qquad (x \geq 0; \ \lambda \text{ is a positive constant})$$

Show that the area below the graph of f over $[0, \infty)$ is equal to 1. (See Fig. 11.3.)

Solution   For $b > 0$, the area below the graph of f over $[0, b]$ is equal to

$$\int_0^b \lambda e^{-\lambda x} \, dx = \Big|_0^b \left(-e^{-\lambda x}\right) = -e^{-\lambda b} + 1$$

As $b \to \infty$, so $-e^{-\lambda b} + 1$ approaches 1. Therefore,

$$\int_0^\infty \lambda e^{-\lambda x} \, dx = \lim_{b \to \infty} \int_0^b \lambda e^{-\lambda x} \, dx = \lim_{b \to \infty} \left(-e^{-\lambda b} + 1\right) = 1$$

Example 11.8

Show that

$$\int_1^\infty \frac{1}{x^a} \, dx = \frac{1}{a - 1} \qquad \text{(for } a > 1\text{)} \tag{1}$$

Then study the case $a \leq 1$.

Solution   For $a \neq 1$ and $b > 1$,

$$\int_1^b \frac{1}{x^a} \, dx = \int_1^b x^{-a} \, dx = \Big|_1^b \frac{1}{1-a} x^{1-a} = \frac{1}{1-a}(b^{1-a} - 1) \tag{2}$$

FIGURE 11.3   Area A has an unbounded base, but the height decreases to 0 so rapidly that the total area is 1.

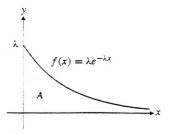

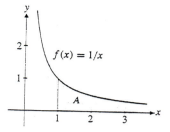

FIGURE 11.4 "$A = \int_1^\infty (1/x)\,dx = \infty$." $1/x$ does not approach 0 fast enough, so the improper integral diverges.

For $a > 1$, one has $b^{1-a} = 1/b^{a-1} \to 0$ as $b \to \infty$. Hence, [1] follows from [2] by letting $b \to \infty$.

For $a = 1$, we have $\int_1^b (1/x)\,dx = \ln b - \ln 1 = \ln b$, which tends to ∞ as b tends to ∞, so $\int_1^\infty (1/x)\,dx$ diverges. See Fig. 11.4.

For $a < 1$, the last expression in [2] tends to ∞ as b tends to ∞. Hence, the integral diverges in this case.

If both limits of integration are infinite, the improper integral of a continuous function f on $(-\infty, \infty)$ is defined by

$$\int_{-\infty}^{\infty} f(x)\,dx = \int_{-\infty}^{0} f(x)\,dx + \int_{0}^{\infty} f(x)\,dx \qquad [11.8]$$

If *both* integrals on the right-hand side converge, the improper integral $\int_{-\infty}^{\infty} f(x)\,dx$ is said to *converge*; otherwise, it *diverges*. Instead of using 0 as the point of sub-division, one could use an arbitrary fixed real number c. The value assigned to the integral will always be the same, provided that the integral does converge.

It is important to note that definition [11.8] requires both integrals on the right-hand side to converge. Note in particular that

$$\lim_{b \to \infty} \int_{-b}^{b} f(x)\,dx \qquad [*]$$

is *not* the definition of $\int_{-\infty}^{+\infty} f(x)\,dx$. Problem 4 provides an example in which [*] exists, yet the integral in [11.8] diverges. So [*] is not an acceptable definition, whereas [11.8] is.

Example 11.9

For $c > 0$, examine the convergence of

$$\int_{-\infty}^{+\infty} xe^{-cx^2}\,dx$$

Solution   Let us begin with the indefinite integral $\int xe^{-cx^2}\,dx$. Making the substitution $u = -cx^2$, we have $du = -2cx\,dx$ and so

$$\int xe^{-cx^2}\,dx = -\frac{1}{2c}\int e^u\,du = -\frac{1}{2c}e^u + C = -\frac{1}{2c}e^{-cx^2} + C$$

According to [11.8], provided both integrals on the right side exist, one has

$$\int_{-\infty}^{\infty} xe^{-cx^2}\,dx = \int_{-\infty}^{0} xe^{-cx^2}\,dx + \int_{0}^{\infty} xe^{-cx^2}\,dx \qquad [*]$$

But now

$$\int_{-\infty}^{0} xe^{-cx^2}\,dx = \lim_{a \to -\infty}\int_{a}^{0} xe^{-cx^2}\,dx = \lim_{a \to -\infty}\left. -\frac{1}{2c}e^{-cx^2}\right|_{a}^{0} = -\frac{1}{2c}$$

In the same way, we see that the second integral in [*] is $1/2c$, so

$$\int_{-\infty}^{\infty} xe^{-cx^2}\,dx = -\frac{1}{2c} + \frac{1}{2c} = 0 \qquad (c > 0) \qquad [**]$$

(This result is very important in statistics. See Problem 13.)

Integrals of Unbounded Functions

We turn next to improper integrals where the *integrand* is not bounded.
Consider first the function $f(x) = 1/\sqrt{x}$, with $x \in (0, 2]$. (See Fig. 11.5.) Note that $f(x) \to \infty$ as $x \to 0^+$. The function f is continuous in the interval $[h, 2]$

FIGURE 11.5 The "height" of the domain is unbounded, but $y = 1/\sqrt{x}$ approaches the y-axis so quickly that the total area is finite.

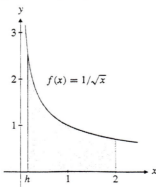

for an arbitrary fixed number h in $(0, 2)$. Therefore, the definite integral of f over the interval $[h, 2]$ exists, and

$$\int_h^2 \frac{1}{\sqrt{x}}\, dx = \Big|_h^2\ 2\sqrt{x} = 2\sqrt{2} - 2\sqrt{h}$$

The limit of this expression as $h \to 0^+$ is $2\sqrt{2}$. Then, by definition,

$$\int_0^2 \frac{1}{\sqrt{x}}\, dx = 2\sqrt{2}$$

The improper integral is said to converge in this case, and the area below the graph of f over the interval $(0, 2]$ is $2\sqrt{2}$. The area of $1/\sqrt{x}$ over the interval $(h, 2]$ is shown in Fig. 11.5.

   More generally, suppose that f is a continuous function in the interval $(a, b]$, but $f(x)$ is not defined at $x = a$. Then we define

$$\int_a^b f(x)\, dx = \lim_{h \to 0^+} \int_{a+h}^b f(x)\, dx \qquad [11.9]$$

if the limit exists, and the improper integral of f is said to converge in this case. If $f(x) \geq 0$ in $(a, b]$, we identify the integral as the *area under the graph* of f over the interval $(a, b]$. In the same way,

$$\int_a^b f(x)\, dx = \lim_{h \to 0^+} \int_a^{b-h} f(x)\, dx \qquad [11.10]$$

if the limit exists, in which case the improper integral of f is said to converge.

   Suppose f is continuous in (a, b). We may not even have f defined at a or b. For instance, suppose $f(x) \to -\infty$ as $x \to a^+$ and $f(x) \to +\infty$ as $x \to b^-$. In this case, f is said to be *integrable* in (a, b), and we can define

$$\int_a^b f(x)\, dx = \int_a^c f(x)\, dx + \int_c^b f(x)\, dx \qquad [11.11]$$

provided that both integrals on the right-hand side of [11.11] converge. Here c is an arbitrary fixed number in (a, b), and neither the convergence of the integral nor its value depends on the choice of c. If either of the integrals on the right-hand side of [11.11] does not converge, the left-hand side is not well defined.

   Suppose that S is a union of a finite number of intervals of the form

$$S = (a_1, b_1) \cup (a_2, b_2) \cup \cdots \cup (a_n, b_n)$$

where $a_1 < b_1 \leq a_2 < b_2 \leq \cdots \leq a_n < b_n$, and $a_1 = -\infty$ and/or $b_n = \infty$ are allowed. Provided that f is integrable in each of the intervals $(a_1, b_1), \ldots, (a_n, b_n)$

according to the earlier definitions in this section, then f is said to be *integrable over S*. We define the *integral* over S as:

$$\int_S f(x)\,dx = \sum_{k=1}^{n} \int_{a_k}^{b_k} f(x)\,dx \qquad [11.12]$$

A Comparison Test for Convergence

The following convergence test for integrals is frequently useful because it does not require evaluation of the integral.

Theorem 11.1   (A Comparison Test for Convergence)
Suppose that f and g are continuous for all $x \geq a$ and

$$|f(x)| \leq g(x) \qquad \text{(for all } x \geq a)$$

If $\int_a^\infty g(x)\,dx$ converges, then $\int_a^\infty f(x)\,dx$ converges, and

$$\left| \int_a^\infty f(x)\,dx \right| \leq \int_a^\infty g(x)\,dx$$

Considering the case in which $f(x) \geq 0$, Theorem 11.1 can be interpreted as follows: If the area below the graph of g is finite, then the area below the graph of f is finite as well, because at no point in $[a, \infty)$ does the graph of f lie above the graph of g. (Draw a figure.) This result seems quite plausible and we shall not give an analytical proof. A corresponding theorem holds for the case where the lower limit of integration is $-\infty$. Also, similar comparison tests can be proved for unbounded functions defined on bounded intervals.

Example 11.10
Integrals of the form

$$\int_{t_0}^\infty U\big(c(t)\big)e^{-\alpha t}\,dt \qquad [1]$$

often appear in economic growth theory. Here $c(t)$ denotes consumption at time t, U is an instantaneous utility function, and α is a positive discount rate. Suppose that there exist numbers M and β, with $\beta < \alpha$, such that

$$|U\big(c(t)\big)| \leq Me^{\beta t} \qquad [2]$$

for all $t \geq t_0$ and for each possible consumption level $c(t)$ at time t. Thus, the absolute value of the utility of consumption is growing at a rate less than the discount rate α. Prove that then [1] converges.

Solution   From [2],

$$|U(c(t))e^{-\alpha t}| \le M e^{-(\alpha-\beta)t} \qquad \text{(for all } t \ge t_0)$$

Moreover,

$$\int_{t_0}^{T} M e^{-(\alpha-\beta)t}\, dt = \left. \frac{-M}{\alpha-\beta} e^{-(\alpha-\beta)t}\right|_{t_0}^{T} = \frac{M}{\alpha-\beta}\left[e^{-(\alpha-\beta)t_0} - e^{-(\alpha-\beta)T}\right]$$

Because $\alpha - \beta > 0$, the last expression tends to $[M/(\alpha - \beta)]\, e^{-(\alpha-\beta)t_0}$ as $T \to \infty$. From Theorem 11.1, it follows that [1] converges.

Example 11.11

The function $f(x) = e^{-x^2}$ is extremely important in statistics, because it is the basis of the *Gaussian*, or *normal*, distribution. It is possible to show that the improper integral

$$\int_{-\infty}^{+\infty} e^{-x^2}\, dx \tag{1}$$

converges. Note that according to [11.4] in Section 11.2, the function $f(x) = e^{-x^2}$ has no indefinite integral that we can find. Because $f(x) = e^{-x^2}$ is symmetric about the y-axis, it suffices to prove that $\int_0^\infty e^{-x^2}\, dx$ converges. To this end, subdivide the interval of integration so that

$$\int_0^\infty e^{-x^2}\, dx = \int_0^1 e^{-x^2}\, dx + \int_1^\infty e^{-x^2}\, dx \tag{2}$$

Of course, $\int_0^1 e^{-x^2}\, dx$ presents no problem because it is the integral of a continuous function over a bounded interval. For $x \ge 1$, one has $0 \le e^{-x^2} \le e^{-x}$. Now $\int_1^\infty e^{-x}\, dx$ converges (to $1/e$), so according to Theorem 11.1, the integral $\int_1^\infty e^{-x^2}\, dx$ must also converge. From [2], it follows that $\int_0^\infty e^{-x^2}\, dx$ converges. Thus, the integral [1] does converge, but we have not found its value. In fact, more advanced techniques of integration show that

$$\int_{-\infty}^{+\infty} e^{-x^2}\, dx = \sqrt{\pi} \tag{11.13}$$

Problems

1. Determine the following integrals, if they converge. Indicate those that diverge.

   a. $\displaystyle\int_1^\infty \frac{1}{x^3}\, dx$ **b.** $\displaystyle\int_1^\infty \frac{1}{\sqrt{x}}\, dx$

c. $\displaystyle\int_{-\infty}^{0} e^x \, dx$ d. $\displaystyle\int_{0}^{a} \frac{x \, dx}{\sqrt{a^2 - x^2}}$ $(a > 0)$

2. Define f for all x by $f(x) = 1/(b-a)$ for $x \in [a, b]$, $f(x) = 0$ for $x \notin [a, b]$. (In statistics, f is called the *rectangular* (or *uniform*) *distribution*). Find the following:

a. $\displaystyle\int_{-\infty}^{+\infty} f(x) \, dx$ b. $\displaystyle\int_{-\infty}^{+\infty} xf(x) \, dx$ c. $\displaystyle\int_{-\infty}^{+\infty} x^2 f(x) \, dx$

3. In connection with Example 11.7, find the following:

a. $\displaystyle\int_{0}^{\infty} x\lambda e^{-\lambda x} \, dx$ b. $\displaystyle\int_{0}^{\infty} (x - 1/\lambda)^2 \, \lambda e^{-\lambda x} \, dx$

c. $\displaystyle\int_{0}^{\infty} (x - 1/\lambda)^3 \, \lambda e^{-\lambda x} \, dx$

(The three numbers you obtain are called respectively the expectation, the variance, and the third central moment of the exponential distribution.)

4. Prove that $\int_{-\infty}^{+\infty} x/(1 + x^2) \, dx$ diverges, but that $\lim_{b\to\infty} \int_{-b}^{b} x/(1 + x^2) \, dx$ converges.

5. The function f is defined for $x > 0$ by $f(x) = (\ln x)/x^3$.
   a. Find the maximum and minimum points of f, if there are any.
   b. Examine the convergence of $\int_{0}^{1} f(x) \, dx$ and $\int_{1}^{\infty} f(x) \, dx$.

6. Use the comparison test of Theorem 11.1 to prove the convergence of

$$\int_{1}^{\infty} \frac{1}{1 + x^2} \, dx$$

7. Show that

$$\int_{-2}^{3} \left(\frac{1}{\sqrt{x + 2}} + \frac{1}{\sqrt{3 - x}} \right) dx = 4\sqrt{5}$$

8. R. E. Hall and D. W. Jorgenson, in their article on "Tax Policy and Investment Behavior," use the integral

$$z = \int_{0}^{\infty} e^{-rs} D(s) \, ds$$

to represent the present discounted value, at interest rate r, of the time-dependent stream of depreciation allowances $D(s)$ $(0 \le s < \infty)$. Find z as a function of τ in the following cases:
   a. $D(s) = 1/\tau$ for $0 \le s \le \tau$, $D(s) = 0$ for $s > \tau$. (Constant depreciation over τ years.)
   b. $D(s) = 2(\tau - s)/\tau^2$ for $0 \le s \le \tau$, $D(s) = 0$ for $s > \tau$. (Straight-line depreciation.)

9. Suppose you evaluate $\int_{-1}^{+1} (1/x^2)\, dx$ by using definition [10.12] in Section 10.3 of the definite integral without thinking. You get a negative answer even though the integrand is never negative. What has gone wrong?

10. Prove that the following integral converges and find its value:

$$\int_0^1 \frac{\ln x}{\sqrt{x}}\, dx$$

Harder Problems

11. Find the integral

$$I_k = \int_1^\infty \left(\frac{k}{x} - \frac{k^2}{1+kx} \right) dx \qquad (k \text{ is a positive constant})$$

Find the limit of I_k as $k \to \infty$, if it exists.

12. Use the results in Example 11.8 to prove [6.18] in Section 6.5. (*Hint:* Draw the graph of $f(x) = x^{-p}$ in $[1, \infty)$, and interpret each of the sums $\sum_{n=1}^\infty n^{-p}$ and $\sum_{n=2}^\infty n^{-p}$ geometrically as sums of an infinite number of rectangles.)

13. In statistics, the normal, or Gaussian, density function is defined by

$$f(x) = \frac{1}{\sigma\sqrt{2\pi}} e^{-(x-\mu)^2/2\sigma^2}$$

in the interval $(-\infty, \infty)$.[2] Prove that

(a) $\int_{-\infty}^{+\infty} f(x)\, dx = 1$ (b) $\int_{-\infty}^{+\infty} x f(x)\, dx = \mu$

(c) $\int_{-\infty}^{+\infty} x^2 f(x)\, dx = \sigma^2 + \mu^2$

(*Hint:* Use the substitution $u = (x - \mu)/\sqrt{2}\sigma$, together with [11.13] and the result in Example 11.9.)

11.4 A Note on Income Distribution and Lorenz Curves

In Section 10.4 it was explained how, if $f(r)$ is the income distribution function for a population of n individuals, then $n \int_a^b f(r)\, dr$ represents the number of individuals with incomes in the interval $[a, b]$—see Equation [10.27]. In addition, $n \int_a^b r f(r)\, dr$ represents the total income of these individuals—see Equation [10.28].

---

[2] This function, its bell-shaped graph, and a portrait of its inventor Carl Friedrich Gauss (1777–1855), appear on the German 10-mark currency note issued in early 1989.

TABLE 11.1 *Shares of total income*

Income group	United States 1980	United States 1990	Netherlands 1959	Netherlands 1985	World 1989
Lowest fifth	5.2	4.6	5.0	7.8	1.4
Second fifth	11.5	10.8	11.9	13.9	1.9
Third fifth	17.5	16.6	17.4	18.1	2.3
Fourth fifth	24.3	23.8	22.7	23.4	11.7
Highest fifth	41.5	44.3	43.0	36.7	82.7

A statistical device for describing some important features of any such income distribution is the **Lorenz Curve**.[3] This curve is based on the shares of total income that accrue to different groups of individuals in the population, starting with the poorest and working up to the richest. Consider, for example, the data in Table 11.1.[4] It may be apparent already that inequality increased in the United States during the 1980s, and that it decreased in the Netherlands during the much longer period 1959–1985. The distribution in the Netherlands in 1959 is quite close to that in the United States for 1980. The reported distribution for the world as a whole is close to an extreme.

These preliminary insights are confirmed by a rather more careful analysis based on Lorenz curves. To construct these, we first cumulate the incomes of different fifths of the population so that the five new groups we consider are respectively the lowest 20%, then the lowest 40%, the lowest 60%, the lowest 80%, followed by the whole population. This gives Table 11.2.[5]

Figure 11.6 illustrates two of the resulting Lorenz curves, found by fitting smoothed curves to the data points in the second and fifth columns of Table 11.2.

The question we ask now is this: If the income distribution is really described by the continuous density function $f(r)$, as in Section 10.4, how does one find the Lorenz curve? To answer this, we first need to consider the *cumulative distribution function $F(r)$* of Section 10.4, whose value for each income level r represents the proportion of the population having incomes $\leq r$. Thus, the value of this function

[3]Named after the American statistician Max Otto Lorenz, who introduced it as one of the "Methods for Measuring Concentration of Wealth" (rather than income) in an article published in the *Journal of the American Statistical Association*, 1905.

[4]Data for the United States are taken from the Bureau of the Census. Those for the Netherlands come originally from the Dutch Central Bureau of Statistics. World income data are taken from the UN Development Program's *Human Development Report* for 1992. Actually, data of this kind for the world as a whole do not exist. The reported figures represent what the world distribution of income would be if the gross domestic product of each nation were perfectly equally distributed as income to all the inhabitants of that nation. Nevertheless, there is no reason to think that the resulting figures seriously exaggerate the true extent of world inequality.

[5]As is often the case with data of this kind, rounding errors mean that the totals of the figures in Table 11.1 are not exactly 100% in every case.

TABLE 11.2 *Cumulative incomes*

Income group	United States 1980	United States 1990	Netherlands 1959	Netherlands 1985	World 1989
Lowest 20%	5.2	4.6	5.0	7.8	1.4
Lowest 40%	16.7	15.4	16.9	21.7	3.3
Lowest 60%	34.2	32.0	34.3	39.8	5.6
Lowest 80%	58.5	55.8	57.0	63.2	17.3
Lowest 100%	100.0	100.0	100.0	100.0	100.0

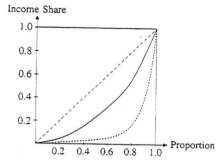

FIGURE 11.6 **Approximate Lorenz curves for the U.S. in 1990 (solid curve) and the whole world in 1989 (dotted curve). The dashed curve represents perfect equality.**

is given by the integral

$$F(r) = \int_0^r f(x)\,dx$$

which evidently satisfies $F'(r) = f(r)$ for all income levels r. We assume that $f(r) > 0$ at all income levels $r \geq 0$, implying that $F(r)$ is strictly increasing. Moreover, assuming that everybody has some income, even if only a little, it must be true that $F(0) = 0$. Also $F(\infty) = 1$, because everybody has a finite income, even if some individuals may have extremely large incomes. Here $F(\infty) = 1$ is a shorthand notation for $F(r) \to 1$ as $r \to \infty$.

Along the horizontal axis of the graph of the Lorenz curve, the variable is the proportion $p = F(r)$ of the population having incomes $\leq r$. Constructing the Lorenz curve requires considering the inverse of this function, $r = R(p)$, which is also strictly increasing.

The function $R(p)$ can be given an important interpretation. For each $p \in [0, 1]$, the value $R(p)$ is that income level for which the exact fraction or proportion p of the population has income $r \leq R(p)$; this must be true because, by the definition of an inverse function, $F(R(p)) = p$. When $p = 1/2$, for example, the income level $R(1/2)$ has the property that half the population has income $r \leq R(1/2)$, whereas the other half has income $r > R(1/2)$; this "middle" income level is generally called the *median* of the distribution $f(r)$. Ranges of income between different values of $R(p)$ also receive appropriate names—for example, the interval $[R(0.2), R(0.4)]$ is called the *second quintile*, $[R(0.6), R(0.7)]$ is called the *seventh decile*, and so on. The different values of $R(p)$ are generally known as *percentiles*, and also as *order statistics*.

By the usual rule for differentiating the inverse of a function (see [7.24] in Section 7.6), we have

$$R'(p) = \frac{1}{F'(r)} = \frac{1}{f(r)} = \frac{1}{f(R(p))} \qquad [11.14]$$

This is valid for all $p \in (0, 1)$ because we assumed that $f(r) > 0$ at all income levels r.

The Lorenz curve is the graph of the function $L(p)$ whose value for each p represents the share of total income accruing to the poorest fraction p of the population. Now, total income is given by $n \int_0^\infty r\, f(r)\, dr$, where n is the total number of individuals in the population. Because $R(p)$ is the income level of the richest person in the poorest fraction p of the population, the total income of this group is $n \int_0^{R(p)} r\, f(r)\, dr$. Thus, we have

$$L(p) = \frac{n \int_0^{R(p)} r\, f(r)\, dr}{n \int_0^\infty r\, f(r)\, dr} = \frac{1}{m} \int_0^{R(p)} r\, f(r)\, dr \qquad [11.15]$$

where m is the mean income $\int_0^\infty r\, f(r)\, dr$. Because $0 \le \int_0^{R(p)} rf(r)\, dr \le \int_0^\infty rf(r)\, dr$, Equation [11.15] implies that $0 \le L(p) \le 1$ for all $p \in [0, 1]$. The slope of the Lorenz curve can be found by making use of the differentiation rule (10.22) in Section 10.3. In fact,

$$L'(p) = \frac{1}{m} R(p) f(R(p)) R'(p) = \frac{R(p)}{m}$$

where the second equality follows from [11.14]. Thus, the slope of the Lorenz curve is equal to the ratio of the income level $R(p)$ to mean income m. This slope increases steadily from $0 = R(0)$ when $p = 0$, to "$\infty = R(1)$" when $p = 1$. In particular, differentiating a second time gives

$$L''(p) = \frac{R'(p)}{m} = \frac{1}{mf(R(p))} > 0$$

for all $p \in (0, 1)$, implying that a Lorenz curve is strictly convex. And, as Fig. 11.6 illustrates, each Lorenz curve has a horizontal tangent at $p = 0$, together with a vertical tangent at $p = 1$. Finally, $L'(p) = 1$ at the unique point where $R(p) = m$ and so for $p = F(m)$. For $0 < p < F(m)$, one has $L'(p) < 1$, so that the Lorenz curve initially rises more slowly than the $45°$ line. At $p = F(m)$, the horizontal distance between the Lorenz curve and the 45° line reaches a maximum. For $F(m) < p < 1$, one has $L'(p) > 1$, so that the Lorenz curve ends by rising faster than the 45° line until the two intersect once again when $p = 1$. In particular, this shows that $L(p) < p$ throughout the open interval $p \in (0, 1)$.

The Lorenz curve can also be used to define a common measure G of income inequality, generally known as the **Gini coefficient**.[6] Geometrically, G is twice the area of the set lying below the 45° line and above the Lorenz curve. But this area can be represented as the difference between the two integrals $\int_0^1 p \, dp = 1/2$ and $\int_0^1 L(p) \, dp$. So

$$G = 2 \left[\frac{1}{2} - \int_0^1 L(p) dp \right] = 1 - 2 \int_0^1 L(p) \, dp \qquad \text{(\textbf{Gini coefficient})} \qquad [11.16]$$

From this it follows that $0 < G < 1$. The low extreme $G = 0$ is approached as the Lorenz curve shifts up closer to the 45° line. This occurs as income becomes distributed more equally, with each poorest fraction p of the population getting closer to receiving its full share p of the total available income. The other extreme $G = 1$ is approached as the Lorenz curve shifts down further away from the 45° line. This occurs as income becomes distributed more unequally, with each poorest fraction p of the population getting closer to a zero share of the total available income, and a decreasingly small fraction of very prosperous people getting closer to having all available income. Generally, as the Lorenz curve shifts down, the income distribution becomes more unequal, and the Gini coefficient increases.

Problems

1. Draw the Lorenz curves for the first, third, and fourth columns of Table 11.2.

2. Estimate values of the Gini coefficients for all five distributions reported in Table 11.2.

---

[6]This is named after the Italian Corrado Gini, who first proposed it in 1912, and apparently discovered the Lorenz curve independently of Lorenz. His definition was the double integral $G = (1/2m) \int_0^\infty \int_0^\infty |r - r'| f(r) f(r') \, dr \, dr'$, but this is equivalent to the definition given here. We do not show this because we do not consider double integrals in this book.

12

Linear Algebra: Vectors and Matrices

At first sight it is curious that a subject as pure and passionless as mathematics can have anything useful to say about that messy, ill-structured, chancy world in which we live. —Fortunately we find that whenever we comprehend what was previously mysterious, there is at the centre of everything order, pattern and common sense.
—B. H. P. Rivett (1978)

Most mathematical models used by economists ultimately involve a system of several equations. If these equations are all linear, the study of such systems belongs to an area of mathematics called **linear algebra**.

Input–output analysis is one prominent area of economics that uses systems of linear equations. Models such as those based on Wassily Leontief's pioneering work *The Structure of American Economy, 1919–1939* have systems with hundreds of equations containing hundreds of unknowns. This model, and similar ones developed in the former Soviet Union by Leonid Kantorovich, were intended to help plan the production of military equipment and other supplies during the Second World War.

In order to comprehend such enormous systems of equations, it is convenient to work with a number of concepts such as vectors, matrices, and determinants. These are introduced in this chapter and in the next two, where we demonstrate their use in economics. Actually, the usefulness of linear algebra extends far beyond its ability to solve systems of linear equations. For instance, in the theory of differential and difference equations, in linear and nonlinear optimization theory, in statistics and econometrics, the methods of linear algebra are used extensively. In fact, from now on almost every chapter of this book makes some use of these methods.

12.1 Systems of Linear Equations

Large systems of simultaneous equations are easier to study systematically with notation that is suitable for a general system of m linear equations with n unknowns. If the unknowns are denoted by $x_1, \ldots, x_n$, we usually write such a system in the form

$$
\begin{aligned}
a_{11}x_1 + a_{12}x_2 + \cdots + a_{1n}x_n &= b_1 \\
a_{21}x_1 + a_{22}x_2 + \cdots + a_{2n}x_n &= b_2 \\
&\cdots\cdots\cdots\cdots\cdots\cdots\cdots\cdots\cdots\cdots\cdots\cdots \\
a_{m1}x_1 + a_{m2}x_2 + \cdots + a_{mn}x_n &= b_m
\end{aligned}
\qquad [12.1]
$$

where $a_{11}, a_{12}, \ldots, a_{mn}$ are called the *coefficients* of the system, and $b_1, \ldots, b_m$ are called the *right-hand sides*.

Note carefully the arrangement of the subscripts. For instance, a_{21} is the coefficient in the second equation of the first variable (x_1). In general, a_{ij} is the coefficient in the ith equation of the jth variable (x_j). One or more of these coefficients may be 0—indeed, a high proportion of them may be.

A **solution** of system [12.1] is an ordered set of numbers $s_1, s_2, \ldots, s_n$ that satisfies all the equations simultaneously when we put $x_1 = s_1$, $x_2 = s_2$, $\ldots, x_n = s_n$. Usually, a solution is written as $(s_1, s_2, \ldots, s_n)$. Note that the order in which we write the components is essential in the sense that if $(s_1, s_2, \ldots, s_n)$ satisfies [12.1], then $(s_n, s_{n-1}, \ldots, s_1)$, say, will usually *not* be a solution.

If system [12.1] has at least one solution, it is said to be **consistent**. When the system has no solution, it is said to be **inconsistent**.

There are computer programs that make it easy to check whether a system like [12.1] has solutions, and to find possible solutions, even if there are thousands of equations and unknowns. Still, economists need to understand the general theory of such equation systems so that they can follow theoretical arguments and conclusions related to linear models of this kind.

Leontief Models

In order to illustrate why linear systems of equations are important in economics, we briefly discuss a simple example of the input–output model due to Leontief.

Example 12.1

An economy has three industries—fishing, forestry, and boatbuilding.

To produce 1 ton of fish requires the services of α fishing boats.

To produce 1 ton of timber requires β tons of fish, in order to feed the foresters.

To produce 1 fishing boat requires γ tons of timber.

These are the only inputs needed for each of these three industries. Suppose there is no final (external) demand for fishing boats. Find what gross outputs each of the three industries must produce in order to meet the final demands of d_1 tons of fish and d_2 tons of timber.

Solution   Let x_1 denote the total number of tons of fish to be produced, x_2 the total number of tons of timber, and x_3 the total number of fishing boats.

Consider fish first. Because βx_2 tons of fish are needed to produce x_2 units of timber, and because final demand for fish is d_1, we must have $x_1 = \beta x_2 + d_1$. (Producing fishing boats does not require fish consumption, so there is no term with x_3.) Concerning timber production, the equation $x_2 = \gamma x_3 + d_2$ must be satisfied. Finally, for boatbuilding, only the fishing industry needs boats; there is no final demand in this case and so $x_3 = \alpha x_1$. Thus, the following three equations must be satisfied:

$$x_1 = \beta x_2 + d_1$$
$$x_2 = \gamma x_3 + d_2 \qquad\qquad [1]$$
$$x_3 = \alpha x_1$$

Inserting $x_3 = \alpha x_1$ into the second equation gives $x_2 = \gamma \alpha x_1 + d_2$, which inserted into the first equation yields

$$x_1 = \beta \gamma \alpha x_1 + \beta d_2 + d_1$$

Solving this last equation for x_1 gives

$$x_1 = \frac{d_1 + \beta d_2}{1 - \alpha \beta \gamma} \qquad\qquad [2]$$

The corresponding expressions for the two other variables are

$$x_2 = \frac{\alpha \gamma d_1 + d_2}{1 - \alpha \beta \gamma} \qquad x_3 = \frac{\alpha d_1 + \alpha \beta d_2}{1 - \alpha \beta \gamma} \qquad [3]$$

Clearly, this solution for (x_1, x_2, x_3) only makes sense when $\alpha \beta \gamma < 1$. For if $\alpha \beta \gamma \geq 1$, it is impossible for this economy to meet any final demands for fish and timber—production in the economy is too inefficient.

More generally, the Leontief model describes an economy with n inter-linked industries, each of which produces a single good using only one process of production. To produce its good, each industry must use inputs from at least some other industries. For example, the steel industry needs goods from the coal industry as well as from many other industries. In addition to supplying its own good to other industries that need it, each industry also faces external demand for its product from consumers, governments, foreigners, and so on. The amount needed to meet this external demand is called the *final demand*.

Let x_i denote the total number of units of good i that industry i is going to produce in a certain year. Furthermore, let

$$a_{ij} = \begin{cases} \text{the number of units of good } i \text{ needed} \\ \text{to produce one unit of good } j \end{cases} \qquad [12.2]$$

We assume that input requirements are directly proportional to the amount of the output produced. Then

$$a_{ij}x_j = \begin{cases} \text{the number of units of good } i \text{ needed} \\ \text{to produce } x_j \text{ units of good } j \end{cases} \qquad [12.3]$$

In order that x_1 units of good 1, x_2 units of good 2, ..., x_n units of good n can all be produced, industry i needs to supply a total of

$$a_{i1}x_1 + a_{i2}x_2 + \cdots + a_{in}x_n$$

units of good i. If we require industry i also to supply b_i units to meet final demand, then equilibrium between supply and demand requires that

$$x_i = a_{i1}x_1 + a_{i2}x_2 + \cdots + a_{in}x_n + b_i$$

This goes for all $i = 1, 2, \ldots, n$. So we arrive at the following system of equations:

$$x_1 = a_{11}x_1 + a_{12}x_2 + \cdots + a_{1n}x_n + b_1$$
$$x_2 = a_{21}x_1 + a_{22}x_2 + \cdots + a_{2n}x_n + b_2$$
$$\cdots\cdots\cdots\cdots\cdots\cdots\cdots\cdots\cdots\cdots\cdots\cdots\cdots\cdots\cdots \qquad [12.4]$$
$$x_n = a_{n1}x_1 + a_{n2}x_2 + \cdots + a_{nn}x_n + b_n$$

Note that in the first equation, x_1 appears on the left-hand side as well as in the first term on the right-hand side. In the second equation, x_2 appears on the left-hand side as well as in the second term on the right-hand side, and so on. Moving all terms involving $x_1, \ldots, x_n$ to the left-hand side and rearranging gives the system of equations

$$
\begin{aligned}
(1 - a_{11})x_1 - \quad a_{12}x_2 - \cdots - \quad a_{1n}x_n &= b_1 \\
-a_{21}x_1 + (1 - a_{22})x_2 - \cdots - \quad a_{2n}x_n &= b_2 \\
&\cdots\cdots\cdots\cdots\cdots\cdots\cdots\cdots\cdots\cdots\cdots\cdots\cdots\cdots\cdots \\
-a_{n1}x_1 - \quad a_{n2}x_2 - \cdots + (1 - a_{nn})x_n &= b_n
\end{aligned}
$$

[12.5]

This is called the **Leontief system**. The numbers a_{11}, a_{12}, $\ldots$, a_{nn} are called **input** (or **technical**) **coefficients**. Given any collection of final demand quantities $(b_1, b_2, \ldots, b_m)$, a solution $(x_1, x_2, \ldots, x_n)$ of [12.5] will give outputs for each industry such that the combined interindustry and final demands just can be met. Of course, only nonnegative values for the x_i make sense.

Problems

1. Consider an economy divided into an agricultural sector (A) and an industrial sector (I). To produce one unit in sector A requires $1/6$ unit from A and $1/4$ unit from I. To produce one unit in sector I requires $1/4$ unit from A and $1/4$ unit from I. Suppose final demands in each of the two sectors are 60 units.
   a. Write down the Leontief system for this economy.
   b. Find the number of units that has to be produced in each sector in order to meet the final demands.

2. In the Leontief system [12.5]:
   a. What is the interpretation of the condition that $a_{ii} = 0$ for all i?
   b. What is the intepretation of the sum $a_{i1} + a_{i2} + \cdots + a_{in}$?
   c. What is the intepretation of the input coefficients $(a_{1j}, a_{2j}, \ldots, a_{nj})$?
   d. Can you give any interpretation to the sum $a_{1j} + a_{2j} + \cdots + a_{nj}$?

3. Write down system [12.5] when $n = 2$, $a_{11} = 0.2$, $a_{12} = 0.3$, $a_{21} = 0.4$, $a_{22} = 0.1$, $b_1 = 120$, and $b_2 = 90$. What is the solution to this system?

4. Consider an input–output model with three sectors. Sector 1 is heavy industry, sector 2 is light industry, and sector 3 is agriculture. Suppose that the input requirements are given by the following table:

	Heavy industry	Light industry	Agriculture
Units of heavy industry goods	$a_{11} = 0.1$	$a_{12} = 0.2$	$a_{13} = 0.1$
Units of light industry goods	$a_{21} = 0.3$	$a_{22} = 0.2$	$a_{23} = 0.2$
Units of agri- cultural goods	$a_{31} = 0.2$	$a_{32} = 0.2$	$a_{33} = 0.1$

Suppose the final demands for the three goods are 85, 95, and 20 units, respectively. If x_1, x_2, and x_3 denote the number of units that have to be produced in the three sectors, write down the Leontief model for the problem. Verify that $x_1 = 150$, $x_2 = 200$, and $x_3 = 100$ is a solution.

12.2 Vectors

Suppose a warehouse has n different goods (commodities) denoted by $V_1, V_2, \ldots, V_n$. Each month the number of units $a_1, a_2, \ldots, a_n$ of each good in stock is recorded. It is convenient to represent these stock quantities by

either a row: $(a_1, a_2, \ldots, a_n)$ or a column: $\begin{pmatrix} a_1 \\ a_2 \\ \vdots \\ a_n \end{pmatrix}$ [*]

Such an ordered set of numbers, which is distinguished not only by the elements it contains, but also by the order in which they appear, is called a **vector**. In particular, the first vector in [*] is called a **row vector** whereas the second is a **column vector**.

Vectors will appear in bold type. For row vectors we write

$$\mathbf{a} = (a_1, a_2, \ldots, a_n)$$

The numbers $a_1, a_2, \ldots, a_n$ are called the **components** (or **coordinates**) of the vector, and a_i is its ith component or ith coordinate. If we want to emphasize that a vector has n components, we refer to it as an n**-vector**. (The term "n-tuple" is often used as well.) Alternatively, if $\mathbf{a}$ is an n-vector, then we say that it has **dimension** n. Note that any solution of the linear system of m equations [12.1] is an n-vector. On the other hand, the numbers $b_1, b_2, \ldots, b_m$ that make up the right-hand sides of these m equations constitute an m-vector. Of course, m and n can be different.

It is clear that the row vector $(7, 13, 4)$ and the column vector

$$\begin{pmatrix} 7 \\ 13 \\ 4 \end{pmatrix}$$

contain exactly the same information—the numbers and their order are the same, only the arrangement of the numbers is different. It becomes more important to distinguish between row and column vectors when we study matrices.

Operations on Vectors

Two n-vectors $\mathbf{a}$ and $\mathbf{b}$ are said to be **equal** if all their corresponding components are equal; then we write $\mathbf{a} = \mathbf{b}$. If two vectors are not equal, we use the symbol $\neq$. Note that equality is possible only between vectors of the same dimension.

Example 12.2

   (a) $(x, y, z) = (2, -1, 3)$ if and only if $x = 2$, $y = -1$, and $z = 3$.
   (b) $(1, -1, 3) \neq (-1, 1, 3)$.
   (c) $(1, 1, 2) \neq (1, 1, 2, 2)$ because the two vectors do not have the same number of components.

If **a** and **b** are two n-vectors, the **sum** of **a** and **b**, denoted by **a** + **b**, is the n-vector obtained by adding each component of **a** to the corresponding component of **b**.[1] In symbols (for row vectors),

$$(a_1, a_2, \ldots, a_n) + (b_1, b_2, \ldots, b_n) = (a_1 + b_1, a_2 + b_2, \ldots, a_n + b_n) \quad [12.6]$$

If **a** is an n-vector and t is a real number, we define t**a** as the n-vector whose components are t times the corresponding components in **a**. In symbols,

$$t(a_1, a_2, \ldots, a_n) = (ta_1, ta_2, \ldots, ta_n) \quad [12.7]$$

This is called *multiplication by a scalar* (the scalar being the number t that is used to "scale" vector **a**). Note in particular that if t is a natural number, then t**a** is the sum of t copies of the vector **a**. For instance,

$$3\mathbf{a} = \mathbf{a} + \mathbf{a} + \mathbf{a}$$

If **a** and **b** are both n-vectors, then the **difference** between **a** and **b** is defined by

$$\mathbf{a} - \mathbf{b} = \mathbf{a} + (-1)\mathbf{b}$$

This implies that

$$(a_1, a_2, \ldots, a_n) - (b_1, b_2, \ldots, b_n) = (a_1 - b_1, a_2 - b_2, \ldots, a_n - b_n) \quad [12.8]$$

Thus, **a** − **b** is obtained by subtracting each component of **b** from the corresponding component of **a**.

For each n-vector **a**, the difference **a** − **a** is the vector consisting of only zeros. This is called the **zero-vector**:

$$\mathbf{0} = (0, 0, \ldots, 0) \quad [12.9]$$

Note that $\mathbf{a} - \mathbf{b} = \mathbf{0} \iff \mathbf{a} = \mathbf{b}$.

Example 12.3

   If $\mathbf{a} = (3, -2, 5)$ and $\mathbf{b} = (-2, 10, -3)$, compute $\mathbf{a} + \mathbf{b}$, $\mathbf{a} - \mathbf{b}$, $3\mathbf{a}$, $-\sqrt{2}\,\mathbf{b}$, and $3\mathbf{a} + 4\mathbf{b}$.

---

[1] If two vectors do not have the same dimension, their sum is simply not defined, nor is the difference.

Solution

$$\mathbf{a} + \mathbf{b} = \big(3 + (-2), -2 + 10, 5 + (-3)\big) = (1, 8, 2)$$

$$\mathbf{a} - \mathbf{b} = \big(3 - (-2), -2 - 10, 5 - (-3)\big) = (5, -12, 8)$$

$$3\mathbf{a} = 3(3, -2, 5) = (3 \cdot 3, 3(-2), 3 \cdot 5) = (9, -6, 15)$$

$$-\sqrt{2}\,\mathbf{b} = \big(2\sqrt{2}, -10\sqrt{2}, 3\sqrt{2}\big)$$

$$3\mathbf{a} + 4\mathbf{b} = 3(3, -2, 5) + 4(-2, 10, -3) = (9, -6, 15) + (-8, 40, -12)$$

$$= (1, 34, 3)$$

If $\mathbf{a}$ and $\mathbf{b}$ are two n-vectors and t and s are real numbers, the n-vector $t\mathbf{a} + s\mathbf{b}$ is said to be a **linear combination** of $\mathbf{a}$ and $\mathbf{b}$. In symbols, using column vectors,

$$t\begin{pmatrix} a_1 \\ a_2 \\ \vdots \\ a_n \end{pmatrix} + s\begin{pmatrix} b_1 \\ b_2 \\ \vdots \\ b_n \end{pmatrix} = \begin{pmatrix} ta_1 + sb_1 \\ ta_2 + sb_2 \\ \vdots \\ ta_n + sb_n \end{pmatrix}$$

We can interpret such linear combinations in the context of the warehouse example (in the case when t and s are positive integers): If t persons all buy the same commodity vector $\mathbf{a}$ and s persons all buy commodity vector $\mathbf{b}$, then the vector $t\mathbf{a} + s\mathbf{b}$ represents the total commodity vector that is sold by the warehouse.

More generally, if $\mathbf{a}_1, \mathbf{a}_2, \ldots, \mathbf{a}_n$ are all m-vectors and $x_1, x_2, \ldots, x_n$ are real numbers, then the m-vector

$$x_1\mathbf{a}_1 + x_2\mathbf{a}_2 + \cdots + x_n\mathbf{a}_n \tag{12.10}$$

is called a **linear combination** of $\mathbf{a}_1, \mathbf{a}_2, \ldots, \mathbf{a}_n$.

Example 12.4

Consider the general system of linear equations [12.1]. Suppose we introduce the column vectors:

$$\mathbf{a}_1 = \begin{pmatrix} a_{11} \\ a_{21} \\ \vdots \\ a_{m1} \end{pmatrix}, \quad \mathbf{a}_2 = \begin{pmatrix} a_{12} \\ a_{22} \\ \vdots \\ a_{m2} \end{pmatrix}, \ldots, \quad \mathbf{a}_n = \begin{pmatrix} a_{1n} \\ a_{2n} \\ \vdots \\ a_{mn} \end{pmatrix}, \quad \mathbf{b} = \begin{pmatrix} b_1 \\ b_2 \\ \vdots \\ b_m \end{pmatrix}$$

Then [12.1] can be written in the form

$$x_1\mathbf{a}_1 + x_2\mathbf{a}_2 + \cdots + x_n\mathbf{a}_n = \mathbf{b} \tag{12.11}$$

Because [12.11] is equivalent to [12.1], we see that *system [12.1] is consistent (has a solution) if and only if* $\mathbf{b}$ *can be expressed as a linear combination of*

$\mathbf{a}_1, \mathbf{a}_2, \ldots, \mathbf{a}_n$. As a concrete example, the system

$$3x_1 - 4x_2 = 10$$
$$x_1 + 5x_2 = -3$$

[1]

is equivalent to the vector equation

$$x_1 \begin{pmatrix} 3 \\ 1 \end{pmatrix} + x_2 \begin{pmatrix} -4 \\ 5 \end{pmatrix} = \begin{pmatrix} 10 \\ -3 \end{pmatrix}$$

The solution to [1] is $x_1 = 2$ and $x_2 = -1$. So in this case

$$\begin{pmatrix} 10 \\ -3 \end{pmatrix}$$

can be written as a linear combination

$$2 \begin{pmatrix} 3 \\ 1 \end{pmatrix} + (-1) \begin{pmatrix} -4 \\ 5 \end{pmatrix}$$

of

$$\begin{pmatrix} 3 \\ 1 \end{pmatrix} \text{ and } \begin{pmatrix} -4 \\ 5 \end{pmatrix}$$

Several rules for addition of vectors and multiplication of a vector by a scalar follow immediately from these definitions. The most important are as follows:

Rules for Vector Addition and Multiplication by Scalars

If $\mathbf{a}, \mathbf{b}$, and $\mathbf{c}$ are arbitrary n-vectors and α, β are arbitrary numbers, then

$$(\mathbf{a} + \mathbf{b}) + \mathbf{c} = \mathbf{a} + (\mathbf{b} + \mathbf{c}) \qquad \text{(a)}$$

$$\mathbf{a} + \mathbf{b} = \mathbf{b} + \mathbf{a} \qquad \text{(b)}$$

$$\mathbf{a} + \mathbf{0} = \mathbf{a} \qquad \text{(c)}$$

$$\mathbf{a} + (-\mathbf{a}) = \mathbf{0} \qquad \text{(d)}$$

$$(\alpha + \beta)\mathbf{a} = \alpha\mathbf{a} + \beta\mathbf{a} \qquad \text{(e)}$$

$$\alpha(\mathbf{a} + \mathbf{b}) = \alpha\mathbf{a} + \alpha\mathbf{b} \qquad \text{(f)}$$

$$\alpha(\beta\mathbf{a}) = (\alpha\beta)\mathbf{a} \qquad \text{(g)}$$

$$1\mathbf{a} = \mathbf{a} \qquad \text{(h)}$$

[12.12]

Equations (a) and (b) are called the **associative** and **commutative** laws, respectively. These two rules make it possible to arrange the terms of a sum in any order we wish, and to group them in any fashion. In particular, instead of the expressions in (a), we might as well write $\mathbf{a} + \mathbf{b} + \mathbf{c}$, dropping the parentheses.

The point of exhibiting all the rules in [12.12] is that they allow us to manipulate vectors in much the same way as ordinary numbers, without having to bother about each separate component. The next example makes this point clearer.

Example 12.5

Given two n-vectors $\mathbf{a}$ and $\mathbf{b}$, find the n-vector $\mathbf{x}$ such that $3\mathbf{x} + 2\mathbf{a} = 5\mathbf{b}$.

Solution   When two vectors are equal, we can add the same vector $(-2\mathbf{a})$ to each side, of course, and still have the equality

$$(3\mathbf{x} + 2\mathbf{a}) + (-2\mathbf{a}) = 5\mathbf{b} + (-2\mathbf{a})$$

According to rule [12.12] (a), the left-hand side of the previous equation is

$$(3\mathbf{x} + 2\mathbf{a}) + (-2\mathbf{a}) = 3\mathbf{x} + (2\mathbf{a} + (-2\mathbf{a})) = 3\mathbf{x} + \mathbf{0} = 3\mathbf{x}$$

where we have also used [12.12] (d) and (c). Hence,

$$3\mathbf{x} = 5\mathbf{b} + (-2\mathbf{a})$$

Multiplying each side by $1/3$ yields

$$\tfrac{1}{3}(3\mathbf{x}) = \tfrac{1}{3}[5\mathbf{b} + (-2\mathbf{a})]$$

Hence, using [12.12] (f), (g), and (h) gives

$$\mathbf{x} = \tfrac{5}{3}\mathbf{b} - \tfrac{2}{3}\mathbf{a}$$

as the only vector $\mathbf{x}$ that satisfies the equation $3\mathbf{x} + 2\mathbf{a} = 5\mathbf{b}$.

Problems

1. Compute $\mathbf{a} + \mathbf{b}$, $\mathbf{a} - \mathbf{b}$, $2\mathbf{a} + 3\mathbf{b}$, and $-5\mathbf{a} + 2\mathbf{b}$ when

$$\mathbf{a} = \begin{pmatrix} 2 \\ -1 \end{pmatrix} \quad \text{and} \quad \mathbf{b} = \begin{pmatrix} 3 \\ 4 \end{pmatrix}$$

2. Let $\mathbf{a} = (1, 2, 2)$, $\mathbf{b} = (0, 0, -3)$, and $\mathbf{c} = (-2, 4, -3)$. Find the following:

$$\mathbf{a} + \mathbf{b} + \mathbf{c}, \qquad \mathbf{a} - 2\mathbf{b} + 2\mathbf{c}, \qquad 3\mathbf{a} + 2\mathbf{b} - 3\mathbf{c}, \qquad -\mathbf{a} - \mathbf{b} - \mathbf{c}$$

3. Find the components a_1, a_2, and a_3 when

$$3 \begin{pmatrix} a_1 \\ a_2 \\ a_3 \end{pmatrix} = \begin{pmatrix} 0 \\ 1 \\ 3 \end{pmatrix}$$

4. If $3(x, y, z) + 5(-1, 2, 3) = (4, 1, 3)$, find x, y, and z.

5. a. If $\mathbf{x} + \mathbf{0} = \mathbf{0}$, what do you know about the components of $\mathbf{x}$?
   b. If $0\mathbf{x} = \mathbf{0}$, what do you know about the components of $\mathbf{x}$?

6. a. Show that vector equation

$$x \begin{pmatrix} 3 \\ -4 \end{pmatrix} + y \begin{pmatrix} -2 \\ 3 \end{pmatrix} = \begin{pmatrix} -1 \\ 2 \end{pmatrix}$$

represents two equations in two unknowns, x and y. Find the solution.
   b. Show that there are no numbers x and y such that

$$x \begin{pmatrix} 2 \\ -3 \end{pmatrix} + y \begin{pmatrix} 4 \\ -6 \end{pmatrix} = \begin{pmatrix} 1 \\ 0 \end{pmatrix}$$

7. Solve the vector equation $4\mathbf{x} - 7\mathbf{a} = 2\mathbf{x} + 8\mathbf{b} - \mathbf{a}$ for $\mathbf{x}$ in terms of $\mathbf{a}$ and $\mathbf{b}$.

8. Express the vector $(4, -11)$ as a linear combination of $(2, -1)$ and $(1, 4)$.

9. An oil company can convert one barrel of crude oil into three different kinds of fuel. Without any lead additives, its outputs of the three kinds of fuel from one barrel of crude are given by the vector $(2, 2, 4)$. With the legally permitted maximum amount of lead additives, its outputs from one barrel of crude are $(5, 0, 3)$. Assume that the effects of lead additives are proportional, so that using a fraction θ of the maximum permitted amount (with $0 \leq \theta \leq 1$) yields output vector $(1 - \theta)(2, 2, 4) + \theta(5, 0, 3)$.
   a. Is it possible for the company to produce the following output vectors?
   (i) $(3\frac{1}{2}, 1, 3\frac{1}{2})$ (ii) $(4, \frac{1}{3}, 3\frac{1}{3})$ (iii) $(1, 6, 9)$
   b. If it is possible, what proportion of legally permitted amounts of lead should be used in each case? Do any of your answers change if output can be thrown away?

12.3 Geometric Interpretations of Vectors

The word "vector" is originally Latin and was used to mean both "carrier" and "passenger," or "one who is carried." In particular, the word is related to the act of moving a person or object from one place to another. In the xy-plane, any such shift can be described by the distance a_1 moved in the x-direction and by the distance a_2 moved in the y-direction. A movement in the plane is therefore uniquely determined by an ordered pair or 2-vector (a_1, a_2). Geometrically, such a movement

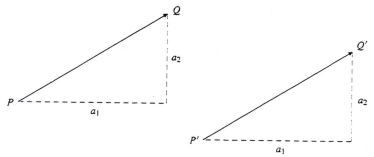

FIGURE 12.1

can be illustrated by an elongated arrow from the start point P to the end point Q, as in Fig. 12.1. If we make a parallel displacement of the arrow so that it starts at P' and ends at Q', the resulting arrow will represent the same movement, because the x and y components are still a_1 and a_2, respectively. See Fig. 12.1 again.

The vector from P to Q is denoted by $\overrightarrow{PQ}$, and we refer to it as a **geometric vector** or *directed line segment*. Two geometric vectors that have the same direction and the same length are said to be equal (in much the same way as the two fractions 2/6 and 1/3 represent the same number).

Suppose that the geometric vector **a** involves a movement from $P = (p_1, p_2)$ to $Q = (q_1, q_2)$. Then the pair (a_1, a_2) that describes the movement in both the x and y directions is given by $a_1 = q_1 - p_1$, $a_2 = q_2 - p_2$, or by $(a_1, a_2) = (q_1, q_2) - (p_1, p_2)$. This is illustrated in Fig. 12.2.

On the other hand, if the pair (a_1, a_2) is given, the corresponding movement is obtained by moving a_1 units in the direction of the x-axis and a_2 units in the direction of the y-axis. If we start at the point $P = (p_1, p_2)$, then we arrive at the point Q with coordinates $(q_1, q_2) = (p_1 + a_1, p_2 + a_2)$, also shown in Fig. 12.2.

The correspondence just explained makes it merely a matter of convenience whether we think of a vector as an ordered pair of numbers (a_1, a_2), or as a directed line segment such as $\overrightarrow{PQ}$ in Fig. 12.2.

FIGURE 12.2

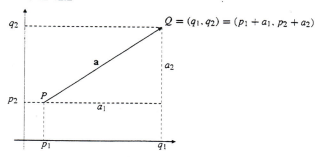

Geometric Interpretations of Vector Operations

If we represent vectors by directed line segments, the vector operations $\mathbf{a} + \mathbf{b}$, $\mathbf{a} - \mathbf{b}$, and $t\mathbf{a}$ can be given interesting geometric interpretations. Let $\mathbf{a} = (a_1, a_2)$ and $\mathbf{b} = (b_1, b_2)$ both start at the origin $(0, 0)$ of the coordinate system.

The sum $\mathbf{a} + \mathbf{b}$ shown in Fig. 12.3 is the diagonal in the parallelogram determined by the two sides $\mathbf{a}$ and $\mathbf{b}$. The geometric reason for this can be seen from Fig. 12.4, in which the two triangles OSR and PTQ are congruent. Thus, OR is parallel to PQ and has the same length, so $OPQR$ is a parallelogram. (This parallelogram law of adding vectors will be familiar to those who have studied physics. If $\mathbf{a}$ and $\mathbf{b}$ represent two forces acting on a particle at O, then the single combined force $\mathbf{a} + \mathbf{b}$ acting on the particle will produce the same result.) The parallelogram law of addition is also illustrated in Fig. 12.5. One way of interpreting this figure is that if $\mathbf{a}$ takes you from O to P and $\mathbf{b}$ takes you on from P to Q, then the combined movement $\mathbf{a} + \mathbf{b}$ takes you from O to Q.

Figure 12.6 gives a geometric interpretation to the vector $\mathbf{a} - \mathbf{b}$. Note carefully the direction of the geometric vector $\mathbf{a} - \mathbf{b}$. And note that $\mathbf{b} + (\mathbf{a} - \mathbf{b}) = \mathbf{a}$.

The geometric interpretation of $t\mathbf{a}$, where t is any real number, is also straightforward. If $t > 0$, then $t\mathbf{a}$ is the vector with the same direction as $\mathbf{a}$

FIGURE 12.3

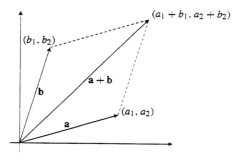

FIGURE 12.4

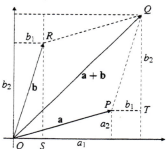

FIGURE 12.5

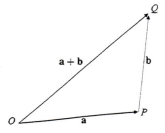

FIGURE 12.6

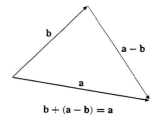

$\mathbf{b} + (\mathbf{a} - \mathbf{b}) = \mathbf{a}$

and whose length is t times the length of **a**. If $t < 0$, the direction is reversed and the length is multiplied by the absolute value of t. Indeed, multiplication by t is like rescaling the vector **a**; that is why the number t is often called a **scalar**.

Geometric Interpretations of Vectors in 3-Space and n-Space

We represent a point or a vector in a plane (also called 2-space and denoted R^2) by a pair of real numbers using two mutually orthogonal coordinate lines. In a similar way, points or vectors in 3-space R^3 can be represented by triples of real numbers using three mutually orthogonal coordinate lines. In Fig. 12.7, we have drawn such a coordinate system. The three lines that are orthogonal to each other and intersect at the point O in Fig. 12.7 are called *coordinate axes*. They are usually called the x-axis, y-axis, and z-axis. We often think of the plane spanned by the x-axis and the y-axis as horizontal, with the z-axis passing vertically through it. We choose units to measure the length along each axis, and select a positive direction on each of them as indicated by the arrows.

Every point P in space now has an associated triple of numbers (a_1, a_2, a_3) that describes its location, as suggested in Fig. 12.7. Conversely, it is clear that every triple of numbers also represents a point in space in this way. Note in particular that when a_3 is negative, the point (a_1, a_2, a_3) lies below the xy-plane in which $z = 0$. In Fig. 12.8, we have constructed the point with coordinates $(-2, 3, -4)$.

Now any 3-vector (a_1, a_2, a_3) can be considered in an obvious way as a geometric vector or movement in 3-space R^3. As with ordered pairs in the plane, there is a natural correspondence between ordered triples (a_1, a_2, a_3) and geometric vectors regarded as directed line segments. The parallelogram law of addition

FIGURE 12.7

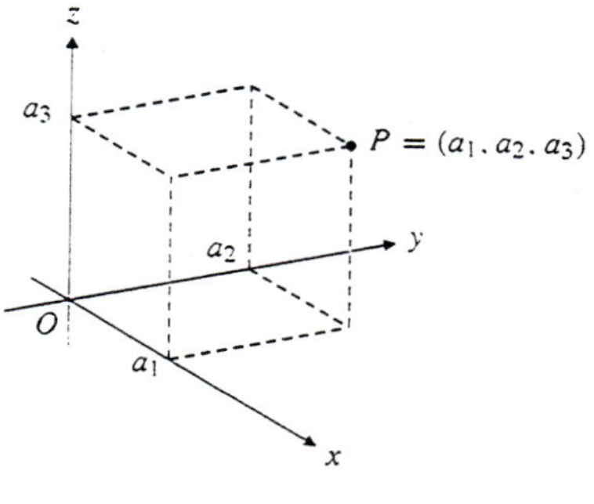

FIGURE 12.8

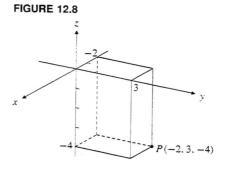

remains valid in R^3, as does the geometric interpretation of the multiplication of a vector by a scalar.

Although the set R^n of all n-vectors has no natural spatial interpretation when $n \geq 4$, we still use geometric language when we discuss properties of R^n, because many properties of R^2 and R^3 carry over to R^n.

Problems

1. Let $\mathbf{a} = (5, -1)$ and $\mathbf{b} = (-2, 4)$. Compute $\mathbf{a} + \mathbf{b}$, $-\frac{1}{2}\mathbf{a}$, and illustrate with geometric vectors starting at the origin.

2. Let $\mathbf{a} = (3, 1)$ and $\mathbf{b} = (-1, 2)$. Define $\mathbf{x} = (1 - \lambda)\mathbf{a} + \lambda\mathbf{b}$.
   a. Compute $\mathbf{x}$ when $\lambda = 0, 1/4, 1/2, 3/4$, and 1. Illustrate.
   b. As λ runs through all real numbers between 0 and 1, what set of points does $\mathbf{x}$ trace out? Show that if λ runs through *all* real numbers, then $\mathbf{x}$ traces out the whole straight line through $(3, 1)$ and $(-1, 2)$.

3. Let $\mathbf{a} = (1, 2, 1)$ and $\mathbf{b} = (-3, 0, -2)$.
   a. Find real numbers x_1 and x_2 such that $x_1\mathbf{a} + x_2\mathbf{b} = (5, 4, 4)$.
   b. Prove that there are no real numbers x_1 and x_2 satisfying $x_1\mathbf{a} + x_2\mathbf{b} = (-3, 6, 1)$.

4. Draw a three-dimensional coordinate system and mark the points

$$P = (3, 0, 0), \qquad Q = (0, 2, 0), \qquad R = (0, 0, -4), \qquad S = (3, -2, 4)$$

(For S, you should make a drawing similar to that in Fig. 12.8.)

5. Describe the locations of the points (x, y, z) in three dimensions where
   a. $y = 2$, $z = 3$ (x varies freely)   b. $y = x$ (z varies freely)

12.4 The Scalar Product

Consider again the warehouse example in Section 12.2. Suppose now that the prices per unit of the n different commodities are $p_1, p_2, \ldots, p_n$, respectively. Then the value of quantity x_j of the jth commodity at the appropriate price p_j must be $p_j x_j$. And so the total value of the entire commodity vector $\mathbf{a} = (a_1, a_2, \ldots, a_n)$ is

$$p_1 a_1 + p_2 a_2 + \cdots + p_n a_n \qquad [*]$$

If the vector of prices is $\mathbf{p} = (p_1, p_2, \ldots, p_n)$, then the number in $[*]$ is called the **scalar product** of $\mathbf{p}$ and $\mathbf{a}$. This is often written as $\mathbf{p} \cdot \mathbf{a}$ (and sometimes called the "dot product" for this reason). In general, we have the following definition (formulated for row vectors):

Scalar Product

The scalar product of any two n-vectors $\mathbf{a} = (a_1, a_2, \ldots, a_n)$ and $\mathbf{b} = (b_1, b_2, \ldots, b_n)$ is defined as

$$\mathbf{a} \cdot \mathbf{b} = a_1 b_1 + a_2 b_2 + \cdots + a_n b_n = \sum_{i=1}^{n} a_i b_i \qquad [12.13]$$

Note that the scalar product of two vectors is not a vector but a *number* (or scalar). It is obtained by simply multiplying all the pairs (a_j, b_j) of the corresponding components in the two vectors $\mathbf{a}$ and $\mathbf{b}$, and then finally adding the results. Note that $\mathbf{a} \cdot \mathbf{b}$ is *only defined* if $\mathbf{a}$ and $\mathbf{b}$ are both of the same dimension.

Example 12.6

If $\mathbf{a} = (1, -2, 3)$ and $\mathbf{b} = (-3, 2, 5)$, compute $\mathbf{a} \cdot \mathbf{b}$.

Solution

$$\mathbf{a} \cdot \mathbf{b} = 1 \cdot (-3) + (-2) \cdot 2 + 3 \cdot 5 = 8$$

Example 12.7

Person A goes to a fruit stall and buys 3 kg of cherries, 4 kg of pears, 3 kg of oranges, and 5 kg of apples. Person B buys 2 kg of cherries, no pears, 2 kg of oranges, and 4 kg of apples. Suppose the prices for 1 kg of each are cherries: $0.75, pears: $0.60, oranges: $0.50, and apples: $0.40. Let $\mathbf{x}_A$ and $\mathbf{x}_B$ denote the vectors of purchases of persons A and B, respectively, and let $\mathbf{p} = (0.75, 0.60, 0.50, 0.40)$ be the vector of prices.

(a) What is the total vector bought by A and B together? How much does it cost?

(b) Verify that the cost of A's order plus the cost of B's order is the amount you found in part (a).

Solution

(a) The total basket bought by A and B is given by the vector

$$\mathbf{x}_A + \mathbf{x}_B = (3, 4, 3, 5) + (2, 0, 2, 4)$$
$$= (5, 4, 5, 9)$$

whose dollar cost is

$$\mathbf{p} \cdot (\mathbf{x}_A + \mathbf{x}_B) = (0.75, 0.60, 0.50, 0.40) \cdot (5, 4, 5, 9)$$
$$= 0.75 \cdot 5 + 0.60 \cdot 4 + 0.50 \cdot 5 + 0.40 \cdot 9$$

which amounts to \$12.25.

(b) The cost of A's purchase is

$$\mathbf{p} \cdot \mathbf{x}_A = 0.75 \cdot 3 + 0.60 \cdot 4 + 0.50 \cdot 3 + 0.40 \cdot 5 = 8.15$$

whereas the cost of B's order is

$$\mathbf{p} \cdot \mathbf{x}_B = 0.75 \cdot 2 + 0.60 \cdot 0 + 0.50 \cdot 2 + 0.40 \cdot 4 = 4.10$$

and $8.15 + 4.10 = 12.25$.

Example 12.8

You want to drive from city A to city C. There are many roads you can take, but all of them pass over one of the three bridges, B_1, B_2, and B_3. In Fig. 12.9, the numbers indicate how many different roads connect these cities to the different bridges. For instance, five roads join A and B_2. The number of different roads can be represented by vectors. Let $\mathbf{P} = (3, 5, 2)$ represent the number of roads from A to B_1, B_2, and B_3, respectively. Let $\mathbf{Q} = (4, 2, 1)$ represent the number of roads from each of B_1, B_2, and B_3 to C. How many different choices are there for getting directly from A to C without crossing more than one bridge?

Solution   You can get from A to B_1 along one of three different roads. For each of these roads, you have four choices of road to get from B_1 to C. Hence, there are $3 \cdot 4$ possibilities of getting from A to C via B_1. Arguing this way for bridges B_2 and B_3 as well shows that the total number of different

FIGURE 12.9

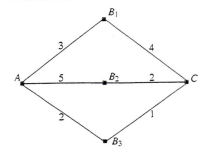

routes is

$$3 \cdot 4 + 5 \cdot 2 + 2 \cdot 1 = 24$$

which is precisely the scalar product of **P** and **Q**.

Important properties of the scalar product follow:

Rules for the Scalar Product

If **a**, **b**, and **c** are n-vectors and α is a scalar, then

$$\mathbf{a} \cdot \mathbf{b} = \mathbf{b} \cdot \mathbf{a} \qquad \text{(a)}$$

$$\mathbf{a} \cdot (\mathbf{b} + \mathbf{c}) = \mathbf{a} \cdot \mathbf{b} + \mathbf{a} \cdot \mathbf{c} \qquad \text{(b)}$$ [12.14]

$$(\alpha \mathbf{a}) \cdot \mathbf{b} = \mathbf{a} \cdot (\alpha \mathbf{b}) = \alpha(\mathbf{a} \cdot \mathbf{b}) \qquad \text{(c)}$$

$$\mathbf{a} \cdot \mathbf{a} > 0 \iff \mathbf{a} \neq \mathbf{0} \qquad \text{(d)}$$

Rules (a) and (c) are trivial. To prove rule (b), consider the vectors $\mathbf{a} = (a_1, \ldots, a_n)$, $\mathbf{b} = (b_1, \ldots, b_n)$, and $\mathbf{c} = (c_1, \ldots, c_n)$. Then

$$\mathbf{a} \cdot (\mathbf{b} + \mathbf{c}) = (a_1, \ldots, a_n) \cdot (b_1 + c_1, \ldots, b_n + c_n)$$

$$= a_1(b_1 + c_1) + \cdots + a_n(b_n + c_n)$$

$$= a_1 b_1 + \cdots + a_n b_n + a_1 c_1 + \cdots + a_n c_n$$

$$= \mathbf{a} \cdot \mathbf{b} + \mathbf{a} \cdot \mathbf{c}$$

To prove rule (d), it suffices to note that $\mathbf{a} \cdot \mathbf{a} = a_1^2 + a_2^2 + \cdots + a_n^2$. This is always nonnegative, and is zero only if all the a_i's are 0.

Lengths of Vectors and the Cauchy–Schwarz Inequality

If $\mathbf{a} = (a_1, a_2, \ldots, a_n)$, we define the **length** (or **norm**) of the vector **a**, denoted by $||\mathbf{a}||$, as $||\mathbf{a}|| = \sqrt{\mathbf{a} \cdot \mathbf{a}}$, or

$$||\mathbf{a}|| = \sqrt{a_1^2 + a_2^2 + \cdots + a_n^2} \qquad [12.15]$$

Using [12.15], we define the (Euclidean) **distance** between the two n-vectors $\mathbf{a} = (a_1, a_2, \ldots, a_n)$ and $\mathbf{b} = (b_1, b_2, \ldots, b_n)$ as

$$||\mathbf{a} - \mathbf{b}|| = \sqrt{(a_1 - b_1)^2 + (a_2 - b_2)^2 + \cdots + (a_n - b_n)^2} \qquad [12.16]$$

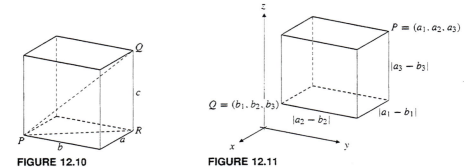

FIGURE 12.10   **FIGURE 12.11**

For $n = 2$, this definition agrees with the usual concept of distance. (See [2.2] in Section 2.3.) For $n = 3$, we can confirm definition [12.16] by studying Figs. 12.10 and 12.11.

Let us first compute the length of the diagonal of a rectangular box with sides of length a, b, and c, as shown in Fig. 12.10. According to Pythagoras' theorem, $(PR)^2 = a^2 + b^2$, and then $(PQ)^2 = (PR)^2 + (RQ)^2 = a^2 + b^2 + c^2$, so the diagonal $PQ = \sqrt{a^2 + b^2 + c^2}$.

In Fig. 12.11, we want to find the distance between the points P and Q with coordinates (a_1, a_2, a_3) and (b_1, b_2, b_3), respectively. We see that these points lie precisely at diagonally opposite vertices of a rectangular box with sides of length $a = |a_1 - b_1|$, $b = |a_2 - b_2|$, and $c = |a_3 - b_3|$. Hence, $(PQ)^2$, the square of the distance between P and Q, is $a^2 + b^2 + c^2 = |a_1 - b_1|^2 + |a_2 - b_2|^2 + |a_3 - b_3|^2 = (a_1 - b_1)^2 + (a_2 - b_2)^2 + (a_3 - b_3)^2$. Thus, the distance between (a_1, a_2, a_3) and (b_1, b_2, b_3) is

$$d = \sqrt{(a_1 - b_1)^2 + (a_2 - b_2)^2 + (a_3 - b_3)^2}$$

which agrees with [12.16]

In Problem 12. Section 3.1, you were asked to prove a famous inequality. By using the notation we have just introduced, [3.5] can be expressed as

$$|\mathbf{a} \cdot \mathbf{b}| \leq ||\mathbf{a}|| \cdot ||\mathbf{b}|| \qquad \textbf{(Cauchy–Schwarz inequality)} \qquad [12.17]$$

Example 12.9

For the two vectors $\mathbf{a} = (1, -2, 3)$ and $\mathbf{b} = (-3, 2, 5)$ in Example 12.6, check the Cauchy–Schwarz inequality.

Solution   We find that

$$||\mathbf{a}|| = \sqrt{1^2 + (-2)^2 + 3^2} = \sqrt{14}. \qquad ||\mathbf{b}|| = \sqrt{(-3)^2 + 2^2 + 5^2} = \sqrt{38}$$

In Example 12.6 we found the scalar product of these vectors to be 8. So inequality [12.17] says that $8 \leq \sqrt{14}\sqrt{38}$, which is certainly true.

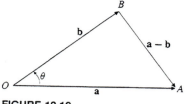

FIGURE 12.12

Orthogonality

Consider Fig. 12.12, which exhibits three vectors, $\mathbf{a}$, $\mathbf{b}$, and $\mathbf{a} - \mathbf{b}$ in R^2 or R^3. According to Pythagoras' theorem, angle θ between the two vectors $\mathbf{a}$ and $\mathbf{b}$ is a right angle ($= 90°$) if and only if $(OA)^2 + (OB)^2 = (AB)^2$, or $||\mathbf{a}||^2 + ||\mathbf{b}||^2 = ||\mathbf{a} - \mathbf{b}||^2$. This implies that $\theta = 90°$ if and only if

$$\mathbf{a} \cdot \mathbf{a} + \mathbf{b} \cdot \mathbf{b} = (\mathbf{a} - \mathbf{b}) \cdot (\mathbf{a} - \mathbf{b})$$
$$= \mathbf{a} \cdot \mathbf{a} - \mathbf{a} \cdot \mathbf{b} - \mathbf{b} \cdot \mathbf{a} + \mathbf{b} \cdot \mathbf{b} \qquad [*]$$

Because $\mathbf{a} \cdot \mathbf{b} = \mathbf{b} \cdot \mathbf{a}$, equality [*] requires $2\mathbf{a} \cdot \mathbf{b} = 0$, and so $\mathbf{a} \cdot \mathbf{b} = 0$. When the angle between two vectors $\mathbf{a}$ and $\mathbf{b}$ is 90°, they are said to be **orthogonal**, and we write $\mathbf{a} \perp \mathbf{b}$. Thus, we have proved that two vectors in R^2 or R^3 are orthogonal if and only if their scalar product is 0. In symbols:

$$\mathbf{a} \perp \mathbf{b} \iff \mathbf{a} \cdot \mathbf{b} = 0 \qquad [12.18]$$

For pairs of vectors in R^n, we *define* orthogonality between $\mathbf{a}$ and $\mathbf{b}$ by [12.18]. The concept of orthogonality is often used in econometrics. In this book, it will reappear in Section 12.5 and in Section 14.6, where we consider "orthogonal matrices."

Note: (This relies on some elementary trigonometry—see Appendix C.) Let $\mathbf{a}$ and $\mathbf{b}$ be two vectors in R^n. Define the *angle* θ between them by

$$\cos \theta = \frac{\mathbf{a} \cdot \mathbf{b}}{||\mathbf{a}|| \cdot ||\mathbf{b}||} \qquad (\theta \in [0, \pi]) \qquad [12.19]$$

Definition [12.19] makes sense because [12.17] implies that the right-hand side has an absolute value ≤ 1. Note also that according to [12.19], $\cos \theta = 0$ iff $\mathbf{a} \cdot \mathbf{b} = 0$. This agrees with [12.18] because, for $\theta \in [0, \pi]$, we have $\cos \theta = 0$ iff $\theta = \pi/2$.

Problems

1. If

$$\mathbf{a} = \begin{pmatrix} 2 \\ -1 \end{pmatrix} \text{ and } \mathbf{b} = \begin{pmatrix} 3 \\ 4 \end{pmatrix}$$

   compute $\mathbf{a} \cdot \mathbf{a}$, $\mathbf{a} \cdot \mathbf{b}$, and $\mathbf{a} \cdot (\mathbf{a} + \mathbf{b})$. Verify that $\mathbf{a} \cdot \mathbf{a} + \mathbf{a} \cdot \mathbf{b} = \mathbf{a} \cdot (\mathbf{a} + \mathbf{b})$.

2. Let $\mathbf{a} = (1, 2, 2)$, $\mathbf{b} = (0, 0, -3)$, and $\mathbf{c} = (-2, 4, -3)$.
   a. Compute $\mathbf{a} \cdot \mathbf{b}$, $\mathbf{b} \cdot \mathbf{a}$, $(\mathbf{a} + \mathbf{b}) \cdot \mathbf{c}$, $\mathbf{a} \cdot \mathbf{c} + \mathbf{b} \cdot \mathbf{c}$, $\mathbf{a} \cdot (3\mathbf{b})$, and $3\mathbf{a} \cdot \mathbf{b}$. Then verify all the properties in [12.14].
   b. Compute $||\mathbf{a}||$, $||\mathbf{b}||$, and $||\mathbf{c}||$.
   c. Verify that [12.17] holds for the vectors $\mathbf{a}$ and $\mathbf{b}$.

3. Check which of these pairs of vectors are orthogonal:
   a. $(1, 2)$ and $(-2, 1)$ b. $(1, -1, 1)$ and $(-1, 1, -1)$
   c. $(a, -b, 1)$ and $(b, a, 0)$

4. For what values of x is the scalar product of $(x, x - 1, 3)$ and $(x, x, 3x)$ equal to 0?

5. For what values of x are $(x, -x - 8, x, x)$ and $(x, 1, -2, 1)$ orthogonal?

6. A construction company has an order for three types of houses: 5 of type A, 7 of type B, and 12 of type C. Write down a three-dimensional vector $\mathbf{x}$ whose coordinates give the number of houses of each type. Suppose that each house of type A requires 20 units of timber, type B requires 18 units, and type C requires 25 units. Write down a vector $\mathbf{u}$ that gives the different quantities required of the different types A, B, and C. Find the total timber requirement by computing the scalar product $\mathbf{u} \cdot \mathbf{x}$.

7. Show that if $\mathbf{a}$ and $\mathbf{b}$ are n-vectors, then

$$(\mathbf{a} + \mathbf{b}) \cdot (\mathbf{a} + \mathbf{b}) = \mathbf{a} \cdot \mathbf{a} + 2\mathbf{a} \cdot \mathbf{b} + \mathbf{b} \cdot \mathbf{b}$$

8. If $\mathbf{a}$ and $\mathbf{b}$ are n-vectors, prove the *triangle inequality* $||\mathbf{a} + \mathbf{b}|| \leq ||\mathbf{a}|| + ||\mathbf{b}||$. (*Hint:* Start from $||\mathbf{a} + \mathbf{b}||^2 = (\mathbf{a} + \mathbf{b})(\mathbf{a} + \mathbf{b})$. You may also need to use [12.17].)

9. A firm produces the nonnegative output quantities $z_1, z_2, \ldots, z_n$ of n different goods, using as inputs the nonnegative quantities $x_1, x_2, \ldots, x_n$ of the same n goods. For each good i ($i = 1, \ldots, n$), define $y_i = z_i - x_i$ as the *net output* of good i, and let p_i be the price of good i. Let $\mathbf{p} = (p_1, \ldots, p_n)$, $\mathbf{x} = (x_1, \ldots, x_n)$ (the **input vector**), $\mathbf{y} = (y_1, \ldots, y_n)$ (the **net output vector**), and $\mathbf{z} = (z_1, \ldots, z_n)$ (the **output vector**).
   a. Calculate the firm's revenue and its costs.

b. Show that the firm's profit is given by the scalar product $\mathbf{p} \cdot \mathbf{y}$. What if $\mathbf{p} \cdot \mathbf{y}$ is negative?

10. A firm has two plants that produce outputs of three goods. Its total labor force is fixed. When a fraction λ of its labor force is allocated to its first plant and a fraction $1 - \lambda$ to its second (with $0 \leq \lambda \leq 1$), the total outputs of the three goods are given by the vector

$$\lambda \begin{pmatrix} 8 \\ 4 \\ 4 \end{pmatrix} + (1 - \lambda) \begin{pmatrix} 2 \\ 6 \\ 10 \end{pmatrix}$$

a. Is it possible for the firm to produce either of the two output vectors

(i) $\begin{pmatrix} 5 \\ 5 \\ 7 \end{pmatrix}$ (ii) $\begin{pmatrix} 7 \\ 5 \\ 5 \end{pmatrix}$

if outputs cannot be thrown away?

b. How do your answers to part (a) change if outputs can be thrown away?

c. How will the revenue-maximizing choice of the fraction λ depend upon the selling prices (p_1, p_2, p_3) of the three goods? What condition must be satisfied by these prices if both plants are to remain in use?

11. A firm produces the first of two goods as its output using the second good as its input, and its net output vector (see Problem 9) is

$$\begin{pmatrix} 2 \\ -1 \end{pmatrix}$$

The price vector it faces is $(1, 3)$. Find the firm's: (a) input vector, (b) output vector, (c) costs, (d) revenue, (e) value of net output, and (f) profit or loss.

12.5 Lines and Planes

Let $\mathbf{a} = (a_1, a_2, a_3)$ and $\mathbf{b} = (b_1, b_2, b_3)$ be two vectors in R^3. Think of them as arrows from the origin to the points with coordinates (a_1, a_2, a_3) and (b_1, b_2, b_3). The straight line L passing through these points is shown in Fig. 12.13.

Let t be a real number and put $\mathbf{x} = \mathbf{a} + t(\mathbf{b} - \mathbf{a}) = (1 - t)\mathbf{a} + t\mathbf{b}$. Then $t = 0$ gives $\mathbf{x} = \mathbf{a}$ and $t = 1$ gives $\mathbf{x} = \mathbf{b}$. In general, by the geometric rule for adding vectors, we see that as t runs through all the real numbers, so $\mathbf{x}$ describes the whole straight line L.

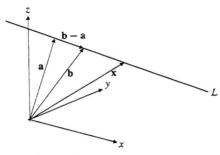

FIGURE 12.13

For R^n, we introduce the following definition:

A Line in R^n

The line L through $\mathbf{a} = (a_1, \ldots, a_n)$ and $\mathbf{b} = (b_1, \ldots, b_n)$ is the set of all $\mathbf{x} = (x_1, \ldots, x_n)$ satisfying

$$\mathbf{x} = (1 - t)\mathbf{a} + t\mathbf{b}$$ [12.20]

for some real number t.

By using the coordinates of $\mathbf{a}$ and $\mathbf{b}$, [12.20] is equivalent to

$$x_1 = (1 - t)a_1 + tb_1, \; x_2 = (1 - t)a_2 + tb_2, \ldots, x_n = (1 - t)a_n + tb_n \quad [12.21]$$

Example 12.10

Describe the straight line in R^3 through the two points $(1, 2, 2)$ and $(-1, -1, 4)$. Where does it meet the $x_1 x_2$-plane?

Solution   According to [12.21], the straight line is given by the equations:

$$x_1 = (1 - t) \cdot 1 + t(-1) = 1 - 2t$$
$$x_2 = (1 - t) \cdot 2 + t(-1) = 2 - 3t$$
$$x_3 = (1 - t) \cdot 2 + t \cdot 4 = 2 + 2t$$

This line intersects the $x_1 x_2$-plane when $x_3 = 0$. Then $2 + 2t = 0$, so $t = -1$, implying that $x_1 = 3$ and $x_2 = 5$. Thus, the line meets the $x_1 x_2$-plane at the point $(3, 5, 0)$, as shown in Fig. 12.14.

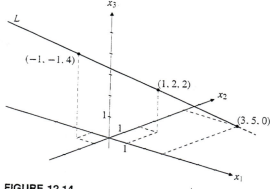

FIGURE 12.14

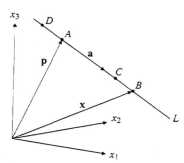

FIGURE 12.15

Suppose $\mathbf{p} = (p_1, \ldots, p_n)$ is a point in R^n. The straight line L passing through $(p_1, \ldots, p_n)$ in the same direction as the vector $\mathbf{a} = (a_1, \ldots, a_n)$ is given by

$$\mathbf{x} = \mathbf{p} + t\mathbf{a} \qquad (t \text{ is any real number}) \qquad [12.22]$$

This should be apparent from Fig. 12.15, where A is $\mathbf{p}$, B is $\mathbf{x} = \mathbf{p} + \mathbf{a}$, C is $\mathbf{p} + \frac{3}{4}\mathbf{a}$, D is $\mathbf{p} - \frac{1}{4}\mathbf{a}$, and so on.

Hyperplanes

Consider first a plane $\mathcal{P}$ in R^3 passing through point $\mathbf{a} = (a_1, a_2, a_3)$ and having the vector $\mathbf{p} = (p_1, p_2, p_3) \neq (0, 0, 0)$ as its normal. This is shown in Fig. 12.16. To say that $\mathbf{p}$ is **normal** to plane $\mathcal{P}$ means that $\mathbf{p}$ is normal (orthogonal or perpendicular) to any line in the plane. Thus, if $\mathbf{x} = (x_1, x_2, x_3)$ is any other point in $\mathcal{P}$, then $\mathbf{x} - \mathbf{a}$ is orthogonal to $\mathbf{p}$. Therefore, the scalar product of $\mathbf{p}$ and $\mathbf{x} - \mathbf{a}$ must be 0, so that

$$\mathbf{p} \cdot (\mathbf{x} - \mathbf{a}) = 0$$

FIGURE 12.16

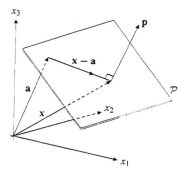

Using the coordinate representation of the vectors, this is equivalent to

$$(p_1, p_2, p_3) \cdot (x_1 - a_1, x_2 - a_2, x_3 - a_3) = 0 \qquad [12.23]$$

So [12.23] is the general equation of a plane in R^3 passing through $\mathbf{a} = (a_1, a_2, a_3)$. Note that the coefficients (p_1, p_2, p_3) of x_1, x_2, x_3 represent a nonzero vector that is normal to the plane.

Example 12.11

Find the equation for the plane in R^3 through $\mathbf{a} = (2, 1, -1)$ with $\mathbf{p} = (-1, 1, 3)$ as a normal. Does the line in Example 12.10 intersect this plane?

Solution   Using [12.23], the equation is

$$-1 \cdot (x_1 - 2) + 1 \cdot (x_2 - 1) + 3(x_3 - (-1)) = 0$$

or

$$-x_1 + x_2 + 3x_3 = -4$$

If the line given by the three equations $x_1 = 1 - 2t$, $x_2 = 2 - 3t$, and $x_3 = 2 + 2t$ meets this plane, then we must have

$$-(1 - 2t) + (2 - 3t) + 3(2 + 2t) = -4$$

Solving this equation for t yields $t = -11/5$, and so the point of intersection is given by

$$x_1 = 1 - 2 \cdot (-11/5) = 27/5,$$
$$x_2 = 2 - 3 \cdot (-11/5) = 43/5, \text{ and}$$
$$x_3 = 2 + 2 \cdot (-11/5) = -12/5.$$

Motivated by this characterization of a plane in R^3, we introduce the following general definition in R^n.

A Hyperplane in R^n

A hyperplane through $\mathbf{a} = (a_1, \ldots, a_n)$ that is orthogonal to a vector $\mathbf{p} = (p_1, \ldots, p_n) \neq \mathbf{0}$ is the set of all points $\mathbf{x} = (x_1, \ldots, x_n)$ satisfying

$$\mathbf{p} \cdot (\mathbf{x} - \mathbf{a}) = 0 \qquad [12.24]$$

Note that if the normal vector $\mathbf{p}$ is replaced by the scalar multiple $s\mathbf{p}$, where $s \neq 0$, then precisely the same set of vectors $\mathbf{x}$ will satisfy the hyperplane equation.

Using the coordinate representation of the vectors, the hyperplane has the equation

$$p_1(x_1 - a_1) + p_2(x_2 - a_2) + \cdots + p_n(x_n - a_n) = 0 \qquad [12.25]$$

or $p_1 x_1 + p_2 x_2 + \cdots + p_n a_n = A$, where $A = p_1 a_1 + p_2 a_2 + \cdots + p_n a_n$.

Example 12.12

A person who has an amount m to spend on n different commodities, whose prices per unit are $p_1, p_2, \ldots, p_n$, respectively, can afford any commodity vector $\mathbf{x} = (x_1, x_2, \ldots, x_n)$ that satisfies the budget inequality

$$p_1 x_1 + p_2 x_2 + \cdots + p_n x_n \leq m \qquad [12.26]$$

When [12.26] is satisfied with equality, it describes the *budget (hyper) plane* whose normal is the price vector $(p_1, p_2, \ldots, p_n)$.

Usually, it is implicitly assumed that $x_1 \geq 0, x_2 \geq 0, \ldots, x_n \geq 0$. See Fig. 15.4 of Section 15.2 for the case $n = 3$. Note that in Fig. 15.4, the vector (p, q, r) is normal to the plane.

Problems

1. Find the equation for the line:
   a. that passes through points $(3, -2, 2)$ and $(10, 2, 1)$.
   b. that passes through point $(1, 3, 2)$ and has the same direction as $(0, -1, 1)$.
2. The line L is given by $x_1 = -t + 2$, $x_2 = 2t - 1$, and $x_3 = t + 3$.
   a. Verify that the point $\mathbf{a} = (2, -1, 3)$ lies on L, but that $(1, 1, 1)$ does not.
   b. Determine the direction of L.
   c. Find the equation for the plane through $\mathbf{a}$ that is orthogonal to L.
   d. Find the point where L intersects the plane $3x_1 + 5x_2 - x_3 = 6$.
3. Find the equation for the plane through the points $(3, 4, -3)$, $(5, 2, 1)$, and $(2, -1, 4)$.
4. **a.** Show that $\mathbf{a} = (-2, 1, -1)$ is a point in the plane $-x + 2y + 3z = 1$.
   b. Find the equation for the normal at $\mathbf{a}$ to the plane in part (a).

12.6 Matrices and Matrix Operations

A **matrix** is simply a rectangular array of numbers considered as an entity. It is usually enclosed in either parentheses or brackets. With m **rows** and n **columns** in the array, we have an *m-by-n* matrix (written as $m \times n$). We usually denote a matrix with bold capital letters such as **A**, **B**, and so on. However, where a matrix has only one row, it will often be regarded as a row vector and denoted by a bold lowercase letter. Similarly, matrices with only one column can be regarded as column vectors. In general, an $m \times n$ matrix is of the form

$$\mathbf{A} = \begin{pmatrix} a_{11} & a_{12} & \cdots & a_{1n} \\ a_{21} & a_{22} & \cdots & a_{2n} \\ \vdots & \vdots & & \vdots \\ a_{m1} & a_{m2} & \cdots & a_{mn} \end{pmatrix} \qquad [12.27]$$

This matrix is said to have **order** $m \times n$. The mn numbers that constitute $\mathbf{A}$ are called its **elements** or **entries**. In particular, a_{ij} denotes the element in the ith row and the jth column. Note the important convention by which (a) the number of *rows* precedes the number of *columns* and (b) the *row* number precedes the *column* number. For brevity, the $m \times n$ matrix in [12.27] is often expressed as $(a_{ij})_{m \times n}$, or more simply as (a_{ij}), if the order $m \times n$ is either obvious or unimportant.

Example 12.13

$$\mathbf{A} = \begin{pmatrix} 3 & -2 \\ 5 & 8 \end{pmatrix}, \quad \mathbf{B} = (-1, \quad 2, \quad \sqrt{3}, \quad 16), \quad \mathbf{C} = \begin{pmatrix} -1 & 2 \\ 8 & 5 \\ 7 & 6 \\ 1 & 1 \end{pmatrix}$$

are matrices. Of these, $\mathbf{A}$ is 2×2, $\mathbf{B}$ is 1×4, and $\mathbf{C}$ is 4×2. Also $a_{21} = 5$ and $c_{32} = 6$. Note that b_{23} is undefined because $\mathbf{B}$ only has one row.

Example 12.14
Construct the 4×3 matrix $\mathbf{A} = (a_{ij})_{4 \times 3}$ with $a_{ij} = 2i - j$.

Solution   Matrix $\mathbf{A}$ has $4 \cdot 3 = 12$ entries. Because $a_{ij} = 2i - j$, $a_{11} = 2 \cdot 1 - 1 = 1$, $a_{12} = 2 \cdot 1 - 2 = 0$, $a_{13} = 2 \cdot 1 - 3 = -1$, and so on. The complete matrix is

$$\mathbf{A} = \begin{pmatrix} 2 \cdot 1 - 1 & 2 \cdot 1 - 2 & 2 \cdot 1 - 3 \\ 2 \cdot 2 - 1 & 2 \cdot 2 - 2 & 2 \cdot 2 - 3 \\ 2 \cdot 3 - 1 & 2 \cdot 3 - 2 & 2 \cdot 3 - 3 \\ 2 \cdot 4 - 1 & 2 \cdot 4 - 2 & 2 \cdot 4 - 3 \end{pmatrix} = \begin{pmatrix} 1 & 0 & -1 \\ 3 & 2 & 1 \\ 5 & 4 & 3 \\ 7 & 6 & 5 \end{pmatrix}$$

If $m = n$, so that the matrix has the same number of columns as rows, it is called a **square matrix** of order n. If $\mathbf{A} = (a_{ij})_{n \times n}$, then the elements $a_{11}, a_{22}, \ldots, a_{nn}$ constitute the **main diagonal** that runs from the top left (a_{11}) to the bottom right (a_{nn}). For instance, the matrix $\mathbf{A}$ in Example 12.13 is a square matrix of order 2. The main diagonal consists of the numbers 3 and 8.

Example 12.15

Consider the general linear system

$$
\begin{aligned}
a_{11}x_1 + a_{12}x_2 + \cdots + a_{1n}x_n &= b_1 \\
a_{21}x_1 + a_{22}x_2 + \cdots + a_{2n}x_n &= b_2 \\
&\cdots\cdots\cdots\cdots\cdots\cdots\cdots\cdots\cdots\cdots\cdots\cdots\cdots\cdots\cdots\cdots\cdots\cdots\cdots \\
a_{m1}x_1 + a_{m2}x_2 + \cdots + a_{mn}x_n &= b_m
\end{aligned}
\qquad [*]
$$

of m equations in n unknowns. It is natural to represent the coefficients of the x's in [*] by the $m \times n$ matrix **A** that is arranged as in [12.27]. Then **A** is called the **coefficient matrix** of [*]. For instance, the coefficient matrix of

$$
\begin{aligned}
3x_1 - 2x_2 + 6x_3 &= 5 \\
5x_1 + x_2 + 2x_3 &= -2
\end{aligned}
\quad \text{is} \quad
\begin{pmatrix} 3 & -2 & 6 \\ 5 & 1 & 2 \end{pmatrix}
$$

Example 12.16

Consider a chain of stores with four outlets, B_1, B_2, B_3, and B_4, each selling eight different commodities, $V_1, V_2, \ldots, V_8$. Let a_{ij} denote the dollar value of the sales of commodity V_i at outlet B_j during a certain month. A suitable way of recording this data is in the 8×4 matrix or "spreadsheet"

$$
\mathbf{A} = \begin{pmatrix}
a_{11} & a_{12} & a_{13} & a_{14} \\
a_{21} & a_{22} & a_{23} & a_{24} \\
\vdots & \vdots & \vdots & \vdots \\
a_{81} & a_{82} & a_{83} & a_{84}
\end{pmatrix}
$$

The eight rows refer to the eight commodities, whereas the four columns refer to the four outlets. For instance, if $a_{73} = 225$, this means that the sales of commodity 7 at outlet 3 were worth \$225 for the month in question.

Matrix Operations

So far matrices have been regarded as just rectangular arrays of numbers that can be useful for storing information. The real motivation for introducing matrices, however, is that there are useful rules for manipulating them that correspond (to some extent) with the familiar rules of ordinary algebra.

First, let us agree how to define equality between matrices. If $\mathbf{A} = (a_{ij})_{m \times n}$ and $\mathbf{B} = (b_{ij})_{m \times n}$ are two $m \times n$ matrices, then **A** and **B** are said to be **equal**, and we write $\mathbf{A} = \mathbf{B}$, provided that $a_{ij} = b_{ij}$ for all $i = 1, 2, \ldots, m$, and $j = 1, 2, \ldots, n$. Thus, two matrices **A** and **B** are equal if they have the same dimensions *and* if all their corresponding entries are equal. If **A** and **B** are *not* equal, then we write $\mathbf{A} \neq \mathbf{B}$.

Example 12.17

When is $\begin{pmatrix} 3 & t-1 \\ 2t & u \end{pmatrix} = \begin{pmatrix} t & 2v \\ u+1 & t+w \end{pmatrix}$?

Solution   Both are 2×2 matrices. So equality requires $3 = t$, $t-1 = 2v$, $2t = u+1$, and $u = t+w$. By solving these simultaneous equations, it follows that the two matrices are equal if and only if $t = 3$, $v = 1$, $u = 5$, and $w = 2$. Then both matrices are equal to

$$\begin{pmatrix} 3 & 2 \\ 6 & 5 \end{pmatrix}$$

Addition and Multiplication by a Scalar

Let us return to Example 12.16, where the 8×4 matrix $\mathbf{A}$ represents the dollar values of total sales of the eight commodities at the four outlets in a certain month. Suppose that the dollar values of sales for the next month are given by a corresponding 8×4 matrix $\mathbf{B} = (b_{ij})_{8 \times 4}$. The total sales revenues from each commodity in each of the outlets in the course of these two months combined would then be given by a new 8×4 matrix $\mathbf{C} = (c_{ij})_{8 \times 4}$, where $c_{ij} = a_{ij} + b_{ij}$ for $i = 1, \ldots, 8$ and for $j = 1, \ldots, 4$. Matrix $\mathbf{C}$ is called the "sum" of $\mathbf{A}$ and $\mathbf{B}$ and we write $\mathbf{C} = \mathbf{A} + \mathbf{B}$.

In general, if $\mathbf{A} = (a_{ij})_{m \times n}$ and $\mathbf{B} = (b_{ij})_{m \times n}$, we define the **sum** of $\mathbf{A}$ and $\mathbf{B}$ as the $m \times n$ matrix $(a_{ij} + b_{ij})_{m \times n}$. Thus,

$$\mathbf{A} + \mathbf{B} = (a_{ij})_{m \times n} + (b_{ij})_{m \times n}$$
$$= (a_{ij} + b_{ij})_{m \times n} \qquad [12.28]$$

So we add two matrices of the same order by adding their corresponding entries.

If α is a real number, we define $\alpha \mathbf{A}$ by

$$\alpha \mathbf{A} = \alpha (a_{ij})_{m \times n} = (\alpha a_{ij})_{m \times n} \qquad [12.29]$$

Thus, to multiply a matrix by a scalar, multiply each entry in the matrix by that scalar. Returning to the chain of stores, the matrix equation $\mathbf{B} = 2\mathbf{A}$ would mean that all the entries in $\mathbf{B}$ are twice the corresponding elements in $\mathbf{A}$—that is, the sales revenue for each commodity in each of the outlets has exactly doubled from one month to the next. (Of course, this is a rather unlikely event.)

Example 12.18

Compute $\mathbf{A} + \mathbf{B}$, $3\mathbf{A}$, and $(-\frac{1}{2})\mathbf{B}$, if

$$\mathbf{A} = \begin{pmatrix} 1 & 2 & 0 \\ 4 & -3 & -1 \end{pmatrix} \quad \text{and} \quad \mathbf{B} = \begin{pmatrix} 0 & 1 & 2 \\ 1 & 0 & 2 \end{pmatrix}$$

Solution

$$A + B = \begin{pmatrix} 1 & 3 & 2 \\ 5 & -3 & 1 \end{pmatrix}$$

$$3A = \begin{pmatrix} 3 & 6 & 0 \\ 12 & -9 & -3 \end{pmatrix}$$

$$(-\tfrac{1}{2})B = \begin{pmatrix} 0 & -\tfrac{1}{2} & -1 \\ -\tfrac{1}{2} & 0 & -1 \end{pmatrix}$$

The matrix $(-1)A$ is usually denoted by $-A$, and the difference between the two matrices A and B of the same dimension, $A - B$, means the same as $A + (-1)B$. In our chain store example, $B - A$ denotes the (net) change in sales revenue for each commodity from each outlet between one month and the next. Positive components represent increases and negative components represent decreases.

With the definitions given earlier, it is easy to derive some useful rules. Let A, B, and C be arbitrary $m \times n$ matrices, and let α and β be real numbers. Also, let 0 denote the $m \times n$ matrix consisting only of zeros, called the **zero matrix**. Then:

Rules for Matrix Addition and Multiplication by Scalars

$$(A + B) + C = A + (B + C) \qquad \text{(a)}$$

$$A + B = B + A \qquad \text{(b)}$$

$$A + 0 = A \qquad \text{(c)}$$

$$A + (-A) = 0 \qquad \text{(d)}$$

$$(\alpha + \beta)A = \alpha A + \beta A \qquad \text{(e)}$$

$$\alpha(A + B) = \alpha A + \alpha B \qquad \text{(f)}$$

[12.30]

Each of these rules follows directly from the definitions and the corresponding rules for ordinary numbers.

Because of rule [12.30](a), there is no need to put parentheses in expressions like $A + B + C$. Note also that definitions [12.28] and [12.29] imply that $A + A + A$ is equal to $3A$.

Problems

1. Construct the matrix $A = (a_{ij})_{3 \times 3}$, where $a_{ii} = 1$ for $i = 1, 2, 3$, and $a_{ij} = 0$ for $i \neq j$.

2. Construct the two matrices $\mathbf{A} = (a_{ij})_{2\times3}$, where (a) $a_{ij} = i + j$ and (b) $a_{ij} = (-1)^{i+j}$.

3. For what values of u and v are the following two matrices equal?

$$\begin{pmatrix} (1-u)^2 & v^2 & 3 \\ v & 2u & 5 \\ 6 & u & -1 \end{pmatrix} = \begin{pmatrix} 4 & 4 & u \\ v & -3v & u-v \\ 6 & v+5 & -1 \end{pmatrix}$$

4. Evaluate $\mathbf{A} + \mathbf{B}$ and $3\mathbf{A}$ when

$$\mathbf{A} = \begin{pmatrix} 0 & 1 \\ 2 & 3 \end{pmatrix} \quad \text{and} \quad \mathbf{B} = \begin{pmatrix} 1 & -1 \\ 5 & 2 \end{pmatrix}$$

5. Evaluate $\mathbf{A} + \mathbf{B}$, $\mathbf{A} - \mathbf{B}$, and $5\mathbf{A} - 3\mathbf{B}$ when

$$\mathbf{A} = \begin{pmatrix} 0 & 1 & -1 \\ 2 & 3 & 7 \end{pmatrix} \quad \text{and} \quad \mathbf{B} = \begin{pmatrix} 1 & -1 & 5 \\ 0 & 1 & 9 \end{pmatrix}$$

12.7 Matrix Multiplication

The matrix operations introduced so far should seem quite natural. The way in which we define matrix multiplication is not so straightforward.[2] An important motivation for this definition is the way it helps certain key manipulations of linear equations.

Consider, for example, the following two systems of linear equations

$$z_1 = a_{11}y_1 + a_{12}y_2 + a_{13}y_3$$
$$z_2 = a_{21}y_1 + a_{22}y_2 + a_{23}y_3 \qquad [1]$$

$$y_1 = b_{11}x_1 + b_{12}x_2$$
$$y_2 = b_{21}x_1 + b_{22}x_2 \qquad [2]$$
$$y_3 = b_{31}x_1 + b_{32}x_2$$

The coefficient matrices of these two systems of equations are, respectively,

$$\mathbf{A} = \begin{pmatrix} a_{11} & a_{12} & a_{13} \\ a_{21} & a_{22} & a_{23} \end{pmatrix} \quad \text{and} \quad \mathbf{B} = \begin{pmatrix} b_{11} & b_{12} \\ b_{21} & b_{22} \\ b_{31} & b_{32} \end{pmatrix} \qquad [3]$$

---

[2] It is tempting to define the product of two matrices $\mathbf{A} = (a_{ij})_{m\times n}$ and $\mathbf{B} = (b_{ij})_{m\times n}$ of the same dimensions this way: The product of $\mathbf{A}$ and $\mathbf{B}$ is simply the matrix $\mathbf{C} = (c_{ij})_{m\times n}$, where $c_{ij} = a_{ij}b_{ij}$ is obtained by multiplying the entries of the two matrices term by term. This is a respectable matrix operation and, in fact, matrix $\mathbf{C}$ is called the *Hadamard product* of $\mathbf{A}$ and $\mathbf{B}$. However, the definition of matrix multiplication that we give is the one used by far the most in linear algebra.

System [1] expresses the z variables in terms of the y's, whereas in [2], the y's are expressed in terms of the x's. So the z variables must be related to the x variables. Indeed, take the expressions for y_1, y_2, and y_3 in [2] and insert them into [1]. This gives

$$z_1 = a_{11}(b_{11}x_1 + b_{12}x_2) + a_{12}(b_{21}x_1 + b_{22}x_2) + a_{13}(b_{31}x_1 + b_{32}x_2)$$
$$z_2 = a_{21}(b_{11}x_1 + b_{12}x_2) + a_{22}(b_{21}x_1 + b_{22}x_2) + a_{23}(b_{31}x_1 + b_{32}x_2)$$

Rearranging the terms yields

$$z_1 = (a_{11}b_{11} + a_{12}b_{21} + a_{13}b_{31})x_1 + (a_{11}b_{12} + a_{12}b_{22} + a_{13}b_{32})x_2$$
$$z_2 = (a_{21}b_{11} + a_{22}b_{21} + a_{23}b_{31})x_1 + (a_{21}b_{12} + a_{22}b_{22} + a_{23}b_{32})x_2 \qquad [4]$$

The coefficient matrix of this system is, therefore,

$$\mathbf{C} = \begin{pmatrix} a_{11}b_{11} + a_{12}b_{21} + a_{13}b_{31} & a_{11}b_{12} + a_{12}b_{22} + a_{13}b_{32} \\ a_{21}b_{11} + a_{22}b_{21} + a_{23}b_{31} & a_{21}b_{12} + a_{22}b_{22} + a_{23}b_{32} \end{pmatrix} \qquad [5]$$

Note that $\mathbf{A}$ is 2×3 and $\mathbf{B}$ is 3×2. Thus, $\mathbf{B}$ *has as many rows as* $\mathbf{A}$ *has columns.* Matrix $\mathbf{C}$ is 2×2. Letting $\mathbf{C} = (c_{ij})_{2 \times 2}$, we see that c_{11} is equal to the scalar product of the first row vector in $\mathbf{A}$ and the first column vector in $\mathbf{B}$. Moreover, c_{12} is the scalar product of the first row vector in $\mathbf{A}$ and the second column vector in $\mathbf{B}$, and so on. Thus, c_{ij} is the scalar product of the ith row in $\mathbf{A}$ with the jth column in $\mathbf{B}$.

The matrix $\mathbf{C}$ in [5] is called the **(matrix) product** of $\mathbf{A}$ and $\mathbf{B}$ and we write $\mathbf{C} = \mathbf{AB}$. Here is a numerical example.

Example 12.19

$$\begin{pmatrix} 1 & 0 & 3 \\ 2 & 1 & 5 \end{pmatrix} \begin{pmatrix} 1 & 3 \\ 2 & 5 \\ 6 & 2 \end{pmatrix} = \begin{pmatrix} 1 \cdot 1 + 0 \cdot 2 + 3 \cdot 6 & 1 \cdot 3 + 0 \cdot 5 + 3 \cdot 2 \\ 2 \cdot 1 + 1 \cdot 2 + 5 \cdot 6 & 2 \cdot 3 + 1 \cdot 5 + 5 \cdot 2 \end{pmatrix}$$

$$= \begin{pmatrix} 19 & 9 \\ 34 & 21 \end{pmatrix}$$

In order to generalize the arguments related to the preceding Equations [1] to [5], assume that as in [1], the variables $z_1, \ldots, z_m$ are expressed linearly in terms of $y_1, \ldots, y_n$, and that as in [2], the variables $y_1, \ldots, y_n$ are expressed linearly in terms of $x_1, \ldots, x_p$. Then $z_1, \ldots, z_m$ can be expressed linearly in terms of $x_1, \ldots, x_p$.

The result we get leads directly to the following definition:

Matrix Multiplication

Suppose that $\mathbf{A} = (a_{ij})_{m \times n}$ and that $\mathbf{B} = (b_{ij})_{n \times p}$. Then the product $\mathbf{C} = \mathbf{AB}$ is the $m \times p$ matrix $\mathbf{C} = (c_{ij})_{m \times p}$ whose element in the ith row and the jth column is the scalar product

$$c_{ij} = a_{i1}b_{1j} + a_{i2}b_{2j} + \cdots + a_{in}b_{nj} \qquad [12.31]$$

of the ith row of $\mathbf{A}$ with the jth column of $\mathbf{B}$.

One way of visualizing matrix multiplication is this:

$$
\begin{pmatrix}
a_{11} & \cdots & a_{1k} & \cdots & a_{1n} \\
& \vdots & & \vdots & \vdots \\
\boxed{a_{i1} \ \cdots \ a_{ik} \ \cdots \ a_{in}} \\
& \vdots & & \vdots & \vdots \\
a_{m1} & \cdots & a_{mk} & \cdots & a_{mn}
\end{pmatrix}
\cdot
\begin{pmatrix}
b_{11} & \cdots & \boxed{b_{1j}} & \cdots & b_{1p} \\
\vdots & & \vdots & & \vdots \\
b_{k1} & \cdots & b_{kj} & \cdots & b_{kp} \\
\vdots & & \vdots & & \vdots \\
b_{n1} & \cdots & b_{nj} & \cdots & b_{np}
\end{pmatrix}
=
\begin{pmatrix}
c_{11} & \cdots & c_{1j} & \cdots & c_{1p} \\
\vdots & & \vdots & & \vdots \\
c_{i1} & \cdots & \boxed{c_{ij}} & \cdots & c_{ip} \\
\vdots & & \vdots & & \vdots \\
c_{m1} & \cdots & c_{mj} & \cdots & c_{mp}
\end{pmatrix}
$$

Note that the product $\mathbf{AB}$ is defined only if the number of columns in $\mathbf{A}$ is equal to the number of rows in $\mathbf{B}$. Also, if $\mathbf{A}$ and $\mathbf{B}$ are two matrices, then $\mathbf{AB}$ might be defined, even if $\mathbf{BA}$ is not. For instance, if $\mathbf{A}$ is 6×3 and $\mathbf{B}$ is 3×5, then $\mathbf{AB}$ is defined (and is 6×5), whereas $\mathbf{BA}$ is not defined. There is no way of forming scalar products from the five-component row vectors of $\mathbf{B}$ and the six-component column vectors of $\mathbf{A}$.

Example 12.20

Suppose matrices $\mathbf{A}$ and $\mathbf{B}$ are

$$
\mathbf{A} = \begin{pmatrix} 0 & 1 & 2 \\ 2 & 3 & 1 \\ 4 & -1 & 6 \end{pmatrix} \qquad \text{and} \qquad \mathbf{B} = \begin{pmatrix} 3 & 2 \\ 1 & 0 \\ -1 & 1 \end{pmatrix}
$$

Compute the matrix product $\mathbf{AB}$. Is the product $\mathbf{BA}$ defined?

Solution $\mathbf{A}$ is 3×3 and $\mathbf{B}$ is 3×2, so $\mathbf{AB}$ is a 3×2 matrix:

$$
\mathbf{AB} = \begin{pmatrix} 0 & 1 & 2 \\ \boxed{2 \quad 3 \quad 1} \\ 4 & -1 & 6 \end{pmatrix} \begin{pmatrix} \boxed{3} & 2 \\ \boxed{1} & 0 \\ \boxed{-1} & 1 \end{pmatrix} = \begin{pmatrix} -1 & 2 \\ \boxed{8} & 5 \\ 5 & 14 \end{pmatrix}
$$

(We have indicated how the element in the second row and first column of
AB is found. It is the scalar product of the second row vector in **A** and the
first column vector in **B**; this is $2 \cdot 3 + 3 \cdot 1 + 1 \cdot (-1) = 8$.) The product **BA**
is not defined because the number of columns in **B** ($= 2$) is not equal to the
number of rows in **A** ($= 3$).

Note: In the example, **AB** was defined but **BA** was not. Even in cases in which
AB and **BA** are both defined, they are usually not equal. See Problem 1 and the
last subsection "Errors to Avoid" in Section 12.8. When we write **AB**, we say that
we **premultiply B** by **A**, whereas in **BA** we **postmultiply B** by **A**.

Example 12.21

Initially, three firms A, B, and C (also numbered 1, 2, and 3), share the
market for a certain commodity. Firm A has 20% of the market, B has 60%,
and C has 20%. In the course of the next year, the following changes occur:

$$\begin{cases} A \text{ keeps } 85\% \text{ of its customers, while losing } 5\% \text{ to } B \text{ and } 10\% \text{ to } C \\ B \text{ keeps } 55\% \text{ of its customers, while losing } 10\% \text{ to } A \text{ and } 35\% \text{ to } C \\ C \text{ keeps } 85\% \text{ of its customers, while losing } 10\% \text{ to } A \text{ and } 5\% \text{ to } B \end{cases} \quad [1]$$

A *market share vector* is defined as a column vector **s** whose components
are all nonnegative and sum to 1. Define the matrix **T** and the initial share
vector **s** by

$$\mathbf{T} = \begin{pmatrix} 0.85 & 0.10 & 0.10 \\ 0.05 & 0.55 & 0.05 \\ 0.10 & 0.35 & 0.85 \end{pmatrix} \quad \text{and} \quad \mathbf{s} = \begin{pmatrix} 0.2 \\ 0.6 \\ 0.2 \end{pmatrix}$$

Notice that t_{ij} is the percentage of j's customers who become i's customers
in the next period. So **T** is called the *transition matrix*.

Compute the vector **Ts**, show that it is also a market share vector, and
give an interpretation. What is the interpretation of $\mathbf{T}(\mathbf{Ts})$, $\mathbf{T}(\mathbf{T}(\mathbf{Ts}))$, ...?

Solution

$$\mathbf{Ts} = \begin{pmatrix} 0.85 & 0.10 & 0.10 \\ 0.05 & 0.55 & 0.05 \\ 0.10 & 0.35 & 0.85 \end{pmatrix} \begin{pmatrix} 0.2 \\ 0.6 \\ 0.2 \end{pmatrix} = \begin{pmatrix} 0.25 \\ 0.35 \\ 0.40 \end{pmatrix} \quad [2]$$

Because $0.25 + 0.35 + 0.40 = 1$, **Ts** is also a market share vector. The first
entry in **Ts** is obtained from the calculation

$$0.85 \cdot 0.2 + 0.10 \cdot 0.6 + 0.10 \cdot 0.2 = 0.25 \quad [3]$$

Here $0.85 \cdot 0.2$ is A's share of the market that it retains after 1 year, $0.10 \cdot 0.6$
is the share A gains from B, and $0.10 \cdot 0.2$ is the share A gains from C.

The sum in [3] is therefore A's total share of the market after 1 year. The other entries in **Ts** have corresponding interpretations, so **Ts** must be the new market share vector after 1 year. Then **T(Ts)** is the market share vector after one more year—that is, after 2 years, and so on. (In Problem 4, you are asked to compute **T(Ts)**.)

Systems of Equations in Matrix Form

The definition [12.31] of matrix multiplication was introduced in order to allow systems of equations to be manipulated. Indeed, it turns out that we can write linear systems of equations very compactly by means of matrix multiplication. For instance, consider the system:

$$3x_1 + 4x_2 = 5$$
$$7x_1 - 2x_2 = 2$$
[1]

Now define

$$\mathbf{A} = \begin{pmatrix} 3 & 4 \\ 7 & -2 \end{pmatrix}, \qquad \mathbf{x} = \begin{pmatrix} x_1 \\ x_2 \end{pmatrix}, \qquad \text{and} \qquad \mathbf{b} = \begin{pmatrix} 5 \\ 2 \end{pmatrix}$$
[2]

Then we see that

$$\mathbf{Ax} = \begin{pmatrix} 3 & 4 \\ 7 & -2 \end{pmatrix} \begin{pmatrix} x_1 \\ x_2 \end{pmatrix} = \begin{pmatrix} 3x_1 + 4x_2 \\ 7x_1 - 2x_2 \end{pmatrix}$$

So [1] is equivalent to the matrix equation

$$\mathbf{Ax} = \mathbf{b}$$

Consider the general linear system [12.1]. Suppose we define

$$\mathbf{A} = \begin{pmatrix} a_{11} & a_{12} & \cdots & a_{1n} \\ a_{21} & a_{22} & \cdots & a_{2n} \\ \vdots & \vdots & & \vdots \\ a_{m1} & a_{m2} & \cdots & a_{mn} \end{pmatrix}, \qquad \mathbf{x} = \begin{pmatrix} x_1 \\ x_2 \\ \vdots \\ x_n \end{pmatrix}, \qquad \mathbf{b} = \begin{pmatrix} b_1 \\ b_2 \\ \vdots \\ b_m \end{pmatrix}$$
[12.32]

So **A** is $m \times n$ and **x** is $n \times 1$. The matrix product **Ax** is then defined by [12.31] and is $m \times 1$. It follows that

$a_{11}x_1 + a_{12}x_2 + \cdots + a_{1n}x_n = b_1$

$a_{21}x_1 + a_{22}x_2 + \cdots + a_{2n}x_n = b_2$ can be written as $\mathbf{Ax} = \mathbf{b}$ [12.33]

....

$a_{m1}x_1 + a_{m2}x_2 + \cdots + a_{mn}x_n = b_m$

This very concise notation turns out to be extremely useful.

Problems

1. Compute the products **AB** and **BA**, if possible, for the following:

   a. $A = \begin{pmatrix} 0 & -2 \\ 3 & 1 \end{pmatrix}$ $B = \begin{pmatrix} -1 & 4 \\ 1 & 5 \end{pmatrix}$

   b. $A = \begin{pmatrix} 8 & 3 & -2 \\ 1 & 0 & 4 \end{pmatrix}$ $B = \begin{pmatrix} 2 & -2 \\ 4 & 3 \\ 1 & -5 \end{pmatrix}$

   c. $A = \begin{pmatrix} 0 \\ -2 \\ 4 \\ 1 \end{pmatrix}$ $B = (0, \ -2, \ 3, \ 1)$

   d. $A = \begin{pmatrix} -1 & 0 \\ 2 & 4 \end{pmatrix}$ $B = \begin{pmatrix} 3 & 1 \\ -1 & 1 \\ 0 & 2 \end{pmatrix}$

2. Let

$$A = \begin{pmatrix} 1 & 2 & -3 \\ 5 & 0 & 2 \\ 1 & -1 & 1 \end{pmatrix}, \qquad B = \begin{pmatrix} 3 & -1 & 2 \\ 4 & 2 & 5 \\ 2 & 0 & 3 \end{pmatrix}, \qquad C = \begin{pmatrix} 4 & 1 & 2 \\ 0 & 3 & 2 \\ 1 & -2 & 3 \end{pmatrix}$$

Find the matrices $A + B$, $A - B$, **AB**, **BA**, **A(BC)**, and **(AB)C**.

3. Find all matrices **B** that "commute" with $A = \begin{pmatrix} 1 & 2 \\ 2 & 3 \end{pmatrix}$ in the sense that **BA = AB**.

4. In Example 12.21, compute **T(Ts)**.

12.8 Rules for Matrix Multiplication

The algebraic rules related to addition of matrices and multiplication of a matrix by a scalar were all natural and easy to verify. Matrix multiplication is a more complicated operation and we must carefully examine what rules apply. We have already noticed that the commutative law **AB = BA** does *not* hold in general. The following three important rules *are* generally valid, however.

If **A**, **B**, and **C** are matrices whose dimensions are such that the given operations are defined, then:

$(AB)C = A(BC)$	**(associative law)**	[12.34]
$A(B + C) = AB + AC$	**(left distributive law)**	[12.35]
$(A + B)C = AC + BC$	**(right distributive law)**	[12.36]

Note that both left and right distributive laws are stated here because, unlike for numbers, matrix multiplication is not commutative.

Example 12.22

Verify [12.34], [12.35], and [12.36] for the following matrices:

$$\mathbf{A} = \begin{pmatrix} 1 & 2 \\ 0 & 1 \end{pmatrix}, \qquad \mathbf{B} = \begin{pmatrix} 0 & -1 \\ 3 & 2 \end{pmatrix}, \qquad \mathbf{C} = \begin{pmatrix} 1 & 1 \\ 2 & 1 \end{pmatrix}$$

Solution   All multiplication and addition operations are defined, with

$$\mathbf{AB} = \begin{pmatrix} 6 & 3 \\ 3 & 2 \end{pmatrix}, \qquad (\mathbf{AB})\mathbf{C} = \begin{pmatrix} 6 & 3 \\ 3 & 2 \end{pmatrix} \begin{pmatrix} 1 & 1 \\ 2 & 1 \end{pmatrix} = \begin{pmatrix} 12 & 9 \\ 7 & 5 \end{pmatrix}$$

$$\mathbf{BC} = \begin{pmatrix} -2 & -1 \\ 7 & 5 \end{pmatrix}, \qquad \mathbf{A}(\mathbf{BC}) = \begin{pmatrix} 1 & 2 \\ 0 & 1 \end{pmatrix} \begin{pmatrix} -2 & -1 \\ 7 & 5 \end{pmatrix} = \begin{pmatrix} 12 & 9 \\ 7 & 5 \end{pmatrix}$$

Thus, $(\mathbf{AB})\mathbf{C} = \mathbf{A}(\mathbf{BC})$ in this case. Moreover,

$$\mathbf{B} + \mathbf{C} = \begin{pmatrix} 1 & 0 \\ 5 & 3 \end{pmatrix}, \qquad \mathbf{A}(\mathbf{B} + \mathbf{C}) = \begin{pmatrix} 1 & 2 \\ 0 & 1 \end{pmatrix} \begin{pmatrix} 1 & 0 \\ 5 & 3 \end{pmatrix} = \begin{pmatrix} 11 & 6 \\ 5 & 3 \end{pmatrix}$$

and

$$\mathbf{AC} = \begin{pmatrix} 5 & 3 \\ 2 & 1 \end{pmatrix}, \qquad \mathbf{AB} + \mathbf{AC} = \begin{pmatrix} 6 & 3 \\ 3 & 2 \end{pmatrix} + \begin{pmatrix} 5 & 3 \\ 2 & 1 \end{pmatrix} = \begin{pmatrix} 11 & 6 \\ 5 & 3 \end{pmatrix}$$

So $\mathbf{A}(\mathbf{B} + \mathbf{C}) = \mathbf{AB} + \mathbf{AC}$. You should now verify the right distributive law [12.36] for yourself.

Proof of [12.34]   Suppose $\mathbf{A} = (a_{ij})_{m \times n}$, $\mathbf{B} = (b_{ij})_{n \times p}$, and $\mathbf{C} = (c_{ij})_{p \times q}$. It is easy to verify that these dimensions imply that $(\mathbf{AB})\mathbf{C}$ and $\mathbf{A}(\mathbf{BC})$ are both defined as $m \times q$ matrices. We have to prove that their corresponding elements are all equal.

Consider first $(\mathbf{AB})\mathbf{C}$. The rs element in $(\mathbf{AB})\mathbf{C}$ is the scalar product of the rth row in $\mathbf{AB}$ and the sth column in $\mathbf{C}$. But the rth row of $\mathbf{D} = \mathbf{AB}$ is $(d_{r1}, d_{r2}, \ldots, d_{rp})$, where d_{rj} is the scalar product of the rth row of $\mathbf{A}$ and the jth column of $\mathbf{B}$. So

$$d_{rj} = a_{r1}b_{1j} + a_{r2}b_{2j} + \cdots + a_{rn}b_{nj}$$

$$= \sum_{i=1}^{n} a_{ri}b_{ij}$$

The elements in the sth column of $\mathbf{C}$ are $c_{1s}, c_{2s}, \ldots, c_{ps}$. Hence, the rs

element in $(\mathbf{AB})\mathbf{C}$ is

$$d_{r1}c_{1s} + d_{r2}c_{2s} + \cdots + d_{rp}c_{ps} = \sum_{j=1}^{p} d_{rj}c_{js} = \sum_{j=1}^{p}\left(\sum_{i=1}^{n} a_{ri}b_{ij}\right)c_{js}$$

$$= \sum_{j=1}^{p}\left(\sum_{i=1}^{n} a_{ri}b_{ij}c_{js}\right) \qquad [1]$$

Consider next $\mathbf{A}(\mathbf{BC})$. The rs element in this matrix is the scalar product of the rth row of $\mathbf{A}$ and the sth column of $\mathbf{BC}$. Row r in $\mathbf{A}$ is $(a_{r1}, a_{r2}, \dots, a_{rn})$. Column s in $\mathbf{BC}$ is $(e_{1s}, e_{2s}, \dots, e_{ns})$, where

$$e_{is} = b_{i1}c_{1s} + b_{i2}c_{2s} + \cdots + b_{ip}c_{ps}$$

$$= \sum_{j=1}^{p} b_{ij}c_{js}$$

is the scalar product of row i in $\mathbf{B}$ with column s in $\mathbf{C}$. Thus, the rs element in $\mathbf{A}(\mathbf{BC})$ is

$$a_{r1}e_{1s} + a_{r2}e_{2s} + \cdots + a_{rn}e_{ns} = \sum_{i=1}^{n} a_{ri}e_{is} = \sum_{i=1}^{n} a_{ri}\left(\sum_{j=1}^{p} b_{ij}c_{js}\right)$$

$$= \sum_{i=1}^{n}\left(\sum_{j=1}^{p} a_{ri}b_{ij}c_{js}\right) \qquad [2]$$

Looking more closely at the last expressions in [1] and [2], we see that they are equal because both are equal to the double sum of all terms of the form $a_{ri}b_{ij}c_{js}$, as i ranges from 1 to n and j ranges from 1 to p. This proves [12.34].

Because of [12.34], parentheses are not required in a matrix product such as $\mathbf{ABC}$. Of course, a corresponding result is valid for products of more factors.

We leave the reader to prove [12.35]. It will probably be best first to show [12.35] for the case when $\mathbf{A}$, $\mathbf{B}$, and $\mathbf{C}$ are all 2×2 matrices, after which it may be clearer how to treat the general case. The proof of [12.36] is similar.

Proving [12.34] involved examining in detail all the elements of the relevant matrices, and a corresponding examination is necessary to prove [12.35] and [12.36]. A useful technique in matrix algebra is to prove new results by using [12.34] to [12.36], rather than examining individual elements. For instance, suppose we are asked to prove that if $\mathbf{A} = (a_{ij})$ and $\mathbf{B} = (b_{ij})$ are both $n \times n$ matrices, then

$$(\mathbf{A} + \mathbf{B})(\mathbf{A} + \mathbf{B}) = \mathbf{AA} + \mathbf{AB} + \mathbf{BA} + \mathbf{BB} \qquad [*]$$

According to [12.35],

$$(A + B)(A + B) = (A + B)A + (A + B)B$$

By [12.36], one has $(A+B)A = AA+BA$ and $(A+B)B = AB+BB$, from which we see that [*] follows.

Powers of Matrices

If A is a square matrix, we write AA as A^2, and AAA as A^3, and so on. In general,

$$A^n = AA \cdots A \qquad (A \text{ is repeated } n \text{ times}) \qquad [12.37]$$

Example 12.23

Let $A = \begin{pmatrix} 1 & -1 \\ 0 & 1 \end{pmatrix}$. Compute A^2 and A^3. Guess the general form of A^n, and prove your guess by induction on n. (For induction, see Section B.5 of Appendix B.)

Solution   We find that

$$A^2 = AA = \begin{pmatrix} 1 & -2 \\ 0 & 1 \end{pmatrix}, \quad A^3 = A^2A = \begin{pmatrix} 1 & -3 \\ 0 & 1 \end{pmatrix}, \quad A^4 = A^3A = \begin{pmatrix} 1 & -4 \\ 0 & 1 \end{pmatrix}$$

We guess, therefore, that for all natural numbers n,

$$A^n = \begin{pmatrix} 1 & -n \\ 0 & 1 \end{pmatrix} \qquad [*]$$

We confirm this by induction on n. Formula [*] *is* correct for $n = 1$. *Suppose* it is correct for $n = k$—that is,

$$A^k = \begin{pmatrix} 1 & -k \\ 0 & 1 \end{pmatrix}$$

Then

$$A^{k+1} = A^kA = \begin{pmatrix} 1 & -k \\ 0 & 1 \end{pmatrix}\begin{pmatrix} 1 & -1 \\ 0 & 1 \end{pmatrix} = \begin{pmatrix} 1 & -k-1 \\ 0 & 1 \end{pmatrix}$$

which is precisely the result we obtain in [*] by putting $n = k + 1$. If the induction hypothesis [*] is valid for $n = k$, we have shown that it is also valid for $n = k + 1$. So [*] is indeed generally valid.

Example 12.24

Suppose P and Q are $n \times n$ matrices such that $PQ = Q^2P$. Prove that $(PQ)^2 = Q^6P^2$.

Solution   The proof is simple if we use the associative law [12.34] and $PQ = Q^2P$ repeatedly:

$$(PQ)^2 = (PQ)(PQ) = (Q^2P)(Q^2P) = (Q^2P)Q(QP) = Q^2(PQ)(QP)$$

$$= Q^2(Q^2P)(QP) = Q^2Q^2(PQ)P = Q^2Q^2(Q^2P)P = Q^2Q^2Q^2P^2 = Q^6P^2$$

It would be essentially impossible to prove this equality by looking at individual elements. (Note carefully that $(PQ)^2$ is generally *not* equal to P^2Q^2. In fact, $(PQ)^2 = (PQ)(PQ) = P(QP)Q = P(PQ)Q = P^2Q^2$ if $PQ = QP$, but this last condition is not necessary.)

The Identity Matrix

The **identity matrix** of order n, denoted by I_n (or often just by I), is the $n \times n$ matrix having ones along the main diagonal and zeros elsewhere:

$$I_n = \begin{pmatrix} 1 & 0 & \cdots & 0 \\ 0 & 1 & \cdots & 0 \\ \vdots & \vdots & \ddots & \vdots \\ 0 & 0 & \cdots & 1 \end{pmatrix}_{n \times n} \qquad \textbf{(identity matrix)} \qquad [12.38]$$

If A is any $m \times n$ matrix, it is easy to verify that $AI_n = A$. Likewise, if B is any $n \times m$ matrix, then $I_nB = B$. In particular,

$$AI_n = I_nA = A \qquad \text{(for every } n \times n \text{ matrix } A) \qquad [12.39]$$

Thus, I_n is the matrix equivalent to 1 in the real number system. In fact, it is the only matrix with this property. To prove this, suppose E is an arbitrary $n \times n$ matrix such that $AE = A$ for all $n \times n$ matrices A. Putting $A = I_n$ in particular yields $I_nE = I_n$. But $I_nE = E$ according to [12.39]. So $I_n = E$.

Errors to Avoid

The rules of matrix algebra make many arguments very easy, but one has to be extremely careful to use only valid rules. Look at [∗] following the proof of [12.34], for instance. It is tempting to simplify the expression $AA + AB + BA + BB$ on the right-hand side to $AA + 2AB + BB$. This is wrong! Even when AB and BA are both defined, AB is not necessarily equal to BA. Matrix multiplication is *not* commutative.

Example 12.25

Let A and B be the matrices

$$A = \begin{pmatrix} 2 & 0 \\ 0 & 3 \end{pmatrix} \qquad B = \begin{pmatrix} 0 & 1 \\ 1 & 0 \end{pmatrix}$$

Show that $AB \neq BA$.

Solution

$$AB = \begin{pmatrix} 0 & 2 \\ 3 & 0 \end{pmatrix} \quad \text{and} \quad BA = \begin{pmatrix} 0 & 3 \\ 2 & 0 \end{pmatrix}$$

Hence, $AB \neq BA$.

If a and b are real numbers, then $ab = 0$ implies that either a or b is 0. The corresponding result is not true for matrices. In fact, AB can be the zero matrix even if neither A nor B is the zero matrix.

Example 12.26

Let $A = \begin{pmatrix} 3 & 1 \\ 6 & 2 \end{pmatrix}$ $B = \begin{pmatrix} 1 & 2 \\ -3 & -6 \end{pmatrix}$. Compute AB.

Solution

$$AB = \begin{pmatrix} 3 & 1 \\ 6 & 2 \end{pmatrix} \begin{pmatrix} 1 & 2 \\ -3 & -6 \end{pmatrix} = \begin{pmatrix} 0 & 0 \\ 0 & 0 \end{pmatrix}$$

For real numbers, if $ab = ac$ and $a \neq 0$, then $b = c$, because we can cancel by multiplying each side of the equation by $1/a$. The corresponding cancellation "rule" is not valid for matrices. Example 12.26 illustrates this point also: There $AB = A0$ and $A \neq 0$, yet $B \neq 0$.

So we have found examples showing that in general:

$$AB \neq BA \qquad \text{[12.40]}$$

$$AB = 0 \quad \text{does not imply that either } A \text{ or } B \text{ is } 0 \qquad \text{[12.41]}$$

$$AB = AC \text{ and } A \neq 0 \quad \text{do not imply that } B = C \qquad \text{[12.42]}$$

Here [12.40] says that matrix multiplication is not commutative in general, whereas [12.42] shows us that the cancellation law is generally invalid for matrix multiplication. (The cancellation law *is valid* if A has a so-called inverse. See Section 13.6.)

Problems

1. Verify the distributive law $A(B + C) = AB + AC$ when

$$A = \begin{pmatrix} 1 & 2 \\ 3 & 4 \end{pmatrix}, \quad B = \begin{pmatrix} 2 & -1 & 1 & 0 \\ 3 & -1 & 2 & 1 \end{pmatrix}, \quad C = \begin{pmatrix} -1 & 1 & 1 & 2 \\ -2 & 2 & 0 & -1 \end{pmatrix}$$

2. Compute the product

$$(x, y, z) \begin{pmatrix} a & d & e \\ d & b & f \\ e & f & c \end{pmatrix} \begin{pmatrix} x \\ y \\ z \end{pmatrix}$$

3. Verify by actual multiplication that $(\mathbf{AB})\mathbf{C} = \mathbf{A}(\mathbf{BC})$ if

$$\mathbf{A} = \begin{pmatrix} a_{11} & a_{12} \\ a_{21} & a_{22} \end{pmatrix}, \qquad \mathbf{B} = \begin{pmatrix} b_{11} & b_{12} \\ b_{21} & b_{22} \end{pmatrix}, \qquad \mathbf{C} = \begin{pmatrix} c_{11} & c_{12} \\ c_{21} & c_{22} \end{pmatrix}$$

4. If $\mathbf{A}$ and $\mathbf{B}$ are square matrices of order n, prove that

$$(\mathbf{A} + \mathbf{B})(\mathbf{A} - \mathbf{B}) \neq \mathbf{AA} - \mathbf{BB} \qquad [1]$$

$$(\mathbf{A} - \mathbf{B})(\mathbf{A} - \mathbf{B}) \neq \mathbf{AA} - 2\mathbf{AB} + \mathbf{BB} \qquad [2]$$

except in special cases. Find a necessary and sufficient condition for equality to hold in each case.

5. Compute: (a) $\begin{pmatrix} 1 & 0 & 0 \\ 0 & 1 & 0 \\ 0 & 0 & 1 \end{pmatrix} \begin{pmatrix} 5 & 3 & 1 \\ 2 & 0 & 9 \\ 1 & 3 & 3 \end{pmatrix}$ (b) $(1, \quad 2, \quad -3) \begin{pmatrix} 1 & 0 & 0 \\ 0 & 1 & 0 \\ 0 & 0 & 1 \end{pmatrix}$

6. Let $\mathbf{A}$ be the 3×3 matrix

$$\mathbf{A} = \begin{pmatrix} 1 & 1 & 1 \\ -1 & -1 & -1 \\ 1 & 1 & 1 \end{pmatrix}$$

    a. Find a 3-vector $\mathbf{x}_0$ for which $\mathbf{Ax}_0 = \mathbf{x}_0$ and $\mathbf{x}_0$ has length 1.
    b. Compute $\mathbf{A}^n \mathbf{x}_0$ for $n = 1, 2, \ldots$.

7. A square matrix $\mathbf{A}$ is said to be **idempotent** if $\mathbf{AA} = \mathbf{A}$.
    a. Show that the following matrix is idempotent:

$$\begin{pmatrix} 2 & -2 & -4 \\ -1 & 3 & 4 \\ 1 & -2 & -3 \end{pmatrix}$$

    b. Show that if $\mathbf{AB} = \mathbf{A}$ and $\mathbf{BA} = \mathbf{B}$, then $\mathbf{A}$ and $\mathbf{B}$ are both idempotent.
    c. Show that if $\mathbf{A}$ is idempotent, then $\mathbf{A}^n = \mathbf{A}$ for all positive integers n.

Harder Problems

8. Suppose $\mathbf{A} = \begin{pmatrix} a & b \\ c & d \end{pmatrix}$.
    a. Show that $\mathbf{A}^2 = (a + d)\mathbf{A} - (ad - bc)\mathbf{I}_2$.
    b. Use part (a) to show that $\mathbf{A}^3 = \mathbf{0}$ implies $\mathbf{A}^2 = \mathbf{0}$. (*Hint:* Multiply the equality in part (a) by $\mathbf{A}$, and use the equality $\mathbf{A}^3 = \mathbf{0}$ to derive an equation, which you should then multiply by $\mathbf{A}$ once again.)
    c. Give an example of a matrix $\mathbf{A}$ such that $\mathbf{A}^2 = \mathbf{A}^3 = \mathbf{0}$, but $\mathbf{A} \neq \mathbf{0}$.

12.9 The Transpose

Suppose we interchange the rows and columns of an $m \times n$ matrix $\mathbf{A}$ so that the first row becomes the first column, and so on. We call the new matrix the **transpose** of $\mathbf{A}$. This new matrix is of order $n \times m$ and is denoted by $\mathbf{A}'$ (or $\mathbf{A}^T$). Thus,

$$\mathbf{A} = \begin{pmatrix} a_{11} & a_{12} & \cdots & a_{1n} \\ a_{21} & a_{22} & \cdots & a_{2n} \\ \vdots & \vdots & & \vdots \\ a_{m1} & a_{m2} & \cdots & a_{mn} \end{pmatrix} \implies \mathbf{A}' = \begin{pmatrix} a_{11} & a_{21} & \cdots & a_{m1} \\ a_{12} & a_{22} & \cdots & a_{m2} \\ \vdots & \vdots & & \vdots \\ a_{1n} & a_{2n} & \cdots & a_{mn} \end{pmatrix} \quad [12.43]$$

So we can write $\mathbf{A}' = (a'_{ij})$, where $a'_{ij} = a_{ji}$. The subscripts i and j have to be interchanged.

Example 12.27

Let

$$\mathbf{A} = \begin{pmatrix} -1 & 0 \\ 2 & 3 \\ 5 & -1 \end{pmatrix}, \qquad \mathbf{B} = \begin{pmatrix} 1 & -1 & 0 & 4 \\ 2 & 1 & 1 & 1 \end{pmatrix}$$

Find $\mathbf{A}'$ and $\mathbf{B}'$.

Solution

$$\mathbf{A}' = \begin{pmatrix} -1 & 2 & 5 \\ 0 & 3 & -1 \end{pmatrix}, \qquad \mathbf{B}' = \begin{pmatrix} 1 & 2 \\ -1 & 1 \\ 0 & 1 \\ 4 & 1 \end{pmatrix}$$

The following rules apply to transpose matrices:

Rules for Transposition

$$(\mathbf{A}')' = \mathbf{A} \qquad \text{(a)}$$

$$(\mathbf{A} + \mathbf{B})' = \mathbf{A}' + \mathbf{B}' \qquad \text{(b)} \qquad [12.44]$$

$$(\alpha\mathbf{A})' = \alpha\mathbf{A}' \qquad \text{(c)}$$

$$(\mathbf{AB})' = \mathbf{B}'\mathbf{A}' \qquad \text{(d)}$$

Verifying the first three rules is very easy, and you should prove them in detail. To prove rule (d), suppose that $\mathbf{A}$ is $m \times n$ and $\mathbf{B}$ is $n \times p$. Then $\mathbf{A}'$ is $n \times m$, $\mathbf{B}'$ is $p \times n$,

AB is $m \times p$, $(\mathbf{AB})'$ is $p \times m$, and $\mathbf{B}'\mathbf{A}'$ is $p \times m$. Thus, $(\mathbf{AB})'$ and $\mathbf{B}'\mathbf{A}'$ have the same order. It remains to prove that corresponding elements in the two matrices are equal.

The rs element in $(\mathbf{AB})'$ is the sr element in **AB**, which is the following scalar product of the sth row vector in **A** with the rth column vector in **B**:

$$a_{s1}b_{1r} + a_{s2}b_{2r} + \cdots + a_{sn}b_{nr} \qquad [1]$$

On the other hand, the rs element in $\mathbf{B}'\mathbf{A}'$ is the following scalar product of the rth row vector in $\mathbf{B}'$ (which is the rth column $(b_{1r}, b_{2r}, \ldots, b_{nr})$ of **B**) by the sth column vector in $\mathbf{A}'$ (which is the sth row $(a_{s1}, a_{s2}, \ldots, a_{sn})$ of **A**):

$$b_{1r}a_{s1} + b_{2r}a_{s2} + \cdots + b_{nr}a_{sn} \qquad [2]$$

The two sums in [1] and [2] are clearly equal; indeed, [2] is also the scalar product of the sth row vector in **A** with the rth column vector in **B**. So we have proved rule [12.44](d).

Symmetric Matrices

Square matrices with the property that they are symmetric about the main diagonal are called **symmetric**. For example,

$$\begin{pmatrix} -3 & 2 \\ 2 & 0 \end{pmatrix}, \qquad \begin{pmatrix} 2 & -1 & 5 \\ -1 & -3 & 2 \\ 5 & 2 & 8 \end{pmatrix}, \qquad \begin{pmatrix} a & b & c \\ b & d & e \\ c & e & f \end{pmatrix}$$

are all symmetric. Symmetric matrices are characterized by the fact that they are equal to their own transposes:

The matrix **A** is **symmetric** $\iff$ $\mathbf{A} = \mathbf{A}'$ $\qquad$ [12.45]

Hence, matrix $\mathbf{A} = (a_{ij})_{n \times n}$ is symmetric iff $a_{ij} = a_{ji}$ for all i, j.

Example 12.28

If **X** is an arbitrary $m \times n$ matrix, show that $\mathbf{XX}'$ and $\mathbf{X}'\mathbf{X}$ are both symmetric.

Solution First, note that $\mathbf{XX}'$ is $m \times m$, whereas $\mathbf{X}'\mathbf{X}$ is $n \times n$. Let **Z** denote $\mathbf{X}'$. We obtain

$$(\mathbf{XX}')' = (\mathbf{XZ})' = \mathbf{Z}'\mathbf{X}' = (\mathbf{X}')'\mathbf{X}' = \mathbf{XX}'$$

$$(\mathbf{X}'\mathbf{X})' = (\mathbf{ZX})' = \mathbf{X}'\mathbf{Z}' = \mathbf{X}'(\mathbf{X}')' = \mathbf{X}'\mathbf{X}$$

where we have used the transposition rules [12.44](d) and (a). It follows that $\mathbf{X}'\mathbf{X}$ and $\mathbf{XX}'$ are symmetric.

Problems

1. Find the transposes of $\mathbf{A} = \begin{pmatrix} 3 & 5 & 8 & 3 \\ -1 & 2 & 6 & 4 \end{pmatrix}$ $\mathbf{B} = \begin{pmatrix} 0 \\ 1 \\ -1 \\ 2 \end{pmatrix}$

2. Let $\mathbf{A} = \begin{pmatrix} 3 & 2 \\ -1 & 5 \end{pmatrix}$, $\mathbf{B} = \begin{pmatrix} 0 & 2 \\ 2 & 2 \end{pmatrix}$, $\alpha = -2$. Compute $\mathbf{A}'$, $\mathbf{B}'$, $(\mathbf{A} + \mathbf{B})'$, $(\alpha\mathbf{A})'$, $\mathbf{AB}$, $(\mathbf{AB})'$, $\mathbf{B}'\mathbf{A}'$, and $\mathbf{A}'\mathbf{B}'$. Then verify all the rules in [12.44] for these particular values of $\mathbf{A}$, $\mathbf{B}$, and α.

3. Show that $\mathbf{A} = \begin{pmatrix} 3 & 2 & 3 \\ 2 & -1 & 1 \\ 3 & 1 & 0 \end{pmatrix}$ and $\mathbf{B} = \begin{pmatrix} 0 & 4 & 8 \\ 4 & 0 & 13 \\ 8 & 13 & 0 \end{pmatrix}$ are symmetric.

4. For what values of a is $\begin{pmatrix} a & a^2 - 1 & -3 \\ a+1 & 2 & a^2+4 \\ -3 & 4a & -1 \end{pmatrix}$ symmetric?

5. Is the product of two symmetric matrices necessarily symmetric?

6. **a.** If $\mathbf{A}_1$, $\mathbf{A}_2$, and $\mathbf{A}_3$ are matrices for which the given products are defined, show that

$$(\mathbf{A}_1\mathbf{A}_2\mathbf{A}_3)' = \mathbf{A}_3'\mathbf{A}_2'\mathbf{A}_1'$$

   b. Show by induction that

$$(\mathbf{A}_1\mathbf{A}_2 \cdots \mathbf{A}_n)' = \mathbf{A}_n' \cdots \mathbf{A}_2'\mathbf{A}_1'$$

   when all the matrix products are defined.

7. An $n \times n$ matrix $\mathbf{P}$ is said to be **orthogonal** if $\mathbf{P}'\mathbf{P} = \mathbf{I}_n$.

   a. For $\lambda = 1/\sqrt{2}$ show that $\mathbf{P} = \begin{pmatrix} \lambda & 0 & \lambda \\ \lambda & 0 & -\lambda \\ 0 & 1 & 0 \end{pmatrix}$ is orthogonal.

   b. Show that the 2×2 matrix $\begin{pmatrix} p & -q \\ q & p \end{pmatrix}$ is orthogonal iff $p^2 + q^2 = 1$.

   c. Show that the product of two orthogonal matrices is orthogonal.

   d. Show that any two different columns of an orthogonal matrix are orthogonal vectors, as are any two different rows. (*Hint:* Recall definition [12.18] in Section 12.4.)

Harder Problems

8. If $\mathbf{A} = (a_{ij})$ is an $n \times n$ matrix, the **trace** $\mathrm{tr}(\mathbf{A})$ of $\mathbf{A}$ is defined by

$$\mathrm{tr}(\mathbf{A}) = \sum_{i=1}^{n} a_{ii}$$

Thus, $\mathrm{tr}(\mathbf{A})$ is the sum of the diagonal elements of $\mathbf{A}$. Show that if $\mathbf{A}$ and $\mathbf{B}$ are $n \times n$ matrices, then:

   a. $\mathrm{tr}(\mathbf{A} + \mathbf{B}) = \mathrm{tr}(\mathbf{A}) + \mathrm{tr}(\mathbf{B})$

   b. $\mathrm{tr}(c\mathbf{A}) = c\ \mathrm{tr}(\mathbf{A})$ (c is a scalar)

   c. $\mathrm{tr}(\mathbf{AB}) = \mathrm{tr}(\mathbf{BA})$

   d. $\mathrm{tr}(\mathbf{A}') = \mathrm{tr}(\mathbf{A})$

9. Let $\mathbf{A}$ be a 2×2 matrix for which $\mathbf{A}^2 = \mathbf{0}$. Show that $\mathrm{tr}(\mathbf{A}) = 0$.

13

Determinants and Matrix Inversion

Cayley's matrices (1857) have flourished and today constitute a very important and useful instrument in mathematics.
—Howard Eves (1979)

This chapter continues the study of linear algebra. The first topic discussed is *determinants*. Though some economists have claimed that determinants are almost useless, we shall see that they do in fact play an important role in several areas of mathematics that are of interest to economists.

After introducing determinants, we consider the fundamentally important concept of the *inverse* of a square matrix and its main properties. Cramer's rule for the solution of a system of n linear equations and n unknowns is discussed next. Although it is not efficient for solving systems of equations with more than three unknowns, Cramer's rule is often used in theoretical studies.

13.1 Determinants of Order 2

Consider the system of linear equations:

$$a_{11}x_1 + a_{12}x_2 = b_1$$
$$a_{21}x_1 + a_{22}x_2 = b_2$$

[13.1]

Its associated coefficient matrix is

$$\mathbf{A} = \begin{pmatrix} a_{11} & a_{12} \\ a_{21} & a_{22} \end{pmatrix} \qquad [13.2]$$

Solving the equation system [13.1] in the usual way (see Section A.9) yields

$$x_1 = \frac{b_1 a_{22} - b_2 a_{12}}{a_{11} a_{22} - a_{21} a_{12}}, \qquad x_2 = \frac{b_2 a_{11} - b_1 a_{21}}{a_{11} a_{22} - a_{21} a_{12}} \qquad [13.3]$$

The two fractions have a common denominator. This number, $a_{11}a_{22} - a_{21}a_{12}$, is called the **determinant** of the matrix **A**. Note that if this number is zero, then the expressions for x_1 and x_2 become meaningless—indeed, in this case, the equation system [13.1] has either no solutions or else infinitely many solutions.

The determinant of **A** is denoted by either det(**A**) or |**A**|. Thus,

$$|\mathbf{A}| = \begin{vmatrix} a_{11} & a_{12} \\ a_{21} & a_{22} \end{vmatrix} = a_{11}a_{22} - a_{21}a_{12} \qquad [13.4]$$

for any 2×2 matrix **A**. Such a determinant is said to have **order** 2. For the special case of order 2 determinants, the rule for calculating |**A**| is: (a) multiply the diagonal elements, (b) multiply the off-diagonal elements, and (c) subtract the product of the off-diagonal elements from the product of the diagonal elements.

Example 13.1

$$\begin{vmatrix} 4 & 1 \\ 3 & 2 \end{vmatrix} = 4 \cdot 2 - 3 \cdot 1 = 5, \qquad \begin{vmatrix} b_1 & a_{12} \\ b_2 & a_{22} \end{vmatrix} = b_1 a_{22} - b_2 a_{12}, \qquad \begin{vmatrix} a_{11} & b_1 \\ a_{21} & b_2 \end{vmatrix} = b_2 a_{11} - b_1 a_{21}$$

Note: Geometrically, each of the two equations represents [13.1] represents the graph of a straight line. If |**A**| $\neq$ 0, the two lines intersect at a unique point. If |**A**| $= 0$, either the two lines are parallel and there are no solutions, or the two lines coincide and there is an infinite number of solutions.

From Example 13.1, we see that the *numerators* of the expressions for x_1 and x_2 in [13.3] can also be written as determinants. If |**A**| $\neq$ 0, then

$$x_1 = \frac{\begin{vmatrix} b_1 & a_{12} \\ b_2 & a_{22} \end{vmatrix}}{|\mathbf{A}|}, \qquad x_2 = \frac{\begin{vmatrix} a_{11} & b_1 \\ a_{21} & b_2 \end{vmatrix}}{|\mathbf{A}|} \qquad [13.5]$$

This is a special case of a result referred to as **Cramer's rule** (named after the Swiss mathematician G. Cramer, 1704–1752). It turns out that a similar rule applies to three equations with three unknowns (see the next section). Later in Section 13.8, we shall generalize the rule to n equations in n unknowns.

Example 13.2

Use [13.5] to find the solutions of

$$2x_1 + 4x_2 = 7$$
$$2x_1 - 2x_2 = -2$$

Solution

$$x_1 = \frac{\begin{vmatrix} 7 & 4 \\ -2 & -2 \end{vmatrix}}{\begin{vmatrix} 2 & 4 \\ 2 & -2 \end{vmatrix}} = \frac{-6}{-12} = \frac{1}{2}, \qquad x_2 = \frac{\begin{vmatrix} 2 & 7 \\ 2 & -2 \end{vmatrix}}{\begin{vmatrix} 2 & 4 \\ 2 & -2 \end{vmatrix}} = \frac{-18}{-12} = \frac{3}{2}$$

Check by substitution that $x_1 = 1/2$, $x_2 = 3/2$ really is a solution.

Example 13.3

Use [13.5] to find Q_1^D and Q_2^D in terms of the parameters when

$$2(b + \beta_1)Q_1^D + bQ_2^D = a - \alpha_1$$
$$bQ_1^D + 2(b + \beta_2)Q_2^D = a - \alpha_2$$

Solution   The determinant of the coefficient matrix is

$$\Delta = \begin{vmatrix} 2(b + \beta_1) & b \\ b & 2(b + \beta_2) \end{vmatrix} = 4(b + \beta_1)(b + \beta_2) - b^2$$

Provided $\Delta \neq 0$, by [13.5] the solutions are

$$Q_1^D = \frac{\begin{vmatrix} a - \alpha_1 & b \\ a - \alpha_2 & 2(b + \beta_2) \end{vmatrix}}{\Delta} = \frac{2(b + \beta_2)(a - \alpha_1) - b(a - \alpha_2)}{\Delta}$$

$$Q_2^D = \frac{\begin{vmatrix} 2(b + \beta_1) & a - \alpha_1 \\ b & a - \alpha_2 \end{vmatrix}}{\Delta} = \frac{2(b + \beta_1)(a - \alpha_2) - b(a - \alpha_1)}{\Delta}$$

This example illustrates the convenience of Cramer's rule when several parameters are involved.

A Geometric Interpretation

Determinants of order 2 have a nice geometric interpretation, as shown in Fig. 13.1. If the two vectors are situated as in Fig. 13.1, then the determinant is equal to the shaded area of the parallelogram. If we interchange the two row vectors in the

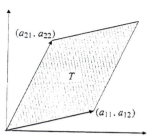

FIGURE 13.1   Area =

$$\pm \begin{vmatrix} a_{11} & a_{12} \\ a_{21} & a_{22} \end{vmatrix}.$$

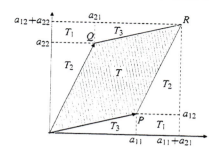

FIGURE 13.2

determinant, then it becomes a negative number whose absolute value is equal to the shaded area.

Figure 13.2 illustrates why the result claimed in Fig. 13.1 is true. We want to find area T. Note that $2T_1 + 2T_2 + 2T_3 + T = (a_{11} + a_{21})(a_{12} + a_{22})$, where $T_1 = a_{12}a_{21}$, $T_2 = \frac{1}{2}a_{21}a_{22}$, and $T_3 = \frac{1}{2}a_{11}a_{12}$. Then $T = a_{11}a_{22} - a_{21}a_{12}$, by elementary algebra.

Problems

1. Compute the following determinants:

   a. $\begin{vmatrix} 3 & 0 \\ 2 & 6 \end{vmatrix}$ **b.** $\begin{vmatrix} a & a \\ b & b \end{vmatrix}$ **c.** $\begin{vmatrix} a+b & a-b \\ a-b & a+b \end{vmatrix}$ **d.** $\begin{vmatrix} 3^t & 2^t \\ 3^{t-1} & 2^{t-1} \end{vmatrix}$

2. Illustrate the geometric interpretation in Fig. 13.1 for the determinant in Problem 1(a).

3. Use Cramer's rule [13.5] to solve the following systems of equations for x and y. Test the answers by substitution.

   a. $3x_1 - x_2 = 8$ **b.** $x + 3y = 1$ **c.** $ax - by = 1$

       $x_1 - 2x_2 = 5$ $3x - 2y = 14$ $bx + ay = 2$

4. Let

   $$A = \begin{pmatrix} a_{11} & a_{12} \\ a_{21} & a_{22} \end{pmatrix} \quad \text{and} \quad B = \begin{pmatrix} b_{11} & b_{12} \\ b_{21} & b_{22} \end{pmatrix}$$

   Show that $|AB| = |A| \cdot |B|$.

5. Find two 2×2 matrices A and B such that $|A + B| \neq |A| + |B|$.

6. Use Cramer's rule to find Y and C when

   $$Y = C + I_0 + G_0 \qquad C = a + bY$$

   where Y is national product and C is private consumption. The symbols I_0 (private investment), G_0 (public consumption and investment), a, and b all represent constants, with $b < 1$. (Actually, this is a typical case in which one should *not* use Cramer's rule, because Y and C can be found much more simply. How?)

7. Consider the following linked macroeconomic model of two nations, $i = 1, 2$, that trade with each other:

$$Y_1 = C_1 + A_1 + X_1 - M_1, \qquad C_1 = c_1 Y_1, \qquad M_1 = m_1 Y_1$$
$$Y_2 = C_2 + A_2 + X_2 - M_2, \qquad C_2 = c_2 Y_2, \qquad M_2 = m_2 Y_2$$

Here, for $i = 1, 2$, Y_i is income, C_i is consumption, A_i is (exogenous) autonomous expenditure, X_i denotes exports, and M_i denotes imports of country i.

   a. Interpret the two equations $X_1 = M_2$ and $X_2 = M_1$.

   b. Given the equations in part (a), calculate the corresponding equilibrium values of Y_1 and Y_2 as functions of the exogenous variables.

   c. How does an increase in A_1 affect Y_2? Interpret your answer.

8. Let the matrix $\mathbf{A}(t)$ be defined for every t by $\mathbf{A}(t) = \begin{pmatrix} t^2 & 2t - 1 \\ 2t & 2 \end{pmatrix}$.

   Evaluate the determinant $|\mathbf{A}(t)|$ and find the values of t for which $|\mathbf{A}(t)| = 0$.

9. Let $a(t)$ and $b(t)$ be twice differentiable functions. Prove that

$$\frac{d}{dt} \begin{vmatrix} a(t) & b(t) \\ a'(t) & b'(t) \end{vmatrix} = \begin{vmatrix} a(t) & b(t) \\ a''(t) & b''(t) \end{vmatrix}$$

Verify this rule for the determinant $|\mathbf{A}(t)|$ in Problem 8.

13.2 Determinants of Order 3

Consider the system of three linear equations in three unknowns:

$$a_{11}x_1 + a_{12}x_2 + a_{13}x_3 = b_1$$
$$a_{21}x_1 + a_{22}x_2 + a_{23}x_3 = b_2 \qquad \text{[13.6]}$$
$$a_{31}x_1 + a_{32}x_2 + a_{33}x_3 = b_3$$

Here the coefficient matrix $\mathbf{A}$ is 3×3. By applying the method of elimination along with some rather heavy algebraic computation, eventually this system can be solved for x_1, x_2, and x_3. The resulting expression for x_1 is

$$x_1 = \frac{b_1 a_{22} a_{33} - b_1 a_{23} a_{32} - b_2 a_{12} a_{33} + b_2 a_{13} a_{32} + b_3 a_{12} a_{23} - b_3 a_{22} a_{13}}{a_{11} a_{22} a_{33} - a_{11} a_{23} a_{32} + a_{12} a_{23} a_{31} - a_{12} a_{21} a_{33} + a_{13} a_{21} a_{32} - a_{13} a_{22} a_{31}}$$

We shall not triple the demands on the reader's patience and eyesight by giving the corresponding expressions for x_2 and x_3. However, we do claim that these expressions share the same denominator as that given for x_1. This common denominator is called the **determinant** of $\mathbf{A}$, denoted by $\det(\mathbf{A})$ or $|\mathbf{A}|$. It is defined as

$$
|\mathbf{A}| = \begin{vmatrix} a_{11} & a_{12} & a_{13} \\ a_{21} & a_{22} & a_{23} \\ a_{31} & a_{32} & a_{33} \end{vmatrix}
$$

$$
= \begin{cases} a_{11}a_{22}a_{33} - a_{11}a_{23}a_{32} + a_{12}a_{23}a_{31} \\ \quad - a_{12}a_{21}a_{33} + a_{13}a_{21}a_{32} - a_{13}a_{22}a_{31} \end{cases} \tag{13.7}
$$

Expansion by Cofactors

Consider the sum of the six terms in [13.7]. It looks quite messy, but the method of expansion by cofactors makes it easy to write down all the terms. First, note that each of the three elements a_{11}, a_{12}, and a_{13} in the first row of $\mathbf{A}$ appears in exactly two terms of [13.7]. In fact, $|\mathbf{A}|$ can be written as

$$
|\mathbf{A}| = a_{11}(a_{22}a_{33} - a_{23}a_{32}) - a_{12}(a_{21}a_{33} - a_{23}a_{31}) + a_{13}(a_{21}a_{32} - a_{22}a_{31})
$$

which is the same as

$$
|\mathbf{A}| = a_{11}\begin{vmatrix} a_{22} & a_{23} \\ a_{32} & a_{33} \end{vmatrix} - a_{12}\begin{vmatrix} a_{21} & a_{23} \\ a_{31} & a_{33} \end{vmatrix} + a_{13}\begin{vmatrix} a_{21} & a_{22} \\ a_{31} & a_{32} \end{vmatrix} \tag{13.8}
$$

In this way, the computation of a determinant of order 3 can be reduced to calculating three determinants of order 2. Note that a_{11} is multiplied by the second-order determinant obtained by deleting the *first* row and the *first* column of $|\mathbf{A}|$. Likewise, a_{12}, with a minus sign attached to it, is multiplied by the determinant obtained by deleting the *first* row and the *second* column of $|\mathbf{A}|$. Finally, a_{13} is multiplied by the determinant obtained by deleting the *first* row and the *third* column of $|\mathbf{A}|$.

Example 13.4

Use [13.8] to compute

$$
|\mathbf{A}| = \begin{vmatrix} 3 & 0 & 2 \\ -1 & 1 & 0 \\ 5 & 2 & 3 \end{vmatrix}
$$

Solution

$$
|\mathbf{A}| = 3 \cdot \begin{vmatrix} 1 & 0 \\ 2 & 3 \end{vmatrix} - 0 \cdot \begin{vmatrix} -1 & 0 \\ 5 & 3 \end{vmatrix} + 2 \cdot \begin{vmatrix} -1 & 1 \\ 5 & 2 \end{vmatrix}
$$

$$
= 3 \cdot 3 - 0 + 2 \cdot (-2 - 5) = -5
$$

Example 13.5

Use [13.8] to prove that

$$|\mathbf{A}| = \begin{vmatrix} 1 & a & a^2 \\ 1 & b & b^2 \\ 1 & c & c^2 \end{vmatrix}$$

$$= (b - a)(c - a)(c - b)$$

Solution

$$|\mathbf{A}| = 1 \cdot \begin{vmatrix} b & b^2 \\ c & c^2 \end{vmatrix} - a \cdot \begin{vmatrix} 1 & b^2 \\ 1 & c^2 \end{vmatrix} + a^2 \cdot \begin{vmatrix} 1 & b \\ 1 & c \end{vmatrix}$$

$$= bc^2 - b^2c - ac^2 + ab^2 + a^2c - a^2b$$

You are not expected to see at once that these six terms can be written as $(b - a)(c - a)(c - b)$. Rather, you should expand $(b - a)[(c - a)(c - b)]$ and verify the equality in that way.

A determinant can be expanded in terms of the elements of any row or column. We shall give a full discussion of this in Section 13.5.

A careful study of the numerator in the expression for x_1 in the beginning of this section reveals that it can also be written as a determinant. The same is true of the corresponding formulas for x_2 and x_3. In fact, if $|\mathbf{A}| \neq 0$, then one has

$$x_1 = \frac{\begin{vmatrix} b_1 & a_{12} & a_{13} \\ b_2 & a_{22} & a_{23} \\ b_3 & a_{32} & a_{33} \end{vmatrix}}{|\mathbf{A}|}, \quad x_2 = \frac{\begin{vmatrix} a_{11} & b_1 & a_{13} \\ a_{21} & b_2 & a_{23} \\ a_{31} & b_3 & a_{33} \end{vmatrix}}{|\mathbf{A}|}, \quad x_3 = \frac{\begin{vmatrix} a_{11} & a_{12} & b_1 \\ a_{21} & a_{22} & b_2 \\ a_{31} & a_{32} & b_3 \end{vmatrix}}{|\mathbf{A}|}$$

$$[13.9]$$

This is Cramer's rule for the solution of [13.6] (see Section 13.8).

Note: In the determinants appearing in the numerators of x_1, x_2, and x_3 of [13.9], observe how the right-hand column in [13.6],

$$\begin{pmatrix} b_1 \\ b_2 \\ b_3 \end{pmatrix}$$

shifts from the first column when solving for x_1, to the second column when solving for x_2, and then to the third column when solving for x_3. This makes it very easy to remember Cramer's rule.

Example 13.6

Solve the following system of equations by using [13.9]:

$$
\begin{aligned}
2x_1 + 2x_2 - x_3 &= -3 \\
4x_1 + 2x_3 &= 8 \\
6x_2 - 3x_3 &= -12
\end{aligned}
$$

Solution   In this case, the determinant $|A|$ in [13.9] is

$$
|A| = \begin{vmatrix} 2 & 2 & -1 \\ 4 & 0 & 2 \\ 0 & 6 & -3 \end{vmatrix} = -24
$$

The numerators in [13.9] are

$$
\begin{vmatrix} -3 & 2 & -1 \\ 8 & 0 & 2 \\ -12 & 6 & -3 \end{vmatrix} = -12, \quad
\begin{vmatrix} 2 & -3 & -1 \\ 4 & 8 & 2 \\ 0 & -12 & -3 \end{vmatrix} = 12, \quad
\begin{vmatrix} 2 & 2 & -3 \\ 4 & 0 & 8 \\ 0 & 6 & -12 \end{vmatrix} = -72
$$

Hence, [13.9] yields the solution $x_1 = (-12)/(-24) = 1/2$, $x_2 = 12/(-24) = -1/2$, and $x_3 = (-72)/(-24) = 3$. Inserting this into the original system of equations confirms that this is a correct answer.

A Geometric Interpretation

Like determinants of order 2, those of order 3 also have a geometric interpretation that is shown and explained in Fig. 13.3.

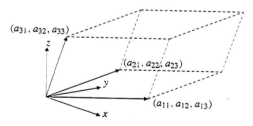

FIGURE 13.3 $\pm \begin{vmatrix} a_{11} & a_{12} & a_{13} \\ a_{21} & a_{22} & a_{23} \\ a_{31} & a_{32} & a_{33} \end{vmatrix} = \left\{ \begin{array}{l} \text{the volume of the} \\ \text{"box" spanned by} \\ \text{the three vectors} \end{array} \right.$

Sarrus' Rule

Here is an alternative way of evaluating determinants of order 3 that many people find convenient. Write down the determinant twice, except that the second time the last column of the second determinant should be omitted:

$$
\begin{vmatrix}
a_{11} & a_{12} & a_{13} & a_{11} & a_{12} \\
a_{21} & a_{22} & a_{23} & a_{21} & a_{22} \\
a_{31} & a_{32} & a_{33} & a_{31} & a_{32}
\end{vmatrix} \qquad\qquad [13.10]
$$

First, multiply along the three lines falling to the right, giving all these products a plus sign:

$$ a_{11}a_{22}a_{33} + a_{12}a_{23}a_{31} + a_{13}a_{21}a_{32} \qquad\qquad [*] $$

Then multiply along the three lines rising to the right, giving all these products a minus sign:

$$ -a_{31}a_{22}a_{13} - a_{32}a_{23}a_{11} - a_{33}a_{21}a_{12} \qquad\qquad [**] $$

The sum of the terms in [*] and [**] is exactly equal to $|\mathbf{A}|$. (It is important to note that this rule, known as *Sarrus' rule*, *does not generalize* to determinants of order higher than 3.)

Problems

1. Compute the following:

   a. $\begin{vmatrix} 1 & -1 & 0 \\ 1 & 3 & 2 \\ 1 & 0 & 0 \end{vmatrix}$
   b. $\begin{vmatrix} 1 & -1 & 0 \\ 1 & 3 & 2 \\ 1 & 2 & 1 \end{vmatrix}$
   c. $\begin{vmatrix} a & b & c \\ 0 & d & e \\ 0 & 0 & f \end{vmatrix}$
   d. $\begin{vmatrix} a & 0 & b \\ 0 & e & 0 \\ c & 0 & d \end{vmatrix}$

2. Let

   $$ \mathbf{A} = \begin{pmatrix} 1 & -1 & 0 \\ 1 & 3 & 2 \\ 1 & 2 & 1 \end{pmatrix} \quad \text{and} \quad \mathbf{B} = \begin{pmatrix} 1 & 2 & 3 \\ 2 & 3 & 4 \\ 0 & 1 & -1 \end{pmatrix} $$

   Compute $\mathbf{AB}$, $|\mathbf{A}|$, $|\mathbf{B}|$, $|\mathbf{A}| \cdot |\mathbf{B}|$, and $|\mathbf{AB}|$.

3. Use Cramer's rule to solve the following systems of equations. Check your answers.

   a. $x_1 - x_2 + x_3 = 2$
   $x_1 + x_2 - x_3 = 0$
   $-x_1 - x_2 - x_3 = -6$

   b. $x_1 - x_2 = 0$
   $x_1 + 3x_2 + 2x_3 = 0$
   $x_1 + 2x_2 + x_3 = 0$

   c. $x + 3y - 2z = 1$
   $3x - 2y + 5z = 14$
   $2x - 5y + 3z = 1$

4. Show that

$$
\begin{vmatrix}
1+a & 1 & 1 \\
1 & 1+b & 1 \\
1 & 1 & 1+c
\end{vmatrix} = abc + ab + ac + bc
$$

5. Consider the simple macro model described by the three equations

$$Y = C + A_0, \qquad C = a + b(Y - T), \qquad T = d + tY$$

where Y is income, C is consumption, T is tax revenue, A_0 is the constant (exogenous) autonomous expenditure, and a, b, d, and t are all positive parameters. Find the equilibrium values of the endogenous variables Y, C, and T by

(a) successive elimination or substitution

(b) writing the equations in matrix form and applying Cramer's rule.

6. Prove that

$$\begin{vmatrix} a_{11} & a_{12} & a_{13} \\ a_{31} & a_{32} & a_{33} \\ a_{21} & a_{22} & a_{23} \end{vmatrix} = - \begin{vmatrix} a_{11} & a_{12} & a_{13} \\ a_{21} & a_{22} & a_{23} \\ a_{31} & a_{32} & a_{33} \end{vmatrix}$$

(Thus, interchanging rows 2 and 3 of the determinant changes its sign.)

13.3 Determinants of Order *n*

This section gives an alternative definition of a determinant that is particularly useful when proving general results. If you are not so interested in these proofs, you might skip this section and rely instead on expansions by cofactors in all your work on determinants, as explained in Section 13.5.

For a 3×3 matrix $\mathbf{A} = (a_{ij})_{3\times3}$, [13.7] defined the determinant $|\mathbf{A}|$ as

$$a_{11}a_{22}a_{33} - a_{11}a_{23}a_{32} + a_{12}a_{23}a_{31} - a_{12}a_{21}a_{33} + a_{13}a_{21}a_{32} - a_{13}a_{22}a_{31} \qquad [*]$$

A closer examination of this sum reveals a definite pattern. Each term is the product of three different elements of the matrix. Each product contains one element from each row of $\mathbf{A}$ and one element from each column of $\mathbf{A}$. In fact, the elements in the six terms are chosen from the matrix $\mathbf{A}$ according to the pattern shown in Fig. 13.4 (disregard the lines for a moment).

In a 3×3 matrix, there are precisely six different ways of picking three elements with one element from each row and one element from each column. All the six corresponding products appear in [*]. How do we determine the sign of

FIGURE 13.4

the terms in [∗]? By using the lines drawn in each of the six boxes, the following rule emerges:[1]

The Sign Rule

To determine the sign of any term in the sum, mark in the array all the elements appearing in that term. We could join all possible pairs of these elements with lines. These lines will then either fall or rise. Now mark only those lines that rise toward the right. If the number of these rising lines is even, then the corresponding term is assigned a plus sign; if it is odd, it is assigned a minus sign.

[13.11]

Let us apply this rule to the six boxes in Fig. 13.4: In the first box, no lines rise, so $a_{11}a_{22}a_{33}$ has a plus sign. In the fourth box, exactly one line rises, so $a_{12}a_{21}a_{33}$ has a minus sign. And so on.

Suppose $\mathbf{A} = (a_{ij})_{n \times n}$ is an arbitrary $n \times n$ matrix. Suppose we pick n elements from $\mathbf{A}$, including exactly one element from each row and exactly one element from each column. Take the product of these n elements, giving an expression of the form $a_{1r_1}a_{2r_2}\cdots a_{nr_n}$. Here $r_1, r_2, \ldots, r_n$ represents a reshuffling (or permutation) of the numbers $1, 2, \ldots, n$. The numbers $1, 2, \ldots, n$ can be permuted in $n! = 1 \cdot 2 \cdots (n-1)n$ different ways: For the first element, there are n choices; for each of these first choices, there are $n - 1$ choices for the second element; and so on.

Now we define the determinant of $\mathbf{A}$, $\det \mathbf{A}$ or $|\mathbf{A}|$, as follows:

$|\mathbf{A}|$ is a sum of $n!$ terms where:

1. Each term is the product of n elements of the matrix, with one element from each row and one element from each column. Moreover, every product of exactly n factors, in which each row and each column is represented exactly once, must appear in this sum.

2. The sign of each term is found by applying the sign rule [13.11].

[13.12]

---

[1]The sign rule in [13.11] is described in a somewhat unusual way. However, it is equivalent to the sign rule based on the concepts of even and odd permutations that is used in most books on linear algebra.

In symbols, one has

$$|\mathbf{A}| = \begin{vmatrix} a_{11} & a_{12} & \cdots & a_{1n} \\ a_{21} & a_{22} & \cdots & a_{2n} \\ \vdots & \vdots & \ddots & \vdots \\ a_{n1} & a_{n2} & \cdots & a_{nn} \end{vmatrix}$$

$$= \sum (\pm) a_{1r_1} a_{2r_2} \cdots a_{nr_n}$$

[13.13]

Example 13.7

Consider the determinant of an arbitrary 4×4 matrix $\mathbf{A} = (a_{ij})_{4\times4}$:

$$|\mathbf{A}| = \begin{vmatrix} a_{11} & a_{12} & a_{13} & a_{14} \\ a_{21} & a_{22} & a_{23} & a_{24} \\ a_{31} & a_{32} & a_{33} & a_{34} \\ a_{41} & a_{42} & a_{43} & a_{44} \end{vmatrix}$$

It consists of $4! = 4 \cdot 3 \cdot 2 \cdot 1 = 24$ terms. One of these terms is $a_{13}a_{21}a_{32}a_{44}$, and the corresponding factors are the boxed elements in the array. What sign should this term have? According to the sign rule [13.11], the term should have a plus sign because there are exactly two lines that rise to the right. Check that the four indicated terms in the following sum have been given the correct sign:

$$|\mathbf{A}| = a_{11}a_{22}a_{33}a_{44} - a_{12}a_{21}a_{33}a_{44} + \cdots + a_{13}a_{21}a_{32}a_{44} - \cdots + a_{14}a_{23}a_{32}a_{41}$$

Note that there are 20 other terms that we have left out.

The determinant of an $n \times n$ matrix is called a **determinant of order** n. In general, it is difficult to evaluate determinants by using definition [13.12], even if n is only 4 or 5. If $n > 5$, the work is usually enormous. For example, if $n = 6$, then $n! = 720$, and so there are 720 terms in the sum defining the determinant. Fortunately, other methods are available that reduce the work considerably. Most computers have standard programs for evaluating determinants.

In a few special cases, it is easy to evaluate a determinant even if the order is high. For instance, it is easy to see that

$$\begin{vmatrix} a_{11} & a_{12} & \cdots & a_{1n} \\ 0 & a_{22} & \cdots & a_{2n} \\ \vdots & \vdots & \ddots & \vdots \\ 0 & 0 & \cdots & a_{nn} \end{vmatrix} = a_{11}a_{22}\ldots a_{nn}$$

[13.14]

Here all the elements *below* the main diagonal are 0, and the determinant is the product of all the elements on the main diagonal. To see why, note that in order to have a term that is not 0, we have to choose a_{11} from column 1. From column 2, we cannot choose a_{12}, because we have already picked an element from the first row (a_{11}). Hence, from column 2, we have to pick a_{22} in order to have a term different from 0. From the third column, we have to pick a_{33}, and so on. Thus, only the term $a_{11}a_{22} \cdots a_{nn}$ can be $\neq 0$. The sign of this term is plus because none of the lines between the elements in the term rises.

The matrix whose determinant is given in [13.14] is called *upper triangular*. If a matrix is a transpose of an upper triangular matrix, so that all elements above the diagonal are 0, then the matrix is *lower triangular*. The determinant of a lower triangular matrix is also equal to the product of the elements on its main diagonal.

Problems

1. Use the definition of determinant to compute the following:

a.
$$\begin{vmatrix} 1 & 0 & 0 & 0 \\ 0 & 2 & 0 & 0 \\ 0 & 0 & 3 & 0 \\ 0 & 0 & 0 & 4 \end{vmatrix}$$

b.
$$\begin{vmatrix} 0 & 0 & 0 & 1 \\ 0 & 0 & 1 & 0 \\ 0 & 1 & 0 & 0 \\ 1 & 0 & 0 & 0 \end{vmatrix}$$

c.
$$\begin{vmatrix} 1 & 0 & 0 & 1 \\ 0 & 1 & 0 & 0 \\ 0 & 0 & 1 & 0 \\ a & b & c & d \end{vmatrix}$$

d.
$$\begin{vmatrix} 1 & 0 & 0 & 2 \\ 0 & 1 & 0 & -3 \\ 0 & 0 & 1 & 4 \\ 2 & 3 & 4 & 11 \end{vmatrix}$$

2. The determinant of the following 5×5 matrix consists of $5! = 120$ terms. One of them is the product of the boxed elements. Write this term with its correct sign.

$$\begin{vmatrix} a_{11} & \boxed{a_{12}} & a_{13} & a_{14} & a_{15} \\ a_{21} & a_{22} & \boxed{a_{23}} & a_{24} & a_{25} \\ a_{31} & a_{32} & a_{33} & a_{34} & \boxed{a_{35}} \\ \boxed{a_{41}} & a_{42} & a_{43} & a_{44} & a_{45} \\ a_{51} & a_{52} & a_{53} & \boxed{a_{54}} & a_{55} \end{vmatrix}$$

3. Write the term indicated by the boxes with its correct sign. (See the previous problem.)

$$\begin{vmatrix} a_{11} & a_{12} & a_{13} & a_{14} & \boxed{a_{15}} \\ a_{21} & a_{22} & a_{23} & \boxed{a_{24}} & a_{25} \\ a_{31} & \boxed{a_{32}} & a_{33} & a_{34} & a_{35} \\ a_{41} & a_{42} & \boxed{a_{43}} & a_{44} & a_{45} \\ \boxed{a_{51}} & a_{52} & a_{53} & a_{54} & a_{55} \end{vmatrix}$$

13.4 Basic Rules for Determinants

Based on definition [13.12] of the determinant of an $n \times n$ matrix **A**, one can prove a number of important properties. Certainly, many of these are mainly of theoretical interest, but they also make it simpler to evaluate determinants.

Theorem 13.1   (Rules for Determinants)

1. If each of the entries in one or more rows or columns of **A** is 0, then $|\mathbf{A}| = 0$.

2. The determinant of the transpose of **A** is the same as the determinant of the matrix itself: $|\mathbf{A}| = |\mathbf{A}'|$.

3. If **B** is the matrix obtained by multiplying each entry of one row (or column) of **A** by the same number α, then $|\mathbf{B}| = \alpha |\mathbf{A}|$.

4. If two rows (or columns) of **A** are interchanged, then the determinant changes its sign, but keeps its absolute value.

5. If two rows (or columns) of **A** are equal, then $|\mathbf{A}| = 0$.

6. If two rows (or columns) of **A** are proportional, then $|\mathbf{A}| = 0$.

7. If a scalar multiple of one row (or column) is added to another row (or column), then the value of the determinant does not change.

8. The determinant of the product of two $n \times n$ matrices **A** and **B** is the product of the determinants of each of the factors:

$$|\mathbf{AB}| = |\mathbf{A}| \cdot |\mathbf{B}|$$

[13.15]

9. If **A** is an $n \times n$ matrix and α is a real number, then

$$|\alpha \mathbf{A}| = \alpha^n |\mathbf{A}|$$

[13.16]

Rules 3, 4, and 7 implicitly assume that all other rows (or columns) remain unchanged. It should also be recalled that the determinant of a sum is (usually) *not* the sum of the determinants:

$$|\mathbf{A} + \mathbf{B}| \neq |\mathbf{A}| + |\mathbf{B}|$$

An example of this general inequality was asked for in Problem 5 of Section 13.1.
    Proofs for most of these properties are given at the end of this section. First, however, let us illustrate them in some special cases:

Rule 1: $\begin{vmatrix} a_{11} & a_{12} \\ 0 & 0 \end{vmatrix} = a_{11} \cdot 0 - a_{12} \cdot 0 = 0$

Rule 2: $|\mathbf{A}| = \begin{vmatrix} a_{11} & a_{12} \\ a_{21} & a_{22} \end{vmatrix} = a_{11}a_{22} - a_{12}a_{21}, \quad |\mathbf{A}'| = \begin{vmatrix} a_{11} & a_{21} \\ a_{12} & a_{22} \end{vmatrix} = a_{11}a_{22} - a_{12}a_{21}$

We see that $|\mathbf{A}'|$ has exactly the same terms as $|\mathbf{A}|$. In particular, $|\mathbf{A}'| = |\mathbf{A}|$.

Rule 3: $\begin{vmatrix} a_{11} & a_{12} \\ \alpha a_{21} & \alpha a_{22} \end{vmatrix} = a_{11}(\alpha a_{22}) - a_{12}(\alpha a_{21})$

$$= \alpha(a_{11}a_{22} - a_{12}a_{21}) = \alpha \begin{vmatrix} a_{11} & a_{12} \\ a_{21} & a_{22} \end{vmatrix}$$

Rule 4: $\begin{vmatrix} a_{21} & a_{22} \\ a_{11} & a_{12} \end{vmatrix} = a_{21}a_{12} - a_{11}a_{22} = -(a_{11}a_{22} - a_{12}a_{21}) = - \begin{vmatrix} a_{11} & a_{12} \\ a_{21} & a_{22} \end{vmatrix}$

Rule 5: $\begin{vmatrix} a_{11} & a_{12} \\ a_{11} & a_{12} \end{vmatrix} = a_{11}a_{12} - a_{12}a_{11} = 0$

Let us also see how rule 5 helps to confirm the result in Example 13.5 of Section 13.2. Note that the product $(b - a)(c - a)(c - b)$ is 0 if $b = a$, $c = a$, or $c = b$, and in each of these three cases, two rows of the matrix are equal.

Rule 6: $\begin{vmatrix} a_{11} & a_{12} \\ \beta a_{11} & \beta a_{12} \end{vmatrix} = a_{11}(\beta a_{12}) - a_{12}(\beta a_{11}) = \beta(a_{11}a_{12} - a_{11}a_{12}) = 0$

Rule 7: Multiply each entry in the first row of a determinant of order 2 by α and add the results pairwise to the entries in the second row. Then the determinant does not change its value. (Note carefully how we indicate this operation.)

$$\begin{vmatrix} a_{11} & a_{12} \\ a_{21} & a_{22} \end{vmatrix} \overset{\alpha}{\longleftarrow} = \begin{vmatrix} a_{11} & a_{12} \\ a_{21} + \alpha a_{11} & a_{22} + \alpha a_{12} \end{vmatrix}$$

$$= a_{11}(a_{22} + \alpha a_{12}) - a_{12}(a_{21} + \alpha a_{11})$$

$$= a_{11}a_{22} + \alpha a_{11}a_{12} - a_{12}a_{21} - \alpha a_{12}a_{11} = a_{11}a_{22} - a_{12}a_{21}$$

$$= \begin{vmatrix} a_{11} & a_{12} \\ a_{21} & a_{22} \end{vmatrix}$$

This rule is particularly useful for evaluating determinants. We give two examples.

Example 13.8

$$\begin{vmatrix} 1 & 5 & -1 \\ -1 & 1 & 3 \\ 3 & 2 & 1 \end{vmatrix} \overset{1}{\longleftarrow} = \begin{vmatrix} 1 & 5 & -1 \\ -1+1 & 1+5 & 3+(-1) \\ 3 & 2 & 1 \end{vmatrix} = \begin{vmatrix} 1 & 5 & -1 \\ 0 & 6 & 2 \\ 3 & 2 & 1 \end{vmatrix} \overset{-3}{\longleftarrow}$$

$$= \begin{vmatrix} 1 & 5 & -1 \\ 0 & 6 & 2 \\ 0 & -13 & 4 \end{vmatrix} \overset{13/6}{\longleftarrow} = \begin{vmatrix} 1 & 5 & -1 \\ 0 & 6 & 2 \\ 0 & 0 & 25/3 \end{vmatrix}$$

$$= 1 \cdot 6 \cdot \frac{25}{3} = 50$$

Here, 1 times the first row has been added to the second in order to obtain a zero in the first column. Then (-3) times the first row has been added to the third, which gives a second zero in the first column. Thereafter, 13/6 times the second row has been added to the third, which adds a zero to the second column. Note the way in which we have indicated these operations. In the end, they produce an upper triangular matrix that we evaluate by means of [13.14].

In the next example, the first two steps involve more than one operation simultaneously.

Example 13.9

$$\begin{vmatrix} a+b & a & a \\ a & a+b & a \\ a & a & a+b \end{vmatrix} = \begin{vmatrix} 3a+b & 3a+b & 3a+b \\ a & a+b & a \\ a & a & a+b \end{vmatrix}$$

$$= (3a+b) \begin{vmatrix} 1 & 1 & 1 \\ a & a+b & a \\ a & a & a+b \end{vmatrix} = (3a+b) \begin{vmatrix} 1 & 1 & 1 \\ 0 & b & 0 \\ 0 & 0 & b \end{vmatrix}$$

$$= (3a+b) \cdot 1 \cdot b \cdot b = b^2(3a+b)$$

Rule 8: This is also an important property. If you have done Problem 4 of Section 13.1, you have already proved it for 2×2 matrices. Here is an example involving 3×3 matrices.

Example 13.10

Check that $|\mathbf{A}\mathbf{B}| = |\mathbf{A}| \cdot |\mathbf{B}|$ when

$$\mathbf{A} = \begin{pmatrix} 1 & 5 & -1 \\ -1 & 1 & 3 \\ 3 & 2 & 1 \end{pmatrix} \qquad \mathbf{B} = \begin{pmatrix} 3 & 0 & 2 \\ -1 & 1 & 0 \\ 5 & 2 & 3 \end{pmatrix}$$

Solution   Here $|\mathbf{A}| = 50$ (as in Example 13.8) and $|\mathbf{B}| = -5$. But

$$\mathbf{A}\mathbf{B} = \begin{pmatrix} -7 & 3 & -1 \\ 11 & 7 & 7 \\ 12 & 4 & 9 \end{pmatrix}$$

So we find that $|\mathbf{A}\mathbf{B}| = -250 = |\mathbf{A}| \cdot |\mathbf{B}|$.

Rule 9:
$$\begin{vmatrix} \alpha a_{11} & \alpha a_{12} \\ \alpha a_{21} & \alpha a_{22} \end{vmatrix} = \alpha a_{11} \alpha a_{22} - \alpha a_{12} \alpha a_{21} = \alpha^2(a_{11}a_{22} - a_{12}a_{21})$$

$$= \alpha^2 \begin{vmatrix} a_{11} & a_{12} \\ a_{21} & a_{22} \end{vmatrix}$$

Theorem 13.1 exhibits some of the most important rules for determinants. Confidence in dealing with them comes only from doing many problems.

On the proof of Theorem 13.1:

Rule 1: Each of the $n!$ terms in the determinant is a product that includes an element from at least one row (or column) in which every entry is 0. Hence, each term in the determinant is 0, and so the whole determinant is 0.

Rule 2: Each term in $|\mathbf{A}|$ is the product of entries chosen from $\mathbf{A}$ to include exactly one element from each row and one element from each column. Exactly the same terms, therefore, must appear in $|\mathbf{A}'|$ also.

What about the signs? Consider the following special case, with $n = 5$:

$$|\mathbf{A}| = \begin{vmatrix} a_{11} & a_{12} & a_{13} & a_{14} & a_{15} \\ a_{21} & a_{22} & a_{23} & a_{24} & a_{25} \\ a_{31} & a_{32} & a_{33} & a_{34} & a_{35} \\ a_{41} & a_{42} & a_{43} & a_{44} & a_{45} \\ a_{51} & a_{52} & a_{53} & a_{54} & a_{55} \end{vmatrix}$$

$$|\mathbf{A}'| = \begin{vmatrix} a_{11} & a_{21} & a_{31} & a_{41} & a \\ a_{12} & a_{22} & a_{32} & a_{42} & a_{52} \\ a_{13} & a_{23} & a_{33} & a_{43} & a_{53} \\ a_{14} & a_{24} & a_{34} & a_{44} & a_{54} \\ a_{15} & a_{25} & a_{35} & a_{45} & a_{55} \end{vmatrix}$$

The term $a_{12}a_{23}a_{35}a_{41}a_{54}$ appears in both $|\mathbf{A}|$ and in $|\mathbf{A}'|$. Of those lines joining pairs of entries in $|\mathbf{A}|$, the number that rise to the right is 4, as is the corresponding number of lines in $|\mathbf{A}'|$. This is true in general. Transposing means reflection about the main diagonal $a_{11}a_{22}\ldots a_{nn}$. If the line L joining any two entries in one of the terms of $|\mathbf{A}|$ rises to the right (as it does between a_{41} and a_{35} in the illustration), then the mirror image L' of this line, which joins the same two entries in the corresponding term in $|\mathbf{A}'|$, will also rise to the right and vice versa.

Rule 3: Each term in the sum defining $|\mathbf{B}|$ is α multiplied by the corresponding term in the sum defining $|\mathbf{A}|$. Hence, $|\mathbf{B}| = \alpha|\mathbf{A}|$.

Rule 4: First, consider the case in which two adjacent rows of $|\mathbf{A}|$ are interchanged, namely, rows i and $i + 1$, in order to obtain $|\mathbf{A}_c|$ as indicated in the following display:

$$|\mathbf{A}| = \begin{vmatrix} a_{11} & a_{12} & \cdots & a_{1n} \\ \vdots & \vdots & & \vdots \\ a_{i1} & a_{i2} & \cdots & a_{in} \\ a_{i+1,1} & a_{i+1,2} & \cdots & a_{i+1,n} \\ \vdots & \vdots & & \vdots \\ a_{n1} & a_{n2} & \cdots & a_{nn} \end{vmatrix}$$

$$|\mathbf{A}_c| = \begin{vmatrix} a_{11} & a_{12} & \cdots & \boxed{a_{1n}} \\ \vdots & \vdots & & \vdots \\ a_{i+1.1} & a_{i+1.2} & \cdots & a_{i+1.n} \\ a_{i1} & \boxed{a_{i2}} & \cdots & a_{in} \\ \vdots & \vdots & & \vdots \\ a_{n1} & a_{n2} & \cdots & a_{nn} \end{vmatrix}$$

Using the definitions of $|\mathbf{A}|$ and $|\mathbf{A}_c|$, it is clear that any term appearing in $|\mathbf{A}|$ also appears in $|\mathbf{A}_c|$, and vice versa. What about the sign? Think of the positions of the individual entries of a term in $|\mathbf{A}|$ and of the corresponding term in $|\mathbf{A}_c|$. All the lines joining entries that have not changed their positions have the same slope as before. The same is true for lines joining entries whose positions do not change to entries in the two rows that are interchanged. (Look, for example, at the line joining a_{1n} to a_{i2} in the two previously displayed determinants.) It remains to consider the lines joining two entries in the rows that *are* interchanged. They must clearly change from rising to falling as one goes to the right. Because each term in $|\mathbf{A}|$ and in $|\mathbf{A}_c|$ contains exactly one pair of entries from these two rows, and because the line joining these two entries has changed from rising to falling as one goes to the right, the number of lines that rise to the right in these two determinants must differ by exactly 1. Hence, $|\mathbf{A}| = -|\mathbf{A}_c|$.

Suppose next that two non-adjacent rows are to be interchanged. Start by interchanging the upper one of these rows with the row immediately below it, then with the row next down, and so on. Suppose that s interchanges are needed to bring the previous upper row into its new position. The second of the two rows to be interchanged is now immediately above its original position. Interchange it successively with the row directly above it exactly $(s - 1)$ times to bring it to its final new position. In all, we have performed $s + s - 1 = 2s - 1$ interchanges of neighboring rows. Each of these interchanges changes the sign of the determinant, and in all, we have an odd number of sign changes. Hence, the determinant *has* changed its sign by interchanging two rows.

Rule 5: If we interchange the two rows that are equal, the determinant will be exactly the same. But according to rule 4, the determinant has changed its sign. Hence, $|\mathbf{A}| = -|\mathbf{A}|$, which means that $|\mathbf{A}| = 0$.

Rule 6: This follows immediately from rules 3 and 5.

Rule 7: Symbolically, the proof of this rule is as follows, for the case when the scalar multiple α of row i is added to row j:

$$\sum (\pm) a_{1r_1} \cdots a_{ir_i} \cdots (a_{jr_j} + \alpha a_{ir_j}) \cdots a_{nr_n}$$

$$= \sum (\pm) a_{1r_1} \cdots a_{ir_i} \cdots a_{jr_j} \cdots a_{nr_n} + \alpha \sum (\pm) a_{1r_1} \cdots a_{ir_i} \cdots a_{ir_j} \cdots a_{nr_n}$$

$$= |\mathbf{A}| + \alpha \cdot 0 = |\mathbf{A}|$$

(The last sum is zero because it is equal to a determinant with rows i and j equal.)

Rule 8: The proof of this rule for the case $n = 2$ is the object of Problem 4 in Section 13.1. Here Problem 11, suggests a proof of the general case.

Rule 9: The matrix $\alpha \mathbf{A}$ is obtained by multiplying *each* entry in $\mathbf{A}$ by α. By rule 3, $|\alpha \mathbf{A}|$ is then equal to $\alpha^n |\mathbf{A}|$, because there are n rows each of which has α as a factor in each entry.

Problems

1. Let $\mathbf{A} = \begin{pmatrix} 1 & 2 \\ 3 & 4 \end{pmatrix}$ $\mathbf{B} = \begin{pmatrix} 3 & 4 \\ 5 & 6 \end{pmatrix}$

    a. Compute $\mathbf{AB}$, $\mathbf{BA}$, $\mathbf{A'B'}$, and $\mathbf{B'A'}$.

    b. Show that $|\mathbf{A}| = |\mathbf{A'}|$ and $|\mathbf{A}\,\mathbf{B}| = |\mathbf{A}| \cdot |\mathbf{B}|$. Is $|\mathbf{A'B'}| = |\mathbf{A'}| \cdot |\mathbf{B'}|$?

2. Let $\mathbf{A} = \begin{pmatrix} 2 & 1 & 3 \\ 1 & 0 & 1 \\ 1 & 2 & 5 \end{pmatrix}$.

    Compute $\mathbf{A'}$, and show next that $|\mathbf{A}| = |\mathbf{A'}|$.

3. Evaluate the following determinants as simply as possible:

    a. $\begin{vmatrix} 3 & 0 & 1 & 2 \\ 1 & 0 & -1 & 8 \\ 2 & 0 & 5 & 6 \\ -1 & 0 & -11 & 2 \end{vmatrix}$ **b.** $\begin{vmatrix} 1 & 2 & 3 & 4 \\ 0 & -1 & 2 & 4 \\ 0 & 0 & 3 & -1 \\ -3 & -6 & -9 & -12 \end{vmatrix}$

    c. $\begin{vmatrix} a & 1 & 1 & 2a \\ 1 & -a & 3 & 0 \\ a & 2 & a & 1 \\ 3a & 1 & 0 & 0 \end{vmatrix}$

4. Prove that each of the following determinants is zero:

    a. $\begin{vmatrix} 1 & 2 & 3 \\ 2 & 4 & 5 \\ 3 & 6 & 8 \end{vmatrix}$ **b.** $\begin{vmatrix} 1 & a & b+c \\ 1 & b & c+a \\ 1 & c & a+b \end{vmatrix}$ **c.** $\begin{vmatrix} x-y & x-y & x^2-y^2 \\ 1 & 1 & x+y \\ y & 1 & x \end{vmatrix}$

5. Let $\mathbf{X} = \begin{pmatrix} 1 & 0 & 0 \\ 1 & 1 & 1 \\ 1 & 2 & 0 \\ 1 & 0 & 1 \end{pmatrix}$.

    Compute $\mathbf{X'X}$ and $|\mathbf{X'X}|$.

6. Let $\mathbf{A}$ and $\mathbf{B}$ be 3×3 matrices with $|\mathbf{A}| = 3$ and $|\mathbf{B}| = -4$. Where possible, find the numerical values of $|\mathbf{AB}|$, $3|\mathbf{A}|$, $|-2\mathbf{B}|$, $|\mathbf{A}| + |\mathbf{B}|$, and $|\mathbf{A} + \mathbf{B}|$.

7. Show that an orthogonal matrix (see Problem 7 of Section 12.9) must have determinant 1 or -1.

8. A square matrix $\mathbf{A}$ of order n is called **involutive** if $\mathbf{A}^2 = \mathbf{I}_n$.

    a. Show that the determinant of an involutive matrix is 1 or -1.

    b. Show that $\begin{pmatrix} -1 & 0 \\ 0 & -1 \end{pmatrix}$ and $\begin{pmatrix} a & 1-a^2 \\ 1 & -a \end{pmatrix}$ are involutive (for all a).

    c. Show that $\mathbf{A}$ is involutive $\iff (\mathbf{I}_n - \mathbf{A})(\mathbf{I}_n + \mathbf{A}) = \mathbf{0}$.

Harder Problems

9. Without computing the determinants, show that

$$\begin{vmatrix} b^2 + c^2 & ab & ac \\ ab & a^2 + c^2 & bc \\ ac & bc & a^2 + b^2 \end{vmatrix} = \begin{vmatrix} 0 & c & b \\ c & 0 & a \\ b & a & 0 \end{vmatrix}^2$$

10. Prove that

$$D_n = \begin{vmatrix} a + b & a & \cdots & a \\ a & a + b & \cdots & a \\ \vdots & \vdots & \ddots & \vdots \\ a & a & \cdots & a + b \end{vmatrix} = b^{n-1}(na + b)$$

(*Hint:* Study Example 13.9.)

11. **a.** Let

$$|\mathbf{A}| = \begin{vmatrix} a_{11} & a_{12} \\ a_{21} & a_{22} \end{vmatrix} \qquad |\mathbf{B}| = \begin{vmatrix} b_{11} & b_{12} \\ b_{21} & b_{22} \end{vmatrix}$$

Prove that

$$|\mathbf{A}| \cdot |\mathbf{B}| = \begin{vmatrix} a_{11} & a_{12} & 0 & 0 \\ a_{21} & a_{22} & 0 & 0 \\ -1 & 0 & b_{11} & b_{12} \\ 0 & -1 & b_{21} & b_{22} \end{vmatrix}$$

$$= \begin{vmatrix} 0 & 0 & a_{11}b_{11} + a_{12}b_{21} & a_{11}b_{12} + a_{12}b_{22} \\ 0 & 0 & a_{21}b_{11} + a_{22}b_{21} & a_{21}b_{12} + a_{22}b_{22} \\ -1 & 0 & b_{11} & b_{12} \\ 0 & -1 & b_{21} & b_{22} \end{vmatrix}$$

$$= |\mathbf{AB}|$$

(We have indicated the operations you should use to obtain the second equality.)

b. Try to generalize the method in part (a) so that it applies when **A** and **B** are arbitrary $n \times n$ matrices, and thus give a proof of rule 8 in Theorem 13.1.

13.5 Expansion by Cofactors

According to definition [13.12], the determinant of an $n \times n$ matrix $\mathbf{A} = (a_{ij})$ is a sum of $n!$ terms. Each term contains one element from each row and one element from each column. Consider in particular row i and pick out all the terms that have a_{i1} as a factor, then all terms that have a_{i2} as a factor, and so on. Because all the terms have one and only one element from row i, in this way we get all the terms of $|\mathbf{A}|$. So we can write

$$|\mathbf{A}| = a_{i1}C_{i1} + a_{i2}C_{i2} + \cdots + a_{ij}C_{ij} + \cdots + a_{in}C_{in} \qquad [13.17]$$

This is called the *expansion of* $|\mathbf{A}|$ *in terms of the elements of the* ith *row.* The coefficients $C_{i1}, \ldots, C_{in}$ are the **cofactors** of the elements $a_{i1}, \ldots, a_{in}$.[2]

In the same way, we can expand $|\mathbf{A}|$ in terms of the elements of the jth column:

$$|\mathbf{A}| = a_{1j}C_{1j} + a_{2j}C_{2j} + \cdots + a_{ij}C_{ij} + \cdots + a_{nj}C_{nj} \qquad [13.18]$$

What makes expansions [13.17] and [13.18] extremely useful is that in general each cofactor C_{ij} can be found by applying the following procedure to the determinant $|\mathbf{A}|$. First, delete row i and column j to arrive at a determinant A_{ij} of order $n-1$, which is called a **minor**. Multiply the minor by the factor $(-1)^{i+j}$. This gives the cofactor.

In symbols, it turns out that the cofactor C_{ij} must be given by

$$C_{ij} = (-1)^{i+j} \begin{vmatrix} a_{11} & \cdots & a_{1,j-1} & a_{1j} & a_{1,j+1} & \cdots & a_{1n} \\ a_{21} & \cdots & a_{2,j-1} & a_{2j} & a_{2,j+1} & \cdots & a_{2n} \\ \vdots & & \vdots & \vdots & \vdots & & \vdots \\ a_{i1} & \cdots & a_{i,j-1} & a_{ij} & a_{i,j+1} & \cdots & a_{in} \\ \vdots & & \vdots & \vdots & \vdots & & \vdots \\ a_{n1} & \cdots & a_{n,j-1} & a_{nj} & a_{n,j+1} & \cdots & a_{nn} \end{vmatrix} \qquad [13.19]$$

where lines have been drawn through row i and column j, which are to be deleted from the matrix.

A proof of [13.19] will be given at the end of this section. If we look back at [13.8] in Section 13.2, however, it confirms [13.19] in a special case. Indeed, put $|\mathbf{A}| = a_{11}C_{11} + a_{12}C_{12} + a_{13}C_{13}$. Then [13.8] implies that

$$C_{11} = (-1)^{1+1}\begin{vmatrix} a_{22} & a_{23} \\ a_{32} & a_{33} \end{vmatrix}, \quad C_{12} = (-1)^{1+2}\begin{vmatrix} a_{21} & a_{23} \\ a_{31} & a_{33} \end{vmatrix}, \quad C_{13} = (-1)^{1+3}\begin{vmatrix} a_{21} & a_{22} \\ a_{31} & a_{32} \end{vmatrix}$$

precisely in accordance with [13.19].

Generally, formula [13.19] is rather complicated. Test your understanding of it by studying the following example.

---

[2]The expansions in [13.17] and [13.18] are also called *cofactor expansions* of the determinant, which is a special case of the general Laplace expansion.

Example 13.11

Check that the cofactor of the element c in the determinant

$$|\mathbf{A}| = \begin{vmatrix} 3 & 0 & 0 & 2 \\ 6 & 1 & \boxed{c} & 2 \\ -1 & 1 & 0 & 0 \\ 5 & 2 & 0 & 3 \end{vmatrix} \quad \text{is} \quad C_{23} = (-1)^{2+3} \begin{vmatrix} 3 & 0 & 2 \\ -1 & 1 & 0 \\ 5 & 2 & 3 \end{vmatrix}$$

Find the value of $|\mathbf{A}|$ by using Example 13.4 in Sec. 13.2.

Solution   Because the element c is in row 2 and column 3, its cofactor has been written correctly. To find the numerical value of $|\mathbf{A}|$, we use [13.18] and expand in terms of the elements of the *third column* of $|\mathbf{A}|$ (because it has so many zeros). This yields

$$|\mathbf{A}| = a_{23}C_{23} = c\,(-1)^{2+3} \begin{vmatrix} 3 & 0 & 2 \\ -1 & 1 & 0 \\ 5 & 2 & 3 \end{vmatrix} = c\,(-1)(-5) = 5c$$

Example 13.11 shows a simple case in which we can evaluate a determinant by using cofactor expansion. The example is particularly simple because there are many zeros in the third column. If the zeros are not there initially, we can often create them by appealing to rule 7 in Theorem 13.1 of Section 13.4. Two examples illustrate the method.[3]

Example 13.12

$$\begin{vmatrix} 3 & -1 & 2 \\ 0 & -1 & -1 \\ 6 & 1 & 2 \end{vmatrix} = \begin{vmatrix} 3 & -1 & 2 \\ 0 & -1 & -1 \\ 0 & 3 & -2 \end{vmatrix} \overset{(1)}{=} 3 \begin{vmatrix} -1 & -1 \\ 3 & -2 \end{vmatrix} = 3(2+3) = 15$$

To derive the equality labelled (1), expand by column 1.

Example 13.13

$$\begin{vmatrix} 2 & 0 & 3 & -1 \\ 0 & 4 & 0 & 0 \\ 0 & 1 & -1 & 2 \\ 3 & 2 & 5 & -3 \end{vmatrix} \overset{(1)}{=} (-1)^{2+2} \cdot 4 \begin{vmatrix} 2 & 3 & -1 \\ 0 & -1 & 2 \\ 3 & 5 & -3 \end{vmatrix}$$

$$= 4 \begin{vmatrix} 2 & 3 & -1 \\ 0 & -1 & 2 \\ 0 & 1/2 & -3/2 \end{vmatrix} \overset{(2)}{=} 4 \cdot 2 \begin{vmatrix} -1 & 2 \\ 1/2 & -3/2 \end{vmatrix} = 8\left(\tfrac{3}{2} - \tfrac{2}{2}\right) = 4$$

For equality (1), expand by row 2. For equality (2), expand by column 1.

[3]To compute a general 10×10 determinant using definition [13.12] requires no fewer than 36,287,999 operations of addition or multiplication! Systematic use of rule 7 in Theorem 13.1 can reduce the required number of operations to about 380.

Expansion by Alien Cofactors

According to [13.17] and [13.18], if the elements of any row (or column) of a determinant are multiplied by the cofactors of the elements in that row (or column) and the products are added, the result is the value of the determinant. What happens if we multiply the elements of a row (or column) by the cofactors of a different (alien) row (or column)? Consider the following example.

Example 13.14

If $\mathbf{A} = (a_{ij})_{3 \times 3}$, then the expansion of $|\mathbf{A}|$ in terms of the elements in the second row is

$$|\mathbf{A}| = a_{21}C_{21} + a_{22}C_{22} + a_{23}C_{23}$$

Suppose we change the elements a_{21}, a_{22}, and a_{23} to a, b, and c. Then C_{21}, C_{22}, and C_{23} are unchanged. So, the new determinant is

$$\begin{vmatrix} a_{11} & a_{12} & a_{13} \\ a & b & c \\ a_{31} & a_{32} & a_{33} \end{vmatrix} = aC_{21} + bC_{22} + cC_{23} \qquad [*]$$

In particular, if we replace a, b, and c by a_{11}, a_{12}, and a_{13} or by a_{31}, a_{32}, and a_{33}, then the determinant in $[*]$ is 0 because two rows are equal. Hence,

$$a_{11}C_{21} + a_{12}C_{22} + a_{13}C_{23} = 0$$

$$a_{31}C_{21} + a_{32}C_{22} + a_{33}C_{23} = 0$$

Thus, the sum of the products of the elements in either row 1 or row 3 multiplied by the cofactors of the elements in row 2 is zero.

Obviously, the argument used in this example can be generalized: If we multiply the elements of a row (or a column) by the cofactors of a different row (or column) and then add the products, the result is 0.

We summarize all the results in this section in the following theorem:

Theorem 13.2 (Cofactor Expansion of a Determinant)   Let $\mathbf{A} = (a_{ij})_{n \times n}$. Suppose that the cofactors C_{ij} are defined as in [13.19]. Then:

$$a_{i1}C_{i1} + a_{i2}C_{i2} + \cdots + a_{in}C_{in} = |\mathbf{A}|$$

$$a_{i1}C_{k1} + a_{i2}C_{k2} + \cdots + a_{in}C_{kn} = 0 \qquad (k \neq i)$$

[13.20]

$$a_{1j}C_{1j} + a_{2j}C_{2j} + \cdots + a_{nj}C_{nj} = |\mathbf{A}|$$

$$a_{1j}C_{1k} + a_{2j}C_{2k} + \cdots + a_{nj}C_{nk} = 0 \qquad (k \neq j)$$

[13.21]

Theorem 13.2 says that an expansion of a determinant by row i in terms of the cofactors of row k vanishes when $k \neq i$, and is equal to $|\mathbf{A}|$ if $k = i$. Likewise, an expansion by column j in terms of the cofactors of column k vanishes when $k \neq j$, and is equal to $|\mathbf{A}|$ if $k = j$.

Proof of formula [13.19]:   The definition of cofactor C_{ij} (see [13.17]) implies that C_{ij} is a sum of terms, each equal to the product of $n - 1$ elements from the matrix $\mathbf{A}$, chosen in such a way that there is one element from each row except row i, and one element from each column except column j. It follows that, except for a possible change in sign, C_{ij} is the determinant of the submatrix formed from $\mathbf{A}$ by crossing out row i and column j.

It remains only to determine the correct sign. Look first at C_{11}. The determinant obtained by crossing out row 1 and column 1 is

$$\begin{vmatrix} a_{22} & a_{23} & \cdots & a_{2n} \\ a_{32} & a_{33} & \cdots & a_{3n} \\ \vdots & \vdots & \ddots & \vdots \\ a_{n2} & a_{n3} & \cdots & a_{nn} \end{vmatrix} \qquad [*]$$

The signs of the terms in C_{11} are the same as the signs of the corresponding terms in $a_{11}C_{11}$. The signs of the terms in $a_{11}C_{11}$ are determined by the number of lines joining pairs of elements that rise as they go to the right, including all those that rise up to a_{11}. However, there cannot be any lines that rise up to a_{11}, so C_{11} is *equal* to the determinant [*].

Consider next C_{ij}. Move row i to row 1 by $i - 1$ interchanges of two adjacent rows. The $i - 1$ previous rows, while retaining their old order, are moved one position down. By performing $j - 1$ interchanges, the new column j is moved left to the position of column 1. Because we have interchanged $i - 1 + j - 1 = i + j - 2$ rows and columns in all, the determinant has changed sign $i + j - 2$ times. Because $(-1)^{i+j-2} = (-1)^{i+j}$, $|\mathbf{A}|$ must be given by

$$|\mathbf{A}| = (-1)^{i+j} \begin{vmatrix} a_{ij} & a_{i1} & \cdots & a_{i,j-1} & a_{i,j+1} & \cdots & a_{in} \\ a_{1j} & a_{11} & \cdots & a_{1,j-1} & a_{1,j+1} & \cdots & a_{1n} \\ \vdots & \vdots & & \vdots & \vdots & & \vdots \\ a_{i-1,j} & a_{i-1,1} & \cdots & a_{i-1,j-1} & a_{i-1,j+1} & \cdots & a_{i-1,n} \\ a_{i+1,j} & a_{i+1,1} & \cdots & a_{i+1,j-1} & a_{i+1,j+1} & \cdots & a_{i+1,n} \\ \vdots & \vdots & & \vdots & \vdots & & \vdots \\ a_{nj} & a_{n1} & \cdots & a_{n,j-1} & a_{n,j+1} & \cdots & a_{nn} \end{vmatrix} \qquad [**]$$

As with [*], the cofactor of the element a_{ij} in [**] is equal to the determinant in [13.19], because by crossing out row 1 and column 1 in [**] we get the same result as by crossing out row i and column j in the original determinant. Hence, the complement of a_{ij} in the expansion of $|\mathbf{A}|$ is given by [13.19].

Problems

1. Use the method in Examples 13.12 and 13.13 to compute the following determinants:

a. $\begin{vmatrix} 1 & 2 & 4 \\ 1 & 3 & 9 \\ 1 & 4 & 16 \end{vmatrix}$ **b.** $\begin{vmatrix} 1 & 2 & 3 & 4 \\ 0 & -1 & 0 & 11 \\ 2 & -1 & 0 & 3 \\ -2 & 0 & -1 & 3 \end{vmatrix}$ **c.** $\begin{vmatrix} 2 & 1 & 3 & 3 \\ 3 & 2 & 1 & 6 \\ 1 & 3 & 0 & 9 \\ 2 & 4 & 1 & 12 \end{vmatrix}$

2. Compute the following determinants:

a. $\begin{vmatrix} 0 & 0 & a \\ 0 & b & 0 \\ c & 0 & 0 \end{vmatrix}$ **b.** $\begin{vmatrix} 0 & 0 & 0 & a \\ 0 & 0 & b & 0 \\ 0 & c & 0 & 0 \\ d & 0 & 0 & 0 \end{vmatrix}$ **c.** $\begin{vmatrix} 0 & 0 & 0 & 0 & 1 \\ 0 & 0 & 0 & 5 & 1 \\ 0 & 0 & 3 & 1 & 2 \\ 0 & 4 & 0 & 3 & 4 \\ 6 & 2 & 3 & 1 & 2 \end{vmatrix}$

Harder Problems

3. One can prove that for all $n = 2, 3, \ldots$,

$$\begin{vmatrix} 1 & x_1 & x_1^2 & \cdots & x_1^{n-1} \\ 1 & x_2 & x_2^2 & \cdots & x_2^{n-1} \\ \vdots & \vdots & \vdots & \ddots & \vdots \\ 1 & x_n & x_n^2 & \cdots & x_n^{n-1} \end{vmatrix} = \prod_{1 \leq j < i \leq n} (x_i - x_j)$$

This is the **Vandermonde determinant**. The product symbol $\prod$ means that we take the product of all factors of form $x_i - x_j$ for $i > j$, where i and j vary from 1 to n. (If $n = 3$, then $\prod_{1 \leq j < i \leq 3}(x_i - x_j) = (x_2 - x_1)(x_3 - x_1)(x_3 - x_2)$. See Example 13.5 in Section 13.2.) Prove the equality for $n = 4$. (*Hint:* Multiply each of the third, second, and first columns successively by $-x_1$, before adding the results to the following column in each case. Then use the result for $n = 3$.)

13.6 The Inverse of a Matrix

Suppose that α is a real number satisfying $\alpha \neq 0$. Then there is a unique number α^{-1} with the property that $\alpha\alpha^{-1} = \alpha^{-1}\alpha = 1$. We call α^{-1} the (multiplicative) inverse of α. We saw in Section 12.8 that the identity matrix **I** (with 1's along the main diagonal and 0's elsewhere) is the matrix equivalent of 1 in the real number system.[4] This makes the following terminology seem natural.

Given matrix **A**, if there exists a matrix **X** such that

$$\mathbf{AX} = \mathbf{XA} = \mathbf{I} \tag{13.22}$$

---

[4]From now on, we write **I** instead of $\mathbf{I}_n$ whenever the dimension n of the identity matrix seems obvious.

then we say that $\mathbf{X}$ is an **inverse** of $\mathbf{A}$. Moreover, $\mathbf{A}$ is said to be **invertible** in this case. Because $\mathbf{XA} = \mathbf{AX} = \mathbf{I}$, the matrix $\mathbf{A}$ is also an inverse of $\mathbf{X}$—that is, $\mathbf{A}$ and $\mathbf{X}$ are inverses of each other. Note that both the two matrix products $\mathbf{AX}$ and $\mathbf{XA}$ are defined and can also be equal only if $\mathbf{A}$ and $\mathbf{X}$ are square matrices of the same order. *Thus, only square matrices can have inverses.* But not even all square matrices have inverses, as the following example shows.

Example 13.15

(a) Show that

$$\mathbf{A} = \begin{pmatrix} 5 & 6 \\ 5 & 10 \end{pmatrix} \quad \text{and} \quad \mathbf{X} = \begin{pmatrix} 1/2 & -3/10 \\ -1/4 & 1/4 \end{pmatrix}$$

are inverses of each other.

(b) Show that $\mathbf{A} = \begin{pmatrix} 1 & 0 \\ 0 & 0 \end{pmatrix}$ has no inverse.

Solution

(a) $\begin{pmatrix} 5 & 6 \\ 5 & 10 \end{pmatrix} \begin{pmatrix} 1/2 & -3/10 \\ -1/4 & 1/4 \end{pmatrix} = \begin{pmatrix} 5/2 - 6/4 & -15/10 + 6/4 \\ 5/2 - 10/4 & -15/10 + 10/4 \end{pmatrix}$

$$= \begin{pmatrix} 1 & 0 \\ 0 & 1 \end{pmatrix}$$

and likewise we verify that $\mathbf{XA} = \mathbf{I}$.

(b) Observe that for all real numbers x, y, z, and w,

$$\begin{pmatrix} 1 & 0 \\ 0 & 0 \end{pmatrix} \begin{pmatrix} x & y \\ z & w \end{pmatrix} = \begin{pmatrix} x & y \\ 0 & 0 \end{pmatrix}$$

So there is no way of choosing x, y, z, and w to make the product of these two matrices equal to $\mathbf{I}$. Thus, $\begin{pmatrix} 1 & 0 \\ 0 & 0 \end{pmatrix}$ has no inverse.

The following questions arise:

1. Which matrices have inverses?
2. Can a given matrix have more than one inverse?
3. How do we find the inverse if it exists?

As for question 1, it is easy to find a *necessary* condition for a matrix $\mathbf{A}$ to have an inverse. In fact, from [13.22] and rule 8 in Theorem 13.1, it follows that $|\mathbf{AX}| = |\mathbf{A}| \cdot |\mathbf{X}| = |\mathbf{I}|$. Using [13.14] of Section 13.3, we see that the identity matrix of any dimension has determinant 1. Thus, if $\mathbf{X}$ is an inverse of $\mathbf{A}$, then

$$|\mathbf{A}| \cdot |\mathbf{X}| = 1 \qquad\qquad [*]$$

We conclude from this equation that $|\mathbf{A}| \neq 0$ is a necessary condition for $\mathbf{A}$ to have an inverse, because $|\mathbf{A}| = 0$ would violate [∗]. As we shall see in the next section, the condition $|\mathbf{A}| \neq 0$ is also *sufficient* for $\mathbf{A}$ to have an inverse. Hence:

$$\text{A square matrix } \mathbf{A} \text{ has an inverse} \iff |\mathbf{A}| \neq 0 \qquad \text{[13.23]}$$

A square matrix $\mathbf{A}$ is said to be **singular** if $|\mathbf{A}| = 0$ and **nonsingular** if $|\mathbf{A}| \neq 0$. According to [13.23], a matrix has an inverse iff it is nonsingular.

Concerning question 2, the answer is no—a matrix cannot have more than one inverse. Indeed, suppose that $\mathbf{X}$ satisfies [13.22] and moreover $\mathbf{AY} = \mathbf{I}$ for some other square matrix $\mathbf{Y}$. Then

$$\mathbf{Y} = \mathbf{IY} = (\mathbf{XA})\mathbf{Y} = \mathbf{X}(\mathbf{AY}) = \mathbf{XI} = \mathbf{X}$$

A similar argument shows that if $\mathbf{YA} = \mathbf{I}$, then $\mathbf{Y} = \mathbf{X}$. *Thus, the inverse of $\mathbf{A}$ is unique if it exists.*

The inverse is usually written $\mathbf{A}^{-1}$. Whereas for numbers, we can write $a^{-1} = 1/a$, the symbol $\mathbf{I}/\mathbf{A}$ has *no* meaning; there are no rules for dividing matrices. Note also that even if the product $\mathbf{A}^{-1}\mathbf{B}$ is defined, it is usually quite different from $\mathbf{BA}^{-1}$ because matrix multiplication does not commute.

The full answer to question 3 is given in the next section. Here we only consider the case of 2×2 matrices.

Example 13.16

Find the inverse of $\mathbf{A} = \begin{pmatrix} a & b \\ c & d \end{pmatrix}$ (when it exists).

Solution   We shall find a 2×2 matrix $\mathbf{X}$ such that $\mathbf{AX} = \mathbf{XA} = \mathbf{I}$. This requires looking for numbers x, y, z, and w such that

$$\begin{pmatrix} a & b \\ c & d \end{pmatrix} \begin{pmatrix} x & y \\ z & w \end{pmatrix} = \begin{pmatrix} 1 & 0 \\ 0 & 1 \end{pmatrix}$$

Matrix multiplication implies that

$$ax + bz = 1, \qquad ay + bw = 0$$
$$cx + dz = 0, \qquad cy + dw = 1$$

Note that we have two systems of equations here, one given by the two equations on the left, and the other given by the two equations on the right. Both systems have $\mathbf{A}$ as a common coefficient matrix. If $|\mathbf{A}| = ad - bc \neq 0$, solving them using Cramers' rule ([13.5] of Section 13.1) or otherwise yields

$$x = \frac{d}{ad - bc}, \qquad z = \frac{-c}{ad - bc}, \qquad y = \frac{-b}{ad - bc}, \qquad w = \frac{a}{ad - bc}$$

Hence, we have proved that if $|\mathbf{A}| = ad - bc \neq 0$, then

$$\mathbf{A} = \begin{pmatrix} a & b \\ c & d \end{pmatrix} \implies \mathbf{A}^{-1} = \frac{1}{ad - bc} \begin{pmatrix} d & -b \\ -c & a \end{pmatrix} \qquad [13.24]$$

For square matrices of order 3, one can use Cramers' rule [13.9] to derive a formula for the inverse. Again, the requirement for the inverse to exist is that the determinant of the coefficient matrix is not 0. Full details will be given in Section 13.7.

Some Useful Implications

If $\mathbf{A}^{-1}$ is the inverse of $\mathbf{A}$, then $\mathbf{A}^{-1}\mathbf{A} = \mathbf{I}$ *and* $\mathbf{A}\mathbf{A}^{-1} = \mathbf{I}$. Actually, each of these equations implies the other, in the sense that

$$\mathbf{AX} = \mathbf{I} \implies \mathbf{X} = \mathbf{A}^{-1} \qquad [13.25]$$

$$\mathbf{YA} = \mathbf{I} \implies \mathbf{Y} = \mathbf{A}^{-1} \qquad [13.26]$$

To prove [13.25], suppose $\mathbf{AX} = \mathbf{I}$. Then $|\mathbf{A}| \cdot |\mathbf{X}| = 1$, so $|\mathbf{A}| \neq 0$, and then by [13.23], $\mathbf{A}^{-1}$ exists. Multiplying $\mathbf{AX} = \mathbf{I}$ from the left by $\mathbf{A}^{-1}$ yields $\mathbf{X} = \mathbf{A}^{-1}$. The proof of [13.26] is almost the same.

These implications are used repeatedly in proving properties of the inverse. Note also how we use [13.25] in the next example.

Example 13.17
Find the inverse of the $n \times n$ matrix $\mathbf{A}$ if $\mathbf{A} - \mathbf{A}^2 = \mathbf{I}$.

Solution   The matrix equation $\mathbf{A} - \mathbf{A}^2 = \mathbf{I}$ yields $\mathbf{A}(\mathbf{I} - \mathbf{A}) = \mathbf{I}$. But then it follows from [13.25] that $\mathbf{A}$ has the inverse $\mathbf{A}^{-1} = \mathbf{I} - \mathbf{A}$.

Properties of the Inverse

We shall now prove some useful rules for the inverse.

Theorem 13.3   (Properties of the Inverse)   Let $\mathbf{A}$ and $\mathbf{B}$ be invertible $n \times n$ matrices. Then:

(a) $\mathbf{A}^{-1}$ is invertible, and $(\mathbf{A}^{-1})^{-1} = \mathbf{A}$.
(b) $\mathbf{AB}$ is invertible, and $(\mathbf{AB})^{-1} = \mathbf{B}^{-1}\mathbf{A}^{-1}$.
(c) The transpose $\mathbf{A}'$ is invertible, and $(\mathbf{A}')^{-1} = (\mathbf{A}^{-1})'$.
(d) $(c\mathbf{A})^{-1} = c^{-1}\mathbf{A}^{-1}$ whenever c is a number $\neq 0$.

Proof　In each case, we use [13.25]:

(a) We have $\mathbf{A}^{-1}\mathbf{A} = \mathbf{I}$, so $\mathbf{A} = (\mathbf{A}^{-1})^{-1}$.

(b) To prove that $\mathbf{X} = \mathbf{B}^{-1}\mathbf{A}^{-1}$ is the inverse of $\mathbf{AB}$, we just have to verify that $(\mathbf{AB})\mathbf{X}$ is equal to $\mathbf{I}$. But

$$(\mathbf{AB})\mathbf{X} = (\mathbf{AB})(\mathbf{B}^{-1}\mathbf{A}^{-1}) = \mathbf{A}(\mathbf{BB}^{-1})\mathbf{A}^{-1}$$

$$= \mathbf{AIA}^{-1} = \mathbf{AA}^{-1} = \mathbf{I}$$

(c) Transposing the equation $\mathbf{A}^{-1}\mathbf{A} = \mathbf{I}$ in accordance with [12.44](d) in Section 12.9 gives $(\mathbf{A}^{-1}\mathbf{A})' = \mathbf{A}'(\mathbf{A}^{-1})' = \mathbf{I}' = \mathbf{I}$. Hence, $(\mathbf{A}')^{-1} = (\mathbf{A}^{-1})'$.

(d) Here $(c\mathbf{A})(c^{-1}\mathbf{A}^{-1}) = cc^{-1}\mathbf{AA}^{-1} = 1 \cdot \mathbf{I} = \mathbf{I}$, so $c^{-1}\mathbf{A}^{-1} = (c\mathbf{A})^{-1}$.

Notes

1. It is important to think carefully through the implications of the four rules in Theorem 13.3 and to understand their uses. A somewhat dramatic story might help you to appreciate rule (c). Some years ago a team of (human) calculators was working in a central bureau of statistics. After 3 weeks of hard work, they finally found the inverse $\mathbf{A}^{-1}$ of a 20×20 matrix $\mathbf{A}$. Then the boss came along and said: "Sorry, I was really interested in the inverse of the transpose of $\mathbf{A}$." Panic—until they realized that property (c) would save them from having to redo all the calculations. They simply transposed the inverse matrix that it had taken 3 weeks to find, because according to (c), the inverse of the transpose is the transpose of the inverse.

2. Suppose that $\mathbf{A}$ is invertible and also symmetric—that is, $\mathbf{A}' = \mathbf{A}$. Then rule (c) implies that $(\mathbf{A}^{-1})' = (\mathbf{A}')^{-1} = \mathbf{A}^{-1}$, so $\mathbf{A}^{-1}$ is symmetric. *The inverse of a symmetric matrix is symmetric.*

3. Rule (b) can be extended to products of several matrices. For instance, if $\mathbf{A}$, $\mathbf{B}$, and $\mathbf{C}$ are all invertible $n \times n$ matrices, then

$$(\mathbf{ABC})^{-1} = \big((\mathbf{AB})\mathbf{C}\big)^{-1} = \mathbf{C}^{-1}(\mathbf{AB})^{-1}$$

$$= \mathbf{C}^{-1}(\mathbf{B}^{-1}\mathbf{A}^{-1}) = \mathbf{C}^{-1}\mathbf{B}^{-1}\mathbf{A}^{-1}$$

where rule (b) has been used twice. Note the assumption in (b) that $\mathbf{A}$ and $\mathbf{B}$ are both $n \times n$ matrices. In statistics and econometrics, we often consider products of the form $\mathbf{XX}'$, where $\mathbf{X}$ is $n \times m$. Then $\mathbf{XX}'$ is $n \times n$. If the determinant $|\mathbf{XX}'|$ is not 0, then $(\mathbf{XX}')^{-1}$ exists, but (b) does not apply because $\mathbf{X}^{-1}$ and $\mathbf{X}'^{-1}$ are only defined if $n = m$.

4. It is a common fallacy to misinterpret (d). For instance, a correct application of (d) is this: $(\tfrac{1}{2}\mathbf{A})^{-1} = 2\mathbf{A}^{-1}$.

Solving Equations by Matrix Inversion

Let $\mathbf{A}$ be an $n \times n$ matrix. If $\mathbf{B}$ is an arbitrary matrix, we consider whether there are matrices $\mathbf{X}$ and $\mathbf{Y}$ of suitable dimensions such that

$$\mathbf{AX} = \mathbf{B} \tag{1}$$

$$\mathbf{YA} = \mathbf{B} \tag{2}$$

In case [1], the matrix $\mathbf{B}$ must have n rows, and in case [2], $\mathbf{B}$ must have n columns. Provided these conditions are satisfied, we have the following result:

Theorem 13.4   If $|\mathbf{A}| \neq 0$, then:

$$\mathbf{AX} = \mathbf{B} \iff \mathbf{X} = \mathbf{A}^{-1}\mathbf{B} \tag{13.27}$$

$$\mathbf{YA} = \mathbf{B} \iff \mathbf{Y} = \mathbf{BA}^{-1} \tag{13.28}$$

Proof   Multiply each side of the equation $\mathbf{AX} = \mathbf{B}$ in [13.27] on the left by $\mathbf{A}^{-1}$. This yields $\mathbf{A}^{-1}(\mathbf{AX}) = \mathbf{A}^{-1}\mathbf{B}$. Because $(\mathbf{A}^{-1}\mathbf{A})\mathbf{X} = \mathbf{I}_n\mathbf{X} = \mathbf{X}$, we conclude that $\mathbf{X} = \mathbf{A}^{-1}\mathbf{B}$ is the only possible solution of the equation. On the other hand, by substituting $\mathbf{X} = \mathbf{A}^{-1}\mathbf{B}$ into $\mathbf{AX} = \mathbf{B}$, we see that it really satisfies the equation.

The proof of [13.28] is similar—multiply each side of $\mathbf{YA} = \mathbf{B}$ on the right by $\mathbf{A}^{-1}$.

Example 13.18

Solve the following system of equations by using Theorem 13.4:

$$2x + y = 3$$
$$2x + 2y = 4 \tag{1}$$

Solution   Suppose we define

$$\mathbf{A} = \begin{pmatrix} 2 & 1 \\ 2 & 2 \end{pmatrix}, \qquad \mathbf{X} = \begin{pmatrix} x \\ y \end{pmatrix}, \qquad \mathbf{B} = \begin{pmatrix} 3 \\ 4 \end{pmatrix}$$

Then [1] is equivalent to the matrix equation $\mathbf{AX} = \mathbf{B}$. Because $|\mathbf{A}| = 2 \neq 0$, matrix $\mathbf{A}$ has an inverse, and according to Theorem 13.4, $\mathbf{X} = \mathbf{A}^{-1}\mathbf{B}$. The inverse of $\mathbf{A}$ is found from [13.24], and we obtain

$$\begin{pmatrix} x \\ y \end{pmatrix} = \mathbf{A}^{-1}\begin{pmatrix} 3 \\ 4 \end{pmatrix} = \begin{pmatrix} 1 & -1/2 \\ -1 & 1 \end{pmatrix}\begin{pmatrix} 3 \\ 4 \end{pmatrix} = \begin{pmatrix} 1 \\ 1 \end{pmatrix}$$

The solution of [1] is, therefore, $x = 1$, $y = 1$. (Check by substitution that this really is the correct solution.)

Problems

1. Prove that the inverse of $\begin{pmatrix} 3 & 0 \\ 2 & -1 \end{pmatrix}$ is $\begin{pmatrix} 1/3 & 0 \\ 2/3 & -1 \end{pmatrix}$.

2. Prove that the inverse of $\begin{pmatrix} 1 & 1 & -3 \\ 2 & 1 & -3 \\ 2 & 2 & 1 \end{pmatrix}$ is $\begin{pmatrix} -1 & 1 & 0 \\ 8/7 & -1 & 3/7 \\ -2/7 & 0 & 1/7 \end{pmatrix}$.

3. Find numbers a and b that make $\mathbf{A}$ the inverse of $\mathbf{B}$ when

$$\mathbf{A} = \begin{pmatrix} 2 & -1 & -1 \\ a & 1/4 & b \\ 1/8 & 1/8 & -1/8 \end{pmatrix} \quad \text{and} \quad \mathbf{B} = \begin{pmatrix} 1 & 2 & 4 \\ 0 & 1 & 6 \\ 1 & 3 & 2 \end{pmatrix}$$

4. Solve the following systems of equations by using Theorem 13.4. (See Example 13.18.)

   a. $2x - 3y = 3$ **b.** $2x - 3y = 8$ **c.** $2x - 3y = 0$

       $3x - 4y = 5$ $3x - 4y = 11$ $3x - 4y = 0$

5. Let $\mathbf{A} = \dfrac{1}{2} \begin{pmatrix} -1 & -\sqrt{3} \\ \sqrt{3} & -1 \end{pmatrix}$. Show that $\mathbf{A}^3 = \mathbf{I}$. Use this to find $\mathbf{A}^{-1}$.

6. Given matrix $\mathbf{A} = \begin{pmatrix} 0 & 1 & 0 \\ 0 & 1 & 1 \\ 1 & 0 & 1 \end{pmatrix}$

   a. Compute $|\mathbf{A}|$, $\mathbf{A}^2$, and $\mathbf{A}^3$. Show that $\mathbf{A}^3 - 2\mathbf{A}^2 + \mathbf{A} - \mathbf{I} = \mathbf{0}$, where $\mathbf{I}$ is the identity matrix of order 3, and $\mathbf{0}$ is the zero matrix.

   b. Show that $\mathbf{A}$ has an inverse and $\mathbf{A}^{-1} = (\mathbf{A} - \mathbf{I})^2$.

   c. Find a matrix $\mathbf{P}$ such that $\mathbf{P}^2 = \mathbf{A}$. Are there other matrices with this property?

7. **a.** Let $\mathbf{A} = \begin{pmatrix} 2 & 1 & 4 \\ 0 & -1 & 3 \end{pmatrix}$. Compute $\mathbf{AA}'$, $|\mathbf{AA}'|$, and $(\mathbf{AA}')^{-1}$.

   b. The matrices $\mathbf{AA}'$ and $(\mathbf{AA}')^{-1}$ in part (a) are both symmetric. Is this a coincidence?

8. Suppose that $\mathbf{A}$, $\mathbf{P}$, and $\mathbf{D}$ are square matrices such that $\mathbf{A} = \mathbf{PDP}^{-1}$.

   a. Show that $\mathbf{A}^2 = \mathbf{PD}^2\mathbf{P}^{-1}$.

   b. Show by induction that $\mathbf{A}^m = \mathbf{PD}^m\mathbf{P}^{-1}$ for any positive integer m.

9. Given $\mathbf{B} = \begin{pmatrix} -1/2 & 5 \\ 1/4 & -1/2 \end{pmatrix}$, compute $\mathbf{B}^2 + \mathbf{B}$, $\mathbf{B}^3 - 2\mathbf{B} + \mathbf{I}$, and then $\mathbf{B}^{-1}$.

10. **a.** Let $\mathbf{C}$ be a square matrix of order n that satisfies $\mathbf{C}^2 + \mathbf{C} = \mathbf{I}$. Show that $\mathbf{C}$ has an inverse and $\mathbf{C}^{-1} = \mathbf{I} + \mathbf{C}$.

   b. Show that $\mathbf{C}^3 = -\mathbf{I} + 2\mathbf{C}$ and $\mathbf{C}^4 = 2\mathbf{I} - 3\mathbf{C}$.

11. a. Suppose that $\mathbf{X}$ is an $m \times n$ matrix and that $|\mathbf{X}'\mathbf{X}| \neq 0$. Show that the matrix

$$\mathbf{A} = \mathbf{I}_m - \mathbf{X}(\mathbf{X}'\mathbf{X})^{-1}\mathbf{X}'$$

is idempotent—that is, $\mathbf{A}^2 = \mathbf{A}$. (See Problem 7 of Section 12.8.)

b. Check the result in part (a) for the particular matrix $\mathbf{X} = \begin{pmatrix} 1 & 1 \\ 1 & 2 \\ 1 & 1 \end{pmatrix}$

12. Let the matrices $\mathbf{A}$ and $\mathbf{T}$ be defined by

$$\mathbf{A} = \begin{pmatrix} 1 & 2 & 3 \\ 2 & 1 & 3 \\ 3 & 2 & 1 \end{pmatrix} \quad \text{and} \quad \mathbf{T} = \frac{1}{12}\begin{pmatrix} s & t & 3 \\ 7 & -8 & 3 \\ 1 & t & -3 \end{pmatrix}$$

where s and t are real numbers.

a. Prove that $\mathbf{T} = \mathbf{A}^{-1}$ for suitable values of s and t.

b. Suppose that the matrix $\mathbf{X}$ satisfies the equation $\mathbf{BX} = 2\mathbf{X} + \mathbf{C}$, where

$$\mathbf{B} = \begin{pmatrix} 3 & 2 & 3 \\ 2 & 3 & 3 \\ 3 & 2 & 3 \end{pmatrix} \quad \text{and} \quad \mathbf{C} = \begin{pmatrix} 2 & 3 & 0 & 1 \\ 1 & 0 & 3 & 1 \\ 0 & 5 & -4 & 1 \end{pmatrix}$$

Use the result in part (a) to find $\mathbf{X}$.

13. Let $\mathbf{D}$ be an $n \times n$ matrix such that $\mathbf{D}^2 = 2\mathbf{D} + 3\mathbf{I}$. Prove that $\mathbf{D}^3 = a\mathbf{D} + b\mathbf{I}$ for suitable values of a and b. Find similar expressions for $\mathbf{D}^6$ and $\mathbf{D}^{-1}$ (that is, expressed in the form $\alpha\mathbf{D} + \beta\mathbf{I}$).

13.7 A General Formula for the Inverse

The previous section certainly presents the most important facts about the inverse and its properties, and as such is "what every economist should know." It is less important for most economists to know a lot about how to compute the inverses of large matrices, because powerful computer programs are available.

Nevertheless, this section presents an explicit formula for the inverse of any nonsingular $n \times n$ matrix $\mathbf{A}$. Though this formula is extremely inefficient for computing inverses of large matrices, it does have theoretical interest. The key to this formula is Theorem 13.2 of Section 13.5 on the expansion of determinants by cofactors.

Let $C_{11}, \ldots, C_{nn}$ denote the cofactors of the elements in $\mathbf{A}$. Then by [13.20] (the rule for expansion by cofactors), one has

$$a_{i1}C_{k1} + a_{i2}C_{k2} + \cdots + a_{in}C_{kn} = \begin{cases} |\mathbf{A}| & \text{if } i = k \\ 0 & \text{if } i \neq k \end{cases} \qquad [*]$$

The sums on the left-hand side look very much like those appearing in matrix products. In fact, the n^2 different equations in [∗] reduce to the single matrix equation

$$
\begin{pmatrix}
a_{11} & a_{12} & \cdots & a_{1n} \\
\vdots & \vdots & & \vdots \\
a_{i1} & a_{i2} & \cdots & a_{in} \\
\vdots & \vdots & & \vdots \\
a_{n1} & a_{n2} & \cdots & a_{nn}
\end{pmatrix}
\begin{pmatrix}
C_{11} & \cdots & C_{k1} & \cdots & C_{n1} \\
C_{12} & \cdots & C_{k2} & \cdots & C_{n2} \\
\vdots & & \vdots & & \vdots \\
C_{1n} & \cdots & C_{kn} & \cdots & C_{nn}
\end{pmatrix}
=
\begin{pmatrix}
|\mathbf{A}| & 0 & \cdots & 0 \\
0 & |\mathbf{A}| & \cdots & 0 \\
\vdots & \vdots & \ddots & \vdots \\
0 & 0 & \cdots & |\mathbf{A}|
\end{pmatrix}
$$

Here the right-hand side matrix is equal to $|\mathbf{A}| \cdot \mathbf{I}$. Let $\mathbf{C}^+ = (C_{ij})$ denote the matrix of cofactors. Then the second matrix in the product on the left-hand side is the matrix $\mathbf{C}^+$ with its row and column indices interchanged. Thus, it is the *transpose* $(\mathbf{C}^+)'$ of that matrix, which is called the **adjoint** of $\mathbf{A}$, and denoted by adj ($\mathbf{A}$). Thus,

$$
\text{adj}\,(\mathbf{A}) = (\mathbf{C}^+)' =
\begin{pmatrix}
C_{11} & \cdots & C_{k1} & \cdots & C_{n1} \\
C_{12} & \cdots & C_{k2} & \cdots & C_{n2} \\
\vdots & & \vdots & & \vdots \\
C_{1n} & \cdots & C_{kn} & \cdots & C_{nn}
\end{pmatrix}
\qquad [13.29]
$$

The previous equation, therefore, can be written as $\mathbf{A}\,\text{adj}\,(\mathbf{A}) = |\mathbf{A}| \cdot \mathbf{I}$. In case $|\mathbf{A}| \neq 0$, this evidently implies that $\mathbf{A}^{-1} = (1/|\mathbf{A}|) \cdot \text{adj}\,(\mathbf{A})$. We have proved:

Theorem 13.5   (General Formula for the Inverse)   Any square matrix $\mathbf{A} = \left(a_{ij}\right)_{n \times n}$ with determinant $|\mathbf{A}| \neq 0$ has a unique inverse $\mathbf{A}^{-1}$ satisfying $\mathbf{A}\mathbf{A}^{-1} = \mathbf{A}^{-1}\mathbf{A} = \mathbf{I}$, which is given by

$$
\mathbf{A}^{-1} = \frac{1}{|\mathbf{A}|} \cdot \text{adj}\,(\mathbf{A})
\qquad [13.30]
$$

If $|\mathbf{A}| = 0$, then there is no matrix $\mathbf{X}$ such that $\mathbf{AX} = \mathbf{XA} = \mathbf{I}$.

Example 13.19
   Let

$$
\mathbf{A} = \begin{pmatrix}
2 & 3 & 4 \\
4 & 3 & 1 \\
1 & 2 & 4
\end{pmatrix}
$$

Show that $\mathbf{A}$ has an inverse and find the inverse.

Solution   According to Theorem 13.5, **A** has an inverse iff $|\mathbf{A}| \neq 0$. Here some calculation shows that $|\mathbf{A}| = -5$, so the inverse exists. The cofactors are

$$C_{11} = \begin{vmatrix} 3 & 1 \\ 2 & 4 \end{vmatrix} = 10, \quad C_{12} = -\begin{vmatrix} 4 & 1 \\ 1 & 4 \end{vmatrix} = -15, \quad C_{13} = \begin{vmatrix} 4 & 3 \\ 1 & 2 \end{vmatrix} = 5$$

$$C_{21} = -\begin{vmatrix} 3 & 4 \\ 2 & 4 \end{vmatrix} = -4, \quad C_{22} = \begin{vmatrix} 2 & 4 \\ 1 & 4 \end{vmatrix} = 4, \quad C_{23} = -\begin{vmatrix} 2 & 3 \\ 1 & 2 \end{vmatrix} = -1$$

$$C_{31} = \begin{vmatrix} 3 & 4 \\ 3 & 1 \end{vmatrix} = -9, \quad C_{32} = -\begin{vmatrix} 2 & 4 \\ 4 & 1 \end{vmatrix} = 14, \quad C_{33} = \begin{vmatrix} 2 & 3 \\ 4 & 3 \end{vmatrix} = -6$$

Hence, the inverse of **A** is

$$\mathbf{A}^{-1} = \frac{1}{|\mathbf{A}|} \begin{pmatrix} C_{11} & C_{21} & C_{31} \\ C_{12} & C_{22} & C_{32} \\ C_{13} & C_{23} & C_{33} \end{pmatrix} = -\frac{1}{5} \begin{pmatrix} 10 & -4 & -9 \\ -15 & 4 & 14 \\ 5 & -1 & -6 \end{pmatrix}$$

(Check the result by showing that $\mathbf{A}\mathbf{A}^{-1} = \mathbf{I}$.)

Finding Inverses by Elementary Row Operations

Theorem 13.5 presented a general formula for the inverse of a nonsingular matrix. Although this formula is important theoretically, it is computationally useless for matrices much larger than 2×2. We shall briefly discuss a method for finding the inverse that is very efficient. Versions of it are generally used by computers to find inverses.

The following operations on a matrix are called **elementary row operations**:

(a) interchanging any two rows

(b) multiplying each element of a row by any scalar $\alpha \neq 0$

(c) adding to each element of the ith row, α times the corresponding element of the jth row

Now, in order to invert an $n \times n$ matrix **A**, first form the $n \times 2n$ matrix $(\mathbf{A} : \mathbf{I})$ by writing down the n columns of **A** followed by the n columns of **I**. Then apply elementary row operations to this matrix in order to transform it to an $n \times 2n$ matrix $(\mathbf{I} : \mathbf{B})$ whose first n columns are all the columns of **I**. It will follow that $\mathbf{B} = \mathbf{A}^{-1}$. If it is impossible to perform such row operations, then **A** has no inverse.[5] The method is illustrated by the following example.

---

[5] It is not difficult to prove that this procedure works, but we omit the proof.

Example 13.20

Find the inverse of $\mathbf{A} = \begin{pmatrix} 1 & 3 & 3 \\ 1 & 3 & 4 \\ 1 & 4 & 3 \end{pmatrix}$

Solution   First, write down the 3×6 matrix whose first three columns are the columns of $\mathbf{A}$ and whose next three columns are the columns of the 3×3 identity matrix:

$$\left(\begin{array}{ccc:ccc} 1 & 3 & 3 & 1 & 0 & 0 \\ 1 & 3 & 4 & 0 & 1 & 0 \\ 1 & 4 & 3 & 0 & 0 & 1 \end{array} \right)$$

The idea is now systematically to use elementary operations on this matrix so that, in the end, the three first columns constitute an identity matrix. Then the last three columns constitute the inverse of $\mathbf{A}$.

First, multiply the first row by -1 and add the result to the second row. This gives a zero in the second row and the first column. You should be able then to understand the other operations used and why they are chosen.

$$\left(\begin{array}{ccc:ccc} 1 & 3 & 3 & 1 & 0 & 0 \\ 1 & 3 & 4 & 0 & 1 & 0 \\ 1 & 4 & 3 & 0 & 0 & 1 \end{array} \right) \overset{-1}{\longleftarrow} \sim \left(\begin{array}{ccc:ccc} 1 & 3 & 3 & 1 & 0 & 0 \\ 0 & 0 & 1 & -1 & 1 & 0 \\ 1 & 4 & 3 & 0 & 0 & 1 \end{array} \right) \overset{-1}{\longleftarrow}$$

$$\sim \left(\begin{array}{ccc:ccc} 1 & 3 & 3 & 1 & 0 & 0 \\ 0 & 0 & 1 & -1 & 1 & 0 \\ 0 & 1 & 0 & -1 & 0 & 1 \end{array} \right) \overset{-3}{\longleftarrow} \sim \left(\begin{array}{ccc:ccc} 1 & 0 & 3 & 4 & 0 & -3 \\ 0 & 0 & 1 & -1 & 1 & 0 \\ 0 & 1 & 0 & -1 & 0 & 1 \end{array} \right) \overset{-3}{\longleftarrow}$$

$$\sim \left(\begin{array}{ccc:ccc} 1 & 0 & 0 & 7 & -3 & -3 \\ 0 & 0 & 1 & -1 & 1 & 0 \\ 0 & 1 & 0 & -1 & 0 & 1 \end{array} \right) \overset{}{\underset{\longleftarrow}{\longleftarrow}} \sim \left(\begin{array}{ccc:ccc} 1 & 0 & 0 & 7 & -3 & -3 \\ 0 & 1 & 0 & -1 & 0 & 1 \\ 0 & 0 & 1 & -1 & 1 & 0 \end{array} \right)$$

We conclude that

$$\mathbf{A}^{-1} = \begin{pmatrix} 7 & -3 & -3 \\ -1 & 0 & 1 \\ -1 & 1 & 0 \end{pmatrix}$$

(Check that $\mathbf{A}\mathbf{A}^{-1} = \mathbf{I}$.)

Problems

1. Use Theorem 13.5 to compute the inverses of the following matrices, if they exist:

   a. $\begin{pmatrix} 2 & 3 \\ 4 & 5 \end{pmatrix}$ b. $\begin{pmatrix} 1 & 0 & 2 \\ 2 & -1 & 0 \\ 0 & 2 & -1 \end{pmatrix}$ c. $\begin{pmatrix} 1 & 0 & 0 \\ -3 & -2 & 1 \\ 4 & -16 & 8 \end{pmatrix}$

2. Find the inverse of $\begin{pmatrix} -2 & 3 & 2 \\ 6 & 0 & 3 \\ 4 & 1 & -1 \end{pmatrix}$

3. Let $\mathbf{A} = \begin{pmatrix} 0.2 & 0.6 & 0.2 \\ 0 & 0.2 & 0.4 \\ 0.2 & 0.2 & 0 \end{pmatrix}$. Find $(\mathbf{I} - \mathbf{A})^{-1}$.

4. Consider the following problem. Repeated observations of a phenomenon lead to a number of equations with the same square coefficient matrix (a_{ij}), but with different right-hand sides:

$$a_{11}x_1 + \cdots + a_{1n}x_n = b_{i1}$$
$$\cdots\cdots\cdots\cdots\cdots\cdots\cdots\cdots\cdots \qquad (i = 1, \ldots, p) \qquad [*]$$
$$a_{n1}x_1 + \cdots + a_{nn}x_n = b_{in}$$

Explain how to find the solutions of all the systems by using row operations to get

$$\begin{pmatrix} a_{11} & \cdots & a_{1n} & b_{11} & \cdots & b_{p1} \\ \vdots & \ddots & \vdots & \vdots & \ddots & \vdots \\ a_{n1} & \cdots & a_{nn} & b_{1n} & \cdots & b_{pn} \end{pmatrix} \sim \begin{pmatrix} 1 & \cdots & 0 & b_{11}^* & \cdots & b_{p1}^* \\ \vdots & \ddots & \vdots & \vdots & \ddots & \vdots \\ 0 & \cdots & 1 & b_{1n}^* & \cdots & b_{pn}^* \end{pmatrix}$$

What then is the solution of the system of equations [*] for $i = k$?

5. Use the method in Example 13.20 to compute the inverses of the following matrices (check each result by verifying that $\mathbf{AA}^{-1} = \mathbf{I}$).

   a. $\begin{pmatrix} 1 & 2 \\ 3 & 4 \end{pmatrix}$
   b. $\begin{pmatrix} 1 & 2 & 3 \\ 2 & 4 & 5 \\ 3 & 5 & 6 \end{pmatrix}$
   c. $\begin{pmatrix} 3 & 2 & -1 \\ -1 & 5 & 8 \\ -9 & -6 & 3 \end{pmatrix}$

13.8 Cramer's Rule

Cramer's rule for solving n linear equations in n unknowns is a direct generalization of the same rule for systems of equations with two or three unknowns. Consider the system $\mathbf{Ax} = \mathbf{b}$, or

$$a_{11}x_1 + a_{12}x_2 + \cdots + a_{1n}x_n = b_1$$
$$a_{21}x_1 + a_{22}x_2 + \cdots + a_{2n}x_n = b_2$$
$$\cdots\cdots\cdots\cdots\cdots\cdots\cdots\cdots\cdots \qquad\qquad [13.31]$$
$$a_{n1}x_1 + a_{n2}x_2 + \cdots + a_{nn}x_n = b_n$$

Let D_j denote the determinant obtained from $|\mathbf{A}|$ by replacing the jth column vector with the column vector whose components are $b_1, b_2, \ldots, b_n$. Thus,

$$D_j = \begin{vmatrix} a_{11} & \cdots & a_{1j-1} & b_1 & a_{1j+1} & \cdots & a_{1n} \\ a_{21} & \cdots & a_{2j-1} & b_2 & a_{2j+1} & \cdots & a_{2n} \\ \vdots & & \vdots & \vdots & \vdots & & \vdots \\ a_{n1} & \cdots & a_{nj-1} & b_n & a_{nj+1} & \cdots & a_{nn} \end{vmatrix} \qquad (j = 1, \ldots, n) \qquad [13.32]$$

Note that expanding D_j by its jth column gives

$$D_j = C_{1j}b_1 + C_{2j}b_2 + \cdots + C_{nj}b_n \qquad [*]$$

where the cofactors C_{ij} are given by [13.19] of Section 13.5. Now we can prove the following result:

Theorem 13.6 (Cramer's Rule) The general linear system [13.31] of n equations in n unknowns has a unique solution if $\mathbf{A}$ is nonsingular ($|\mathbf{A}| \neq 0$). The solution is

$$x_1 = \frac{D_1}{|\mathbf{A}|}, \quad x_2 = \frac{D_2}{|\mathbf{A}|}, \quad \ldots, \quad x_n = \frac{D_n}{|\mathbf{A}|} \qquad [13.33]$$

where $D_1, D_2, \ldots, D_n$ are defined by [13.32].

Proof System [13.31] can be written in the form

$$\begin{pmatrix} a_{11} & a_{12} & \cdots & a_{1n} \\ a_{21} & a_{22} & \cdots & a_{2n} \\ \vdots & \vdots & \ddots & \vdots \\ a_{n1} & a_{n2} & \cdots & a_{nn} \end{pmatrix} \begin{pmatrix} x_1 \\ x_2 \\ \vdots \\ x_n \end{pmatrix} = \begin{pmatrix} b_1 \\ b_2 \\ \vdots \\ b_n \end{pmatrix} \qquad [1]$$

Using formula [13.30] for the inverse of the coefficient matrix $\mathbf{A}$ yields

$$\begin{pmatrix} x_1 \\ x_2 \\ \vdots \\ x_n \end{pmatrix} = \frac{1}{|\mathbf{A}|} \cdot \begin{pmatrix} C_{11} & C_{21} & \cdots & C_{n1} \\ C_{12} & C_{22} & \cdots & C_{n2} \\ \vdots & \vdots & \ddots & \vdots \\ C_{1n} & C_{2n} & \cdots & C_{nn} \end{pmatrix} \cdot \begin{pmatrix} b_1 \\ b_2 \\ \vdots \\ b_n \end{pmatrix} \qquad [2]$$

where the cofactors C_{ij} are given by [13.19] of Section 13.5. From [2], we have in particular that

$$x_j = \frac{1}{|\mathbf{A}|}(C_{1j}b_1 x \cdots + C_{nj}b_x) = \frac{D_j}{|\mathbf{A}|} \qquad (j = 1, 2, \ldots, n) \qquad [3]$$

where the last equality follows from the previous equation [∗]. This proves [13.33].

Example 13.21

Examine for which values of p the following system of equations has solutions, and find these solutions.

$$
\begin{aligned}
px + y\phantom{{}+z} &= 1 \\
x - y + z &= 0 \\
2y - z &= 3
\end{aligned}
$$

Solution   The coefficient matrix has determinant

$$
|\mathbf{A}| = \begin{vmatrix} p & 1 & 0 \\ 1 & -1 & 1 \\ 0 & 2 & -1 \end{vmatrix} = 1 - p
$$

According to Theorem 13.6, the system has a unique solution if $1 - p \neq 0$ — that is, if $p \neq 1$. In this case, the determinants in [13.32] are

$$
D_1 = \begin{vmatrix} 1 & 1 & 0 \\ 0 & -1 & 1 \\ 3 & 2 & -1 \end{vmatrix}, \qquad
D_2 = \begin{vmatrix} p & 1 & 0 \\ 1 & 0 & 1 \\ 0 & 3 & -1 \end{vmatrix}, \qquad
D_3 = \begin{vmatrix} p & 1 & 1 \\ 1 & -1 & 0 \\ 0 & 2 & 3 \end{vmatrix}
$$

We find that $D_1 = 2$, $D_2 = 1 - 3p$, and $D_3 = -1 - 3p$, so [13.33] yields

$$
x = \frac{D_1}{|\mathbf{A}|} = \frac{2}{1-p}, \qquad
y = \frac{D_2}{|\mathbf{A}|} = \frac{1-3p}{1-p}, \qquad
z = \frac{D_3}{|\mathbf{A}|} = \frac{-1-3p}{1-p}
$$

when $p \neq 1$. When $p = 1$, however, adding the last two of the original equations implies that $x + y = 3$. This contradicts the first equation, which becomes $x + y = 1$. So there is no solution in this case.

Homogeneous Systems of Equations

We end this chapter by studying the special case in which the right-hand side of the system of equations [13.31] consists only of zeros. The system is then called **homogeneous**. A homogeneous system will always have the so-called **trivial solution** $x_1 = x_2 = \cdots = x_n = 0$. In many problems, one is interested in knowing when a homogeneous system has **nontrivial** solutions.

Theorem 13.7   (Nontrivial Solutions of Homogeneous Systems)   The
homogeneous linear system of equations with n equations and n unknowns

$$a_{11}x_1 + a_{12}x_2 + \cdots + a_{1n}x_n = 0$$

$$a_{21}x_1 + a_{22}x_2 + \cdots + a_{2n}x_n = 0$$

$$\dots\dots\dots\dots\dots\dots\dots\dots\dots$$ [13.34]

$$a_{n1}x_1 + a_{n2}x_2 + \cdots + a_{nn}x_n = 0$$

has nontrivial solutions if and only if the coefficient matrix $\mathbf{A} = \left(a_{ij}\right)_{n \times n}$ is
singular (that is, iff $|\mathbf{A}| = 0$).

Partial Argument: Suppose that $|\mathbf{A}| \neq 0$. Then, by Cramer's rule, $x_1, \ldots, x_n$ are
given by [13.33]. But the numerator in each of these fractions is 0, because each of
the determinants $D_1, \ldots, D_n$ contains a column consisting entirely of zeros. Then
the system only has the trivial solution. In other words: *System [13.34] can only
have nontrivial solutions if the determinant $|\mathbf{A}|$ vanishes.* One can also prove that
if $|\mathbf{A}| = 0$, then system [13.34] does have nontrivial solutions.[6]

Example 13.22

Examine for which values of λ the following system of equations has nontrivial solutions:

$$5x + 2y + z = \lambda x$$

$$2x + \ y \quad\quad = \lambda y$$ [1]

$$x \quad\quad + z = \lambda z$$

Solution   The variables x, y, and z appear on both sides of the equations,
so we start by putting the system into standard form:

$$(5 - \lambda)x + \quad\quad 2y + \quad\quad z = 0$$

$$2x + (1 - \lambda)y \quad\quad\quad = 0$$ [2]

$$x \quad\quad\quad\quad + (1 - \lambda)z = 0$$

According to Theorem 13.7, system [2] has a nontrivial solution iff the coefficient matrix is singular:

$$\begin{vmatrix} 5 - \lambda & 2 & 1 \\ 2 & 1 - \lambda & 0 \\ 1 & 0 & 1 - \lambda \end{vmatrix} = 0$$

---

[6]See Theorem 14.5 of Section 14.3: If $|\mathbf{A}| = 0$, then the rank of $\mathbf{A}$ is less than n, and system
[13.34] has at least 1 degree of freedom, so it has an infinite number of solutions.

The value of the determinant is $\lambda(1 - \lambda)(\lambda - 6)$. Hence, system [1] has nontrivial solutions iff $\lambda = 0$, 1, or 6.

Problems

1. Use Cramer's rule to solve the following two systems of equations:

   a.
   $$x + 2y - z = -5$$
   $$2x - y + z = 6$$
   $$x - y - 3z = -3$$

   b.
   $$x + y \qquad = 3$$
   $$x \qquad + z = 2$$
   $$y + z + u = 6$$
   $$y \qquad + u = 1$$

2. Use Theorem 13.7 to prove that the following system of equations has a unique solution for all values of b_1, b_2, b_3, and find the solution.

$$3x_1 + x_2 \qquad = b_1$$
$$x_1 - x_2 + 2x_3 = b_2$$
$$2x_1 + 3x_2 - x_3 = b_3$$

3. Prove that the homogeneous system of equations

$$ax + by + cz = 0$$
$$bx + cy + az = 0$$
$$cx + ay + bz = 0$$

has a nontrivial solution if and only if $a^3 + b^3 + c^3 - 3abc = 0$.

Further Topics in Linear Algebra

*Professional mathematicians use the word "obvious"
to indicate that it is obvious how to give a complete
proof. To use "obvious" to mean "I am sure it's true,
but I can't prove it," is not a commendable practice.*
— *C. Clark* (1982)

In an economic model described by a linear system of equations, it is important to know when that system has a solution, and when the solution is unique. General conditions for existence and uniqueness are most easily stated by using the concepts of linearly dependent and linearly independent sets of vectors. These concepts are now introduced, along with the related concept of the rank of a matrix. This chapter also discusses eigenvalues and the spectral theorem for symmetric matrices. These concepts will be useful in Chapter 17, where we treat second-order conditions for multivariable optimization.

14.1 Linear Independence

Recall that any system of linear equations can be written as a vector equation. For instance, the system in Example 13.6 of Section 13.2 was

$$
\begin{aligned}
2x_1 + 2x_2 - x_3 &= -3 \\
4x_1 \quad\quad + 2x_3 &= 8 \\
6x_2 - 3x_3 &= -12
\end{aligned}
\qquad [1]
$$

This system can be written as the vector equation

$$x_1 \mathbf{a}_1 + x_2 \mathbf{a}_2 + x_3 \mathbf{a}_3 = \mathbf{b} \qquad [2]$$

where

$$\mathbf{a}_1 = \begin{pmatrix} 2 \\ 4 \\ 0 \end{pmatrix}, \quad \mathbf{a}_2 = \begin{pmatrix} 2 \\ 0 \\ 6 \end{pmatrix}, \quad \mathbf{a}_3 = \begin{pmatrix} -1 \\ 2 \\ -3 \end{pmatrix}, \quad \mathbf{b} = \begin{pmatrix} -3 \\ 8 \\ -12 \end{pmatrix} \qquad [3]$$

According to [2], system [1] has a solution iff **b** can be written as a linear combination of the column vectors of the coefficient matrix **A**. In fact, from Example 13.6, we see that $\mathbf{b} = (1/2)\mathbf{a}_1 + (-1/2)\mathbf{a}_2 + 3\mathbf{a}_3$, because $x_1 = 1/2$, $x_2 = -1/2$, and $x_3 = 3$ solve [1]. In this case, we say that **b** is *linearly dependent* on the vectors $\mathbf{a}_1$, $\mathbf{a}_2$, and $\mathbf{a}_3$.

More generally, if one particular member of a set of vectors in R^m can be expressed as a linear combination of the other vectors in the set, that vector is said to be *linearly dependent* on the others, and the whole set of vectors is said to be *linearly dependent*. But if no vector in the set can be expressed as a linear combination of the others, then the set of vectors is *linearly independent*.

It is convenient to have an equivalent but more symmetric definition of linearly dependent and independent vectors.

The n vectors $\mathbf{a}_1$, $\mathbf{a}_2$, $\ldots$, $\mathbf{a}_n$ in R^m are **linearly dependent** if there exist numbers $c_1, c_2, \ldots, c_n$ not all zero such that

$$c_1 \mathbf{a}_1 + c_2 \mathbf{a}_2 + \cdots + c_n \mathbf{a}_n = \mathbf{0} \qquad [14.1]$$

If this equation holds only when $c_1 = c_2 = \cdots = c_n = 0$, then the vectors are said to be **linearly independent**.

So a linear combination of linearly independent vectors can only be the **0** vector if all the coefficients in the linear combination are zero.

Example 14.1

(a) Prove that $\mathbf{a}_1 = \begin{pmatrix} 3 \\ 1 \end{pmatrix}$ and $\mathbf{a}_2 = \begin{pmatrix} 6 \\ 2 \end{pmatrix}$ are linearly dependent. Illustrate.

(b) Prove that $\mathbf{a}_1 = \begin{pmatrix} 3 \\ 1 \end{pmatrix}$ and $\mathbf{a}_2 = \begin{pmatrix} 1 \\ 2 \end{pmatrix}$ are linearly independent. Illustrate.

Solution

(a) Here $\mathbf{a}_2 = 2\mathbf{a}_1$, so $2\mathbf{a}_1 - \mathbf{a}_2 = \mathbf{0}$. Choosing $c_1 = 2$ and $c_2 = -1$ yields $c_1\mathbf{a}_1 + c_2\mathbf{a}_2 = \mathbf{0}$, so according to definition [14.1], $\mathbf{a}_1$ and $\mathbf{a}_2$ are linearly

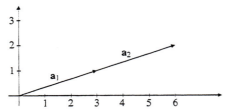

FIGURE 14.1   Vectors a_1 and a_2 are linearly dependent.

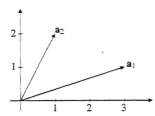

FIGURE 14.2   Vectors a_1 and a_2 are linearly independent.

dependent. The vector $\mathbf{a}_2$ points in the same direction as $\mathbf{a}_1$, and its length is twice that of $\mathbf{a}_1$. See Fig. 14.1.

(b) The equation $c_1\mathbf{a}_1 + c_2\mathbf{a}_2 = \mathbf{0}$ reduces in this case to

$$3c_1 + c_2 = 0$$
$$c_1 + 2c_2 = 0$$

This system has only the solution $c_1 = c_2 = 0$. Thus, $\mathbf{a}_1$ and $\mathbf{a}_2$ are linearly independent. See Fig. 14.2.

The formal definition of linear dependence given earlier might seem rather odd. However, we can very easily prove the following equivalence:
Any set of n vectors $\mathbf{a}_1, \mathbf{a}_2, \ldots, \mathbf{a}_n$ in R^m is linearly dependent if at least one of them can be written as a linear combination of the others.

Proof: First, suppose that $\mathbf{a}_1, \mathbf{a}_2, \ldots, \mathbf{a}_n$ are linearly dependent. Then the equation $c_1\mathbf{a}_1 + c_2\mathbf{a}_2 + \cdots + c_n\mathbf{a}_n = \mathbf{0}$ holds with at least *one* of the c_i's different from 0. After reordering the vectors $\mathbf{a}_i$ and the corresponding scalars c_i, if necessary, we can suppose, for example, that $c_1 \neq 0$. Solving the equation for $\mathbf{a}_1$ yields

$$\mathbf{a}_1 = -\frac{c_2}{c_1}\mathbf{a}_2 - \cdots - \frac{c_n}{c_1}\mathbf{a}_n$$

Thus, $\mathbf{a}_1$ has been expressed as a linear combination of the other vectors.

Suppose on the other hand that $\mathbf{a}_1$, say, can be written as a linear combination of the others, with $\mathbf{a}_1 = d_2\mathbf{a}_2 + d_3\mathbf{a}_3 + \cdots + d_n\mathbf{a}_n$. This equation can be written as

$$(-1)\mathbf{a}_1 + d_2\mathbf{a}_2 + d_3\mathbf{a}_3 + \cdots + d_n\mathbf{a}_n = \mathbf{0}$$

At least one of the coefficients is not 0, so the set $\mathbf{a}_1, \ldots, \mathbf{a}_n$ is linearly dependent.

A set of vectors which is not linearly dependent is linearly independent. Hence, the following is true.

Any set of vectors $\mathbf{a}_1, \mathbf{a}_2, \ldots, \mathbf{a}_n$ *in* R^m *is linearly independent iff none of them can be written as a linear combination of the others.*

It is very helpful to have a geometric feeling for the meaning of linear dependence and independence. For the case of R^2, Example 14.1 illustrated the possibilities. In R^3, let $\mathbf{a}_1$ and $\mathbf{a}_2$ be two non-parallel 3-vectors starting at the origin. If t_1 and t_2 are real numbers, then the vector $\mathbf{x} = t_1\mathbf{a}_1 + t_2\mathbf{a}_2$ is a linear combination of $\mathbf{a}_1$ and $\mathbf{a}_2$. Geometrically, the set of all linear combinations of $\mathbf{a}_1$ and $\mathbf{a}_2$ is called the plane **spanned** by $\mathbf{a}_1$ and $\mathbf{a}_2$. Any vector in the plane spanned by $\mathbf{a}_1$ and $\mathbf{a}_2$ is linearly dependent on $\mathbf{a}_1$ and $\mathbf{a}_2$.

Suppose we take another 3-vector $\mathbf{a}_3$ that is *not* in the plane spanned by $\mathbf{a}_1$ and $\mathbf{a}_2$. Then the three vectors $\mathbf{a}_1$, $\mathbf{a}_2$, and $\mathbf{a}_3$ are linearly independent, because no vector in the set can be written as a linear combination of the others. In general, three vectors in R^3 are linearly dependent iff they all lie in the same plane. Three vectors in R^3 are linearly independent iff there is no plane that contains all three vectors. Figures 14.3 and 14.4 give geometric illustrations of these statements.

In R^m, the two m-vectors $\mathbf{a}_1$ and $\mathbf{a}_2$ are linearly dependent iff one of the vectors, say, $\mathbf{a}_1$, is proportional to the other, so that $\mathbf{a}_1 = c\mathbf{a}_2$. If $c \neq 0$, the two vectors are called **parallel**.

FIGURE 14.3 Vectors $\mathbf{a}_1$, $\mathbf{a}_2$, and $\mathbf{a}_3$ are linearly dependent.

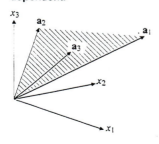

FIGURE 14.4 Vectors $\mathbf{a}_1$, $\mathbf{a}_2$, and $\mathbf{a}_3$ are linearly independent.

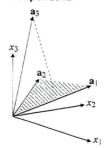

Linear Dependence and Systems of Linear Equations

Consider the general system of m equations in n unknowns, written both in its usual form and also as a vector equation:

$$a_{11}x_1 + \cdots + a_{1n}x_n = b_1$$
$$\cdots\cdots\cdots\cdots\cdots\cdots \iff x_1\mathbf{a}_1 + \cdots + x_n\mathbf{a}_n = \mathbf{b} \qquad [14.2]$$
$$a_{m1}x_1 + \cdots + a_{mn}x_n = b_m$$

Here $\mathbf{a}_1, \ldots, \mathbf{a}_n$ are the column vectors of coefficients, and $\mathbf{b}$ is the column vector with components $b_1, \ldots, b_m$. (See Example 12.4 of Section 12.2.)

Suppose that [14.2] has two solutions $(u_1, \ldots, u_n)$ and $(v_1, \ldots, v_n)$. Then

$$u_1\mathbf{a}_1 + \cdots + u_n\mathbf{a}_n = \mathbf{b} \qquad \text{and} \qquad v_1\mathbf{a}_1 + \cdots + v_n\mathbf{a}_n = \mathbf{b}$$

Subtracting the second equation from the first yields

$$(u_1 - v_1)\mathbf{a}_1 + \cdots + (u_n - v_n)\mathbf{a}_n = \mathbf{0} \qquad [*]$$

Let $c_1 = u_1 - v_1, \ldots, c_n = u_n - v_n$. The condition that the solutions are different is equivalent to the condition that $c_1, \ldots, c_n$ are not all equal to 0. We conclude that if system [14.2] has more than one solution, then column vectors $\mathbf{a}_1, \ldots, \mathbf{a}_n$ are linearly dependent. Equivalently: If column vectors $\mathbf{a}_1, \ldots, \mathbf{a}_n$ are linearly independent, then system [14.2] has at most one solution. Without saying more about the right-hand side vector $\mathbf{b}$, however, we cannot know if there are any solutions at all, in general.

Example 14.2

Consider n vectors $\mathbf{a}_1, \mathbf{a}_2, \ldots, \mathbf{a}_n$ in R^n, and let $\mathbf{A}$ be the $n \times n$ matrix with these n vectors as columns:

$$\mathbf{A} = \begin{pmatrix} a_{11} & a_{12} & \cdots & a_{1n} \\ a_{21} & a_{22} & \cdots & a_{2n} \\ \vdots & \vdots & \ddots & \vdots \\ a_{n1} & a_{n2} & \cdots & a_{nn} \end{pmatrix} \qquad \text{where} \qquad \mathbf{a}_j = \begin{pmatrix} a_{1j} \\ a_{2j} \\ \vdots \\ a_{nj} \end{pmatrix} \qquad [14.3]$$

Prove that the n column vectors are linearly independent iff $|\mathbf{A}| \neq 0$.

Solution The vectors $\mathbf{a}_1, \mathbf{a}_2, \ldots, \mathbf{a}_n$ are linearly independent iff the vector equation $x_1\mathbf{a}_1 + x_2\mathbf{a}_2 + \cdots + x_n\mathbf{a}_n = \mathbf{0}$ has only the trivial solution $x_1 = x_2 = \cdots = x_n = 0$. This vector equation is equivalent to the homogeneous system [13.34] in Theorem 13.7 of Section 13.8, and this theorem shows that [13.34] has only the trivial solution iff $|\mathbf{A}| \neq 0$.

Note: Two vectors $\mathbf{a}_1$ and $\mathbf{a}_2$ in R^2 are linearly dependent iff the determinant $|\mathbf{a}_1\mathbf{a}_2|$ of the matrix with columns $\mathbf{a}_1$ and $\mathbf{a}_2$ is zero, which is true iff the area shown in Fig. 13.1 collapses to zero. A similar statement is true if $|\mathbf{a}_1\mathbf{a}_2\mathbf{a}_3| = 0$, where $\mathbf{a}_1$, $\mathbf{a}_2$, and $\mathbf{a}_3$ are three vectors in R^3 (see Fig. 13.3 of Section 13.2).

Problems

1. Express $\begin{pmatrix} 8 \\ 9 \end{pmatrix}$ as a linear combination of $\begin{pmatrix} 2 \\ 5 \end{pmatrix}$ and $\begin{pmatrix} -1 \\ 3 \end{pmatrix}$.

2. Decide which of the following pairs of vectors are linearly independent:

   a. $\begin{pmatrix} -1 \\ 2 \end{pmatrix}$, $\begin{pmatrix} 3 \\ -6 \end{pmatrix}$ **b.** $\begin{pmatrix} 2 \\ -1 \end{pmatrix}$, $\begin{pmatrix} 3 \\ 4 \end{pmatrix}$ **c.** $\begin{pmatrix} -1 \\ 1 \end{pmatrix}$, $\begin{pmatrix} 1 \\ -1 \end{pmatrix}$

3. Prove that $\begin{pmatrix} 1 \\ 0 \\ 1 \end{pmatrix}$, $\begin{pmatrix} 2 \\ 1 \\ 0 \end{pmatrix}$, and $\begin{pmatrix} 0 \\ 1 \\ 1 \end{pmatrix}$ are linearly independent. (Use the result in Example 14.2.)

4. Prove that vectors $(1, 1, 1)$, $(2, 1, 0)$, $(3, 1, 4)$, and $(1, 2, -2)$ are linearly dependent.

5. If $\mathbf{a}$, $\mathbf{b}$, and $\mathbf{c}$ are linearly independent vectors in R^m, prove that $\mathbf{a} + \mathbf{b}$, $\mathbf{b} + \mathbf{c}$, and $\mathbf{a} + \mathbf{c}$ are also linearly independent. Is the same true for $\mathbf{a} - \mathbf{b}$, $\mathbf{b} + \mathbf{c}$, and $\mathbf{a} + \mathbf{c}$?

6. **a.** Suppose that $\mathbf{a}, \mathbf{b}, \mathbf{c} \in R^3$ are all different from $\mathbf{0}$, and that $\mathbf{a} \perp \mathbf{b}$, $\mathbf{b} \perp \mathbf{c}$, $\mathbf{a} \perp \mathbf{c}$. Prove that $\mathbf{a}$, $\mathbf{b}$, and $\mathbf{c}$ are linearly independent.

   b. Suppose that $\mathbf{a}_1, \ldots, \mathbf{a}_n$ are vectors in R^m, all different from $\mathbf{0}$. Suppose that $\mathbf{a}_i \perp \mathbf{a}_j$ for all $i \neq j$. Prove that $\mathbf{a}_1, \ldots, \mathbf{a}_n$ are linearly independent.

7. Prove the following results:

   a. If a set of vectors is linearly dependent, then any *larger* set (that is, any set containing the original) is also linearly dependent.

   b. If a set of vectors is linearly independent, then any subset (that is, any set contained in the original) is linearly independent.

14.2 The Rank of a Matrix

Associated with any matrix is an important number called its *rank*. An $m \times n$ matrix $\mathbf{A}$ has n column vectors, each with m components. The largest number of such column vectors in $\mathbf{A}$ that form a linearly independent set is called the **rank** of $\mathbf{A}$, denoted by $r(\mathbf{A})$.

> The **rank** of a matrix $\mathbf{A}$, written $r(\mathbf{A})$, is the maximum number of linearly independent column vectors in $\mathbf{A}$. If $\mathbf{A}$ is any $\mathbf{0}$ matrix, we put $r(\mathbf{A}) = 0$.   [14.4]

Knowing the rank of a matrix gives very useful information. In particular, it is of central importance in stating the main results concerning the existence and multiplicity of solutions to linear systems of equations discussed in the next section.

Example 14.3

Let A be a square matrix of order n. Because the matrix has only n columns, the rank must be less than or equal to n. In fact, according to Example 14.2, the n column vectors of A are linearly independent iff $|A| \neq 0$. We conclude that a square matrix A of order n has rank n iff $|A| \neq 0$.

The rank of a matrix can be characterized in terms of the nonvanishing minors of the matrix. In general, a **minor** of order k in A is obtained by deleting all but k rows and k columns of A, and then taking the determinant of the resulting $k \times k$ matrix.

Example 14.4

Describe all the minors of the matrix $A = \begin{pmatrix} 1 & 0 & 2 & 1 \\ 0 & 2 & 4 & 2 \\ 0 & 2 & 2 & 1 \end{pmatrix}$.

Solution   There are:

(a) *4 minors of order 3.* These are obtained by deleting any one of the 4 columns:

$$\begin{vmatrix} 1 & 0 & 2 \\ 0 & 2 & 4 \\ 0 & 2 & 2 \end{vmatrix}, \quad \begin{vmatrix} 1 & 0 & 1 \\ 0 & 2 & 2 \\ 0 & 2 & 1 \end{vmatrix}, \quad \begin{vmatrix} 1 & 2 & 1 \\ 0 & 4 & 2 \\ 0 & 2 & 1 \end{vmatrix}, \quad \begin{vmatrix} 0 & 2 & 1 \\ 2 & 4 & 2 \\ 2 & 2 & 1 \end{vmatrix}$$

(b) *18 minors of order 2.* These are obtained by deleting one row and two columns, in all possible ways. Two of them are:

$$\begin{vmatrix} 1 & 0 \\ 0 & 2 \end{vmatrix}$$ (deleting the third row and the third and fourth columns)

$$\begin{vmatrix} 0 & 1 \\ 2 & 1 \end{vmatrix}$$ (deleting the second row and the first and third columns)

(c) *12 minors of order 1.* These are all the 12 individual elements of A.

The relation between the rank and the minors is expressed in the following theorem:

Theorem 14.1   The rank $r(A)$ of matrix A is equal to the order of the largest minor of A that is different from 0.

If $\mathbf{A}$ is a square matrix of order n, then the largest minor of $\mathbf{A}$ is $|\mathbf{A}|$ itself. So $r(\mathbf{A}) = n$ iff $|\mathbf{A}| \neq 0$. This accords with Example 14.2.[1]

Example 14.5

Find the ranks of the following matrices:

(a) $\begin{pmatrix} 1 & 0 & 2 & 1 \\ 0 & 2 & 4 & 2 \\ 0 & 2 & 2 & 1 \end{pmatrix}$ (b) $\begin{pmatrix} -1 & 0 & 2 & 1 \\ -2 & 2 & 4 & 2 \\ -3 & 1 & 6 & 3 \end{pmatrix}$ (c) $\begin{pmatrix} -1 & 0 & 2 & 1 \\ -2 & 0 & 4 & 2 \\ -3 & 0 & 6 & 3 \end{pmatrix}$

Solution   None of the matrices has a rank higher than 3, because there are no minors of order 4 or higher in any of the three matrices.

(a) The rank is 3 because the following minor of order 3 is $\neq 0$:

$$\begin{vmatrix} 1 & 0 & 2 \\ 0 & 2 & 4 \\ 0 & 2 & 2 \end{vmatrix} = -4$$

(b) All minors of order 3 are 0, whereas $\begin{vmatrix} -1 & 0 \\ -2 & 2 \end{vmatrix}$, say, equals -2, so the rank is 2.

(c) All minors of order 3 and 2 are 0. Because not all elements are 0, the rank is 1.

Example 14.6

Determine the rank of the following matrix, for all values of x:

$$\mathbf{A} = \begin{pmatrix} 5 - x & 2 & 1 \\ 2 & 1 - x & 0 \\ 1 & 0 & 1 - x \end{pmatrix}$$

Solution   Expanding $|\mathbf{A}|$ by the third column, we see that

$$|\mathbf{A}| = 1[-(1 - x)] + (1 - x)[(5 - x)(1 - x) - 4] = x(1 - x)(x - 6)$$

If $x \neq 0$, $x \neq 1$, and $x \neq 6$, then the rank is 3. Because the minor

$$\begin{vmatrix} 5 - x & 2 \\ 1 & 0 \end{vmatrix} = -2 \neq 0$$

whatever the value of x, we see that the rank of the matrix is 2 when x is 0, 1, or 6.

[1] Proofs of Theorem 14.1 are given in most books on linear algebra, for example, Hadley (1973).

Recall that the determinant of a matrix is equal to the determinant of its transpose. The following result is therefore not surprising:

Theorem 14.2   The rank of a matrix **A** is equal to the rank of its transpose: $r(\mathbf{A}) = r(\mathbf{A}')$.

Proof   Suppose $|\mathbf{D}|$ is a minor of **A**. Then $|\mathbf{D}'|$ is a minor of $\mathbf{A}'$, and vice versa. Because $|\mathbf{D}'| = |\mathbf{D}|$, the result follows from Theorem 14.1.

It follows from [14.4] and Theorem 14.2 that the rank of a matrix can also be characterized as the maximal number of linearly independent rows of **A**. So we have three ways of showing that $r(\mathbf{A}) = k$:

(a) Find one set of k columns that is linearly independent, and then show that no set of *more* than k columns is linearly independent.

(b) Find one set of k rows that is linearly independent, and then show that no set of *more* than k rows is linearly independent.

(c) Find one minor of order k that is not 0, and then show that *all* minors of order higher than k are 0.

An Efficient Way of Finding the Rank of a Matrix

None of the methods described earlier for finding the rank of a matrix is very efficient. A better method is based on the fact that the rank of a matrix is not affected by elementary operations. (See, for example, Hadley (1973).) At the end of Section 13.7, we defined elementary row operations. If the corresponding operations are performed on the columns, we call them elementary column operations. Elementary row and column operations, which were useful for computing determinants and for finding inverses, are also convenient when we wish to determine the rank of a matrix. In the following, if matrix **A** can be transformed into **B** by using elementary operations, then we write $\mathbf{A} \sim \mathbf{B}$.

Example 14.7

Find the rank of $\begin{pmatrix} 1 & 2 & 3 & 2 \\ 2 & 3 & 5 & 1 \\ 1 & 3 & 4 & 5 \end{pmatrix}$.

Solution   Here

$$\begin{pmatrix} 1 & 2 & 3 & 2 \\ 2 & 3 & 5 & 1 \\ 1 & 3 & 4 & 5 \end{pmatrix} \xleftarrow[\quad]{-2 \quad -1} \sim \begin{pmatrix} 1 & 2 & 3 & 2 \\ 0 & -1 & -1 & -3 \\ 0 & 1 & 1 & 3 \end{pmatrix} \xleftarrow{1}$$

$$\sim \begin{pmatrix} 1 & 2 & 3 & 2 \\ 0 & -1 & -1 & -3 \\ 0 & 0 & 0 & 0 \end{pmatrix}$$

The rank of the last matrix is obviously 2, because there are precisely two linearly independent rows. So the original matrix has rank 2.

Problems

1. Determine the rank of the following matrices:

a. $\begin{pmatrix} 1 & 2 \\ 8 & 16 \end{pmatrix}$
   b. $\begin{pmatrix} 1 & 3 & 4 \\ 2 & 0 & 1 \end{pmatrix}$

c. $\begin{pmatrix} 1 & 2 & -1 & 3 \\ 2 & 4 & -4 & 7 \\ -1 & -2 & -1 & -2 \end{pmatrix}$
   d. $\begin{pmatrix} 1 & 3 & 0 & 0 \\ 2 & 4 & 0 & -1 \\ 1 & -1 & 2 & 2 \end{pmatrix}$

e. $\begin{pmatrix} 2 & 1 & 3 & 7 \\ -1 & 4 & 3 & 1 \\ 3 & 2 & 5 & 11 \end{pmatrix}$
   f. $\begin{pmatrix} 1 & -2 & -1 & 1 \\ 2 & 1 & 1 & 2 \\ -1 & 1 & -1 & -3 \\ -2 & -5 & -2 & 0 \end{pmatrix}$

2. Determine the rank of the following matrices for all values of the parameters:

a. $\begin{pmatrix} x & 0 & x^2 - 2 \\ 0 & 1 & 1 \\ -1 & x & x - 1 \end{pmatrix}$
   b. $\begin{pmatrix} t+3 & 5 & 6 \\ -1 & t-3 & -6 \\ 1 & 1 & t+4 \end{pmatrix}$

c. $\begin{pmatrix} 1 & x & y & 0 \\ 0 & z & w & 1 \\ 1 & x & y & 0 \\ 0 & z & w & 1 \end{pmatrix}$

3. Give an example where $r(\mathbf{AB}) \neq r(\mathbf{BA})$. (*Hint:* Try some 2×2 matrices.)

14.3 Main Results on Linear Systems of Equations

Consider the general linear system of m simultaneous equations in n unknowns:

$$
\begin{aligned}
a_{11}x_1 + a_{12}x_2 + \cdots + a_{1n}x_n &= b_1 \\
a_{21}x_1 + a_{22}x_2 + \cdots + a_{2n}x_n &= b_2 \\
&\cdots \cdots \\
a_{m1}x_1 + a_{m2}x_2 + \cdots + a_{mn}x_n &= b_m
\end{aligned}
\qquad [14.5]
$$

or

$$\mathbf{Ax} = \mathbf{b}$$

where $\mathbf{A}$ is the $m \times n$ coefficient matrix.

Define a new $m \times (n + 1)$ **augmented** matrix $\mathbf{A_b}$ that contains $\mathbf{A}$ in the first n columns and $\mathbf{b}$ in column $n + 1$:

$$\mathbf{A} = \begin{pmatrix} a_{11} & a_{12} & \cdots & a_{1n} \\ a_{21} & a_{22} & \cdots & a_{2n} \\ \vdots & \vdots & & \vdots \\ a_{m1} & a_{m2} & \cdots & a_{mn} \end{pmatrix} \quad \text{and} \quad \mathbf{A_b} = \begin{pmatrix} a_{11} & a_{12} & \cdots & a_{1n} & b_1 \\ a_{21} & a_{22} & \cdots & a_{2n} & b_2 \\ \vdots & \vdots & & \vdots & \vdots \\ a_{m1} & a_{m2} & \cdots & a_{mn} & b_m \end{pmatrix}$$

It turns out that the relationship between the ranks of $\mathbf{A}$ and $\mathbf{A_b}$ is crucial in determining whether or not system [14.5] has a solution. Because all the columns in $\mathbf{A}$ occur in $\mathbf{A_b}$, the rank of $\mathbf{A}$ is certainly less than or equal to the rank of $\mathbf{A_b}$. Moreover, because $\mathbf{A_b}$ contains only one more column than $\mathbf{A}$, the number $r(\mathbf{A_b})$ cannot be greater than $r(\mathbf{A}) + 1$.

Theorem 14.3 A necessary and sufficient condition for a linear system of equations to be consistent (that is, to have at least one solution) is that the rank of the coefficient matrix is equal to the rank of the augmented matrix. Briefly:

$$\mathbf{Ax = b} \quad \text{has a solution} \quad \Longleftrightarrow \quad r(\mathbf{A}) = r(\mathbf{A_b})$$

Proof Let the column vectors in $\mathbf{A_b}$ be $\mathbf{a}_1, \mathbf{a}_2, \ldots, \mathbf{a}_n, \mathbf{b}$. and suppose that [14.5] has a solution $(x_1, \ldots, x_n)$ such that $x_1\mathbf{a}_1 + \cdots + x_n\mathbf{a}_n = \mathbf{b}$. Multiplying the first n columns in $\mathbf{A_b}$ by $-x_1, \ldots, -x_n$, respectively, and adding the sum of the resulting column vectors to the last column in $\mathbf{A_b}$, it follows that $\mathbf{A_b} \sim [\mathbf{a}_1, \ldots, \mathbf{a}_n, \mathbf{0}]$. Evidently, this matrix has the same rank as $\mathbf{A}$, so $r(\mathbf{A_b}) = r(\mathbf{A})$, because elementary column operations preserve the rank.

Suppose on the other hand that $r(\mathbf{A}) = r(\mathbf{A_b}) = k$. Then k of the columns of $\mathbf{A}$ are linearly independent. To simplify notation, suppose that the first k columns $\mathbf{a}_1, \ldots, \mathbf{a}_k$ are linearly independent. Because $r(\mathbf{A_b}) = k$, vector $\mathbf{b}$ can be written as a linear combination $\mathbf{b} = x_1^0\mathbf{a}_1 + \cdots + x_k^0\mathbf{a}_k$ of $\mathbf{a}_1, \ldots, \mathbf{a}_k$. otherwise $\mathbf{A_b}$ would have rank $k + 1$. But then $(x_1^0, \ldots, x_k^0, 0, \ldots, 0)$ is a solution of $\mathbf{Ax = b}$.

Theorem 14.3 yields a very simple test for deciding whether or not a linear system of equations has solutions. The system has at least one solution iff $r(\mathbf{A}) = r(\mathbf{A_b})$. For instance, if $m = 5$, $n = 10$, and $r(\mathbf{A}) = r(\mathbf{A_b}) = 2$, then the system has at least one solution.

Example 14.8

Apply Theorem 14.3 to the system

$$2x_1 - x_2 = 3$$
$$4x_1 - 2x_2 = 5$$

Solution   Here

$$\mathbf{A} = \begin{pmatrix} 2 & -1 \\ 4 & -2 \end{pmatrix} \quad \text{and} \quad \mathbf{A_b} = \begin{pmatrix} 2 & -1 & 3 \\ 4 & -2 & 5 \end{pmatrix}$$

We see that $|\mathbf{A}| = 0$, so $r(\mathbf{A}) < 2$. Because not all the elements in $\mathbf{A}$ are 0, it follows that $r(\mathbf{A}) = 1$. But $r(\mathbf{A_b}) = 2$, because the minor obtained by deleting the first column is equal to 1. Thus, $r(\mathbf{A}) \neq r(\mathbf{A_b})$, so the system has no solutions. We confirm this result by elimination. From the first equation, $x_2 = 2x_1 - 3$, which inserted into the second equation yields $4x_1 - 4x_1 + 6 = 5$, and so we have the contradiction $6 = 5$.

Superfluous Equations

Consider the case where $r(\mathbf{A}) = r(\mathbf{A_b}) = k$ with $k < m$, so that the common rank of $\mathbf{A}$ and $\mathbf{A_b}$ is less than the number of equations. The maximum number of linearly independent row vectors in $\mathbf{A_b}$ is k, so there exist k row vectors in $\mathbf{A_b}$ that are linearly independent, and any other row vector in $\mathbf{A_b}$ is a linear combination of those k vectors. We will now prove that, if the vector $(x_1^0, x_2^0, \ldots, x_n^0)$ satisfies the k equations corresponding to the k linearly independent row vectors in $\mathbf{A_b}$, then it also satisfies any other equation corresponding to a row in $\mathbf{A_b}$ that is a linear combination of these k rows.

To simplify notation, assume that the first k row vectors in $\mathbf{A_b}$ are linearly independent. For $s = k + 1, \ldots, m$, we can then put

$$(a_{s1}, a_{s2}, \ldots, a_{sn}, b_s) = \sum_{l=1}^{k} \lambda_{sl}(a_{l1}, a_{l2}, \ldots, a_{ln}, b_l) \qquad [*]$$

for suitable constants $\lambda_{s1}, \lambda_{s2}, \ldots, \lambda_{sk}$. Suppose that $\sum_{j=1}^{n} a_{lj} x_j^0 = b_l$, for $l = 1, \ldots, k$, so that $(x_1^0, \ldots, x_n^0)$ satisfies the k first equations in [14.5]. From [*], we see in particular that $a_{sj} = \sum_{l=1}^{k} \lambda_{sl} a_{lj}$ and that $b_s = \sum_{l=1}^{k} \lambda_{sl} b_l$. For $s = k + 1, \ldots, m$, we therefore obtain

$$\sum_{j=1}^{n} a_{sj} x_j^0 = \sum_{j=1}^{n} \left(\sum_{l=1}^{k} \lambda_{sl} a_{lj} \right) x_j^0$$

$$= \sum_{l=1}^{k} \lambda_{sl} \left(\sum_{j=1}^{n} a_{lj} x_j^0 \right) = \sum_{l=1}^{k} \lambda_{sl} b_l = b_s$$

This confirms that if $(x_1^0, \ldots, x_n^0)$ satisfies the first k equations in [14.5], then it is automatically a solution of the last $m - k$ equations in [14.5].

Theorem 14.4   Suppose that system [14.5] has solutions and that the common rank $r(\mathbf{A}) = r(\mathbf{A_b}) = k < m$. Then there exist $m - k$ of the equations that are superfluous, in the sense that any solution that satisfies the other k equations will also satisfy these $m - k$ equations. The $m - k$ equations can be ignored, therefore, when solving the system.

Degrees of Freedom

Consider the case where $r(\mathbf{A}) = r(\mathbf{A_b}) = k$, with k less than the number of variables in the system. Because $r(\mathbf{A}) = k$, we know that there exists at least one minor of order k in $\mathbf{A}$ that is different from 0 (Theorem 14.1). After renumbering the equations and the variables (if necessary), we can assume that the $k \times k$ matrix

$$\begin{pmatrix} a_{11} & a_{12} & \cdots & a_{1k} \\ a_{21} & a_{22} & \cdots & a_{2k} \\ \vdots & \vdots & \ddots & \vdots \\ a_{k1} & a_{k2} & \cdots & a_{kk} \end{pmatrix}$$

in the upper left-hand corner of $\mathbf{A}$ has a nonzero determinant. If $k < m$, then the last $m - k$ equations in [14.5] are superfluous and the whole system [14.5] has exactly the same solutions as the first k equations on their own:

$$\begin{aligned} a_{11}x_1 + \cdots + a_{1k}x_k + a_{1,k+1}x_{k+1} + \cdots + a_{1n}x_n &= b_1 \\ a_{21}x_1 + \cdots + a_{2k}x_k + a_{2,k+1}x_{k+1} + \cdots + a_{2n}x_n &= b_2 \\ &\cdots\cdots\cdots\cdots\cdots\cdots\cdots\cdots\cdots\cdots\cdots\cdots\cdots\cdots \\ a_{k1}x_1 + \cdots + a_{kk}x_k + a_{k,k+1}x_{k+1} + \cdots + a_{kn}x_n &= b_k \end{aligned}$$

[1]

We introduce the following helpful notation:

$$\mathbf{C} = \begin{pmatrix} a_{11} & \cdots & a_{1k} \\ \vdots & \ddots & \vdots \\ a_{k1} & \cdots & a_{kk} \end{pmatrix}, \qquad \mathbf{R} = \begin{pmatrix} a_{1,k+1} & \cdots & a_{1n} \\ \vdots & & \vdots \\ a_{k,k+1} & \cdots & a_{kn} \end{pmatrix}$$

$$\mathbf{y} = \begin{pmatrix} x_1 \\ \vdots \\ x_k \end{pmatrix}, \qquad \mathbf{z} = \begin{pmatrix} x_{k+1} \\ \vdots \\ x_n \end{pmatrix}, \qquad \mathbf{b}^* = \begin{pmatrix} b_1 \\ \vdots \\ b_k \end{pmatrix}$$

Then system [1] can be written in matrix form:

$$\mathbf{Cy} + \mathbf{Rz} = \mathbf{b}^* \qquad \text{or} \qquad \mathbf{Cy} = \mathbf{b}^* - \mathbf{Rz}$$

[2]

Because we assumed that $|\mathbf{C}| \neq 0$, the matrix $\mathbf{C}$ has an inverse $\mathbf{C}^{-1}$. Multiply each side of the second equation in [2] on the left by $\mathbf{C}^{-1}$ to obtain

$$\mathbf{y} = \mathbf{C}^{-1}\mathbf{b}^* - \mathbf{C}^{-1}\mathbf{R}\mathbf{z} \qquad [3]$$

Suppose we choose an arbitrary vector $\mathbf{z}$, with components $x_{k+1}, x_{k+2}, \ldots, x_n$. Then the vector $\mathbf{y}$, and thus $x_1, x_2, \ldots, x_k$, are all uniquely determined, with the latter as linear functions of $x_{k+1}, x_{k+2}, \ldots, x_n$. We have the following theorem:

Theorem 14.5   Suppose that system [14.5] has solutions and that $r(\mathbf{A}) = r(\mathbf{A_b}) = k < n$. Then there exist $n - k$ of the variables that can be chosen freely, whereas the remaining k variables are uniquely determined by the choice of these $n - k$ free variables. We say that the system has $n - k$ **degrees of freedom**.

Example 14.9

Decide whether the following system of equations has any solutions, and if it has, find the number of degrees of freedom.

$$
\begin{aligned}
x_1 + x_2 - 2x_3 + x_4 + 3x_5 &= 1 \\
2x_1 - x_2 + 2x_3 + 2x_4 + 6x_5 &= 2 \\
3x_1 + 5x_2 - 10x_3 - 3x_4 - 9x_5 &= 3 \\
3x_1 + 2x_2 - 4x_3 - 3x_4 - 9x_5 &= 3
\end{aligned}
$$

Solution   Here

$$
\mathbf{A} = \begin{pmatrix}
1 & 1 & -2 & 1 & 3 \\
2 & -1 & 2 & 2 & 6 \\
3 & 5 & -10 & -3 & -9 \\
3 & 2 & -4 & -3 & -9
\end{pmatrix}
$$

and

$$
\mathbf{A_b} = \begin{pmatrix}
1 & 1 & -2 & 1 & 3 & 1 \\
2 & -1 & 2 & 2 & 6 & 2 \\
3 & 5 & -10 & -3 & -9 & 3 \\
3 & 2 & -4 & -3 & -9 & 3
\end{pmatrix}
$$

In general, $r(\mathbf{A_b}) \geq r(\mathbf{A})$. All minors of order 4 in $\mathbf{A_b}$ are equal to 0 (note that several pairs of columns are proportional), so that $r(\mathbf{A_b}) \leq 3$. Now, there are minors of order 3 that are different from 0. For example, the minor formed by the first, third, and fourth columns, and by the first, second, and fourth rows, is different from 0 because

$$\begin{vmatrix} 1 & -2 & 1 \\ 2 & 2 & 2 \\ 3 & -4 & -3 \end{vmatrix} = -36 \qquad [*]$$

Hence, $r(\mathbf{A}) = 3$. Because $3 \geq r(\mathbf{A_b}) \geq r(\mathbf{A})$, we have $r(\mathbf{A}) = r(\mathbf{A_b}) = 3$, and the system has solutions. There is one superfluous equation. Because the first, second, and fourth rows in $\mathbf{A_b}$ are linearly independent, the third equation can be dropped. The number of variables is 5, and because $r(\mathbf{A}) = r(\mathbf{A_b}) = 3$, there are *2 degrees of freedom*.

Next we find all the solutions to the system of equations. The determinant in $[*]$ is different from 0, so we rewrite the subsystem of three independent equations in the form

$$\begin{aligned} x_1 &- 2x_3 + x_4 + x_2 + 3x_5 = 1 \\ 2x_1 &+ 2x_3 + 2x_4 - x_2 + 6x_5 = 2 \\ 3x_1 &- 4x_3 - 3x_4 + 2x_2 - 9x_5 = 3 \end{aligned} \qquad [**]$$

or, in matrix form, as

$$\begin{pmatrix} 1 & -2 & 1 \\ 2 & 2 & 2 \\ 3 & -4 & -3 \end{pmatrix} \begin{pmatrix} x_1 \\ x_3 \\ x_4 \end{pmatrix} + \begin{pmatrix} 1 & 3 \\ -1 & 6 \\ 2 & -9 \end{pmatrix} \begin{pmatrix} x_2 \\ x_5 \end{pmatrix} = \begin{pmatrix} 1 \\ 2 \\ 3 \end{pmatrix}$$

The 3×3 coefficient matrix corresponding to x_1, x_3, and x_4 in $[**]$ has a determinant different from 0, so it has an inverse. Therefore,

$$\begin{pmatrix} x_1 \\ x_3 \\ x_4 \end{pmatrix} = \begin{pmatrix} 1 & -2 & 1 \\ 2 & 2 & 2 \\ 3 & -4 & -3 \end{pmatrix}^{-1} \begin{pmatrix} 1 \\ 2 \\ 3 \end{pmatrix} - \begin{pmatrix} 1 & -2 & 1 \\ 2 & 2 & 2 \\ 3 & -4 & -3 \end{pmatrix}^{-1} \begin{pmatrix} 1 & 3 \\ -1 & 6 \\ 2 & -9 \end{pmatrix} \begin{pmatrix} x_2 \\ x_5 \end{pmatrix}$$

Now it is easy to verify that

$$\begin{pmatrix} 1 & -2 & 1 \\ 2 & 2 & 2 \\ 3 & -4 & -3 \end{pmatrix}^{-1} = \frac{1}{18} \begin{pmatrix} -1 & 5 & 3 \\ -6 & 3 & 0 \\ 7 & 1 & -3 \end{pmatrix}$$

Then, after some routine algebra, we have

$$\begin{pmatrix} x_1 \\ x_3 \\ x_4 \end{pmatrix} = \begin{pmatrix} 1 \\ 0 \\ 0 \end{pmatrix} - \begin{pmatrix} 0 \\ -\frac{1}{2}x_2 \\ 3x_5 \end{pmatrix} = \begin{pmatrix} 1 \\ \frac{1}{2}x_2 \\ -3x_5 \end{pmatrix}$$

So, if $x_2 = a$ and $x_5 = b$ are arbitrary real numbers, then there is a solution

$$x_1 = 1, \quad x_2 = a, \quad x_3 = \tfrac{1}{2}a, \quad x_4 = -3b, \quad x_5 = b$$

This confirms that there are 2 degrees of freedom. (You should verify that the values found for $x_1, \ldots, x_5$ do satisfy the original system of equations for all possible values of a and b.)

The concept of degrees of freedom that was introduced in Theorem 14.5 is very important. Note that if a linear system of equations has k degrees of freedom, then there *exist* k variables that can be chosen freely. It is not necessarily the first k variables that can be chosen freely. For instance, in Example 14.9 there are 2 degrees of freedom, but x_1 cannot be chosen freely because $x_1 = 1$.

Problems

1. Use Theorems 14.3 to 14.5 in order to examine whether the following systems of equations have solutions. If they do, determine the number of degrees of freedom. Find all the solutions. Check the results by elimination.

   a. $-2x_1 - 3x_2 + x_3 = 3$
   $\quad\;\; 4x_1 + 6x_2 - 2x_3 = 1$

   b. $x_1 + x_2 - x_3 + x_4 = 2$
   $\quad\;\; 2x_1 - x_2 + x_3 - 3x_4 = 1$

   c. $x_1 - x_2 + 2x_3 + x_4 = 1$
   $\quad\; 2x_1 + x_2 - x_3 + 3x_4 = 3$
   $\quad\;\; x_1 + 5x_2 - 8x_3 + x_4 = 1$
   $\quad\; 4x_1 + 5x_2 - 7x_3 + 7x_4 = 7$

   d. $x_1 + x_2 + 2x_3 + x_4 = 5$
   $\quad\; 2x_1 + 3x_2 - x_3 - 2x_4 = 2$
   $\quad\; 4x_1 + 5x_2 + 3x_3 \quad\;\;\; = 7$

   e. $x_1 - x_2 + x_3 = 0$
   $\quad\;\; x_1 + 2x_2 - x_3 = 0$
   $\quad\; 2x_1 + x_2 + 3x_3 = 0$

   f. $x_1 + x_2 + x_3 + x_4 = 0$
   $\quad\;\; x_1 + 3x_2 + 2x_3 + 4x_4 = 0$
   $\quad\; 2x_1 + x_2 \quad\quad - x_4 = 0$

2. Prove that the system

$$2x + 3y = k$$
$$x + cy = 1$$

has a unique solution, except for one particular value c^* of c. Find this solution. Prove also that for $c = c^*$, the system has no solution except for a special value k^* of k. Find the solution for $k = k^*$.

3. Discuss the solutions of

$$x + 2y + 3z = 1$$
$$-x + ay - 21z = 2$$
$$3x + 7y + az = b$$

for different values of a and b.

4. Let $\mathbf{Ax} = \mathbf{b}$ be a linear system of equations in matrix form. Prove that if $\mathbf{x}_1$ and $\mathbf{x}_2$ are both solutions of the system, then so is $(1 - \lambda)\mathbf{x}_1 + \lambda\mathbf{x}_2$ for all real numbers λ. Use this fact to prove that a linear system of equations that is consistent has either one solution or infinitely many solutions. (For instance, it cannot have exactly three solutions.)

5. Consider the system

$$\begin{array}{rcrcrcr} x_1 & + & x_2 & + & x_3 & = & 2q \\ 2x_1 & - & 3x_2 & + & 2x_3 & = & 4q \\ 3x_1 & - & 2x_2 & + & px_3 & = & q \end{array}$$

where p and q are arbitrary constants.

a. For what values of p and q does this system have a unique solution, several solutions, or no solution?

b. Determine for each value of p the set of all vectors $\mathbf{z}$ that are orthogonal to the three vectors

$$\begin{pmatrix} 1 \\ 1 \\ 1 \end{pmatrix}, \quad \begin{pmatrix} 2 \\ -3 \\ 2 \end{pmatrix}, \quad \begin{pmatrix} 3 \\ -2 \\ p \end{pmatrix}$$

c. Let $\mathbf{a}_1, \ldots, \mathbf{a}_n$ be n linearly independent vectors in R^n. Prove that if a vector $\mathbf{b}$ in R^n is orthogonal to all vectors $\mathbf{a}_1, \ldots, \mathbf{a}_n$, then $\mathbf{b} = \mathbf{0}$.

6. Let the matrix $\mathbf{A}_t$ be defined for all real numbers t by

$$\mathbf{A}_t = \begin{pmatrix} 1 & 3 & 2 \\ 2 & 5 & t \\ 4 & 7-t & -6 \end{pmatrix}$$

a. For what values of t does $\mathbf{A}_t$ have an inverse?
b. Find the rank of $\mathbf{A}_t$ for each value of t.
c. When $t = -3$, find all the vectors $\mathbf{x}$ that satisfy the vector equation

$$\mathbf{A}_{-3}\mathbf{x} = \begin{pmatrix} 11 \\ 3 \\ 6 \end{pmatrix}$$

d. When $t = 2$, determine a vector $\mathbf{z} \neq \mathbf{0}$ that is orthogonal to each vector of the form $\mathbf{A}_2\mathbf{x}$, where $\mathbf{x}$ is an arbitrary vector in R^3.

14.4 Eigenvalues

In Section 12.8 we introduced the powers $\mathbf{A}^n$, $n = 1, 2, \ldots$ of a square matrix $\mathbf{A}$. Such powers appear in many applied problems. If $\mathbf{A}$ is a matrix of high order, then computing $\mathbf{A}^5$, or even worse $\mathbf{A}^{100}$, is usually a major problem. But suppose there happens to be a nonzero vector **x** and a scalar λ with the special property that

$$\mathbf{Ax} = \lambda \mathbf{x} \qquad [*]$$

In this case, we would have $\mathbf{A^2x} = \mathbf{A(Ax)} = \mathbf{A}(\lambda \mathbf{x}) = \lambda \mathbf{Ax} = \lambda\lambda \mathbf{x} = \lambda^2 \mathbf{x}$. By induction on n, it follows that any matrix power $\mathbf{A}^n$ satisfies

$$\mathbf{A}^n\mathbf{x} = \lambda^n \mathbf{x}$$

Then many of the properties of $\mathbf{A}^n$ can be deduced by studying the number λ raised to the same power, which is vastly simpler.

A nonzero vector **x** that solves [*] is called an **eigenvector**, and the associated λ is called an **eigenvalue**. Zero solutions are not very interesting, of course, because $\mathbf{A0} = \lambda \mathbf{0}$ for every scalar λ.

In optimization theory, in the theory of linear difference and differential equations, in statistics, in population dynamics, and in many other applications of mathematics, arguments and results based on eigenvalues are important. Here is a formal definition:

Eigenvalues and Eigenvectors

If **A** is an $n \times n$ matrix, then the scalar λ is an **eigenvalue** of **A** if there is a nonzero vector $\mathbf{x} \in R^n$ such that

$$\mathbf{Ax} = \lambda \mathbf{x} \qquad [14.6]$$

Then **x** is an **eigenvector** of **A** (associated with λ).

It should be noted that if **x** is an eigenvector associated with the eigenvalue λ, then $\alpha \mathbf{x}$ is another eigenvector for every scalar $\alpha \neq 0$. Eigenvalues and eigenvectors are also called **characteristic values** and **characteristic vectors**, respectively.

Example 14.10

In Example 12.21 of Section 12.7, we studied the market shares of three firms. We now ask whether there exists a distribution of market shares that will remain the same next year, assuming that the transition matrix in that example prevails. The problem can be formulated this way: Is it possible to find an initial market share vector **v** to satisfy the following equation?

$$\mathbf{Tv} = \mathbf{v}$$

In other words, is $\lambda = 1$ an eigenvalue of the matrix **T** for some eigenvector **v**?

The answer is yes. The vector **v** with components 0.4, 0.1, and 0.5 is an eigenvector because

$$
\begin{pmatrix} 0.85 & 0.10 & 0.10 \\ 0.05 & 0.55 & 0.05 \\ 0.10 & 0.35 & 0.85 \end{pmatrix} \begin{pmatrix} 0.4 \\ 0.1 \\ 0.5 \end{pmatrix} = \begin{pmatrix} 0.4 \\ 0.1 \\ 0.5 \end{pmatrix}
$$

(Problem 5 studies this example more closely.)

How to Find Eigenvalues

The eigenvalue equation [14.6] can be written as

$$
(\mathbf{A} - \lambda \mathbf{I})\mathbf{x} = \mathbf{0} \tag{14.7}
$$

where **I** denotes the identity matrix of order n. According to Theorem 13.7 of Section 13.8, this homogeneous linear system of equations has a nontrivial solution $\mathbf{x} \neq \mathbf{0}$ iff the coefficient matrix has determinant *equal* to 0—that is, iff

$$
|\mathbf{A} - \lambda \mathbf{I}| = 0 \tag{$*$}
$$

Letting $p(\lambda) = |\mathbf{A} - \lambda \mathbf{I}|$ where $\mathbf{A} = (a_{ij})_{n \times n}$, we have the equation

$$
p(\lambda) = \begin{vmatrix} a_{11} - \lambda & a_{12} & \cdots & a_{1n} \\ a_{21} & a_{22} - \lambda & \cdots & a_{2n} \\ \vdots & \vdots & \ddots & \vdots \\ a_{n1} & a_{n2} & \cdots & a_{nn} - \lambda \end{vmatrix} = 0 \tag{14.8}
$$

This is called the **characteristic equation** (or **eigenvalue equation**) of **A**. From the definition of a determinant, it follows that $p(\lambda)$ is a polynomial in λ. The roots of this **characteristic polynomial** are precisely the eigenvalues of **A**.[2]

If the components of vector **x** are $x_1, \ldots, x_n$, then [14.7] can be written as

$$
\begin{aligned}
(a_{11} - \lambda)x_1 + a_{12}x_2 + \cdots + a_{1n}x_n &= 0 \\
a_{21}x_1 + (a_{22} - \lambda)x_2 + \cdots + a_{2n}x_n &= 0 \\
\cdots\cdots\cdots\cdots\cdots\cdots\cdots\cdots\cdots\cdots\cdots\cdots\cdots\cdots & \\
a_{n1}x_1 + a_{n2}x_2 + \cdots + (a_{nn} - \lambda)x_n &= 0
\end{aligned} \tag{14.9}
$$

An eigenvector associated with λ is a nontrivial solution $(x_1, \ldots, x_n)$ of [14.9].

---

[2] According to the fundamental theorem of algebra, Equation [14.8] has n roots, real or complex. The complex roots are also called eigenvalues, but this book primarily considers cases in which the roots are all real.

Example 14.11

Find the real eigenvalues and associated eigenvectors of the following:

(a) $\mathbf{A} = \begin{pmatrix} 1 & 2 \\ 3 & 0 \end{pmatrix}$

(b) $\mathbf{B} = \begin{pmatrix} 0 & 1 \\ -1 & 0 \end{pmatrix}$

Solution

(a) The characteristic equation is

$$|\mathbf{A} - \lambda\mathbf{I}| = \begin{vmatrix} 1 - \lambda & 2 \\ 3 & -\lambda \end{vmatrix}$$

$$= \lambda^2 - \lambda - 6 = 0$$

with solutions $\lambda_1 = -2$ and $\lambda_2 = 3$, which are the eigenvalues of $\mathbf{A}$. For $\lambda = \lambda_1 = -2$, [14.9] gives

$$3x_1 + 2x_2 = 0$$
$$3x_1 + 2x_2 = 0$$

Choosing $x_2 = t$, we have $x_1 = -\frac{2}{3}t$. The eigenvectors associated with $\lambda_1 = -2$ are, therefore,

$$\mathbf{x} = t \begin{pmatrix} -2/3 \\ 1 \end{pmatrix} \qquad (t \in R)$$

For $\lambda_2 = 3$, [14.9] implies that $x_1 = x_2$, so the eigenvectors are

$$\mathbf{x} = s \begin{pmatrix} 1 \\ 1 \end{pmatrix} \qquad (s \in R)$$

(b) The characteristic equation is

$$|\mathbf{B} - \lambda\mathbf{I}| = \begin{vmatrix} -\lambda & 1 \\ -1 & -\lambda \end{vmatrix}$$

$$= \lambda^2 + 1 = 0$$

which does not have any real roots, so the matrix has no real eigenvalues.

Example 14.12

Find the real eigenvalues and associated eigenvectors of the following:

(a) $\mathbf{A} = \begin{pmatrix} 0 & 0 & 6 \\ 1/2 & 0 & 0 \\ 0 & 1/3 & 0 \end{pmatrix}$

(b) $\mathbf{B} = \begin{pmatrix} 5 & -6 & -6 \\ -1 & 4 & 2 \\ 3 & -6 & -4 \end{pmatrix}$

Solution

(a) The characteristic equation is

$$|\mathbf{A} - \lambda\mathbf{I}| = \begin{vmatrix} -\lambda & 0 & 6 \\ 1/2 & -\lambda & 0 \\ 0 & 1/3 & -\lambda \end{vmatrix}$$

$$= -\lambda^3 + 1 = 0$$

which has $\lambda = 1$ as its only real root. The eigenvectors associated with $\lambda = 1$ satisfy [14.9], which becomes

$$
\begin{aligned}
-x_1 \qquad\quad + 6x_3 &= 0 \\
\tfrac{1}{2}x_1 - \quad x_2 \qquad &= 0 \\
\tfrac{1}{3}x_2 - \quad x_3 &= 0
\end{aligned}
$$

This gives the eigenvectors

$$\mathbf{x} = t\begin{pmatrix} 6 \\ 3 \\ 1 \end{pmatrix} \qquad (t \in R]$$

(b) The characteristic equation is

$$|\mathbf{B} - \lambda\mathbf{I}| = \begin{vmatrix} 5-\lambda & -6 & -6 \\ -1 & 4-\lambda & 2 \\ 3 & -6 & -4-\lambda \end{vmatrix} = -(\lambda-2)^2(\lambda-1) = 0$$

Thus, $\lambda_1 = 1$ and $\lambda_2 = 2$ are the eigenvalues. For $\lambda_1 = 1$, system [14.9] is

$$
\begin{aligned}
4x_1 - 6x_2 - 6x_3 &= 0 \\
-x_1 + 3x_2 + 2x_3 &= 0 \\
3x_1 - 6x_2 - 5x_3 &= 0
\end{aligned}
$$

Solving this system by elimination gives the eigenvectors

$$\mathbf{x} = t\begin{pmatrix} 3 \\ -1 \\ 3 \end{pmatrix} \qquad (t \in R)$$

For $\lambda_2 = 2$, [14.9] gives

$$3x_1 - 6x_2 - 6x_3 = 0$$
$$-x_1 + 2x_2 + 2x_3 = 0$$
$$3x_1 - 6x_2 - 6x_3 = 0$$

The first and the third equations are identical. Choosing $x_2 = s$ and $x_3 = t$ freely, we have $x_1 = 2s + 2t$. The eigenvectors associated with $\lambda_2 = 2$, therefore, are all the vectors of the form

$$\mathbf{x} = \begin{pmatrix} 2s + 2t \\ s \\ t \end{pmatrix} = \begin{pmatrix} 2 \\ 1 \\ 0 \end{pmatrix} s + \begin{pmatrix} 2 \\ 0 \\ 1 \end{pmatrix} t \qquad (s \in R, \ t \in R)$$

Example 14.13

Let $\mathbf{D} = \text{diag}(c_1, \ldots, c_n)$ denote an $n \times n$ diagonal matrix with diagonal elements $c_1, \ldots, c_n$. Then the characteristic equation is

$$|\mathbf{D} - \lambda\mathbf{I}| = \begin{vmatrix} c_1 - \lambda & 0 & \cdots & 0 \\ 0 & c_2 - \lambda & \cdots & 0 \\ \vdots & \vdots & \ddots & \vdots \\ 0 & 0 & \cdots & c_n - \lambda \end{vmatrix}$$
$$= (c_1 - \lambda)(c_2 - \lambda) \cdots (c_n - \lambda)$$

Hence, the eigenvalues of $\mathbf{D}$ are precisely the diagonal elements. Because $\mathbf{D}\mathbf{e}_j = c_j\mathbf{e}_j$ (where $\mathbf{e}_j$ is the jth **unit vector** in R^n, having all components 0, except for the jth component that is 1), it follows that $\mathbf{e}_j$ is an eigenvector associated with the eigenvalue c_j of $\mathbf{D}$.

Example 14.14

Let

$$\mathbf{A} = \begin{pmatrix} a_{11} & a_{12} \\ a_{21} & a_{22} \end{pmatrix}$$

be a 2×2 matrix. When are its eigenvalues real? What are the signs of its eigenvalues when they are real?

Solution The eigenvalues are the roots of the characteristic equation

$$0 = |\mathbf{A} - \lambda\mathbf{I}| = \begin{vmatrix} a_{11} - \lambda & a_{12} \\ a_{21} & a_{22} - \lambda \end{vmatrix} = (a_{11} - \lambda)(a_{22} - \lambda) - a_{12}a_{21}$$
$$= \lambda^2 - (a_{11} + a_{22})\lambda + (a_{11}a_{22} - a_{12}a_{21})$$

The roots of this quadratic equation are

$$\lambda = \tfrac{1}{2}(a_{11} + a_{22}) \pm \sqrt{\tfrac{1}{4}(a_{11} + a_{22})^2 - (a_{11}a_{22} - a_{12}a_{21})}$$

These roots are real iff $(a_{11} + a_{22})^2 \geq 4(a_{11}a_{22} - a_{12}a_{21})$, which is equivalent to $(a_{11} - a_{22})^2 + 4a_{12}a_{21} \geq 0$. In particular, both eigenvalues are real if the matrix is symmetric, because then $a_{12} = a_{21}$ and so we have a sum of squares on the left-hand side of this last inequality.

If the real eigenvalues are λ_1 and λ_2, then

$$\lambda^2 - (a_{11} + a_{22})\lambda + (a_{11}a_{22} - a_{12}a_{21}) = (\lambda - \lambda_1)(\lambda - \lambda_2)$$

$$= \lambda^2 - (\lambda_1 + \lambda_2)\lambda + \lambda_1\lambda_2$$

Thus, the sum $\lambda_1 + \lambda_2$ of the eigenvalues is equal to $a_{11} + a_{22}$, the sum of the diagonal elements (also called the *trace* of the matrix—see Problem 8, Section 12.9). The product $\lambda_1\lambda_2$ of the eigenvalues is equal to the determinant $a_{11}a_{22} - a_{12}a_{21} = |\mathbf{A}|$. It follows that:

1. both eigenvalues are positive iff $a_{11} + a_{22} > 0$ and $|\mathbf{A}| > 0$
2. both eigenvalues are negative iff $a_{11} + a_{22} < 0$ and $|\mathbf{A}| > 0$
3. the two eigenvalues have different signs iff $|\mathbf{A}| < 0$

Moreover, there is a zero eigenvalue iff $|\mathbf{A}| = 0$. Then the other eigenvalue is equal to $a_{11} + a_{22}$.

Problems

1. Find the eigenvalues and eigenvectors of the following:

   a. $\begin{pmatrix} 2 & -7 \\ 3 & -8 \end{pmatrix}$ **b.** $\begin{pmatrix} 2 & 4 \\ -2 & 6 \end{pmatrix}$ **c.** $\begin{pmatrix} 1 & 4 \\ 6 & -1 \end{pmatrix}$

   d. $\begin{pmatrix} 2 & 0 & 0 \\ 0 & 3 & 0 \\ 0 & 0 & 4 \end{pmatrix}$ **e.** $\begin{pmatrix} 2 & 1 & -1 \\ 0 & 1 & 1 \\ 2 & 0 & -2 \end{pmatrix}$ **f.** $\begin{pmatrix} 1 & -1 & 0 \\ -1 & 2 & -1 \\ 0 & -1 & 1 \end{pmatrix}$

2. Prove that λ is an eigenvalue of the matrix $\mathbf{A}$ iff λ is an eigenvalue of $\mathbf{A}'$.

3. Suppose $\mathbf{A}$ is a square matrix and let λ be an eigenvalue of $\mathbf{A}$. Prove that if $|\mathbf{A}| \neq 0$, then $\lambda \neq 0$, and then show that $1/\lambda$ is an eigenvalue of the inverse $\mathbf{A}^{-1}$.

4. Let matrices $\mathbf{A}$ and $\mathbf{X}$ be defined by

$$\mathbf{A} = \begin{pmatrix} a & a & 0 \\ a & a & 0 \\ 0 & 0 & b \end{pmatrix} \quad \text{and} \quad \mathbf{X} = \begin{pmatrix} x \\ y \\ z \end{pmatrix} \quad (a \text{ and } b \text{ are real numbers})$$

    a. Compute $X'AX$, A^2, and A^3.
    b. Find all the eigenvalues of A.
    c. Express the characteristic polynomial $p(\lambda)$ as a cubic function of λ. Show that if we replace λ by A, then $p(A)$ is the zero matrix.[3]

Harder Problems

    5. Compute the eigenvalues of the matrix T in Example 14.10. (*Hint:* We know already that $\lambda = 1$ is an eigenvalue.) If v is an eigenvector associated with $\lambda = 1$, compute $T^n v$, where n is a natural number.

    6. Prove that if A and B are both invertible $n \times n$ matrices, then AB and BA have the same eigenvalues.

    7. Let $A = (a_{ij})_{n \times n}$ be a matrix where all column sums are 1, that is, $\sum_{i=1}^{n} a_{ij} = 1$ for $j = 1, 2, \ldots, n$. Prove that $\lambda = 1$ is an eigenvalue of A. (*Hint:* Consider first the case $n = 2$.)

14.5 Diagonalization

Diagonal matrices are simple to work with. For example,

$$
D = \begin{pmatrix} d_1 & 0 & 0 \\ 0 & d_2 & 0 \\ 0 & 0 & d_3 \end{pmatrix}, \quad E = \begin{pmatrix} e_1 & 0 & 0 \\ 0 & e_2 & 0 \\ 0 & 0 & e_3 \end{pmatrix} \implies DE = \begin{pmatrix} d_1 e_1 & 0 & 0 \\ 0 & d_2 e_2 & 0 \\ 0 & 0 & d_3 e_3 \end{pmatrix}
$$

Also, for each natural number m,

$$
D^m = \begin{pmatrix} d_1^m & 0 & 0 \\ 0 & d_2^m & 0 \\ 0 & 0 & d_3^m \end{pmatrix}
$$

In general, an $n \times n$ matrix A is called **diagonalizable** if there exists an invertible $n \times n$ matrix P and a diagonal matrix D such that

$$
P^{-1}AP = D = \mathrm{diag}\,(d_1, d_2, \ldots, d_n) \tag{14.10}
$$

where $d_1, d_2, \ldots, d_n$ are the diagonal elements. As pointed out in Section 14.4, if A is a square matrix of high order, then computing a large power of A is usually a major problem. However, suppose that A is diagonalizable, so that [14.10] holds. Multiplying [14.10] on the left by P and on the right by P^{-1} yields

$$
A = PDP^{-1} \tag{1}
$$

---

[3] The fact that $p(A)$ is the zero matrix is a special case of the *Cayley–Hamilton theorem*, which states that any square matrix satisfies its own characteristic equation.

Suppose m is a natural number. According to Problem 8 in Section 13.6,

$$\mathbf{A}^m = \mathbf{P}\mathbf{D}^m\mathbf{P}^{-1} \qquad [2]$$

Because $\mathbf{D}$ is a diagonal matrix, it is easy to calculate $\mathbf{D}^m$, and [2] then yields a simple way of finding $\mathbf{A}^m$. So the remaining problem is to find the matrices $\mathbf{P}$ and $\mathbf{D}$ needed in [1]. We note first the following result:

$\mathbf{A}$ and $\mathbf{P}^{-1}\mathbf{A}\mathbf{P}$ have the same eigenvalues $\qquad\qquad$ [14.11]

This is because these two matrices have the same characteristic polynomial, as

$$|\mathbf{P}^{-1}\mathbf{A}\mathbf{P} - \lambda\mathbf{I}| = |\mathbf{P}^{-1}\mathbf{A}\mathbf{P} - \mathbf{P}^{-1}\lambda\mathbf{I}\mathbf{P}| = |\mathbf{P}^{-1}(\mathbf{A} - \lambda\mathbf{I})\mathbf{P}| = |\mathbf{P}^{-1}||\mathbf{A} - \lambda\mathbf{I}||\mathbf{P}|$$

$$= |\mathbf{A} - \lambda\mathbf{I}|$$

(This chain of equalities uses the facts that the determinant of a product is the product of the determinants and that the determinant of an inverse matrix is the reciprocal of the determinant of the matrix.) Now the eigenvalues of a diagonal matrix are equal to the diagonal elements (see Example 14.13 of Section 14.4). It follows that if $\mathbf{A}$ is diagonalizable so that [14.10] holds, then $\mathbf{P}^{-1}\mathbf{A}\mathbf{P} = \text{diag } (\lambda_1, \ldots, \lambda_n)$, where $\lambda_1, \ldots, \lambda_n$ are the eigenvalues of $\mathbf{A}$, written in the appropriate order. Here the eigenvalues are not necessarily all distinct.

These useful properties prompt two questions:

1. Which square matrices are diagonalizable?
2. If $\mathbf{A}$ is diagonalizable, how do we find the matrix $\mathbf{P}$ in [14.10]?

The answers are given in the next theorem.

Theorem 14.6 $\qquad$ An $n \times n$ matrix $\mathbf{A}$ is diagonalizable iff $\mathbf{A}$ has a set of n linearly independent eigenvectors $\mathbf{x}_1, \ldots, \mathbf{x}_n$. In this case,

$$\mathbf{P}^{-1}\mathbf{A}\mathbf{P} = \begin{pmatrix} \lambda_1 & 0 & \ldots & 0 \\ 0 & \lambda_2 & \ldots & 0 \\ \vdots & \vdots & \ddots & \vdots \\ 0 & 0 & \ldots & \lambda_n \end{pmatrix} \qquad [14.12]$$

where $\mathbf{P}$ is the matrix with $\mathbf{x}_1, \ldots, \mathbf{x}_n$ as its columns, and $\lambda_1, \ldots, \lambda_n$ are the associated eigenvalues.

Proof   The $n \times n$ matrix **A** is diagonalizable iff there exists an invertible matrix $\mathbf{P} = (p_{ij})_{n \times n}$ such that [14.10] holds, or, equivalently, such that $\mathbf{AP} = \mathbf{P}\,\text{diag}\,(\lambda_1, \ldots, \lambda_n)$. This last equation can be written as

$$
\mathbf{AP} = \begin{pmatrix} p_{11} & p_{12} & \cdots & p_{1n} \\ p_{21} & p_{22} & \cdots & p_{2n} \\ \vdots & \vdots & \ddots & \vdots \\ p_{n1} & p_{n2} & \cdots & p_{nn} \end{pmatrix} \cdot \begin{pmatrix} \lambda_1 & 0 & \cdots & 0 \\ 0 & \lambda_2 & \cdots & 0 \\ \vdots & \vdots & \ddots & \vdots \\ 0 & 0 & \cdots & \lambda_n \end{pmatrix}
$$

$$
= \begin{pmatrix} \lambda_1 p_{11} & \lambda_2 p_{12} & \cdots & \lambda_n p_{1n} \\ \lambda_1 p_{21} & \lambda_2 p_{22} & \cdots & \lambda_n p_{2n} \\ \vdots & \vdots & \ddots & \vdots \\ \lambda_1 p_{n1} & \lambda_2 p_{n2} & \cdots & \lambda_n p_{nn} \end{pmatrix} = (\lambda_1 \mathbf{x}_1, \lambda_2 \mathbf{x}_2, \ldots, \lambda_n \mathbf{x}_n)
$$

[1]

where the last equality follows from the fact that the columns of **P** are $\mathbf{x}_1, \mathbf{x}_2, \ldots, \mathbf{x}_n$. Moreover, $\mathbf{AP} = (\mathbf{Ax}_1, \mathbf{Ax}_2, \ldots, \mathbf{Ax}_n)$. Thus, [1] is equivalent to the n equations

$$
\mathbf{Ax}_k = \lambda_k \mathbf{x}_k \qquad (k = 1, 2, \ldots, n)
$$

[2]

But these equations say that $\mathbf{x}_1, \ldots, \mathbf{x}_n$ are eigenvectors of the matrix **A** with $\lambda_1, \ldots, \lambda_n$ as the corresponding eigenvalues. Because **P** has an inverse iff $|\mathbf{P}| \neq 0$, and so iff $\mathbf{x}_1, \ldots, \mathbf{x}_n$ are linearly independent, the proof of Theorem 14.6 is complete.

Example 14.15
Verify Theorem 14.6 for

$$
\mathbf{A} = \begin{pmatrix} 1 & 2 \\ 3 & 0 \end{pmatrix}
$$

(See Example 14.11(a) of Section 14.4.)

Solution   The eigenvalues are $\lambda_1 = -2$ and $\lambda_2 = 3$, and as corresponding eigenvectors, we can choose the vectors

$$
\begin{pmatrix} 2 \\ -3 \end{pmatrix} \qquad \text{and} \qquad \begin{pmatrix} 1 \\ 1 \end{pmatrix}
$$

So we take

$$
\mathbf{P} = \begin{pmatrix} 2 & 1 \\ -3 & 1 \end{pmatrix} \qquad \text{for which} \qquad \mathbf{P}^{-1} = \begin{pmatrix} 1/5 & -1/5 \\ 3/5 & 2/5 \end{pmatrix}
$$

With some routine algebra, we find that $\mathbf{P}^{-1}\mathbf{AP}$ is the matrix diag $(-2, 3)$, which confirms Theorem 14.6.

Example 14.16
Verify Theorem 14.6 for matrix **B** in Example 14.12 of Section 14.4.

Solution   The eigenvalues were $\lambda_1 = 1$ and $\lambda_2 = 2$. Moreover, we found the three eigenvectors

$$\mathbf{x}_1 = \begin{pmatrix} 3 \\ -1 \\ 3 \end{pmatrix}, \qquad \mathbf{x}_2 = \begin{pmatrix} 2 \\ 1 \\ 0 \end{pmatrix}, \qquad \text{and} \qquad \mathbf{x}_3 = \begin{pmatrix} 2 \\ 0 \\ 1 \end{pmatrix}$$

These vectors are linearly independent, so $\mathbf{B}$ *is* diagonalizable. If we choose

$$\mathbf{P} = \begin{pmatrix} 3 & 2 & 2 \\ -1 & 1 & 0 \\ 3 & 0 & 1 \end{pmatrix}, \quad \text{we find that} \quad \mathbf{P}^{-1} = \begin{pmatrix} -1 & 2 & 2 \\ -1 & 3 & 2 \\ 3 & -6 & -5 \end{pmatrix}$$

and a routine calculation confirms that $\mathbf{P}^{-1}\mathbf{B}\mathbf{P} = \operatorname{diag}(1, 2, 2)$.

Not all matrices are diagonalizable. Nor is it always easy to verify the necessary and sufficient conditions in Theorem 14.6 for a matrix to be diagonalizable. Indeed, easy necessary and sufficient conditions for a matrix to be diagonalizable do not exist. One can prove that if $\mathbf{A}$ is an $n \times n$ matrix with n different eigenvalues, then $\mathbf{A}$ is diagonalizable. Yet, Example 14.16 shows that this condition is not necessary, because the matrix there is diagonalizable and yet the eigenvalues are not all distinct.

Problems

1. If $\mathbf{D} = \operatorname{diag}(1/2, 1/3, 1/4)$, compute $\mathbf{D}^2$ and $\mathbf{D}^n$, for any natural number $n \geq 3$. What is the limit of $\mathbf{D}^n$ as $n \to \infty$?

2. Are the following matrices diagonalizable?
   a. The matrix $\mathbf{A}$ in Example 14.12(a) of Section 14.4.
   b. The matrices in Problems 1(e) and (f) of Section 14.4.

3. Show that the following matrices are diagonalizable, find a suitable matrix $\mathbf{P}$ (this matrix is not unique), and then verify [14.12]:

   a. $\begin{pmatrix} 2 & 1 \\ 0 & -1 \end{pmatrix}$ **b.** $\begin{pmatrix} 6 & -14 & 0 \\ 0 & -3 & -6 \\ 0 & -3 & 0 \end{pmatrix}$ **c.** $\begin{pmatrix} 1 & 3 & 0 \\ 3 & -2 & -1 \\ 0 & -1 & 1 \end{pmatrix}$

14.6 The Spectral Theorem for Symmetric Matrices

Many of the square matrices encountered in economic applications are symmetric. In particular, second-order conditions for extrema of functions of many variables involve quadratic forms, which can be expressed in terms of symmetric matrices. So we turn now to a special study of eigenvalues of symmetric matrices. In Example 14.14 of Section 14.4, we have already seen that a symmetric 2×2 matrix has real eigenvalues. In fact, this is a general property of symmetric matrices, because of the following:

Theorem 14.7   Suppose $\mathbf{A}$ is a symmetric $n \times n$ matrix (with real entries), so that $\mathbf{A} = \mathbf{A}'$. Then:

(a) The characteristic polynomial of $\mathbf{A}$ has only real roots, that is, all the eigenvalues of $\mathbf{A}$ are real.

(b) If $\mathbf{x}$ and $\mathbf{y}$ are eigenvectors associated with two different eigenvalues λ and μ, then $\mathbf{x}$ and $\mathbf{y}$ are orthogonal (in the sense that $\mathbf{x}'\mathbf{y} = 0$).

Proof

(a) Proving (a) is quite advanced, so we refer to Hadley (1973).

(b) Suppose that $\mathbf{Ax} = \lambda \mathbf{x}$ and $\mathbf{Ay} = \mu \mathbf{y}$. Multiplying these two equalities on the left by $\mathbf{y}'$ and $\mathbf{x}'$, respectively, yields:

$$[1] \quad \mathbf{y}'\mathbf{Ax} = \lambda \mathbf{y}'\mathbf{x} \qquad\qquad [2] \quad \mathbf{x}'\mathbf{Ay} = \mu \mathbf{x}'\mathbf{y}$$

Because $\mathbf{A}$ is symmetric, transposing each side of [1] yields $\mathbf{x}'\mathbf{Ay} = \lambda \mathbf{x}'\mathbf{y}$. Hence, [2] implies that $\lambda\mathbf{x}'\mathbf{y} = \mu\mathbf{x}'\mathbf{y}$ or that $(\lambda - \mu)\mathbf{x}'\mathbf{y} = 0$. In case $\lambda \neq \mu$, it follows that $\mathbf{x}'\mathbf{y} = 0$, so $\mathbf{x}$ and $\mathbf{y}$ are orthogonal.

The Spectral Theorem

The following theorem is a very important result in linear algebra.

Theorem 14.8   (The Spectral Theorem)   Suppose that $\mathbf{A}$ is a symmetric $n \times n$ matrix. Then there exists an orthogonal matrix $\mathbf{U}$ (that is, with $\mathbf{U}^{-1} = \mathbf{U}'$) such that

$$\mathbf{U}^{-1}\mathbf{AU} = \operatorname{diag}(\lambda_1, \lambda_2, \ldots, \lambda_n) \qquad\qquad [14.13]$$

where $\lambda_1, \lambda_2, \ldots, \lambda_n$ are the eigenvalues of $\mathbf{A}$.

Proof (in a special case):   According to Theorem 14.7, all the eigenvalues are real. If they also happen to be all different, then Theorem 14.6 shows that $\mathbf{A}$ is diagonalizable and that the matrix $\mathbf{P}$ in [14.12] of Theorem 14.6 is $\mathbf{P} = (\mathbf{x}_1, \ldots, \mathbf{x}_n)$, where $\mathbf{x}_1, \ldots, \mathbf{x}_n$ are the eigenvectors corresponding to $\lambda_1, \ldots, \lambda_n$. We can make all these eigenvectors have length 1 by replacing them with $\mathbf{x}_1 / \| \mathbf{x}_1 \|, \ldots, \mathbf{x}_n / \| \mathbf{x}_n \|$. According to Theorem 14.7, the vectors $\mathbf{x}_1$, $\ldots, \mathbf{x}_n$ are mutually orthogonal. Then the matrix $\mathbf{P}$ is also orthogonal (see

Problem 3). If we let $\mathbf{U} = \mathbf{P}$, then we have proved Theorem 14.8 for the case when all the eigenvalues are distinct. For the proof of the general case, we refer to Hadley (1973).

Problems

1. By finding $\mathbf{U}$ explicitly, verify [14.13] for the following matrices:

   a. $\mathbf{A} = \begin{pmatrix} 2 & 1 \\ 1 & 2 \end{pmatrix}$ b. $\mathbf{A} = \begin{pmatrix} 1 & 1 & 0 \\ 1 & 1 & 0 \\ 0 & 0 & 2 \end{pmatrix}$ c. $\mathbf{A} = \begin{pmatrix} 1 & 3 & 4 \\ 3 & 1 & 0 \\ 4 & 0 & 1 \end{pmatrix}$

2. Verify Theorems 14.6 and 14.7 for the following matrices:

   a. $\mathbf{A} = \begin{pmatrix} 1 & 2 \\ 2 & -2 \end{pmatrix}$ b. $\mathbf{A} = \begin{pmatrix} 0 & 0 & 1 \\ 0 & 0 & 1 \\ 1 & 1 & -1 \end{pmatrix}$

3. Prove that if $\mathbf{P}$ is an $n \times n$ matrix whose column vectors are all of length 1 and mutually orthogonal, then $\mathbf{P}$ is orthogonal.

=15=

Functions of Several Variables

You know we all became mathematicians
for the same reason: We were lazy.
—*Max Rosenlicht* (1949)

So far, we have mostly studied functions of one variable—that is, functions whose domain is a set of real numbers and whose range is also a set of real numbers. Yet a realistic description of many economic phenomena requires considering a large number of variables simultaneously. For example, the demand for a good depends on consumer tastes, the price of that good, on different consumers' incomes, and on the prices of complements and substitutes, among other things. This requires a function of several variables to be considered.

Much of what economists need consists of relatively simple generalizations of functions of one variable and their properties. Most of the difficulties already arise in the transition from one variable to two variables. Therefore, it may be sensible in the following to concentrate on functions of two variables before trying to tackle the material dealing with functions of more than two variables. However, there are many interesting economic problems that can only be represented mathematically by functions of a large number of variables.

15.1 Functions of Two or More Variables

We begin with the following definition:

> A **function** f **of two variables** x **and** y with domain D is a rule that assigns a specified number $f(x, y)$ to each point (x, y) in D.

[15.1]

489

Example 15.1

Consider the function f that, to every pair of numbers (x, y), assigns the number $2x + x^2 y^3$. The function f is thus defined by

$$f(x, y) = 2x + x^2 y^3$$

What are $f(1, 0)$, $f(0, 1)$, $f(-2, 3)$, and $f(a + 1, b)$?

Solution $f(1, 0) = 2 \cdot 1 + 1^2 \cdot 0^3 = 2$, $f(0, 1) = 2 \cdot 0 + 0^2 \cdot 1^3 = 0$, and $f(-2, 3) = 2(-2) + (-2)^2 \cdot 3^3 = -4 + 4 \cdot 27 = 104$. Finally, we find $f(a+1, b)$ by replacing x with $a+1$ and y with b in the formula for $f(x, y)$, giving $f(a + 1, b) = 2(a + 1) + (a + 1)^2 b^3$.

Example 15.2

A study of the demand for milk by R. Frisch and T. Haavelmo found the relationship

$$x = A \frac{r^{2.08}}{p^{1.5}} \qquad (A \text{ is a positive constant}) \qquad [*]$$

where x is milk consumption, p is the relative price of milk, and r is income per family. This equation defines x as a function of p and r. Note that milk consumption goes up when income r increases, and goes down when the price of milk increases, which seems reasonable.

Example 15.3

A function of two variables appearing in many economic models is

$$F(x, y) = Ax^a y^b \qquad (A, a, \text{ and } b \text{ are constants}) \qquad [15.2]$$

Usually, one assumes that F is defined only for $x > 0$ and $y > 0$; sometimes for $x \geq 0$ and $y \geq 0$. Then F is generally called a **Cobb–Douglas function**.[1] Note that the function defined in $[*]$ of Example 15.2 is a Cobb–Douglas function, because we have $x = Ap^{-1.5} r^{2.08}$.

As another example of a Cobb–Douglas function, here is an estimated production function for a certain lobster fishery:

$$F(S, E) = 2.26 \, S^{0.44} E^{0.48} \qquad [**]$$

where S denotes the stock of lobster, E the harvesting effort, and $F(S, E)$ the catch.

---

[1] The function in [15.2] is named after two American researchers. C. W. Cobb and P. H. Douglas, who applied it (with $a + b = 1$) in a paper on the estimation of production functions that appeared in 1927. Actually, the function should properly be called a "Wicksell function," because the Swedish economist Knut Wicksell (1851–1926) introduced such production functions before 1900. See B. Sandelin, "On the origin of the Cobb–Douglas production function," *Economy and History*, 19 (1976), 117–123.

Example 15.4

For the function F given in [15.2], find an expression for $F(2x, 2y)$ and for $F(tx, ty)$, where t is an arbitrary positive number. What is $F(tS, tE)$ for the function in [**]?

Solution

$$F(2x, 2y) = A(2x)^a (2y)^b = A2^a x^a 2^b y^b = 2^a 2^b Ax^a y^b = 2^{a+b} F(x, y)$$

$$F(tx, ty) = A(tx)^a (ty)^b = At^a x^a t^b y^b = t^{a+b} Ax^a y^b = t^{a+b} F(x, y)$$

$$F(tS, tE) = 2.26(tS)^{0.44} (tE)^{0.48} = 2.26 \, t^{0.44} S^{0.44} t^{0.48} E^{0.48} = t^{0.92} F(S, E)$$

The last calculation shows that if we multiply both S and E by the factor t, then the catch will be $t^{0.92}$ times as big. If $t = 2$, for example, then this formula shows that doubling both the stock and the harvesting effort leads to a catch that is a little less than twice as big. (It is $2^{0.92} \approx 1.89$ times as big.)

Functions of More Than Two Variables

Many of the most important functions we study in economics, such as the gross domestic product (GDP) of a country, depend in a complicated way on a large number of variables. In some abstract models, it may be sufficient to ascertain that such a connection exists without specifying the dependence more closely. In this case, we say only that the GDP is a *function* of the different variables. The function concept we use is a direct generalization of definition [15.1].

A **function** f of n variables $x_1, \ldots, x_n$ with domain D is a rule that assigns a specified number $f(x_1, \ldots, x_n)$ to each n-vector $(x_1, \ldots, x_n)$ in D.   [15.3]

Let us look at some examples of functions of several variables in economics.

Example 15.5

(a) The demand for sugar in the United States in the period 1929–1935 was estimated by T. W. Schultz, who found that it could be described approximately by the formula

$$x = 108.83 - 6.0294p + 0.164w - 0.4217t$$

Here the demand x for sugar is a function of three variables: p (the price of sugar), w (a production index), and t (the date, where $t = 0$ corresponds to 1929).

(b) R. Stone estimated the following formula for the demand for beer in England:

$$x = 1.058\, x_1^{0.136} x_2^{-0.727} x_3^{0.914} x_4^{0.816}$$

Here the quantity demanded x is a function of four variables: x_1 (the income of the individual), x_2 (the price of beer), x_3 (a general price index for all other commodities), and x_4 (the strength of the beer).

The simplest of the functions in Example 15.5 is (a). The variables p, w, and t occur here only to the first power, and they are only multiplied by constants, not by each other. Such functions are called *linear*. In general,

$$f(x_1, x_2, \ldots, x_n) = a_1 x_1 + a_2 x_2 + \cdots + a_n x_n + b \qquad [15.4]$$

(where a_1, a_2, ..., a_n and b are constants) is a **linear function**[2] in n variables. Example 15.5(b) is a special case of the general Cobb–Douglas function

$$F(x_1, x_2, \ldots, x_n) = A x_1^{a_1} x_2^{a_2} \ldots x_n^{a_n} \qquad (A, a_1, \ldots, a_n \text{ are constants; } A > 0) \qquad [15.5]$$

defined for $x_1 > 0, x_2 > 0, \ldots, x_n > 0$. We encounter this function many times in this book.

Note: If we compare the linear function in [15.4] with the Cobb–Douglas function [15.5], the latter function is, of course, more complicated. Suppose, however, that $A > 0$ and $x_1 > 0, \ldots, x_n > 0$. Then taking the natural logarithm of each side in [15.5] gives

$$\ln F = \ln A + a_1 \ln x_1 + a_2 \ln x_2 + \cdots + a_n \ln x_n \qquad [15.6]$$

This shows that the Cobb–Douglas function is *log-linear* (or ln-linear), because $\ln F$ is a linear function of $\ln x_1$, $\ln x_2$, ..., $\ln x_n$.

Example 15.6

Suppose that the results of n observations of a quantity are given by n positive numbers x_1, x_2, ..., x_n. In statistics, several different measures for their average value are used. The most common are

the **arithmetic** mean: $\bar{x}_A = \dfrac{1}{n}(x_1 + x_2 + \cdots + x_n)$ [1]

the **geometric** mean: $\bar{x}_G = \sqrt[n]{x_1 x_2 \ldots x_n}$ [2]

the **harmonic** mean: $\bar{x}_H = \dfrac{1}{\dfrac{1}{n}\left(\dfrac{1}{x_1} + \dfrac{1}{x_2} + \cdots + \dfrac{1}{x_n}\right)}$ [3]

---

[2]This is rather common terminology, although mathematicians would insist that f should really be called *affine* if $b \neq 0$, and *linear* only if $b = 0$.

Note that $\bar{x}_A$ is a linear function of $x_1, \ldots, x_n$, whereas $\bar{x}_G$ and $\bar{x}_H$ are nonlinear functions. ($\bar{x}_G$ is log-linear.)

For example, if the results of four observations are $x_1 = 1$, $x_2 = 2$, $x_3 = 3$, and $x_4 = 4$, then $\bar{x}_A = (1+2+3+4)/4 = 2.5$, $\bar{x}_G = \sqrt[4]{1 \cdot 2 \cdot 3 \cdot 4} = \sqrt[4]{24} \approx 2.21$, and $\bar{x}_H = \left[(1/1 + 1/2 + 1/3 + 1/4)/4\right]^{-1} = 48/25 = 1.92$. In this case, $\bar{x}_H \leq \bar{x}_G \leq \bar{x}_A$, and it turns out that these inequalities are valid in general:

$$\bar{x}_H \leq \bar{x}_G \leq \bar{x}_A \qquad [4]$$

For $n = 2$, we showed that $\bar{x}_G \leq \bar{x}_A$ in Example 1.3 in Section 1.4. See also Problems 9 and 10 as a motivation for $\bar{x}_H$ and Problem 11 concerning a proof of the inequalities in [4].

Domains

For functions studied in economics, there are usually explicit or implicit restrictions on the domain of variation for the variables. For instance, we usually assume that the quantity x_i of a commodity is nonnegative, so $x_i \geq 0$. In economics, it is often crucially important to be clear what are the domains of the functions being used.

As for functions of one variable, we assume, unless otherwise stated, that the domain of a function defined by a formula is the largest domain in which the formula gives a meaningful and unique value.

For functions of two variables x and y, the domain is a set of points in the xy-plane. Sometimes it is helpful to draw a picture of the domain in the xy-plane. Let us look at some examples.

Example 15.7

Determine the domains of the functions given by the following formulas and draw the sets in the xy-plane.

   (a) $f(x, y) = \sqrt{x - 1} + \sqrt{y}$

   (b) $g(x, y) = \dfrac{2}{\sqrt{x^2 + y^2 - 4}} + \sqrt{9 - (x^2 + y^2)}$

Solution

   (a) We must require that $x \geq 1$ and $y \geq 0$, for only then do $\sqrt{x - 1}$ and $\sqrt{y}$ have any meaning. The domain is indicated in Fig. 15.1.

   (b) $\sqrt{x^2 + y^2 - 4}$ is only defined if $x^2 + y^2 \geq 4$. Moreover, we must have $x^2 + y^2 \neq 4$; otherwise, the denominator is equal to 0. Furthermore, we must require that $9 - (x^2 + y^2) \geq 0$, or $x^2 + y^2 \leq 9$. All in all, therefore, we must have $4 < x^2 + y^2 \leq 9$. Because the graph of $x^2 + y^2 = r^2$ consists of all the points on the circle with center at the origin and radius r, the domain is the set of

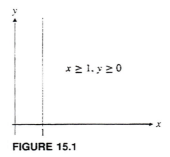

$x \geq 1, y \geq 0$

FIGURE 15.1

points (x, y) that lie outside (but not on) the circle $x^2 + y^2 = 4$, and inside or on the circle $x^2 + y^2 = 9$. This set is shown in Fig. 15.2.

Example 15.8

An individual must decide what quantities of n different commodities to buy during a given time period. Utility theory assumes that the individual has a utility function $U(x_1, x_2, \ldots, x_n)$ representing preferences, and that this measures the satisfaction the individual obtains by acquiring x_1 units of good no. 1, x_2 units of good no. 2, and so on. This is an important economic example of a function of n variables, to which we return several times.

Some economic models assume that

$$U(x_1, x_2, \ldots, x_n) = a_1 \ln(x_1 - c_1) + a_2 \ln(x_2 - c_2) + \cdots + a_n \ln(x_n - c_n)$$

where the parameters or constants $c_1, c_2, \ldots, c_n$ represent the minimum "subsistence" quantities that the consumer must have of the different commodities in order to survive. (Some or even many of the constants c_i could be equal to 0.) Because $\ln z$ is only defined when $z > 0$, we see that $x_1 > c_1$, $x_2 > c_2, \ldots, x_n > c_n$ is the requirement for U to be defined.

FIGURE 15.2

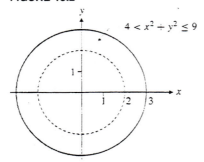

$4 < x^2 + y^2 \leq 9$

Problems

1. Let $f(x, y) = xy^2$. Compute $f(0, 1)$, $f(-1, 2)$, and $f(a, a)$.

2. Let $f(x, y) = 3x^2 - 2xy + y^3$. Compute $f(1, 1)$, $f(-2, 3)$, $f(1/x, 1/y)$, $[f(x + h, y) - f(x, y)]/h$, and $[f(x, y + k) - f(x, y)]/k$.

3. Let $f(x, y) = x^2 + 2xy + y^2$.
   a. Find $f(-1, 2)$, $f(a, a)$, and $f(a + h, b) - f(a, b)$.
   b. Show that $f(2x, 2y) = 2^2 f(x, y)$ and, in general, $f(tx, ty) = t^2 f(x, y)$ for all t.

4. Let $F(K, L) = 10K^{1/2}L^{1/3}$, $K \geq 0$, $L \geq 0$.
   a. Find $F(1, 1)$, $F(4, 27)$, $F(9, 1/27)$, $F(3, \sqrt{2})$, $F(100, 1000)$, and $F(2K, 2L)$.
   b. Find a constant a such that $F(tK, tL) = t^a F(K, L)$ for all $t > 0$, $K \geq 0$, and $L \geq 0$.

5. Some studies in agricultural economics employ production functions of the form $Y = F(K, L, T)$, where Y is the size of the harvest, K capital invested, L labor, and T the area of agricultural land used to grow the crop.
   a. Explain the meaning of $F(K + 1, L, T) - F(K, L, T)$.
   b. Many studies assume that F is Cobb–Douglas. What form does F then have?
   c. If F is Cobb–Douglas, find $F(tK, tL, tT)$ expressed in terms of t and $F(K, L, T)$.

6. A study of milk production found that

$$y = 2.90 \, x_1^{0.015} x_2^{0.250} x_3^{0.350} x_4^{0.408} x_5^{0.030}$$

where y is the output of milk, and $x_1, \ldots, x_5$ are the quantities of five different input factors. (For instance, x_1 is work effort and x_3 is grass consumption.)
   a. If all the factors of production were doubled, what would happen to y?
   b. Write the relation in log-linear form.

7. Examine for which (x, y) the functions given by the following formulas are defined and draw the domains in the xy-plane for (b) and (c).
   a. $\dfrac{x^2 + y^3}{y - x + 2}$ b. $\sqrt{2 - (x^2 + y^2)}$ c. $\sqrt{(4 - x^2 - y^2)(x^2 + y^2 - 1)}$

8. For which pairs of numbers (x, y) are the functions given by the following formulas defined?
   a. $\ln(x + y)$ b. $\sqrt{x^2 - y^2} + \sqrt{x^2 + y^2 - 1}$ c. $\sqrt{y - x^2} - \sqrt{\sqrt{x} - y}$

9. On a drive to a neighboring city center, you spend 5 minutes stopped at traffic lights at an average speed of 0 kilometers per hour, 10 minutes driving on local roads at an average speed of 30 kph, 20 minutes on an expressway at an average speed of 60 kph, and 15 minutes on a freeway driving at an average

speed of 80 kph. How far do you drive, and what is your average speed for the whole journey?

Harder Problems

10. Suppose that n machines A_1, A_2, ..., A_n produce the same product in the time span T and that the production times per unit are respectively t_1, t_2, ..., t_n. Show that if all the machines had been equally efficient and together had produced exactly the same total amount in the time span T, then each machine's production time per unit would have been precisely the harmonic mean $\bar{t}_H$ of t_1, t_2, ..., t_n.

11. In this problem, we refer to Example 15.6 and the definitions given there. Also, if $f(x)$ is concave over an interval I, and x_1, x_2, ..., x_n belong to I, then by Jensen's inequality ([9.18] in Section 9.6),

$$f\left(\frac{1}{n}(x_1 + x_2 + \cdots + x_n)\right) \geq \frac{1}{n}f(x_1) + \frac{1}{n}f(x_2) + \cdots + \frac{1}{n}f(x_n) \qquad [*]$$

a. Show that if $x_1 = x_2 = \cdots = x_n$, then $\bar{x}_H = \bar{x}_G = \bar{x}_A$.
b. Let $f(x) = \ln x$. Then f is concave on $(0, \infty)$. Show that $\bar{x}_G \leq \bar{x}_A$ by using inequality $[*]$.
c. In the inequality $\bar{x}_G \leq \bar{x}_A$, replace x_1 by $1/x_1$, x_2 by $1/x_2$, ..., and x_n by $1/x_n$. Prove that $\bar{x}_H \leq \bar{x}_G$.

15.2 Geometric Representations of Functions of Several Variables

This section considers how to visualize functions of several variables, in particular functions of two variables.

Surfaces in Three-Dimensional Space

An equation such as $f(x, y) = c$ in *two* variables x and y can be represented by a point set in the plane, called the **graph** of the equation. In a similar way, an equation $g(x, y, z) = c$ in *three* variables x, y, and z can be represented by a point set in 3-space, also called the **graph** of the equation. (For a discussion of 3-space, see Section 12.3.) This graph consists of all triples (x, y, z) satisfying the equation, and will usually form what can be called a **surface** in space. Three simple cases are given by the equations

$$(a) \quad x = a, \qquad (b) \quad y = b, \qquad (c) \quad z = c$$

where it is understood that there are no requirements on the variables other than those mentioned. The points (x, y, z) in space satisfying $x = a$ (with no require-

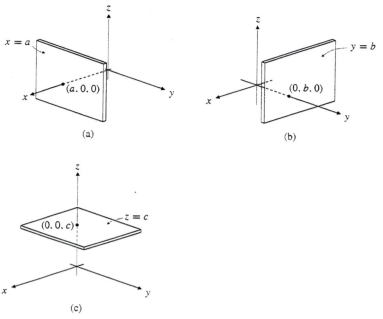

FIGURE 15.3

ment on y and z) lie in the plane indicated in Fig. 15.3(a); Figs. 15.3(b) and (c) show pieces of the two others.

Some more interesting examples of equations in three variables x, y, and z that represent surfaces in space are the following:

$$\text{(d)} \quad px + qy + rz = m, \qquad \text{(e)} \quad x^2 + y^2 + z^2 = 4$$

Equation (d) can be given an economic interpretation. Suppose a person spends an amount m on the purchase of three commodities, whose prices are respectively p, q, and r per unit. If the person buys x units of the first, y units of the second, and z units of the third commodity, then the total cost is $px + qy + rz$. Hence, (d) is the individual's *budget equation*: Only triples (x, y, z) that satisfy (d) can be bought if expenditure is m. As explained in Section 12.5, Equation (d) represents a *plane* in space, the **budget plane**. Because in most cases one also has $x \geq 0$, $y \geq 0$, and $z \geq 0$, the interesting part of the plane described by (d) is the triangle with vertices at $P = (m/p, 0, 0)$, $Q = (0, m/q, 0)$, and $R = (0, 0, m/r)$, as shown in Fig. 15.4.

Consider Equation (e) next. According to the discussion in Section 12.4 (see [12.16]), the expression $x^2 + y^2 + z^2 = (x - 0)^2 + (y - 0)^2 + (z - 0)^2$ is the square of the distance from the origin $(0, 0, 0)$ to the point (x, y, z). So the graph of (e) consists of those points (x, y, z) whose distance from the origin is 2. Thus, it

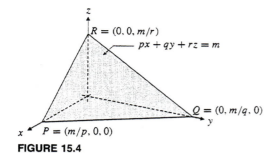

FIGURE 15.4

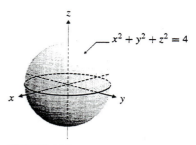

FIGURE 15.5

represents a sphere centered at $(0, 0, 0)$ and with radius 2, as shown in Fig. 15.5. If (e) were replaced by the inequality $x^2 + y^2 + z^2 \leq 4$, it would represent a solid ball.

The Graph of a Function of Two Variables

Suppose that $z = f(x, y)$ represents a function of two variables defined in a set A in the xy-plane. By the graph of the function f, we understand the graph of the equation $z - f(x, y) = 0$. If f is a sufficiently "nice" function, the graph of f is a smooth surface in space, like the one shown in Fig. 15.6.

This method of representing a function of two variables helps us to visualize its behavior in broad outline. However, it requires considerable artistic ability to represent in only two dimensions the graph of $z = f(x, y)$ that lies in three-dimensional space. It is certainly difficult to use the resulting drawing for quantitative measurements. (By using modern computer graphics, however, complicated functions of two variables can be drawn fairly easily.) We now describe a second method that often does better.

FIGURE 15.6 The graph of $y = f(x, y)$.

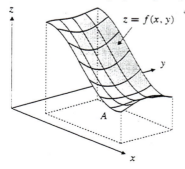

Level Curves for z = f(x, y)

Map makers can describe some topographical features of the earth's surface such as hills and valleys even on a plane map. To do so, they draw a set of *level curves* or contours connecting points on the map that represent places on the earth's surface with the same elevation above sea level. For instance, there may be such contours corresponding to 100 meters above sea level, others for 200, 300, and 400 meters above sea level, and so on. Where the contours are close together, there is a steep slope. Studying the contour map gives a good idea of altitude variations on the ground.

The same idea can be used to give a geometric representation of an arbitrary function $z = f(x, y)$. The graph of the function in three-dimensional space is visualized as being cut by horizontal planes parallel to the xy-plane. The resulting intersections between the planes and the graph are then projected onto the xy-plane. If the intersecting plane is $z = c$, then the projection of the intersection onto the xy-plane is called the **level curve at height c for f**. This level curve will consist of points satisfying the equation

$$f(x, y) = c$$

Figure 15.7 illustrates such a level curve.

Example 15.9

Consider the function of two variables defined by the equation

$$z = x^2 + y^2 \qquad [1]$$

What are the level curves? Draw both a set of level curves and the graph of the function.

Solution   The variable z can only assume values ≥ 0. The level curves have the equation

$$x^2 + y^2 = c \qquad [2]$$

FIGURE 15.7   The graph of z = f(x, y) and one of its level curves.

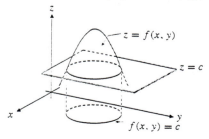

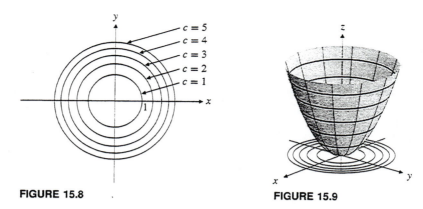

FIGURE 15.8   **FIGURE 15.9**

where $c \geq 0$. We see that these are circles in the xy-plane centered at the origin and with radius $\sqrt{c}$. See Fig. 15.8.

Concerning the graph of [1], all the level curves are circles. For $y = 0$, we have $z = x^2$. This shows that the graph of [1] cuts the xz-plane (where $y = 0$) in a parabola. Similarly, we see that for $x = 0$ one has $z = y^2$, which is the graph of a parabola in the yz-plane. It follows that the graph of [1] is obtained by rotating the parabola $z = x^2$ around the z-axis. The surface is called a **paraboloid** (of revolution), as shown in Fig. 15.9, which also shows the level curves in the xy-plane.

Example 15.10

Suppose $F(K, L)$ denotes the number of units produced by a firm when the input of capital is K and that of labor is L. A level curve for the function is a curve in the KL-plane given by

$$F(K, L) = Y_0 \qquad (Y_0 \text{ is a constant})$$

This curve is called an **isoquant** (indicating "equal quantity"). For a Cobb–Douglas function $F(K, L) = AK^a L^b$ with $a + b < 1$ and $A > 0$, Figs. 15.10 and 15.11 show a part of the graph and some of the isoquants. (Here it is convenient to view the surface from a perspective other than that used for most other figures in this section.)

Example 15.11

Show that all points (x, y) satisfying $xy = 3$ lie on a level curve for the function

$$g(x, y) = \frac{3(xy + 1)^2}{x^4 y^4 - 1}$$

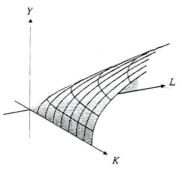

FIGURE 15.10

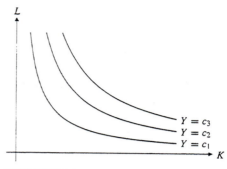

FIGURE 15.11

Solution   By substituting $xy = 3$ in the expression for g, we find

$$g(x, y) = \frac{3(xy + 1)^2}{(xy)^4 - 1} = \frac{3(3 + 1)^2}{3^4 - 1} = \frac{48}{80} = \frac{3}{5}$$

For all (x, y) where $xy = 3$, the value of $g(x, y)$ is a constant 3/5. This means that $xy = 3$ is on a level curve (at height 3/5) for g.

In fact, for any value of c other than -1 or 1, $xy = c$ is the equation of a level curve for g because $g(x, y) = 3(c + 1)^2/(c^4 - 1)$ when $xy = c$.

Some Other Surfaces in Three-Dimensional Space

It is usually not at all simple to draw the graphs of equations in three variables. Yet, in recent years, a number of powerful computer programs for drawing surfaces in three-dimensional space have been developed. Two surfaces that can be drawn in this way appear in Figs. 15.12 and 15.13. (Figure 15.12 looks like a rugby football.)

FIGURE 15.12 $x^2/a^2 + y^2/b^2 + z^2/c^2 = 1.$

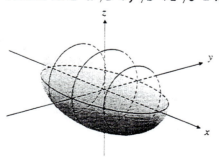

FIGURE 15.13 $z = x^4 - 3x^2y^2 + y^4.$

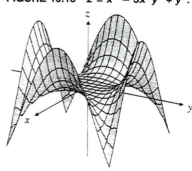

Functions of n Variables and the Euclidean n-Dimensional Space R^n

No concrete geometric interpretation is possible for functions of n variables in the general case when $n \geq 3$. Yet economists still use *geometric language* when dealing with functions of n variables, even though they may not think of themselves as doing geometry. It is usual to call the set of all possible n-tuples $(x_1, x_2, \ldots, x_n)$ of real numbers the **Euclidean n-dimensional space**, or **n-space**, and to denote it by R^n. For $n = 1$, 2, and 3, we have geometric interpretations of R^n as a line, a plane, and a 3-dimensional space, respectively. But for $n \geq 4$, there is no geometric interpretation.

If $z = f(x_1, x_2, \ldots, x_n)$ represents a function of n variables, we let the **graph** of f be the set of all points $\left(x_1, x_2, \ldots, x_n, f(x_1, x_2, \ldots, x_n)\right)$ in R^{n+1} for which $(x_1, x_2, \ldots, x_n)$ belongs to the domain of f. We also call the graph a **surface** (or sometimes a **hypersurface**) in R^{n+1}. For $z = z_0$ (constant), the set of points in R^n satisfying $f(x_1, x_2, \ldots, x_n) = z_0$ is called a **level surface** of f.

In production theory, it is usual to give level surfaces a different name. If $x = f(v_1, v_2, \ldots, v_n)$ is the amount produced when the input quantities of n different factors of production are respectively $v_1, v_2, \ldots, v_n$, the level surfaces where $f(v_1, v_2, \ldots, v_n) = x_0$ (constant) are called *isoquants*, as in Example 15.10.

Continuity

The concept of continuity for functions of one variable may be generalized to functions of several variables. Roughly speaking, a function of n variables is continuous if small changes in the independent variables give small changes in the function value. Just as in the one-variable case, we have the following useful rule:

Any function of n variables that can be constructed from continuous functions by combining the operations of addition, subtraction, multiplication, division, and functional composition is continuous wherever it is defined.

If a function of one variable is continuous, it will also be continuous when considered as a function of several variables. For example, $f(x, y, z) = x^2$ is a continuous function of x, y, and z. (Small changes in x, y, and z give at most small changes in x^2.)

Example 15.12

Where are the functions given by the following formulas continuous?

(a) $f(x, y, z) = x^2 y + 8x^2 y^5 z - xy + 8z$

(b) $g(x, y) = \dfrac{xy - 3}{x^2 + y^2 - 4}$

Solution

(a) As the sum of products of powers, f is defined and continuous for all x, y, and z.

(b) The function g is defined and continuous for all (x, y) except those that lie on the circle $x^2 + y^2 = 4$. There the denominator is zero, and so $g(x, y)$ is not defined.

Problems

1. Draw the graphs of the following functions in three-dimensional space, and draw a set of level curves for each of them:

   a. $z = 3 - x - y$ **b.** $z = \sqrt{3 - x^2 - y^2}$

2. Show that $x^2 + y^2 = 6$ is a level curve of $f(x, y) = \sqrt{x^2 + y^2} - x^2 - y^2 + 2$, and that all the level curves of f must be circles centered at the origin.

3. Show that $x^2 - y^2 = c$, for all values of the constant c lies on a level curve for $f(x, y) = e^{x^2}e^{-y^2} + x^4 - 2x^2y^2 + y^4$.

4. Let $f(x)$ represent a function of one variable. If we let $g(x, y) = f(x)$, then we have defined a function of two variables, but y is not present in its formula. Explain how the graph of g is obtained from the graph of f. Illustrate with $f(x) = -x^3$.

5. Explain why two level curves of $z = f(x, y)$ corresponding to different function values of z cannot intersect.

15.3 Partial Derivatives with Two Variables

When we study a function $y = f(x)$ of one variable, the derivative $f'(x)$ measures the function's rate of change as x changes. For functions of two variables, such as $z = f(x, y)$, we also want to examine how quickly the value of the function changes with respect to changes in the values of the independent variables. For example, if $f(x, y)$ is a firm's profit when it uses quantities x and y of two different inputs, we want to know whether and by how much profits increase as x and y are varied.

Consider the function

$$z = x^3 + 2y^2 \tag{1}$$

Suppose, first, that y is held constant. Then $2y^2$ is constant, and the rate of change of z with respect to x is given by

$$\frac{dz}{dx} = 3x^2$$

On the other hand, we can keep x fixed in [1] and examine how z varies as y varies. This involves taking the derivative of z with respect to y while keeping x constant. The result is

$$\frac{dz}{dy} = 4y$$

Of course, there are other variations we could study. For example, x and y could vary simultaneously. But in this section, we restrict our attention to variations in *either x or y*.

When we consider functions of two or more variables, we shall write $\partial z/\partial x$ instead of dz/dx for the derivative of z with respect to x. In the same way, we write $\partial z/\partial y$ instead of dz/dy. Hence, we have

$$z = x^3 + 2y^2 \implies \frac{\partial z}{\partial x} = 3x^2 \quad \text{and} \quad \frac{\partial z}{\partial y} = 4y$$

In general, we introduce the following definitions:

Suppose $z = f(x, y)$. Let $\partial z/\partial x$, called the **partial derivative of z or f with respect to x**, be the derivative of $f(x, y)$ with respect to x when y is held constant. Also, let $\partial z/\partial y$, called the **partial derivative of z or f with respect to y**, be the derivative of $f(x, y)$ with respect to y when x is held constant. [15.7]

When $z = f(x, y)$, we also denote the derivative $\partial z/\partial x$ by $\partial f/\partial x$. In the same way, $\partial z/\partial y = \partial f/\partial y$. Note that $\partial f/\partial x$ is the rate of change of $f(x, y)$ with respect to x, when y is constant, and correspondingly for $\partial f/\partial y$.

It is usually easy to find the partial derivatives of a function $z = f(x, y)$. To compute $\partial f/\partial x$, just think of y as a constant and differentiate $f(x, y)$ with respect to x as if f were a function only of x. All the rules for finding derivatives of functions of one variable can be used when we want to compute $\partial f/\partial x$. The same is true for $\partial f/\partial y$. Let us look at some further examples.

Example 15.13

Compute the partial derivatives of the following:

(a) $f(x, y) = x^3y + x^2y^2 + x + y^2$
(b) $f(x, y) = xy/(x^2 + y^2)$

Solution

(a) We find

$$\frac{\partial f}{\partial x} = 3x^2y + 2xy^2 + 1 \qquad \text{(holding } y \text{ constant)}$$

$$\frac{\partial f}{\partial y} = x^3 + 2x^2y + 2y \qquad \text{(holding } x \text{ constant)}$$

(b) For this function, the quotient gives

$$\frac{\partial f}{\partial x} = \frac{y(x^2 + y^2) - 2xxy}{(x^2 + y^2)^2} = \frac{y^3 - x^2y}{(x^2 + y^2)^2}, \qquad \frac{\partial f}{\partial y} = \frac{x^3 - y^2x}{(x^2 + y^2)^2}$$

Observe that the function in (b) is symmetric in x and y, in the sense that the function value is unchanged if we interchange x and y. By interchanging x and y in the formula for $\partial f/\partial x$, therefore, we will find the correct formula for $\partial f/\partial y$. (Compute $\partial f/\partial y$ in the usual way and check that the foregoing answer is correct.)

Other forms of notation are often used to indicate the partial derivatives of $z = f(x, y)$. Some of the most common are

$$\frac{\partial f}{\partial x} = \frac{\partial z}{\partial x} = z'_x = f'_x(x, y) = f'_1(x, y) = \frac{\partial f(x, y)}{\partial x}$$

$$\frac{\partial f}{\partial y} = \frac{\partial z}{\partial y} = z'_y = f'_y(x, y) = f'_2(x, y) = \frac{\partial f(x, y)}{\partial y}$$

Among these, $f'_1(x, y)$ and $f'_2(x, y)$ are the most satisfactory. Here the numerical subscripts refer to positions of the argument in the function. Thus, f'_1 indicates the partial derivative w.r.t. the first variable, and f'_2 w.r.t. the second variable. We are also reminded that the partial derivatives themselves are functions of x and y. Finally, $f'_1(a, b)$ and $f'_2(a, b)$ are suitable designations of the values of the partial derivatives at point (a, b) instead of at (x, y). For example, for the function in Example 15.13(a),

$$f(x, y) = x^3y + x^2y^2 + x + y^2 \implies f'_1(x, y) = 3x^2y + 2xy^2 + 1$$

Hence, $f'_1(0, 0) = 1$ and $f'_1(-1, 2) = 3(-1)^2 2 + 2(-1)2^2 + 1 = -1$.

The notations $f'_x(x, y)$ and $f'_y(x, y)$ are often used, but especially in connection with composite functions, these notations are sometimes too ambiguous. For instance, what is the meaning of $f'_x(x^2y, x - y)$?

Higher-Order Partial Derivatives

If $z = f(x, y)$, then $\partial f / \partial x$ and $\partial f / \partial y$ are called **first-order partial derivatives**. These partial derivatives are themselves functions of two variables. From $\partial f / \partial x$, we can generate two new functions by taking the partial derivatives with respect to x and y. In the same way, we can take the partial derivatives of $\partial f / \partial y$ with respect to x and y. The four functions we obtain in this way are called **second-order partial derivatives** of $f(x, y)$. They are expressed as

$$\frac{\partial}{\partial x}\left(\frac{\partial f}{\partial x}\right) = \frac{\partial^2 f}{\partial x^2}, \qquad \frac{\partial}{\partial y}\left(\frac{\partial f}{\partial x}\right) = \frac{\partial^2 f}{\partial y \partial x}$$

$$\frac{\partial}{\partial x}\left(\frac{\partial f}{\partial y}\right) = \frac{\partial^2 f}{\partial x \partial y}, \qquad \frac{\partial}{\partial y}\left(\frac{\partial f}{\partial y}\right) = \frac{\partial^2 f}{\partial y^2}$$

For brevity, we sometimes refer to the first- and second-order "partials," suppressing the word "derivatives."

Example 15.14

For the function in Example 15.13(a), we obtain

$$\frac{\partial^2 f}{\partial x^2} = 6xy + 2y^2, \qquad \frac{\partial^2 f}{\partial y \partial x} = 3x^2 + 4xy = \frac{\partial^2 f}{\partial x \partial y}, \qquad \frac{\partial^2 f}{\partial y^2} = 2x^2 + 2$$

Several other kinds of notation are also frequently used for the second-order partial derivatives. For example, $\partial^2 f / \partial x^2$ is also denoted by $f''_{11}(x, y)$ or $f''_{xx}(x, y)$. In the same way, $\partial^2 f / \partial y \partial x$ can also be written as $f''_{12}(x, y)$ or $f''_{xy}(x, y)$. Note that $f''_{12}(x, y)$ means that we differentiate $f(x, y)$ first with respect to the first argument x and then with respect to the second argument y. To find $f''_{21}(x, y)$, we must differentiate in the reverse order. In Example 15.14, these two "mixed" second-order partial derivatives (or "cross-partials") are equal. For most functions $z = f(x, y)$ used in practical applications, it will actually be the case that

$$\frac{\partial^2 f}{\partial x \partial y} = \frac{\partial^2 f}{\partial y \partial x} \qquad [15.8]$$

Sufficient conditions for the equality in [15.8] are given in Theorem 15.1 of Section 15.5.

It is very important to note the exact meaning of the different symbols that have been introduced. If we consider [15.8], for example, it would be a serious mistake to believe that the two expressions are equal because $\partial x \partial y$ is the same as $\partial y \partial x$. Here the expression on the left-hand side is in fact the derivative of $\partial f / \partial y$ with respect to x, and the right-hand side is the derivative of $\partial f / \partial x$ with respect to y. It is a remarkable fact, and not a triviality, that the two are usually equal. As another example, we observe that $\partial^2 z / \partial x^2$ is quite different from $(\partial z / \partial x)^2$. For example, if $z = x^2 + y^2$, then $\partial z / \partial x = 2x$. Therefore, $\partial^2 z / \partial x^2 = 2$, whereas $(\partial z / \partial x)^2 = 4x^2$.

Analogously, we define partial derivatives of the third, fourth, and higher orders. For example, we obtain $\partial^4 z / \partial x \partial y^3 = z'''_{yyyx}$ when we first differentiate z three times with respect to y and then differentiate the result once more with respect to x.

Here is an additional example.

Example 15.15

If $f(x, y) = x^3 e^{y^2}$, find the first- and second-order partial derivatives at $(x, y) = (1, 0)$.

Solution   To find $f'_1(x, y)$, we differentiate $x^3 e^{y^2}$ with respect to x while treating y as a constant. When y is a constant, so is e^{y^2}. Hence,

$$f'_1(x, y) = 3x^2 e^{y^2} \qquad \text{and so} \qquad f'_1(1, 0) = 3 \cdot 1^2 e^{0^2} = 3$$

To find $f'_2(x, y)$, we differentiate $f(x, y)$ with respect to y while treating x as a constant:

$$f'_2(x, y) = x^3 2y e^{y^2} = 2x^3 y e^{y^2} \qquad \text{and so} \qquad f'_2(1, 0) = 0$$

To find the second-order partial $f''_{11}(x, y)$, we must differentiate $f'_1(x, y)$ with respect to x once more, while treating y as a constant:

$$f''_{11}(x, y) = 6x e^{y^2} \qquad \text{and so} \qquad f''_{11}(1, 0) = 6 \cdot 1 e^{0^2} = 6$$

To find $f''_{22}(x, y)$, we must differentiate $f'_2(x, y) = 2x^3 y e^{y^2}$ with respect to y once more, while treating x as a constant. Because $y e^{y^2}$ is a product of two functions, each involving y, we use the product rule to obtain

$$f''_{22}(x, y) = (2x^3)(1 \cdot e^{y^2} + y 2y e^{y^2}) = 2x^3 e^{y^2} + 4x^3 y^2 e^{y^2}$$

Evaluating this at $(1, 0)$ gives $f''_{22}(1, 0) = 2$. Moreover,

$$f''_{12}(x, y) = \frac{\partial}{\partial y}\left[f'_1(x, y)\right] = \frac{\partial}{\partial y}(3x^2 e^{y^2}) = 3x^2 2y e^{y^2} = 6x^2 y e^{y^2}$$

and

$$f''_{21}(x, y) = \frac{\partial}{\partial x}\left[f'_2(x, y)\right] = \frac{\partial}{\partial x}(2x^3 y e^{y^2}) = 6x^2 y e^{y^2}$$

Hence, $f''_{12}(1, 0) = f''_{21}(1, 0) = 0$.

Approximations to Partial Derivatives

Recall how, when x is a single variable, we can often get a good approximation to $f'(x)$ by computing $f(x + 1) - f(x)$ (see Example 4.5 in Section 4.3). Because $f_x'(x, y)$ is simply the derivative of $f(x, y)$ with respect to x when y is held constant, we obtain the corresponding approximation

$$f_x'(x, y) \approx f(x + 1, y) - f(x, y)$$

In words:

The partial derivative $f_x'(x, y)$ is approximately equal to the change in $f(x, y)$ that results from increasing x by one unit while holding y constant.   [15.9]

The partial derivative $f_y'(x, y)$ is approximately equal to the change in $f(x, y)$ that results from increasing y by one unit while holding x constant.   [15.10]

The number $f_x'(x, y)$ measures the rate of change of f with respect to x. If $f_x'(x, y) > 0$, then a small increase in x will lead to an increase in $f(x, y)$. When the approximation in [15.9] is permissible, we can say that $f_x'(x, y) > 0$ means that a unit increase in x will lead an increase in $f(x, y)$. Similarly, $f_x'(x, y) < 0$ means that a unit increase in x will lead to a decrease in $f(x, y)$.

Note: The approximations in [15.9] and [15.10] must be used with caution. Roughly speaking, they will not be too inaccurate provided that the partial derivatives do not vary too much over the actual intervals.

Example 15.16

In Example 15.2, we studied the function $x = Ap^{-1.5}r^{2.08}$. Compute the partial derivatives of x with respect to p and r, and discuss their signs.

Solution   We find

$$\frac{\partial x}{\partial p} = -1.5Ap^{-2.5}r^{2.08}, \qquad \frac{\partial x}{\partial r} = 2.08Ap^{-1.5}r^{1.08}$$

Because A, p, and r are positive, $\partial x / \partial p < 0$ and $\partial x / \partial r > 0$. These signs accord with the final remarks in Example 15.2.

Problems

1. Find $\partial z / \partial x$ and $\partial z / \partial y$ for the following:

   a. $z = x^2 + 3y^2$ **b.** $z = xy$ **c.** $z = 5x^4y^2 - 2xy^5$ **d.** $z = e^{x+y}$

   e. $z = e^{xy}$ **f.** $z = e^x/y$ **g.** $z = \ln(x+y)$ **h.** $z = \ln(xy)$

2. Find $f_1'(x, y)$, $f_2'(x, y)$, and $f_{12}''(x, y)$ for the following:

   a. $f(x, y) = x^7 - y^7$ **b.** $f(x, y) = x^5 \ln y$ **c.** $f(x, y) = (x^2 - 2y^2)^5$

3. Find all first- and second-order partial derivatives of the following:

   a. $z = 3x + 4y$ **b.** $z = x^3 y^2$ **c.** $z = x^5 - 3x^2 y + y^6$

   d. $z = x/y$ **e.** $z = (x-y)/(x+y)$ **f.** $z = \sqrt{x^2 + y^2}$

4. Let $F(S, E) = 2.26 \, S^{0.44} E^{0.48}$ (see Example 15.3).

   a. Compute $F_S'(S, E)$ and $F_E'(S, E)$.

   b. Show that $S F_S' + E F_E' = kF$ for a suitable constant k.

5. Prove that if $z = (ax + by)^2$, then $x z_x' + y z_y' = 2z$.

6. Find all the first- and second-order partial derivatives of the following:

   a. $z = x^2 + e^{2y}$ **b.** $z = y \ln x$ **c.** $z = xy^2 - e^{xy}$

7. Let $f(x, y) = x \ln y - y^2 2^{xy}$. Find all the first- and second-order partial derivatives at $(x, y) = (1, 1)$.

8. Let $z = \dfrac{1}{2} \ln(x^2 + y^2)$. Show that $\partial^2 z/\partial x^2 + \partial^2 z/\partial y^2 = 0$.

Harder Problems

9. Compute $\partial^{p+q} z/\partial y^q \partial x^p$ at $(0, 0)$ for the following:

   a. $z = e^x \ln(1 + y)$ **b.** $z = e^{x+y}(xy + y - 1)$

10. Prove that if $u = Ax^a y^b$, then

$$\frac{1}{u_x'} \frac{\partial}{\partial x}\left(\frac{u_{xy}''}{u_x' u_y'}\right) = \frac{1}{u_y'} \frac{\partial}{\partial y}\left(\frac{u_{xy}''}{u_x' u_y'}\right)$$

15.4 Partial Derivatives and Tangent Planes

Partial derivatives of the first order have an interesting geometric interpretation. Let $z = f(x, y)$ be a function of two variables, with graph as shown in Fig. 15.14. Let us keep the value of y fixed at y_0. The points (x, y) on the graph of f that have $y = y_0$ are those that lie on the curve K_y indicated in the figure. The partial derivative $f_x'(x_0, y_0)$ is the derivative of $z = f(x, y_0)$ with respect to x at the point $x = x_0$, and is therefore the slope of the tangent line l_y to the curve K_y at $x = x_0$. In the same way, $f_y'(x_0, y_0)$ is the slope of the tangent line l_x to the curve K_x at $y = y_0$.

    This geometric interpretation of the two partial derivatives can be explained in another way. Imagine that the graph of f describes a mountain, and suppose that we are standing at point P with coordinates $\left(x_0, y_0, f(x_0, y_0)\right)$ in three

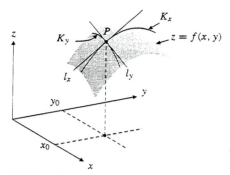

FIGURE 15.14

dimensions, where the height is $f(x_0, y_0)$ units above the xy-plane. The slope of the terrain at P depends on the direction in which we look. In particular, let us look in the direction parallel to the positive x-axis. Then $f_x'(x_0, y_0)$ is a measure of the "steepness" in this direction. In the figure, $f_x'(x_0, y_0)$ is negative, because moving from P in the direction given by the positive x-axis will take us downwards. In the same way, we see that $f_y'(x_0, y_0)$ is a measure of the "steepness" in the direction parallel to the positive y-axis. We also see that $f_y'(x_0, y_0)$ is positive, meaning that the slope is upward in this direction.

Let us now briefly consider the geometric interpretation of the "direct" second-order derivatives f_{xx}'' and f_{yy}''. Consider the curve K_y on the graph of f in the figure. It seems that along this curve, $f_{xx}''(x, y_0)$ is negative, because $f_x'(x, y_0)$ decreases as x increases. In particular, $f_{xx}''(x_0, y_0) < 0$. In the same way, we see that moving along K_x makes $f_y'(x_0, y)$ decrease as y increases, so $f_{yy}''(x_0, y) < 0$ along K_x. In particular, $f_{yy}''(x_0, y_0) < 0$.

Example 15.17

Consider Fig. 15.15, showing some level curves of a function $z = f(x, y)$. On the basis of this figure, answer the following questions:

   (a) What are the signs of $f_x'(x, y)$ and $f_y'(x, y)$ at P and Q?
   (b) What are the solutions of the two equations: (i) $f(3, y) = 4$ and (ii) $f(x, 4) = 6$?
   (c) What is the largest value that $f(x, y)$ can attain when $x = 2$, and for which y value does this maximum occur?

Solution

   (a) If you stand at P, you are on the level curve $f(x, y) = 2$. If you look in the direction of the positive x-axis (along the line $y = 4$), then you will see the terrain sloping upwards, because the (nearest) level curves

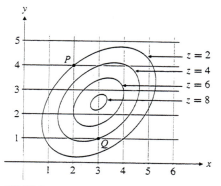

FIGURE 15.15

correspond to larger z values. Hence, $f'_x > 0$. If you stand at P and look in the direction of the positive y-axis (along $x = 2$), the terrain will slope downwards. Thus, at P, we must have $f'_y < 0$. At Q, we find similarly that $f'_x < 0$ and $f'_y > 0$.

(b) Equation (i) has the solutions $y = 1$ and $y = 4$, because the line $x = 3$ cuts the level curve $f(x, y) = 4$ at $(3, 1)$ and at $(3, 4)$. Equation (ii) has no solutions, because the line $y = 4$ does not meet the level curve $f(x, y) = 6$ at all.

(c) The highest value of c for which the level curve $f(x, y) = c$ has a point in common with the line $x = 2$ is $c = 6$. The largest value of $f(x, y)$ when $x = 2$ is therefore 6, and we see that this maximum value is attained when $y \approx 2.2$.

Tangent Planes

Look back at Fig. 15.14. The two tangent lines l_x and l_y determine a unique plane through the point $P = (x_0, y_0, f(x_0, y_0))$. This plane is called the *tangent plane* to the surface at P. From [12.23] in Section 12.5, the general equation for a plane in three-dimensional space passing through a point (x_0, y_0, z_0) is $a(x - x_0) + b(y - y_0) + c(z - z_0) = 0$. If $c = 0$, then this plane is parallel to the z-axis. If $c \neq 0$ and we define $A = -a/c$, $B = -b/c$, then solving the equation for $z - z_0$ gives

$$z - z_0 = A(x - x_0) + B(y - y_0) \qquad [1]$$

So the tangent plane to the surface at P must have this form. It remains to determine A and B. Now, line l_y lies in the plane. Because the slope of the line is $f'_1(x_0, y_0)$, the points (x, y, z) that lie on l_y are characterized by the two equations $y = y_0$ and $z - z_0 = f'_1(x_0, y_0)(x - x_0)$. All these points (x, y, z) lie in the plane

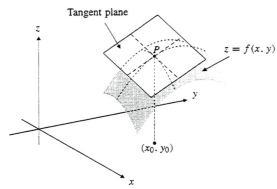

FIGURE 15.16   **The graph of a function $z = f(x, y)$ and its tangent plane at P.**

[1] only if $A = f'_1(x_0, y_0)$. In a similar way, we see that $B = f'_2(x_0, y_0)$. The conclusion is as follows:

The **tangent plane** to $z = f(x, y)$ at the point (x_0, y_0, z_0), with $z_0 = f(x_0, y_0)$, has the equation

$$z - z_0 = f'_1(x_0, y_0)(x - x_0) + f'_2(x_0, y_0)(y - y_0)$$ [15.11]

The tangent plane is illustrated in Fig. 15.16.

Example 15.18

Find the tangent plane at $(x_0, y_0, z_0) = (1, 1, 5)$ to the graph of

$$f(x, y) = x^2 + 2xy + 2y^2$$

Solution   Because $f(1, 1) = 5$, the given point lies on the graph of f. We find that

$$f'_1(x, y) = 2x + 2y, \qquad f'_2(x, y) = 2x + 4y$$

Hence, $f'_1(1, 1) = 4$ and $f'_2(1, 1) = 6$. Thus, [15.11] yields

$$z - 5 = 4(x - 1) + 6(y - 1) \qquad \text{or} \qquad z = 4x + 6y - 5$$

Problems

1. In Fig. 15.17, we have drawn some level curves for a function $z = f(x, y)$, together with the line $2x + 3y = 12$.

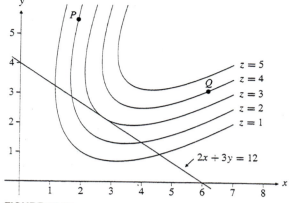

FIGURE 15.17

    a. What are the signs of f_x' and f_y' at P and Q?

    b. Find possible solutions of the two equations (i) $f(1, y) = 2$ and (ii) $f(x, 2) = 2$.

    c. What is the largest value of $f(x, y)$ among those (x, y) that satisfy $2x + 3y = 12$?

2. Suppose $F(x, y)$ is a function about which all we know is that $F(0, 0) = 0$, $F_1'(x, y) \geq 2$ for all (x, y), and $F_2'(x, y) \leq 1$ for all (x, y). What can be said about the relative sizes of $F(0, 0)$, $F(1, 0)$, $F(2, 0)$, $F(0, 1)$, and $F(1, 1)$? Write down the inequalities that have to hold between these numbers.

3. Find the tangent planes to the following surfaces at the indicated points:

    a. $z = x^2 + y^2$ at $(1, 2, 5)$ **b.** $z = (y - x^2)(y - 2x^2)$ at $(1, 3, 2)$

4. Prove that all tangent planes to $z = xf(y/x)$ pass through the origin.

15.5 Partial Derivatives with Many Variables

The functions economists study usually have many variables, so we need to extend the concept of partial derivatives to such functions.

> If $z = f(x_1, x_2, \ldots, x_n)$, then $\partial f/\partial x_i$ is the derivative of $f(x_1, x_2, \ldots, x_n)$ with respect to x_i when all the other variables x_j ($j \neq i$) are held constant.   [15.12]

These n partial derivatives are of the first order. Other notation used for the first-order partials of $z = f(x_1, x_2, \ldots, x_n)$ includes

$$\frac{\partial f}{\partial x_i} = \frac{\partial z}{\partial x_i} = \partial z/\partial x_i = z_i' = f_i'(x_1, x_2, \ldots, x_n)$$

As in [15.9] and [15.10] in Section 15.3, we have the following rough approximation:

The partial derivative $\partial z / \partial x_i$ is approximately equal to the change in $z = f(x_1, x_2, \ldots, x_n)$ caused by an increase in x_i of one unit, while all the other x_j $(j \neq i)$ are held constant.   [15.13]

In symbols:

$$f_i'(x_1, \ldots, x_n)$$
$$\approx f(x_1, \ldots, x_{i-1}, x_i + 1, x_{i+1}, \ldots, x_n) - f(x_1, \ldots, x_{i-1}, x_i, x_{i+1}, \ldots, x_n)$$

For each of the n first-order partials of f, we have n second-order partials:

$$\frac{\partial}{\partial x_j} \left(\frac{\partial f}{\partial x_i} \right) = \frac{\partial^2 f}{\partial x_j \partial x_i} = z_{ij}''$$

Here both i and j may take any value $1, 2, \ldots, n$, so there are altogether n^2 second-order partial derivatives. The $n \times n$ matrix of second-order partials

$$\begin{pmatrix} f_{11}''(\mathbf{x}) & f_{12}''(\mathbf{x}) & \cdots & f_{1n}''(\mathbf{x}) \\ f_{21}''(\mathbf{x}) & f_{22}''(\mathbf{x}) & \cdots & f_{2n}''(\mathbf{x}) \\ \vdots & \vdots & \ddots & \vdots \\ f_{n1}''(\mathbf{x}) & f_{n2}''(\mathbf{x}) & \cdots & f_{nn}''(\mathbf{x}) \end{pmatrix}$$ [15.14]

is the **Hessian** (or **Hessian matrix**) of f evaluated at $\mathbf{x} = (x_1, x_2, \ldots, x_n)$. Because usually $f_{ij}''(\mathbf{x}) = f_{ji}''(\mathbf{x})$ for all i and j, the number of different partials is reduced from n^2 to at most $\frac{1}{2}n(n + 1)$, and the Hessian is symmetric. (See Theorem 15.1, which follows.)

Example 15.19

Find the first-order partials with respect to A, B, and T for the function $a(A, B, T) = 122 + 3A - 25T - 75B^2 - A/B$. Also find the Hessian of $a(A, B, T)$.

Solution

$$\partial a / \partial A = 3 - 1/B, \qquad \partial a / \partial B = -150B + A/B^2, \qquad \partial a / \partial T = -25$$

and the Hessian is

$$
\begin{pmatrix}
\dfrac{\partial^2 a}{\partial A^2} & \dfrac{\partial^2 a}{\partial A \partial B} & \dfrac{\partial^2 a}{\partial A \partial T} \\[2ex]
\dfrac{\partial^2 a}{\partial B \partial A} & \dfrac{\partial^2 a}{\partial B^2} & \dfrac{\partial^2 a}{\partial B \partial T} \\[2ex]
\dfrac{\partial^2 a}{\partial T \partial A} & \dfrac{\partial^2 a}{\partial T \partial B} & \dfrac{\partial^2 a}{\partial T^2}
\end{pmatrix}
=
\begin{pmatrix}
0 & \dfrac{1}{B^2} & 0 \\[2ex]
\dfrac{1}{B^2} & -150 - 2\dfrac{A}{B^3} & 0 \\[2ex]
0 & 0 & 0
\end{pmatrix}
$$

Young's Theorem

We mentioned earlier that if $z = f(x_1, x_2, \ldots, x_n)$, then z_{ij}'' and z_{ji}'' are usually equal; this implies that the order of differentiation does not matter. The next theorem makes precise a more general result.

Theorem 15.1   (Young's Theorem)   Suppose that two mth-order partial derivatives of the function $f(x_1, x_2, \ldots, x_n)$ involve the same number of differentiations with respect to each of the variables, and are both continuous in an open set S. Then the two partial derivatives are necessarily equal at all points in S.

The content of this result can be explained as follows: Let $m = m_1 + \cdots + m_n$, and suppose that $f(x_1, x_2, \ldots, x_n)$ is differentiated m_1 times with respect to x_1, m_2 times with respect to x_2, $\ldots$, and m_n times with respect to x_n. Suppose that the continuity condition is satisfied for these mth-order partial derivatives. Then we end up with the same result no matter what is the order of differentiation, because each of the final partial derivatives is equal to

$$
\frac{\partial^m f}{\partial x_1^{m_1} \partial x_2^{m_2} \cdots \partial x_n^{m_n}}
$$

In particular, for the case when $m = 2$,

$$
\frac{\partial^2 f}{\partial x_j \partial x_i} = \frac{\partial^2 f}{\partial x_i \partial x_j} \qquad (i = 1, 2, \ldots, n, \quad j = 1, 2, \ldots, n)
$$

if both these partials are continuous. An example where this equality is not satisfied is presented in Problem 6. (A proof of Young's theorem is given in most advanced calculus books.)

Formal Definitions of Partial Derivatives

So far in this chapter, the functions have been given by explicit formulas and we have found the partial derivatives by using the ordinary rules for differentiation. If these rules of differentiation cannot be used, however, we must resort directly to the formal definition of partial derivatives. This corresponds closely to the definition for ordinary derivatives of functions of one variable, because partial derivatives are merely ordinary derivatives that are obtained by keeping all but one of the variables constant.

If $z = f(x_1, \ldots, x_n)$, then with $g(x_i) = f(x_1, \ldots, x_{i-1}, x_i, x_{i+1}, \ldots, x_n)$, we have $\partial z / \partial x_i = g'(x_i)$. (Here we think of all the variables x_j other than x_i as constants.) If we use the definition of $g'(x_i)$ (see [4.3] of Section 4.2), we obtain

$$\frac{\partial z}{\partial x_i} = \lim_{h \to 0} \frac{f(x_1, \ldots, x_i + h, \ldots, x_n) - f(x_1, \ldots, x_i, \ldots, x_n)}{h} \qquad [15.15]$$

(If we consider $h = 1$ as a number close to 0, we obtain the approximation in [15.13].) If the limit in [15.15] does not exist, then we say that $\partial z / \partial x_i$ *does not exist*, or that z is not differentiable with respect to x_i at the point. For instance, if a function describes the height of a pyramid, the partial derivatives will not exist at the point corresponding to the top of the pyramid.

Almost all the functions we consider will have continuous partial derivatives everywhere in their domains. If $z = f(x_1, x_2, \ldots, x_n)$ has continuous partial derivatives of the first order in a domain A, we call f **continuously differentiable** in A.[3] In this case, f is called a C^1 **function** on A. If all partial derivatives up to order k exist and are continuous, f is called a C^k **function**.

Problems

1. Calculate all first-order partials of the following functions:
   a. $f(x, y, z) = x^2 + y^3 + z^4$ **b.** $f(x, y, z) = 5x^2 - 3y^3 + 3z^4$
   c. $f(x, y, z) = xyz$ **d.** $f(x, y, z) = x^4/yz$
   e. $f(x, y, z) = (x^2 + y^3 + z^4)^6$ **f.** $f(x, y, z) = e^{xyz}$

2. For $F(x, y, z) = x^2 e^{xz} + y^3 e^{xy}$ calculate $F_1'(1, 1, 1)$, $F_2'(1, 1, 1)$, and $F_3'(1, 1, 1)$.

3. Let x and y be the populations of two cities and d the distance between them. Suppose that the number of travelers T between the cities is given by

$$T = k\frac{xy}{d^n} \qquad (k \text{ and } n \text{ are positive constants})$$

Compute $\partial T/\partial x$, $\partial T/\partial y$, and $\partial T/\partial d$, and discuss their signs.

[3]This seems appropriate, even though it is not quite standard mathematical terminology.

4. Find all the first- and second-order partials of the function $w(x, y, z) = 3xyz + x^2 y - xz^3$.

5. Find all the first-order partial derivatives of the following:

   a. $E(p, q) = ap^2 e^{bq}$

   b. $R(p_1, p_2) = \alpha p_1^{\beta} + \gamma e^{p_1 p_2}$

   c. $x(v_1, \ldots, v_n) = \sum_{i=1}^{n} a_i v_i$

Harder Problems

6. Define the function $f(x, y) = xy(x^2 - y^2)/(x^2 + y^2)$ when $(x, y) \neq (0, 0)$, and $f(0, 0) = 0$. Show that Young's theorem does not apply at $(0, 0)$ by finding $f_1'(0, y)$ and $f_2'(x, 0)$, then showing that $f_{12}''(0, 0) = 1$ and that $f_{21}''(0, 0) = -1$. Show that Young's theorem is not contradicted because both f_{12}'' and f_{21}'' are discontinuous at $(0, 0)$.

7. Find all the first-order partial derivatives of $f(u, v, w) = u^{v^{w}}$.

15.6 Partial Derivatives in Economics

This section considers a number of economic examples of partial derivatives.

Example 15.20

Consider an agricultural production function $Y = F(K, L, T)$, where Y is the number of units produced, K capital invested, L labor input, and T the area of agricultural land that is used. Then $\partial Y / \partial K = F_K'$ is called the **marginal product of capital**. It is the rate of change of output Y with respect to K when L and T are held fixed. Similarly, $\partial Y / \partial L = F_L'$ and $\partial Y / \partial T = F_T'$ are the **marginal products of labor and of land**, respectively. For example, if K is the value of capital equipment measured in dollars, and $\partial Y / \partial K = 5$, then increasing capital input by 1 dollar would increase output by approximately 5 units.

Suppose, in particular, that F is the Cobb–Douglas function

$$F(K, L, T) = AK^a L^b T^c \qquad (A, a, b, \text{ and } c \text{ are positive constants}) \qquad [1]$$

Find the marginal products, and the second-order partials. Discuss their signs.

Solution   The marginal products are

$$F_K' = AaK^{a-1}L^b T^c$$

$$F_L' = AbK^a L^{b-1} T^c \qquad [2]$$

$$F_T' = AcK^a L^b T^{c-1}$$

Assuming K, L, and T are all positive, the marginal products are positive. Thus, an increase in capital, labor, or land will increase the number of units produced.

The mixed second-order partials (or cross-partials) are

$$F''_{KL} = AabK^{a-1}L^{b-1}T^c$$

$$F''_{KT} = AacK^{a-1}L^bT^{c-1} \qquad\qquad [3]$$

$$F''_{LT} = AbcK^aL^{b-1}T^{c-1}$$

Check for yourself that F''_{LK}, F''_{TK}, and F''_{TL} give, respectively, the same results as in [3]. Note that these partials are positive. We call each pair of factors *complementary*, because more of one increases the marginal product of the other.

The direct second-order partials are

$$F''_{KK} = Aa(a-1)K^{a-2}L^bT^c$$

$$F''_{LL} = Ab(b-1)K^aL^{b-2}T^c$$

$$F''_{TT} = Ac(c-1)K^aL^bT^{c-2}$$

For instance, F''_{KK} is the partial derivative of the marginal product of capital (F'_K) with respect to K. If $a < 1$, then $F''_{KK} < 0$, and there is a diminishing marginal product of capital—that is, a small increase in the capital invested will lead to a decrease in the marginal product of capital. We can interpret this to mean that although small increases in capital cause output to rise $(F'_K > 0)$, this rise occurs at a decreasing rate $(F''_{KK} < 0)$. Similarly for labor (if $b < 1$), and for land (if $c < 1$).

Example 15.21

Let x be an index of the total amount of goods produced and consumed in a society, and let z be a measure of the level of pollution. If $u(x, z)$ measures the total well-being of the society (not a very easy function to estimate!), what signs do you expect $u'_x(x, z)$ and $u'_z(x, z)$ to have? Can you guess what economists usually assume about the sign of $u''_{xz}(x, z)$?

Solution   It is reasonable to expect that well-being increases as the amount of goods increases, but decreases as the level of pollution increases. Hence, we will usually have $u'_x(x, z) > 0$ and $u'_z(x, z) < 0$. According to [15.13] of Section 15.5, $u''_{xz} = (\partial/\partial z)(u'_x)$ is approximately equal to the change in u'_x when the level of pollution increases by one unit. Here $u'_x \approx$ the increase in welfare obtained by a unit increase in x. It is often assumed that $u''_{xz} < 0$. This implies that the increase in welfare obtained by an extra unit of x will decrease when the level of pollution increases. (An analogy: When I sit in a smoke-filled room, my increase in satisfaction from getting an extra piece of cake will decrease if the concentration of smoke increases too much.)

Example 15.22

The following modified version of the Cobb–Douglas function has been used in some economic studies:

$$F(K, L) = AK^a L^b e^{cK/L} \qquad (A, a, b, \text{ and } c \text{ are positive constants})$$

Compute the marginal products F'_K and F'_L and discuss their signs.

Solution   Differentiating with respect to K while keeping L constant, AL^b is also constant, so

$$F'_K = AL^b \frac{\partial}{\partial K} \left(K^a e^{cK/L} \right)$$

We must now use the product rule for differentiation. According to the chain rule, the derivative of $e^{cK/L}$ with respect to K is $(c/L)e^{cK/L}$, so

$$F'_K = AL^b \left[aK^{a-1} e^{cK/L} + K^a (c/L)e^{cK/L} \right]$$

$$= \left(\frac{a}{K} + \frac{c}{L} \right) F(K, L)$$

In the same way,

$$F'_L = AK^a \left[bL^{b-1} e^{cK/L} + L^b (-cK/L^2)e^{cK/L} \right]$$

$$= \left(\frac{b}{L} - \frac{cK}{L^2} \right) F(K, L)$$

If K and L are positive, then F'_K is always positive, but F'_L is positive only if $b > cK/L$. (If $b < cK/L$, then $F'_L < 0$, so an increase in labor leads to a reduction of output. The function is, therefore, most suitable as a production function in a domain where $b > cK/L$.)

Example 15.23

For the general Cobb–Douglas function F in logarithmic form,

$$\ln F = \ln A + a_1 \ln x_1 + a_2 \ln x_2 + \cdots + a_n \ln x_n \qquad [*]$$

(see [15.6] in Section 15.1), show that

$$\sum_{i=1}^{n} x_i \frac{\partial F}{\partial x_i} = (a_1 + a_2 + \cdots + a_n)F$$

Solution   Differentiating each side of [∗] partially with respect to x_i by means of the chain rule gives

$$\frac{1}{F}\frac{\partial F}{\partial x_i} = a_i \frac{1}{x_i} \qquad \text{or} \qquad x_i \frac{\partial F}{\partial x_i} = a_i F$$

for $i = 1, 2, \ldots, n$. So

$$\sum_{i=1}^{n} x_i \frac{\partial F}{\partial x_i} = \sum_{i=1}^{n} a_i F = \left(\sum_{i=1}^{n} a_i\right) F = (a_1 + a_2 + \cdots + a_n)F$$

Example 15.24

In Example 15.8 of Section 15.1 the function $U(x_1, x_2, \ldots, x_n)$ is a measure of the satisfaction or "utility" that an individual obtains by consuming the respective quantities $x_1, x_2, \ldots, x_n$ of n different goods. The partial derivative $\partial U / \partial x_i$ is called the **marginal utility** of the ith good. Usually, all the n marginal utilities are positive, because we expect utility to increase as the individual obtains more of a commodity.

For the function $U = a_1 \ln(x_1 - c_1) + a_2 \ln(x_2 - c_2) + \cdots + a_n \ln(x_n - c_n)$ specified in that example, we find

$$\frac{\partial U}{\partial x_1} = \frac{a_1}{x_1 - c_1}, \quad \frac{\partial U}{\partial x_2} = \frac{a_2}{x_2 - c_2}, \ldots, \frac{\partial U}{\partial x_n} = \frac{a_n}{x_n - c_n}$$

If the parameters $a_1, \ldots, a_n$ are all positive and $x_1 > c_1, \ldots, x_n > c_n$, then we see that all the marginal utilities are positive.

Problems

1. The demand for money M in the United States for the period 1929–1952 has been estimated as

$$M = 0.14Y + 76.03(r - 2)^{-0.84} \qquad (r > 2)$$

where Y is the annual national income, and r is the interest rate (in percent per year). Compute $\partial M / \partial Y$ and $\partial M / \partial r$ and discuss their signs.

2. If a and b are constants, compute the expression $KY'_K + LY'_L$ for the following:

   a. $Y = AK^a + BL^a$ **b.** $Y = AK^a L^b$ **c.** $Y = \dfrac{K^2 L^2}{aL^3 + bK^3}$

3. Let $F(K, L, M) = AK^a L^b M^c$. Show then that $KF'_K + LF'_L + MF'_M = (a + b + c)F$.

4. Let $D(p, q)$ and $E(p, q)$ be the demands for two commodities when the prices per unit are p and q, respectively. Suppose the commodities are *substitutes* in consumption, such as butter and margarine. What are the normal signs of the partial derivatives of D and E with respect to p and q?

5. Compute $\partial U/\partial x_i$ when $U(x_1, x_2, \ldots, x_n) = 100 - e^{-x_1} - e^{-x_2} - \cdots - e^{-x_n}$.

Harder Problems

6. Compute the expression $KY'_K + LY'_L$ if $Y = Ae^{\lambda t}\left[\delta K^{-\rho} + (1-\delta)L^{-\rho}\right]^{-m/\rho}$.

15.7 Linear Models with Quadratic Objectives

In this section, we consider some simple optimization models that lead to the problem of maximizing or minimizing a quadratic objective function in two variables.

Example 15.25 (Discriminating Monopolist)

Consider a firm that sells a product in two isolated geographical areas. If it wants to, it can then charge different prices in the two different areas because what is sold in one area cannot easily be resold in the other. As an example, it seems that express mail or courier services find it possible to charge much higher prices in Europe than they can in North America. Suppose that such a firm also has some monopoly power to influence the different prices it faces in the two separate markets by adjusting the quantity it sells in each. Economists generally use the term "discriminating monopolist" to describe a firm having this power.

Faced with two such isolated markets, the discriminating monopolist has two independent demand curves. Suppose that, in inverse form, these are

$$P_1 = a_1 - b_1 Q_1, \qquad P_2 = a_2 - b_2 Q_2 \qquad [1]$$

for market areas 1 and 2, respectively. Suppose, too, that the total cost function is

$$C(Q) = \alpha(Q_1 + Q_2)$$

with total cost proportional to total production.[4]

As a function of Q_1 and Q_2, total profits are

$$\pi(Q_1, Q_2) = P_1 Q_1 + P_2 Q_2 - C(Q_1 + Q_2)$$
$$= (a_1 - b_1 Q_1)Q_1 + (a_2 - b_2 Q_2)Q_2 - \alpha(Q_1 + Q_2)$$
$$= (a_1 - \alpha)Q_1 + (a_2 - \alpha)Q_2 - b_1 Q_1^2 - b_2 Q_2^2$$

---

[4] It is true that this cost function neglects transport costs, but the point to be made is that, even though supplies to the two areas are perfect substitutes in production, the monopolist will generally charge different prices, if allowed.

We want to find the values of Q_1 and Q_2 that maximize profits. To solve this problem as in Section 3.2 by completing the square is quite simple; we just treat Q_1 and Q_2 as separate variables. Indeed,

$$\pi = -b_1\left[Q_1 - \frac{(a_1 - \alpha)}{2b_1}\right]^2 - b_2\left[Q_2 - \frac{(a_2 - \alpha)}{2b_2}\right]^2$$
$$+ \frac{(a_1 - \alpha)^2}{4b_1} + \frac{(a_2 - \alpha)^2}{4b_2} \qquad [2]$$

So the solution involves the optimal quantities

$$Q_1^* = (a_1 - \alpha)/2b_1, \qquad Q_2^* = (a_2 - \alpha)/2b_2$$

The corresponding prices can be found by inserting these values in [1] to get

$$P_1^* = a_1 - b_1 Q_1^* = \tfrac{1}{2}(a_1 + \alpha), \qquad P_2^* = a_2 - b_2 Q_2^* = \tfrac{1}{2}(a_2 + \alpha)$$

From [2], maximum profits must be

$$\pi^* = \frac{(a_1 - \alpha)^2}{4b_1} + \frac{(a_2 - \alpha)^2}{4b_2}$$

This solution is valid as long as $a_1 \geq \alpha$ and $a_2 \geq \alpha$. In this case, P_1^* and P_2^* are both no less than α. This implies that there is no "cross subsidy" with the price in one market less than cost, and the losses in that market being subsidized by profits in the other market. Nor is there any "dumping," with price less than cost in one of the two markets. It is notable that the optimal prices are independent of b_1 and b_2. More important, note that the prices are *not* the same in the two markets, except in the special case when $a_1 = a_2$. Indeed, $P_1^* > P_2^*$ iff $a_1 > a_2$. This says that the price is higher in the market where consumers are willing to pay a higher price for each unit when the quantity is close to zero.

The foregoing analysis was simple because of the "separability" of the quadratic function $\pi(Q_1, Q_2)$, which took the form of the sum of a quadratic function $\pi_1(Q_1) = (a_1 - \alpha - b_1 Q_1)Q_1$ of Q_1 and a quadratic function $\pi_2(Q_2) = (a_2 - \alpha - b_2 Q_2)Q_2$ of Q_2, without any term in $Q_1 Q_2$. If we allowed the discriminating monopolist to have a quadratic cost function $C(Q) = \alpha Q + \beta Q^2$, where $Q = Q_1 + Q_2$ is total output, then the profit function $\pi(Q_1, Q_2)$ could still be maximized by completing squares. However, the analysis would become much more complicated, so we leave it out.

Example 15.26 (Discriminating Monopsonist)

A monopolist is a firm facing a downward sloping demand curve. A *discriminating monopolist* such as in Example 15.25 faces separate downward-sloping demand curves in two or more isolated markets. A *monopsonist*, on the other hand, is a firm facing an upward-sloping supply curve for one or more of its factors of production, and a *discriminating monopsonist* faces two or more upward-sloping supply curves for different kinds of the same input—for example, workers of different race or gender. Of course, discrimination by race or gender is illegal in many countries. The following analysis, however, suggests one possible reason why discrimination has had to be outlawed, and why firms might wish to discriminate if they are allowed to.

Indeed, consider a firm using quantities L_1 and L_2 of two types of labor as its only input in order to produce output Q according to the simple production function

$$Q = L_1 + L_2$$

Thus, both output and labor supply are measured so that each unit of labor produces one unit of output. Note especially how the two types of labor are essentially indistinguishable, because each unit of each type makes an equal contribution to the firm's output. Suppose, however, that there are two segmented labor markets, with different inverse supply functions specifying the wage that must be paid to attract a given labor supply. Specifically, suppose that

$$w_1 = \alpha_1 + \beta_1 L_1, \qquad w_2 = \alpha_2 + \beta_2 L_2$$

Assume that the firm is competitive in its output market, taking price P as fixed. Then the firm's profits are

$$
\begin{aligned}
\pi(L_1, L_2) &= PQ - w_1 L_1 - w_2 L_2 \\
&= P(L_1 + L_2) - (\alpha_1 + \beta_1 L_1)L_1 - (\alpha_2 + \beta_2 L_2)L_2 \\
&= (P - \alpha_1)L_1 - \beta_1 L_1^2 + (P - \alpha_2)L_2 - \beta_2 L_2^2 \\
&= -\beta_1\left(L_1 - \frac{P - \alpha_1}{2\beta_1}\right)^2 - \beta_2\left(L_2 - \frac{P - \alpha_2}{2\beta_2}\right)^2 \\
&\quad + \frac{(P - \alpha_1)^2}{4\beta_1} r + \frac{(P - \alpha_2)^2}{4\beta_2}
\end{aligned}
$$

It follows that the optimal labor demands are

$$L_1^* = \frac{P - \alpha_1}{2\beta_1}, \qquad L_2^* = \frac{P - \alpha_2}{2\beta_2}$$

These yield the maximum profit

$$\pi^* = \frac{(P - \alpha_1)^2}{4\beta_1} + \frac{(P - \alpha_2)^2}{4\beta_2}$$

The corresponding wages are

$$w_1^* = \alpha_1 + \beta_1 L_1^* = \tfrac{1}{2}(P + \alpha_1), \qquad w_2^* = \alpha_2 + \beta_2 L_2^* = \tfrac{1}{2}(P + \alpha_2)$$

Hence, $w_1^* = w_2^*$ only if $\alpha_1 = \alpha_2$. Generally, the wage is higher for the type of labor that demands a higher wage for very low levels of labor supply—perhaps this is the type of labor with better job prospects elsewhere.

Example 15.27 (Econometrics: Linear Regression)
Most applied economics is concerned with analyzing data in order to try to discern some pattern that helps in understanding the past, and possibly in predicting the future. For example, price and quantity data for a particular commodity such as natural gas may be used in order to try to estimate a demand curve that can be used to predict how demand will respond to future price changes. The most common technique for doing this is *linear regression*.

Suppose it is thought that variable y—say, the quantity demanded—depends upon variable x—say, price or income. Suppose that we have observations (x_t, y_t) of both variables at times $t = 1, 2, \ldots, T$. Then the technique of linear regression seeks to fit a linear function

$$y = \alpha + \beta x$$

to the data, as indicated in Fig. 15.18. Of course, an exact fit is possible only if there exist numbers α and β for which

$$y_t = \alpha + \beta x_t \qquad (t = 1, 2, \ldots, T)$$

This is rarely possible. Generally, one has instead

$$y_t = \alpha + \beta x_t + e_t \qquad (t = 1, 2, \ldots, T)$$

where e_t is an *error* or *disturbance* term.

FIGURE 15.18

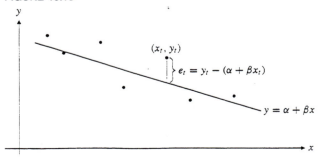

Obviously, one hopes that the errors will be small, on average. So the parameters α and β are chosen somehow to make the errors as "small as possible." One idea would be to make the sum $\sum_{t=1}^{T}(y_t - \alpha - \beta x_t)$ equal to zero. However, in this case, large positive discrepancies would cancel large negative discrepancies. Indeed, the sum of errors could be zero even though the line is very far from giving a perfect or even a good fit. We must somehow prevent large positive errors from canceling large negative errors. Usually, this is done by minimizing the "loss" function

$$L(\alpha, \beta) = \frac{1}{T} \sum_{t=1}^{T} e_t^2 = \frac{1}{T} \sum_{t=1}^{T}(y_t - \alpha - \beta x_t)^2 \qquad [1]$$

that is the average of the squares of the errors. Expanding the square gives[5]

$$L(\alpha, \beta) = T^{-1} \sum_{t}(y_t^2 + \alpha^2 + \beta^2 x_t^2 - 2\alpha y_t - 2\beta x_t y_t + 2\alpha\beta x_t)$$

This is a quadratic function of α and β. We shall show how to complete the squares of this function, and so how to derive the *ordinary least-squares* estimates of α and β. Before doing so, however, it helps to introduce some standard notation. Write

$$\mu_x = \frac{x_1 + \cdots + x_T}{T} = T^{-1} \sum_{t} x_t, \qquad \mu_y = \frac{y_1 + \cdots + y_T}{T} = T^{-1} \sum_{t} y_t \qquad [2]$$

for the *statistical means* of x_t and y_t, respectively. And write

$$\sigma_{xx} = T^{-1} \sum_{t}(x_t - \mu_x)^2$$

$$\sigma_{yy} = T^{-1} \sum_{t}(y_t - \mu_y)^2 \qquad [3]$$

$$\sigma_{xy} = T^{-1} \sum_{t}(x_t - \mu_x)(y_t - \mu_y)$$

for the *statistical variances* of x_t and y_t and for the *covariance*, respectively. Also note how the foregoing definition of σ_{xx} implies that

$$\sigma_{xx} = T^{-1} \sum_{t}(x_t^2 - 2\mu_x x_t + \mu_x^2) = T^{-1} \sum_{t} x_t^2 - 2\mu_x T^{-1} \sum_{t} x_t + \mu_x^2$$

$$= T^{-1} \sum_{t} x_t^2 - 2\mu_x^2 + \mu_x^2 = T^{-1} \sum_{t} x_t^2 - \mu_x^2$$

[5]From now on. we often use $\sum_t$ to denote $\sum_{t=1}^{T}$.

Similarly,

$$\sigma_{yy} = T^{-1} \sum_t y_t^2 - \mu_y^2, \qquad \sigma_{xy} = T^{-1} \sum_t x_t y_t - \mu_x \mu_y$$

(You should check the last as an exercise.) Then the expression for $L(\alpha, \beta)$ becomes

$$L(\alpha, \beta) = (\sigma_{yy} + \mu_y^2) + \alpha^2 + \beta^2(\sigma_{xx} + \mu_x^2) - 2\alpha\mu_y - 2\beta(\sigma_{xy} + \mu_x\mu_y) + 2\alpha\beta\mu_x$$

$$= \alpha^2 + \mu_y^2 + \beta^2\mu_x^2 - 2\alpha\mu_y - 2\beta\mu_x\mu_y + 2\alpha\beta\mu_x + \beta^2\sigma_{xx} - 2\beta\sigma_{xy} + \sigma_{yy}$$

Completing the squares then gives

$$L(\alpha, \beta) = (\mu_y - \alpha - \beta\mu_x)^2 + \sigma_{xx}\left(\beta - \frac{\sigma_{xy}}{\sigma_{xx}}\right)^2 + \sigma_{yy} - \frac{\sigma_{xy}^2}{\sigma_{xx}}$$

From this, it follows that the "ordinary least-squares" (or OLS) estimates that minimize $L(\alpha, \beta)$ with respect to α and β are given by

$$\hat{\beta} = \sigma_{xy}/\sigma_{xx}, \qquad \hat{\alpha} = \mu_y - \hat{\beta}\mu_x = \mu_y - (\sigma_{xy}/\sigma_{xx})\mu_x \qquad [4]$$

Note in particular that $\hat{\alpha}$ is chosen to make the estimated straight line

$$y = \hat{\alpha} + \hat{\beta}x$$

go through the mean (μ_x, μ_y) of the observed pairs (x_t, y_t), $t = 1, \ldots, T$.

Problems

1. Suppose a monopolist is practicing price discrimination in the sale of a product by charging different prices in two separate markets. Suppose the demand curves are

$$P_1 = 100 - Q_1, \qquad P_2 = 80 - Q_2$$

   and suppose that the cost function is $C = 6(Q_1 + Q_2)$. How much should be sold in the two markets to maximize profits? What are the prices charged? How much profit is lost if price discrimination is made illegal?

2. Calculate the loss of profit if the discriminating monopolist of Example 15.25 is not allowed to discriminate.

3. Calculate the loss of profit if the discriminating monopsonist of Example 15.26 is not allowed to discriminate.

4. With reference to Example 15.27, find an expression for $\hat{L}$, the minimum value of $L(\alpha, \beta)$.

15.8 Quadratic Forms in Two Variables

Sections 3.1 and 3.2 presented some examples where quadratic functions in one variable could be optimized by completing the square. Examples 15.25 to 15.27 illustrate how completing squares can also work for quadratic functions of several variables. It must be admitted, however, that calculus techniques would save quite a bit of algebra in many cases. Nevertheless, even the calculus techniques that are presented in Chapter 17, especially the second-order conditions, at some stage involve examining properties of particular quadratic functions called "quadratic forms."

A **quadratic form** of two variables is a function

$$f(x, y) = ax^2 + 2bxy + cy^2 \qquad [15.16]$$

where a, b, and c are three real constants. Using matrix notation, we can write (see Problem 4)

$$f(x, y) = (x, y) \begin{pmatrix} a & b \\ b & c \end{pmatrix} \begin{pmatrix} x \\ y \end{pmatrix}$$

The second-order partials of f are $f_{11}'' = 2a$, $f_{12}'' = f_{21}'' = 2b$, and $f_{22}'' = 2c$, so according to [15.14] of Section 15.5, the Hessian of f is

$$2 \begin{pmatrix} a & b \\ b & c \end{pmatrix}$$

The quadratic form $f(x, y) = ax^2 + 2bxy + cy^2$ is said to be **positive definite** if $f(x, y) > 0$ for all $(x, y) \neq (0, 0)$, and **positive semidefinite** if $f(x, y) \geq 0$ for all (x, y).

Next, $f(x, y)$ is **negative definite** if $f(x, y) < 0$ for all $(x, y) \neq (0, 0)$, and **negative semidefinite** if $f(x, y) \leq 0$ for all (x, y).

Finally, $f(x, y)$ is **indefinite** if there are two different pairs (x^-, y^-) and (x^+, y^+) such that $f(x^-, y^-) < 0$ and $f(x^+, y^+) > 0$.

Example 15.28

Discuss the definiteness properties of the five quadratic forms:

(a) $x^2 + y^2$ (b) $(x + y)^2$ (c) $-x^2 - y^2$ (d) $-(x + y)^2$ (e) $x^2 - y^2$

Solution

(a) $x^2 + y^2 > 0$ for all $(x, y) \neq (0, 0)$, so $x^2 + y^2$ is positive definite.

(b) $(x + y)^2 \geq 0$ for all (x, y), but $(x + y)^2 = 0$ when $(x, y) = (1, -1)$, for instance. So $(x + y)^2$ is positive semidefinite, but not positive definite.

(c) and (d) are simply (a) and (b) with the signs reversed; the quadratic forms are respectively negative definite and negative semidefinite.

(e) $x^2 - y^2 > 0$ if $(x, y) = (1, 0)$, and $x^2 - y^2 < 0$ if $(x, y) = (0, 1)$. Hence, the quadratic form is indefinite.

Note that $f(0, 0) = 0$ whatever the constants a, b, and c may be, so the preceding definitions of positive and negative definiteness have to exclude the point $(0, 0)$.

These definitions evidently imply that (a) a positive definite or semidefinite quadratic form has a minimum at $(0, 0)$, (b) a negative definite or semidefinite quadratic form has a maximum at $(0, 0)$, and (c) an *indefinite* quadratic form has no maximum or minimum anywhere. When the form is definite (positive or negative), the minimum or maximum is *strict*.

The definiteness of a quadratic form depends entirely on the values of the coefficients a, b, and c. In fact, we shall prove the following very important results:

The **quadratic form** $f(x, y) = ax^2 + 2bxy + cy^2$ is

positive definite	$\Longleftrightarrow$	$a > 0$, $c > 0$, and $\begin{vmatrix} a & b \\ b & c \end{vmatrix} > 0$	[15.17]
positive semidefinite	$\Longleftrightarrow$	$a \geq 0$, $c \geq 0$, and $\begin{vmatrix} a & b \\ b & c \end{vmatrix} \geq 0$	[15.18]
negative definite	$\Longleftrightarrow$	$a < 0$, $c < 0$, and $\begin{vmatrix} a & b \\ b & c \end{vmatrix} > 0$	[15.19]
negative semidefinite	$\Longleftrightarrow$	$a \leq 0$, $c \leq 0$, and $\begin{vmatrix} a & b \\ b & c \end{vmatrix} \geq 0$	[15.20]
indefinite	$\Longleftrightarrow$	$\begin{vmatrix} a & b \\ b & c \end{vmatrix} < 0$	[15.21]

(Recall that

$$\begin{vmatrix} a & b \\ b & c \end{vmatrix} = ac - b^2$$

by the definition of a 2×2 determinant (see [13.4] in Section 13.1).)

Proof   We prove [15.18] first. Suppose that $f(x, y)$ is positive semidefinite. Then, in particular, $f(1, 0) = a \geq 0$ and $f(0, 1) = c \geq 0$. If $a = 0$, then $f(x, 1) = 2bx + c$, which can only be ≥ 0 for all x provided $b = 0$. (If $b > 0$, choosing x as a large negative number makes $f(x, 1)$ negative. If $b < 0$, choosing x as a large positive number makes $f(x, 1)$ negative.) Thus, $ac - b^2 = 0$. If $a > 0$, then $f(-b, a) = ab^2 - 2ab^2 + ca^2 = a(ac - b^2)$, which must be nonnegative, so $ac - b^2 \geq 0$.

To prove the reverse implication in [15.18], suppose that $a \geq 0$, $c \geq 0$, and $ac - b^2 \geq 0$. If $a = 0$, then $ac - b^2 \geq 0$ implies $b = 0$, and then $f(x, y) = cy^2 \geq 0$ for all (x, y). If $a > 0$, then we can write

$$f(x, y) = a\left(x + \frac{b}{a}y\right)^2 + \left(c - \frac{b^2}{a}\right)y^2 \qquad [*]$$

Because $c - b^2/a \geq 0$ and $a > 0$, we see that $f(x, y) \geq 0$ for all (x, y).

The equivalence in [15.20] is proved in the same way as [15.18] after reversing signs.

To prove [15.17], suppose $f(x, y)$ is positive definite. Then $f(1, 0) = a > 0$ and $f(0, 1) = c > 0$. But then [*] yields $f(-b/a, 1) = c - b^2/a = (ac - b^2)/a > 0$, so $ac - b^2 > 0$. To prove the reverse implication in [15.17], suppose $a > 0$ and $ac - b^2 > 0$. By [*], $f(x, y) \geq 0$ for all (x, y). If $f(x, y) = 0$, then $x + by/a = 0$ and $y = 0$, so $x = y = 0$. Hence, $f(x, y)$ is positive definite. The equivalence in [15.19] is proved in the same way—just reverse signs.

Finally, we prove [15.21]. Suppose $f(x, y)$ is indefinite. Because neither the inequalities in [15.18] nor those in [15.20] are satisfied, either a and c have opposite signs or $ac - b^2 < 0$. But if a and c do have opposite signs, then $ac < 0 \leq b^2$ anyway, so $ac - b^2 < 0$ in all cases.

To prove the reverse implication in [15.21], suppose $ac - b^2 < 0$. If $a \neq 0$, then $f(1, 0) = a$ and $f(-b, a) = a(ac - b^2)$ have opposite signs, so $f(x, y)$ is indefinite. If $a = 0$ and $c = 0$, then $f(1, 1) = 2b$ and $f(-1, 1) = -2b$. Because $ac - b^2 < 0$ implies $b^2 > 0$ in this case, one has $b \neq 0$ and so $f(x, y)$ is indefinite. If $a = 0$ and $c \neq 0$, then $f(0, 1) = c$ and $f(c, -b) = -b^2 c$ have different signs, so $f(x, y)$ is indefinite.

General Quadratic Functions in Two Variables

Adding any linear function $px + qy + r$ of x and y to the terms in [15.16] gives

$$f(x, y) = ax^2 + 2bxy + cy^2 + px + qy + r \qquad [15.22]$$

This is the general quadratic function of x and y. It can be expressed as

$$f(x, y) = a(x + \xi)^2 + 2b(x + \xi)(y + \eta) + c(y + \eta)^2 + d \qquad [15.23]$$

provided that we arrange to have

$$2a\xi + 2b\eta = p, \qquad 2b\xi + 2c\eta = q, \qquad a\xi^2 + 2b\xi\eta + c\eta^2 + d = r$$

so that the coefficients of x and y match, as well as the constant term. This involves choosing

$$\xi = \frac{cp - bq}{2(ac - b^2)}, \qquad \eta = \frac{aq - bp}{2(ac - b^2)}, \qquad d = r - (a\xi^2 + 2b\xi\eta + c\eta^2) \qquad [15.24]$$

which is possible provided that $ac \neq b^2$. If $ac = b^2 \neq 0$, then

$$f(x, y) = a\left(x + \sqrt{\frac{c}{a}}y\right)^2 + px + qy + r$$

and it is easy to study the quadratic function directly. A similar transformation works if $ac = b^2 = 0$ and either a or c is $\neq 0$. If $a = b = c = 0$, the function is not even quadratic.

Thus, the only interesting cases arise when, after changing variables if necessary by replacing x with $x + \xi$ and y with $y + \eta$, the function f can be written in the form

$$f(x, y) = ax^2 + 2bxy + cy^2 + d$$

Of course, the constant d does not change the essential behavior of $f(x, y)$. Thus, in all interesting cases, the general quadratic function [15.22] is reduced to the quadratic form [15.16] that was studied in detail earlier.

Quadratic Forms with Linear Constraints

Consider the quadratic form $Q = ax^2 + 2bxy + cy^2$ and assume that the variables are subject to the linear constraint $px + qy = 0$, where $q \neq 0$. Solving the constraint for y, we have $y = -px/q$, and substituting this value for y into the expression for Q yields

$$Q = ax^2 + 2bx\left(-\frac{px}{q}\right) + c\left(-\frac{px}{q}\right)^2 = \frac{1}{q^2}(aq^2 - 2bpq + cp^2)x^2 \qquad [*]$$

We say that $Q(x, y)$ is **positive (negative) definite subject to the constraint** $px + qy = 0$ provided Q is positive (negative) for all $(x, y) \neq (0, 0)$ satisfying the constraint $px + qy = 0$. By expanding the determinant, it is easy to verify that

$$aq^2 - 2bpq + cp^2 = -\begin{vmatrix} 0 & p & q \\ p & a & b \\ q & b & c \end{vmatrix} \qquad [**]$$

Combining this result with [*] gives

$$\left.\begin{array}{l} Q = ax^2 + 2bxy + cy^2 \text{ is positive definite} \\ \text{subject to the constraint } px + qy = 0 \end{array}\right\} \iff \begin{vmatrix} 0 & p & q \\ p & a & b \\ q & b & c \end{vmatrix} < 0 \quad [15.25]$$

Problems

1. Use [15.17] to [15.21] to determine the definiteness of the following quadratic forms:

   a. $4x^2 + 8xy + 5y^2$ **b.** $-x^2 + xy - 3y^2$ **c.** $x^2 - 6xy + 9y^2$

   d. $4x^2 - y^2$ **e.** $\frac{1}{2}x^2 - xy + \frac{1}{4}y^2$ **f.** $6xy - 9y^2 - x^2$

2. Show that the following quadratic functions can be expressed in the form [15.23] by using [15.24]:
   a. $f(x, y) = 2x^2 - 4xy + y^2 - 3x + 4y$
   b. $f(x, y) = -x^2 - xy + y^2 - x - y + 5$
3. Examine the definiteness of the following quadratic forms subject to the given linear constraint:
   a. $x^2 - 2xy + y^2$ subject to $x + y = 0$.
   b. $2x^2 - 4xy + y^2$ subject to $3x + 4y = 0$.
   c. $-x^2 + xy - y^2$ subject to $5x - 2y = 0$.
4. Verify the matrix equation that was displayed following Equation [15.16].

15.9 Quadratic Forms in Many Variables

We often encounter quadratic forms in more than two variables, such as that in three variables with $Q(x_1, x_2, x_3) = 2x_1^2 + 4x_1x_2 - x_1x_3 + x_2^2 + 5x_2^2 - x_3^2$. The sum of the exponents of the variables in each term is 2.

A general **quadratic form** in n variables is a function $Q = Q(x_1, \ldots, x_n)$ given by the double sum

$$Q = \sum_{i=1}^{n} \sum_{j=1}^{n} a_{ij} x_i x_j$$

[15.26]

$$= a_{11}x_1^2 + a_{12}x_1x_2 + \cdots + a_{ij}x_ix_j + \cdots + a_{nn}x_n^2$$

Suppose we put

$$\mathbf{x} = \begin{pmatrix} x_1 \\ x_2 \\ \vdots \\ x_n \end{pmatrix}, \qquad \mathbf{A} = \begin{pmatrix} a_{11} & a_{12} & \cdots & a_{1n} \\ a_{21} & a_{22} & \cdots & a_{2n} \\ \vdots & \vdots & \ddots & \vdots \\ a_{n1} & a_{n2} & \cdots & a_{nn} \end{pmatrix}$$

Then it follows from the definition of matrix multiplication that

$$Q(x_1, \ldots, x_n) = Q(\mathbf{x}) = \mathbf{x}'\mathbf{A}\mathbf{x}$$

[15.27]

Of course, $x_ix_j = x_jx_i$, so we can write $a_{ij}x_ix_j + a_{ji}x_jx_i = (a_{ij} + a_{ji})x_ix_j$. If we replace a_{ij} and a_{ji} by $\frac{1}{2}(a_{ij} + a_{ji})$, then a_{ij} and a_{ji} become equal without changing $Q(x_1, \ldots, x_n)$. Thus, we can assume in [15.26] that

$$a_{ij} = a_{ji} \qquad \text{(for all } i \text{ and } j\text{)}$$

[15.28]

which means that matrix $\mathbf{A}$ is symmetric.

Example 15.29
Write

$$Q(x_1, x_2, x_3) = 5x_1^2 + x_1x_2 - 3x_1x_3 + 3x_2x_1 + x_2^2 - 2x_2x_3 + 5x_3x_1 + 2x_3x_2 + x_3^2$$

in the form [15.27], both with **A** not symmetric and **A** symmetric.

Solution

$$Q(x_1, x_2, x_3) = (x_1, x_2, x_3) \begin{pmatrix} 5 & 1 & -3 \\ 3 & 1 & -2 \\ 5 & 2 & 1 \end{pmatrix} \begin{pmatrix} x_1 \\ x_2 \\ x_3 \end{pmatrix}$$

$$= (x_1, x_2, x_3) \begin{pmatrix} 5 & 2 & 1 \\ 2 & 1 & 0 \\ 1 & 0 & 1 \end{pmatrix} \begin{pmatrix} x_1 \\ x_2 \\ x_3 \end{pmatrix}$$

The Sign of a Quadratic Form

We are particularly interested in conditions ensuring that Q is always positive or always negative, thus generalizing some of the results from the previous section.

In general, a symmetric $n \times n$ matrix **A** and its associated quadratic form Q are both said to be **positive definite** if

$$Q(x_1, \ldots, x_n) = \mathbf{x}'\mathbf{A}\mathbf{x} > 0 \qquad \text{for all } (x_1, \ldots, x_n) \neq (0, \ldots, 0) \qquad [15.29]$$

They are said to be **negative definite** if

$$Q(x_1, \ldots, x_n) = \mathbf{x}'\mathbf{A}\mathbf{x} < 0 \qquad \text{for all } (x_1, \ldots, x_n) \neq (0, \ldots, 0) \qquad [15.30]$$

If we replace $>$ in [15.29] with ≥ 0, then **A** is **positive semidefinite**, and **A** is **negative semidefinite** if we replace $<$ in [15.30] with $\leq$. Finally, **A** is **indefinite** if it is neither positive semidefinite nor negative semidefinite. (In this case, there must exist a vector $\mathbf{x}_0$ and a vector $\mathbf{y}_0$ such that $\mathbf{x}_0'\mathbf{A}\mathbf{x}_0 < 0$ and $\mathbf{y}_0'\mathbf{A}\mathbf{y}_0 > 0$.) Note that $Q(0, \ldots, 0) = 0$ whatever the constants a_{ij} may be, so the foregoing definitions of positive and negative definiteness have to exclude the point $(0, \ldots, 0)$.

Example 15.30
Let $\mathbf{D} = \text{diag}(\lambda_1, \ldots, \lambda_n)$ be an $n \times n$ diagonal matrix. When is the matrix **D**: (a) negative definite, (b) positive semidefinite, and (c) indefinite?

Solution   **D** is a symmetric matrix whose associated quadratic form is

$$Q = (x_1, x_2, \ldots, x_n) \begin{pmatrix} \lambda_1 & 0 & \cdots & 0 \\ 0 & \lambda_2 & \cdots & 0 \\ \vdots & \vdots & \ddots & \vdots \\ 0 & 0 & \cdots & \lambda_n \end{pmatrix} \begin{pmatrix} x_1 \\ x_2 \\ \vdots \\ x_n \end{pmatrix}$$

$$= (x_1, x_2, \ldots, x_n) \begin{pmatrix} \lambda_1 x_1 \\ \lambda_2 x_2 \\ \vdots \\ \lambda_n x_n \end{pmatrix} = \sum_{i=1}^{n} \lambda_i x_i^2$$

(a) This quadratic form is obviously negative definite if $\lambda_i < 0$ for $i = 1, 2, \ldots, n$. Conversely, if $\lambda_i \geq 0$ for any i, then $Q \geq 0$ when $\mathbf{x}$ is the unit vector $\mathbf{e}_i$ whose ith component is 1, but all other components are zero. So if $\mathbf{D}$ is negative definite, then $\lambda_i < 0$ for $i = 1, 2, \ldots, n$.

(b) $\mathbf{D}$ is evidently positive semidefinite iff $\lambda_i \geq 0$ for $i = 1, 2, \ldots, n$.

(c) $\mathbf{D}$ is evidently indefinite iff there is at least one positive diagonal element as well as at least one negative diagonal element.

By Example 14.13 of Section 14.4, the diagonal elements of a diagonal matrix are its eigenvalues. So Example 15.30 shows that the definiteness properties of a quadratic form depends upon those eigenvalues. The same is true for the general 2×2 symmetric matrix

$$\mathbf{A} = \begin{pmatrix} a & b \\ b & c \end{pmatrix}$$

By Example 14.14, the eigenvalues λ_1 and λ_2 of $\mathbf{A}$ are real, with $\lambda_1 + \lambda_2 = a + c$ and $\lambda_1 \lambda_2 = \det(\mathbf{A})$. By [15.18], $\mathbf{A}$ is positive semidefinite iff $a \geq 0$, $c \geq 0$, and $\det(\mathbf{A}) \geq 0$. But because $\det(\mathbf{A}) \geq 0$ ensures that a and c cannot have opposite signs, $\mathbf{A}$ is positive semidefinite iff $\lambda_1 + \lambda_2 = a + c \geq 0$ and $\det(\mathbf{A}) = \lambda_1 \lambda_2 \geq 0$. It follows that $\mathbf{A}$ is positive semidefinite iff λ_1 and λ_2 are both nonnegative. The cases of negative semidefinite, of positive or negative definite, and of indefinite matrices, are entirely similar. Indeed, the sign of any quadratic form in n variables is determined by the signs of the eigenvalues of the associated matrix, because of the following:

Theorem 15.2   Suppose $\mathbf{A}$ is a symmetric matrix. Then:

(a) $\mathbf{A}$ is positive definite $\Longleftrightarrow$ all eigenvalues of $\mathbf{A}$ are positive.

(b) $\mathbf{A}$ is positive semidefinite $\Longleftrightarrow$ all eigenvalues of $\mathbf{A}$ are ≥ 0.

(c) $\mathbf{A}$ is negative definite $\Longleftrightarrow$ all eigenvalues of $\mathbf{A}$ are negative.

(d) $\mathbf{A}$ is negative semidefinite $\Longleftrightarrow$ all eigenvalues of $\mathbf{A}$ are ≤ 0.

(e) $\mathbf{A}$ is indefinite $\Longleftrightarrow$ $\mathbf{A}$ has at least two eigenvalues with opposite signs.

Proof   Let λ be any eigenvalue of $\mathbf{A}$. Then there is a corresponding eigenvector $\mathbf{x}_\lambda \neq \mathbf{0}$ such that $\mathbf{A}\mathbf{x}_\lambda = \lambda \mathbf{x}_\lambda$. So $Q(\mathbf{x}_\lambda) = \mathbf{x}_\lambda' \mathbf{A}\mathbf{x}_\lambda = \mathbf{x}_\lambda' \lambda \mathbf{x}_\lambda = \lambda \mathbf{x}_\lambda' \mathbf{x}_\lambda$, which has the same sign as λ. Now, if $\mathbf{A}$ is positive definite, then $Q(\mathbf{x}_\lambda) = \mathbf{x}_\lambda' \mathbf{A}\mathbf{x}_\lambda = \lambda \mathbf{x}_\lambda' \mathbf{x}_\lambda > 0$ for all eigenvectors $\mathbf{x}_\lambda \neq \mathbf{0}$ and so for all eigenvalues

λ. Thus, **A** can have only positive eigenvalues. This also holds for negative definite, for positive or negative semidefinite, and for indefinite matrices.

Conversely, by Theorem 14.8 in Section 14.6, there exists an orthogonal matrix **U** (with $\mathbf{U}^{-1} = \mathbf{U}'$) such that

$$\mathbf{U}'\mathbf{A}\mathbf{U} = \text{diag }(\lambda_1, \ldots, \lambda_n) = \mathbf{D}$$

where $\lambda_1, \ldots, \lambda_n$ are the eigenvalues of **A**. Hence,

$$\mathbf{A} = (\mathbf{U}')^{-1}(\mathbf{U}'\mathbf{A}\mathbf{U})\mathbf{U}^{-1} = (\mathbf{U}')^{-1}\mathbf{D}\mathbf{U}^{-1} = \mathbf{U}\mathbf{D}\mathbf{U}'$$

But now, for any **x** in R^n, it must be true that

$$\mathbf{x}'\mathbf{A}\mathbf{x} = \mathbf{x}'\mathbf{U}\mathbf{D}\mathbf{U}'\mathbf{x} = (\mathbf{U}'\mathbf{x})'\mathbf{D}(\mathbf{U}'\mathbf{x}) = \mathbf{y}'\mathbf{D}\mathbf{y} = \sum_{k=1}^{n}\lambda_k y_k^2$$

where $\mathbf{y} = \mathbf{U}'\mathbf{x}$. Moreover, if $\mathbf{x} \neq \mathbf{0}$, then $\mathbf{y} \neq \mathbf{0}$ because $\mathbf{x} = \mathbf{U}\mathbf{y}$. So now, in case (a), when all eigenvalues of **A** are positive, then $\mathbf{y}'\mathbf{D}\mathbf{y} > 0$ for all $\mathbf{y} \neq \mathbf{0}$, and so $\mathbf{x}'\mathbf{A}\mathbf{x} > 0$ for all $\mathbf{x} \neq \mathbf{0}$, implying that **A** is positive definite. The proofs for the cases (b) to (e) are entirely similar.

Example 15.31

Check the sign of the quadratic form in Example 15.29.

Solution   The characteristic equation of the corresponding symmetric matrix is

$$\begin{vmatrix} 5 - \lambda & 2 & 1 \\ 2 & 1 - \lambda & 0 \\ 1 & 0 & 1 - \lambda \end{vmatrix} = 0$$

Thus, $(5 - \lambda)(1 - \lambda)^2 - 4(1 - \lambda) - (1 - \lambda) = 0$, which reduces to $\lambda(1 - \lambda)(\lambda - 6) = 0$. So the eigenvalues are 0, 1, and 6. From (b) in Theorem 15.2, the quadratic form is positive semidefinite.

In order to apply Theorem 15.2, we have to compute the eigenvalues of the associated matrix. The next theorem makes it possible to decide the definiteness of a matrix **A** by checking the signs of certain minors of **A**.

Let $\mathbf{A} = (a_{ij})$ be any $n \times n$ matrix. The **leading principal minors** of **A** are the n determinants:

$$D_k = \begin{vmatrix} a_{11} & a_{12} & \cdots & a_{1k} \\ a_{21} & a_{22} & \cdots & a_{2k} \\ \vdots & \vdots & \ddots & \vdots \\ a_{k1} & a_{k2} & \cdots & a_{kk} \end{vmatrix} \qquad (k = 1, \ldots, n) \qquad [15.31]$$

Note that D_k is obtained from $|\mathbf{A}|$ by crossing out the last $n - k$ columns and the corresponding last $n - k$ rows. Thus, for $k = 1, 2, 3, \ldots, n$, the leading principal minors are, respectively,

$$a_{11}, \quad \begin{vmatrix} a_{11} & a_{12} \\ a_{21} & a_{22} \end{vmatrix}, \quad \begin{vmatrix} a_{11} & a_{12} & a_{13} \\ a_{21} & a_{22} & a_{23} \\ a_{31} & a_{32} & a_{33} \end{vmatrix}, \dots, \quad \begin{vmatrix} a_{11} & a_{12} & \dots & a_{1n} \\ a_{21} & a_{22} & \dots & a_{2n} \\ \vdots & \vdots & \ddots & \vdots \\ a_{n1} & a_{n2} & \dots & a_{nn} \end{vmatrix} \qquad [15.32]$$

One can prove the following result:[6]

Theorem 15.3   Let $\mathbf{A} = (a_{ij})_{n \times n}$ be a symmetric matrix, with leading principal minors D_k $(k = 1, 2, \dots, n)$ defined by [15.31]. Then:
  (a) $\mathbf{A}$ is positive definite $\iff$ $D_k > 0$ for $k = 1, 2, \dots, n$.
  (b) $\mathbf{A}$ is negative definite $\iff$ $(-1)^k D_k > 0$ for $k = 1, 2, \dots, n$.

Though the proof of Theorem 15.3 is too advanced for this book, it can easily be illustrated for the case when $\mathbf{A}$ is a diagonal matrix with $\mathbf{A} = \text{diag}(\lambda_1, \dots, \lambda_n)$. For then Example 14.13 of Section 14.4 and Theorem 15.2 imply that $\mathbf{A}$ is positive definite iff $\lambda_i > 0$ for $i = 1, 2, \dots, n$. However, the leading principal minors of $\mathbf{A}$ are $\lambda_1, \lambda_1 \lambda_2, \lambda_1 \lambda_2 \lambda_3, \dots, \lambda_1 \lambda_2 \lambda_3 \dots \lambda_n$, which are all positive iff $\lambda_i > 0$ for $i = 1, 2, \dots, n$. So case (a) of Theorem 15.3 is verified. On the other hand, $\mathbf{A}$ is negative definite iff $\lambda_i < 0$ for $i = 1, 2, \dots, n$. However, the leading principal minors alternate in sign iff $\lambda_i < 0$ for $i = 1, 2, \dots, n$, which is case (b) of Theorem 15.3.

Also, when $\mathbf{A}$ is a 2×2 matrix, conditions [15.17] and [15.19] of Section 15.8 are the appropriate versions of Theorem 15.3. This is because

$$\begin{vmatrix} a & b \\ b & c \end{vmatrix} > 0$$

implies that $ac > b^2 \geq 0$, so $ac > 0$, implying that a and c must have the same sign.

Example 15.32
  Prove that the following matrix is negative definite:

$$\mathbf{A} = \begin{pmatrix} -3 & 2 & 0 \\ 2 & -3 & 0 \\ 0 & 0 & -5 \end{pmatrix}$$

Solution   In this case,

$$-3 < 0, \quad \begin{vmatrix} -3 & 2 \\ 2 & -3 \end{vmatrix} = 5 > 0, \quad \begin{vmatrix} -3 & 2 & 0 \\ 2 & -3 & 0 \\ 0 & 0 & -5 \end{vmatrix} = -25 < 0$$

---

[6]See, for example, Hadley (1973).

By Theorem 15.3 (b), we see that **A** is negative definite. As an exercise, you should also apply the eigenvalue test, Theorem 15.2.

The Semidefinite Case

It is tempting to conjecture that a matrix will be positive semidefinite iff all the strict inequalities in Theorem 15.3(a) are replaced by weak inequalities. This is wrong. The quadratic form $Q(x_1, x_2) = 0x_1^2 + 0 \cdot x_1 x_2 - x_2^2 = -x_2^2$ is negative semidefinite, not positive semidefinite. Yet the leading principal minors of the associated matrix

$$\begin{pmatrix} 0 & 0 \\ 0 & -1 \end{pmatrix}$$

are both ≥ 0 (in fact, both $= 0$).

In order to check semidefiniteness by calculating minors, one has to consider the signs of *all* the principal minors of **A**, not only the leading principal minors. An arbitrary principal minor of order $(n - r) \times (n - r)$ in **A** is obtained by crossing out any r rows and the corresponding r columns—not necessarily the last r rows and columns. *One can prove that a quadratic form* $\mathbf{x}'\mathbf{A}\mathbf{x}$ *is positive semidefinite iff all the principal minors in* **A** *are* ≥ 0. For the 2×2 case, [15.18] of Section 15.8 confirms this result. Also, *one can prove that* $\mathbf{x}'\mathbf{A}\mathbf{x}$ *is negative semidefinite iff all the principal minors of order k in* **A** *have the same sign as* $(-1)^k$. For the 2×2 case, [15.20] confirms this.

Another case in which it is easy to confirm these two results occurs when **A** is diagonal. For then **A** is positive semidefinite iff all its diagonal elements are nonnegative; the principal minors of **A**, which are products of its diagonal elements, will also be nonnegative iff all its diagonal elements are nonnegative. There is an obvious corresponding argument when **A** is negative semidefinite.

Problems

1. Write the quadratic form [15.26] in full when $n = 3$.

2. Write the following quadratic forms in the matrix form [15.27] with **A** symmetric:

   a. $x^2 + 2xy + y^2$ **b.** $3x_1^2 - 2x_1 x_2 + 3x_1 x_3 + x_2^2 - 4x_2 x_3 + 3x_3^2$

3. Use Theorem 15.3 to classify the following quadratic forms in the three variables x_1, x_2, and x_3:

   a. $x_1^2 + 2x_2^2 + 8x_3^2$ **b.** $x_2^2 + 8x_3^2$ **c.** $-3x_1^2 + 2x_1 x_2 - x_2^2 + 4x_2 x_3 - 8x_3^2$

4. Suppose **A** is positive semidefinite and symmetric. Prove that **A** is positive definite if $|\mathbf{A}| \neq 0$.

=16

Tools for Comparative Statics

Mere power and mere knowledge exalt
human nature but do not bless it.
—*Francis Bacon* (The Advancement of Learning)

The ultimate aim of this chapter is to study properties of functions defined implicitly by a system of simultaneous equations. In particular, we are interested in how economic variables like demand and supply respond to changes in parameters like price. This is the subject of comparative statics, in which the general question is: What happens to an optimal solution when the parameters of the problem change? A large proportion of economic analysis relies on comparative statics, so this topic is extremely important.

16.1 The Chain Rule

Many economic models involve composite functions. These are functions of one or several variables in which the variables are themselves functions of other basic variables. For example, output could be a function of capital and labor, both of which are functions of time. How does output vary with time? More generally, what happens to the value of a composite function as its basic variables change? This is the general problem we discuss in this and the next section. The results obtained also generalize the chain rule of Section 5.2 to partial derivatives. This section considers the simplest case.

Suppose z is a function of x and y, with

$$z = F(x, y) \qquad [1]$$

where x and y both are functions of a variable t, with

$$x = f(t), \qquad y = g(t) \tag{2}$$

Substituting for x and y in [1] gives

$$z = F(f(t), g(t)) \tag{3}$$

so that z is a function of t alone. A change in t will in general lead to changes in both $f(t)$ and $g(t)$, and as a result, z changes. *How* does z change when t changes? For example, will a small increase in t lead to an increase or a decrease in z? The answer to such questions will be easier if we can find an expression for dz/dt, the rate of change of z with respect to t. This is given by the following rule:

The Chain Rule

When $z = F(x, y)$ with $x = f(t)$ and $y = g(t)$, then

$$\frac{dz}{dt} = F_1'(x, y)\frac{dx}{dt} + F_2'(x, y)\frac{dy}{dt} \tag{16.1}$$

It is important to understand precisely the content of [16.1]. It gives the derivative of $z = F(x, y)$ with respect to t when x and y are both differentiable functions of t. This derivative is usually called the **total derivative** of z with respect to t. According to [16.1], one contribution to the total derivative occurs because the first variable in $F(x, y)$, namely x, depends on t. This contribution is $F_1'(x, y)\,dx/dt$. A second contribution arises because the second variable in $F(x, y)$, namely y, also depends on t. This contribution is $F_2'(x, y)\,dy/dt$. The total derivative dz/dt is the *sum* of the two contributions.

Here is a simple example.

Example 16.1

Use [16.1] to compute dz/dt when $z = F(x, y) = x^2 + y^3$ with $x = t^2$ and $y = 2t$.

Solution   We get

$$F_1'(x, y) = 2x, \qquad F_2'(x, y) = 3y^2, \qquad \frac{dx}{dt} = 2t, \qquad \frac{dy}{dt} = 2$$

Then formula [16.1] gives

$$\frac{dz}{dt} = 2x \cdot 2t + 3y^2 \cdot 2 = 4tx + 6y^2 = 4t^3 + 24t^2$$

where the last equality comes from substituting the appropriate functions of t for x and y respectively. In this case, we can test the chain rule by substituting $x = t^2$ and $y = 2t$ in the formula for $F(x, y)$ and then differentiating with respect to t. The result is

$$z = x^2 + y^3 = (t^2)^2 + (2t)^3 = t^4 + 8t^3 \implies \frac{dz}{dt} = 4t^3 + 24t^2$$

as before.

Example 16.2

Suppose two commodities are sold on a market where prices per unit are respectively p and q. Suppose that the demands for the two commodities depend on these prices. (All other factors that might influence demand are assumed to be constant.) In particular, let $D_1 = D_1(p, q)$ denote demand for the first commodity.

Suppose that prices p and q vary with time t, so that $p = p(t)$ and $q = q(t)$. Then demand can be determined as a function $D_1 = D_1\big(p(t), q(t)\big)$ of t alone, and it is interesting to ask how D_1 changes with t. This problem is precisely the same as that posed earlier—only the symbols are different. Changing the symbols as appropriate, and then using the chain rule [16.1] implies that

$$\frac{dD_1}{dt} = \frac{\partial D_1(p, q)}{\partial p} \dot{p}(t) + \frac{\partial D_1(p, q)}{\partial q} \dot{q}(t)$$

where we have denoted time derivatives by "dots." The first term on the right-hand side gives the effect on demand that arises because the price p is changing, and the second term gives the effect of the change in q.

Example 16.3

Example 15.10 of Section 15.2 considered the production function $Y = F(K, L)$, where Y is output, K is capital, and L is labor. Suppose that K and L are functions of time. Then [16.1] tells us that

$$\dot{Y} = \frac{\partial Y}{\partial K} \dot{K} + \frac{\partial Y}{\partial L} \dot{L} \tag{1}$$

Thus, total output increases at a rate found by multiplying the marginal product of each input by the rate of change of that input, and then summing over the inputs.

In the special case of the Cobb–Douglas function $F(K, L) = AK^a L^b$, one has

$$\dot{Y} = aAK^{a-1}L^b\dot{K} + bAK^a L^{b-1}\dot{L} \tag{2}$$

Dividing each term in [2] by $Y = AK^a L^b$ yields

$$\frac{\dot{Y}}{Y} = a\frac{\dot{K}}{K} + b\frac{\dot{L}}{L}$$

The relative rate of change of output is, therefore, a linear combination of the relative rates of change of capital and labor.

Here is a rather typical example of one way economists use [16.1].

Example 16.4

Let $u(x, z)$ denote the "total well-being" of a society, where x is an index of the total amount of goods produced and consumed, and z is a measure of the level of pollution. Assume that $u_x'(x, z) > 0$ and $u_z'(x, z) < 0$. (See Example 15.21 of Section 15.6.) Suppose the level of pollution z is some increasing function $z = h(x)$ of x, with $h'(x) > 0$. Then total well-being becomes a function

$$U(x) = u(x, h(x))$$

of x alone. Find a necessary condition for $U(x)$ to have a maximum at $x = x^* > 0$, and give this condition an economic interpretation.

Solution   A necessary condition for $U(x)$ to have a maximum at $x^* > 0$ is that $U'(x^*) = 0$. In order to compute $U'(x)$, we use the chain rule [16.1]:

$$U'(x) = u_x'(x, h(x)) + u_z'(x, h(x))h'(x)$$

So $U'(x^*) = 0$ requires that

$$u_x'(x^*, h(x^*)) = -u_z'(x^*, h(x^*))h'(x^*) \tag{*}$$

Suppose we think of increasing x^* by one unit. How much do we gain directly? Approximately $u_x'(x^*, h(x^*))$ (see [15.9] of Section 15.3). On the other hand, if we increase x^* by one unit, the level of pollution increases by about $h'(x^*)$ units. For each unit increase in pollution, we lose $u_z'(x^*, h(x^*))$ in well-being, so in all we lose about $u_z'(x^*, h(x^*))h'(x^*)$ from a unit increase in x^*. Equation [*] just states that what we gain directly from a unit increase in x^* equals what we lose indirectly through increased pollution.

In fact, the chain rule [16.1] has many implications. In particular, all the general rules for differentiating functions of one variable turn out to be just special cases of this result (see Problem 4).

Directional Derivatives

If $z = f(x, y)$, the partial derivatives $f_1'(x, y)$ and $f_2'(x, y)$ measure the rates of change of $f(x, y)$ in the directions of the x-axis and of the y-axis, respectively. We also want to measure the rate of change of the function in other directions.

Choose a particular point (x_0, y_0) in the domain. Any nonzero vector (h, k) is then a *direction* in which we can move away from (x_0, y_0) in a straight line to points of the form

$$(x, y) = (x(t), y(t)) = (x_0 + th, y_0 + tk)$$

Given the point (x_0, y_0) and the direction $(h, k) \neq (0, 0)$, define the *directional function g* by

$$g(t) = f(x_0 + th, y_0 + tk) \qquad [1]$$

This is a function of one variable, recording what happens to f as one moves away from (x_0, y_0) in the direction (h, k), or in the reverse direction $(-h, -k)$. (See Fig. 16.1.) By using the chain rule, the derivative of this directional function can be calculated as

$$g'(t) = f_1'(x, y)\frac{dx}{dt} + f_2'(x, y)\frac{dy}{dt}$$

$$= f_1'(x_0 + th, y_0 + tk)h + f_2'(x_0 + th, y_0 + tk)k \qquad [2]$$

Letting $t = 0$ gives

$$g'(0) = f_1'(x_0, y_0)h + f_2'(x_0, y_0)k \qquad [3]$$

For the case when the vector (h, k) has length 1, the derivative of f in the direction (h, k) is called *the directional derivative of f in the direction (h, k) at (x_0, y_0)*. It

FIGURE 16.1

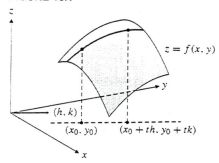

$z = f(x, y)$

(h, k)

(x_0, y_0) $(x_0 + th, y_0 + tk)$

is denoted by $D_{h,k} f(x_0, y_0)$, so we have the following:

Directional Derivative

The directional derivative of $f(x, y)$ at (x_0, y_0) in the direction of the unit vector (h, k) (that is, $h^2 + k^2 = 1$) is

$$D_{h,k} f(x_0, y_0) = f_1(x_0, y_0) h + f_2(x_0, y_0) k \qquad [16.2]$$

Note that only when (h, k) has length 1 does the derivative of the directional function have the following convenient property: A move of one unit away from (x_0, y_0) in direction (h, k) changes the value of f by approximately $D_{h,k} f(x_0, y_0)$. The vector $(f_1(x_0, y_0), f_2(x_0, y_0))$ is called the **gradient** of $f(x, y)$ at (x_0, y_0). Thus, [16.2] says that the directional derivative in direction (h, k) is the scalar product of the gradient with the vector (h, k).

Let us also compute the second derivative of the directional function g. To find $g''(t)$, we have to differentiate [2] with respect to t, thus obtaining

$$g''(t) = \frac{d}{dt} f_1'(x, y)h + \frac{d}{dt} f_2'(x, y)k \qquad [4]$$

where $x = x_0 + th$, and $y = y_0 + tk$. Again, we must use the chain rule [16.1]. We get

$$\frac{d}{dt} f_1'(x, y) = f_{11}''(x, y)\frac{dx}{dt} + f_{12}''(x, y)\frac{dy}{dt} = f_{11}''(x, y)h + f_{12}''(x, y)k$$

$$\frac{d}{dt} f_2'(x, y) = f_{21}''(x, y)\frac{dx}{dt} + f_{22}''(x, y)\frac{dy}{dt} = f_{21}''(x, y)h + f_{22}''(x, y)k$$

Assuming that $f_{12}'' = f_{21}''$, insertion into [4] gives

$$g''(t) = f_{11}''(x, y)h^2 + 2f_{12}''(x, y)hk + f_{22}''(x, y)k^2 \qquad [5]$$

where $x = x_0 + th$, and $y = y_0 + tk$. Letting $t = 0$ and assuming again that (h, k) has length 1, we obtain the following **second directional derivative**:

$$D_{h,k}^2 f(x_0, y_0) = f_{11}''(x_0, y_0)h^2 + 2f_{12}''(x_0, y_0)hk + f_{22}''(x_0, y_0)k^2 \qquad [16.3]$$

Example 16.5

Let $f(x, y) = xy$. Compute the first and second directional derivatives of f at (x_0, y_0) in the directions: (a) $(h, k) = (1/\sqrt{2}, 1/\sqrt{2})$ and (b) $(h, k) = (1/\sqrt{2}, -1/\sqrt{2})$.

Solution   We have

$$f_1'(x, y) = y, \quad f_2'(x, y) = x, \quad f_{11}''(x, y) = 0,$$
$$f_{12}''(x, y) = f_{21}''(x, y) = 1, \quad f_{22}''(x, y) = 0$$

Thus, if $(h, k) = (1/\sqrt{2}, 1/\sqrt{2})$, then

$$D_{h,k} f(x_0, y_0) = y_0 \frac{1}{\sqrt{2}} + x_0 \frac{1}{\sqrt{2}} = \frac{1}{\sqrt{2}} (x_0 + y_0)$$

and

$$D_{h,k}^2 f(x_0, y_0) = 0 \left(\frac{1}{\sqrt{2}} \right)^2 + 2 \frac{1}{\sqrt{2}} \frac{1}{\sqrt{2}} + 0 \left(\frac{1}{\sqrt{2}} \right)^2 = 1$$

If $(h, k) = (1/\sqrt{2}, -1/\sqrt{2})$, then

$$D_{h,k} f(x_0, y_0) = y_0 \frac{1}{\sqrt{2}} + x_0 \frac{-1}{\sqrt{2}} = \frac{1}{\sqrt{2}} (y_0 - x_0)$$

and

$$D_{h,k}^2 f(x_0, y_0) = 2 \left(\frac{1}{\sqrt{2}} \right) \left(\frac{-1}{\sqrt{2}} \right) = -1$$

A Rough Argument for the Chain Rule

In order to show that the chain rule is valid, none of the earlier rules for derivatives can be applied. Instead, we must go all the way back to the definition of derivative. Letting $\phi(t)$ denote $F(f(t), g(t))$, we must examine the limit as $\Delta t \to 0$ of the Newton quotient

$$\frac{\phi(t + \Delta t) - \phi(t)}{\Delta t} = \frac{F(f(t + \Delta t), g(t + \Delta t)) - F(f(t), g(t))}{\Delta t} \qquad [1]$$

Because $x = f(t)$ and $y = g(t)$, we define $\Delta x = f(t + \Delta t) - f(t)$ and $\Delta y = g(t + \Delta t) - g(t)$, so that $f(t + \Delta t) = x + \Delta x$, $g(t + \Delta t) = y + \Delta y$. Substituting the last two expressions into [1], then subtracting and adding $F(x, y + \Delta y)$, we obtain

$$\frac{\phi(t + \Delta t) - \phi(t)}{\Delta t} = \frac{F(x + \Delta x, y + \Delta y) - F(x, y + \Delta y) + F(x, y + \Delta y) - F(x, y)}{\Delta t}$$

$$[2]$$

Now assume that Δx and Δy are different from 0 for all Δt close to 0. Then some simple algebraic manipulation suggests that, for all Δt close to 0, we have

$$\frac{\phi(t + \Delta t) - \phi(t)}{\Delta t} = \frac{F(x + \Delta x, y + \Delta y) - F(x, y + \Delta y)}{\Delta x} \frac{\Delta x}{\Delta t}$$
$$+ \frac{F(x, y + \Delta y) - F(x, y)}{\Delta y} \frac{\Delta y}{\Delta t}$$ [3]

When $\Delta t \to 0$, then $\Delta x / \Delta t \to dx/dt = f'(t)$, and $\Delta y / \Delta t \to dy/dt = g'(t)$. In particular, $\Delta x \to 0$ and $\Delta y \to 0$. From the definition of partial derivatives (see [15.15] of Section 15.5), we see that $(F(x + \Delta x, y + \Delta y) - F(x, y + \Delta y))/\Delta x$ tends to $F_1'(x, y + \Delta y)$ as $\Delta x \to 0$, and that $(F(x, y + \Delta y) - F(x, y))/\Delta y$ tends to $F_2'(x, y)$ as $\Delta y \to 0$. As $\Delta t \to 0$, both Δx and Δy tend to 0, and because F_1' is a continuous function, $F_1'(x, y + \Delta y) \to F_1'(x, y)$.[1] Finally, taking all the limits as $\Delta t \to 0$ gives

$$\phi'(t) = \lim_{\Delta t \to 0} \frac{\phi(t + \Delta t) - \phi(t)}{\Delta t} = F_1'(x, y) \frac{dx}{dt} + F_2'(x, y) \frac{dy}{dt}$$ [4]

as required.

Problems

1. In the following cases, find dz/dt by using the chain rule [16.1]:
   a. $F(x, y) = x + y^2$, $x = t^2$, $y = t^3$.
   b. $F(x, y) = x \ln y + y \ln x$, $x = t + 1$, $y = \ln t$.
   c. Check the answers by first substituting the expressions for x and y and then differentiating.

2. If $z = F(t, y)$ and $y = g(t)$, find a formula for dz/dt. Consider in particular the case where $z = t^2 + ye^y$ and $y = t^2$.

3. With reference to Example 16.3, let $Y = 10KL - \sqrt{K} - \sqrt{L}$, and suppose $K = 0.2t + 5$ and $L = 5e^{0.1t}$. Find dY/dt for $t = 0$.

4. What do you get if you apply the chain rule [16.1] when $F(x, y)$ is as follows?

   (a) $x + y$ (b) $x - y$ (c) $x \cdot y$ (d) x/y (e) $G(x)$

   Here $x = f(t)$, $y = g(t)$, and $G(x)$ are differentiable functions.

5. Consider Example 16.4 and let $u(x, z) = A \ln [1 + (x/z)^\alpha]$. Let $z = h(x) = \sqrt[3]{ax^4 + b}$, with the constants A, α, a, and b all positive. Find the optimal level of production x^* in this case.

---

[1] There is a small technical point in connection with the last limit. When $\Delta t \to 0$, then both Δx and Δy approach 0 together. We ought really to show that the expression $[F(x + \Delta x, y + \Delta y) - F(x, y + \Delta y)]/\Delta x$ tends to $F_1'(x, y)$ as $\Delta t \to 0$, and not just as first $\Delta x \to 0$ and then second as $\Delta y \to 0$.

6. A function is given by

$$F(x, y) = \tfrac{2}{3} \ln x + \tfrac{1}{3} \ln y$$

    a. Determine the domain of $F(x, y)$. Draw the level curve $F(x, y) = 0$ and indicate where $F(x, y) > 0$. (Use the fact that $F(x, y) = \tfrac{1}{3} \ln(x^2 y)$.)

    b. Find dz/dt when $z = F(x, y)$, $x = e^{3t}$, and $y = 1 + e^{-3t}$. Determine $\lim_{t \to \infty} dz/dt$.

7. Compute the directional derivatives of the following functions at the given point and in the given direction.

    a. $f(x, y) = 2x + y - 1$ at $(2, 1)$, in the direction of $(1, 1)$.

    b. $g(x, y) = xe^{yx} - xy$ at $(1, 1)$, in the direction of $(3, 4)$.

Harder Problems

8. If $z = F(x, y)$, $x = f(t)$, and $y = g(t)$, prove that

$$\frac{d^2z}{dt^2} = \frac{\partial z}{\partial x}\frac{d^2x}{dt^2} + \frac{\partial z}{\partial y}\frac{d^2y}{dt^2} + \frac{\partial^2 z}{\partial x^2}\left(\frac{dx}{dt}\right)^2 + 2\frac{\partial^2 z}{\partial x \partial y}\left(\frac{dx}{dt}\right)\left(\frac{dy}{dt}\right) + \frac{\partial^2 z}{\partial y^2}\left(\frac{dy}{dt}\right)^2$$

under appropriate assumptions on F, f, and g.

16.2 More General Chain Rules

It is easy to generalize the chain rule to the situation where

$$z = F(x, y), \qquad x = f(t, s), \qquad y = g(t, s)$$

In this case, z is a function of both t and s, with

$$z = F(f(t, s), g(t, s))$$

Thus, it makes sense to look for both partial derivatives $\partial z/\partial t$ and $\partial z/\partial s$. If we keep s fixed, then z is a function of t alone, and we can therefore use the chain rule [16.1]. In the same way, by keeping t fixed, we can differentiate z with respect to s by using [16.1]. The result is the following:

The Chain Rule

When $z = F(x, y)$ with $x = f(t, s)$ and $y = g(t, s)$, then

    (a) $\dfrac{\partial z}{\partial t} = F_1'(x, y)\dfrac{\partial x}{\partial t} + F_2'(x, y)\dfrac{\partial y}{\partial t}$ [16.4]

    (b) $\dfrac{\partial z}{\partial s} = F_1'(x, y)\dfrac{\partial x}{\partial s} + F_2'(x, y)\dfrac{\partial y}{\partial s}$

Example 16.6

Find $\partial z/\partial t$ and $\partial z/\partial s$ when $z = F(x, y) = x^2 + 2y^2$, with $x = t - s^2$ and $y = ts$.

Solution   We obtain

$$F_1'(x, y) = 2x, \quad F_2'(x, y) = 4y, \quad \frac{\partial x}{\partial t} = 1, \quad \frac{\partial x}{\partial s} = -2s, \quad \frac{\partial y}{\partial t} = s, \quad \frac{\partial y}{\partial s} = t$$

Formulas [16.4] (a) and (b) therefore give:

$$\frac{\partial z}{\partial t} = 2x \cdot 1 + 4y \cdot s = 2(t - s^2) + 4tss = 2t - 2s^2 + 4ts^2$$

$$\frac{\partial z}{\partial s} = 2x \cdot (-2s) + 4y \cdot t = 2(t - s^2)(-2s) + 4tst = -4ts + 4s^3 + 4t^2s$$

Check the answers by first expressing z as a function of t and s, and then differentiating.

The General Case

Economists sometimes use a more general version of the chain rule. Suppose that

$$z = F(x_1, \ldots, x_n) \text{ with } x_1 = f_1(t_1, \ldots, t_m), \ldots, x_n = f_n(t_1, \ldots, t_m) \qquad [16.5]$$

Substituting the x_i's as functions of the t_j's into the formula for z gives z as a **composite function** of $t_1, t_2, \ldots, t_m$. An obvious generalization of [16.1] and [16.4] is as follows:

The General Chain Rule

When [16.5] is true, then

$$\frac{\partial z}{\partial t_j} = \frac{\partial z}{\partial x_1} \frac{\partial x_1}{\partial t_j} + \frac{\partial z}{\partial x_2} \frac{\partial x_2}{\partial t_j} + \cdots + \frac{\partial z}{\partial x_n} \frac{\partial x_n}{\partial t_j}, \quad (j = 1, 2, \ldots, m) \qquad [16.6]$$

This is an important formula that every economist should understand. A small change in a basic variable t_j gives rise to a chain reaction. First, every x_i depends on t_j in general and hence changes when t_j is changed. In its turn, z is affected. The contribution to the total derivative of z with respect to t_j, resulting from the change in x_i, is $(\partial z/\partial x_i)(\partial x_i/\partial t_j)$. Formula [16.6] shows that $\partial z/\partial t_j$ is the sum of all these contributions.

Note: For [16.6] to hold, we must make some assumptions about the functions involved. The following requirements are sufficient: F is a continuous function with continuous partial derivatives in an open domain A in R^n, and $f_1, f_2, \ldots, f_n$

all have continuous partial derivatives with respect to $t_1, t_2, \ldots, t_m$ in a domain B in R^m. We also suppose that $(t_1, t_2, \ldots, t_m) \in B \Rightarrow (x_1, x_2, \ldots, x_n) \in A$.

Leibniz's Formula

Section 10.3 showed how to differentiate integrals with respect to a parameter appearing in the limits of integration. Actually, a generalization of the formulas presented there is much used in economics:[2]

Leibniz's Formula

Suppose that $f(t, x)$, $a(t)$, and $b(t)$ are differentiable functions, and that

$$F(t) = \int_{a(t)}^{b(t)} f(t, x)\, dx \qquad [16.7]$$

Then the derivative of F is given by

$$F'(t) = f\big(t, b(t)\big) b'(t) - f\big(t, a(t)\big) a'(t) + \int_{a(t)}^{b(t)} \frac{\partial f(t, x)}{\partial t}\, dx \qquad [16.8]$$

Note that when t changes in [16.7], the limits of integration $a(t)$ and $b(t)$ both change, and moreover the integrand $f(t, x)$ changes for each x. Formula [16.8] captures the total effect on the integral of all these changes.

We discuss briefly the rationale behind the Leibniz's formula. Let H be the function of three variables:

$$H(t, u, v) = \int_u^v f(t, x)\, dx$$

Then with $u = a(t)$ and $v = b(t)$, we have $F(t) = H(t, a(t), b(t))$. So, by the chain rule for differentiating composite functions,

$$F'(t) = H'_t + H'_u a'(t) + H'_v b'(t) \qquad [*]$$

where H'_t is the derivative of H w.r.t. t when u and v are constant. It is reasonable to guess that we can differentiate H partially w.r.t. t by differentiating under the integral sign, giving $H'_t = \int_u^v f'_t(t, x)\, dx$. Moreover, according to [10.20] and [10.21] in Section 10.3, $H'_u = -f(t, u)$ and $H'_v = f(t, v)$. Inserting these results into [*] yields [16.8]. Note that if $f(t, x)$ is independent of t, then $\partial f(t, x)/\partial t = 0$, so [16.8] reduces to [10.22].[3]

---

[2]In Richard Feynman's *Surely You're Joking, Mr. Feynman!* (Bantam Books, New York, 1986), the late Nobel laureate vividly describes the usefulness of this result to physicists: it is equally useful for economists.

[3]For a more detailed discussion of Leibniz's formula, see Bartle (1976), Section 31.

Example 16.7

Use [16.8] to compute $F'(t)$ when $F(t) = \int_t^{t^2} \frac{1}{2}x^2 t \, dx$. Check the answer by calculating the integral first and then differentiating.

Solution   We obtain

$$F'(t) = \frac{1}{2}(t^2)^2 t \cdot 2t - \frac{1}{2}t^2 t \cdot 1 + \int_t^{t^2} \frac{1}{2}x^2 \, dx$$

$$= t^6 - \frac{1}{2}t^3 + \left| \frac{1}{t} \frac{1}{6}x^3 \right| = t^6 - \frac{1}{2}t^3 + \frac{1}{6}\left[(t^2)^3 - t^3\right] = \frac{7}{6}t^6 - \frac{2}{3}t^3$$

In this case, the integral $F(t)$ is easy to calculate explicitly:

$$F(t) = \frac{1}{2}t \int_t^{t^2} x^2 \, dx = \frac{1}{2}t \left| \frac{1}{t} \frac{1}{3}x^3 \right| = \frac{1}{6}(t^7 - t^4)$$

Differentiating yields the same expression for $F'(t)$ as before.

Example 16.8

Suppose that a small business earns a net profit $y(t)$ at each time $t \in [0, T]$. At time $s \in [0, T]$, the discounted value (DV) of future profits is

$$V(s, r) = \int_s^T y(t)e^{-r(t-s)} \, dt$$

where r is the constant rate of discount. (See [10.34] of Section 10.4.) Compute $V_s'(s, r)$ by using Leibniz's rule.

Solution   We get

$$V_s'(s, r) = -y(s) + \int_s^T y(t)re^{-r(t-s)} \, dt = -y(s) + rV(s, r) \qquad [*]$$

where the last equality was obtained by moving the constant r outside the integral.

Solving equation [*] for r yields

$$r = \frac{y(s) + V_s'(s, r)}{V(s, r)} \qquad [**]$$

This has an important interpretation. At time s, the business owner earns $y(s)$, and the DV of future profits is increasing at the instantaneous rate $V_s'(s, r)$. The ratio on the right-hand side of [**] is known as the *proportional instantaneous rate of return* of the investment. Equation [**] requires this ratio to be equal to r. In fact, if r were the proportional instantaneous rate of return on a (relatively) safe asset like government bonds, and if the left-hand side of [**] were higher than the right-hand side, then the business owner would be better off selling the business for the amount $V(s, r)$, which it is worth at time s, and holding bonds instead. But if the left-hand side of [**] were lower than the right-hand side, then existing bondholders would do better to sell their bonds and buy clones of this small business.

Problems

1. Use [16.4] to find $\partial z/\partial t$ and $\partial z/\partial s$ for the following cases:
   a. $z = xy^2$, $\quad x = t + s^2$, $\quad y = t^2 s$
   b. $z = \frac{x-y}{x+y}$, $\quad x = e^{t+s}$, $\quad y = e^{ts}$

2. Find expressions for $\partial z/\partial t_1$ and $\partial z/\partial t_2$ when $z = F(x)$ and $x = f(t_1, t_2)$.

3. a. Find $\partial u/\partial x_i$ when $u = F(U)$, where $U = f(x_1, x_2, \ldots, x_n)$.
   b. Use the result in (a) when $F(U) = U^\delta$ and $U = \sum_{j=1}^{n} A_j x_j^{\alpha_j}$, where δ, A_j, and α_j are all constants, and the variables x_j are all positive.

4. a. If $u = \ln(x^3 + y^3 + z^3 - 3xyz)$, show that

$$\text{(i)} \quad x\frac{\partial u}{\partial x} + y\frac{\partial u}{\partial y} + z\frac{\partial u}{\partial z} = 3 \qquad \text{(ii)} \quad (x + y + z)\left(\frac{\partial u}{\partial x} + \frac{\partial u}{\partial y} + \frac{\partial u}{\partial z}\right) = 3$$

   b. If $z = f(x^2 y)$, show that $x\dfrac{\partial z}{\partial x} = 2y\dfrac{\partial z}{\partial y}$

5. a. Find a formula for $\partial u/\partial r$ when $u = f(x, y, z, w)$ and x, y, z, and w all are functions of two variables r and t.
   b. Let $u = xyzw$, $x = r + s$, $y = r - s$, $z = rs$, and $w = r/s$, and compute $\partial u/\partial r$ when $(r, s) = (2, 1)$.

6. Find $F'(\alpha)$ when $F(\alpha) = \int_0^1 x e^{\alpha x^2} \, dx$ $(\alpha \neq 0)$ by using [16.8]. Check the answer by finding an explicit expression for $F(\alpha)$ and then differentiating.

7. Find $F'(t)$ in the following cases:
   a. $F(t) = \displaystyle\int_t^{2t} x^2 \, dx$ \qquad b. $F(t) = \displaystyle\int_1^2 \frac{e^{tx}}{x} \, dx$ \qquad c. $F(t) = \displaystyle\int_t^{2t} \frac{e^{tx}}{x} \, dx$

8. In a growth model studied by N. Kaldor and J. A. Mirrlees, a function N is defined by

$$N(t) = \int_{t-T(t)}^{t} n(\tau) e^{-\delta(t - T(t))} \, d\tau$$

where $T = T(t)$ is a given differentiable positive function. Compute $\dot{N}(t)$.

9. Suppose that f is a continuous function and g is a differentiable function. Evaluate

$$\frac{d}{d\rho} \int_0^{g(\rho)} e^{-\rho t} f(t) \, dt$$

10. Define

$$z(t) = \int_t^{2t} x(\tau) \exp\left[-\int_t^{\tau} r(s)\,ds\right]d\tau, \qquad p(t) = \exp\left[-\int_t^{2t} r(s)\,ds\right]$$

where the functions $x(\tau)$ and $r(s)$ are both differentiable. Prove that

$$\dot{z}(t) - r(t)z(t) = 2p(t)x(2t) - x(t)$$

11. Let $\mathbf{x}^0$ be a fixed vector in R^n and $\mathbf{h} \neq \mathbf{0}$ a fixed direction in R^n. Suppose that the function $f(\mathbf{x})$ has continuous partial derivatives of the first and second order in an open set containing $\mathbf{x}^0$. Define $g(t) = f(\mathbf{x}^0 + t\mathbf{h})$.
   a. Prove that $g'(t) = \sum_{i=1}^{n} f_i'(\mathbf{x}^0 + t\mathbf{h})h_i$.
   b. Prove that $g''(t) = \sum_{i=1}^{n}\sum_{j=1}^{n} f_{ij}''(\mathbf{x}^0 + t\mathbf{h})h_i h_j$.
      (If $\|\mathbf{h}\| = 1$, then $g'(0) = \sum_{i=1}^{n} f_i'(\mathbf{x}^0)h_i$ is called the *directional derivative* of f at $\mathbf{x}^0$ in the direction $\mathbf{h}$, and $g''(0) = \sum_{i=1}^{n}\sum_{j=1}^{n} f_{ij}''(\mathbf{x}^0)h_i h_j$ is called the *second directional derivative*.)

Harder Problems

12. A firm faces uncertain demand D and has existing inventory I. There are different costs per unit for having too much stock and too little. So the firm wants to choose its stock level Q in order to minimize the function

$$g(Q) = c(Q - I) + h\int_0^Q (Q - D)f(D)\,dD + p\int_Q^a (D - Q)f(D)\,dD$$

where c, I, h, p, and a are positive constants with $p > c$, and f is a given nonnegative function that satisfies $\int_0^a f(D)\,dD = 1$ (which means that f can be interpreted as a probability distribution function).
   a. Compute $g'(Q)$ and $g''(Q)$, and prove that g is convex.
   b. Define $F(Q*) = \int_0^{Q*} f(D)\,dD$, where $Q*$ is the minimum point of $g(Q)$. Use the first-order conditions for minimization of g to find an equation for $F(Q*)$, the probability that demand D does not exceed $Q*$. Use this equation to find the value of $F(Q*)$ when $Q*$ is optimal.

16.3 Derivatives of Functions Defined Implicitly

We often need to differentiate functions that are defined implicitly by one equation or by a system of simultaneous equations. In Section 5.3 we considered some simple cases; it is a good idea to review those examples now. Here we study the problem from a more general point of view. We begin by discussing the techniques of implicit differentiation. Some important theoretical problems must be taken into account, but these will be left until the end of this section.

Let F be a function of two variables, and consider the equation

$$F(x, y) = c \qquad (c \text{ is a constant}) \qquad [1]$$

Thus, [1] represents a level curve for F. (See Section 15.2.) Suppose this equation defines y as a function $y = f(x)$ of x in some interval I. (See Fig. 16.2.) This means that

$$F(x, f(x)) = c \qquad \text{for all } x \in I \qquad [2]$$

If f is differentiable, what is the derivative of $y = f(x)$? If the graph of f looks like the one given in Fig. 16.2, the geometric problem is to find the slope of the graph at a point P.

To find an expression for the slope, introduce the auxiliary function u defined for all $x \in I$ by $u(x) = F(x, f(x))$. Then, according to the chain rule [16.1], $u'(x) = F_1'(x, f(x)) \cdot 1 + F_2'(x, f(x)) \cdot f'(x)$. Now, [2] states that $u(x) = c$ for all $x \in I$. The derivative of a constant is 0, so we have

$$u'(x) = F_1'(x, f(x)) + F_2'(x, f(x)) \cdot f'(x) = 0$$

If $F_2'(x, f(x)) \neq 0$, then $f'(x) = -F_1'(x, f(x))/F_2'(x, f(x))$. Thus, after simplifying notation, we have

$$F(x, y) = c \implies \frac{dy}{dx} = -\frac{F_1'(x, y)}{F_2'(x, y)} \qquad (F_2'(x, y) \neq 0) \qquad [16.9]$$

This is an important result. Note that when [1] defines y implicitly as a function of x, formula [16.9] gives the derivative of y w.r.t. x even when it is impossible to solve the equation explicitly for y.

FIGURE 16.2 What is the slope at P?

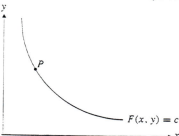

Example 16.9

Use [16.9] to compute y' when $xy^{1/2} = 2$.

Solution   We put $F(x, y) = xy^{1/2}$. Then $F_1'(x, y) = y^{1/2}$ and $F_2'(x, y) = \frac{1}{2}xy^{-1/2}$. Hence, [16.9] becomes

$$y' = \frac{dy}{dx} = -\frac{F_1'(x, y)}{F_2'(x, y)} = -\frac{y^{1/2}}{\frac{1}{2}xy^{-1/2}} = -\frac{2y}{x}$$

This confirms the result in the introductory example in Section 5.3.

Example 16.10

For the curve given by

$$x^3 + x^2y - 2y^2 - 10y = 0$$

find the slope of and equation for the tangent at the point $(x, y) = (2, 1)$.

Solution   First, note that $x = 2$ and $y = 1$ satisfy the equation, so that $(2, 1)$ is a point on the curve. Let $F(x, y) = x^3 + x^2y - 2y^2 - 10y$. Then the given equation is equivalent to $F(x, y) = 0$, which is a level curve for F. Here $F_1'(x, y) = 3x^2 + 2xy$ and $F_2'(x, y) = x^2 - 4y - 10$. So [16.9] implies that

$$y' = -\frac{3x^2 + 2xy}{x^2 - 4y - 10}$$

For $x = 2$ and $y = 1$ in particular, one has $y' = 8/5$. Then the point-slope formula [2.6] of Section 2.5 implies that the tangent at $(2, 1)$ must have the equation $y - 1 = (8/5)(x - 2)$, or $y = (1/5)(8x - 11)$.

Example 16.11

Assume that the equation $e^{xy^2} - 2x - 4y = c$ defines y as a differentiable function $y = f(x)$ of x. Find a value of the constant c such that $f(0) = 1$, and compute y' at $(x, y) = (0, 1)$.

Solution   When $x = 0$ and $y = 1$, the equation becomes $1 - 4 = c$, so $c = -3$. Let $F(x, y) = e^{xy^2} - 2x - 4y$. Then $F_1'(x, y) = y^2e^{xy^2} - 2$, and $F_2'(x, y) = 2xye^{xy^2} - 4$. Thus, from [16.9], we have

$$y' = -\frac{F_1'(x, y)}{F_2'(x, y)} = -\frac{y^2e^{xy^2} - 2}{2xye^{xy^2} - 4}$$

When $x = 0$ and $y = 1$, we find $y' = -1/4$. (Note that in this example it is impossible to solve $e^{xy^2} - 2x - 4y = -3$ explicitly for y. Still we found an explicit expression for the derivative of y with respect to x.)

Here is an important economic example using a function defined implicitly by an equation.

Example 16.12

We generalize Example 5.9 of Section 5.3, and assume that $D = f(t, P)$ is the demand for a commodity that depends on the price P before tax, as well as on the sales tax per unit, denoted by t. Suppose that $S = g(P)$ is the supply function. Of course, in general, the equilibrium price $P = P(t)$ depends on t. Indeed, $P = P(t)$ should satisfy the equation

$$f(t, P) = g(P) \qquad [*]$$

for all t in some relevant interval. Suppose that [*] defines P implicitly as a differentiable function of t, and find an expression for dP/dt; then discuss its sign.

Solution   Let $F(t, P) = f(t, P) - g(P)$. Then equation [*] becomes $F(t, P) = 0$, so formula [16.9] yields

$$\frac{dP}{dt} = -\frac{F_t'(t, P)}{F_P'(t, P)} = -\frac{f_t'(t, P)}{f_P'(t, P) - g'(P)} = \frac{f_t'(t, P)}{g'(P) - f_P'(t, P)} \qquad [**]$$

It is reasonable to assume that $g'(P) > 0$ (meaning that supply increases if price increases) and that $f_t'(t, P)$ and $f_P'(t, P)$ are both < 0 (meaning that demand decreases if either the tax or the price increases). Then [**] tells us that $dP/dt < 0$, implying that the pre-tax price faced by suppliers decreases as the tax increases. Thus, suppliers, as well as consumers, are adversely affected if taxes on their products rise.

Of course, we can also derive formula [**] by implicit differentiation of [*] with respect to t, regarding P as a function of t:

$$f_t'(t, P) \cdot 1 + f_P'(t, P)\frac{dP}{dt} = g'(P)\frac{dP}{dt}$$

Solving this equation for dP/dt yields [**] again.

The General Equation for the Tangent to F(x, y) = c

If point P in Fig. 16.3 has coordinates (x_0, y_0), and if $F_2'(x_0, y_0) \neq 0$, then the slope of the tangent at P is given by $-F_1'(x_0, y_0)/F_2'(x_0, y_0)$. By using the point–slope formula [2.6] of Section 2.5, the tangent at P, therefore, has the equation

$$y - y_0 = -\left[F_1'(x_0, y_0)/F_2'(x_0, y_0)\right](x - x_0)$$

This can be written more symmetrically as

$$F_1'(x_0, y_0)(x - x_0) + F_2'(x_0, y_0)(y - y_0) = 0 \qquad [16.10]$$

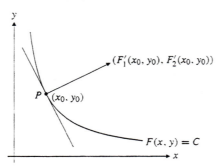

FIGURE 16.3 **The gradient is orthogonal to the tangent at P.**

which remains valid even if $F_2'(x_0, y_0) = 0$ and the tangent at P is vertical.

Example 16.13

Find the tangent to the curve in Example 16.10 at $(2, 1)$ by using [16.10].

Solution Here $F_1'(x, y) = 3x^2 + 2xy = 3 \cdot 2^2 + 2 \cdot 2 \cdot 1 = 16$ at $(2, 1)$, and $F_2'(x, y) = x^2 - 4y - 10 = 2^2 - 4 \cdot 1 - 10 = -10$ at $(2, 1)$. Thus, [16.10] yields

$$16(x - 2) + (-10)(y - 1) = 0, \qquad \text{or} \qquad y = (1/5)(8x - 11)$$

This is the same result as in Example 16.10.

The vector $(F_1'(x_0, y_0), F_2'(x_0, y_0))$, also denoted by $\nabla F(x_0, y_0)$, is the **gradient** of $F(x, y)$ at (x_0, y_0). Using the notation for a scalar product, [16.10] can be written as

$$(F_1'(x_0, y_0), F_2'(x_0, y_0)) \cdot (x - x_0, y - y_0) = 0 \qquad [*]$$

This shows that the gradient is orthogonal to the tangent, as illustrated in Fig. 16.3.

If (h, k) is a unit vector, and $\nabla F(x_0, y_0) \neq (0, 0)$, then according to [16.2] in Section 16.1, the scalar product $D = \nabla F(x_0, y_0) \cdot (h, k)$ is the directional derivative of $F(x, y)$ at (x_0, y_0) in the direction (h, k). A movement of one unit away from (x_0, y_0) in direction (h, k) changes the value of $F(x_0, y_0)$ by approximately D. Now, according to [12.19] in Section 12.4,

$$D = ||\nabla F(x_0, y_0)|| \cdot ||(h, k)|| \cdot \cos \phi$$

where ϕ is the angle between the vectors $\nabla F(x_0, y_0)$ and (h, k). Hence, D attains its maximum value when $\phi = 0$, because then $\cos \phi = 1$. (Recall that $\cos \phi$ is always less than or equal to 1.) When $\phi = 0$, the vector $\nabla F(x_0, y_0)$ points in the same direction as (h, k). Consequently, $\nabla F(x_0, y_0)$ points in the direction of maximal increase of $F(x, y)$. So we have the following:

Properties of the Gradient

If $\nabla F(x, y) \neq (0, 0)$, then:

1. $\nabla F(x, y)$ is orthogonal to the level curve $F(x, y) = C$.
2. $\nabla F(x, y)$ points in the direction of maximal increase of $F(x, y)$.

[16.11]

Note. [16.11] can be generalized. If $f(\mathbf{x}) = f(x_1, \ldots, x_n)$ is differentiable, then one can prove that its gradient, $\nabla f(\mathbf{x}) = (\partial f(\mathbf{x})/\partial x_1, \ldots, \partial f(\mathbf{x})/\partial x_n)$, is orthogonal to the level suface $f(\mathbf{x}) = C$ and that $\nabla f(\mathbf{x})$ points in the direction of maximal increase of $f(\mathbf{x})$.

A Formula for the Second Derivative

Formula [16.9] gives the slope of the level curve $F(x, y) = c$. Sometimes we need to know if the level curve is convex or concave, and so we need to compute y''. By [16.9], we have $y' = -F_1'(x, y)/F_2'(x, y)$. Write $G(x) = F_1'(x, y)$ and $H(x) = F_2'(x, y)$, where y is a function of x. Our aim now is to differentiate the quotient

$$y' = -\frac{G(x)}{H(x)}$$

with respect to x. According to the rule for differentiating quotients,

$$y'' = -\frac{G'(x)H(x) - G(x)H'(x)}{[H(x)]^2} \quad [*]$$

Keeping in mind that y is a function of x, both $G(x)$ and $H(x)$ are composite functions. So we differentiate them both by using the chain rule [16.1], thereby obtaining

$$G'(x) = F_{11}''(x, y) \cdot 1 + F_{12}''(x, y) \cdot y'$$
$$H'(x) = F_{21}''(x, y) \cdot 1 + F_{22}''(x, y) \cdot y'$$

We assume that $F_{12}'' = F_{21}''$. Replace y' in both the preceding equations by the quotient in [16.9], and then insert the results into [*]. After some algebraic simplifications, this yields

$$y'' = -\frac{1}{(F_2')^3}\left[F_{11}''(F_2')^2 - 2F_{12}''F_1'F_2' + F_{22}''(F_1')^2\right] \quad [16.12]$$

Finally, after making use of [**] at the end of Section 15.8, we can write the result in the somewhat more memorizable form:

$$F(x, y) = c \implies y'' = \frac{d^2 y}{dx^2} = \frac{1}{(F_2')^3} \begin{vmatrix} 0 & F_1' & F_2' \\ F_1' & F_{11}'' & F_{12}'' \\ F_2' & F_{21}'' & F_{22}'' \end{vmatrix}$$ [16.13]

valid for $F_2' \neq 0$.

Example 16.14

Use [16.12] to find y'' when $xy^{1/2} = 2$. (See Example 16.9 and Example 5.10 of Section 5.3.)

Solution   When $F(x, y) = xy^{1/2}$, $F_1'(x, y) = y^{1/2}$ and $F_2'(x, y) = \frac{1}{2}xy^{-1/2}$. Furthermore, $F_{11}'' = 0$, $F_{12}'' = \frac{1}{2}y^{-1/2}$, and $F_{22}'' = -\frac{1}{4}xy^{-3/2}$. Thus, according to [16.12],

$$y'' = -\frac{1}{(\frac{1}{2}xy^{-1/2})^3}\left[-2(\tfrac{1}{2}y^{-1/2})y^{1/2}(\tfrac{1}{2}xy^{-1/2}) + (-\tfrac{1}{4}xy^{-3/2})(y^{1/2})^2\right]$$

This simplifies to $y'' = 6y/x^2$, the same result we obtained more easily in Example 5.10 of Section 5.3.

Theoretical Considerations

So far, this section has presented the technique of implicit differentiation. In particular, *provided that* $F(x, y) = c$ defines y as a differentiable function of x, we were able to derive the formula $y' = -F_1'(x, y)/F_2'(x, y)$. Yet it is easy to construct examples in which this formula makes no sense at all. For instance, consider the equation

$$x^2 + e^{xy} = 0$$ [1]

With $F(x, y) = x^2 + e^{xy}$ and $c = 0$, [1] reduces to the equation $F(x, y) = c$. Then formula [16.9] suggests that

$$y' = -\frac{F_1'(x, y)}{F_2'(x, y)} = -\frac{2x + ye^{xy}}{xe^{xy}}$$ [2]

whenever $F_2'(x, y) = xe^{xy} \neq 0$. However, a closer look at [1] reveals that its left-hand side is always positive, so no pair (x, y) satisfies the equation. Thus, the graph of the equation is empty, and the "result" in [2] is complete nonsense.

Even if the level curve $F(x, y) = c$ is not the graph of one function $y = f(x)$, it can almost always be considered as a composite graph of several functions. An example is shown in Fig 16.4. Most vertical lines cut the curve in Fig. 16.4 three times, so the curve is not the graph of a function. However, the graph in Fig. 16.4 is put together from three different function graphs. Figure 16.5 shows the graph of the middle of these three. There is in addition a "bottom function" whose range consists of smaller values of y, and whose graph is the part of the curve below and to the right of P in Fig. 16.4. There is also a third "top function" whose graph is the part of the curve above and to the left of Q. The argument leading up to [16.9] applies to each of the three functions that constitute the graph. Hence, we have found the slope of the tangent to the level curve in Fig. 16.4 at an arbitrary point (x, y) on the curve, except at the particular points P and Q where $F_2'(x, y) = 0$ and so the gradient is parallel to the x-axis. At these points, the curve has a vertical tangent.

It is quite difficult to find conditions on F and c sufficient to guarantee that the equation $F(x, y) = c$ defines y as a differentiable function of x. Any advanced calculus book discusses this problem, however. Briefly expressed, according to the *implicit function theorem*, if F is continuously differentiable, $F(x_0, y_0) = c$, and $F_2'(x_0, y_0) \neq 0$, then the equation $F(x, y) = c$ *will* define y as a continuously differentiable function of x in a (small) rectangle centered at (x_0, y_0). Moreover, the derivative is given by $y' = -F_1'(x, y)/F_2'(x, y)$.[4]

The crucial condition in this theorem is that $F_2'(x_0, y_0) \neq 0$. This is satisfied at point R in Fig. 16.6. So we can find a rectangle centered at R such that the curve passing through this rectangle is cut exactly once by each vertical line that intersects the rectangle. On the other hand, there is no rectangle centered at P such that the curve passing through this rectangle is cut exactly once by each vertical line that intersects the rectangle—however we draw the rectangle, the part of the curve contained within it is cut at least twice by some such vertical lines, and not at all by others.

We have discussed conditions for $F(x, y) = c$ to define y as a differentiable function of x. We might as well ask for conditions for the equation to define x as a differentiable function of y. In fact, because of the obvious symmetry, if F is continuously differentiable, $F(x_0, y_0) = c$, and $F_1'(x_0, y_0) \neq 0$, then the equation

FIGURE 16.4

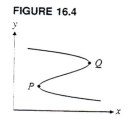

FIGURE 16.5

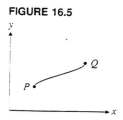

FIGURE 16.6

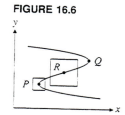

[4]Actually, if F is n times continuously differentiable, then y as a function of x is also n times continuously differentiable. In the terminology used at the end of Section 15.5, if F is a C^n function, then y is a C^n function of x as well.

$F(x, y) = c$ *will* define x as a continuously differentiable function of y in a (small) interval centered at y_0, and the derivative is given by $x' = -F_2'(x, y)/F_1'(x, y)$.

Problems

1. Use the formula in [16.9] to find y' when y is defined implicitly by the equation $2x^2 + 6xy + y^2 = 18$. Let $F(x, y) = 2x^2 + 6xy + y^2$ and $c = 18$. Check the result in Problem 2 of Section 5.3.

2. Use formulas [16.9] and [16.12] to find y' and y'' for the following:

   a. $xy = 1$ **b.** $x - y + 3xy = 2$ **c.** $y^6 - x^5 = 0$

3. **a.** Find the slope of the level curve $F(x, y) = 0$ when $F(x, y) = x^2 - y^2$. Which point must be excluded? Draw the level curve(s) in the xy-plane.
   b. Find the slope of the level curve $F(x, y) = 0$ when $F(x, y) = y^3 - x^2$. Which point must be excluded? Draw the level curve in the xy-plane.

4. A curve in the xy-plane is given by the equation

$$2x^2 + xy + y^2 - 8 = 0$$

   a. Find the equation for the tangent at the point $(2, 0)$.
   b. Which points on the curve have a horizontal tangent?

5. Let f be a function with $f(x) > 0$, $f'(x) > 0$, and $f''(x) < 0$ for all $x > 0$.
   a. The equation $[f(x)/f'(x)] - x = t$ defines x implicitly as a function of t. Find dx/dt and show that it is > 0.
   b. Show that the elasticity $\mathrm{El}_t \, f'(x) = -t/(t + x)$.

6. The equation $y^2 + 5x = xe^{x(y-2)}$ represents a curve in the xy-plane. Explain why the curve passes through the point $(-1, 2)$, and show that the slope of the tangent at this point is equal to $-4/3$. Also find the equation for the tangent here.

Harder Problems

7. A function $U(x, y)$ is called *separable* in the domain S if there exist functions F, f, and g such that

$$U(x, y) = F\big(f(x) + g(y)\big) \qquad \text{for all } (x, y) \in S \qquad [1]$$

   a. Show that with appropriate requirements on F, f, and g, one must then have

$$\frac{\partial^2}{\partial x \partial y}\left[\ln \frac{U_x'(x, y)}{U_y'(x, y)}\right] = 0 \qquad \text{for all } (x, y) \in S \qquad [2]$$

   b. Show that $U(x, y) = Ax^a y^b$ satisfies [2] for all $x > 0$ and $y > 0$, then show (explicitly) how this function can be written in the form [1]. (One can show that with certain mild restrictions on U, [2] will in general imply [1].)

16.4 Partial Elasticities

Section 5.6 introduced the concept of elasticity for functions of one variable. Here we study the corresponding concept for functions of several variables. This enables us to distinguish between, for instance, the price and income elasticities of demand, as well as between own and cross price elasticities.

If $z = f(x_1, x_2, \ldots, x_n)$, we define the **partial elasticity** of z (or of f) with respect to x_i as the elasticity of z with respect to x_i when all the other variables are held constant. Thus,

$$\text{El}_i \, z = \frac{x_i}{f(x_1, x_2, \ldots, x_n)} \frac{\partial f(x_1, x_2, \ldots, x_n)}{\partial x_i} = \frac{x_i}{z} \frac{\partial z}{\partial x_i} \qquad [16.14]$$

The number $\text{El}_i \, z$ is approximately equal to the percentage change in z caused by a 1% increase in x_i, keeping all the other x_j ($j \neq i$) constant (see Section 5.6). Among other forms of notation commonly used instead of $\text{El}_i \, z$, we mention

$$\text{El}_i \, f(x_1, x_2, \ldots, x_n), \qquad \text{El}_{x_i} \, z, \qquad \hat{z}_i \text{ ("z hat } i\text{"}), \qquad \text{and} \qquad e_i \text{ or } \epsilon_i$$

Example 16.15

Find the elasticity of $z = xye^{x+y}$ w.r.t. x (with x and y both positive).

Solution If you have not studied the rules for elasticities in Problem 7 of Section 5.6, you can argue as follows: Take the natural logarithm of both sides to get $\ln z = \ln x + \ln y + \ln e^{x+y} = \ln x + \ln y + x + y$. Differentiating this equation partially w.r.t. x yields $z'_x/z = 1/x + 1$. Hence,

$$\text{El}_x \, z = \frac{x}{z} z'_x = x \frac{z'_x}{z} = x \left(\frac{1}{x} + 1 \right) = 1 + x$$

Example 16.16

Let $D_1 = D_1(p, q)$ denote demand for a product as a function of prices p and q. Then, as in Example 16.2,

$$\frac{dD_1}{dt} = \frac{\partial D_1(p, q)}{\partial p} \dot{p}(t) + \frac{\partial D_1(p, q)}{\partial q} \dot{q}(t)$$

It follows that

$$\frac{1}{D_1} \frac{dD_1}{dt} = \frac{p}{D_1} \frac{\partial D_1}{\partial p} \frac{\dot{p}}{p} + \frac{q}{D_1} \frac{\partial D_1}{\partial q} \frac{\dot{q}}{q} = \text{El}_p \, D_1 \frac{\dot{p}}{p} + \text{El}_q \, D_1 \frac{\dot{q}}{q}$$

So the rate of growth of demand is the elasticity weighted sum of the proportional rates of price increase.

Example 16.17

Suppose $D = A x_1^{a_1} x_2^{a_2} \cdots x_n^{a_n}$ is a demand function (where $A > 0$, a_1, a_2, $\ldots$, a_n are constants and $x_1 > 0$, $x_2 > 0$, $\ldots$, $x_n > 0$). Compute the elasticity of D with respect to x_1 and x_i.

Solution   Take the natural logarithm of both sides to get

$$\ln D = \ln A + a_1 \ln x_1 + \cdots + a_n \ln x_n$$

Differentiation w.r.t. x_1 yields

$$\frac{D_1'}{D} = \frac{a_1}{x_1}, \qquad \text{so} \qquad \text{El}_1 D = \frac{x_1 D_1'}{D} = a_1$$

Similarly, $\text{El}_i D = a_i$, for $i = 1, 2, \ldots, n$.

As a special case of Example 16.17, let $D_i = A m^{\alpha} p_i^{-\beta} p_j^{\gamma}$, where m is income, p_i is own price, and p_j is the price of a substitute good. Then α is the income elasticity of demand, $-\beta$ is the own price elasticity, and γ is the cross price elasticity. However, because own price elasticities of demand are usually negative, one often describes β rather than $-\beta$ as being the own price elasticity of demand. Usually, there is no confusion—except among economics students struggling to understand elasticity!

Elasticities of Composite Functions

Sections 16.1 and 16.2 presented the derivatives of composite functions. Now we see how to find their elasticities. Let us consider the general case directly and formulate the following result, which is valid with appropriate requirements on the functions involved:

$$z = F(x_1, \ldots, x_n), \quad x_i = f_i(t_1, \ldots, t_m), \quad i = 1, \ldots, n$$

$$\implies \text{El}_{t_j} z = \sum_{i=1}^{n} \text{El}_i F(x_1, \ldots, x_n) \, \text{El}_j x_i \qquad [16.15]$$

Let us call F the main function, $x_1, \ldots, x_n$ the intermediate variables, and $t_1, \ldots, t_m$ the basic variables. Then [16.15] tells us how to find the elasticities of the main dependent variable z in terms of the elasticities of the main function with respect to the intermediate variables, and the elasticities of the intermediate variables with respect to the basic variables. Formulate the result in your own words.

The proof of [16.15] follows directly from the corresponding result for the derivative, that is the chain rule [16.6] in Section 16.2. Indeed, assume that z and $x_1, \ldots, x_n$ are all not zero. Then, if we multiply each side of the equation in [16.6] by t_j/z, we get

$$\frac{t_j}{z}\frac{\partial z}{\partial t_j} = \frac{t_j}{z}\sum_{i=1}^{n} F_i'(x_1, \ldots, x_n)\frac{\partial x_i}{\partial t_j} = \sum_{i=1}^{n}\frac{x_i}{z}F_i'(x_1, \ldots, x_n)\frac{t_j}{x_i}\frac{\partial x_i}{\partial t_j}$$

Note that we have used a little trick to derive the last equality. We see at once that [16.15] must be true.

Example 16.18

Aukrust and Bjerke have estimated that the growth in the national product of Norway can be described by the production function

$$Y(t) = 2.262\big[K(t)\big]^{0.203}\big[L(t)\big]^{0.763}e^{0.0181t} \tag{1}$$

As usual $Y(t)$, $K(t)$, and $L(t)$ denote respectively net national product, real capital stock, and labor used in year t. The factor $e^{0.0181t}$ is due to "technical progress." Find an expression for the elasticity of Y with respect to t.

Solution In order to find $\text{El}_t\, Y(t)$, we express the production function as

$$Y = 2.262K^{0.203}L^{0.763}T \qquad \text{with } K = K(t),\ L = L(t),\ T = e^{0.0181t}$$

Using [16.15] together with the rules for manipulating elasticities (see Problem 7 of Section 5.6), we have

$$\text{El}_t\, Y(t) = 0.203\text{El}_t\, K(t) + 0.763\text{El}_t\, L(t) + 0.0181t$$

The Elasticity of Substitution

Consider a level curve $F(x, y) = c$ for a function F of two variables. In Section 16.3, we found the slope of the level curve to be $y' = -F_1'(x, y)/F_2'(x, y)$. Economists often denote $-y'$ by R_{yx}, and give this fraction a special name.

The **marginal rate of substitution** between y and x is

$$R_{yx} = \frac{F_1'(x, y)}{F_2'(x, y)} \tag{16.16}$$

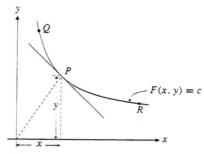

FIGURE 16.7

Note that $R_{yx} \approx -\Delta y / \Delta x$ when we move along the level curve $F(x, y) = c$. If $\Delta x = -1$ in particular, then $R_{yx} \approx \Delta y$. Thus, R_{yx} is approximately the quantity of y we must add per unit of x removed, if we are to stay on the same level curve.

Consider Fig. 16.7. The number R_{yx} varies along the level curve $F(x, y) = c$. At point Q, the slope of the tangent is a large negative number, and so R_{yx} is a large positive number. At P, the number R_{yx} is about 1.5, and at R it is about 0.5. When we move along the level curve from left to right, R_{yx} will be strictly decreasing with values in some positive interval I. For each value of R_{yx} in I, there corresponds a certain point (x, y) on the level curve $F(x, y) = c$, and thus a certain value of y/x. The fraction y/x is therefore a function of R_{yx}, and we define the following:

When $F(x, y) = c$, the **elasticity of substitution** between y and x is

$$\sigma_{yx} = \mathrm{El}_{R_{yx}}\left(\frac{y}{x}\right) \qquad [16.17]$$

Thus, σ_{yx} is the elasticity of the fraction y/x with respect to the marginal rate of substitution. Roughly speaking, σ_{yx} is the percentage change in the fraction y/x when we move along the level curve $F(x, y) = c$ far enough so that R_{yx} increases by 1%. In Problem 10, the elasticity of substitution is expressed in terms of the partials of the function F.

Example 16.19

Compute σ_{KL} for the Cobb–Douglas function $F(K, L) = AK^a L^b$.

Solution The marginal rate of substitution between K and L is

$$R_{KL} = \frac{F_L'}{F_K'} = \frac{bAK^a L^{b-1}}{aAK^{a-1} L^b} = \frac{b}{a}\frac{K}{L}$$

Thus, $K/L = (a/b) R_{KL}$. The elasticity of the last expression w.r.t. R_{KL} is 1. Hence, $\sigma_{KL} = 1$ for the Cobb–Douglas function.

Example 16.20

Compute the elasticity of substitution for

$$F(K, L) = A\left(aK^{-\varrho} + bL^{-\varrho}\right)^{-m/\varrho} \qquad [1]$$

where A, a, and b are positive constants, and $\varrho \neq 0$ with $\varrho > -1$.

Solution   Here

$$F'_K = A(-m/\varrho)\left(aK^{-\varrho} + bL^{-\varrho}\right)^{(-m/\varrho)-1} a(-\varrho)K^{-\varrho-1}$$

$$F'_L = A(-m/\varrho)\left(aK^{-\varrho} + bL^{-\varrho}\right)^{(-m/\varrho)-1} b(-\varrho)L^{-\varrho-1}$$

Hence,

$$R_{KL} = \frac{F'_L}{F'_K} = \frac{b}{a}\frac{L^{-\varrho-1}}{K^{-\varrho-1}} = \frac{b}{a}\left(\frac{K}{L}\right)^{\varrho+1}$$

so that

$$\frac{K}{L} = \left(\frac{a}{b}\right)^{1/(\varrho+1)} (R_{KL})^{1/(\varrho+1)}$$

Recalling that the elasticity of Ax^b w.r.t. x is b, definition [16.17] implies that

$$\sigma_{KL} = \mathrm{El}_{R_{KL}}\left(\frac{K}{L}\right) = \frac{1}{\varrho + 1} \qquad [2]$$

We have shown thus that the function F defined by [1] has constant elasticity of substitution $1/(\varrho + 1)$. For this reason, F is usually called the **CES function** (where CES stands for "constant elasticity of substitution").

Note from [2] that the elasticity of substitution for the CES function tends to 1 as $\varrho \to 0$, and this is precisely the elasticity of substitution for the Cobb–Douglas function in the previous example. See Problem 11 for further details.

Problems

1. Find the partial elasticities of z with respect to x and y in the following cases:
   a. $z = xy$ **b.** $z = x^2 y^5$ **c.** $z = x^n e^x y^n e^y$ **d.** $z = x + y$

2. Let $z = (a_1 x_1^d + a_2 x_2^d + a_3 x_3^d)^g$, where a_1, a_2, a_3, d, and g are constants. Compute $\mathrm{El}_1 z + \mathrm{El}_2 z + \mathrm{El}_3 z$.

3. Let $z = x_1^p \cdots x_n^p \exp(a_1 x_1 + \cdots + a_n x_n)$, where a_1, ..., a_n, and p are constants. Find the partial elasticities of z with respect to x_1, ..., x_n.

4. Find the elasticity of z with respect to t for the following:
   a. $z = x^{20} y^{30}$, $x = t + 1$ and $y = (t + 1)^2$
   b. $z = x^2 + y^2$, $x = \ln t$ and $y = e^{-t} t^2$

5. If $y/x = \ln(xy)$, find the elasticity of y with respect to x.

6. The following system of equations defines y and z as differentiable functions of x:

$$z = e^{ax+by}, \qquad x^a y^b z^c = 1$$

where a, b, and c are positive constants. Find the elasticities of y and z with respect to x.

7. **a.** Find the marginal rate of substitution between y and x for

$$F(x, y) = x^a + y^a \qquad (a \text{ is a constant} \neq 0 \text{ and } 1)$$

   b. Compute the elasticity of substitution between y and x.

8. J. W. Kendrick and R. Sato have studied the production function

$$Y = A_0 e^{0.021t} \frac{KL}{(aL^{2/3} + bK^{2/3})^{3/2}}$$

where A_0, a, and b are positive constants. Find the elasticity of substitution σ_{KL} between K and L.

Harder Problems

9. M. Brown and J. S. De Cani in a paper on technical progress and income distribution use the production function

$$F(K, N) = \gamma_1 \left(\frac{N^\alpha K^\alpha}{N^\alpha + \gamma_2 K^\alpha} \right)^{v/\alpha}$$

where α, v, γ_1, and γ_2 are positive constants. Compute σ_{KN}.

10. The elasticity of substitution defined in [16.17] can be expressed in terms of the partial derivatives of the function F as:

$$\sigma_{yx} = \frac{-F_1' F_2'(x F_1' + y F_2')}{xy\left[(F_2')^2 F_{11}'' - 2F_1' F_2' F_{12}'' + (F_1')^2 F_{22}''\right]}$$

Use this formula to derive the result in Example 16.19.

11. Consider the function $F(K, L) = A\left(aK^{-\varrho} + bL^{-\varrho}\right)^{-1/\varrho}$ for the case $b = 1 - a$. Apply l'Hôpital's rule to $z = \ln[F(K, L)/A]$ in order to show that, as $\varrho \to 0$, so the CES-function $A\left[aK^{-\varrho} + (1-a)L^{-\varrho}\right]^{-1/\varrho}$ tends to the Cobb–Douglas function $AK^a L^{1-a}$.

16.5 Homogeneous Functions of Two Variables

One class of especially important functions in economics consists of the homogeneous functions. The function f of two variables x and y defined in a domain D is said to be **homogeneous of degree** k if, for all (x, y) in D,

$$f(tx, ty) = t^k f(x, y) \qquad \text{for all } t > 0 \qquad\qquad [16.18]$$

Multiplication of both variables by a positive factor t will thus multiply the value of the function by the factor t^k. (In this section, it is always to be understood that, if (x, y) is in D, then (tx, ty) must be in D for all $t > 0$.)

The degree of homogeneity of a function can be an arbitrary number—positive, zero, or negative. Earlier we determined the homogeneity of several particular functions. For instance, we found in Example 15.4 of Section 15.1 that

$$F(S, E) = 2.26 S^{0.44} E^{0.48} \quad \text{is homogeneous of degree } 0.44 + 0.48 = 0.92$$

and more generally that the Cobb–Douglas function

$$F(x, y) = A x^a y^b \quad \text{is homogeneous of degree } a + b$$

Example 16.21

Show that the following function, which is defined for all x and y, is homogeneous of degree 3:

$$f(x, y) = 3x^2 y - y^3$$

Solution   If we replace x by tx and y by ty in the formula for $f(x, y)$, we obtain

$$f(tx, ty) = 3(tx)^2(ty) - (ty)^3 = 3t^2 x^2 ty - t^3 y^3 = t^3(3x^2 y - y^3)$$
$$= t^3 f(x, y)$$

This confirms that f is homogeneous of degree 3. If we let $t = 2$, then $f(2x, 2y) = 2^3 f(x, y) = 8 f(x, y)$. After doubling x and y, the value of this function increases by a factor of 8.

Note that the sum of the exponents in each term in the polynomial in Example 16.21 is equal to 3. In general, a polynomial is homogeneous of degree k if and only if the sum of the exponents in each term is k. Other types of polynomial, such as $f(x, y) = x^3 + xy$, are not homogeneous of any degree. (See Problem 5.)

Let us mention some important properties of homogeneous functions of two variables that are of interest in economic applications. The first is **Euler's theorem,** which says that

$$f(x, y) \text{ is homogeneous of degree } k \iff x\frac{\partial f}{\partial x} + y\frac{\partial f}{\partial y} = kf(x, y) \qquad [16.19]$$

It is easy to demonstrate that when f is homogeneous of degree k, then the right-hand side of [16.19] is true. For differentiating each side of [16.18] w.r.t. t, using the chain rule to differentiate the left-hand side, gives

$$xf_1'(tx, ty) + yf_2'(tx, ty) = kt^{k-1}f(x, y)$$

Putting $t = 1$ gives $xf_1'(x, y) + yf_2'(x, y) = kf(x, y)$ immediately. Theorem 16.1 in the next section also proves the converse, and considers the case of n variables.

Euler's theorem shows that a function $z = f(x, y)$ is homogeneous of degree k iff the expression $xz_x' + yz_y'$ is equal to kz. For example, Problem 5 of Section 15.3 asked you to prove that if $z = (ax + by)^2$, then $xz_x' + yz_y' = 2z$; from [16.19], it follows that z is homogeneous of degree 2 as a function of x and y. Definition [16.18] confirms this.

We note three other interesting properties of a function $f(x, y)$ that is homogeneous of degree k:

$$f_1'(x, y) \text{ and } f_2'(x, y) \text{ are both homogeneous of degree } k - 1 \qquad [16.20]$$

$$f(x, y) = x^k f(1, y/x) = y^k f(x/y, 1) \qquad (\text{for } x > 0, y > 0) \qquad [16.21]$$

$$x^2 f_{11}''(x, y) + 2xy f_{12}''(x, y) + y^2 f_{22}''(x, y) = k(k - 1)f(x, y) \qquad [16.22]$$

To prove [16.20], keep t and y constant and differentiate Equation [16.18] partially w.r.t. x. Then $tf_1'(tx, ty) = t^k f_1'(x, y)$, so $f_1'(tx, ty) = t^{k-1}f_1'(x, y)$, thus showing that $f_1'(x, y)$ is homogeneous of degree $k - 1$. A corresponding argument shows that $f_2'(x, y)$ is homogeneous of degree $k - 1$.

We can prove the two equalities in [16.21] by replacing t in [16.18] by $1/x$ and by $1/y$, respectively.

Finally, to show [16.22] (assuming that $f(x, y)$ is a C^2 function), we note first that because $f_1'(x, y)$ and $f_2'(x, y)$ are both homogeneous of degree $k - 1$, Euler's theorem can be applied to f_1' and f_2'. It implies that

$$\begin{aligned} xf_{11}''(x, y) + yf_{12}''(x, y) &= (k - 1)f_1'(x, y) \\ xf_{21}''(x, y) + yf_{22}''(x, y) &= (k - 1)f_2'(x, y) \end{aligned} \qquad [*]$$

Let us now multiply the first of these equations by x, the second by y, and then add. Because f is a c^2 function $f''_{12} = f''_{21}$, so the result is

$$x^2 f''_{11}(x, y) + 2xy f''_{12}(x, y) + y^2 f''_{22}(x, y) = (k - 1)[x f'_1(x, y) + y f'_2(x, y)]$$

According to Euler's theorem, however, $x f'_1(x, y) + y f'_2(x, y) = k f(x, y)$. So [16.22] is verified.

Example 16.22

Check [16.19] to [16.22] for $f(x, y) = 3x^2 y - y^3$.

Solution   We find

$$f'_1(x, y) = 6xy \qquad \text{and} \qquad f'_2(x, y) = 3x^2 - 3y^2 \qquad [1]$$

Hence,

$$x f'_1(x, y) + y f'_2(x, y) = 6x^2 y + 3x^2 y - 3y^3 = 3(3x^2 y - y^3)$$
$$= 3f(x, y)$$

Example 16.21 showed that f is homogeneous of degree 3, so this confirms [16.19].

From [1], both f'_1 and f'_2 are homogeneous of degree 2, which confirms [16.20]. As for [16.21], in this case it takes the form

$$3x^2 y - y^3 = x^3 [3(y/x) - (y/x)^3] = y^3 [3(x/y)^2 - 1]$$

Finally, to show [16.22], first compute the second-order partial derivatives:

$$f''_{11}(x, y) = 6y, \qquad f''_{12}(x, y) = 6x, \qquad f''_{22}(x, y) = -6y$$

Hence,

$$x^2 f''_{11}(x, y) + 2xy f''_{12}(x, y) + y^2 f''_{22}(x, y) = 6x^2 y + 12x^2 y - 6y^3$$
$$= 6(3x^2 y - y^3) = 3 \cdot 2 f(x, y)$$

which confirms [16.22] as well.

Geometric Aspects of Homogeneous Functions

Homogeneous functions in two variables have some interesting geometric properties. Let $f(x, y)$ be homogeneous of degree k. Consider a ray in the xy-plane from the origin $(0, 0)$ through the point $(x_0, y_0) \neq (0, 0)$. An arbitrary point on this ray is of the form (tx_0, ty_0) for some positive number t. If we let $f(x_0, y_0) = c$, then $f(tx_0, ty_0) = t^k f(x_0, y_0) = t^k c$. Above any ray in the xy-plane through a point (x_0, y_0), the relevant portion of the graph of f therefore consists of the

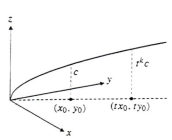

FIGURE 16.8

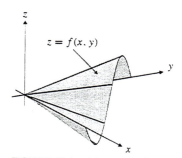

FIGURE 16.9 *f* **is homogeneous of degree 1.**

curve $z = t^k c$, where t measures the distance along the ray from the origin, and $c = f(x_0, y_0)$. A function that is homogeneous of degree k is therefore completely determined if its value is known at one point on each ray through the origin. (See Fig. 16.8.) In particular, let $k = 1$ so that $f(x, y)$ is homogeneous of degree 1. The curve $z = t^k c$ lying vertically above each relevant ray through the origin is then the straight line $z = tc$. Because of this, it is often said that *the graph of a homogeneous function of degree 1 is generated by straight lines through the origin.* Figure 16.9 illustrates this.

We have seen how it is often convenient to consider the level curves of a function $f(x, y)$ of two variables instead of its graph. What can we say about the level curves of a function if the function is homogeneous? It turns out that *for a homogeneous function, even if only one of its level curves is known, then so are all its other level curves.*

To see this, consider a function $f(x, y)$ that is homogeneous of degree k, and let $f(x, y) = c$ be one of its level curves, as illustrated in Fig. 16.10. We now explain how to construct the level curve through an arbitrary point A not lying on $f(x, y) = c$: First, draw the ray through the origin and the point A. This ray intersects the level curve $f(x, y) = c$ at a point (x_1, y_1). The coordinates of A will then be of the form (tx_1, ty_1) for some value of t. (In the figure, $t \approx 2$.)

FIGURE 16.10

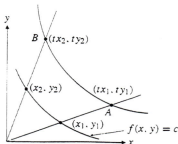

In order to construct a new point on the same level curve as A, draw a new ray through the origin. This ray intersects the original level curve $f(x, y) = c$ at (x_2, y_2). Now use the value of t found earlier to determine the new point B with coordinates (tx_2, ty_2). This new point B is on the same level curve as A because $f(tx_2, ty_2) = t^k f(x_2, y_2) = t^k c = t^k f(x_1, y_1) = f(tx_1, ty_1)$. By repeating this construction for different rays through the origin that intersect the level curve $f(x, y) = c$, we can find as many points as we wish on the new level curve.

The foregoing argument shows that if $f(x, y)$ is homogeneous, then the whole form of the function is determined by any one of its level curves and by the degree of homogeneity of the function. The shape of each level curve of a homogeneous function is often determined by specifying its elasticity of substitution, as defined in [16.17].

Problems

1. Show that $f(x, y) = x^4 + x^2 y^2$ is homogeneous of degree 4 by using [16.18].

2. Find the degree of homogeneity of $x(p, r) = Ap^{-1.5} r^{2.08}$.

3. Show that $f(x, y) = xy^2 + x^3$ is homogeneous of degree 3. Verify that the four properties [16.19] to [16.22] all hold.

4. See whether the function $f(x, y) = xy/(x^2 + y^2)$ is homogeneous, and check Euler's theorem if it is.

5. Show that $f(x, y) = x^3 + xy$ is not homogeneous of any degree. (*Hint:* Let $x = y = 1$. Apply [16.18] with $t = 2$ and $t = 4$ to get a contradiction.)

6. If $g(x, y)$ is homogeneous of degree 1, show that $f(x, y) = a \ln[g(x, y)/x]$ is homogeneous of degree 0.

7. Use [*] in the proof of [16.22] to show that if $f(x, y)$ is homogeneous of degree 1 for $x > 0$ and $y > 0$, then $f_{11}''(x, y) f_{22}''(x, y) - [f_{12}''(x, y)]^2 \equiv 0$.

8. If F is a function of one variable that is homogeneous of degree $k \neq 0$, and if F^{-1} exists, prove that F^{-1} is homogeneous of degree $1/k$. Test the result by applying it to $F(x) = \sqrt{x}$.

16.6 General Homogeneous and Homothetic Functions

Suppose that f is a function of n variables defined in a domain D. Suppose that whenever $(x_1, x_2, \ldots, x_n) \in D$ and $t > 0$, then $(tx_1, tx_2, \ldots, tx_n)$ also lies in D. (A set D with this property is called a **cone**.) We say that f is **homogeneous of degree k** on D if

$$f(tx_1, tx_2, \ldots, tx_n) = t^k f(x_1, x_2, \ldots, x_n) \qquad \text{(for all } t > 0) \qquad [16.23]$$

The constant k can be any number—positive, zero, or negative.

Example 16.23

Test the homogeneity of

$$f(x_1, x_2, x_3, x_4) = \frac{x_1 + 2x_2 + 3x_3 + 4x_4}{x_1^2 + x_2^2 + x_3^2 + x_4^2}$$

Solution   Here f is homogeneous of degree -1 because

$$f(tx_1, tx_2, tx_3, tx_4) = \frac{tx_1 + 2tx_2 + 3tx_3 + 4tx_4}{(tx_1)^2 + (tx_2)^2 + (tx_3)^2 + (tx_4)^2}$$

$$= \frac{t(x_1 + 2x_2 + 3x_3 + 4x_4)}{t^2(x_1^2 + x_2^2 + x_3^2 + x_4^2)} = t^{-1} f(x_1, x_2, x_3, x_4)$$

Euler's theorem can be generalized to functions of n variables:

Theorem 16.1   (Euler's Theorem)   Suppose f is a function of n variables with continuous partial derivatives in an open domain D, where $t > 0$ and $(x_1, x_2, \ldots, x_n) \in D$ imply $(tx_1, tx_2, \ldots, tx_n) \in D$. Then f is homogeneous of degree k in D if and only if the following equation holds for all $(x_1, x_2, \ldots, x_n) \in D$:

$$\sum_{i=1}^{n} x_i f_i'(x_1, x_2, \ldots, x_n) = kf(x_1, x_2, \ldots, x_n) \qquad [16.24]$$

Proof   Suppose f is homogeneous of degree k so [16.23] holds. Differentiating this equation with respect to t (with $(x_1, x_2, \ldots, x_n)$ fixed) yields

$$\sum_{i=1}^{n} x_i f_i'(tx_1, tx_2, \ldots, tx_n) = kt^{k-1} f(x_1, x_2, \ldots, x_n)$$

Setting $t = 1$ gives [16.24] immediately.

To prove the converse, assume that [16.24] is valid for all $\mathbf{x} = (x_1, x_2, \ldots, x_n)$ in D. Keep $\mathbf{x}$ fixed and define the function g for all $t > 0$ by

$$g(t) = t^{-k} f(tx_1, tx_2, \ldots, tx_n) - f(x_1, x_2, \ldots, x_n) \qquad [1]$$

Then differentiation with respect to t gives

$$g'(t) = -kt^{-k-1} f(tx_1, tx_2, \ldots, tx_n) + t^{-k} \sum_{i=1}^{n} x_i f_i'(tx_1, tx_2, \ldots, tx_n) \qquad [2]$$

Because $(tx_1, tx_2, \ldots, tx_n)$ lies in D, [16.24] must also be valid when each x_i is replaced by tx_i. Therefore,

$$\sum_{i=1}^{n} (tx_i) f_i'(tx_1, tx_2, \ldots, tx_n) = kf(tx_1, tx_2, \ldots, tx_n)$$

Applying this to the last term of [2] implies that, for all $t > 0$,

$$g'(t) = -kt^{-k-1} f(tx_1, tx_2, \ldots, tx_n) + t^{-k-1} kf(tx_1, tx_2, \ldots, tx_n) = 0$$

It follows that $g(t)$ must be a constant C. Obviously, $g(1) = 0$, so $C = 0$, implying that $g(t) \equiv 0$. According to the definition of g in [1], this proves that

$$f(tx_1, tx_2, \ldots, tx_n) = t^k f(x_1, x_2, \ldots, x_n)$$

Thus, f is indeed homogeneous of degree k.

The results in [16.20] to [16.22] can also be generalized to functions of n variables. The proofs are similar to those in Section 16.5, so they can be safely left to the reader.

Thus, if $f(x_1, \ldots, x_n)$ is homogeneous of degree k, then (with suitable assumptions on f):

$$f_i'(x_1, \ldots, x_n) \text{ is homogeneous of degree } k - 1, \qquad i = 1, \ldots, n \qquad [16.25]$$

$$f(x_1, \ldots, x_n) = (x_1)^k f(1, x_2/x_1, \ldots, x_n/x_1)$$

$$\vdots \qquad\qquad [16.26]$$

$$= (x_n)^k f(x_1/x_n, \ldots, x_{n-1}/x_n, 1)$$

provided that $x_1, x_2, \ldots, x_n > 0$.

$$\sum_{i=1}^{n} \sum_{j=1}^{n} x_i x_j f_{ij}''(x_1, x_2, \ldots, x_n) = k(k-1) f(x_1, x_2, \ldots, x_n) \qquad [16.27]$$

An interesting version of the Euler equation [16.24] is obtained by dividing each term of the equation by $f(x_1, x_2, \ldots, x_n)$, provided this number is not 0. Recalling the definition [16.14] of partial elasticity, we have

$$\text{El}_1(x_1, \ldots, x_n) + \text{El}_2(x_1, \ldots, x_n) + \cdots + \text{El}_n(x_1, \ldots, x_n) = k \qquad [16.28]$$

Thus, the sum of the partial elasticities of a function of n variables that is homogeneous of degree k must be equal to k.

Economic Applications

Let us consider some typical examples of homogeneous functions in economics.

Example 16.24

Let $f(v_1, \ldots, v_n)$ denote the output of a production process when the input quantities are $v_1, \ldots, v_n$. It is often assumed that if all the input quantities are scaled by a factor t, then t times as much output as before is produced, so that

$$f(tv_1, \ldots, tv_n) = tf(v_1, \ldots, v_n) \qquad \text{(for all } t > 0)$$

This implies that f is homogeneous of degree 1. Production functions with this property are said to exhibit *constant returns to scale*. A production function that is homogeneous of degree $k < 1$ has *decreasing returns to scale*, whereas it has *increasing returns to scale* if $k > 1$.

The general Cobb–Douglas function $F(v_1, \ldots, v_n) = A v_1^{a_1} \cdots v_n^{a_n}$ (see [15.5] in Section 15.1) is often used as an example of a production function. As an exercise, show that it is homogeneous, and examine when it has constant/decreasing/increasing returns to scale.

Example 16.25

In a market with three commodities whose prices per unit are respectively p, q, and r, suppose that the demand for one of the commodities by a consumer with income m is given by $x(p, q, r, m)$. Suppose that the three prices and income m are all multiplied by some $t > 0$. (Imagine, for example, that the prices of all commodities rise by 10%, but that the consumer's income also rises by 10%.) Then the consumer's budget constraint $px + qy + rz \leq m$ becomes $tpx + tqy + trz \leq tm$, which is exactly the same constraint. It is therefore natural to assume that the consumer's demand remains unchanged, with

$$x(tp, tq, tr, tm) = x(p, q, r, m) \qquad [1]$$

Requiring [1] to be valid for all $t > 0$ means that the demand function x is homogeneous of degree 0. In this case, it is often said that demand is not influenced by "money illusion." A concrete example of such a function that has been used in demand ·analysis is

$$x(p, q, r, m) = \frac{mp^b}{p^{b+1} + q^{b+1} + r^{b+1}} \qquad (b \text{ is a constant})$$

This function is homogeneous of degree 0 because

$$x(tp, tq, tr, tm) = \frac{(tm)(tp)^b}{(tp)^{b+1} + (tq)^{b+1} + (tr)^{b+1}} = \frac{t^{1+b}}{t^{b+1}} x(p, q, r, m)$$
$$= x(p, q, r, m)$$

In some cases, we encounter nonhomogeneous functions of several variables that are, however, homogeneous when regarded as functions of some of the variables only, with the other variables fixed. Naturally, we say that $f(x_1, \ldots, x_n, y_1, \ldots, y_m)$ is *homogeneous of degree k in the variables* $y_1, \ldots, y_m$ (at the point $(x_1, \ldots, x_n)$) if the "partial" function g defined by $g(y_1, \ldots, y_m) = f(x_1, \ldots, x_n, y_1, \ldots, y_m)$ is homogeneous of degree k in the usual sense.

Homothetic Functions

Let f be a function of n variables $\mathbf{x} = (x_1, \ldots, x_n)$ defined in a cone K. Then f is called **homothetic** provided that

$$\mathbf{x}, \mathbf{y} \in K, \qquad f(\mathbf{x}) = f(\mathbf{y}), \quad t > 0 \implies f(t\mathbf{x}) = f(t\mathbf{y}) \qquad [16.29]$$

For instance, if f is some consumer's utility function, [16.29] requires that whenever the consumer is indifferent between the two commodity bundles $\mathbf{x}$ and $\mathbf{y}$, then she is also indifferent after they have been magnified or shrunk in the same proportion.

A homogeneous function f of any degree k is homothetic. To see this, note that if $f(\mathbf{x}) = f(\mathbf{y})$ and $t > 0$, then homogeneity implies that

$$f(t\mathbf{x}) = t^k f(\mathbf{x}) = t^k f(\mathbf{y}) = f(t\mathbf{y})$$

It is easy to prove a more general result. Define the function $F(\mathbf{x})$ by

$$F(\mathbf{x}) = H(f(\mathbf{x})), \quad \text{where} \quad \begin{cases} H \text{ is strictly increasing} \\ \text{and } f \text{ is homogeneous of degree } k \end{cases} \qquad [16.30]$$

We claim that $F(\mathbf{x})$ is homothetic. To prove this, suppose that $F(\mathbf{x}) = F(\mathbf{y})$, or equivalently, that $H(f(\mathbf{x})) = H(f(\mathbf{y}))$. Because H is strictly increasing, this implies that $f(\mathbf{x}) = f(\mathbf{y})$. Because f is homogeneous of degree k, if $t > 0$, then

$$F(t\mathbf{x}) = H(f(t\mathbf{x})) = H(t^k f(\mathbf{x})) = H(t^k f(\mathbf{y})) = H(f(t\mathbf{y})) = F(t\mathbf{y})$$

which proves that $F(\mathbf{x})$ is homothetic. Hence, any strictly increasing function of a homogeneous function is homothetic. It is actually quite common to take [16.30] as the definition of a homothetic function, usually with $k = 1$.[5]

The next example shows that not all homothetic functions are homogeneous.

---

[5] One can prove that if $f(\mathbf{x})$ is a continuous homothetic function (according to definition [16.29]) such that, for each $x_0 \in K$, $f(tx_0)$ is a strictly increasing function of t, then f can be written in the form [16.30] with $k = 1$.

Example 16.26

Define $F(x, y) = a \ln x + b \ln y = \ln(x^a y^b)$, for all $x > 0$ and $y > 0$, where a and b are any positive parameters. The $\ln$ function *is* strictly increasing, and $x^a y^b$ is homogeneous of degree $a + b$. So $F(x, y)$ is a strictly increasing function of a homogeneous function, and thus it is homothetic. But F is not homogeneous because

$$F(tx, ty) = \ln \left[(tx)^a (ty)^b \right] = \ln(t^{a+b} x^a y^b) = (a + b) \ln t + \ln(x^a y^b)$$

which cannot be written as $t^k \ln(x^a y^b)$ for any (fixed) value of k. (See also Problem 6.)

Note that this particular function F can be written as a strictly increasing function of a function that is homogeneous of any given degree k. Simply define the new function $f(x, y) = \left(x^{ka} y^{kb} \right)^{1/(a+b)}$, which is easily seen to be homogeneous of degree k. Then note that $F(x, y) = [(a + b)/k] \ln f(x, y)$.

Problems

1. Examine which of the following functions are homogeneous, and find, if possible, the degree of homogeneity:

   a. $f(x, y) = 3x + 4y$ b. $g(x, y) = 3x + 4y - 2$

   c. $h(x, y, z) = \dfrac{\sqrt{x} + \sqrt{y} + \sqrt{z}}{x + y + z}$ d. $G(x, y) = \sqrt{xy} \ln \dfrac{x^2 + y^2}{xy}$

   e. $H(x, y) = \ln x + \ln y$ f. $p(x_1, x_2, \ldots, x_n) = \displaystyle\sum_{i=1}^{n} x_i^n$

2. Examine the homogeneity of the following:

   a. $F(x_1, x_2, x_3) = \dfrac{(x_1 x_2 x_3)^2}{x_1^4 + x_2^4 + x_3^4} \left(\dfrac{1}{x_1} + \dfrac{1}{x_2} + \dfrac{1}{x_3} \right)$

   b. $G(x_1, x_2, x_3) = \left(a x_1^d + b x_2^d + c x_3^d \right)^g$

3. Examine the homogeneity of the function in Example 15.5 (b) of Section 15.1.

4. Consider $\bar{x}_A$, $\bar{x}_G$, and $\bar{x}_H$, as defined in Example 15.6 of Section 15.1. Are these homogeneous of any degree?

5. D. W. Katzner has considered a utility function $u(x_1, \ldots, x_n)$ with continuous partial derivatives that for some constant a satisfy

$$\sum_{i=1}^{n} x_i \frac{\partial u}{\partial x_i} = a \qquad \text{(for all } x_1 > 0, \ldots, x_n > 0)$$

Show that the function $v(x_1, \ldots, x_n) = u(x_1, \ldots, x_n) - a \ln(x_1 + \cdots + x_n)$ is homogeneous of degree 0. (*Hint*: Use Euler's Theorem 16.1.)

6. Prove that the function F in Example 16.26 is not homogeneous by using Euler's theorem.

7. Prove that if $F(x, y)$ is homogenous of degree 1, then the elasticity of substitution can be expressed as $\sigma_{yx} = F_1' F_2' / F F_{12}''$. (*Hint:* Use Euler's theorem [16.19], together with [∗] in the proof of [16.22], and the result in Problem 10 of Section 16.4.)

8. Suppose that $f(x_1, \ldots, x_n)$ and $g(x_1, \ldots, x_n)$ are homogeneous of degree r and s, respectively. Examine whether the following functions $h(x_1, \ldots, x_n)$ are homogeneous. Determine the degree of homogeneity in each case.
   - **a.** $h(x_1, x_2, \ldots, x_n) = f(x_1^m, x_2^m, \ldots, x_n^m)$
   - **b.** $h(x_1, x_2, \ldots, x_n) = \left[g(x_1, x_2, \ldots, x_n) \right]^p$
   - **c.** $h = f + g$ **d.** $h = f \cdot g$ **e.** $h = f/g$

9. Show that no generalization of the concept of a homogeneous function emerges if one replaces t^k in [16.23] by an arbitrary function $g(t)$. (*Hint:* Differentiate the new [16.23] with respect to t, and let $t = 1$. Then use Euler's theorem.)

16.7 More on Implicit Differentiation

Section 16.3 explained how to differentiate functions defined implicitly, concentrating on the case with only two variables. More general cases are now discussed.

Consider the equation $F(x, y, z) = c$, where c is a constant. In general, this equation determines a surface in three-dimensional space consisting of all the triples (x, y, z) that satisfy the equation. This is called the **graph** of the equation. Suppose that $z = f(x, y)$ defines a function that, for all (x, y) in some domain A, satisfies the equation $F(x, y, z) = c$. Then

$$F\big(x, y, f(x, y)\big) = c \qquad \text{for all } (x, y) \in A$$

Suppose F and f are differentiable. Because the function g defined by $g(x, y) = F\big(x, y, f(x, y)\big)$ is equal to the constant c for all $(x, y) \in A$, the partial derivatives g_x' and g_y' must both be 0. However, $g(x, y)$ is a composite function of x and y whose partial derivatives can be found by using the chain rule [16.6] in Section 16.2. Therefore,

$$g_x' = F_x' \cdot 1 + F_z' \cdot z_x' = 0, \qquad g_y' = F_y' \cdot 1 + F_z' \cdot z_y' = 0$$

This implies the following expressions for the partial derivatives of $z = f(x, y)$:

$$F(x, y, z) = c \implies z_x' = -\frac{F_x'}{F_z'}, \quad z_y' = -\frac{F_y'}{F_z'} \qquad (F_z' \neq 0) \qquad [16.31]$$

Using [16.31] allows formulas for z'_x and z'_y to be found even if it is impossible to solve the equation $F(x, y, z) = c$ explicitly for z as a function of x and y.

Example 16.27

The equation

$$x - 2y - 3z + z^2 = -2 \qquad [1]$$

defines z as a twice differentiable function of x and y about the point $(x, y, z) = (0, 0, 2)$. Compute z'_x and z'_y, and then z''_{xx}, z''_{xy}, and z''_{yy}. Find also the numerical values of all these partial derivatives at $(0, 0)$.

Solution   Let $F(x, y, z) = x - 2y - 3z + z^2$ and $c = -2$. Then

$$F'_x = 1, \qquad F'_y = -2, \qquad F'_z = 2z - 3$$

Formula [16.31] cannot be applied when $F'_z = 0$, so we assume that $z \neq 3/2$. Then [16.31] gives

$$z'_x = -\frac{1}{2z - 3}, \qquad z'_y = -\frac{-2}{2z - 3} = \frac{2}{2z - 3} \qquad [2]$$

For $x = 0$, $y = 0$, and $z = 2$ in particular, we obtain $z'_x = -1$ and $z'_y = 2$.

We find z''_{xx} by differentiating the expression for z'_x partially with respect to x. Keeping in mind that z is a function of x and y, we get

$$z''_{xx} = \frac{\partial}{\partial x}\left(-\frac{1}{2z - 3}\right) = \frac{\partial}{\partial x}\left[-(2z - 3)^{-1}\right] = (2z - 3)^{-2}2z'_x$$

Using the expression for z'_x from [2], we have

$$z''_{xx} = \frac{-2}{(2z - 3)^3}$$

Correspondingly, we have

$$z''_{xy} = \frac{\partial}{\partial y}z'_x = \frac{\partial}{\partial y}\left[-(2z - 3)^{-1}\right] = (2z - 3)^{-2}2z'_y = \frac{4}{(2z - 3)^3}$$

and

$$z''_{yy} = \frac{\partial}{\partial y}z'_y = \frac{\partial}{\partial y}\left[2(2z - 3)^{-1}\right] = -2(2z - 3)^{-2}2z'_y = \frac{-8}{(2z - 3)^3}$$

For $x = y = 0$ and $z = 2$, we get $z''_{xx} = -2$, $z''_{xy} = 4$, and $z''_{yy} = -8$.

The General Case

The foregoing can be extended to any number of variables. Suppose z is defined implicitly as a differentiable function of the n variables $x_1, \ldots, x_n$ by the equation

$$F(x_1, x_2, \ldots, x_n, z) = c \qquad (c \text{ is a constant}) \qquad \text{[16.32]}$$

The proof of the following result is a direct extension of the argument we gave for [16.31] and so is left to the reader:

$$\frac{\partial z}{\partial x_i} = -\frac{\partial F/\partial x_i}{\partial F/\partial z}, \qquad (i = 1, 2, \ldots, n) \qquad \text{[16.33]}$$

assuming that $\partial F/\partial z \neq 0$.

Problems

1. Find $\partial z/\partial x$ for the following:

   a. $3x + y - z = 0$ **b.** $xyz + xz^3 - xy^2z^5 = 1$ **c.** $e^{xyz} = xyz$

2. Compute z'_x, z'_y, and z''_{xy} when $x^3 + y^3 + z^3 - 3z = 0$.

3. The equation $x^y + y^z + z^x = k$, where k is a positive constant, defines z as a function of x and y, for $x > 0$ and $y > 0$. Find the partial derivatives of z with respect to x and y.

4. Let $D = f(r, P)$ denote the demand for an agricultural commodity when the price is P and r is the producers' total advertising expenditure. Let supply be given by $S = g(w, P)$, where w is an index for how favorable the weather has been. Assume $g'_w(w, P) > 0$. Equilibrium now requires $f(r, P) = g(w, P)$. Assume that this equation defines P implicitly as a differentiable function of r and w. Compute P'_w, and comment on the sign.

5. With appropriate requirements on the function f, prove that $z = xf(x/y)$ implies $xz'_x + yz'_y = z$.

6. Let f be a differentiable function of one variable, and let a and b be two constants. Suppose that the equation $x - az = f(y - bz)$ defines z as a differentiable function of x and y. Prove that z satisfies $az'_x + bz'_y = 1$.

16.8 Linear Approximations and Differentials

Section 5.4 discussed linear approximations to functions of one variable. Geometrically, we approximated the graph of the function by its tangent. In a similar way, linear approximations to functions of two variables come from using the tangent plane instead of the true graph of the function. According to [15.11] in Section 15.4, the equation for the tangent plane to $z = f(x, y)$ at the point $(a, b, f(a, b))$ of its graph is

$$z = f(a, b) + f_1'(a, b)(x - a) + f_2'(a, b)(y - b)$$

Hence:

The **linear approximation** to $f(x, y)$ about (a, b) is

$$f(x, y) \approx f(a, b) + f_1'(a, b)(x - a) + f_2'(a, b)(y - b)$$ [16.34]

Example 16.28

Find the linear approximation to $f(x, y) = e^{x+y}(xy - 1)$ about $(0, 0)$.

Solution   Here

$$f_1'(x, y) = e^{x+y}(xy - 1) + e^{x+y}y, \qquad f_2'(x, y) = e^{x+y}(xy - 1) + e^{x+y}x$$

so that $f(0, 0) = -1$, $f_1'(0, 0) = -1$, and $f_2'(0, 0) = -1$. Hence, [16.34] gives

$$e^{x+y}(xy - 1) \approx -1 - x - y$$

For x and y close to 0, the complicated function $z = e^{x+y}(xy - 1)$ is approximated by the simple linear function $z = -1 - x - y$.

The Differential of a Function of Two Variables

Let $z = f(x, y)$ be a differentiable function of two variables. If dx and dy are arbitrary real numbers (not necessarily small), we define the **differential** of $z = f(x, y)$ at (x, y), denoted by dz or df, so that

---

$$z = f(x, y) \implies dz = f_1'(x, y)\, dx + f_2'(x, y)\, dy$$ [16.35]

When x is changed to $x + dx$ and y is changed to $y + dy$, then the actual change in the value of the function is the **increment**

$$\Delta z = f(x + dx, y + dy) - f(x, y)$$

If dx and dy are small in absolute value, then Δz can be approximated by dz:

$$\Delta z \approx dz = f_1'(x, y)\, dx + f_2'(x, y)\, dy$$ [16.36]

Note: By using the mean-value theorem, one can prove that the difference between Δz and the differential dz can be written as

$$\Delta z - dz = \epsilon_1 \, dx + \epsilon_2 \, dy$$

where ϵ_1 and ϵ_2 are functions of dx and dy that both tend to 0 as $dx \to 0$ and $dy \to 0$. Thus, if dx and dy are both very small, the difference $\Delta z - dz$ is "very, very small."

The approximation in [16.36] can be given a geometric interpretation. The error that arises from replacing Δz by dz results from "following the tangent plane rather than the surface," as illustrated in Fig. 16.11. Here is an analytical argument. Let

$$Z - f(x, y) = f_1'(x, y)(X - x) + f_2'(x, y)(Y - y)$$

be the equation for the set of points (X, Y, Z) in the tangent plane at the point $P = (x, y, f(x, y))$. Letting $X = x + dx$ and $Y = y + dy$, we obtain

$$Z = f(x, y) + f_1'(x, y) \, dx + f_2'(x, y) \, dy = f(x, y) + dz$$

The length of the line segment QS in the figure *is*, therefore, $f(x, y) + dz$.

Example 16.29

Let $Y = F(K, L)$ be a production function with K and L as capital and labor inputs, respectively. Then F_K' and F_L' are the marginal products of capital and labor. (See Example 15.20 of Section 15.6.) If dK and dL are arbitrary increments in K and L, respectively, the *differential* of $Y = F(K, L)$ is

$$dY = F_K' \, dK + F_L' \, dL$$

FIGURE 16.11   The geometric interpretation of Δz and the differential dz.

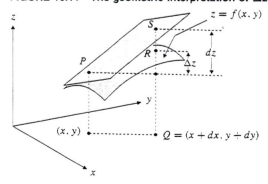

The increment $\Delta Y = F(K + dK, L + dL) - F(K, L)$ in Y can be approximated by dY provided dK and dL are small (in absolute value), and so

$$\Delta Y = F(K + dK, L + dL) - F(K, L) \approx F'_K \, dK + F'_L \, dL$$

Generally, approximation [16.36] can be used to estimate $f(x + dx, y + dy)$ when dx and dy are small and the values of $f(x, y)$, $f'_1(x, y)$, and $f'_2(x, y)$ are known:

$$f(x + dx, y + dy) \approx f(x, y) + f'_1(x, y) \, dx + f'_2(x, y) \, dy \qquad [16.37]$$

Example 16.30 .

Let $f(x, y) = xy^3 - 2x^3$. Then $f(2, 3) = 38$. Use [16.37] to estimate the value of $f(2.01, 2.98)$.

Solution　　Here $f'_1(x, y) = y^3 - 6x^2$ and $f'_2(x, y) = 3xy^2$. With $x = 2$, $y = 3$, $dx = 0.01$, and $dy = -0.02$, we have $f'_1(2, 3) = 3$ and $f'_2(2, 3) = 54$. Thus, [16.37] gives

$$f(2.01, 2.98) \approx f(2, 3) + f'_1(2, 3) \cdot 0.01 + f'_2(2, 3) \cdot (-0.02)$$

$$= 38 + 3(0.01) + 54(-0.02) = 36.95$$

The correct value to four decimal places is $f(2.01, 2.98) = 36.9506$. The change in f is -1.0494 instead of -1.05, so the error in the change is -0.0006.

If $z = f(x, y)$, we can always compute the differential $dz = df$ by first finding the partial derivatives $f'_1(x, y)$ and $f'_2(x, y)$, and then using the definition of dz. Conversely, once we know the differential of a function of two variables, then we have the partial derivatives because

$$dz = A \, dx + B \, dy \implies \frac{\partial z}{\partial x} = A \quad \text{and} \quad \frac{\partial z}{\partial y} = B$$

Note: In the literature on mathematics for economists, it is quite common to require that dx and dy be "infinitesimals," or infinitely small, in the definition of the differential $dz = f'_1(x, y) \, dx + f'_2(x, y) \, dy$. In this case, it is often claimed, Δz becomes equal to dz. Imprecise ideas of this sort have caused confusion over the centuries since Leibniz first introduced them, and they have largely been abandoned in mathematics.[6]

---

[6]In nonstandard analysis, a respectable part of modern mathematics, it is shown that a modified version of Leibniz's ideas about infinitesimals can be made precise. There even have been some interesting applications of nonstandard analysis to theoretical economics.

Rules for Differentials

Section 5.4 developed several rules for working with differentials of functions of one variable. The same rules apply to functions of several variables. Indeed, suppose that $f(x, y)$ and $g(x, y)$ are differentiable. By [16.35], their differentials are $df = f_1' dx + f_2' dy$ and $dg = g_1' dx + g_2' dy$. If $d(\ )$ denotes the differential of whatever is inside the parentheses, then the following rules are exactly the same as [5.8]:

Rules for Differentials

$$d(af + bg) = a\, df + b\, dg \qquad (a \text{ and } b \text{ are constants})$$

$$d(f \cdot g) = g\, df + f\, dg \qquad\qquad\qquad\qquad\qquad [16.38]$$

$$d\left(\frac{f}{g}\right) = \frac{g\, df - f\, dg}{g^2} \qquad (\text{when } g \neq 0)$$

These rules are also quite easy to prove. For example, consider the product rule applied to the function $f \cdot g$ defined by $(f \cdot g)(x, y) = f(x, y) \cdot g(x, y)$. We have

$$d(f \cdot g) = \frac{\partial}{\partial x}\left[f(x, y) \cdot g(x, y)\right] dx + \frac{\partial}{\partial y}\left[f(x, y) \cdot g(x, y)\right] dy$$

$$= (f_x' \cdot g + f \cdot g_x')\, dx + (f_y' \cdot g + f \cdot g_y')\, dy$$

$$= g(f_x' dx + f_y' dy) + f(g_x' dx + g_y' dy) = g \cdot df + f \cdot dg$$

There is also a chain rule for differentials. Suppose that $z = F(x, y) = g\big(f(x, y)\big)$, where g is a differentiable function of one variable. Then

$$dz = F_x' dx + F_y' dy = g'\big(f(x, y)\big) f_x' dx + g'\big(f(x, y)\big) f_y' dy$$

$$= g'\big(f(x, y)\big)(f_x' dx + f_y' dy) = g'\big(f(x, y)\big)\, df$$

because $F_x' = g' f_x'$, $F_y' = g' f_y'$, and $df = f_x' dx + f_y' dy$. Briefly formulated:

$$z = g\big(f(x, y)\big) \implies dz = g'\big(f(x, y)\big)\, df \qquad\qquad [16.39]$$

Example 16.31

Find an expression for dz in terms of dx and dy for the following:

(a) $z = Ax^a + By^b$

(b) $z = e^{xu}$ with $u = u(x, y)$

(c) $z = \ln(x^2 + y)$

Solution

(a) $dz = A\,d(x^a) + B\,d(y^b) = Aax^{a-1}\,dx + Bby^{b-1}\,dy$

(b) $dz = e^{xu}\,d(xu) = e^{xu}(x\,du + u\,dx)$

$$= e^{xu}\big\{x\big[u_1'(x, y)\,dx + u_2'(x, y)\,dy\big] + u\,dx\big\}$$

$$= e^{xu}\big\{\big[xu_1'(x, y) + u\big]\,dx + xu_2'(x, y)\,dy\big\}$$

(c) $dz = d\ln(x^2 + y) = \dfrac{d(x^2 + y)}{x^2 + y} = \dfrac{2x\,dx + dy}{x^2 + y}$

Invariance of the Differential

Suppose that

$$z = F(x, y), \qquad x = f(t, s), \qquad y = g(t, s) \tag{1}$$

where F, f, and g are all differentiable functions. Thus, z is a composite function of t and s. Suppose that t and s are changed by dt and ds, respectively. The differential of z, regarded as a function of t and s, is then

$$dz = z_t'\,dt + z_s'\,ds \tag{2}$$

Using the expressions for z_t' and z_s' in the chain rule [16.4], of Section 16.2 gives

$$dz = \big[F_1'(x, y)x_t' + F_2'(x, y)y_t'\big]\,dt + \big[F_1'(x, y)x_s' + F_2'(x, y)y_s'\big]\,ds$$

$$= F_1'(x, y)(x_t'\,dt + x_s'\,ds) + F_2'(x, y)(y_t'\,dt + y_s'\,ds) \tag{3}$$

$$= F_1'(x, y)\,dx + F_2'(x, y)\,dy$$

where dx and dy denote the differentials of $x = f(t, s)$ and $y = g(t, s)$, respectively, as functions of t and s. Note that the expression for dz in [3] is precisely the definition of the differential of $z = F(x, y)$ when x and y are changed by dx and dy, respectively. *Thus, the differential of z has the same form whether x and y are free variables, or whether they depend on other variables t and s.* This property is referred to as the **invariance** of the differential.

The Differential of a Function of n Variables

The differential of a function $z = f(x_1, x_2, \ldots, x_n)$ of n variables is defined in the obvious way as

$$dz = df = f_1'\,dx_1 + f_2'\,dx_2 + \cdots + f_n'\,dx_n \tag{16.40}$$

If the absolute values of $dx_1, \ldots, dx_n$ are all small, then again $\Delta z \approx dz$, where Δz is the actual increment of z when $(x_1, \ldots, x_n)$ is changed to $(x_1+dx_1, \ldots, x_n+dx_n)$.

The rules for differentials in [16.38] are valid for functions of n variables, and there is also a general rule for invariance of the differential: *The differential of $z = F(x_1, \ldots, x_n)$ has the same form whether $x_1, \ldots, x_n$ are free variables or depend on other, basic variables.* The proofs are easy extensions of those for two variables.

Example 16.32

Compute dz when $z = A x_1^{a_1} x_2^{a_2} \cdots x_n^{a_n}$, where $x_1 > 0$, $x_2 > 0$, $\ldots$, $x_n > 0$, and $A, a_1, a_2, \ldots, a_n$ are all constants with A positive. (*Hint:* First, take the natural logarithm of each side.)

Solution   Taking the logarithm of each side yields

$$\ln z = \ln A + a_1 \ln x_1 + a_2 \ln x_2 + \cdots + a_n \ln x_n$$

Hence,

$$\frac{1}{z} dz = a_1 \frac{1}{x_1} dx_1 + a_2 \frac{1}{x_2} dx_2 + \cdots + a_n \frac{1}{x_n} dx_n$$

so that

$$dz = z \left(\frac{a_1}{x_1} dx_1 + \frac{a_2}{x_2} dx_2 + \cdots + \frac{a_n}{x_n} dx_n \right)$$

Problems

1. Find the linear approximation about $(0, 0)$ for the following:
   a. $f(x, y) = \sqrt{1 + x + y}$ **b.** $f(x, y) = e^x \ln(1 + y)$
   c. $f(x, y) = A(x + 1)^a (y + 1)^b$

2. Suppose that

$$g^*(\mu, \varepsilon) = \left[(1 + \mu)(1 + \varepsilon)^\alpha \right]^{1/(1-\beta)} - 1 \qquad (\alpha \text{ and } \beta \text{ are constants})$$

Show that if μ and ε are close to 0, then

$$g^*(\mu, \varepsilon) \approx \frac{1}{1 - \beta} \mu + \frac{\alpha}{1 - \beta} \varepsilon$$

3. Let $f(x, y) = 3x^2 + xy - y^2$.
   a. Compute $f(1.02, 1.99)$.
   b. Let $f(1.02, 1.99) = f(1 + 0.02, 2 - 0.01)$ and use [16.37] to find an approximate value for $f(1.02, 1.99)$. How large is the error caused by this approximation?

4. Let $f(x, y) = 3x^2 y + 2y^3$. Then $f(1, -1) = -5$. Use [16.37] to estimate the value of $f(0.98, -1.01)$. How large is the error caused by this approximation?

5. Suppose that $v(1, 0) = -1$, $v_1'(1, 0) = -4/3$, and $v_2'(1, 0) = 1/3$. Use [16.37] to find an approximate value for $v(1.01, 0.02)$

6. Determine the differential of $z = xy^2 + x^3$ by:
   a. computing $\partial z/\partial x$ and $\partial z/\partial y$ and then using the definition of dz.
   b. using the rules in [16.38].

7. Compute the differentials of the following:
   a. $z = x^3 + y^3$
   b. $z = xe^{y^2}$
   c. $z = \ln(x^2 - y^2)$

8. Compute the differentials of the following:
   a. $U = a_1 u_1^2 + \cdots + a_n u_n^2$
   b. $U = A\left(\delta_1 u_1^{-\varrho} + \cdots + \delta_n u_n^{-\varrho}\right)^{-1/\varrho}$
   where $a_1, \ldots, a_n, A, \delta_1, \ldots, \delta_n$, and ϱ are positive constants.

9. Find dz expressed in terms of dx and dy when $u = u(x, y)$ and
   a. $z = x^2 u$
   b. $z = u^2$
   c. $z = \ln(xy + yu)$

10. Find an approximate value for $T = [(2.01)^2 + (2.99)^2 + (6.02)^2]^{1/2}$ by using the approximation $\Delta T \approx dT$.

11. Find dU expressed in terms of dx and dy when $U = U(x, y)$ satisfies the equation

$$U e^U = x\sqrt{y}$$

12. a. Differentiate the equation $X = AN^\beta e^{\varrho t}$, where A, β, and ϱ are constants.
    b. Differentiate the equation $X_1 = BX^E N^{1-E}$, where B and E are constants.

Harder Problems

13. The differential dz defined in [16.40] is called the *differential of the first order*. If f has continuous partial derivatives of the second order, we define the *differential of the second order* as the differential of dz, so that

$$d^2 z = d(dz) = \sum_{j=1}^{n} \frac{\partial}{\partial x_j}\left(\sum_{i=1}^{n} f_i' \, dx_i\right) dx_j = \sum_{j=1}^{n}\sum_{i=1}^{n} f_{ij}'' \, dx_i \, dx_j$$

    a. Compute $d^2 z$ for $z = xy + y^2$.
    b. Suppose that $x = t$ and $y = t^2$. Compute dz expressed in terms of dt for the function in part (a). Compute also $d^2 z$. (This example shows that there is no rule of invariance for the second differential.)

14. Define $g(t) = f(x_1^0 + t \, dx_1, \ldots, x_n^0 + t \, dx_n)$. Use the approximation $g(1) \approx g(0) + g'(0)$ to derive a generalization of [16.37].

16.9 Systems of Equations

As remarked previously, economic models often involve systems of simultaneous equations. In this section, we see how differentials can provide an efficient way of finding the partial derivatives of functions defined implicitly by such systems.

Degrees of Freedom

Let $x_1, x_2, \ldots, x_n$ be n variables. If there are no restrictions placed on them, we say, by definition, that there are n *degrees of freedom*, because all the n variables can be freely chosen. If the variables are required to satisfy *one* equation of the form $f_1(x_1, x_2, \ldots, x_n) = 0$, then the number of degrees of freedom is, in general, reduced by 1. Whenever one further "independent" restriction is introduced, the number of degrees of freedom is again reduced by 1. In general, introducing $m < n$ independent restrictions on $x_1, x_2, \ldots, x_n$ means that the variables satisfy a system of independent equations having the form

$$f_1(x_1, x_2, \ldots, x_n) = 0$$

$$f_2(x_1, x_2, \ldots, x_n) = 0$$

$$\cdots\cdots\cdots\cdots\cdots\cdots\cdots$$

$$f_m(x_1, x_2, \ldots, x_n) = 0$$

[16.41]

Then, provided that $m < n$, the remaining number of degrees of freedom is $n - m$. The rule that emerges from these considerations is a rather rough one, especially as it is hard to explain precisely what it means for equations to be "independent." Nevertheless, the following is much used in economics and statistics:

The Counting Rule

To find the number of degrees of freedom for a system of equations, count the number of variables, n, and the number of "independent" equations, m. If $n > m$, there are $n - m$ degrees of freedom in the system. If $n < m$, there is no solution to the system.

[16.42]

This rule of counting variables and equations is used in justifying the following economic proposition: "The number of independent targets that a government can pursue cannot possibly exceed the number of available policy instruments." For example, a government seeking simultaneous low inflation, low unemployment, and stability of exchange rates needs at least three independent policy instruments.

It should be noted that the counting rule is not generally valid. For example, if 100 variables $x_1, \ldots, x_{100}$ are restricted to satisfy one equation, the rule says that the number of degrees of freedom should be 99. However, if the equation happens to be

$$x_1^2 + x_2^2 + \cdots + x_{100}^2 = 0$$

then there is only one solution, $x_1 = x_2 = \cdots = x_{100} = 0$, and so there are no degrees of freedom at all.

It is obvious that the word "independent" cannot be dropped from the statement of the counting rule. For instance, if we just repeat an equation that has appeared before, the number of degrees of freedom will certainly not be reduced.

The concept of degrees of freedom introduced earlier needs to be generalized. *A system of equations in n variables is said to have k* **degrees of freedom** *if there is a set of k variables that can be freely chosen, while the remaining n − k variables are uniquely determined once the k free variables have been assigned specific values.* Thus, the system must define $n - k$ of the variables as functions of the remaining k free variables. If the n variables are restricted to vary in a set A in R^n, we say that the system has k *degrees of freedom in A.*

In order to qualify as a system with k degrees of freedom, it suffices that there *exist* k of the variables that can be freely chosen. We do not require that *any* set of k variables can be chosen freely.

Suppose we have a *linear* system of m equations in n unknowns, $\mathbf{Ax} = \mathbf{b}$. According to Theorem 14.3 of Section 14.3, the system has a solution iff the rank of the coefficient matrix $\mathbf{A}$ is equal to the rank of the argumented matrix. In this case, the counting rule gives the correct result iff the m row vectors in $\mathbf{A}$ are linearly independent, because then the rank of $\mathbf{A}$ is equal to m. (See Theorem 14.5.) So linear independence among the row vectors of the coefficient matrix is what is needed for the counting rule to apply. The meaning of "independent" equations in the case of nonlinear equations is a bit more complicated, so we do not discuss it here.

So far, we have discussed the two cases $m < n$ and $m > n$. What about the case $m = n$, in which the number of equations is equal to the number of unknowns? Even in the simplest case of one equation in one variable, $f(x) = 0$, such an equation might have any number of solutions. Consider, for instance, the following four different single equations in one variable:

$$x^2 + 1 = 0, \qquad x - 1 = 0, \qquad (x - 1)(x - 2) \cdots (x - p) = 0, \qquad \sin x = 0$$

These have 0, 1, p, and an infinite number of solutions, respectively.

In general, a system with as many equations as unknowns is usually consistent (that is, has solutions), but it may have several solutions. These solutions are usually "separated" or "isolated" from each other, as points in R^n.

We are often interested in models with systems of equations having a unique, economically meaningful solution, because then the model purports to predict the values of particular economic variables. Based on the earlier discussion, we can at least formulate the following rough rule: *A system of equations does not, in general, have a unique solution unless there are exactly as many equations as unknowns.*

To establish the existence of a unique solution of a system involving non-linear equations is usually very difficult. So-called "fixed-point theorems" and other results from "global analysis" can sometimes be used to establish uniqueness.

Finding Partial Derivatives from Differentials

We begin with an example.

Example 16.33

Consider the system of equations

$$u^2 + v = xy$$

$$uv = -x^2 + y^2 \qquad [1]$$

(a) What has the counting rule to say about this system? Find the differentials of u and v expressed in terms of dx and dy.

(b) Find the partial derivatives of u and v with respect to x and y.

(c) $(x, y, u, v) = (1, 0, 1, -1)$ satisfies system [1]. If $x_0 = 1$ is increased by 0.01 and $y_0 = 0$ is increased by 0.02, what is (approximately) the new value of u?

Solution

(a) There are four variables and two equations, so there should be 2 degrees of freedom. Suppose we choose fixed values for x and y. Then there are two equations for determining the two remaining variables, u and v. For example, if $x = 1$ and $y = 0$, then [1] reduces to $u^2 = -v$ and $uv = -1$, from which we find $u = 1$ and $v = -1$. For other values of x and y, it is more difficult to find solutions for u and v. However, it seems reasonable to assume that system [1] defines $u = u(x, y)$ and $v = v(x, y)$ as differentiable functions of x and y, at least if the domains of the variables are suitably restricted.[7]

Because u and v are functions of x and y, so is $u^2 + v$, and it is equal to xy for all x and y. Then the differential of the left-hand side

---

[7]The implicit function theorem in the next section tells the precise story.

must be equal to the differential of the right-hand side, so $d(u^2 + v) = d(xy)$. In the same way, $d(uv) = d(-x^2 + y^2)$. Using the rules for differentials, we obtain

$$
\begin{aligned}
2u\,du + dv &= y\,dx + x\,dy \\
v\,du + u\,dv &= -2x\,dx + 2y\,dy
\end{aligned}
\qquad [2]
$$

Note that by the rule for the invariance of the differential, system [2] is valid whichever pair of variables are independent.

We want to solve system [2] for du and dv. There are two equations in the two unknowns du and dv of the form

$$
A\,du + B\,dv = C
$$

$$
D\,du + E\,dv = F
$$

where, for instance, $A = 2u$, $C = y\,dx + x\,dy$, and so on. Using Cramer's rule or otherwise, we find that

$$
du = \frac{yu + 2x}{2u^2 - v}\,dx + \frac{xu - 2y}{2u^2 - v}\,dy
\qquad [3]
$$

$$
dv = \frac{-4xu - yv}{2u^2 - v}\,dx + \frac{4uy - xv}{2u^2 - v}\,dy
\qquad [4]
$$

(b) From [3], we obtain immediately that

$$
\frac{\partial u}{\partial x} = \frac{yu + 2x}{2u^2 - v}, \qquad \frac{\partial u}{\partial y} = \frac{xu - 2y}{2u^2 - v}
$$

Also, the partial derivatives of v with respect to x and y are the coefficients of dx and dy, respectively, in [4]. In this way, we have found all the first-order partial derivatives.

(c) We use the approximation

$$
u(x + dx, y + dy) \approx u(x, y) + du
$$

Letting $x = 1$, $y = 0$, $dx = 0.01$, and $dy = 0.02$, we obtain

$$
u(1 + 0.01, 0 + 0.02) \approx u(1, 0) + u_1'(1, 0) \cdot 0.01 + u_2'(1, 0) \cdot 0.02
$$

$$
= 1 + \tfrac{2}{3} \cdot 0.01 + \tfrac{1}{3} \cdot 0.02 \approx 1 + 0.0133 = 1.0133
$$

Note that in this case, it is not easy to find the exact value of $u(1.01, 0.02)$.

Example 16.34

Consider the following macroeconomic model:

$$Y = C + I + G \tag{1}$$

$$C = f(Y - T) \tag{2}$$

$$I = h(r) \tag{3}$$

$$r = m(M) \tag{4}$$

Here Y is national income, C consumption, I investment, G public expenditure, T tax revenue, r interest rate, and M money supply. Check the number of degrees of freedom. If we assume that f, h, and m are differentiable functions with $0 < f' < 1$, $h' < 0$, and $m' < 0$, then these equations will determine Y, C, I, and r as differentiable functions of M, T, and G. Differentiate the system and express the differentials of Y, C, I, and r in terms of the differentials of M, T, and G. Find $\partial Y / \partial T$ and $\partial C / \partial T$, and comment on their signs.

Suppose $P_0 = (M_0, T_0, G_0, Y_0, C_0, I_0, r_0)$ is an initial equilibrium point for the system. If the money supply M, tax revenue T, and public expenditure G are all slightly changed, find the approximate changes in national income Y and in consumption C.

Solution   There are seven variables, Y, C, I, r, M, T, and G, and four equations. Thus, there should be 3 degrees of freedom. Differentiating the system yields

$$
\begin{aligned}
dY &= dC + dI + dG \\
dC &= f'(Y - T)(dY - dT) \\
dI &= h'(r)\, dr \\
dr &= m'(M)\, dM
\end{aligned}
\tag{5}
$$

We wish to solve this linear system for the differential changes dY, dC, dI, and dr in the endogenous variables Y, C, I, and r, expressing these in terms of the differential changes dM, dT, and dG in the exogenous policy variables M, T, and G. From the last two equations in [5], we can find dI and dr immediately.[8] In fact

$$dr = m'(M)\, dM, \qquad dI = h'(r)m'(M)\, dM \tag{6}$$

---

[8] It is *not* a good idea to use Cramer's rule to solve system [5]. which has four unknowns.

Inserting the expression for dI from [6] into the first two equations in [5] gives

$$dY - dC = h'(r)m'(M)\, dM \qquad\qquad\qquad + dG$$
$$f'(Y - T)dY - dC = \qquad\qquad\qquad f'(Y - T)\, dT \qquad [7]$$

These are two equations to determine the two unknowns dY and dC. Using Cramer's rule and simplifying notation, we have

$$dY = \frac{h'm'}{1 - f'}\, dM - \frac{f'}{1 - f'}\, dT + \frac{1}{1 - f'}\, dG$$
$$dC = \frac{f'h'm'}{1 - f'}\, dM - \frac{f'}{1 - f'}\, dT + \frac{f'}{1 - f'}\, dG \qquad [8]$$

We have now found the differentials dY, dC, dI, and dr expressed linearly in terms of the differentials dM, dT, and dG. From [8] and [6], we can at once compute the partial derivatives of Y, C, I, and r with respect to M, T, and G. For example, $\partial Y/\partial T = -f'/(1 - f')$ and $\partial r/\partial T = 0$. Note that because $0 < f' < 1$, we have $\partial Y/\partial T = -f'/(1 - f') < 0$. Thus, a small increase in the tax level (keeping M and G constant) decreases national income in this model, but not if the extra tax revenue is all spent by the government. For if $dT = dG = dx$ (and $dM = 0$), then $dY = dx$ and $dC = dI = dr = 0$.

If dM, dT, and dG are small in absolute value, then

$$\Delta Y = Y(M_0 + dM, T_0 + dT, G_0 + dG) - Y(M_0, T_0, G_0) \approx dY$$

Note that when computing dY in this case, the partial derivatives have to be evaluated at the initial equilibrium point P_0.

Problems

1. Consider the system of equations:

$$xu^3 + v = y^2$$
$$3uv - x = 4 \qquad [*]$$

   a. Differentiate the system. Solve for du and dv in terms of dx and dy.
   b. Compute u'_x and v'_x by using the results in part (a).
   c. $(x, y, u, v) = (0, 1, 4/3, 1)$ satisfies [*]. Compute u'_x and v'_x at this point.

2. Suppose that y_1 and y_2 are implicitly defined as differentiable functions of x_1 and x_2 by

$$f_1(x_1, x_2, y_1, y_2) = 3x_1 + x_2^2 - y_1 - 3y_2^3 = 0$$
$$f_2(x_1, x_2, y_1, y_2) = x_1^3 - 2x_2 + 2y_1^3 - y_2 = 0$$

Compute $\partial y_1/\partial x_1$ and $\partial y_2/\partial x_1$.

3. Suppose that the system $F(x, y, u, v) = 0$ and $G(x, y, u, v) = 0$ defines u and v as differentiable functions of x and y. Explain how to find u'_x, and find an expression for this partial derivative.

4. Compute $\partial^2 u/\partial x^2$ when u and v are defined as functions of x and y by the equations $xy + uv = 1$ and $xu + yv = 0$.

5. A version of the "IS–LM" macroeconomic model originally devised by J. R. Hicks leads to the system of equations

$$[1] \ I(r) = S(Y) \quad [2] \ aY + L(r) = M$$

where a is a parameter, and I, S, and L are given differentiable functions.[9] Suppose that the system defines Y and r implicitly as differentiable functions of a and M. Find expressions for $\partial Y/\partial M$ and $\partial r/\partial M$.

Harder Problems

6. Suppose that $F(x, y, z) = 0$ and $w = G(x, y, z)$. Prove that, with appropriate requirements on the functions F and G,

$$\left(\frac{\partial w}{\partial x}\right)_y = \left(\frac{\partial w}{\partial x}\right)_{y, z} + \left(\frac{\partial w}{\partial z}\right)_{x, y} \left(\frac{\partial z}{\partial x}\right)_y$$

(Subscripts refer to the variables that are held constant.)

7. In demand theory, we encounter systems of the form

$$U'_1(x_1, x_2) = \lambda p_1 \qquad\qquad\qquad [1]$$

$$U'_2(x_1, x_2) = \lambda p_2 \qquad\qquad\qquad [2]$$

$$p_1 x_1 + p_2 x_2 = m \qquad\qquad\qquad [3]$$

where $U(x_1, x_2)$ is a given utility function. Suppose that the system defines x_1, x_2, and λ as differentiable functions of p_1, p_2, and m. Find an expression for $\partial x_1/\partial p_1$.

16.10 The Implicit Function Theorem (Optional)

System [16.41] in the previous section is a general system of equations in which all the variables appear symmetrically. When economists deal with systems of equations, notably in comparative static analysis, the variables are usually classified

---

[9]Equation [1] is the IS equation involving the investment function I and savings function S. Equation [2], the LM equation, involves the liquidity preference function I (the demand for money) and the money supply, M. The variable Y denotes national income, and r denotes interest rate.

a priori into two types: **endogenous** variables the model is intended to explain, and **exogenous** variables that are supposed to be determined by "forces" outside the model. This classification depends on the model in question. A variable like public expenditure, for example, might be exogenous in one model, but endogenous in another.

Such models often give rise to a general system of **structural equations** having the form

$$f_1(x_1, x_2, \ldots, x_n, y_1, y_2, \ldots, y_m) = 0$$

$$f_2(x_1, x_2, \ldots, x_n, y_1, y_2, \ldots, y_m) = 0$$

$$\cdots\cdots\cdots\cdots\cdots\cdots\cdots\cdots\cdots\cdots\cdots\cdots\cdots\cdots$$

$$\qquad\qquad\qquad\qquad\qquad\qquad\qquad\qquad\qquad\qquad\text{[16.43]}$$

$$f_m(x_1, x_2, \ldots, x_n, y_1, y_2, \ldots, y_m) = 0$$

where $x_1, \ldots, x_n$ are the exogenous variables, whereas $y_1, \ldots, y_m$ are the endogenous variables. An "equilibrium" solution $(\mathbf{x}^0, \mathbf{y}^0) = (x_1^0, \ldots, x_n^0, y_1^0, \ldots, y_m^0)$ is frequently known, or else assumed to exist. This equilibrium might, for instance, represent a state in which there is equality between supply and demand for each good.

Note that if the counting rule applies, then system [16.43] with m equations in $n + m$ unknowns has $n + m - m = n$ degrees of freedom. Suppose it defines $y_1, \ldots, y_m$ as C^1 functions of $x_1, \ldots, x_n$ in a neighborhood of $(\mathbf{x}^0, \mathbf{y}^0)$. Then the system can be solved "in principle" for $y_1, \ldots, y_m$ in terms of $x_1, \ldots, x_n$ to give

$$y_1 = \varphi_1(x_1, \ldots, x_n), \ldots, y_m = \varphi_m(x_1, \ldots, x_n) \qquad\qquad \text{[16.44]}$$

In this case, [16.44] is said to be the **reduced form** of the structural equation system [16.43]. The endogenous variables have all been expressed as functions of the exogenous variables.

Now, at the initial equilibrium $(\mathbf{x}^0, \mathbf{y}^0)$, we usually have some information about system [16.43]. For instance, we might know the signs of some partial derivatives of the functions f_i. The questions that naturally arise are: (1) Under what conditions is it possible to put [16.43] into its reduced form? (2) What are the properties of the functions φ_j?

The implicit function theorem has answers to both these questions. Even though the precise statement and proof are rather complicated, its main message is easy to grasp. Note that even if the functions $f_1, \ldots, f_m$ are completely specified, it is seldom possible, except in the linear case, to express $y_1, \ldots, y_m$ as elementary functions of $x_1, \ldots, x_n$. Even in the linear case, a large matrix may have to be inverted.

Suppose that $f_1, \ldots, f_m$ are C^1 functions, and *assume* for a moment that the functions φ_j in [16.44] are also C^1. If we insert this solution into [16.43] and take the differential of each equation, we get

$$\frac{\partial f_1}{\partial x_1}dx_1 + \cdots + \frac{\partial f_1}{\partial x_n}dx_n + \frac{\partial f_1}{\partial y_1}dy_1 + \cdots + \frac{\partial f_1}{\partial y_m}dy_m = 0$$

$$\cdots\cdots\cdots\cdots\cdots\cdots\cdots\cdots\cdots\cdots\cdots\cdots\cdots\cdots\cdots\cdots\cdots\cdots\cdots \qquad [16.45]$$

$$\frac{\partial f_m}{\partial x_1}dx_1 + \cdots + \frac{\partial f_m}{\partial x_n}dx_n + \frac{\partial f_m}{\partial y_1}dy_1 + \cdots + \frac{\partial f_m}{\partial y_m}dy_m = 0$$

Moving the first n terms in each equation over to the right-hand side gives

$$\frac{\partial f_1}{\partial y_1}dy_1 + \cdots + \frac{\partial f_1}{\partial y_m}dy_m = -\frac{\partial f_1}{\partial x_1}dx_1 - \cdots - \frac{\partial f_1}{\partial x_n}dx_n$$

$$\cdots\cdots\cdots\cdots\cdots\cdots\cdots\cdots\cdots\cdots\cdots\cdots\cdots\cdots\cdots\cdots\cdots\cdots\cdots \qquad [16.46]$$

$$\frac{\partial f_m}{\partial y_1}dy_1 + \cdots + \frac{\partial f_m}{\partial y_m}dy_m = -\frac{\partial f_m}{\partial x_1}dx_1 - \cdots - \frac{\partial f_m}{\partial x_n}dx_n$$

Solving this linear system of m equations for the m unknowns $dy_1, \ldots, dy_m$ in terms of $dx_1, \ldots, dx_n$ would give us all the partials of $y_1, \ldots, y_m$ with respect to $x_1, \ldots, x_n$. In fact, the equations in [16.46] can be uniquely solved for $dy_1, \ldots, dy_m$ provided that the following **Jacobian determinant** of system [16.43] is different from 0:

$$\frac{\partial(f_1, \ldots, f_n)}{\partial(y_1, \ldots, y_m)} = \begin{vmatrix} \dfrac{\partial f_1}{\partial y_1} & \cdots & \dfrac{\partial f_1}{\partial y_m} \\ \vdots & \ddots & \vdots \\ \dfrac{\partial f_m}{\partial y_1} & \cdots & \dfrac{\partial f_m}{\partial y_m} \end{vmatrix} \qquad [16.47]$$

We *assumed* that [16.43] defines $y_1, \ldots, y_m$ as C^1 functions of $x_1, \ldots, x_n$. It turns out that *if $f_1, \ldots, f_m$ are C^1 functions and if the Jacobian determinant [16.47] is not singular at $(\mathbf{x}^0, \mathbf{y}^0)$, then [16.43] will define $y_1, \ldots, y_m$ as C^1 functions of $x_1, \ldots, x_n$ in a neighborhood of $(\mathbf{x}^0, \mathbf{y}^0)$.* In essence, this is the implicit function theorem.

Example 16.35

Consider system [1] in Example 16.33 in Section 16.9, with u and v as the endogenous variables. Here $(1, 0, 1, -1)$ is an equilibrium point and the Jacobian determinant is $2u^2 - v$. At $(1, 0, 1, -1)$, the Jacobian determinant is 2, so system [1] does define u and v as C^1 functions of x and y in a neighborhood of $(1, 0, 1, -1)$.

Problems

1. Consider the macroeconomic model

$$Y = C + I + G$$
$$C = f(Y, T, r)$$
$$I = h(Y, r)$$

where f and h are continuously differentiable, with $f_Y' > 0$, $f_T' < 0$, $f_r' < 0$, $h_Y' > 0$, $h_r' < 0$, and $f_Y' + h_Y' < 1$ (see also Example 16.34 in Section 16.9).

   a. Differentiate the system, and express dY in terms of dT, dG, and dr.

   b. What happens to Y if T increases? Or if T and G undergo equal increases?

2. Consider the following system of equations:

$$y^2 - z + u - v - w^3 = -1$$
$$-2x + y - z^2 + u + v^3 - w = -3$$
$$x^2 + z - u - v + w^3 = 3$$

The point $P = (x, y, z, u, v, w) = (1, 1, 0, -1, 0, 1)$ is a solution. Apply the implicit function theorem to prove that the system defines u, v, and w as continuously differentiable functions of x, y, and z in a neighborhood of P. Find u_x', v_x', and w_x' at P.

=17=

Multivariable Optimization

Logic merely sanctions the conquests of the intuition.
—*J. Hadamard* (1945)

Chapter 9 was concerned with optimization problems for functions of one variable. Most interesting economic optimization problems involve several variables, however. For example, a profit-maximizing firm chooses the quantities of several different inputs as well as its output. A consumer chooses to buy quantities of many different goods.

Optimization problems usually can be cast in the following mathematical form. There is an **objective function** $f(x_1, \ldots, x_n)$, a real-valued function of n variables whose value should be maximized (or minimized). For example, a firm's profits are a function of its input and output quantities. There is also a **constraint set** or **opportunity set** S that is some subset of R^n. For example, a consumer cannot buy larger quantities of different goods than is allowed by the budget constraint, given the prices that have to be paid and the wealth there is available to spend. Then the problem is to find maximum or minimum points of f in S, provided such points exist.

By specifying the set S appropriately, several different types of optimization problem can be covered. If f has an optimum at an interior point of S, we talk about the *classical case*, which is discussed in this chapter. If S is the set of all points $(x_1, \ldots, x_n)$ that satisfy a number of equations, we have the *Lagrangean problem* of maximizing (or minimizing) a function subject to equality constraints. The *general programming problem* is obtained if S consists of all points $(x_1, \ldots, x_n)$ in R^n that satisfy m constraints in the form of inequalities (including, possibly, nonnegativity conditions on $x_1, \ldots, x_n$). A typical eco-

595

nomic example of such a problem is that of allocating m scarce resources between competing divisions of a firm in order to maximize overall profit while also meeting certain requirements. Chapter 18 considers optimization problems with constraints. If the objective function and all the constraints are linear in $(x_1, \ldots, x_n)$, then we have a *linear programming problem*, which is the topic of Chapter 19.

The next section presents some basic facts concerning two-variable optimization problems. The rest of the chapter then gives a more systematic introduction to multivariable optimization.

17.1 Simple Two-Variable Optimization

Consider a function $z = f(x, y)$ defined on a set S in the xy-plane R^2. Suppose that f attains its largest value (its maximum) at an interior point (x_0, y_0) of S, as indicated in Figure 17.1. If we keep y fixed at y_0, then the function $g(x) = f(x, y_0)$ depends only on x and has its maximum at $x = x_0$. (Geometrically, if P is the highest point on the surface in Figure 17.1, then P is certainly also the highest point on the curve through P that has $y = y_0$.) From Chapter 9, we know that $g'(x_0) = 0$. But for all x, the derivative $g'(x)$ is exactly the same as the partial derivative $f_1'(x, y_0)$, so $f_1'(x_0, y_0) = 0$. In the same way, we see that (x_0, y_0) must satisfy $f_2'(x_0, y_0) = 0$, because the function $h(y) = f(x_0, y)$ has its maximum at $y = y_0$. We have therefore shown that the point (x_0, y_0) must satisfy the two equations

$$f_1'(x, y) = 0, \qquad f_2'(x, y) = 0 \qquad\qquad [17.1]$$

In general, points where both equations in [17.1] hold are called **stationary points** of f. An interior point of S that is a maximum of f must be a stationary point. A similar argument shows that an interior minimum must also satisfy [17.1].

FIGURE 17.1 The function $f(x, y)$ has maximum at (x_0, y_0), because P is the highest point on the surface. $f_1'(x_0, y_0) = f_2'(x_0, y_0) = 0$.

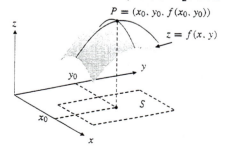

Hence:

Theorem 17.1 (First-Order Conditions; Two Variables)   A necessary condition for a differentiable function $f(x, y)$ to have a maximum or a minimum at an interior point (x_0, y_0) of its domain is that (x_0, y_0) is a stationary point of f—that is,

$$f_1'(x_0, y_0) = 0, \quad f_2'(x_0, y_0) = 0$$

In Fig. 17.2, the three points P, Q, and R are all stationary points, but only P is a maximum. (Later, we shall call Q a *local maximum*, whereas R is a *saddle point*.)

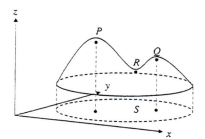

FIGURE 17.2   Point P is a maximum, Q is a local maximum, and R is a saddle point.

Example 17.1

A firm produces two different types A and B of a commodity. The daily cost of producing x units of A and y units of B is

$$C(x, y) = 0.04x^2 + 0.01xy + 0.01y^2 + 4x + 2y + 500$$

Suppose that the firm sells all its output at a price per unit of \$15 for A and \$9 for B. Find the production levels x and y that maximize profit.

Solution   Profit is $\pi(x, y) = 15x + 9y - C(x, y)$, so

$$\pi(x, y) = 15x + 9y - 0.04x^2 - 0.01xy - 0.01y^2 - 4x - 2y - 500$$

If $x > 0$ and $y > 0$ maximize profits, then (x, y) must be a stationary point of the function $\pi(x, y)$, with

$$\frac{\partial \pi}{\partial x} = 15 - 0.08x - 0.01y - 4 = 0, \qquad \frac{\partial \pi}{\partial y} = 9 - 0.01x - 0.02y - 2 = 0$$

These two linear equations in x and y give $x = 100$, $y = 300$, with $\pi(100, 300) = 1100$. (We have not yet proved that this actually is a maximum. See Problem 7 of Section 17.8.)

Example 17.2

Suppose that $Y = F(K, L)$ is a production function with K as the capital input and L as the labor input. Let the price per unit of output be p, let the cost (or rental) per unit of capital be r, and let the price (or wage rate) per unit of labor be w, where p, r, and w are all positive. The profit from producing and selling $F(K, L)$ units is then

$$\pi(K, L) = pF(K, L) - rK - wL \qquad [17.2]$$

If F is differentiable and π has a maximum with $K > 0$, $L > 0$, then by Theorem 17.1, the partials of π must vanish. So the first-order conditions (FOCs) are

$$\pi'_K(K, L) = pF'_K(K, L) - r = 0$$
$$\pi'_L(K, L) = pF'_L(K, L) - w = 0 \qquad [*]$$

Thus, a necessary condition for profit to be a maximum when $K = K^*$ and $L = L^*$ is that

$$pF'_K(K^*, L^*) = r, \qquad pF'_L(K^*, L^*) = w \qquad [17.3]$$

Suppose we think of increasing capital input from the level K^* by 1 unit. How much would be gained? We would increase production by approximately $F'_K(K^*, L^*)$ units. Because each of these units is priced at p, the gain in revenue is approximately $pF'_K(K^*, L^*)$. How much is lost by increasing capital input by one unit? We lose r, because this is the price for one unit of capital. These two must be equal. The second equation in [17.3] has a similar interpretation: Increasing labor input by one unit from level L^* will lead to the approximate gain $pF'_L(K^*, L^*)$ in revenue, whereas the extra labor cost is w. The profit-maximizing pair (K^*, L^*) thus has the property that the extra revenue from increasing each input by one unit is just offset by the extra cost.

Note that the conditions in [17.3] are necessary, but generally not sufficient for an interior maximum. Sufficient conditions for an optimum are discussed in Sections 17.4 and 17.7 to 17.9.

Example 17.3

Consider the special case of the previous model in which

$$F(K, L) = 6K^{1/2}L^{1/3}$$

with $p = 0.5$, $r = 0.1$, and $w = 1$. Find the maximum profit in this case.

Solution   The profit function is

$$\pi(K, L) = 0.5 \cdot 6K^{1/2}L^{1/3} - 0.1K - 1 \cdot L = 3K^{1/2}L^{1/3} - 0.1K - L$$

The first-order conditions are

$$\pi'_K(K, L) = 1.5 \cdot K^{-1/2}L^{1/3} - 0.1 = 0, \qquad \pi'_L(K, L) = K^{1/2}L^{-2/3} - 1 = 0$$

The first equation gives $K^{1/2} = 15L^{1/3}$. Inserting this value of $K^{1/2}$ into the second equation yields $15L^{1/3}L^{-2/3} = 1$. So $15L^{-1/3} = 1$, or $L = 15^3$. It follows that, in order to maximize profits, we have to choose

$$L = 15^3 = 3375 \qquad \text{and} \qquad K = 15^2L^{2/3} = 15^4 = 50,625$$

The value of the profit function is $\pi = 3(15^4)^{1/2}(15^3)^{1/3} - 0.1 \cdot 15^4 - 15^3 = 0.5 \cdot 15^3 = 1687.5$. (See Example 17.20 of Section 17.8 for a proof that this is indeed a maximum point.)

This section concludes with one last example showing how a transformation can be used to convert the problem into the form we have been discussing.

Example 17.4

A firm has three factories each of which produces the same item. Let x, y, and z denote the respective numbers of units that are produced at the three factories in order to cover a total order for 2000 units. Hence, $x + y + z = 2000$. The cost functions for the three factories are

$$C_1(x) = 200 + \frac{1}{100}x^2, \qquad C_2(y) = 200 + y + \frac{1}{300}y^3, \qquad C_3(z) = 200 + 10z$$

The total cost of covering the order is thus

$$C = C_1(x) + C_2(y) + C_3(z)$$

Find the values of x, y, and z that minimize C. (*Hint:* Reduce the problem to one with only two variables by solving $x + y + z = 2000$ for z.)

Solution   Solving the equation $x + y + z = 2000$ for z yields $z = 2000 - x - y$. Substituting this expression for z in the expression for C yields, after simplifying,

$$C = \frac{1}{100}x^2 - 10x + \frac{1}{300}y^3 - 9y + 20,600$$

Stationary points for C must satisfy the equations

$$\frac{\partial C}{\partial x} = \frac{1}{50}x - 10 = 0, \qquad \frac{\partial C}{\partial y} = \frac{1}{100}y^2 - 9 = 0$$

The only solution is $x = 500$ and $y = 30$, implying that $z = 1470$. The corresponding value of C is $17,920$. (In Example 17.19 of Section 17.8, we prove that this *is* a minimum.)

Problems

1. The function f defined for all (x, y) by $f(x, y) = -2x^2 - y^2 + 4x + 4y - 3$ has a maximum. Find the corresponding values of x and y.

2. The function f defined for all (x, y) by

$$f(x, y) = -2x^2 - 2xy - 2y^2 + 36x + 42y - 158$$

has a maximum point. What is it?

3. **a.** The function f defined for all (x, y) by $f(x, y) = x^2 + y^2 - 6x + 8y + 35$ has a minimum point. What is it?
   b. Show that $f(x, y)$ can be written in the form

$$f(x, y) = (x - 3)^2 + (y + 4)^2 + 10.$$

   Explain why this shows that you have really found the minimum in part (a).

4. Yearly profits (in millions of dollars) for a firm are given by

$$P(x, y) = -x^2 - y^2 + 22x + 18y - 102$$

   where x is the amount spent on research (in millions of dollars), and y is the amount spent on advertising (in millions of dollars).
   a. Find the profits when $x = 10$, $y = 8$ and when $x = 12$, $y = 10$.
   b. Find the values of x and y that maximize profits, and the corresponding profit.

5. The discriminating monopolist of Example 15.25 of Section 15.7 had the profit function

$$\pi(Q_1, Q_2) = (a_1 - \alpha)Q_1 + (a_2 - \alpha)Q_2 - b_1 Q_1^2 - b_2 Q_2^2$$

   Find the only positive values of Q_1 and Q_2 that can possibly maximize profits. Compare your results with those in Example 15.25.

6. Find the smallest value of $x^2 + y^2 + z^2$ when we require that $4x + 2y - z = 5$. (Geometric interpretation: Find the point in the plane $4x + 2y - z = 5$ that is closest to the origin.)

7. The discriminating monopsonist of Example 15.26 of Section 15.7 had the profit function

$$\pi(L_1, L_2) = (P - \alpha_1)L_1 - \beta_1 L_1^2 + (P - \alpha_2)L_2 - \beta_2 L_2^2$$

Find the only positive values of L_1 and L_2 that can possibly maximize profits. Compare your results with those in Example 15.26.

8. For the profit function discussed in Example 17.2, let $p = 1$, $r = 0.65$, $w = 1.2$, and

$$F(K, L) = 80 - (K - 3)^2 - 2(L - 6)^2 - (K - 3)(L - 6)$$

Find the values of K and L that satisfy [17.3] in this case.

9. If x, y, and z are positive numbers such that $x + 3y + 4z = 108$, find the maximum value of the product $P = xyz$. (*Hint:* Make P a function of y and z by eliminating the variable x.) Economic interpretation: xyz is the "utility" of a person from consuming x, y, and z units, respectively, of three commodities. The prices per unit of the three commodities are 1, 3, and 4; income is 108.

Harder Problems

10. Find the values of x, y, and z that maximize the function $Ax^a y^b z^c$ subject to $px + qy + rz = m$. (The constants A, a, b, c, p, q, and r are all positive, and $a + b + c \leq 1$.)

11. Find the values of x, y, and z that maximize the function $x^a + y^a + z^a$ subject to $px + qy + rz = m$. (The constants a, p, q, and r are positive, and $a < 1$.)

17.2 Maxima and Minima, with a Dash of Topology

The previous section presented some simple optimization problems for functions of two variables. The rest of this chapter extends the theory in many directions. Because most interesting economic optimization problems involve functions of many variables, not just one or two, we formulate most of the basic results for such functions.

Definition of Maximum and Minimum

Let f be a function of n variables $x_1, \ldots, x_n$ defined over a set S in R^n. Suppose that $\mathbf{c} = (c_1, \ldots, c_n)$ belongs to S and gives a value to f that is larger than or equal to the values attained by f at all other points $\mathbf{x} = (x_1, \ldots, x_n)$ of S. Thus, in symbols,

$$f(\mathbf{x}) \leq f(\mathbf{c}) \qquad \text{for all } \mathbf{x} \text{ in } S \qquad [17.4]$$

Then $\mathbf{c}$ is called a (global) **maximum point** for f in S and $f(\mathbf{c})$ is called the **maximum value**. In the same way, we define **minimum point** and **minimum value** by reversing the inequality sign in [17.4]. As collective names, we use **extreme points** and **extreme values** to indicate either maxima or minima. For the case when f is a function of two variables, geometric interpretations of these concepts were provided in the previous section.

Suppose that f is a function of n variables defined over a set S in R^n and that $f(\mathbf{x}) \leq f(\mathbf{c})$ for all $\mathbf{x}$ in S, so $\mathbf{c}$ maximizes f over S. Then $-f(\mathbf{x}) \geq -f(\mathbf{c})$ for all $\mathbf{x}$ in S. Thus, $\mathbf{c}$ maximizes f over S iff $\mathbf{c}$ minimizes $-f$ over S. We can use this simple observation to convert maximization problems to minimization problems and vice versa. (Recall the one variable illustration in Fig. 9.1.)

A Useful Result

A simple result, which is nevertheless of considerable interest in theoretical economics, is often expressed as follows: *Maximizing a function is equivalent to maximizing a (strictly) increasing transformation of that function.* For instance, suppose we want to find all pairs (x, y) that maximize $f(x, y)$ over a set S in the xy-plane. Then we can just as well try to find those (x, y) that maximize over S any one of the following alternative objective functions:

$$[1] \ af(x, y) + b \quad (a > 0) \quad [2] \ e^{f(x,y)} \quad [3] \ \ln f(x, y)$$

(In case [3], it must be true that $f(x, y) > 0$ over S.) The maximum *points* are exactly the same. But the maximum *values* are, of course, quite different. As a concrete example, the problem

$$\text{maximize } e^{x^2+2xy^2-y^3} \text{ subject to } (x, y) \in S$$

has the same solutions for x and y as the problem

$$\text{maximize } x^2 + 2xy^2 - y^3 \text{ subject to } (x, y) \in S$$

because the function $u \to e^u$ is strictly increasing. In general, it is easy to prove the following result:

Theorem 17.2   Let $f(\mathbf{x}) = f(x_1, \ldots, x_n)$ be defined over a set S in R^n and let F be a function of one variable defined over the range of f. Define g over S by

$$g(x_1, \ldots, x_n) = F\big(f(x_1, \ldots, x_n)\big) \qquad [17.5]$$

Then:

(a) If F is increasing and $\mathbf{c} = (c_1, \ldots, c_n)$ maximizes (minimizes) f over S, then $\mathbf{c}$ also maximizes (minimizes) g over S.

(b) If F is strictly increasing, then $\mathbf{c}$ maximizes (minimizes) f over S if and only if $\mathbf{c}$ maximizes (minimizes) g over S.

Proof   (For the maximization case—the argument in the minimization case is entirely similar.)

(a) Because $\mathbf{c}$ maximizes f over S, we have $f(\mathbf{x}) \leq f(\mathbf{c})$ for all $\mathbf{x}$ in S. But then $g(\mathbf{x}) = F\big(f(\mathbf{x})\big) \leq F\big(f(\mathbf{c})\big) = g(\mathbf{c})$ for all $\mathbf{x}$ in S, because F is increasing. It follows that $\mathbf{c}$ maximizes g over S.

(b) If F is also strictly increasing and $f(\mathbf{x}) > f(\mathbf{c})$, then it must be true that $g(\mathbf{x}) = F\big(f(\mathbf{x})\big) > F\big(f(\mathbf{c})\big) = g(\mathbf{c})$. So $g(\mathbf{x}) \leq g(\mathbf{c})$ for all $\mathbf{x}$ in S implies that $f(\mathbf{x}) \leq f(\mathbf{c})$ for all $\mathbf{x}$ in S.

Note: The proof of Theorem 17.2 is extremely simple. It is based only on the concepts of maximum/minimum, and of increasing/strictly increasing functions. Some people appear to distrust such simple, direct arguments and replace them by inefficient or even insufficient arguments based on "differentiating everything in sight" in order to use first- or second-order conditions. Such distrust merely makes matters unnecessarily complicated and risks introducing errors. Note that in Theorem 17.2 no continuity or differentiability assumptions are required.

Topology in the Plane

For many of the results concerning functions of one variable that were presented in Chapter 9, it was important to distinguish between different types of domain for the functions. For functions of several variables, the distinction between different types of domain is no less important. In the one-variable case, most functions were defined over intervals, and there are not many different types of interval. For functions of several variables, there are many different types of domain. Fortunately, the relevant distinctions can be made using only a few concepts from elementary topology.

We start with sets in the plane. A point (a, b) is called an **interior point** of a set S in the plane if there exists a circle centered at (a, b) such that all points inside the circle lie in S. A set is called **open** if it consists of only interior points. The point (a, b) is called a **boundary point** of a set S if *every* circle centered at (a, b) contains points inside S as well as points outside S. A boundary point of S does not necessarily lie in S. However, if S contains all its boundary points, then S is called **closed**. These concepts are illustrated in Figs. 17.3 and 17.4. Note

FIGURE 17.3

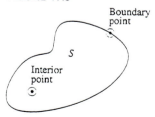

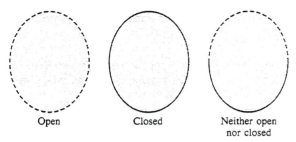

| Open | Closed | Neither open nor closed |

FIGURE 17.4

that a set that contains some but not all its boundary points, like the last of those illustrated in Fig. 17.4, is neither open nor closed. In fact, a set is closed iff its complement is open.

Figures 17.3 and 17.4 give only very loose indications of what it means for a set to be either open or closed. Of course, if a set is not even precisely defined, it is impossible to decide conclusively whether it is open or closed.

In many of the optimization problems we consider, sets are defined by one or more inequalities, and boundary points occur where one or more of these inequalities are satisfied with equality. For instance, provided that p, q, and m are positive parameters, the (budget) set of points (x, y) that satisfy the inequalities

$$px + qy \leq m, \quad x \geq 0, \quad y \geq 0 \qquad [1]$$

is closed. This set is a triangle, as shown in Figure 2.41 of Section 2.5. Its boundary consists of the three sides of the triangle. Each of the three sides corresponds to having one of the inequalities in [1] be satisfied with equality. On the other hand, the set obtained by replacing $\leq$ by $<$ and $\geq$ by $>$ is open.

In general, if $g(x, y)$ is a continuous function and c is a real number, then the three sets

$$\{(x, y) : g(x, y) \geq c\}, \qquad \{(x, y) : g(x, y) \leq c\}, \qquad \{(x, y) : g(x, y) = c\}$$

are all closed. If $\geq$ is replaced by $>$ or $\leq$ is replaced by $<$, then the corresponding sets are open.

A set is **bounded** if the whole set is contained within a sufficiently large circle. The sets in Fig. 17.4 and in Fig. 2.41 are all bounded. The set of all (x, y) satisfying

$$x \geq 1 \qquad \text{and} \qquad y \geq 0 \qquad [2]$$

is a closed, but unbounded set. (See Fig. 15.1.) The set is closed because it contains all its boundary points. How would you characterize the set in Figure 15.2? (In fact, it is neither open nor closed, but it is bounded.) A set in the plane that is both closed and bounded is often called **compact**.

Economists often have to consider sets defined in quite complicated ways. It is difficult to imagine how the presence or absence of a particular boundary point has any practical relevance. Nevertheless, the distinction is needed because of the mathematical results that can then be demonstrated.

Topology in R^n

It is very easy to generalize to R^n the topological concepts just introduced. Recall that in Section 12.4, the distance between any two n-vectors $\mathbf{a} = (a_1, \ldots, a_n)$ and $\mathbf{b} = (b_1, \ldots, b_n)$ was defined as $\|\mathbf{a} - \mathbf{b}\| = \sqrt{(a_1 - b_1)^2 + \cdots + (a_n - b_n)^2}$.

An *n-ball* centered at $\mathbf{a} = (a_1, \ldots, a_n)$ and with radius r is the set of all $\mathbf{x} = (x_1, \ldots, x_n)$ such that $\|\mathbf{x} - \mathbf{a}\| < r$. If we now replace the word "circle" by "n-ball," then the definitions above of interior point, open set, boundary point, closed set, bounded set, and compact set are all valid for sets in R^n. A **neighborhood** N of a point a is a set containing an n-ball centered at a.

If $g(\mathbf{x}) = g(x_1, \ldots, x_n)$ is a continuous function of n variables, and c is a real number, then the three sets

$$\{\mathbf{x} : g(\mathbf{x}) \geq c\}, \qquad \{\mathbf{x} : g(\mathbf{x}) \leq c\}, \qquad \{\mathbf{x} : g(\mathbf{x}) = c\}$$

are all closed. If $\geq$ is replaced by $>$ or $\leq$ is replaced by $<$, then the corresponding sets are open.

If A is an arbitrary set in R^n, we define the **interior** of A as the set of interior points of A. If A is open, the interior of A is equal to the set A itself.

Problems

1. For the following two functions, find the maximum or minimum values (or show that they do not exist) by a direct argument:

   a. $f(x, y) = (x + 1)^2 + (y - 3)^2 - 10$

   b. $f(x, y) = 3 - \sqrt{2 - (x^2 + y^2)}$

2. Prove that provided $A > 0$ and $x_1 > 0, \ldots, x > 0$, the problem

   $$\text{maximize } Ax_1^{a_1} \cdots x_n^{a_n} \qquad \text{subject to } x_1 + \ldots + x_n = 1$$

   has the same solution as the problem

   $$\text{maximize } \ln A + a_1 \ln x_1 + \cdots + a_n \ln x_n \qquad \text{subject to } x_1 + \ldots = x_n = 1$$

3. Simplify the following problem:

   $$\text{maximize } \tfrac{1}{2}\left[e^{x^2 + y^2 - 2x} - e^{-(x^2 + y^2 - 2x)} \right] \qquad \text{when } (x, y) \in S$$

4. Let $g(x, y) = F(f(x, y))$, where f and F are continuously differentiable with $F' > 0$. Prove that (x_0, y_0) is a stationary point for f iff it is a stationary point for g.

5. Give an example of a discontinuous function g of one variable such that the set $\{x : g(x) \leq 1\}$ is not closed.

Harder Problems

6. **a.** Show that the set S of all (x, y) such that $x^2 + xy + y^2 = 3$ is closed.
    b. Show that S is bounded. (*Hint:* Consider the equivalent equation $(x + y/2)^2 + 3y^2/4 = 3$. Hence, $3y^2/4 \leq 3$, so that $-2 \leq y \leq 2$. Using symmetry, show that $-2 \leq x \leq 2$.)
    c. Show that the set of all (x, y) such that $x^2 + xy - y^2 = 3$ is closed, but not bounded. (*Hint:* Any pair (x, y) with $x = \frac{1}{2}(\sqrt{5t^2 + 12} - t)$ and $y = t$ satisfies the equation. But $x \to \infty$ and $y \to \infty$ as $t \to \infty$.)

7. In each of the four cases illustrated Fig. 17.5, can there possibly be a strictly increasing function F such that $g(x) = F(f(x))$?

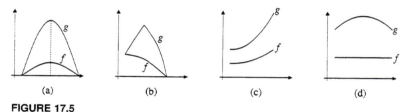

    (a)   (b)   (c)   (d)

FIGURE 17.5

17.3 The Extreme-Value Theorem and How to Use It

As with functions of one variable, it is easy to find examples of functions of several variables that do not have any maximum or minimum points. For providing sufficient conditions to ensure that extreme points do exist, however, the extreme-value theorem (Theorem 7.3 of Section 7.2) was very useful for functions of one variable. It can be directly generalized to functions of several variables.

Theorem 17.3   (Extreme-Value Theorem)   If f is a continuous function over a closed, bounded set S in R^n, then there exist both a maximum $\mathbf{c} = (c_1, \ldots, c_n)$ and a minimum point $\mathbf{d} = (d_1, \ldots, d_n)$ in S—that is, there exist $\mathbf{c}$ and $\mathbf{d}$ in S such that

$$f(\mathbf{d}) \leq f(\mathbf{x}) \leq f(\mathbf{c}) \qquad \text{for all } \mathbf{x} \text{ in } S$$

Theorem 17.3 is a *pure existence theorem*. It does not tell us *how to find* the extreme points. The proof is found in most advanced calculus books. Also, even though the conditions of the theorem are *sufficient* to ensure existence of extreme points, they are far from necessary. See Section 7.2 for our earlier warning in connection with functions of one variable.

Finding Maxima and Minima

Section 17.1 presented some simple cases where we can find the maximum and minimum points of a function of two variables by finding its stationary points. For a function of n variables, vector $\mathbf{c} = (c_1, \ldots, c_n)$ is called a **stationary point** of $f(x_1, \ldots, x_n)$ if $\mathbf{x} = \mathbf{c}$ is a solution to the n equations

$$\frac{\partial f}{\partial x_1}(\mathbf{x}) = 0, \qquad \frac{\partial f}{\partial x_2}(\mathbf{x}) = 0, \quad \ldots, \quad \frac{\partial f}{\partial x_n}(\mathbf{x}) = 0 \qquad [17.6]$$

Now Theorem 17.1 can easily be generalized to functions of n variables.

Theorem 17.4 **(Necessary First-Order Conditions)** Let f be defined in a set S in R^n and let $\mathbf{c} = (c_1, \ldots, c_n)$ be an interior point in S at which f is differentiable. A necessary condition for $\mathbf{c}$ to be a maximum or minimum point for f is that $\mathbf{c}$ is a stationary point for f—that is,

$$f_i'(\mathbf{c}) = 0 \qquad (i = 1, \ldots, n)$$

Proof Keep i ($1 \leq i \leq n$) fixed and define the function $g(x_i) = f(c_1, \ldots, c_{i-1}, x_i, c_{i+1}, \ldots, c_n)$, whose domain consists of those x_i such that $(c_1, \ldots, c_{i-1}, x_i, c_{i+1}, \ldots, c_n)$ belongs to S. If $\mathbf{c} = (c_1, \ldots, c_n)$ is a maximum (or minimum) point for f, then the function g of one variable must attain a maximum (or minimum) at $x_i = c_i$. Because $\mathbf{c}$ is an interior point of S, it follows that c_i is also an interior point in the domain of g. Hence, according to Theorem 7.4 of Section 7.2, we must have $g'(c_i) = 0$. But $g'(c_i) = f_i'(c_1, \ldots, c_n)$, and so the conclusion follows.

If $f(x_1, \ldots, x_n)$ is defined over a set S in R^n, then the maximum and minimum points (if there are any) must lie either in the interior of S or on the boundary of S. According to Theorem 17.4, if f is differentiable, then any maximum or minimum points in the interior must satisfy the first-order conditions [17.6]. Most of the functions we study are differentiable everywhere. The procedure set out in the following frame, therefore, covers many of the optimization problems we encounter.

Problem   Find the maximum and minimum values of a differentiable function $f(\mathbf{x})$ defined on a closed, bounded set S in R^n.

Solution

1. Find all stationary points of f in the interior of S.
2. Find the largest and the smallest value of $f(\mathbf{x})$ on the boundary of S. (If it is convenient to subdivide the boundary into several pieces, find the largest and the smallest value on each piece of the boundary.)
3. Compute the values of the function at all the points found in 1 and in 2.
4. The largest function value in 3 is the maximum value of f in S.
5. The smallest function value in 3 is the minimum value of f in S.

[17.7]

Let us try out this procedure on the function whose graph is depicted in Figure 17.6 below. (Because the function is not specified analytically, we are only able to give a rough geometric argument.)

In the interior of the rectangular domain S, there is only one stationary point for f, namely, (x_0, y_0), which corresponds to point P of the graph. The boundary of S consists of four straight-line segments. The point R vertically above one corner point of S represents the maximum value of f along the boundary; similarly, Q represents the minimum value of f along the boundary. The only candidates for a maximum/minimum are, therefore, the three points P, Q, and R. By comparing the values of f at these points, we see that P represents the minimum value, whereas R represents the maximum value of f in S.

The reader will be glad to hear that for most optimization problems in economics, especially those appearing in textbooks, the difficulties tackled by the

FIGURE 17.6

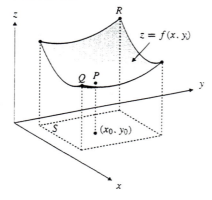

recipe do not arise. Usually, there is an interior optimum that can be found by equating the first-order partial derivatives to zero. Conditions that are sufficient for this easier approach to work are discussed later in this chapter. Nevertheless, we consider some examples to illustrate the recipe in [17.7].

Example 17.5

Find the extreme points and extreme values for $f(x, y)$ defined over S when

$$f(x, y) = x^2 + y^2 + y - 1, \qquad S = \{(x, y) : x^2 + y^2 \le 1\}$$

Solution   The set S consists of all the points on or inside the circle of radius 1 centered at the origin, as shown in Figure 17.7. The continuous function f will attain a maximum and minimum over S, by the extreme-value theorem.

According to the preceding recipe, we start by finding all the stationary points in the interior of S. These stationary points satisfy the two equations

$$f_x'(x, y) = 2x = 0, \qquad f_y'(x, y) = 2y + 1 = 0$$

So $(x, y) = (0, -1/2)$ is the only stationary point, and it is in the interior of S, with $f(0, -1/2) = -5/4$.

The boundary of S consists of the circle $x^2 + y^2 = 1$. Note that if (x, y) lies on this circle, then in particular both x and y lie in the interval $[-1, 1]$. Inserting $x^2 + y^2 = 1$ into the expression for $f(x, y)$ shows that, *along the boundary of S*, the value of f is determined by the following function of one variable:

$$g(y) = 1 + y - 1 = y \qquad (y \in [-1, 1])$$

The maximum value of g is 1 for $y = 1$, and then $x = 0$. The minimum value is -1 when $y = -1$, and then again $x = 0$.

FIGURE 17.7   The domain in Example 17.5.

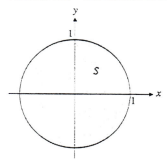

We have now found the only three possible candidates for extreme points, namely, $(0, -1/2)$, $(0, 1)$, and $(0, -1)$. But $f(0, -1/2) = -5/4$, $f(0, 1) = 1$, and $f(0, -1) = -1$. We conclude that the *maximum value* of f in S is 1, attained at $(0, 1)$, whereas the *minimum value* is $-5/4$, attained at $(0, -1/2)$.

Example 17.6

In one study of the quantities x and y of natural gas that continental Europe should import from Norway and Siberia, respectively, it was assumed that the benefits were given by $f(x, y) = 9x + 8y - 6(x + y)^2$. The term $-6(x + y)^2$ arises because the world price of natural gas rises as more is imported in total. Because of capacity constraints, x and y must satisfy $0 \leq x \leq 5$ and $0 \leq y \leq 3$. Finally, for political reasons, it was felt that imports from Norway should not provide too small a fraction of total imports at the margin, so that $x \geq 2(y - 1)$, or $-x + 2y \leq 2$. Thus, the optimization problem was cast as

$$\max \ f(x, y) = 9x + 8y - 6(x + y)^2 \ \text{subject to } 0 \leq x \leq 5, \ 0 \leq y \leq 3, \ -x + 2y \leq 2$$

Draw in the xy-plane the set S of all points satisfying the three constraints, and then solve the problem.

Solution   The set S is shown in Fig. 17.8. It is clearly closed and bounded, so the continuous function f has a maximum in S.

We look first for stationary points in the interior of S. Any such points must solve the two equations

$$\frac{\partial f}{\partial x} = 9 - 12(x + y) = 0, \qquad \frac{\partial f}{\partial y} = 8 - 12(x + y) = 0$$

Thus, $12(x + y) = 9$ and also $12(x + y) = 8$, which is impossible. Hence, there are no stationary points. The maximum value of f must therefore

FIGURE 17.8   The domain in Example 17.6.

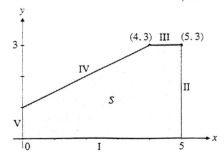

occur at the boundary, which consists of five parts. Either the maximum value occurs at one of the five corners or "extreme points" of the boundary, or else at an interior point of one of five straight "edges." The function values at the five corners are

$$f(0,0) = 0, \quad f(5,0) = -105, \quad f(5,3) = -315, \quad f(4,3) = -234, \quad f(0,1) = 2$$

We proceed to examine the behavior of f at interior points of each of the five edges, which are indicated by roman numerals in Fig. 17.8:

(I) On edge (I), $y = 0$, $x \in (0,5)$. Here the behavior of f is determined by the function $g_1(x) = f(x,0) = 9x - 6x^2$ for $x \in (0,5)$. If this function has a maximum in $(0,5)$, it must occur at a point where $g_1'(x) = 9 - 12x = 0$, and so at $x = 3/4$. We find that $g_1(3/4) = f(3/4, 0) = 27/8$.

(II) On edge (II), $x = 5$, $y \in (0,3)$. Define the function $g_2(y) = f(5,y) = 45 + 8y - 6(5+y)^2$ for $y \in (0,3)$. Here $g_2'(y) = 8 - 12(5+y) = -52 - 12y$, which is negative throughout $(0,3)$, so there are no stationary points on this edge.

(III) On edge (III), $y = 3$, $x \in (4,5)$. Define the function $g_3(x) = f(x,3) = 9x + 24 - 6(x+3)^2$ for $x \in (4,5)$. Here $g_3'(x) = 9 - 12(x+3) = -27 - 12x$, which is negative throughout $(4,5)$, so there are no stationary points on this edge either.

(IV) On edge (IV), $-x + 2y = 2$, or $y = x/2 + 1$, with $x \in (0,4)$. Define the function

$$g_4(x) = f(x, x/2 + 1) = 9x + 8(x/2 + 1) - 6(x + x/2 + 1)^2$$
$$= -27x^2/2 - 5x + 2$$

for $x \in (0,4)$. Here $g_4'(x) = -27x - 5$, which is negative in $(0,4)$, so there are no stationary points here.

(V) On edge (V), $x = 0$, $y \in (0,1)$. Define the function $g_5(y) = f(0,y) = 8y - 6y^2$. Then $g_5'(y) = 8 - 12y = 0$ at $y = 2/3$, with $g_5(2/3) = f(0, 2/3) = 8/3$.

After comparing the values of f at the five corners of the boundary and at the two points found on the edges labeled (I) and (V), we conclude that the maximum value of f is 27/8, which is achieved at $(3/4, 0)$.

Problems

1. Let $f(x, y) = 4x - 2x^2 - 2y^2$, $S = \{(x, y) : x^2 + y^2 \le 25\}$.

a. Compute $f_1'(x, y)$ and $f_2'(x, y)$, then find the only stationary point for f.

b. Find the extreme points for f over S.

2. Find the maximum and minimum points for $f(x, y)$ defined over S for the following:

   a. $f(x, y) = x^3 + y^3 - 9xy + 27$ subject to $0 \le x \le 4, 0 \le y \le 4$.

   b. $f(x, y) = x^2 + 2y^2 - x$ subject to $x^2 + y^2 \le 1$.

   c. $f(x, y) = 3 + x^3 - x^2 - y^2$ subject to $x^2 + y^2 \le 1$ and $x \ge 0$.

   d. $f(x, y) = (x-2)e^{x^2-x}(2y-1)e^{(y-2)^2}$ subject to $0 \le x \le 2, 0 \le y \le 1/2$.

3. Let the domain of the function h be the set of all (x, y) satisfying both $1 \le x \le 2$ and $0 \le y \le x - 1$, and let $h(x, y) = x^2 y(x - y - 1)$. Prove that h has global extreme points, and find them.

4. Let f be a function of two variables given by

$$f(x, y) = (x + y)e^{-(x+y^2)/4}$$

and let D be the domain consisting of the points (x, y) satisfying $x + y \ge 1$, $y \ge 0$.

   a. Draw the domain D in the xy-plane, and find the first-order partials of f.

   b. Take it for granted that f attains a maximum in the domain D. Find the maximum point and the maximum value.

Harder Problems

5. Solve the problem

$$\text{maximize } (x^3 + y^2)^{1/4} \text{ subject to } x \ge 0, \ y \ge 0, \ x + y \le k$$

where k is a positive number.

6. Consider the function f defined for all (x, y) by

$$f(x, y) = 3(x^2 + y^2)^{3/2} - 4(x^2 + y^2)^{1/2} + y$$

   a. Find the stationary points of f. (Remember that $(y^2)^{1/2} = |y|$.)

   b. Let $S = \{(x, y) : x \ge 0 \text{ and } x^2 + y^2 \le 1\}$. Explain why f must attain a maximum and a minimum over S, and find the corresponding points.

17.4 Local Extreme Points

Sometimes one is interested in studying *local* extreme points of a function. The point $\mathbf{c} = (c_1, \ldots, c_n)$ is said to be a **local maximum** point of f in S if $f(\mathbf{x}) \le f(\mathbf{c})$ for all $\mathbf{x}$ in S sufficiently close to $\mathbf{c}$. More precisely, the requirement is that there exists a positive number r for which

$$f(\mathbf{x}) \le f(\mathbf{c}) \text{ for all } \mathbf{x} \text{ in } S \text{ with } \ \|\mathbf{x} - \mathbf{c}\| < r \qquad [17.8]$$

A **local minimum** point is defined in the obvious way, and it is also clear what we mean by *local maximum and minimum values, local extreme points*, and *local extreme values*. Note how these definitions imply that a global extreme point is also a local extreme point, but the converse is not true, of course.

In searching for maximum and minimum points, Theorem 17.4 on necessary first-order conditions was very useful. The same result also applies to the local extreme points: *At a local extreme point in the interior of the domain of a differentiable function, all the first-order partial derivatives are 0.* This observation follows because the proof of Theorem 17.4 only considered the behavior of the function in a small neighborhood of the optimal point.

These first-order conditions are necessary for a differentiable function to have a local extreme point. However, a stationary point does not have to be a local extreme point. A stationary point $\mathbf{c}$ of f that is neither a local maximum nor a local minimum point is called a **saddle point** of f.

Example 17.7
Show that $(0, 0)$ is a saddle point of $f(x, y) = x^2 - y^2$.

Solution   It is easy to check that $(0, 0)$ is a stationary point at which $f(0, 0) = 0$. Moreover, $f(x, 0) = x^2$, so $f(x, y)$ takes positive values arbitrarily close to the origin. In addition, $f(0, y) = -y^2$, so $f(x, y)$ also takes negative values arbitrarily close to the origin. Hence, $(0, 0)$ is a saddle point. The graph of the function is shown in Fig. 17.9.

These concepts can be illustrated by thinking of the mountains in the Himalayas. Every peak is a local maximum, but only the highest (Mount Everest) is the (global) maximum. The deepest points of the lakes are local minima, and the mountain passes correspond to saddle points. The stationary points of a function

FIGURE 17.9   The graph of $f(x, y) = x^2 - y^2$. Point $(0, 0)$ is a saddle point.

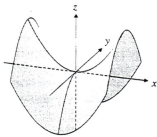

thus can be put into three categories:

---

1. local maximum points
2. local minimum points
3. saddle points

[17.9]

To help decide whether a given stationary point is of type 1, 2, or 3, one can use the *second-derivative test*. Let us look at the case of functions of two variables, and leave the general case until Section 17.9.

Second-Order Conditions for Functions of Two Variables

Consider a function $z = f(x, y)$ defined on a domain S. Let (x_0, y_0) be an interior point of S that is also a stationary point of f, so that

$$f_1'(x_0, y_0) = 0 \quad \text{and} \quad f_2'(x_0, y_0) = 0$$

Then (x_0, y_0) is either a local maximum point, a local minimum point, or a saddle point. How do we distinguish between these three cases?

Consider first the case when $z = f(x, y)$ has a local maximum at (x_0, y_0). The functions $g(x) = f(x, y_0)$ and $h(y) = f(x_0, y)$ describe the behavior of f along the straight lines $y = y_0$ and $x = x_0$, respectively (see Fig. 17.1). These functions must achieve maxima at x_0 and y_0, respectively. Therefore, $g''(x_0) = f_{11}''(x_0, y_0) \leq 0$ and $h''(y_0) = f_{22}''(x_0, y_0) \leq 0$. On the other hand, if $g''(x_0) < 0$ and $h''(y_0) < 0$, then we know that g and h really do achieve local maxima at x_0 and y_0, respectively. Stated differently, the conditions $f_{11}''(x_0, y_0) < 0$ and $f_{22}''(x_0, y_0) < 0$ will ensure that $f(x, y)$ has a local maximum in the directions through (x_0, y_0) that are parallel to the x-axis and the y-axis.

However, note that the signs of $f_{11}''(x_0, y_0)$ and $f_{22}''(x_0, y_0)$ on their own do not reveal much about the behavior of the graph of $z = f(x, y)$ when we move away from (x_0, y_0) in directions other than the two mentioned. Let us consider an example.

Example 17.8

Study the behavior of $f(x, y) = 3xy - x^2 - y^2$ along the lines $y = 0$, $x = 0$, and $y = x$.

Solution We see that $f(x, 0) = -x^2$ has a maximum at $x = 0$ and $f(0, y) = -y^2$ has maximum at $y = 0$. But if we let $y = x$, then $f(x, x) = x^2$, which has a minimum at $x = 0$. This function has a maximum at the origin in both the x and y directions, yet it has a minimum at the origin in the direction $y = x$. The origin is a stationary point for f that is a saddle point. Yet we find that $f_{11}''(0, 0) = -2$ and $f_{22}''(0, 0) = -2$.

It turns out that in order to have a correct second-derivative test for functions $f(x, y)$ of two variables, the mixed second-order partial $f_{12}''(x_0, y_0)$ must also be considered. One has the following result:[1]

Theorem 17.5 (Second-Derivative Test for Functions of Two Variables)
Let $f(x, y)$ be a function with continuous partial derivatives of the first and second order in a domain S, and let (x_0, y_0) be an interior point of S that is a stationary point for f. Write

$$A = f_{11}''(x_0, y_0), \quad B = f_{12}''(x_0, y_0), \quad \text{and} \quad C = f_{22}''(x_0, y_0) \qquad [17.10]$$

Now:

(a) If $A < 0$ and $AC - B^2 > 0$, then (x_0, y_0) is a local maximum point.
(b) If $A > 0$ and $AC - B^2 > 0$, then (x_0, y_0) is a local minimum point.
(c) If $AC - B^2 < 0$, then (x_0, y_0) is a saddle point.
(d) If $AC - B^2 = 0$, then (x_0, y_0) could be a local maximum, a local minimum, or a saddle point.

Note that the conditions $A < 0$ and $AC - B^2 > 0$ in (a) imply also that $AC > B^2 \geq 0$ and so $AC > 0$; dividing this last inequality by the negative number A implies that $C < 0$. The condition $f_{22}''(x_0, y_0) < 0$ is thus (indirectly) included in the assumptions in (a). The corresponding observation is also valid for (b).

The conditions in (a), (b), and (c) are usually called *second-order conditions*. Note that these are sufficient conditions for a stationary point to be respectively a *local* maximum point, a *local* minimum point, or a saddle point. None of these conditions is necessary. The result in Problem 6 will confirm (d), because it shows that a stationary point where $AC - B^2 = 0$ can fall into any of the three categories.

Example 17.9

Find the stationary points of $f(x, y)$ and classify them when

$$f(x, y) = -x^3 + xy + y^2 + x$$

Solution   The stationary points must satisfy the two equations

$$f_1'(x, y) = -3x^2 + y + 1 = 0 \quad \text{and} \quad f_2'(x, y) = x + 2y = 0$$

The second equation implies that $y = -x/2$. Inserting this into the first equation yields $-3x^2 - x/2 + 1 = 0$, or $6x^2 + x - 2 = 0$. This is a quadratic

---

[1] Theorem 17.5 deals only with second-order conditions for local extrema of a function of two variables. Results on global extrema of such functions are given in Section 17.8. Results for functions of n variables are the subject of Section 17.9, where proofs are also given.

equation with solutions $x = 1/2$ and $x = -2/3$. The corresponding values of y can be found from $y = -x/2$, and we conclude that $(1/2, -1/4)$ and $(-2/3, 1/3)$ are the only stationary points. Furthermore, $f_{11}''(x, y) = -6x$, $f_{12}''(x, y) = 1$, and $f_{22}''(x, y) = 2$. A convenient way of classifying the stationary points is to make a table like Table 17.1.

TABLE 17.1

Point	A	B	C	$AC - B^2$	Classification
$(1/2, -1/4)$	-3	1	2	-7	Saddle point
$(-2/3, 1/3)$	4	1	2	7	Local minimum

A rather more complicated example is the following:

Example 17.10

Classify the stationary points of $f(x, y) = (x - 2)e^{x^2 - x}e^{(y-2)^2}$.

Solution   Here we find that

$$f_1'(x, y) = \left[e^{x^2 - x} + (x - 2)(2x - 1)e^{x^2 - x} \right] e^{(y-2)^2} = (2x^2 - 5x + 3)e^{x^2 - x}e^{(y-2)^2}$$

$$f_2'(x, y) = (x - 2)e^{x^2 - x}2(y - 2)e^{(y-2)^2} = 2(x - 2)(y - 2)e^{x^2 - x}e^{(y-2)^2}$$

Note that $f_1'(x, y) = 0$ iff $2x^2 - 5x + 3 = 0$. Solving this equation, we see that there are only two possibilities: $x = 1$ or $x = 3/2$. If x has either of these two values, then $f_2'(x, y) = 0$ only for $y = 2$. We conclude that $(1, 2)$ and $(3/2, 2)$ are the only stationary points.

The second-order partials are (there is no point in simplifying the answers here)

$$f_{11}''(x, y) = \left[(4x - 5)e^{x^2 - x} + (2x^2 - 5x + 3)(2x - 1)e^{x^2 - x} \right] e^{(y-2)^2}$$

$$f_{12}''(x, y) = (2x^2 - 5x + 3)e^{x^2 - x}2(y - 2)e^{(y-2)^2}$$

$$f_{22}''(x, y) = 2(x - 2)e^{x^2 - x} \left[e^{(y-2)^2} + (y - 2)2(y - 2)e^{(y-2)^2} \right]$$

Table 17.2 shows the classification of the stationary points.

TABLE 17.2

Point	A	B	C	$AC - B^2$	Classification
$(1, 2)$	-1	0	-2	2	Local maximum
$(3/2, 2)$	$e^{3/4}$	0	$-e^{3/4}$	$-e^{3/2}$	Saddle point

Problems

1. Consider the function f defined for all (x, y) by $f(x, y) = x^2 + 2xy^2 + 2y^2$.

    a. Compute the first- and second-order partials of f.
    b. Show that the stationary points are $(0, 0)$, $(-1, 1)$, $(-1, -1)$, and classify them.

2. Find all the stationary points of the following functions and examine what the second-derivative test says about them:

    a. $f(x, y) = x^3 + y^3 - 3xy$ **b.** $f(x, y) = x^2 - xy + y^2 + 3x - 2y + 1$

    c. $f(x, y) = x^2 y^3 (6 - x - y)$ **d.** $f(x, y) = \sqrt{1 - x^2 - y^2} + x^2 - 2y^2$

    e. $f(x, y) = x^4 + 2y^2 - 2xy$ **f.** $f(x, y) = \ln(1 + x^2 y)$

3. **a.** Determine values of the constants a, b, and c such that

$$f(x, y) = ax^2 y + bxy + 2xy^2 + c$$

    has a local minimum at the point $(2/3, 1/3)$ with local minimum value $-1/9$.

    b. With the values of a, b, and c found in part (a), find the maximum and minimum values of f over the domain in the xy-plane determined by the inequalities $x \geq 0$, $y \geq 0$, and $2x + y \leq 4$.

4. The function g is given by $g(x, y) = (x - 1)^2 y e^{x+3y}$.
    a. Find the level curves $g(x, y) = 0$. Where is $g(x, y) > 0$?
    b. Compute g_1' and g_2'. Find the stationary points and classify them.
    c. Decide whether g has global extreme points.

5. Let the function f be defined for all x, y by $f(x, y) = xe^{-x}(y^2 - 4y)$.
    a. Find all stationary points of f and classify them by using the second-derivative test.
    b. Show that f has neither a global maximum nor a global minimum.
    c. Let $S = \{(x, y) : 0 \leq x \leq 5, \ 0 \leq y \leq 4\}$. Prove that f has global maximum and minimum points in S and find them.
    d. Find the slope of the tangent to the level curve $xe^{-x}(y^2 - 4y) = e - 4$ at the point where $x = 1$ and $y = 4 - e$.

6. Consider the three functions:

    (a) $z = -x^4 - y^4$ (b) $z = x^4 + y^4$ (c) $z = x^3 + y^3$

    Prove that the origin is a stationary point for each one of these functions, and that $AC - B^2 = 0$ at the origin in each case. By studying the functions directly, prove that the origin is respectively a maximum point for (a), a minimum point for (b), and a saddle point for (c).

Harder Problems

7. The production function for a firm depends on capital, K, and the number of workers, L. It is given by

$$f(K, L) = \sqrt{\sqrt{K} + \sqrt{L}}$$

The price per unit of the product is p, the cost of capital is r, and the wage rate is w, so that profit is

$$\pi(K, L) = p\sqrt{\sqrt{K} + \sqrt{L}} - rK - wL, \qquad (K \geq 0, \ L \geq 0)$$

a. Suppose that $\pi(K, L)$ has a maximum in its domain, and find the maximum point. What is the maximum when $p = 32\sqrt{2}$ and $w = r = 1$?

b. Suppose now that the firm becomes worker-controlled, and seeks to maximize value added per worker, that is, $[\pi(K, L) + wL]/L$. If we let $k = K/L$, explain why the value added per worker is

$$h(L, k) = p\sqrt{1 + \sqrt{k}} \cdot L^{-3/4} - rk$$

c. Let $p = 32\sqrt{2}$, $r = 1$, and suppose that the corresponding function $h(L, k)$ has a maximum in the domain A consisting of all (L, k) with $L \geq 16$ and $k > 0$. Call the maximum point $(\bar{L}, \bar{k})$. Find $\bar{L}$ and show that $\bar{k} = 1$. Find the maximum value of h.

8. Consider the function f defined by $f(x, y) = (y - x^2)(y - 2x^2)$ for all (x, y).

a. The graph of $z = f(x, y)$ divides the xy-plane $z = 0$ into two parabolas. In the xy-plane, draw the domain where f is negative.

b. Show that $(0, 0)$ is the only stationary point. Use part (a) to show that it is a saddle point.

c. Let $(h, k) \neq (0, 0)$ be any direction vector. Let $g(t) = f(th, tk)$ and show that g has a local minimum at $t = 0$, whatever the direction (h, k) may be. (Thus, although $(0, 0)$ is a saddle point, the function has a local minimum at the origin in each direction through the origin.)

9. Let the function h be given by

$$h(x, y) = x^4 y^4 + 2x^2 y^2 - 2x^2 - 2y^2$$

Find the stationary points of h and classify them as local maxima, local minima, global maxima, or global minima.

17.5 Convex Sets

A set of points S in the plane is called **convex** if each pair of points in S can be joined by a line segment lying entirely within S. Examples are given in Fig. 17.10.

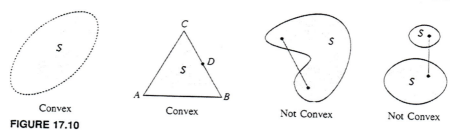

FIGURE 17.10

This definition of a convex set can be extended to sets in R^n. Let $\mathbf{x}$ and $\mathbf{y}$ be any two points in R^n. Define the **line segment** joining $\mathbf{x}$ and $\mathbf{y}$ as the set

$$[\mathbf{x}, \mathbf{y}] = \{\mathbf{z} : \text{there exists } \lambda \in [0, 1] \text{ such that } \mathbf{z} = (1 - \lambda)\mathbf{x} + \lambda\mathbf{y}\} \qquad [17.11]$$

whose members are *convex combinations* $\mathbf{z} = (1 - \lambda)\mathbf{x} + \lambda\mathbf{y}$, with $0 \leq \lambda \leq 1$, of the two end points $\mathbf{x}$ and $\mathbf{y}$.

If $\mathbf{z} = (1 - \lambda)\mathbf{x} + \lambda\mathbf{y}$ and $\lambda = 0$, then $\mathbf{z} = \mathbf{x}$. At the other extreme, $\lambda = 1$ gives $\mathbf{z} = \mathbf{y}$, and $\lambda = 1/2$ gives $\mathbf{z} = \frac{1}{2}\mathbf{x} + \frac{1}{2}\mathbf{y}$, the midpoint between $\mathbf{x}$ and $\mathbf{y}$. Note that if we let λ run through *all* real values, then $\mathbf{z}$ describes the whole of the straight line L through $\mathbf{x}$ and $\mathbf{y}$. (See Fig. 17.11 and [12.20] in Section 12.5.)

The definition of a convex set in R^n is now easy to formulate.

A set S in R^n is **convex** if

$$\mathbf{x} \in S, \mathbf{y} \in S, \text{ and } \lambda \in [0, 1] \implies (1 - \lambda)\mathbf{x} + \lambda\mathbf{y} \in S \qquad [17.12]$$

Note in particular that the empty set and also any set consisting of one single point are convex. Intuitively speaking, a convex set must be "connected" and without "holes"; its boundary must not "bend inwards" at any point.

In economics, convex sets are important. Consider the following typical example.

Example 17.11

Let $U(\mathbf{x}) = U(x_1, \ldots, x_n)$ denote the utility function for an individual. If $U(\mathbf{x}^0) = a$, then the **upper-level set** $\Gamma_a = \{\mathbf{x} : U(\mathbf{x}) \geq a\}$ consists of all

FIGURE 17.11

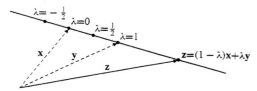

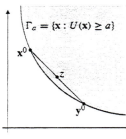

FIGURE 17.12 Γ_a is a convex set.

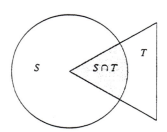

FIGURE 17.13 $S \cap T$ is convex.

commodity vectors that the individual values at least as much as $\mathbf{x}^0$. In consumer theory, Γ_a is often assumed to be a convex set. Figure 17.12 shows a typical upper-level set for the case of two goods.

If S and T are two convex sets in R^n, then their intersection $S \cap T$ is also convex (see Fig. 17.13). More generally:

$$S_1, \ldots, S_m \text{ convex in } R^n \implies S_1 \cap \cdots \cap S_m \text{ convex}$$ [17.13]

Proof: (One of the world's simplest!) Suppose that $\mathbf{x}$ and $\mathbf{y}$ both lie in the set $S = S_1 \cap \cdots \cap S_m$. Then $\mathbf{x}$ and $\mathbf{y}$ both lie in S_i for each $i = 1, \ldots, m$. Because S_i is convex, the line segment $[\mathbf{x}, \mathbf{y}]$ must lie in S_i for each $i = 1, \ldots, m$ and hence in the intersection $S_1 \cap \cdots \cap S_m = S$. This means that S is convex.

Problems

1. Decide which of the four sets shown in Fig. 17.14 are convex.

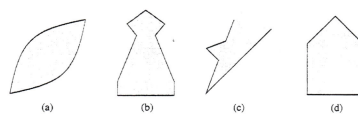

(a)   (b)   (c)   (d)

FIGURE 17.14

2. Decide which of the following sets are convex by drawing each in the xy-plane.

    a. $\{(x, y) : x^2 + y^2 < 2\}$ **b.** $\{(x, y) : x \geq 0, \ y \geq 0\}$

    c. $\{(x, y) : x^2 + y^2 > 8\}$ **d.** $\{(x, y) : x \geq 0, \ y \geq 0, \ xy \geq 1\}$

    e. $\{(x, y) : xy \leq 1\}$ **f.** $\{(x, y) : \sqrt{x} + \sqrt{y} \leq 2\}$

3. Suppose that S is a convex set in R^n with a finite number of elements. How many members can S have?

4. If S and T are two sets in R^n and a and b are numbers, then denote by $aS + bT$ the set of all points taking the form $a\mathbf{x} + b\mathbf{y}$, where $\mathbf{x} \in S$ and $\mathbf{y} \in T$. Prove that if S and T are both convex, then so is $aS + bT$.

5. If S and T are any two sets, the **Cartesian product** of S and T is defined by $S \times T = \{(s, t) : s \in S, t \in T\}$, as illustrated in Fig. 17.15 for the case when S and T are intervals of the real line. Prove that if S and T are both convex sets in R^n, then $S \times T$ is also convex.

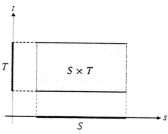

FIGURE 17.15

17.6 Concave and Convex Functions

Sections 9.5 and 9.6 presented concave and convex functions of one variable. We now generalize these concepts to functions of many variables whose domains are convex sets. First, consider the function of two variables, $z = f(x, y)$, as shown in Fig. 17.16. This function is concave according to the following obvious adaptation of definition [9.14] in Section 9.6:

The function $f(x, y)$ is **concave (convex)** if its domain is convex and the line segment joining any two points on the graph is never above (below) the graph.   [17.14]

This definition is often difficult to check. After all, for a function that is specified by a complicated formula, it is far from evident whether the geometric condition [17.14] is satisfied or not. We turn to algebra instead and look for tests of concavity or convexity that generalize [9.15] and [9.16] in Section 9.6. In fact, it is easy to see that the following definition [17.15] is equivalent to [17.14].

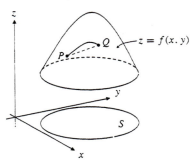

FIGURE 17.16 The function $f(x, y)$ is concave; the entire line segment PQ lies below the graph of f.

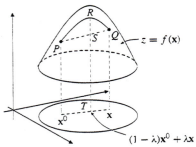

FIGURE 17.17 $TR = f((1 - \lambda)x^0 + \lambda x) \geq TS = (1 - \lambda)f(x^0) + \lambda f(x)$. The function $f(x)$ defined over S is concave.

Definition of Concave and Convex Functions

The general definition of a concave function is entirely similar to the definition of a concave function of one variable (see Fig. 17.17):

Definition of a Concave Function

A function $f(\mathbf{x}) = f(x_1, \ldots, x_n)$ defined on a convex set S is **concave** in S if

$$f((1 - \lambda)\mathbf{x}^0 + \lambda \mathbf{x}) \geq (1 - \lambda)f(\mathbf{x}^0) + \lambda f(\mathbf{x}) \qquad [17.15]$$

for all $\mathbf{x}^0, \mathbf{x} \in S$, and all $\lambda \in (0, 1)$.

If we have a *strict* inequality whenever $\mathbf{x} \neq \mathbf{x}^0$ in [17.15], then f is **strictly concave**. For a strictly concave function of two variables, the line segment between two arbitrary points on the graph will lie strictly below the graph (except at the end points). The function whose graph is drawn in Fig. 17.17 is, therefore, strictly concave.

The function f is **convex** in S if $-f$ is concave, so that [17.15] is valid with $\geq$ replaced by $\leq$. Furthermore, f is **strictly convex** if $-f$ is strictly concave.

Here are some examples where these definitions can be used fairly easily.

Example 17.12

Consider the linear function

$$f(\mathbf{x}) = \mathbf{a} \cdot \mathbf{x} + b = a_1 x_1 + \cdots + a_n x_n + b$$

where $\mathbf{a} = (a_1, \ldots, a_n)$ is a constant vector, and b is a constant. Show that f is both concave and convex.

Solution   For all $\mathbf{x}^0$, $\mathbf{x}$, and all $\lambda \in [0, 1]$, the definition of f and the rules for scalar products ([12.14] in Section 12.4) imply that

$$f((1 - \lambda)\mathbf{x}^0 + \lambda\mathbf{x}) = \mathbf{a} \cdot [(1 - \lambda)\mathbf{x}^0 + \lambda\mathbf{x}] + b$$

$$= (1 - \lambda)\mathbf{a} \cdot \mathbf{x}^0 + \lambda\mathbf{a} \cdot \mathbf{x} + (1 - \lambda)b + \lambda b$$

$$= (1 - \lambda)(\mathbf{a} \cdot \mathbf{x}^0 + b) + \lambda(\mathbf{a} \cdot \mathbf{x} + b)$$

$$= (1 - \lambda)f(\mathbf{x}^0) + \lambda f(\mathbf{x})$$

(Note how we also used the fact that $b = (1 - \lambda)b + \lambda b$.) Hence, [17.15] is satisfied with equality, and so f is both concave and convex (but not strictly concave or strictly convex).

Example 17.13

Suppose that $g(x)$ is a concave (convex) function of one variable in the interval I. Define $f(x, y) = g(x)$ for all $x \in I$ and all y in some interval J. Prove that $f(x, y)$ is concave (convex) for $x \in I$ and $y \in J$.

Suppose now that $g(x)$ is strictly concave (strictly convex). Will $f(x, y)$ also be strictly concave (strictly convex)?

Solution   First, note that the domain of f is the Cartesian product $I \times J$, which is convex because I and J are convex intervals (see Problem 5 of Section 17.5). Suppose g is (say) concave and let x_1 and x_2 belong to I, whereas y_1 and y_2 belong to J, and $\lambda \in [0, 1]$. Then

$$f((1 - \lambda)x_1 + \lambda x_2, (1 - \lambda)y_1 + \lambda y_2) = g((1 - \lambda)x_1 + \lambda x_2)$$

$$\geq (1 - \lambda)g(x_1) + \lambda g(x_2)$$

$$= (1 - \lambda)f(x_1, y_1) + \lambda f(x_2, y_2)$$

which proves that $f(x, y)$ is concave. However, when $x_1 = x_2 = x$, the inequality becomes an equality and so

$$f((1 - \lambda)x_1 + \lambda x_2, (1 - \lambda)y_1 + \lambda y_2) = (1 - \lambda)f(x_1, y_1) + \lambda f(x_2, y_2)$$

even when $g(x)$ is strictly concave (strictly convex) and $y_1 \neq y_2$, while $0 < \lambda < 1$. See Fig. 17.18. So $f(x, y)$ is *not* strictly concave (strictly convex) (except in the trivial case when J is a single point).

Note: The result in Example 17.13 can be generalized: If $f(x_1, \ldots, x_p)$ is concave (convex) in $(x_1, \ldots, x_p)$, then $F(x_1, \ldots, x_p, x_{p+1}, \ldots, x_n) = f(x_1, \ldots, x_p)$ is concave (convex) in $(x_1, \ldots, x_n)$, where $n \geq p$. However, F will not be strictly concave (strictly convex) when $n > p$, except in trivial cases.

There is a characterization of concavity/convexity that is sometimes useful and easy to prove (see Problem 4). Consider a concave function f and let M_f

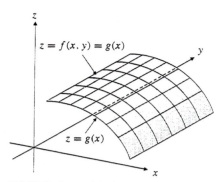

FIGURE 17.18 The function $g(x)$ is strictly concave, but $f(x, y)$ is not.

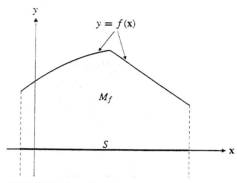

FIGURE 17.19 The function $f(x)$ is concave iff M_f is convex.

denote the set of all points on or below its graph (as illustrated in Fig. 17.19). Then the function f is concave iff M_f is a convex set. A similar statement is true for convex functions and we have

$$f \text{ is concave} \iff M_f = \{(\mathbf{x}, y) : \mathbf{x} \in S \text{ and } y \leq f(\mathbf{x})\} \text{ is convex}$$

$$f \text{ is convex} \iff N_f = \{(\mathbf{x}, y) : \mathbf{x} \in S \text{ and } y \geq f(\mathbf{x})\} \text{ is convex}$$

[17.16]

Jensen's Inequality

Jensen's inequality for concave functions of one variable ([9.18] in Section 9.6) can easily be generalized to functions of several variables:

Jensen's Inequality (Discrete Version)

A function f of n variables is concave on a convex set S in R^n iff the following inequality is satisfied for all $\mathbf{x}_1, \ldots, \mathbf{x}_m$ in S and all $\lambda_1 \geq 0, \ldots,$ $\lambda_m \geq 0$ with $\lambda_1 + \cdots + \lambda_m = 1$:

$$f(\lambda_1 \mathbf{x}_1 + \cdots + \lambda_m \mathbf{x}_m) \geq \lambda_1 f(\mathbf{x}_1) + \cdots + \lambda_m f(\mathbf{x}_m)$$

[17.17]

Nonnegative real numbers that sum to one are called **convex weights**. By letting $\mathbf{x}^0 = \mathbf{x}_1$, $\mathbf{x} = \mathbf{x}_2$, $1 - \lambda = \lambda_1$, and $\lambda = \lambda_2$, definition [17.15] of a concave function reduces to [17.17] for $m = 2$. In particular, if [17.17] holds, then f *is* concave. It remains to prove that if f is concave, then [17.17] holds for all $m \geq 3$. To prove [17.17] for $m = 3$, suppose λ_1, λ_2, and λ_3 are convex weights and let $\mathbf{x}_1, \mathbf{x}_2, \mathbf{x}_3 \in R^n$. Assume, too, that $\lambda_2 + \lambda_3 > 0$; otherwise, if $\lambda_2 = \lambda_3 = 0$, then $\lambda_1 = 1$ and [17.17] holds trivially. Now $\lambda_2 + \lambda_3 = 1 - \lambda_1$, and so, because

$\lambda_2 + \lambda_3 > 0$ and because [17.17] must hold for $m = 2$ with the convex weights $\lambda_2/(\lambda_2 + \lambda_3)$ and $\lambda_3/(\lambda_2 + \lambda_3)$, we have

$$f(\lambda_1 \mathbf{x}_1 + \lambda_2 \mathbf{x}_2 + \lambda_3 \mathbf{x}_3) = f\left(\lambda_1 \mathbf{x}_1 + (1 - \lambda_1)\frac{\lambda_2 \mathbf{x}_2 + \lambda_3 \mathbf{x}_3}{\lambda_2 + \lambda_3}\right)$$

$$\geq \lambda_1 f(\mathbf{x}_1) + (1 - \lambda_1) f\left(\frac{\lambda_2 \mathbf{x}_2 + \lambda_3 \mathbf{x}_3}{\lambda_2 + \lambda_3}\right)$$

$$\geq \lambda_1 f(\mathbf{x}_1) + (1 - \lambda_1)\left[\frac{\lambda_2}{\lambda_2 + \lambda_3} f(\mathbf{x}_2) + \frac{\lambda_3}{\lambda_2 + \lambda_3} f(\mathbf{x}_3)\right]$$

$$= \lambda_1 f(\mathbf{x}_1) + \lambda_2 f(\mathbf{x}_2) + \lambda_3 f(\mathbf{x}_3)$$

To prove [17.17] in the general case, one can use mathematical induction on m, the number of vectors.

There is also a continuous version of Jensen's inequality that involves integrals. We restrict our attention to functions of one real variable. A proof of the next theorem is suggested in Problem 3 of Section 17.7.[2]

Jensen's Inequality (Continuous Version)

Let $x(t)$ and $\lambda(t)$ be continuous functions in the interval $[a, b]$, with $\lambda(t) \geq 0$ and $\int_a^b \lambda(t) \, dt = 1$. If f is a concave function defined on the range of $x(t)$, then

$$f\left(\int_a^b \lambda(t) x(t) \, dt\right) \geq \int_a^b \lambda(t) f(x(t)) \, dt \qquad [17.18]$$

Note: Jensen's inequality is important in statistics. One application is this: If f is concave in an interval I and if X is a random variable with finite expectation $E(X)$, then $f(E(X)) \geq E(f(X))$.

Example 17.14   (Consumption Smoothing in Continuous Time)

Suppose that a consumer expects to live from now when time $t = 0$ until time T. Let $c(t)$ denote consumption expenditure at time t, and $y(t)$ the given income flow. Suppose that W_0 is wealth at time 0. Assume that the consumer would like to choose $c(t)$ so as to maximize the *lifetime intertemporal utility function*

$$\int_0^T e^{-\alpha t} u(c(t)) \, dt \qquad [1]$$

where $\alpha > 0$ is the *rate of impatience or of utility discount*, and $u(c)$ is a strictly increasing concave utility function (such as $\ln c$ or $-c^{-2}$). Suppose

---

[2] If f is convex, the inequalities in [17.17] and [17.18] are obviously reversed.

that r is the instantaneous rate of interest on savings, and that the consumer is not allowed to pass time T in debt. The initial wealth together with the present discounted value (PDV) of future income is

$$W_T = W_0 + \int_0^T e^{-rt} y(t) \, dt$$

The *intertemporal budget constraint* is expressed by the requirement that the PDV of consumption cannot exceed W_T:

$$\int_0^T e^{-rt} c(t) \, dt \leq W_T \qquad \text{(for all admissible } c(t)) \qquad [2]$$

Finding an optimal time path of consumption for a problem like this generally involves techniques from optimal control theory—an advanced topic that we do not discuss in this book. In the special case when $r = \alpha$, however, an optimal time path can be shown easily by means of Jensen's inequality. Let $\bar{c}$ be the (constant) level of consumption that satisfies the equation

$$\int_0^T e^{-rt} \bar{c} \, dt = W_T = W_0 + \int_0^T e^{-rt} y(t) \, dt \qquad [3]$$

Note how $\bar{c} = \bar{y}$ in the special case when $W_0 = 0$ and $y(t) = \bar{y}$ for all t. Our claim is that an optimal path is to choose $c(t) = \bar{c}$ for all t, which we call "consumption smoothing" because all fluctuations in income are smoothed out through saving and borrowing in a way that leaves consumption constant over time.

To establish this claim, define the constant $\bar{\alpha} = \int_0^T e^{-rt} \, dt$. Then [3] implies $\bar{c} = W_T/\bar{\alpha}$. Now apply Jensen's inequality to the concave function u with weights $\lambda(t) = (1/\bar{\alpha})e^{-rt}$. This yields

$$u\left(\int_0^T (1/\bar{\alpha})e^{-rt} c(t) \, dt \right) \geq \int_0^T (1/\bar{\alpha})e^{-rt} u(c(t)) \, dt$$
$$= (1/\bar{\alpha}) \int_0^T e^{-rt} u(c(t)) \, dt \qquad [4]$$

Inequalities [4] and [2], together with the fact that $\bar{c} = W_T/\bar{\alpha}$ and the definition of $\bar{\alpha}$, respectively, imply that

$$\int_0^T e^{-rt} u(c(t)) \, dt \leq \bar{\alpha} \, u\left(\frac{1}{\bar{\alpha}} \int_0^T e^{-rt} c(t) \, dt \right)$$
$$\leq \bar{\alpha} \, u\left(\frac{W_T}{\bar{\alpha}} \right) = \bar{\alpha} u(\bar{c}) = \int_0^T e^{-rt} u(\bar{c}) \, dt \qquad [5]$$

Thus, we have proved that no other consumption plan satisfying budget constraint [2] can yield a higher value of lifetime utility, given by [1], than does the "smoothed consumption" path with $c(t) = \bar{c}$ for all t.[3]

Problems

1. Which of the functions whose graphs are shown in Fig. 17.20 are convex/concave, strictly concave/strictly convex?

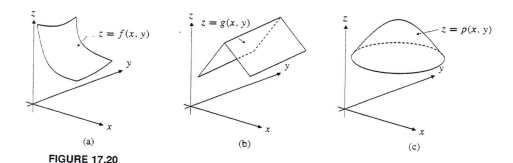

(a)   (b)   (c)

FIGURE 17.20

2. Show that a function f defined in a convex set S in R^n is both concave and convex iff it is linear.

3. Define the function f for all $\mathbf{x} \in R^n$ by $f(\mathbf{x}) = ||\mathbf{x}|| = (x_1^2 + \cdots + x_n^2)^{1/2}$. Show that f is a convex function. (*Hint:* Use the triangle inequality in Problem 8 of Section 12.4.)

4. Prove properties [17.16].

17.7 Useful Conditions for Concavity and Convexity

The following results can sometimes be used to check whether a given function is concave or convex.

---

[3]This is actually quite an important topic in economics. The level of consumption that can be sustained without change is how J. R. Hicks defined "income." M. Friedman called a similar measure "permanent income," and enunciated the "permanent income hypothesis" according to which a measure of "permanent consumption" equals permanent income.

Theorem 17.6   Let f and g be functions defined over a convex set S in R^n. Then:

(a) f and g concave and $a \geq 0$, $b \geq 0 \implies af + bg$ concave.

(b) f and g convex and $a \geq 0$, $b \geq 0 \implies af + bg$ convex.

(c) $\left.\begin{array}{l} f(\mathbf{x}) \text{ concave and } F(u) \\ \text{concave and increasing} \end{array}\right\} \implies U(\mathbf{x}) = F(f(\mathbf{x}))$ concave.

(d) $\left.\begin{array}{l} f(\mathbf{x}) \text{ convex and } F(u) \\ \text{convex and increasing} \end{array}\right\} \implies U(\mathbf{x}) = F(f(\mathbf{x}))$ convex.

(e) f and g concave $\implies h(\mathbf{x}) = \min\{\, f(\mathbf{x}), g(\mathbf{x})\,\}$ is concave.

(f) f and g convex $\implies H(\mathbf{x}) = \max\{\, f(\mathbf{x}), g(\mathbf{x})\,\}$ is convex.

Proof   We prove parts (a). (c), and (e). The proofs of parts (b), (d), and (f) are similar, with an obvious change of each inequality sign.

(a) Let $G(\mathbf{x}) = af(\mathbf{x}) + bg(\mathbf{x})$. If $\lambda \in (0, 1)$ and $\mathbf{x}^0, \mathbf{x} \in S$, then

$$
\begin{aligned}
G((1 - \lambda)\mathbf{x}^0 + \lambda\mathbf{x}) &= af((1 - \lambda)\mathbf{x}^0 + \lambda\mathbf{x}) + bg((1 - \lambda)\mathbf{x}^0 + \lambda\mathbf{x}) \\
&\geq a\big[(1 - \lambda)f(\mathbf{x}^0) + \lambda f(\mathbf{x})\big] + b\big[(1 - \lambda)g(\mathbf{x}^0) + \lambda g(\mathbf{x})\big] \\
&= (1 - \lambda)\big[af(\mathbf{x}^0) + bg(\mathbf{x}^0)\big] + \lambda\big[af(\mathbf{x}) + bg(\mathbf{x})\big] \\
&= (1 - \lambda)G(\mathbf{x}^0) + \lambda G(\mathbf{x})
\end{aligned}
$$

Here we use the definition of G first, and then the definition of concavity of f and g together with $a \geq 0$, $b \geq 0$. The implied inequality

$$
G((1 - \lambda)\mathbf{x}^0 + \lambda\mathbf{x}) \geq (1 - \lambda)G(\mathbf{x}^0) + \lambda G(\mathbf{x})
$$

says that G is concave.

(c) Let $\mathbf{x}^0, \mathbf{x} \in S$, and let $\lambda \in (0, 1)$. Then

$$
\begin{aligned}
U((1 - \lambda)\mathbf{x}^0 + \lambda\mathbf{x}) &= F\big(f((1 - \lambda)\mathbf{x}^0 + \lambda\mathbf{x})\big) \\
&\geq F\big((1 - \lambda)f(\mathbf{x}^0) + \lambda f(\mathbf{x})\big) \\
&\geq (1 - \lambda)F(f(\mathbf{x}^0)) + \lambda F(f(\mathbf{x})) \\
&= (1 - \lambda)U(\mathbf{x}^0) + \lambda U(\mathbf{x})
\end{aligned}
$$

The first inequality uses the concavity of f and the fact that F is increasing. The second inequality is due to the concavity of F.

(e) The function h assigns to $\mathbf{x}$ the smaller of the numbers $f(\mathbf{x})$ and $g(\mathbf{x})$. In the notation of [17.16], it follows that $M_h = M_f \cap M_g$ (draw the graphs to convince yourself that this is true). The intersection of convex sets is convex, so it follows that M_h is convex and so h is concave.

Note: If $f(\mathbf{x}) = \mathbf{a} \cdot \mathbf{x} + b$, so that f is a linear function of $\mathbf{x}$, then in (c) and (d), the assumption that F is increasing can be dropped. Indeed, in the proof of (c), the first inequality used the concavity of f and the fact that F was increasing. When f is linear, this inequality becomes an equality, and the rest of the argument is as before. Thus:

A concave (convex) function of a linear function is concave (convex)   [17.19]

Example 17.15

Examine the concavity/convexity of the following functions:

    (a) $f(x, y, z) = ax^2 + by^2 + cz^2$ (a, b, and c are nonnegative)
    (b) $g(x, y, z) = e^{ax^2 + by^2 + cz^2}$ (a, b, and c are nonnegative)
    (c) $h(x_1, \ldots, x_n) = \ln(a_1 x_1 + \cdots + a_n x_n)$ ($a_1 x_1 + \cdots + a_n x_n$ is positive)

Solution   The function f is convex as a sum of convex functions. The function g is also convex. In fact, $g(x, y, z) = e^u$, with $u = ax^2 + by^2 + cz^2$. Here the transformation $u \to e^u$ is convex and increasing, and u is convex, so by Theorem 17.6(d), g is convex. Finally, h is concave as an increasing concave function ($u \to \ln u$) of a linear (and thus concave) function.

The next result discussed in this section has an obvious geometric interpretation. Consider Fig. 17.16 in Section 17.6 and take any point P on the graph. The tangent plane to the graph at P is seen to lie above the graph. In fact, it is reasonable to expect that this geometric property characterizes differentiable concave functions. The next theorem is an algebraic statement of this important property:[4]

Theorem 17.7   Suppose that $f(\mathbf{x}) = f(x_1, \ldots, x_n)$ has continuous partial derivatives in an open, convex set S in R^n. Then:

(a) f is concave in S iff for all $\mathbf{x}^0, \mathbf{x} \in S$

$$f(\mathbf{x}) - f(\mathbf{x}^0) \le \sum_{i=1}^{n} \frac{\partial f(\mathbf{x}^0)}{\partial x_i}(x_i - x_i^0) \qquad [17.20]$$

(b) f is strictly concave iff the inequality in (a) is strict for all $\mathbf{x} \ne \mathbf{x}^0$.
(c) The corresponding result for convex (or strictly convex) functions is obtained by replacing $\le$ (or $<$) by $\ge$ (or $>$) in the inequality in (a) (or (b)).

---

[4]The inequality in [17.20] is actually valid whenever f is concave and has partial derivatives at $\mathbf{x}^0$.

Proof   (a) Assume, first, that f is concave, and let $\mathbf{x}^0$, $\mathbf{x} \in S$. Rearranging the terms in inequality [17.15] of Section 17.6 implies that, for all $\lambda \in (0, 1)$, we have

$$f(\mathbf{x}) - f(\mathbf{x}^0) \leq \frac{f((1 - \lambda)\mathbf{x}^0 + \lambda \mathbf{x}) - f(\mathbf{x}^0)}{\lambda} \tag{1}$$

Define the function g by $g(\lambda) = f((1 - \lambda)\mathbf{x}^0 + \lambda \mathbf{x}) = f(\mathbf{x}^0 + \lambda(\mathbf{x} - \mathbf{x}^0))$. Then $g(0) = f(\mathbf{x}^0)$, so the right-hand side of [1] is $[g(\lambda) - g(0)]/\lambda$. By Problem 11 of Section 16.2, this tends to $g'(0) = \sum_{i=1}^{n} \left[\partial f(\mathbf{x}^0)/\partial x_i\right]$ $(x_i - x_i^0)$ as $\lambda \to 0^-$. Thus, passing to the limit in [1] as $\lambda \to 0^+$ gives inequality [17.20].

To prove the reverse implication, suppose that $\mathbf{x}^0$, $\mathbf{x} \in S$ and $\lambda \in (0, 1)$. We introduce vector notation and define the row vectors:

$$\nabla f(\mathbf{x}) = (f_1'(\mathbf{x}), \ldots, f_n'(\mathbf{x})) \qquad \text{and} \qquad \mathbf{x} - \mathbf{x}^0 = (x_1 - x_1^0, \ldots, x_n - x_n^0) \tag{2}$$

where $\nabla f(\mathbf{x})$ is the **gradient** of f at $\mathbf{x}$. (See Section 16.3 for the case $n = 2$.) Let $\mathbf{z} = (1 - \lambda)\mathbf{x}^0 + \lambda \mathbf{x}$. Then $\mathbf{z} \in S$, and according to the inequality in part (a) of [17.20], with $\mathbf{z}$ replacing $\mathbf{x}^0$, one has

$$f(\mathbf{x}) - f(\mathbf{z}) \leq \nabla f(\mathbf{z}) \cdot (\mathbf{x} - \mathbf{z}) \tag{3}$$

Because part (a) of [17.20] is assumed to hold throughout S, inequality [3] is also true when $\mathbf{x}$ is replaced by $\mathbf{x}^0$, and so

$$f(\mathbf{x}^0) - f(\mathbf{z}) \leq \nabla f(\mathbf{z}) \cdot (\mathbf{x}^0 - \mathbf{z}) \tag{4}$$

Now multiply [4] by $1 - \lambda > 0$ and [3] by $\lambda > 0$, then add. The result is

$$(1 - \lambda)[f(\mathbf{x}^0) - f(\mathbf{z})] + \lambda[f(\mathbf{x}) - f(\mathbf{z})]$$
$$\leq \nabla f(\mathbf{z})\left[(1 - \lambda)(\mathbf{x}^0 - \mathbf{z}) + \lambda(\mathbf{x} - \mathbf{z})\right] \tag{5}$$

The left-hand side of [5] is $(1 - \lambda)f(\mathbf{x}^0) + \lambda f(\mathbf{x}) - f(\mathbf{z})$, and the expression in the square bracket on the right-hand side is $(1 - \lambda)\mathbf{x}^0 + \lambda \mathbf{x} - \mathbf{z} = \mathbf{0}$. Thus, [5] shows that f is concave.

(b) Suppose f is strictly concave in S. Then [1] holds with strict inequality for $\mathbf{x}^0 \neq \mathbf{x}$. For $\mathbf{z} = (1 - \lambda)\mathbf{x}^0 + \lambda \mathbf{x}$, we have

$$f(\mathbf{x}) - f(\mathbf{x}^0) < \frac{f(\mathbf{z}) - f(\mathbf{x}^0)}{\lambda} \leq \frac{\nabla f(\mathbf{x}^0) \cdot (\mathbf{z} - \mathbf{x}^0)}{\lambda} = \nabla f(\mathbf{x}^0) \cdot (\mathbf{x} - \mathbf{x}^0)$$

using the already proved part (a) of Theorem 17.7, as well as the fact that $\mathbf{z} - \mathbf{x}^0 = \lambda(\mathbf{x} - \mathbf{x}^0)$. Thus, part (a) of [17.20] is valid with strict inequality.

If on the other hand [17.20] holds with strict inequality for $\mathbf{x} \neq \mathbf{x}^0$, then [3], [4], and [5] all hold with $\leq$ replaced by $<$, and it follows that f is strictly concave.

(c) This is proved by replacing f with $-f$.

Theorem 17.7 has a very important application in optimization theory. Suppose $f(\mathbf{x}) = f(x_1, \ldots, x_n)$ is differentiable and concave in a convex set S, and suppose $\mathbf{x}^0$ is an interior point in S at which all the first-order partials of f vanish. Then, thinking geometrically about the case of two variables, the tangent plane to the graph of f at $\mathbf{x}^0$ is horizontal. Because the graph lies below the tangent plane, it can never be higher than at $\mathbf{x}^0$. So $\mathbf{x}^0$ is a global maximum point. A similar result is valid for convex functions. The formal statement and proof are as follows:

Theorem 17.8   Suppose that $f(\mathbf{x})$ has continuous partial derivatives in a convex set S in R^n, and let $\mathbf{x}^0$ be an interior point in S. Now:

(a) If f is concave, then $\mathbf{x}^0$ is a (global) maximum point of f in S iff $\mathbf{x}^0$ is a stationary point of f.

(b) If f is convex, then $\mathbf{x}^0$ is a (global) minimum point of f in S iff $\mathbf{x}^0$ is a stationary point of f.

Proof   If f has a maximum or a minimum at $\mathbf{x}^0$, then $\mathbf{x}^0$ must be a stationary point—that is, all partials the first order must vanish.

Suppose on the other hand that $\mathbf{x}^0$ is a stationary point and that f is concave. We apply Theorem 17.7. Because $f_i'(\mathbf{x}^0) = 0$ for $i = 1, \ldots, n$, it follows from the inequality in part (a) of [17.20] that $f(\mathbf{x}) \leq f(\mathbf{x}^0)$ for all $\mathbf{x} \in S$. This shows that $\mathbf{x}^0$ is a maximum point. The case when f is convex is proved in the same way.

It is sometimes difficult to use the results in this section to decide whether a given function is concave, convex, or neither. For a more practical approach, we will turn to second-derivative tests in the next section.

Problems

1. Prove that $f(x, y, z) = (x + 2y + 3z)^2$ is convex. (*Hint:* Use [17.19].)

2. To what extent do parts (a), (c), and (e) of Theorem 17.6 remain true if one considers strictly concave instead of concave functions?

3. Prove Jensen's inequality [17.18] in Section 17.6 for the case in which f is differentiable by using the following idea: By [17.20], concavity of f implies that $f(x(t)) - f(z) \leq f'(z)[x(t) - z]$. Multiply both sides of this inequality by $\lambda(t)$ and integrate w.r.t. t. Then let $z = \int_a^b \lambda(t) x(t)\, dt$.

17.8 Second-Derivative Tests for Concavity/Convexity: The Two-Variable Case

For twice differentiable functions of one variable, Section 9.5 showed that the sign of the second derivative reveals the concavity or convexity of the function. For functions of two variables, there is a corresponding characterization. (For a proof, see the next section.)

Theorem 17.9   Let $z = f(x, y)$ be a function with continuous partial derivatives of the first and second order, defined over an open convex set S in the plane. Then:

(a) f is concave $\iff$ $f_{11}'' \leq 0,\ f_{22}'' \leq 0$, and $\begin{vmatrix} f_{11}'' & f_{12}'' \\ f_{21}'' & f_{22}'' \end{vmatrix} \geq 0$

(b) f is convex $\iff$ $f_{11}'' \geq 0,\ f_{22}'' \geq 0$, and $\begin{vmatrix} f_{11}'' & f_{12}'' \\ f_{21}'' & f_{22}'' \end{vmatrix} \geq 0$

where all the inequalities should hold throughout S.

Example 17.16

Let $f(x, y) = 2x - y - x^2 + 2xy - y^2$ for all (x, y). Is f concave/convex?

Solution   Here $f_1' = 2 - 2x + 2y$ and $f_2' = -1 + 2x - 2y$, so

$$f_{11}'' = -2, \qquad f_{12}'' = f_{21}'' = 2, \qquad \text{and} \qquad f_{22}'' = -2$$

Hence,

$$f_{11}'' \leq 0, \qquad f_{22}'' \leq 0, \qquad \text{and} \qquad \begin{vmatrix} f_{11}'' & f_{12}'' \\ f_{21}'' & f_{22}'' \end{vmatrix} = \begin{vmatrix} -2 & 2 \\ 2 & -2 \end{vmatrix} = 0 \geq 0$$

We conclude that $f(x, y)$ is concave.

Example 17.17

Show that the CES function f defined for $K > 0$, $L > 0$ by

$$f(K, L) = A\left[\delta K^{-\rho} + (1 - \delta)L^{-\rho}\right]^{-1/\rho} \qquad (A > 0,\ \rho \neq 0,\ 0 \leq \delta \leq 1)$$

is concave for $\rho \geq -1$ and convex for $\rho \leq -1$.

Solution   After a fair amount of work, we find that

$$f''_{KK} = -(\rho + 1)\delta(1 - \delta)AK^{-\rho-2}L^{-\rho}\left[\delta K^{-\rho} + (1 - \delta)L^{-\rho}\right]^{-(1/\rho)-2}$$

$$f''_{LL} = -(\rho + 1)\delta(1 - \delta)AK^{-\rho}L^{-\rho-2}\left[\delta K^{-\rho} + (1 - \delta)L^{-\rho}\right]^{-(1/\rho)-2}$$

$$f''_{KL} = (\rho + 1)\delta(1 - \delta)AK^{-\rho-1}L^{-\rho-1}\left[\delta K^{-\rho} + (1 - \delta)L^{-\rho}\right]^{-(1/\rho)-2}$$

It follows that for $\rho \geq -1$, we have $f''_{KK} \leq 0$ and $f''_{LL} \leq 0$, whereas for $\rho \leq -1$, we have $f''_{KK} \geq 0$ and $f''_{LL} \geq 0$. Moreover, $f''_{KK}f''_{LL} - (f''_{KL})^2 \equiv 0$. (This is also a consequence of f being homogeneous of degree 1—see Problem 7 of Section 16.5.) The conclusion follows from parts (a) and (b) of Theorem 17.9.

A variant of this theorem gives *sufficient* conditions for *strict* concavity/convexity. (For a proof, see the next section.)

Theorem 17.10   Let $z = f(x, y)$ be a function with continuous partial derivatives of the first and second order, defined over an open convex set S in the plane. Then:

(a) $f''_{11} < 0$ and $\begin{vmatrix} f''_{11} & f''_{12} \\ f''_{21} & f''_{22} \end{vmatrix} > 0 \implies f$ is strictly concave

(b) $f''_{11} > 0$ and $\begin{vmatrix} f''_{11} & f''_{12} \\ f''_{21} & f''_{22} \end{vmatrix} > 0 \implies f$ is strictly convex

where all the inequalities should hold throughout S.

Note 1: The implications in parts (a) and (b) cannot be reversed. For example, it is easy to show that $f(x, y) = -x^4 - y^4$ is strictly concave in the whole plane, even though $f''_{11}(0, 0) = 0$.

Note 2: From the two sufficient conditions already specified in part (a), it follows that $f''_{22}(x, y) < 0$. And from the two conditions in part (b), it follows that $f''_{22}(x, y) > 0$.

Example 17.18

Show that the Cobb–Douglas function $Y = AK^aL^b$, defined for all $K > 0$ and $L > 0$, is concave if $A > 0$, $a \geq 0$, $b \geq 0$, and $a + b \leq 1$, and is strictly concave if a and b are positive with $a + b < 1$.

Solution   Here one has $Y''_{KK} = a(a-1)AK^{a-2}L^b$, $Y''_{KL} = Y''_{LK} = abAK^{a-1}L^{b-1}$, and $Y''_{LL} = b(b-1)AK^aL^{b-2}$. Moreover,

$$\begin{vmatrix} Y''_{KK} & Y''_{KL} \\ Y''_{LK} & Y''_{LL} \end{vmatrix} = a(a-1)AK^{a-2}L^b b(b-1)AK^aL^{b-2} - (abAK^{a-1}L^{b-1})^2$$

$$= abA^2K^{2a-2}L^{2b-2}\big[(a-1)(b-1) - ab\big]$$

$$= abA^2K^{2a-2}L^{2b-2}\big[1 - (a+b)\big]$$

The conclusions follow immediately from Theorems 17.9 (a) and 17.10 (a).

The foregoing results have a number of interesting implications in optimization theory. Combining Theorems 17.8 and 17.9 gives the following useful result.

Theorem 17.11   (**Sufficient Conditions for Global Extreme Points**)
Let $f(x, y)$ be a function with continuous partial derivatives of the first and second order in a convex domain S, and let (x_0, y_0) be an interior point of S at which f is stationary.

(a) If, for all (x, y) in S, one has $f''_{11}(x, y) \leq 0$, $f''_{22}(x, y) \leq 0$, and $f''_{11}(x, y)f''_{22}(x, y) - \big[f''_{12}(x, y)\big]^2 \geq 0$, then (x_0, y_0) is a *maximum point* for $f(x, y)$ in S.

(b) If, for all (x, y) in S, one has $f''_{11}(x, y) \geq 0$, $f''_{22}(x, y) \geq 0$, and $f''_{11}(x, y)f''_{22}(x, y) - \big[f''_{12}(x, y)\big]^2 \geq 0$, then (x_0, y_0) is a *minimum point* for $f(x, y)$ in S.

Example 17.19
Consider the function

$$C(x, y) = \frac{1}{100}x^2 - 10x + \frac{1}{300}y^3 - 9y + 20,600$$

defined for $x \geq 0$ and $y \geq 0$. In Example 17.4, we proved that the only stationary point is $(x, y) = (500, 30)$. Prove that this is a *minimum* point.

Solution   Here

$$C''_{11}(x, y) = \frac{1}{50}, \qquad C''_{12}(x, y) = 0, \qquad \text{and} \qquad C''_{22}(x, y) = \frac{1}{50}y$$

Here $C''_{11}(x, y) \geq 0$, $C''_{22}(x, y) \geq 0$, and $C''_{11}(x, y)C''_{22}(x, y) - [C''_{12}(x, y)]^2 = y/2500 \geq 0$ for all $x \geq 0$, $y \geq 0$. Hence, Theorem 17.11 (b) shows that $(500, 30)$ is a minimum point.

Example 17.20

Show that we found the maximum in Example 17.3.

Solution   For $\pi(K, L) = 3K^{1/2}L^{1/3} - 0.1K - L$ with $K > 0$ and $L > 0$, we have

$$\pi''_{KK} = -\tfrac{3}{4}K^{-3/2}L^{1/3}, \qquad \pi''_{KL} = \tfrac{1}{2}K^{-1/2}L^{-2/3}, \qquad \text{and} \qquad \pi''_{LL} = -\tfrac{2}{3}K^{1/2}L^{-5/3}$$

Hence, $\pi''_{KK} < 0$ and $\pi''_{LL} < 0$ for all $K > 0$ and $L > 0$; moreover,

$$\pi''_{KK}\pi''_{LL} - (\pi''_{KL})^2 = \tfrac{1}{2}K^{-1}L^{-4/3} - \tfrac{1}{4}K^{-1}L^{-4/3} = \tfrac{1}{4}K^{-1}L^{-4/3} > 0$$

It follows from part (a) in Theorem 17.11 that the stationary point $(K, L) = (50,625, 3375)$ does maximize profits.

Problems

1. Let f be defined for all x, y by $f(x, y) = x - y - x^2$.
   a. Show that f is concave: (i) by using Theorem 17.9; (ii) by using Theorem 17.6 of Section 17.7.
   b. Show that $-e^{-f(x,y)}$ is concave.

2. a. Show that the general quadratic function

$$f(x, y) = ax^2 + 2bxy + cy^2 + px + qy + r$$

is strictly concave if $ac - b^2 > 0$ and $a < 0$, whereas it is strictly convex if $ac - b^2 > 0$ and $a > 0$. (Using the terminology from Section 15.8, this means in particular that if the quadratic form $ax^2 + 2bxy + cy^2$ is negative (positive) definite, then it is a strictly concave (convex) function.)
   b. Find necessary and sufficient conditions for $f(x, y)$ to be concave/convex.

3. Decide for which values of the constant a the following function is concave, convex, or neither:

$$f(x, y) = -6x^2 + (2a + 4)xy - y^2 + 4ay$$

4. Examine the convexity/concavity of the following functions:
   a. $f(x, y) = x + y - e^x - e^{x+y}$ b. $g(x, y) = e^{x+y} + e^{x-y} - \frac{3}{2}x - \frac{1}{2}y$

5. Define the function f over $[-1, 1]$ by $f(-1) = f(1) = 2$ and $f(x) = |x|$ for $|x| < 1$. Draw the graph of f and explain why f is convex. Note that f is discontinuous at $x = -1$ and at $x = 1$, and not differentiable at $x = 0$.

6. Find the largest convex domain S in the xy-plane on which the function $f(x, y) = x^2 - y^2 - xy - x^3$ is concave.

7. Use Theorem 17.11 to confirm that the solution to Example 17.1 indeed maximizes profits.

8. Use Theorem 17.11 to show that the function f defined by

$$f(x, y) = -2x^2 - y^2 + 4x + 4y - 3$$

for all (x, y) has a maximum at $(x, y) = (1, 2)$.

9. Show that the stationary points you found give maxima in Problems 4, 7, and 8, all in Section 17.1.

10. Each of two firms A and B produces its own version, X and Y, of a commodity in amounts x and y, and these are sold at prices p and q per unit, respectively. Each firm determines its own price and produces exactly as much as is demanded. The demands for the two commodities are given by

$$x = 29 - 5p + 4q, \qquad y = 16 + 4p - 6q$$

Firm A has total costs $5 + x$, and firm B has total costs $3 + 2y$. (Assume that the functions to be maximized have maxima, and at positive prices.)

a. Initially, the two firms cooperate as one monopolist would in order to maximize their combined profit. Find the prices (p, q), the production levels (x, y), and the profits of firms A and B.

b. Then cooperation breaks down, with each producer maximizing its own profit.
   If q is fixed, how will A choose p? (Find p as a function $p = p_A(q)$ of q.)
   If p is fixed, how will B choose q? (Find q as a function $q = q_B(p)$ of p.)

c. Under the assumptions in part (b), what constant equilibrium prices are possible? What are the production levels and the net incomes in this case?

d. Draw a diagram with p along the horizontal axis and q along the vertical axis, and draw the "reaction" curves $p_A(q)$ and $q_B(p)$. Show on the diagram how the prices change over time if A breaks the cooperation first by maximizing its profit, taking B's initial price as fixed, then B answers by maximizing its profit with A's price fixed, then A responds, and so on.

Harder Problem

11. Consider the function $f(x, y) = (\ln x)^a (\ln y)^b$ defined for $x > 1$ and $y > 1$. Here $a > 0$, $b > 0$, and $a + b < 1$. Show that f is strictly concave.

17.9 Second-Derivative Tests for Concavity/Convexity: The *n*-Variable Case

The results in Theorems 17.9 and 17.10 on concavity/convexity of functions of two variables can be generalized to functions of n variables. Suppose that $z = f(\mathbf{x}) = f(x_1, \dots, x_n)$ is a C^2 function in a domain S in R^n. Recall from Section 15.5 that the matrix

$$\mathbf{H}(\mathbf{x}) = [f_{ij}''(\mathbf{x})]_{n \times n} \qquad [17.21]$$

is called the *Hessian*, or *Hessian matrix*, of f at $\mathbf{x}$. In the terminology of Section 15.9, the n determinants

$$D_k(\mathbf{x}) = \begin{vmatrix} f_{11}''(\mathbf{x}) & f_{12}''(\mathbf{x}) & \cdots & f_{1k}''(\mathbf{x}) \\ f_{21}''(\mathbf{x}) & f_{22}''(\mathbf{x}) & \cdots & f_{2k}''(\mathbf{x}) \\ \vdots & \vdots & \ddots & \vdots \\ f_{k1}''(\mathbf{x}) & f_{k2}''(\mathbf{x}) & \cdots & f_{kk}''(\mathbf{x}) \end{vmatrix} \qquad (k = 1, \dots, n) \qquad [17.22]$$

are called the *leading principal minors* of $\mathbf{H}(\mathbf{x})$. Theorem 17.10 can then be generalized as follows:

$(-1)^k D_k(\mathbf{x}) > 0$ for $k = 1, \dots, n$ and for all $\mathbf{x} \in S \implies$

f is strictly concave in S [17.23]

$D_k(\mathbf{x}) > 0$ for $k = 1, \dots, n$ and for all $\mathbf{x} \in S \implies$

f is strictly convex in S [17.24]

For $n = 2$, the conditions in [17.23] reduce to $D_1(\mathbf{x}) < 0$ and $D_2(\mathbf{x}) > 0$. But

$$D_1(\mathbf{x}) = f_{11}''(\mathbf{x}) \qquad \text{and} \qquad D_2(\mathbf{x}) = \begin{vmatrix} f_{11}''(\mathbf{x}) & f_{12}''(\mathbf{x}) \\ f_{21}''(\mathbf{x}) & f_{22}''(\mathbf{x}) \end{vmatrix}$$

So the conditions in [17.23] reduce to those in part (a) of Theorem 17.10 in Section 17.8, and the conditions in [17.24] reduce to those in part (b) (with $\mathbf{x} = (x, y)$ in each case).

Theorem 17.9 can also be generalized. To do so, however, we must consider the signs of *all* the principal minors of $\mathbf{H}(\mathbf{x})$, not only the leading principal minors. An arbitrary principal minor of order r in $\mathbf{H}(\mathbf{x})$, denoted by $\Delta_r(\mathbf{x})$, is obtained by crossing out both $n - r$ of the rows and the corresponding $n - r$ columns.

Example 17.21

If $n = 2$, the Hessian matrix is

$$\mathbf{H}(x_1, x_2) = \begin{pmatrix} f_{11}''(x_1, x_2) & f_{12}''(x_1, x_2) \\ f_{21}''(x_1, x_2) & f_{22}''(x_1, x_2) \end{pmatrix}$$

The principal minors of order 1 are the diagonal elements $f_{11}''(x_1, x_2)$ and $f_{22}''(x_1, x_2)$. Note that the element $f_{12}''(x_1, x_2)$ cannot be obtained by crossing out one row and the corresponding column. The only principal minor of order 2 is $|\mathbf{H}(x_1, x_2)| = f_{11}''(x_1, x_2) f_{22}''(x_1, x_2) - [f_{12}''(x_1, x_2)]^2$.

Briefly formulated, if $f(\mathbf{x}) = f(x_1, \ldots, x_n)$ is a C^2 function defined in an open, convex set S in R^n, then:

$$f \text{ is concave in } S \iff \begin{cases} \text{for all } \Delta_r(\mathbf{x}) \text{ and all } \mathbf{x} \in S, \\ (-1)^r \Delta_r(\mathbf{x}) \geq 0 \text{ for } r = 1, \ldots, n. \end{cases} \qquad [17.25]$$

$$f \text{ is convex in } S \iff \begin{cases} \text{for all } \Delta_r(\mathbf{x}) \text{ and all } \mathbf{x} \in S, \\ \Delta_r(\mathbf{x}) \geq 0 \text{ for } r = 1, \ldots, n. \end{cases} \qquad [17.26]$$

For $n = 2$, it follows from Example 17.21 that the conditions in [17.25] and [17.26] are exactly the same as the conditions in Theorem 17.9.

Second-Order Conditions for Local Extreme Points

We state briefly the second-order conditions for local extreme points for a function of n variables:

Theorem 17.12   (Necessary/Sufficient Conditions for Local Extreme Points)   Suppose $f(x_1, \ldots, x_n)$ is a C^2-function in a set S in R^n and let $\mathbf{x}^0$ be an interior stationary point in S—that is,

$$f_i'(\mathbf{x}^0) = 0 \quad (i = 1, \ldots, n)$$

Let $D_k(\mathbf{x}^0)$ be defined by [17.22], and let $\Delta_r(\mathbf{x}^0)$ denote an arbitrary principal minor of order r of the Hessian matrix. Then:

(a) $\mathbf{x}^0$ local maximum point $\implies$ $\begin{cases} (-1)^r \Delta_r(\mathbf{x}^0) \geq 0 \text{ for} \\ \text{all principal minors} \\ \Delta_r(\mathbf{x}^0) \text{ of order } r = \\ 1, \ldots, n. \end{cases}$

(b) $(-1)^k D_k(\mathbf{x}^0) > 0$, $k = 1, \ldots, n \implies \mathbf{x}^0$ local maximum point.

(c) $\mathbf{x}^0$ local minimum point $\implies$ $\begin{cases} \Delta_r(\mathbf{x}^0) \geq 0 \text{ for} \\ \text{all principal minors} \\ \Delta_r(\mathbf{x}^0) \text{ of order } r = \\ 1, \ldots, n. \end{cases}$

(d) $D_k(\mathbf{x}^0) > 0$, $k = 1, \ldots, n \implies \mathbf{x}^0$ local minimum point.

Here parts (b) and (d) are the most useful results. Note that all the determinants are evaluated at $\mathbf{x}^0$. From the continuity of the second-order partials and the definition of a determinant, it follows that if the determinant inequalities in (say) part (b) hold at $\mathbf{x}^0$, then they also hold in some small neighborhood N of this point. Then [17.23] implies that f is (strictly) concave in N, and the conclusion in part (b) follows from Theorem 17.8 (a) in Section 17.7.

Recall that a stationary point $\mathbf{x}^0$ of f that is neither a local maximum nor a local minimum point is called a **saddle point**. The following result gives sufficient conditions for a saddle point (for a proof, see Problem 3):

Saddle Point Test

If $D_n(\mathbf{x}^0) \neq 0$ and neither the determinant conditions in (b) nor in (d) of Theorem 17.12 are satisfied, then a stationary point $\mathbf{x}^0$ of f is a saddle point.

[17.27]

Example 17.22

The following function has stationary points $(-2, -2, -2)$ and $(0, 0, 0)$:

$$f(x, y, z) = x^3 + 3xy + 3xz + y^3 + 3yz + z^3$$

Classify these stationary points by using Theorem 17.12 and [17.27].

Solution   The Hessian matrix is

$$\begin{pmatrix} f_{11}'' & f_{12}'' & f_{13}'' \\ f_{21}'' & f_{22}'' & f_{23}'' \\ f_{31}'' & f_{32}'' & f_{33}'' \end{pmatrix} = \begin{pmatrix} 6x & 3 & 3 \\ 3 & 6y & 3 \\ 3 & 3 & 6z \end{pmatrix}$$

At $(-2, -2 - 2)$, the leading principal minors are

$$6(-2) = -12, \quad \begin{vmatrix} 6(-2) & 3 \\ 3 & 6(-2) \end{vmatrix} = 135, \quad \begin{vmatrix} 6(-2) & 3 & 3 \\ 3 & 6(-2) & 3 \\ 3 & 3 & 6(-2) \end{vmatrix} = -1350$$

So $(-2, -2, -2)$ is a local maximum point.

At $(0, 0, 0)$, the leading principal minors are

$$6 \cdot 0 = 0, \quad \begin{vmatrix} 0 & 3 \\ 3 & 0 \end{vmatrix} = -9, \quad \begin{vmatrix} 0 & 3 & 3 \\ 3 & 0 & 3 \\ 3 & 3 & 0 \end{vmatrix} = 54$$

Neither the conditions in (b) nor those in (d) are satisfied. Moreover, $D_3(0, 0, 0) = 54 \neq 0$. According to [17.27], $(0, 0, 0)$ is a saddle point.

So far we have stated the main results in this section in terms of determinants because the determinant criteria appear to be most commonly used in economics. Yet these results can also be expressed as tests based on the definiteness properties of the quadratic form whose associated matrix is the Hessian matrix. In fact, the natural way of proving these results is to study the properties of these quadratic forms.

Theorem 17.13   Let $z = f(\mathbf{x})$ be a C^2 function in an open convex set S in R^n. If $\mathbf{H}(\mathbf{x})$ denotes the Hessian matrix of f, then:

(a) f is concave $\Longleftrightarrow$ $\mathbf{H}(\mathbf{x})$ is negative semidefinite for all $\mathbf{x} \in S$.
(b) f is convex $\Longleftrightarrow$ $\mathbf{H}(\mathbf{x})$ is positive semidefinite for all $\mathbf{x} \in S$.

Proof   (a) Suppose f is concave. Given any $\mathbf{x} \in S$ and $\mathbf{h} \in R^n$, let $\mathbf{x}(t)$ denote $\mathbf{x} + t\mathbf{h}$, for each real number t. Because S is an open set, there exists a positive number δ such that $\mathbf{x}(t) = \mathbf{x} + t\mathbf{h} \in S$ for all $|t| < \delta$. Let I be the open interval $(-\delta, \delta)$, and define $g(t)$ for $t \in I$ by

$$g(t) = f(\mathbf{x}(t)) = f(\mathbf{x} + t\mathbf{h})$$

Because f is a C^2 function, Problem 11 of Section 16.2 implies that g is twice differentiable, with $g''(t) = \mathbf{h}'\mathbf{H}(\mathbf{x}(t))\mathbf{h}$. Because g is a concave function f of the linear function $\mathbf{x}(t)$ of t, the result in [17.19] says that g is concave. Hence, $g''(t) \le 0$ in I. For $t = 0$, one has $\mathbf{x}(0) = \mathbf{x}$, so this gives $\mathbf{h}'\mathbf{H}(\mathbf{x})\mathbf{h} \le 0$. This is true for all $\mathbf{x} \in S$ and all $\mathbf{h} \in R^n$, so $\mathbf{H}(\mathbf{x})$ is negative semidefinite for all $\mathbf{x} \in S$.

Conversely, suppose $\mathbf{H}(\mathbf{x})$ is negative semidefinite throughout S. Take any two points $\mathbf{x}^0$ and $\mathbf{x}^1$ in S. For all $t \in [0, 1]$, define $\mathbf{x}(t) = \mathbf{x}^0 + t(\mathbf{x}^1 - \mathbf{x}^0) = (1 - t)\mathbf{x}^0 + t\mathbf{x}^1$. Because S is convex, it follows that $\mathbf{x}(t) \in S$, and so we can define

$$g(t) = f(\mathbf{x}(t)) = f(\mathbf{x}^0 + t(\mathbf{x}^1 - \mathbf{x}^0)) \qquad [1]$$

Then Problem 11 of Section 16.2, with $\mathbf{h} = \mathbf{x}^1 - \mathbf{x}^0$, again implies that

$$g''(t) = (\mathbf{x}^1 - \mathbf{x}^0)' \, \mathbf{H}(\mathbf{x}(t))(\mathbf{x}^1 - \mathbf{x}^0) \qquad [2]$$

For all $t \in [0, 1]$, this is ≤ 0 by the hypothesis that $\mathbf{H}(\mathbf{x})$ is negative semidefinite throughout S. Therefore, g is concave on $[0, 1]$. In particular,

$$f((1 - t)\mathbf{x}^0 + t\mathbf{x}^1) = g(t) = g((1 - t) \cdot 0 + t \cdot 1) \ge (1 - t)g(0) + tg(1)$$
$$= (1 - t)f(\mathbf{x}^0) + tf(\mathbf{x}^1) \qquad [3]$$

Thus, $f((1 - t)\mathbf{x}^0 + t\mathbf{x}^1) \ge (1 - t)f(\mathbf{x}^0) + tf(\mathbf{x}^1)$ for all $\mathbf{x}^0, \mathbf{x}^1 \in S$ and all $t \in [0, 1]$, so f must be concave.

To prove part (b), replace f by $-f$ in the proof of part (a).

Theorem 17.14   Let $z = f(\mathbf{x})$ be a C^2 function in an open convex set S in R^n. If $\mathbf{H}(\mathbf{x})$ denotes the Hessian matrix of f, then:

(a) f is strictly concave if $\mathbf{H}(\mathbf{x})$ is negative definite for all $\mathbf{x} \in S$.
(b) f is strictly convex if $\mathbf{H}(\mathbf{x})$ is positive definite for all $\mathbf{x} \in S$.

Proof   (a) Take any two points $\mathbf{x}$ and $\mathbf{x}_0$ in S with $\mathbf{x} \ne \mathbf{x}_0$, and define g for $t \in [0, 1]$ as in [1]. If $\mathbf{H}(\mathbf{x})$ is negative definite in S, then according to [2], $g''(t) < 0$ for all $t \in (0, 1)$, and so g is strictly concave. But then there is strict inequality in [3] when $t \in (0, 1)$. We conclude that f is strictly concave.

Our previous results on strict concavity/convexity and concavity/convexity in terms of the signs of certain minors now follow immediately from Theorems 17.13

and 17.14 by using the tests for negative/positive definiteness and semidefiniteness discussed in Sections 15.8 and 15.9.

Recall also that the positive or negative (semi-) definiteness of the Hessian matrix can be discerned from the signs of its eigenvalues, as was discussed in Theorem 15.2 of Section 15.9. Thus, part (a) of Theorem 17.13 can be restated so that (when f is a C^2 function on an open convex set S) f is concave iff $\mathbf{H}(\mathbf{x})$ has nonpositive eigenvalues for all $\mathbf{x} \in S$. And part (a) of Theorem 17.14 so that f is strictly concave if $\mathbf{H}(\mathbf{x})$ has negative eigenvalues for all $\mathbf{x} \in S$. There are obvious corresponding eigenvalue conditions for f to be convex, or strictly convex.

Problems

1. The following function is defined in all of R^3 and has only one stationary point. Prove that it is a local minimum point.

$$f(x_1, x_2, x_3) = x_1^2 + x_2^2 + 3x_3^2 - x_1 x_2 + 2x_1 x_3 + x_2 x_3$$

2. Classify the stationary points of the following:
   a. $f(x, y, z) = x^2 + 2y^2 + 3z^2 + 2xy + 2xz$
   b. $f(x, y, z) = x^3 + y^3 + z^3 - 9xy - 9xz + 27x$
   c. $f(x_1, x_2, x_3, x_4) = 20x_2 + 48x_3 + 6x_4 + 8x_1 x_2 - 4x_1^2 - 12x_3^2 - x_4^2 - 4x_2^3$

Harder Problems

3. Prove [17.27]. (*Hint:* $D_n(\mathbf{x}^0) \neq 0$ implies that 0 is not an eigenvalue of the Hessian matrix. If neither the determinant conditions in (b) nor in (d) of Theorem 17.12 are satisfied, then (using Theorems 15.2 and 15.3 of Section 15.9). Thus, the Hessian matrix must have positive as well as negative eigenvalues. Thus, the Hessian matrix is indefinite.)

17.10 Quasi-Concave and Quasi-Convex Functions

Let $f(\mathbf{x})$ be a function defined over a convex set S in R^n. For each real number a, define the set P_a by

$$P_a = \{\mathbf{x} \in S : f(\mathbf{x}) \geq a\} \qquad [17.28]$$

Then P_a is a subset of S that is called an **upper level set** for f. This is illustrated in Fig. 17.22 for a function of two variables.

The function whose graph is shown in Fig. 17.21 is not concave. For example, the line segment between points P and Q on the graph lies *above* the graph of f, not below. On the other hand, it is a typical example of a quasi-concave

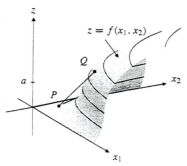

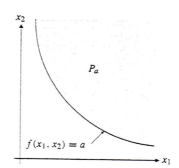

**FIGURE 17.21   The graph
of a quasi-concave function
$z = f(x_1, x_2)$.**

FIGURE 17.22
$P_a = \{(x_1, x_2) : f(x_1, x_2) \geq a\}$
**is an upper level set for
the function $f(x_1, x_2)$ in
Figure 17.21.**

function. A typical upper level set for the function is shown in Fig. 17.22. Note that all the upper level sets of the function are convex. We introduce the following definition:

The function f, defined over a convex set $S \subset R^n$, is **quasi-concave** if the upper level set $P_a = \{\mathbf{x} \in S : f(\mathbf{x}) \geq a\}$ is convex for each number a.

[17.29]

We say that f is **quasi-convex** if $-f$ is quasi-concave. So f is quasi-convex iff the **lower level set** $P^a = \{\mathbf{x} : f(\mathbf{x}) \leq a\}$ is convex for each number a.

Figure 17.21 shows an example of a quasi-concave function that is not concave. On the other hand, a concave (convex) function defined on a convex set S is always quasi-concave (quasi-convex):

If $f(\mathbf{x})$ is concave, then $f(\mathbf{x})$ is quasi-concave.
If $f(\mathbf{x})$ is convex, then $f(\mathbf{x})$ is quasi-convex.

[17.30]

To prove the first statement in [17.30], suppose f is concave in the set S. Take any two points $\mathbf{x}$ and $\mathbf{y} \in P_a$ and let $\lambda \in [0, 1]$. Because S is convex, $(1-\lambda)\mathbf{x} + \lambda\mathbf{y} \in S$. Moreover, because $f(\mathbf{x}) \geq a$, $f(\mathbf{y}) \geq a$, and $\lambda \in [0, 1]$, the definition of concavity of f implies that

$$f((1-\lambda)\mathbf{x} + \lambda\mathbf{y}) \geq (1-\lambda)f(\mathbf{x}) + \lambda f(\mathbf{y}) \geq (1-\lambda)a + \lambda a = a$$

This shows that $(1-\lambda)\mathbf{x} + \lambda\mathbf{y} \in P_a$. Hence, the upper level set P_a is convex.

The second statement in [17.30] follows by applying the first statement to $-f(x)$, as usual.

The following simple characterization of quasi-concave functions is useful.

Theorem 17.15   Let f be a function of n variables defined over a convex set S in R^n. Then f is quasi-concave iff, for all $\mathbf{x}, \mathbf{x}^0 \in S$, and all $\lambda \in [0, 1]$, one has

$$f(\mathbf{x}) \geq f(\mathbf{x}^0) \implies f((1-\lambda)\mathbf{x} + \lambda\mathbf{x}^0) \geq f(\mathbf{x}^0) \qquad [17.31]$$

Proof   Suppose that f is quasi-concave, that $\mathbf{x}, \mathbf{x}^0 \in S$, and $\lambda \in [0, 1]$. Suppose that $f(\mathbf{x}) \geq f(\mathbf{x}^0)$ and let $a = f(\mathbf{x}^0)$. We see then that both $\mathbf{x}$ and $\mathbf{x}^0$ belong to the upper level set $P_a = \{\mathbf{u} \in S : f(\mathbf{u}) \geq a\}$. Because P_a is convex, $(1-\lambda)\mathbf{x} + \lambda\mathbf{x}^0 \in P_a$, which implies that $f((1-\lambda)\mathbf{x} + \lambda\mathbf{x}^0) \geq a = f(\mathbf{x}^0)$.

Conversely, suppose that [17.31] holds, and let a be an arbitrary number. We must show that $P_a = \{\mathbf{u} \in S : f(\mathbf{u}) \geq a\}$ is convex. If P_a is empty or only consists of one point, then P_a is convex. If P_a contains more than one point, take two arbitrary points $\mathbf{x}$ and $\mathbf{x}^0$ in P_a and let $\lambda \in [0, 1]$. Suppose, for example, that $f(\mathbf{x}) \geq f(\mathbf{x}^0)$. Then by [17.31], $f((1-\lambda)\mathbf{x} + \lambda\mathbf{x}^0) \geq f(\mathbf{x}^0)$. Because $f(\mathbf{x}^0) \geq a$, it follows that $(1-\lambda)\mathbf{x} + \lambda\mathbf{x}^0 \in P_a$, and so P_a is convex.

Some useful properties of quasi-concave (quasi-convex) functions are these:

Theorem 17.16

(a) A sum of quasi-concave (quasi-convex) functions is not necessarily quasi-concave (quasi-convex).

(b) If $f(\mathbf{x})$ is quasi-concave (quasi-convex) and F is strictly increasing, then $F(f(\mathbf{x}))$ is quasi-concave (quasi-convex).

(c) If $f(\mathbf{x})$ is quasi-concave (quasi-convex) and F is strictly decreasing, then $F(f(\mathbf{x}))$ is quasi-convex (quasi-concave).

Proof   Convince yourself that part (a) is true, while doing Problem 3 at the same time.

The proofs of parts (b) and (c) are almost identical, so we prove only part (b). Suppose that $f(\mathbf{x})$ is quasi-concave and F is strictly increasing. If $F(f(\mathbf{x})) \geq F(f(\mathbf{x}^0))$, then $f(\mathbf{x}) \geq f(\mathbf{x}^0)$, because F is strictly increasing. Now Theorem 17.15 implies that $f((1-\lambda)\mathbf{x} + \lambda\mathbf{x}^0) \geq f(\mathbf{x}^0)$ for all $\lambda \in [0, 1]$, because f is quasi-concave. So $F(f((1-\lambda)\mathbf{x} + \lambda\mathbf{x}^0)) \geq F(f(\mathbf{x}^0))$, because F is increasing. This proves that $F(f(\mathbf{x}))$ is quasi-concave. The quasi-convex case is proved in the same way.

Example 17.23

Show that $f(x) = e^{-x^2}$ is quasi-concave. Let $F_1(u) = \ln u$ for $u > 0$, and $F_2(u) = 1/u$ for $u > 0$. Check to see if Theorem 17.16 (b) and (c) are confirmed in this case.

Solution   The upper level sets of f are defined by $\{x : e^{-x^2} \geq a\}$. The maximum of f is 1 at $x = 0$. So if $a = 1$, the upper level set consists of the single number 0. If $a > 1$, the upper level set is empty. If $a < 1$, then $e^{-x^2} \geq a$ iff $-x^2 \geq \ln a$ iff $x^2 \leq -\ln a$, and the values of x satisfying this inequality lie in an interval. Thus, all level sets are convex, and so f is quasi-concave.

The function $F_1(u) = \ln u$ is strictly increasing for $u > 0$. Moreover, $F_1(f(x)) = \ln(e^{-x^2}) = -x^2$, which is concave and therefore quasi-concave.

The function $F_2(u) = 1/u$ is strictly decreasing for $u > 0$. Moreover, $F_2(f(x)) = 1/e^{-x^2} = e^{x^2}$, which is convex and therefore quasi-convex. (If $y = e^{x^2}$, then $y' = 2xe^{x^2}$, and so $y'' = 2e^{x^2} + 4x^2e^{x^2} > 0$ for all x.)

These results accord with Theorem 17.16.

Example 17.24

The Cobb–Douglas function is defined for all $x_1 > 0, \ldots, x_n > 0$ by

$$z = Ax_1^{a_1}x_2^{a_2} \cdots x_n^{a_n} \qquad (a_1, a_2, \ldots, a_n \text{ and } A \text{ are positive}) \qquad [1]$$

Taking ln of each side yields

$$\ln z = \ln A + a_1 \ln x_1 + \cdots + a_n \ln x_n$$

As a sum of concave functions, $\ln z$ is concave, and hence quasi-concave. Now, $z = e^{\ln z}$, and the function $u \to e^u$ is increasing. Hence, z is an increasing function of a quasi-concave function, and thus quasi-concave. (Note that the *only* restriction on constants $a_1, \ldots, a_n$ is that they are all positive.)

For $a_1 + \cdots + a_n < 1$, the Cobb–Douglas function is strictly concave. (See Example 17.18 for the case $n = 2$ and Problem 6 of this section for the general case.) For $a_1 + \cdots + a_n > 1$, it is not concave. (If we let $x_1 = \cdots = x_n = x$, then $z = Ax^{a_1 + \cdots + a_n}$, which is strictly convex in x for $a_1 + \cdots + a_n > 1$. Thus, the function is strictly convex along the ray $x_1 = \cdots = x_n = x$.)

If $a_1 + \cdots + a_n \leq 1$, the Cobb–Douglas function is not only quasi-concave, but concave as well.[5] The following display sets out some of the most important properties of the Cobb–Douglas function.

---

[5]When $f(x_1, \ldots, x_n)$ is homogeneous of degree $q \in (0, 1]$, it can be shown that f is concave iff it is quasi-concave. See P. Newman, "Some properties of concave functions." *Journal of Economic Theory* 1, (1969): 291–314.

The Cobb–Douglas function $z = A x_1^{a_1} \cdots x_n^{a_n}$, defined for $x_1 > 0, \ldots,$ $x_n > 0$, with A and $a_1, \ldots, a_n$ positive, is:

   (a) homogeneous of degree $a_1 + \cdots + a_n$

   (b) quasi-concave for all $a_1, \ldots, a_n > 0$

   (c) concave for $a_1 + \cdots + a_n \leq 1$

   (d) strictly concave for $a_1 + \cdots + a_n < 1$

[17.32]

In Example 17.11 of Section 17.5, we pointed out that the upper level sets of a utility function are often assumed to be convex, which means that the utility function is quasi-concave. A slightly more restrictive assumption is that the utility function is strictly quasi-concave according to the following definition:

A function $f(\mathbf{x})$ is **strictly quasi-concave** if

$$f(\mathbf{x}) \geq f(\mathbf{x}^0), \ \mathbf{x} \neq \mathbf{x}^0, \ \text{and} \ 0 < \lambda < 1 \implies f((1-\lambda)\mathbf{x} + \lambda\mathbf{x}^0) > f(\mathbf{x}^0)$$

[17.33]

It follows immediately from this definition and Theorem 17.15 that if $f(\mathbf{x})$ is strictly quasi-concave, then $f(\mathbf{x})$ is quasi-concave.

Example 17.25

A function $f(\mathbf{x})$ is quasi-concave, but not necessarily concave, if its upper level sets have the right shape. Recall that the problem of maximizing $f(\mathbf{x})$ is equivalent to that of maximizing $F(f(\mathbf{x}))$ whenever F is a strictly increasing function of one variable (see Theorem 17.2 of Section 17.2). The issue arises whether, by choosing a strictly increasing transformation F, a quasi-concave function $f(\mathbf{x})$ can be "concavified" or converted into a concave function $F(f(\mathbf{x}))$. The function whose graph is shown in Fig. 17.23 shows that this may not be possible.

The analytic definition of the function is

$$f(x) = \begin{cases} x, & \text{if } 0 \leq x \leq 1 \\ 1, & \text{if } 1 < x \leq 2 \\ x - 1, & \text{if } x > 2 \end{cases}$$

The function f is quasi-concave because it is increasing. (The sets $\{x \in R : f(x) \geq a\}$ are the convex intervals $[a, \infty)$ for $a \leq 1$, and $[1+a, \infty)$ for $a \geq 1$.) But any strictly increasing transformation, $F(f(\mathbf{x}))$, yields a function that is strictly increasing for $x < 1$, constant for $1 \leq x \leq 2$, and strictly increasing for $x > 2$; no such function can be concave.

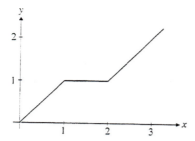

FIGURE 17.23 The function f is quasi-concave, but cannot be "concavified" by a strictly increasing transformation.

A Determinant Criterion for Quasi-Concavity

This section ends with a criterion for checking the quasi-concavity of a function by examining the signs of certain determinants, called **bordered Hessians**. The ordinary Hessians used for examining concavity of a function are "bordered" by an extra row and column consisting of the first-order partials of the function.

Theorem 17.17   Let f be a C^2 function defined in an open, convex set S in R^n. Define the bordered Hessian determinants $D_r(\mathbf{x})$, $r = 1, \ldots, n$, by

$$D_r(\mathbf{x}) = \begin{vmatrix} 0 & f_1'(\mathbf{x}) & \cdots & f_r'(\mathbf{x}) \\ f_1'(\mathbf{x}) & f_{11}''(\mathbf{x}) & \cdots & f_{1r}''(\mathbf{x}) \\ \vdots & \vdots & \ddots & \vdots \\ f_r'(\mathbf{x}) & f_{r1}''(\mathbf{x}) & \cdots & f_{rr}''(\mathbf{x}) \end{vmatrix}$$

(a) A necessary condition for f to be quasi-concave is that $(-1)^r D_r(\mathbf{x}) \geq 0$ for $r = 1, \ldots, n$, and all $\mathbf{x} \in S$.

(b) A sufficient condition for f to be quasi-concave is that $(-1)^r D_r(\mathbf{x}) > 0$ for $r = 1, \ldots, n$, and all $\mathbf{x} \in S$.

Example 17.26

We know already from Example 17.24 that the Cobb–Douglas function defined for all $x_1 > 0, \ldots, x_n > 0$ by $z = A x_1^{a_1} x_2^{a_2} \cdots x_n^{a_n}$ is quasi-concave wherever $A, a_1, \ldots, a_n$ are all positive. We use Theorem 17.17 to confirm this result. We consider the case $n = 3$, but the following argument is easily generalized. The first- and second-order partials can be expressed as

$$z_i' = \frac{a_i}{x_i} z, \qquad z_{ii}'' = \frac{a_i(a_i - 1)}{x_i^2} z, \qquad z_{ij}'' = \frac{a_i a_j}{x_i x_j} z \quad (i \neq j)$$

So the determinant $D_3 = D_3(x_1, x_2, x_3)$ is

$$
\begin{vmatrix}
0 & a_1 z/x_1 & a_2 z/x_2 & a_3 z/x_3 \\
a_1 z/x_1 & a_1(a_1 - 1)z/x_1^2 & a_1 a_2 z/x_1 x_2 & a_1 a_3 z/x_1 x_3 \\
a_2 z/x_2 & a_2 a_1 z/x_2 x_1 & a_2(a_2 - 1)z/x_2^2 & a_2 a_3 z/x_2 x_3 \\
a_3 z/x_3 & a_3 a_1 z/x_3 x_1 & a_3 a_2 z/x_3 x_2 & a_3(a_3 - 1)z/x_3^2
\end{vmatrix}
$$

$$
= \frac{a_1 a_2 a_3}{(x_1 x_2 x_3)^2} z^4
\begin{vmatrix}
0 & 1 & 1 & 1 \\
a_1 & a_1 - 1 & a_1 & a_1 \\
a_2 & a_2 & a_2 - 1 & a_2 \\
a_3 & a_3 & a_3 & a_3 - 1
\end{vmatrix}
$$

Note how we have systematically removed common factors from each row and column. In the last determinant, add the sum of all the other rows to the first row. The resulting determinant has $a_1 + a_2 + a_3$ as a common element throughout its first row, so it can be expressed as

$$
(a_1 + a_2 + a_3)
\begin{vmatrix}
1 & 1 & 1 & 1 \\
a_1 & a_1 - 1 & a_1 & a_1 \\
a_2 & a_2 & a_2 - 1 & a_2 \\
a_3 & a_3 & a_3 & a_3 - 1
\end{vmatrix}
$$

In the new last determinant, subtract the first column from each of the last three, to obtain

$$
\begin{vmatrix}
1 & 0 & 0 & 0 \\
a_1 & -1 & 0 & 0 \\
a_2 & 0 & -1 & 0 \\
a_3 & 0 & 0 & -1
\end{vmatrix} = (-1)^3
$$

Thus,

$$
D_3 = (-1)^3 \frac{a_1 a_2 a_3 (a_1 + a_2 + a_3)}{(x_1 x_2 x_3)^2} z^4
$$

If A, a_1, a_2, and a_3 are all positive, then

$$
(-1)^3 D_3 = (-1)^6 \frac{a_1 a_2 a_3 (a_1 + a_2 + a_3)}{(x_1 x_2 x_3)^2} z^4 > 0
$$

Similar but easier calculations show that

$$
(-1)^2 D_2 = \frac{a_1 a_2 (a_1 + a_2)}{(x_1 x_2)^2} z^3 > 0 \quad \text{and} \quad (-1)^1 D_1 = \frac{a_1^2}{x_1^2} z^2 > 0
$$

We conclude from Theorem 17.17 (b) that the Cobb–Douglas function $z = A x_1^{a_1} x_2^{a_2} x_3^{a_3}$ is quasi-concave, provided only that A, a_1, a_2, and a_3 are all positive.

Problems

1. Decide which of the following functions are quasi-concave:
   a. $f(x) = 3x + 4$
   b. $f(x, y) = ye^x$, $(y > 0)$
   c. $f(x, y) = -x^2 y^3$, $(x > 0, \ y > 0)$
   d. $f(x) = x^3 + x^2 + 1$ if $x < 0$. $f(x) = 1$ if $x \geq 0$

2. Show that any increasing (or decreasing) function of one variable defined on an interval is quasi-concave.

3. Show by an example that the sum of quasi-concave functions is not in general quasi-concave.

4. Use Theorem 17.15 to show that $f(\mathbf{x})$ is quasi-concave iff

$$f((1 - \lambda)\mathbf{x} + \lambda\mathbf{x}^0) \geq \min \{ f(\mathbf{x}), f(\mathbf{x}^0) \} \text{ for all } \lambda \in [0, 1], \text{ and all } \mathbf{x}, \mathbf{x}^0 \in S$$

5. What does Theorem 17.17 (b) say about functions of one variable?

Harder Problems

6. Consider the Cobb–Douglas function $z = Ax_1^{a_1} x_2^{a_2} \cdots x_n^{a_n}$ of Example 17.24.
   a. Compute the kth leading principal minors of the Hessian $\mathbf{H}(\mathbf{x})$ as in [17.22] of Section 17.9 and prove that its value is

$$D_k = \frac{a_1 \cdots a_k}{(x_1 \cdots x_k)^2} z^k \begin{vmatrix} a_1 - 1 & a_1 & \cdots & a_1 \\ a_2 & a_2 - 1 & \cdots & a_2 \\ \vdots & \vdots & \ddots & \vdots \\ a_k & a_k & \cdots & a_k - 1 \end{vmatrix}$$

   b. Prove that

$$D_k = (-1)^{k-1} \left(\sum_{i=1}^{k} a_i - 1 \right) z^k \frac{a_1 \cdots a_k}{(x_1 \cdots x_k)^2}$$

   (*Hint:* Add the sum of all the other rows to the first row; extract the factor $\sum_{i=1}^{k} a_i - 1$; and then subtract the first column in the new determinant from all the other columns.)

   c. Prove that the function is strictly concave for $a_1 + \cdots + a_n < 1$.

7. Suppose $F(x, y)$ is a C^2 function and suppose the equation $F(x, y) = c$ implicitly defines $y = \phi(x)$ as a C^2 function of x. Prove that if F is quasi-concave and $F_2'(x, y) > 0$, then ϕ is convex. (*Hint:* You will need [16.13] in Section 16.3, and Theorem 17.17.)

18

Constrained Optimization

*Mathematics is removed from this turmoil of
human life, but its methods and the relations
are a mirror, an incredibly pure mirror, of
the relations that link facts of our existence.*
—*Konrad Knopp* (1928)

In economic optimization problems, the variables involved are almost always required to satisfy certain constraints. For instance, prices and quantities are often nonnegative by definition, and scarcities dictate that consumption quantities are usually bounded from above. In addition, production quotas, budget limitations, and other constraints might restrict the range of choice.

This chapter starts by considering the problem of maximizing or minimizing a function whose variables are restricted to satisfy one or more equality constraints. A typical economic example concerns a consumer who chooses how much of the available income m to spend on a good x whose price is p, and how much income to leave over for expenditure y on other goods. Note that the consumer then faces the budget constraint $px + y = m$. Suppose that preferences are represented by the utility function $u(x, y)$. In mathematical terms, therefore, the consumer faces the problem of choosing (x, y) in order to maximize $u(x, y)$ subject to $px + y = m$. This is a typical *constrained maximization problem*. In this case, because $y = m - px$, the same problem can be expressed as the *unconstrained maximization* of the function $f(x) = u(x, m - px)$ with respect to the single variable x. Indeed, this method of reducing a constrained optimization problem to an unconstrained one was used repeatedly in Section 17.1.

Consider more generally a consumer who is faced with the problem of deciding how much to buy of n different commodities in a certain period. Denote

650

the utility function by $U(x_1, \ldots, x_n)$ (see Example 15.8 of Section 15.1). Let the price per unit of commodity i be fixed and equal to p_i, so that $p_1 x_1 + \cdots + p_n x_n$ is the amount required to buy the commodity vector $(x_1, \ldots, x_n)$. Assume moreover that the consumer intends to spend an amount m on the n commodities. Then it is possible to purchase any commodity vector $(x_1, \ldots, x_n)$ that satisfies the *budget constraint* $p_1 x_1 + \cdots + p_n x_n = m$. The problem facing the consumer is, among all commodity vectors $(x_1, \ldots, x_n)$ that satisfy the budget constraint, find one which maximizes utility. Briefly formulated, the problem is

$$\max_{x_1, \ldots, x_n} U(x_1, \ldots, x_n) \quad \text{subject to } p_1 x_1 + \cdots + p_n x_n = m \qquad [18.1]$$

It is also tacitly assumed that $x_1 \geq 0, \ldots, x_n \geq 0$. Again, because we can solve the budget constraint for x_n, say, in terms of $x_1, \ldots, x_{n-1}$, problem [18.1] can also be expressed as an unconstrained maximization problem.

When the constraint is a complicated function, or when there are several equality constraints to consider, this substitution method might be difficult or impossible to carry out in practice. In such cases, other techniques should be used. In particular, economists make much use of the **method of Lagrange multipliers**. Actually, the same method is sometimes used by economists even for problems that are quite easy to express as unconstrained problems. The reason is that Lagrange multipliers have important economic interpretations.[1]

Optimization problems in which the constraints take the form of inequalities rather than equalities are usually called **programming problems.** These have been systematically studied only fairly recently. In fact, all the main results have been obtained during the last 40 to 50 years. We give a brief introduction to nonlinear programming problems in Sections 18.8 to 18.10. Linear programs, in which all the relevant functions are linear, are the subject of Chapter 19.

18.1 Two Variables, One Equality Constraint

Consider the problem of maximizing (or minimizing) a function $f(x, y)$ when x and y are restricted to satisfy an equation $g(x, y) = c$. In case we want to maximize $f(x, y)$, the problem is

$$\max f(x, y) \quad \text{subject to } g(x, y) = c \qquad [18.2]$$

Problem [18.2] can be given a geometric interpretation, as in Fig. 18.1.

---

[1] The method is named after its discoverer, the French mathematician Joseph Louis Lagrange (1736–1813). The Danish economist Harald Westergaard seems to have been the first who used it in economics, in 1876. (See Thorkild Davidsen, "Westergaard, Edgeworth and the use of Lagrange multipliers in economics," *Economic Journal* 96 (1986): 808–811.)

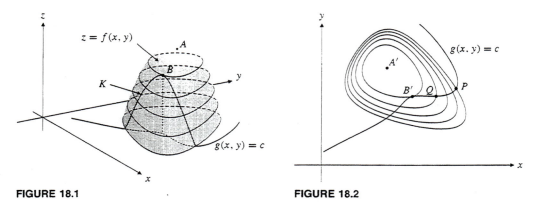

FIGURE 18.1   **FIGURE 18.2**

The graph of f is a surface like a bowl, whereas the equation $g(x, y) = c$ represents a curve in the xy-plane. The curve K on the bowl is the one that lies directly above the curve $g(x, y) = c$. (The latter curve is the projection of K onto the xy-plane.) Maximizing $f(x, y)$ without taking the constraint into account gets us to the peak A in Fig. 18.1. The solution to problem [18.2], however, is at B, which is the highest point on the curve K. If we think of the graph of f as representing a mountain, and K as a mountain path, then we seek the highest point on the path, which is B. Analytically, the problem is to find the coordinates of B.

In Fig. 18.2, we show some of the level curves for f, and also indicate the constraint curve $g(x, y) = c$. Now A' represents the point at which $f(x, y)$ has its unconstrained (free) maximum. The closer a level curve of f is to point A', the higher is the value of f along that level curve. We are seeking that point on the constraint curve $g(x, y) = c$ where f has its highest value. If we start at point P on the constraint curve and move along that curve toward A', we encounter level curves with higher and higher values of f. Obviously, point Q indicated in Fig. 18.2 is not the point on $g(x, y) = c$ at which f has its highest value, because the constraint curve passes *through* the level curve of f at that point. Therefore, we can proceed along the constraint curve and attain higher values of f. However, when we reach point B', we cannot go any higher. It is intuitively clear that B' is the point with the property that the constraint curve touches (without intersecting) a level curve for f. This observation implies that the slope of the tangent to the curve $g(x, y) = c$ at (x, y) is equal to the slope of the tangent to the level curve of f at that point.

Recall from Section 16.3 that the slope of the level curve $F(x, y) = c$ is given by $dy/dx = -F_1'(x, y)/F_2'(x, y)$. Thus, the condition that the slope of the tangent to $g(x, y) = c$ is equal to the slope of a level curve for $f(x, y)$ can be expressed analytically as follows:[2]

$$-g_1'(x, y)/g_2'(x, y) = -f_1'(x, y)/f_2'(x, y)$$

---

[2]Disregard for a moment points (x, y) at which one or both partials of f and g with respect to y vanish. See Theorem 18.1 for a precise result.

or

$$\frac{f_1'(x, y)}{f_2'(x, y)} = \frac{g_1'(x, y)}{g_2'(x, y)} \qquad [18.3]$$

A corresponding argument for the problem of minimizing $f(x, y)$ subject to $g(x, y) = c$ gives the same condition [18.3]. It follows that a necessary condition for (x, y) to solve problem [18.2] (or the corresponding minimization problem) is that (x, y) satisfies both [18.3] and $g(x, y) = c$. These give two equations for determining the two unknowns x and y.

Example 18.1

Find the only possible solution to the problem

$$\max \; xy \quad \text{subject to } 2x + y = m$$

Solution   Comparing the problem with [18.2], we see that $f(x, y) = xy$, $g(x, y) = 2x + y$, and $c = m$. So $f_1'(x, y) = y$, $f_2'(x, y) = x$, $g_1'(x, y) = 2$, and $g_2'(x, y) = 1$. Hence, [18.3] yields

$$\frac{y}{x} = \frac{2}{1} \qquad \text{or} \qquad y = 2x$$

Inserting $y = 2x$ into the constraint $2x + y = m$ gives $2x + 2x = m$. Thus, $x = m/4$ and so $y = m/2$. (Solving the constraint equation for y yields $y = m - 2x$, and then $xy = x(m - 2x) = -2x^2 + mx$, whose graph is a parabola with a maximum at $x = m/4$. So $x = m/4$ and $y = m/2$ solve the maximization problem.)

Example 18.2

Find the only possible solution to the consumer demand problem

$$\max \; x^\alpha y^\beta \quad \text{subject to} \quad px + y = m \qquad [1]$$

where α and β are positive constants.

Solution   With $f(x, y) = x^\alpha y^\beta$ and $g(x, y) = px + y$, we have $f_1'(x, y) = \alpha x^{\alpha-1} y^\beta$, $f_2'(x, y) = \beta x^\alpha y^{\beta-1}$, $g_1'(x, y) = p$, and $g_2'(x, y) = 1$. So [18.3] yields

$$\frac{\alpha x^{\alpha-1} y^\beta}{\beta x^\alpha y^{\beta-1}} = \frac{p}{1} \qquad \text{or} \qquad \frac{\alpha}{\beta} \frac{y}{x} = p$$

(Note how we have canceled $x^{\alpha-1}$ and $y^{\beta-1}$ from the first fraction.) Solving the latter equation for y gives $y = (\beta/\alpha) px$, which inserted into the budget constraint yields $px + (\beta/\alpha) px = m$ or $px(\alpha + \beta) = \alpha m$. Therefore,

$$px = \frac{\alpha}{\alpha + \beta} m \,, \qquad y = \frac{\beta}{\alpha + \beta} m \qquad [2]$$

This solution is very sensible. It says that the consumer should spend the fraction $\alpha/(\alpha + \beta)$ of income on the first good and the fraction $\beta/(\alpha + \beta)$ on everything else. (For a proof that this is really the solution, see Problem 3, Section 18.10. For an alternative (and much easier) proof, study the sign variation of the derivative of the one-variable function $x^{\alpha}(m - px)^{\beta}$.)

In the few problems that accompany this section, you are supposed to solve some particular constrained optimization problems by using condition [18.3]. The next section then explains the Lagrange multiplier method, which is actually the most convenient technique for solving most problems of this type.

Problems

Find the only possible solutions to the following constrained optimization problems:

1. **a.** max $f(x, y) = x + y$ subject to $g(x, y) = x^2 + y = 1$.
   b. min $f(x, y) = x^2 + y^2$ subject to $x + 2y = 4$.
2. **a.** max(min) $3xy$ subject to $x^2 + y^2 = 8$.
   b. max(min) $x + y$ subject to $x^2 + 3xy + 3y^2 = 3$.
3. max $f(x, y) = 10x^{1/2}y^{1/3}$ subject to $g(x, y) = 2x + 4y = 9$.

18.2 The Lagrange Multiplier Method

Recall the constrained optimization problem in [18.2], which is to maximize $f(x, y)$ subject to $g(x, y) = c$. The first-order condition [18.3] can be expressed in a way that is easy both to remember and generalize. First, rearrange [18.3] to obtain

$$\frac{f_1'(x, y)}{g_1'(x, y)} = \frac{f_2'(x, y)}{g_2'(x, y)} \qquad [*]$$

If (x_0, y_0) solves problem [18.2], then the left- and right-hand sides of [*] are equal at (x_0, y_0). The common value λ of these fractions is called a **Lagrange multiplier**, and equation [*] can then be expressed as

$$f_1'(x, y) - \lambda g_1'(x, y) = 0, \qquad f_2'(x, y) - \lambda g_2'(x, y) = 0 \qquad [18.4]$$

Now define the **Lagrangean function** $\mathcal{L}$ by

$$\mathcal{L}(x, y) = f(x, y) - \lambda(g(x, y) - c) \qquad [18.5]$$

The partials of $\mathcal{L}(x, y)$ with respect to x and y are $\mathcal{L}_1'(x, y) = f_1'(x, y) - \lambda g_1'(x, y)$ and $\mathcal{L}_2'(x, y) = f_2'(x, y) - \lambda g_2'(x, y)$, respectively. Thus, Equation [18.4] is the

first-order condition expressing the requirement that the partials of $\mathcal{L}$ vanish. This argument supports the following procedure:

The Lagrangean Method

To find the solutions of the problem

$$\max(\min) \; f(x, y) \; \text{subject to} \; g(x, y) = c$$

proceed as follows:

1. Write down the Lagrangean function

$$\mathcal{L}(x, y) = f(x, y) - \lambda\big(g(x, y) - c\big)$$

   where λ is a constant.

2. Differentiate $\mathcal{L}$ with respect to x and y, and equate the partials to 0.

3. The two equations in **2** together with the constraint yield the following three equations:

$$f_1'(x, y) = \lambda g_1'(x, y)$$
$$f_2'(x, y) = \lambda g_2'(x, y)$$
$$g(x, y) = c$$

4. Solve these three equations for the three unknowns x, y, and λ.

This method will in general give us all pairs of numbers (x, y) that can possibly solve the problem. As a bonus, we get the corresponding value of the Lagrange multiplier λ. We shall see shortly that λ has a very interesting interpretation that is useful in many economic optimization problems.[3]

Example 18.3

Use Lagrange's method for the problem in Example 18.1.

Solution   The Lagrangean is

$$\mathcal{L}(x, y) = xy - \lambda(2x + y - m)$$

So the necessary conditions for the solution of the problem are

$$\mathcal{L}_1'(x, y) = y - 2\lambda = 0, \qquad \mathcal{L}_2'(x, y) = x - \lambda = 0, \qquad 2x + y = m \quad [*]$$

---

[3] Some prefer to consider the Lagrangean as a function of three variables, $\mathcal{L}(x, y, \lambda)$. Then $\partial\mathcal{L}/\partial\lambda = -[g(x, y) - c]$, so equating this partial to 0 yields the constraint $g(x, y) = c$. Later in Section 18.8, when inequality constraints are being discussed, some dangers of this procedure will be pointed out.

The first two equations imply that $y = 2\lambda$ and $x = \lambda$. So $y = 2x$. Inserting this into the constraint yields $2x + 2x = m$. Therefore, $x = m/4$, $y = m/2$, and $\lambda = x = m/4$. This is the same solution for x and y as we found in Example 18.1.

Example 18.4

Solve the problem

$$\max(\min)\ \ f(x, y) = x^2 + y^2\ \ \text{subject to}\ \ g(x, y) = x^2 + xy + y^2 = 3 \quad [1]$$

Solution   The Lagrangean in this case is

$$\mathcal{L}(x, y) = x^2 + y^2 - \lambda(x^2 + xy + y^2 - 3)$$

The three equations to consider are

$$\mathcal{L}'_1(x, y) = 2x - \lambda(2x + y) = 0 \quad [2]$$

$$\mathcal{L}'_2(x, y) = 2y - \lambda(x + 2y) = 0 \quad [3]$$

$$x^2 + xy + y^2 - 3 = 0 \quad [4]$$

The solutions x, y, and λ of these three equations can be found in several ways. Here is a simple method: First, add equations [2] and [3]. This yields

$$2(x + y) = 3\lambda(x + y) \quad [5]$$

Suppose $x + y \neq 0$. Then by [5], $\lambda = 2/3$. Inserted into [2], this gives $x = y$, and then [4] gives $x^2 = 1$, or $x = \pm 1$. Hence, we have the two solution candidates $(x, y, \lambda) = (1, 1, 2/3)$ and $(-1, -1, 2/3)$.
Suppose $x + y = 0$, implying that $y = -x$. Then by [4], $x^2 = 3$, and [2] gives $\lambda = 2$. Hence, we have the two candidates $(x, y, \lambda) = (\sqrt{3}, -\sqrt{3}, 2)$ and $(-\sqrt{3}, \sqrt{3}, 2)$.

We have found the only four points (x, y) that can solve problem [1]. Furthermore,

$$f(1, 1) = f(-1, -1) \doteq 2, \qquad f(\sqrt{3}, -\sqrt{3}) = f(-\sqrt{3}, \sqrt{3}) = 6 \quad [6]$$

We conclude that if problem [1] has solutions, then $(1, 1)$ and $(-1, -1)$ solve the minimization problem, whereas $(\sqrt{3}, -\sqrt{3})$ and $(-\sqrt{3}, \sqrt{3})$ solve the maximization problem.

How can we be certain that the problem has solutions? The function $f(x, y) = x^2 + y^2$ is continuous and the set of all (x, y) satisfying the constraint $x^2 + xy + y^2 = 3$ is a closed, bounded set (see Problem 6, Section 17.2). The extreme-value theorem (Theorem 17.3) therefore assures us that problem [1] has solutions. (Geometrically, the constraint describes an

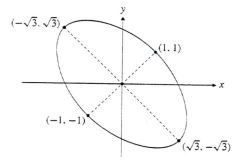

FIGURE 18.3

ellipse and problem [1] is to find the smallest and the largest distance from the origin to a point on the ellipse. See Fig. 18.3.)

An alternative way of proving that we have found the solution is the following, although this method works only in special cases. We shall prove that $(x, y) = (1, 1)$ minimizes $f(x, y) = x^2 + y^2$ subject to the constraint $x^2 + xy + y^2 = 3$. (The other points are treated in the same way.) Let $x = 1 + h$ and $y = 1 + k$. Then

$$f(x, y) = (1 + h)^2 + (1 + k)^2 = 2 + 2(h + k) + h^2 + k^2 \qquad [7]$$

If $(x, y) = (1 + h, 1 + k)$ satisfies the constraint, then

$$(1 + h)^2 + (1 + h)(1 + k) + (1 + k)^2 = 3$$

so

$$h + k = -hk/3 - (h^2 + k^2)/3$$

Inserting this expression for $h + k$ into [7] yields

$$f(x, y) = 2 + 2\left[-\tfrac{1}{3}hk - \tfrac{1}{3}(h^2 + k^2)\right] + h^2 + k^2 = 2 + \tfrac{1}{3}(h - k)^2$$

Because $\tfrac{1}{3}(h - k)^2 \geq 0$ for all (h, k), so $f(x, y) \geq 2$ for all values of (x, y). But because $f(1, 1) = 2$, this means that $(1, 1)$ really does minimize $f(x, y)$ subject to the constraint.

Economic Interpretations of the Lagrange Multiplier

Consider again the problem

$$\max f(x, y) \text{ subject to } g(x, y) = c$$

Suppose x^* and y^* are the values of x and y that solve this problem. In general, x^* and y^* depend on c. We *assume* that $x^* = x^*(c)$ and $y^* = y^*(c)$ are differentiable functions of c. The associated value f^* of $f(x, y)$ is then also a function of c, with

$$f^*(c) = f(x^*(c), y^*(c)) \qquad [18.6]$$

Here $f^*(c)$ is called the **(optimal) value function** for the problem. When using the Lagrangean method, the associated value $\lambda(c)$ of the Lagrange multiplier also depends on c. Provided that certain regularity conditions are satisfied, we have the remarkable result that

$$\frac{df^*(c)}{dc} = \lambda(c) \qquad [18.7]$$

Thus, *the Lagrange multiplier $\lambda = \lambda(c)$ is the rate at which the optimal value of the objective function changes with respect to changes in the constraint constant c.*

Proof of [18.7], assuming that $f^*(c)$ is differentiable: Taking the differential of [18.6] gives

$$df^*(c) = df(x^*, y^*) = f_1'(x^*, y^*)\, dx^* + f_2'(x^*, y^*)\, dy^* \qquad [1]$$

But from the first-order conditions [18.4], $f_1'(x^*, y^*) = \lambda g_1'(x^*, y^*)$ and $f_2'(x^*, y^*) = \lambda g_2'(x^*, y^*)$, so [1] can be written as

$$df^*(c) = \lambda g_1'(x^*, y^*)\, dx^* + \lambda g_2'(x^*, y^*)\, dy^* \qquad [2]$$

Moreover, taking the differential of the identity $g(x^*(c), y^*(c)) = c$ yields

$$g_1'(x^*, y^*)\, dx^* + g_2'(x^*, y^*)\, dy^* = dc$$

so [2] implies $df^*(c) = \lambda\, dc$.

In particular, if dc is a small change in c, then

$$f^*(c + dc) - f^*(c) \approx \lambda(c)\, dc \qquad [18.8]$$

In economic applications, c often denotes the available stock of some resource, and $f(x, y)$ denotes utility or profit. Then $\lambda(c)\, dc$, for $dc > 0$, measures approximately the increase in utility or profit that can be obtained from dc units more of the resource. Economists call λ a **shadow price** of the resource.

Example 18.5

Consider the problem max xy subject to $2x + y = m$ in Example 18.3. With the notation introduced earlier, the solution is $x^*(m) = m/4$, $y^*(m) = m/2$, and $\lambda(m) = m/4$. So the value function is $f^*(m) = (m/4)(m/2) = m^2/8$.

Here $df^*(m)/dm = m/4 = \lambda(m)$. Thus, [18.7] is confirmed. Suppose in particular that $m = 100$. Then $f^*(100) = 100^2/8$. What happens to the value function if $m = 100$ is increased by 1? Its new value is $f^*(101) = 101^2/8$, so we have $f^*(101) - f^*(100) = 101^2/8 - 100^2/8 = 1275.125 - 1250 = 25.125$. Note how formula [18.8] predicts that $f^*(101) - f^*(100) \approx \lambda(100) \cdot 1 = 25 \cdot 1 = 25$, which is a good approximation to the true value 25.125.

Example 18.6

A firm uses inputs K and L of capital and labor, respectively, to produce a single output Q according to the production function $Q = F(K, L) = K^{1/2}L^{1/4}$. The prices of capital and labor are r and w, respectively.

(a) Find the cost minimizing inputs of K and L, and also the minimum cost C, as functions of r, w, and Q. Denote the cost minimizing values by K^*, L^*, and C^*.

(b) Verify that

$$K^* = \frac{\partial C^*}{\partial r}, \qquad L^* = \frac{\partial C^*}{\partial w}, \qquad \lambda = \frac{\partial C^*}{\partial Q}, \qquad \frac{\partial K^*}{\partial w} = \frac{\partial L^*}{\partial r}$$

where λ denotes the Lagrange multiplier.

Solution (a) The firm faces the cost minimization problem

$$\min C = rK + wL \text{ subject to } K^{1/2}L^{1/4} = Q$$

The Lagrangean here is $\mathcal{L}(K, L) = rK + wL - \lambda(K^{1/2}L^{1/4} - Q)$. Equating the partials to zero yields

$$\frac{\partial \mathcal{L}}{\partial K} = r - \frac{1}{2}\lambda K^{-1/2}L^{1/4} = 0, \qquad \frac{\partial \mathcal{L}}{\partial L} = w - \frac{1}{4}\lambda K^{1/2}L^{-3/4} = 0$$

Thus, $r = \frac{1}{2}\lambda K^{-1/2}L^{1/4}$ and $w = \frac{1}{4}\lambda K^{1/2}L^{-3/4}$. Solving both these equations for λ, then equating the two expressions obtained, yields

$$\lambda = 2rK^{1/2}L^{-1/4} = 4wK^{-1/2}L^{3/4} \tag{1}$$

Gathering terms on each side of the last equality (or multiplying both sides by $K^{1/2}L^{1/4}$) implies that $2rK = 4wL$, so $L = (r/2w)K$. Inserting this into the constraint $K^{1/2}L^{1/4} = Q$ gives $K^{1/2}(r/2w)^{1/4}K^{1/4} = Q$ so

$$K^{3/4} = 2^{1/4}r^{-1/4}w^{1/4}Q$$

Raising each side of the last equality to the power 4/3 yields (using $*$ superscripts)

$$K^* = 2^{1/3} r^{-1/3} w^{1/3} Q^{4/3}$$

and so

$$L^* = (r/2w) K^* = 2^{-2/3} r^{2/3} w^{-2/3} Q^{4/3}$$

The corresponding minimal cost is

$$C^* = r K^* + w L^* = 3 \cdot 2^{-2/3} r^{2/3} w^{1/3} Q^{4/3} \qquad [2]$$

Finally, using [1] again, we find that $\lambda = 2^{4/3} r^{2/3} w^{1/3} Q^{1/3}$. (For a proof that K^* and L^* really solve the minimization problem, see Example 18.8 of Section 18.4.)

(b) From [2], we find in particular that

$$\frac{\partial C^*}{\partial r} = 3 \cdot 2^{-2/3} \frac{2}{3} r^{-1/3} w^{1/3} Q^{4/3} = 2^{1/3} r^{-1/3} w^{1/3} Q^{4/3} = K^*$$

Note that the third equality in (b) is a special case of [18.7], and we find that the common value is $\lambda = \partial C^* / \partial Q = 2^{4/3} r^{2/3} w^{1/3} Q^{1/3}$. The other equalities are also easily verified.

Note: One of the most frequently occurring errors in the economics literature concerning the Lagrangean method is the claim that it transforms a constrained optimization problem into one of finding an unconstrained optimum of the Lagrangean. Problem 4 shows that this is wrong.

Problems

1. Consider the problem max $f(x, y) = x + y$ subject to $g(x, y) = x^2 + y = 1$.
   a. Write down the Lagrangean function for the problem and solve the necessary conditions in this case.
   b. Explain the solution geometrically by drawing appropriate level curves for $f(x, y)$ together with the graph of the parabola $x^2 + y = 1$. Does the associated minimization problem have a solution?
   c. Replace the constraint by $x^2 + y = 1.1$, and solve the problem in this case. Find the corresponding change in the optimal value of $f(x, y) = x + y$, and check to see if this change is approximately equal to $\lambda \cdot 0.1$, as suggested by [18.8].

2. Consider the problem

$$\min f(x, y) = x^2 + y^2 \text{ subject to } x + 2y = a \qquad (a \text{ is a constant})$$

   a. Solve the problem by first using the constraint to eliminate y. Prove that you have really found the minimum.

b. Write down the Lagrangean function for the problem and solve the necessary conditions in this case.

c. Also solve the problem by studying the level curves of $f(x, y) = x^2 + y^2$ together with the graph of the straight line $x + 2y = a$ in the same diagram. Can you give a geometric interpretation of the problem? Does the associated maximization problem have a solution?

d. Verify equation [18.7] for this problem.

3. Solve the following problems by the Lagrangean method. Prove, in each case, that you have found the optimal solution.

    a. max $x^2 + 3xy + y^2$ subject to $x + y = 100$.

    b. max $12x\sqrt{y}$ subject to $3x + 4y = 12$.

4. Consider the problem max xy subject to $x + y = 2$. Using the Lagrangean method, prove that $(x, y) = (1, 1)$ solves the problem with $\lambda = 1$. Prove also that $(1, 1)$ does not maximize the associated Lagrangean function $\mathcal{L}(x, y) = xy - 1 \cdot (x + y - 2)$ with $\lambda = 1$.

5. Consider the problem max $10x^{1/2}y^{1/3}$ subject to $2x + 4y = m$.

    a. Write down the necessary conditions in this case, and solve them for x, y, and λ as functions of m.

    b. Verify [18.7].

6. Consider the problem max $U(x, y) = 100 - e^{-x} - e^{-y}$ subject to $px + qy = m$.

    a. Write down the necessary conditions for the solution of the problem and solve them for x, y, and λ as functions of p, q, and m.

    b. Prove that x and y are homogeneous of degree 0 as functions of p, q, and m. Explain how one can arrive at this conclusion just by looking at the given problem. (What happens to the constraint when p, q, and m are replaced by tp, tq, and tm, respectively, for some $t > 0$?)

7. Let p be a fixed real number and consider the problem

$$\min x + 2y \text{ subject to } p(x^2 + y^2) + x^2y^2 - 4 = 0 \qquad [*]$$

    a. For $p = 0$, find the solution to the problem if we assume $x \geq 0$ and $y \geq 0$.

    b. For p arbitrary, prove that in order for a point (x, y) with $x > 0$ and $y > 0$ to solve problem $[*]$, then (x, y) must satisfy the equations

$$2px - py + 2xy^2 - x^2y = 0, \qquad px^2 + py^2 + x^2y^2 = 4 \qquad [**]$$

    c. Assume that $[**]$ defines x and y as continuously differentiable functions of p in a certain interval around $p = 0$. By implicit differentiation of $[**]$, find the derivatives $x'(p)$ and $y'(p)$ at $p = 0$.

d. Let $h(p) = x(p) + 2y(p)$. Find $h'(0)$.

8. An oil producer starts production on an oil field at time $t = 0$. Suppose that all the oil will be extracted in a time span $[0, y]$ and that the production per unit of time at time $t \in [0, y]$ is $xt(y - t)$. Assume that the producer can choose the size of x as well as that of y. The total amount of oil extracted in the given time span is thus given by the following function of x and y:

$$g(x, y) = \int_0^y xt(y - t)\, dt$$

Assume further that the sales price p per unit of oil is an increasing function of time, $p = 1 + t$, and that the cost per unit of oil extracted is equal to αy^2, where α is a positive constant. The net income per unit of time is then $(1 + t - \alpha y^2)xt(y - t)$, so that the total net income in the time span $[0, y]$ is a function of x and y given by

$$f(x, y) = \int_0^y (1 + t - \alpha y^2)\, xt\, (y - t)\, dt$$

If the total amount of extractable oil in the field is M, the producer can only choose values of x and y such that $g(x, y) = M$. Its problem is thus

$$\max\ f(x, y) \text{ subject to } g(x, y) = M \qquad [*]$$

a. Find explicit expressions for $f(x, y)$ and $g(x, y)$ by calculating the given integrals, and then solve problem [*].
b. As $\alpha \to 0$, the value of y that maximizes net income will tend to ∞. Why?
c. Verify Equation [18.7] in this case.

18.3 An Analytical Proof of the Lagrangean Method (Optional)

The discussion in Section 18.2 did not make precise the conditions under which the Lagrangean method works. Actually, some optimization problems can cause trouble unless we take greater care. A case in point is the following problem:

Example 18.7

$$\max\ f(x, y) = 2x + 3y \text{ subject to } g(x, y) = \sqrt{x} + \sqrt{y} = 5$$

Solution   The Lagrangean is $\mathcal{L}(x, y) = 2x + 3y - \lambda(\sqrt{x} + \sqrt{y} - 5)$. So, the three conditions for (x, y) to be a solution appear to be

$$\mathcal{L}'_1(x, y) = 2 - \lambda \frac{1}{2\sqrt{x}} = 0$$

$$\mathcal{L}'_2(x, y) = 3 - \lambda \frac{1}{2\sqrt{y}} = 0 \qquad\qquad [1]$$

$$\sqrt{x} + \sqrt{y} = 5$$

The first two equations of [1] give $\lambda = 4\sqrt{x} = 6\sqrt{y}$. Squaring and then eliminating λ^2 gives $16x = 36y$, which implies $y = 4x/9$. Inserting this equation into the constraint gives $(5/3)\sqrt{x} = 5$, and so $x = 9$. It follows that $y = 4$. Thus, the Lagrangean method suggests the solution $(x, y) = (9, 4)$. Here $f(9, 4) = 2 \cdot 9 + 3 \cdot 4 = 30$. But, for instance, $(x, y) = (25, 0)$ also satisfies the constraint, and $f(25, 0) = 50$. Hence, $(9, 4)$ does *not* solve the given problem.

Is there a solution to the maximization problem? Yes. In fact, the set of points satisfying the constraint is the curve indicated in Fig. 18.4, and this is a closed, bounded set. The continuous function $f(x, y) = 2x + 3y$ therefore attains both a maximum and minimum on this curve, by the extreme-value theorem. How this fits in with the Lagrangean method is explained in what follows.

The solution to the problem can be obtained by studying the level curves of $f(x, y) = 2x + 3y$, which are all straight lines. The minimum value of $f(x, y)$ subject to the given constraint is at the point P, which was previously found to be $(x, y) = (9, 4)$. The maximum is attained at the point $(0, 25)$, with $f(0, 25) = 75$. The Lagrangean method cannot find this extreme point, however.

FIGURE 18.4   Point P minimizes $2x + 3y$ when $\sqrt{x} + \sqrt{y} = 5$, whereas $(0, 25)$ is the maximum point.

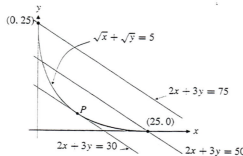

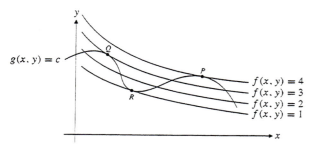

FIGURE 18.5 **Level curves for** $z = f(x, y)$ **are shown, together with the graph of** $g(x, y) = c$.

The argument supporting condition [18.3], which was the basis for the Lagrangean method, is also valid for local extreme points of $f(x, y)$ subject to $g(x, y) = c$. Figure 18.5 illustrates the concepts of local and global extreme points in this setting. The point R is a local minimum point for $f(x, y)$ subject to $g(x, y) = c$, and Q and P are local maximum points. The global maximum of $f(x, y)$ subject to $g(x, y) = c$ is attained only at P. Each of the points P, Q, and R in Fig. 18.5 satisfies the necessary condition [18.3]. A precise result is as follows:

Theorem 18.1 (Lagrange's Theorem)   Suppose that $f(x, y)$ and $g(x, y)$ have continuous partial derivatives in a domain A of the xy-plane, and that (x_0, y_0) is both an interior point of A and a local extreme point for $f(x, y)$ subject to the constraint $g(x, y) = c$. Suppose further that $g_1'(x_0, y_0)$ and $g_2'(x_0, y_0)$ are not both 0. Then there exists a unique number λ such that the Lagrangean function

$$\mathcal{L}(x, y) = f(x, y) - \lambda \left(g(x, y) - c \right)$$

has a stationary point at (x_0, y_0).

Proof   Suppose $g_2'(x_0, y_0) \neq 0$. By the implicit function theorem (see the Note at the end of Section 16.3), the equation $g(x, y) = c$ defines y as a differentiable function of x in some neighborhood of (x_0, y_0). If this function is denoted by $y = h(x)$, then

$$y' = h'(x) = -g_1'(x, y)/g_2'(x, y)$$

With $g(x, y) = c$ replaced by $y = h(x)$, the constrained maximization problem [18.2] is reduced to the problem of maximizing $z = f(x, y) = f(x, h(x))$ with respect to the single variable x. A necessary condition for a maximum is that the total derivative of z with respect to x is 0. But

$$\frac{dz}{dx} = f_1'(x, y) + f_2'(x, y)y' \qquad \text{(with } y' = h'(x)\text{)}$$

Substituting the previous expression for $h'(x)$ gives the following necessary condition for (x_0, y_0) to be a local extreme point:

$$\frac{dz}{dx} = f_1'(x_0, y_0) - f_2'(x_0, y_0)\frac{g_1'(x_0, y_0)}{g_2'(x_0, y_0)} = 0 \qquad [18.9]$$

Introducing $\lambda = f_2'(x_0, y_0)/g_2'(x_0, y_0)$, we see that the earlier stationarity conditions [18.4] are both satisfied at (x_0, y_0), so the Lagrangean has a stationary point at (x_0, y_0).

We assumed that $g_2'(x_0, y_0) \neq 0$. If instead $g_2'(x_0, y_0) = 0$, the hypotheses imply that $g_1'(x_0, y_0) \neq 0$. Then the implicit function theorem tells us that $g(x, y) = c$ defines x as a differentiable function of y in a neighborhood of (x_0, y_0). The rest of the argument goes along the same lines, with x and y interchanged throughout.

In the light of Theorem 18.1, let us now reconsider the difficulty we encountered in Example 18.7. The function $f(x, y) = 2x + 3y$ is continuously differentiable everywhere. The constraint function $g(x, y) = \sqrt{x} + \sqrt{y}$, however, is defined only for $x \geq 0$ and $y \geq 0$. Its partial derivatives are $g_1'(x, y) = 1/2\sqrt{x}$ and $g_2'(x, y) = 1/2\sqrt{y}$, and we see that g is continuously differentiable only on the set A of (x, y) such that $x > 0$ and $y > 0$. Note that g_1' and g_2' are different from 0 at all points of the open set A. Theorem 18.1 tells us that a point in A that lies on the constraint curve and solves our problem must satisfy [1] in Example 18.7. We found only one point with this property, namely, $(9, 4)$. However, there are two other points outside A to examine: the boundary points $(25, 0)$ and $(0, 25)$ on the constraint curve. Because $f(9, 4) = 30$, $f(25, 0) = 50$, and $f(0, 25) = 75$, we conclude that the minimum point is $(9, 4)$ and the maximum point is $(0, 25)$. (From the argument in Example 18.7, we do know that the maximum and minimum are attained.)

Problems

1. The following text taken from a book on mathematics for management contains *grave* errors. Sort them out. "Consider the general problem of finding the extreme points of $z = f(x, y)$ subject to the constraint $g(x, y) = 0$. Clearly the extreme points must satisfy the pair of equations $f_x'(x, y) = 0$, $f_y'(x, y) = 0$ in addition to the constraint $g(x, y) = 0$. Thus, there are three equations that must be satisfied by the pair of unknowns x, y. Because there are more equations than unknowns, the system is said to be overdetermined and, in general, is difficult to solve. In order to facilitate computation ... " (A description of the Lagrangean method follows.)

2. Consider the problem

$$\min f(x, y) = (x - 1)^2 + y^2 \text{ subject to } y^2 - 8x = 0$$

    a. Try to solve the problem by reducing it to a minimization problem in (i) the x variable; (ii) the y variable. Comment.
    b. Solve the problem by using the Lagrangean method.
    c. Give a geometric interpretation of the problem.

Harder Problems

3. Let the functions f and g be defined by

$$f(x, y) = (x + 2)^2 + y^2 \quad \text{and} \quad g(x, y) = y^2 - x(x + 1)^2$$

Find the minimum value of $f(x, y)$ subject to $g(x, y) = 0$. (*Hint:* Draw a graph. Be sure to include all points satisfying $g(x, y) = 0$.)

18.4 Sufficient Conditions

Under the hypotheses of Theorem 18.1, the Lagrange multiplier method for the problem

$$\max(\min) f(x, y) \text{ subject to } g(x, y) = c \qquad [18.10]$$

gives *necessary* conditions for the solution of the problem. In order to ascertain that we have really found the solution, more arguments are needed. Sometimes we can rely on the extreme-value theorem (as in Examples 18.4 and 18.7), or ad hoc methods (as at the end of Example 18.4).

    If (x_0, y_0) does solve problem [18.10], then Theorem 18.1 implies that the Lagrangean function $\mathcal{L}(x, y) = f(x, y) - \lambda(g(x, y) - c)$ is stationary at (x_0, y_0), but $\mathcal{L}$ does not necessarily have a maximum (minimum) at (x_0, y_0) (see Problem 4, Section 18.2). Suppose, however, that (x_0, y_0) happens to maximize $\mathcal{L}(x, y)$ among *all* (x, y). Then

$$\mathcal{L}(x_0, y_0) = f(x_0, y_0) - \lambda(g(x_0, y_0) - c)$$
$$\geq \mathcal{L}(x, y) \qquad [*]$$
$$= f(x, y) - \lambda(g(x, y) - c)$$

for all (x, y). If (x_0, y_0) also satisfies the constraint $g(x_0, y_0) = c$, then $[*]$ reduces to $f(x_0, y_0) \geq f(x, y)$ for all (x, y) such that $g(x, y) = c$. Hence, (x_0, y_0) really does solve the maximization problem [18.10]. A corresponding result is obtained for the minimization problem in [18.10], provided that (x_0, y_0) minimizes $\mathcal{L}(x, y)$ among all pairs (x, y). Combining this observation with Theorem 17.8 in

Section 17.7 gives the following:

Theorem 18.2 (Global Sufficiency)   Suppose that $f(x, y)$ and $g(x, y)$ in problem [18.10] are continuously differentiable functions on an open convex set A in R^2, and let $(x_0, y_0) \in A$ be an interior stationary point for the Lagrangean function

$$\mathcal{L}(x, y) = f(x, y) - \lambda(g(x, y) - c)$$

Suppose further that $g(x_0, y_0) = c$. Then

$$\mathcal{L}(x, y) \text{ concave} \implies \begin{cases} (x_0, y_0) \text{ solves the maximization} \\ \text{problem in [18.10]} \end{cases}$$

$$\mathcal{L}(x, y) \text{ convex} \implies \begin{cases} (x_0, y_0) \text{ solves the minimization} \\ \text{problem in [18.10]} \end{cases}$$

Note that $\mathcal{L}(x, y) = f(x, y) - \lambda(g(x, y) - c)$ is *concave* if $f(x, y)$ is concave and $\lambda g(x, y)$ is convex, because then $\mathcal{L}(x, y) = f(x, y) + [-\lambda g(x, y)] + \lambda c$ is a sum of concave functions.

Example 18.8

Consider Example 18.6 of Section 18.2. The linear function $rK + wL$ is convex, and the Cobb–Douglas function $K^{1/2}L^{1/4}$ is concave (see Example 17.18, Section 17.8). Because $\lambda \geq 0$, the Lagrangean

$$\mathcal{L}(K, L) = rK + wL + (-\lambda)(K^{1/2}L^{1/4} - Q)$$

is a sum of two convex functions, and hence convex. By Theorem 18.2, the pair (K^*, L^*) *is* cost-minimizing.

Local Sufficient Conditions

Consider the local constrained maximization (or minimization) problem

$$\text{local max(min) } f(x, y) \text{ subject to } g(x, y) = c \qquad [18.11]$$

Our argument for the first-order conditions is essentially as follows. Where $g_2'(x, y) \neq 0$, the objective $z = f(x, y)$ is, in effect, a function of x alone, because of the presence of the constraint. By computing dz/dx and taking into account how y depends on x, we obtain a necessary condition for local extreme points. To find a sufficient condition for local extreme points, we consider the sign of d^2z/dx^2. Now [18.9] implies that

$$\frac{dz}{dx} = f_1'(x, y) - f_2'(x, y)\frac{g_1'(x, y)}{g_2'(x, y)} \qquad [1]$$

The derivative d^2z/dx^2 is just the total derivative of dz/dx w.r.t. x. Assuming that f and g are twice continuously differentiable functions and recalling that y is a function of x, we obtain

$$\frac{d^2z}{dx^2} = f_{11}'' + f_{12}''y' - (f_{21}'' + f_{22}''y')\frac{g_1'}{g_2'} - f_2'\frac{(g_{11}'' + g_{12}''y')g_2' - (g_{21}'' + g_{22}''y')g_1'}{(g_2')^2}$$

Because f and g are twice continuously differentiable functions, $f_{12}'' = f_{21}''$ and $g_{12}'' = g_{21}''$. Moreover, $y' = -g_1'/g_2'$. Also $f_1' = \lambda g_1'$ and $f_2' = \lambda g_2'$, because these are the first-order conditions. Using these relationships to eliminate y' and f_2', as well as some elementary algebra, we obtain

$$\frac{d^2z}{dx^2} = \frac{1}{(g_2')^2}\left[(f_{11}'' - \lambda g_{11}'')(g_2')^2 - 2(f_{12}'' - \lambda g_{12}'')g_1'g_2' + (f_{22}'' - \lambda g_{22}'')(g_1')^2\right] \qquad [2]$$

It turns out that the rather lengthy expression in square brackets can be written in a symmetric form that is much easier to remember. In fact, using the result in [**] at the end of Section 15.8, if we define $D(x, y)$ by

$$D(x, y) = \begin{vmatrix} 0 & g_1'(x, y) & g_2'(x, y) \\ g_1'(x, y) & f_{11}''(x, y) - \lambda g_{11}''(x, y) & f_{12}''(x, y) - \lambda g_{12}''(x, y) \\ g_2'(x, y) & f_{21}''(x, y) - \lambda g_{21}''(x, y) & f_{22}''(x, y) - \lambda g_{22}''(x, y) \end{vmatrix} \qquad [18.12]$$

then

$$\frac{d^2z}{dx^2} = -\frac{1}{[g_2'(x, y)]^2}D(x, y) \qquad [18.13]$$

Note that the 2×2 matrix at the bottom right of [18.12] is the Hessian of the Lagrangean function. So the determinant is naturally called a **bordered Hessian**. We have arrived at the following result:

A sufficient condition for (x_0, y_0) to solve problem [18.11] is that (x_0, y_0) satisfies the first-order conditions and, moreover, that the bordered Hessian $D(x_0, y_0)$ given by [18.12] is > 0 in the maximization case, and is < 0 in the minimization case. [18.14]

The conditions on the sign of the determinant $D(x, y)$ are called the (local) *second-order conditions* for problem [18.11].

Example 18.9

Consider the problem

$$\text{local max (min) } f(x, y) = x^2 + y^2$$

$$\text{subject to } g(x, y) = x^2 + xy + y^2 = 3$$

(see Example 18.4). The first-order conditions give the points $(1, 1)$ and $(-1, -1)$ with $\lambda = 2/3$, as well as $(\sqrt{3}, -\sqrt{3})$ and $(-\sqrt{3}, \sqrt{3})$ with $\lambda = 2$. Check the second-order conditions in this case.

Solution   In this case, $f_{11}'' = 2$, $f_{12}'' = 0$, $f_{22}'' = 2$, $g_{11}'' = 2$, $g_{12}'' = 1$, and $g_{22}'' = 2$, so

$$D(x, y) = \begin{vmatrix} 0 & 2x+y & x+2y \\ 2x+y & 2-2\lambda & -\lambda \\ x+2y & -\lambda & 2-2\lambda \end{vmatrix}$$

Evaluating the four relevant determinants of order 3 when $\lambda = 2/3$ or 2, as appropriate, yields $D(1, 1) = D(-1, -1) = -24$ and $D(\sqrt{3}, -\sqrt{3}) = D(-\sqrt{3}, \sqrt{3}) = 24$. We conclude that $(1, 1)$ and $(-1, -1)$ are local minimum points, whereas $(\sqrt{3}, -\sqrt{3})$ and $(-\sqrt{3}, \sqrt{3})$ are local maximum points. (In Example 18.4, we actually proved that these points were *global* extreme points.)

Problems

1. Use Theorem 18.2 to check the optimal solution in Problem 5, Section 18.2.
2. Consider the problem min $x^2 + y^2$ subject to $x + 2y = a$. Compute $D(x, y)$ in [18.12] in this case. Compare with the result in Problem 2, Section 18.2.

18.5 More General Lagrangean Problems

Constrained optimization problems in economics usually involve more than just two variables. We begin by considering the problem

$$\text{max(min) } f(x_1, \dots, x_n) \text{ subject to } g(x_1, \dots, x_n) = c \qquad [18.15]$$

Lagrange's method from the previous sections can be easily generalized. As before, associate a Lagrangean multiplier λ with the constraint and form the Lagrangean

$$\mathcal{L}(x_1, \dots, x_n) = f(x_1, \dots, x_n) - \lambda\big(g(x_1, \dots, x_n) - c\big) \qquad [18.16]$$

Next, compute the partial derivatives of $\mathcal{L}$ and equate them to zero, so that

$$f_1'(x_1, \ldots, x_n) - \lambda g_1'(x_1, \ldots, x_n) = 0$$

$$\cdots\cdots\cdots\cdots\cdots\cdots\cdots\cdots\cdots\cdots\cdots\cdots\cdots\cdots \qquad [18.17]$$

$$f_n'(x_1, \ldots, x_n) - \lambda g_n'(x_1, \ldots, x_n) = 0$$

These n equations together with the constraint form $n + 1$ equations to determine the $n + 1$ unknowns $x_1, \ldots, x_n$, and λ.

Note: This method will (in general) fail to give correct necessary conditions if all the partials of $g(x_1, \ldots, x_n)$ vanish at the stationary point of the Lagrangean. Otherwise, the proof is an easy generalization of that for Theorem 18.1. If, say, $\partial g / \partial x_n \neq 0$, "solve" $g(x_1, \ldots, x_n) = c$ for x_n and reduce the problem to an unconstrained problem in $x_1, \ldots, x_{n-1}$. (See Problem 11 for the case $n = 3$.)

Example 18.10

Find the only possible solution to the problem

$$\max\ x^2 y^3 z \quad \text{subject to}\ x + y + z = 12 \qquad [1]$$

Solution   The Lagrangean is

$$\mathcal{L}(x, y, z) = x^2 y^3 z - \lambda(x + y + z - 12) \qquad [2]$$

The first-order conditions [18.17] become

$$\frac{\partial \mathcal{L}}{\partial x} = 2x y^3 z - \lambda = 0$$

$$\frac{\partial \mathcal{L}}{\partial y} = 3x^2 y^2 z - \lambda = 0 \qquad [3]$$

$$\frac{\partial \mathcal{L}}{\partial z} = x^2 y^3 - \lambda = 0$$

If *any* of the variables x, y, and z is 0, then $x^2 y^3 z = 0$, which is *not* the maximum value. So suppose that x, y, and z are all $\neq 0$. From the two first equations in [3], we have $2x y^3 z = 3x^2 y^2 z$, so $y = 3x/2$. The first and third equations in [3] likewise give $z = x/2$. Inserting $y = 3x/2$ and $z = x/2$ into the constraint yields $x + 3x/2 + x/2 = 12$, so $x = 4$. Then $y = 6$ and $z = 2$. Thus, the only possible solution is $(x, y, z) = (4, 6, 2)$.

Example 18.11

For problem [18.1] in the introduction, the Lagrangean function is

$$\mathcal{L}(x_1, \ldots, x_n) = U(x_1, \ldots, x_n) - \lambda(p_1 x_1 + \cdots + p_n x_n - m)$$

so

$$\mathcal{L}_i'(x_1, \ldots, x_n) = U_i'(x_1, \ldots, x_n) - \lambda p_i \qquad (i = 1, \ldots, n)$$

Writing $\mathbf{x} = (x_1, \ldots, x_n)$, we have

$$\frac{U_1'(\mathbf{x})}{p_1} = \frac{U_2'(\mathbf{x})}{p_2} = \cdots = \frac{U_n'(\mathbf{x})}{p_n} = \lambda \qquad [18.18]$$

Apart from the last equation, which serves only to determine the Lagrangean multiplier λ, we have $n - 1$ equations. (For $n = 2$, there is one equation; for $n = 3$, there are two equations; and so on.) In addition, the constraint must hold. Thus, we have n equations to determine the values of $x_1, \ldots, x_n$. The partial derivative $U_i'(\mathbf{x}) = \partial U / \partial x_i$ is called the **marginal utility** of the ith commodity. Equation [18.18] say that *if* $\mathbf{x} = (x_1, \ldots, x_n)$ *maximizes utility subject to the budget constraint, then the ratio between the marginal utility of a commodity and its price per unit must be the same for all the commodities.*

Assume that the system consisting of the equations in [18.18] plus the budget constraint is solved for $x_1, \ldots, x_n$ as functions of $p_1, \ldots, p_n$ and m, giving $x_i = D_i(p_1, \ldots, p_n, m)$, for $i = 1, \ldots, n$. Then $D_i(p_1, \ldots, p_n, m)$ gives the amount of the ith commodity demanded by the individual when facing prices $p_1, \ldots, p_n$ and income m. Therefore, $D_1, \ldots, D_n$ are called the **(individual) demand functions**.

Example 18.12

An individual purchases quantities a, b, and c of three different commodities whose prices are p, q, and r, respectively. The consumer's (exogenous) income is m, where $m > 2p$, and the utility function is given as $U(a, b, c) = a + \ln(bc)$. Find the consumer's demand for each good as a function of prices p, q, r, and income m. Show that expenditure on each of the second and the third goods is always equal to p.

Solution Here $U_1'(a, b, c) = 1$, $U_2'(a, b, c) = (1/bc)c = 1/b$, and $U_3'(a, b, c) = (1/bc)b = 1/c$. Equations [18.18] imply that

$$\frac{1}{p} = \frac{1/b}{q} = \frac{1/c}{r} = \lambda.$$

From the first equality, we get $qb = p$, and from the second, $rc = p$, so expenditure on each of the second and the third goods *is* equal to p. Inserting $qb = p$ and $rc = p$ into the budget constraint yields $pa + p + p = m$, so $a = m/p - 2$. This is positive when $m > 2p$. Thus, for $m > 2p$, the demand functions are $a = m/p - 2$, $b = p/q$, and $c = p/r$.

The General Case

Sometimes economists need to consider optimization problems with more than one equality constraint. The corresponding general Lagrangean problem is

$$\max(\min) f(x_1, \ldots, x_n) \text{ subject to } \begin{cases} g_1(x_1, \ldots, x_n) = c_1 \\ \ldots\ldots\ldots\ldots\ldots \\ g_m(x_1, \ldots, x_n) = c_m \end{cases} \qquad [18.19]$$

The method of Lagrange multipliers can be extended to treat problem [18.19]. Associate **Lagrange multipliers** with each of the m constraints, and define the new **Lagrangean function** by

$$\mathcal{L}(x_1, \ldots, x_n) = f(x_1, \ldots, x_n) - \sum_{j=1}^{m} \lambda_j \left(g_j(x_1, \ldots, x_n) - c_j \right) \qquad [18.20]$$

The necessary first-order conditions for an optimum are that the partial derivatives of the Lagrangean w.r.t. each x_i vanish, so that[4]

$$\frac{\partial \mathcal{L}}{\partial x_i} = \frac{\partial f(x_1, \ldots, x_n)}{\partial x_i} - \sum_{j=1}^{m} \lambda_j \frac{\partial g_j(x_1, \ldots, x_n)}{\partial x_i} = 0, \qquad i = 1, 2, \ldots, n \qquad [18.21]$$

Together with the m equality constraints, these n equations form a total of $n + m$ equations in the $n + m$ unknowns $x_1, \ldots, x_n, \lambda_1, \ldots, \lambda_m$.

Example 18.13

Solve the problem

$$\max(\min) x^2 + y^2 + z^2 \text{ subject to } \begin{cases} x + 2y + z = 1 & [1] \\ 2x - y - 3z = 4 & [2] \end{cases}$$

Solution   The Lagrangean function is

$$\mathcal{L}(x, y, z) = x^2 + y^2 + z^2 - \lambda_1(x + 2y + z - 1) - \lambda_2(2x - y - 3z - 4)$$

The first-order conditions [18.21] require that

$$\frac{\partial \mathcal{L}}{\partial x} = 2x - \lambda_1 - 2\lambda_2 = 0 \qquad [3]$$

$$\frac{\partial \mathcal{L}}{\partial y} = 2y - 2\lambda_1 + \lambda_2 = 0 \qquad [4]$$

$$\frac{\partial \mathcal{L}}{\partial z} = 2z - \lambda_1 + 3\lambda_2 = 0 \qquad [5]$$

---

[4]In Theorem 18.1, we assumed that g_1' and g_2' did not both vanish. The corresponding condition here is that the gradient vectors of $g_1, \ldots, g_m$ are linearly independent in R^n.

So there are five equations, [1] to [5], to determine the five unknowns x, y, z, λ_1, and λ_2.

Solving [3] and [4] simultaneously for λ_1 and λ_2 gives

$$\lambda_1 = \frac{2}{5}x + \frac{4}{5}y, \qquad \lambda_2 = \frac{4}{5}x - \frac{2}{5}y \qquad [6]$$

Inserting these expressions for λ_1 and λ_2 into [5] and rearranging yields

$$x - y + z = 0 \qquad [7]$$

This equation together with [1] and [2] constitutes a system of three linear equations in the unknowns x, y, and z. Solving this system by Cramer's rule (or better, elimination) gives

$$x = \frac{16}{15}, \qquad y = \frac{1}{3}, \qquad z = -\frac{11}{15} \qquad [8]$$

The corresponding values of the multipliers are $\lambda_1 = 52/75$ and $\lambda_2 = 54/75$.

Here is a geometric argument that might convince you that [8] solves the minimization problem. Each of the two constraints represents a plane in R^3, and the points satisfying both constraints consequently lie on the straight line where the two planes intersect. Now $x^2 + y^2 + z^2$ is the square of the distance from the origin to the point (x, y, z). Therefore, our problem is to find the minimum and the maximum distances from the origin to the points on a straight line. No maximum distance can possibly exist, but it is geometrically obvious that there is a minimum distance, and that it must be attained at the point we have found.

Problems

1. Consider the problem min $x^2 + y^2 + z^2$ subject to $x + y + z = 1$.
   a. Write down the Lagrangean for this problem, and find the only point (x, y, z) that satisfies the necessary conditions.
   b. Give a geometric argument for the existence of a solution. Has the corresponding maximization problem any solution?

2. Solve the problem min $x + 4y + 3z$ subject to $x^2 + 2y^2 + \frac{1}{3}z^2 = b$. (Suppose that $b > 0$ and take it for granted that the problem has a solution.)

3. Each week an individual consumes quantities x and y of two goods, and works for ℓ hours. These quantities are chosen to maximize the utility function

$$U(x, y, \ell) = \alpha \ln x + \beta \ln y + (1 - \alpha - \beta) \ln(L - \ell)$$

which is defined for $0 \le \ell < L$ and for $x, y > 0$. Here α and β are positive parameters satisfying $\alpha + \beta < 1$. The individual faces the budget constraint $p x + q y = w \ell + m$, where $m \ (\geq 0)$ denotes unearned income.

a. Assuming that

$$m \leq \left(\frac{\alpha + \beta}{1 - \alpha - \beta} \right) w L \qquad\qquad [*]$$

find the individual's demands x, y, and labor supply ℓ as functions of p, q, r, and m.

b. What happens if the inequality $[*]$ is violated?

4. For the problem in Example 18.13, let $(x, y, z) = (\frac{16}{15} + h, \frac{1}{3} + k, -\frac{11}{15} + \ell)$. Show that if (x, y, z) satisfies both constraints, then $k = -h$ and $\ell = h$. Then show that $f(x, y, z) = (16/15)^2 + (1/3)^2 + (-11/15)^2 + 3h^2$. Conclusion?

5. Solve the following problem, assuming that it has a solution:

$$\min x^2 - 2x + 2y^2 + z^2 + z \quad \text{subject to} \quad \begin{cases} x + y + z = 1 \\ 2x - y - z = 5 \end{cases}$$

6. a. By using Lagrange's method, find *possible* solutions to the problem

$$\max \, (\min) \, x + y + z \quad \text{subject to} \quad \begin{cases} x^2 + y^2 + z^2 = 1 \\ x - y - z = 1 \end{cases}$$

b. Give a geometric interpretation of the constraints, and use the extreme-value theorem to prove that maximum and minimum values exist. Find the maximum and minimum points.

7. Solve the problem

$$\max \, (\min) \, x + y \quad \text{subject to} \quad \begin{cases} x^2 + 2y^2 + z^2 = 1 \\ x + y + z = 1 \end{cases}$$

8. A statistical problem requires solving

$$\min a_1^2 x_1^2 + a_2^2 x_2^2 + \cdots + a_n^2 x_n^2 \quad \text{subject to} \quad x_1 + x_2 + \cdots + x_n = 1$$

Solve the problem, taking it for granted that the minimum value exists.

Harder Problems

9. a. Solve the problem (taking it for granted that there is a solution)

$$\min \, f(x, y, z) = (y + z - 3)^2 \quad \text{subject to} \quad \begin{cases} x^2 + y + z = 2 \\ x + y^2 + 2z = 2 \end{cases}$$

b. The necessary conditions in part (a) have two solutions. It is tempting to believe that the one that does not solve the minimization problem must solve the maximization problem. Show that this is not the case here.

10. Consider the problem in Example 18.11. Find the demand functions when (cf. Problems 10 and 11 in Section 17.1):

    a. $U(x_1, \ldots, x_n) = Ax_1^{a_1} \cdots x_n^{a_n}$ $(A > 0, a_1 > 0, \cdots, a_n > 0)$

    b. $U(x_1, \ldots, x_n) = x_1^a + \cdots + x_n^a$ $(0 < a < 1)$

11. Consider the problem max (min) $f(x_1, x_2, x_3)$ subject to $g(x_1, x_2, x_3) = c$. Suppose that the constraint equation defines x_3 as a continuously differentiable function of x_1 and x_2. Derive [18.17] for $n = 3$ by using the idea in the analytical proof of [18.9] in Section 18.3. (*Hint:* Let $\lambda = f_3'/g_3'$.)

12. Consider the problem $\max \mathbf{x}'\mathbf{A}\mathbf{x} = \sum_{i=1}^{n} \sum_{j=1}^{n} a_{ij} x_i x_j$ subject to $\mathbf{x}'\mathbf{x} = \sum x_i^2 = 1$ (with $\mathbf{A}$ symmetric). Prove that any solution vector $\mathbf{x}_0$ must be an eigenvector for $\mathbf{A}$. If λ_0 is the associated eigenvalue, show that $\lambda_0 = \mathbf{x}_0'\mathbf{A}\mathbf{x}_0$. Thus, the maximum value of $\mathbf{x}'\mathbf{A}\mathbf{x}$ subject to the given constraint is the largest eigenvalue of $\mathbf{A}$. (*Hint:* Consider, first, the case $n = 2$.) What about the corresponding minimization problem?

18.6 Economic Interpretations of Lagrange Multipliers

Section 18.2 showed how the Lagrange multiplier for the problem of maximizing $f(x, y)$ subject to $g(x, y) = c$ can be given an interesting marginal value interpretation. This section generalizes this result. By using the vector notation $\mathbf{x} = (x_1, \ldots, x_n)$, the general Lagrangean problem [18.19] can be formulated more concisely as

$$\max(\min) f(\mathbf{x}) \quad \text{subject to } g_j(\mathbf{x}) = c_j, \quad j = 1, \ldots, m \qquad [18.22]$$

Let $x_1^*, \ldots, x_n^*$ be the values of $x_1, \ldots, x_n$ that satisfy the necessary conditions for the solution to [18.22]. In general, $x_1^*, \ldots, x_n^*$ depend on the values of $c_1, \ldots, c_m$. We assume that $x_i^* = x_i^*(c_1, \ldots, c_m)$ $(i = 1, \ldots, n)$ are differentiable functions of $c_1, \ldots, c_m$. The associated value f^* of f is then a function of $c_1, \ldots, c_m$ as well. Indeed, if we put $\mathbf{x}^* = (x_1^*, \ldots, x_n^*)$ and $\mathbf{c} = (c_1, \ldots, c_m)$, then

$$f^*(\mathbf{c}) = f(\mathbf{x}^*(\mathbf{c})) = f(x_1^*(\mathbf{c}), \ldots, x_n^*(\mathbf{c})) \qquad [18.23]$$

The function f^* is called the (**optimal**) **value function** for problem [18.22]. The Lagrange multipliers associated with $\mathbf{x}^*$ also depend on $c_1, \ldots, c_m$. Provided that certain regularity conditions are satisfied, we have

$$\frac{\partial f^*(\mathbf{c})}{\partial c_i} = \lambda_i(\mathbf{c}) \qquad (i = 1, \ldots, m) \tag{18.24}$$

The Lagrange multiplier $\lambda_i = \lambda_i(\mathbf{c})$ for the ith constraint is the rate at which the optimal value of the objective function changes w.r.t. changes in the constant c_i. The number λ_i is referred to as a **shadow price** (or **marginal value**) imputed to a unit of resource i.

A rough argument for [18.24]: Taking the differential of [18.23] gives

$$df^*(\mathbf{c}) = df(\mathbf{x}^*(\mathbf{c})) = \sum_{i=1}^{n} f_i'(\mathbf{x}^*(\mathbf{c})) \, dx_i^*(\mathbf{c})$$

But the first-order conditions [18.21] of Section 18.5 imply that

$$f_i'(\mathbf{x}^*(\mathbf{c})) = \sum_{j=1}^{m} \lambda_j \frac{\partial g_j(\mathbf{x}^*(\mathbf{c}))}{\partial x_i} \qquad (i = 1, \ldots, n)$$

Also, differentiating each identity $g_j(\mathbf{x}^*(\mathbf{c})) = c_j$ gives

$$\sum_{i=1}^{n} \frac{\partial g_j(\mathbf{x}^*(\mathbf{c}))}{\partial x_i} \, dx_i^*(\mathbf{c}) = dc_j \qquad (j = 1, \ldots, m)$$

Therefore,

$$df^*(\mathbf{c}) = \sum_{i=1}^{n} \sum_{j=1}^{m} \lambda_j \frac{\partial g_j(\mathbf{x}^*(\mathbf{c}))}{\partial x_i} dx_i^*(\mathbf{c})$$

$$= \sum_{j=1}^{m} \lambda_j \sum_{i=1}^{n} \frac{\partial g_j(\mathbf{x}^*(\mathbf{c}))}{\partial x_i} dx_i^*(\mathbf{c})$$

$$= \sum_{j=1}^{m} \lambda_j \, dc_j$$

Suppose we change $\mathbf{c} = (c_1, \ldots, c_m)$ by $\mathbf{dc} = (dc_1, \ldots, dc_m)$. According to Section 16.8, if $dc_1, \ldots, dc_m$ are small in absolute value, then

$$f^*(\mathbf{c} + \mathbf{dc}) - f^*(\mathbf{c}) \approx \lambda_1(\mathbf{c}) \, dc_1 + \cdots + \lambda_m(\mathbf{c}) \, dc_m \tag{18.25}$$

Example 18.14

For Example 18.11, Section 18.5, let $U^*(p_1, \ldots, p_n, m)$ denote the maximum utility obtainable when prices are $p_1, \ldots, p_n$ and the income is m. This U^* is called the *indirect* utility function. Using [18.24], we see that

$$\lambda = \frac{\partial U^*}{\partial m} \qquad [18.26]$$

Thus, λ is approximately the increase in maximum utility from increasing income by one unit. Therefore, λ is generally called the **marginal utility of income.**

Example 18.15

Consider the problem in Example 18.13 of Section 18.5, and suppose we change the first constraint to $x + 2y + z = 0.9$ and the second constraint to $2x - y - 3z = 4.1$. Estimate the corresponding change in the value function by using [18.25]. Find the new value of the value function.

Solution   Using the notation in [18.22] to [18.25] and the results in Example 18.13, we have $c_1 = 1$, $c_2 = 4$, $dc_1 = -0.1$, $dc_2 = 0.1$, $\lambda_1(1, 4) = 52/75$, $\lambda_2(1, 4) = 54/75$, and

$$f^*(c_1, c_2) = f^*(1, 4) = (16/15)^2 + (1/3)^2 + (-11/15)^2$$
$$= 402/225$$

Then [18.25] yields

$$f^*(1 - 0.1, 4 + 0.1) - f^*(1, 4) \approx \lambda_1(1, 4)\, dc_1 + \lambda_2(1, 4)\, dc_2$$
$$= (52/75)(-0.1) + (54/75)(0.1)$$
$$= 0.2/75$$

Thus, $f^*(0.9, 4.1) = f^*(1-0.1, 4+0.1) \approx 402/225 - 0.2/75 = 401.4/225 = 1.784$. To find the exact value of $f^*(0.9, 4.1)$, observe that [7] in Example 18.13 is still valid. Thus, we have the three equations

$$x + 2y + z = 0.9, \qquad 2x - y - 3z = 4.1, \qquad x - y + z = 0$$

whose solutions for x, y, and z are 1.06, 0.3, and -0.76, respectively. Therefore, $f^*(0.9, 4.1) = (1.06)^2 + (0.3)^2 + (-0.76)^2 = 1.7912$.

Problems

1. Verify [18.24] for Problem 2, Section 18.5.

2. Consider the problem

$$\max f(x, y, z) = 4z - x^2 - y^2 - z^2$$
$$\text{subject to } g(x, y, z) = z - xy = 0 \qquad\qquad [*]$$

   a. Use Lagrange's method to find necessary conditions for the solution of the problem, and find all triples (x, y, z) that satisfy these conditions.
   b. The point $(1, 1, 1)$ is a maximum point in [*]. Find an approximate value for the change in the maximum value of f if we change the constraint from $z - xy = 0$ to $z - xy = 0.1$.

3. Consider the problem

$$\max x_1 + x_2 + x_3 + x_4 \text{ subject to } \begin{cases} \frac{1}{3}x_1 + \frac{1}{3}x_2 + \frac{1}{8}x_3 + \frac{1}{8}x_4 = 3 & [1] \\ x_1 x_2 x_3 x_4 = 144 & [2] \\ x_1, \ldots, x_4 \text{ are all } \geq 0 & [3] \end{cases}$$

   a. Write down the necessary conditions for the solution of this problem.
   b. Show that the necessary conditions imply $x_1 = x_2$ and $x_3 = x_4$. Find the solution. (Assume that the problem has a solution.)
   c. Suppose that constraint [2] is changed to $x_1 x_2 x_3 x_4 = 145$. Can you give (approximately) the change in the optimal value of $x_1 + x_2 + x_3 + x_4$, without redoing the whole problem?

18.7 Envelope Results

Optimization problems in economics usually involve functions that depend on a number of parameters, like prices, tax rates, income levels, and so on. Although these parameters are held constant during optimization, they vary according to the economic situation. For example, we may calculate a firm's profit maximum treating the prices it faces as parameters, but then want to know how the profit maximum responds to changes in those prices. So it is important to know what happens to the optimal solution when the situation changes—that is, if the parameters change. The Lagrange multipliers considered in the previous section gave some information of this kind.

   More generally, consider the problem

$$\max_{\mathbf{x}} f(\mathbf{x}, \mathbf{r}) \text{ subject to } g_j(\mathbf{x}, \mathbf{r}) = 0, \quad j = 1, \ldots, m \qquad [18.27]$$

where $\mathbf{r} = (r_1, \ldots, r_k)$ is a vector of parameters. Here $\mathbf{r}$ is kept constant during the maximization w.r.t. $\mathbf{x} = (x_1, \ldots, x_n)$. Note that the parameters may appear in the objective as well as in the constraint functions. The maximum value of $f(\mathbf{x}, \mathbf{r})$ obtained in [18.27] will depend on $\mathbf{r}$, and we denote it by $f^*(\mathbf{r})$. Assuming that the maximum value exists,

$$f^*(\mathbf{r}) = \max \{ f(\mathbf{x}, \mathbf{r}) : g_j(\mathbf{x}, \mathbf{r}) = 0, \ j = 1, \ldots, m \} \qquad [18.28]$$

Thus, $f^*(\mathbf{r})$ is the maximum value of all numbers $f(\mathbf{x}, \mathbf{r})$ as $\mathbf{x}$ runs through all $\mathbf{x}$ where $g_j(\mathbf{x}, \mathbf{r}) = 0$, $j = 1, \ldots, m$. The function $f^*(\mathbf{r})$ is called the **value function** for problem [18.27]. If we let $x_1^*(\mathbf{r}), \ldots, x_n^*(\mathbf{r})$ denote the values of $x_1, \ldots, x_n$ for which the maximum value in [18.28] is obtained, then

$$f^*(\mathbf{r}) = f(\mathbf{x}^*(\mathbf{r}), \mathbf{r}) = f(x_1^*(\mathbf{r}), \ldots, x_n^*(\mathbf{r}), r_1, \ldots, r_k) \qquad [18.29]$$

First, consider the case in which there are no constraints. When $n = 1$, the construction of the function $f^*(r)$ as the "envelope" of all the different $f(x, r)$ functions is indicated in Fig. 18.6.

The following result shows in general how to differentiate the value function:

If $f^*(\mathbf{r}) = \max_{\mathbf{x}} f(\mathbf{x}, \mathbf{r})$ and $\mathbf{x}^*(\mathbf{r})$ is the value of $\mathbf{x}$ that maximizes $f(\mathbf{x}, \mathbf{r})$, then

$$\frac{\partial f^*(\mathbf{r})}{\partial r_j} = \frac{\partial f(\mathbf{x}^*(\mathbf{r}), \mathbf{r})}{\partial r_j} \qquad (j = 1, \ldots, k) \qquad [18.30]$$

Economists call this an **envelope theorem**. It is a very useful result that should be studied carefully. Note that if r_j is changed, then $f^*(\mathbf{r})$ changes for two reasons: First, a change in r_j changes the vector $\mathbf{r}$ and thus it changes $f(\mathbf{x}, \mathbf{r})$ directly. Second, a change in r_j changes all the functions $x_1^*(\mathbf{r}), \ldots, x_n^*(\mathbf{r})$, and, hence, $f(\mathbf{x}^*(\mathbf{r}), \mathbf{r})$ is changed indirectly. The result in [18.30] shows that the total effect on the value function of a small change in r_j is found by simply computing the partial derivative of $f(\mathbf{x}^*(\mathbf{r}), \mathbf{r})$ w.r.t. r_j, ignoring the indirect effect of the depen-

FIGURE 18.6 The function $f^*(r)$ is the "envelope" of all the different $f(x, r)$ functions.

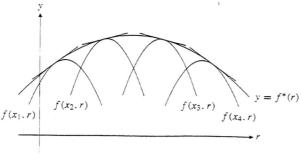

dence of $\mathbf{x}^*$ on $\mathbf{r}$ altogether. At first sight, this seems very surprising. On further reflection, however, you may realize that the first-order conditions for $\mathbf{x}^*(\mathbf{r})$ to maximize $f(\mathbf{x}, \mathbf{r})$ w.r.t. $\mathbf{x}$ imply that small changes in $\mathbf{x}$ induced by a small change in $\mathbf{r}$ have negligible effects on the value of $f(\mathbf{x}^*, \mathbf{r})$. This is confirmed in the proof that follows.

Consider next the more general problem [18.27] and suppose that $\lambda_i = \lambda_i(\mathbf{r})$, $i = 1, \ldots, m$, are the Lagrange multipliers obtained from the first-order conditions for the problem. Let $\mathcal{L}(\mathbf{x}, \mathbf{r}) = f(\mathbf{x}, \mathbf{r}) - \sum_{j=1}^{m} \lambda_j g_j(\mathbf{x}, \mathbf{r})$ be the corresponding Lagrange function. Then:

$$\frac{\partial f^*(\mathbf{r})}{\partial r_j} = \frac{\partial \mathcal{L}(\mathbf{x}^*(\mathbf{r}), \mathbf{r})}{\partial r_j} \qquad (j = 1, \ldots, k) \qquad [18.31]$$

According to this result, the total effect on the value of $f^*(\mathbf{r})$ of a small change in r_j is found by simply differentiating the Lagrangean $\mathcal{L}(\mathbf{x}, \mathbf{r})$ partially w.r.t. r_j, treating the x's as well as the λ's as constants. This is the (general) **envelope theorem**. The following proof *assumes* that $f^*(\mathbf{r})$ is differentiable; it is very similar to the rough argument we gave for [18.24].

Proof of [18.31]: Using the chain rule to differentiate [18.29] w.r.t. r_h yields

$$\frac{\partial f^*(\mathbf{r})}{\partial r_h} = \sum_{i=1}^{n} \frac{\partial f(\mathbf{x}^*(\mathbf{r}), \mathbf{r})}{\partial x_i} \frac{\partial x_i^*(\mathbf{r})}{\partial r_h} + \frac{\partial f(\mathbf{x}^*(\mathbf{r}), \mathbf{r})}{\partial r_h} \qquad [1]$$

From the first-order conditions for problem [18.27], for all $i = 1, \ldots, n$,

$$\frac{\partial f(\mathbf{x}^*(\mathbf{r}), \mathbf{r})}{\partial x_i} = \sum_{j=1}^{m} \lambda_j \frac{\partial g_j(\mathbf{x}^*(\mathbf{r}), \mathbf{r})}{\partial x_i}$$

So [1] can be written as

$$\frac{\partial f^*(\mathbf{r})}{\partial r_h} = \sum_{i=1}^{n} \left[\sum_{j=1}^{m} \lambda_j \frac{\partial g_j(\mathbf{x}^*(\mathbf{r}), \mathbf{r})}{\partial x_i} \right] \frac{\partial x_i^*(\mathbf{r})}{\partial r_h} + \frac{\partial f(\mathbf{x}^*(\mathbf{r}), \mathbf{r})}{\partial r_h}$$

$$= \sum_{j=1}^{m} \lambda_j \left[\sum_{i=1}^{n} \frac{\partial g_j(\mathbf{x}^*(\mathbf{r}), \mathbf{r})}{\partial x_i} \frac{\partial x_i^*(\mathbf{r})}{\partial r_h} \right] + \frac{\partial f(\mathbf{x}^*(\mathbf{r})\mathbf{r})}{\partial r_h} \qquad [2]$$

Now, using the chain rule to differentiate the identity $g_j(\mathbf{x}^*(\mathbf{r}), \mathbf{r}) = 0$ w.r.t. r_h yields

$$\sum_{i=1}^{n} \frac{\partial g_j(\mathbf{x}^*(\mathbf{r}), \mathbf{r})}{\partial x_i} \frac{\partial x_i^*(\mathbf{r})}{\partial r_h} + \frac{\partial g_j(\mathbf{x}^*(\mathbf{r}), \mathbf{r})}{\partial r_h} = 0$$

which holds for all $j = 1, \ldots, m$. So [2] can be written as

$$\frac{\partial f^*(\mathbf{r})}{\partial r_h} = -\sum_{j=1}^{m} \lambda_j \frac{\partial g_j(\mathbf{x}^*(\mathbf{r}), \mathbf{r})}{\partial r_h} + \frac{\partial f(\mathbf{x}^*(\mathbf{r}), \mathbf{r})}{\partial r_h} = \frac{\partial \mathcal{L}(\mathbf{x}^*(\mathbf{r}), \mathbf{r})}{\partial r_h}$$

Because the difference between the two subscripts h and j is of no significance, this proves [18.31].

Note: This proof used only the first-order conditions for problem [18.27]. Therefore, the results in [18.30] and [18.31] are equally valid if we minimize rather than maximize $f(\mathbf{x}, \mathbf{r})$ w.r.t. $\mathbf{x}$.

Example 18.16

Consider the problem

$$\min C = rK + wL \quad \text{subject to} \quad K^{1/2}L^{1/4} = Q$$

studied in Example 18.6 of Section 18.2. Let $C^* = C(r, w, Q)$ denote the value function for the problem and let $\mathcal{L} = rK + wL - \lambda(K^{1/2}L^{1/4} - Q)$ denote the Lagrangean. Verify directly the first three equalities in Example 18.6(b).

Solution   Note that the partial derivatives of $\mathcal{L}$ w.r.t. r, w, and Q are $\partial \mathcal{L}/\partial r = K$, $\partial \mathcal{L}/\partial w = L$, and $\partial \mathcal{L}/\partial Q = \lambda$. So according to [18.31],

$$\frac{\partial C^*}{\partial r} = K, \qquad \frac{\partial C^*}{\partial w} = L, \qquad \frac{\partial C^*}{\partial Q} = \lambda$$

This accords with the results in Example 18.6.

Problems

1. Consider the problem: max $U(x, y) = 10x^{1/2}y^{1/2}$ subject to $px + qy = m$. Let $U^*(p, q, m)$ be the optimal value function and write down the results obtained from [18.31]. Using the Lagrangean method, find the values of x and y (as functions of p, q, and m) that solve the problem, and verify [18.31] directly.

2. Explain why [18.24] is a special case of [18.31].

3. Consider the problem

$$\max x_1^a x_2^{b-a}(x_1 + b - a)^{-b} \quad \text{subject to} \quad p_1 x_1 + p_2 x_2 = m$$

with a and b as constants.

   a. Solve the problem and thereby find the two demand functions $x_1 = D_1(p_1, p_2, m)$ and $x_2 = D_2(p_1, p_2, m)$.

b. Check the signs of the partials of x_1 and x_2 w.r.t. p_1, p_2, and m.

c. Verify that D_1 and D_2 are homogeneous of degree 0.

18.8 Nonlinear Programming: A Rough Guide

So far this chapter has considered how to maximize or minimize a function subject to equality constraints. The final sections concern nonlinear programming problems, which involve *inequality* constraints. Some particularly simple inequality constraints are those requiring certain variables to be nonnegative. These often have to be imposed in order that the solution should make economic sense. In addition, bounds on the availability of resources are often expressed as inequalities rather than equalities.

A fairly general nonlinear programming problem is the following:

$$\max \ f(x_1, \ldots, x_n) \ \text{ subject to } \ \begin{cases} g_1(x_1, \ldots, x_n) \le c_1 \\ \ldots\ldots\ldots\ldots\ldots \\ g_m(x_1, \ldots, x_n) \le c_m \end{cases} \quad [18.32]$$

The set of vectors $\mathbf{x} = (x_1, \ldots, x_n)$ that satisfies all the constraints is called the **constraint set**, the **admissible set**, or, more often, the **feasible set**.

Note that minimizing $f(x_1, \ldots, x_n)$ and maximizing $-f(x_1, \ldots, x_n)$ are equivalent. Also an inequality constraint of the form $g_j(x_1, \ldots, x_n) \ge c_j$ can be rewritten as $-g_j(x_1, \ldots, x_n) \le -c_j$, whereas an equality constraint $g_j(x_1, \ldots, x_n) = c_j$ is equivalent to the double inequality constraint $g_j(x_1, \ldots, x_n) \le c_j$ and $-g_j(x_1, \ldots, x_n) \le -c_j$. In this way, most constrained optimization problems can be expressed in the form [18.32].

In principle, such problems can be solved by the classical methods used in Section 17.3. These involved examining the stationary points of f in the interior of the feasible set S, and the behavior of f on the boundary of S. However, since the 1950s, economists have generally tackled such problems by using an extension of the Lagrangean multiplier method due originally to H. W. Kuhn and A. W. Tucker.

A Simple Case

Consider first the simple nonlinear programming problem

$$\max \ f(x, y) \ \text{ subject to } \ g(x, y) \le c \quad [18.33]$$

In fact, what we do first is to write down a recipe giving all the points (x, y) that can possibly solve problem [18.33], except in some bizarre cases. The recipe closely resembles the one we used to solve the Lagrangean problem max $f(x, y)$ subject to $g(x, y) = c$.

Recipe for Solving max $f(x, y)$ **subject to** $g(x, y) \leq c$

1. Associate a constant Lagrange multiplier λ with the constraint $g(x, y) \leq c$, and define the Lagrangean function

$$\mathcal{L}(x, y) = f(x, y) - \lambda \big(g(x, y) - c \big)$$

[18.34]

2. Equate the partials of $\mathcal{L}(x, y)$ to zero:

$$\mathcal{L}'_1(x, y) = f'_1(x, y) - \lambda g'_1(x, y) = 0$$
$$\mathcal{L}'_2(x, y) = f'_2(x, y) - \lambda g'_2(x, y) = 0$$

[18.35]

3. Introduce the **complementary slackness condition**

$$\lambda \geq 0 \ (= 0 \ \text{if} \ g(x, y) < c)$$

[18.36]

4. Require (x, y) to satisfy the constraint

$$g(x, y) \leq c$$

If we find all the pairs (x, y) (together with suitable values of λ) that satisfy all these conditions, then we have all the candidates for the solution of problem [18.33]. Note that conditions 1 and 2 are exactly the conditions used in the Lagrangean method of Section 18.2. Condition 4 obviously has to be satisfied, so the only new feature is condition 3.

In fact, condition 3 is rather tricky. It requires that λ is nonnegative, and moreover that $\lambda = 0$ if $g(x, y) < c$. Thus, if $\lambda > 0$, we must have $g(x, y) = c$. An alternative formulation of this condition is that

$$\lambda \geq 0, \qquad \lambda \cdot [g(x, y) - c] = 0$$

[18.37]

Later we shall see that even in nonlinear programming, the Lagrange multiplier λ can be interpreted as a "price" associated with increasing the right-hand side c of the "resource constraint" $g(x, y) \leq c$ by one unit. With this interpretation, prices are nonnegative, and if the resource constraint is not binding because $g(x, y) < c$ at the optimum, this means that the price associated with increasing c by one unit is 0.

Note that it is possible to have *both* $\lambda = 0$ *and* $g(x, y) = c$ in [18.36]. The two inequalities $\lambda \geq 0$ and $g(x, y) \leq c$ are **complementary** inequalities in the sense that at most one can be "slack"—that is, at most one can hold with inequality. Equivalently, at least one must be an equality.

Warning: With equality constraints, setting the partial derivative $\partial \mathcal{L}/\partial \lambda$ equal to zero just recovers the constraint $g(x, y) = c$, and so is a valid procedure for deriving a first-order condition (as was pointed out in the footnote following the discussion of the Lagrangean method in Section 18.2). With an inequality constraint, however, one can have $\partial \mathcal{L}/\partial \lambda = -g(x, y) + c > 0$ if the constraint is slack or inactive at an optimum. For this reason, we recommend against differentiating the Lagrangean w.r.t. the multiplier λ, even though several other books advocate this procedure.

Example 18.17

Solve the problem

$$\max f(x, y) = x^2 + y^2 + y - 1 \quad \text{subject to } g(x, y) = x^2 + y^2 \leq 1$$

Solution   The Lagrangean is

$$\mathcal{L}(x, y) = x^2 + y^2 + y - 1 - \lambda(x^2 + y^2 - 1) \qquad [1]$$

Here the first-order conditions are

$$\mathcal{L}'_1(x, y) = 2x - 2\lambda x = 0 \qquad [2]$$

$$\mathcal{L}'_2(x, y) = 2y + 1 - 2\lambda y = 0 \qquad [3]$$

The complementary slackness condition is

$$\lambda \geq 0 \ (= 0 \text{ if } x^2 + y^2 < 1) \qquad [4]$$

We want to find all pairs (x, y) that satisfy these conditions for some suitable value of λ.

We begin by looking at condition [2], which is $2x(1 - \lambda) = 0$. There are two possibilities: $\lambda = 1$ or $x = 0$. If $\lambda = 1$, then [3] yields $1 = 0$, a contradiction. *Hence, $x = 0$.*

Suppose $x^2 + y^2 = 1$ and so $y = \pm 1$ because $x = 0$. Choose $y = 1$ first. Then [3] implies $\lambda = 3/2$ and so [4] is satisfied. Thus, $(0, 1)$ *with* $\lambda = 3/2$ *is a candidate for optimality* (because all the conditions [2]–[4] are satisfied). Next, choose $y = -1$. Then condition [3] yields $\lambda = 1/2$ and [4] is again satisfied. Thus, $(0, -1)$ *with $\lambda = 1/2$ is a candidate for optimality.*

Finally, consider the case when $x = 0$ and also $x^2 + y^2 = y^2 < 1$—that is, $-1 < y < 1$. Then [4] implies that $\lambda = 0$, and so [3] yields $y = -1/2$. Hence, $(0, -1/2)$ *with $\lambda = 0$ is a candidate for optimality.*

We conclude that there are three candidates for optimality. Now

$$f(0, 1) = 1, \qquad f(0, -1) = -1, \qquad f(0, -1/2) = -5/4 \qquad [5]$$

Because we want to maximize a continuous function over a closed, bounded set, by the extreme-value theorem there is a solution to the problem. Because the only possible solutions are the three points already found, we conclude from [5] that $x = 0$ and $y = 1$ solve the problem. (The point $(0, -1/2)$ solves the corresponding minimization problem. We solved both these problems in Example 17.5 in Section 17.3.)

Why Do the Recipe Conditions 1 to 4 Work?

Suppose (x^*, y^*) solves problem [18.33]. Then either $g(x^*, y^*) < c$, in which case the constraint $g(x, y) \leq c$ is said to be **inactive** or **slack** at (x^*, y^*), or else $g(x^*, y^*) = c$, in which case the same inequality constraint is said to be **active** or **binding** at (x^*, y^*). The two different cases are illustrated in Figs. 18.7 and 18.8. The objective function increases as the level curves shrink. In Fig. 18.7, the solution (x^*, y^*) to problem [18.33] is an interior point of the feasible set. On the other hand, in Fig. 18.8, the solution (x^*, y^*) is at the boundary of the feasible set.

In case the solution (x^*, y^*) satisfies $g(x^*, y^*) < c$, as in Fig. 18.7, the point (x^*, y^*) is usually an interior maximum of the function f. Then it is a stationary point at which $f'_1(x^*, y^*) = f'_2(x^*, y^*) = 0$. In this case, if we set $\lambda = 0$, then conditions [18.35] to [18.36] of the recipe are all satisfied.

On the other hand, in the case when the constraint is binding at (x^*, y^*), as in Fig. 18.8, the point (x^*, y^*) solves the Lagrangean problem

$$\max \; f(x, y) \; \text{subject to} \; g(x, y) = c \tag{18.38}$$

with an equality constraint. Provided that the conditions of Theorem 18.1 are all satisfied, there will exist a Lagrange multiplier λ such that the Lagrangean function [18.34] satisfies the first-order conditions [18.35] at (x^*, y^*). It remains to be shown that this Lagrange multiplier λ satisfies $\lambda \geq 0$, thus ensuring that [18.36] is also satisfied at (x^*, y^*).

To see why $\lambda \geq 0$ in this case, note that the first-order conditions can be expressed as

$$\nabla f(x^*, y^*) = \lambda \nabla g(x^*, y^*)$$

so that the gradient vector of f at (x^*, y^*) is proportional to that of g. According

FIGURE 18.7   **The point P = (x^*, y^*) is an interior point of the feasible set.**

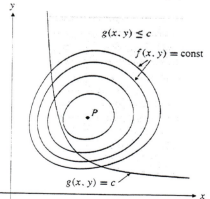

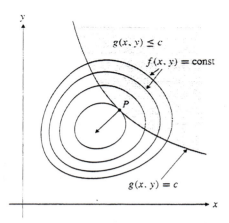

FIGURE 18.8 **The constraint $g(x, y) \leq c$ is binding at P $= (x^*, y^*)$.**

to (16.11) of Section 16.3, the gradient points in a direction of increasing function values. Now, if λ were negative, the vectors ∇f and ∇g at (x^*, y^*) would point in opposite directions. So moving away from (x^*, y^*) in the direction ∇f a small distance would increase f while decreasing g. Thus it would take us to a point (x, y) with $f(x, y) > f(x^*, y^*)$ and $g(x, y) < g(x^*, y^*) = c$. So (x^*, y^*) could not be an optimal solution. Thus $\lambda \geq 0$ after all. In fact, in Fig. 18.8, both $\nabla f(x^*, y^*)$ and $\nabla g(x^*, y^*)$ must point in the indicated direction.

An alternative explanation, which generalizes more easily to the case of many variables and many constraints, requires considering the two value functions

$$v(b) = \max\{f(x, y) : g(x, y) \leq b\}$$

$$f^*(b) = \max\{f(x, y) : g(x, y) = b\}$$

[18.39]

for the versions of problem [18.33] in which the constant c has been replaced by the variable parameter b, and where $f^*(b)$ arises from the problem where the inequality constraint has been replaced by the corresponding equality constraint. Recall from [18.7] that $\lambda = df^*(c)/dc$ if f^* is differentiable at c. We shall now show that f^* is nondecreasing at $b = c$, thus implying that $\lambda \geq 0$—at least when f^* is differentiable.

Indeed, [18.39] implies that $f^*(b) \leq v(b)$ for all b, because the equality constraint is more stringent than the (weak) inequality constraint, and imposing a more stringent constraint never allows a higher maximum value. But also, in case $b < c$, constraint $g(x, y) \leq b$ is more stringent than $g(x, y) \leq c$, from which it follows that $v(b) \leq v(c)$. Finally, because we are discussing the case when constraint $g(x^*, y^*) = c$ binds at the solution to problem [18.33], we must have $v(c) = f^*(c)$. Thus, the chain $f^*(b) \leq v(b) \leq v(c) = f^*(c)$ is satisfied whenever $b < c$. From this it follows that $f^*(b) \leq f^*(c)$, so $f^*(b)$ is increasing at $b = c$, and finally $\lambda = df^*(c)/dc \geq 0$, as required.

The General Case

It is now very easy to write down a recipe for solving the general nonlinear programming problem [18.32].

Recipe for Solving the General Nonlinear Programming Problem

$$\max (\min) f(\mathbf{x}) \text{ subject to } g_j(\mathbf{x}) \leq c_j \qquad (j = 1, \ldots, m)$$

where $\mathbf{x}$ denotes $(x_1, \ldots, x_n)$.

1. Write down the Lagrangean

$$\mathcal{L}(\mathbf{x}) = f(\mathbf{x}) - \sum_{j=1}^{m} \lambda_j (g_j(\mathbf{x}) - c_j)$$

   with $\lambda_1, \ldots, \lambda_m$ as the Lagrange multipliers associated with the m constraints.

2. Equate all the first-order partials of $\mathcal{L}(\mathbf{x})$ to 0:

$$\frac{\partial \mathcal{L}(\mathbf{x})}{\partial x_i} = \frac{\partial f(\mathbf{x})}{\partial x_i} - \sum_{j=1}^{m} \lambda_j \frac{\partial g_j(\mathbf{x})}{\partial x_i} = 0 \qquad (i = 1, \ldots, n)$$

3. Impose the complementary slackness conditions:

$$\lambda_j \geq 0 \; (= 0 \text{ if } g_j(\mathbf{x}) < c_j) \qquad (j = 1, \ldots, m)$$

4. Require $\mathbf{x}$ to satisfy the constraints

$$g_j(\mathbf{x}) \leq c_j \qquad (j = 1, \ldots, m)$$

Find all $\mathbf{x}$, together with associated values of $\lambda_1, \ldots, \lambda_m$, which satisfy all these conditions. These are the solution candidates, at least one of which solves the problem (if it has a solution).

Steps 2 to 4 are often called the **Kuhn–Tucker conditions**. Note that these are (essentially) *necessary* conditions for the solution of problem [18.32]. In general, they are far from sufficient. Indeed, suppose one can find a point $\mathbf{x}^0$ at which f is stationary and $g_j(\mathbf{x}) < c_j$ for $j = 1, \ldots, m$. Then the Kuhn–Tucker conditions 2 to 4 will automatically be satisfied by $\mathbf{x}^0$ together with the Lagrange multipliers $\lambda_1 = \cdots = \lambda_m = 0$. Yet then $\mathbf{x}^0$ could be a local or global minimum or maximum, or some kind of saddle point. Nothing more is known unless second-order conditions of some kind are also considered. Sufficient conditions for a maximum are discussed in Section 18.10.

Example 18.18

A firm has L units of labor and produces three goods. The production of x, y, and z units of the goods requires αx^2, βy^2, and γz^2 units of labor, respectively. Solve the problem

$$\max ax + by + cz \text{ subject to } \alpha x^2 + \beta y^2 + \gamma z^2 \leq L \qquad [1]$$

when the coefficients a, b, c, α, β, and γ are all positive constants.

Solution   The Lagrangean is

$$\mathcal{L}(x, y, z) = ax + by + cz - \lambda(\alpha x^2 + \beta y^2 + \gamma z^2 - L)$$

The necessary conditions for (x^*, y^*, z^*) to solve the problem are

$$\frac{\partial \mathcal{L}}{\partial x} = a - 2\lambda \alpha x^* = 0 \qquad [2]$$

$$\frac{\partial \mathcal{L}}{\partial y} = b - 2\lambda \beta y^* = 0 \qquad [3]$$

$$\frac{\partial \mathcal{L}}{\partial z} = c - 2\lambda \gamma z^* = 0 \qquad [4]$$

$$\lambda \geq 0 \ (= 0 \text{ if } \alpha(x^*)^2 + \beta(y^*)^2 + \gamma(z^*)^2 < L) \qquad [5]$$

Because a, b, and c are all nonzero, it follows from [2] to [4] that λ, x^*, y^*, and z^* are all not 0. Hence, [2] to [4] imply that $\lambda = a/2\alpha x^* = b/2\beta y^* = c/2\gamma z^*$. So

$$y^* = \frac{\alpha}{\beta}\frac{b}{a}x^*, \qquad z^* = \frac{\alpha}{\gamma}\frac{c}{a}x^* \qquad [6]$$

Also, because $\lambda \neq 0$, the complementary slackness condition [5] implies that

$$\alpha(x^*)^2 + \beta(y^*)^2 + \gamma(z^*)^2 = L \qquad [7]$$

Inserting the expressions for y^* and z^* from [6] into [7] yields

$$\alpha(x^*)^2 + \frac{\alpha^2}{\beta}\frac{b^2}{a^2}(x^*)^2 + \frac{\alpha^2}{\gamma}\frac{c^2}{a^2}(x^*)^2 = L$$

Accordingly, after a little more algebra the positive solution is found to be

$$x^* = a\sqrt{L}/\alpha\mu \qquad [8]$$

where μ denotes the constant $\mu = \sqrt{a^2/\alpha + b^2/\beta + c^2/\gamma}$. Similarly,

$$y^* = b\sqrt{L}/\beta\mu, \qquad z^* = c\sqrt{L}/\gamma\mu \qquad [9]$$

The constraint $\alpha x^2 + \beta y^2 + \gamma z^2 \leq L$ defines a closed, bounded set (in fact, an ellipsoid), so by the extreme-value theorem, there is a solution. Because the values of x^*, y^*, and z^* in [8] and [9] are the only positive solutions to the Kuhn–Tucker conditions, they solve the problem. (The argument in Example 18.21 of Section 18.10 also proves optimality.)

In more complicated nonlinear programming problems, it is sometimes hard to know where to begin "attacking" the necessary conditions. In the next example, we use a systematic procedure for locating all the candidates.

Example 18.19
Solve the problem

$$\max 4z - x^2 - y^2 - z^2 \text{ subject to } \begin{cases} \leq xy & [1] \\ x^2 + y^2 + z^2 & \leq 3 & [2] \end{cases}$$

Solution   Here $f(x, y, z) = 4z - x^2 - y^2 - z^2$. We represent the constraints by

$$g_1(x, y, z) = z - xy \leq 0, \qquad g_2(x, y, z) = x^2 + y^2 + z^2 \leq 3$$

and introduce the Lagrangean

$$\mathcal{L}(x, y, z) = 4z - x^2 - y^2 - z^2 - \lambda(z - xy) - \mu(x^2 + y^2 + z^2 - 3)$$

The necessary conditions are

$$\frac{\partial \mathcal{L}}{\partial x} = -2x + \lambda y - 2\mu x = 0 \tag{3}$$

$$\frac{\partial \mathcal{L}}{\partial y} = -2y + \lambda x - 2\mu y = 0 \tag{4}$$

$$\frac{\partial \mathcal{L}}{\partial z} = 4 - 2z - \lambda - 2\mu z = 0 \tag{5}$$

$$\lambda \geq 0 \ (= 0 \text{ if } z < xy) \tag{6}$$

$$\mu \geq 0 \ (= 0 \text{ if } x^2 + y^2 + z^2 < 3) \tag{7}$$

For each of the two constraints, we either have equality (if the constraint is *active*) or inequality (if the constraint is *inactive*). Thus, there are four distinct cases:

Case I: [1] and [2] are both inactive—that is, $z < xy$ and $x^2 + y^2 + z^2 < 3$. Then by [6] and [7], $\lambda = \mu = 0$. Inserted into Equations [3] to [5], this yields $x = y = 0$ and $z = 2$, which contradicts [2]. *No solution candidates*.
Case II: [1] is inactive, [2] is active. Then $\lambda = 0$, by [6]. So [3] yields $2x(1 + \mu) = 0$. Hence, $x = 0$, because $\mu \geq 0$. Inserted into [4], this gives

$y(1 + \mu) = 0$, so $y = 0$. From $x^2 + y^2 + z^2 = 3$ it follows that $z = \pm\sqrt{3}$. But $z \leq xy = 0$ by [1], so $z = -\sqrt{3}$ and then [5] yields $4 + 2\sqrt{3} = -2\sqrt{3}\mu$, which contradicts $\mu \geq 0$. *No solution candidates.*

Case III: [1] is active, [2] is inactive. Then $xy = z$ and $\mu = 0$.

Now, if $x \neq 0$, then from [4], $\lambda = 2y/x$. Inserted into [3], this yields $2x = 2y^2/x$, so $x^2 = y^2$, or $y = \pm x$. But then $\lambda = 2y/x = \pm 2$, and because $\lambda \geq 0$, so $\lambda = 2$. Therefore, $y = x$. From [5], $z = 1$, so [1] being active implies that $x^2 = y^2 = 1$. Then $x^2 + y^2 + z^2 = 3$, which contradicts the hypothesis that [2] is inactive.

So the only possibility in this case is that $x = 0$. Because of [4], $2(1 + \mu)y = 0$ and so $y = 0$. Then $z = 0$ because [1] is active, so [5] implies $\lambda = 4$. Then all the conditions [1] to [7] are satisfied. Thus, $(0, 0, 0)$ with $\lambda = 4$ and $\mu = 0$ is a candidate.

Case IV: [1] and [2] are both active. Then $xy = z$ and $x^2 + y^2 + z^2 = 3$. From [3] and [4], we get $-2x + \lambda y - 2\mu x = -2y + \lambda x - 2\mu y$, or $(y - x)(2 + \lambda + 2\mu) = 0$. Because $2 + \lambda + 2\mu > 0$, one has $y = x$. Thus, $z = x^2$ and $x^2 + x^2 + x^4 = 3$ or $(x^2)^2 + 2(x^2) - 3 = 0$, implying that $x^2 = -1 \pm \sqrt{4} = -1 \pm 2$. For x real, the only possibility is $x^2 = 1$, and so $x = \pm 1$. Then $y = x = \pm 1$ and $z = xy = 1$. Now [3] and [4] both imply that $(-2 + \lambda - 2\mu)x = 0$ and so $-2 + \lambda - 2\mu = 0$, because $x \neq 0$. But [5] implies that $2 - \lambda - 2\mu = 0$ because $z = 1$. Adding these two equations in λ and μ gives $-4\mu = 0$. So $\mu = 0$ and $\lambda = 2$. This leaves the *two solution candidates* $(1, 1, 1)$ *and* $(-1, -1, 1)$, *both with $\lambda = 2$ and $\mu = 0$.*

Now

$$f(0, 0, 0) = 0, \qquad f(1, 1, 1) = 1, \qquad f(-1, -1, 1) = 1$$

so $(1, 1, 1)$ and $(-1, -1, 1)$ both solve the problem. (Again the extreme-value theorem tells us that there is a solution.)

Note: The general method for finding all candidates for optimality in a nonlinear programming problem can be formulated as follows: First, examine the case in which none of the constraints is active; then examine all cases in which only one constraint is active; then all cases in which exactly two are active; and so on. In the end, examine the case in which all constraints are active. At each step, we find all vectors **x**, with associated values of the Lagrangean multipliers, that satisfy all the relevant conditions—if there are any. Then we search through all the possibilities to find the best.

Problems

1. Consider the problem

$$\max x^2 + 2y^2 - x \text{ subject to } x^2 + y^2 \leq 1$$

    a. Write down the Lagrangean function and the first-order conditions in [18.35].

    b. What is the complementary slackness condition?

    c. Find all pairs (x, y) that satisfy all the necessary conditions. (There are five candidates.) Find the solution to the problem.

2. Solve the following problems, assuming they have solutions:

    a. max $\frac{1}{2}x - y$ subject to $x + e^{-x} \le y, x \ge 0$.

    b. max $x^2 + 2y$ subject to $x^2 + y^2 \le 5, \ y \ge 0$.

3. Solve the following problems, assuming they have solutions:

    a. max $y - x^2$ subject to $y \ge 0, \ y - x \ge -2, \ y^2 \le x$.

    b. max $xe^{y-x} - 2ey$ subject to $x \ge 0, \ 0 \le y \le 1 + x/2$.

4. Consider the problem

$$\max x + ay \quad \text{subject to} \quad x^2 + y^2 \le 1, \ x + y \ge 0 \qquad (a \text{ is a constant})$$

    a. Write down the necessary conditions.

    b. Find the solution for all values of the constant a.

5. Consider the problem

$$\max \ln x_1 (x_2 + x_3) + \text{subject to} \begin{cases} x_1 + x_2 + x_3 & \le 1 \\ x_1 & \ge 1 \\ x_1^2 + x_2^2 & \le 2 \end{cases}$$

    a. Write down the necessary conditions.

    b. Find *all* points satisfying the necessary conditions. (*Hint:* There are infinitely many.) What is the solution to the problem?

Harder Problems

6. Solve the problem

$$\max \ln(x^2 + 2y) - \tfrac{1}{2}x^2 - y \quad \text{subject to} \quad 2 \le xy, \ x \ge 1, \ y \ge 1$$

18.9 More on Nonlinear Programming (Optional)

This section considers first the case in which all the variables are assumed to be nonnegative, and states the modified Kuhn–Tucker conditions for this case. Then it discusses some economic interpretations of nonlinear programming.

Nonnegativity Conditions on the Variables

Consider the general nonlinear programming problem [18.32] once again. Often, variables involved in economic optimization problems must be nonnegative by their very nature. It is not difficult to incorporate such constraints in the formulation of [18.32]. If $x_1 \geq 0$, for example, this can be represented by the new constraint $g_{m+1}(x_1, \ldots, x_n) = -x_1 \leq 0$, and we introduce an additional Lagrange multiplier to go with it. But in order not to have too many Lagrange multipliers to handle, the necessary conditions for the solution of nonlinear programming problems with nonnegativity constraints are sometimes formulated in a slightly different way.

Consider first the problem

$$\max \ f(x, y) \ \text{subject to} \ g(x, y) \leq c, \ x \geq 0, \ y \geq 0 \qquad [18.40]$$

Here we introduce the functions $g_1(x, y) = -x$ and $g_2(x, y) = -y$, so that the constraints in problem [18.40] become $g(x, y) \leq c, g_1(x, y) \leq 0$, and $g_2(x, y) \leq 0$. Applying the recipe for solving [18.32], we introduce the Lagrangean

$$\mathcal{L}(x, y) = f(x, y) - \lambda(g(x, y) - c) - \mu_1(-x) - \mu_2(-y)$$

The Kuhn–Tucker conditions are

$$\frac{\partial \mathcal{L}}{\partial x} = f_1'(x, y) - \lambda g_1'(x, y) + \mu_1 = 0 \qquad [1]$$

$$\frac{\partial \mathcal{L}}{\partial y} = f_2'(x, y) - \lambda g_2'(x, y) + \mu_2 = 0 \qquad [2]$$

$$\lambda \geq 0 \quad (= 0 \ \text{if} \ g(x, y) < c) \qquad [3]$$

$$\mu_1 \geq 0 \quad (= 0 \ \text{if} \ x > 0) \qquad [4]$$

$$\mu_2 \geq 0 \quad (= 0 \ \text{if} \ y > 0) \qquad [5]$$

From [1], we have $f_1'(x, y) - \lambda g_1'(x, y) = -\mu_1$. From [4], we have $-\mu_1 \leq 0$ and $-\mu_1 = 0$ if $x > 0$. Thus, [1] and [4] are together equivalent to

$$f_1'(x, y) - \lambda g_1'(x, y) \leq 0 \quad (= 0 \ \text{if} \ x > 0) \qquad [6]$$

In the same way, [2] and [5] are together equivalent to

$$f_2'(x, y) - \lambda g_2'(x, y) \leq 0 \quad (= 0 \ \text{if} \ y > 0) \qquad [7]$$

So the new Kuhn–Tucker conditions are [6], [7], and [3]. Note that after replacing [1] and [4] by [6], as well as [2] and [5] by [7], only the multiplier λ associated with $g(x, y) \leq c$ remains.

The same idea can obviously be extended to the n-variable problem

$$\max \ f(x_1, \ldots, x_n) \ \text{s.t.} \ \begin{cases} g_1(x_1, \ldots, x_n) \leq c_1 \\ \ldots\ldots\ldots\ldots\ldots \\ g_m(x_1, \ldots, x_n) \leq c_m \end{cases}, \ x_1 \geq 0, \ldots, x_n \geq 0 \qquad [18.41]$$

Briefly formulated, the necessary conditions for the solution of [18.41] are that, for each $i = 1, \ldots, n$:

$$\frac{\partial f(\mathbf{x})}{\partial x_i} - \sum_{j=1}^{m} \lambda_j \frac{\partial g_j(\mathbf{x})}{\partial x_i} \leq 0 \quad (= 0 \text{ if } x_i > 0) \qquad [18.42]$$

$$\lambda_j \geq 0 \quad (= 0 \text{ if } g_j(\mathbf{x}) < c_j) \qquad (j = 1, \ldots, m) \qquad [18.43]$$

Example 18.20   (Peak Load Pricing)

Consider a producer who generates electricity by burning a fuel such as coal or natural gas. The demand for electricity varies between peak periods, during which all the generating capacity is used, and off-peak periods. We consider a certain time interval (say, a year) divided into n periods of equal length. Let the sales of electric power in these n periods be $x_1, x_2, \ldots, x_n$. Assume that a regulatory authority fixes the corresponding prices at levels equal to $p_1, p_2, \ldots, p_n$. The total operating cost over all n periods is $C(x_1, \ldots, x_n)$, and k is the output capacity in each period. Let $D(k)$ denote the cost of maintaining output capacity k. The producer's total profit is then

$$\pi(x_1, \ldots, x_n, k) = \sum_{i=1}^{n} p_i x_i - C(x_1, \ldots, x_n) - D(k) \qquad [1]$$

Because the producer cannot exceed capacity k in any period, it faces the constraints

$$x_1 \leq k, \quad \ldots, \quad x_n \leq k \qquad [2]$$

We consider the problem of finding $x_1 \geq 0, \ldots, x_n \geq 0$ and $k \geq 0$ so that profit is maximized subject to the capacity constraints [2].

This is a nonlinear programming problem with $n + 1$ variables and n constraints. The Lagrangean function $\mathcal{L}$ is

$$\mathcal{L}(x_1, \ldots, x_n, k) = \sum_{i=1}^{n} p_i x_i - C(x_1, \ldots, x_n) - D(k) - \sum_{i=1}^{n} \lambda_i (x_i - k)$$

The choice $(x_1^0, \ldots, x_n^0, k^0) \geq 0$ can solve the problem only if there exist Lagrange multipliers $\lambda_1 \geq 0, \ldots, \lambda_n \geq 0$ such that

$$\frac{\partial \mathcal{L}}{\partial x_i} = p_i - C_i'(x_1^0, \ldots, x_n^0) - \lambda_i \leq 0 \quad (= 0 \text{ if } x_i^0 > 0) \qquad (i = 1, \ldots, n) \quad [3]$$

$$\frac{\partial \mathcal{L}}{\partial k} = -D'(k^0) + \sum_{i=1}^{n} \lambda_i \leq 0 \quad (= 0 \text{ if } k^0 > 0) \qquad [4]$$

$$\lambda_i \geq 0 \quad (= 0 \text{ if } x_i^0 < k^0) \qquad (i = 1, \ldots, n) \qquad [5]$$

Suppose i is such that $x_i^0 > 0$. Then [3] implies that

$$p_i = C_i'(x_1^0, \ldots, x_n^0) + \lambda_i \qquad [6]$$

If period i is an off-peak period, then $x_i^0 < k^0$ and so $\lambda_i = 0$ by [5]. From [6], it follows that $p_i = C_i'(x_1^0, \ldots, x_n^0)$. Thus, we see that *the profit-maximizing pattern of outputs* $(x_1^0, \ldots, x_n^0)$ *will bring about equality between the regulator's price in any off-peak period and the corresponding marginal operating cost.*

On the other hand λ_j might be positive in a peak period when $x^0 j = k^0$. If $k^0 > 0$, it follows from [4] that $\sum_{i=1}^{n} \lambda_i = D'(k^0)$. We conclude that the output pattern will be such that *in peak periods the price set by the regulator will exceed the marginal operating costs by an additional amount* λ_i, *which is really the "shadow price" of the capacity constraint* $x_i \leq k$. *The sum of these shadow prices over all peak periods is equal to the marginal capacity cost.*

An Economic Interpretation of Nonlinear Programming Problems

Consider a firm producing some final product by using n different intermediate "production processes." In production, m different resources are required whose total supplies are $c_1, \ldots, c_m$. Let $f(x_1, \ldots, x_n)$ denote the number of units of the commodity produced when the n production processes are run at the levels $x_1, \ldots, x_n$. Let $g_j(x_1, \ldots, x_n)$ be the corresponding number of units of resource number j required ($j = 1, \ldots, m$). Problem [18.41] can then be formulated as follows:

Find nonnegative activity levels at which to operate the production processes in order to obtain the largest possible output of the produced commodity, taking into account the impossibility of using more of any resource than its total supply.

For each resource j, specify a shadow price of λ_j per unit. To produce $f(x_1, \ldots, x_n)$ units of the commodity requires $g_j(x_1, \ldots, x_n)$ units of resource j at a shadow cost of $\lambda_j g_j(x_1, \ldots, x_n)$. If we let the shadow price per unit of the produced commodity be 1, then the function $\pi(x_1, \ldots, x_n)$ defined by

$$\pi(x_1, \ldots, x_n) = f(x_1, \ldots, x_n) - \sum_{j=1}^{m} \lambda_j g_j(x_1, \ldots, x_n) \qquad [18.44]$$

indicates the *shadow profit* from running the processes at the vector $(x_1, \ldots, x_n)$ of activity levels. Suppose that we find an activity vector $\mathbf{x}^0 = (x_1^0, \ldots, x_n^0)$ and nonnegative shadow prices $\lambda_1, \ldots, \lambda_m$ such that:

1. $\mathbf{x}^0$ maximizes shadow profit among all nonnegative vectors of activity levels.
2. $\mathbf{x}^0$ satisfies each resource constraint $g_j(\mathbf{x}^0) \leq c_j$, $j = 1, \ldots, m$.

3. If the jth resource is not fully used because $g_j(\mathbf{x}^0) < c_j$, then the shadow price λ_j of that resource is 0.

Under these conditions, we can prove that $\mathbf{x}^0$ solves problem [18.41]:

Theorem 18.3   Consider the problem

$$\max f(\mathbf{x}) \quad \text{subject to} \quad g_j(\mathbf{x}) \leq c_j, \ j = 1, \ldots, m, \ \mathbf{x} \geq \mathbf{0}$$

Suppose there exist numbers $\lambda_1, \ldots, \lambda_m$ and a feasible vector $\mathbf{x}^0 = (x_1^0, \ldots, x_n^0)$ such that

(a) $f(\mathbf{x}^0) - \sum\limits_{j=1}^{m} \lambda_j g_j(\mathbf{x}^0) \geq f(\mathbf{x}) - \sum\limits_{j=1}^{m} \lambda_j g_j(\mathbf{x})$ for all $\mathbf{x} \geq \mathbf{0}$

(b) $\lambda_j \geq 0 \ (= 0 \text{ if } g_j(\mathbf{x}^0) < c_j) \text{ for } j = 1, \ldots, m$

Then $\mathbf{x}^0$ solves the problem.

Proof   Let S denote the feasible set of vectors $\mathbf{x}$ satisfying constraints $g_j(\mathbf{x}) \leq c_j$ for $j = 1, \ldots, m$, and $\mathbf{x} \geq \mathbf{0}$. (The single "vector inequality" $\mathbf{x} \geq \mathbf{0}$ expresses the requirement that all n inequalities $x_1 \geq 0, \ldots, x_n \geq 0$ be satisfied simultaneously.) Rearranging the terms in (a) gives[5]

$$f(\mathbf{x}^0) - f(\mathbf{x}) \geq \sum_{j=1}^{m} \lambda_j (g_j(\mathbf{x}^0) - g_j(\mathbf{x})) \quad \text{for all } \mathbf{x} \geq \mathbf{0} \qquad [*]$$

But (b) and the feasibility condition $g_j(\mathbf{x}) \leq c_j$ together imply that $\lambda_j g_j(\mathbf{x}^0) = \lambda_j c_j$ for $j = 1, \ldots, m$. (If $\lambda_j = 0$, the equality is obvious. If $\lambda_j > 0$, then (b) together with feasibility implies that $g_j(\mathbf{x}^0) = c_j$, and so $\lambda_j g_j(\mathbf{x}^0) = \lambda_j c_j$.) Summing these equalities over j gives

$$\sum_{j=1}^{m} \lambda_j g_j(\mathbf{x}^0) = \sum_{j=1}^{m} \lambda_j c_j \qquad [18.45]$$

Therefore, [*] implies that

$$f(\mathbf{x}^0) - f(\mathbf{x}) \geq \sum_{j=1}^{m} \lambda_j (c_j - g_j(\mathbf{x})) \quad \text{for all } \mathbf{x} \in S \qquad [**]$$

---

[5]It is actually enough to assume that [*] holds for all $\mathbf{x}$ satisfying the constraints.

However, feasibility and $\lambda_j \geq 0$ imply that $\lambda_j (c_j - g_j(\mathbf{x})) \geq 0$ for $j = 1, \ldots, m$, and so the right-hand side of [**] is ≥ 0. Thus, $f(\mathbf{x}^0) \geq f(\mathbf{x})$ for all $\mathbf{x} \in S$.

No regularity conditions on f or $g_1, \ldots, g_m$ are required in Theorem 18.3, except that we assumed implicitly that the functions are all defined for $\mathbf{x} \geq \mathbf{0}$.

Note how, using our economic terminology, [18.45] tells us that, at the given shadow prices for the resources, *the total value of the resources used at the optimum* $\mathbf{x}^0$ *is equal to the total shadow value of the initial stocks.*

Theorem 18.3 provides sufficient conditions for $\mathbf{x}^0$ to solve problem [18.41]. Are these conditions necessary as well? That is, if $\mathbf{x}^0 = (x_1^0, \ldots, x_n^0)$ solves problem [18.41], is it always possible to find nonnegative prices $\lambda_1, \ldots, \lambda_m$ such that (a) and (b) in Theorem 18.3 are satisfied? The answer is no. However, if the function π in [18.44] is concave, and if we impose a weak additional condition on the constraint set, then one can prove the existence of such prices $\lambda_1, \ldots, \lambda_m$.[6]

Properties of the Value Function

Let us now return to the general nonlinear programming problem [18.32] without explicit nonnegativity constraints. The optimal value of the objective $f(\mathbf{x})$ obviously depends on $\mathbf{c} = (c_1, \ldots, c_m)$. The function defined by

$$v(\mathbf{c}) = \max\{ f(\mathbf{x}) : g_j(\mathbf{x}) \leq c_j, \ j = 1, \ldots, m \} \qquad [18.46]$$

assigns to each vector $\mathbf{c}$ the optimal value $v(\mathbf{c})$ of f. It is called the **value function** for the problem.

The following three properties of v are very useful:

1. $v(\mathbf{c})$ is nondecreasing in each variable $c_1, \ldots, c_m$.
2. If $\partial v(\mathbf{c})/\partial c_j$ exists, then it is equal to $\lambda_j(\mathbf{c})$, $\quad j = 1, \ldots, m$.
3. If $f(\mathbf{x})$ is concave and $g_1(\mathbf{x}), \ldots, g_m(\mathbf{x})$ are all convex, then $v(\mathbf{c})$ is concave.

Here property 1 follows immediately because if c_j increases, and all the other variables are fixed, then the feasible set becomes larger; hence, $v(\mathbf{c})$ cannot decrease. Concerning property 2, each $\lambda_j(\mathbf{c})$ is a Lagrange multiplier coming from the Kuhn–Tucker conditions. However, there is a catch: The value function v need not be differentiable. Even if f and $g_1, \ldots, g_m$ are all differentiable, the value function can have sudden changes of slope.[7] We give a proof of property 3, which is important in many economic applications.

---

[6]See Dixit (1990).

[7]For a discussion of the properties of the value function, see Luenberger (1973), Section 10.6, and Dixit (1990).

Proof of Property 3:   Let $x(c)$ denote an optimal solution to the problem when the vector of right-hand sides in the inequalities is $c = (c_1, \ldots, c_m)$. Suppose that c' and c'' are two arbitrary right-hand side vectors. Then $v(c') = f(x(c'))$ and $v(c'') = f(x(c''))$, with $g_j(x(c')) \leq c'_j$ and $g_j(x(c'')) \leq c''_j$, for $j = 1, \ldots, m$. Let $t \in [0, 1]$. Corresponding to the right-hand side vector $(1 - t)c' + tc''$, there is an optimal solution $x((1 - t)c' + tc'')$ for which

$$v((1 - t)c' + tc'') = f(x((1 - t)c' + tc''))$$

Define $\hat{x} = (1 - t)x(c') + tx(c'')$. Convexity of g_j implies that, for $j = 1, \ldots, m$, one has

$$g_j(\hat{x}) \leq (1 - t)g_j(x(c')) + tg_j(x(c'')) \leq (1 - t)c'_j + tc''_j$$

where the latter inequality follows from feasibility of the two vectors $x(c')$ and $x(c'')$. Thus, $\hat{x}$ is feasible for the problem where the right-hand side vector is $(1 - t)c' + tc''$. By definition, $x((1 - t)c' + tc'')$ is optimal for this problem. Hence,

$$f(\hat{x}) \leq f(x((1 - t)c' + tc'')) = v((1 - t)c' + tc'') \qquad [*]$$

Also, concavity of f implies that

$$f(\hat{x}) \geq (1 - t)f(x(c')) + tf(x(c'')) = (1 - t)v(c') + tv(c'') \qquad [**]$$

Now concavity of v follows from the inequalities $[*]$ and $[**]$.

Problems

1. Solve the problem max $1 - x^2 - y^2$ subject to $x \geq 0$, $y \geq 0$ by (a) a direct argument and (b) using the Kuhn–Tucker conditions from the previous section.

2. Use conditions [18.42] and [18.43] to solve the gas import problem in Example 17.6, Section 17.3–namely,

$$\max\ 9x + 8y - 6(x + y)^2 \text{ subject to } \begin{cases} x & \leq 5 \\ & y & \leq 3 \\ -x + 2y & \leq 2 \end{cases} \quad x \geq 0, \ y \geq 0$$

3. Suppose that optimal capacity utilization by a firm requires that its output quantities x_1 and x_2, and capacity level k should be chosen to solve the

problem

$$\max \ x_1 + 3x_2 - x_1^2 - x_2^2 - k^2 \ \text{ subject to } \begin{cases} x_1 \le k \\ x_2 \le k \end{cases}, \quad x_1 \ge 0, \ x_2 \ge 0, \ k \ge 0$$

Show that $k = 0$ cannot be optimal, and then find the solution.

Harder Problems

4. Suppose that $\mathbf{x}^0 = (x_1^0, \ldots, x_n^0) \ge \mathbf{0}$ and $\lambda = \mathbf{p} = (\lambda_1, \ldots, \lambda_m) \ge \mathbf{0}$ satisfy the sufficient conditions (a) and (b) in Theorem 18.3, so that $\mathbf{x}^0$ solves problem [18.41]. Suppose that $\widehat{\mathbf{x}} = (\hat{x}_1, \ldots, \hat{x}_n) \ge \mathbf{0}$ also solves the problem. Prove that, *for the same $\lambda_1, \ldots, \lambda_m$ as those associated with $\mathbf{x}^0$*, the vector $\widehat{\mathbf{x}}$ will also satisfy (a) and (b), but with $\mathbf{x}^0$ replaced by $\widehat{\mathbf{x}}$.

5. Consider the problem

$$\max_{\mathbf{x}} f(\mathbf{x}, \mathbf{r}) \ \text{ subject to } g_j(\mathbf{x}, \mathbf{r}) \le 0, \ j = 1, \ldots, m$$

Suppose that f is concave in $(\mathbf{x}, \mathbf{r})$, and each $g_j(\mathbf{x}, \mathbf{r})$ is convex in $(\mathbf{x}, \mathbf{r})$. Show that $v(\mathbf{r})$, the optimal value of f as a function of $\mathbf{r}$, is concave in $\mathbf{r}$. (*Hint:* Use the same approach as in the earlier proof of property 3.)

6. For problem [18.41], define $\mathcal{L}(\mathbf{x}, \lambda) = f(\mathbf{x}) - \sum_{j=1}^{m} \lambda_j (g_j(\mathbf{x}) - c_j)$. Say that $\mathcal{L}$ has a **saddle point** at $(\mathbf{x}^*, \lambda^*)$, with $\mathbf{x}^* \ge \mathbf{0}$, $\lambda^* \ge \mathbf{0}$, if

$$\mathcal{L}(\mathbf{x}, \lambda^*) \le \mathcal{L}(\mathbf{x}^*, \lambda^*) \le \mathcal{L}(\mathbf{x}^*, \lambda) \ \text{ for all } \mathbf{x} \ge \mathbf{0} \text{ and all } \lambda \ge \mathbf{0} \qquad [*]$$

a. Show that, if $\mathcal{L}$ has a saddle point at $(\mathbf{x}^*, \lambda^*)$, then $\mathbf{x}^*$ solves problem [18.41]. (*Hint:* Use the second inequality in [*] to show that $g_j(\mathbf{x}^*) \le c_j$ for $j = 1, \ldots, m$. Show next that $\sum_{j=1}^{m} \lambda_j^* (g_j(\mathbf{x}^*) - c_j) = 0$. Then use the first inequality in [*] to finish the proof.)

b. Suppose that there exist a feasible vector $\mathbf{x}^* \ge \mathbf{0}$ and prices $\lambda^* \ge \mathbf{0}$ such that $\mathcal{L}(\mathbf{x}, \lambda^*) \le \mathcal{L}(\mathbf{x}^*, \lambda^*)$ whenever $\mathbf{x}$ is feasible, and with $\lambda_j = 0$ if $g_j(\mathbf{x}^*) < c_j$ for $j = 1, \ldots, m$. Show that $\mathcal{L}(\mathbf{x}, \lambda)$ has a saddle point at $(\mathbf{x}^*, \lambda^*)$ in this case.

18.10 Precise Results (Optional)

We begin by showing that, provided suitable concavity/convexity conditions are satisfied, the Kuhn–Tucker conditions are sufficient for optimality.[8]

---

[8]The classical reference is H. W. Kuhn and A. W. Tucker. "Nonlinear Programming." in *Proceedings of the Second Berkeley Symposium on Mathematical Statistics and Probability*. J. Neyman (editor). pp. 481–492. University of California Press. Berkeley. (1951). See also Dixit (1990).

Theorem 18.4   (Kuhn–Tucker Sufficient Conditions)   Consider the nonlinear programming problem

$$\max \ f(\mathbf{x}) \text{ subject to } g_j(\mathbf{x}) \le c_j, \ j = 1, \dots, m \qquad [18.47]$$

where f and $g_1, \dots, g_m$ are continuously differentiable with f concave and $g_1, \dots, g_m$ all convex. Suppose that there exist numbers $\lambda_1, \dots, \lambda_m$ and a feasible vector $\mathbf{x}^0$ such that

(a) $\dfrac{\partial f(\mathbf{x}^0)}{\partial x_i} - \displaystyle\sum_{j=1}^{m} \lambda_j \dfrac{\partial g_j(\mathbf{x}^0)}{\partial x_i} = 0 \qquad (i = 1, \dots, n)$

(b) $\lambda_j \ge 0 \ \ (= 0 \text{ if } g_j(\mathbf{x}^0) < c_j) \qquad (j = 1, \dots, m)$

Then $\mathbf{x}^0$ solves the problem.

Proof   The Lagrangean function $\mathcal{L}(\mathbf{x})$ can be written as

$$f(\mathbf{x}) + \lambda_1(-g_1(\mathbf{x}) + c_1) + \cdots + \lambda_m(-g_m(\mathbf{x}) + c_m)$$

This is concave as a sum of concave functions. By (a), $\partial \mathcal{L}(\mathbf{x}^0)/\partial x_i = 0$ for $i = 1, \dots, n$, and so Theorem 17.8 of Section 17.7 implies that $\mathbf{x}^0$ maximizes $\mathcal{L}(\mathbf{x})$. The result follows from Theorem 18.3 (which is still true without the nonnegativity constraints $\mathbf{x} \ge \mathbf{0}$).

Note: It is easy to prove that Theorem 18.4 is valid for problem [18.41], with nonnegativity constraints on the variables, provided that (a) and (b) are replaced by [18.42] and [18.43].

Example 18.21
What has Theorem 18.4 to say about the problem in Example 18.18?

Solution   The objective function $f(x, y, z) = ax + by + cz$ is linear and hence concave. Also, $g(x, y, z) = \alpha x^2 + \beta y^2 + \gamma z^2$ is a sum of convex functions (for $\alpha \ge 0$, $\beta \ge 0$, and $\gamma \ge 0$), and hence convex. Because the values of x^*, y^*, and z^* given by [8] and [9] are solutions to conditions (a) and (b) of Theorem 18.4, we know that they are optimal.

When its assumptions are satisfied, Theorem 18.4 is very convenient. However, concavity of f and convexity of the functions g_j are certainly restrictive assumptions. For instance, in Example 18.17 of Section 18.8, the objective function $f(x, y)$ is not concave, and in Example 18.19, constraint function $g_1(x, y, z) = z - xy$ is not convex.

In many economic applications, the following generalization of Theorem 18.4 is often useful.[9]

Theorem 18.5 (Sufficient Conditions for Quasi-Concave Programming)
Consider the problem in Theorem 18.4 where functions f and $g_1, \ldots, g_m$ are continuously differentiable. Suppose there exist numbers $\lambda_1, \ldots, \lambda_m$ and a vector $\mathbf{x}^0$ such that

(a) $\mathbf{x}^0$ is feasible and (a) and (b) in Theorem 18.4 are satisfied.
(b) $(f_1'(\mathbf{x}^0), \ldots, f_n'(\mathbf{x}^0)) \neq (0, \ldots, 0)$.
(c) $f(\mathbf{x})$ is quasi-concave, and $\lambda_j g_j(\mathbf{x})$ is quasi-convex for $j = 1, \ldots, m$.

Then $\mathbf{x}^0$ solves the problem.

Condition (b) is a significant addition to the corresponding conditions in Theorem 18.4. It excludes points $\mathbf{x}^0$ at which f is stationary. This is necessary because a stationary point for the quasi-concave function f might not even be a local maximum, let alone a solution to the constrained maximization problem. (See Problem 5.)

Example 18.22

Consider the following standard problem in consumer demand theory in which we allow the consumer to underspend:

$$\max U(x_1, \ldots, x_n) \text{ subject to } p_1 x_1 + \cdots + p_n x_n \leq m \qquad [1]$$

Assume that the utility function U is continuously differentiable and quasi-concave, and that prices $p_1, \ldots, p_n$ are nonnegative. Suppose that $\mathbf{x}^0 = (x_1^0, \ldots, x_n^0)$ satisfies the budget constraint, as well as (a) and (b) in Theorem 18.4, so that

$$U_i'(\mathbf{x}^0) = \lambda p_i \qquad (i = 1, \ldots, n) \qquad [2]$$

$$\lambda \geq 0 \quad (= 0 \text{ if } p_1 x_1^0 + \cdots + p_n x_n^0 < m) \qquad [3]$$

In addition, assume that not all the partials $U_1'(\mathbf{x}^0), \ldots, U_n'(\mathbf{x}^0)$ are zero. Then [2] implies that $\lambda > 0$, and so $p_1 x_1^0 + \cdots + p_n x_n^0 = m$. Thus, the budget is fully utilized and $\mathbf{x}^0$ solves problem [1]. (To take into account explicitly the constraints $x_1 \geq 0, \ldots, x_n \geq 0$, use the Note to Theorem 18.4.)

---

[9]See K. J. Arrow and A. C. Enthoven. "Quasi-concave programming." *Econometrica* 26 (1959): 522–552.

Necessary Conditions

So far, this section has discussed sufficient conditions for optimality in nonlinear programming. We turn next to necessary conditions.

The recipe in Section 18.8 for problem [18.32] gives us all the candidates for optimality, except in "bizarre cases." In order to obtain conditions that are truly necessary, we have to introduce a new condition:[10]

A Constraint Qualification

The functions g_j $(j = 1, \dots, m)$ corresponding to constraints that are active at $\mathbf{x}^0$ have linearly independent gradients at $\mathbf{x}^0$.

[18.48]

Example 18.23, which follows, shows that the constraint qualification cannot be dropped from Theorem 18.6.

Theorem 18.6 (Kuhn–Tucker Necessary Conditions)   Suppose $\mathbf{x} = (x_1^0, \dots, x_n^0)$ solves the problem

$$\max f(\mathbf{x}) \text{ subject to } g_j(\mathbf{x}) \le c_j, \quad j = 1, \dots, m$$

where f and $g_1, \dots, g_m$ are continuously differentiable functions. Suppose further that constraint qualification [18.48] holds. Then there exist unique numbers $\lambda_1, \dots, \lambda_m$ such that

(a) $\dfrac{\partial f(\mathbf{x}^0)}{\partial x_i} - \sum_{j=1}^{m} \lambda_j \dfrac{\partial g_j(\mathbf{x}^0)}{\partial x_i} = 0 \qquad (i = 1, \dots, n)$

(b) $\lambda_j \ge 0 \ \ (= 0 \text{ if } g_j(\mathbf{x}^0) < c_j) \qquad (j = 1, \dots, m)$

Example 18.23

Consider the problem

$$\max f(x, y) = xy \text{ subject to } g(x, y) = (x + y - 2)^2 \le 0$$

Because $(x + y - 2)^2$ is always nonnegative, the constraint is equivalent to $x + y - 2 = 0$, so the solution is $x = 1$ and $y = 1$ (see Problem 4,

---

[10]Note the similarity between this condition and the corresponding condition for the Lagrangean problem in footnote 4 to [18.21] in Section 18.5. For a proof of Theorem 18.6, see Luenberger (1973).

Section 18.2). Condition (a) in Theorem 18.6 reduces to

$$y - 2\lambda(x + y - 2) = 0, \qquad x - 2\lambda(x + y - 2) = 0$$

Letting $x = 1$ and $y = 1$ yields the contradiction $1 = 0$ in each case.
    Note that $g_1'(x, y) = g_2'(x, y) = 2(x + y - 2) = 0$ for $x = y = 1$, so the gradient of g at $(1, 1)$ is $(0, 0)$, which is not a linearly independent set of vectors. Thus, the constraint qualification fails to hold at $(1, 1)$.

According to Theorem 18.6, if $\mathbf{x}^0$ solves problem [18.32] and the constraint qualification is satisfied at $\mathbf{x}^0$, then conditions (a) and (b) hold. This means that if the constraint qualification does not hold at $\mathbf{x}^0$, then $\mathbf{x}^0$ can be a solution to the problem and yet not satisfy (a) and (b) (as was the case with $\mathbf{x}^0 = (1, 1)$ in the previous example). The correct method for finding *all* candidates for optimality in problem [18.32] is therefore as follows:

1. Find all feasible points where conditions (a) and (b) are satisfied.
2. Find also all feasible points where the constraint qualification fails.

If we know that the problem has a solution, then steps 1 and 2 will find all possible solution candidates for us. After evaluating f at all these candidates, we can pick out the one (or ones) that maximizes f.
Note: A common error when using Theorem 18.6 is the following: From conditions (a) and (b) in the theorem, a unique solution candidate $\mathbf{x}^0$ is found. Then the constraint qualification is checked at $\mathbf{x}^0$. The error consists in not checking whether the constraint qualification fails at *other* feasible points. If it does, these points are also solution candidates, and the true optimum might occur at one of them. This possibility is illustrated by Problem 6.

Problems

1. Consider the problem

$$\max f(x, y) = 2 - (x - 1)^2 - e^{y^2} \text{ subject to } x^2 + y^2 \leq a$$

   where a is a positive constant.
   a. Prove that $f(x, y)$ is concave.
   b. Write down the Kuhn–Tucker conditions for the solution of the problem. Find the only possible solution (which will depend on the size of a), and prove optimality by using Theorem 18.4.

2. **a.** Solve the following problem by a geometric argument.

$$\max 2x + y \quad \text{subject to} \quad \begin{cases} (x + 1)^2 + y^2 \leq 4 \\ x^2 + (y + 1)^2 \leq 4 \end{cases} \qquad x \geq 0, \ y \geq 0$$

b. Write down the Kuhn–Tucker conditions. By using the Note to Theorem 18.4, prove that the point you found in part (a) solves the problem.

c. Suppose the constraint $x^2+(y+1)^2 \leq 4$ is replaced by $x^2+(y+1)^2 \leq 4.1$. Estimate the approximate change in the optimal value of $2x + y$.

3. Consider the problem in Example 18.2. Use Theorem 18.5 to prove that you have found the solution. (*Hint:* Use [17.32](b) in Section 17.10.)

4. Consider the problem $\max f(x)$ subject to $x \in [a, b]$, $a < b$.

   a. By letting $g_1(x) = a - x \leq 0$ and $g_2(x) = x - b \leq 0$ be the constraints, check what the Kuhn–Tucker conditions have to say about a point x^* that solves the problem. (Consider the three cases $x^* = a$, $x^* \in (a, b)$, and $x^* = b$.

   b. Suppose $f(x)$ is concave. Then the Kuhn–Tucker conditions are sufficient for optimality. Illustrate the three cases that can occur.

5. Consider the problem

$$\max (x - 1)^3 \text{ subject to } g_1(x) = -x \leq 0, \quad g_2(x) = x \leq 2$$

   a. Find the solution graphically.

   b. Prove that with $x^0 = 1$ and $\lambda_1 = \lambda_2 = 0$, conditions (a) and (c) in Theorem 18.5 are satisfied. Is (b) satisfied at $x^0 = 1$? Is x^0 the optimal solution?

6. Consider the problem

$$\max 3x + y \text{ subject to } y \leq (1 - x)^3, \quad x \geq 0, \quad y \geq 0$$

   a. Find the solution graphically, and show that the constraint qualification [18.48] is violated.

   b. Prove that the only solution to (a) and (b) of Theorem 18.6 is $x = 0$ and $y = 1$, with corresponding Lagrange multipliers $(1, 0, 0)$. (Note that, even though the constraint qualification is satisfied at $(x, y) = (0, 1)$, this is not the optimum.)

=19= Linear Programming

If one would take statistics about which mathematical problem is using up most of the computer time in the world, then (not counting database handling problems like sorting and searching) the answer would probably be linear programming.
—*L. Lovász* (1980)

Linear programming is the name used for problems in which the objective is to maximize or minimize a linear function subject to linear inequality constraints.

As the opening quotation from Lovász indicates, linear programming is a mathematical technique of immense practical importance. Since its origins in the 1940s, there have been important theoretical and computational developments, and its methods are now used every day in many parts of the world.

Because of its extensive use in economic decision problems, all economists should have some basic knowledge of this theory. However, its importance extends even beyond its practical applications. In particular, the duality theory of linear programming is a basis for understanding more complicated optimization problems with even more interesting economic applications.

In principle, *any* linear programming problem (often called an LP problem) can be solved, if a solution exists. The *simplex method* introduced in 1947 by G. B. Dantzig is a very efficient numerical procedure that finds the solution in a finite number of operations. This method will not be discussed in this book. In fact, for economists, it is probably more important to understand the duality theory of LP than the details of the simplex method. After all, faced with a nontrivial LP problem, it is natural to use one of the great number of available LP computer programs to find the solution.

19.1 Preliminaries

A general linear programming problem with only two decision variables involves maximizing or minimizing a linear function

$$z = c_1 x_1 + c_2 x_2 \qquad \text{(criterion function)}$$

subject to m constraints

$$a_{11} x_1 + a_{12} x_2 \leq b_1$$
$$a_{21} x_1 + a_{22} x_2 \leq b_2$$
$$\cdots \cdots \cdots \cdots \cdots \cdots \qquad \text{(inequality constraints)}$$
$$a_{m1} x_1 + a_{m2} x_2 \leq b_m$$

Usually, we also impose explicit nonnegativity constraints on x_1 and x_2:

$$x_1 \geq 0, \quad x_2 \geq 0 \qquad \text{(nonnegativity constraints)}$$

Note that the direction of the inequalities in the inequality constraints is a convention in the sense that any inequality of the form $ax_1 + bx_2 \geq c$ is equivalent to the inequality $-ax_1 - bx_2 \leq -c$.

A Graphical Approach to Simple LP Problems

LP problems with only two decision variables can be solved by a simple geometric method.

Example 19.1

A baker has 150 kilograms of flour, 22 kilos of sugar, and 27.5 kilos of butter with which to make two types of cake. Suppose that making one dozen A cakes requires 3 kilos of flour, 1 kilo of sugar, and 1 kilo of butter, whereas making one dozen B cakes requires 6 kilos of flour, 0.5 kilo of sugar, and 1 kilo of butter. Suppose that the profit from one dozen A cakes is 20 and from one dozen B cakes is 30. How many dozen A cakes (x_1) and how many dozen B cakes (x_2) will maximize the baker's profit?

Solution   An output of x_1 dozen A cakes and x_2 dozen B cakes would need $3x_1 + 6x_2$ kilos of flour. Because there are only 150 kilos of flour, the inequality

$$3x_1 + 6x_2 \leq 150 \qquad \text{(flour constraint)} \qquad [1]$$

must hold. Similarily, for sugar,

$$x_1 + 0.5x_2 \leq 22 \qquad \text{(sugar constraint)} \qquad [2]$$

and for butter,

$$x_1 + x_2 \leq 27.5 \qquad \text{(butter constraint)} \qquad [3]$$

Of course, $x_1 \geq 0$ and $x_2 \geq 0$. The profit obtained from producing x_1 dozen A cakes and x_2 dozen B cakes is

$$z = 20x_1 + 30x_2 \qquad [4]$$

In short, the problem is to

$$\max z = 20x_1 + 30x_2 \quad \text{s.t.} \quad \begin{cases} 3x_1 + 6x_2 \leq 150 \\ x_1 + 0.5x_2 \leq 22 \\ x_1 + x_2 \leq 27.5 \end{cases} \quad x_1 \geq 0, \, x_2 \geq 0 \qquad [5]$$

This problem will now be solved graphically.

The output pair (x_1, x_2) is called *feasible* (or *admissible*) for problem [5] if all the five constraints are satisfied. Look at the flour constraint, which is $3x_1 + 6x_2 \leq 150$. If we use all the flour, then $3x_1 + 6x_2 = 150$, and we call this the *flour border*. We can find similar "borders" for the other inputs. Figure 19.1 shows the straight lines that represent the flour border, the sugar border, and the butter border. In order for (x_1, x_2) to be feasible, it has to be on or below (to the "southwest" of) *each* of the three borders simultaneously. Because constraints $x_1 \geq 0$ and $x_2 \geq 0$ restrict (x_1, x_2) to the nonnegative quadrant, the set of feasible pairs for problem [5], called the *feasible* (or *admissible*) *region*, is the shaded set S shown in Fig. 19.2. (This set S is a so-called *convex polyhedron*, and the five corner points O, A, B, C, and D are called *extreme points* of the set S.)

FIGURE 19.1

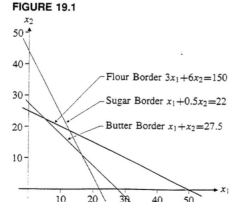

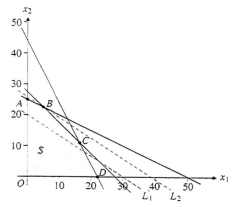

FIGURE 19.2

In principle, the baker can find the point in the feasible region that maximizes profit by calculating $20x_1 + 30x_2$ at each point of S and picking the highest value. In practice, this is impossible because there are infinitely many feasible points. Let us argue this way instead. Can the baker obtain a profit of 600? If so, the straight line $20x_1 + 30x_2 = 600$ must have points in common with S. This line is represented in Fig. 19.2 by dashed line L_1. It does have points in common with S. (One of them is $(x_1, x_2) = (0, 20)$, where no A cakes are produced, but 20 dozen B cakes are, and the profit *is* $20 \cdot 0 + 30 \cdot 20 = 600$.) Can the baker do better? Yes. For instance, the straight line $20x_1 + 30x_2 = 601$ also has points in common with S and the profit is 601. In fact, the straight lines

$$20x_1 + 30x_2 = c \qquad (c \text{ is a constant}) \qquad [6]$$

are all parallel to $20x_1 + 30x_2 = 600$. As c increases, the line given by [6] moves out farther and farther to the northeast. It is clear that the straight line [6] that has the highest value of c and still has a point in common with S is dashed line L_2 in the figure. It touches set S at point B. Note that B is at the intersection of the flour border and the butter border. Its coordinates, therefore, satisfy the two equations:

$$3x_1 + 6x_2 = 150 \qquad \text{and} \qquad x_1 + x_2 = 27.5$$

Solving these two simultaneous equations yields $x_1 = 5$ and $x_2 = 22.5$. So the baker maximizes profit by baking 5 dozen A cakes and 22.5 dozen B cakes. This uses all the available flour and butter, but $22 - 5 - 0.5 \cdot 22.5 = 5.75$ kilos of sugar are left over. The profit earned is $20x_1 + 30x_2 = 775$.

Our next example is a minimization problem.

Example 19.2

A firm is producing two goods, A and B. It has two factories that jointly produce the two goods in the following quantities (per hour):

	Factory 1	Factory 2
Good A	10	20
Good B	25	25

The firm receives an order for 300 units of A and 500 units of B. The costs of operating the two factories are 10,000 and 8000 per hour. Formulate the linear programming problem of minimizing the total cost of meeting this order.

Solution   Let u_1 and u_2 be the number of hours that the two factories operate to produce the order. Then $10u_1 + 20u_2$ units of good A are produced, and $25u_1 + 25u_2$ units of good B. Because 300 units of A and 500 units of B are required,

$$10u_1 + 20u_2 \geq 300$$
$$25u_1 + 25u_2 \geq 500 \qquad [1]$$

In addition, of course, $u_1 \geq 0$ and $u_2 \geq 0$. The total costs of operating the two factories for u_1 and u_2 hours, respectively, are $10,000\,u_1 + 8000\,u_2$. The problem is, therefore,

$$\min 10,000\,u_1 + 8000\,u_2 \text{ subject to } \begin{cases} 10u_1 + 20u_2 \geq 300 \\ 25u_1 + 25u_2 \geq 500 \end{cases} \quad u_1 \geq 0, \, u_2 \geq 0$$

The feasible set S is shown in Fig. 19.3. Because the inequalities in [1] are of the $\geq$ type, the feasible set lies to the northeast. We show some of

FIGURE 19.3

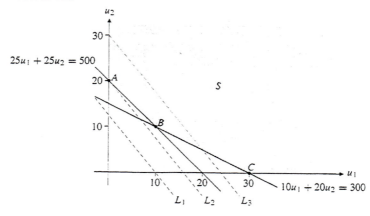

the level curves $10{,}000u_1 + 8000u_2 = c$, marked L_1, L_2, and L_3. These three correspond to the values 100,000; 160,000; and 240,000 of the cost level c. As c increases, the level curve moves farther and farther to the northeast.

The solution to the minimization problem is clearly the level curve that touches the feasible set S at point A with coordinates $(0, 20)$. Hence, the optimal solution is to operate factory 2 for 20 hours and not to use factory 1 at all. The minimum cost of producing the order is 160,000.

The graphical method of solving linear programming problems works well when there are only two decision variables. It is possible in principle to extend the method to the case with three decision variables. Then the feasible set is a convex polyhedron in 3-space, and the level surfaces of the criterion function are planes in 3-space. However, it is not easy to visualize the solution in such cases. For more than three decision variables, no geometric method is available. (By using duality theory, however, one can solve LP problems geometrically when *either* the number of unknowns or the number of constraints is less than or equal to 3; see Section 19.5.)

Both the previous examples had optimal solutions. If the feasible region is unbounded, however, a (finite) optimal solution might not exist, as is the case in Problem 2.

The General LP Problem

The general LP problem is that of maximizing or minimizing

$$z = c_1 x_1 + \cdots + c_n x_n \qquad \textbf{(criterion, or objective, function)} \qquad [19.1]$$

with $c_1, \ldots, c_n$ as given constants, subject to m constraints

$$
\begin{aligned}
a_{11}x_1 + \cdots + a_{1n}x_n &\le b_1 \\
a_{21}x_1 + \cdots + a_{2n}x_n &\le b_2 \\
&\cdots\cdots\cdots\cdots\cdots\cdots\cdots\cdots \\
a_{m1}x_1 + \cdots + a_{mn}x_n &\le b_m
\end{aligned}
\qquad \textbf{(inequality constraints)} \qquad [19.2]
$$

where elements a_{ij} and b_k are given constants. Usually, we assume explicitly that

$$x_1 \ge 0, \ldots, x_n \ge 0 \qquad \textbf{(nonnegativity constraints)} \qquad [19.3]$$

There is no essential difference between a minimization problem and a maximization problem, because the optimal solution $(x_1^*, \ldots, x_n^*)$ that minimizes [19.1] subject to [19.2] and [19.3] also maximizes $-z$, and $\min z = -\max(-z)$. An n-vector $(x_1, \ldots, x_n)$ that satisfies [19.2] and [19.3] is called **feasible**.

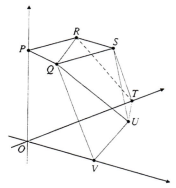

FIGURE 19.4

The set of feasible points is a *convex polyhedron* in the *nonnegative orthant* of *n*-space. An example in 3-space is shown in Fig. 19.4. The flat portions of the boundary are called *faces* and the points O, P, Q, R, S, T, U, and V are called *extreme points*. In *n*-space, a convex polyhedron also has faces and extreme points. If *n* and *m* are large, the number of extreme points can be astronomical.[1]

If an LP problem has a solution, then it must have a solution at an extreme point. The simplex method is a procedure that allows us to move from one extreme point to another in such a way that the value of the criterion function never decreases, until we come to a point such that by moving to another extreme point it is impossible to increase the value of the criterion function. We have then reached the optimal solution.

Problems

1. Use the graphical method to solve the following LP problems:

    a. max $3x_1 + 4x_2$ s.t. $\begin{cases} 3x_1 + 2x_2 \le 6 \\ x_1 + 4x_2 \le 4 \end{cases}$ $x_1 \ge 0$, $x_2 \ge 0$

    b. min $10u_1 + 27u_2$ s.t. $\begin{cases} u_1 + 3u_2 \ge 11 \\ 2u_1 + 5u_2 \ge 20 \end{cases}$ $u_1 \ge 0$, $u_2 \ge 0$

    c. max $2x_1 + 5x_2$ s.t. $\begin{cases} -2x_1 + 3x_2 \le 6 \\ 7x_1 - 2x_2 \le 14 \\ x_1 + x_2 \le 5 \end{cases}$ $x_1 \ge 0$, $x_2 \ge 0$

    d. max $8x_1 + 9x_2$ s.t. $\begin{cases} x_1 + 2x_2 \le 8 \\ 2x_1 + 3x_2 \le 13 \\ x_1 + x_2 \le 6 \end{cases}$ $x_1 \ge 0$, $x_2 \ge 0$

    e. max $-2x_1 + x_2$ s.t. $0 \le x_1 - 3x_2 \le 3$, $x_1 \ge 2$, $x_1 \ge 0$, $x_2 \ge 0$

---

[1] Because an extreme point typically involves *n* of the *n* + *m* inequality constraints holding with equality, there can be as many as $(n + m)!/n!m!$ extreme points. For example, if $n = 50$ and $m = 60$ (which is quite small by the standards of the problems that can be solved numerically), then there can be as many as $110!/50!60!$ or more than $6 \cdot 10^{31}$ extreme points.

2. **a.** Is there a solution to the following problem?

$$\max x_1 + x_2 \text{ s.t. } \begin{cases} -x_1 + x_2 \leq -1 \\ -x_1 + 3x_2 \leq 3 \end{cases} \quad x_1 \geq 0, \ x_2 \geq 0$$

   b. Is there a solution if the criterion function is $z = -x_1 - x_2$?

3. Set A consists of all (x_1, x_2) satisfying

$$-2x_1 + x_2 \leq 2$$
$$x_1 + 2x_2 \leq 8$$
$$x_1 \geq 0, \ x_2 \geq 0$$

   Solve the following problems with A as the feasible set:

   a. max x_2 **b.** max x_1 **c.** max $3x_1 + 2x_2$

   d. min $2x_1 - 2x_2$ **e.** max $2x_1 + 4x_2$ **f.** min $-3x_1 - 2x_2$

4. A firm produces two types of television sets, an inexpensive type (A) and an expensive type (B). The firm earns a profit of 700 from each TV of type A, and 1000 for each TV of type B. There are three stages of the production process. Stage I requires 3 hours of labor on each set of type A and 5 hours of labor on each set of type B. The total available number of hours is 3900. Stage II requires 1 hour of labor on each set of type A and 3 hours on each set of type B. The total labor they have is 2100 hours. At stage III, 2 hours of labor are needed for both types, and 2200 hours of labor are available. How many TV sets of each type should the firm produce to maximize its profit?

5. Replace the criterion function in Example 19.1 by $20x_1 + tx_2$. For what values of t will the maximum profit still be at $x_1 = 5$ and $x_2 = 22.5$?

19.2 Introduction to Duality Theory

Confronted with an optimization problem involving scarce resources, an economist will often ask: What happens to the optimal solution if the availability of the resources changes? For linear programs, answers to questions of this type are intimately related to the so-called duality theory of LP. As a point of departure, let us again consider the baker's problem in Example 19.1.

Example 19.3

Suppose the baker were to receive (free of charge) one extra kilo of flour. How much would this extra kilo add to his maximum profit? How much would an extra kilo of sugar contribute to profit? Or an extra kilo of butter?

Solution   If the baker receives one extra kilo of flour, his flour border would become $3x_1 + 6x_2 = 151$. It is clear from Fig. 19.2 that the feasible set S will expand slightly and point B will move up to the left a little along the butter border. The new optimal point B' will be at the intersection of the lines $3x_1 + 6x_2 = 151$ and $x_1 + x_2 = 27.5$. Solving these equations gives $x_1 = 14/3$ and $x_2 = 137/6$. Then the criterion function becomes equal to $20(14/3) + 30(137/6) = 2335/3 = 775 + 10/3$. So profit rises by $10/3$.

If the baker receives an extra kilo of sugar, the feasible set will expand, but the optimal point is still at B. Recall that at the optimum in the original problem, the baker had 5.75 kilos of unused sugar. There is no extra profit.

An extra kilo of butter would give a new optimal point at the intersection of the lines $3x_1 + 6x_2 = 150$ and $x_1 + x_2 = 28.5$. Solving these equations gives $x_1 = 7$ and $x_2 = 21.5$ with $20x_1 + 30x_2 = 775 + 10$. Profit rises by 10. These results can be summarized as follows:

a. An extra kilo of flour would increase the optimal z by $10/3$.

b. An extra kilo of sugar would increase the optimal z by 0.

c. An extra kilo of butter would increase the optimal z by 10.

The three numbers $u_1^* = 10/3$, $u_2^* = 0$ and $u_3^* = 10$ are related to the flour, sugar, and butter constraints, respectively. They are the *marginal* profits from an extra kilo of each ingredient. Actually, these numbers have many interesting properties.

Suppose (x_1, x_2) is a feasible pair in the problem, so that constraints [1], [2], and [3] in Example 19.1 are satisfied. Multiply [1] by $10/3$, [2] by 0, and [3] by 10. Because the multipliers are all ≥ 0, the inequalities are preserved. That is,

$$(10/3)(3x_1 + 6x_2) \leq (10/3) \cdot 150$$

$$0(x_1 + 0.5x_2) \leq 0 \cdot 22$$

$$10(x_1 + x_2) \leq 10 \cdot 27.5$$

Now add all these inequalities, using the obvious fact that if $A \leq B, C \leq D$, and $E \leq F$, then $A + C + E \leq B + D + F$. The result is

$$10x_1 + 20x_2 + 10x_1 + 10x_2 \leq \frac{10}{3} \cdot 150 + 10 \cdot 27.5$$

which reduces to

$$20x_1 + 30x_2 \leq 775$$

Thus, using the "magic" numbers u_1^*, u_2^*, and u_3^* defined before, we have proved that if (x_1, x_2) is any feasible pair, then the criterion function has to be less than or equal to 775. Because $x_1 = 5$ and $x_2 = 22.5$ give z the value 775, we have in this way *proved algebraically* that $(5, 22.5)$ *is* the solution.

The pattern revealed in this example turns up in all linear programming problems. In fact, the numbers u_1^*, u_2^*, and u_3^* are solutions to a new LP problem called the *dual* of the original problem.

The Dual Problem

Consider once again the baker's problem, which is

$$\max 20x_1 + 30x_2 \text{ subject to } \begin{cases} 3x_1 + 6x_2 \leq 150 \\ x_1 + 0.5x_2 \leq 22 \\ x_1 + x_2 \leq 27.5 \end{cases} \quad x_1, x_2 \geq 0 \quad [1]$$

Suppose the baker gets tired of running the business. (After all, there must be many complaints about the rather plain cakes.) Somebody else wants to take over and buy all the baker's ingredients. The baker intends to charge a price u_1 for each kilo of flour, u_2 for each kilo of sugar, and u_3 for each kilo of butter.

Because one dozen A cakes requires 3 kilos of flour and 1 kilo each of sugar and butter, the baker will charge $3u_1 + u_2 + u_3$ for the ingredients needed to produce a dozen A cakes. The baker originally had a profit of 20 for each dozen A cakes, and he wants to earn at least as much from these ingredients if he quits. Hence, the baker insists that the prices (u_1, u_2, u_3) must satisfy

$$3u_1 + u_2 + u_3 \geq 20$$

Otherwise, it would be more profitable to use the ingredients himself to produce A cakes. If the baker also wants to earn at least as much as before for the ingredients needed to produce a dozen B cakes, the requirement is

$$6u_1 + 0.5u_2 + u_3 \geq 30$$

Presumably, the entrant wants to buy the baker's resources as inexpensively as possible. The total cost of 150 kilos of flour, 22 kilos of sugar, and 27.5 kilos of butter is $150u_1 + 22u_2 + 27.5u_3$. In order to pay as little as possible while having the baker accept the offer, the entrant should suggest prices $u_1 \geq 0$, $u_2 \geq 0$, and $u_3 \geq 0$, which solve

$$\min 150u_1 + 22u_2 + 27.5u_3 \text{ subject to } \begin{cases} 3u_1 + u_2 + u_3 \geq 20 \\ 6u_1 + 0.5u_2 + u_3 \geq 30 \end{cases} \quad [2]$$

with $u_1 \geq 0$, $u_2 \geq 0$, and $u_3 \geq 0$.

An interesting question is this: If the baker lets the entrant take over the business and solve problem [2], will the baker earn as much as before? It turns out that the answer is yes. The solution to [2] is $u_1^* = 10/3$, and $u_2^* = 0$, and $u_3^* = 10$, and the amount the baker gets for selling the resources is $150u_1^* + 22u_2^* + 27.5u_3^* = 775$, which is precisely the maximum value of the criterion function in problem [1].

The entrant pays for each ingredient exactly the marginal profit for that ingredient which was calculated previously. In particular, the price of sugar is zero, because the baker has more than he can use optimally.

Problem [2] is called the *dual* of problem [1]. The two problems turn out to be closely related. Let us explain in general how to construct the dual of an LP problem.

The General Case

Consider the general LP problem

$$\max c_1 x_1 + \cdots + c_n x_n \text{ subject to } \begin{cases} a_{11} x_1 + \cdots + a_{1n} x_n \le b_1 \\ \cdots\cdots\cdots\cdots\cdots\cdots\cdots\cdots \\ a_{m1} x_1 + \cdots + a_{mn} x_n \le b_m \end{cases} \quad [19.4]$$

with nonnegativity constraints $x_1 \ge 0, \ldots, x_n \ge 0$.

The **dual** of [19.4] is the LP problem

$$\min b_1 u_1 + \cdots + b_m u_m \text{ subject to } \begin{cases} a_{11} u_1 + \cdots + a_{m1} u_m \ge c_1 \\ \cdots\cdots\cdots\cdots\cdots\cdots\cdots\cdots \\ a_{1n} u_1 + \cdots + a_{mn} u_m \ge c_n \end{cases} \quad [19.5]$$

with nonnegativity constraints $u_1 \ge 0, \ldots, u_m \ge 0$. Note that problem [19.5] is constructed using exactly the same coefficients $c_1, \ldots, c_n, a_{11}, \ldots, a_{mn}$, and $b_1, \ldots, b_m$ as in [19.4].

In problem [19.4], which we now refer to as the **primal** problem, there are n variables $x_1, \ldots, x_n$ and m constraints (disregarding the nonnegativity constraints). In the dual [19.5], there are m variables $u_1, \ldots, u_m$ and n constraints. Whereas the primal is a maximization problem, the dual is a minimization problem. In both problems, all variables are nonnegative. The m constraints in the primal problem are of the "less than or equal to" type, whereas the n constraints in the dual are of the "greater than or equal to" type. The coefficients of the criterion function in either problem are the right-hand side elements of the constraints in the other problem. Finally, the two matrices formed by the coefficients of the variables in the constraints in the primal and dual problems are transposes of each other, because they take the form

$$\mathbf{A} = \begin{pmatrix} a_{11} & a_{12} & \cdots & a_{1n} \\ a_{21} & a_{22} & \cdots & a_{2n} \\ \vdots & \vdots & & \vdots \\ a_{m1} & a_{m2} & \cdots & a_{mn} \end{pmatrix} \quad \text{and} \quad \mathbf{A}' = \begin{pmatrix} a_{11} & a_{21} & \cdots & a_{m1} \\ a_{12} & a_{22} & \cdots & a_{m2} \\ \vdots & \vdots & & \vdots \\ a_{1n} & a_{2n} & \cdots & a_{mn} \end{pmatrix} \quad [19.6]$$

Check carefully that problem [2] is the dual of problem [1] in the sense we have just explained. Due to the symmetry between the two problems, we call either the dual of the other.

Matrix Formulation

Let us introduce the following column vectors (matrices):

$$\mathbf{x} = \begin{pmatrix} x_1 \\ \vdots \\ x_n \end{pmatrix}, \quad \mathbf{c} = \begin{pmatrix} c_1 \\ \vdots \\ c_n \end{pmatrix}, \quad \mathbf{b} = \begin{pmatrix} b_1 \\ \vdots \\ b_m \end{pmatrix}, \quad \mathbf{u} = \begin{pmatrix} u_1 \\ \vdots \\ u_m \end{pmatrix} \quad [19.7]$$

Then the primal can be written as follows (with $\mathbf{A}$ and $\mathbf{A}'$ given by [19.6]):

$$\max \mathbf{c}'\mathbf{x} \quad \text{subject to} \quad \mathbf{Ax} \leq \mathbf{b}, \ \mathbf{x} \geq \mathbf{0} \qquad [19.8]$$

And the dual can be written as min $\mathbf{b}'\mathbf{u}$ subject to $\mathbf{A}'\mathbf{u} \geq \mathbf{c}$, $\mathbf{u} \geq \mathbf{0}$. It is more convenient, however, to write the dual in a slightly different way. Transposing $\mathbf{A}'\mathbf{u} \geq \mathbf{c}$ using the rules in [12.44] of Section 12.9 yields $\mathbf{u}'\mathbf{A} \geq \mathbf{c}'$, and moreover $\mathbf{b}'\mathbf{u} = \mathbf{u}'\mathbf{b}$. So the dual can be written as

$$\min \mathbf{u}'\mathbf{b} \quad \text{subject to} \quad \mathbf{u}'\mathbf{A} \geq \mathbf{c}', \ \mathbf{u} \geq \mathbf{0} \qquad [19.9]$$

Problems

1. Consider Problem 1(a) in Section 19.1.
   a. Replace the constraint $3x_1 + 2x_2 \leq 6$ by $3x_1 + 2x_2 \leq 7$. Find the new optimal solution and compute the increase u_1^* in the criterion function.
   b. Replace the constraint $x_1 + 4x_2 \leq 4$ by $x_1 + 4x_2 \leq 5$. Find the new optimal solution and compute the increase u_2^* in the criterion function.
   c. By the same argument as in Example 19.3, prove that if (x_1, x_2) is feasible in the original problem, then the criterion function can never be larger than 36/5.

2. Write down the dual to Problems 1(a) and (b) in Section 19.1.

3. Write down the dual to Problem 1(d) in Section 19.1.

19.3 The Duality Theorem

This section presents the main results relating the two solutions to an LP problem and its dual. We begin by considering the baker's problem yet again.

Example 19.4

Consider problems [1] and [2] in Section 19.2. Suppose that (x_1, x_2) is an arbitrary feasible pair in [1], which means that $x_1 \geq 0$, $x_2 \geq 0$, and the three $\leq$ inequalities in [1] are satisfied. Let (u_1, u_2, u_3) be an arbitrary feasible triple in [2]. Multiply the $\leq$ inequalities in [1] by the nonnegative numbers u_1, u_2, and u_3, respectively, and then add the inequalities. The result is the new inequality

$$(3x_1 + 6x_2)u_1 + (x_1 + 0.5x_2)u_2 + (x_1 + x_2)u_3 \leq 150u_1 + 22u_2 + 27.5u_3$$

Rearranging the terms on the left-hand side yields

$$(3u_1 + u_2 + u_3)x_1 + (6u_1 + 0.5u_2 + u_3)x_2 \leq 150u_1 + 22u_2 + 27.5u_3 \qquad [*]$$

In a corresponding way, we multiply the $\geq$ inequalities in [2] by the non-negative numbers x_1 and x_2, respectively, and add the results. This gives

$$(3u_1 + u_2 + u_3)x_1 + (6u_1 + 0.5u_2 + u_3)x_2 \geq 20x_1 + 30x_2 \qquad [**]$$

From [*] and [**] together, it follows that

$$150u_1 + 22u_2 + 27.5u_3 \geq 20x_1 + 30x_2 \qquad [***]$$

for all feasible (x_1, x_2) in problem [1] and for all feasible (u_1, u_2, u_3) in problem [2]. We conclude that in this example, the criterion function in the dual problem is always greater than or equal to the criterion function of the primal problem, whatever feasible (x_1, x_2) and (u_1, u_2, u_3) are chosen.

The inequality [***] is valid for the feasible pair $(x_1, x_2) = (5, 22.5)$ in particular. For each feasible triple (u_1, u_2, u_3), we therefore obtain

$$150u_1 + 22u_2 + 27.5u_3 \geq 20 \cdot 5 + 30 \cdot 22.5 = 775$$

It follows that if we can find a feasible triple (u_1^*, u_2^*, u_3^*) for problem [2] such that $150u_1^* + 22u_2^* + 27.5u_3^* = 775$, then (u_1^*, u_2^*, u_3^*) must solve problem [2], because no lower value of the criterion function is obtainable. In Section 19.2, we saw that for $(u_1^*, u_2^*, u_3^*) = (10/3, 0, 10)$, the criterion function in the dual did have the value 775. Hence, $(10/3, 0, 10)$ solves the dual problem.

The first general result we prove is the following:

Theorem 19.1   If $(x_1, \ldots, x_n)$ is feasible in the primal problem [19.4] and $(u_1, \ldots, u_m)$ is feasible in the dual problem [19.5], then

$$b_1u_1 + \cdots + b_mu_m \geq c_1x_1 + \cdots + c_nx_n \qquad [19.10]$$

So the dual criterion function has a value that is always at least as large as that of the primal.

Proof   Multiply the m inequalities in [19.4] by the nonnegative numbers $u_1, \ldots, u_m$, then add. Also, multiply the n inequalities in [19.5] by the nonnegative numbers $x_1, \ldots, x_n$, then add. These two operations yield the two inequalities

$$(a_{11}x_1 + \cdots + a_{1n}x_n)u_1 + \cdots + (a_{m1}x_1 + \cdots + a_{mn}x_n)u_m \leq b_1u_1 + \cdots + b_mu_m$$

$$(a_{11}u_1 + \cdots + a_{m1}u_m)x_1 + \cdots + (a_{1n}u_1 + \cdots + a_{mn}u_m)x_n \geq c_1x_1 + \cdots + c_nx_n$$

By rearranging the terms on the left-hand side of each inequality, we see that each is equal to the double sum $\sum_{i=1}^{m} \sum_{j=1}^{n} a_{ij}u_ix_j$. Then [19.10] follows immediately.

From Theorem 19.1 another interesting result is obtained:

Theorem 19.2   Suppose that $(x_1^*, \ldots, x_n^*)$ and $(u_1^*, \ldots, u_m^*)$ are feasible in problems [19.4] and [19.5], respectively, and that

$$c_1x_1^* + \cdots + c_nx_n^* = b_1u_1^* + \cdots + b_mu_m^* \qquad [19.11]$$

Then $(x_1^*, \ldots, x_n^*)$ solves problem [19.4] and $(u_1^*, \ldots, u_m^*)$ solves problem [19.5].

Proof   Let $(x_1, \ldots, x_n)$ be an arbitrary feasible n-vector for problem [19.4]. Using [19.10] with $u_1 = u_1^*, \ldots, u_m = u_m^*$, as well as [19.11], we obtain

$$c_1x_1 + \cdots + c_nx_n \leq b_1u_1^* + \cdots + b_mu_m^*$$

$$= c_1x_1^* + \cdots + c_nx_n^*$$

This proves that $(x_1^*, \ldots, x_n^*)$ solves [19.4].

Suppose that $(u_1, \ldots, u_m)$ is feasible for problem [19.5]. Then [19.10] and [19.11] together imply that

$$b_1u_1 + \cdots + b_mu_m \geq c_1x_1^* + \cdots + c_nx_n^*$$

$$= b_1u_1^* + \cdots + b_mu_m^*$$

This proves that $(u_1^*, \ldots, u_m^*)$ solves [19.5].

Theorem 19.2 shows that if we are able to find *feasible* solutions for problems [19.4] and [19.5] that give the same value to the criterion function in each of the two problems, then these feasible solutions are, in fact, *optimal* solutions.

The most important result in duality theory is the following:

Theorem 19.3 (The Duality Theorem)   Suppose the primal problem [19.4] has a (finite) optimal solution. Then the dual problem [19.5] also has a (finite) optimal solution, and the corresponding values of the criterion functions are equal. If the primal has no bounded optimum, then the dual has no feasible solution.

The proofs of Theorems 19.1 and 19.2 were very simple. It is much more difficult to prove the first statement in Theorem 19.3 concerning the existence of a solution to the dual, and so we shall not attempt to provide a proof here. The last statement in Theorem 19.3, however, follows readily from inequality [19.10]. For if $(u_1, \ldots, u_n)$ is any feasible solution to the dual problem, then $b_1 u_1 + \cdots + b_m u_m$ is a finite number greater than or equal to *any* number $c_1 x_1 + \cdots + c_n x_n$ when $(x_1, \ldots, x_n)$ is feasible in the primal. This puts an upper bound on the possible values of $c_1 x_1 + \cdots + c_n x_n$.

Note: It is a useful exercise to formulate and prove Theorems 19.1 and 19.2 using matrix algebra. Let us do so for Theorem 19.1. Suppose $\mathbf{x}$ is feasible in [19.8] and $\mathbf{u}$ is feasible in [19.9]. Then

$$\mathbf{u}'\mathbf{b} \geq \mathbf{u}'(\mathbf{A}\mathbf{x}) = (\mathbf{u}'\mathbf{A})\mathbf{x} \geq \mathbf{c}'\mathbf{x}$$

You should note carefully how these inequalities correspond to those we established in the earlier proof of Theorem 19.1.

Problems

1. Consider the problem

$$\max 2x + 7y \text{ subject to } \begin{cases} 4x + 5y \leq 20 \\ 3x + 7y \leq 21 \end{cases} \quad x \geq 0, \ y \geq 0$$

   a. Solve it by a geometric argument.
   b. Write down the dual and solve it by a geometric argument.
   c. Are the values of the criterion functions equal? (If not, then according to Theorem 19.3, you have made a mistake.)

2. Write down the dual to the problem in Example 19.2 and solve it. Check that the optimal values of the criterion functions are equal.

3. A firm produces small and medium television sets. The profit is 400 for each small and 500 for each medium television set. Each television has to be processed in three different divisions. Each small television requires respectively 2, 1, and 1 hour in divisions 1, 2, and 3. The corresponding numbers for the medium television sets are 1, 4, and 2. Suppose divisions 1

and 2 both have a capacity of at most 16 hours per day, and division 3 has a capacity of at most 11 hours per day. Let x_1 and x_2 denote the number of small and medium television sets that are produced per day.

a. Show that in order to maximize profits per day, one must solve the following problem:

$$\text{max } 400x_1 + 500x_2 \text{ subject to } \begin{cases} 2x_1 + x_2 \leq 16 \\ x_1 + 4x_2 \leq 16 \\ x_1 + 2x_2 \leq 11 \end{cases} \quad x_1 \geq 0, \, x_2 \geq 0$$

b. Solve this problem graphically.

c. If the firm could increase its capacity by 1 hour a day in just one of the three divisions, which should be the first to have its capacity increased?

19.4 A General Economic Interpretation

This section gives a general economic interpretation of the LP problem [19.4] and its dual [19.5]. Think of a firm that produces one or several outputs using m different **resources** as inputs. There are n different **activities** (or processes) involved in the production process. A typical activity is characterized by the fact that running it at unit level requires a certain amount of each resource. If a_{ij} is the number of units of resource i that are needed to run activity j at unit level, the vector with components $a_{1j}, a_{2j}, \ldots, a_{mj}$ expresses the m different total resource requirements for running activity j at unit level. If we run the activities at levels $x_1, \ldots, x_n$, the total resource requirement can be expressed as the column vector

$$x_1 \begin{pmatrix} a_{11} \\ \vdots \\ a_{m1} \end{pmatrix} + \cdots + x_n \begin{pmatrix} a_{1n} \\ \vdots \\ a_{mn} \end{pmatrix}$$

If the available resources are $b_1, \ldots, b_m$, then the feasible activity levels are those that satisfy the m constraints in [19.4]. The nonnegativity constraints reflect the fact that we cannot run the activities at negative levels.

Each activity brings a certain "reward." Let c_j be a measure of the reward (or value) created by running activity j at unit level. The total reward obtained by running the activities at levels $x_1, \ldots, x_n$ is then $c_1x_1 + \cdots + c_nx_n$. The problem of the firm is therefore to solve the following LP problem: *Find those levels for the n activities that maximize the total reward, subject to the given resource constraints.*

The problem in Example 19.1 can be interpreted in this way. There are two activities of making each of the two types of cake, and there are three resources— flour, sugar, and butter.

Let us turn to the dual problem [19.5]. In order to be in business, the firm has to use some resources. Each resource, therefore, has a value or price. Let u_j

be the price associated with one unit of resource j. Rather than think of u_j as a market price for resource j, we should think of it as (somehow) measuring the relative contribution that one unit of resource j makes to the total economic result. These prices are not real prices, so they are often called **shadow prices**.

Because $a_{1j}, a_{2j}, \ldots, a_{mj}$ are the numbers of units of each of the m resources needed to run activity j at unit level, $a_{1j}u_1 + a_{2j}u_2 + \cdots + a_{mj}u_m$ is the total (shadow) cost of running activity j at unit level. Because c_j is the reward (value) of running activity j at unit level,

$$c_j - (a_{1j}u_1 + a_{2j}u_2 + \cdots + a_{mj}u_m)$$

can be regarded as the (shadow) *profit* of running activity j at unit level. Note that the jth constraint in the dual problem [19.5] says that the (shadow) profit from running activity j at unit level is ≤ 0.

The criterion function $Z = b_1u_1 + \cdots + b_mu_m$ in the dual LP problem measures the (shadow) value of the initial stock of all the resources. The dual problem is, therefore, the following: *Among all choices of nonnegative shadow prices $u_1, \ldots, u_m$ such that the profit of running each activity at unit level is ≤ 0, find one that minimizes the (shadow) value of the initial resources.*

The Optimal Dual Variables as Shadow Prices

Consider again the primal problem

$$\max c_1x_1 + \cdots + c_nx_n \text{ subject to } \begin{cases} a_{11}x_1 + \cdots + a_{1n}x_n \leq b_1 \\ \cdots\cdots\cdots\cdots\cdots\cdots\cdots \\ a_{m1}x_1 + \cdots + a_{mn}x_n \leq b_m \end{cases} \quad [*]$$

with $x_1 \geq 0, \ldots, x_n \geq 0$. What happens to the optimal value of the criterion function if the numbers $b_1, \ldots, b_m$ change? If the changes $\Delta b_1, \ldots, \Delta b_m$ are positive, then the feasible set increases and the new optimal value of the criterion function cannot be smaller. (Usually it increases.) The following analysis also applies when some or all the changes $\Delta b_1, \ldots, \Delta b_m$ are negative.

How big is the change in the optimal value? Suppose $(x_1^*, \ldots, x_n^*)$ and $(x_1^* + \Delta x_1, \ldots, x_n^* + \Delta x_n)$ are optimal solutions to the primal when the right-hand side is respectively $(b_1, \ldots, b_m)$ and $(b_1 + \Delta b_1, \ldots, b_m + \Delta b_m)$. If $\Delta b_1, \ldots, \Delta b_m$ are all sufficiently small, the duals of the two problems often have the same optimal solution $u_1^*, \ldots, u_m^*$. Then, according to Theorem 19.3, one has

$$c_1x_1^* + \cdots + c_nx_n^* = b_1u_1^* + \cdots + b_mu_m^*$$
$$c_1(x_1^* + \Delta x_1) + \cdots + c_n(x_n^* + \Delta x_n) = (b_1 + \Delta b_1)u_1^* + \cdots + (b_m + \Delta b_m)u_m^*$$

Hence, by subtraction,

$$c_1\Delta x_1 + \cdots + c_n\Delta x_n = u_1^*\Delta b_1 + \cdots + u_m^*\Delta b_m$$

Here the left-hand side is the change we obtain in the criterion function in [*] when $b_1, \ldots, b_m$ are changed by $\Delta b_1, \ldots, \Delta b_m$, respectively. Denoting this change in z by Δz^*, we obtain

$$\Delta z^* = u_1^* \Delta b_1 + \cdots + u_m^* \Delta b_m \qquad [19.12]$$

Note: The assumption underlying [19.12] is that the changes in the b's do not cause the optimal dual variables to change.

Problems

1. Consider Problem 1 in Section 19.3,

$$\max 2x + 7y \text{ subject to } \begin{cases} 4x + 5y \leq 20 \\ 3x + 7y \leq 21 \end{cases} \quad x \geq 0, \ y \geq 0$$

We found that the optimal solution of this problem was $x^* = 0$, and $y^* = 3$, with $z^* = 2x^* + 7y^* = 21$. The optimal solution of the dual was $u_1^* = 0$ and $u_2^* = 1$. Suppose we change 20 to 20.1 and 21 to 20.8. What is the corresponding change in the criterion function?

19.5 Complementary Slackness

Consider again the baker's problem [1] in Section 19.2 and its dual [2]. The solution to [1] was $x_1^* = 5$ and $x_2^* = 22.5$, with the first and the third inequalities both satisfied with equality. The solution to the dual was $u_1^* = 10/3$, $u_2^* = 0$, and $u_3^* = 10$, with both inequalities in the dual satisfied with equality. Thus, in this example,

$$x_1^* > 0, \ x_2^* > 0 \Longrightarrow \begin{cases} \text{the first and second inequalities} \\ \text{in the dual are satisfied with equality} \end{cases} \qquad [1]$$

$$u_1^* > 0, \ u_3^* > 0 \Longrightarrow \begin{cases} \text{the first and third inequalities} \\ \text{in the primal are satisfied with equality} \end{cases} \qquad [2]$$

We interpret [2] this way: Because the shadow prices of flour and butter are positive, in the optimal solution, all the available flour and butter are used. We do not use all the available sugar, so its shadow price is zero—it is not a scarce resource. These results hold more generally.

Indeed, first, consider the problem

$$\max c_1 x_1 + c_2 x_2 \text{ subject to } \begin{cases} a_{11}x_1 + a_{12}x_2 \leq b_1 \\ a_{21}x_1 + a_{22}x_2 \leq b_2 \\ a_{31}x_1 + a_{32}x_2 \leq b_3 \end{cases} \quad x_1 \geq 0, \ x_2 \geq 0 \quad [3]$$

and its dual

$$\min\ b_1u_1 + b_2u_2 + b_3u_3 \text{ subject to } \begin{cases} a_{11}u_1 + a_{21}u_2 + a_{31}u_3 & \geq c_1 \\ a_{12}u_1 + a_{22}u_2 + a_{32}u_3 & \geq c_2 \end{cases} \qquad [4]$$

with u_1, u_2, and $u_3 \geq 0$. Suppose (x_1^*, x_2^*) solves [3] whereas (u_1^*, u_2^*, u_3^*) solves [4]. Then

$$\text{(a)} \quad \begin{array}{c} a_{11}x_1^* + a_{12}x_2^* \leq b_1 \\ a_{21}x_1^* + a_{22}x_2^* \leq b_2 \\ a_{31}x_1^* + a_{32}x_2^* \leq b_3 \end{array} \qquad \text{(b)} \quad \begin{array}{c} a_{11}u_1^* + a_{21}u_2^* + a_{31}u_3^* \geq c_1 \\ a_{12}u_1^* + a_{22}u_2^* + a_{32}u_3^* \geq c_2 \end{array} \qquad [5]$$

Multiply the three inequalities in [5](a) by the three nonnegative numbers u_1^*, u_2^*, and u_3^*, respectively. Then add the results. This yields the inequality

$$(a_{11}x_1^* + a_{12}x_2^*)u_1^* + (a_{21}x_1^* + a_{22}x_2^*)u_2^* + (a_{31}x_1^* + a_{32}x_2^*)u_3^* \leq b_1u_1^* + b_2u_2^* + b_3u_3^* \quad [6]$$

Multiply the two inequalities in [5](b) by x_1^* and x_2^*, respectively, and then add. This gives

$$(a_{11}u_1^* + a_{21}u_2^* + a_{31}u_3^*)x_1^* + (a_{12}u_1^* + a_{22}u_2^* + a_{32}u_3^*)x_2^* \geq c_1x_1^* + c_2x_2^* \qquad [7]$$

Looking closely at the left-hand sides of the two inequalities in [6] and [7] reveals that they are equal. Moreover, by the duality theorem of LP (Theorem 19.3), the right-hand sides of [6] and [7] are equal. Hence, both inequalities in [6] and [7] can be replaced by *equalities*. Thus, replacing $\leq$ by $=$ in [6] and rearranging, we obtain

$$(a_{11}x_1^* + a_{12}x_2^* - b_1)u_1^* + (a_{21}x_1^* + a_{22}x_2^* - b_2)u_2^* + (a_{31}x_1^* + a_{32}x_2^* - b_3)u_3^* = 0 \quad [8]$$

Each term in the parentheses within [8] is ≤ 0 because (x_1^*, x_2^*) is feasible. So, because u_1^*, u_2^*, and u_3^* are all ≥ 0, the three terms in [8] are ≤ 0. If any were < 0, their sum would be < 0. Because their sum is 0, each of them must be 0. Thus,

$$(a_{j1}x_1^* + a_{j2}x_2^* - b_j)u_j^* = 0 \qquad (j = 1, 2, 3)$$

We conclude that

$$a_{j1}x_1^* + a_{j2}x_2^* \leq b_j \ (= b_j \text{ if } u_j^* > 0) \qquad (j = 1, 2, 3) \qquad [9]$$

Using the fact that $\geq$ in [7] can be replaced by $=$, and reasoning in exactly the same way as before, we also get

$$a_{1i}u_1^* + a_{2i}u_2^* + a_{3i}u_3^* \geq c_i \ (= c_i \text{ if } x_i^* > 0) \qquad (i = 1, 2, 3) \qquad [10]$$

The results in [9] and [10] are called the *complementary slackness conditions*. The arguments used to show that these conditions are necessary extend in a straightforward way to the general case. Furthermore. the same complementary slackness conditions are also sufficient for optimality. Here is a general statement and proof:

Theorem 19.4   (Complementary Slackness)   Suppose that the primal problem [19.4] of Section 19.2 has an optimal solution $\mathbf{x}^* = (x_1^*, \ldots, x_n^*)$, whereas the dual [19.5] has an optimal solution $\mathbf{u}^* = (u_1^*, \ldots, u_m^*)$. Then for $i = 1, \ldots, n$, and $j = 1, \ldots, m$,

$$a_{1i}u_1^* + \cdots + a_{mi}u_m^* \geq c_i \ \ (= c_i \text{ if } x_i^* > 0) \tag{19.13}$$

$$a_{j1}x_1^* + \cdots + a_{jn}x_n^* \leq b_j \ \ (= b_j \text{ if } u_j^* > 0) \tag{19.14}$$

Conversely, if $\mathbf{x}^*$ and $\mathbf{u}^*$ have all their components nonnegative and satisfy [19.13] and [19.14], then $\mathbf{x}^*$ and $\mathbf{u}^*$ solve the primal problem [19.4] and the dual [19.5], respectively.

Proof   Suppose $\mathbf{x}^*$ solves [19.4] and $\mathbf{u}^*$ solves [19.5]. Then. in particular (see [19.8] and [19.9]).

$$\mathbf{Ax}^* \leq \mathbf{b} \quad \text{and} \quad (\mathbf{u}^*)'\mathbf{A} \geq \mathbf{c}' \tag{1}$$

Multiplying the first inequality in [1] on the left by $(\mathbf{u}^*)' \geq \mathbf{0}$ and the second inequality on the right by $\mathbf{x}^* \geq \mathbf{0}$ yields

$$(\mathbf{u}^*)'\mathbf{Ax}^* \leq (\mathbf{u}^*)'\mathbf{b} \quad \text{and} \quad (\mathbf{u}^*)'\mathbf{Ax}^* \geq \mathbf{c}'\mathbf{x}^* \tag{2}$$

According to Theorem 19.3. $(\mathbf{u}^*)'\mathbf{b} = \mathbf{c}'\mathbf{x}^*$. So both inequalities in [2] must be equalities. They can be written as

$$(\mathbf{u}^*)'(\mathbf{Ax}^* - \mathbf{b}) = 0 \quad \text{and} \quad ((\mathbf{u}^*)'\mathbf{A} - \mathbf{c}')\mathbf{x}^* = 0 \tag{3}$$

But these two equations are equivalent to

$$\sum_{j=1}^{m} u_j^*(a_{j1}x_1^* + \cdots + a_{jn}x_n^* - b_j) = 0 \tag{4}$$

and

$$\sum_{i=1}^{n}(a_{1i}u_1^* + \cdots + a_{mi}u_m^* - c_i)x_i^* = 0 \tag{5}$$

For $j = 1, \ldots, m$ one has both $u_j^* \geq 0$ and $a_{j1}x_1^* + \cdots + a_{jn}x_n^* - b_j \leq 0$. So each term in the sum [4] is ≤ 0. The sum of all the terms is 0. so there can be no negative term. because there is no positive term to cancel it. Hence, each term in the sum [4] must be 0. Therefore.

$$u_j^*(a_{j1}x_1^* + \cdots + a_{jn}x_n^* - b_j) = 0 \qquad (j = 1, \ldots, m) \qquad [6]$$

Now [19.14] follows immediately. Property [19.13] is proved in the same way by noting how [5] implies that

$$x_i^*(a_{1i}u_1^* + \cdots + a_{mi}u_m^* - c_i) = 0 \qquad (i = 1, \ldots, n) \qquad [7]$$

Suppose on the other hand that $\mathbf{x}^*$ and $\mathbf{u}^*$ have all their components nonnegative and satisfy [19.13] and [19.14]. It follows immediately that [6] and [7] are satisfied. So summing over j and i, respectively, we obtain [4] and [5]. From these equalities, it follows that $\sum_{j=1}^{m} b_j u_j^* = \sum_{j=1}^{m} \sum_{i=1}^{n} a_{ji} x_i^* u_j^*$ and also $\sum_{i=1}^{n} c_i x_i^* = \sum_{i=1}^{n} \sum_{j=1}^{m} a_{ji} u_j^* x_i^*$. But the two double sums are equal. Hence, $\sum_{j=1}^{m} b_j u_j^* = \sum_{i=1}^{n} c_i x_i^*$, so according to Theorem 19.2, the vector $(x_1^*, \cdots, x_n^*)$ solves problem [1] and $(u_1^*, \cdots, u_m^*)$ solves the dual.

Note: Using the general economic interpretations we gave in Section 19.4, conditions [19.13] and [19.14] can be interpreted as follows:
If the optimal solution of the primal problem implies that activity i is in operation $(x_i^* > 0)$, *then the (shadow) profit from running that activity at unit level is 0.*
If the shadow price of resource j is positive $(u_j^* > 0)$, *then all the available stock of resource j must be used in any optimum.*

How Complementary Slackness Can Help Solve LP Problems

If the solution to either the primal or the dual problem is known, then the complementary slackness conditions can help find the solution to the other problem by determining which constraints are slack. Let us look at an example.

Example 19.5

Consider the problem

$$\text{max } 3x_1 + 4x_2 + 6x_3 \text{ subject to } \begin{cases} 3x_1 + x_2 + x_3 \le 2 \\ x_1 + 2x_2 + 6x_3 \le 1 \end{cases} \qquad [1]$$

with $x_1 \ge 0$, $x_2 \ge 0$, and $x_3 \ge 0$. Write down the dual problem and solve it by a geometric argument. Then use complementary slackness to solve [1].

Solution The dual problem is

$$\text{min } 2u_1 + u_2 \text{ subject to } \begin{cases} 3u_1 + u_2 \ge 3 \\ u_1 + 2u_2 \ge 4 \\ u_1 + 6u_2 \ge 6 \end{cases} \quad u_1, u_2 \ge 0 \qquad [2]$$

Using the geometric solution technique shown in Example 19.2, we find the solution $u_1^* = 2/5$, and $u_2^* = 9/5$. Then $3u_1^* + u_2^* = 3$, $u_1^* + 2u_2^* = 4$, and $u_1^* + 6u_2^* > 6$.

What do we know about the solution (x_1^*, x_2^*, x_3^*) to [1]? According to [19.14], because $u_1^* > 0$ and $u_2^* > 0$, both inequalities in [1] are satisfied with equality. So

$$3x_1^* + x_2^* + x_3^* = 2 \quad \text{and} \quad x_1^* + 2x_2^* + 6x_3^* = 1 \quad [3]$$

Now x_3^* cannot be > 0, otherwise [19.13] would imply $u_1^* + 6u_2^* = 6$. Hence, $x_3^* = 0$. Letting $x_3^* = 0$ in [3] and solving for x_1^* and x_2^* gives

$$x_1^* = 3/5, \qquad x_2^* = 1/5, \qquad x_3^* = 0$$

This is the solution to problem [1]. Note that the optimal values of the criterion functions in the two problems are indeed equal: $2u_1^* + u_2^* = 13/5$ and $3x_1^* + 4x_2^* + 6x_3^* = 13/5$, just as they should be according to the duality theorem.

The Kuhn–Tucker Theorem Applied to Linear Programs

Consider the general linear programming problem

$$\max c_1 x_1 + \cdots + c_n x_n \quad \text{s.t.} \quad \begin{cases} a_{11} x_1 + \cdots + a_{1n} x_n \leq b_1 \\ \dots\dots\dots\dots\dots\dots\dots\dots \\ a_{m1} x_1 + \cdots + a_{mn} x_n \leq b_m \end{cases} \quad x_1 \geq 0, \ \dots, \ x_n \geq 0$$

$$[1]$$

This problem is obviously a special case of the general nonlinear programming problem

$$\max f(x_1, \dots, x_n) \quad \text{s.t.} \quad \begin{cases} g_1(x_1, \dots, x_n) \leq c_1 \\ \dots\dots\dots\dots\dots\dots \\ g_m(x_1, \dots, x_n) \leq c_m \end{cases} \quad x_1 \geq 0, \ \dots, \ x_n \geq 0 \quad [2]$$

which was studied in Section 18.9. Note that the functions f and g_j in [1] are all linear, so are concave as well as convex. Thus, the Kuhn–Tucker conditions [18.42] and [18.43] are sufficient for optimality of a vector $\mathbf{x} = (x_1, x_2, \dots, x_n)$ satisfying the constraints specified in [1]. Let us see what form these conditions take in the linear case.

If we let $\lambda_j = u_j$ for $j = 1, \dots, m$, conditions [18.42] and [18.43] become

$$c_i - (a_{1i} u_1 + \cdots + a_{mi} u_m) \leq 0 \quad (= 0 \text{ if } x_i > 0) \qquad (i = 1, \dots, n) \qquad [3]$$

$$u_j \geq 0 \quad (= 0 \text{ if } a_{j1} x_1 + \cdots + a_{jn} x_n < b_j) \qquad (j = 1, \dots, m) \qquad [4]$$

When combined with the requirement that **x** satisfy the constraints in problem [1], these conditions are precisely the complementary slackness conditions in Theorem 19.4.

Duality When Some Constraints are Equalities

Suppose that one of the constraints in the primal problem is the equality

$$a_{i1}x_1 + \cdots + a_{in}x_n = b_i \qquad [*]$$

Then we can replace it by the two inequalities

$$a_{i1}x_1 + \cdots + a_{in}x_n \le b_i \quad \text{and} \quad -a_{i1}x_1 - \cdots - a_{in}x_n \le -b_i \qquad [**]$$

in order to put the problem into standard form. Constraint [*] thus gives rise to two dual variables u_i' and u_i''. In the matrix describing the dual constraints, the two columns associated with u_i' and u_i'' are equal except for opposite signs everywhere. Therefore, we can replace the two variables u_i' and u_i'' with $u_i = u_i' - u_i''$, but then there is no restriction on the sign of u_i. We see that *if the ith constraint in the primal is an equality, then the ith dual variable has an unrestricted sign.* This is consistent with the economic interpretation we have given. If we are forced to use all of resource i, then it is not surprising that the resource may command a negative shadow price—it may be something that is harmful in excess. For instance, if the baker of Example 19.1 was forced to include all the stock of sugar in the cakes, the best point in Fig. 19.2 would be B, not C. Some profit would be lost.

From the symmetry between the primal and the dual, we realize now that *if one of the variables in the primal has an unrestricted sign, then the corresponding constraint in the dual is an equality.*

Problems

1. Consider Problem 1 of Section 19.3. The optimal solution of the primal was $x^* = 0$, and $y^* = 3$, whereas $u_1^* = 0$, $u_2^* = 1$ was the optimal solution of the dual. Verify that [19.13] and [19.14] are satisfied in this case.

2. **a.** Solve the following problem geometrically:

$$\min y_1 + 2y_2 \text{ subject to } \begin{cases} y_1 + 6y_2 \ge 15 \\ y_1 + y_2 \ge 5 \\ -y_1 + y_2 \ge -5 \\ y_1 - 2y_2 \ge -20 \end{cases} \quad y_1 \ge 0, \ y_2 \ge 0$$

b. Write down the dual problem and solve it.

c. What happens to the optimal dual variables if the constraint $y_1 + 6y_2 \ge 15$ is changed to $y_1 + 6y_2 \ge 15.1$?

3. A firm produces two commodities A and B. The firm has three factories that jointly produce both commodities in the amounts per hour given in the following table:

	Factory 1	Factory 2	Factory 3
Commodity A	10	20	20
Commodity B	20	10	20

The firm receives an order for 300 units of A and 500 units of B. The cost per hour of running factories 1, 2, and 3 are respectively 10,000; 8000; and 11,000.

a. Let y_1, y_2, and y_3, respectively, denote the number of hours for which the three factories are used. Write down the linear programming problem of minimizing the costs of fulfilling the order.

b. Show that the dual of the problem in part (a) is

$$\max 300x_1 + 500x_2 \text{ s.t.} \begin{cases} 10x_1 + 20x_2 \le 10,000 \\ 20x_1 + 10x_2 \le 8000 \\ 20x_1 + 20x_2 \le 11,000 \end{cases} \qquad x_1 \ge 0. \, x_2 \ge 0$$

Solve this problem and then find the solution of the problem in part (a).

c. By how much will the minimum cost of production increase if the cost per hour in factory 1 increases by 100?

Harder Problems

4. The following problem has arisen in production theory:

$$\max x^1 + x^2 + \cdots + x^N \text{ s.t.} \begin{cases} \xi_1^1 x^1 + \xi_1^2 x^2 + \cdots + \xi_1^N x^N \le V_1 \\ \xi_2^1 x^1 + \xi_2^2 x^2 + \cdots + \xi_2^N x^N \le V_2 \\ x^1 \qquad\qquad\qquad\qquad \le \bar{x}^1 \\ \qquad x^2 \qquad\qquad\qquad \le \bar{x}^2 \\ \qquad\qquad \ddots \qquad\qquad \vdots \\ \qquad\qquad\qquad\qquad x^N \le \bar{x}^N \end{cases} \qquad [1]$$

where variables x^1, x^2, ..., x^N are all ≥ 0. Here ξ_i^j, V_1, V_2, $\bar{x}^1$, ..., $\bar{x}^N$ are fixed constants. (Superscripts $i = 1, \ldots, N$ refer to production units; V_1 and V_2 are available quantities of two resources; each $\bar{x}^j$ is a capacity constraint on the output of unit j.) Write down the dual to problem [1], with q_1 and q_2 denoting the dual prices associated with the first two constraints in [1], whereas r^1, r^2, ..., r^N are the dual variables associated with the last N constraints. Let the values of the variables that solve the two problems be those indicated with a hat. Show that if [1] has a finite optimum, then

$$\hat{x}^i > 0 \implies \xi_1^i \hat{q}_1 + \xi_2^i \hat{q}_2 + r^i = 1 \qquad (i = 1, \ldots, N) \qquad \text{[i]}$$

$$\xi_1^i \hat{q}_1 + \xi_2^i \hat{q}_2 + r^i > 1 \implies x^i = 0 \qquad (i = 1, \ldots, N) \qquad \text{[ii]}$$

$$\hat{q}_j > 0 \implies \xi_j^1 \hat{x}^1 + \cdots + \xi_j^N \hat{x}^N = V_j \qquad (j = 1, 2) \qquad \text{[iii]}$$

$$\xi_j^1 \hat{x}^1 + \cdots + \xi_j^N \hat{x}^N < V_j \implies \hat{q}_j = 0 \qquad (j = 1, 2) \qquad \text{[iv]}$$

$$\hat{r}^i > 0 \implies \hat{x}^i = \bar{x}^i \qquad (i = 1, \ldots, N) \qquad \text{[v]}$$

$$\hat{x}^i < \bar{x}^i \implies \hat{r}^i = 0 \qquad (i = 1, \ldots, N) \qquad \text{[vi]}$$

5. Consider the LP problem

$$\max 3x_1 + 2x_2 \text{ subject to } \begin{cases} x_1 + x_2 & \leq 3 \\ 2x_1 + x_2 - x_3 & \leq 1 \\ x_1 + 2x_2 - 2x_3 & \leq 1 \end{cases} \quad x_1 \geq 0, x_2 \geq 0, x_3 \geq 0$$

a. Suppose x_3 is a fixed number. Solve the problem if $x_3 = 0$ and if $x_3 = 3$.
b. Solve the problem for any fixed value of x_3 in $[0, \infty)$. The maximal value of $3x_1 + 2x_2$ becomes a function of x_3. Find this function and maximize it.
c. Do the results in part (b) say anything about the solution to the original problem in which x_3 can also be chosen?

20

Difference Equations

> *Mathematics is not a careful march down a well-cleared highway, but a journey into a strange wilderness, where the explorers often get lost.*
> —W. S. Anglin (1992)

Economists often study the development through time of economic variables like national income, the interest rate, the money supply, the production of oil, and the price of wheat. The laws governing the behavior of these variables are usually expressed in terms of one or more equations.

If time is taken to be a discrete (or integer valued) variable and the equations relate the values of such variables at different points of time, then we are confronted with *difference equations* or *recurrence relations*. In this case, time is usually measured by simply counting forward the number of periods that have elapsed after an initial time $t = 0$. Sometimes, however, we also consider negative times, in which case $t = 0$ should be thought of as the *origin* of our time measure.

If time is regarded as a continuous variable and the equations involve unknown functions and their derivatives, we find ourselves considering *differential equations*.

This chapter deals with first- and second-order difference equations, whereas the next chapter deals with the elementary theory of differential equations.

20.1 First-Order Difference Equations

Changes in many of the quantities economists study (such as income, consumption, and savings) are usually observed at fixed time intervals (for example, each day, week, or year). These quantities are then dated according to the period to which they refer, and the behavior of these economic variables is studied at discrete moments of time. Equations that relate such quantities at different times are called **difference equations**. For example, such an equation might relate the amount of national income in one period to the national income in one or more previous periods.

Let $f(t, x)$ be a function defined for all positive integers t and all real numbers x. A fairly general difference equation of the *first order* is[1]

$$x_t = f(t, x_{t-1}) \qquad (t = 1, 2, \ldots) \qquad [20.1]$$

This is a first-order equation because it relates the value of a function in each period t to the value of the same function in the previous period $t - 1$ only. (When we deal with functions defined for discrete time periods, we usually let x_t (rather than $x(t)$) denote the value of the variable at time t.)

Note: Some people refer to equations of type [20.1] as **recurrence relations** and would insist that a difference equation is one where the difference $\Delta x_t = x_t - x_{t-1}$ is specified as a function of t and x_{t-1}. But Equation [20.1] is evidently equivalent to the difference equation $\Delta x_t = f(t, x_{t-1}) - x_{t-1}$. Conversely, given a difference equation $\Delta x_t = g(t, x_{t-1})$, there is a corresponding recurrence relation $x_t = x_{t-1} + g(t, x_{t-1})$. Because of this obvious correspondence between recurrence relations and difference equations, there seems no good reason to maintain a distinction between the two. So we will refer to [20.1] as a difference equation.

Suppose x_0 is given. Then successive insertions into [20.1] yield

$$x_1 = f(1, x_0)$$
$$x_2 = f(2, x_1) = f(2, f(1, x_0))$$
$$x_3 = f(3, x_2) = f(3, f(2, f(1, x_0)))$$

and so on. *For a given value of x_0, we can compute x_t for any value of t.* Formally, we state this simple result as a theorem:

Theorem 20.1 (Existence and Uniqueness Theorem) Consider the difference equation $x_t = f(t, x_{t-1})$, $t = 1, 2, \ldots$, where f is defined for all values of the variables. If x_0 is an arbitrary fixed number, then there exists a uniquely determined function x_t that is a solution of the equation and has the given value for $t = 0$.

In general, for each choice of x_0, there is a different corresponding unique solution of [20.1]. Consequently, there are infinitely many solutions.

---

[1]The *general* difference equation of the first order is $F(t, x_{t-1}, x_t) = 0$. If this equation can be solved for x_t in terms of t and x_{t-1}, we have Equation [20.1].

The existence and uniqueness theorem for [20.1] is almost trivial. It implies that when x_0 is given, the successive values of x_t can be computed for any natural number t. Does this not tell us the whole story? Why do we need more?

We do, in fact, need to know more. In economic applications, we are usually interested in establishing qualitative results concerning the solutions. For example, we might be interested in the behavior of the solution when t becomes very large; we might be interested in how changes in the parameters entering into the difference equation affect its solution; and so on. Such questions are difficult or impossible to handle if we base our discussion on the "insertion method" alone. Actually, the insertion method suffers from another defect in connection with numerical computations. For example, suppose that we have a difference equation of the type [20.1], and we want to compute x_{100}. A time-consuming process of successive insertions will finally yield an expression for x_{100}. However, computational errors can easily occur, and if we work with approximate numbers (as we usually do in serious applications), the approximation error might well explode and in the end give an entirely misleading answer. So there really is a need for a more systematic theory of difference equations. Preferably, the solutions should be expressed in terms of elementary functions. Unfortunately, this is possible only for rather restricted classes of equations.

First-Order Equations with a Constant Coefficient

We study first the *linear difference equation*

$$x_t = ax_{t-1} + b_t \qquad (t = 1, 2, \ldots) \qquad [20.2]$$

Starting with a given x_0, it is possible to calculate x_t algebraically for small t. Indeed,

$$x_1 = ax_0 + b_1$$

$$x_2 = ax_1 + b_2 = a(ax_0 + b_1) + b_2 = a^2 x_0 + ab_1 + b_2$$

$$x_3 = ax_2 + b_3 = a(a^2 x_0 + ab_1 + b_2) + b_3 = a^3 x_0 + a^2 b_1 + ab_2 + b_3$$

Here are two more values of x_t, without the benefit of each step being explained:

$$x_4 = a^4 x_0 + a^3 b_1 + a^2 b_2 + ab_3 + b_4$$

$$x_5 = a^5 x_0 + a^4 b_1 + a^3 b_2 + a^2 b_3 + ab_4 + b_5$$

This makes the pattern clear. In each case, the formula for x_t begins with the term $a^t x_0$, and then adds the terms $a^{t-1} b_1, a^{t-2} b_2, \ldots, ab_{t-1}, b_t$ in turn, to give the overall sum $a^t x_0 + \sum_{k=1}^{t} a^{t-k} b_k$. We thus arrive at the following hypothesis (which is true for $t = 1, 2, 3, 4, 5$):

The difference equation

$$x_t = ax_{t-1} + b_t \qquad (t = 1, 2, \ldots)$$

has the solution

$$x_t = a^t x_0 + \sum_{k=1}^{t} a^{t-k} b_k \qquad (t = 1, 2, \ldots) \qquad [20.3]$$

(Remember that $a^{t-k} = a^0 = 1$ when $t = k$.) Indeed, one can check that [20.3] really is a solution of [20.2]. Substituting the expression suggested by [20.3] for x_{t-1} into the right-hand side of [20.2] yields

$$ax_{t-1} + b_t = a\left(a^{t-1}x_0 + \sum_{k=1}^{t-1} a^{t-1-k}b_k\right) + b_t = a^t x_0 + \sum_{k=1}^{t-1} a^{t-k}b_k + b_t$$

$$= a^t x_0 + \sum_{k=1}^{t} a^{t-k}b_k$$

This matches our expression for x_t, so [20.3] does solve the difference equation. Consider the special case when $b_k = b$ for all $k = 1, 2, \ldots$. Then

$$\sum_{k=1}^{t} a^{t-k}b_k = b\sum_{k=1}^{t} a^{t-k} = b(a^{t-1} + a^{t-2} + \cdots + a + 1)$$

Because of the summation formula [6.10] in Section 6.5 for a geometric series, we have $1 + a + a^2 + \cdots + a^{t-1} = (1 - a^t)/(1 - a)$, for $a \neq 1$. Thus, for $t = 1, 2, \ldots,$

$$x_t = ax_{t-1} + b \iff x_t = a^t\left(x_0 - \frac{b}{1-a}\right) + \frac{b}{1-a}, \qquad (a \neq 1) \qquad [20.4]$$

For $a = 1$, we have $1 + a + \cdots + a^{t-1} = t$ and $x_t = x_0 + tb$ for $t = 1, 2, \ldots$.

Example 20.1

Solve the difference equations:

$$\textbf{(a)} \ \ x_t = \tfrac{1}{2}x_{t-1} + 3 \qquad \textbf{(b)} \ \ x_t = -3x_{t-1} + 4$$

Solution   Using [20.4] and letting $a = 1/2$ and $b = 3$ gives the following solution of (a):

$$x_t = \left(\tfrac{1}{2}\right)^t (x_0 - 6) + 6$$

To solve (b), we use [20.4] again. Letting $a = -3$ and $b = 4$ gives

$$x_t = (-3)^t (x_0 - 1) + 1$$

Example 20.2   (A Model of Growth)

Let Y_t denote national income, I_t total investment, and S_t total saving—all in period t. Suppose that saving is proportional to national income, and investment is proportional to the change in income. Then, for $t = 1, 2, \ldots$,

$$S_t = \alpha Y_t \tag{1}$$

$$I_t = \beta(Y_t - Y_{t-1}) \tag{2}$$

$$S_t = I_t \tag{3}$$

Here [3] is the familiar equilibrium condition, whereas α and β are positive constants. Assume that $\beta > \alpha > 0$. Deduce a difference equation determining the path of Y_t, given Y_0, and solve it.

Solution   From [3] and [1], $I_t = \alpha Y_t$. Inserted into [2], this yields $\alpha Y_t = \beta(Y_t - Y_{t-1})$ or $(\alpha - \beta)Y_t = -\beta Y_{t-1}$. Thus,

$$Y_t = \frac{\beta}{\beta - \alpha} Y_{t-1} \qquad (t = 1, 2, \ldots) \tag{4}$$

Using [20.4] gives the solution

$$Y_t = \left(\frac{\beta}{\beta - \alpha}\right)^t Y_0 \qquad (t = 1, 2, \ldots) \tag{5}$$

The difference equation [4] constitutes an instance of the equation

$$Y_t = \left(1 + \frac{p}{100}\right) Y_{t-1} = (1 + g)Y_{t-1} \qquad (t = 1, 2, \ldots) \tag{6}$$

The solution of [6] is $Y_t = (1 + g)^t Y_0$. Note that g $(= p\%)$ is the constant proportional growth rate, because $g = (Y_{t+1} - Y_t)/Y_t$. In [5], the proportional growth rate is $g = \alpha/(\beta - \alpha)$.

Equilibrium States and Stability

Consider the solution of $x_t = ax_{t-1} + b$ given in [20.4]. If $x_0 = b/(1-a)$, then $x_t = b/(1-a)$ for all t. In fact, if $x_s = b/(1-a)$ for some $s \geq 0$, then

$$x_{s+1} = a\frac{b}{1-a} + b = \frac{b}{1-a}$$

Also $x_{s+2} = b/(1-a)$, and so on. We conclude that if x_s ever becomes equal to $b/(1-a)$ at some time s, then x_t will remain at this constant level for each $t \geq s$. The constant

$$x^* = \frac{b}{1-a} \qquad [20.5]$$

is called an **equilibrium** (or **stationary**) state for $x_t = ax_{t-1} + b$ when $a \neq 1$. *Note:* An alternative way of finding x^* is to seek a solution of $x_t = ax_{t-1} + b$ with $x_t = x^*$ for all t. Such a solution must satisfy $x_t = x_{t-1} = x^*$ and so $x^* = ax^* + b$. Therefore, for $a \neq 1$, we obtain $x^* = b/(1-a)$ again.

Definition [20.5] allows us to rewrite [20.4] as

$$x_t - x^* = a(x_{t-1} - x^*) \quad \Longleftrightarrow \quad x_t - x^* = a^t(x_0 - x^*) \qquad [20.6]$$

Note that $x_t - x^*$ is the deviation of x_t from its equilibrium value. So [20.6] shows that this deviation grows (or shrinks) at the constant proportional rate $a - 1$.

Suppose the constant a is less than 1 in absolute value—that is, $|a| < 1$, or $-1 < a < 1$. Then $a^t \to 0$ as $t \to \infty$, so [20.4] implies that

$$x_t \to x^* = \frac{b}{1-a} \qquad \text{as} \qquad t \to \infty$$

Hence, if $|a| < 1$, the solution in [20.4] converges to the equilibrium state when $t \to \infty$. The equation is then called **stable**. Two cases of stability are shown in Fig. 20.1 (a) and (b). In the first case, x_t converges monotonically down to the equilibrium state. In the second case, x_t exhibits decreasing fluctuations around the equilibrium state. In this case, we have **damped oscillations**.

If $|a| > 1$, then the absolute value of a^t approaches ∞ as $t \to \infty$. From [20.4], it follows that x_t moves farther and farther away from the equilibrium state, except when $x_0 = b/(1-a)$. Two cases of this phenomenon are illustrated in Fig. 20.1 (c) and (d). In the first case, x_t tends to $-\infty$, and in the second case, x_t exhibits increasing fluctuations around the equilibrium state. In the latter instance, we say that there are **explosive oscillations**.

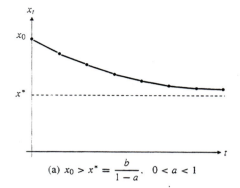

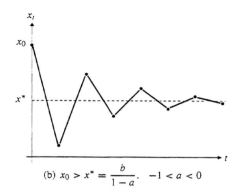

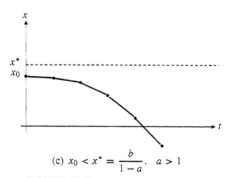

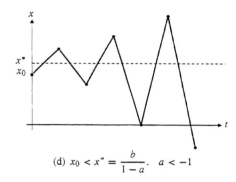

FIGURE 20.1

Example 20.3

Equation [a] in Example 20.1 is stable because $a = 1/2$. The equilibrium state is $b/(1-a) = 3/(1-1/2) = 6$. We see from the solution given in that example that $x_t \to 6$ as $t \to \infty$.

Equation [b] in Example 20.1 is not stable because $|a| = |-3| = 3 > 1$. The solution does *not* converge to the equilibrium state $x^* = 1$ as $t \to \infty$, except if $x_0 = 1$—in fact, there are explosive oscillations.

Example 20.4 (The Hog Cycle: A Cobweb Model)

Assume that the total cost of raising q pigs is $C(q) = \alpha q + \beta q^2$. Suppose there are N identical pig farms. Let the demand curve for pigs be given by $D(p) = \gamma - \delta p$, as a function of price p, where the constants α, β, γ, and δ are all positive. Suppose, too, that each farmer behaves competitively, taking price p as given and maximizing profits $\pi(q) = pq - C(q) = pq - \alpha q - \beta q^2$.

Then the quantity $q > 0$ can only maximize profits if

$$\pi'(q) = p - \alpha - 2\beta q = 0 \qquad \text{and so} \qquad q = \frac{p - \alpha}{2\beta} \qquad [1]$$

We see from [1] that $\pi'(q) > 0$ for $q < (p - \alpha)/2\beta$, and $\pi'(q) < 0$ for $q > (p - \alpha)/2\beta$. Thus, $q = (p - \alpha)/2\beta$ maximizes profits provided $p > \alpha$. In aggregate, the supply of pigs from all N farms is

$$S = \frac{N(p - \alpha)}{2\beta} \qquad (p > \alpha)$$

Now, suppose it takes one period to raise each pig, and that when choosing the number of pigs to raise for sale at time t, each farmer remembers the price p_{t-1} at time $t - 1$ and expects p_t to be the same as p_{t-1}. Then the aggregate supply at time t will be $S_t = N(p_{t-1} - \alpha)/2\beta$.

Equilibrium of supply and demand in all periods requires that $S_t = D(p_t)$, so

$$\frac{N(p_{t-1} - \alpha)}{2\beta} = \gamma - \delta p_t \qquad (t = 1, 2, \ldots)$$

Solving for p_t in terms of p_{t-1} and the parameters gives the difference equation

$$p_t = -\frac{N}{2\beta\delta} p_{t-1} + \frac{\alpha N + 2\beta\gamma}{2\beta\delta} \qquad (t = 1, 2, \ldots) \tag{2}$$

The stationary state occurs when the price p^* satisfies

$$p_t = p_{t-1} = p^* = \frac{\alpha N + 2\beta\gamma}{2\beta\delta + N}$$

The solution to [2] is

$$p_t = p^* + (-a)^t (p_0 - p^*) \qquad (a = N/2\beta\delta) \tag{3}$$

Equation [2] is stable if $|-a| < 1$, which happens when $N < 2\beta\delta$. In this case, $p_t \to p^*$ as $t \to \infty$. The solution in this case is illustrated in Fig. 20.2. Here, S_0 is the supply of pigs at time 0. The price at which all these can be sold is p_0. This determines the supply S_1 one period later which then determines P_1, and so on. The resulting price cycles are damped and both price and quantity converge to a steady-state equilibrium at (S^*, p^*). This is also an equilibrium of supply and demand. If $N > 2\beta\delta$, however, then the oscillations explode, and eventually p_t becomes less than α. Then the pig farms go out of business, and the solution has to be described in a different way. There is no convergence to a steady state. A third intermediate case occurs when $N = 2\beta\delta$ and $a = 1$. Then the pair (S_t, p_t) oscillates perpetually between the two values $(\gamma - \delta p_0, p_0)$ and $(\delta(p_0 - \alpha), \alpha + \gamma/\delta - p_0)$.

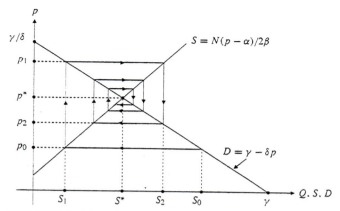

FIGURE 20.2 The cobweb model in Example 20.4—the convergent case.

Problems

1. Find the solutions to the following difference equations with the given values of x_0:

   a. $x_t = 2x_{t-1} + 4,$ $x_0 = 1$
   b. $3x_t = x_{t-1} + 2,$ $x_0 = 2$
   c. $2x_t + 3x_{t-1} + 2 = 0,$ $x_0 = -1$
   d. $x_t - x_{t-1} + 3 = 0,$ $x_0 = 3$

2. Consider the difference equation in [20.4] and explain how its solution behaves in each of the following cases, with $x^* = b/(1 - a)$ (for $a \neq 1$):

   a. $0 < a < 1,$ $x_0 < x^*$ **b.** $-1 < a < 0,$ $x_0 < x^*$
   c. $a > 1,$ $x_0 > x^*$ **d.** $a < -1,$ $x_0 > x^*$
   e. $a \neq 1,$ $x_0 = x^*$ **f.** $a = -1,$ $x_0 \neq x^*$
   g. $a = 1,$ $b > 0$ **h.** $a = 1,$ $b < 0$
   i. $a = 1,$ $b = 0$

3. Show that if A_t is a given function of t, then the difference equation

$$ x_t = ax_{t-1} + A_t \qquad (t = 1, 2, \ldots) \tag{1} $$

has the solution

$$ x_t = a^t x_0 + (a^{t-1} A_1 + a^{t-2} A_2 + \cdots + A_t) \tag{2} $$

In particular, let $A_t = bc^t$ for $t = 0, 1, \ldots$, and use the summation formula for a geometric series to find an expression for the sum in the parentheses in [2] in this case. Hence, find the solution of the difference equation for $a \neq c$ and for $a = c$.

4. Consider the difference equation

$$y_{t+1}(a + by_t) = cy_t \qquad (t = 0, 1, \ldots)$$

where we assume that a, b, and c are positive constants, and $y_0 > 0$.
a. Show that $y_t > 0$ for all $t = 0, 1, \ldots$.
b. Define a new function x_t by $x_t = 1/y_t$. Show that by using this substitution, the new difference equation is of the type in [20.4]. Next solve the difference equation

$$y_{t+1}(2 + 3y_t) = 4y_t$$

assuming that $y_0 = 1/2$. What is the limit of y_t as $t \to \infty$?

5. Consider the difference equation $x_t = \sqrt{x_{t-1} - 1}$ with $x_0 = 5$. Compute x_1, x_2, and x_3. What about x_4? (This problem illustrates the need to take care if the domain of the function f in [20.1] is restricted in any way.)

Harder Problems

6. The authors Frisch, Haavelmo, Norregaard-Rasmussen, and Zeuthen, in their study of the "wage—price spiral" of inflation, considered the following system for $t = 0, 1, \ldots$:

$$\frac{W_{t+2} - W_{t+1}}{W_{t+1}} = \frac{P_{t+1} - P_t}{P_t} \qquad \text{and} \qquad P_t = \gamma + \beta W_t \qquad [1]$$

Here W_t denotes the wage level, P_t the price index at time t, and γ and β are constants. The first equation states that the proportional increase in wages is equal to the proportional increase in the price index one period earlier, whereas the second equation relates prices to current wages.
a. Deduce from [1] the following equation for W_t:

$$\frac{W_{t+2}}{\gamma + \beta W_{t+1}} = \frac{W_{t+1}}{\gamma + \beta W_t} \qquad (t = 0, 1, \ldots) \qquad [2]$$

b. Use [2] to prove that

$$W_{t+1} = c(\gamma + \beta W_t) \qquad (t = 0, 1, \ldots) \qquad [3]$$

where $c = W_1/P_0$, and find a general expression for W_t when $c\beta \neq 1$.
c. Under what conditions will [3] be stable and what is the limit of W_t as $t \to \infty$ in this case?

20.2 Compound Interest and Present Discounted Values

The theory in the previous section can be applied to describe the effect of compound interest on a savings account with deposits and withdrawals. Let w_t, c_t, and y_t respectively denote the size of the account (or wealth), and the amounts withdrawn for consumption and deposited as income in period t. If the interest rate per period is a constant r, the relevant difference equation is

$$w_t = (1+r)w_{t-1} + (y_t - c_t) \qquad (t = 1, 2, \ldots) \qquad [20.7]$$

The result in [20.3] implies that the solution of [20.7] is

$$w_t = (1+r)^t w_0 + \sum_{k=1}^{t} (1+r)^{t-k}(y_k - c_k) \qquad (t = 1, 2, \ldots) \qquad [20.8]$$

because $a = 1 + r$ and $b_t = y_t - c_t$.

Let us multiply each term in [20.8] by $(1+r)^{-t}$. This is a multiplier of sufficient economic importance that is generally called the **discount factor**. The result is

$$(1+r)^{-t} w_t = w_0 + \sum_{k=1}^{t} (1+r)^{-k}(y_k - c_k) \qquad [20.9]$$

If time 0 is now, then the left-hand side is the **present discounted value (PDV)** of the assets in the account at time t. Equation [20.9] says that this is equal to

a. initial assets w_0

b. plus the total PDV of all future deposits, $\sum_{k=1}^{t} (1+r)^{-k} y_k$

c. *minus* the total PDV of all future withdrawals $\sum_{k=1}^{t} (1+r)^{-k} c_k$

In the case when $w_0 = w_t = 0$, so that the first deposit opens the account at time 0, and the last withdrawal closes it at time t, we have

$$\sum_{k=1}^{t} (1+r)^{-k} c_k = \sum_{k=1}^{t} (1+r)^{-k} y_k$$

This requires the total PDV of all withdrawals to equal the total PDV of all deposits.

If time t is now, the formula for w_t in [20.8] can be interpreted as follows: *Current assets w_t reflect the interest earned on initial assets w_0, with adjustments for the interest earned on all later deposits, or foregone because of later withdrawals.*

Example 20.5   (Mortgage Repayments)

A particular case of the difference equation [20.7] occurs when a family borrows an amount B at time 0 as a home mortgage. Suppose there is a fixed interest rate of r per period (usually paid each month rather than once per year). Suppose, too, that there are equal repayments of amount z each period, until the mortgage is paid off after T periods (for example, 30 years, or 360 months). The outstanding balance or *principal* b_t on the loan in period t satisfies the difference equation

$$b_t = (1+r)b_{t-1} - z \qquad \text{with } b_0 = B \text{ and } b_T = 0 \tag{1}$$

This difference equation can be solved by using [20.4] with $x_t = b_t$, $a = 1 + r$, $b = -z$, and $b_0 = B$. We obtain

$$b_t = (1+r)^t \left(B - \frac{z}{r} \right) + \frac{z}{r} \tag{2}$$

But $b_t = 0$ when $t = T$, so $0 = (1+r)^T (B - z/r) + z/r$. Solving for B yields

$$B = \frac{z}{r}[1 - (1+r)^{-T}] = z \sum_{t=1}^{T} (1+r)^{-t} \tag{3}$$

The original loan is, therefore, equal to the PDV of T equal repayments of amount z each period, starting in period 1.

Solving [3] for z instead yields

$$z = \frac{rB}{1 - (1+r)^{-T}} = rB + \frac{(1+r)^{-T}rB}{1 - (1+r)^{-T}} \tag{4}$$

Hence, the repayment each period is slightly larger than just the interest rB on the original loan B; there are principal as well as interest payments each period. This distinction is of some importance in tax jurisdictions like the U.S., where the interest part rb_{t-1} of each mortgage repayment is usually deductible from taxable income, whereas principal repayments are not deductible.

Notice that from [3], $B - z/r = -(z/r)(1+r)^{-T}$. Inserted into [2], this yields

$$b_t = \frac{z}{r}[1 - (1+r)^{t-T}] \tag{5}$$

as the remaining principal at time t. Thus, at time t, the interest payment on this principal at time $t - 1$ is

$$rb_{t-1} = z[1 - (1+r)^{t-1-T}]$$

Because z is the total payment, it follows that the principal repayment in period t is

$$z - rb_{t-1} = z(1+r)^{t-1-T}$$

This is an amount that starts out very small but then grows exponentially at the rate $1 + r$. In the last period, when $t = T$, the interest payment is

$$z \left(1 - \frac{1}{1+r} \right) = \frac{rz}{1+r}$$

whereas the principal repayment is $z/(1+r)$. But when $t = 1$ and the first payment z is due, only the amount $z(1+r)^{-T}$ repays principal; all the rest is interest.

Problems

1. Find the solution of [20.7] for $r = 0.2$, $w_0 = 1000$, $y_t = 100$, and $x_t = 50$.

2. Suppose that at time $t = 0$, you borrow \$100,000 at the fixed interest rate $r = 0.07$ per year. You are supposed to repay the loan in 30 equal repayments so that after $T = 30$ years, the mortgage is paid off. How much is the yearly repayment? How much of this is interest and how much is principal: (a) in the first year and (b) in the last year?

3. A loan of amount \$$L$ is taken out on January 1 of year 0. Installment payments for the principal and interest are made annually, commencing on January 1 of year 1. Let the interest rate be $r < 2$, so that the interest amounts to rL for the first payment. The contract states that the principal share of the repayment will be half the size of the interest share.
   a. Show that the debt after January 1 of year n is $(1 - r/2)^n L$.
   b. Find r when it is known that exactly half the original loan is paid after 10 years.
   c. What will the remaining payments be each year if the contract is not changed?

20.3 Linear Equations with a Variable Coefficient

Sometimes economists need to consider a more general form of the linear difference equation [20.2], where coefficient a can vary over time. This will be the case in Example 20.6 concerning the present value of an income stream when the interest rate varies.

The general first-order linear difference equation takes the form

$$x_t = a_t x_{t-1} + b_t \qquad (t = 1, 2, \ldots) \qquad [20.10]$$

where a_t depends on t. Proceeding as before, we calculate x_t explicitly for the first few values of t, starting with a given x_0 when $t = 0$. We have

$$x_1 = a_1 x_0 + b_1$$

$$x_2 = a_2 x_1 + b_2 = a_2(a_1 x_0 + b_1) + b_2 = a_2 a_1 x_0 + a_2 b_1 + b_2$$

Then, omitting the details of the next two calculations, we have

$$x_3 = a_3 a_2 a_1 x_0 + a_3 a_2 b_1 + a_3 b_2 + b_3$$

$$x_4 = a_4 a_3 a_2 a_1 x_0 + a_4 a_3 a_2 b_1 + a_4 a_3 b_2 + a_4 b_3 + b_4$$

This is considerably more complicated than when a_t was independent of t, yet you should still be able to discern a pattern. Indeed, the successive coefficients of x_0 are

$$a_1, \quad a_1 a_2, \quad a_1 a_2 a_3, \quad a_1 a_2 a_3 a_4$$

These can be expressed as (see Section B.4 for an explanation of the product notation)

$$\prod_{s=1}^{t} a_s \quad \text{for } t = 1, 2, 3, 4 \qquad [20.11]$$

In fact, the general formula for x_t becomes

$$x_t = \left(\prod_{s=1}^{t} a_s \right) x_0 + \left(\prod_{s=2}^{t} a_s \right) b_1 + \left(\prod_{s=3}^{t} a_s \right) b_2 + \cdots + \left(\prod_{s=t}^{t} a_s \right) b_{t-1} + b_t$$

This can be written as

$$x_t = \left(\prod_{s=1}^{t} a_s \right) x_0 + \sum_{k=1}^{t} \left(\prod_{s=k+1}^{t} a_s \right) b_k \qquad [20.12]$$

provided we agree that the product $\prod_{s=t+1}^{t} a_s$ of zero terms is 1. A formal proof of [20.12] is possible using mathematical induction.

Example 20.6 (Compound Interest and PDVs with Variable Interest Rates)
We can now modify our previous compound interest and present discounted value calculations in Section 20.2 to allow interest rates r_t that vary from period to period. The relevant difference equation becomes

$$w_t = (1 + r_t) w_{t-1} + y_t - c_t \qquad (t = 1, 2, \ldots) \qquad [1]$$

Formula [20.12] yields

$$w_t = \left[\prod_{s=1}^{t} (1 + r_s) \right] w_0 + \sum_{k=1}^{t} \left[\prod_{s=k+1}^{t} (1 + r_s) \right] (y_k - c_k) \qquad [2]$$

Define the **discount factor** D_t by

$$D_t = \frac{1}{\prod_{s=1}^{t}(1 + r_s)} = \prod_{s=1}^{t}(1 + r_s)^{-1} \qquad [3]$$

Note that when $r_s = r$ for all s, then $D_t = (1 + r)^{-t}$, the discount factor used in Section 20.2 (see [20.9]). Multiplying each term of [2] by D_t yields

$$D_t w_t = w_0 + \sum_{k=1}^{t} \left[\frac{\prod_{s=k+1}^{t}(1 + r_s)}{\prod_{s=1}^{t}(1 + r_s)} \right] (y_k - c_k)$$

But

$$\frac{\prod_{s=k+1}^{t}(1 + r_s)}{\prod_{s=1}^{t}(1 + r_s)} = \frac{(1 + r_{k+1}) \cdots (1 + r_t)}{(1 + r_1) \cdots (1 + r_k)(1 + r_{k+1}) \cdots (1 + r_t)}$$

$$= \frac{1}{(1 + r_1) \cdots (1 + r_k)} = D_k$$

Hence,

$$D_t w_t = w_0 + \sum_{k=1}^{t} D_k(y_k - c_k) \qquad (t = 1, 2, \ldots) \qquad [4]$$

The interpretation in terms of present discounted values (PDVs) is exactly the same as before (see formula [20.9]).

In the special case of no deposits or withdrawals, one has

$$w_t = w_0/D_t \doteq w_0 \prod_{k=1}^{t}(1 + r_k)$$

just as one would expect. After all, w_0 invested initially becomes $w_0(1 + r_1)$ after one period, then $w_0(1 + r_1)(1 + r_2)$ after two periods, and so on. So the discount factors have an entirely appropriate form. Indeed, introduce the **interest factor** R_k defined by

$$R_k = \frac{D_k}{D_t} = \prod_{s=k+1}^{t}(1 + r_s) \qquad [5]$$

Then formula [2] can be written as

$$w_t = R_0 w_0 + \sum_{k=1}^{t} R_k (y_k - c_k) \qquad [6]$$

which is the appropriate generalization of formula [20.8].

Problems

1. Work through the mortgage example in Example 20.5 once again when interest rates are variable. Note that, in practice, variable interest mortgages
   have repayments that increase when the interest rate increases, and decrease
   when it decreases. Why is this? What would happen if there were a large
   unforeseen increase in interest rates without any increase in repayments?

20.4 Second-Order Equations

So far this chapter has considered first-order difference equations, in which each
value x_t of a function is related to the value x_{t-1} of the function in the previous
period only. Next we present a typical example from economics, where it is
necessary to consider second-order difference equations.

Example 20.7   (A Multiplier-Accelerator Model)
Let Y_t denote national income, C_t total consumption, and I_t total investment
in a country at time t. Assume that for $t = 0, 1, \ldots,$

$$Y_t = C_t + I_t \qquad [1]$$

$$C_{t+1} = aY_t + b \qquad [2]$$

$$I_{t+1} = c(C_{t+1} - C_t) \qquad [3]$$

where a, b, and c are constants.

Equation [1] simply states that national income is divided between consumption and investment. Equation [2] is the assumption that consumption
in period $t + 1$ is a linear function of national income in the previous period. This is the "multiplier" part of the model. Finally, Equation [3] states
that investment in period $t + 1$ is proportional to the change in consumption
from the previous period. The idea is that the existing capital stock provides
enough capacity for production to meet current consumption. So investment
is only needed when consumption increases. This is the "accelerator" part
of the model. The combined "multiplier-accelerator" model has been studied
by several economists, notably P. A. Samuelson.

Assume that consumption C_0 and investment I_0 are known in the initial
period $t = 0$. Then by [1], $Y_0 = C_0 + I_0$, and by [2], $C_1 = aY_0 + b$. From [3],

we obtain $I_1 = c(C_1 - C_0)$, and then [1] in turn gives $Y_1 = C_1 + I_1$. Hence, Y_1, C_1, and I_1 are all known. Turning to [2] again, we find C_2, then [3] gives us the value of I_2, and [1] in turn produces the value of Y_2. Obviously, in this way, we can obtain expressions for C_t, Y_t, and I_t for all t in terms of C_0, Y_0, and the constants a, b, and c. However, the expressions derived get increasingly complicated.

Another method of studying the system is usually more enlightening. It consists of eliminating two of the unknown functions so as to end up with one difference equation in one unknown. Here we use this method to end up with a difference equation in Y_t. To do so, note that equations [1] to [3] are valid for all $t = 0, 1, \ldots$. Replace t with $t + 1$ in [2] and [3] and t with $t + 2$ in [1] to obtain

$$C_{t+2} = aY_{t+1} + b \tag{4}$$

$$I_{t+2} = c(C_{t+2} - C_{t+1}) \tag{5}$$

$$Y_{t+2} = C_{t+2} + I_{t+2} \tag{6}$$

Inserting [4] and [2] into [5] yields $I_{t+2} = ac(Y_{t+1} - Y_t)$. Inserting this result and [4] into [6] gives $Y_{t+2} = aY_{t+1} + b + ac(Y_{t+1} - Y_t)$. Rearranging gives

$$Y_{t+2} - a(1 + c)Y_{t+1} + acY_t = b \qquad (t = 0, 1, \ldots) \tag{7}$$

This is a second-order difference equation with Y_t as the unknown function. The next section sets out a general method for solving such equations.

Most second-order difference equations can be written in the form

$$x_{t+2} = f(t, x_t, x_{t+1}) \qquad (t = 0, 1, \ldots) \tag{20.13}$$

Suppose that f is defined for all possible values of the variables (t, x_t, x_{t+1}). Suppose x_0 and x_1 have fixed values. Letting $t = 0$ in [20.13], we see that $x_2 = f(0, x_0, x_1)$. Letting $t = 1$ in [20.13] yields $x_3 = f(1, x_1, f(0, x_0, x_1))$. By successively inserting $t = 2$, $t = 3$, … into [20.13], the values of x_t for *all* t are uniquely determined in terms of x_0 and x_1. Hence, we have the following result, which is similar to Theorem 20.1.

Theorem 20.2 (Existence and Uniqueness Theorem) Consider the difference equation $x_{t+2} = f(t, x_t, x_{t+1})$, $t = 0, 1, \ldots$, where f is defined for all values of the variables. If x_0 and x_1 are arbitrary fixed numbers, then there exists a uniquely determined function x_t that is a solution of the equation and has the given values for $t = 0$ and $t = 1$.

In general, for each different choice of x_0 and x_1, there is a different corresponding unique solution of Equation [20.13]. Consequently, there are infinitely many solutions. As already explained, we can find any value of x_t by successively substituting values of t. Even so, the arguments set out just after Theorem 20.1, for developing a theory of first-order difference equations, are no less valid for difference equations of the second order.

Consider again equation [20.13] and assume that f is defined on all of R^3. A solution of the equation is then uniquely determined by its values for the first two periods. By definition, the **general** (or complete) solution of [20.13] is a function

$$x_t = g(t, A, B) \qquad [20.14]$$

that depends on two arbitrary constants, and has the property that an arbitrary solution of [20.13] can be obtained from [20.14] by choosing appropriate values of A and B. Thus, [20.14] is the general solution of [20.13] provided that, given arbitrary values of x_0 and x_1, the system

$$g(0, A, B) = x_0, \qquad g(1, A, B) = x_1 \qquad [20.15]$$

has unique solutions for A and B.

Example 20.8

The difference equation

$$x_{t+2} - \tfrac{1}{6}x_{t+1} - \tfrac{1}{6}x_t = 0$$

is of second order. By direct substitution, it is easy to check that the function $x_t = A\,(1/2)^t + B\,(-1/3)^t$ satisfies the equation for all values of A and B. (How to find this particular function is explained in the next section.) Let x_0 and x_1 be arbitrary numbers. In this case, system [20.15] is

$$A + B = x_0, \qquad \tfrac{1}{2}A - \tfrac{1}{3}B = x_1$$

It follows that $A = \tfrac{2}{5}x_0 + \tfrac{6}{5}x_1$ and $B = \tfrac{3}{5}x_0 - \tfrac{6}{5}x_1$. Therefore, $x_t = A(1/2)^t + B(-1/3)^t$ is the general solution of the given equation.

We assumed in Theorem 20.2 that the function f in [20.13] was defined on all of R^3. If this is not the case for a particular difference equation, it is possible that there is no solution at all (see, for example, Problem 5 in Section 20.1).

Linear Equations

The general second-order linear difference equation is

$$x_{t+2} + a_t x_{t+1} + b_t x_t = c_t \qquad [20.16]$$

where a_t, b_t, and c_t are given functions of t. The associated **homogeneous** equation

$$x_{t+2} + a_t x_{t+1} + b_t x_t = 0 \qquad\qquad [20.17]$$

is obtained from [20.16] by replacing c_t with 0. We claim that if the two functions $u_t^{(1)}$ and $u_t^{(2)}$ of t both satisfy [20.17], then $x_t = A u_t^{(1)} + B u_t^{(2)}$ also satisfies [20.17] for all choices of constants A and B. In fact, $x_{t+1} = A u_{t+1}^{(1)} + B u_{t+1}^{(2)}$ and $x_{t+2} = A u_{t+2}^{(1)} + B u_{t+2}^{(2)}$. Inserting these expressions for x_{t+1} and x_{t+2} into the left-hand side of [20.17] yields

$$A u_{t+2}^{(1)} + B u_{t+2}^{(2)} + a_t \left[A u_{t+1}^{(1)} + B u_{t+1}^{(2)} \right] + b_t \left[A u_t^{(1)} + B u_t^{(2)} \right]$$

$$= A \left[u_{t+2}^{(1)} + a_t u_{t+1}^{(1)} + b_t u_t^{(1)} \right] + B \left[u_{t+2}^{(2)} + a_t u_{t+1}^{(2)} + b_t u_t^{(2)} \right]$$

It was assumed that $u_t^{(1)}$ and $u_t^{(2)}$ satisfy [20.17], so the two expressions in the square brackets on the RHS of this last equation must both be 0; so, too, must the whole RHS. Thus, we have proved that the function $x_t = A u_t^{(1)} + B u_t^{(2)}$ satisfies [20.17] for all values of constants A and B.

Suppose that somehow we manage to find two solutions $u_t^{(1)}$ and $u_t^{(2)}$ of [20.17]. Then $x_t = A u_t^{(1)} + B u_t^{(2)}$ satisfies [20.17] for all values of A and B. Is this the general solution? No; in order to be sure that $A u_t^{(1)} + B u_t^{(2)}$ really is the general solution of [20.17], we must also require that $u_t^{(1)}$ and $u_t^{(2)}$ be linearly independent—that is, that they are not proportional. Thus:

The homogeneous difference equation

$$x_{t+2} + a_t x_{t+1} + b_t x_t = 0$$

has the **general solution**

$$x_t = A u_t^{(1)} + B u_t^{(2)} \qquad\qquad [20.18]$$

where $u_t^{(1)}$ and $u_t^{(2)}$ are any two linearly independent solutions, and A and B are arbitrary constants.

Proof   In view of the discussion following Theorem 20.2, it suffices to prove that, for arbitrarily given values of x_0 and x_1, there exist constants A and B satisfying

$$A u_0^{(1)} + B u_0^{(2)} = x_0, \qquad A u_1^{(1)} + B u_1^{(2)} = x_1$$

According to Cramer's rule, this system can be solved uniquely for A and B

provided that the determinant

$$W = \begin{vmatrix} u_0^{(1)} & u_0^{(2)} \\ u_1^{(1)} & u_1^{(2)} \end{vmatrix}$$ [1]

is different from 0. To prove that $W \neq 0$, we show that $W = 0$ leads to a contradiction.

If $W = 0$, then the columns in W are linearly dependent. Therefore, there must exist numbers λ_1 and λ_2, not both 0, such that

$$\lambda_1 u_0^{(1)} + \lambda_2 u_0^{(2)} = 0$$
$$\lambda_1 u_1^{(1)} + \lambda_2 u_1^{(2)} = 0$$ [2]

Define $\bar{x}_t = \lambda_1 u_t^{(1)} + \lambda_2 u_t^{(2)}$. Then $\bar{x}_t$ satisfies [20.17] (because $u_t^{(1)}$ and $u_t^{(2)}$ both are solutions). Moreover, [2] tells us that $\bar{x}_0 = 0$ and $\bar{x}_1 = 0$. According to Theorem 20.2, there is only one function $\bar{x}_t$ that satisfies [20.17] and has $\bar{x}_0 = 0$ and $\bar{x}_1 = 0$. Obviously, this must be $\bar{x}_t \equiv 0$ for all t. Hence, $\lambda_1 u_t^{(1)} + \lambda_2 u_t^{(2)} \equiv 0$. But this contradicts the assumption that $u_t^{(1)}$ and $u_t^{(2)}$ are linearly independent. This contradiction tells us that $W \neq 0$ after all.

Our next result concerns the structure of the general solution of the nonhomogeneous equation [20.16]. Suppose we are able to find some **particular solution** u_t^* of [20.16]. If x_t is an arbitrary solution of [20.16], then it is easy to see that the difference $x_t - u_t^*$ is a solution of the associated homogeneous equation [20.17]. According to [20.18], therefore, we have $x_t - u_t^* = Au_t^{(1)} + Bu_t^{(2)}$, where $u_t^{(1)}$ and $u_t^{(2)}$ are two linearly independent solutions of [20.17], and A and B are arbitrary constants. Hence:

The nonhomogeneous difference equation

$$x_{t+2} + a_t x_{t+1} + b_t x_t = c_t$$

has the **general solution**

$$x_t = Au_t^{(1)} + Bu_t^{(2)} + u_t^*$$ [20.19]

where $Au_t^{(1)} + Bu_t^{(2)}$ is the general solution of the associated homogeneous equation (with c_t replaced by zero), and u_t^* is a particular solution of the nonhomogeneous equation.

Note: In order to use [20.18] and [20.19], we really need to decide when two functions are linearly independent. The following sufficient condition is easy to apply (and generalizes easily to the case of n functions):

$$\begin{vmatrix} u_0^{(1)} & u_0^{(2)} \\ u_1^{(1)} & u_1^{(2)} \end{vmatrix} \neq 0 \implies u_t^{(1)} \text{ and } u_t^{(2)} \text{ are linearly independent} \qquad [20.20]$$

Proof Suppose $u_t^{(1)}$ and $u_t^{(2)}$ are linearly *dependent*. Then there exist numbers A and B. not both 0. such that $Au_t^{(1)} + Bu_t^{(2)} = 0$ for all $t = 0. 1. \ldots$. In particular. letting $t = 0$ and $t = 1$ gives

$$Au_0^{(1)} + Bu_0^{(2)} = 0. \qquad Au_1^{(1)} + Bu_1^{(2)} = 0$$

According to Theorem 13.7 of Section 13.8. this homogeneous system of linear equations has a nontrivial solution iff the determinant of the system is 0. This determinant is precisely the one in [20.20]. So we have proved that if $u_t^{(1)}$ and $u_t^{(2)}$ are linearly dependent, then the determinant in [20.20] is 0. We conclude that if the determinant is not 0. then $u_t^{(1)}$ and $u_t^{(2)}$ are linearly independent.

Example 20.9
Find the general solution of

$$x_{t+2} - 5x_{t+1} + 6x_t = 2t - 3 \qquad (t = 0, 1, \ldots) \qquad [1]$$

Solution This is an equation of the form [20.16]. The associated homogeneous equation is

$$x_{t+2} - 5x_{t+1} + 6x_t = 0 \qquad [2]$$

It is easy to verify that $u_t^{(1)} = 2^t$ and $u_t^{(2)} = 3^t$ both satisfy [2]. (In the next section, we see how to make such a clever guess.) The functions 2^t and 3^t are linearly independent because the determinant in [20.20] is $3 - 2 = 1$, so $x_t = A2^t + B3^t$ is the general solution of [2].

The form of the RHS of [1] suggests that a function of the type $u_t^* = at+b$ might be a solution. The following method of undetermined coefficients can be used to find a and b. In fact, $u_{t+1}^* = a(t + 1) + b$ and $u_{t+2}^* = a(t + 2) + b$. Inserting these into [1] yields

$$a(t + 2) + b - 5[a(t + 1) + b] + 6(at + b) = 2t - 3$$

for all $t = 0. 1. \ldots$. After simplifying the LHS, we obtain

$$2at - 3a + 2b = 2t - 3 \qquad \text{for all } t = 0. 1. \ldots$$

Equating the coefficients of t and the constant term, we conclude that $2a = 2$ and that $-3a + 2b = -3$. Thus, $a = 1$ and $b = 0$, so $u_t^* = t$ is a solution of

[1]. According to [20.19], the general solution of [1] is

$$x_t = A2^t + B3^t + t$$

There is no universally applicable method of discovering the two linearly independent solutions of [20.17] that we need in order to find the general solution of the equation. However, in the special case when the coefficients a_t and b_t are both constants independent of t, then it is always possible to find the two solutions required. The next section shows how to do this.

Problems

1. Prove by direct substitution that the following functions of t are solutions of the associated difference equation (A and B are constants):
   a. $x_t = A + 2t$, $x_{t+1} = x_t + 2$
   b. $x_t = A3^t + B4^t$, $x_{t+2} - 7x_{t+1} + 12x_t = 0$
2. Prove that $x_t = A + Bt$ is the general solution of $x_{t+2} - 2x_{t+1} + x_t = 0$.
3. Prove that $x_t = A3^t + B4^t$ is the general solution of $x_{t+2} - 7x_{t+1} + 12x_t = 0$. (See Problem 1(b).)
4. Prove that $x_t = A2^t + Bt2^t + 1$ is the general solution of $x_{t+2} - 4x_{t+1} + 4x_t = 1$.

Harder Problems

5. Consider the difference equation

$$x_{t+1} - e^{-2at}x_t = e^{-at^2} \qquad (t = 0, 1, \ldots, a \neq 0)$$

   a. Find the general solution $\tilde{x}_t$ of the associated homogeneous equation expressed as a function of t and $\tilde{x}_0$.
   b. Prove that

$$u_t^* = \frac{1}{1 - e^{-a}} e^{-a(t-1)^2}$$

   is a particular solution of the given nonhomogeneous equation, and find, in turn, the general solution of the given equation.

20.5 Second-Order Equations with Constant Coefficients

Consider the homogeneous equation

$$x_{t+2} + ax_{t+1} + bx_t = 0 \qquad\qquad [20.21]$$

where a and b are arbitrary constants, $b \neq 0$, and x_t is the unknown function.

According to [20.18], finding the general solution of [20.21] requires us to discover two solutions $u_t^{(1)}$ and $u_t^{(2)}$ that are linearly independent. On the basis of experience gained in some of the previous examples and problems, it should come as no surprise that we try to find solutions of [20.21] having the form $x_t = m^t$. Then $x_{t+1} = m^{t+1} = m \cdot m^t$ and $x_{t+2} = m^{t+2} = m^2 \cdot m^t$. So inserting these expressions into [20.21] yields $m^t(m^2 + am + b) = 0$. If $m \neq 0$, then m^t satisfies [20.21] provided m satisfies the equation

$$m^2 + am + b = 0 \qquad\qquad [20.22]$$

This equation is called the **characteristic equation** of the difference equation. Its solutions are

$$m_1 = -\tfrac{1}{2}a + \sqrt{\tfrac{1}{4}a^2 - b}, \qquad m_2 = -\tfrac{1}{2}a - \sqrt{\tfrac{1}{4}a^2 - b} \qquad [20.23]$$

Generally, there are three different cases to consider, which are summed up in the following frame:

The **general solution** of

$$x_{t+2} + ax_{t+1} + bx_t = 0$$

(with $b \neq 0$) is determined as follows

1. For $\tfrac{1}{4}a^2 - b > 0$, when the characteristic equation has two different real roots, the solution is

$$x_t = Am_1^t + Bm_2^t, \qquad m_{1,2} = -\tfrac{1}{2}a \pm \sqrt{\tfrac{1}{4}a^2 - b}$$

2. For $\tfrac{1}{4}a^2 - b = 0$, when the characteristic equation has one real double root, the solution is

$$x_t = (A + Bt)m^t, \qquad m = -\tfrac{1}{2}a$$

3. For $\tfrac{1}{4}a^2 - b < 0$, when the characteristic equation has no real roots, the solution is, with $\theta \in [0, \pi]$,

$$x_t = Ar^t \cos(\theta t + \omega), \qquad r = \sqrt{b}, \qquad \cos\theta = -a/(2\sqrt{b})$$

The case $\tfrac{1}{4}a^2 - b > 0$ is the simplest. Then m_1 and m_2 are real and different, so m_1^t and m_2^t are solutions of [20.21]. The determinant in [20.20] is

$$\begin{vmatrix} u_0^{(1)} & u_0^{(2)} \\ u_1^{(1)} & u_1^{(2)} \end{vmatrix} = \begin{vmatrix} 1 & 1 \\ m_1 & m_2 \end{vmatrix} = m_2 - m_1 \neq 0$$

So the two solutions are linearly independent, and the general solution is consequently as given in 1.

If $\frac{1}{4}a^2 - b = 0$, then $m = -\frac{1}{2}a$ is a double root of [20.22]. This means that $m^2 + am + b = (m + \frac{1}{2}a)^2$. In addition to m^t, the function tm^t also satisfies [20.21] (see Problem 6). Moreover, these two functions are linearly independent because the determinant in [20.20] is equal to m. The general solution is, therefore, as indicated in 2.

If $\frac{1}{4}a^2 - b < 0$, the roots of [20.22] are complex. The suggested solution can be expressed in another way. According to Problem 3 in Section C.1,

$$Ar^t \cos(\theta t + \omega) = C_1 r^t \cos(\theta t) + C_2 r^t \sin(\theta t) \qquad [*]$$

provided we define $C_1 = A \cos \omega$ and $C_2 = -A \sin \omega$. The two functions $u_t^{(1)} = r^t \cos(\theta t)$ and $u_t^{(2)} = r^t \sin(\theta t)$ are linearly independent. Indeed, determinant [20.20] is

$$\begin{vmatrix} 1 & 0 \\ r \cos \theta & r \sin \theta \end{vmatrix} = r \sin \theta = \sqrt{b} \sqrt{1 - \cos^2 \theta}$$

$$= \sqrt{b} \sqrt{1 - a^2/4b} = \sqrt{b - \tfrac{1}{4}a^2} > 0$$

Moreover, direct substitution can be used to show that both these functions satisfy [20.21], although the algebra required is quite heavy.

We see that when the characteristic equation has complex roots, the solution of [20.21] involves oscillations. Quantity Ar^t is the **amplitude** at time t and r is called the **growth factor**. The number $\theta/2\pi$ is called the **frequency** of the oscillation and ω is its **phase**. Note that when $|r| < 1$, then $|Ar^t| \to 0$ as $t \to \infty$ and the oscillations are called **damped**. If $|r| > 1$, the oscillations are called **explosive**, and in the case $|r| = 1$, we have undamped oscillations. Note also that the amplitude and the phase, in general, both depend on the initial conditions (the values of x_0 and x_1), whereas the frequency and the growth factor are independent of the initial conditions and depend only on the coefficients a and b in the original difference equation.

Let us now consider some examples of difference equations of the form [20.21].

Example 20.10

Find the general solutions of

(a) $x_{t+2} - 3.9x_{t+1} + 3.78x_t = 0$ (b) $x_{t+2} - 6x_{t+1} + 9x_t = 0$
(c) $x_{t+2} - x_{t+1} + x_t = 0$

Solution

(a) The characteristic equation is $m^2 - 3.9m + 3.78 = 0$, with solutions $m_1 = 1.8$ and $m_2 = 2.1$, so the general solution is

$$x_t = A(1.8)^t + B(2.1)^t$$

(b) The characteristic equation is $m^2 - 6m + 9 = (m - 3)^2 = 0$, so $m = 3$ is a double root. The general solution is

$$x_t = (A + Bt)3^t$$

(c) The characteristic equation is $m^2 - m + 1 = 0$, with complex roots. Here $r = \sqrt{b} = 1$ and $\cos\theta = 1/2$, so $\theta = \frac{1}{3}\pi$. The general solution is

$$x_t = A\cos(\tfrac{1}{3}\pi t + \omega)$$

The frequency is $(\pi/3)/2\pi = 1/6$, and the growth factor is 1, so the oscillations are undamped.

The Nonhomogeneous Case

Let us now consider the nonhomogeneous equation

$$x_{t+2} + ax_{t+1} + bx_t = c_t \qquad (b \neq 0) \qquad\qquad [20.24]$$

According to [20.19], the general solution of [20.24] is

$$x_t = Au_t^{(1)} + Bu_t^{(2)} + u_t^* \qquad\qquad [20.25]$$

where $Au_t^{(1)} + Bu_t^{(2)}$ is the general solution of the associated homogeneous equation [20.21], and u_t^* is a particular solution of [20.24]. We know how to find $Au_t^{(1)} + Bu_t^{(2)}$. How do we find u_t^*? In some cases, it is easy. For example, consider the case in which $c_t = c$, where c is a constant, so that [20.24] takes the form

$$x_{t+2} + ax_{t+1} + bx_t = c \qquad (c \text{ is a constant}) \qquad\qquad [20.26]$$

Let us try to find a solution of the form $x_t = C$, where C is a constant. Then $x_{t+1} = x_{t+2} = C$, so insertion of $x_t = C$ into the equation gives $C + aC + bC = c$, that is, $C = c/(1 + a + b)$. It follows that if $1 + a + b \neq 0$, then $c/(1 + a + b)$ is a solution of [20.26]. (If $1 + a + b = 0$, no constant function satisfies [20.26]. To handle this case, see Problem 5.)

Consider more generally the case in which c_t in [20.24] is a linear combination of terms in the form

$$a^t, \qquad t^m, \qquad \cos(bt), \qquad \sin(bt)$$

or products of such terms. Then the method of undetermined coefficients can be used to obtain a special solution of [20.24]. If the function c_t in [20.24] happens to satisfy the homogeneous equation, the function to test must be modified.[2]

---

[2]For general details. we refer to S. Goldberg. *Introduction to Difference Equations.* John Wiley. New York. 1961. Sec. 3.4. or F. B. Hildebrand. *Finite-Difference Equations and Simulations.* Prentice Hall. Englewood Cliffs. New Jersey. 1968. Sec. 1.8.

Example 20.11

Solve the equation $x_{t+2} - 5x_{t+1} + 6x_t = 4^t + t^2 + 3$.

Solution The associated homogeneous equation has $m^2 - 5m + 6 = 0$ as its characteristic equation, with the two roots $m_1 = 2$ and $m_2 = 3$. Its general solution is, therefore, $A2^t + B3^t$. To find a particular solution, we try to adjust undetermined coefficients C, D, E, and F so that

$$u_t^* = C4^t + Dt^2 + Et + F$$

is a solution. (You cannot put $E = 0$.) We get

$$C4^{t+2} + D(t+2)^2 + E(t+2) + F - 5[C4^{t+1} + D(t+1)^2 + E(t+1) + F]$$
$$+ 6(C4^t + Dt^2 + Et + F) = 4^t + t^2 + 3$$

Expanding and rearranging yield

$$2C4^t + 2Dt^2 + (-6D + 2E)t + (-D - 3E + 2F) = 4^t + t^2 + 3$$

Because the four functions 4^t, t^2, t, and 1 are linearly independent, this can hold for all $t = 0, 1, \ldots$ only if $2C = 1$, $2D = 1$, $-6D + 2E = 0$, and $-D - 3E + 2F = 3$, so that $C = 1/2$, $D = 1/2$, $E = 3/2$, and $F = 4$. The general solution of the equation is, therefore,

$$x_t = A2^t + B3^t + \tfrac{1}{2}4^t + \tfrac{1}{2}t^2 + \tfrac{3}{2}t + 4$$

The method of finding a special solution of [20.24] that was used in the last example usually will not work unless the right-hand side is of the form explained before.

Stability

Suppose an economy evolves according to some difference equation (or system of difference equations). If the right number of initial conditions is imposed, there is a unique solution of the system. Also, if one or more initial conditions are changed, the solution changes. An important question is this: Will small changes in the initial conditions have any effect on the long-run behavior of the solution, or will the effect "die out" as $t \to \infty$? In the latter case, the system is called **stable**. On the other hand, if small changes in the initial conditions might lead to significant differences in the behavior of the solution in the long run, then the system is **unstable**. Because an initial state cannot be pinpointed exactly, but only approximately, stability in the sense indicated before is usually a minimum requirement for a model to yield meaningful long-run predictions.

Consider in particular the second-order nonhomogeneous difference equation

$$x_{t+2} + ax_{t+1} + bx_t = c_t \qquad (b \neq 0) \qquad [*]$$

The general solution of [*] is in the form

$$x_t = Au_t^{(1)} + Bu_t^{(2)} + u_t^* \qquad [**]$$

Equation [*] is called **globally asymptotically stable** (**stable** for short) if the general solution $Au_t^{(1)} + Bu_t^{(2)}$ of the associated homogeneous equation approaches 0 as $t \to \infty$, for all values of A and B. Then any solution of the equation approaches the particular solution u_t^*, which is independent of the initial conditions. So the effect of the initial conditions "dies out" as $t \to \infty$.

If $Au_t^{(1)} + Bu_t^{(2)}$ approaches 0 as $t \to \infty$, for all values of A and B, then, in particular, $u_t^{(1)} \to 0$ as $t \to \infty$ (choose $A = 1$, $B = 0$), and $u_t^{(2)} \to 0$ as $t \to \infty$ (choose $A = 0$, $B = 1$). On the other hand, these two conditions are surely sufficient for $Au_t^{(1)} + Bu_t^{(2)}$ to approach 0 as $t \to \infty$.

We claim that $u_t^{(1)} \to 0$ and $u_t^{(2)} \to 0$ as $t \to \infty$ iff the moduli of the roots of $m^2 + am + b = 0$ are both less than 1. (A brief introduction to complex numbers, including a definition of the modulus of a complex number, is given in Section C.3. Note that if m is a real number, then the modulus is equal to the absolute value of m.) Suppose the characteristic polynomial has complex roots $m = \alpha \pm i\beta$. Then $\alpha = -a/2$ and $\beta = \sqrt{b - \frac{1}{4}a^2}$. So the modulus of either root is equal to $|m| = \sqrt{\alpha^2 + \beta^2} = \sqrt{\frac{1}{4}a^2 + b - \frac{1}{4}a^2} = \sqrt{b}$. We argued before that the two solutions $r^t \cos(\theta t)$ and $r^t \sin(\theta t)$ approach 0 as t approaches infinity iff $r = \sqrt{b} < 1$—that is, $b < 1$.

If the characteristic polynomial has two real roots, $m_1 \neq m_2$, then the two solutions are $u_t^{(1)} = m_1^t$ and $u_t^{(2)} = m_2^t$. In this case, we see that $u_t^{(1)} \to 0$ and $u_t^{(2)} \to 0$ as $t \to \infty$ iff $|m_1| < 1$ and $|m_2| < 1$. Finally, if the characteristic polynomial has a real double root, $m = -a/2$, then the two linearly independent solutions are m^t and tm^t. Again, $|m| < 1$ is a necessary and sufficient condition for these two solutions to approach 0 as $t \to \infty$. (Certainly, if $|m| \geq 1$, then tm^t does not approach 0 as $t \to \infty$. On the other hand, suppose $|m| = 1/\delta$, where $\delta > 1$. Then $|tm^t| = t|m|^t = t/\delta^t \to 0$ as $t \to \infty$ because of [8.18] in Section 8.3.) Thus:

Equation [*] is stable if and only if both roots of the characteristic equation $m^2 + am + b = 0$ have moduli strictly less than 1.   [20.27]

To determine the stability of [*], all we have to do is to check the moduli of the characteristic roots. One can give a criterion also in terms of the coefficients of [*].

$x_{t-2} + ax_{t-1} + bx_t = c_t$ is stable $\iff |a| < 1 + b$ and $b < 1$ [20.28]

To see why these conditions are necessary and sufficient, consider first the case of complex roots. Then we saw that [*] is stable iff $b < 1$. Thus, the inequality conditions in [20.28] are sufficient. In the complex case, the graph of the parabola $f(m) = m^2 + am + b$ does not intersect the m axis. In particular, $f(1) = 1 + a + b$ and $f(-1) = 1 - a + b$ must both be positive. But $1 + a + b > 0$ and $1 - a + b > 0$ are equivalent to $|a| < 1 + b$, so the inequality conditions are also necessary. Problem 10 asks you to analyze the case of real roots, and prove [20.28] in this case.

Example 20.12

Check the stability of the equation:

$$x_{t+2} - \tfrac{1}{6}x_{t+1} - \tfrac{1}{6}x_t = c_t$$

Solution   In this case, $a = -1/6$ and $b = -1/6$, so $|a| = 1/6$ and $1 + b = 5/6$. Thus, according to [20.28], the equation is stable. This conclusion can be confirmed by looking at the general solution of the associated homogeneous equation, which is $x_t = A(1/2)^t + B(-1/3)^t$ (see Example 20.8 in Section 20.4). Clearly, $x_t \to 0$ irrespective of the values of A and B, so the given equation is stable.

Example 20.13

Check the stability of the model in Example 20.7 of Section 20.4, with a and c positive,

$$Y_{t+2} - a(1 + c)Y_{t+1} + acY_t = b$$

Solution   From [20.28], it follows that the equation is stable iff $a(1+c) < 1 + ac$ and $ac < 1$—that is, iff $a < 1$ and $ac < 1$. (See also Problem 3.)

Problems

Find the general solutions of the difference equations in Problems 1 and 2.

1. **a.** $x_{t+2} - 6x_{t+1} + 8x_t = 0$ **b.** $x_{t+2} - 8x_{t+1} + 16x_t = 0$
   c. $x_{t+2} + 2x_{t+1} + 3x_t = 0$ **d.** $3x_{t+2} + 2x_t = 4$

2. **a.** $x_{t+2} + 2x_{t+1} + x_t = 9 \cdot 2^t$ **b.** $x_{t+2} - 3x_{t+1} + 2x_t = 3 \cdot 5^t + \sin\left(\tfrac{1}{2}\pi t\right)$

3. In Example 20.13, we studied the difference equation

$$Y_{t+2} - a(1 + c)Y_{t+1} + acY_t = b$$

Assume that $a > 0$, $c > 0$, and $a \neq 1$.
   a. Find a special solution of the equation.

b. Find the characteristic equation of the associated homogeneous equation and determine when it has two different real roots, a double real root, and two complex roots.

4. In a model on location theory, the following difference equation is encountered

$$D_{n+2} - 4(ab + 1)D_{n+1} + 4a^2b^2 D_n = 0 \qquad (n = 0, 1, \ldots)$$

where a and b are constants, and D_n is the unknown function. Find the solution of this equation assuming that $1 + 2ab > 0$.

5. Consider Equation [20.26] and assume that $1 + a + b = 0$. If $a \neq -2$, find a constant D such that Dt satisfies [20.26]. If $a = -2$, find a constant D such that Dt^2 satisfies [20.26].

6. Consider Equation [20.21] assuming that $\frac{1}{4}a^2 - b = 0$, so that the characteristic equation has a real double root $m = -a/2$. Let $x_t = u_t(-a/2)^t$ and prove that x_t satisfies [20.21] provided that u_t satisfies the equation $u_{t+2} - 2u_{t+1} + u_t = 0$. Use the result in Problem 2 of Section 20.4 to find x_t.

7. Check the stability of the following equations by using [20.28].

    a. $x_{t+2} - \frac{1}{3}x_t = \sin t$ **b.** $x_{t+2} - x_{t+1} - x_t = 0$

    c. $x_{t+2} - \frac{1}{8}x_{t+1} + \frac{1}{6}x_t = t^2 e^t$ **d.** $x_{t+2} + 3x_{t+1} - 4x_t = t - 1$

8. a. A model due to B. J. Ball and E. Smolensky is based on the following system:

$$C_t = cY_{t-1}, \qquad K_t = \sigma Y_{t-1}, \qquad Y_t = C_t + K_t - K_{t-1}$$

where C_t denotes consumption, K_t capital stock, Y_t net national product, and c and σ are positive constants. Give an economic interpretation of the equations.

  b. Derive a difference equation of the second order for Y_t. Find necessary and sufficient conditions for the solution of this equation to have explosive oscillations.

9. a. A model due to J. R. Hicks uses the following difference equation:

$$Y_{t+2} - (b + k)Y_{t+1} + kY_t = a(1 + g)^t \qquad (t = 0, 1, \ldots)$$

where a, b, g, and k are constants. Find a special solution Y_t^* of the equation.

  b. Give conditions for the characteristic equation to have two complex roots.

  c. Find the growth factor r of the oscillations when the conditions obtained in part (b) are satisfied, and determine when the oscillations are damped.

Harder Problems

10. Prove [20.28] for the case when the characteristic polynomial has real roots by studying the parabola $f(m) = m^2 + am + b$. (Hint: Consider the values of $f(-1)$, $f(1)$, $f'(-1)$, and $f'(1)$.)

11. The following equation appears in a paper by Akerlof and Stiglitz:

$$K_{t+2} + \left(\frac{\sigma\beta}{\alpha} - 2\right)K_{t+1} + (1 - \sigma\beta)K_t = d$$

where the constants α, β, and σ are positive.
  a. Find a condition for the roots of the characteristic equation to be complex.
  b. Find a necessary and sufficient condition for stability.

12. a. Consider the equation

$$x_{t+2} + a_t x_{t+1} + b_t x_t = c_t \qquad (t = 0, 1, 2, \ldots) \qquad [*]$$

  Suppose $u_t^{(1)}$ and $u_t^{(2)}$ are two linearly independent solutions of [*] and define

$$D_{i+1} = u_{i+1}^{(1)} u_{i+2}^{(2)} - u_{i+2}^{(1)} u_{i+1}^{(2)}$$

  Prove that the general solution of [*] is

$$x_t = Au_t^{(1)} + Bu_t^{(2)} - u_t^{(1)} \sum_{i=0}^{t-1} \frac{c_i u_{i+1}^{(2)}}{D_{i+1}} + u_t^{(2)} \sum_{i=0}^{t-1} \frac{c_i u_{i+1}^{(1)}}{D_{i+1}} \qquad [**]$$

  where A and B are arbitrary constants.
  b. The following difference equation appears in a stochastic model by L. R. Klein and R. S. Preston:

$$p_t + \lambda_1 p_{t-1} + \lambda_2 p_{t-2} = u_t \qquad (t = 2, 3, \ldots)$$

  where λ_1 and λ_2 are constants, and u_t is a given function. Use [**] to find p_t for the case in which $r_1 \neq r_2$ are the roots of the characteristic equation.

21

Differential Equations

...the task of the theory of ordinary differential equations is to reconstruct the past and predict the future of the process from a knowledge of this local law of evolution.
—*V. I. Arnold* (1973)

The theory of differential equations is one of the most fascinating fields of mathematics, and also one of great practical importance. Differential equations play a fundamental role in physics, because they can express many of the laws of nature. Indeed, this is why systematic studies of differential equations were begun by Newton and Leibniz in the seventeenth century. Differential equations are also often used by economists.

21.1 First-Order Differential Equations

What is a differential equation? As the name suggests, it is an equation. Unlike ordinary algebraic equations, in a differential equation:

1. The unknown is a function (often of time), not a number.
2. The equation includes one or more of the derivatives of the function.

An *ordinary* differential equation is one for which the unknown is a function of only one variable, for example, $dx/dt = f(x, t)$, where $x = x(t)$ is the unknown function. For a *partial differential equation*, the unknown is a function of two or more variables, and one or more of the partial derivatives of the function are included. For example, $x\,\partial z/\partial x + y\,\partial z/\partial y = kz$ is a partial differential equation in the unknown function $z = z(x, y)$.[1]

For the first part of this chapter, we restrict attention to first-order (ordinary) differential equations—that is, equations where only the first-order derivatives of the unknown functions of one variable are included. Typical examples are

$$\frac{dx(t)}{dt} = x(t) + t \tag{a}$$

$$\frac{dK(t)}{dt} = \alpha\sigma K(t) + H_0 e^{\mu t} \tag{b}$$

$$\frac{dk}{dt} = sf(k) - \lambda k \tag{c}$$

Later in Examples 21.13 (in Section 21.5) and 21.17 (in Section 21.7), the last two equations will be given interesting economic interpretations, both concerning the evolution of an economy's capital stock.

Solving equation [a] means finding all functions $x(t)$ such that, for every value of t, the derivative $\dot{x}(t)$ of $x(t)$ is equal to $x(t) + t$. (Recall that we often use dot notation for the derivative, $\dot{x} = dx/dt$, especially when the independent variable is time t.) In equation [b], $K(t)$ is the unknown function, whereas α, σ, H_0, and μ are constants. In equation [c], $f(k)$ is a given function, whereas s and λ are constants. The unknown function is $k = k(t)$.

Note: We often use t to denote the independent variable. This is because most of the differential equations that appear in economics have time as their independent variable. The following theory is, of course, valid even if the independent variable is not time.

Example 21.1

The simplest kind of differential equation is the following:

$$\dot{x} = f(t) \tag{*}$$

This equation can be solved by ordinary integration, because

$$\dot{x} = f(t) \quad \Longleftrightarrow \quad x = \int f(t)\,dt + C$$

---

[1] This partial differential equation was solved in Section 16.5 (see [16.19]): its solutions are all homogeneous functions of degree k.

where C is an arbitrary constant. For example, if $f(t) = t^2 - 1$, then

$$\dot{x} = t^2 - 1 \quad \Longleftrightarrow \quad x = \int (t^2 - 1)\, dt + C = \tfrac{1}{3}t^3 - t + C$$

More generally, a first-order differential equation can usually be written as

$$\dot{x} = F(t, x) \qquad [21.1]$$

where F is a given function of two variables, and $x = x(t)$ is the unknown function. A differentiable function $x = x(t)$ that is defined in an open interval I of the real line and satisfies [21.1] for all t in I is called a **solution** of [21.1] in I. The graph of any solution is called an **integral curve**.

All of equations [a], [b], and [c] are of the form [21.1]. For example, if we let $x = x(t)$, we see that [a] becomes $dx/dt = F(t, x)$ with $F(t, x) = x + t$.

Example 21.2
Consider the differential equation

$$\dot{x} = x + t \qquad [*]$$

(a) Show that $x = -t - 1$ and $x = e^t - t - 1$ are two particular solutions of the equation over the entire real line.

(b) More generally, show that $x = Ce^t - t - 1$ is a solution of [*] for all t, whatever the choice of the constant C. (To see why this solution has been suggested, see Section 21.5 and especially Problem 1 in that Section.)

(c) Show that $x = e^t - 1$ is not a solution of [*].

Solution

(a) If $x = -t - 1$, then $\dot{x} = -1$ and $x + t = (-t - 1) + t = -1$. Hence, $\dot{x} = x + t$ for all t in this case. If $x = e^t - t - 1$, then $\dot{x} = e^t - 1$ and $x + t = (e^t - t - 1) + t = e^t - 1$. Once again we see that [*] is satisfied for all t.

(b) When $x = Ce^t - t - 1$, we have $\dot{x} = Ce^t - 1 = x + t$ for all t.

(c) When $x = e^t - 1$, one has $\dot{x} = e^t$ and $x + t = e^t + t - 1$. In this case, $\dot{x}$ is only equal to $x + t$ for $t = 1$, so $x = e^t - 1$ is *not* a solution of equation [*] on any open interval.

Examples 21.1 and 21.2 illustrate the fact that a differential equation usually has infinitely many solutions. In Example 21.2, we found that $x = Ce^t - t - 1$ was a solution of $\dot{x} = x + t$ for each choice of the constant C, and we shall see (Problem 1, Section 21.5) that no other function satisfies the equation.

The set of all solutions of any differential equation is called the **general** (or **complete**) solution of the equation. A first-order differential equation usually has a general solution that depends on *one* constant.[2] If we require the solution to pass through a given point in the tx-plane, then the constant is determined uniquely, except in special cases.

Example 21.3

Find the solution of $\dot{x} = x + t$ that passes through the point $(t, x) = (0, 1)$.

Solution   The general solution is $x(t) = Ce^t - t - 1$. If we want to make it pass through $(t, x) = (0, 1)$, we must arrange that $x(0) = 1$. Hence, $1 = Ce^0 - 0 - 1$, implying that $C = 2$. The required solution is, therefore, $x(t) = 2e^t - t - 1$.

The problem in Example 21.3 can be formulated as follows: Find the unique function $x(t)$ such that

$$\dot{x}(t) = x(t) + t \qquad \text{and} \qquad x(0) = 1 \qquad\qquad [*]$$

If $t = 0$ denotes the initial time, then $x(0) = 1$ is called an **initial condition** and we call [*] an **initial-value problem**.

Such initial-value problems arise naturally in many economic models. For instance, suppose an economic growth model involves a first-order differential equation for the accumulation of capital over time. The initial stock of capital is often historically given, and therefore helps to determine the unique solution of the equation.

Qualitative Theory of Differential Equations

When the theory of differential equations was first developed, mathematicians primarily tried to find explicit solutions of special types of equation. It became increasingly obvious, however, that only very few equations could be solved this way. In many cases, it is not necessary to obtain explicit formulas for the solution. Instead, it suffices to discover some important properties of the solution. As a result, the theory of differential equations includes many results concerning the general behavior of the solutions. This is the so-called *qualitative theory*. Its main results include existence and uniqueness theorems, sensitivity analysis, and investigations of the stability of equilibria. Such topics are of both theoretical interest and practical importance.

Along with this qualitative theory, much work has been put into developing useful numerical methods for finding approximate solutions of differential equations. Computers have played an important role here, but these developments are not discussed in this book.

[2]Problem 5 shows why we must use the word "usually" in this statement.

Problems

1. Show that $x(t) = Ce^{-t} + \frac{1}{2}e^{t}$ is a solution of the equation $\dot{x}(t) + x(t) = e^{t}$, for all values of C.

2. Consider the differential equation $t\dot{x} = 2x$.
   a. Show that $x = Ct^{2}$ is a solution for all choices of constant C.
   b. Find in particular the integral curve through $(1, 2)$.

3. Show that any function $x = x(t)$ that satisfies the equation $xe^{tx} = C$ is a solution of the differential equation $(1 + tx)\dot{x} = -x^{2}$. (*Hint:* Differentiate $xe^{tx} = C$ implicitly w.r.t. t.)

4. In each of the following cases, show that any function $x = x(t)$ that satisfies the equation on the left is a solution of the corresponding differential equation on the right.
   a. $x^{2} + 2\sqrt{1 - t^{2}} = 0$, $\dot{x} = \dfrac{t}{x\sqrt{1 - t^{2}}}$
   b. $\frac{1}{2}e^{t^{2}} + e^{-x}(x + 1) + C = 0$, $x\dot{x} = te^{t^{2}+x}$
   c. $(1 - t)x^{2} = t^{3}$, $2t^{3}\dot{x} = x(x^{2} + 3t^{2})$

5. Show that $x = Ct - C^{2}$ is a solution of the differential equation $\dot{x}^{2} = t\dot{x} - x$, for all values of the constant C. Then show that it is not the general solution because $x = \frac{1}{4}t^{2}$ is also a solution.

6. The function $x = x(t)$ satisfies $x(0) = 0$ and the differential equation $\dot{x} = (1 + x^{2})t$, for all t. Prove that $t = 0$ is a global minimum ·point for $x(t)$, and that the function $x(t)$ is convex for all t. (*Hint:* You do not have to solve the equation.)

21.2 The Direction Is Given: Find the Path!

Consider again the differential equation $\dot{x} = x + t$, which was studied in Example 21.2. If $x = x(t)$ is a solution, then the slope of the tangent to the graph (or integral curve) at the point (t, x) is equal to $x + t$. At the point $(t, x) = (0, 0)$, the slope is therefore equal to $0 + 0 = 0$, and at $(1, 2)$, the slope is $1 + 2 = 3$, and so on. In Fig. 21.1, we have drawn several small straight-line segments with slopes $x + t$ through points in the (t, x)-plane. This gives us a so-called **direction diagram** (or **slope field**) for the differential equation $\dot{x} = x + t$. If an integral curve passes through one of these points, it will have the corresponding line segment as its tangent. Therefore, we can draw curves that follow the direction of the line segments, and hence get a general impression of what the integral curves of $\dot{x} = x + t$ look like.

A direction diagram like this can be drawn for any differential equation of the form $\dot{x} = F(t, x)$. In cases where it is impossible to solve the equation explicitly, a direction diagram can give a rough but useful indication of how the integral curves behave. In a nutshell, the problem of solving the differential equation $\dot{x} = F(t, x)$ can be put like this: The direction is given, find the path!

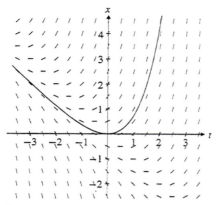

FIGURE 21.1   A direction diagram for $\dot{x} = x + t$. The integral curve through $(0,0)$ is shown.

Problems

1. Draw a direction diagram for the differential equation $\dot{x} = x/t$ and draw some integral curves.

2. Draw a direction diagram for the differential equation $\dot{x} = -t/x$ and draw the integral curve through $(2, 0)$.

21.3 Separable Differential Equations I

Suppose that $F(t, x)$ can be written as a product $f(t)g(x)$ of two functions, one of which depends only on t and the other only on x. Then the differential equation $\dot{x} = F(t, x)$ takes the special form

$$\dot{x} = f(t)g(x) \qquad\qquad [21.2]$$

In this case, we say that the differential equation is **separable**. For instance, the equation $\dot{x} = -2tx^2$ is evidently separable.

It is important to learn to distinguish between separable and nonseparable equations. The reason is that separable equations are among those that can be solved in terms of integrals of known functions.

Example 21.4

Decide which of the following differential equations are separable:

(a) $\dot{x} = t^2 - 1$ **(b)** $\dot{x} = xt + t$ **(c)** $\dot{x} = xt + t^2$

(d) $x\dot{x} = e^{x+t}\sqrt{1 + t^2}$ **(e)** $\dot{x} = \sqrt[4]{t^2 + x}$ **(f)** $\dot{x} = F(t) + G(x)$

Solution

(a) Separable. Let $f(t) = t^2 - 1$ and $g(x) = 1$.

(b) Separable, because $xt + t = t(x + 1)$.

(c) Not separable. It is impossible to write the sum $xt + t^2$ in the form $f(t)g(x)$. Note that $t(x + t)$ does not count as a separation because both factors would then depend on t.

(d) Separable. Because $e^{x+t} = e^x e^t$, we can put $f(t) = e^t \sqrt{1 + t^2}$ and $g(x) = e^x / x$.

(e) Not separable. It is impossible to write $\sqrt[4]{t^2 + x}$ in the form $f(t)g(x)$.

(f) Not separable in general. (The equation looks simple enough, but no method is known for solving this equation, except numerically or in special cases such as when G is a linear function of x.)

Before explaining how to solve the separable equation $\dot{x} = f(t)g(x)$ in general, we point out a special solution that arises if $g(x)$ has a zero at $x = a$, so that $g(a) = 0$. In fact, $x(t) \equiv a$ will be a solution of the equation in this case, because the right- and left-hand sides of the equation are both 0 for all t.

Now, suppose that $x = \varphi(t)$ is a function defined in an interval I such that $g(\varphi(t)) \neq 0$ throughout I. Then $x = \varphi(t)$ will solve [21.2] iff

$$\frac{\dot{\varphi}(t)}{g(\varphi(t))} = f(t)$$

for all t in I. But these two functions are equal in I iff

$$\int \frac{\dot{\varphi}(t)}{g(\varphi(t))} \, dt = \int f(t) \, dt + C \qquad [*]$$

for some constant C. Suppose we substitute $x = \varphi(t)$, so that $dx = \dot{\varphi}(t) \, dt$ in the integral on the left-hand side. Then according to the rule of integration by substitution (see Section 11.2), equation [*] is equivalent to

$$\int \frac{dx}{g(x)} = \int f(t) \, dt + C$$

Thus,

$$G(x) = F(t) + C \qquad [**]$$

where the derivative of $G(x)$ w.r.t. x is $1/g(x)$, and the derivative of $F(t)$ w.r.t. t is $f(t)$. This is valid in any interval I throughout which $g(x) \neq 0$. If g is also continuous in I, it can never change sign, so that $G'(x) = 1/g(x)$ is either strictly increasing or strictly decreasing, hence invertible. So [**] has a solution $x = G^{-1}(F(t) + C)$.

By using differential notation, the preceding method can be expressed as:

Method for Solving Separable Differential Equations

1. Equation [21.2] can be written as

$$\frac{dx}{dt} = f(t)g(x) \qquad\qquad [*]$$

2. Separate the variables:

$$\frac{dx}{g(x)} = f(t)\,dt$$

3. Integrate:

$$\int \frac{dx}{g(x)} = \int f(t)\,dt + C$$

4. Evaluate (if possible) the two integrals and you obtain (possibly in implicit form) a solution of [*].
5. In addition, every zero $x = a$ of $g(x)$ gives rise to the constant solution $x(t) \equiv a$.

Example 21.5

Solve the differential equation

$$\frac{dx}{dt} = \frac{t^3}{x^6 + 1}$$

Solution   We use the previous method, with $f(t) = t^3$ and $g(x) = 1/(x^6 + 1)$. Because $g(x)$ is never 0, there are no constant solutions. We proceed as follows:

Separate: $(x^6 + 1)\,dx = t^3\,dt$

Integrate: $\int (x^6 + 1)\,dx = \int t^3\,dt + C$

Evaluate: $\frac{1}{7}x^7 + x = \frac{1}{4}t^4 + C$

The desired functions $x = x(t)$ are those that satisfy the last equation for all t.

Note: We usually say that we have solved a differential equation even if the unknown function (as shown in Example 21.5) cannot be expressed explicitly. The important point is that we have found an equation involving the unknown function where the derivative of that function does not appear.

Example 21.6 (Compound Interest)

Suppose that $w = w(t) > 0$ is the wealth in an account at time t, and that $r(t)$ is the interest rate, with interest compounded continuously. Then

$$\dot{w} = r(t)w \qquad [1]$$

which is a separable equation. Separating the variables and integrating yields

$$\int \frac{dw}{w} = \int r(t)\,dt + C_1$$

Therefore,

$$\ln w = R(t) + C_1 \qquad \text{where} \qquad R(t) = \int r(t)\,dt$$

So the solution is

$$w(t) = e^{R(t)+C_1} = e^{C_1}e^{R(t)} = Ce^{R(t)} \qquad [2]$$

after introducing the new constant $C = e^{C_1}$. Suppose the initial value of the account is $w(0)$. Then [2] implies that $w(0) = Ce^{R(0)}$, so $C = w(0)e^{-R(0)}$ and [2] becomes $w(t) = w(0)e^{R(t)-R(0)}$. But $R(t) - R(0) = \int_0^t r(s)\,ds$, and so

$$w(t) = w(0)e^{\int_0^t r(s)\,ds}$$

$$= w(0)\exp \int_0^t r(s)\,ds \qquad [3]$$

This is the unique solution of [1] with $w(0)$ as the size of the account at time $t = 0$.

Example 21.7

Solve the differential equation

$$\frac{dx}{dt} = -2x^2 t \qquad [1]$$

and find the integral curve that passes through $(t, x) = (0, -1/2)$.

Solution   We observe first that $x(t) \equiv 0$ is one (trivial) solution. But this does not go through $(0, -1/2)$, so we follow the recipe:

Separate: $$-\frac{dx}{x^2} = 2t \, dt$$

Integrate: $$-\int \frac{dx}{x^2} = \int 2t \, dt + C$$

Evaluate: $$\frac{1}{x} = t^2 + C$$

It follows that the general solution is

$$x = \frac{1}{t^2 + C} \qquad\qquad [2]$$

To find the integral curve through $(0, -1/2)$, we must determine the correct value of C. Because we require $x = -1/2$ for $t = 0$, it follows from [2] that $-1/2 = 1/C$, so $C = -2$. Thus, the integral curve passing through $(0, -1/2)$ is $x = 1/(t^2 - 2)$.

Figure 21.2 shows integral curves of the form [2] for $C = -2, -1$, 0, 1/2, 1, and 2. (The value of C can be inferred from the fact that each curve passes through the point $(t, x) = (0, 1/C)$.) The constant of integration crucially affects the shape of the curve as well as its position.

Suppose we ask for a differentiable solution of [1] that is valid throughout the interval $[0, \infty)$. If we require $x(0) = 0$, the only solution is $x(t) \equiv 0$. If $x(0) = x_0 > 0$, constant C in equation [2] becomes $C = 1/x_0 > 0$. Hence, the required solution is

$$x(t) = \frac{1}{t^2 + 1/x_0} \qquad\qquad [3]$$

FIGURE 21.2

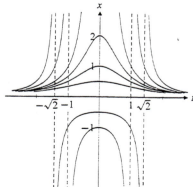

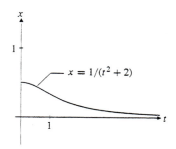

FIGURE 21.3

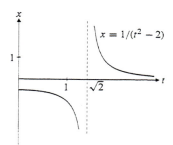

FIGURE 21.4

For instance, if $x_0 = 1/2$, then $x(t) = 1/(t^2 + 2)$, whose graph is shown in Fig. 21.3. On the other hand, if $x_0 < 0$, then the function in [3] is not defined when $t^2 + 1/x_0 = 0$, and so when $t = \pm\sqrt{-1/x_0}$. For instance, if $x_0 = -1/2$, then $x(t) = 1/(t^2 - 2)$, whose graph on $[0, \sqrt{2})$ is shown in Fig. 21.4. When $t \to (\sqrt{2})^-$, then $x(t) \to -\infty$. For $t > \sqrt{2}$, the graph of $x(t) = 1/(t^2 - 2)$ is also shown in Fig. 21.4. This is a solution of [1] in the interval $(\sqrt{2}, \infty)$. Note in particular that if $x_0 < 0$, then there is no differentiable function that satisfies [1] on the whole of $[0, \infty)$.

Problems

1. Solve the equation $x^2\dot{x} = t + 1$. Find the integral curve through $(t, x) = (1, 1)$.

2. Solve the following differential equations:
   a. $\dot{x} = t^3 - t$ b. $\dot{x} = te^t - t$ c. $e^x\dot{x} = t + 1$

3. a. Find the solution of $\dot{x} = \frac{1}{2}x$. Find, in particular, the integral curve through $(0, 1)$.
   b. Find the solution of $\dot{x} = ax$. Find, in particular, the integral curve through (t_0, x_0).

4. Explain why biological populations that develop as suggested in Fig. 21.5(a) or (b) *cannot* be described by differential equations of the form $\dot{N}/N = f(N)$, no matter how function f is chosen. ($N(t)$ is the size of the population at time t.)

5. Find the complete solution of $\dot{x} + a(t)x = 0$. In particular, when $a(t) = a + bc^t$ (a, b, and c are positive; $c \neq 1$) show that the solution of the equation can be written in the form $x = Cp^t q^{c^t}$, where p and q are constants determined by a, b, and c, whereas C is an arbitrary constant. (This is Gompertz–Makeham's law of mortality.)

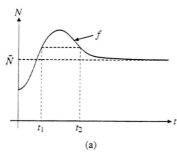

(a)

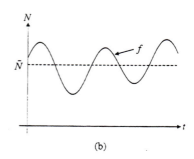

(b)

FIGURE 21.5

6. Find $x = x(t)$ when $\text{El}_t \, x$, the elasticity $t\dot{x}/x$ of $x(t)$ w.r.t. t, satisfies the following equations for all t:

    a. $\text{El}_t \, x = a$ **b.** $\text{El}_t \, x = at + b$ **c.** $\text{El}_t \, x = ax + b$

7. The following differential equations have been studied in economics. Solve them.

    a. $\dot{K} = (A n_0^\alpha a^b) K^{b-c} e^{(\alpha v + \varepsilon)t}$, $b - c \neq 1, \ \alpha v + \varepsilon \neq 0$

    b. $\dot{x} = \dfrac{(\beta - \alpha x)(x - a)}{x}$, $\alpha > 0, \ \beta > 0, \ a > 0, \ \alpha a \neq \beta$

    Hint: For (b): $\dfrac{x}{(\beta - \alpha x)(x - a)} = \dfrac{1}{\beta - \alpha a}\left(\dfrac{\beta}{\beta - \alpha x} + \dfrac{a}{x - a}\right)$

Harder Problems

8. Differential equations of the form $\dot{x} = g(x/t)$, where the RHS depends only on the ratio x/t, are called **homogeneous**. Prove that if we substitute $z = x/t$, a homogeneous equation becomes a separable equation with z as the unknown function. Use this method to solve the equation $3tx^2\dot{x} = x^3 + t^3$.

21.4 Separable Differential Equations II

Consider once again the separable equation $\dot{x} = f(t)g(x)$. A solution of this equation passing through a particular point can be found by the method used in Example 21.7: First, find the general solution, and then determine the appropriate value of the constant. Alternatively, we might argue as follows: Suppose φ is a function defined in an interval $[t_0, t_1]$ such that $g(\varphi(s)) \neq 0$ in this interval. Then φ is a solution of the equation in this interval iff

$$\int_{t_0}^{t} \frac{\dot{\varphi}(s)}{g(\varphi(s))}\, ds = \int_{t_0}^{t} f(s)\, ds$$

for all $t \in [t_0, t_1]$. Now make the substitution $\xi = \varphi(s)$, so that $d\xi = \dot{\varphi}(s)\, ds$. Then let $x_0 = \varphi(t_0)$ and $x = \varphi(t)$. This yields the following result:

The unique solution of the initial-value problem

$$\dot{x} = f(t)g(x), \qquad x(t_0) = x_0$$

is found by solving the following equation for x:

$$\int_{x_0}^{x} \frac{d\xi}{g(\xi)} = \int_{t_0}^{t} f(s)\, ds \qquad\qquad [21.3]$$

Example 21.8
Find the unique solution of the initial-value problem

$$\dot{x} = -2x^2 t, \qquad x(0) = -1/2$$

Solution   Let $g(\xi) = -\xi^2$, $f(s) = 2s$, $t_0 = 0$, and $x_0 = -1/2$. Then [21.3] yields

$$\int_{-1/2}^{x} \frac{d\xi}{-\xi^2} = \int_{0}^{t} 2s\, ds \qquad \text{or} \qquad \left.\frac{1}{\xi}\right|_{-1/2}^{x} = \left.s^2\right|_{0}^{t}$$

Therefore,

$$\frac{1}{x} - \frac{1}{(-1/2)} = t^2 \qquad \text{or} \qquad \frac{1}{x} = t^2 - 2$$

It follows that

$$x = \frac{1}{t^2 - 2}$$

which is the result we found in Example 21.7.

Example 21.9
Let $X = X(t)$ denote the national product, $K = K(t)$ the capital stock, and $L = L(t)$ the number of workers in a country at time t. Suppose that, for all $t \geq 0$,

$$X = AK^{1-\alpha}L^{\alpha} \qquad\qquad [a]$$

$$\dot{K} = sX \qquad\qquad [b]$$

$$L = L_0 e^{\lambda t} \qquad\qquad [c]$$

where A, α, s, L_0, and λ are all positive constants, with $0 < \alpha < 1$. Derive from these equations a single differential equation to determine $K = K(t)$, and find the solution of that equation when $K(0) = K_0 > 0$. (This model is generalized in Example 21.17 in Section 21.7. In [a] we have a Cobb–Douglas production function, [b] says that aggregate investment is proportional to output, whereas [c] implies that the labor force grows exponentially.)

Solution   From [a] to [c], we derive the single differential equation

$$\dot{K} = \frac{dK}{dt} = sAK^{1-\alpha}L^{\alpha} = sAL_0^{\alpha}e^{\alpha\lambda t}K^{1-\alpha}$$

This is clearly separable. Separating the variables yields

$$K^{\alpha-1}\,dK = sAL_0^{\alpha}e^{\alpha\lambda t}\,dt$$

Using [21.3] gives

$$\int_{K_0}^{K} \xi^{\alpha-1}\,d\xi = \int_0^t sAL_0^{\alpha}e^{\alpha\lambda\tau}\,d\tau$$

Evaluating the integrals gives

$$\left. \frac{1}{\alpha}\xi^{\alpha} \right|_{K_0}^{K} = \left. \frac{1}{\alpha\lambda}sAL_0^{\alpha} \right|_0^t e^{\alpha\lambda\tau}$$

or

$$\frac{1}{\alpha}(K^{\alpha} - K_0^{\alpha}) = \frac{1}{\alpha\lambda}sAL_0^{\alpha}(e^{\alpha\lambda t} - 1)$$

Solving for K yields

$$K = \left[K_0^{\alpha} + (s/\lambda)AL_0^{\alpha}(e^{\alpha\lambda t} - 1) \right]^{1/\alpha}$$

See Problem 5 for a closer examination of this model.

We close this section with an example of "logistic growth," which has many applications.

Example 21.10

Solve the following differential equation when $a \neq b$:

$$\frac{dx}{dt} = B(x - a)(x - b) \tag{1}$$

Find, in particular, the solution when $B = -1$, $a = -1$, and $b = 2$, and draw some integral curves in this case.

Solution   Observe that both $x \equiv a$ and $x \equiv b$ are trivial solutions of the equation. In order to find the other solutions, separate the variables as follows. First, put all terms involving x on the left-hand side, and all terms involving t on the right-hand side. Then integrate, to get

$$\int \frac{1}{(x-a)(x-b)} \, dx = \int B \, dt$$

The next step is to transform the integrand on the left. We find that

$$\frac{1}{(x-a)(x-b)} = \frac{1}{b-a} \left(\frac{1}{x-b} - \frac{1}{x-a} \right)$$

Hence,

$$\int \frac{1}{(x-a)(x-b)} \, dx = \frac{1}{b-a} \left(\int \frac{1}{x-b} \, dx - \int \frac{1}{x-a} \, dx \right)$$

Except for a constant, the right-hand side equals

$$\frac{1}{b-a} \left(\ln|x-b| - \ln|x-a| \right) = \frac{1}{b-a} \ln \frac{|x-b|}{|x-a|}$$

So, for some constant C_1, the solution is

$$\frac{1}{b-a} \ln \frac{|x-b|}{|x-a|} = Bt + C_1 \qquad \text{or} \qquad \ln \left| \frac{x-b}{x-a} \right| = B(b-a)t + C_2$$

with $C_2 = C_1(b-a)$. So

$$\left| \frac{x-b}{x-a} \right| = e^{B(b-a)t+C_2} = e^{B(b-a)t} e^{C_2} \tag{2}$$

After defining the new constant $C = \pm e^{C_2}$, we have

$$\frac{x-b}{x-a} = \pm e^{C_2} e^{B(b-a)t} = C e^{B(b-a)t} \tag{3}$$

Solving this last equation for x finally gives

$$x = \frac{b - aC e^{B(b-a)t}}{1 - C e^{B(b-a)t}} = a + \frac{b-a}{1 - C e^{B(b-a)t}} \tag{4}$$

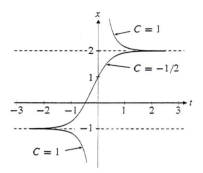

FIGURE 21.6

For $B = -1$, $a = -1$, and $b = 2$, equation [1] is $\dot{x} = -(x+1)(x-2)$. Note that $\dot{x}$ is positive for x between -1 and 2. Hence, the integral curves are rising with t in the horizontal strip between lines $x = -1$ and $x = 2$. In the same way, we can see directly from the differential equation that the integral curves are decreasing above and below this strip. In addition to the constant solutions $x = -1$ and $x = 2$, we see from [4] that the general solution of the equation $\dot{x} = -(x+1)(x-2)$ is

$$x = -1 + \frac{3}{1 - Ce^{-3t}}$$

Two of the associated integral curves are shown in Fig. 21.6.

Note: It follows from [2] that, on any integral curve, $|(x-b)/(x-a)|$ is not zero for any t. Because the fraction is a continuous function of t, it cannot jump from positive to negative values, and it must, therefore, have a constant sign.

Problems

Find the complete solutions of the differential equations in Problems 1 and 2. Also find the integral curves through the indicated points by using [21.3].

1. **a.** $t\dot{x} = x(1-t)$, $(t_0, x_0) = (1, 1/e)$
    b. $(1 + t^3)\dot{x} = t^2 x$, $(t_0, x_0) = (0, 2)$
2. **a.** $x\dot{x} = t$, $(t_0, x_0) = (\sqrt{2}, 1)$
    b. $e^{2t}(dx/dt) - x^2 - 2x - 1 = 0$. $(t_0, x_0) = (0, 0)$
3. Show that the logistic differential equation

$$f'(t) = rf(t)[1 - f(t)/K]$$ (r and K are positive constants)

is a special case of Equation [1] in Example 21.10, and use [4] to find the nonconstant solution.

Harder Problems

4. In connection with a study of CES (constant elasticity of substitution) production functions, Arrow, Chenery, Minhas, and Solow were led to consider the differential equation

$$\frac{dy}{dx} = \frac{y(1 - \alpha y^{\varrho})}{x} \qquad (\alpha \text{ and } \varrho \text{ are constants; } \varrho \neq 0; \ x > 0; \ y > 0) \quad [1]$$

Use the identity

$$\frac{1}{y} + \frac{\alpha y^{\varrho - 1}}{1 - \alpha y^{\varrho}} = \frac{1}{y(1 - \alpha y^{\varrho})}$$

to show that the general solution of [1] is

$$y = (\beta x^{-\varrho} + \alpha)^{-1/\varrho} \qquad [2]$$

Suppose we let $x = K/L$, $y = Y/L$, and define new constants A and a by $A = (\alpha + \beta)^{-1/\varrho}$ and $a = \beta/(\alpha + \beta)$. Then $1 - a = \alpha/(\alpha + \beta)$ and $\alpha + \beta = A^{-\varrho}$, so $\alpha = (1 - a)A^{-\varrho}$ and $\beta = aA^{-\varrho}$. Now it follows from [2] that $Y = A\left[aK^{-\varrho} + (1 - a)L^{-\varrho}\right]^{-1/\varrho}$, which is a special form of the CES production function (see Example 16.20 in Section 16.4).

5. a. With reference to Example 21.9, show that K/L tends to $(sA/\lambda)^{1/\alpha}$ as $t \to \infty$. Compute the limit for X/L as $t \to \infty$.

b. Replace equation [c] in Example 21.9 with [c'] $L = b(t+a)^p$, where a, b, and p are positive constants. From [a], [b], and [c'], derive a differential equation for $K = K(t)$. Solve the equation when $K(0) = K_0$, and examine the behavior of K/L as $t \to \infty$.

21.5 First-Order Linear Differential Equations I

A **first-order linear differential equation** is one that can be written in the form

$$\dot{x} + a(t)x = b(t) \qquad [21.4]$$

where a and b are continuous functions of t in a certain interval, and $x = x(t)$ is the unknown function. Equation [21.4] is called "linear" because the left-hand side is a linear function of x and $\dot{x}$.

The following are all examples of first-order linear equations:

[a] $\dot{x} + x = t$ \qquad [b] $\dot{x} + 2tx = 4t$ \qquad [c] $(t^2 + 1)\dot{x} + e^t x = t \ln t$

The first two equations are obviously of the form [21.4]. The last one can be put into this form if we divide each term by $t^2 + 1$ to get

$$\dot{x} + \frac{e^t}{t^2 + 1} x = \frac{t \ln t}{t^2 + 1}$$

An interesting example of a linear equation is the continuous time analog of the compound interest equation for an account with deposits and withdrawals that was studied in Section 20.2 and Example 20.6 of Section 20.3. Consider first the case of a constant interest rate r. Then the wealth $w = w(t)$ in the account evolves according to the equation

$$\dot{w} = rw + y(t) - c(t) \tag{21.5}$$

where $y(t)$ is the flow of savings from income, and $c(t)$ is the flow of consumption withdrawals at time t. This is clearly a first-order linear differential equation.

If there are no deposits to or withdrawals from the account, then $y(t) = c(t) = 0$ and so [21.5] reduces to the separable equation $\dot{w} = rw$. The general solution is $w = Ae^{rt}$ or $e^{-rt}w(t) = A$. In the presence of the terms $y(t)$ and $c(t)$, Equation [21.5] is not separable. Just as it helped in Section 20.2 to multiply Equation [20.8] by the discount factor $(1 + r)^{-t}$ in discrete time, here we multiply by the appropriate discount factor for continuous time, which is e^{-rt}. Then [21.5] can be written as

$$e^{-rt}[\dot{w}(t) - rw(t)] = e^{-rt}[y(t) - c(t)] \tag{1}$$

Now the key step is to note that the left-hand side is simply the derivative of $e^{-rt}w(t)$:

$$\frac{d}{dt}[e^{-rt}w(t)] = e^{-rt}\dot{w}(t) - re^{-rt}w(t)$$

So [1] can be written as

$$\frac{d}{dt}[e^{-rt}w(t)] = e^{-rt}[y(t) - c(t)] \tag{2}$$

Hence, for some constant C,

$$e^{-rt}w(t) = \int e^{-rt}[y(t) - c(t)]\,dt + C$$

Multiplying this last equation by e^{rt} yields the solution

$$w(t) = Ce^{rt} + e^{rt} \int e^{-rt}[y(t) - c(t)]\,dt \tag{3}$$

The definite integral form of this solution may be more useful. In general, if $\dot{F}(t) = f(t)$, then $F(t) = F(0) + \int_0^t f(s)\,ds$. Thus, because $e^{-r \cdot 0} = 1$, it follows from Equation [2] that

$$e^{-rt} w(t) = w(0) + \int\limits_0^t e^{-rs} [y(s) - c(s)] \, ds \qquad [4]$$

where s has replaced t as the variable of integration in order to avoid any confusion. Equation [4] states that $e^{-rt} w(t)$, the PDV of assets at time t, is the sum of the initial assets $w(0)$ and $\int_0^t e^{-rs} y(s) \, ds$, the total PDV of all deposits, minus $\int_0^t e^{-rs} c(s) \, ds$, the total PDV of all withdrawals.

The discount factor e^{-rt}, that featured in the trick enabling us to solve [21.5], is called an **integrating factor**.

If we multiply Equation [4] by e^{rt} and rearrange, we obtain the following solution of [21.5]:

$$w(t) = e^{rt} w(0) + e^{rt} \int\limits_0^t e^{-rs} [y(s) - x(s)] \, ds \qquad [21.6]$$

Generally, when the function $a(t)$ in [21.4] is a constant a, the equation is equivalent to [21.5]. Then [3] allows us to deduce the following result (where e^{at} is the integrating factor in this case):

$$\dot{x} + ax = b(t) \iff x = e^{-at} \left[C + \int e^{at} b(t) \, dt \right] \qquad (C \text{ is a constant}) \qquad [21.7]$$

In particular, if $b(t)$ is also a constant b, then $\int e^{at} b \, dt = (b/a) e^{at}$ and so

$$\dot{x} + ax = b \iff x = Ce^{-at} + \frac{b}{a} \qquad (C \text{ is a constant}) \qquad [21.8]$$

If we let $C = 0$ in [21.8], we obtain the solution $x(t) = b/a$. Then we say that $x = b/a$ is an *equilibrium state*, or a *stationary state*, for the equation. Observe how this solution can be obtained from $\dot{x} + ax = b$ by letting $\dot{x} = 0$ and then solving the resulting equation for x. If constant a is positive, then it follows that the solution $x = Ce^{-at} + b/a$ indicated by [21.8] converges to b/a as $t \to \infty$. In this case, the equation is said to be *stable*, because every solution of the equation converges to an equilibrium as t approaches infinity.

Example 21.11

Find the general solution of

$$\dot{x} + 2x = 8$$

and determine whether the equation is stable.

Solution   By [21.8], the solution is

$$x = Ce^{-2t} + 4$$

Here the equilibrium state is $x = 4$, and the equation is stable because $a = 2 > 0$, so $x \to 4$ as $t \to \infty$.

Linear differential equations appear in many economic models. Here are two examples.

Example 21.12

When the price of a commodity is P, let $D(P) = a - bP$ denote the demand and $S(P) = \alpha + \beta P$ the supply. Here a, b, α, and β are positive constants (see Example 2.19, Section 2.5). Assume that the price $P = P(t)$ varies with time, and that $\dot{P}$ is proportional to excess demand $D(P) - S(P)$. Thus,

$$\dot{P} = \lambda[D(P) - S(P)]$$

where λ is a positive constant. Inserting the expressions for $D(P)$ and $S(P)$ into this equation gives $\dot{P} = \lambda(a - bP - \alpha - \beta P)$. Rearranging, we then obtain

$$\dot{P} + \lambda(b + \beta)P = \lambda(a - \alpha)$$

According to [21.8], the solution is

$$P = Ce^{-\lambda(b+\beta)t} + \frac{a - \alpha}{b + \beta}$$

Because $\lambda(b + \beta)$ is positive, as t tends to infinity, P converges to the equilibrium price $P^e = (a - \alpha)/(b + \beta)$ for which $D(P^e) = S(P^e)$. Thus, the equation is stable.

Example 21.13

Consider the following model of economic growth in a developing country:

$$X(t) = \sigma K(t) \tag{1}$$

$$\dot{K}(t) = \alpha X(t) + H(t) \tag{2}$$

$$N(t) = N_0 e^{\rho t} \tag{3}$$

where $X(t)$ is the total production per year, $K(t)$ is the capital stock, $H(t)$ is the flow of foreign aid per year, and $N(t)$ is the size of the population, all measured at time t. In [1], we assume that the volume of production is simply proportional to the capital stock, with the factor of proportionality

σ being called the *average productivity of capital*. In [2], we assume that the total growth of capital per year is equal to internal savings plus foreign aid. We assume that savings are proportional to production, with the factor of proportionality α being called the *savings rate*. Finally, [3] tells us that population increases at a constant proportional rate of growth ρ.

Derive from these equations a differential equation for $K(t)$. Assume that $H(t) = H_0 e^{\mu t}$, and find the solution of the differential equation in this case, given that $K(0) = K_0$ and $\alpha\sigma \neq \mu$. Find an expression for $x(t) = X(t)/N(t)$, which is production per head.

Solution   From [1] and [2], it follows that $K(t)$ must satisfy the linear differential equation

$$\dot{K}(t) = \alpha\sigma K(t) + H(t) \tag{4}$$

Put $H(t) = H_0 e^{\mu t}$ and use [21.7] to obtain

$$K(t) = Ce^{\alpha\sigma t} + e^{\alpha\sigma t} \int e^{-\alpha\sigma t} H_0 e^{\mu t}\, dt = Ce^{\alpha\sigma t} + e^{\alpha\sigma t} \int H_0 e^{(\mu-\alpha\sigma)t}\, dt$$

$$= Ce^{\alpha\sigma t} + e^{\alpha\sigma t} \frac{H_0}{\mu - \alpha\sigma} e^{(\mu-\alpha\sigma)t} = Ce^{\alpha\sigma t} + \frac{H_0}{\mu - \alpha\sigma} e^{\mu t}$$

For $t = 0$, we obtain $K(0) = K_0 = C + H_0/(\mu - \alpha\sigma)$. This gives $C = K_0 - H_0/(\mu - \alpha\sigma)$. Thus, the solution is

$$K(t) = \left(K_0 - \frac{H_0}{\mu - \alpha\sigma} \right) e^{\alpha\sigma t} + \frac{H_0}{\mu - \alpha\sigma} e^{\mu t} \tag{5}$$

Per capita production is equal to $x(t) = X(t)/N(t) = \sigma K(t)/N_0 e^{\rho t}$. If we use the expression for $K(t)$ in [5], an easy calculation shows that

$$x(t) = x(0)e^{(\alpha\sigma-\rho)t} + \left(\frac{\sigma}{\alpha\sigma - \mu} \right) \frac{H_0}{N_0} e^{(\alpha\sigma-\rho)t} \left[1 - e^{(\mu-\alpha\sigma)t} \right] \tag{6}$$

In Problem 7 you are asked to study this model more closely.

Problems

1. Find the general solution of $\dot{x} = x + t$. (See Example 21.2.)

2. Use the formula in [21.8] to find the general solution of $\dot{x} + \frac{1}{2}x = \frac{1}{4}$. Determine the equilibrium state of the equation, and examine whether it is stable. Also draw some typical integral curves.

3. In a macroeconomic model, $C(t)$, $I(t)$, and $Y(t)$ denote respectively the consumption, investment, and national income in a country at time t. Assume

that, for all t:

[1] $\quad C(t) + I(t) = Y(t)$ [2] $\quad I(t) = k\dot{C}(t)$ [3] $\quad C(t) = aY(t) + b$

where a, b, and k are positive constants, with $a < 1$.

a. Derive the following differential equation for $Y(t)$:

$$\dot{Y}(t) = \frac{1-a}{ka} Y(t) - \frac{b}{ka}$$

b. Solve this equation when $Y(0) = Y_0 > b/(1-a)$, and then find the corresponding function $I(t)$.

c. Compute $\lim_{t \to \infty}[Y(t)/I(t)]$.

4. The equation in [21.8] is separable. Solve it as a separable differential equation, and show that you obtain the same solution as that indicated in [21.8].

5. Find the general solutions of the following differential equations, and in each case, find the integral curve through $(t, x) = (0, 1)$:

   a. $\dot{x} - 3x = 5$ **b.** $3\dot{x} + 2x + 16 = 0$ **c.** $\dot{x} + 2x = t^2$

Harder Problems

6. Let $N = N(t)$ denote the size of a certain population, $X = X(t)$ the total production, and $x(t) = X(t)/N(t)$ the production per capita at time t. T. Haavelmo[3] studied the model described by the equations:

[1] $\quad \dfrac{\dot{N}}{N} = \alpha - \beta \dfrac{N}{X}$ [2] $\quad X = AN^a$

where α, β, and a are positive constants, with $a \neq 1$. Show that this leads to a differential equation of the form [21.8] for $x = x(t)$. Solve this equation and then find expressions for $N = N(t)$ and $X = X(t)$. Examine the limits for $x(t)$, $N(t)$, and $X(t)$ as $t \to \infty$ in the case $0 < a < 1$.

7. Consider the model in Example 21.13.

   a. Let $H_0 = 0$ and then find the condition for the production per capita to increase with time. A common estimate for σ in developing countries is 0.3. If the population increases at the rate 3% per year ($\rho = 0.03$), how high must the savings rate α be for $x(t)$ to increase with time?

   b. Show that, when $H_0 > 0$ and $\mu \neq \alpha\sigma$, [6] implies that $x(t)$ is always larger than $x(0)e^{(\alpha\sigma - \rho)t}$. (Look at the two cases $\alpha\sigma - \mu > 0$ and $\alpha\sigma - \mu < 0$ separately.) Why was this to be expected?

   c. Assume that $\alpha\sigma < \rho$. Find a necessary and sufficient condition to obtain *sustained* growth in production per capita. Give an economic interpretation.

[3]T. Haavelmo. *A Study in the Theory of Economic Evolution.* North-Holland. Amsterdam. 1964.

21.6 First-Order Linear Differential Equations II

This section studies the solution of the general linear equation $\dot{x} + a(t)x = b(t)$, in which the coefficient $a(t)$ of x is not constant. As economic motivation for the solution procedure we are about to present, consider the compound interest example of Equation [21.5], but with a variable interest rate $r(t)$:

$$\dot{w} = r(t)w + y(t) - c(t) \qquad\qquad [21.9]$$

In Example 21.6 of Section 21.3, we saw how to solve this equation for the case when there were no deposits or withdrawals. Indeed, for some constant C,

$$\dot{w} = r(t)w \quad\Longleftrightarrow\quad w = Ce^{R(t)}, \qquad \text{where} \qquad R(t) = \int r(t)\,dt$$

This suggests trying the variable discount factor $e^{-R(t)}$ as a suitable integrating factor. We see that

$$\frac{d}{dt}\left[e^{-R(t)}w\right] = e^{-R(t)}\dot{w} - \dot{R}(t)e^{-R(t)}w = e^{-R(t)}[\dot{w} - r(t)w]$$

Therefore,

$$\frac{d}{dt}\left[e^{-R(t)}w\right] = e^{-R(t)}[y(t) - c(t)] \qquad\qquad [*]$$

Integrating equation [*] yields

$$e^{-R(t)}w(t) = \int e^{-R(t)}[y(t) - c(t)]\,dt + C$$

and so

$$w(t) = Ce^{R(t)} + e^{R(t)}\int e^{-R(t)}[y(t) - c(t)]\,dt, \quad \text{with} \quad R(t) = \int r(t)\,dt \quad [21.10]$$

This is very much like Equation [3] near the beginning of Section 21.5, except that e^{rt} has been replaced by $e^{R(t)} = \exp\left[\int r(t)\,dt\right]$.

The solution of the general linear equation [21.4] is found from [21.10] by substituting x for w, $-a(t)$ for $r(t)$, and $b(t)$ for $y(t) - c(t)$. The result is

$$\dot{x} + a(t)x = b(t) \quad\Longleftrightarrow\quad x = e^{-\int a(t)\,dt}\left[C + \int e^{\int a(t)\,dt}b(t)\,dt\right] \qquad [21.11]$$

Example 21.14

Find the general solution of

$$\dot{x} + 2tx = 4t$$

and the integral curve through $(t, x) = (0, -2)$.

Solution We see that the formula in [21.11] can be used with $a(t) = 2t$ and $b(t) = 4t$. Then $\int a(t)\,dt = \int 2t\,dt = t^2 + C_1$. We choose $C_1 = 0$ so that $\int a(t)\,dt = t^2$ (choosing another value for C_1 instead gives the same general solution). Then [21.11] gives

$$x = e^{-t^2}\left(C + \int e^{t^2} 4t\,dt\right) = Ce^{-t^2} + e^{-t^2} 2e^{t^2} = Ce^{-t^2} + 2$$

If $x = -2$ for $t = 0$, then $-2 = Ce^0 + 2$, and so $C = -4$. The integral curve through $(0, -2)$, therefore, has the equation $x = 2 - 4e^{-t^2}$.

The Solution of the General Linear Equation When $x(t_0) = x_0$ Is Given

Assume that the value of $x(t)$ is known for $t = t_0$. Then the constant C in [21.11] is determined. As it is often useful to have the formula for the corresponding solution of the equation, we derive it here.

Let F be a function such that $\dot{F}(t) = b(t)e^{A(t)}$, where $A(t) = \int a(t)\,dt$ and so, $A(t) - A(s)$. The solution in [21.11] can then be written as

$$x(t) = Ce^{-A(t)} + e^{-A(t)} F(t)$$

Now let $t = t_0$ and solve for C to get $C = x(t_0)e^{A(t_0)} - F(t_0)$. Hence,

$$x(t) = x(t_0)e^{-[A(t) - A(t_0)]} + e^{-A(t)} [F(t) - F(t_0)]$$

From the definition of $F(t)$, we find that $F(t) - F(t_0) = \int_{t_0}^{t} b(s)e^{A(s)}\,ds$. So

$$e^{-A(t)} [F(t) - F(t_0)] = e^{-A(t)} \int_{t_0}^{t} b(s)e^{A(s)}\,ds = \int_{t_0}^{t} b(s)e^{-[A(t) - A(s)]}\,ds$$

(We can include $e^{-A(t)}$ in the integrand, because we are integrating w.r.t. s.) Finally, therefore, we have the following result when $x(t_0) = x_0$:

$$\dot{x} + a(t)x = b(t) \iff x = x_0 e^{-\int_{t_0}^{t} a(\xi)\,d\xi} + \int_{t_0}^{t} b(s)e^{-\int_{s}^{t} a(\xi)\,d\xi}\,ds \qquad [21.12]$$

Problems

1. Find the general solutions of the following differential equations:

    a. $t\dot{x} + 2x + t = 0$ $(t \neq 0)$ **b.** $\dot{x} - \dfrac{1}{t}x = t$ $(t > 0)$

    c. $\dot{x} - \dfrac{t}{t^2 - 1}x = t$ $(t > 1)$ **d.** $\dot{x} - \dfrac{2}{t}x + \dfrac{2a^2}{t^2} = 0$ $(t > 0)$

2. For the differential equation

$$\dot{x} = 2tx + t(1 + t^2)$$

    show that the solution $x(t)$ that passes through $(t, x) = (0, 0)$ has a local minimum at $t = 0$. Examine whether the limit $\lim_{t \to \infty} x(t)$ exists.

3. Solve the linear differential equation

$$\dot{p} + \dfrac{1}{t^2}p = \dfrac{1}{t^3}   (t > 0)$$

    Find, in particular, the solution that satisfies the requirement $p(1) = 0$. Check the answer by direct substitution.

4. Prove that differential equations of the form

$$\dot{x} = Q(t)x + R(t)x^n   \textbf{(Bernoulli's equation)}$$

    can be transformed into a linear equation by substituting $z = x^{1-n}$.

5. Solve the following instances of Bernoulli's equation:

    a. $\dot{x} = -tx + t^3x^3$ **b.** $t\dot{x} + 2x = tx^2$ $(t \neq 0)$

    c. $\dot{x} = 4x + 2e^t\sqrt{x}$ $(x > 0)$

6. An economic growth model leads to the Bernoulli equation

$$\dot{K} = \alpha A(n_0)^a e^{(av+\varepsilon)t}K^b - \alpha\delta K$$

    where A, n_0, a, b, v, α, δ, and ε are positive constants. Find the general solution of the equation when $av + \varepsilon + \alpha\delta(1 - b) \neq 0$.

7. Generally, differential equations of the type

$$\dot{x} = P(t) + Q(t)x + R(t)x^2   \textbf{(Riccati's equation)}$$

    can only be solved numerically. But if we happen to know one special solution $u = u(t)$ of the equation, the substitution $x = u + 1/z$ will turn the equation into a linear equation in z as a function of t. Verify this, and illustrate by finding a formula for the general solution of

$$t\dot{x} = x - (x - t)^2$$

(*Hint:* $x = t$ is a special solution.)

21.7 Qualitative Theory and Stability

Most of the differential equations considered so far have had explicit solutions in terms of elementary functions. In such cases, it is usually easy to study the properties of the solution. Of course, it is convenient when economic phenomena can be described by models involving differential equations that can be solved explicitly. Because most kinds of first-order differential equation do not have this nice property, however, many applications will involve differential equations whose solutions cannot be expressed in terms of elementary functions.

The theory we have discussed so far is insufficient for another reason. In a model designed to illustrate some special economic phenomenon, one must introduce a number of assumptions. It is often desirable to make these assumptions as weak as possible without losing the essential aspect of the problem. If a differential equation appears in the model, it therefore typically contains unspecified parameters.

As a result, when a differential equation is used to describe some particular economic phenomenon, the typical situation is as follows:

1. It is impossible to obtain an explicit solution of the equation.
2. The equation contains unspecified parameters (or even unspecified functions).

These observations raise numerous questions. In this section, we merely discuss the stability problem for first-order differential equations.

Stability and Phase Diagrams

One of the most important properties of a differential equation is whether it has any *equilibrium states*. They correspond to solutions of the equation that do not change over time. In many economic applications, it is also very important to know whether an equilibrium state is stable. This can often be settled even if we cannot find explicit solutions of the equation. For instance, the rest position of a pendulum (hanging downward and motionless) is stable; if it is slightly disturbed while in this position, it will swing around it and gradually approach the equilibrium state of rest. To use a common analogy, in applied problems, we do not expect to find an unstable equilibrium for the same reason that a razor blade will not balance on its edge.

Let us take a closer look at the stability of the equation

$$\dot{x} = F(x) \qquad\qquad [21.13]$$

This is a special example of the equation $\dot{x} = F(t, x)$, where t does not explicitly appear on the right-hand side. For this reason, the equation in [21.13] is called **autonomous.**

In general, we say that a point a represents an **equilibrium state** or a **stationary state** for Equation [21.13] if $F(a) = 0$. In this case, $x(t) = a$ (for all t) is a solution of the equation. If $x(t_0) = a$ for some value t_0 of t, then $x(t)$ is equal to a for all t.

To examine the stability properties of the equilibrium states for [21.13], it is useful to study its **phase diagram.** This is obtained by putting $y = \dot{x}$ and drawing the curve $y = F(x)$ in the xy-plane (or $x\dot{x}$-plane). An example is indicated in Fig. 21.7. Any solution $x = x(t)$ of [21.13] has an associated $\dot{x} = \dot{x}(t)$. For every t, the pair $(x(t), \dot{x}(t))$ is a point on the curve in the phase diagram. What can be said generally about this point when t increases? If we consider a point on the curve (graph) lying above the x-axis, then $F(x(t)) > 0$ and therefore $\dot{x}(t) = F(x(t)) > 0$, so that $x(t)$ increases with t. *It follows from this observation that the point $(x(t), \dot{x}(t))$ moves from left to right in the diagram if we are above the x-axis. If, on the other hand, we are at a point on the graph below the x-axis, then $\dot{x}(t) < 0$, and $x(t)$ decreases with t, so we move from right to left.*

In the example of Fig. 21.7, we have indicated the direction of movement with arrows. There are two equilibrium states here, a_1 and a_2. If we are at one of these states, then we will remain there. However, there is an important difference between the two. If $x(t)$ is close to a_1, but not equal to a_1, then $x(t)$ will approach a_1 as t increases. On the other hand, if $x(t)$ is close to, but not equal to a_2, then $x(t)$ will start to move away from a_2 as t increases. Indeed, $x(t)$ will move away with increasing speed, because x changes more quickly the further the corresponding point $(x, \dot{x})$ is from the x-axis (because $|\dot{x}|$ is larger). We say that a_1 is a **stable equilibrium state,** whereas a_2 is **unstable.**

Look at Fig. 21.7 again. Note that at the stable point a_1, the graph of $\dot{x} = F(x)$ has a negative slope, whereas the slope is positive at a_2. Suppose that a is an equilibrium state for $\dot{x} = F(x)$, so that $F(a) = 0$. If $F'(a) < 0$, then $F(x)$ is positive to the left of $x = a$, and negative to the right. The situation around a is then similar to that around a_1, and a is therefore stable. On the other hand, if

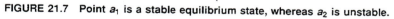

FIGURE 21.7 Point a_1 is a stable equilibrium state, whereas a_2 is unstable.

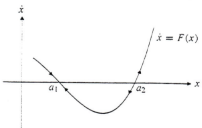

$F'(a) > 0$, then the situation around a is similar to the situation around a_2 in the figure. Hence, a is unstable. We have the following result:

(a) $F(a) = 0$ and $F'(a) < 0 \implies$

$\quad\quad\quad\quad\quad\quad$ a is a stable equilibrium state for $\dot{x} = F(x)$

(b) $F(a) = 0$ and $F'(a) > 0 \implies$

$\quad\quad\quad\quad\quad\quad$ a is an unstable equilibrium state for $\dot{x} = F(x)$

[21.14]

If a is an equilibrium state for $\dot{x} = F(x)$ at which $F'(a) = 0$, then we must examine the situation more closely. You should now give examples showing that a can be stable or unstable in this case.

Example 21.15

Consider the equation

$$\dot{x} + ax = b \quad\quad (a \neq 0)$$

which was studied in Section 21.5. If we let $F(x) = b - ax$, we see that the equation is a special case of [21.13]. In this case, there is *one* equilibrium state, which is $x = b/a$, where $F'(x) = -a$. According to [21.14], the equilibrium state $x = b/a$ will then be stable if $a > 0$, but unstable if $a < 0$. Compare this result with the discussion following Equation [21.8].

Example 21.16

We generalize Example 21.12 in Section 21.5 so that the price $P = P(t)$ satisfies the differential equation

$$\dot{P} = H(D(P) - S(P)) \quad\quad [*]$$

Thus, $\dot{P}$ is a function of the excess demand $D(P) - S(P)$. We assume that the function H satisfies $H(0) = 0$ and $H' > 0$, so that H is strictly increasing. If demand is larger than supply when the price is P, then $D(P) - S(P) > 0$, so $\dot{P} > 0$, and the price increases. On the other hand, the price decreases when $D(P) - S(P) < 0$. Equation [*] therefore represents what can be called a *price adjustment mechanism*.

Let P^e be an equilibrium price for [*], so that $H(D(P^e) - S(P^e)) = 0$, and hence $D(P^e) - S(P^e) = 0$. At the equilibrium price P^e, demand is equal to supply. If we put $F(P) = H(D(P) - S(P))$, then $F'(P) = H'(D(P) - S(P))(D'(P) - S'(P))$. Because $H' > 0$, we see that $F'(P)$ has the same sign as $D'(P) - S'(P)$. Using [21.14] leads to the conclusion that the equilibrium price is *stable* if $D'(P^e) - S'(P^e) < 0$. This condition is usually satisfied because we expect that $D' < 0$ and $S' > 0$.

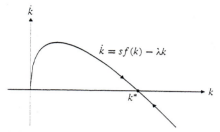

FIGURE 21.8   Phase diagram for [21.15], with appropriate conditions on f.

Example 21.17

The Solow model of "neoclassical" growth theory is based on the differential equation

$$\dot{k} = sf(k) - \lambda k \qquad [21.15]$$

Here the unknown function $k = k(t)$ denotes capital per worker, s the constant rate of saving, f a production function (national product per worker as a function of capital per worker), and λ the constant proportional rate of growth of the number of workers.

Note that [21.15] is a separable equation. But because f is not specified, we still cannot find an explicit solution of the equation. Assume that the phase diagram for equation [21.15] is as shown in Fig. 21.8.[4] Then there is a unique equilibrium state with $k^* \neq 0$. It is given by

$$sf(k^*) = \lambda k^* \qquad [21.16]$$

By studying Fig. 21.8, we see that k^* is stable. No matter what the initial capital per worker $k(0)$ may be, $k(t) \to k^*$ as $t \to \infty$.

Let us briefly discuss sufficient conditions for the existence and uniqueness of an equilibrium in the Solow model. It is usual to assume that $f(0) = 0$, as well as that $f'(k) > 0$ and $f''(k) < 0$ for all $k > 0$. It is also common to postulate the so-called *Inada conditions*,[5] according to which $f'(k) \to \infty$ as $k \to 0$ and also $f'(k) \to 0$ as $k \to \infty$.

To see why these conditions are sufficient, define $G(k) = sf(k) - \lambda k$. Then $G'(k) = sf'(k) - \lambda$, and Equation [21.15] changes to $\dot{k} = G(k)$. The

---

[4]For details see, for instance, H. Y. Wan Jr., *Economic Growth*, Harcourt Brace Jovanovich, 1971.

[5]Named after the Japanese economist K.-I. Inada, who introduced them into growth theory.

assumptions imposed on f imply that $G(0) = 0$, $G'(k) \to \infty$ as $k \to 0$, $G'(k) \to -\lambda < 0$ as $k \to \infty$, and $G''(k) = sf''(k) < 0$ for all $k > 0$. So G has a unique stationary point $\hat{k} > 0$ at which $G'(\hat{k}) = 0$. Moreover, $G(\hat{k}) > 0$, obviously. But now $G'(k) < 0$ for all $k > \hat{k}$, and also $G'(k) < -\frac{1}{2}\lambda < 0$ for all large enough k. It follows that $G(k) \to -\infty$ as $k \to \infty$, and so there is a unique point k^* with $G(k^*) = 0$. In addition, $G'(k^*) < 0$. According to [21.14], this is a sufficient condition for the stability of Equation [21.15].

Here is a more detailed model that leads to Equation [21.15]. Let $X(t)$ denote national income, $K(t)$ capital, and $L(t)$ the number of workers in a country at time t. Assume that

$$X(t) = F(K(t), L(t)) \tag{1}$$

$$\dot{K}(t) = sX(t) \tag{2}$$

$$L(t) = L_0 e^{\lambda t} \tag{3}$$

where F is a production function, and s is the rate of savings. Assume that F is homogeneous of degree 1, so that $F(K, L) = LF(K/L, 1)$ for all K and L. Define $k(t) = K(t)/L(t) = $ capital per worker, and $f(k) = F(k, 1) = F(K/L, 1) = F(K, L)/L = $ output per worker, expressed as a function of k. Then $\dot{k}/k = (d/dt)(\ln k) = (d/dt)(\ln K - \ln L)$, and so

$$\frac{\dot{k}}{k} = \frac{\dot{K}}{K} - \frac{\dot{L}}{L} = \frac{sF(K, L)}{K} - \lambda = \frac{sLf(k)}{K} - \lambda = \frac{sf(k)}{k} - \lambda \tag{4}$$

from which [21.15] follows at once.

The concepts of stable and unstable equilibrium states for Equation [21.13] have not been precisely defined in this section, but these descriptions should give the correct general idea.

Problems

Draw phase diagrams associated with the differential equations in Problems 1 and 2 and determine the nature of the possible equilibrium states.

1. **a.** $\dot{x} = x - 1$ **b.** $\dot{x} + 2x = 24$ **c.** $\dot{x} = x^2 - 9$

2. **a.** $\dot{x} = x^3 + x^2 - x - 1$ **b.** $\dot{x} = 3x^2 + 1$ **c.** $\dot{x} = xe^x$

3. The model described by equations [a] to [c] in Example 21.9 is a special case of that described by [1] to [3] in Example 21.17. Compare the results in Problem 5(a) of Section 21.4 with those in Example 21.17.

4. Consider the differential equation $\dot{x} = \frac{1}{2}(x^2 - 1)$.

a. Find the solution of this separable differential equation, and draw some integral curves in the tx-plane. What happens to the solution as $t \to \infty$ for different initial points x_0?

b. Draw the phase diagram for the equation. Find the two equilibrium states. Decide whether they are stable. Compare with the results in part (a).

Harder Problems

5. a. The stationary state k^* defined by [21.16] in Example 21.17 depends on s and λ. Find expressions for $\partial k^*/\partial s$ and $\partial k^*/\partial \lambda$ and determine the signs of these derivatives when f is strictly concave. (Show that in this case $sf'(k^*) < \lambda$.) Give an economic interpretation of the result. Prove that $F_K'(K, L) = f'(k)$.

b. Consumption per worker c is defined by $c = (X - \dot{K})/L$. Show that when $k = k^*$, then $c = f(k^*) - \lambda k^*$. Use this to show that if consumption per worker in the stationary state is to be maximized, it is necessary that $f'(k^*) = \lambda$, that is, $\partial F/\partial K = \lambda$. *Thus, the marginal product of capital $\partial F/\partial K$ must equal the relative rate of growth of the number of workers.* (This is often called "the golden rule of accumulation.")

c. Show that in the stationary state, $\dot{K}/K$ and $\dot{L}/L$ are both equal to λ.

21.8 Second-Order Differential Equations

So far this chapter has considered first-order differential equations. Many economic models are based on differential equations in which second- or higher-order derivatives appear. For example, in an important area of dynamic optimization called the calculus of variations, the first-order condition for optimality involves a second-order differential equation. This and the next section briefly introduce second-order equations.

Second-order differential equations can usually be written in the form

$$\ddot{x} = F(t, x, \dot{x}) \qquad [21.17]$$

where F is a given fixed function, $x = x(t)$ is the unknown function, and $\dot{x} = dx/dt$. The new feature is the presence of $\ddot{x} = d^2x/dt^2$. The simplest type of second-order equation is considered in the following example.

Example 21.18

Find the most general solution of

$$\ddot{x} = k \qquad (k \text{ is a constant}) \qquad [*]$$

Solution   Because $\ddot{x} = (d/dt)\dot{x}$, direct integration implies that [∗] is equivalent to the equation $\dot{x} = kt + A$, for some constant A. After integrating once more, we see that [∗] is satisfied iff

$$x = \tfrac{1}{2}kt^2 + At + B \qquad \text{(A and B are arbitrary constants)} \qquad [\ast]$$

Geometrically, [∗] represents a collection of parabolas in the tx-plane whose axes are all parallel to the x-axis.

Example 21.19

How would you go about finding the solutions of

$$\ddot{x} = G(t, \dot{x}) \qquad\qquad [21.18]$$

where G is a given function? In particular, solve the equation $\ddot{x} = \dot{x} + t$.

Solution   Note that x is missing from [21.18]. Introduce the new variable $u = \dot{x}$. Then [21.18] becomes $\dot{u} = G(t, u)$, which is a first-order equation. Suppose we manage to find the general solution $u(t)$ of this first-order equation. Then integrating $\dot{x}(t) = u(t)$ will yield the general solution $x(t)$ to [21.18].

Substituting $u = \dot{x}$ in the particular equation $\ddot{x} = \dot{x} + t$ yields $\dot{u} = u + t$. This first-order equation has the general solution $u = Ae^t - t - 1$, where A is a constant (see Example 21.2). Hence, $\dot{x} = Ae^t - t - 1$. Integrating this equation yields $x = \int (Ae^t - t - 1)\, dt = Ae^t - \tfrac{1}{2}t^2 - t + B$, where B is a second arbitrary constant.

Solving Equation [21.17] becomes more difficult if the right-hand side includes both the unknown function and its derivative. In fact, only rather special cases have explicit solutions; generally, one has to resort to numerical solutions for given initial conditions.

Even so, it turns out that the *existence* of a solution can be established for almost all the equations that are likely to appear in applications. According to the *existence and uniqueness theorem*, if the three functions F, F'_x, and $F'_{\dot{x}}$ are all continuous in the three variables $(t, x, \dot{x})$ throughout an open domain S in R^3, then for each point (t_0, x_0, a) in S, there is one and only one function satisfying the equation $\ddot{x} = F(t, x, \dot{x})$ whose integral curve passes through the point (t_0, x_0) and whose derivative has the value a at that point. In fact, the general solution of the equation will depend on two arbitrary constants, as it did in Examples 21.18 and 21.19; that is,

$$\ddot{x} = F(t, x, \dot{x}) \iff x = x(t, A, B)$$

The constants A and B are determined by the two requirements that $x(t_0, A, B) = x_0$ and $\dot{x}(t_0, A, B) = a$.

Example 21.20

Solve the problem

$$\ddot{x} = \dot{x} + t, \quad x(0) = 1, \ \dot{x}(0) = 2$$

Solution   According to Example 21.19, the general solution of this second-order equation is $x = Ae^t - \frac{1}{2}t^2 - t + B$. Letting $x(0) = 1$ yields $1 = A + B$. Moreover, $\dot{x} = Ae^t - t - 1$, so $\dot{x}(0) = 2$ implies that $2 = A - 1$. Thus, $A = 3$, so $B = -2$, and the unique solution of the problem is $x = 3e^t - \frac{1}{2}t^2 - t - 2$.

Linear Equations

The general second-order linear differential equation is

$$\ddot{x} + a(t)\dot{x} + b(t)x = f(t) \qquad [21.19]$$

where $a(t)$, $b(t)$, and $f(t)$ are all continuous functions of t. In contrast to first-order linear equations, in the general case [21.19] has no explicit solution in terms of functions we consider in this book. However, something useful can be said about the structure of the general solution.

Let us begin with the **homogeneous** equation

$$\ddot{x} + a(t)\dot{x} + b(t)x = 0 \qquad [21.20]$$

which is obtained from [21.19] by replacing $f(t)$ by 0. We claim that if $u_1 = u_1(t)$ and $u_2 = u_2(t)$ both satisfy [21.20], then $x = Au_1 + Bu_2$ also satisfies [21.20] for all choices of constants A and B. In fact, direct differentiation gives $\dot{x} = A\dot{u}_1 + B\dot{u}_2$ and $\ddot{x} = A\ddot{u}_1 + B\ddot{u}_2$. Inserting these expressions for $\dot{x}$ and $\ddot{x}$ into the left-hand side of [21.20] yields

$$\ddot{x} + a(t)\dot{x} + b(t)x = A\ddot{u}_1 + B\ddot{u}_2 + a(t)(A\dot{u}_1 + B\dot{u}_2) + b(t)(Au_1 + Bu_2)$$

$$= A[\ddot{u}_1 + a(t)\dot{u}_1 + b(t)u_1] + B[\ddot{u}_2 + a(t)\dot{u}_2 + b(t)u_2]$$

It was assumed that u_1 and u_2 satisfy [21.20], so this last expression is 0. Thus, we have proved that the function $x = Au_1 + Bu_2$ satisfies [21.20] for all values of constants A and B.

Suppose then that we have somehow managed to find two solutions u_1 and u_2 of [21.20]. Then $x = Au_1 + Bu_2$ satisfies [21.20] for all values of A and B. Is this the general solution? No; in order to be sure that $Au_1 + Bu_2$ is the general solution of [21.20], we must require u_1 and u_2 not to be constant multiples of each other—that is, they must not be proportional. The following result is proved in most textbooks on differential equations:

The homogeneous differential equation

$$\ddot{x} + a(t)\dot{x} + b(t)x = 0$$

has the **general solution**

$$x = Au_1(t) + Bu_2(t)$$

where $u_1(t)$ and $u_2(t)$ are two solutions that are not proportional, and A and B are arbitrary constants.

[21.21]

Example 21.21

Investigate the general solutions of the two homogeneous equations

(a) $\ddot{x} = x$ **(b)** $\ddot{x} = -x$

Solution

(a) The problem is to find the functions that do not change when differentiated twice. You probably recall that $x = e^t$ has this property, as does $x = 2e^t$. But these two functions are proportional. So we need to find another function with the property that differentiating it twice leaves it unchanged. After some thought, you might come up with the idea of trying $x = e^{-t}$. In fact, $\dot{x} = -e^{-t}$, and so $\ddot{x} = e^{-t}$. Because e^t and e^{-t} are not proportional, we have

$$\ddot{x} = x \quad\Longleftrightarrow\quad x = Ae^t + Be^{-t} \quad \text{(A and B are arbitrary constants)} \quad [21.22]$$

(b) This equation is a little trickier, because you have to know the rules for differentiating trigonometric functions in order to find the solution. (See Section C.2.) In fact, if $u_1 = \sin t$ and $u_2 = \cos t$, then $\dot{u}_1 = \cos t$ and $\dot{u}_2 = -\sin t$. Differentiating once more gives $\ddot{u}_1 = -\sin t = -u_1$ and $\ddot{u}_2 = -\cos t = -u_2$. As $u_1 = \sin t$ and $u_2 = \cos t$ are not constant multiples of each other, we conclude that

$$\ddot{x} = -x \quad\Longleftrightarrow\quad x = A\sin t + B\cos t \quad \text{(A and B are arbitrary constants)}$$
$$[21.23]$$

Equation [21.19] is called a *nonhomogeneous equation*. The homogeneous equation associated with it is [21.20]. Suppose we are able to find *some* **particular solution** $u^* = u^*(t)$ of [21.19]. If $x(t)$ is an arbitrary solution of [21.19], then it is easy to see that the difference $x(t) - u^*(t)$ is a solution of the homogeneous equation [21.20]. In fact, if $v(t) = x(t) - u^*(t)$, then $\dot{v}(t) = \dot{x}(t) - \dot{u}^*(t)$ and

$\ddot{v}(t) = \ddot{x}(t) - \ddot{u}^*(t)$, so

$$\ddot{v}(t) + a(t)\dot{v}(t) + b(t)v(t) = \ddot{x}(t) - \ddot{u}^*(t) + a(t)[\dot{x}(t) - \dot{u}^*(t)] + b(t)[x(t) - u^*(t)]$$

$$= \ddot{x}(t) + a(t)\dot{x}(t) + b(t)x(t)$$

$$- [\ddot{u}^*(t) + a(t)\dot{u}^*(t) + b(t)u^*(t)]$$

$$= f(t) - f(t) = 0$$

Thus, $x(t) - u^*(t)$ is a solution of the homogeneous equation. According to [21.21], therefore, we have $x(t) - u^*(t) = Au_1(t) + Bu_2(t)$, where $u_1(t)$ and $u_2(t)$ are two nonproportional solutions of [21.20], and A and B are arbitrary constants. Hence:

The nonhomogeneous differential equation

$$\ddot{x} + a(t)\dot{x} + b(t)x = f(t)$$

has the **general solution**

$$x = Au_1(t) + Bu_2(t) + u^*(t)$$

[21.24]

where $Au_1(t) + Bu_2(t)$ is the general solution of the associated homogeneous equation (with $f(t)$ replaced by zero), and $u^*(t)$ is a particular solution of the nonhomogeneous equation.

Example 21.22

Find the general solution of

$$\ddot{x} + x = e^t$$

[1]

(*Hint:* Verify that there is a particular solution of the form $u^* = Ae^t$.)

Solution This is an equation of the form [21.19] with $a(t) = 0$, $b(t) = 1$, and $f(t) = e^t$. The associated homogeneous equation was solved in Example 21.21(b).

If $u^* = Ae^t$, then $\dot{u}^* = Ae^t$ and $\ddot{u}^* = Ae^t$, so inserting these results into [1] yields $Ae^t + Ae^t = e^t$. This equality holds for all t only if $A = 1/2$. Thus, $u^* = \frac{1}{2}e^t$ is a particular solution and the general solution is

$$x = A \sin t + B \cos t + \tfrac{1}{2}e^t$$

[2]

There is no general and simple method of discovering the two solutions of [21.20] that we need in order to find the general solution of the equation. However, in the special case when coefficients $a(t)$ and $b(t)$ are both constants, then it is always possible to find the two solutions required. The next section shows how to do this for a wide variety of examples.

Problems

1. By arguing as in Example 21.18, find the general solutions of the following:

    a. $\ddot{x} = t$ **b.** $\ddot{x} = \sin t$ **c.** $\ddot{x} = e^t + t^2$

2. a. Prove that $u_1 = e^t$ and $u_2 = te^t$ both satisfy $\ddot{x} - 2\dot{x} + x = 0$. Show that u_1 and u_2 are not proportional, and, hence, find the general solution of the equation.

    b. Find the general solution of $\ddot{x} - 2\dot{x} + x = 3$.

3. a. Prove that $u_1 = e^{2t}$ and $u_2 = e^{-3t}$ both solve $\ddot{x} + \dot{x} - 6x = 0$. What is the general solution?

    b. Find the general solution of $\ddot{x} + \dot{x} - 6x = 6t$. (*Hint:* The equation has a particular solution of the form $Ct + D$.)

4. A study of the optimal exhaustion of a natural resource uses the equation

$$\ddot{x} - \frac{2-\alpha}{1-\alpha}a\,\dot{x} + \frac{a^2}{1-\alpha}\,x = 0 \qquad (\alpha \neq 0,\ \alpha \neq 1,\ a \neq 0)$$

Prove that $u_1 = e^{at}$ and $u_2 = e^{at/(1-\alpha)}$ are both solutions. What is the general solution?

5. Let $a \neq b$ be two real numbers. Prove that the differential equation

$$(t+a)(t+b)\ddot{x} + 2(2t+a+b)\dot{x} + 2x = 0$$

has two solutions of the form $(t+k)^{-1}$ for appropriate choices of k. Find the general solution of the equation. (*Hint:* Let $x = (t+k)^{-1}$ and then adjust k until the function satisfies the differential equation.)

21.9 Second-Order Equations with Constant Coefficients

Consider the *homogeneous* equation

$$\ddot{x} + a\dot{x} + bx = 0 \qquad\qquad [21.25]$$

where a and b are arbitrary constants, and $x = x(t)$ is the unknown function. According to [21.21], finding the general solution of [21.25] requires us to discover two solutions, $u_1(t)$ and $u_2(t)$, that are not proportional. Because the coefficients in [21.25] are constants, it seems a good idea to try possible solutions x with the property that x, $\dot{x}$, and $\ddot{x}$ are all constant multiples of each other. The exponential function $x = e^{rt}$ has this property, because $\dot{x} = re^{rt} = rx$ and $\ddot{x} = r^2 e^{rt} = r^2 x$. So we try adjusting the constant r in order that $x = e^{rt}$ should satisfy [21.25]. This requires that $r^2 e^{rt} + are^{rt} + be^{rt} = 0$. Canceling the (positive) factor e^{rt} tells us that $x = e^{rt}$ satisfies [21.25] iff r satisfies the equation

$$r^2 + ar + b = 0 \qquad [21.26]$$

This is the **characteristic equation** of the differential equation [21.25]. It is a quadratic equation whose roots are real iff $\frac{1}{4}a^2 - b \geq 0$. Solving [21.26] by the quadratic formula in this case yields the two **characteristic roots**

$$r_1 = -\tfrac{1}{2}a + \sqrt{\tfrac{1}{4}a^2 - b}, \qquad r_2 = -\tfrac{1}{2}a - \sqrt{\tfrac{1}{4}a^2 - b} \qquad [21.27]$$

Generally, there are three different cases to consider that are summed up in the following frame:

The **general solution** of

$$\ddot{x} + a\dot{x} + bx = 0$$

is as follows:

(a) For the case $\frac{1}{4}a^2 - b > 0$ (when the characteristic equation has two distinct real roots):

$$x = Ae^{r_1 t} + Be^{r_2 t}, \quad \text{where} \quad r_{1,2} = -\tfrac{1}{2}a \pm \sqrt{\tfrac{1}{4}a^2 - b}$$

[21.28]

(b) For the case $\frac{1}{4}a^2 - b = 0$ (when the characteristic equation has one real double root):

$$x = (A + Bt)e^{rt}, \quad \text{where} \quad r = -\tfrac{1}{2}a$$

(c) For the case $\frac{1}{4}a^2 - b < 0$ (when the characteristic equation has no real roots):

$$x = Ae^{\alpha t}\cos(\beta t + B), \quad \text{where} \quad \alpha = -\tfrac{1}{2}a, \quad \beta = \sqrt{b - \tfrac{1}{4}a^2}$$

The case $\frac{1}{4}a^2 - b > 0$ is the simplest, because it gives real and distinct characteristic roots r_1 and r_2. The functions $e^{r_1 t}$ and $e^{r_2 t}$ both satisfy [21.25]. These functions are not proportional when $r_1 \neq r_2$, so the general solution is $Ae^{r_1 t} + Be^{r_2 t}$ in this case.

If $\frac{1}{4}a^2 - b = 0$, then $r = -\frac{1}{2}a$ is a double root of [21.26], and $u_1 = e^{rt}$ satisfies [21.25]. Problem 10 is devoted to this case. For the moment, notice that $u_2 = te^{rt}$ also satisfies [21.25]. This is because $\dot{u}_2 = e^{rt} + tre^{rt}$ and $\ddot{u}_2 = re^{rt} + re^{rt} + tr^2 e^{rt}$.

Inserting these derivatives into the left-hand side of [21.25] gives

$$\ddot{u}_2 + a\dot{u}_2 + bu_2 = re^{rt} + re^{rt} + tr^2e^{rt} + ae^{rt} + atre^{rt} + bte^{rt}$$

$$= e^{rt}(a + 2r) + te^{rt}(r^2 + ar + b)$$

after simplifying. But the last expression is 0 because $r = -\frac{1}{2}a$ and $r^2 + ar + b = 0$. Thus, e^{rt} and te^{rt} are indeed both solutions of Equation [21.25]. These two solutions are not proportional, so the general solution is $Ae^{rt} + Bte^{rt}$ in this case.

If $\frac{1}{4}a^2 - b < 0$, the characteristic equation has no real roots. An example is the equation $\ddot{x} + x = 0$, which occurred in Example 21.21(b); then $a = 0$ and $b = 1$, so $\frac{1}{4}a^2 - b = -1$. The general solution was $A \sin t + B \cos t$. It should, therefore, come as no surprise that when $\frac{1}{4}a^2 - b < 0$, the solution of [21.25] involves trigonometric functions.

In fact, if $x = Ae^{\alpha t} \cos(\beta t + B)$, with A and B as arbitrary constants, then the product rule implies that $\dot{x} = A\alpha e^{\alpha t} \cos(\beta t + B) + Ae^{\alpha t}[-\beta \sin(\beta t + B)]$. So

$$\dot{x} = Ae^{\alpha t}[\alpha \cos(\beta t + B) - \beta \sin(\beta t + B)]$$

$$\ddot{x} = Ae^{\alpha t}[(\alpha^2 - \beta^2) \cos(\beta t + B) - 2\alpha\beta \sin(\beta t + B)]$$

Then

$$\ddot{x} + a\dot{x} + bx = Ae^{\alpha t}[(\alpha^2 - \beta^2 + \alpha a + b) \cos(\beta t + B) - (2\alpha + a)\beta \sin(\beta t + B)]$$

Substituting the values of α and β given by case (c) of [21.28], we see that $2\alpha + a = 0$ and also $\alpha^2 - \beta^2 + \alpha a + b = \frac{1}{4}a^2 - (b - \frac{1}{4}a^2) - \frac{1}{2}a^2 + b = 0$, so $x = Ae^{\alpha t} \cos(\beta t + B)$ does satisfy [21.25].

For this last case, too, we have therefore found a function that depends on two arbitrary constants A and B, and satisfies Equation [21.25] for all t. Problem 7 asks you to find an alternative expression for this solution that will make it more obvious that we have indeed found the general solution of [21.25].

Note: (For those of you who need to read about complex numbers, see Section C.3 for a brief introduction.) Suppose $\frac{1}{4}a^2 - b < 0$. Then the characteristic equation $r^2 + ar + b = 0$ has two complex roots, $r_1 = \alpha + i\beta$ and $r_2 = \alpha - i\beta$, where α and β are given by case (c) of [21.28]. Now the two exponential functions $e^{r_1 t} = e^{\alpha t}(\cos \beta t + i \sin \beta t)$ and $e^{r_2 t} = e^{\alpha t}(\cos \beta t - i \sin \beta t)$ both satisfy [21.25]; so, too, will any linear combination of these functions. In particular, both $(e^{r_1 t} + e^{r_2 t})/2 = e^{\alpha t} \cos \beta t$ and $(e^{r_1 t} - e^{r_2 t})/2i = e^{\alpha t} \sin \beta t$ satisfy [21.25], and these functions are not proportional. So the general solution really is $x = Ae^{\alpha t} \cos \beta t + Be^{\alpha t} \sin \beta t$.

Example 21.23

Find the general solutions of the following equations:

(a) $\ddot{x} - 3x = 0$ (b) $\ddot{x} - 4\dot{x} + 4x = 0$ (c) $\ddot{x} - 6\dot{x} + 13x = 0$

Solution

(a) The characteristic equation $r^2 - 3 = 0$ has two real roots $r_1 = -\sqrt{3}$ and $r_2 = \sqrt{3}$. The general solution is

$$x = Ae^{-\sqrt{3}t} + Be^{\sqrt{3}t}$$

(b) The characteristic equation $r^2 - 4r + 4 = (r-2)^2 = 0$ has the double root $r = 2$. Hence, the general solution is

$$x = (A + Bt)e^{2t}$$

(c) The characteristic equation $r^2 - 6r + 13 = 0$ has no real roots. According to case (c) in [21.28], $\alpha = -a/2 = -(-6)/2 = 3$ and $\beta = \sqrt{13 - \frac{1}{4}(-6)^2} = 2$, so the general solution is

$$x = Ae^{3t}\cos(2t + B)$$

The Nonhomogeneous Equation

Consider next the *nonhomogeneous* equation

$$\ddot{x} + a\dot{x} + bx = f(t) \qquad [21.29]$$

where $f(t)$ is an arbitrary continuous function. According to [21.24] in the previous section, the general solution of [21.29] is given by

$$x = x(t) = Au_1(t) + Bu_2(t) + u^*(t) \qquad [21.30]$$

We have explained how to find the terms $Au_1(t) + Bu_2(t)$ by solving the corresponding homogeneous equation. But how do we find a particular solution $u^* = u^*(t)$ of [21.29]? In fact, there is a simple *method of undetermined coefficients* that works in many cases.

If $b = 0$ in [21.29], then the term in x is missing and the substitution $u = \dot{x}$ transforms the equation into a linear equation of the first order (see Example 21.19). So we may assume $b \neq 0$. Consider the following special choices of $f(t)$:

(I) $f(t) = A$ **(a constant)**   In this case, Equation [21.29] must have a solution that is constant, $u^* = c$. Then $\dot{u}^* = \ddot{u}^* = 0$, so the equation reduces to $bc = A$. Hence, $c = A/b$. Thus, for $b \neq 0$:

$$\boxed{\ddot{x} + a\dot{x} + bx = A \text{ has a particular solution } u^* = A/b} \qquad [21.31]$$

(II) $f(x)$ **is a polynomial**   Suppose $f(t)$ is a polynomial of degree n. Then a reasonable guess is that [21.29] has a particular solution that is also a polynomial of degree n, of the form $u^* = A_n t^n + A_{n-1} t^{n-1} + \cdots + A_1 t + A_0$. The undetermined coefficients $A_n, A_{n-1}, \ldots, A_0$ get determined by requiring u^* to satisfy [21.29] and equating coefficients of like powers of t.

Example 21.24

Find a particular solution of

$$\ddot{x} - 4\dot{x} + 4x = t^2 + 2 \qquad\qquad [*]$$

Solution   The right-hand side is a polynomial of degree 2. So we let $u^* = At^2 + Bt + C$ and try adjusting A, B, and C to give a solution. We obtain $\dot{u}^* = 2At + B$, and so $\ddot{u}^* = 2A$. Inserting these expressions for u^*, $\dot{u}^*$, and $\ddot{u}^*$ into [*] yields the equation $2A - 4(2At + B) + 4(At^2 + Bt + C) = t^2 + 2$. Collecting like terms on the LHS gives $4At^2 + (4B - 8A)t + (2A - 4B + 4C) = t^2 + 2$. Equating coefficients of like powers of t yields $4A = 1$, $4B - 8A = 0$, and $2A - 4B + 4C = 2$. Solving these three equations gives $A = 1/4$, $B = 1/2$, and $C = 7/8$. Hence, $u^* = \frac{1}{4}t^2 + \frac{1}{2}t + \frac{7}{8}$ is a particular solution of [*]. Using [21.24] and the result of Example 21.23(b), we see that the general solution of [*] is

$$x = (A + Bt)e^{2t} + \tfrac{1}{4}t^2 + \tfrac{1}{2}t + \tfrac{7}{8}$$

Note that the right-hand side of [*] is $t^2 + 2$, without any t term. Yet no function of the form $Ct^2 + D$ will satisfy it; any solution must include the term $\frac{1}{2}t$.

(III) $f(t) = pe^{qt}$ A natural choice of particular solution would seem to be $u^* = Ae^{qt}$. Then $\dot{u}^* = Aqe^{qt}$, $\ddot{u}^* = Aq^2 e^{qt}$, and substitution into [21.29] yields $Ae^{qt}(q^2 + aq + b) = pe^{qt}$. Hence, if $q^2 + aq + b \neq 0$, it follows that $A = p/(q^2 + aq + b)$ and so a particular solution is

$$u^* = \frac{p}{q^2 + aq + b} e^{qt}$$

The condition $q^2 + aq + b \neq 0$ means that q is not a solution of the characteristic equation [21.26]—that is, that e^{qt} is not a solution of [21.25]. If q is a simple root of $q^2 + aq + b = 0$, we look for a constant B such that Bte^{qt} satisfies [21.29]. If q is a double root, then $Ct^2 e^{qt}$ satisfies [21.29] for some constant C.

(IV) $f(t) = p\sin rt + q\cos rt$ Again the method of undetermined coefficients works. Let $u^* = A\sin rt + B\cos rt$ and adjust constants A and B so that the coefficients of $\sin rt$ and $\cos rt$ match. If $f(t)$ is itself a solution of the homogeneous equation, then $u^* = At\sin rt + Bt\cos rt$ will be a particular solution for suitable choices of constants A and B.

Example 21.25

Find a particular solution of

$$\ddot{x} - 4\dot{x} + 4x = 2\cos 2t$$

Solution   In this case, it is natural to suggest a particular solution of the form $u = A\cos 2t$. Note, however, that the term $-4\dot{u}$ gives us a $\sin 2t$ term on the left-hand side, and no matching term occurs on the right-hand side of the equation. So we try $u^* = A\sin 2t + B\cos 2t$ instead, and adjust constants A and B appropriately. We have $\dot{u}^* = 2A\cos 2t - 2B\sin 2t$ and $\ddot{u}^* = -4A\sin 2t - 4B\cos 2t$. Inserting these expressions into the equation and rearranging, we get $8B\sin 2t - 8A\cos 2t = 2\cos 2t$. Thus, letting $B = 0$ and $A = -1/4$, we see that the given equation is satisfied for all t. So $u^* = (-1/4)\sin 2t$ is a particular solution of the equation. By using [21.24] and the result in Example 21.23(b), the general solution can be determined.

The technique for obtaining particular solutions described before applies also if the right hand side $f(t)$ is a sum, difference, or product of polynomials, exponential functions, or trigonometric functions of the type mentioned. For instance, if $f(t) = (t^2 + 1)e^{3t} + \sin 2t$, let $u^* = (At^2 + Bt + C)e^{3t} + D\sin 2t + E\cos 2t$. On the other hand, if $f(t)$ in [21.29] is an entirely different type of function such as $t\ln t$, the method of undetermined coefficients does not work.

Stability

The stability concepts and results for second-order linear differential equation are closely related to those for difference equations discussed at the end of Section 20.5. If small changes in the initial conditions have no effect on the long-run behavior of the solution, the system is called **stable**. On the other hand, if small changes in the initial conditions can lead to significant differences in the long-run behavior of the solution, then the system is **unstable**.

Consider in particular the second-order nonhomogeneous differential equation

$$\ddot{x} + a(t)\dot{x} + b(t)x = f(t) \qquad [*]$$

Recall that the general solution of [*] is

$$x = Au_1(t) + Bu_2(t) + u^*(t) \qquad [**]$$

where $Au_1(t) + Bu_2(t)$ is the general solution of the associated homogeneous equation (with $f(t)$ replaced by zero), and $u^*(t)$ is a particular solution of the nonhomogeneous equation. Equation [*] is called **globally asymptotically stable** (or just **stable** for short) if the general solution $Au_1(t) + Bu_2(t)$ of the associated homogeneous equation approaches 0 as $t \to \infty$, for all values of A and B. Then any solution of the equation approaches the particular solution $u^*(t)$, which is independent of the initial conditions. So the effect of the initial conditions "dies out" as $t \to \infty$.

As was the case for difference equations, if $Au_1(t) + Bu_2(t)$ approaches 0 as $t \to \infty$, for all values of A and B, then in particular $u_1(t) \to 0$ as $t \to \infty$ (choose $A = 1$, $B = 0$), and $u_2(t) \to 0$ as $t \to \infty$ (choose $A = 0$, $B = 1$). On the other hand, the two conditions that $u_1(t)$ and $u_2(t)$ both approach 0 as t approaches infinity are obviously sufficient for $Au_1(t) + Bu_2(t)$ to approach 0 as $t \to \infty$.

Assume that coefficients $a(t)$ and $b(t)$ in [∗] are constants. Then $u_1(t) \to 0$ and $u_2(t) \to 0$ as $t \to \infty$ iff the real parts of the roots of $r^2 + ar + b = 0$ are both negative. To prove this statement, suppose first that the characteristic polynomial has complex roots, $r = \alpha \pm i\beta$, where $\alpha = -\frac{1}{2}a$ and $\beta = \sqrt{b - \frac{1}{4}a^2}$. Then two linearly independent solutions of the homogeneous equation are $u_1(t) = e^{\alpha t} \cos \beta t$ and $u_2(t) = e^{\alpha t} \sin \beta t$. Here $u_1(t)$ and $u_2(t)$ both approach 0 iff $\alpha < 0$. If the solutions to the characteristic equation are real, again it is easy to see that the equation is stable iff both roots (or the only root if it is a double root) are negative. Hence:

The equation $\ddot{x} + a\dot{x} + bx = f(t)$ is stable iff both roots of the characteristic equation $r^2 + ar + b = 0$ have negative real parts.   [21.32]

So, to determine the stability of the linear differential equation with constant coefficients, all we have to do is to check the real parts of the characteristic roots. One can also give a direct criterion in terms of the coefficients of the equation:

$\ddot{x} + a\dot{x} + bx = f(t)$ is stable $\Longleftrightarrow$ $a > 0$ and $b > 0$ [21.33]

To see why the conditions $a > 0$ and $b > 0$ are necessary and sufficient for stability, let r_1 and r_2 be the roots of the characteristic polynomial. Then $r_1 + r_2 = -a$ and $r_1 r_2 = b$ (see (A.37) in Sec. A.8).

If r_1 and r_2 are real and negative, then $a = -r_1 - r_2$ and $b = r_1 r_2$ are both positive. On the other hand, if $a > 0$ and $b > 0$, then $r_1 + r_2 = -a$ implies that at least one of the roots is negative. Thus, because $r_1 r_2 = b$, it follows that both roots must be negative.

If $r_1 = \alpha + i\beta$ and $r_2 = \alpha - i\beta$, then $r_1 + r_2 = 2\alpha = -a$ and $r_1 r_2 = \alpha^2 + \beta^2 = b$. It follows that r_1 and r_2 both have a negative real part (that is, $\alpha < 0$) iff a and b are both positive. This proves [21.33].

Example 21.26
Check the stability of

$$\ddot{v} + \left(\mu - \frac{\lambda}{a}\right)\dot{v} + \lambda\gamma v = -\frac{\lambda}{a}\dot{b}(t)$$

where μ, λ, γ, and a are constants, and $\dot{b}(t)$ is a given function.

Solution   This is a second-order differential equation in the function $v(t)$ with constant coefficients. According to [21.33], it is stable iff $\mu > \lambda/a$ and $\lambda\gamma > 0$.

Problems

Find the general solutions of the following equations in Problems 1 and 2 and decide which of them are stable.

1. **a.** $\ddot{x} - 3x = 0$ **b.** $\ddot{x} + 4\dot{x} + 8x = 0$ **c.** $3\ddot{x} + 8\dot{x} = 0$
    d. $4\ddot{x} + 4\dot{x} + x = 0$ **e.** $\ddot{x} + \dot{x} - 6x = 8$ **f.** $\ddot{x} + 3\dot{x} + 2x = e^{5t}$
2. **a.** $\ddot{x} - x = \sin t$ **b.** $\ddot{x} - x = e^{-t}$ **c.** $3\ddot{x} - 30\dot{x} + 75x = 2t + 1$
3. Solve the following differential equations for the specific initial conditions:
    a. $\ddot{x} + 2\dot{x} + x = t^2$, $x(0) = 0$, $\dot{x}(0) = 1$
    b. $\ddot{x} + 4x = 4t + 1$, $x(\pi/2) = 0$, $\dot{x}(\pi/2) = 0$
4. Find the general solution of $4\ddot{x} - 15x + 14x = t + \sin t$.
5. Find a particular solution of the differential equation

    $$\ddot{L} + \gamma[\beta + \alpha(1 - \beta)]\dot{L} - \gamma\delta^*L = -\gamma\delta^*kt - \gamma\delta^*L_0 \qquad (\gamma\delta^* \neq 0)$$

    and determine when the solution displays oscillations.
6. Let n be an integer and let $x = f(t)$ be a solution of $\ddot{x} + t^{n-2}x = 0$.
    a. Prove that $x = tf(1/t)$ is a solution of $\ddot{x} + t^{-n-2}x = 0$.
    b. Then solve the differential equation $t^4\ddot{x} + x = 0$.
7. Explain how the general solution of $\ddot{x} + a\dot{x} + bx = 0$ in the case $\frac{1}{4}a^2 - b < 0$ can be written as $x = Ce^{\alpha t}\cos\beta t + De^{\alpha t}\sin\beta t$ for suitable constants C and D. (Use the result in Problem 3 in Section C.1.)
8. An economic model due to T. Haavelmo leads to the differential equation

    $$\ddot{p}(t) = \gamma(a - \alpha)p(t) + k \qquad (\gamma, \alpha, a, \text{ and } k \text{ are constants})$$

    Solve the equation. Is it possible to choose the constants so that the equation is stable?
9. A business cycle model due to F. Dresch incorporates the equation

    $$\dot{p}(t) = a\int_{-\infty}^{t}\big[D(p(\tau)) - S(p(\tau))\big]\,d\tau \qquad (a > 0) \qquad [*]$$

where $p(t)$ denotes a price index at time t, and $D(p)$ and $S(p)$ are aggregate demand and supply, respectively. Thus, [*] says that the rate of price increase is proportional to the accumulated total of all past excess demand. In the case when $D(p) = d_0 + d_1 p$ and $S(p) = s_0 + s_1 p$, with $d_1 < 0$ and $s_1 > 0$, differentiate [*] w.r.t. t in order to deduce a second-order differential equation for $p(t)$. Then find the general solution of this equation.

10. Consider the equation $\ddot{x} + a\dot{x} + bx = 0$ when $\frac{1}{4}a^2 - b = 0$, so that the characteristic equation has a double root $r = -a/2$. Let $x(t) = u(t)e^{rt}$ and prove that this function is a solution provided that $\ddot{u} = 0$. Conclude that the general solution is $x = (A + Bt)e^{rt}$ in this case.

A

Elementary Algebra

This appendix is for students who need to review elementary algebra. To save time, you should quickly glance through the sections, and do some of the problems. (Answers to all the problems in this appendix are given in the back of the book.) If you have difficulties with any of these problems, read the preceding theory carefully and then redo the problems. If you have considerable difficulties with this appendix, turn to a more elementary book on algebra.

A.1 Powers

You probably recall that instead of the product $3 \cdot 3 \cdot 3 \cdot 3$, we often write 3^4, that $\frac{1}{2} \cdot \frac{1}{2} \cdot \frac{1}{2} \cdot \frac{1}{2} \cdot \frac{1}{2}$ can be written as $\left(\frac{1}{2}\right)^5$, and that $(-10)^3 = (-10)(-10)(-10) = -1000$. If a is any number and n is any natural number, then a^n is defined by

$$a^n = \underbrace{a \cdot a \cdots a}_{n \text{ times}} \qquad (a \text{ occurs as a factor } n \text{ times}) \qquad \text{[A.1]}$$

In fact, a^n is called the *nth power of a*; a is the *base*, and n is the *exponent*. We have, for example, $a^1 = a$, $a^2 = a \cdot a$, $x^4 = x \cdot x \cdot x \cdot x$, and

$$\left(\frac{p}{q}\right)^5 = \frac{p}{q} \cdot \frac{p}{q} \cdot \frac{p}{q} \cdot \frac{p}{q} \cdot \frac{p}{q}$$

where $a = p/q$, and $n = 5$. A further example:

$$(r + 1)^3 = (r + 1) \cdot (r + 1) \cdot (r + 1) \qquad \text{(where } a = r + 1 \text{, and } n = 3)$$

The product $(r + 1) \cdot (r + 1) \cdot (r + 1)$ can be expanded further. See Example A.5 in Section A.3. We usually drop the multiplication sign if this is unlikely to create misunderstanding. For example, we write abc instead of $a \cdot b \cdot c$.

We define further

$$a^0 = 1 \qquad \text{for } a \neq 0 \qquad\qquad \text{[A.2]}$$

Thus, $5^0 = 1$, $(-16.2)^0 = 1$, and $(x \cdot y)^0 = 1$ (if $x \cdot y \neq 0$). But if $a = 0$, we do not assign a numerical value to a^0; the expression 0^0 is *undefined*.

We also need to define powers with negative exponents. What do we mean by 3^{-2}? It turns out that the sensible definition is to set 3^{-2} equal to $1/3^2 = 1/9$. In general, we define

$$a^{-n} = \frac{1}{a^n} \qquad\qquad \text{[A.3]}$$

whenever n is a natural number and $a \neq 0$. For example,

$$a^{-1} = \frac{1}{a}, \qquad 8^{-3} = \frac{1}{8^3} = \frac{1}{512}, \qquad (x^2 + 5)^{-16} = \frac{1}{(x^2 + 5)^{16}}$$

Note: Students often make serious mistakes by misplacing parentheses or by interpreting them incorrectly. The following examples highlight some common sources of confusion over the use of parentheses.

1. There is an important difference between $(-10)^2 = (-10)(-10) = 100$, and $-10^2 = -(10 \cdot 10) = -100$. The square of minus 10 is not equal to minus the square of 10.

2. Note that $(2x)^{-1} = 1/2x$, whereas $2x^{-1} = 2 \cdot (1/x) = 2/x$.

3. As we shall see in what follows, $1000 \cdot (1.08)^5$ is the amount you will have in your account after 5 years if you invest $1000 at 8% interest per year. Using a calculator, you quickly find that you will have approximately $1469.33. One student put $1000 \cdot (1.08)^5 = (1000 \cdot 1.08)^5 = (1080)^5$, which is a horrible mistake because it is 10^{12} (or a trillion) times the right answer.

4. The area of a square with sides of length x is x^2. What is the area if the sides are doubled? *Solution:* The area expands to $(2x)^2 = (2x)(2x) = 4x^2$, so it grows four times. If $(2x)^2$ is incorrectly replaced by $2x^2$, the result would only be a doubling of the area. (Use a drawing to prove that the latter is wrong.)

5. The volume of a ball with radius r is $\frac{4}{3}\pi r^3$. What is the volume if the radius is doubled? *Solution:* The new volume is $\frac{4}{3}\pi (2r)^3 = \frac{4}{3}\pi (2r)(2r)(2r) =$

$\frac{4}{3}\pi 8r^3 = 8(\frac{4}{3}\pi r^3)$, so the volume is eight times as large. (If we make the mistake of "simplifying" $(2r)^3$ to $2r^3$, the result would imply only a doubling of the volume; this should be contrary to common sense.)

Properties of Exponents

The following properties of exponents are very important and must be memorized.

General Properties of Exponents

$$a^n \cdot a^m = a^{n+m} \tag{a}$$

$$a^n / a^m = a^{n-m} \tag{b}$$

$$(a^n)^m = a^{n \cdot m} \tag{c}$$

$$(a \cdot b)^n = a^n \cdot b^n \tag{d}$$

$$\left(\frac{a}{b}\right)^n = \frac{a^n}{b^n} \tag{e}$$

[A.4]

Here $a^n \cdot a^m = a^{n+m}$ and $(a^n)^m = a^{n \cdot m}$ are the fundamental rules, because all the others follow from these two and from the definitions of powers. Here are some examples indicating why the rules in [A.4] are valid:

$$a^3 \cdot a^2 = (a \cdot a \cdot a) \cdot (a \cdot a) = a \cdot a \cdot a \cdot a \cdot a = a^5 = a^{3+2}$$

$$a^3 \div a^2 = \frac{a^3}{a^2} = \frac{a \cdot a \cdot a}{a \cdot a} = a = a^{3-2}$$

$$(a^2)^3 = (a^2)(a^2)(a^2) = a^{2+2+2} = a^6 = a^{2 \cdot 3}$$

$$(a \cdot b)^3 = (a \cdot b)(a \cdot b)(a \cdot b) = a \cdot a \cdot a \cdot b \cdot b \cdot b = a^3 b^3$$

$$\left(\frac{a}{b}\right)^4 = \left(\frac{a}{b}\right) \cdot \left(\frac{a}{b}\right) \cdot \left(\frac{a}{b}\right) \cdot \left(\frac{a}{b}\right) = \frac{a^4}{b^4}$$

Property [A.4](a) says that exponents with the same base are multiplied by adding the exponents. Try to formulate the other properties in words as well. Study the examples carefully.

The properties in [A.4] hold also if m and/or n are negative integers. For example,

$$a^{-3} \cdot a^5 = a^{-3+5} = a^2, \qquad (x \cdot y)^{-2} = x^{-2} \cdot y^{-2}$$

Also, using the rules for fractions (see Section A.5), we get

$$\left(\frac{a}{b}\right)^{-n} = \frac{a^{-n}}{b^{-n}} = \frac{1/a^n}{1/b^n} = \frac{(1/a^n) \cdot a^n \cdot b^n}{(1/b^n) \cdot a^n \cdot b^n} = \frac{b^n}{a^n} \tag{A.5}$$

This result can be applied whenever a fraction is raised to a negative power. For example,

$$\left(\frac{5}{4}\right)^{-3} = \frac{4^3}{5^3} = \frac{64}{125}$$

Example A.1

If $ab^2 = 2$, compute the following:

(a) a^2b^4 (b) $a^{-4}b^{-8}$ (c) $a^3b^6 + a^{-1}b^{-2}$

Solution

(a) $a^2b^4 = (ab^2)^2 = 2^2 = 4$

(b) $a^{-4}b^{-8} = (ab^2)^{-4} = 2^{-4} = 1/2^4 = 1/16$

(c) $a^3b^6 + a^{-1}b^{-2} = (ab^2)^3 + (ab^2)^{-1} = 2^3 + 2^{-1} = 8 + 1/2 = 17/2$

Note: An important motivation for introducing definitions [A.2] and [A.3] is that we would like the properties in [A.4] to be valid for all exponents. For example, consider the consequences of requiring [A.4](a) to be valid for $a^5 \cdot a^0$. We obtain $a^{5+0} = a^5$, so that $a^5 \cdot a^0 = a^5$, and hence we must choose $a^0 = 1$. If [A.4](a) is to be valid for $m = -n$, we must have $a^n \cdot a^{-n} = a^{n+(-n)} = a^0 = 1$. Because $a^n \cdot (1/a^n) = 1$, we *must* define a^{-n} by [A.3].

Compound Interest

Powers are used in practically every branch of applied mathematics, including economics. To illustrate their use, consider how they are needed to calculate compound interest.

Suppose you deposit $1000 in a bank at 8% interest per year.[1] After one year you will have earned $1000 \cdot 0.08 = $80 in interest, so the amount in your bank account at the end of the year will be $1080. This can be rewritten as

$$1000 + \frac{1000 \cdot 8}{100} = 1000\left(1 + \frac{8}{100}\right) = 1000 \cdot 1.08$$

If this new amount of $1000 \cdot 1.08$ is left in the bank for another year at an interest

---

[1] Remember that 1% means one in a hundred, or 0.01. To calculate, say, 23% of $4000, we write

$$\frac{4000 \cdot 23}{100} = 920 \qquad \text{or} \qquad 4000 \cdot 0.23 = 920$$

rate of 8%, after a second year, the amount will have grown to a total of

$$1000 \cdot 1.08 + \frac{(1000 \cdot 1.08) \cdot 8}{100} = 1000 \cdot 1.08 \left(1 + \frac{8}{100}\right) = 1000 \cdot (1.08)^2$$

Each year the amount will increase by the factor 1.08, and we see that at the end of t years, it will have grown to $\$1000 \cdot (1.08)^t$. If the original amount is $\$K$ and the interest rate is $p\%$ per year, by the end of the first year, the amount will be $K + K \cdot p/100 = K(1 + p/100)$ dollars. The growth factor per year is thus $1 + p/100$. In general, after t (whole) years, the original investment of $\$K$ will have grown to an amount

$$K \left(1 + \frac{p}{100}\right)^t$$

when the interest rate is $p\%$ per year (and interest is added to the capital every year—that is, compound interest).

If you see an expression like $(1.08)^t$, you should immediately be able to recognize it as the amount to which $\$1$ has grown after t years when the interest rate is 8% per year. What would be the interpretation of $(1.08)^0$? You deposit $\$1$ at 8% per year, and leave the amount for 0 years. Then you still have only $\$1$, because there has been no time to accumulate any interest, so that $(1.08)^0$ *must* equal 1.

Are Negative Exponents Useful?

How much money should you have deposited in the bank 5 years ago in order to have $\$1000$ today, given that the interest rate has been 8% per year over this period? If we call this amount x, the requirement is that $x \cdot (1.08)^5$ must equal $\$1000$, or that

$$x \cdot (1.08)^5 = 1000$$

The solution for x is

$$x = \frac{1000}{(1.08)^5} = 1000 \cdot (1.08)^{-5}$$

(which is approximately $\$681$). It turns out that $\$(1.08)^{-5}$ is what you should have deposited 5 years ago in order to have $\$1$ today, given the constant interest rate of 8%.

In general, $\$P(1 + p/100)^{-t}$ is what you should have deposited t years ago in order to have $\$P$ today if the interest rate has been $p\%$ every year.

Problems

1. Compute the following:

    a. 6^3 **b.** $\left(\frac{2}{3}\right)^2$ **c.** $(-1)^5$ **d.** $(0.3)^2$

    e. $(4.5 - 2.5)^4$ **f.** $2^2 \cdot 2^4$ **g.** $2^2 \cdot 3^2 \cdot 4^2$ **h.** $(2^2 \cdot 3^2)^3$

2. Express the following as powers:

   a. $15 \cdot 15 \cdot 15$ **b.** $\left(-\frac{1}{3}\right)\left(-\frac{1}{3}\right)\left(-\frac{1}{3}\right)$ **c.** $\frac{1}{10}$

   d. 0.0000001 **e.** $t\,t\,t\,t\,t\,t$ **f.** $(a-b)(a-b)(a-b)$

   g. $a\,a\,b\,b\,b\,b$ **h.** $(-a)(-a)(-a)$

3. Simplify:

   a. $a^4 \cdot a^2$ **b.** $(a^4)^2$ **c.** $x^6 \div x^3$ **d.** $\dfrac{b^2}{b^5}$

   e. $(x^2 y^3)^3$ **f.** $\dfrac{x^n \cdot x}{x^{n-1}}$ **g.** $\dfrac{z^2 \div z^5}{z^3 \cdot z^{-4}}$ **h.** $\dfrac{3^3 \cdot 3^{-2}}{3^2 \cdot 3^5}$

4. Compute the following:

   a. $2^0 \cdot 2^1 \cdot 2^2 \cdot 2^3$ **b.** $\left(\dfrac{4}{3}\right)^3$ **c.** $\dfrac{4^2 \cdot 6^2}{3^3 \cdot 2^3}$

   d. $x^5 x^4$ **e.** $y^5 y^4 y^3$ **f.** $(2xy)^3$

   g. $\dfrac{10^2 \cdot 10^{-4} \cdot 10^3}{10^0 \cdot 10^{-2} \cdot 10^5}$ **h.** $\dfrac{(k^2)^3 k^4}{(k^3)^2}$ **i.** $\dfrac{(x+1)^3 (x+1)^{-2}}{(x+1)^2 (x+1)^{-3}}$

5. Which of the following expressions are defined and what are their values?

   a. $\dfrac{0}{26}$ **b.** $\dfrac{2-x}{0}$ **c.** $0 \cdot 0$ **d.** 0^{25}

   e. $(0+2)^0$ **f.** 0^{-2} **g.** $\dfrac{(10)^0}{(0+1)^0}$ **h.** $\dfrac{(0+1)^0}{(0+2)^0}$

6. Find the solution x of the following equations:

   a. $5^2 \cdot 5^x = 5^7$ **b.** $10^x = 1$ **c.** $10^x \div 10^5 = 10^{-2}$

   d. $(25)^2 = 5^x$ **e.** $2^{10} - 2^2 \cdot 2^x = 0$ **f.** $(x+3)^2 = x^2 + 3^2$

7. Which of the following equalities are correct?

   a. $3^5 = 5^3$ **b.** $(5^2)^3 = 5^{2^3}$ **c.** $(3^3)^4 = (3^4)^3$

   d. $0^3 \cdot 4^0 = 0$ **e.** $(0^{-2})(-2)^0 = 1$ **f.** $(5+7)^2 = 5^2 + 7^2$

   g. $\dfrac{2x+4}{2} = x + 4$ **h.** $2(x - y) = x \cdot 2 - y \cdot 2$ **i.** $-x + y = y - x$

8. Which of the following equalities are true and which are false? Justify your answer. (Note: a and b are positive, m and n are integers.)

   a. $a^0 = 0$ **b.** $(a+b)^{-n} = 1/(a+b)^n$ **c.** $a^m \cdot a^m = a^{2m}$

   d. $a^m \cdot b^m = (ab)^{2m}$ **e.** $(a+b)^m = a^m + b^m$ **f.** $a^n \cdot b^m = (ab)^{n+m}$

9. Complete the following:

   a. $xy = 3 \Longrightarrow x^3 y^3 = \cdots$

   b. $ab = -2 \Longrightarrow (ab)^4 = \cdots$

   c. $a^2 = 4 \Longrightarrow (a^{20})^0 = \cdots$

d. n integer $\implies (-1)^{2n} = \cdots$

e. $x^{-1}y^{-1} = 3 \implies x^3 y^3 = \cdots$

f. $x^7 = 2 \implies (x^{-3})^6 (x^2)^2 = \cdots$

g. $\left(\frac{xy}{z}\right)^{-2} = 3 \implies \left(\frac{z}{xy}\right)^6 = \cdots$

h. $a^{-1}b^{-1}c^{-1} = 1/4 \implies (abc)^4 = \cdots$

10. Compute the following:

a. $(2x)^4$

b. $(2^{-1} - 4^{-1})^{-1}$

c. $\dfrac{24x^3 y^2 z^3}{4x^2 yz^2}$

d. $\left[-(-ab^3)^{-3}(a^6 b^6)^2\right]^3$

e. $\dfrac{a^5 \cdot a^3 \cdot a^{-2}}{a^{-3} \cdot a^6}$

f. $\left[\left(\dfrac{x}{2}\right)^3 \cdot \dfrac{8}{x^{-2}}\right]^{-3}$

g. $\dfrac{a^{2n+3}}{a^{2n-1}}$

h. $\dfrac{5^{pq+p} 5^{2p}}{5^{q+3p} 5^{pq}}$

11. Compute the following:

a. 13% of 150

b. 6% of 2400

c. 5.5% of 200

12. A box containing 5 balls costs \$8.50. If the balls are bought individually, they cost \$2.00 each. How much cheaper is it, in percentage terms, to buy the box as opposed to buying 5 individual balls?

13. Give economic interpretations for each of the following expressions and then use a calculator to find the approximate values:

a. $50 \cdot (1.11)^8$

b. $10\,000 \cdot (1.12)^{20}$

c. $5000 \cdot (1.07)^{-10}$

14. Compute 2^{10}. Is 2^{10} bigger than 10^3? Explain on the basis of your answer why 2^{30} is bigger than 10^9. Check by using a calculator.

A.2 Square Roots

So far the power a^x has been defined for integer exponents—that is, when $x = 0$, ± 1, ± 2, ± 3, ... If $a \geq 0$ and $x = 1/2$, then we define $a^x = a^{1/2}$ as equal to $\sqrt{a}$, the **square root** of a. Thus, $a^{1/2} = \sqrt{a}$ is defined as the nonnegative number that when multiplied by itself gives a. This definition makes sense because $a^{1/2} \cdot a^{1/2} = a^{1/2+1/2} = a^1 = a$. Note that a real number multiplied by itself must always be ≥ 0, whether that number is positive, negative, or zero. Therefore, we do not define square roots of negative numbers. For example, $(16)^{1/2} = \sqrt{16} = 4$ because $4 \cdot 4 = 16$, and $(1/9)^{1/2} = \sqrt{1/9} = 1/3$ because $(1/3)(1/3) = 1/9$, while $(-25)^{1/2} = \sqrt{-25}$ is not defined. Usually, the square root of a natural number is an irrational number. For example, $\sqrt{2} \approx 1.414$, $\sqrt{3} \approx 1.732$ are irrational numbers.

Properties [A.4](d) and (e) are also valid for square roots. For instance,

$$\sqrt{16 \cdot 25} = \sqrt{16} \cdot \sqrt{25} = 4 \cdot 5 = 20, \qquad \sqrt{\frac{9}{4}} = \frac{\sqrt{9}}{\sqrt{4}} = \frac{3}{2}$$

These can be formulated alternatively as

$$(16 \cdot 25)^{1/2} = (16)^{1/2} \cdot (25)^{1/2} = 4 \cdot 5 = 20, \qquad \left(\frac{9}{4}\right)^{1/2} = \frac{9^{1/2}}{4^{1/2}} = \frac{3}{2}$$

In general, if a and b are nonnegative numbers with $b \neq 0$, then

$$\text{(a)} \ \ \sqrt{a \cdot b} = \sqrt{a}\sqrt{b} \qquad \text{(b)} \ \ \sqrt{\frac{a}{b}} = \frac{\sqrt{a}}{\sqrt{b}} \qquad\qquad \text{[A.6]}$$

Note that the formulas in [A.6] are not valid if a or b or both are negative. For example, $\sqrt{(-1)(-1)} = \sqrt{1} = 1$, whereas $\sqrt{-1} \cdot \sqrt{-1}$ is not defined.

By using a calculator, we find that $\sqrt{2} \div \sqrt{3} \approx 0.816$. Without a calculator, the division $\sqrt{2} \div \sqrt{3} \approx 1.414 \div 1.732$ would be tedious. It becomes easier if we rationalize the denominator—that is, if we multiply both numerator and denominator by the same term in order to remove expressions with roots in the denominator. Thus,

$$\frac{\sqrt{2}}{\sqrt{3}} = \frac{\sqrt{2} \cdot \sqrt{3}}{\sqrt{3} \cdot \sqrt{3}} = \frac{\sqrt{2 \cdot 3}}{3} = \frac{\sqrt{6}}{3} \approx \frac{2.448}{3} = 0.816$$

Example A.2

Rationalize the denominators: (a) $\dfrac{5}{\sqrt{5}}$ (b) $\dfrac{(a+1)\sqrt{a}}{\sqrt{a+1}}$.

Solution

(a) $\dfrac{5}{\sqrt{5}} = \dfrac{5 \cdot \sqrt{5}}{\sqrt{5} \cdot \sqrt{5}} = \dfrac{5 \cdot \sqrt{5}}{5} = \sqrt{5}$

(b) $\dfrac{(a+1) \cdot \sqrt{a}}{\sqrt{a+1}} = \dfrac{(a+1) \cdot \sqrt{a} \cdot \sqrt{a+1}}{\sqrt{a+1} \cdot \sqrt{a+1}} = \dfrac{(a+1) \cdot \sqrt{a} \cdot \sqrt{a+1}}{a+1}$

$$= \sqrt{a} \cdot \sqrt{a+1} = \sqrt{a(a+1)}$$

Note: One of the most common errors committed in elementary algebra is to replace $\sqrt{a+b}$ by $\sqrt{a} + \sqrt{b}$. For example, $\sqrt{9+16} = \sqrt{25} = 5$, whereas $\sqrt{9} + \sqrt{16} = 3 + 4 = 7$. Thus, we have

$$\sqrt{a+b} \neq \sqrt{a} + \sqrt{b}$$

The following statistics illustrate just how frequently this error occurs. During an examination for a basic course in mathematics for economists, 43 out of 190 students simplified $\sqrt{1/16 + 1/25}$ incorrectly and claimed that it was equal to $1/4 + 1/5 = 9/20$. (The correct answer is $\sqrt{41/400} = \sqrt{41}/20$.)

Problems

1. Compute the following:

   a. $\sqrt{9}$ **b.** $\sqrt{1600}$ **c.** $(100)^{1/2}$ **d.** $\sqrt{9+16}$

   e. $(36)^{-1/2}$ **f.** $(0.49)^{1/2}$ **g.** $\sqrt{0.01}$ **h.** $\sqrt{\dfrac{1}{25}}$

2. Solve for x:

   a. $\sqrt{x} = 9$ **b.** $\sqrt{x} \cdot \sqrt{4} = 4$ **c.** $\sqrt{x+2} = 25$

   d. $\sqrt{3} \cdot \sqrt{5} = \sqrt{x}$ **e.** $2^{2-x} = 8$ **f.** $2^x - 2^{x-1} = 4$

3. Rationalize the denominator and simplify:

   a. $\dfrac{6}{\sqrt{7}}$ **b.** $\dfrac{\sqrt{32}}{\sqrt{2}}$ **c.** $\dfrac{\sqrt{3}}{4\sqrt{2}}$ **d.** $\dfrac{\sqrt{54}-\sqrt{24}}{\sqrt{6}}$

   e. $\dfrac{2}{\sqrt{3}\sqrt{8}}$ **f.** $\dfrac{4}{\sqrt{2y}}$ **g.** $\dfrac{x}{\sqrt{2x}}$ **h.** $\dfrac{x(\sqrt{x}+1)}{\sqrt{x}}$

4. Decide whether each "?" should be replaced by $=$ or $\neq$. Justify your answer. (*Note*: a and b are positive.)

   a. $\sqrt{25 \cdot 16}$? $\sqrt{25} \cdot \sqrt{16}$ **b.** $\sqrt{25+16}$? $\sqrt{25}+\sqrt{16}$

   c. $(a+b)^{1/2}$? $a^{1/2}+b^{1/2}$ **d.** $(a+b)^{-1/2}$? $(\sqrt{a+b})^{-1}$

A.3 Rules of Algebra

You are probably already familiar with the most common rules of algebra. Nevertheless, it may be useful at this stage to recall those that are most important. If a, b, and c are arbitrary real numbers, then:

(a) $a+b = b+a$	(g) $1 \cdot a = a$
(b) $(a+b)+c = a+(b+c)$	(h) $aa^{-1} = 1$ for $a \neq 0$
(c) $a+0 = a$	(i) $(-a)b = a(-b) = -ab$
(d) $a+(-a) = 0$	(j) $(-a)(-b) = ab$
(e) $ab = ba$	(k) $a(b+c) = ab+ac$
(f) $(ab)c = a(bc)$	(l) $(a+b)c = ac+bc$

[A.7]

These rules are used in the following examples:

$$5 + x^2 = x^2 + 5$$
$$x\tfrac{1}{3} = \tfrac{1}{3}x$$
$$(-3)5 = 3(-5) = -(3 \cdot 5) = -15$$
$$3x(y+2z) = 3xy + 6xz$$

$$(a+2b)+3b = a+(2b+3b) = a+5b$$
$$(xy)y^{-1} = x(yy^{-1}) = x$$
$$(-6)(-20) = 120$$
$$(t^2+2t)4t^3 = t^2 4t^3 + 2t4t^3 = 4t^5 + 8t^4$$

Rules [A.7](k) and (l) can be combined with the others in several ways to give:

$$\text{(m)} \quad a(b - c) = a[b + (-c)] = ab + a(-c) = ab - ac$$

$$\text{(n)} \quad x(a + b - c + d) = xa + xb - xc + xd \qquad \text{[A.8]}$$

$$(a + b)(c + d) = ac + ad + bc + bd$$

A geometric argument for [A.8] (0) requires considering areas in Fig. A.1.

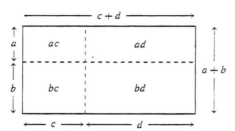

FIGURE A.1

We often encounter parentheses with a minus sign in front. Because $(-1)x = -x$, using (n) gives

$$-(a + b - c + d) = -a - b + c - d \qquad \text{[A.9]}$$

In words: *When removing a pair of parentheses with a minus in front, change the signs of all the terms within the parentheses—do not leave any out.*

Some Important Identities

Three special cases of equation [A.8] are so important that you should memorize them.

$$(a + b)^2 = a^2 + 2ab + b^2 \qquad \text{[A.10]}$$

$$(a - b)^2 = a^2 - 2ab + b^2 \qquad \text{[A.11]}$$

$$(a + b)(a - b) = a^2 - b^2 \qquad \text{[A.12]}$$

Formula [A.12] is often called the *difference-of-squares formula*. (Proof of [A.10]: $(a + b)^2$ means $(a + b)(a + b)$, which according to [A.8] is equal to $aa + ab + ba + bb = a^2 + 2ab + b^2$. Prove [A.11] and [A.12] yourself.)

Example A.3

Use [A.10] to [A.12] to expand each of the following:

(a) $(2x + 3y)^2$ (b) $\left(1 - \frac{1}{2}z\right)^2$ (c) $\left(\sqrt{3} + \sqrt{6}\right)\left(\sqrt{3} - \sqrt{6}\right)$

Solution

(a) $(2x + 3y)^2 = (2x)^2 + 2 \cdot 2x \cdot 3y + (3y)^2 = 4x^2 + 12xy + 9y^2$

(b) $\left(1 - \frac{1}{2}z\right)^2 = 1^2 - 2 \cdot 1 \cdot \frac{1}{2}z + \left(\frac{1}{2}z\right)^2 = 1 - z + \frac{1}{4}z^2$

(c) $\left(\sqrt{3} + \sqrt{6}\right)\left(\sqrt{3} - \sqrt{6}\right) = \left(\sqrt{3}\right)^2 - \left(\sqrt{6}\right)^2 = 3 - 6 = -3$

Example A.4

Expand $\left(\sqrt{x+1} - \sqrt{x+1}\right)^2$.

Solution   Set $a = \sqrt{x} + 1$ and $b = \sqrt{x+1}$. Then using [A.11] and [A.10] gives

$$
\begin{aligned}
\left[(\sqrt{x}+1) - \sqrt{x+1}\right]^2 &= (a-b)^2 = a^2 - 2ab + b^2 \\
&= (\sqrt{x}+1)^2 - 2(\sqrt{x}+1)\sqrt{x+1} + (\sqrt{x+1})^2 \\
&= x + 2\sqrt{x} + 1 - 2\sqrt{x}\sqrt{x+1} - 2\sqrt{x+1} + x + 1 \\
&= 2\left(x + 1 + \sqrt{x} - \sqrt{x}\sqrt{x+1} - \sqrt{x+1}\right)
\end{aligned}
$$

Alternatively, set $\left(\sqrt{x} + 1 - \sqrt{x+1}\right)^2 = (a+b)^2$, where $a = \sqrt{x}$ and $b = 1 - \sqrt{x+1}$; then use [A.10] and [A.12]. Do you get the same solution?

In [A.8], we multiplied two factors, $(a+b)$ and $(c+d)$. How do we compute such products when there are several factors? Consider the following:

$$
\begin{aligned}
(a+b)(c+d)(e+f) &= \left[(a+b)(c+d)\right](e+f) \\
&= \left(ac + ad + bc + bd\right)(e+f) \\
&= (ac + ad + bc + bd)e + (ac + ad + bc + bd)f \\
&= ace + ade + bce + bde + acf + adf + bcf + bdf
\end{aligned}
$$

Alternatively, write $(a+b)(c+d)(e+f) = (a+b)\left[(c+d)(e+f)\right]$, then expand and show that you get the same answer.

Example A.5

Compute $(r+1)^3$.

Solution

$$(r+1)^3 = \left[(r+1)(r+1)\right](r+1) = (r^2 + 2r + 1)(r+1) = r^3 + 3r^2 + 3r + 1$$

Let us illustrate this last result with an example. A ball with radius r meters has a volume of $\frac{4}{3}\pi r^3$. By how much does the volume expand if the radius increases by 1 meter? The solution is

$$\frac{4}{3}\pi (r+1)^3 - \frac{4}{3}\pi r^3 = \frac{4}{3}\pi (r^3 + 3r^2 + 3r + 1) - \frac{4}{3}\pi r^3 = \frac{4}{3}\pi (3r^2 + 3r + 1)$$

Algebraic Expressions

Expressions such as $3xy - 5x^2y^3 + 2xy + 6y^3x^2 - 3x + 5yx$ are called *algebraic expressions*. We call $3xy$, $-5x^2y^3$, $2xy$, $6y^3x^2$, $-3x$, and $5yx$ the *terms* in the expression that is formed by adding all the terms together. The numbers 3, -5, 2, 6, -3, and 5 are the *numerical coefficients* of the terms. Two terms where only the numerical coefficients are different, such as $-5x^2y^3$ and $6y^3x^2$, are called *terms of the same type*. In order to simplify expressions, we usually collect terms of the same type. Then within each term, we usually put numerical coefficients first and place the letters in alphabetical order. Thus,

$$3xy - 5x^2y^3 + 2xy + 6y^3x^2 - 3x + 5yx = x^2y^3 + 10xy - 3x$$

Example A.6
Expand and simplify:

(a) $(2pq - 3p^2)(p + 2q) - (q^2 - 2pq)(2p - q)$
(b) $(xy - 3y^2)(x^2y - x^3 + 3xy^2)$

Solution

(a) $(2pq - 3p^2)(p + 2q) - (q^2 - 2pq)(2p - q)$

$$= 2pqp + 2pq2q - 3p^3 - 6p^2q - (q^2 2p - q^3 - 4pqp + 2pq^2)$$

$$= 2p^2q + 4pq^2 - 3p^3 - 6p^2q - 2pq^2 + q^3 + 4p^2q - 2pq^2$$

$$= -3p^3 + q^3$$

(b) $(xy - 3y^2)(x^2y - x^3 + 3xy^2)$

$$= xyx^2y - xyx^3 + xy3xy^2 - 3y^2x^2y + 3y^2x^3 - 3y^2 3xy^2$$

$$= x^3y^2 - x^4y + 3x^2y^3 - 3x^2y^3 + 3x^3y^2 - 9xy^4$$

$$= -x^4y + 4x^3y^2 - 9xy^4$$

Problems

1. Simplify the following:

   a. $-3 + (-4) - (-8)$ **b.** $(-3)(2-4)$ **c.** $(-3)(-12)\left(-\frac{1}{2}\right)$
   d. $-3[4 - (-2)]$ **e.** $-3(-x - 4)$ **f.** $(5x - 3y)9$

g. $2x \left(\dfrac{3}{2x} \right)$ **h.** $0 \cdot (1 - x)$ **i.** $-7x \dfrac{2}{14x}$

In Problems 2–6, expand and collect terms.

2. a. $5a^2 - 3b - (-a^2 - b) - 3(a^2 + b)$
   b. $-x(2x - y) + y(1 - x) + 3(x + y)$
   c. $12t^2 - 3t + 16 - 2(6t^2 - 2t + 8)$
   d. $r^3 - 3r^2s + 3rs^2 + s^3 - (-s^3 - r^3 + 3r^2s)$

3. a. $-3(n^2 - 2n + 3)$ **b.** $x^2(1 + x^3)$
   c. $(4n - 3)(n - 2)$ **d.** $6a^2b(5ab - 3ab^2)$
   e. $(a^2b - ab^2)(a + b)$ **f.** $(x - y)(x - 2y)(x - 3y)$

4. a. $a(a - 1)$ **b.** $(x - 3)(x + 7)$ **c.** $-\sqrt{3}\left(\sqrt{3} - \sqrt{6}\right)$
   d. $(1 - \sqrt{2})^2$ **e.** $(x - 1)^3$ **f.** $(1 - b^2)(1 + b^2)$
   g. $(1 + x + x^2 + x^3)(1 - x)$ **h.** $(1 + x)^4$

5. a. $3(x - y) + (3y - x)$ **b.** $(a - 2b)^2$
   c. $\left(\tfrac{1}{2}x - \tfrac{1}{3}y\right)\left(\tfrac{1}{2}x + \tfrac{1}{3}y\right)$ **d.** $2x^2y - 3x - (2 + 3x^2y)$
   e. $(x + a)(x + b)$ **f.** $(x - 2y)^3$

6. a. $(2t - 1)(t^2 - 2t + 1)$ **b.** $(a + 1)^2 + (a - 1)^2 - 2(a + 1)(a - 1)$
   c. $(x + y + z)^2$ **d.** $(x + y + z)^2 - (x - y - z)^2$

7. Use [A.10] to [A.12] to expand each of the following:

   a. $(3x + 2y)^2$ **b.** $\left(\sqrt{3} + \sqrt{2}\right)^2$
   c. $(-3u + 8v)^2$ **d.** $(u - 5v)(u + 5v)$

8. Compute $(1000)^2/[(252)^2 - (248)^2]$ without using a calculator.

9. Expand and collect terms:

   a. $(x^2 - y^2)^2$ **b.** $\dfrac{1}{\left(\sqrt{5} + \sqrt{3}\right)\left(\sqrt{5} - \sqrt{3}\right)}$ **c.** $(a - b + 1)^2$
   d. $(\sqrt{a} - \sqrt{b})^2$ **e.** $\left[(\sqrt{2} + 1)(\sqrt{2} - 1)\right]^{100}$ **f.** $(n - 1)^4$

10. Expand and collect terms:

   a. $(ax + b)(cx + d)$ **b.** $(2 - t^2)(2 + t^2)$
   c. $(a + b + c)^2$ **d.** $(a^5 - b^5)(a^5 + b^5)$
   e. $(\sqrt{3} + \sqrt{5} + \sqrt{7})(\sqrt{3} + \sqrt{5} - \sqrt{7})$ **f.** $(u - v)^2(u + v)^2$

11. Use the diagrams in Fig. A.2 to give a geometric interpretation of [A.10] and [A.11].

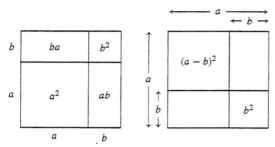

FIGURE A.2

Harder Problems

12. Show that

$$(a - b)(a + b) = a^2 - b^2$$
$$(a - b)(a^2 + ab + b^2) = a^3 - b^3$$
$$(a - b)(a^3 + a^2b + ab^2 + b^3) = a^4 - b^4$$
$$(a - b)(a^4 + a^3b + a^2b^2 + ab^3 + b^4) = a^5 - b^5$$

Guess the result of the division $(a^{10} - b^{10})/(a - b)$, and try to verify your guess.

A.4 Factors

When we write $49 = 7 \cdot 7$, $125 = 5 \cdot 5 \cdot 5$, or $672 = 2 \cdot 3 \cdot 4 \cdot 4 \cdot 7$, we say that we have *factored* these numbers. Algebraic expressions can often be factored in a similar way. For example,

$$6x^2y = 2 \cdot 3 \cdot x \cdot x \cdot y \quad \text{and} \quad 5x^2y^3 - 15xy^2 = 5 \cdot x \cdot y \cdot y(xy - 3)$$

Example A.7

Factor each of the following:

(a) $5x^2 + 15x$ (b) $-18b^2 + 9ab$

(c) $K(1 + r) + K(1 + r)r$ (d) $\delta L^{-3} + (1 - \delta)L^{-2}$

Solution

(a) $5x^2 + 15x = 5x(x + 3)$

(b) $-18b^2 + 9ab = 9ab - 18b^2 = 3 \cdot 3b(a - 2b)$

(c) $K(1 + r) + K(1 + r)r = K(1 + r)(1 + r) = K(1 + r)^2$

(d) $\delta L^{-3} + (1 - \delta)L^{-2} = L^{-3}[\delta + (1 - \delta)L]$

Formulas [A.10] to [A.12] can often be used "in reverse" for factorization. They sometimes enable us to factor expressions that otherwise appear to have no factors.

Example A.8

Factor each of the following:

(a) $16a^2 - 1$ (b) $x^2y^2 - 25z^2$ (c) $4u^2 + 8u + 4$ (d) $x^2 - x + \frac{1}{4}$

Solution

(a) $16a^2 - 1 = (4a + 1)(4a - 1)$ $\qquad$ (apply [A.12])

(b) $x^2y^2 - 25z^2 = (xy + 5z)(xy - 5z)$ $\qquad$ (apply [A.12])

(c) $4u^2 + 8u + 4 = (2u + 2)^2 = 4(u + 1)^2$ $\qquad$ (apply [A.10])

(d) $x^2 - x + \frac{1}{4} = (x - \frac{1}{2})^2$ $\qquad$ (apply [A.11])

Usually, it is easy to verify that an algebraic expression has been factored correctly by simply multiplying the factors. For example, we check that

$$x^2 - (a + b)x + ab = (x - a)(x - b) \qquad [A.13]$$

by expanding $(x - a)(x - b)$. Formula [A.13] itself is important because it can often be used to factor quadratic expressions.

Example A.9

Factor (if possible) the following:

(a) $x^2 - 8x + 15$ (b) $x^2 + 5x + 6$ (c) $x^2 + 2x + 2$

Solution

(a) Comparing this with [A.13], we see that making $x^2 - 8x + 15$ equal to $(x - a)(x - b)$ requires that $a + b = 8$ and $ab = 15$. We need to find two numbers, a and b, whose sum is 8 and whose product is 15. Such numbers are $a = 3$ and $b = 5$ (or $a = 5$ and $b = 3$), so the factorization is

$$x^2 - 8x + 15 = (x - 3)(x - 5)$$

(b) In a similar way, we find that $x^2 + 5x + 6 = (x + 2)(x + 3)$.

(c) In this case, we need two numbers, a and b, whose sum is -2 and whose product is 2. Because there is no pair of real numbers with these properties, factorization is not possible.

Section A.8 will investigate factorization of expressions like $ax^2 + bx + c$ more systematically.

We conclude this section with some examples where a suitable grouping of terms is the crucial point.

Example A.10

Try to factor the following:

(a) $x^2 + 2xy^2 + xy + 2y^3$ (b) $a^3 - 4b^3 - 4ab^2 + a^2b$

Solution

(a) This is quite simple:

$$\begin{aligned}
x^2 + 2xy^2 + xy + 2y^3 &= (x^2 + 2xy^2) + (xy + 2y^3) \\
&= (x + 2y^2)x + (x + 2y^2)y \\
&= (x + 2y^2)(x + y)
\end{aligned}$$

(b) This demands some careful rearrangement of terms:

$$\begin{aligned}
a^3 - 4b^3 - 4ab^2 + a^2b &= a^3 - 4ab^2 + a^2b - 4b^3 \\
&= a(a^2 - 4b^2) + b(a^2 - 4b^2) \\
&= (a + b)(a^2 - 4b^2) \\
&= (a + b)(a + 2b)(a - 2b)
\end{aligned}$$

Note: If we write $15 + 25 = 3 \cdot 5 + 5 \cdot 5$, then we have factored 15 and 25, but *not* the sum $15 + 25$. Correspondingly, $9x^2 - 25y^2 = 3 \cdot 3 \cdot x \cdot x - 5 \cdot 5 \cdot y \cdot y$ is *not* a factorization of $9x^2 - 25y^2$. (The correct factorization is $9x^2 - 25y^2 = (3x - 5y)(3x + 5y)$.)

Problems

In Problems 1 to 3, factor the given expressions.

1. a. $28a^2b^3$ **b.** $4x + 8y - 24z$ **c.** $2x^2 - 6xy$
     d. $4a^2b^3 + 6a^3b^2$ **e.** $7x^2 - 49xy$ **f.** $5xy^2 - 45x^3y^2$
     g. $16 - b^2$ **h.** $3x^2 - 12$

2. **a.** $x^2 - 4x + 4$ **b.** $4t^2 s - 8ts^2$

      c. $16a^2 + 16ab + 4b^2$ **d.** $5x^4 - 10x^2 y^2$

3. **a.** $K^3 - K^2 L$ **b.** $KL^3 + KL$ **c.** $L^2 - K^2$

      d. $K^2 - 2KL + L^2$ **e.** $K^3 L - 4K^2 L^2 + 4KL^3$ **f.** $K^{-\rho} - K^{-2\rho}$

4. Use the method in Example A.9 to factor the following:

      a. $x^2 + 5x + 6$ **b.** $x^2 + 2x - 15$ **c.** $p^2 - 3p + 2$

      d. $2q^2 + 16q - 66$ **e.** $3x^2 - 12x - 15$ **f.** $-p^2 - p + 20$

5. Factor (see Example A.10) the following:

      a. $5(x + 2y) + a(x + 2y)$ **b.** $(a + b)c - d(a + b)$

      c. $ax + ay + 2x + 2y$ **d.** $2x^2 - 5yz + 10xz - xy$

      e. $p^2 - q^2 + p - q$ **f.** $u^3 + v^3 - u^2 v - v^2 u$

6. Factor the following:

      a. $p + prt$ **b.** $\pi r^2 + 2\pi rh$ **c.** $\frac{1}{4}mnr - \frac{1}{4}mn$

      d. $PR^2 - PQR$ **e.** $(1 + r)^2 + (1 + r)^3$ **f.** $\frac{1}{2}gh^4 - \frac{1}{8}g^3 h^2$

Harder Problems

7. Factor the following:

      a. $a^{2n} - 25$ **b.** $(a + b)^2 - c^2$ **c.** $(a + b + c)^2 - (a + b)^2$

      d. $x^4 - y^4$ **e.** $81 - c^4$ **f.** $x^6 - y^6$

      (Hint for (d): $x^4 - y^4 = (x^2 + y^2)(x^2 - y^2)$ and so on.)

A.5 Fractions

Recall that

$$a \div b = \frac{a}{b} \quad \begin{matrix} \leftarrow \text{numerator} \\ \leftarrow \text{denominator} \end{matrix}$$

For example, $5 \div 8 = \frac{5}{8}$. For typographical reasons, we often write 5/8 instead of $\frac{5}{8}$. Of course, $5 \div 8 = 0.625$, and $5/8 = 0.625$. In this case, we have written the fraction as a decimal number. Fraction 5/8 is called a *proper fraction* because 5 is less than 8. Fraction 19/8 is an *improper fraction* because the numerator is larger than (or equal to) the denominator. An improper fraction can be written as a *mixed number*:

$$\tfrac{19}{8} = 2 + \tfrac{3}{8} = 2\tfrac{3}{8}$$

Note: $2\frac{3}{8}$ means 2 *plus* 3/8. On the other hand, $2 \cdot \frac{3}{8} = \frac{2 \cdot 3}{8} = \frac{3}{4}$ (by the rules reviewed in what follows). Note, however, that $2\frac{x}{8}$ means $2 \cdot \frac{x}{8}$; the notation $\frac{2x}{8}$

or $2x/8$ is obviously preferable in this case. Indeed, $\frac{19}{8}$ is probably better than $2\frac{3}{8}$ because it also helps avoid ambiguity.

Note that $0 \div 5 = 0$. In general, $0 \div b = 0$ whatever the number b, except if $b = 0$. On the other hand, $b \div 0$ is not defined for any number b.

$$\frac{0}{b} = 0 \quad (b \neq 0), \qquad \frac{b}{0} \text{ is not defined}$$

Reducing and Extending Fractions

You should know that

$$\frac{a \cdot c}{b \cdot c} = \frac{a}{b} \quad (b \neq 0 \text{ and } c \neq 0) \tag{A.14}$$

In general, we reduce fractions by factoring the numerator and the denominator and canceling *common factors* (that is, dividing both the numerator and denominator by the same nonzero quantity). Thus:

(a) $\dfrac{189}{135} = \dfrac{3 \cdot 3 \cdot 3 \cdot 7}{3 \cdot 3 \cdot 3 \cdot 5} = \dfrac{7}{5}$

(b) $\dfrac{5x^2yz^3}{25xy^2z} = \dfrac{5 \cdot x \cdot x \cdot x \cdot z \cdot z \cdot z}{5 \cdot 5 \cdot x \cdot x \cdot y \cdot z} = \dfrac{xz^2}{5y}$

(c) $\dfrac{x^2 + xy}{x^2 - y^2} = \dfrac{x(x + y)}{(x - y)(x + y)} = \dfrac{x}{x - y}$

(d) $\dfrac{4 - 4a + a^2}{a^2 - 4} = \dfrac{(a - 2)(a - 2)}{(a - 2)(a + 2)} = \dfrac{a - 2}{a + 2}$

When we use property [A.14] in reverse, we are *expanding* the fraction:

$$\frac{5}{8} = \frac{5 \cdot 125}{8 \cdot 125} = \frac{625}{1000} = 0.625$$

$$\frac{1}{\sqrt{5} + \sqrt{3}} = \frac{\sqrt{5} - \sqrt{3}}{(\sqrt{5} + \sqrt{3})(\sqrt{5} - \sqrt{3})} = \frac{\sqrt{5} - \sqrt{3}}{5 - 3} = \frac{1}{2}(\sqrt{5} - \sqrt{3})$$

Note the trick we used in the last example to make the denominator rational.

When we simplify fractions, only common factors can be removed. Two frequently occurring errors are illustrated in the following examples:

$$\textbf{Wrong!} \quad \rightarrow \quad \frac{2x + 3y}{xy} = \frac{2 + 3x}{x} = \frac{2 + 3}{1} = 5$$

and

$$\textbf{Wrong!} \quad \rightarrow \quad \frac{x - 1}{x^2 - 1} = \frac{x - 1}{(x - 1)(x + 1)} = \frac{0}{x + 1} = 0$$

In the first case, we cannot simplify the expression because the numerator and the denominator do not have common factors. In the second case, the correct way of reducing the fraction gives the answer $1/(x+1)$.

Sign Rules

The following sign rules are important:

$$\frac{-a}{-b} = \frac{(-a) \cdot (-1)}{(-b) \cdot (-1)} = \frac{a}{b} \quad \text{and} \quad -\frac{a}{b} = (-1)\frac{a}{b} = \frac{(-1)a}{b} = \frac{-a}{b} \quad \text{[A.15]}$$

These equalities are derived from [A.14], the equation $-x = (-1)x$, and property [A.19], which follows.

Addition of Fractions

Here are three basic rules for adding fractions:

$$\frac{a}{c} + \frac{b}{c} = \frac{a+b}{c} \qquad \text{[A.16]}$$

$$\frac{a}{b} + \frac{c}{d} = \frac{a \cdot d + b \cdot c}{b \cdot d} \qquad \text{[A.17]}$$

$$a + \frac{c}{d} = \frac{a \cdot d + c}{d} \qquad \text{[A.18]}$$

Because $a/1 = a$, [A.18] follows from [A.17] by letting $b = 1$. Formula [A.17] follows from [A.14] and [A.16]:

$$\frac{a}{b} + \frac{c}{d} = \frac{a \cdot d}{b \cdot d} + \frac{c \cdot b}{d \cdot b} = \frac{a \cdot d + b \cdot c}{b \cdot d}$$

Example A.11

(a) $\dfrac{5}{3} + \dfrac{13}{3} = \dfrac{18}{3} = 6$

(b) $\dfrac{3}{5} + \dfrac{1}{6} = \dfrac{3 \cdot 6 + 5 \cdot 1}{5 \cdot 6} = \dfrac{23}{30}$

(c) $\dfrac{a-1}{6a} + \dfrac{a}{6a} + \dfrac{1}{6a} = \dfrac{a-1+a+1}{6a} = \dfrac{2a}{6a} = \dfrac{2 \cdot a}{2 \cdot 3 \cdot a} = \dfrac{1}{3}$

Combining [A.16], [A.17], and [A.18] with [A.15] gives

(d) $\dfrac{a}{c} + \dfrac{b}{c} - \dfrac{d}{c} = \dfrac{a+b-d}{c}$

(e) $\dfrac{a}{b} - \dfrac{c}{d} + \dfrac{e}{f} = \dfrac{adf}{bdf} - \dfrac{cbf}{bdf} + \dfrac{ebd}{bdf} = \dfrac{adf - cbf + ebd}{bdf}$

If the numbers b, d, and f have common factors, the computation carried out in (e) involves unnecessarily large numbers. We can simplify the process by first finding the least common denominator (LCD) of the fractions. To do so, factor each denominator completely; the LCD is the product of all the distinct factors that appear in any denominator, each raised to the highest power to which it gets raised in any denominator. The use of the LCD is demonstrated in the following example.

Example A.12

Simplify the following:

$$\text{(a)} \quad \frac{1}{2} - \frac{1}{3} + \frac{1}{6} \qquad \text{(b)} \quad \frac{2+a}{a^2b} + \frac{1-b}{ab^2} - \frac{2b}{a^2b^2}$$

$$\text{(c)} \quad \frac{x-y}{x+y} - \frac{x}{x-y} + \frac{3xy}{x^2-y^2}$$

Solution

(a) The LCD is 6 and so

$$\frac{1}{2} - \frac{1}{3} + \frac{1}{6} = \frac{1 \cdot 3}{2 \cdot 3} - \frac{1 \cdot 2}{2 \cdot 3} + \frac{1}{2 \cdot 3} = \frac{3 - 2 + 1}{6} = \frac{2}{6} = \frac{1}{3}$$

(b) The LCD is a^2b^2 and so

$$\frac{2+a}{a^2b} + \frac{1-b}{ab^2} - \frac{2b}{a^2b^2} = \frac{(2+a)b}{a^2b^2} + \frac{(1-b)a}{a^2b^2} - \frac{2b}{a^2b^2}$$

$$= \frac{2b + ab + a - ba - 2b}{a^2b^2} = \frac{a}{a^2b^2} = \frac{1}{ab^2}$$

(c) The LCD is $(x+y)(x-y)$ and so

$$\frac{x-y}{x+y} - \frac{x}{x-y} + \frac{3xy}{x^2-y^2} = \frac{(x-y)(x-y)}{(x-y)(x+y)} - \frac{x(x+y)}{(x-y)(x+y)} + \frac{3xy}{(x-y)(x+y)}$$

$$= \frac{x^2 - 2xy + y^2 - x^2 - xy + 3xy}{(x-y)(x+y)} = \frac{y^2}{x^2-y^2}$$

An Important Note

What do we mean by $1 - \frac{5-3}{2}$? It means that from the number 1, we subtract the number $\frac{5-3}{2} = \frac{2}{2} = 1$. Therefore, $1 - \frac{5-3}{2} = 0$. Alternatively,

$$1 - \frac{5-3}{2} = \frac{2}{2} - \frac{(5-3)}{2} = \frac{2-(5-3)}{2} = \frac{2-5+3}{2} = \frac{0}{2} = 0$$

In the same way,

$$\frac{2+b}{ab^2} - \frac{a-2}{a^2b}$$

means that we subtract

$$\frac{a-2}{a^2b} \quad \text{from} \quad \frac{2+b}{ab^2}$$

$$\frac{2+b}{ab^2} - \frac{a-2}{a^2b} = \frac{(2+b)a}{a^2b^2} - \frac{(a-2)b}{a^2b^2} = \frac{(2+b)a-(a-2)b}{a^2b^2} = \frac{2(a+b)}{a^2b^2}$$

It is a good idea first to enclose in parentheses the numerators of the fractions that are being subtracted.

Example A.13

Simplify the expression

$$\frac{x-1}{x+1} - \frac{1-x}{x-1} - \frac{-1+4x}{2(x+1)}$$

Solution

$$\frac{x-1}{x+1} - \frac{1-x}{x-1} - \frac{-1+4x}{2(x+1)} = \frac{(x-1)}{x+1} - \frac{(1-x)}{x-1} - \frac{(-1+4x)}{2(x+1)}$$

$$= \frac{2(x-1)^2 - 2(1-x)(x+1) - (-1+4x)(x-1)}{2(x+1)(x-1)}$$

$$= \frac{2(x^2-2x+1) - 2(1-x^2) - (4x^2-5x+1)}{2(x+1)(x-1)}$$

$$= \frac{(x-1)}{2(x+1)(x-1)} = \frac{1}{2(x+1)}$$

Multiplication and Division of Fractions

Here are three basic rules for multiplication and division of fractions:

$$a \cdot \frac{b}{c} = \frac{a \cdot b}{c} \qquad \text{[A.19]}$$

$$\frac{a}{b} \cdot \frac{c}{d} = \frac{a \cdot c}{b \cdot d} \qquad \text{[A.20]}$$

$$\frac{a}{b} \div \frac{c}{d} = \frac{a}{b} \cdot \frac{d}{c} = \frac{a \cdot d}{b \cdot c} \qquad \text{[A.21]}$$

Example of [A.19]:

$$3 \cdot \frac{b}{c} = \frac{b}{c} + \frac{b}{c} + \frac{b}{c} = \frac{b+b+b}{c} = \frac{3b}{c}$$

We prove [A.21] by writing $(a/b) \div (c/d)$ as a ratio of fractions:

$$\frac{a}{b} \div \frac{c}{d} = \frac{\frac{a}{b}}{\frac{c}{d}} = \frac{b \cdot d \cdot \frac{a}{b}}{b \cdot d \cdot \frac{c}{d}} = \frac{\frac{\cancel{b} \cdot d \cdot a}{\cancel{b}}}{\frac{b \cdot \cancel{d} \cdot c}{\cancel{d}}} = \frac{d \cdot a}{b \cdot c} = \frac{a \cdot d}{b \cdot c} = \frac{a}{b} \cdot \frac{d}{c}$$

Example A.14

Simplify the following:

(a) $6 \cdot \dfrac{5}{13}$ (b) $\dfrac{4}{7} \cdot \dfrac{5}{8}$ (c) $\dfrac{3}{8} \div \dfrac{6}{14}$ (d) $2xy^2 \cdot \dfrac{x + 2y}{3xy^3}$

(e) $\dfrac{1 - 36x^2}{18x + 9y} \div \dfrac{(2 - 12x)(1 + 6x)}{16x^2 - 4y^2}$ (f) $\dfrac{\dfrac{a}{2} - \dfrac{a}{5}}{\dfrac{a}{5} - \dfrac{a}{6}}$

Solution

(a) $6 \cdot \dfrac{5}{13} = \dfrac{6 \cdot 5}{13} = \dfrac{30}{13} = 2\dfrac{4}{13}$

(b) $\dfrac{4}{7} \cdot \dfrac{5}{8} = \dfrac{4 \cdot 5}{7 \cdot 8} = \dfrac{\cancel{4} \cdot 5}{7 \cdot 2 \cdot \cancel{4}} = \dfrac{5}{14}$

(c) $\dfrac{3}{8} \div \dfrac{6}{14} = \dfrac{3}{8} \cdot \dfrac{14}{6} = \dfrac{\cancel{3} \cdot \cancel{2} \cdot 7}{\cancel{2} \cdot 2 \cdot 2 \cdot 2 \cdot \cancel{3}} = \dfrac{7}{8}$

(d) $2xy^2 \cdot \dfrac{x + 2y}{3xy^3} = \dfrac{2x\cancel{x}^{\cancel{2}}(x + 2y)}{3\cancel{x}y^{\cancel{3}}} = \dfrac{2(x + 2y)}{3y}$

(e) $\dfrac{1 - 36x^2}{18x + 9y} \div \dfrac{(2 - 12x)(1 + 6x)}{16x^2 - 4y^2}$

$= \dfrac{(1 - 36x^2)}{(18x + 9y)} \cdot \dfrac{(16x^2 - 4y^2)}{(2 - 12x)(1 + 6x)}$

$= \dfrac{(1 - 36x^2) \cdot 4(4x^2 - y^2)}{9(2x + y) \cdot 2 \cdot (1 - 6x)(1 + 6x)}$

$= \dfrac{(1 - 6x)(1 + 6x) \cdot 4(2x - y)(2x + y)}{9(2x + y) \cdot 2 \cdot (1 - 6x)(1 + 6x)} = \dfrac{2(2x - y)}{9}$

(f) $\dfrac{\dfrac{a}{2} - \dfrac{a}{5}}{\dfrac{a}{5} - \dfrac{a}{6}} = \dfrac{\dfrac{5a}{10} - \dfrac{2a}{10}}{\dfrac{6a}{30} - \dfrac{5a}{30}} = \dfrac{\dfrac{3a}{10}}{\dfrac{a}{30}} = \dfrac{\dfrac{3a}{10} \cdot 30}{\dfrac{a}{30} \cdot 30} = \dfrac{9a}{a} = 9$

When we deal with fractions of fractions, we should be sure to emphasize which is the fraction line of the dominant fraction. For example,

$$\frac{a}{\dfrac{b}{c}} \quad \text{means} \quad a \div \left(\frac{b}{c}\right) = \frac{ac}{b} \quad \text{whereas} \quad \frac{\dfrac{a}{b}}{c} \quad \text{means} \quad \frac{a}{b} \div c = \frac{a}{bc}$$

However, the first should be written as $\frac{a}{b/c}$, and the second as $\frac{a/b}{c}$.

Problems

In Problems 1 to 3, simplify the various expressions.

1. **a.** $\dfrac{3}{7} + \dfrac{4}{7} - \dfrac{5}{7}$ **b.** $\dfrac{3}{4} + \dfrac{4}{3} - 1$ **c.** $\dfrac{3}{12} - \dfrac{1}{24}$ **d.** $\dfrac{1}{5} - \dfrac{2}{25} - \dfrac{3}{75}$

e. $3\dfrac{3}{5} - 1\dfrac{4}{5}$ **f.** $\dfrac{3}{5} \cdot \dfrac{5}{6}$ **g.** $\left(\dfrac{3}{5} \div \dfrac{2}{15}\right) \cdot \dfrac{1}{9}$ **h.** $\dfrac{\frac{2}{3} + \frac{1}{4}}{\frac{3}{4} + \frac{3}{2}}$

2. **a.** $\dfrac{x}{10} - \dfrac{3x}{10} + \dfrac{17x}{10}$ **b.** $\dfrac{9a}{10} - \dfrac{a}{2} + \dfrac{a}{5}$ **c.** $\dfrac{b+2}{10} - \dfrac{3b}{15} + \dfrac{b}{10}$

d. $\dfrac{x+2}{3} + \dfrac{1-3x}{4}$ **e.** $\dfrac{3}{2b} - \dfrac{5}{3b}$ **f.** $\dfrac{3a-2}{3a} - \dfrac{2b-1}{2b} + \dfrac{4b+3a}{6ab}$

3. **a.** $\dfrac{1}{x-2} - \dfrac{1}{x+2}$ **b.** $\dfrac{6x+25}{4x+2} - \dfrac{6x^2+x-2}{4x^2-1}$

c. $\dfrac{18b^2}{a^2-9b^2} - \dfrac{a}{a+3b} + 2$ **d.** $\dfrac{1}{8ab} - \dfrac{1}{8b(a+2)} + \dfrac{1}{b(a^2-4)}$

e. $\dfrac{2t-t^2}{t+2} \cdot \left(\dfrac{5t}{t-2} - \dfrac{2t}{t-2}\right)$ **f.** $2 - \dfrac{a\left(1 - \frac{1}{2a}\right)}{0.25}$

4. If $x = 3/7$ and $y = 1/14$, find the simplest forms of these fractions:

a. $x + y$ **b.** $\dfrac{x}{y}$ **c.** $\dfrac{x-y}{x+y}$ **d.** $\dfrac{13(2x-3y)}{2x+1}$

5. Reduce the following expressions by making the denominators rational:

a. $\dfrac{1}{\sqrt{7} + \sqrt{5}}$ **b.** $\dfrac{\sqrt{5} - \sqrt{3}}{\sqrt{5} + \sqrt{3}}$ **c.** $\dfrac{x}{\sqrt{3} - 2}$

d. $\dfrac{x\sqrt{y} - y\sqrt{x}}{x\sqrt{y} + y\sqrt{x}}$ **e.** $\dfrac{h}{\sqrt{x+h} - \sqrt{x}}$ **f.** $\dfrac{1 - \sqrt{x+1}}{1 + \sqrt{x+1}}$

6. Simplify the following:

a. $\dfrac{2}{x} + \dfrac{1}{x+1} - 3$ **b.** $\dfrac{t}{2t+1} - \dfrac{t}{2t-1}$ **c.** $\dfrac{3x}{x+2} - \dfrac{4x}{2-x} - \dfrac{2x-1}{x^2-4}$

d. $\dfrac{\dfrac{1}{x}+\dfrac{1}{y}}{\dfrac{1}{xy}}$ **e.** $\dfrac{\dfrac{1}{(x+h)^2}-\dfrac{1}{x^2}}{h}$ **f.** $\dfrac{\dfrac{10x^2}{x^2-1}}{\dfrac{5x}{x+1}}$

7. Prove that $x^2 + 2xy - 3y^2 = (x+3y)(x-y)$, and then simplify:

$$\frac{x-y}{x^2+2xy-3y^2} - \frac{2}{x-y} - \frac{7}{x+3y}$$

8. Simplify the following expressions:

   a. $n - \dfrac{n}{1-\dfrac{1}{n}}$ **b.** $\dfrac{\dfrac{1}{x-1}+\dfrac{1}{x^2-1}}{x-\dfrac{2}{x+1}}$

9. Simplify the following expressions:

   a. $\left(\dfrac{1}{4}-\dfrac{1}{5}\right)^{-2}$ **b.** $\dfrac{1}{1+x^{p-q}}+\dfrac{1}{1+x^{q-p}}$ **c.** $\dfrac{a^{-2}-b^{-2}}{a^{-1}-b^{-1}}$

10. Reduce the following fractions:

   a. $\dfrac{25a^3b^2}{125ab}$ **b.** $\dfrac{x^2-y^2}{x+y}$ **c.** $\dfrac{4a^2-12ab+9b^2}{4a^2-9b^2}$ **d.** $\dfrac{4x-x^3}{4-4x+x^2}$

A.6 Simple Equations and How to Solve Them

Some equations can be solved easily. Consider, for example, the equation $3x+10 = 28$. To solve this, we ask: What number must be added to 10 to get 28? Answer: 18. Hence, $3x = 18$. Because 3 times x is 18, x must be 6. There are no other solutions.

   In more complicated cases, we need a more systematic procedure for solving equations. Two equations that have exactly the same solutions are called *equivalent*. The main principles used in solving equations are summarized as follows:

We get equivalent equations if on both sides of the equality sign we do the following:

   (a) add the same number
   (b) subtract the same number
   (c) multiply by the same number $\neq 0$
   (d) divide by the same number $\neq 0$

[A.22]

In order to solve simple equations, we can use [A.22] as follows. First, apply rules (a) and (b) to isolate all terms containing the unknown on the same side of the equality sign. Next, combine all the terms containing the unknown. Finally, use rules (c) and (d) to find the unknown.

The principle is illustrated by the following examples.

Example A.15

Solve the equation $3x + 10 = x + 4$.

Solution   By using the rules in [A.22] systematically, we obtain:

$$3x + 10 = x + 4$$
$$3x + 10 - 10 = x + 4 - 10$$
$$3x = x - 6$$
$$3x - x = x - x - 6$$
$$2x = -6$$
$$\frac{2x}{2} = \frac{-6}{2}$$
$$x = -3$$

With experience, it is possible to shorten the number of steps involved:

$$3x + 10 = x + 4 \iff 3x - x = 4 - 10 \iff 2x = -6 \iff x = -3$$

Here the *equivalence arrow* $\iff$ means: "has the same solutions as."

When faced with more complicated equations involving parentheses and fractions, we usually begin by multiplying out the parentheses, and then we multiply both sides of the equation by the common denominator for all the fractions. We illustrate the procedure in the following example.

Example A.16

Solve the equation $6p - \frac{1}{2}(2p - 3) = 3(1 - p) - \frac{7}{6}(p + 2)$.

Solution

$$6p - p + \frac{3}{2} = 3 - 3p - \frac{7}{6}p - \frac{7}{3}$$
$$36p - 6p + 9 = 18 - 18p - 7p - 14$$
$$55p = -5$$
$$p = -\frac{5}{55} = -\frac{1}{11}$$

The next two examples show that at times great care is needed to find the right solutions.

Example A.17

Solve the equation

$$\frac{x+2}{x-2} - \frac{8}{x^2 - 2x} = \frac{2}{x}$$

Solution   The equation is equivalent to

$$\frac{x+2}{x-2} - \frac{8}{x(x-2)} = \frac{2}{x}$$

We see that $x = 2$ and $x = 0$ both make the equation absurd, because at least one of the denominators becomes 0. If $x \neq 0$ and $x \neq 2$, we can multiply both sides of the equation by the common denominator $x(x-2)$ to obtain

$$\frac{x+2}{x-2} \cdot x(x-2) - \frac{8}{x(x-2)} \cdot x(x-2) = \frac{2}{x} \cdot x(x-2)$$

$$(x+2)x - 8 = 2(x-2)$$

$$x^2 + 2x - 8 = 2x - 4$$

$$x^2 = 4$$

Because $2^2 = 4$ and $(-2)^2 = (-2)(-2) = 4$, both $x = 2$ and $x = -2$ satisfy the last equation. But because $x = 2$ makes the original equation absurd, *only $x = -2$ is a solution.*

Example A.18

Solve the equation

$$\frac{z}{z-5} + \frac{1}{3} = \frac{-5}{5-z}$$

Solution   We see that z cannot be 5. In order to remember this, we often write

$$\frac{z}{z-5} + \frac{1}{3} = \frac{-5}{5-z} \qquad (z \neq 5)$$

We continue by multiplying both sides by $3(z-5)$. This gives

$$3z + z - 5 = 15$$

which has the unique solution $z = 5$. Because we had to assume $z \neq 5$, we must conclude that no solution exists for this equation.

It is often the case that in order to solve a problem, especially in economics, you must first formulate an appropriate algebraic equation.

Example A.19

A firm manufactures a commodity that costs $20 per unit to produce. In addition, the firm has fixed costs of $2000. Each unit is sold for $75. How many units must be sold if the firm is to have a profit of $14,500?

Solution   If the number of units produced and sold is denoted by Q, then the revenue of the firm is $75Q$ and the total cost of production is $20Q + 2000$. Because profit is the difference between total revenue and total cost, it can be written as

$$75Q - (20Q + 2000)$$

Because we want the profit to be 14,500, the equation

$$75Q - (20Q + 2000) = 14,500$$

must be satisfied. It is easy to find the solution $Q = 16,500/55 = 300$ units.

Problems

In Problems 1 to 3, solve the equations.

1. **a.** $5x - 10 = 15$
   b. $2x - (5 + x) = 16 - (3x + 9)$
   c. $-5(3x - 2) = 16(1 - x)$
   d. $4x + 2(x - 4) - 3 = 2(3x - 5) - 1$
   e. $\frac{2}{3}x = -8$
   f. $(8x - 7)5 - 3(6x - 4) + 5x^2 = (x + 1)(5x + 2)$
   g. $x^2 + 10x + 25 = 0$
   h. $(3x - 1)^2 + (4x + 1)^2 = (5x - 1)(5x + 1) + 1$

2. **a.** $3x + 2 = 11$ **b.** $-3x = 21$

   c. $3x = \frac{1}{4}x - 7$ **d.** $\frac{x - 3}{4} + 2 = 3x$

   e. $\frac{1}{2x + 1} = \frac{1}{x + 2}$ **f.** $\sqrt{2x + 14} = 16$

3. **a.** $\frac{x - 3}{x + 3} = \frac{x - 4}{x + 4}$ **b.** $\frac{3}{x - 3} - \frac{2}{x + 3} = \frac{x^2}{x^2 - 9} - 1$

   c. $\frac{6x}{5} - \frac{5}{x} = \frac{2x - 3}{3} + \frac{8x}{15}$

4. Solve the following problems by first formulating an equation:
   a. The sum of twice a number and 5 is equal to the difference between the number and 3. Find the number.
   b. The sum of three successive natural numbers is 10 more than twice the smallest of them.

    c. Ann receives double pay for every hour she works over and above 38 hours per week. Last week, she worked 48 hours and earned a total of $812. What is Ann's regular hourly wage?

    d. John has invested $15,000 at an annual interest rate of 10%. How much additional money should he invest at the interest rate of 12% if he wants the total interest income earned by the end of the year to equal $2100?

    e. When Mr. Barne passed away, his estate was divided in the following manner: 2/3 of the estate was left to his wife, 1/4 to his children, and the remainder, $1000, was donated to a charitable organization. How big was Mr. Barne's estate?

5. Solve the following equations:

    a. $\dfrac{3y-1}{4} - \dfrac{1-y}{3} + 2 = 3y$

    b. $\dfrac{4}{x} + \dfrac{3}{x+2} = \dfrac{2x+2}{x^2+2x} + \dfrac{7}{2x+4}$

    c. $\dfrac{2 - \dfrac{z}{1-z}}{1+z} = \dfrac{6}{2z+1}$

    d. $\dfrac{1}{2}\left(\dfrac{p}{2} - \dfrac{3}{4}\right) - \dfrac{1}{4}\left(1 - \dfrac{p}{3}\right) - \dfrac{1}{3}(-p+1) = -\dfrac{1}{3}$

6. A swimming pooling can be filled by any one of three different hosepipes in 20, 30, and 60 minutes, respectively. How long will it take to fill the pool if all three hosepipes are used at the same time?

A.7 Inequalities

The real numbers consist of the positive numbers, 0, and the negative numbers. If a is a positive number, we write $a > 0$ (or $0 < a$), and we say that a is greater than zero. A fundamental property of the set of positive numbers is

$$a > 0 \text{ and } b > 0 \text{ imply } a + b > 0 \text{ and } a \cdot b > 0 \qquad \text{[A.23]}$$

If the number c is negative, we write $c < 0$ (or $0 > c$).

    In general, we say that *the number a is greater than the number b*, and we write $a > b$ (or $b < a$), if $a - b$ is positive:

$$a > b \qquad \text{means that} \qquad a - b > 0 \qquad \text{[A.24]}$$

Thus, $4.11 > 3.12$ because $4.11 - 3.12 = 0.99 > 0$, and $-3 > -5$ because $-3 - (-5) = 2 > 0$. On the number line (see Fig. A.3), $a > b$ means that a lies to right of b.

When $a > b$, we often say that a *is strictly greater than b* in order to emphasize that $a = b$ is ruled out. If $a > b$ or $a = b$, then we write $a \geq b$ (or $b \leq a$) and say that a is *greater than or equal to b.*

$$a \geq b \qquad \text{means that} \qquad a - b \geq 0 \qquad \text{[A.25]}$$

For example, $4 \geq 4$ and $4 \geq 2$. Note in particular that it *is* correct to write $4 \geq 2$, because $4 - 2$ *is* positive or 0.

One can prove a number of important properties of $>$ and $\geq$. For example,

$$a > b \text{ and } c \text{ arbitrary implies } a + c > b + c \qquad \text{[A.26]}$$

The argument is simple: For all a, b, and c, $(a+c)-(b+c) = a+c-b-c = a-b$. Hence, if $a - b > 0$, then $a + c - (b + c) > 0$. So [A.26] follows from [A.24]. On the number line in Fig. A.3, [A.26] is:

FIGURE A.3

At the risk of being trivial, here is another interpretation of [A.26]. If one day the temperature in Paris is higher than that in London, and the temperature at both places then increases (or decreases) by the same number of degrees, then the ensuing Paris temperature is still higher than that in London.

In order to find when a given inequality is satisfied, property [A.26] is basic.

Example A.20
Find the values of x satisfying $2x - 5 > x - 3$.

Solution   Adding 5 to both sides of the inequality yields

$$2x - 5 + 5 > x - 3 + 5 \qquad \text{or} \qquad 2x > x + 2$$

Adding $(-x)$ to both sides yields $2x - x > x - x + 2$, so the solution is $x > 2$.

Further Properties of Inequalities

To deal with more complicated inequalities involves using the following further properties:

$$a > b \quad \text{and} \quad b > c \implies a > c \qquad \text{[A.27]}$$

$$a > b \quad \text{and} \quad c > 0 \implies ac > bc \qquad \text{[A.28]}$$

$$a > b \quad \text{and} \quad c < 0 \implies ac < bc \qquad \text{[A.29]}$$

$$a > b \quad \text{and} \quad c > d \implies a + c > b + d \qquad \text{[A.30]}$$

The corresponding properties are valid when each $>$ is replaced by $\geq$. These four properties all follow easily from [A.23]. For example, [A.29] is proved in this way. Suppose $a > b$ and $c < 0$. Then $a - b > 0$ and $-c > 0$, so according to [A.23], $(a - b)(-c) > 0$. Hence, $-ac + bc > 0$ and, therefore, $ac < bc$.

According to [A.28], if an inequality is multiplied by a positive number, the direction of the inequality is preserved. On the other hand, according to [A.29], *if we multiply an inequality by a negative number, the direction of the inequality is reversed.* It is important that you understand these rules, and realize that they correspond to everyday experience. For instance, [A.28] can be interpreted this way: given two rectangles with the same base, the one with the larger height has the larger area.

Sign Diagrams

We often need to find the values of a variable for which a given inequality is satisfied.

Example A.21

Check whether the inequality $(x - 1)(3 - x) > 0$ is satisfied for $x = -3$, $x = 2$, and $x = 5$. Then find all the values x that satisfy the same inequality.

Solution   For $x = -3$, we have $(x - 1)(3 - x) = (-4) \cdot 6 = -24 < 0$; for $x = 2$, we have $(x - 1)(3 - x) = 1 \cdot 1 = 1 > 0$; and for $x = 5$, we have $(x - 1)(3 - x) = 4 \cdot (-2) = -8 < 0$. Hence, the inequality is satisfied for $x = 2$, but not for $x = -3$ or $x = 5$.

To find the entire solution set, we use a sign diagram. The sign variation for each factor in the product is determined. For example, the factor $x - 1$ is negative when $x < 1$, is 0 when $x = 1$, and is positive when $x > 1$. This sign variation is represented in the diagram below. The dashed line to the left of the vertical line $x = 1$ indicates that $x - 1 < 0$ if $x < 1$; the small circle indicates that $x - 1 = 0$ when $x = 1$; and the solid line to the right of $x = 1$ indicates that $x - 1 > 0$ if $x > 1$. In a similar way, we represent the sign variation for $3 - x$. The sign variation of the product is obtained as follows. When $x < 1$, then $x - 1$ is negative and $3 - x$ is positive, so the product is negative. When $1 < x < 3$, both factors are positive, so the product is positive. When $x > 3$, then $x - 1$ is positive and $3 - x$ is negative, so the product is negative. Conclusion: The solution set consists of those x's that are greater than 1, but less than 3. So $(x - 1)(3 - x) > 0$ if and only if $1 < x < 3$.

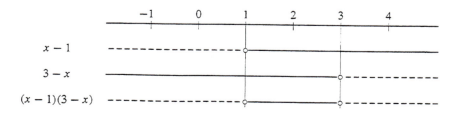

Example A.22

Find the solution set of

$$\frac{2p-3}{p-1} > 3 - p$$

Solution   It is tempting to begin by multiplying each side of the inequality by $p-1$. However, then we must distinguish between the two cases, $p-1 > 0$ and $p-1 < 0$. If we multiply through by $p-1$ when $p-1 < 0$, we have to reverse the inequality sign. There is an alternative method that can be used, which makes it unnecessary to distinguish between two different cases. We begin by adding $p-3$ to both sides. This yields

$$\frac{2p-3}{p-1} + p - 3 > 0$$

Making $p-1$ the common denominator gives

$$\frac{2p-3+(p-3)(p-1)}{p-1} > 0 \qquad \text{or} \qquad \frac{p(p-2)}{p-1} > 0$$

because $2p-3+(p-3)(p-1) = 2p-3+p^2-4p+3 = p^2-2p = p(p-2)$. To find the solution set of this inequality, we again use a sign diagram. On the basis of the sign variations for p, $p-2$, and $p-1$, the sign variation for $p(p-2)/(p-1)$ is determined. For example, if $0 < p < 1$, then p is positive and $(p-2)$ is negative, so $p(p-2)$ is negative. But $p-1$ is also negative on this interval, so $p(p-2)/(p-1)$ is positive. Arguing this way for all the relevant intervals leads to the following conclusion: The fraction $p(p-2)/(p-1)$ is positive if and only if $0 < p < 1$ or $p > 2$. (The original inequality has no meaning when $p = 1$. This is symbolized by a cross in the diagram.) So the original inequality is satisfied if and only if $0 < p < 1$ or $p > 2$.

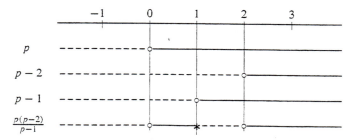

Warning 1: The most common error committed in solving inequalities is precisely the one that was indicated in Example A.22: If we multiply by $p-1$, the inequality is *only* preserved if $p-1$ is positive, that is, if $p > 1$.

Warning 2: It is vital that you really understand the method of sign diagrams. A standard error is illustrated by the following example. Find the solution set for

$$\frac{(x-2)+3(x+1)}{x+3} \leq 0$$

"Solution": We construct the sign diagram:

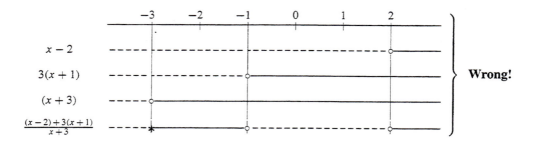

According to this diagram, the inequality should be satisfied for $x < -3$ and for $-1 \leq x \leq 2$. However, for $x = -4$ (< -3), the fraction reduces to 15, which is positive. What went wrong? Suppose $x < -3$. Then $x - 2 < 0$ and $3(x + 1) < 0$ and, therefore, the numerator $(x - 2) + 3(x + 1)$ is negative. Because the denominator $x + 3$ is also negative for $x < -3$, the fraction is positive. The sign variation for the fraction in the diagram above is, therefore, completely wrong. We obtain a correct solution to the given problem by first collecting terms in the numerator so that the inequality becomes $(4x + 1)/(x + 3) \leq 0$. A sign diagram for this inequality reveals the correct answer, which is $-3 < x \leq -1/4$.

Double Inequalities

Two inequalities that are valid simultaneously are often written as a double inequality. If, for example, $a \leq z$ and moreover $z < b$, it is natural to write $a \leq z < b$. (On the other hand, if $a \leq z$ and $z > b$, but we do not know which is the larger of a and b, then we cannot write $a \leq b < z$ or $b \leq a \leq z$, and we do *not* write $a \leq z > b$.)

Example A.23

One day, the lowest temperature in a certain city is 50°F, and the highest is 77°F. What is the corresponding temperature variation in degrees Celsius? (If F denotes degrees Fahrenheit and C denotes degrees Celsius, then $F = \frac{9}{5}C + 32$.)

Solution

$$50 \leq F \leq 77$$
$$50 \leq \tfrac{9}{5}C + 32 \leq 77$$
$$50 - 32 \leq \tfrac{9}{5}C \leq 77 - 32$$
$$18 \leq \tfrac{9}{5}C \leq 45$$
$$90 \leq 9C \leq 225$$
$$10 \leq C \leq 25$$

The temperature varied between 10 and 25°C.

Problems

1. Decide which of the following inequalities are true:

    a. $-6.15 > -7.16$ **b.** $6 \geq 6$ **c.** $(-5)^2 \leq 0$ **d.** $-\tfrac{1}{2}\pi < -\tfrac{1}{3}\pi$

    e. $\dfrac{4}{5} > \dfrac{6}{7}$ **f.** $2^3 < 3^2$ **g.** $2^{-3} < 3^{-2}$ **h.** $\dfrac{1}{2} - \dfrac{2}{3} < \dfrac{1}{4} - \dfrac{1}{3}$

Find the solution sets for the inequalities in Problems 2 to 5.

2. **a.** $3x + 5 < x - 13$ **b.** $3x - (x - 1) \geq x - (1 - x)$

    c. $\dfrac{2x - 4}{3} \leq 7$ **d.** $\tfrac{1}{3}(1 - x) \geq 2(x - 3)$

    e. $\dfrac{t}{24} - (t + 1) + \dfrac{3t}{8} < \dfrac{5}{12}(t + 1) - \dfrac{7}{6}$ **f.** $\dfrac{x + 2}{x + 4} \leq 3$

3. **a.** $\dfrac{x + 2}{x - 1} < 0$ **b.** $\dfrac{2x + 1}{x - 3} > 1$ **c.** $5a^2 \leq 125$

    d. $2 < \dfrac{3x + 1}{2x + 4}$ **e.** $\dfrac{120}{n} + 1.1 \leq 1.85$ **f.** $g^2 - 2g \leq 0$

    g. $\dfrac{1}{p - 2} + \dfrac{3}{p^2 - 4p + 4} \geq 0$ **h.** $\dfrac{-n - 2}{n + 4} > 2$ **i.** $x^4 < x^2$

4. **a.** $(x - 1)(x + 4) > 0$ **b.** $(x - 1)^2(x + 4) > 0$

    c. $(x - 1)(x - 2)(x - 3) \leq 0$ **d.** $(5x - 1)^{10}(x - 1) < 0$

    e. $(5x - 1)^{11}(x - 1) < 0$ **f.** $\dfrac{3x - 1}{x} > x + 3$

    g. $\dfrac{x - 3}{x + 3} < 2x - 1$ **h.** $x^2 + 4x - 5 \leq 0$

    i. $-\tfrac{1}{3}x^3 - x^2 + 6x \leq 0$

5. a. $1 \leq \frac{1}{3}(2x - 1) + \frac{8}{3}(1 - x) < 16$ **b.** $-5 < \frac{1}{x} < 0$ **c.** $\dfrac{\frac{1}{x} - 1}{\frac{1}{x} + 1} \geq 1$

6. Decide whether the following inequalities are valid for all x and y:

   a. $x + 1 > x$ **b.** $x^2 > x$ **c.** $x + x > x$ **d.** $x^2 + y^2 \geq 2xy$

7. In 1993, there was a fixed charge of approximately \$120 per year for having a telephone in Zimbabwe, and an additional \$0.167 per call unit used.

   a. What was the total cost for 1 year in which x call units are used?

   b. What were the smallest and largest numbers of call units one could use if the annual telephone bill were to be between \$170.10 and \$186.80?

8. a. The temperature for storing potatoes should be between 4 and 6°C. What are the corresponding temperatures in degrees Fahrenheit?

   b. The freshness of a bottle of milk is guaranteed for 7 days if it is kept at between 36 and 40°F. Find the corresponding temperature variation in degrees Celsius.

A.8 Quadratic Equations

This section reviews the method for solving quadratic equations. An example of such an equation is $12x^2 - 16x - 3 = 0$. We could, of course, try to find the values of x that satisfy the equation by trial and error. However, then it is not easy to find the only two solutions, which are $x = 3/2$ and $x = -1/6$.

Note: The methods for solving equations we have used so far are based on [A.22] in Section A.6. Many students try to use similar ideas to solve quadratic equations like $12x^2 - 16x - 3 = 0$. One attempt is this: $12x^2 - 16x - 3 = 0$, so $12x^2 - 16x = 3$, and $2x(6x - 8) = 3$. Thus, the product of $2x$ and $6x - 8$ must be 3. But there are infinitely many pairs of numbers whose product is 3, so this is of very little help in finding x.

Some others first try to divide each term by x. Then $12x^2 - 16x - 3 = 0$ yields $12x - 16 = 3/x$. Because the unknown x now occurs on both sides of the equation, we are stuck. Evidently, we need a completely new idea in order to find the solution.

The general quadratic equation has the form

$$ax^2 + bx + c = 0 \qquad (a \neq 0) \qquad \text{[A.31]}$$

where a, b, and c are given constants, and x is the unknown. Some simple examples:

   (a) $x^2 - 4 = 0$ ($a = 1$, $b = 0$, and $c = -4$)

   (b) $5x^2 - 8x = 0$ ($a = 5$, $b = -8$, and $c = 0$)

   (c) $x^2 + 3 = 0$ ($a = 1$, $b = 0$, and $c = 3$)

In each case, we are interested in finding the solutions (if there are any).

(a) The equation yields $x^2 = 4$, and, hence, $x = \pm\sqrt{4} = \pm 2$, which means that x is either 2 or -2. (Alternatively: $x^2 - 4 = (x+2)(x-2) = 0$, so $x = 2$ or $x = -2$.)

(b) Here x is a common factor on the left-hand side, so $x(5x - 8) = 0$. But the product of two numbers is 0 if and only if at least one of the factors is 0. Hence, there are two possibilities: either $x = 0$ or $5x - 8 = 0$, so $x = 0$ or $x = 8/5$.

(c) Because x^2 is always ≥ 0, the equation $x^2 + 3 = 0$ has no solution.

Now we turn to two examples of equations that are more difficult to solve.

Example A.24

$$x^2 + 8x - 9 = 0 \qquad [1]$$

It is natural to begin by moving 9 to the right-hand side:

$$x^2 + 8x = 9 \qquad [2]$$

However, because x occurs in two terms, it is not obvious how to proceed. A method called *completing the square*, one of the oldest tricks in mathematics, turns out to work. To see how, recall from [A.10] that

$$(x + a)^2 = x^2 + 2ax + a^2 \qquad [*]$$

where $x^2 + 2ax + a^2$ is called a *complete square*. Now look at the expression $x^2 + 8x$ on the left-hand side of [2]. What must be added to this expression to make it a complete square? Comparing the left-hand side of [2] with the right-hand side of [*], we see that we should have $2a = 8$ and, hence, $a = 4$. Thus, $a^2 = 4^2$, and by adding 4^2 to the left-hand side of [2], we complete the square of $x^2 + 8x$ to get

$$x^2 + 8x + 4^2 = (x + 4)^2$$

Let us now add 4^2 to both sides of Equation [2]. We then obtain an equation that has precisely the same solutions as [2] and where, moreover, the left-hand side is a complete square:

$$x^2 + 8x + 4^2 = 9 + 4^2$$

Thus, [2] is equivalent to

$$(x + 4)^2 = 25 \qquad [3]$$

Now, the equation $z^2 = 25$ has two solutions, $z = \sqrt{25} = 5$ and $z =$

$-\sqrt{25} = -5$. Thus, from [3], either $x + 4 = 5$ or $x + 4 = -5$. The solutions to Equation [1] are, therefore, $x = 1$ and $x = -9$.

Equation [3] can be written as

$$(x + 4)^2 - 5^2 = 0 \qquad\qquad [4]$$

Then, using the difference of squares formula [A.12] yields

$$(x + 4 - 5)(x + 4 + 5) = 0 \qquad \text{or} \qquad (x - 1)(x + 9) = 0$$

So we have the following *factorization* of the left-hand side of [1]:

$$x^2 + 8x - 9 = (x - 1)(x + 9)$$

Example A.25

Solve

$$12x^2 - 16x - 3 = 0$$

and factor the left-hand side.

Solution The given equation is equivalent to

$$12 \left(x^2 - \tfrac{4}{3}x - \tfrac{1}{4} \right) = 0 \qquad\qquad [1]$$

This equation clearly has the same solutions as

$$x^2 - \tfrac{4}{3}x = \tfrac{1}{4} \qquad\qquad [2]$$

Now complete the square for $x^2 - \tfrac{4}{3}x = x^2 + \left(-\tfrac{4}{3}\right)x$. One-half of the coefficient of x is $-\tfrac{2}{3}$, and, therefore, we add the square of $-\tfrac{2}{3}$ to each side of [2], thus obtaining

$$x^2 - \tfrac{4}{3}x + \left(-\tfrac{2}{3}\right)^2 = \tfrac{1}{4} + \left(-\tfrac{2}{3}\right)^2 = \tfrac{1}{4} + \tfrac{4}{9}$$

$$\left(x - \tfrac{2}{3} \right)^2 = \tfrac{25}{36} \qquad\qquad [3]$$

Hence, $x - \tfrac{2}{3} = \sqrt{\tfrac{25}{36}} = \tfrac{5}{6}$ or $x - \tfrac{2}{3} = -\sqrt{\tfrac{25}{36}} = -\tfrac{5}{6}$. The two solutions are, therefore, $x = \tfrac{2}{3} + \tfrac{5}{6} = \tfrac{9}{6} = \tfrac{3}{2}$ and $x = \tfrac{2}{3} - \tfrac{5}{6} = -\tfrac{1}{6}$.

As demonstrated in Example A.24, we see that [3] can be written as

$$\left(x - \tfrac{2}{3} - \tfrac{5}{6} \right)\left(x - \tfrac{2}{3} + \tfrac{5}{6} \right) = 0 \qquad \text{or} \qquad \left(x - \tfrac{3}{2} \right)\left(x + \tfrac{1}{6} \right) = 0$$

Hence, we obtain the factorization

$$12 \left(x^2 - \tfrac{4}{3}x - \tfrac{1}{4} \right) = 12 \left(x - \tfrac{3}{2} \right)\left(x + \tfrac{1}{6} \right) \qquad\qquad [4]$$

Check that this is correct by expanding the right-hand side.

The General Case

We will now apply the method of completing the square to the general quadratic equation [A.31]. We begin by taking the nonzero coefficient of x^2 outside the parentheses so that [A.31] becomes

$$a \left(x^2 + \frac{b}{a}x + \frac{c}{a} \right) = 0 \qquad \text{[A.32]}$$

Because $a \neq 0$ this equation has the same solutions as

$$x^2 + \frac{b}{a}x = -\frac{c}{a}$$

One-half of the coefficient of x is $b/2a$. Adding the square of this number to each side of the equation yields

$$x^2 + \frac{b}{a}x + \left(\frac{b}{2a} \right)^2 = -\frac{c}{a} + \left(\frac{b}{2a} \right)^2$$

or

$$\left(x + \frac{b}{2a} \right)^2 = \frac{b^2 - 4ac}{4a^2} \qquad \text{[A.33]}$$

Note that $a^2 > 0$ and, if $b^2 - 4ac < 0$, then the right-hand side of [A.33] is negative. Because $(x + b/2a)^2$ is nonnegative for all choices of x, we conclude that if $b^2 - 4ac < 0$, then equation [A.33] has no solutions. On the other hand, if $b^2 - 4ac \geq 0$, then [A.33] yields two possibilities:

$$x + \frac{b}{2a} = \frac{\sqrt{b^2 - 4ac}}{2a} \qquad \text{or} \qquad x + \frac{b}{2a} = -\frac{\sqrt{b^2 - 4ac}}{2a}$$

Then the values of x are easily found. In conclusion:

For $b^2 - 4ac \geq 0$, $a \neq 0$,

$$ax^2 + bx + c = 0 \iff x = \frac{-b \pm \sqrt{b^2 - 4ac}}{2a} \qquad \text{[A.34]}$$

It is a good idea to spend 10 minutes to memorize this formula thoroughly. Once you have done so, you can immediately write the solutions of any quadratic equation. Only if $b^2 - 4ac \geq 0$ are the solutions real numbers. If we use the formula when $b^2 - 4ac < 0$, the square root of a negative number appears and no real solution exists.

Example A.26

Use [A.34] to find the solutions of

$$2x^2 - 4x - 7 = 0$$

Solution   Write the equation as $2x^2 + (-4)x + (-7) = 0$. Because $a = 2$, $b = -4$, and $c = -7$, formula [A.34] yields

$$x = \frac{-(-4) \pm \sqrt{(-4)^2 - 4 \cdot 2 \cdot (-7)}}{2 \cdot 2} = \frac{4 \pm \sqrt{16 + 56}}{4}$$

$$= \frac{4 \pm \sqrt{72}}{4} = \frac{4 \pm 6\sqrt{2}}{4} = 1 \pm \frac{3}{2}\sqrt{2}$$

The solutions are, therefore, $x = 1 + \frac{3}{2}\sqrt{2}$ and $x = 1 - \frac{3}{2}\sqrt{2}$.

Suppose $b^2 - 4ac \geq 0$. By using the square of the difference formula as we did in Examples A.24 and A.25, it follows that [A.33] is equivalent to

$$\left(x + \frac{b}{2a} - \frac{\sqrt{b^2 - 4ac}}{2a}\right)\left(x + \frac{b}{2a} + \frac{\sqrt{b^2 - 4ac}}{2a}\right) = 0 \qquad \text{[A.35]}$$

Denoting the two solutions in [A.34] by x_1 and x_2, Equation [A.35] can be written as $(x - x_1)(x - x_2) = 0$. Therefore, $x^2 + (b/a)x + c/a = (x - x_1)(x - x_2)$. Hence:

Provided that $b^2 - 4ac \geq 0$ and $a \neq 0$, we have

$$ax^2 + bx + c = a(x - x_1)(x - x_2) \qquad \text{[A.36]}$$

where

$$x_{1,2} = \frac{-b \pm \sqrt{b^2 - 4ac}}{2a}$$

This is a very important result, because it shows how to factor a general quadratic function. If $b^2 - 4ac < 0$, there is no factorization of $ax^2 + bx + c$.

Expanding the right-hand side of the identity $x^2 + (b/a)x + c/a = (x - x_1)(x - x_2)$ yields $x^2 + (b/a)x + c/a = x^2 - (x_1 + x_2)x + x_1 x_2$. Equating like powers of x gives $x_1 + x_2 = -b/a$ and $x_1 x_2 = c/a$. Thus:

If x_1 and x_2 are the roots of $ax^2 + bx + c = 0$, then

$$x_1 + x_2 = -b/a \quad \text{and} \quad x_1 x_2 = c/a \qquad \text{[A.37]}$$

Example A.27

Factor (if possible) the following second-degree polynomials:

$$\text{(a) } \tfrac{1}{3}x^2 + \tfrac{2}{3}x - \tfrac{14}{3} \qquad \text{(b) } -2x^2 + 40x - 600$$

Solution

(a) For $\tfrac{1}{3}x^2 + \tfrac{2}{3}x - \tfrac{14}{3} = 0$, we have $a = \tfrac{1}{3}$, $b = \tfrac{2}{3}$, and $c = -\tfrac{14}{3}$, so [A.34] gives

$$x_{1,2} = \frac{-\tfrac{2}{3} \pm \sqrt{(\tfrac{2}{3})^2 - 4 \cdot (\tfrac{1}{3}) \cdot (-\tfrac{14}{3})}}{2 \cdot (\tfrac{1}{3})} = \frac{-\tfrac{2}{3} \pm \sqrt{\tfrac{4}{9} + \tfrac{56}{9}}}{\tfrac{2}{3}}$$

$$= \frac{-\tfrac{2}{3} \pm \sqrt{60}/3}{\tfrac{2}{3}} = \frac{-2 \pm \sqrt{60}}{2} = \frac{-2 \pm 2\sqrt{15}}{2} = -1 \pm \sqrt{15}$$

The solutions are, therefore, $x_1 = -1 + \sqrt{15}$ and $x_2 = -1 - \sqrt{15}$, so [A.36] yields

$$\tfrac{1}{3}x^2 + \tfrac{2}{3}x - \tfrac{14}{3} = \tfrac{1}{3}\big[x - (-1 + \sqrt{15})\big]\big[x - (-1 - \sqrt{15})\big]$$

(b) For $-2x^2 + 40x - 600 = 0$, $a = -2$, $b = 40$, and $c = -600$, so $b^2 - 4ac = 1600 - 4800 = -3200$. Therefore, no factorization like that in [A.36] exists in this case.

Note: The general formula for the solution of a second-degree equation is very useful. However, if b or c is 0, then it is unnecessary to use the formula.

1. If $ax^2 + bx = 0$ (the quadratic equation lacks the constant term), then factorization yields $x(ax + b) = 0$, which gives the solutions $x = 0$ and $x = -b/a$ directly.

2. If $ax^2 + c = 0$ (the equation lacks the term involving x), then $a(x^2 + c/a) = 0$ and there are two possibilities. If $c/a > 0$, then the equation $x^2 + c/a = 0$ has no solutions. If $c/a < 0$, then the solutions are $x = \pm\sqrt{-c/a}$.

Problems

1. Solve the following quadratic equations (if they have solutions):

   a. $15x - x^2 = 0$ **b.** $p^2 - 16 = 0$ **c.** $(q - 3)(q + 4) = 0$

   d. $2x^2 + 9 = 0$ **e.** $x(x + 1) = 2x(x - 1)$ **f.** $x^2 - 4x + 4 = 0$

2. Solve the following quadratic equations by using the method of completing the square, and factor (if possible) the left-hand side:

   a. $x^2 - 5x + 6 = 0$ **b.** $y^2 - y - 12 = 0$

  c. $2x^2 + 60x + 800 = 0$ **d.** $-\frac{1}{4}x^2 + \frac{1}{2}x + \frac{1}{2} = 0$

  e. $m(m-5) - 3 = 0$ **f.** $0.1p^2 + p - 2.4 = 0$

3. Solve the following quadratic equations:

  a. $r^2 + 11r - 26 = 0$ **b.** $3p^2 + 45p = 48$

  c. $20\,000 = 300K - K^2$ **d.** $r^2 + (\sqrt{3} - \sqrt{2})r = \sqrt{6}$

  e. $0.03x^2 - 0.009x = 0.012$ **f.** $\dfrac{1}{24} = p^2 - \dfrac{1}{12}p$

4. Solve the following equations by using formula [A.34]:

  a. $x^2 - 3x + 2 = 0$ **b.** $5t^2 - t = 3$ **c.** $6x = 4x^2 - 1$

  d. $9x^2 + 42x + 44 = 0$ **e.** $30\,000 = x(x + 200)$ **f.** $3x^2 = 5x - 1$

5. **a.** Find the rectangle whose circumference is 40 cm and area is 75 cm^2.

  b. Find two successive natural numbers whose sum of squares is 13.

  c. In a right-angled triangle, the hypotenuse is 34 cm. One of the short sides is 14 cm longer than the other. Find the lengths of the two short sides.

  d. A motorist drove 80 km. In order to save 16 minutes, he had to drive 10 km/h faster than usual. What was his usual driving speed?

6. Solve the following equations:

  a. $x^3 - 4x = 0$ **b.** $x^4 - 5x^2 + 4 = 0$ **c.** $z^{-2} - 2z^{-1} - 15 = 0$

7. Prove formula [A.34] using the following approach. Multiply Equation [A.31] by $4a$; after rearranging, this yields $4a^2x^2 + 4abx = -4ac$. Now add b^2 to both sides. Notice that the left-hand side is then a complete square.

A.9 Two Equations with Two Unknowns

This section reviews some methods for solving equations with two unknowns.

Example A.28

Find the values of x and y that satisfy the two equations

$$2x + 3y = 18$$
$$3x - 4y = -7$$

[1]

We need to find the values of x and y that satisfy *both* equations. Suppose we start by trying $x = 0$ in the first equation; this implies $y = 6$. Given $x = 0$ and $y = 6$, $2x + 3y = 18$ and $3x - 4y = -24$. Thus, the first equation in [1] *is* satisfied, but not the second. Hence, $x = 0$ and $y = 6$ is *not* a solution to [1]. Only if we are very lucky will we find the solution to [1] by such trial and error.

Fortunately, there exist more systematic methods for solving [1].

Method 1: First, solve one of the equations for one of the variables in terms of the other and then substitute the result into the other equation. This leaves only one equation in one unknown, which is easily solved.

Applying this method to [1], we solve the first equation for y in terms of x: $2x + 3y = 18$ implies that $3y = 18 - 2x$ and, hence, $y = 6 - \frac{2}{3}x$. Substituting this expression for y into the second equation in [1] gives

$$3x - 4\left(6 - \tfrac{2}{3}x\right) = -7$$

$$3x - 24 + \tfrac{8}{3}x = -7$$

$$9x - 72 + 8x = -21$$

$$17x = 51$$

Hence, $x = 3$. Then we find y by using $y = 6 - \frac{2}{3}x$ once again, thus implying that $y = 6 - \frac{2}{3} \cdot 3 = 4$. The solution of [1] is, hence, $x = 3$ and $y = 4$. (Such a solution should always be checked by direct substitution.)

Method 2: This method is based on eliminating one of the variables by adding or subtracting a multiple of one equation from the other. For system [1], suppose we want to eliminate y; a similar method could be used to eliminate x instead. If we multiply the first equation in [1] by 4 and the second by 3, then the coefficients of the y terms in both equations will be the same except for the sign. If we then add the transformed equations together, we obtain

$$
\begin{aligned}
8x + 12y &= 72 \\
9x - 12y &= -21 \\
\hline
17x \phantom{{}+12y} &= 51
\end{aligned}
\qquad [2]
$$

Hence, $x = 3$. To find the value for y, substitute 3 for x in either of the original equations and solve for y. This gives $y = 4$, which agrees with the earlier result.

Some prefer to find both x and y by using the following setup:

$$
\begin{array}{l|c|c}
2x + 3y = 18 & 4 & 3 \\
3x - 4y = -7 & 3 & -2
\end{array}
\qquad [3]
$$

The first column on the right-hand side of [3] suggests that we multiply the first equation by 4 and the second by 3. This leads to the arrangement in [2]. The second column on the right-hand side of [3] suggests that we multiply the first equation by 3 and the second by -2. Doing this yields

$$6x + 9y = 54$$

$$\underline{-6x + 8y = 14}$$

$$17y = 68$$

$$y = 4$$

We end this section by using the elimination method to solve a general linear system of equations with two equations and two unknowns:

$$ax + by = c$$
$$dx + ey = f$$

[A.38]

Here a, b, c, d, e, and f are arbitrary given numbers, whereas x and y are the unknowns. If we let $a = 2$, $b = 3$, $c = 18$, $d = 3$, $e = -4$, and $f = -7$, then [A.38] reduces to system [1]. Using the elimination method for the general case, we obtain

$$\begin{array}{lll} ax + by = c & \quad e & \quad d \\ dx + ey = f & \quad -b & \quad -a \end{array}$$

$$\begin{array}{ll} aex + bey = ce & \qquad adx + bdy = cd \\ \underline{-bdx - bey = -bf} & \qquad \underline{-adx - aey = -af} \\ (ae - bd)x = ce - bf & \qquad (bd - ae)y = cd - af \end{array}$$

which gives

$$x = \frac{ce - bf}{ae - bd} \qquad\qquad y = \frac{cd - af}{bd - ae} = \frac{af - cd}{ae - bd}$$

[A.39]

We have found expressions for both x and y.

The formulas in [A.39] break down if the denominator $ae - bd$ in both fractions is equal to 0. This case requires special attention—see Section 14.3.

Problems

1. Solve each of the following systems of two simultaneous equations:

   (a) $x - y = 5$ (b) $4x - 3y = 1$ (c) $3x + 4y = 2.1$

     $x + y = 11$ $2x + 9y = 4$ $5x - 6y = 7.3$

2. Solve each of the following systems of two simultaneous equations:

   (a) $2K + L = 11.35$ (b) $230p + 450q = 1810$

     $K + 4L = 25.8$ $100p + 150q = 650$

(c) $0.01r + 0.21s = \ \ 0.042$

$-0.25r + 0.55s = -0.47$

3. **a.** Find two numbers whose sum is 52 and whose difference is 26.

   b. Five tables and 20 chairs cost $1800, whereas 2 tables and 3 chairs cost $420. What is the price of each table and each chair?

   c. A firm produces a good in two qualities, A and B. The estimate for the coming year's sales of A is 50% higher than the estimate of the sales of B. The profit per unit sold of the two qualities is $300 for A and $200 for B. If the goal is a profit of $13,000 over the next year, how much of each of the two qualities must be produced?

   d. A person has saved a total of $10,000 in two accounts. The interest rates are 5 and 7.2% per year, respectively. If the person earns $676 interest in 1 year, what was the balance in each of the two accounts?

B

Sums, Products, and Induction

B.1 Summation Notation

Suppose we are interested in the population of a country that is divided into six regions. Let N_i denote the population in region i. Then

$$N_1 + N_2 + N_3 + N_4 + N_5 + N_6$$

is the total population. It is often convenient to have an abbreviated notation for such lengthy sums. The capital Greek letter sigma Σ is used as a **summation symbol**, and the previous sum is written as

$$\sum_{i=1}^{6} N_i$$

This expression means the "sum from $i = 1$ to $i = 6$ of N_i." Suppose, in general, that there are n regions. Then

$$N_1 + N_2 + \cdots + N_n \tag{1}$$

is one possible notation for the total population. Here $\cdots$ indicates that the obvious pattern continues. In summation notation, we write

$$\sum_{i=1}^{n} N_i$$

This notation tells us to form the sum of all the terms that result when we substitute successive integers for i, starting with $i = 1$ and ending with $i = n$. The symbol i is called the **index of summation**. It is a "dummy variable" that can be replaced by any other letter (provided that the letter has not already been used for something else). That is, both $\sum_{j=1}^{n} N_j$ and $\sum_{i=1}^{n} N_i$ represent the same sum [1].

The upper and lower limits of summation can both vary. For example,

$$\sum_{i=30}^{35} N_i = N_{30} + N_{31} + N_{32} + N_{33} + N_{34} + N_{35}$$

is the total population in the six regions numbered from 30 to 35.

More generally, if p and q are integers with $q \geq p$, then

$$\sum_{i=p}^{q} a_i = a_p + a_{p+1} + \cdots + a_q$$

denotes the sum of the terms that result when we substitute successive integers for i, starting with $i = p$ and ending with $i = q$. If the upper and lower limits of summation are the same, then the "sum" reduces to one term. For example,

$$\sum_{i=1}^{1} N_i = N_1, \qquad \sum_{i=3}^{3} \frac{1}{i^2} = \frac{1}{3^2} = \frac{1}{9}$$

And if the upper limit is less than the lower limit, then there are no terms at all, so the "sum" reduces to zero.

Example B.1

Compute the following sums:

(a) $\displaystyle\sum_{i=1}^{5} i^2$ (b) $\displaystyle\sum_{k=3}^{6} (5k - 3)$ (c) $\displaystyle\sum_{j=0}^{2} \frac{1}{(j + 1)(j + 3)}$

Solution

(a) $\displaystyle\sum_{i=1}^{5} i^2 = 1^2 + 2^2 + 3^2 + 4^2 + 5^2 = 1 + 4 + 9 + 16 + 25 = 55$

(b) $\displaystyle\sum_{k=3}^{6}(5k-3) = (5\cdot3-3) + (5\cdot4-3) + (5\cdot5-3) + (5\cdot6-3) = 78$

(c) $\displaystyle\sum_{j=0}^{2}\frac{1}{(j+1)(j+3)} = \frac{1}{1\cdot3} + \frac{1}{2\cdot4} + \frac{1}{3\cdot5} = \frac{40+15+8}{120} = \frac{63}{120}$

$\displaystyle = \frac{21}{40}$

Sums and summation notation occur frequently in books and papers on economics. Often, there are several variables or parameters in addition to the summation index. It is important to be able to read such sums. In each case, the summation symbol tells you that there is a sum of terms. The sum results from substituting successive integers for the summation index, starting with the lower limit and ending with the upper limit.

Example B.2

Expand the following sums:

(a) $\displaystyle\sum_{i=1}^{n} p_t^{(i)} q^{(i)}$ **(b)** $\displaystyle\sum_{j=-2}^{1} x^{5-j} y^{j}$ **(c)** $\displaystyle\sum_{i=1}^{N}(x_{ij} - \bar{x}_j)^2$

Solution

(a) $\displaystyle\sum_{i=1}^{n} p_t^{(i)} q^{(i)} = p_t^{(1)} q^{(1)} + p_t^{(2)} q^{(2)} + \cdots + p_t^{(n)} q^{(n)}$

(b) $\displaystyle\sum_{j=-2}^{1} x^{5-j} y^{j} = x^{5-(-2)} y^{-2} + x^{5-(-1)} y^{-1} + x^{5-0} y^{0} + x^{5-1} y^{1}$

$\displaystyle = x^{7} y^{-2} + x^{6} y^{-1} + x^{5} + x^{4} y$

(c) $\displaystyle\sum_{i=1}^{N}(x_{ij} - \bar{x}_j)^2 = (x_{1j} - \bar{x}_j)^2 + (x_{2j} - \bar{x}_j)^2 + \cdots + (x_{Nj} - \bar{x}_j)^2$

Note that t is *not* an index of summation in (a), and j is *not* an index of summation in (c).

Example B.3

Write the following sums using summation notation:

(a) $1 + 3 + 3^2 + 3^3 + \cdots + 3^{81}$

(b) $a_i^6 + a_i^5 b_j + a_i^4 b_j^2 + a_i^3 b_j^3 + a_i^2 b_j^4 + a_i b_j^5 + b_j^6$

Solution

(a) This is easy if we note that the first two terms of the sum can be written as $3^0 = 1$ and $3^1 = 3$. The general term is 3^i, and we have

$$1 + 3 + 3^2 + 3^3 + \cdots + 3^{81} = \sum_{i=0}^{81} 3^i$$

(b) This is more difficult. Note, however, that the indices i and j never change. Also the exponent for a_i decreases step by step from 6 to 0, whereas that for b_j increases from 0 to 6. The general term has the form $a_i^{6-k} b_j^k$, where k varies from 0 to 6. Thus,

$$a_i^6 + a_i^5 b_j + a_i^4 b_j^2 + a_i^3 b_j^3 + a_i^2 b_j^4 + a_i b_j^5 + b_j^6 = \sum_{k=0}^{6} a_i^{6-k} b_j^k$$

Example B.4

To measure variations in the cost of living, a number of different *price indices* have been suggested.

Consider a "basket" of n commodities. For $i = 1, \ldots, n$, define

$$q^{(i)} = \text{number of units of good } i \text{ in the basket}$$

$$p_0^{(i)} = \text{price per unit of good } i \text{ in year } 0$$

$$p_t^{(i)} = \text{price per unit of good } i \text{ in year } t$$

Then

$$\sum_{i=1}^{n} p_0^{(i)} q^{(i)} = p_0^{(1)} q^{(1)} + p_0^{(2)} q^{(2)} + \cdots + p_0^{(n)} q^{(n)} \qquad [1]$$

is the cost of the basket in year 0, and

$$\sum_{i=1}^{n} p_t^{(i)} q^{(i)} = p_t^{(1)} q^{(1)} + p_t^{(2)} q^{(2)} + \cdots + p_t^{(n)} q^{(n)} \qquad [2]$$

is the cost of the basket in year t. A price index for year t, with year 0 as the base year, is defined as

$$\frac{\displaystyle\sum_{i=1}^{n} p_t^{(i)} q^{(i)}}{\displaystyle\sum_{i=1}^{n} p_0^{(i)} q^{(i)}} \cdot 100 \qquad [B.1]$$

If the cost of the basket is 1032 in year 0 and the price of the same basket in year t is 1548, then the price index is $(1548/1032) \cdot 100 = 150$.

In case the quantities $q^{(i)}$ are levels of consumption in the base year 0, this index is called the **Laspeyres price index**. But if the quantities $q^{(i)}$ are levels of consumption in the year t, this index is called the **Paasche price index**.

Problems

1. Evaluate the following:

   a. $\displaystyle\sum_{i=1}^{10} i$.

   b. $\displaystyle\sum_{k=2}^{6} (5 \cdot 3^{k-2} - k)$

   c. $\displaystyle\sum_{m=0}^{5} (2m + 1)$

   d. $\displaystyle\sum_{l=0}^{2} 2^{2^l}$

   e. $\displaystyle\sum_{i=1}^{10} 2$

   f. $\displaystyle\sum_{j=1}^{4} \frac{j+1}{j}$

2. Expand the following sums:

   a. $\displaystyle\sum_{k=-2}^{2} 2\sqrt{k+2}$

   b. $\displaystyle\sum_{i=0}^{3} (x + 2i)^2$

   c. $\displaystyle\sum_{k=1}^{n} a_{ki} b^{k+1}$

   d. $\displaystyle\sum_{j=0}^{m} f(x_j)\, \Delta x_j$

3. Write these sums by using summation notation:

   a. $4 + 8 + 12 + 16 + \cdots + 4n$

   b. $1^3 + 2^3 + 3^3 + 4^3 + \cdots + n^3$

   c. $1 - \dfrac{1}{3} + \dfrac{1}{5} - \dfrac{1}{7} + \cdots + (-1)^n \dfrac{1}{2n+1}$

   d. $a_{i1} b_{1j} + a_{i2} b_{2j} + \cdots + a_{in} b_{nj}$

   e. $3x + 9x^2 + 27x^3 + 81x^4 + 243x^5 + 729x^6$

   f. $a_i^3 b_{i+3} + a_i^4 b_{i+4} + \cdots + a_i^p b_{i+p}$

   g. $a_i^3 b_{i+3} + a_{i+1}^4 b_{i+4} + \cdots + a_{i+p}^{p+3} b_{i+p+3}$

   h. $81,297 + 81,495 + 81,693 + 81,891$

4. Compute the price index [B.1] if $n = 3$, $p_0^{(1)} = 1$, $p_0^{(2)} = 2$, $p_0^{(3)} = 3$, $p_t^{(1)} = 2$, $p_t^{(2)} = 3$, $p_t^{(3)} = 4$, $q^{(1)} = 3$, $q^{(2)} = 5$, and $q^{(3)} = 7$.

5. a. Expand $\sum_{i=1}^{5} (x_i - \bar{x})$, and prove that it is equal to $\sum_{i=1}^{5} x_i - 5\bar{x}$.

   b. Prove in general that

$$\sum_{i=1}^{n} (x_i - \bar{x}) = \sum_{i=1}^{n} x_i - n\bar{x}$$

6. Consider a country divided into 100 regions. For a certain year, let c_{ij} be the number of persons who move from region i to region j. If, say, $i = 25$

and $j = 10$, then we write $c_{25,10}$ for c_{ij}. Explain the meaning of the sums:

a. $\displaystyle\sum_{j=1}^{100} c_{ij}$
b. $\displaystyle\sum_{i=1}^{100} c_{ij}$

7. Decide which of the following equalities are generally valid:

a. $\displaystyle\sum_{k=1}^{n} ck^2 = c \sum_{k=1}^{n} k^2$
b. $\displaystyle\left(\sum_{i=1}^{n} a_i\right)^2 = \sum_{i=1}^{n} a_i^2$

c. $\displaystyle\sum_{j=1}^{n} b_j + \sum_{j=n+1}^{N} b_j = \sum_{j=1}^{N} b_j$
d. $\displaystyle\sum_{k=3}^{7} 5^{k-2} = \sum_{k=0}^{4} 5^{k+1}$

e. $\displaystyle\sum_{i=0}^{n-1} a_{i,j}^2 = \sum_{k=1}^{n} a_{k-1,j}^2$
f. $\displaystyle\sum_{k=1}^{n} \frac{a_k}{k} = \frac{1}{k} \sum_{k=1}^{n} a_k$

B.2 Rules for Sums

The following algebraic properties of the sigma notation are helpful when manipulating sums:

$$\sum_{i=1}^{n}(a_i + b_i) = \sum_{i=1}^{n} a_i + \sum_{i=1}^{n} b_i \qquad \textbf{(additivity property)} \qquad \text{[B.2]}$$

$$\sum_{i=1}^{n} ca_i = c \sum_{i=1}^{n} a_i \qquad \textbf{(homogeneity property)} \qquad \text{[B.3]}$$

The proofs of these properties are straightforward. For example, [B.3] is proved by noting that

$$\sum_{i=1}^{n} ca_i = ca_1 + ca_2 + \cdots + ca_n = c(a_1 + a_2 + \cdots + a_n) = c \sum_{i=1}^{n} a_i$$

Property [B.3] states that a constant factor can be moved across the summation sign. If $a_i = 1$ for all i in [B.3], then

$$\sum_{i=1}^{n} c = nc \qquad \text{[B.4]}$$

which just states that a constant c summed n times is equal to n times c.

Properties [B.2] to [B.4] are also valid if the lower index of summation is an integer other than 1. For example,

$$\sum_{k=3}^{6} 7 = 7 + 7 + 7 + 7 = 28$$

because the number 7 is summed 4 times.

Rules [B.2] to [B.4] can be applied in combination to give formulas like

$$\sum_{i=1}^{n} (a_i + b_i - c_i + d) = \sum_{i=1}^{n} a_i + \sum_{i=1}^{n} b_i - \sum_{i=1}^{n} c_i + nd$$

Example B.5

Evaluate the sum

$$\sum_{m=2}^{n} \frac{1}{(m-1)m} = \frac{1}{1\cdot 2} + \frac{1}{2\cdot 3} + \frac{1}{3\cdot 4} + \cdots + \frac{1}{(n-1)n}$$

by using the identity

$$\frac{1}{(m-1)m} = \frac{1}{m-1} - \frac{1}{m}$$

Solution

$$\sum_{m=2}^{n} \frac{1}{m(m-1)}$$

$$= \sum_{m=2}^{n} \left(\frac{1}{m-1} - \frac{1}{m} \right) = \sum_{m=2}^{n} \frac{1}{m-1} - \sum_{m=2}^{n} \frac{1}{m}$$

$$= \left(\frac{1}{1} + \frac{1}{2} + \frac{1}{3} + \cdots + \frac{1}{n-1} \right) - \left(\frac{1}{2} + \frac{1}{3} + \cdots + \frac{1}{n-1} + \frac{1}{n} \right)$$

$$= 1 - \frac{1}{n}$$

To derive the last equality, note that all the terms cancel pairwise, except the first term within the first parentheses and the last term within the last parentheses. This is a commonly used and powerful trick for calculating certain kinds of sums.

Example B.6

The **arithmetic mean** $\bar{x}$ of n numbers $x_1, x_2, \ldots, x_n$ is the sum of all the numbers divided by the number of terms, n:

$$\bar{x} = \frac{1}{n} \sum_{i=1}^{n} x_i$$

Prove that

$$\sum_{i=1}^{n} (x_i - \bar{x}) = 0 \quad \text{and} \quad \sum_{i=1}^{n} (x_i - \bar{x})^2 = \sum_{i=1}^{n} x_i^2 - n\bar{x}^2$$

Solution The difference $x_i - \bar{x}$ is the deviation between x_i and the mean. We prove first that the sum of these deviations is 0, using the foregoing definition of $\bar{x}$:

$$\sum_{i=1}^{n} (x_i - \bar{x}) = \sum_{i=1}^{n} x_i - \sum_{i=1}^{n} \bar{x} = \sum_{i=1}^{n} x_i - n\bar{x} = n\bar{x} - n\bar{x} = 0$$

Furthermore,

$$\sum_{i=1}^{n} (x_i - \bar{x})^2 = \sum_{i=1}^{n} (x_i^2 - 2\bar{x}x_i + \bar{x}^2) = \sum_{i=1}^{n} x_i^2 - 2\bar{x} \sum_{i=1}^{n} x_i + \sum_{i=1}^{n} \bar{x}^2$$

$$= \sum_{i=1}^{n} x_i^2 - 2\bar{x}n\bar{x} + n\bar{x}^2 = \sum_{i=1}^{n} x_i^2 - n\bar{x}^2$$

Note: We have considered some useful algebraic properties of sums. A frequent error is a failure to observe that, in general,

$$\sum_{i=1}^{n} x_i^2 \neq \left(\sum_{i=1}^{n} x_i \right)^2$$

It is important to note that the sum of the squares is not generally equal to the square of the sum. For example, $\sum_{i=1}^{2} x_i^2 = x_1^2 + x_2^2$ whereas $\left(\sum_{i=1}^{2} x_i\right)^2 = (x_1 + x_2)^2 = x_1^2 + 2x_1x_2 + x_2^2$, so the two are equal iff $x_1 x_2 = 0$—that is, x_1 or x_2 (or both) must be zero. More generally,

$$\sum_{i=1}^{n} x_i y_i \neq \left(\sum_{i=1}^{n} x_i \right) \left(\sum_{i=1}^{n} y_i \right)$$

so the sum of the cross products is not equal to the products of the individual sums.

Useful Formulas

If you asked a group of 10–12-year-old students to sum all the numbers from 1 to 100, would you expect to have a correct answer within 1 hour? According to reliable sources, Carl F. Gauss solved a similar problem in his tenth year. His teacher asked his students to sum $81,297 + 81,495 + 81,693 + \cdots + 100,899$. There are 100 terms and the difference between successive terms is constant and equal to 198. Obviously, the teacher chose this sum knowing that a trick could yield the answer quickly. Thus, the laboriously derived answers of the students could easily be checked. But Gauss, who later became one of the world's leading mathematicians, gave the right answer, which is 9,109,800, in only a few minutes.

Applied to the easier problem of finding the sum $1 + 2 + \cdots + n$, Gauss' argument was probably as follows: First, write the sum x in two ways

$$x = 1 + 2 + \cdots + (n-1) + n$$
$$x = n + (n-1) + \cdots + 2 + 1$$

Summing vertically gives

$$2x = (1+n) + \left[2 + (n-1)\right] + \cdots + \left[(n-1) + 2\right] + (n+1)$$
$$= (1+n) + (1+n) + \cdots + (1+n) + (1+n)$$
$$= n(1+n)$$

Thus, we have the result:

$$\sum_{i=1}^{n} i = 1 + 2 + \cdots + n = \tfrac{1}{2}n(n+1) \qquad \text{[B.5]}$$

The following two summation formulas are sometimes useful:

$$\sum_{i=1}^{n} i^2 = 1^2 + 2^2 + 3^2 + \cdots + n^2 = \tfrac{1}{6}n(n+1)(2n+1) \qquad \text{[B.6]}$$

$$\sum_{i=1}^{n} i^3 = 1^3 + 2^3 + 3^3 + \cdots + n^3 = \left[\frac{n(n+1)}{2}\right]^2 \qquad \text{[B.7]}$$

Check to see if these formulas are true for $n = 1, 2$, and 3. One way of proving that they are valid generally is to use mathematical induction, as discussed in Section B.5.

Newton's Binomial Formula

We all know that $(a + b)^1 = a + b$ and $(a + b)^2 = a^2 + 2ab + b^2$. Using the latter equality and writing $(a + b)^3 = (a + b)^2(a + b)$ and $(a + b)^4 = (a + b)^2(a + b)^2$, we find that

$$(a + b)^1 = a + b$$

$$(a + b)^2 = a^2 + 2ab + b^2$$

$$(a + b)^3 = a^3 + 3a^2b + 3ab^2 + b^3$$

$$(a + b)^4 = a^4 + 4a^3b + 6a^2b^2 + 4ab^3 + b^4$$

What is the corresponding formula for $(a + b)^m$, where m is an arbitrary positive integer? The answer is given by the Newton binomial formula:

$$(a + b)^m = a^m + \binom{m}{1}a^{m-1}b + \binom{m}{2}a^{m-2}b^2 + \cdots$$
$$+ \binom{m}{m-1}ab^{m-1} + \binom{m}{m}b^m \qquad [\text{B.8}]$$

Here the binomial coefficient

$$\binom{m}{k} = \frac{m(m - 1)\cdots(m - k + 1)}{k!}$$

as explained in Section 7.4. Formula [B.8] is proved in Section 7.4. In general, $\binom{m}{1} = m$ and $\binom{m}{m} = 1$. For $m = 5$, we have

$$\binom{5}{2} = \frac{5 \cdot 4}{1 \cdot 2} = 10, \qquad \binom{5}{3} = \frac{5 \cdot 4 \cdot 3}{1 \cdot 2 \cdot 3} = 10, \qquad \binom{5}{4} = \frac{5 \cdot 4 \cdot 3 \cdot 2}{1 \cdot 2 \cdot 3 \cdot 4} = 5$$

So [B.8] yields

$$(a + b)^5 = a^5 + 5a^4b + 10a^3b^2 + 10a^2b^3 + 5ab^4 + b^5$$

If we study the coefficients in the expansions for the successive powers of $(a + b)$, we have the following pattern, called **Pascal's triangle** (though it was actually known in China by around 1100, long before Blaise Pascal was born):

$$
\begin{array}{ccccccccccccccccccc}
&&&&&&&&& 1 &&&&&&&&& \\
&&&&&&&& 1 && 1 &&&&&&&& \\
&&&&&&& 1 && 2 && 1 &&&&&&& \\
&&&&&& 1 && 3 && 3 && 1 &&&&&& \\
&&&&& 1 && 4 && 6 && 4 && 1 &&&&& \\
&&&& 1 && 5 && 10 && 10 && 5 && 1 &&&& \\
&&& 1 && 6 && 15 && 20 && 15 && 6 && 1 &&& \\
&& 1 && 7 && 21 && 35 && 35 && 21 && 7 && 1 && \\
& 1 && 8 && 28 && 56 && 70 && 56 && 28 && 8 && 1 & \\
1 && 9 && 36 && 84 && 126 && 126 && 84 && 36 && 9 && 1
\end{array}
$$

This table can be continued indefinitely. The numbers in this triangle are the binomial coefficients. For instance, the numbers in row 6 (when the first row is numbered 0) are

$$
\binom{6}{0} \quad \binom{6}{1} \quad \binom{6}{2} \quad \binom{6}{3} \quad \binom{6}{4} \quad \binom{6}{5} \quad \binom{6}{6}
$$

Note, first, that the numbers are symmetric about the middle line. This symmetry can be expressed as

$$
\binom{m}{k} = \binom{m}{m-k} \tag{B.9}
$$

For example, $\binom{6}{2} = 15 = \binom{6}{4}$. Second, the sum of two adjacent numbers in any row is equal to the number between the two in the row below. For instance, the sum of 21 and 35 in the seventh row is equal to 56 in the eighth row. In terms of symbols,

$$
\binom{m}{k} + \binom{m}{k+1} = \binom{m+1}{k+1} \tag{B.10}
$$

In Problem 4, you are asked to prove [B.9] and [B.10].

Problems

1. Use the results in [B.5] and [B.6] to find $\sum_{k=1}^{n}(k^2 + 3k + 2)$.
2. Use Newton's binomial formula [B.8] to find $(a + b)^6$.

3. **a.** Prove that $\sum_{k=1}^{8}(a_{k+1} - a_k) = a_9 - a_1$, and, more generally, that $\sum_{k=1}^{n}(a_{k+1} - a_k) = a_{n+1} - a_1$.

   b. Use the result in (a) to compute the following:

   (i) $\displaystyle\sum_{k=1}^{50}\left(\frac{1}{k} - \frac{1}{k+1}\right)$ (ii) $\displaystyle\sum_{k=1}^{12}\left(3^{k+1} - 3^k\right)$

   (iii) $\displaystyle\sum_{k=1}^{n}\left(ar^{k+1} - ar^k\right)$

4. **a.** Verify that

$$\binom{8}{3} = \binom{8}{8-3} \quad \text{and that} \quad \binom{8}{3} + \binom{8}{3+1} = \binom{8+1}{3+1}$$

   b. Verify [B.9] and [B.10] by using the definition of $\dbinom{m}{k}$.

5. Find the sum

$$\sum_{k=0}^{n-1}\frac{n}{x}\left(\frac{kx}{n}\right)^2$$

6. Prove the summation formula for an arithmetic series,

$$\sum_{i=0}^{n-1}(a+id) = na + \frac{n(n-1)d}{2}$$

   by using the idea in the proof of [B.5]. Then verify the summation result of Gauss mentioned earlier.

B.3 Double Sums

Often one has to combine several summation signs. Consider, for example, the following rectangular array of numbers:

$$
\begin{array}{cccc}
a_{11} & a_{12} & \cdots & a_{1n} \\
a_{21} & a_{22} & \cdots & a_{2n} \\
\vdots & \vdots & & \vdots \\
a_{m1} & a_{m2} & \cdots & a_{mn}
\end{array}
\qquad \text{[B.11]}
$$

A typical number here is of the form a_{ij}, where $1 \le i \le m$ and $1 \le j \le n$. (For example, a_{ij} may indicate the total revenue of a firm from its sales in region i in month j.) There are $n \cdot m$ numbers in all. Let us find the sum of all the numbers in the array by first finding the sum of the numbers in each of the m rows and then adding all these row sums. The m row sums can be written in the form $\sum_{j=1}^{n} a_{1j}$,

$\sum_{j=1}^{n} a_{2j}, \ldots, \sum_{j=1}^{n} a_{mj}$. (In our example, these row sums are the total revenues in each region summed over all the n months.) The sum of these m sums is equal to $\sum_{j=1}^{n} a_{1j} + \sum_{j=1}^{n} a_{2j} + \cdots + \sum_{j=1}^{n} a_{mj}$, which can be written as $\sum_{i=1}^{m} \left(\sum_{j=1}^{n} a_{ij} \right)$.

If we add the numbers in each of the n columns first and then take the sum of these columns, we get instead

$$\sum_{i=1}^{m} a_{i1} + \sum_{i=1}^{m} a_{i2} + \cdots + \sum_{i=1}^{m} a_{in} = \sum_{j=1}^{n} \left(\sum_{i=1}^{m} a_{ij} \right)$$

(How do you interpret this sum in our economic example?) In both these cases, we have calculated the sum of all the numbers in the array, so that we must have

$$\sum_{i=1}^{m} \sum_{j=1}^{n} a_{ij} = \sum_{j=1}^{n} \sum_{i=1}^{m} a_{ij} \qquad \text{[B.12]}$$

where, according to usual practice, we have deleted the parentheses. Formula [B.12] says that *in a (finite) double sum, the order of summation is immaterial*. Here it is important to note that the summation limits for i and j are independent of each other. (See Problem 2 for a case in which the summation limits are not independent.)

Example B.7

Compute

$$\sum_{i=1}^{3} \sum_{j=1}^{4} (i + 2j)$$

Solution

$$\sum_{i=1}^{3} \sum_{j=1}^{4} (i + 2j) = \sum_{i=1}^{3} \left[(i + 2) + (i + 4) + (i + 6) + (i + 8) \right]$$

$$= \sum_{i=1}^{3} (4i + 20) = 24 + 28 + 32 = 84$$

(Perform the summation by first summing over i, and then over j, and show that the result is the same.)

Example B.8

Consider the $m \cdot n$ numbers a_{ij} in [B.11]. Denote the arithmetic mean of them all by $\bar{a}$, and the mean of all the numbers in the jth column by $\bar{a}_j$, so that

$$\bar{a} = \frac{1}{mn} \sum_{r=1}^{m} \sum_{s=1}^{n} a_{rs}, \qquad \bar{a}_j = \frac{1}{m} \sum_{r=1}^{m} a_{rj}$$

Prove that

$$\sum_{r=1}^{m}\sum_{s=1}^{m}(a_{rj}-\bar{a})(a_{sj}-\bar{a}) = m^2(\bar{a}_j-\bar{a})^2 \qquad [*]$$

Solution   Because $a_{rj}-\bar{a}$ is independent of the summation index s, we get

$$\sum_{s=1}^{m}(a_{rj}-\bar{a})(a_{sj}-\bar{a}) = (a_{rj}-\bar{a})\sum_{s=1}^{m}(a_{sj}-\bar{a})$$

for each r, and so

$$\sum_{r=1}^{m}\sum_{s=1}^{m}(a_{rj}-\bar{a})(a_{sj}-\bar{a}) = \left[\sum_{r=1}^{m}(a_{rj}-\bar{a})\right]\left[\sum_{s=1}^{m}(a_{sj}-\bar{a})\right] \qquad [**]$$

Using [B.2] to [B.4] and the previous expression $\bar{a}_j$, we have

$$\sum_{r=1}^{m}(a_{rj}-\bar{a}) = \sum_{r=1}^{m}a_{rj} - \sum_{r=1}^{m}\bar{a} = m\bar{a}_j - m\bar{a} = m(\bar{a}_j-\bar{a}) \qquad [***]$$

Moreover, replacing r with s as the index of summation in [***] gives

$$\sum_{s=1}^{m}(a_{sj}-\bar{a}) = m(\bar{a}_j-\bar{a})$$

Substituting these values into [**] then confirms [*].

Problems

1. Expand the following:

a. $\displaystyle\sum_{i=1}^{3}\sum_{j=1}^{4}i\cdot 3^j$ **b.** $\displaystyle\sum_{s=0}^{2}\sum_{r=2}^{4}\left(\frac{rs}{r+s}\right)^2$ **c.** $\displaystyle\sum_{i=1}^{m}\sum_{j=1}^{n}i\cdot k^j$ $(k\neq 1)$

2. Prove that the sum of all the numbers in the triangular table

$$
\begin{array}{ccccc}
a_{11} & & & & \\
a_{21} & a_{22} & & & \\
a_{31} & a_{32} & a_{33} & & \\
\vdots & \vdots & \vdots & \ddots & \\
a_{m1} & a_{m2} & a_{m3} & \cdots & a_{mm}
\end{array}
$$

can be written as

$$\sum_{i=1}^{m} \left(\sum_{j=1}^{i} a_{ij} \right) \qquad \text{or as} \qquad \sum_{j=1}^{m} \left(\sum_{i=j}^{m} a_{ij} \right)$$

3. Consider a group of individuals each having a certain number of units of m different goods. Let a_{ij} denote the number of units of good i owned by person j ($i = 1, \ldots, m$, $j = 1, \ldots, n$). Explain in words the meaning of the following sums:

a. $\displaystyle\sum_{j=1}^{n} a_{ij}$
   b. $\displaystyle\sum_{i=1}^{m} a_{ij}$
   c. $\displaystyle\sum_{j=1}^{n}\sum_{i=1}^{m} a_{ij}$

B.4 Products

There is a special notation for products, analogous to the $\sum$ notation for sums. If $a_1, a_2, \ldots, a_n$ are numbers, then we write $\prod_{i=1}^{n} a_i$ for the product of the numbers $a_1, a_2, \ldots a_n$. That is,

$$\prod_{i=1}^{n} a_i = a_1 a_2 \cdots a_n \qquad [\text{B}.13]$$

The values of all the a_i as i ranges from 1 to n are multiplied together. More generally, if m and n are integers with $m \leq n$, then we write

$$\prod_{i=m}^{n} a_i = a_m a_{m+1} \cdots a_n \qquad [\text{B}.14]$$

This product consists of $n - m + 1$ factors. For instance, if $n = 6$ and $m = 3$, then $\prod_{i=3}^{6} a_i = a_3 a_4 a_5 a_6$ is a product of $6 - 3 + 1 = 4$ factors.

Example B.9
   Expand the following products:

(a) $\displaystyle\prod_{i=3}^{6} (2i - 1)$
   (b) $\displaystyle\prod_{k=1}^{n} \left(1 + \frac{1}{k}\right)^k$

Solution

(a) $\displaystyle\prod_{i=3}^{6} (2i - 1) = 5 \cdot 7 \cdot 9 \cdot 11 = 3465$

(b) $\displaystyle\prod_{k=1}^{n}\left(1+\frac{1}{k}\right)^{k} = \left(1+\frac{1}{1}\right)^{1}\left(1+\frac{1}{2}\right)^{2}\cdots\left(1+\frac{1}{n}\right)^{n}$

If all the a_i's in [B.13] and [B.14] are equal to the same number a, then

$$\prod_{i=1}^{n} a = a^{n}, \qquad \prod_{i=m}^{n} a = a^{n-m+1} \qquad\qquad \text{[B.15]}$$

In Section 20.3, we consider sums of products. Let us consider a typical example.

Example B.10
Evaluate the expression

$$\sum_{k=1}^{3}\left(\prod_{s=k+1}^{5} x_s\right) y^{k}$$

Solution   Each product in parentheses obviously depends on k. If we let $D_k = \prod_{s=k+1}^{5} x_s$, the sum becomes $\sum_{k=1}^{3} D_k y^{k} = D_1 y^1 + D_2 y^2 + D_3 y^3$, so

$$\sum_{k=1}^{3}\left(\prod_{s=k+1}^{5} x_s\right) y^{k} = \left(\prod_{s=2}^{5} x_s\right) y^1 + \left(\prod_{s=3}^{5} x_s\right) y^2 + \left(\prod_{s=4}^{5} x_s\right) y^3$$

$$= (x_2 x_3 x_4 x_5)y + (x_3 x_4 x_5)y^2 + (x_4 x_5)y^3$$

Problems

1. Evaluate the following:

   a. $\displaystyle\prod_{s=1}^{6} 2^{-s}$ **b.** $\displaystyle\prod_{k=3}^{6} k^{3}$ **c.** $\displaystyle\prod_{j=-2}^{1} \frac{j}{j+3}$ **d.** $\displaystyle\frac{\prod_{s=3}^{5}(1+r_s)}{\prod_{s=1}^{5}(1+r_s)}$

2. Expand the following expressions:

   a. $\displaystyle\prod_{k=1}^{n} \frac{2k}{2k-1}\frac{2k}{2k+1}$ **b.** $\displaystyle\prod_{i=1}^{n} \frac{a_i}{b_i}$ **c.** $\displaystyle\sum_{i=1}^{n}\left(\prod_{s=i+1}^{n} a_s\right) b_i$

3. Which of the following equalities are true?

   a. $\displaystyle\prod_{i=1}^{n} ka_i = k\prod_{i=1}^{n} a_i$ **b.** $\displaystyle\prod_{i=1}^{n} y_i^{3} = \left(\prod_{i=1}^{n} y_i\right)^{3}$

   c. $\displaystyle\prod_{i=1}^{n} x_i y_i = \left(\prod_{i=1}^{n} x_i\right)\left(\prod_{i=1}^{n} y_i\right)$ **d.** $\displaystyle\prod_{i=1}^{n}\left(\prod_{j=1}^{i} a_{ij}\right) = \prod_{j=1}^{n}\left(\prod_{i=j}^{n} a_{ij}\right)$

B.5 Induction

Proof by induction is an important technique for verifying formulas involving natural numbers. For instance, consider the sum of the first n odd numbers. We observe that

$$1 = 1 \; = 1^2$$
$$1 + 3 = 4 \; = 2^2$$
$$1 + 3 + 5 = 9 \; = 3^2$$
$$1 + 3 + 5 + 7 = 16 = 4^2$$
$$1 + 3 + 5 + 7 + 9 = 25 = 5^2$$

This suggests a general pattern, with the sum of the first n odd numbers equal to n^2:

$$1 + 3 + 5 + \cdots + (2n - 1) = n^2 \qquad [*]$$

To prove that this is generally valid, we can proceed as follows. Suppose that the formula in $[*]$ is correct for a certain natural number $n = k$, so that

$$1 + 3 + 5 + \cdots + (2k - 1) = k^2$$

By adding the next odd number $2k + 1$ to each side, we get

$$1 + 3 + 5 + \cdots + (2k - 1) + (2k + 1) = k^2 + (2k + 1) = (k + 1)^2$$

But this is the formula $[*]$ with $n = k + 1$. Hence, we have proved that if the sum of the first k odd numbers is k^2, then the sum of the first $k + 1$ odd numbers equals $(k + 1)^2$. This implication, together with the fact that $[*]$ *is* valid for $n = 1$, implies that $[*]$ is generally valid. For we have just shown that if $[*]$ is true for $n = 1$, then it is true for $n = 2$; that if it is true for $n = 2$, then it is true for $n = 3$; ...; that if it is true for $n = k$, then it is true for $n = k + 1$; and so on.

A proof of this type is called a *proof by induction*. We show that the formula is valid for $n = 1$ and moreover that *if* the formula is valid for $n = k$, then it is also valid for $n = k + 1$. It follows by induction that the formula is valid for all natural numbers n. Our next example requires you to know about differentiation.

Example B.11
Prove by induction that, for all positive integers n,

$$f(x) = x^n \implies f'(x) = nx^{n-1} \qquad [1]$$

Solution   Formula [1] is correct for $n = 1$, because $f(x) = x \Rightarrow f'(x) = 1 = 1 \cdot x^{1-1}$. *Suppose* that [1] is valid for $n = k$. Then

$$f(x) = x^k \Longrightarrow f'(x) = kx^{k-1} \qquad [2]$$

We have to prove that [1] is valid also for $n = k + 1$. To this end, we must differentiate $f(x) = x^{k+1}$. We cannot use [1] for $n = k + 1$, but because we have assumed the correctness of [2], we write $f(x) = x^{k+1} = x^k \cdot x$. Using the product rule for derivatives together with [2], we get

$$f(x) = x^k \cdot x \Longrightarrow f'(x) = kx^{k-1} \cdot x + x^k \cdot 1 = (k + 1)x^k$$

But this result is precisely what we get by replacing the number n in [1] by $k + 1$. Using induction, we have proved [1] for all positive integers.

On the basis of these examples, the general structure of an induction proof can be explained as follows: We want to prove that a mathematical formula $A(n)$ that depends on n is valid for all natural numbers n. In the two previous examples, the respective statements $A(n)$ were

$$A(n) : 1 + 3 + 5 + \cdots + (2n - 1) = n^2$$
$$A(n) : f(x) = x^n \Longrightarrow f'(x) = nx^{n-1}$$

The steps required in each proof are as follows: First, verify that $A(1)$ is valid, which means that the formula is correct for $n = 1$. Then prove that for each natural number k, if $A(k)$ is true, it follows that $A(k + 1)$ must be true. Here $A(k)$ is called *the induction hypothesis*, and the step from $A(k)$ to $A(k + 1)$ is called *the induction step* in the proof. When the induction step is proved for an arbitrary natural number k, then, by induction, statement $A(n)$ is true for all n. The general principle can now be formulated:

The Principle of Mathematical Induction

Suppose that $A(n)$ is a statement for all natural numbers n and that

(a) $A(1)$ is true   [B.16]
(b) if the induction hypothesis $A(k)$ is true, then $A(k + 1)$ is true for each natural number k

Then $A(n)$ is true for all natural numbers n.

The principle of induction seems intuitively evident. If the truth of $A(k)$ for each k implies the truth of $A(k+1)$, then because $A(1)$ is true, $A(2)$ must be true, which, in turn, means that $A(3)$ is true, and so on. (An analogy: Consider a ladder with an infinite number of steps. Suppose you can climb the first step and suppose, moreover, that after each step, you can always climb the next. Then you are able to climb up to any step.)

The principle of mathematical induction can easily be generalized to the case in which we have a statement $A(n)$ for each natural number greater than or equal to an arbitrary natural number n_0. If we can prove that $A(n_0)$ is valid, and moreover we can prove that if $A(k)$ is true, then $A(k+1)$ is true for each $k \geq n_0$, then $A(n)$ is true for all $n \geq n_0$.

Problems

1. Prove statement [B.5] in Sec. B.2 by induction, namely:

$$1 + 2 + 3 + \cdots + n = \tfrac{1}{2}n(n+1) \qquad\qquad [*]$$

2. Prove formulas [B.6] and [B.7] in Section B.2 by induction.

3. Prove the following by induction:

   a. $\dfrac{1}{1 \cdot 2} + \dfrac{1}{2 \cdot 3} + \dfrac{1}{3 \cdot 4} + \cdots + \dfrac{1}{n(n+1)} = \dfrac{n}{n+1}$

   b. $3 + 3^2 + 3^3 + 3^4 + \cdots + 3^n = \tfrac{1}{2}(3^{n+1} - 3)$

4. $1^3 + 2^3 + 3^3 = 36$ is divisible by 9. Prove by induction that the sum $n^3 + (n+1)^3 + (n+2)^3$ of three consecutive cubes is always divisible by 9.

5. Prove by induction that for $k \neq 1$,

$$a + ak + \cdots + ak^{n-1} = a\frac{1 - k^n}{1 - k}$$

(See also (6.10) in Section 6.5.)

6. Let n be a positive integer and consider the expression $s_n = n^2 - n + 41$. Verify that s_n is a prime number (and so has no factor except 1 and itself) for $n = 1, 2, 3, 4$, and 5. With some efforts, one can prove that s_n is a prime number for $n = 6, 7, \ldots$, and 40 as well. Is s_n a prime for all n? (This problem was first suggested by the Swiss mathematician L. Euler.)

Trigonometric Functions

—and mathematics is nourished by dreamers
—as it nourishes them.
—D'Arcy W. Thompson (1940)

Many phenomena, both physical and economic, appear to repeat themselves with predictable regularity. Examples are alternating electric currents in physics, heartbeat and respiration in physiology, and seasonal variations in economics such as increased demand for heating fuel in winter. Many economists have also looked for regular periodic patterns in macroeconomic variables like national output or interest rates. Indeed, that is why the term "business cycle" has come into general use in economics.

There are special "periodic functions" that can be used to describe such phenomena mathematically. Among these, the *trigonometric functions* are the most important. Many will have studied such functions in trigonometry, which is used for computing angles and distances in triangles and in polygons built up from triangles. The results are useful in surveying, astronomy, navigation, and in many other fields. But as far as economics is concerned, trigonometric functions are used primarily to describe periodic phenomena. This appendix provides a brief introduction.

C.1 Basic Definitions and Results

According to our definition in Section 2.1, *any* rule gives a function if it assigns one and only one number in the range to each number in the domain. The rule may be defined in various ways. For trigonometric functions, the way we set out in what follows might strike you as rather odd, yet it does accord with this general definition of a function.

Consider the circle in Fig. C.1 with radius 1 and center at the origin. Let A be the point on the circle with coordinates $(1, 0)$. For each real number x, we measure an arc of length $|x|$ around the circle from A. If $x > 0$, the arc is chosen in the positive direction (that is counterclockwise), but in the negative direction if $x < 0$. This gives a point P_x with certain coordinates (u, v). The arc x is measured with the same unit of length as the radius. Because the radius of the circle is $r = 1$, the circumference equals $2\pi r = 2\pi$. If $x = \pi/2$, we go one-quarter of the way round the circle in a counterclockwise direction to the point $P_{\pi/2}$, which has coordinates $(0, 1)$. For P_π, we go half way round to the point with coordinates $(u, v) = (-1, 0)$; for $P_{3\pi/2}$, we get $(u, v) = (0, -1)$; for $P_0 = P_{2\pi}$, we have $(u, v) = (1, 0)$; and so on. For the point P_x shown in Fig. C.1, we have $u \approx 0.45$ and $v \approx 0.9$.

In general, as x increases, so P_x rotates around the unit circle, and the values of u and v oscillate up and down. They eventually repeat themselves as P_x moves through points where it has been before. In particular, x, $x \pm 2\pi$, $x \pm 4\pi$, and so on, all define the same point on the circle. Thus, $P_x = P_{x+2n\pi}$ for $n = \pm 1, \pm 2, \ldots$. This procedure assigns a point P_x with coordinates (u, v) to each real number x.

The **sine** function is the rule that assigns the number v to the number x.

The **cosine** function is the rule that assigns the number u to the number x.

It is standard to abbreviate *sine* to sin and *cosine* to cos. So we have

$$\sin x = v \quad \text{and} \quad \cos x = u \qquad \text{[C.1]}$$

The domains of the functions sin and cos are thus the set of all real numbers. Both their ranges are the closed interval $[-1, 1]$, because all the values in this interval

FIGURE C.1 $\sin x = v$ and $\cos x = u$.

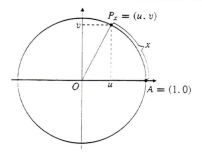

are attained by u and v as P_x runs around the circle. Note also that a small change in x changes point P_x only slightly, so the coordinates u and v will also change only slightly, and $v = \sin x$ and $u = \cos x$ are both continuous functions of x. (In fact, from Fig. C.1, we see that a given change in x implies changes in u and v that are smaller in absolute value.)

If x is any number such that $\cos x \neq 0$, we define the **tangent** function by simply dividing $\sin x$ by $\cos x$. It is standard to abbreviate *tangent* to tan, so that

$$\tan x = \frac{\sin x}{\cos x} \qquad\qquad [C.2]$$

Measuring Angles in Radians

In trigonometry, it is common to define the sin, cos, and tan of *angles*, usually measured in degrees. Figure C.1 shows how the arc length x can be used to measure the angle AOP_x. Then it is said that the angle is measured in **radians**. It is common practice to operate with degrees in elementary geometry and in tables of trigonometric functions, so one must know how to convert degrees into radians and vice versa. Now $360° = 2\pi$ radians, because when $x = 2\pi$, line OP_x has rotated through $360°$. So we have the following:

$$1° = \left(\frac{\pi}{180}\right) \text{ radians} \approx 0.017 \text{ radians}, \quad 1 \text{ radian} = \left(\frac{180}{\pi}\right)° \approx 57.3° \qquad [C.3]$$

For some particularly important angles, the conversions between degrees and radians are given in Fig. C.2. The degree scale for measuring angles is built on an arbitrary choice of unit in that the complete circle is divided into $360°$. This corresponds to the ancient Babylonian calendar that divided the year into 360 days—a rather crude approximation.[1] From a mathematical viewpoint, the radian scale is the most natural one for measuring angles. The reason is that the formulas of calculus are simpler when angles are measured in radians rather than in degrees.

There is no method for finding exact numerical values of the trigonometric functions in the general case. Approximations are given in tables and are also available on most scientific calculators.

For certain special values of x, however, we can compute $\sin x$ and $\cos x$ by using elementary geometry. Consider Fig. C.3. Here we have chosen $x = \pi/6$. Then angle BOP is $30°$, and triangle BOP is a $30° - 60° - 90°$ triangle. Figure C.4 reminds you of a basic fact about such triangles. So in Fig. C.3, line $PB = \frac{1}{2}OP = \frac{1}{2}$. Then Pythagoras' theorem implies that $(OB)^2 = (OP)^2 - (BP)^2 = 1 - \frac{1}{4} = \frac{3}{4}$,

---

[1] It seems that the Babylonians wanted the number of days in the year to be divisible by 12, the number of signs in the Zodiac.

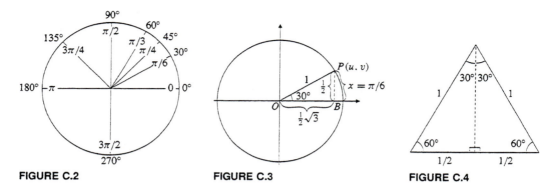

FIGURE C.2   **FIGURE C.3**   **FIGURE C.4**

and so $OB = \frac{1}{2}\sqrt{3}$. The coordinates of P, therefore, must be $u = \frac{1}{2}\sqrt{3}$ and $v = \frac{1}{2}$. From [C.1] and [C.2], we then obtain

$$\sin\frac{\pi}{6} = \frac{1}{2}, \qquad \cos\frac{\pi}{6} = \frac{1}{2}\sqrt{3}, \qquad \tan\frac{\pi}{6} = \frac{1}{3}\sqrt{3}$$

By using similar geometric considerations, we can establish Table C.1.

TABLE C.1   *Special values of the trigonometric functions*

x	0	$\frac{\pi}{6} = 30°$	$\frac{\pi}{4} = 45°$	$\frac{\pi}{3} = 60°$	$\frac{\pi}{2} = 90°$	$\frac{3\pi}{4} = 135°$	$\pi = 180°$	$\frac{3\pi}{2} = 270°$	$2\pi = 360°$
$\sin x$	0	$\frac{1}{2}$	$\frac{1}{2}\sqrt{2}$	$\frac{1}{2}\sqrt{3}$	1	$\frac{1}{2}\sqrt{2}$	0	-1	0
$\cos x$	1	$\frac{1}{2}\sqrt{3}$	$\frac{1}{2}\sqrt{2}$	$\frac{1}{2}$	0	$-\frac{1}{2}\sqrt{2}$	-1	0	1
$\tan x$	0	$\frac{1}{3}\sqrt{3}$	1	$\sqrt{3}$	*	-1	0	•	0

*Not defined.

The Graphs of the Trigonometric Functions

Because the construction illustrated in Fig. C.1 implies that $P_{x+2\pi} = P_x$ for all x, we must have

$$\sin(x + 2\pi) = \sin x, \qquad \cos(x + 2\pi) = \cos x \qquad \text{[C.4]}$$

We say that sin and cos are **periodic** with **period** 2π. Moreover (see Problem 5),

$$\tan(x + \pi) = \tan x \qquad \text{[C.5]}$$

so that tan is **periodic** with **period** π.

We noted before that the ranges of sin and cos were the interval $[-1, 1]$, so

$$-1 \le \sin x \le 1, \qquad -1 \le \cos x \le 1$$

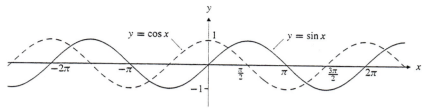

FIGURE C.5

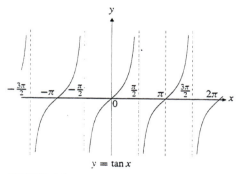

FIGURE C.6

The graphs of sin and cos are shown in Fig. C.5. The cosine curve can be obtained by translating the sine curve $\pi/2$ units to the left. This follows from the relation

$$\sin\left(x + \frac{\pi}{2}\right) = \cos x \qquad\qquad [C.6]$$

(see Problem 5).

The graph of the tangent function is shown in Fig. C.6. Note that its value is positive iff both the sine and the cosine functions have the same sign. Also $\tan x$ is undefined when $x = \frac{1}{2}\pi + n\pi$ for an integer n, because then $\cos x = 0$.

Trigonometric Formulas

There is a large number of trigonometric formulas that have pestered high school students for generations. Here we mention only two of them. (The problems provide some additional formulas and results.)

Write $\sin^2 x$ for $(\sin x)^2$, $\cos^2 x$ for $(\cos x)^2$, and $\tan^2 x$ for $(\tan x)^2$. Similar notation is also used for higher powers of the trigonometric functions. For example, $\cos^3 x = (\cos x)^3$.

The first formula we mention is very simple. Consider the point $P_x = (u, v)$ in Fig. C.1. It lies on the unit circle. Therefore, we have $u^2 + v^2 = 1$. Because

$u = \cos x$ and $v = \sin x$, we conclude that

$$\sin^2 x + \cos^2 x = 1 \qquad\qquad [C.7]$$

Another useful formula is the following:

$$\cos(x - y) = \cos x \cos y + \sin x \sin y \qquad\qquad [C.8]$$

Problem 14 indicates a proof of [C.8]. By using this basic equation, similar formulas for $\cos(x + y)$, $\sin(x + y)$, and $\sin(x - y)$ are quite easy to prove (see Problems 3 and 4).

More Complicated Functions

We have now discussed some important properties of the three basic trigonometric functions: sin, cos, and tan. As mentioned earlier, in economics, they are mainly used in connection with periodic phenomena. It is often the case that more complicated expressions must be used.

We have seen that $y = \sin x$ is periodic with period 2π. The graph of the function shows a wavelike curve that is said to have **period** (or **wavelength**) 2π. If, instead, we represent graphically the function given by $y = \sin(x/2)$, we still get a wavelike curve, but the period is now twice as long, namely, 4π. When x increases from 0 to 4π, then $x/2$ increases from 0 to 2π, so $\sin(x/2)$ is periodic with period 4π. More generally, $y = \sin(ax)$ is periodic with period $2\pi/a$, for when x increases from 0 to $2\pi/a$, then ax increases from 0 to 2π. The value of $y = \sin(ax)$ will still oscillate between -1 and 1, and we say that the **amplitude** is equal to 1. To have a periodic function with amplitude A, just let $y = A \sin ax$, which varies between $-A$ and A. Hence,

$$y = A \sin(ax) \quad \text{has period } 2\pi/a \text{ and amplitude } A$$

The reciprocal, $a/2\pi$, of the period is called the **frequency**. It is the number of oscillations per unit of time.

The graph of $y = A \sin(ax)$ intersects the x-axis at $x = 0$. To get a curve translated a certain distance in the x-direction, let $y = A \sin(ax + b)$. To get a curve translated in the y-direction, let

$$y = A \sin(ax + b) + B \qquad\qquad [C.9]$$

The graph of this function will be a sine curve with amplitude A and period $2\pi/a$. Relative to $y = A \sin(ax)$, it will be translated a distance $-b/a$ in the x-direction and a distance B in the y-direction. See Fig. C.7 (in which $a > 0$ and $b < 0$).

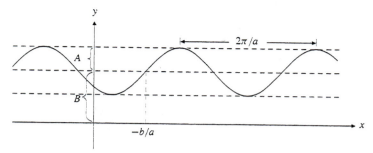

FIGURE C.7

Problems

1. Use a diagram like Fig. C.3 to verify the values in Table C.1 for $x = \pi/4$.

2. Verify that for all x, we have

$$\sin(-x) = -\sin x, \qquad \cos(-x) = \cos x, \qquad \tan(-x) = -\tan x$$

3. Write $\cos(x + y) = \cos[x - (-y)]$, then use the results in Problem 2 and [C.8] to verify that

$$\cos(x + y) = \cos x \cos y - \sin x \sin y$$

4. Use [C.8] to show that $\cos(y - \pi/2) = \sin y$. From this, it follows that $\sin(y - \pi/2) = \cos(y - \pi) = -\cos y$, again using [C.8]. Then let $\sin(x+y) = \cos[x + (y - \pi/2)]$ and so prove that

$$\sin(x + y) = \sin x \cos y + \cos x \sin y, \qquad \sin(x - y) = \sin x \cos y - \cos x \sin y$$

5. Use the results in Problems 3 and 4 to prove [C.5] and [C.6].

6. Find the following values:

    a. $\sin(\pi - \pi/6)$ **b.** $\cos(\pi + \pi/6)$ **c.** $\sin(-3\pi/4)$

    d. $\cos(5\pi/4)$ **e.** $\tan(7\pi/6)$ **f.** $\sin(\pi/12)$

7. Simplify the following expressions:

    a. $\sqrt{2}\sin(x + \pi/4) - \cos x$ **b.** $\dfrac{\sin[\pi - (\alpha + \beta)]}{\cos[2\pi - (\alpha + \beta)]}$

    c. $\dfrac{\sin(a + x) - \sin(a - x)}{\cos(a + x) - \cos(a - x)}$

8. Prove that

$$\sin A - \sin B = 2\cos\frac{A + B}{2}\sin\frac{A - B}{2}$$

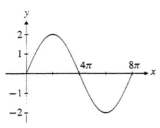

FIGURE C.8

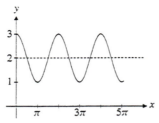

FIGURE C.9

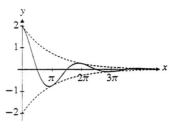

FIGURE C.10

(*Hint:* Let $x + y = A$ and $x - y = B$ in the two formulas in Problem 4, then subtract.)

9. Prove that for all real numbers x and y,

$$\sin(x + y) \sin(x - y) = \sin^2 x - \sin^2 y$$

10. Draw the graphs of the following functions. Then give their periods and amplitudes.

   a. $f(x) = \sin(2x)$ **b.** $g(x) = 3\sin(x/2)$ **c.** $h(x) = 2\sin(3x + 4) + 2$

11. Explain why the following functions represent respectively an oscillation that dies out and an oscillation that explodes.

   a. $f(x) = (1/2)^x \sin x$ **b.** $g(x) = 2^x \cos 2x$

12. Find functions whose graphs are shown in Figs. C.8 to C.10. In Fig. C.10, the dashed-line curves have the equations $y = \pm 2e^{-x/\pi}$.

Harder Problems

13. Consider triangle ABC in Fig. C.11. Because the square of the distance between $A = (b, 0)$ and $B = (a \cos x, a \sin x)$ is equal to c^2, show that the following theorem is true.

FIGURE C.11

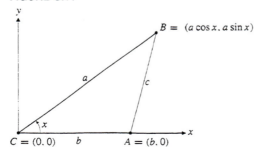

The Extended Pythagorean Theorem

$$c^2 = a^2 + b^2 - 2ab\cos x$$

[C.10]

---

14. Consider Fig. C.12 in which angle POQ is $x - y$. According to [C.10], we have $|QP|^2 = |OQ|^2 + |OP|^2 - 2|OQ||OP|\cos(x - y)$. Use this equality to prove [C.8].

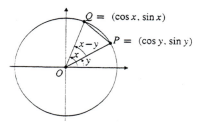

$Q = (\cos x, \sin x)$

$P = (\cos y, \sin y)$

FIGURE C.12

C.2 Derivatives of Trigonometric Functions

Consider the graph of the sine function in Fig. C.5. It is periodic, so its derivative must also be periodic. (Can you explain why?) The slope of the graph of $f(x) = \sin x$ at $x = 0$ seems to be 1, as is the value of $\cos x$ at $x = 0$. Also the slope at $x = \pi/2$ is 0, as is $\cos \pi/2$. Therefore, it should not be surprising that

$$y = \sin x \quad \Rightarrow \quad y' = \cos x$$

[C.11]

To *prove* [C.11] requires considering the Newton quotient of $f(x) = \sin x$, which is

$$\frac{f(x + h) - f(x)}{h} = \frac{\sin(x + h) - \sin x}{h}$$

Using the identity in Problem 8 of Section C.1 gives

$$\frac{\sin(x + h) - \sin x}{h} = \frac{2\cos\left[\frac{1}{2}(x + h + x)\right]\sin\left[\frac{1}{2}(x + h - x)\right]}{h}$$

$$= \cos(x + \tfrac{1}{2}h)\frac{\sin\left(\frac{1}{2}h\right)}{\frac{1}{2}h}$$

[*]

Suppose we could show that $(\sin u)/u \to 1$ as $u \to 0$. Letting $u = \frac{1}{2}h$ and letting $h \to 0$ would give $[\sin(\frac{1}{2}h)]/\frac{1}{2}h \to 1$ as $h \to 0$. So the limit of [*] as $h \to 0$ would be $\cos x$. This would prove [C.11].

We therefore need to show that $(\sin u)/u \to 1$ as $u \to 0$. Table C.2 shows the values of $(\sin u)/u$ for some positive values of u close to 0. (Remember to set your calculator to radians!)

TABLE C.2

u	1	0.5	0.3	0.1	0.01
$\dfrac{\sin u}{u}$	0.841	0.959	0.985	0.998	0.9998

The result $\lim_{u \to 0}(\sin u)/u = 1$ can be proved using Fig. C.13. Clearly,

$$\text{area of triangle } OAB \leq \text{area of sector } OAB \leq \text{area of triangle } OAC$$

Triangle OAB has area $\frac{1}{2}(1 \cdot \sin u) = \frac{1}{2}\sin u$. In Fig. C.13(c), the length of OA is $OC \cdot \cos u$, so $OC = 1/\cos u$. But then $AC = OC \cdot \sin u = \tan u$. Thus, triangle OAC has area $\frac{1}{2}\tan u$. Finally, arc u is a fraction $u/2\pi$ of the distance 2π around the whole circle with radius 1. Hence, sector OAB has an area equal to a fraction $u/2\pi$ of the area π of the whole circle with radius 1—that is, its area is $\frac{1}{2}u$. So

$$\frac{1}{2}\sin u \leq \frac{1}{2}u \leq \frac{1}{2}\tan u = \frac{1}{2}\frac{\sin u}{\cos u}$$

For $u \in (0, \pi/2)$, one has $\cos u > 0$. Therefore, these inequalities imply that $(\sin u)/u \leq 1$ and $\cos u \leq (\sin u)/u$. So

$$\cos u \leq \frac{\sin u}{u} \leq 1 \qquad\qquad [**]$$

The inequalities $[**]$ also hold for $u \in (-\pi/2, 0)$, because $\cos(-u) = \cos u$

FIGURE C.13a

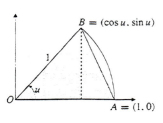

$B = (\cos u, \sin u)$

$A = (1, 0)$

FIGURE C.13b

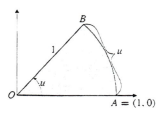

$A = (1, 0)$

FIGURE C.13c

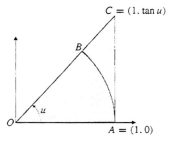

$C = (1, \tan u)$

$A = (1, 0)$

and $\sin(-u) = -\sin u$, so $[\sin(-u)]/(-u) = (\sin u)/u$. Recall that $\cos u \rightarrow 1$ as $u \rightarrow 0$. Thus, using the squeezing rule [6.27] in Section 6.7, we see that

$$\lim_{u \to 0} \frac{\sin u}{u} = 1 \qquad\qquad [C.12]$$

If u is a function of x, the chain rule for differentiation gives

$$y = \sin u, \quad u = u(x) \quad \Rightarrow \quad y' = u' \cos u \qquad\qquad [C.13]$$

Let $g(x) = \cos x$. According to [C.6], we have $g(x) = \sin(x + \pi/2)$, so [C.13] yields $g'(x) = \cos(x + \pi/2)$. But Problem 3 in Section C.1 yields the implication that $\cos(x + \pi/2) = -\sin x$. Hence,

$$y = \cos x \quad \Rightarrow \quad y' = -\sin x \qquad\qquad [C.14]$$

The quotient rule for differentiating $y = \tan x = \sin x / \cos x$ gives (see Problem 2)

$$y = \tan x \quad \Rightarrow \quad y' = \frac{1}{\cos^2 x} = 1 + \tan^2 x \qquad \text{(provided that } \cos x \neq 0\text{)} \quad [C.15]$$

Combining these rules of differentiation with those developed earlier allows us to differentiate many expressions involving trigonometric functions.

Example C.1
Differentiate the following functions:

$\quad$ **(a)** $y = \sin 2x$ $\qquad$ **(b)** $y = \sin^2 x + \cos^2 x$ $\qquad$ **(c)** $y = \dfrac{\sin x}{\cos x + x}$

Solution

(a) Use [C.13] with $u = 2x$ to obtain $y' = 2 \cos u = 2 \cos 2x$.

(b) $y = (\sin x)^2 + (\cos x)^2 \Rightarrow y' = 2(\sin x) \cos x + 2(\cos x)(-\sin x) = 0$. (We see here that $y' \equiv 0$, so that y must be constant. Because $y = 1$ when $x = 0$, the constant must be 1. Hence, we find once again the relation $\sin^2 x + \cos^2 x = 1$.)

(c) Use the quotient rule for differentiation to obtain

$$y' = \frac{(\cos x + x) \cos x - \sin x(-\sin x + 1)}{(\cos x + x)^2}$$

$$= \frac{\cos^2 x + x \cos x + \sin^2 x - \sin x}{(\cos x + x)^2} = \frac{1 + x \cos x - \sin x}{(\cos x + x)^2}$$

Inverse Trigonometric Functions

Consider the problem of solving the equation

$$\sin x = y \qquad\qquad\qquad\qquad \text{[C.16]}$$

for x. Figure C.14 illustrates the problem. If $y > 1$ or $y < -1$, then the equation $\sin x = y$ has no solution, whereas it has infinitely many solutions if $y \in [-1, 1]$.

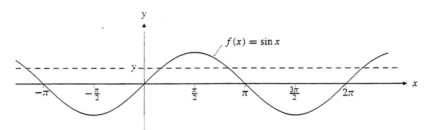

FIGURE C.14

Suppose we require that $x \in [-\pi/2, \pi/2]$. In this interval, $\sin x$ is strictly increasing (because $(\sin x)' = \cos x > 0$ in $(-\pi/2, \pi/2)$). So Equation [C.16] has a unique solution x in this interval for each $y \in [-1, 1]$. We denote this solution by $x = \arcsin y$. In the terminology of Section 7.6, we have now shown that the function $f(x) = \sin x$, with domain $[-\pi/2, \pi/2]$ and range $[-1, 1]$, has an inverse function g. We call this inverse the **arcsine** function. If we use x as a free variable also for the inverse, we have

$$g(x) = \arcsin x, \qquad x \in [-1, 1] \qquad\qquad \text{[C.17]}$$

By definition, $\arcsin x$ is *the number in* $[-\pi/2, \pi/2]$ *whose sine is equal to* x ($\arcsin x$ is "the angle (arc) whose sine is x"). For instance, we have $\arcsin 1/2 = \pi/6$. The graph of $y = \arcsin x$ is shown in Fig. C.15. According to [7.22] in Section 7.6, the graphs of $y = \sin x$ and $y = \arcsin x$ are symmetric about the line $y = x$.

The derivative of $g(x) = \arcsin x$ is found most easily by using implicit differentiation. From the definition of $g(x)$, it follows that $\sin g(x) = x$ for all $x \in (-1, 1)$. If we *assume* that $g(x)$ is differentiable, differentiation using the chain rule gives $\cos[g(x)] \cdot g'(x) = 1$. So

$$g'(x) = \frac{1}{\cos g(x)} = \frac{1}{\sqrt{1 - \sin^2 g(x)}} = \frac{1}{\sqrt{1 - x^2}}$$

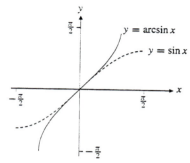

FIGURE C.15

(Alternatively, we could have made use of [7.24] in Section 7.6.) Thus,

$$y = \arcsin x \implies y' = \frac{1}{\sqrt{1 - x^2}} \qquad (-1 < x < 1) \qquad \text{[C.18]}$$

It can be shown in the same way that $y = \cos x$ defined on $[0, \pi]$ has an inverse function $y = \arccos x$ defined on $[-1, 1]$, and that

$$y = \arccos x \implies y' = -\frac{1}{\sqrt{1 - x^2}} \qquad (-1 < x < 1) \qquad \text{[C.19]}$$

Consider, finally, $y = \tan x$ defined in the interval $(-\pi/2, \pi/2)$. Because $y' = 1/\cos^2 x > 0$, the function is strictly increasing, and the range is $(-\infty, \infty)$. The function, therefore, has an inverse function $y = \arctan x$ that is defined in $(-\infty, \infty)$ and has range $(-\pi/2, \pi/2)$. Using implicit differentiation, this time of the equation $\tan y = x$ (so that $y = \arctan x$), yields

$$y = \arctan x \implies y' = \frac{1}{1 + x^2} \qquad (-\infty < x < \infty) \qquad \text{[C.20]}$$

The graph of $y = \arctan x$ is shown in Fig. C.16.

FIGURE C.16

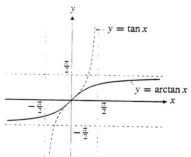

Calculators that have trigonometric functions usually also have their inverses. They are denoted by $\sin^{-1}$, $\cos^{-1}$, and $\tan^{-1}$. If one enters 0.5 and presses the $\boxed{\sin^{-1}}$ key, the answer is 30, because the calculator usually uses degrees. If radians are used, it will give the answer $\pi/6$, or rather 0.5235987.

Problems

1. Find the derivatives of the following functions:

   a. $y = \sin \frac{1}{2}x$ **b.** $y = x \cos x$ **c.** $y = \tan x^2$ **d.** $y = \dfrac{\cos x}{\sin x}$

2. Prove the differentiation rule in [C.15]. (Remember that $\sin^2 x + \cos^2 x = 1$.)

3. Find the derivatives of the following functions:

   a. $y = \sin x + \cos x$ **b.** $y = x^5 \sin x + \sqrt{x} \cos x + 3$ **c.** $y = \dfrac{\sqrt{x} \cos x}{x^2 + 1}$

4. Compute the following:

   a. $\dfrac{d}{dx}(1 - \cos ax)$ **b.** $\dfrac{d}{dt}(at \sin bt)$ **c.** $\dfrac{d}{dt}(\sin\{\cos[\sin(at + b)]\})$

5. Use l'Hôpital's rule, if necessary, to compute

   a. $\lim\limits_{x \to 0} \dfrac{\sin 2x}{x}$ **b.** $\lim\limits_{t \to 0} \dfrac{\sin mt}{\sin nt}$ $(n \neq 0)$

   c. $\lim\limits_{t \to 0} \dfrac{1 - \cos t}{t^2}$ **d.** $\lim\limits_{a \to 0} \dfrac{\sin ax}{x}$ $(x \neq 0)$

6. Find the maximum and minimum of $f(x) = (\sin x - x - 1)^3$ in the interval $I = [0, 3\pi/2]$.

7. Studies of economic cycles often use functions of the form

$$p(t) = C_0 + C_1 \cos \lambda t + C_2 \sin \lambda t$$

   Show that $p''(t) + \lambda^2 p(t)$ is a constant K, and find K.

8. If $y = f(x)$ is a differentiable function that satisfies

$$x \cos y - y \sin x = 0$$

   what is y'? Find the equation for the tangent to the curve at $(\pi, \pi/2)$.

9. Find the derivative of $f(x) = 3 \sin 2x + 4 \cos 4x$.

10. Evaluate the following integrals (for the last two integrals, use integration by parts, as in Section 11.1):

   a. $\displaystyle\int \sin x \, dx$ **b.** $\displaystyle\int_0^{\pi/2} \cos x \, dx$ **c.** $\displaystyle\int \sin^2 x \, dx$ **d.** $\displaystyle\int_0^{\pi} x \cos x \, dx$

11. Evaluate the following integrals by introducing a suitable new variable, as in Section 11.2:

    a. $\int \tan x \, dx = \int \frac{\sin x}{\cos x} \, dx$ **b.** $\int (\cos x) e^{\sin x} \, dx$ **c.** $\int \cos^5 x \sin x \, dx$

12. Determine the following values:

    a. $\arcsin \frac{1}{2}\sqrt{2}$ **b.** $\arccos 0$ **c.** $\arccos \frac{1}{2}\sqrt{3}$ **d.** $\arctan \sqrt{3}$

13. Find the derivatives of the following:

    a. $\arcsin 2x$ **b.** $\arctan(x^2 + 1)$ **c.** $\arccos \sqrt{x}$

14. Show that

$$\frac{d}{dx}\left[\arctan\left(\frac{e^x - e^{-x}}{2}\right)\right] = \frac{2}{e^x + e^{-x}}$$

Harder Problems

15. In Fig. C.17, PP' represents a shoreline. A swimmer in difficulties at A (in the sea) is spotted by the lifeguard at point B (on the land). The guard can swim at v_1 km/h and run at v_2 km/h. Show that in order to get from B to A as quickly as possible, the guard must cross PP' at C, where the position of C is such that

$$\frac{\sin \alpha_1}{v_1} = \frac{\sin \alpha_2}{v_2}$$

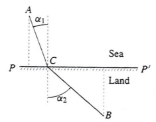

FIGURE C.17

C.3 Complex Numbers

Section 1.4 explained how the concept of numbers can successively be extended from natural numbers via integers and rationals to real numbers. Each of these extensions expands the set of equations that have solutions. Now, simple quadratic equations like $x^2 + 1 = 0$ and $x^2 + 4x + 8 = 0$ have no solution within the real number system. By introducing complex numbers, however, all quadratic equations become soluble. Within the complex number system, *any* algebraic equation

$$a_n x^n + a_{n-1}x^{n-1} + \cdots + a_1 x + a_0 = 0$$

has solutions (provided that the left-hand side is not a constant other than zero).

Definition of Complex Numbers

The standard formula for solving the equation $x^2 + 4x + 8 = 0$ yields the expressions $-2 + \sqrt{-4}$ and $-2 - \sqrt{-4}$. So far, we have not given these any meaning. But if we take the liberty of letting $\sqrt{-4} = \sqrt{4}\sqrt{-1} = 2\sqrt{-1}$, we obtain the "solutions"

$$-2 + 2\sqrt{-1} \qquad \text{and} \qquad -2 - 2\sqrt{-1} \qquad\qquad [*]$$

Here -2 and 2 are well-known numbers, but $\sqrt{-1}$ is not. By pretending that $\sqrt{-1}$ is a number x whose square is -1, we make x satisfy the equation $x^2 = -1$.

By treating these expressions as if they satisfied the usual algebraic rules, with the additional provision that $\sqrt{-1}\sqrt{-1}$ means -1, expressions of the type $a + b\sqrt{-1}$ can be used to solve any quadratic equation without real roots.

This fact motivates the introduction of a new type of number. Let the symbol i denote a "number" satisfying the equation $x^2 + 1 = 0$. (Mathematicians usually prefer to use the symbol i rather than $\sqrt{-1}$.)

By definition, then, the **complex number system** is the set of all symbols of the form $a + bi$, where a and b are real numbers. The number a is called the **real part** and b is called the **imaginary part** of the complex number. Moreover, the respective operations of addition and multiplication are defined by

$$(a + bi) + (c + di) = (a + c) + (b + d)i \qquad\qquad [\text{C.21}]$$

$$(a + bi)(c + di) = (ac - bd) + (ad + bc)i \qquad\qquad [\text{C.22}]$$

Equation [C.22] is precisely what results if we perform the multiplication $(a + bi)(c + di)$ according to the usual algebraic rules, thus obtaining $ac + (ad + bc)i + bdi^2$, and then replace i^2 by -1. When multiplying complex numbers in practice, we usually perform the computation this way, rather than employing rule [C.22] directly.

It is also common practice to denote complex numbers by single letters near the end of the alphabet, such as $z = a + bi$ or $w = c + di$. Two complex numbers like this are said to be equal iff both their real and their imaginary parts are equal—that is, $z = w$ iff $a = c$ and $b = d$. If the imaginary part of a complex number is 0, we let $a + 0i = a$. In fact, complex numbers of the form $a + 0i$ behave just like the corresponding real numbers with respect to addition and multiplication. In particular, the numbers $0 \ (= 0 + 0i)$ and $1 \ (= 1 + 0i)$ obey the same algebraic rules whether we regard them as complex or as real numbers.

If $a + bi$ and $c + di$ are arbitrary complex numbers, the **difference** between them, $(a + bi) - (c + di)$, is the complex number $x + yi$ that, when added to $c + di$, gives $a + bi$; thus, $a + bi = (c + di) + (x + yi)$. It follows that $a + bi = (c + x) + (d + y)i$. By definition of equality for complex numbers, $a = c + x$ and $b = d + y$, so $x = a - c$ and $y = b - d$. Hence, we have

$$(a + bi) - (c + di) = (a - c) + (b - d)i \qquad [\text{C.23}]$$

Suppose $z = a + bi$ and assume that $z \neq 0 + 0i = 0$. We wish to see if there is a complex number that deserves to be called the "inverse" of z. Such a number $x + yi$ must satisfy $(a + bi)(x + yi) = 1$. Expanding the product yields $(ax - by) + (ay + bx)i = 1$, so $ax - by = 1$ and $ay + bx = 0$. Solving these simultaneous equations for x and y yields $x = a/(a^2 + b^2)$ and $y = -b/(a^2 + b^2)$. (Note that because $z \neq 0$, we have $a^2 + b^2 \neq 0$.) With these values of x and y, the complex number $x + yi$ deserves to be called the **inverse** of $z = a + bi$:

$$\frac{1}{a + bi} = \frac{a}{a^2 + b^2} - \frac{b}{a^2 + b^2}i = \frac{a - bi}{a^2 + b^2} \qquad [\text{C.24}]$$

This definition of the inverse of a complex number leads to the following definition of division of complex numbers:

$$\frac{a + bi}{c + di} = (a + bi)\frac{1}{c + di} = (a + bi)\frac{c - di}{c^2 + d^2} = \frac{(ac + bd) + (bc - ad)i}{c^2 + d^2} \qquad [\text{C.25}]$$

A simpler way to obtain [C.25] is to multiply both numerator and denominator by $c - di$, which gives

$$\frac{a + bi}{c + di} = \frac{(a + bi)(c - di)}{(c + di)(c - di)} = \frac{(ac + bd) + (bc - ad)i}{c^2 + d^2}$$

Example C.2

If $z = 3 + 4i$ and $w = 2 - 5i$, simplify the following:

(a) $z + w$ (b) zw (c) z/w

Solution

(a) $z + w = (3 + 4i) + (2 - 5i) = 5 - i$

(b) $zw = (3 + 4i)(2 - 5i) = 6 - 15i + 8i - 20i^2 = 26 - 7i$

(c) $\dfrac{z}{w} = \dfrac{3 + 4i}{2 - 5i} = \dfrac{(3 + 4i)(2 + 5i)}{(2 - 5i)(2 + 5i)} = \dfrac{6 + 15i + 8i - 20}{4 + 25} = \dfrac{-14 + 23i}{29}$

Trigonometric Form of Complex Numbers

Each complex number $z = a + bi$ obviously can be identified with the ordered pair (a, b), and so with the point in the plane represented by this pair. Figure C.18 shows how to represent the complex numbers i, $-i$, and $3 + 2i$. The plane representing complex numbers is called an **Argand diagram**. The horizontal axis, representing numbers of the form $a + 0i$, is called the **real axis**, and the

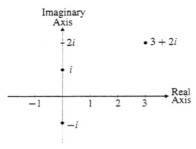

FIGURE C.18   An Argand diagram.

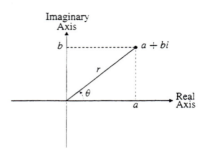

FIGURE C.19   Polar coordinates.

vertical axis, representing numbers of the form $0 + bi$, is called the **imaginary axis.**

Instead of representing a complex number $z = a + bi$ by the pair (a, b), we could use *polar coordinates*. With reference to Fig. C.19, let θ be the angle (measured in radians) between the positive real axis and the vector from the origin to point (a, b), and let r be the distance from the origin to the point. Then $a = r \cos \theta$ and $b = r \sin \theta$, so

$$z = a + bi = r(\cos \theta + i \sin \theta) \qquad \text{[C.26]}$$

The last expression is the **trigonometric (or polar) form** of the complex number z. Angle θ is called the **argument** of the complex number z. Note that the length of the vector from the origin to the pair (a, b) is $r = \sqrt{a^2 + b^2}$. This is called the *modulus* of the complex number, denoted by $|z|$. Hence,

$$|z| = \sqrt{a^2 + b^2} \quad \text{is the **modulus** of } z = a + bi \qquad \text{[C.27]}$$

Multiplication and division of complex numbers have neat geometric interpretations if we represent the numbers in their trigonometric form. Indeed,

$$r_1(\cos \theta_1 + i \sin \theta_1) r_2(\cos \theta_2 + i \sin \theta_2) = r_1 r_2 [\cos(\theta_1 + \theta_2) + i \sin(\theta_1 + \theta_2)] \quad \text{[C.28]}$$

because Problems 3 and 4 in Section C.1 imply the identities $\cos(\theta_1 + \theta_2) = \cos \theta_1 \cos \theta_2 - \sin \theta_1 \sin \theta_2$ and $\sin(\theta_1 + \theta_2) = \sin \theta_1 \cos \theta_2 + \cos \theta_1 \sin \theta_2$. Thus, *the product of two complex numbers is that complex number whose modulus is the product of the moduli, and whose argument is the sum of the arguments of the two factors.*

In a similar way, we can show that

$$\frac{r_1(\cos \theta_1 + i \sin \theta_1)}{r_2(\cos \theta_2 + i \sin \theta_2)} = \frac{r_1}{r_2}[\cos(\theta_1 - \theta_2) + i \sin(\theta_1 - \theta_2)] \qquad \text{[C.29]}$$

If we let $r_1 = r_2 = 1$ and $\theta_1 = \theta_2 = \theta$ in [C.28], then we obtain $(\cos \theta + i \sin \theta)^2 = \cos 2\theta + i \sin 2\theta$. Similarly, $(\cos \theta + i \sin \theta)^3 = (\cos \theta + i \sin \theta)^2 (\cos \theta + i \sin \theta) = $

$(\cos 2\theta + i \sin 2\theta)(\cos \theta + i \sin \theta) = \cos 3\theta + i \sin 3\theta$. By induction, we find the famous result

$$(\cos \theta + i \sin \theta)^n = \cos n\theta + i \sin n\theta \qquad \textbf{(De Moivre's formula)} \qquad [\text{C.30}]$$

which is valid for all $n = 1, 2, 3, \ldots$

Note

This has been a very brief introduction to complex numbers. The need to extend the real number system arose in the sixteenth century when Italian mathematicians systematically studied algebraic equations of degree 2, 3, and 4. For a long time, the complex numbers were regarded as "imaginary," mystical objects. Not any more. Actually, the extension of the number concept from the real numbers to the complex numbers is motivated by the same concern as the extension from the rationals to the reals. In both cases, we want certain equations to have solutions.

Nowadays complex numbers are indispensable in mathematics. Modern science just could not do without them. However, they do not play a very large role in economics. In this book, they allow a convenient description of the solutions to some second-order difference and differential equations. They also facilitate the study of eigenvalues of matrices.

Problems

1. If $z = 2 - 5i$ and $w = 3 + 3i$, simplify the following expressions:

    a. $z + w$ **b.** zw **c.** $\dfrac{z}{w}$ **d.** $|z|$

2. Represent the complex numbers $z = 2 - 2i$, $w = 1 + 3i$, and $z + w$ in an Argand diagram.

3. Write the following numbers in the form $a + bi$:

    a. $\dfrac{3 + 2i}{1 - i}$ **b.** $\dfrac{4 - 3i}{i}$ **c.** $\dfrac{(3 - 2i)(2 - i)}{(-1 - i)(3 + 2i)}$ **d.** $\left(\dfrac{1 - i}{1 + i}\right)^3$

4. Write the following numbers in trigonometric form:

    a. $\sqrt{3} + 3i$ **b.** -1 **c.** $-2 - 2\sqrt{3}i$ **d.** $1 - i$

D

Geometry

Let no one ignorant of geometry enter this door.
—Entrance to Plato's Academy

The following formulas and results are occasionally useful in economics.

Triangles

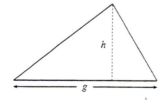 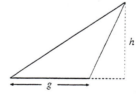 Area: $A = \frac{1}{2}gh$

Circle

Area: $A = \pi r^2$ $\quad$ ($\pi = 3.1415\ldots$)

Circumference: $C = 2\pi r$

Rectangular Solid

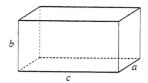

Volume: $V = abc$

Surface Area: $S = 2ab + 2ac + 2bc$

Sphere

Volume: $V = \dfrac{4}{3}\pi r^3$

Surface Area: $S = 4\pi r^2$

Cone

Volume: $V = \dfrac{1}{3}\pi r^2 h$

Surface Area: $S = \pi r^2 + \pi r\sqrt{h^2 + r^2}$

Pyramid

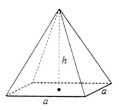

Volume: $V = \dfrac{1}{3}a^2 h$

Surface Area: $S = a^2 + a\sqrt{a^2 + 4h^2}$

Angles

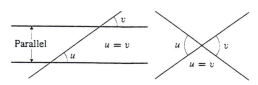

Proportions

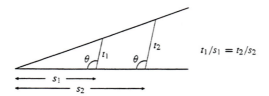

$$t_1/s_1 = t_2/s_2$$

Sum of Angles in Triangles

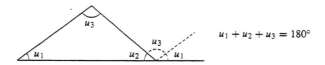

$$u_1 + u_2 + u_3 = 180°$$

Pythagoras' Theorem

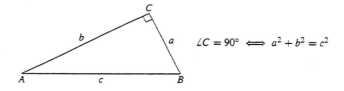

$$\angle C = 90° \iff a^2 + b^2 = c^2$$

Answers to Odd-Numbered Problems

Chapter 1

1.3

1. (a) $p_1x_1 + p_2x_2 + p_3x_3$ (b) $F + bx$ (c) $(F + cx)/x = F/x + c$
(d) After the $p\%$ raise, his salary is $L + pL/100 = L(1 + p/100)$. A $q\%$
raise of this new salary gives the final answer: $L(1 + p/100)(1 + q/100)$.
(e) $V = x(18 - 2x)(18 - 2x) = 4x(9 - x)^2$. (See Figs. 1 and 2.)

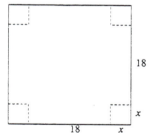

18

x

18   x

FIGURE 1

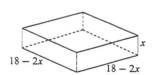

$18 - 2x$ x $18 - 2x$

FIGURE 2

3. (a) $y = \frac{3}{5}(x + 2)$ (b) $x = \dfrac{b + d}{a - c}$ (when $a \neq c$)
(c) Square each side: $A^2K^2L = Y_0^2$. Solving for L yields $L = Y_0^2/A^2K^2$.
(d) $y = \dfrac{m}{q} - \dfrac{p}{q}x$ (when $q \neq 0$)
(e) $\dfrac{1}{1 + r} - a = c\left(\dfrac{1}{1 + r} + b\right)$. Multiplying by $1 + r$ and solving for r
yields $r = \dfrac{(1 - a) - c(1 + b)}{a + bc}$ (f) $Y = \dfrac{I_p + G - ak + b}{1 - a + at}$

5. $2\pi(r+1) - 2\pi r = 2\pi$, where r is the radius of the earth (as an approximate sphere).

7. Let each side have length s. Then the area K is the sum of the areas of the triangles APB, APC, and BPC in Fig. 3, so $\frac{1}{2}sh_1 + \frac{1}{2}sh_2 + \frac{1}{2}sh_3 = K$. Thus, $h_1 + h_2 + h_3 = 2K/s$, which is independent of where P is placed.

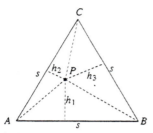

FIGURE 3

1.4

1. (a) Rational (note that this is only an approximation to the irrational number π).

(b) $\sqrt{\frac{9}{2} - \frac{1}{2}} = \sqrt{4} = 2$, a natural number.   (c) $3 - 2 = 1$, a natural number.
(d) $3\pi - 1/4$ is irrational: If $3\pi - 1/4$ were rational, then there would exist integers p and q such that $3\pi - 1/4 = p/q$. Hence, $\pi = (4p + q)/12q$, which would imply that π is rational, a contradiction.

3. (a) $x \neq 4$ (b) $x \neq 0$ and $x \neq -2$ (c) $x \neq -5$ and $x \neq 1$. (The quadratic equation $x^2 + 4x - 5 = 0$ has the solutions $x = -5$ and $x = 1$.)   (d) $x \neq -2$. (The quadratic equation $x^2 + 4x + 4 = (x+2)^2 = 0$ has the solution $x = -2$.)

5. $F/x + c < q$, which yields $x > F/(q - c)$.   For $F = 100,000$, $c = 120$, and $q = 160$: $100,000/x + 120 < 160$, that is, $100,000/x < 40$, and so $x > 100,000/40 = 2500$.

7. (a) $|5 - 3(-1)| = |5 + 3| = 8$, $|5 - 3 \cdot 2| = 1$, $|5 - 3 \cdot 4| = 7$ (b) $x = 5/3$
(c) $|5 - 3x| = 5 - 3x$ for $x \leq 5/3$, $|5 - 3x| = 3x - 5$ for $x > 5/3$

9. (a) $4.999 < x < 5.001$ (b) $|x - 5| < 0.001$

1.5

1. (a) $2x - 4 = 2 \Longrightarrow x = 3$ (b) $x = 3 \Longrightarrow 2x - 4 = 2$ (c) $x = 1 \Longrightarrow$ $x^2 - 2x + 1 = 0$ (d) $x^2 > 4 \Longleftrightarrow x > 2$ or $x < -2$

3. (a) $x \geq 0$ is necessary, but not sufficient.   (b) $x \geq 50$ is sufficient, but not necessary.   (c) $x \geq 4$ is necessary and sufficient.

5. (a) $x = 3$ (b) $x = 0$ or $x = -5$ (c) $x = -3$ or $x = 3$

7. (a) Iff. (Note: $\sqrt{4}$ means 2, not ± 2.) (b) If (c) Only if (d) Iff (e) Only if

9. (a) $x < 0$ or $y < 0$ (b) $x < a$ for at least one x. (c) x and/or y is less than 5. (Is it easier if the statement were: neither Ron nor Rita is less than 5 years old?) (d) There exists an $\varepsilon > 0$ such that B is not satisfied for any $\delta > 0$. (e) Someone may not like cats. (f) Someone never loves anyone.

1.6

1. (b), (d), and (e) all express the same condition. (a) and (c) are different.

3. We should show why the fact that p^2 has 2 as a factor implies that p has 2 as a factor. Assume on the contrary that p does not have 2 as a factor. Then $p = 2m + 1$, for some natural number m. But then $p^2 = (2m + 1)^2 = 4m^2 + 4m + 1 = 2(2m^2 + 2m) + 1$, which is odd and therefore does not have 2 as a factor.

1.7

1. (a) $5 \in C$, $D \subset C$, and $B = C$ are true. The three others are false. (b) $A \cap B = \{2\}$, $A \cup B = \{2, 3, 4, 5, 6\}$, $A \setminus B = \{3, 4\}$, $B \setminus A = \{5, 6\}$, $(A \cup B) \setminus (A \cap B) = \{3, 4, 5, 6\}$, $A \cup B \cup C \cup D = \{2, 3, 4, 5, 6\}$, $A \cap B \cap C = \{2\}$, and $A \cap B \cap C \cap D = \emptyset$

3. (a) $B \subset M$ (b) $F \cap B \cap C \neq \emptyset$ (c) $F \setminus (T \cup C) \subset B$

5. (a) to (e) follow immediately from the definitions and also from obvious Venn diagrams. Both sets in (f) are seen to consist of the areas (1), (2), (3), (4), and (7) in Fig. 1.8 in Section 1.7.

7. The $2^3 = 8$ subsets of $\{a, b, c\}$ are the set itself, the empty set, $\{a\}$, $\{b\}$, $\{c\}$, $\{a, b\}$, $\{a, c\}$, and $\{b, c\}$. The $2^4 = 16$ subsets of $\{a, b, c, d\}$ are the eight preceding sets together with $\{d\}$, $\{a, d\}$, $\{b, d\}$, $\{c, d\}$, $\{a, b, d\}$, $\{a, c, d\}$, $\{b, c, d\}$, and $\{a, b, c, d\}$.

9. (a) Look at Fig. 4. $n(A \cup B)$ is the sum of the numbers of elements in (1), (2), and (3) respectively—that is, $n(A \setminus B)$, $n(A \cap B)$, and $n(B \setminus A)$. $n(A) + n(B)$ is the number of elements in (1) and (2) together, plus the number of elements in (2) and (3) together. Thus, the elements in (2) are counted twice. Hence, you must subtract the number of elements in (2) (that is $n(A \cap B)$) to have equality. (b) Look again at Fig. 4. $n(A \setminus B)$ is the number of elements in (1), and $n(A) - n(A \cap B)$ is the number of elements in (1) and (2) together, minus the number of elements in (2). Hence, it is the number of elements in (1).

FIGURE 4

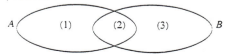

11. (b) is not generally valid. For example, in Problem 1, $(A \cap C) \triangle B = \{2\} \triangle \{2, 5, 6\} = \{5, 6\}$, whereas $(A \triangle B) \cap (C \triangle B) = \{3, 4, 5, 6\} \cap \emptyset = \emptyset$. (Alternatively, use Fig. 1.8 in Section 1.7.)

Chapter 2

2.2

1. (a) $f(0) = 0^2 + 1 = 1$, $f(-1) = (-1)^2 + 1 = 2$, $f(1/2) = 5/4$, and $f(\sqrt{2}) = 3$. (b) (i) For all x. (ii) When $(x + 1)^2 + 1 = (x^2 + 1) + 2$, so $x^2 + 2x + 2 = x^2 + 3$, or $2x + 2 = 3$, or $x = 1/2$. (iii) $x = \pm\sqrt{1/2}$.

3. (a) $f(0) = 0$, $f(a) = a^2$, $f(-a) = a^2 - 4a^2 = -3a^2$, and $f(2a) = 0$ (b) $3f(a) + f(-2a) = 3a^2 + [a^2 - (-2a - a)^2] = 3a^2 + a^2 - 9a^2 = -5a^2$

5. (a) $C(0) = 1000$, $C(100) = 41.000$, and $C(101) - C(100) = 501$ (b) $C(x + 1) - C(x) = 2x + 301 =$ incremental cost of producing one unit more than x.

7. (a) $D(8) = 4$, $D(10) = 3.4$, and $D(10.22) = 3.334$ (b) $P = 10.9$

9. (a) $f(tx) = 100(tx)^2 = 100t^2x^2 = t^2 100x^2 = t^2 f(x)$ (b) $P(tx) = (tx)^{1/2} = t^{1/2}x^{1/2} = t^{1/2}P(x)$

11. (a) $f(a + b) = A(a + b) = Aa + Ab = f(a) + f(b)$ (b) $f(a + b) = 10^{a+b} = 10^a \cdot 10^b = f(a) \cdot f(b)$

13. (a) $x \le 5$ (b) $x \ne 0$ and $x \ne 1$ (c) $-3 < x \le 1$ or $x > 2$ (d) $x > 1$

15. (a) $D_g = [-2, \infty)$, $R_g = (-\infty, 1]$. (The largest value of $g(x)$ is 1 for $x = -2$. As x increases from -2 to ∞, $g(x)$ decreases from 1 to $-\infty$.)

17. $f\left(\dfrac{ax + b}{cx - a}\right) = \dfrac{a\left(\dfrac{ax + b}{cx - a}\right) + b}{c\left(\dfrac{ax + b}{cx - a}\right) - a}$

$$= \frac{a(ax + b) + b(cx - a)}{c(ax + b) - a(cx - a)} = \frac{a^2x + bcx}{a^2 + bc} = x$$

2.3

1. See Fig. 5.

3. See Figs. 6 to 8.

5. (a) $\sqrt{2}$ (b) $\sqrt{29}$ (c) $\frac{1}{2}\sqrt{205}$ (d) $\sqrt{x^2 + 9}$ (e) $2|a|$ (f) $\sqrt{8}$

7. (a) 5.362 (b) $\sqrt{(2\pi)^2 + (2\pi - 1)^2} = \sqrt{8\pi^2 - 4\pi + 1} \approx 8.209$

9. (a) $(x + 5)^2 + (y - 3)^2 = 4$ has center at $(-5, 3)$ and radius 2. (b) $(x + 3)^2 + (y - 4)^2 = 12$ has center at $(-3, 4)$ and radius $\sqrt{12}$.

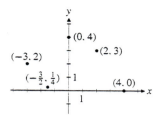

FIGURE 5

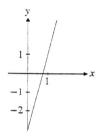

FIGURE 6   **FIGURE 7**   **FIGURE 8**

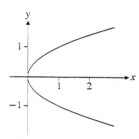

11. The condition is that $\sqrt{(x+2)^2 + y^2} = 2\sqrt{(x-4)^2 + y^2}$, or equivalently $(x-6)^2 + y^2 = 4^2$.

13. (a) The two expressions give total price per unit (product price plus shipping costs) for the product delivered at (x, y) from A and B respectively. (b) The condition is that $p + 10\sqrt{x^2 + y^2} = p + 5\sqrt{(x-60)^2 + y^2}$, which reduces to $(x+20)^2 + y^2 = 40^2$.

15. $x^2 + y^2 + Ax + By + C = 0 \iff x^2 + Ax + y^2 + By + C = 0 \iff$ $x^2 + Ax + (\frac{1}{2}A)^2 + y^2 + By + (\frac{1}{2}B)^2 = \frac{1}{4}(A^2 + B^2 - 4C) \iff (x + \frac{1}{2}A)^2 + (y + \frac{1}{2}B)^2 = \frac{1}{4}(A^2 + B^2 - 4C)$. The last is the equation of a circle centered at $(-\frac{1}{2}A, -\frac{1}{2}B)$ with radius $\frac{1}{2}\sqrt{A^2 + B^2 - 4C}$. If $A^2 + B^2 = 4C$, the graph consists only of the point $(-\frac{1}{2}A, -\frac{1}{2}B)$. For $A^2 + B^2 < 4C$, the solution set is empty.

2.4

1. (a) All x (b) $x = 0$ (c) All x (d) $x = 0$ (For $x > 0$, the equation $y^4 = x$ has *two* solutions.)   (e) $x = \pm 1$ (f) All $x \neq 3$ (g) All x (h) All x

3. Suppose c is positive. Then $f(x) + c$ is obtained by raising the graph of $f(x)$ by c units. $f(x + c)$ is obtained by shifting the graph of $f(x)$ by c units to the left. $-f(x)$ is obtained by reflecting the graph of $f(x)$ in the x-axis. $f(-x)$ is obtained by reflecting the graph of $f(x)$ in the y-axis.

2.5

1. (a) Slope $= (8-3)/(5-2) = 5/3$ (b) $-2/3$ (c) $51/5$

3. L_1 is $y = x+2$, with slope 1; L_2 is $y = -\frac{3}{5}x + 3$, with slope $-3/5$; L_3 is $y = 1$, with slope 0; L_4 is $y = 3x - 14$, with slope 3; L_5 is $y = \frac{1}{9}x + 2$, with slope $1/9$.

5. (a), (b), and (d) are all linear; (c) is not.

7. (a) L_1 is $(y-3) = 2(x-1)$ or $y = 2x+1$ (b) L_2 is $y-2 = \frac{3-2}{3-(-2)}[x-(-2)]$ or $y = x/5 + 12/5$ (c) L_3 is $y = -x/2$ (d) L_4 is $x/a + y/b = 1$, or $y = -bx/a + b$. The graphs are shown in Figs. 9 and 10.

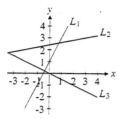

FIGURE 9

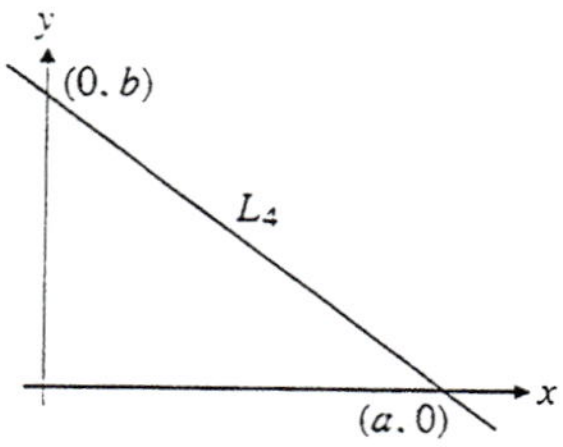

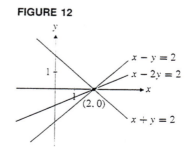

FIGURE 10

9. The point–point formula gives $y - 200 = \dfrac{275 - 200}{150 - 100}(x-100)$ or $y = \frac{3}{2}x + 50$.

11. (a) April 1960 corresponds to $t = 9/4$, when $N(9/4) = -17{,}400 \cdot (9/4) + 151{,}000 = 111{,}850$.   (b) $-17{,}400t + 151{,}000 = 0$ implies $t = 8.68$, which corresponds roughly to September 1966.

13. For (a), shown in Fig. 11, the solution is $x = 3$, $y = -2$. For (b), shown in Fig. 12, the solution is $x = 2$, $y = 0$. For (c), shown in Fig. 13, there are no solutions, because the two lines are parallel.

15. See Fig. 14. $C = 0.8824Y - 1.3941$. The slope is an estimate of the marginal propensity to consume.

17. See Fig. 15. Each arrow shows the side of the line on which the relevant inequality is satisfied. The shaded triangle is the required set.

FIGURE 11

FIGURE 12

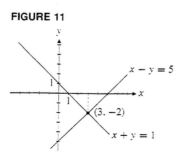

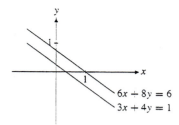

FIGURE 13

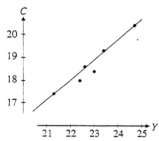

FIGURE 14

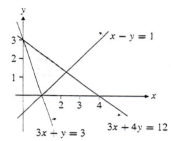

FIGURE 15

Chapter 3

3.1

1. (a)

x			−1	0	1	2	3	4	5
$f(x) = x^2 - 4x$			5	0	−3	−4	−3	0	5

(b) See Fig. 16.   (c) $f(x) = (x-2)^2 - 4$. Minimum at $(2, -4)$.   (d) $x = 0$ and $x = 4$.

FIGURE 16

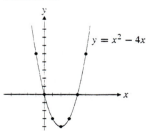

3. (a) $x^2 + 4x = (x+2)^2 - 4$. Minimum -4 for $x = -2$. (b) $x^2 + 6x + 18 = (x+3)^2 + 9$. Minimum 9 for $x = -3$. (c) $-3x^2 + 30x - 30 = -3(x-5)^2 + 45$. Maximum 45 for $x = 5$. (d) $9x^2 - 6x - 44 = 9(x - 1/3)^2 - 45$. Minimum -45 for $x = 1/3$. (e) $-x^2 - 200x + 30,000 = -(x + 100)^2 + 40,000$. Maximum $40,000$ for $x = -100$. (f) $x^2 + 100x - 20,000 = (x+50)^2 - 22,500$. Minimum $-22,500$ for $x = -50$.

5. (a) $x = 2p$ and $x = p$ (b) $x = p$ and $x = q$ (c) $x = -\frac{1}{2}p \pm \sqrt{\frac{1}{4}p^2 - q}$

7. $x = 250$ maximizes A. $(A = -x^2 + 500x = -(x - 250)^2 + 62,500.)$

9. $x = 4(r - 1)/(r^2 + 1)$. (Use [3.4].)

11. Using [3.3], we see that $f(x) = a(x - \bar{x})^2 - A$, with $\bar{x} = -b/2a$, and $A = (b^2 - 4ac)/4a$. Now, $f(\bar{x} - t) = a(\bar{x} - t - \bar{x})^2 - A = a(-t)^2 - A = at^2 - A$, and $f(\bar{x} + t) = a(\bar{x} + t - \bar{x})^2 - A = at^2 - A$. So $f(\bar{x} - t) = f(\bar{x} + t)$ for all t, and the graph is symmetric about the line $x = \bar{x}$.

3.2

1. (a) $\pi(Q) = -\frac{1}{2}Q^2 + (\alpha_1 - \alpha_2 - \gamma)Q$ (b) Using [3.4], $Q^* = \alpha_1 - \alpha_2 - \gamma$ maximizes profits if $\alpha_1 - \alpha_2 - \gamma > 0$. If $\alpha_1 - \alpha_2 - \gamma \le 0$, then $Q^* = 0$. (c) $\pi(Q) = -\frac{1}{2}Q^2 + (\alpha_1 - \alpha_2 - \gamma - t)Q$ and $Q^* = \alpha_1 - \alpha_2 - \gamma - t$ if $\alpha_1 - \alpha_2 - \gamma - t > 0$. (d) Tax revenue $= tQ^* = t(\alpha_1 - \alpha_2 - \gamma - t)$. Then $t = \frac{1}{2}(\alpha_1 - \alpha_2 - \gamma)$ maximizes tax revenues.

3.3

1. (a) 1 and -2 (b) 1, 5, and -5 (c) -1

3. (a) $x + 4$ (b) $x^2 + x + 1$ (c) $-3x^2 - 12x$

5. (a) $x^3 - x - 1$ is not 0 for $x = 1$, so the division leaves a remainder.
(b) $2x^3 - x - 1$ is 0 for $x = 1$, so the division leaves no remainder.
(c) $x^3 - ax^2 + bx - ab$ is 0 for $x = a$, so the division leaves no remainder.
(d) $x^{2n} - 1$ is 0 for $x = -1$, so the division leaves no remainder.

7. (a) $\frac{1}{2}(x + 1)(x - 3)$ (b) $-2(x - 1)(x - 2)(x + 3)$ (c) $\frac{1}{2}(x - 2)^2(x + 3)$

3.4

1. (a) 2 (b) 1/3 (c) 5 (d) 1/8

3. (a) 4/3 (b) 2.5 (c) 1/5

5. (a) $a^{1/5}$ (b) $a^{163/60}$ (c) $9a^7/2$ (d) $a^{1/4}$

7. (b) and (c) are valid; the others are not generally valid.

9. The surface area is $4.84 \cdot (100)^{2/3} \text{ m}^2 \approx 104.27 \text{ m}^2$. You need $104 \cdot 27/5$ or slightly less than 21 liters.

11. (a) $a - b$ (b) $(a + x)/2bx^{3/2}$

3.5

1. The doubling time t^* is determined by the equation $(1.0072)^{t^*} = 2$. Using a calculator, we find $t^* \approx 96.6$.

3. (a) The amount of savings after t years: $100\,(1 + 12/100)^t = 100 \cdot (1.12)^t$
   (b)

x	1	2	5	10	20	30	50
$100 \cdot (1.12)^x$	112	125.44	176.23	310.58	964.63	2995.99	28,900.21

5. The graphs are drawn in Fig. 17.

x	-3	-2	-1	0	1	2	3
2^x	1/8	1/4	1/2	1	2	4	8
2^{-x}	8	4	2	1	1/2	1/4	1/8

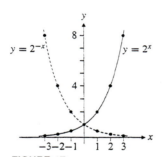

FIGURE 17

7. If $5.1 \cdot (1.035)^t = 3.91 \cdot 10^{11}$, then $(1.035)^t = 3.91 \cdot 10^{11}/5.1 \approx 0.7667 \cdot 10^{11}$. We find (using a calculator) that $t \approx 728$, so the year is $728 + 1969 = 2697$. This is when each Zimbabwean would have only 1 m^2 of land.

9. $(1 + p/100)^{15} = 2$, so $p \approx 4.7\%$

11. (b) and (d) do not define exponential functions. (In (f): $y = (1/2)^x$.)

13. Solve the equation $y = Ab^x$ for A and b by using the two indicated points on each graph. This gives $y = 2 \cdot 2^x$, $y = 2 \cdot 3^x$, and $y = 4(1/2)^x$.

3.6

1. Only (c) does not define a function. (Rectangles with different areas can have the same perimeter.)

3. The function cannot be one-to-one because at least two persons must have the same blood group.

Chapter 4

4.2

1. $f(5+h) - f(5) = 4(5+h)^2 - 4 \cdot 5^2 = 4(25+10h+h^2) - 100 = 40h + 4h^2$.
So $[f(5+h) - f(5)]/h = 40 + 4h \to 40$ as $t \to 0$. Hence, $f'(5) = 40$.
This accords with [4.8] when $a = 4$ and $b = c = 0$.

3. $f'(a) < 0$, $f'(b) = 0$, $f'(c) > 0$, $f'(d) < 0$

5. (a) $f'(0) = 3$ (b) $f'(1) = 2$ (c) $f'(3) = -1/3$ (d) $f'(0) = -2$
(e) $f'(-1) = 0$ (f) $f'(1) = 4$

7. (a) $dD(P)/dP = -b$ (b) $C'(x) = 2qx$

9. (a) $f(x+h) - f(x) = a(x+h)^3 + b(x+h)^2 + c(x+h) + d - (ax^3 + bx^2 + cx + d)$.
Here $(x+h)^3 = x^3 + 3x^2h + 3xh^2 + h^3$ and $(x+h)^2 = x^2 + 2xh + h^2$. Easy algebra then gives $[f(x+h) - f(x)]/h = 3ax^2 + 2bx + c + 3ahx + ah^2 + bh$,
which evidently tends to $3ax^2 + 2bx + c$ as $h \to 0$. (b) If $a = 1$ and
$b = c = d = 0$, then the result in Example 4.3 follows. So does that in
Problem 6 when $a = 0$.

4.3

1. $C'(100) = 203$ and $C'(x) = 2x + 3$.

3. (a) $S'(Y) = b$ (b) $S'(Y) = 4Y + 10$

5. (a) $R'(x) = a$, $C'(x) = 2a_1x + b_1$, and $\pi'(x) = a - 2a_1x - b_1$. The marginal
profit is 0 when $x = (p - b_1)/2a_1$. (b) $R'(x) = 2ax$, $C'(x) = a_1$, and
$\pi'(x) = 2ax - a_1$. The marginal profit is 0 when $x = a_1/2a$. (b) With
$R(x) = ax - bx^3$, $R'(x) = a - 2bx$, $C'(x) = a_1$, and $\pi'(x) = a - 2bx - a_1$.
The marginal profit is 0 when $x = (a - a_1)/2b$.

4.4

1. (a) 3 (b) $-1/2$ (c) $(13)^3 = 2197$ (d) 40 (e) 1 (f) $-3/4$

3. The $\lim_{t \to a} h(t)$ is equal to 0 for $a = -1$, it is 1 for $a = 0$, and it is 3 for
$a = 2$. For $a = 3$ and 4, the limit does not exist.

5. (a) For $h \neq 2$, $\dfrac{\frac{1}{3} - \frac{2}{3h}}{h - 2} = \dfrac{\left(\frac{1}{3} - \frac{2}{3h}\right)3h}{(h-2)3h} = \dfrac{h-2}{(h-2)3h} = \dfrac{1}{3h}$, which tends
to 1/6 as $h \to 2$. (b) $-\infty$ (limit does not exist) (c) 2 (*Hint:* $t - 3$ is a
common factor for $32t - 96$ and $t^2 - 2t - 3$.) (d) $\sqrt{3}/6$ (*Hint:* Multiply
numerator and denominator by $\sqrt{h+3} + \sqrt{3}$.) (e) $-2/3$ (*Hint:* $t + 2$ is a
common factor.) (f) 1/4 (*Hint:* $4 - x = (2 + \sqrt{x})(2 - \sqrt{x})$.)

7. (a) 0.6931 (b) 1.0986 (c) 2.7183

4.5

1. (a) 0 (b) $4x^3$ (c) $90x^9$ (d) 0 (Remember that π is a constant!)

3. (a) $6x^5$ (b) $33x^{10}$ (c) $50x^{49}$ (d) $28x^{-8}$ (e) x^{11} (f) $4x^{-3}$
   (g) $(-3/2)x^{-3/2}$ (h) $3x^{-5/2}$

5. Let $x - a = h$. Then $x = a + h$, and the result follows from [4.3], the ordinary definition of the derivative. For $f(x) = x^2$, the equation gives $f'(a) = 2a$.

7. (a) Let $f(x) = x^2$. Then $f'(x) = 2x$, and the limit is equal to $f'(5) = 2 \cdot 5 = 10$. (b) Let $f(x) = x^5$. Then $f'(x) = 5x^4$, and the limit is equal to $f'(1) = 5 \cdot 1^4 = 5$. (c) Let $f(x) = 5x^2 + 10$. Then $f'(x) = 10x$, and this is the value of the limit.

4.6

1. (a) 1 (b) $1 + 2x$ (c) $15x^4 + 8x^3$ (d) $32x^3 + x^{-1/2}$ (e) $1/2 - 3x + 15x^2$
   (f) $-21x^6$

3. (a) $-6x^{-7}$ (b) $(3/2)x^{1/2} - (1/2)x^{-3/2}$ (c) $(-3/2)x^{-5/2}$ (d) $-2/(x-1)^2$
   (e) $(-4x - 5)/x^6$ (f) $34/(2x + 8)^2$ (g) $-33x^{-12}$
   (h) $(-3x^2 + 2x + 4)/(x^2 + x + 1)^2$

5. $R'(P) = D(P) + PD'(P)$

7. (a) $y = -3x + 4$ (b) $y = x - 1$ (c) $y = (17x - 19)/4$ (d) $y = -(x - 3)/9$

9. (a) $\dfrac{2(AD - BC)p}{(Cp^2 + D)^2}$ (b) $-6y^{-7} - 16y^{-9}$ (c) $-2f'(x)/[1 + f(x)]^2$

11. If $f(x) = 1/x^n$, then by the rule for differentiating a quotient, $f'(x) = (0 \cdot x^n - 1 \cdot nx^{n-1})/(x^n)^2 = -nx^{-n-1}$, which is the power rule.

4.7

1. (a) $y'' = 20x^3 - 36x^2$ (b) $y'' = (-1/4)x^{-3/2}$ (c) $y'' = (-2)(x + 1)^{-3}$

3. (a) $y'' = 18x$ (b) $Y''' = 36$ (c) $d^3z/dt^3 = -2$ (d) $f^{(4)}(1) = 84,000$.

5. $y'' = f''(x)g(x) + 2f'(x)g'(x) + f(x)g''(x)$,
   $y''' = f'''(x)g(x) + 3f''(x)g'(x) + 3f'(x)g''(x) + f(x)g'''(x)$

7. $f(x) = x^{16/3}$ has this property. Successive differentiations eventually yield $f^{(5)}(x) = (16/3)(13/3)(10/3)(7/3)(4/3)x^{1/3}$ for all x, but only for $x \neq 0$ is $f^{(6)}(x) = (16/3)(13/3)(10/3)(7/3)(4/3)(1/3)x^{-2/3}$.

Chapter 5

5.1

1. (a) $f(x) = 9x^4 + 6x^2 + 1$, so $f'(x) = 36x^3 + 12x$.
   (b) Using [5.1]: $f'(x) = 2(3x^2 + 1)^{2-1}6x = 36x^3 + 12x$.

3. (a) $\frac{1}{2}(1+x)^{-1/2}$ (b) $\frac{3}{2}x^2(x^3+1)^{-1/2}$ (c) $-\frac{3}{2}(x-1)^{-2}\left(\dfrac{2x+1}{x-1}\right)^{-1/2}$

   (d) $-66x(1-x^2)^{32}$ (e) $3x^2\sqrt{1-x} - \dfrac{x^3}{2\sqrt{1-x}}$

   (f) $\frac{1}{3}(1+x)^{-2/3}(1-x)^{1/5} - \frac{1}{5}(1+x)^{1/3}(1-x)^{-4/5}$

5. (a) $1 + f'(x)$ (b) $2f(x)f'(x) - 1$ (c) $4[f(x)]^3 f'(x)$

   (d) $2xf(x) + x^2 f'(x) + 3[f(x)]^2 f'(x)$ (e) $f(x) + xf'(x)$ (f) $\dfrac{f'(x)}{2\sqrt{f(x)}}$

   (g) $[2xf(x) - x^2 f'(x)]/[f(x)]^2$ (h) $[2xf(x)f'(x) - 3(f(x))^2]/x^4$

   (i) $\frac{1}{3}\{f(x) + [f(x)]^3 + x\}^{-2/3}\{f'(x) + 3[f(x)]^2 f'(x) + 1\}$

7. $dy/dv = Aapqv^{p-1}(av^p + b)^{q-1}$

9. $f'(x) = m(x-a)^{m-1} \cdot (x-b)^n + n(x-a)^m \cdot (x-b)^{n-1}$. Factoring this expression yields $f'(x) = [m(x-b) + n(x-a)](x-a)^{m-1} \cdot (x-b)^{n-1} = 0$ at $x_0 = (na + mb)/(n+m)$. Clearly, $a < (na + mb)/(n+m) < b$ iff $a(n+m) < na + mb < b(n+m)$. Here $a(n+m) < na + mb$ iff $(a-b)m < 0$, which is true because $a < b$ and m is positive. Moreover, $na + mb < b(n+m)$ iff $0 < n(b-a)$, which is also true.

11. Use the product rule and [5.1]. $m = n = 1$ yields the product rule for derivatives. $m = -n = 1$ yields the quotient rule.

5.2

1. (a) $dy/du = 20u^3$ and $du/dx = 2x$ so $dy/dx = (dy/du) \cdot (du/dx) = 40u^3 x = 40x(1+x^2)^3$

   (b) $dy/dx = (1 - 6u^5)(du/dx) = [1 - 6(1/x + 1)^5](-1/x^2)$

3. (a) $y' = -5(x^2 + x + 1)^{-6}(2x+1)$ (b) $y' = \frac{1}{2}[x + (x + x^{1/2})^{1/2}]^{-1/2}[1 + \frac{1}{2}(x + x^{1/2})^{-1/2}(1 + \frac{1}{2}x^{-1/2})]$ (c) $y' = ax^{a-1}(px + q)^b + x^a bp(px + q)^{b-1}$

5. $dY/dt = F'[h(t)] \cdot h'(t)$

7. $h'(x) = f'(x^2)2x$

9. (a) $\dot{x}/x = 2\dot{a}/a + \dot{b}/b$ (b) $\dot{x}/x = 5\dot{a}/a - \dot{b}/b$

   (c) $\dot{x}/x = (\alpha + \beta)(\alpha a^{\alpha-1}\dot{a} + \beta b^{\beta-1}\dot{b})/(a^\alpha + b^\beta)$ (d) $\dot{x}/x = \alpha\dot{a}/a + \beta\dot{b}/b$

11. (a) $h(x) = f(g(x))$, where $g(x) = 1 + x + x^2$ and $f(u) = u^{1/2}$, so $h'(x) = (1/2)(1 + x + x^2)^{-1/2}(1 + 2x)$.   (b) $h(x) = f(g(x))$, where $g(x) = x^{100} + 28$ and $f(u) = u^{-1}$, so $h'(x) = -(x^{100} + 28)^{-2}100x^{99}$.

13. (a) $y' = 5(x^4)^4 \cdot 4x^3 = 20x^{19}$ (b) $y' = 3(1-x)^2(-1) = -3 + 6x - 3x^2$

15. $dR/dt = (dR/dS)(dS/dK)(dK/dt) = \alpha S^{\alpha-1}\beta\gamma K^{\gamma-1}Apt^{p-1}$

5.3

1. (a) Differentiation w.r.t. x yields $1 \cdot y + xy' = 0$, so $y' = -y/x$. Because $y = 1/x$, this gives $y' = -1/x^2$.   (b) $y' = (1 \div 3y)/(1 - 3x)$. Because

$y = (x-2)/(1-3x)$, this gives $y' = -5/(1-3x)^2$. (c) $y' = 5x^4/6y^5$. Because $y = x^{5/6}$, this gives $y' = (5/6)x^{-1/6}$.

3. $\dfrac{dv}{du} = \dfrac{2u+v}{3v^2-u}$. Hence, $dv/du = 0$ when $v = -2u$. Inserting this value into the original equation implies that $dv/du = 0$ at $(u,v) = (1/8, -1/4)$.

5. $dQ/dP = -19/P^{3/2}$

7. $Y = f(Y) + I + \bar{A} - g(Y)$. Differentiating w.r.t. I using the chain rule yields $dY/dI = f'(Y)(dY/dI) + 1 - g'(Y)(dY/dI)$. Solving for dY/dI gives $dY/dI = 1/[1 - f'(Y) + g'(Y)]$. Imports should increase when income increases, so $g'(Y) > 0$. We find that $dY/dI > 0$.

9. Differentiation w.r.t. x yields $g'(f(x))f'(x) = 1$, so $f'(x) = 1/g'(f(x))$ (provided that $g'(f(x)) \neq 0$).

5.4

1. If $f(x) = \sqrt{1+x}$, then $f'(x) = 1/2\sqrt{1+x}$, so $f(0) = 1$ and $f'(0) = 1/2$. Hence, [5.5] gives $\sqrt{1+x} \approx 1 + \frac{1}{2}(x-0) = 1 + \frac{1}{2}x$. See Fig. 18.

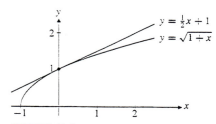

FIGURE 18

3. (a) $1/(1+x) \approx 1 - x$ (b) $(1+x)^5 \approx 1 + 5x$ (c) $(1-x)^{1/4} \approx 1 - x/4$

5. (a) $\sqrt[3]{1.1} = (1+1/10)^{1/3} \approx 1 + (1/3)(1/10) \approx 1.033$ (b) $\sqrt[5]{33} = 2(1+1/32)^{1/5} \approx 2(1+1/160) = 2.0125$ (c) $\sqrt[3]{9} = 2(1+1/8)^{1/3} \approx 2(1+1/24) \approx 2.083$ (d) $(1.02)^{25} = (1+1/50)^{25} \approx 1 + 1/2 = 1.5$ (e) $\sqrt{37} = (36+1)^{1/2} = 6(1+1/36)^{1/2} \approx 6(1+1/72) \approx 6.083$ (f) $(26.95)^{1/3} = (27 - 5/100)^{1/3} = 3(1 - 0.05/27)^{1/3} \approx 3 - 0.05/27 \approx 2.998$

7. $V(r) = (4/3)\pi r^3$. The linear approximation is: $V(2+0.03) - V(2) \approx 0.03 \cdot V'(2) = 0.48\pi$. Actual increase: $V(2.03) - V(2) = 0.487236\pi$.

5.5

1. (a) $(1+x)^5 \approx 1 + 5x + 10x^2$ (b) $AK^\alpha \approx A + \alpha A(K-1) + \frac{1}{2}\alpha(\alpha-1)A(K-1)^2$ (c) $(1 + \frac{3}{2}\varepsilon + \frac{1}{2}\varepsilon^2)^{1/2} \approx 1 + \frac{3}{4}\varepsilon - \frac{1}{32}\varepsilon^2$ (d) $(1-x)^{-1} \approx 1 + x + x^2$

3. Implicit differentiation yields: [*] $3x^2y + x^3y' + 1 = \frac{1}{2}y^{-1/2}y'$. Inserting $x = 0$ and $y = 1$ gives $1 = (\frac{1}{2})1^{-1/2}y'$, so $y' = 2$. Differentiating [*] once

more w.r.t. x yields $6xy + 3x^2y' + 3x^2y' + x^3y'' = -\frac{1}{4}y^{-3/2}(y')^2 + \frac{1}{2}y^{-1/2}y''$.
Inserting $x = 0$, $y = 1$, and $y' = 2$ gives $y'' = 2$. Hence, $y(x) \approx 1 + 2x + x^2$.

5. Use [5.10] with $f(x) = (1+x)^n$ and $x = p/100$. Then $f'(x) = n(i+x)^{n-1}$ and $f''(x) = n(n-1)(1+x)^{n-2}$. The approximation follows.

5.6

1. (a) -3 (b) 100 (c) $1/2$ (d) $-3/2$

3. (a) An increase in prices by 10% leads to a decrease in traffic by approximately 4%. (b) One reason could be that for long-distance travel, more people fly when rail fares go up.

5. $\mathrm{El}_x f(x)^p = \dfrac{x}{f(x)^p} p\,(f(x))^{p-1} f'(x) = p\dfrac{x}{f(x)} f'(x) = p\,\mathrm{El}_x f(x)$

7. (a) $\mathrm{El}_x A = (x/A)(dA/dx) = 0$

(b) $\mathrm{El}_x(fg) = \dfrac{x}{fg}(fg)' = \dfrac{x}{fg}(f'g + fg') = \dfrac{xf'}{f} + \dfrac{xg'}{g} = \mathrm{El}_x f + \mathrm{El}_x g$

(c) $\mathrm{El}_x \dfrac{f}{g} = \dfrac{xg}{f}\left(\dfrac{f}{g}\right)' = \dfrac{xg}{f}\left(\dfrac{gf' - fg'}{g^2}\right) = \dfrac{xf'}{f} - \dfrac{xg'}{g} = \mathrm{El}_x f - \mathrm{El}_x g$

(d) $\mathrm{El}_x(f + g) = \dfrac{x(f' + g')}{f + g} = \dfrac{f\dfrac{xf'}{f} + g\dfrac{xg'}{g}}{f + g} = \dfrac{f\,\mathrm{El}_x f + g\,\mathrm{El}_x g}{f + g}$

(e) Is like (d), but with $+g$ replaced by $-g$, and $+g'$ by $-g'$.

(f) $z = f(g(u))$, $u = g(x) \Rightarrow \mathrm{El}_x z = \dfrac{x}{z}\dfrac{dz}{dx} = \dfrac{x}{u}\dfrac{u}{z}\dfrac{dz}{du}\dfrac{du}{dx} = \mathrm{El}_u f(u)\,\mathrm{El}_x u$

9. (a) $5 + \mathrm{El}_x f(x)$ (b) $\frac{3}{2}\mathrm{El}_x f(x)$ (c) $\dfrac{x + \frac{1}{2}\sqrt{f(x)}\,\mathrm{El}_x f(x)}{x + \sqrt{f(x)}}$ (d) $-\mathrm{El}_x f(x)$

Chapter 6

6.1

1. (a) -4 (b) 0 (c) 2 (d) $-\infty$ (e) ∞ (f) $-\infty$

3. (a) (i) $-\infty$ (ii) ∞ (iii) 0 (iv) A (b) $\lim_{x \to 0} f(x) = B$

5. (a) $y = x - 1$ ($x = -1$ is a vertical asymptote). (b) $y = 2x - 3$ (c) $y = 3x + 5$ ($x = 1$ is a vertical asymptote). (d) $y = 5x$ ($x = 1$ is a vertical asymptote).

6.2

1. (b) and (d) are continuous; the others are not necessarily so. (As for (c), consider Problem 6.)

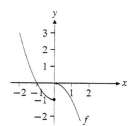

FIGURE 19

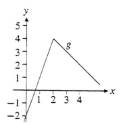

FIGURE 20

3. f is discontinuous at $x = 0$. g is continuous at $x = 2$. The graphs of f and g are shown in Figs. 19 and 20.

5. $a = 5$, so that $\lim_{x \to 1^+} f(x) = 4 = \lim_{x \to 1^-} f(x) = a - 1$.

7. No. Let $f(x) = g(x) = 1$ for $x < a$, let $f(x) = -1$ and $g(x) = 3$ for $x \geq a$. Then f and g are both discontinuous at $x = a$, but $f(x) + g(x) = 2$ for all x, and therefore $f + g$ is continuous for all x. (Draw a figure!) Let $h(x) = -f(x)$ for all x. Then h is also discontinuous at $x = a$, whereas $f(x)h(x) = -1$ for all x, and so $f \cdot h$ is continuous for all x.

6.3

1. $f'(0^+) = 1$ and $f'(0^-) = 0$. See Fig. 21.

3. If $x > 0$, then $f'(x) = \frac{1}{3}x^{-2/3} \to \infty$ as $x \to 0^+$. Also $f'(x) \to -\infty$ as $x \to 0^-$. Hence, the graph has a cusp at $x = 0$. See Fig. 22.

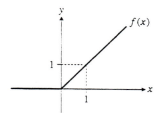

FIGURE 21

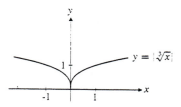

FIGURE 22

6.4

1. (a) $\alpha_n = \dfrac{(3/n) - 1}{2 - (1/n)} \to -\dfrac{1}{2}$ as $n \to \infty$ (b) $\beta_n = \dfrac{1 + (2/n) - (1/n^2)}{3 - (2/n^2)} \to \dfrac{1}{3}$ as $n \to \infty$ (c) $3 \cdot (-1/2) + 4 \cdot (1/3) = -1/6$ (d) $(-1/2) \cdot (1/3) = -1/6$ (e) $(-1/2)/(1/3) = -3/2$ (f) $\sqrt{(1/3) - (-1/2)} = \sqrt{5/6} = \sqrt{30}/6$

6.5

1. $s_n = (3/2)[1 - (1/3)^n] \to 3/2$ as $n \to \infty$, so $\sum_{n=1}^{\infty} \frac{1}{3^{n-1}} = 3/2$.

3. (a) Quotient $k = 1/p$. Converges to $1/(p-1)$ for $|p| > 1$. (b) Quotient $k = 1/\sqrt{x}$. Converges to $x\sqrt{x}/(\sqrt{x} - 1)$ for $\sqrt{x} > 1$, that is, for $x > 1$. (c) Quotient $k = x^2$. Converges to $x^2/(1 - x^2)$ for $|x| < 1$. (d) Quotient $k = 1/(1 + x)$. Converges to $1 + 1/x$ for $|1/(1 + x)| < 1$, that is, for $x > 0$ and for $x < -2$.

5. If x denotes the number of years beyond 1971 that the earth's resources of iron will last, we get $794 + 794 \cdot 1.05 + \cdots + 794 \cdot (1.05)^x = 249 \cdot 10^3$. Using [6.10], we have $794[1 - (1.05)^x]/(1 - 1.05) = 249 \cdot 10^3$ or $1.05^x \approx 16.68$. Using a calculator, we find $x \approx 57.7$, and that the resources will be exhausted part way through the year 2029.

7. (a) A geometric series with quotient $100/101$ that converges to 100. (b) Diverges according to [6.18]. (c) Converges according to [6.18]. (d) Diverges because the nth term $(1 + n)/(4n - 3) \to 1/4$ as $n \to \infty$. (e) Geometric series with quotient $-1/2$ that converges to $-1/3$. (f) Geometric series with quotient $1/\sqrt{3}$ converging to $\sqrt{3}/(\sqrt{3} - 1)$.

6.6

1. Use [6.21] with $n = 15$, $r = 12/100 = 0.12$, and $a = 3500$ to obtain
$$A_{15} = \frac{3500}{0.12}\left[1 - \frac{1}{(1.12)^{15}}\right] \approx 23,838.$$

3. Let $r = p/100$. Then, applying [6.21] with $a = 1000$ and $n = 5$ gives $A_5 = (1000/r)[1 - 1/(1 + r)^5] = 4340$. For $p = 5\%$, the present value is $\$4329.48$; for $p = 4.5\%$, the present value is $\$4389.98$. Because $dA_5/dr < 0$, follows that p is a little less than 5%.

5. Equation [6.23] reduces to $\frac{a}{1+r} + \frac{a}{(1+r)^2} + \cdots = -a_0$. So by [6.22], we have $a/r = -a_0$. Hence, $r = -a/a_0$.

7. By hypothesis, $f(0) = a_0 + a_1 + \cdots + a_{n-1} > 0$. Also, $f(r) \to a_0 < 0$ as $r \to \infty$. Moreover, $f'(r) = -a_1(1 + r)^{-2} - \cdots - (n - 1)a_{n-1}(1 + r)^{-n} < 0$, so $f(r)$ is strictly decreasing. This guarantees that there is a unique internal rate of return, with $r > 0$.

6.7

1. With $f(x) = 5x + 2$, $a = -1$, and $A = -3$, we have $|f(x) - A| = |5x + 2 - (-3)| = |5x + 5| = 5|x + 1|$. Let $\varepsilon > 0$. Choose $\delta = \varepsilon/5$. According to (6.24), the result follows.

3. Because $f(x)$ and $h(x)$ both tend to 2 as x tends to 0, [6.27] implies that $\lim_{x \to 0} g(x) = 2$.

Chapter 7

7.1

1. (a) Let $f(x) = x^7 - 5x^5 + x^3 - 1$. Then f is continuous, $f(-1) = 2$, and $f(1) = -4$, so according to Theorem 7.2, the equation $f(x) = 0$ has a solution in $(-1, 1)$. Parts (b) and (c) are done in the same way.

3. Your height is a continuous function of time. You were once less than 1 meter tall and (unless you are unduly precocious) you are probably now above 1 meter tall. The intermediate value theorem (and common sense) give the conclusion.

5. (a) See Fig. 23.   (b) Define $g(x) = f(x) - x$. Then $g(a) \geq 0$ and $g(b) \leq 0$. If either $g(a)$ or $g(b)$ is 0, we have a fixed point for f. If $g(a) > 0$ and $g(b) < 0$, then $g(x) = 0$ for some x^* in (a, b) by the intermediate-value theorem. This x^* is a fixed point for f.

7.2

1. f is continuous on $[0, 5]$, so the extreme-value theorem applies.

3. f has a maximum at $x = 1$ and a minimum at all $x > 1$. (Draw your own graph.) Yet the function is discontinuous at $x = 1$, and its domain of definition is neither closed nor bounded.

7.3

1. (a) $\xi = 3/2$ (b) $\xi = \sqrt{2}/2$ (c) $\xi = \sqrt{12}$ (d) $\xi = \sqrt{3}$

3. $\xi = \pm 1/\sqrt{27}$. The conditions of the mean-value theorem are not satisfied, because f is not differentiable at $x = 0$. See Fig. 24.

7.4

1. $(1 + x)^{-1} = 1 - x + x^2 - (1 + c)^{-4}x^3$

3. $(1 + 1/8)^{1/3} = 1 + 1/24 - 1/576 + R_3(1/8)$, where $0 < R_3(1/8) < 5/(81 \cdot 8^3)$. Thus, $\sqrt[3]{9} = 2(1 + 1/8)^{1/3} \approx 2.080$, with three correct decimals.

FIGURE 23

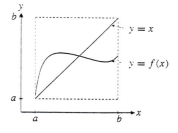

FIGURE 24

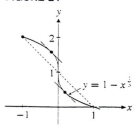

5. The idea is precisely the same as in Problem 4. The expressions get so big that we do not reproduce them here.

7.5

1. (a) $\lim_{x \to 1}(x - 1)/(x^2 - 1) = \lim_{x \to 1} 1/2x = 1/2$ (b) $\lim_{x \to a} 2x/1 = 2a$
   (c) $\lim_{x \to -2}(3x^2 + 6x)/(3x^2 + 10x + 8) = \lim_{x \to -2}(6x + 6)/(6x + 10) = 3$

3. The second fraction is not "0/0". The correct limit is 5/2.

5. Does not exist if $b \neq d$. If $b = d$, the limit is "0/0" and by l'Hôpital's rule, it is $\lim_{x \to 0}[\frac{1}{2}a(ax + b)^{-1/2} - \frac{1}{2}c(cx + d)^{-1/2}]/1 = a/2\sqrt{b} - c/2\sqrt{d} = (a - c)/2\sqrt{b}$.

7. $\sqrt[n]{x^n + a_1 x^{n-1} + \cdots + a_{n-1}x + a_n} - x =$
   $x\left(\sqrt[n]{1 + a_1/x + \cdots + a_n/x^n} - 1\right) = \dfrac{\sqrt[n]{1 + a_1/x + \cdots + a_n/x^n} - 1}{1/x}$.   Now use l'Hôpital's rule.

7.6

1. $p = 64/3 - 10D/3$

3. (a) $x = -y/3$ (b) $x = 1/y$ (c) $x = y^{1/3}$

5. (a) $g(x) = (x^3 + 1)^{1/3}$ (b) $g(x) = (2x + 1)/(x - 1)$
   (c) $g(x) = \left[1 - (x - 2)^5\right]^{1/3}$

7. (a) $f'(x) = 4x - 4x^3 > 0$ for $x \in (0, 1)$, so $R_f = [0, 1]$.
   (b) $g(x) = \sqrt{1 - \sqrt{1 - x}}$

9. (a) $f(x) = x/2$ and $g(x) = 2x$ are inverse functions.   (b) $f(x) = 3x - 2$ and $g(x) = \frac{1}{3}(x+2)$ are inverse functions.   (c) $C = \frac{5}{9}(F - 32)$ and $F = \frac{9}{5}C + 32$ are inverse functions.

11. f^{-1} determines how much it costs to buy a specified number of kilograms of meat.

13. $f'(x) = 4x^2(3 - x^2)/3\sqrt{4 - x^2} > 0$ for $x \in (0, \sqrt{3})$, so f has an inverse on $[0, \sqrt{3}]$. $g'(\sqrt{3}/3) = 1/f'(1) = 3\sqrt{3}/8$.

Chapter 8

8.1

1. (a) $y' = -3e^{-3x}$ (b) $y' = 6x^2 e^{x^3}$ (c) $y' = (-1/x^2)e^{1/x}$
   (d) $y' = 5(4x - 3)e^{2x^2 - 3x + 1}$

3. (a) $f'(x) = e^x + xe^x = e^x(1 + x)$, $f''(x) = e^x(2 + x)$. f is increasing for $x > -1$.   (b) See Fig. 25.

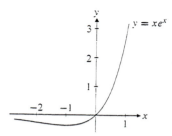

FIGURE 25

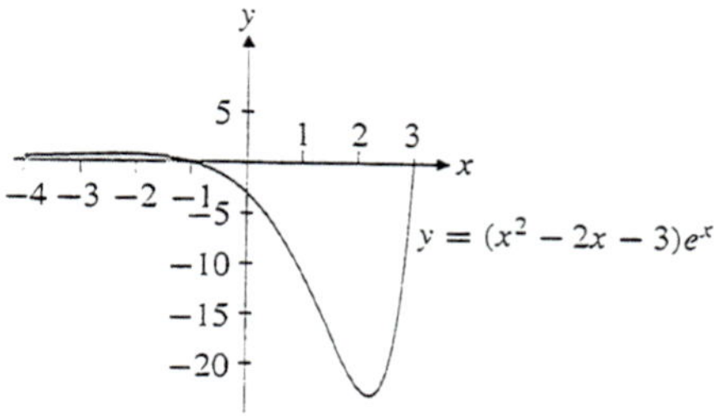

$y = (x^2 - 2x - 3)e^x$

FIGURE 26

5. See Fig. 26.

7. $y = xe^x$ has the derivative $y' = e^x + xe^x = (x + 1)e^x$, so the formula *is* correct for $n = 1$. *Assume* that the kth derivative is $y^{(k)} = (x+k)e^x$. Then by the product rule, $y^{(k+1)} = (d/dx)(x+k)e^x = e^x + (x+k)e^x = [x+(k+1)]e^x$. Thus, the given formula is valid also for $n = k + 1$. By induction, it is valid generally.

8.2

1. (a) $\ln 9 = \ln 3^2 = 2 \ln 3$ (b) $\frac{1}{2} \ln 3$ (c) $\ln \sqrt[5]{3^2} = \ln 3^{2/5} = \frac{2}{5} \ln 3$
(d) $\ln(1/81) = \ln 3^{-4} = -4 \ln 3$

3. (a) $3^x 4^{x+2} = 8$ when $3^x 4^x 4^2 = 8$ or $12^x = 1/2$. Hence, $x = -\ln 2 / \ln 12$.
(b) $\ln x^3 + \ln x^4 = 6$, or $\ln x^7 = 6$, so $7 \ln x = 6$ and then $x = e^{6/7}$.
(c) $4^x(1 - 4^{-1}) = 3^x(3 - 1)$, so $(4/3)^x = 8/3$, implying that
$x = \ln(8/3)/\ln(4/3)$. (Also, $(4/3)^{x-1} = 2$, so an alternative correct answer
is $x = 1 + \ln 2/\ln(4/3)$.)

5. We show how to prove (c) and (e). For (c), when $x > 0$: $\ln(e^3 x^2) = \ln e^3 + \ln x^2 = 3 \ln e + 2 \ln x = 3 + 2 \ln x$. For (e): Note that $p_i \ln(1/p_i) = p_i(\ln 1 - \ln p_i) = -p_i \ln p_i$ when $p_i > 0$.

7. (a) Wrong. (Let $A = e$.) (b) and (c) are right.

9. (a) $x > -1$ (b) $1/3 < x < 1$ (c) $x \neq 0$ (d) $x > 1$ or $x < -1$ (e) $x > 1$
(f) $x \neq e^e$ and $x > 1$

11. (a) $\dfrac{1}{x \ln x}$ (b) $\dfrac{-x}{1 - x^2}$ (c) $e^x \left(\ln x + \dfrac{1}{x} \right)$ (d) $e^{x^3} \left(3x^2 \ln x^2 + \dfrac{2}{x} \right)$
(e) $\dfrac{e^x}{e^x + 1}$ (f) $\dfrac{2x + 3}{x^2 + 3x - 1}$

13. (a) $\ln f(x) = \frac{1}{3}[\ln(x + 1) - \ln(x - 1)]$, so $\dfrac{f'(x)}{f(x)} = \dfrac{1}{3} \left(\dfrac{1}{x + 1} - \dfrac{1}{x - 1} \right) = \dfrac{-2}{3(x^2 - 1)}$ (b) $\ln f(x) = x \ln x$, so $f'(x)/f(x) = \ln x + 1$ (c) $\ln f(x) = \frac{1}{2} \ln(x - 2) + \ln(x^2 + 1) + \ln(x^4 + 6)$, so $\dfrac{f'(x)}{f(x)} = \dfrac{1}{2x - 4} + \dfrac{2x}{x^2 + 1} + \dfrac{4x^3}{x^4 + 6}$

15. (a) $f'(x) = e^{x-1} - 1$ is < 0 for $x < 1$, and > 0 for $x > 1$. But $f(1) = 0$. So $f(x) > 0$ for all $x \neq 0$. See Fig. 27. (b) $f(-1) = e^{-2} + 1 > 1$, $f(1) = 0$, and $f(3) = e^2 - 3 > 1$. By the intermediate-value theorem, there have to be solutions of $f(x) = 1$ in each of the intervals $(-1, 1)$ and $(1, 3)$. Because $f'(x) < 0$ for $x > 1$ and $f'(x) > 0$ for $x > 1$, there is only one solution in each of the two intervals, and these are the only two solutions. (c) g is defined for all $x \neq 1$, $x \neq x_1$, and $x \neq x_2$, where x_1 and x_2 are the two solutions in (b). $g(x) \to 0$ as $x \to \pm\infty$. (d) See Fig. 28.

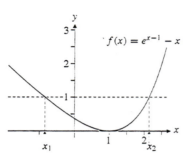

FIGURE 27   **FIGURE 28**

17. (a) $F(x) = e^{-e^{-x}}$ (b) $f(x) = e^{-x}e^{-e^{-x}} = \exp(-x)\exp[-\exp(-x)]$
   (c) $f'(x) = f(x)(e^{-x} - 1)$

19. (a) $xy'/y = ax$ (b) $3 + 2x$ (c) $1 + \dfrac{x}{(x+1)\ln(x+1)}$ (d) $\dfrac{x^{-\delta}}{x^{-\delta} + 1}$

21. $\ln y = v \ln u$, so $y'/y = v' \ln u + vu'/u$.

23. We must solve $x = \frac{1}{2}(e^y - e^{-y})$ for y. Multiply the equation by e^y to get $\frac{1}{2}e^{2y} - \frac{1}{2} = xe^y$ or $e^{2y} - 2xe^y - 1 = 0$. Letting $e^y = z$ yields $z^2 - 2xz - 1 = 0$, with solution $z = x \pm \sqrt{x^2 + 1}$. The minus sign makes z negative, so $z = e^y = x + \sqrt{x^2 + 1}$. This gives $y = \ln(x + \sqrt{x^2 + 1})$ as the inverse function.

8.3

1. (a) $\log_5 25 = \log_5 5^2 = 2 \log_5 5 = 2$ (b) 3/2, because $125 = 5^3$. (c) -2
   (d) -6

3. (a) $y' = 5 \cdot 3^x \ln 3$ (b) $y' = 2^x \ln 2 \ln x + 2^x/x$ (c) $y' = \log_2 x + 1/\ln 2$
   (d) $y' = x/[(1 + x^2)\ln 2]$

5. (a) $0 < x \leq 1/e$ (b) $x^2 - x - 1 \geq 1$, so $x \leq -1$ or $x \geq 2$ (c) One must have $x > 3$. Then $\ln x + \ln(x - 3) = \ln x(x - 3) \leq \ln 4$, and so $x(x - 3) \leq 4$. Thus, $3 < x \leq 4$.

7. Applying l'Hôpital's rule, $\lim_{\lambda \to 0^+} (x^\lambda - y^\lambda)/\lambda = \lim_{\lambda \to 0^+} (x^\lambda \ln x - y^\lambda \ln y)/1 = \ln x - \ln y$.

9. Inserting $e^x \approx 1 + x + \frac{1}{2}x^2 + \frac{1}{6}x^3$ and $e^{-x} \approx 1 - x + \frac{1}{2}x^2 - \frac{1}{6}x^3$ in the given equation yields, after rearranging, $x(x^2 - 1) \approx 0$. So $x = 0$ (exact), $x \approx -1$, and $x \approx 1$.

8.4

1. (a) $\dot{x}/x = 5/(5t + 10)$ (b) $\dot{x}/x = 1/(t + 1)\ln(t + 1)$ (c) $\dot{x}/x = 1$ (d) $\dot{x}/x = \ln 2$ (e) $\dot{x}/x = 2t$ (f) $\dot{x}/x = (e^t - e^{-t})/(e^t + e^{-t})$. So (c) and (d) have a constant relative rate of increase, which accords with [8.22].

3. (a) $P(25) \approx 6595$ (millions)   (b) Doubling time: $t = (\ln 2)/0.02 \approx 34.7$ years.

5. (a) 710   (b) A little more than 21 days.   (c) Yes, after about 35 days, 999 will have or have had influenza, and $N(t) \to 1000$.

7. (a) $f'(x) = k - A\alpha e^{-\alpha x} = 0$ when $x_0 = (1/\alpha)\ln(A\alpha/k)$ (b) $x_0 > 0$ iff $A\alpha > k$. Then $f'(x) < 0$ if $x < x_0$ and $f'(x) > 0$ if $x > x_0$.   (c) x_0 increases as p_0 increases, and as V increases; x_0 decreases as δ increases, and as k increases.

9. $\ln m = -0.02 + 0.19 \ln N$. When $N = 480.000$, then $m \approx 11.77$.

11. $\ln z = \ln 694.500 - 0.3 \ln p$, and $p = (694,500/z)^{10/3}$.

13. (a) See Fig. 29.

T	36.3	35.0	33.9	32.4	24.7	24.2
$\ln n$	5.04	4.89	4.70	4.54	3.64	3.58

(b) $f(T) = 1.99e^{0.12T}$

(c) The fall in temperature that halves the pulse rate is $(\ln 2)/0.12 \approx 5.8$ degrees.

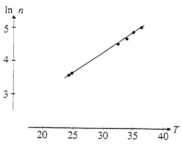

FIGURE 29

15. $t_0 = 1972 + 8000 \ln 0.886$, which gives the approximate date 1004.

8.5

1. (a) (i) $\$1000(1.05)^{10} \approx \$1629$ (ii) $\$1000(1.05)^{50} \approx \$11,467$
   (b) (i) $\$1000(1 + 0.05/12)^{120} \approx \$1647$
   (ii) $\$1000(1 + 0.05/12)^{600} \approx \$12,119$
   (c) (i) $\$1000e^{0.05 \cdot 10} \approx \$1649$ (ii) $\$1000e^{0.05 \cdot 50} \approx \$12,182$.

3. $h'(u) = u/(1 + u)^2 > 0$ for $u > 0$, so $h(u) > 0$ for $u > 0$, implying that $g'(x)/g(x) = h(r/x) > 0$ for all $x > 0$. So $g(x)$ is strictly increasing for $x > 0$. Because $g(x) \to e^r$ as $x \to \infty$, it follows that $g(x) < e^r$ for all $x > 0$. Continuous compounding of interest is best for the lender.

Chapter 9

9.2

1. $y' = 1.06 - 0.08x$. So y has a maximum at $x = 1.06/0.08 = 13.25$.

3. (a) $V'(x) = 12(x - 3)(x - 9)$. So V has maximum 432 at $x = 3$. (b) The box has maximum volume when the square cut out from each corner has a length of 3 cm. (c) Logarithmic differentiation yields $V'(x)/V(x) = 3(3 - x)/x(9 - x)$.

5. (a) Maximum 2 at $x = 0$. No minimum. (b) Maximum 3 at $x = 2$. No minimum. (c) Minimum -3 at $x = -2$. No maximum. (d) Minimum -1 at $x = 0$. No maximum. (e) Maximum 2 at $x = 1$. No minimum. (f) Maximum 1 at $x = 0$. Minimum 1/2 at $x = \pm 1$.

7. $\overline{T}'(Y) = a(bY + c)^{p-1}(pbY - bY - c)/Y^2$, which is 0 for $Y^* = c/b(p - 1)$. This must be the minimum point because $\overline{T}'(Y)$ is negative for $Y < Y^*$ and positive for $Y > Y^*$.

9.3

1. Maximum 80 at $x = 0$. Minimum -20 at $x = 5$. See Fig. 30.

FIGURE 30

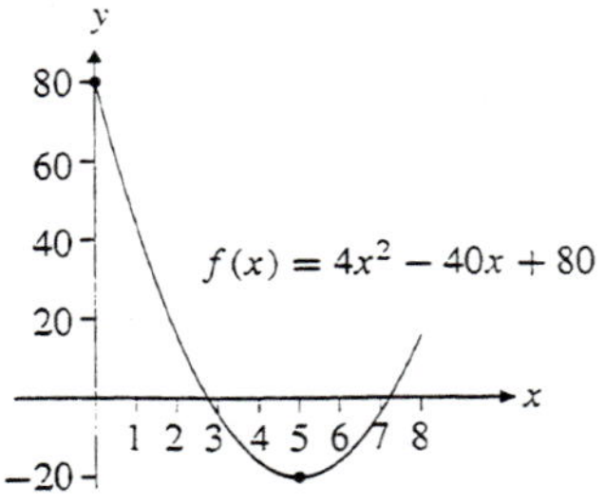

$f(x) = 4x^2 - 40x + 80$

3. Choose both numbers equal to 8. (If $x + y = 16$, then $xy = x(16 - x) = -x^2 + 16x$, with $x \in (0, 16)$, and this function of x has its maximum at $x = 8$.)

5. (a) $Q^* = (p - \beta)/2\gamma$ (b) (i) $Q = 450$ (ii) $Q = 500$ (iii) $Q = 0$

7. $y' = e^{-x}(2x - x^2)$ is positive in $(0, 2)$ and negative in $(2, 4)$, so y has a maximum $4e^{-2} \approx 0.52$ at $x = 2$.

9. $A(Q) = C(Q)/Q = aQ^2 + bQ + c + d/Q$. Then $A'(Q) = 2aQ + b - d/Q^2$, so $A'(Q) \to -\infty$ as $Q \to 0^+$, and $A'(Q) \to \infty$ as $Q \to \infty$. Moreover, $A''(Q) = 2a + 2d/Q^3$, which is positive for all $Q > 0$. Hence, $A'(Q)$ is strictly increasing from $-\infty$ to ∞ in $(0, \infty)$. Thus, there is a unique point Q^* at which $A'(Q^*) = 0$, and Q^* minimizes $A(Q)$. For $b = 0$, $A(Q)$ has a minimum at $Q^* = (d/2a)^{1/3}$.

9.4

1. $f'(x) = 3x^2 - 12 = 0$ at $x = \pm 2$, and $f''(x) = 6x$. So $x = 2$ is a local minimum point, whereas $x = -2$ is a local maximum point.

3. (a) $D_f = [-6, 0) \cup (0, \infty)$; $f(-2) = f(-6) = 0$; moreover $f(x) > 0$ in $(-6, -2) \cup (0, \infty)$. (b) Local maximum $\frac{1}{2}\sqrt{2}$ at $x = -4$. Local minimum $(8/3)\sqrt{3}$ at $x = 6$ and local minimum 0 at $x = -6$ (where $f'(x)$ is undefined). (c) $f(x) \to -\infty$ as $x \to 0^-$, $f(x) \to \infty$ as $x \to 0^+$, $f(x) \to \infty$ as $x \to \infty$, and $f'(x) \to 0$ as $x \to \infty$. f attains neither a maximum nor a minimum.

5. (a) $f(t) = \dfrac{P(t)e^{-rt}}{1 - e^{-rt}} = \dfrac{P(t)}{e^{rt} - 1}$ (b) Here $f'(t) = \dfrac{P'(t)(e^{rt} - 1) - P(t)re^{rt}}{(e^{rt} - 1)^2}$, and $t^* > 0$ can only maximize $f(t)$ if $f'(t^*) = 0$, that is, if $P'(t^*)(e^{rt^*} - 1) = rP(t^*)e^{rt^*}$, which implies that $P'(t^*) = rP(t^*)/(1 - e^{-rt^*})$.

7. a and d are local minimum points, whereas c is a local maximum point for f.

9. (a) $f'(x) = \dfrac{-12x^3 + 6x}{(x^4 - x^2 + 1)^2}$. $x = 0$ is a local minimum point; $x = \pm\sqrt{2}/2$ are global maximum points.   (b) See Fig. 31.

FIGURE 31

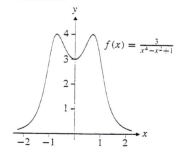

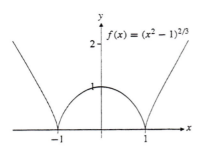

FIGURE 32

11. (a) $f'(x) = 4x/3(x^2 - 1)^{1/3}$ and $f''(x) = 4(x - \sqrt{3})(x + \sqrt{3})/9(x^2 - 1)^{4/3}$.
(b) $x = -1$ and $x = 1$ are local (and global) minimum points. $x = 0$ is a local maximum point. The graph is shown in Fig. 32.

9.5

1. $f'(x) = -(2x/3) + 8$ and $f''(x) = -2/3 < 0$ for all x, so f is concave.

3. (a) $R = p\sqrt{x}$, $C = wx + F$, and $\pi(x) = p\sqrt{x} - wx - F$. (b) $\pi'(x) = p(1/2\sqrt{x}) - w = 0$, or $p(1/2\sqrt{x}) = w$. (Marginal cost = price per unit of output.) (c) $\pi''(x) = -\frac{1}{4}px^{-3/2} < 0$ for all $x > 0$, so profit is maximized. (d) No maximum exists, because $\pi(x) \to \infty$ as $x \to \infty$.

5. (a) $f''(x) = 2x(x^2 - 3)(1 + x^2)^{-3}$, so f is convex in $[-\sqrt{3}, 0]$ and in $[\sqrt{3}, \infty)$. Inflection points are at $x = -\sqrt{3}$, 0, and $\sqrt{3}$. (b) $g''(x) = 4(1 + x)^{-3} > 0$ when $x > -1$, so g is (strictly) convex in $(-1, \infty)$. No inflection points. (c) $h''(x) = (2 + x)e^x$, so h is convex in $[-2, \infty)$ and $x = -2$ is an inflection point.

7. $C''(x) = 6aQ + 2b$, so $C(Q)$ is concave in $[0, -b/3a]$ and convex in $[-b/3a, \infty)$. $Q = -b/3a$ is an inflection point.

9. (a) $f'(v) = \frac{1}{3}(v - 1)^{-2/3}$ is positive in $[0, 1)$ and in $(1, \infty)$. Because $f(v)$ is continuous at $v = 1$, it is (strictly) increasing in $[0, \infty)$. Moreover, $f''(v) = -\frac{2}{9}(v - 1)^{-5/3}$, so $f''(v) > 0$ in $[0, 1)$ and $f''(v) < 0$ in $(1, \infty)$. See Fig. 33. (b) $f'(v_m) = p$, so $v_m = 1 + (3p)^{-3/2}$ (c) See Fig. 33. (d) $\pi(v) = 0$ when $v - 1 = (pv - 1)^3$, or $p^3v^3 - 3p^2v^2 + (3p - 1)v = 0$. This equation always has $v = 0$ as a root. Any other root must satisfy the quadratic equation $p^3v^2 - 3p^2v + 3p - 1 = 0$. For $0 < p < 1/3$, the only positive root is $v = (3 + \sqrt{4/p - 3})/2p$. For $1/3 < p < 4/3$, there are two positive roots, which are $v = (3 \pm \sqrt{4/p - 3})/2p$; for $p = 1/3$, $v = 9$; for $p = 4/3$, $v = 9/8$; for $p > 4/3$, the only root is $v = 0$. (e) The solutions are: For $0 < p < 4/3$, v_m is given by (b). For $p = 4/3$, $v = 0$ and $v = 9/8$. For $p > 4/3$, $v = 0$.

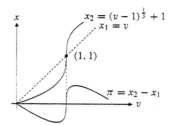

FIGURE 33

9.6

1. (a) Straightforward algebra. (b) $D \geq 0$, so f is concave. (c) $D > 0$ if $\lambda \in (0, 1)$ and $a \neq b$, so f is strictly concave. (d) $f''(x) = -2 < 0$, so according to [9.17], f is strictly concave.

3. (a) Convex, as a sum of convex functions. (b) Concave, as a sum of concave functions. (c) Concave, as a sum of concave functions. (d) Convex, as a sum of convex functions. (See the note immediately preceding Jensen's inequality.)

5. Apply [9.14] to the set shaded in Fig. 34, which is the set of points below the graph of $h(x)$.

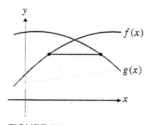

FIGURE 34

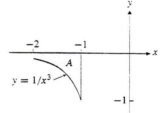

FIGURE 35

Chapter 10

10.1

1. $F(x) = \frac{1}{4}x^4$ and $A = F(1) - F(0) = \frac{1}{4}$.

3. See Fig. 35. $F(x) = -\frac{1}{2}x^{-2}$ so $F(-1) = -\frac{1}{2}(-1)^{-2} = -\frac{1}{2}$ and $F(-2) = -\frac{1}{2}(-2)^{-2} = -\frac{1}{8}$. Because $f(x)$ is negative in $[-2, -1]$, so the area $A = -[F(-1) - F(-2)] = -[-\frac{1}{2} - (-\frac{1}{8})] = \frac{1}{2} - \frac{1}{8} = \frac{3}{8}$.

10.2

1. (a) $\frac{1}{14}x^{14} + C$ (b) $\frac{2}{5}x^2\sqrt{x} + C$ (c) $2\sqrt{x} + C$ (d) $\frac{8}{15}x^{15/8} + C$, because $\sqrt{x\sqrt{x\sqrt{x}}} = x^{7/8}$.

3. (a) $\frac{2}{5}y^2\sqrt{y} - \frac{8}{3}y\sqrt{y} + 8\sqrt{y} + C$ (b) $\frac{1}{3}x^3 - \frac{1}{2}x^2 + x - \ln|x + 1| + C$, because $x^3/(x + 1) = x^2 - x + 1 - 1/(x + 1)$ (c) $\frac{1}{32}(1 + x^2)^{16} + C$

5. Differentiate the right-hand side to get $x\sqrt{ax + b}$.

7. $c(x) = \frac{3}{2}x^2 + 4x + 40$

9. (a) $f'(x) = 2x + 1$ and $f(x) = x^2 + x + 2$ (b) $f'(x) = -1/x + \frac{1}{4}x^4 + 2x - 1$ and $f(x) = -\ln x + (1/20)x^5 + x^2 - x - 1/20$

10.3

1. (a) $\int_0^1 x\,dx = \Big|_0^1 \frac{1}{2}x^2 = (\frac{1}{2})1^2 - (\frac{1}{2})0^2 = 1/2$ (b) $\Big|_1^2 (x^2 + \frac{1}{3}x^3) = 16/3$
   (c) $\Big|_{-2}^3 (\frac{1}{6}x^3 - \frac{1}{12}x^4) = 5/12$

3. (a) $x = 1000\sqrt{3}$ maximizes profits. See Fig. 36.
   (b) $I = \frac{1}{2000} \Big|_{1000}^{3000} (4000x - \frac{1}{2}x^2 - 3,000,000 \ln x) = 2000 - 1500 \ln 3 \approx 352$

5. (a) t^2 (b) $-e^{-t^2}$ (c) $2e^{-t^2}$ (d) $\ln t (1 - t^{-1/2}/4)$ (e) $\frac{1}{3}t^{4/3} - \frac{1}{6}t^{1/6}$
   (f) $2/\sqrt{t^4 + 1}$

7. $A = \int_0^3 (\sqrt{3x} - x^2 + 2x)\,dx = 6$. See Fig. 37.

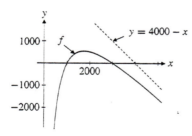

FIGURE 36

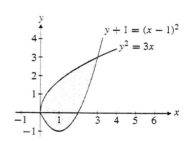

FIGURE 37

9. $W(T) = K(1 - e^{-\rho T})/\rho T$. Here $W(T) \to 0$ as $T \to \infty$, and using l'Hôpital's rule, $W(T) \to K$ as $T \to 0^+$. For $T > 0$, we find $W'(T) = Ke^{-\rho T}(1 + \rho T - e^{\rho T})/\rho T^2 < 0$ because $e^{\rho T} > 1 + \rho T$ (see Problem 14 in Section 8.2). We conclude that $W(T)$ is strictly decreasing and that $W(T) \in (0, K)$.

10.4

1. $x(t) = x_0 - \int_0^t \bar{u} e^{-as} \, ds = x_0 - \bar{u}(1 - e^{-at})/a$. We see that $x(t) \to x_0 - \bar{u}/a$ as $t \to \infty$. If $x_0 \geq \bar{u}/a$, the reservoir will never be empty.

3. (a) $K(5) - K(0) = \int_0^5 (3t^2 + 2t + 5) \, dt = 175$
   (b) $K(T) - K_0 = (T^3 - t_0^3) + (T^2 - t_0^2) + 5(T - t_0)$

5. (a) $\int_0^T a e^{-rt} \, dt = (a/r)(1 - e^{-rT})$ (b) a/r

Chapter 11

11.1

1. (a) Use [11.1] with $f(x) = x$ and $g'(x) = e^{-x}$. Then $g(x) = -e^{-x}$ and $\int x e^{-x} \, dx = x(-e^{-x}) - \int 1 \cdot (-e^{-x}) \, dx = -x e^{-x} - e^{-x} + C$.   (b) Use [11.1] with $f(x) = 3x$ and $g'(x) = e^{4x}$ to get $\frac{3}{4} x e^{4x} - \frac{3}{16} e^{4x} + C$.   (c) Use [11.1] with $f(x) = 1 + x^2$ and $g'(x) = e^{-x}$, as well as the answer to (a), to get $-x^2 e^{-x} - 2x e^{-x} - 3 e^{-x} + C$.   (d) Use [11.1] with $f(x) = \ln x$ and $g'(x) = x$ to get $\frac{1}{2} x^2 \ln x - \frac{1}{4} x^2 + C$.

3. The general formula follows from [11.1]. $\int \ln x \, dx = x \ln x - x + C$.

5. Let $f(x) = \ln x$ and $g'(x) = x^\rho$ and use [11.1].

7. Use [11.2] with $f(u) = u^2$ and $g'(u) = (\bar{u} - u)^{\gamma - 1}$. This gives $g(u) = -(1/\gamma)(\bar{u} - u)^\gamma$, so $T^* = (2k/\gamma) \int_0^{\bar{u}} u(\bar{u} - u)^\gamma \, du$. Then integrate by parts once more to get

$$T^* = -\frac{2k}{\gamma} \left[\left| \frac{u(\bar{u} - u)^{\gamma+1}}{\gamma + 1} \right|_0^{\bar{u}} - \int_0^{\bar{u}} \frac{(\bar{u} - u)^{\gamma+1}}{\gamma + 1} \, du \right] = \frac{2k \bar{u}^{\gamma+2}}{\gamma(\gamma + 1)(\gamma + 2)}$$

11.2

1. (a) $\frac{1}{9}(x^2 + 1)^9 + C$ (Let $f(u) = u^8$, $u = g(x) = x^2 + 1$.)   (b) $\frac{1}{11}(x + 2)^{11} + C$ (Let $u = x + 2$.)   (c) $\ln |x^2 - x + 8| + C$ (Let $u = x^2 - x + 8$.)

3. (a) Substitute $u = \sqrt{1 + x^2}$. Then $u^2 = 1 + x^2$, so $u \, du = x \, dx$. If $x = 0$, then $u = 1$; if $x = 1$, then $u = \sqrt{2}$. Hence, $\int_0^1 x \sqrt{1 + x^2} \, dx = \int_1^{\sqrt{2}} u \, u \, du = \int_1^{\sqrt{2}} u^2 \, du = \left| \frac{1}{3} u^3 \right|_1^{\sqrt{2}} = \frac{1}{3}(2\sqrt{2} - 1)$.   (b) 1/2 (Let $u = \ln y$.)   (c) $\frac{1}{2}(e^2 - e^{2/3})$ (Let $u = 2/x$.)

5. (a) 1/70 (The integrand is $-x^4(x^5 - 1)^{13}$. Let $u = x^5 - 1$.)
   (b) $2\sqrt{x} \ln x - 4\sqrt{x} + C$. (Let $u = \sqrt{x}$.)   (c) 8/3 (Let $u = \sqrt{1 + \sqrt{x}}$.)

7. (a) Make a common denominator on the right-hand side.   (b) (i) $3 \ln 2 - \ln 3$
   (ii) $16 \ln 2 - 7 \ln 3$

9. $I = \dfrac{A(1+C)}{\beta C} \ln\left(\dfrac{1+CD}{1+CDe^{\beta t}}\right) + At.$ (The suggested substitution $x =$
$CDe^{\beta \tau}$ implies $dx = CD\beta e^{\beta \tau}\, d\tau = \beta x\, d\tau$. Moreover,

$$\frac{A(1-De^{\beta \tau})}{1+CDe^{\beta \tau}}\, d\tau = \frac{A(1-x/C)\, dx}{1+x}\ \frac{dx}{\beta x} = \frac{A}{\beta C}\left(\frac{C}{x} - \frac{1+C}{1+x}\right) dx$$

and so on.)

11. (a) $\ln(x + \sqrt{x^2+1}) + C$ (b) $\frac{1}{2}x\sqrt{x^2+1} + \frac{1}{2}\ln(x + \sqrt{x^2+1}) + C$

11.3

1. (a) $\int_1^b (1/x^3)\, dx = \int_1^b x^{-3}\, dx = \big|_1^b(-\frac{1}{2}x^{-2}) = \frac{1}{2} - \frac{1}{2}b^{-2} \to \frac{1}{2}$ as $b \to \infty$.
So $\int_1^\infty (1/x^3)\, dx = \frac{1}{2}$. (b) $\int_1^b x^{-1/2}\, dx = \big|_1^b 2x^{1/2} \to \infty$ as $b \to \infty$, so the
integral diverges. (c) 1 (d) $\int_0^a \dfrac{x\, dx}{\sqrt{a^2-x^2}} = \big|_0^a - \sqrt{a^2 - x^2} = a$

3. Using a simplified notation and the result in Example 11.7, we have:
(a) $\int_0^\infty x\lambda e^{-\lambda x}\, dx = -\big|_0^\infty xe^{-\lambda x} + \int_0^\infty e^{-\lambda x}\, dx = 1/\lambda$
(b) $\int_0^\infty (x - \lambda^{-1})^2 \lambda e^{-\lambda x}\, dx = -\big|_0^\infty (x - \lambda^{-1})^2 e^{-\lambda x} + \int_0^\infty 2(x - \lambda^{-1})$
$e^{-\lambda x}\, dx = \lambda^{-2} + 2\int_0^\infty xe^{-\lambda x}\, dx - 2\lambda^{-1}\int_0^\infty e^{-\lambda x}\, dx = \lambda^{-2} + 2\lambda^{-2} -$
$2\lambda^{-2} = \lambda^{-2}$
(c) $\int_0^\infty (x - \lambda^{-1})^3 \lambda e^{-\lambda x}\, dx = -\big|_0^\infty (x - \lambda^{-1})^3 e^{-\lambda x} + \int_0^\infty 3(x - \lambda^{-1})^2$
$e^{-\lambda x}\, dx = -\lambda^{-3} + 3\lambda^{-1}\int_0^\infty (x - \lambda^{-1})^2 \lambda e^{-\lambda x}\, dx = -\lambda^{-3} + 3\lambda^{-1}\lambda^{-2} = 2\lambda^{-3}$

5. (a) $f'(x) = 1/x^4 - 3\ln x/x^4 = 0$ at $x = e^{1/3}$. $f(x) \to -\infty$ as $x \to 0^+$
and $f(x) \to 0$ as $x \to \infty$. $f(e^{1/3}) = 1/3e > 0$. Hence, f has a
maximum at $(e^{1/3}, 1/3e)$, but no minimum exists. (b) $\int_a^b x^{-3}\ln x\, dx =$
$-\big|_a^b \frac{1}{2}x^{-2}\ln x + \int_a^b \frac{1}{2}x^{-3}\, dx = \big|_a^b(-\frac{1}{2}x^{-2}\ln x - \frac{1}{4}x^{-2})$. This diverges when
$b = 1$ and $a \to 0$. But $\int_1^\infty x^{-3}\ln x\, dx = 1/4$.

7. If both limits exist, the integral is the sum of the following two limits:
$I_1 = \lim_{\epsilon \to 0^+} \int_{-2+\epsilon}^3 (1/\sqrt{x+2})\, dx$ and $I_2 = \lim_{\epsilon \to 0^+} \int_{-2}^{3-\epsilon}(1/\sqrt{3-x})\, dx$.
Here $I_1 = \lim_{\epsilon \to 0^+} \big|_{-2+\epsilon}^3 (2\sqrt{x+2}) = \lim_{\epsilon \to 0^+}(2\sqrt{5} - 2\sqrt{\epsilon}) = 2\sqrt{5}$, and
$I_2 = \lim_{\epsilon \to 0^+} \big|_{-2}^{3-\epsilon}(-2\sqrt{3-x}) = \lim_{\epsilon \to 0^+}(-2\sqrt{\epsilon} + 2\sqrt{5}) = 2\sqrt{5}$. The
answer is $4\sqrt{5}$.

9. $f(x) = 1/x^2$ is not defined at $x = 0$, so f is not continuous in $[-1, 1]$.

11. $\int_1^A [k/x - k^2/(1 + kx)]\, dx = \big|_1^A [k\ln x - k\ln(1+kx)] = \big|_1^A k\ln[x/(1+kx)] =$
$k\ln[A/(1 + kA)] - k\ln[1/(1 + k)] = k\ln[1/(1/A + k)] - k\ln[1/(1 + k)]$,
which tends to $k\ln(1/k) - k\ln[1/(1 + k)] = \ln(1 + 1/k)^k$ as $A \to \infty$. So
$I_k = \ln(1 + 1/k)^k$, which tends to $\ln e = 1$ as $k \to \infty$.

13. The substitution suggested in the hint and [11.13] are useful in all three
cases. For (b), you also need the result in Example 11.7. For (c), the sug-

gested substitution leads to the integral $I = (1/\sqrt{\pi}) \int_{-\infty}^{+\infty} (2\sigma^2 z^2 + 2\sqrt{2}\sigma\mu z + \mu^2)e^{-z^2} dz$. Note that $\int_{-\infty}^{+\infty} e^{-z^2} dz = \sqrt{\pi}$ by [11.13], and $\int_{-\infty}^{+\infty} ze^{-z^2} dz = 0$ by Example 11.9. Finally, integration by parts gives $\int z^2 e^{-z^2} dz = -\frac{1}{2}ze^{-z^2} + \int \frac{1}{2}e^{-z^2} dz$, so $\int_{-\infty}^{+\infty} z^2 e^{-z^2} dz = \frac{1}{2}\sqrt{\pi}$. Thus $I = (1/\sqrt{\pi})(2\sigma^2 \cdot \frac{1}{2}\sqrt{\pi} + 0 + \mu^2\sqrt{\pi}) = \sigma^2 + \mu^2$.

11.4

1. See Fig. 38. The solid curve represents the U.S. income distribution in 1980. The dotted curve gives the distribution in the Netherlands in 1959 (almost the same as the U.S. 1980 curve). The dashed curve gives the distribution in the Netherlands in 1985.

Income Share

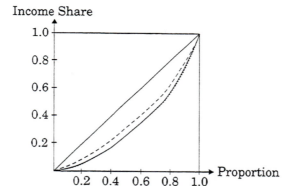

FIGURE 38

Chapter 12

12.1

1. (a) Let x and y denote total production in industries A and I, respectively. Then $x = \frac{1}{6}x + \frac{1}{4}y + 60$ and $y = \frac{1}{4}x + \frac{1}{4}y + 60$. So $\frac{5}{6}x - \frac{1}{4}y = 60$ and $-\frac{1}{4}x + \frac{3}{4}y = 60$. (b) $x = 320/3$ and $y = 1040/9$.

3. $0.8x_1 - 0.3x_2 = 120$ and $-0.4x_1 + 0.9x_2 = 90$, with solution $x_1 = 225$ and $x_2 = 200$.

12.2

1. $\mathbf{a}+\mathbf{b} = \begin{pmatrix} 5 \\ 3 \end{pmatrix}$, $\mathbf{a}-\mathbf{b} = \begin{pmatrix} -1 \\ -5 \end{pmatrix}$, $2\mathbf{a}+3\mathbf{b} = \begin{pmatrix} 13 \\ 10 \end{pmatrix}$, and $-5\mathbf{a}+2\mathbf{b} = \begin{pmatrix} -4 \\ 13 \end{pmatrix}$.

3. $a_1 = 0$, $a_2 = 1/3$, and $a_3 = 1$.

5. (a) $x_i = 0$ for all i. (b) Nothing, because $0 \cdot \mathbf{x} = \mathbf{0}$ for all $\mathbf{x}$.

7. $x = 3a + 4b$

9. (a) (i) Possible, with $\theta = 1/2$.   (ii) Impossible.   (iii) Impossible.
(b) (i) Proportion of lead $\theta = 1/2$.   (ii) If output can be thrown away, the proportion of lead can be $\theta = 2/3$.   (iii) Impossible in any case, because $(1 - \theta)4 + \theta 3 < 9$ for all $\theta \in [0, 1]$.

12.3

1. $a + b = (3, 3)$ and $-\frac{1}{2}a = (-2.5, 0.5)$. See Fig. 39.

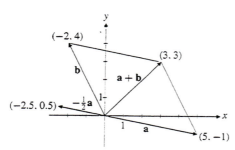

FIGURE 39

3. (a) $x_1 = 2$, $x_2 = -1$.   (b) Suppose $x_1(1, 2, 1) + x_2(-3, 0, -2) = (-3, 6, 1)$. Then $x_1 - 3x_2 = -3$, $2x_1 = 6$, and $x_1 - 2x_2 = 1$. The first two equations yield $x_1 = 3$ and $x_2 = 2$; then the last equation is not satisfied.

5. (a) A straight line through $(0, 2, 3)$ parallel to the x-axis.
(b) A plane parallel to the z-axis through the line $y = x$ in the xy-plane.

12.4

1. $a \cdot a = 5$, $a \cdot b = 2$, and $a \cdot (a + b) = 7$. We see that $a \cdot a + a \cdot b = a \cdot (a + b)$.

3. The pairs of vectors in (a) and (c) are orthogonal.

5. The vectors are orthogonal iff their scalar product is 0, that is iff $x^2 - x - 8 - 2x + x = x^2 - 2x - 8 = 0$, which is the case for $x = -2$ and $x = 4$.

7. Use the rules in [12.14].

9. (a) The firm's revenue is $p \cdot z$. Its costs are $p \cdot x$.   (b) Profit = revenue − costs = $p \cdot z - p \cdot x = p \cdot (z - x) = p \cdot y$. If $p \cdot y < 0$, the firm makes a loss equal to $-p \cdot y$.

11. (a) Input vector = $\begin{pmatrix} 0 \\ 1 \end{pmatrix}$ (b) Output vector = $\begin{pmatrix} 2 \\ 0 \end{pmatrix}$ (c) Cost = $(1, 3)\begin{pmatrix} 0 \\ 1 \end{pmatrix} = 3$
(d) Revenue = $(1, 3)\begin{pmatrix} 2 \\ 0 \end{pmatrix} = 2$ (e) Value of net output = $(1, 3)\begin{pmatrix} 2 \\ -1 \end{pmatrix} = 2 - 3 = -1$ (f) Loss = cost − revenue = $3 - 2 = 1$.

12.5

1. (a) $x_1 = 3 + 7t$, $x_2 = -2 + 4t$, and $x_3 = 2 - t$ (b) $x_1 = 1$, $x_2 = 3 - t$, and $x_3 = 2 + t$

3. $x_1 - 3x_2 - 2x_3 = -3$. (One method: $(5, 2, 1) - (3, 4, -3) = (2, -2, 4)$ and $(2, -1, 4) - (3, 4, -3) = (-1, -5, 7)$ are two vectors in the plane. The normal (p_1, p_2, p_3) must be orthogonal to both these vectors, so $(2, -2, 4) \cdot (p_1, p_2, p_3) = 2p_1 - 2p_2 + 4p_3 = 0$ and $(-1, -5, 7) \cdot (p_1, p_2, p_3) = -p_1 - 5p_2 + 7p_3 = 0$. One solution to these two equations is $(p_1, p_2, p_3) = (1, -3, -2)$. Then using formula [12.23] with $(a_1, a_2, a_3) = (2, -1, 4)$ yields $(1, -3, -2) \cdot (x_1 - 2, x_2 + 1, x_3 - 4) = 0$, which reduces to $x_1 - 3x_2 - 2x_3 = -3$.)

12.6

1. $A = \begin{pmatrix} 1 & 0 & 0 \\ 0 & 1 & 0 \\ 0 & 0 & 1 \end{pmatrix}$

3. $u = 3$ and $v = -2$

5. $A + B = \begin{pmatrix} 1 & 0 & 4 \\ 2 & 4 & 16 \end{pmatrix}$, $A - B = \begin{pmatrix} -1 & 2 & -6 \\ 2 & 2 & -2 \end{pmatrix}$, and $5A - 3B = \begin{pmatrix} -3 & 8 & -20 \\ 10 & 12 & 8 \end{pmatrix}$

12.7

1. (a) $AB = \begin{pmatrix} -2 & -10 \\ -2 & 17 \end{pmatrix}$ and $BA = \begin{pmatrix} 12 & 6 \\ 15 & 3 \end{pmatrix}$

(b) $AB = \begin{pmatrix} 26 & 3 \\ 6 & -22 \end{pmatrix}$ and $BA = \begin{pmatrix} 14 & 6 & -12 \\ 35 & 12 & 4 \\ 3 & 3 & -22 \end{pmatrix}$

(c) $AB = \begin{pmatrix} 0 & 0 & 0 & 0 \\ 0 & 4 & -6 & -2 \\ 0 & -8 & 12 & 4 \\ 0 & -2 & 3 & 1 \end{pmatrix}$ and $BA = (17)$, a 1×1 matrix.

(d) AB is not defined. $BA = \begin{pmatrix} -1 & 4 \\ 3 & 4 \\ 4 & 8 \end{pmatrix}$

3. $B = \begin{pmatrix} w - y & y \\ y & w \end{pmatrix}$, for arbitrary y, w. (*Hint:* Let $B = \begin{pmatrix} x & y \\ z & w \end{pmatrix}$. Then $AB = BA$ iff: [1] $x + 2y = x + 2z$; [2] $2x + 3y = y + 2w$; [3] $z + 2w = 2x + 3z$; and [4] $2z + 3w = 2y + 3w$. Now [1] and [4] are true iff $z = y$. So [2] and [3] are true as well iff $x = w - y$.)

12.8

1. $A(B + C) = AB + AC = \begin{pmatrix} 3 & 2 & 6 & 2 \\ 7 & 4 & 14 & 6 \end{pmatrix}$

3. It is straightforward to show that $(AB)C$ and $A(BC)$ are both equal to the 2×2 matrix $D = (d_{ij})_{2 \times 2}$ with $d_{ij} = a_{i1}b_{11}c_{1j} + a_{i1}b_{12}c_{2j} + a_{i2}b_{21}c_{1j} + a_{i2}b_{22}c_{2j}$ for $i = 1, 2$ and $j = 1, 2$.

5. (a) $\begin{pmatrix} 5 & 3 & 1 \\ 2 & 0 & 9 \\ 1 & 3 & 3 \end{pmatrix}$ (b) $(1, 2, -3)$.

7. (a) Direct verification. (b) $AA = (AB)A = A(BA) = AB = A$, so A is idempotent. Then just interchange A and B to show that B is idempotent. (c) As the induction hypothesis, suppose that $A^k = A$, which is true for $k = 2$. Then $A^{k+1} = A^k A = AA = A$, which completes the proof by induction.

12.9

1. $A' = \begin{pmatrix} 3 & -1 \\ 5 & 2 \\ 8 & 6 \\ 3 & 4 \end{pmatrix}$ and $B' = (0, 1, -1, 2)$

3. $A = A'$ and $B = B'$

5. No! For example: $\begin{pmatrix} 1 & 1 \\ 1 & 2 \end{pmatrix} \begin{pmatrix} 1 & 1 \\ 1 & 1 \end{pmatrix} = \begin{pmatrix} 2 & 2 \\ 3 & 3 \end{pmatrix}$.

7. (a) Direct verification. (b) $\begin{pmatrix} p & q \\ -q & p \end{pmatrix} \begin{pmatrix} p & -q \\ q & p \end{pmatrix} = \begin{pmatrix} p^2 + q^2 & 0 \\ 0 & p^2 + q^2 \end{pmatrix} = \begin{pmatrix} 1 & 0 \\ 0 & 1 \end{pmatrix}$ iff $p^2 + q^2 = 1$. (c) Suppose P and Q are orthogonal, that is, $P'P = I_n$ and $Q'Q = I_n$. Then $(PQ)'(PQ) = (Q'P')(PQ) = Q'(P'P)Q = Q'I_nQ = Q'Q = I_n$, so PQ is orthogonal. (d) If P is orthogonal and c_i and c_j are two different columns of P, then $c_i'c_j$ is the element in row i and column j of $P'P = I$, so $c_i'c_j = 0$. If r_i and r_j are two different rows of P, then $r_i r_j'$ is the element in row i and column j of $PP' = I' = I$, so again $r_i r_j' = 0$.

9. Suppose $\begin{pmatrix} a & b \\ c & d \end{pmatrix} \begin{pmatrix} a & b \\ c & d \end{pmatrix} = \begin{pmatrix} 0 & 0 \\ 0 & 0 \end{pmatrix}$. Then: [1] $a^2 + bc = 0$; [2] $ab + bd = 0$; [3] $ac + cd = 0$; [4] $bc + d^2 = 0$. We claim that tr $(A) = a + d = 0$. Subtracting [4] from [1] yields $a^2 - d^2 = 0$, or $(a - d)(a + d) = 0$. Either $a + d = 0$ and we are through, or $a = d$. But if $a = d$, then [2] implies that $ab = 0$, so [1] implies that $a^3 = -abc = 0$. Hence, $a = 0$ and tr $(A) = a + d = 0$ even when $a = d$.

Chapter 13

13.1

1. (a) 18 (b) 0 (c) $(a+b)^2 - (a-b)^2 = 4ab$ (d) $3^t 2^{t-1} - 3^{t-1} 2^t = 6^{t-1}$

3. (a) $x_1 = 11/5$ and $x_2 = -7/5$ (b) $x = 4$ and $y = -1$ (c) Provided that $a^2 + b^2 \neq 0$, $x = \dfrac{a+2b}{a^2+b^2}$ and $y = \dfrac{2a-b}{a^2+b^2}$.

5. If $\mathbf{A} = \mathbf{B} = \begin{pmatrix} 1 & 0 \\ 0 & 1 \end{pmatrix}$, then $|\mathbf{A} + \mathbf{B}| = 4$, whereas $|\mathbf{A}| + |\mathbf{B}| = 2$. ($\mathbf{A}$ and $\mathbf{B}$ can be chosen almost at random.)

7. (a) $X_1 = M_2$ because nation 1's exports are nation 2's imports. Similarly, $X_2 = M_1$. (b) Substituting for X_1, X_2, M_1, M_2, C_1, and C_2 gives the two equations: [1] $Y_1(1 - c_1 + m_1) - m_2 Y_2 = A_1$; [2] $Y_2(1 - c_2 + m_2) - m_1 Y_1 = A_2$. Using Cramer's rule with $D = (1 - c_2 + m_2)(1 - c_1 + m_1) - m_1 m_2$ yields:

$$Y_1 = \frac{1}{D}[A_2 m_2 + A_1(1 - c_2 + m_2)], \qquad Y_2 = \frac{1}{D}[A_1 m_1 + A_2(1 - c_1 + m_1)]$$

(c) Y_2 depends linearly on A_1. Increasing A_1 by one unit changes Y_2 by the factor m_1/D. Because c_1 is the proportion of income consumed, we can assume that $0 < c_1 < 1$. Likewise, $0 < c_2 < 1$. Because m_1 and m_2 are nonnegative, we see that $D > 0$ and that Y_2 increases when A_1 increases. Here is an economic explanation: An increase in A_1 increases nation 1's income, Y_1. This in turn increases nation 1's imports, M_1. However, nation 1's imports are nation 2's exports, so this causes nation 2's income, Y_2, to increase, and so on.

9. $(d/dt)[a(t)b'(t) - a'(t)b(t)] = a(t)b''(t) - a''(t)b(t)$

13.2

1. (a) -2 (b) -2 (c) adf (d) $e(ad - bc)$

3. (a) $x_1 = 1$, $x_2 = 2$, and $x_3 = 3$ (b) $x_1 = x_2 = x_3 = 0$ (c) $x = 1$, $y = 2$, and $z = 3$

5. (a) Successive substitutions give $Y = C + A_0 = a + b(Y - T) + A_0 = a + bY - b(d + tY) + A_0$. Thus,

$$Y = \frac{A_0 + a - bd}{1 - b + bt}, \qquad C = \frac{a - bd + bA_0 - btA_0}{1 - b + bt},$$

$$T = \frac{d - bd + tA_0 + ta}{1 - b + bt}$$

(b) The matrix equation is

$$\begin{pmatrix} 1 & -1 & 0 \\ -b & 1 & b \\ -t & 0 & 1 \end{pmatrix} \begin{pmatrix} Y \\ C \\ T \end{pmatrix} = \begin{pmatrix} A_0 \\ a \\ d \end{pmatrix}$$

and by Cramer's rule the solution is as in (a).

13.3

1. (a) 24   (b) 1   (c) $d - a$ (d) 0

3. $-a_{15}a_{24}a_{32}a_{43}a_{51}$. (There are nine rising lines.)

13.4

1. (a) $\mathbf{AB} = \begin{pmatrix} 13 & 16 \\ 29 & 36 \end{pmatrix}$, $\mathbf{BA} = \begin{pmatrix} 15 & 22 \\ 23 & 34 \end{pmatrix}$, $\mathbf{A'B'} = \begin{pmatrix} 15 & 23 \\ 22 & 34 \end{pmatrix}$, $\mathbf{B'A'} = \begin{pmatrix} 13 & 29 \\ 16 & 36 \end{pmatrix}$

(b) $|\mathbf{A}| = |\mathbf{A'}| = -2$ and $|\mathbf{B}| = |\mathbf{B'}| = -2$, so $|\mathbf{AB}| = 4 = |\mathbf{A}| \cdot |\mathbf{B}|$, $|\mathbf{A'B'}| = |\mathbf{A'}| \cdot |\mathbf{B'}| = 4$

3. (a) 0 (one column has only zeros).   (b) 0 (rows 1 and 4 are proportional).
(c) Subtract $3a$ times the second column from the first, so that the new fourth row is $(0, 1, 0, 0)$. Interchange the first and fourth rows and then the first and second column. Explain why you can now drop the first row and the first column. The answer is $6a^4 + 29a^2 - 6a - 1$.

5. $\mathbf{X'X} = \begin{pmatrix} 4 & 3 & 2 \\ 3 & 5 & 1 \\ 2 & 1 & 2 \end{pmatrix}$ and $|\mathbf{X'X}| = 10$

7. Because $\mathbf{P'P} = \mathbf{I}_n$, it follows from [13.15] and [13.14] that $|\mathbf{P'}||\mathbf{P}| = |\mathbf{I}_n| = 1$. Because $|\mathbf{P'}| = |\mathbf{P}|$, we get $|\mathbf{P}|^2 = 1$, so $|\mathbf{P}| = \pm 1$.

9. Let $\mathbf{A} = \begin{pmatrix} 0 & c & b \\ c & 0 & a \\ b & a & 0 \end{pmatrix}$. Then compute $\mathbf{A}^2$ and recall [13.15].

11. (a) For the first equality, you can use the definition of a determinant. The second equality is quite easy if you perform the operations indicated. For the last equality, you can again use the definition of a determinant. (From the first column, you have to pick $-1, \ldots$)   (b) If you can do it, you deserve a break.

13.5

1. (a) 2. (Subtract row 1 from both row 2 and row 3 to get a determinant whose first column has elements $1, 0, 0$. Then expand by the first column.)   (b) 30
(c) 0. (Columns 2 and 4 are proportional.)

3. For $n = 4$, the Vandermonde determinant is $\begin{vmatrix} 1 & x_1 & x_1^2 & x_1^3 \\ 1 & x_2 & x_2^2 & x_2^3 \\ 1 & x_3 & x_3^2 & x_3^3 \\ 1 & x_4 & x_4^2 & x_4^3 \end{vmatrix}$

Now multiply the third, the second, and the first columns successively by $-x_1$ and add the results to the next column. This yields the determinant

$$\begin{vmatrix} 1 & 0 & 0 & 0 \\ 1 & x_2 - x_1 & x_2^2 - x_2 x_1 & x_2^3 - x_2^2 x_1 \\ 1 & x_3 - x_1 & x_3^2 - x_3 x_1 & x_3^3 - x_3^2 x_1 \\ 1 & x_4 - x_1 & x_4^2 - x_4 x_1 & x_4^3 - x_4^2 x_1 \end{vmatrix} = (x_2 - x_1)(x_3 - x_1)(x_4 - x_1) \begin{vmatrix} 1 & x_2 & x_2^2 \\ 1 & x_3 & x_3^2 \\ 1 & x_4 & x_4^2 \end{vmatrix}$$

The last equality is obtained by noting that $x_2 - x_1$, $x_3 - x_1$, and $x_4 - x_1$ are common factors in the second, third, and fourth rows, respectively, of the preceding determinant. The last determinant is again a Vandermonde determinant, and the conclusion follows.

13.6

1. $\begin{pmatrix} 3 & 0 \\ 2 & -1 \end{pmatrix} \cdot \begin{pmatrix} 1/3 & 0 \\ 2/3 & -1 \end{pmatrix} = \begin{pmatrix} 1 & 0 \\ 0 & 1 \end{pmatrix}$

3. $\mathbf{AB} = \begin{pmatrix} 1 & 0 & 0 \\ a+b & 2a + 1/4 + 3b & 4a + 3/2 + 2b \\ 0 & 0 & 1 \end{pmatrix} = \mathbf{I}$ iff $a + b = 4a + 3/2 + 2b = 0$ and $2a + 1/4 + 3b = 1$. This is true iff $a = -3/4$ and $b = 3/4$.

5. $\mathbf{A}^{-1} = \mathbf{A}^2 = \frac{1}{2}\begin{pmatrix} -1 & \sqrt{3} \\ -\sqrt{3} & -1 \end{pmatrix}$

7. (a) $\mathbf{AA}' = \begin{pmatrix} 21 & 11 \\ 11 & 10 \end{pmatrix}$, $|\mathbf{AA}'| = 89$, and $(\mathbf{AA}')^{-1} = \frac{1}{89}\begin{pmatrix} 10 & -11 \\ -11 & 21 \end{pmatrix}$.
   (b) No, $\mathbf{AA}'$ is always symmetric (see Note 2 and Example 12.28 in Section 12.9).

9. $\mathbf{B}^2 + \mathbf{B} = \mathbf{I}$ and $\mathbf{B}^3 - 2\mathbf{B} + \mathbf{I} = 0$. From $\mathbf{B}^2 + \mathbf{B} = \mathbf{I}$, we get $\mathbf{B}(\mathbf{B} + \mathbf{I}) = \mathbf{I}$, so $\mathbf{B}^{-1} = \mathbf{B} + \mathbf{I} = \begin{pmatrix} 1/2 & 5 \\ 1/4 & 1/2 \end{pmatrix}$.

11. Let $\mathbf{B} = \mathbf{X}(\mathbf{X}'\mathbf{X})^{-1}\mathbf{X}'$. Then $\mathbf{A}^2 = (\mathbf{I}_m - \mathbf{B})(\mathbf{I}_m - \mathbf{B}) = \mathbf{I}_m - \mathbf{B} - \mathbf{B} + \mathbf{B}^2$. Here $\mathbf{B}^2 = (\mathbf{X}(\mathbf{X}'\mathbf{X})^{-1}\mathbf{X}')(\mathbf{X}(\mathbf{X}'\mathbf{X})^{-1}\mathbf{X}') = \mathbf{X}(\mathbf{X}'\mathbf{X})^{-1}(\mathbf{X}'\mathbf{X})(\mathbf{X}'\mathbf{X})^{-1}\mathbf{X}' = \mathbf{X}(\mathbf{X}'\mathbf{X})^{-1}\mathbf{X}' = \mathbf{B}$. Thus. $\mathbf{A}^2 = \mathbf{I}_m - \mathbf{B} - \mathbf{B} + \mathbf{B} = \mathbf{I}_m - \mathbf{B} = \mathbf{A}$. (b) Direct verification.

13. $\mathbf{D}^3 = \mathbf{D}^2\mathbf{D} = (2\mathbf{D} + 3\mathbf{I}_n)\mathbf{D} = 2\mathbf{D}^2 + 3\mathbf{D} = 2(2\mathbf{D} + 3\mathbf{I}_n) + 3\mathbf{D} = 7\mathbf{D} + 6\mathbf{I}_n$. $\mathbf{D}^6 = \mathbf{D}^3\mathbf{D}^3 = (7\mathbf{D} + 6\mathbf{I}_n)(7\mathbf{D} + 6\mathbf{I}_n) = 49\mathbf{D}^2 + 84\mathbf{D} + 36\mathbf{I}_n = 49(2\mathbf{D} + 3\mathbf{I}_n) + 84\mathbf{D} + 36\mathbf{I}_n = 182\mathbf{D} + 183\mathbf{I}_n$. To find $\mathbf{D}^{-1}$, note that from $\mathbf{D}^2 = 2\mathbf{D} + 3\mathbf{I}_n$, we obtain $\mathbf{D}(\mathbf{D} - 2\mathbf{I}_n) = 3\mathbf{I}_n$, and so $\mathbf{D}\frac{1}{3}(\mathbf{D} - 2\mathbf{I}_n) = \mathbf{I}_n$. Thus, $\mathbf{D}^{-1} = \frac{1}{3}\mathbf{D} - \frac{2}{3}\mathbf{I}_n$.

13.7

1. (a) $\begin{pmatrix} -5/2 & 3/2 \\ 2 & -1 \end{pmatrix}$ (b) $\dfrac{1}{9}\begin{pmatrix} 1 & 4 & 2 \\ 2 & -1 & 4 \\ 4 & -2 & -1 \end{pmatrix}$ (c) The matrix has no inverse.

3. $(\mathbf{I}-\mathbf{A})^{-1} = \dfrac{5}{62}\begin{pmatrix} 18 & 16 & 10 \\ 2 & 19 & 8 \\ 4 & 7 & 16 \end{pmatrix} \approx \begin{pmatrix} 1.45 & 1.29 & 0.81 \\ 0.16 & 1.53 & 0.65 \\ 0.32 & 0.56 & 1.29 \end{pmatrix}$

5. (a) $\begin{pmatrix} -2 & 1 \\ 3/2 & -1/2 \end{pmatrix}$ (b) $\begin{pmatrix} 1 & -3 & 2 \\ -3 & 3 & -1 \\ 2 & -1 & 0 \end{pmatrix}$ (c) There is no inverse.

13.8

1. (a) $x = 1$, $y = -2$, and $z = 2$ (b) $x = -3$, $y = 6$, $z = 5$, and $u = -5$

3. Show that the determinant of the coefficient matrix is equal to the expression $-(a^3 + b^3 + c^3 - 3abc)$, and then use Theorem 13.7.

Chapter 14

14.1

1. $\begin{pmatrix} 8 \\ 9 \end{pmatrix} = x\begin{pmatrix} 2 \\ 5 \end{pmatrix} + y\begin{pmatrix} -1 \\ 3 \end{pmatrix}$ requires $8 = 2x - y$ and $9 = 5x + 3y$. Solving these equations gives $x = 3$ and $y = -2$.

3. The determinant of the matrix with the three vectors as columns is equal to 3, so the vectors are linearly independent.

5. Suppose $\alpha(\mathbf{a}+\mathbf{b}) + \beta(\mathbf{b}+\mathbf{c}) + \gamma(\mathbf{a}+\mathbf{c}) = \mathbf{0}$. Then $(\alpha+\gamma)\mathbf{a} + (\alpha+\beta)\mathbf{b} + (\beta+\gamma)\mathbf{c} = \mathbf{0}$. Because $\mathbf{a}$, $\mathbf{b}$, and $\mathbf{c}$ are linearly independent, $\alpha+\gamma = 0$, $\alpha+\beta = 0$, and $\beta+\gamma = 0$. It follows that $\alpha = \beta = \gamma = 0$, which means that $\mathbf{a}+\mathbf{b}$, $\mathbf{b}+\mathbf{c}$, and $\mathbf{a}+\mathbf{c}$ are linearly independent. The vectors $\mathbf{a}-\mathbf{b}$, $\mathbf{b}+\mathbf{c}$, and $\mathbf{a}+\mathbf{c}$ are linearly *dependent* because $(\mathbf{a}-\mathbf{b}) + (\mathbf{b}+\mathbf{c}) - (\mathbf{a}+\mathbf{c}) = \mathbf{0}$.

7. Both these two statements follow immediately from the definitions.

14.2

1. (a) 1. (The determinant of the matrix is 0, so the rank is less than 2. Because not all entries are 0, the rank is 1.)   (b) 2   (c) 2   (d) 3   (e) 2   (f) 3

3. $\mathbf{A} = \begin{pmatrix} 3 & 1 \\ 6 & 2 \end{pmatrix}$ and $\mathbf{B} = \begin{pmatrix} 1 & 2 \\ -3 & -6 \end{pmatrix}$. Here $r(\mathbf{AB}) = 0$ and $r(\mathbf{BA}) = 1$.

14.3

1. (a) No solutions.   (b) $x_1 = 1 + (2/3)b$, $x_2 = 1 + a - (5/3)b$, $x_3 = a$, and $x_4 = b$, with a, b arbitrary. Two degrees of freedom.   (c) $x_1 = (-1/3)a$,

$x_2 = (5/3)a$, $x_3 = a$, and $x_4 = 1$, with a arbitrary. One degree of freedom. (d) No solutions.   (e) $x_1 = x_2 = x_3 = 0$ is the only solution. There are 0 degrees of freedom.   (f) $x_1 = a$, $x_2 = -a$, $x_3 = -a$, and $x_4 = a$, with a arbitrary. One degree of freedom.

3. For $a \neq 0$ and $a \neq 7$, the system has a unique solution. For $a = 0$ and $b = 9/2$, or for $a = 7$ and $b = 10/3$, the system has an infinite number of solutions. For other values of the parameters, there are no solutions.

5. (a) Unique solution for $p \neq 3$. For $p = 3$ and $q = 0$, there are infinitely many solutions (1 degree of freedom). For $p = 3$ and $q \neq 0$, there are no solutions.   (b) For $p \neq 3$, only $\mathbf{z} = \mathbf{0}$ is orthogonal to the three vectors. For $p = 3$, the vector $\mathbf{z} = (-a, 0, a)$ is orthogonal to the three vectors, for all values of a.   (c) Let the n vectors be $\mathbf{a}_i = (a_{i1}, \ldots, a_{in})$, $i = 1, \ldots, n$. If $\mathbf{b} = (b_1, \ldots, b_n)$ is orthogonal to each of these n vectors, then the scalar product of $\mathbf{b}$ with each $\mathbf{a}_i$ is 0,

$$a_{i1}b_1 + \cdots + a_{in}b_n = 0 \qquad (i = 1, \ldots, n)$$

Because $\mathbf{a}_1, \ldots, \mathbf{a}_n$ are linearly independent, this homogeneous system of equations only has the solution $b_1 = \cdots = b_n = 0$, so $\mathbf{b} = \mathbf{0}$.

14.4

1. With r, s, and t as arbitrary real numbers, we have:

(a) Eigenvalues: $-1, -5$. Eigenvectors: $r \begin{pmatrix} 7 \\ 3 \end{pmatrix}$, $s \begin{pmatrix} 1 \\ 1 \end{pmatrix}$.

(b) No real eigenvalues.

(c) Eigenvalues: $5, -5$. Eigenvectors: $r \begin{pmatrix} 1 \\ 1 \end{pmatrix}$, $s \begin{pmatrix} -2 \\ 3 \end{pmatrix}$.

(d) Eigenvalues: $2, 3, 4$. Eigenvectors: $r \begin{pmatrix} 1 \\ 0 \\ 0 \end{pmatrix}$, $s \begin{pmatrix} 0 \\ 1 \\ 0 \end{pmatrix}$, $t \begin{pmatrix} 0 \\ 0 \\ 1 \end{pmatrix}$.

(e) Eigenvalues: $-1, 0, 2$. Eigenvectors: $r \begin{pmatrix} 1 \\ -1 \\ 2 \end{pmatrix}$, $s \begin{pmatrix} 1 \\ -1 \\ 1 \end{pmatrix}$, $t \begin{pmatrix} 2 \\ 1 \\ 1 \end{pmatrix}$.

(f) Eigenvalues: $0, 1, 3$. Eigenvectors: $r \begin{pmatrix} 1 \\ 1 \\ 1 \end{pmatrix}$, $s \begin{pmatrix} -1 \\ 0 \\ 1 \end{pmatrix}$, $t \begin{pmatrix} 1 \\ -2 \\ 1 \end{pmatrix}$.

3. From [14.8], we see that $\lambda = 0$ is an eigenvalue iff $|\mathbf{A}| = 0$. If $\lambda \neq 0$ is an eigenvalue for $\mathbf{A}$, then $|\mathbf{A} - \lambda\mathbf{I}| = 0$. But we have $|\mathbf{A}^{-1} - (1/\lambda)\mathbf{I}| = |\mathbf{A}^{-1}(\mathbf{I} - (1/\lambda)\mathbf{A})| = |\mathbf{A}^{-1}||1/\lambda||\lambda\mathbf{I} - \mathbf{A}| = 0$, which shows that $1/\lambda$ is an eigenvalue for $\mathbf{A}^{-1}$.

5. The eigenvalues are $\lambda_1 = 1$, $\lambda_2 = 0.75$, and $\lambda_3 = 0.5$. Because $\mathbf{T}(\mathbf{v}) = \mathbf{v}$, it follows that $\mathbf{T}^n(\mathbf{v}) = \mathbf{v}$, for all n.

7. $|\mathbf{A} - \mathbf{I}| = \begin{vmatrix} a_{11} - 1 & a_{12} & \cdots & a_{1n} \\ a_{21} & a_{22} - 1 & \cdots & a_{2n} \\ \vdots & \vdots & \ddots & \vdots \\ a_{n1} & a_{n2} & \cdots & a_{nn} - 1 \end{vmatrix}$. Add all the last $n - 1$ rows

to the first row. Because all the column sums are 1, all entries in the first row are 0. Hence, $|\mathbf{A} - \mathbf{I}| = 0$, so 1 is an eigenvalue for $\mathbf{A}$.

14.5

1. $\mathbf{D}^2 = \text{diag}(1/4, 1/9, 1/16)$, $\mathbf{D}^n = \text{diag}((1/2)^n, (1/3)^n, (1/4)^n)$, $\mathbf{D}^n \to 0$ as $n \to \infty$.

3. (a) The matrix has eigenvalues 2 and -1, with corresponding eigenvectors $(1, 0)$ and $(1, -3)$, respectively. So take $\mathbf{P} = \begin{pmatrix} 1 & 1 \\ 0 & -3 \end{pmatrix}$, and then $\mathbf{P}^{-1}\mathbf{A}\mathbf{P} = \text{diag}(2, -1)$.

(b) $\mathbf{P} = \begin{pmatrix} 14 & 1 & 7 \\ 3 & 0 & 6 \\ -3 & 0 & 3 \end{pmatrix}$ and $\mathbf{P}^{-1}\mathbf{A}\mathbf{P} = \text{diag}(3, 6, -6)$

(c) $\mathbf{P} = \begin{pmatrix} 1 & -3 & 3 \\ 0 & 5 & 2 \\ 3 & 1 & -1 \end{pmatrix}$ and $\mathbf{P}^{-1}\mathbf{A}\mathbf{P} = \text{diag}(1, -4, 3)$.

14.6

1. (a) The matrix has eigenvalues 1 and 3, with corresponding eigenvectors $(1, -1)$ and $(1, 1)$, respectively. After normalizing these eigenvectors, the appropriate orthogonal matrix is $\mathbf{U} = \begin{pmatrix} 1/\sqrt{2} & 1/\sqrt{2} \\ -1/\sqrt{2} & 1/\sqrt{2} \end{pmatrix}$, and then $\mathbf{U}^{-1}\mathbf{A}\mathbf{U} = \text{diag}(1, 3)$.

(b) Matrix $\mathbf{A}$ has only two eigenvalues, which are 0 and 2, but three linearly independent eigenvectors, which are $(1, -1, 0)$, $(1, 1, 0)$, and $(0, 0, 1)$. This suggests taking $\mathbf{U} = \begin{pmatrix} 1/\sqrt{2} & 1/\sqrt{2} & 0 \\ -1/\sqrt{2} & 1/\sqrt{2} & 0 \\ 0 & 0 & 1 \end{pmatrix}$, and then $\mathbf{U}^{-1}\mathbf{A}\mathbf{U} = \text{diag}(0, 2, 2)$.

(c) $\mathbf{U} = \begin{pmatrix} 0 & \sqrt{2}/2 & -\sqrt{2}/2 \\ -4/5 & 3\sqrt{2}/10 & 3\sqrt{2}/10 \\ 3/5 & 2\sqrt{2}/5 & 2\sqrt{2}/5 \end{pmatrix}$, and then $\mathbf{U}^{-1}\mathbf{A}\mathbf{U} = \text{diag}(1, 6, -4)$.

3. Let $\mathbf{p}_1, \mathbf{p}_2, \ldots, \mathbf{p}_n$ be the column vectors of $\mathbf{P}$. Then the diagonal elements of the matrix product $\mathbf{P}'\mathbf{P}$ are all 1, because the length of each column vector is 1. Moreover, the off-diagonal elements are 0 because the column vectors of $\mathbf{P}$ are mutually orthogonal. Hence, $\mathbf{P}'\mathbf{P}$ is the identity matrix, and thus $\mathbf{P}$ is orthogonal.

Chapter 15

15.1

1. $f(0, 1) = 0$, $f(-1, 2) = -4$, and $f(a, a) = a^3$

3. (a) $f(-1, 2) = 1$, $f(a, a) = 4a^2$, and $f(a+h, b) - f(a, b) = 2(a+b)h + h^2$
(b) $f(tx, ty) = (tx)^2 + 2(tx)(ty) + (ty)^2 = t^2(x^2 + 2xy + y^2) = t^2 f(x, y)$

5. (a) $F(K+1, L, M) - F(K, L, M)$ is the increase in output from increasing capital input by one unit. (b) $F(K, L, M) = AK^a L^b M^c$, where A, a, b, and c are positive constants. (c) $F(tK, tL, tM) = t^{a+b+c} F(K, L, M)$

7. (a) $y \neq x - 2$ (b) $x^2 + y^2 \leq 2$ (c) $1 \leq x^2 + y^2 \leq 4$. The sets in cases (b) and (c) are shown in Figs. 40 and 41.

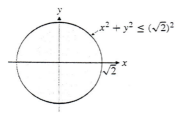

FIGURE 40　　　　　　　　**FIGURE 41**

9. You drive $(5/60) \cdot 0 + (10/60) \cdot 30 + (20/60) \cdot 60 + (15/60) \cdot 80 = 45$ kilometers in $5 + 10 + 20 + 15 = 50$ minutes, so the average speed is $45 \times 60/50 = 54$ kph.

11. (a) Immediate. (b) In this case, $(*)$ becomes: $\ln\left[(1/n)\,(x_1 + \cdots + x_n)\right]$
$\geq (1/n) \ln x_1 + \cdots + (1/n) \ln x_n = \ln x_1^{1/n} + \cdots + \ln x_n^{1/n} = \ln\left(x_1^{1/n} \ldots x_n^{1/n}\right) = \ln \sqrt[n]{x_1 \ldots x_n}$, and the conclusion follows.
(c) The suggested replacements yield the inequality $\sqrt[n]{(1/x_1) \cdots (1/x_n)} \leq (1/n)(1/x_1 + \cdots + 1/x_n)$. This inequality says that $1/\bar{x}_G \leq 1/\bar{x}_H$, so $\bar{x}_H \leq \bar{x}_G$.

15.2

1. See Figs. 42 and 43. (Note that only a portion of the graph is indicated in each case.)

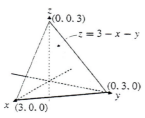

FIGURE 42

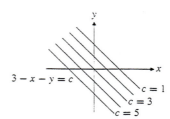

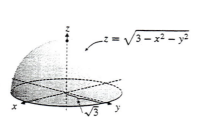

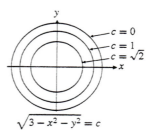

FIGURE 43

3. Note that $f(x, y) = e^{x^2-y^2} + (x^2 - y^2)^2$. Hence, for all pairs (x, y) where $x^2 - y^2 = c$, we have $f(x, y) = e^c + c^2$, so $x^2 - y^2 = c$ lies on a level curve at the height $e^c + c^2$.

5. At the point of intersection, f would have two different values, which is impossible when f is a function.

15.3

1. (a) $\partial z/\partial x = 2x$, $\partial z/\partial y = 6y$ (b) $\partial z/\partial x = y$, $\partial z/\partial y = x$
   (c) $\partial z/\partial x = 20x^3 y^2 - 2y^5$, $\partial z/\partial y = 10x^4 y - 10xy^4$
   (d) $\partial z/\partial x = \partial z/\partial y = e^{x+y}$
   (e) $\partial z/\partial x = ye^{xy}$, $\partial z/\partial y = xe^{xy}$
   (f) $\partial z/\partial x = e^x/y$, $\partial z/\partial y = -e^x/y^2$
   (g) $\partial z/\partial x = \partial z/\partial y = 1/(x + y)$ (h) $\partial z/\partial x = 1/x$, $\partial z/\partial y = 1/y$

3. (a) $z'_x = 3$, $z'_y = 4$, and $z''_{xx} = z''_{xy} = z''_{yx} = z''_{yy} = 0$
   (b) $z'_x = 3x^2 y^2$, $z'_y = 2x^3 y$, $z''_{xx} = 6xy^2$, $z''_{yy} = 2x^3$, and $z''_{xy} = z''_{yx} = 6x^2 y$
   (c) $z'_x = 5x^4 - 6xy$, $z'_y = -3x^2 + 6y^5$, $z''_{xx} = 20x^3 - 6y$, $z''_{yy} = 30y^4$, and $z''_{xy} = z''_{yx} = -6x$
   (d) $z'_x = 1/y$, $z'_y = -x/y^2$, $z''_{xx} = 0$, $z''_{yy} = 2x/y^3$, and $z''_{xy} = z''_{yx} = -1/y^2$
   (e) $z'_x = 2y(x + y)^{-2}$, $z'_y = -2x(x + y)^{-2}$, $z''_{xx} = -4y(x + y)^{-3}$, $z''_{yy} = 4x(x + y)^{-3}$, and $z''_{xy} = z''_{yx} = 2(x - y)(x + y)^{-3}$
   (f) $z'_x = x(x^2 + y^2)^{-1/2}$, $z'_y = y(x^2 + y^2)^{-1/2}$, $z''_{xx} = y^2(x^2 + y^2)^{-3/2}$, $z''_{yy} = x^2(x^2 + y^2)^{-3/2}$, and $z''_{xy} = z''_{yx} = -xy(x^2 + y^2)^{-3/2}$

5. $xz'_x + yz'_y = x[2(ax + by)a] + y[2(ax + by)b] = 2a^2 x^2 + 2abxy + 2abxy + 2b^2 y^2 = 2(ax + by)^2$

7. $f'_1 = \ln y - y^3 2^{xy} \ln 2$ and $f'_2 = (x/y) - 2y2^{xy} - xy^2 2^{xy} \ln 2$, so $f'_1(1, 1) = -2 \ln 2$, $f'_2(1, 1) = -3 - 2 \ln 2$, $f''_{11}(1, 1) = -2(\ln 2)^2$, $f''_{22}(1, 1) = -5 - 8 \ln 2 - 2(\ln 2)^2$, and $f''_{12}(1, 1) = f''_{21}(1, 1) = 1 - 6 \ln 2 - 2(\ln 2)^2$

9. (a) $\partial^{p+q} z/\partial y^q \partial x^p = (-1)^{q-1}(q - 1)! e^x (1 + y)^{-q}$, which, when evaluated at $(x, y) = (0, 0)$, is equal to $(-1)^{q-1}(q - 1)!$ (Begin by differentiating w.r.t. x. Clearly, $\partial^p z/\partial x^p = e^x \ln(1 + y)$. Next, differentiating once w.r.t. y yields

$\partial^{p+1}z/\partial y\partial x^p = e^x(1+y)^{-1}$, then $\partial^{p+2}z/\partial y^2\partial x^p = e^x(-1)(1+y)^{-2}$, and so on.)

(b) $(p+1)q-1$. ($\partial^p z/\partial x^p = e^{x+y}[xy+(p+1)y-1]$ by induction on p. Then $\partial^{p+q}z/\partial y^q\partial x^p = e^{x+y}[xy+(p+1)y+qx+(p+1)q-1]$ by induction on q.)

15.4

1. (a) $f_x' > 0$ and $f_y' < 0$ at P, whereas $f_x' < 0$ and $f_y' > 0$ at Q.
   (b) (i) No solutions. (ii) $x \approx 2$ and $x \approx 6$ (c) 3

3. (a) $z = 2x + 4y - 5$ (b) $z = -10x + 3y + 3$

15.5

1. (a) $f_1' = 2x$, $f_2' = 3y^2$, and $f_3' = 4z^3$ (b) $f_1' = 10x$, $f_2' = -9y^2$, and $f_3' = 12z^3$
   (c) $f_1' = yz$, $f_2' = xz$, and $f_3' = xy$ (d) $f_1' = 4x^3/yz$, $f_2' = -x^4/y^2z$, and $f_3' = -x^4/yz^2$
   (e) $f_1' = 12x(x^2 + y^3 + z^4)^5$, $f_2' = 18y^2(x^2 + y^3 + z^4)^5$, and $f_3' = 24z^3(x^2 + y^3 + z^4)^5$
   (f) $f_1' = yze^{xyz}$, $f_2' = xze^{xyz}$, and $f_3' = xye^{xyz}$

3. $\partial T/\partial x = ky/d^n$ and $\partial T/\partial y = kx/d^n$ are both positive, so that the number of travelers increases if the size of either city increases, which is reasonable. $\partial T/\partial d = -nkxy/d^{n+1}$ is negative, so that the number of travelers decreases if the distance between the cities increases, which is also reasonable.

5. (a) $E_p' = 2ape^{bq}$ and $E_q' = abp^2e^{bq}$ (b) $\partial R/\partial p_1 = \alpha\beta p_1^{\beta-1} + \gamma p_2 e^{p_1 p_2}$ and $\partial R/\partial p_2 = \gamma p_1 e^{p_1 p_2}$ (c) $\partial x/\partial v_i = a_i$, $i = 1, 2, \ldots, n$. (For example, when $n = 3$ and $i = 2$, then $(\partial/\partial v_2)(a_1 v_1 + a_2 v_2 + a_3 v_3) = a_2$.)

7. $f_u' = v^w \cdot u^{v^w-1}$, $f_v' = u^{v^w} \cdot w \cdot v^{w-1} \cdot \ln u$, and $f_w' = u^{v^w} \cdot v^w \cdot \ln u \cdot \ln v$.

15.6

1. (a) We get $\partial M/\partial Y = 0.14$ and $\partial M/\partial r = -0.84 \cdot 76.03(r - 2)^{-1.84} = -63.8652(r - 2)^{-1.84}$, so $\partial M/\partial Y$ is positive and $\partial M/\partial r$ is negative, which accords with standard economic intuition.

3. $F_K' = aF/K$, $F_L' = bF/L$, and $F_M' = cF/M$, so $KF_K' + LF_L' + MF_M' = (a + b + c)F$.

5. $\partial U/\partial x_i = e^{-x_i}$, for $i = 1, \ldots, n$

15.7

1. Profit $= (100 - Q_1)Q_1 + (80 - Q_2)Q_2 - 6(Q_1 + Q_2) = 94Q_1 - Q_1^2 + 74Q_2 - Q_2^2$. This is maximized when $Q_1 = 47$ and $Q_2 = 37$, so $P_1 = 53$ and $P_2 = 43$. Then profit is 3578. If price discrimination is illegal, then $P_1 = P_2 = P$, so $Q_1 = 100 - P$, $Q_2 = 80 - P$, and total demand is

$Q = 180 - 2P$. Thus, inverse demand is $P = 90 - \frac{1}{2}Q$, so profit $=$ $(90 - \frac{1}{2}Q)Q - 6Q = 84Q - \frac{1}{2}Q^2$, which is maximized when $Q = 84$, and so $P = 48$. Then profit is 3528, so lost profit is 50.

3. $w = w_1 = w_2 = \alpha_1 + \beta_1 L_1 = \alpha_2 + \beta_2 L_2$, so that $L_1 = (w - \alpha_1)/\beta_1$ and $L_2 = (w - \alpha_2)/\beta_2$. Thus, total labor supply equals $L = L_1 + L_2 = [(\beta_1 + \beta_2)w - (\alpha_1\beta_2 + \alpha_2\beta_1),]/\beta_1\beta_2$. The inverse labor supply function is $w = (\alpha_1\beta_2 + \alpha_2\beta_1 + \beta_1\beta_2 L)/(\beta_1 + \beta_2)$. The firm's profit is

$$\pi(L) = (P - w)L = \left(P - \frac{\alpha_1\beta_2 + \alpha_2\beta_1}{\beta_1 + \beta_2}\right) L - \frac{\beta_1\beta_2}{\beta_1 + \beta_2}L^2$$

This is maximized at

$$L^* = \frac{\beta_1 + \beta_2}{2\beta_1\beta_2}\left(P - \frac{\alpha_1\beta_2 + \alpha_2\beta_1}{\beta_1 + \beta_2}\right)$$

with

$$\pi(L^*) = \frac{[\beta_1(P - \alpha_2) + \beta_2(P - \alpha_1)]^2}{4\beta_1\beta_2(\beta_1 + \beta_2)}$$

After some manipulation, the loss of profit compared with π^* given in Example 15.26 of Sec. 15.7 can be calculated as $(\alpha_1 - \alpha_2)^2/4(\beta_1 + \beta_2)$. (Note that the loss is zero when $\alpha_1 = \alpha_2$, which is as it should be because then the monopsonist does not want to discriminate anyway.)

15.8

1. (a) The associated symmetric matrix is $\begin{pmatrix} 4 & 4 \\ 4 & 5 \end{pmatrix}$, whose determinant is positive. The quadratic form satisfies [15.17], so is positive definite.

(b) $\begin{pmatrix} -1 & \frac{1}{2} \\ \frac{1}{2} & -3 \end{pmatrix}$ satisfies [15.19], so the quadratic form is negative definite.

(c) $\begin{pmatrix} 1 & -3 \\ -3 & 9 \end{pmatrix}$ satisfies [15.18], but not [15.17], so the quadratic form is positive semidefinite. (d) $\begin{pmatrix} 4 & 0 \\ 0 & -1 \end{pmatrix}$ satisfies [15.21], so the quadratic form is indefinite. (e) Indefinite. (f) Negative semidefinite.

3. (a) $\begin{vmatrix} 0 & 1 & 1 \\ 1 & 1 & -1 \\ 1 & -1 & 1 \end{vmatrix} = -4 < 0$, so positive definite subject to the constraint.

(b) $\begin{vmatrix} 0 & 3 & 4 \\ 3 & 2 & -2 \\ 4 & -2 & 1 \end{vmatrix} = -89 < 0$, so positive definite subject to the constraint.

(c) $\begin{vmatrix} 0 & 5 & -2 \\ 5 & -1 & \frac{1}{2} \\ -2 & \frac{1}{2} & -1 \end{vmatrix} = 19 > 0$, so *negative* definite subject to the constraint.

15.9

1. $a_{11}x_1^2 + a_{12}x_1x_2 + a_{13}x_1x_3 + a_{21}x_2x_1 + a_{22}x_2^2 + a_{23}x_2x_3 + a_{31}x_3x_1 + a_{32}x_3x_2 + a_{33}x_3^2$

3. (a) Positive definite.   (b) Positive semidefinite.   (c) Negative definite. (The associated symmetric matrix is

$$\begin{pmatrix} -3 & 1 & 0 \\ 1 & -1 & 2 \\ 0 & 2 & -8 \end{pmatrix}$$

whose leading principle minors are $D_1 = -3$, $D_2 = 2$, and $D_3 = -4$. Thus, the quadratic form is negative definite.)

Chapter 16

16.1

1. (a) $dz/dt = F_1'(x, y)dx/dt + F_2'(x, y)dy/dt = 1 \cdot 2t + 2y \cdot 3t^2 = 2t + 6t^5$

(b) $\dfrac{dz}{dt} = \left(\ln y + \dfrac{y}{x} \right) \cdot 1 + \left(\dfrac{x}{y} + \ln x \right) \cdot \dfrac{1}{t} = \ln(\ln t) + \dfrac{\ln t}{t+1} + \dfrac{t+1}{t \ln t} + \dfrac{\ln(t+1)}{t}$

3. $dY/dt = (10L - \tfrac{1}{2}K^{-1/2}) \, dK/dt + (10K - \tfrac{1}{2}L^{-1/2}) \, dL/dt = 35 - 7\sqrt{5}/100$ when $t = 0$.

5. $u = A \ln[1 + x^\alpha (ax^4 + b)^{-\alpha/3}]$. It is sufficient to maximize with respect to x either $x^\alpha (ax^4 + b)^{-\alpha/3}$, or $\ln[x^\alpha (ax^4 + b)^{-\alpha/3}] = \alpha[\ln x - \tfrac{1}{3} \ln(ax^4 + b)]$. The first-order condition $1/x - 4ax^3/3(ax^4 + b) = 0$ is satisfied at $x^* = \sqrt[4]{3b/a}$, and $h(x^*) = \sqrt[3]{4b}$.

7. (a) $(2, 1) \cdot (1/\sqrt{2}, 1/\sqrt{2}) = 3\sqrt{2}/2$ (b) $(2e-1, e-1) \cdot (3/5, 4/5) = 2e - 7/5$

16.2

1. (a) $\partial z/\partial t = y^2 + 2xy \cdot 2ts = 5t^4 s^2 + 4t^3 s^4$, and $\partial z/\partial s = y^2 \cdot 2s + 2xyt^2 = 2t^5 s + 4t^4 s^3$

(b) $\dfrac{\partial z}{\partial t} = \dfrac{2(1-s)e^{ts+t+s}}{(e^{t+s} + e^{ts})^2}$ and $\dfrac{\partial z}{\partial s} = \dfrac{2(1-t)e^{ts-t+s}}{(e^{t+s} + e^{ts})^2}$

3. (a) $\partial u/\partial x_i = F'(U) \cdot \partial U/\partial x_i$

(b) $\partial u/\partial x_i = \delta A_i \alpha_i x_i^{\alpha_i - 1} \left(\sum_{j=1}^n A_j x_j^{\alpha_j} \right)^{\delta - 1}$

5. (a) $\dfrac{\partial u}{\partial r} = \dfrac{\partial f}{\partial x} \dfrac{\partial x}{\partial r} + \dfrac{\partial f}{\partial y} \dfrac{\partial y}{\partial r} + \dfrac{\partial f}{\partial z} \dfrac{\partial z}{\partial r} + \dfrac{\partial f}{\partial w} \dfrac{\partial w}{\partial r}$ (b) 28

7. (a) $F'(t) = (2t)^2 \cdot 2 - t^2 \cdot 1 = 7t^2$ (b) $F'(t) = \int_1^2 e^{tx} dx = (e^{2t} - e^t)/t$

(c) $F'(t) = \dfrac{2}{t}(e^{2t^2} - e^{t^2})$. $(F'(t) = \dfrac{e^{2t^2}}{2t} \cdot 2 - \dfrac{e^{t^2}}{t} + \int_t^{2t} \dfrac{\partial}{\partial t}\left(\dfrac{e^{tx}}{x}\right) dx =$

$\dfrac{e^{2t^2}}{t} - \dfrac{e^{t^2}}{t} + \int_t^{2t} e^{tx} dx = \dfrac{e^{2t^2}}{t} - \dfrac{e^{t^2}}{t} + \left.\dfrac{e^{tx}}{t}\right|_t^{2t} = \dfrac{2}{t}(e^{2t^2} - e^{t^2})$.)

9. $e^{-\rho g(\rho)} f(g(\rho))g'(\rho) - \int_0^{g(\rho)} te^{-\rho t} f(t)\, dt$

11. Using the general chain rule [16.6], the results are easy generalizations of [2] and [5] in the discussion of directional derivatives in Section 16.1.

16.3

1. [16.9] yields $y' = -(4x + 6y)/(6x + 2y) = -(2x + 3y)/(3x + y)$.

3. (a) $y' = x/y = \pm 1$. The origin must be excluded. See Fig. 44.
(b) $y' = 2x/3y^2 = (2/3)x^{-1/3}$. The origin must be excluded. See Fig. 45.

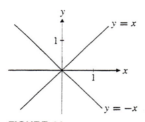

FIGURE 44

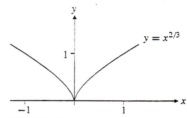

FIGURE 45

5. (a) $\dfrac{dx}{dt} = \dfrac{-[f'(x)]^2}{f(x)f''(x)} > 0$ for all t.   (b) $\mathrm{El}_t\, f'(x) = \dfrac{t}{f'(x)}\dfrac{df'(x)}{dt}$

$= \dfrac{t}{f'(x)} f''(x)\dfrac{dx}{dt} = \dfrac{t}{f'(x)} f''(x)\dfrac{-[f'(x)]^2}{f(x)f''(x)} = -\dfrac{tf'(x)}{f(x)} = -\dfrac{t}{t+x}$

7. (a) $U'_x(x, y) = F'(f(x)+g(y)) f'(x)$, and $U'_y(x, y) = F'(f(x)+g(y))g'(y)$, so $\ln\left[U'_x(x, y)/U'_y(x, y)\right] = \ln\left[f'(x)/g'(y)\right] = \ln f'(x) - \ln g'(y)$. Now the result follows easily.   (b) Confirming [2] is routine. Then $Ax^a y^b = e^{f(x)+g(y)}$, where $f(x) = \ln A + a \ln x$ and $g(y) = b \ln y$.

16.4

1. (a) $\mathrm{El}_x z = 1$ and $\mathrm{El}_y z = 1$ (b) $\mathrm{El}_x z = 2$ and $\mathrm{El}_y z = 5$ (c) $\mathrm{El}_x z = n + x$ and $\mathrm{El}_y z = n + y$ (d) $\mathrm{El}_x z = x/(x + y)$ and $\mathrm{El}_y z = y/(x + y)$

3. $\mathrm{El}_i z = p + a_i x_i$, for $i = 1, \ldots, n$.

5. Differentiate each side of the identity $y/x = \ln(xy)$ w.r.t. x, thus obtaining $\dfrac{y'}{x} - \dfrac{y}{x^2} = \dfrac{1}{x} + \dfrac{y'}{y}$. Solving for y' gives $y' = \dfrac{(x+y)y}{x(y-x)}$, and $\text{El}_x y = \dfrac{xy'}{y} = \dfrac{x+y}{y-x}$.

7. (a) $R_{yx} = (x/y)^{a-1} = (y/x)^{1-a}$ (b) $\sigma_{yx} = 1/(1-a)$

9. $F(K, N) = \gamma_1(K^{-\alpha} + \gamma_2 N^{-\alpha})^{-v/\alpha}$, so $F_K'/F_N' = K^{-\alpha-1}/\gamma_2 N^{-\alpha-1}$, implying that $\sigma_{KN} = 1/(1+\alpha)$.

11. $z = -\ln[aK^{-\varrho} + (1-a)L^{-\varrho}]/\varrho \to$ "0/0" as $\varrho \to 0$. By l'Hôpital's rule,

$$\lim_{\varrho \to 0} z = \lim_{\varrho \to 0} \left[\frac{aK^{-\varrho}\ln K + (1-a)L^{-\varrho}\ln L}{aK^{-\varrho} + (1-a)L^{-\varrho}} \right] /1$$

$$= a\ln K + (1-a)\ln L = \ln K^a L^{1-a}$$

16.5

1. $f(tx, ty) = (tx)^4 + (tx)^2(ty)^2 = t^4 x^4 + t^2 x^2 t^2 y^2 = t^4(x^4 + x^2 y^2) = t^4 f(x, y)$, so f is homogeneous of degree 4.

3. $f(tx, ty) = (tx)(ty)^2 + (tx)^3 = t^3(xy^2 + x^3) = t^3 f(x, y)$, so f is homogeneous of degree 3. [16.19]: $xf_1'(x, y) + yf_2'(x, y) = x(y^2 + 3x^2) + y2xy = 3x^3 + 3xy^2 = 3(x^3 + xy^2) = 3f(x, y)$. [16.20]: It is easy to see that $f_1'(x, y) = y^2 + 3x^2$ and $f_2'(x, y) = 2xy$ are homogeneous of degree 2. [16.21]: $f(x, y) = x^3 + xy^2 = x^3[1 + (y/x)^2] = y^3[(x/y)^3 + x/y]$. [16.22]: $x^2 f_{11}'' + 2xy f_{12}'' + y^2 f_{22}'' = x^2(6x) + 2xy(2y) + y^2(2x) = 6x^3 + 4xy^2 + 2xy^2 = 3 \cdot 2 f(x, y)$.

5. [16.18] requires that $t^3 x^3 + t^2 xy = t^k(x^3 + xy)$ for all $t > 0$. In particular, for $x = y = 1$, we must have $t^3 + t^2 = 2t^k$. For $t = 2$, we get $12 = 2 \cdot 2^k$, or $2^k = 6$. For $t = 4$, we get $80 = 2 \cdot 4^k$, or $4^k = 40$. But 4^k should be the square of 2^k. So the two values of k must be different, implying that f is not homogeneous of any degree.

7. From [*] with $k = 1$, we get $f_{11}'' = (-y/x)f_{12}''$ and $f_{22}'' = (-x/y)f_{21}''$. But $f_{12}'' = f_{21}''$, so $f_{11}'' f_{22}'' - (f_{12}'')^2 = (-y/x)f_{12}''(-x/y)f_{12}'' - (f_{12}'')^2 = 0$.

16.6

1. (a) Homogeneous of degree 1.   (b) Not homogeneous.   (c) Homogeneous of degree $-1/2$.   (d) Homogeneous of degree 1.   (e) Not homogeneous. (f) Homogeneous of degree n.

3. Homogeneous of degree $0.136 + (-0.727) + 0.914 + 0.816 = 1.139$.

5. $v_i' = u_i' - a/(x_1 + \cdots + x_n)$, so $\sum_{i=1}^n x_i v_i' = \sum_{i=1}^n x_i u_i' - \sum_{i=1}^n ax_i/(x_1 + \cdots + x_n) = a - a \sum_{i=1}^n x_i/(x_1 + \cdots + x_n) = a - a = 0$. Hence, by Euler's theorem, v is homogeneous of degree 0.

7. Let C and D denote the numerator and the denominator respectively in the expression for σ_{yx} that is given in Problem 10 of Sec. 16.4. Then, by Euler's theorem, $C = -F_1' F_2'(x F_1' + y F_2') = -F_1' F_2' F$. Using the facts that $x F_{11}'' = -y F_{12}''$ and $y F_{22}'' = -x F_{21}'' = -x F_{12}''$, it follows that D equals
$$xy\left[(F_2')^2 F_{11}'' - 2 F_1' F_2' F_{12}'' + (F_1')^2 F_{22}''\right] = -F_{12}''\left[(y F_2')^2 + 2xy F_1' F_2' + (x F_1')^2\right] =$$
$$-F_{12}''(x F_1' + y F_2')^2 = -F_{12}'' F^2. \text{ Thus } \sigma_{xy} = C/D = (-F_1' F_2' F)/(-F_{12}'' F^2) =$$
$$F_1' F_2'/F F_{12}''.$$

9. Differentiate $f(tx_1, \ldots, tx_n) = g(t) f(x_1, \ldots, x_n)$ w.r.t. t and put $t = 1$, as in the proof of Theorem 16.1. This yields $\sum_{i=1}^{n} x_i f_i'(tx_1, \ldots, tx_n) = g'(1) f(x_1, \ldots, x_n)$. Thus, by Euler's theorem, f must be homogeneous of degree $g'(1)$. In fact, $g(t) = t^k$ where $k = g'(1)$.

16.7

1. (a) $\dfrac{\partial z}{\partial x} = 3$ (b) $\dfrac{\partial z}{\partial x} = -\dfrac{yz + z^3 - y^2 z^5}{xy + 3xz^2 - 5xy^2 z^4}$

   (c) $\dfrac{\partial z}{\partial x} = -\dfrac{yze^{xyz} - 3yz}{xye^{xyz} - 3xy} = -\dfrac{z}{x}$

3. $z_x' = -\dfrac{yx^{y-1} + z^x \ln z}{y^z \ln y + xz^{x-1}}$ and $z_y' = -\dfrac{x^y \ln x + zy^{z-1}}{y^z \ln y + xz^{x-1}}$

5. $z_x' = f(x/y) + xf'(x/y)(1/y)$ and $z_y' = xf'(x/y)(-x/y^2)$, so we have $xz_x' + yz_y' = xf(x/y) + (x^2/y)f'(x/y) + yx(-x/y^2)f'(x/y) = xf(x/y) = z$. Alternatively, note that z is homogeneous of degree 1, so the equality follows from Euler's theorem.

16.8

1. (a) $f(x, y) \approx 1 + x/2 + y/2$ (b) $f(x, y) \approx y$ (c) $f(x, y) \approx A(1 + ax + by)$

3. (a) $f(1.02, 1.99) = 1.1909$ (b) $f(1.02, 1.99) \approx f(1, 2) + (0.02) \cdot 8 + (-0.01) \cdot (-3) = 1.19$. The error is 0.0009.

5. $v(1.01, 0.02) \approx v(1, 0) + v_1'(1, 0) \cdot 0.01 + v_2'(1.0) \cdot 0.02 \approx -1.00667$.

7. (a) $dz = 3x^2\, dx + 3y^2\, dy$ (b) $dz = e^{y^2}(dx + 2xy\, dy)$

   (c) $dz = \dfrac{2(x\, dx - y\, dy)}{x^2 - y^2}$

9. (a) $dz = 2xu\, dx + x^2(u_x'\, dx + u_y'\, dy)$ (b) $dz = 2u(u_x'\, dx + u_y'\, dy)$

   (c) $dz = \left[(y + yu_x')\, dx + (x + u + yu_y')\, dy\right]/(xy + yu)$

11. $dU = \dfrac{\sqrt{y}}{e^U + Ue^U}\, dx + \dfrac{x}{2\sqrt{y}(e^U + Ue^U)}\, dy$

13. (a) $d^2z = 2\, dx\, dy + 2(dy)^2$ (b) $dz = (3t^2 + 4t^3)dt$ and then $d^2z = (6t + 12t^2)(dt)^2$. On the other hand, the expression for d^2z derived from (a) is equal to $(4t + 8t^2)(dt)^2$.

16.9

1. (a) $u^3 dx + x3u^2 du + dv = 2y\,dy$, $3v\,du + 3u\,dv - dx = 0$. Solving for du and dv yields, with $D = 9xu^3 - 3v$, $du = D^{-1}(-3u^4 - 1)\,dx + D^{-1}6yu\,dy$, $dv = D^{-1}(3xu^2 + 3u^3 v)\,dx + D^{-1}(-6yv)\,dy$ (b) $u'_x = D^{-1}(-3u^4 - 1)$, $v'_x = D^{-1}(3xu^2 + 3u^3 v)$ (c) $u'_x = 283/81$ and $v'_x = -64/27$

3. With y fixed, $F'_x\,dx + F'_u\,du + F'_v\,dv = 0$ and $G'_x\,dx + G'_u\,du + G'_v\,dv = 0$. Eliminating dv and solving for du in terms of dx gives the answer $u'_x = -(F'_x G'_v - F'_v G'_x)/(F'_u G'_v - F'_v G'_u)$.

5. With a fixed, $I'(r)\,dr = S'(Y)\,dY$ and $a\,dY + L'(r)\,dr = dM$. Solving for dY and dr in terms of dM gives

$$\frac{\partial Y}{\partial M} = \frac{I'(r)}{aI'(r) + L'(r)S'(Y)} \quad \text{and} \quad \frac{\partial r}{\partial M} = \frac{S'(Y)}{aI'(r) + L'(r)S'(Y)}$$

7. $\dfrac{\partial x_1}{\partial p_1} = \dfrac{\lambda p_2^2 + x_1(p_2 U''_{12} - p_1 U''_{22})}{p_1^2 U''_{22} - 2p_1 p_2 U''_{12} + p_2^2 U''_{11}}$. (Differentiating with $dp_2 = dm = 0$ yields: [1'] $U''_{11}\,dx_1 + U''_{12}\,dx_2 = p_1 d\lambda + \lambda dp_1$; [2'] $U''_{21}\,dx_1 + U''_{22}\,dx_2 = p_2 d\lambda$; and [3'] $p_1\,dx_1 + dp_1 x_1 + p_2\,dx_2 = 0$. Solve for dx_1.)

16.10

1. (a) Differentiation yields: (1') $dY = dC + dI + dG$, (2') $dC = f'_Y\,dY + f'_T\,dT + f'_r\,dr$, (3') $dI = h'_Y\,dY + h'_r\,dr$. Hence, $dY = \left(f'_T\,dT + dG + (f'_r + h'_r)\,dr\right)/(1 - f'_Y - h'_Y)$.
(b) Because $\partial Y/\partial T = f'_T/(1 - f'_Y - h'_Y) < 0$, so Y decreases as T increases. But if $dT = dG$ with $dr = 0$, then $dY = (1 + f'_T)dT/(1 - f'_Y - h'_Y)$, which is positive provided that $f'_T > -1$.

Chapter 17

17.1

1. $x = 1$, $y = 2$ ($f'_1(x, y) = -4x + 4 = 0$, $f'_2(x, y) = -2y + 4 = 0$ for $x = 1$, $y = 2$).

3. (a) $x = 3$, $y = -4$ (b) $f(x, y) = x^2 - 6x + 3^2 + y^2 + 8y + 4^2 + 35 - 3^2 - 4^2 = (x - 3)^2 + (y + 4)^2 + 10 \geq 10$ for all (x, y), whereas $f(3, -4) = 10$.

5. $Q_1 = (a_1 - \alpha)/2b_1$ and $Q_2 = (a_2 - \alpha)/2b_2$. (Solve the following equations for Q_1 and Q_2: $\partial \pi(Q_1, Q_2)/\partial Q_1 = a_1 - \alpha - 2b_1 Q_1 = 0$ and $\partial \pi(Q_1, Q_2)/\partial Q_2 = a_2 - \alpha - 2b_2 Q_2 = 0$.)

7. $L_1 = (P - \alpha_1)/2\beta_1$ and $L_2 = (P - \alpha_2)/2\beta_2$

9. P has maximum 3888 for $x = 36$, $y = 12$, and $z = 9$. (Note that $P = (108 - 3y - 4z)yz$. Then $\partial P/\partial y = 108z - 6yz - 4z^2 = 0$ and

$\partial P/\partial z = 108y - 3y^2 - 8yz = 0$. Because y and z are assumed to be positive, the first-order conditions reduce to $6y + 4z = 108$ and $3y + 8z = 108$, with solution $y = 12$ and $z = 9$.)

11. $x = mp^{-k}/Q$, $y = mq^{-k}/Q$, and $z = mr^{-k}/Q$, where $k = 1/(1-a)$, and $Q = p^{-ak} + q^{-ak} + r^{-ak}$. (The constraint yields $z = (m - px - qy)/r$, so we maximize $P = x^a + y^a + z^a$ w.r.t. x and y. The first-order conditions are $P'_x = ax^{a-1} + az^{a-1}(-p/r) = 0$, and $P'_y = ay^{a-1} + az^{a-1}(-q/r) = 0$. These give [1] $x = p^{-k}r^k z$, [2] $y = q^{-k}r^k z$. It follows that [3] $y = p^k q^{-k} x$. Then [1] implies $x = p^{-k}r^{ak}m - p^{1-k}r^{ak}x - q^{1-k}r^{ak}x$. Solving for x gives $x = mp^{-k}/(p^{-ak} + q^{-ak} + r^{-ak})$. Then [3] gives the correct expression for y, and that for z emerges from [1] or [2].)

17.2

1. (a) Minimum -10 at $(-1, 3)$, because $f(x, y)$ is clearly ≥ -10 for all (x, y), and $f(-1, 3) = -10$. No maximum exists.
   (b) Maximum 3 for all (x, y) satisfying $x^2 + y^2 = 2$. Minimum $3 - \sqrt{2}$ at $(0, 0)$.

3. Because $F(u) = \frac{1}{2}(e^u - e^{-u})$ is strictly increasing, the problem is equivalent to max $(x^2 + y^2 - 2x)$ when $(x, y) \in S$.

5. Let $g(x) = 1$ in $[0, 1)$, $g(x) = 2$ in $[1, 2]$. Then g is discontinuous at $x = 1$ and $\{x : g(x) \leq 1\} = [0, 1)$, which is not closed. (Draw your own graph of g.)

7. (a) Yes. (b) No. (Because F is strictly increasing, f and g must have maxima at the same point in the domain.   (c) Yes.   (d) No. (Because f is a constant, $F(f(x))$ must be a constant.)

17.3

1. (a) $f'_1(x, y) = 4 - 4x$ and $f'_2(x, y) = -4y$. The only stationary point is $(1, 0)$.
   (b) $f(x, y)$ has maximum 2 at $(1, 0)$ and minimum -70 at $(-5, 0)$. (A maximum and minimum exist, by the extreme-value theorem. At the stationary point, $f(1, 0) = 2$. Along the boundary, the function value is $4x - 50$, with $x \in [-5, 5]$. So its maximum along the boundary is -30 at $x = 5$ and its minimum is -70 at $x = -5$.)

3. A maximum and minimum exist, because of Theorem 17.3. The maximum is 1 at $(2, 1/2)$. The minimum is 0 at $(x, 0)$ and $(x, x - 1)$, with x arbitrary in $[1, 2]$.

5. For $k \in (0, 1)$, F has a maximum $\sqrt{k}$ at $(0, k)$. For $k \in (1, \infty)$, F has a maximum $k^{3/4}$ at $(k, 0)$. For $k = 1$, F has a maximum 1 at $(0, 1)$ and at $(1, 0)$.

17.4

1. (a) $f_1' = 2x + 2y^2$, $f_2' = 4xy + 4y$, $f_{11}'' = 2$, $f_{12}'' = f_{21}'' = 4y$, and $f_{22}'' = 4x + 4$.

(b) The stationary points satisfy $x + y^2 = 0$ and $(x+1)y = 0$. Hence, $y = 0$ and $x = 0$, or $x = -1$ and $y = \pm 1$. Now Theorem 17.5 implies that $(0, 0)$ is a local minimum, whereas $(-1, 1)$ and $(-1, -1)$ are saddle points.

3. (a) The first-order conditions $2axy + by + 2y^2 = 0$ and $ax^2 + bx + 4xy = 0$ must have $(x, y) = (2/3, 1/3)$ as a solution. So $a = 1$ and $b = -2$. Also $c = 1/27$, so that $f(2/3, 1/3) = -1/9$. Applying Theorem 17.5 shows that this is a local minimum.   (b) Maximum 193/27 at $(2/3, 8/3)$.   Minimum $-1/9$ at $(2/3, 1/3)$.

5. (a) $(1, 2)$ is a local minimum; $(0, 0)$ and $(0, 4)$ are saddle points.   (b) Study $f(x, 1)$ as $x \to -\infty$, and $f(-1, y)$ as $y \to \infty$.   (c) A maximum and minimum exist because of Theorem 17.3. f has a minimum $-4/e$ at $(1, 2)$, and a maximum 0 at all $(x, 0)$ and $(x, 4)$ satisfying $x \in [0, 5]$, and at all $(0, y)$ satisfying $y \in [0, 4]$.

(d) $y' = -f_x'/f_y' = (x - 1)(y^2 - 4y)/x(2y - 4) = 0$ when $x = 1$ and $y = 4 - e$.

7. (a) $K = w^2 L/r^2$ and $L = 2^{-8/3} p^{4/3} w^{-4/3} r^{2/3} (r + w)^{-2/3}$. For $p = 32\sqrt{2}$, $r = w = 1$, we have $K = L = 16$.   (b) Value added per worker is

$$\frac{\pi + wL}{L} = \frac{p(\sqrt{\sqrt{kL} + \sqrt{L}} - rkL)}{L} = \frac{p\sqrt{1 + \sqrt{k}}}{L^{3/4}} - rk$$

(c) $L = 16$. The maximum of h is $h(16, 1) = 7$.

9. Stationary points are: $(0, 0)$, $(a, -a)$, (a, a), $(-a, a)$, and $(-a, -a)$, where $a = \sqrt{u_0}$, and u_0 is the unique positive solution of the equation $u^3 + u - 1 = 0$. (The first-order conditions are $4x(x^2 y^4 + y^2 - 1) = 0$ and $4y(x^4 y^2 + x^2 - 1) = 0$. One possibility is $(x, y) = (0, 0)$. Otherwise, $x \neq 0 \iff y \neq 0$. If $(x, y) \neq (0, 0)$, we find that $x^2 y^4 + y^2 = 1 = x^4 y^2 + x^2$, so $x^2 = y^2$. Therefore, $y = \pm x$, and so x must satisfy $x^6 + x^2 - 1 = 0$. Let $u = x^2$. The equation $g(u) = u^3 + u - 1 = 0$ has a solution in $(0, 1)$ by the intermediate-value theorem. The solution is unique because $g'(u) = 3u^2 + 1 > 0$ for all u.) Global extreme points do not exist. (Consider $h(x, 0)$ and $h(x, x)$, as x tends to infinity.) $(0, 0)$ gives a local maximum; the others are saddle points.

17.5

1. Only (a) and (d) are convex.

3. At most one point. (If the set had two distinct points, any of the infinitely many points on the line segment between the points would have to belong to the set.)

5. Suppose (s_1, t_1), $(s_2, t_2) \in S \times T$, with $s_1, s_2 \in S$ and $t_1, t_2 \in T$. With $\lambda \in [0, 1]$, we have $(1 - \lambda)(s_1, t_1) + \lambda(s_2, t_2) = ((1 - \lambda)s_1 + \lambda s_2, (1 - \lambda)t_1 + \lambda t_2)$. This belongs to $S \times T$ because $(1 - \lambda)s_1 + \lambda s_2 \in S$ and $(1 - \lambda)t_1 + \lambda t_2 \in T$, by the convexity of S and T, respectively. Hence, $S \times T$ is convex.

17.6

1. (a) Strictly convex. (b) Concave, but not strictly concave. (c) Strictly concave.

3. If $\mathbf{x}^0, \mathbf{x} \in R^n$ and $\lambda \in [0, 1]$, we have $f((1-\lambda)\mathbf{x}^0 + \lambda\mathbf{x}) = ||(1-\lambda)\mathbf{x}^0 + \lambda\mathbf{x}|| \leq ||(1 - \lambda)\mathbf{x}^0|| + ||\lambda\mathbf{x}|| = (1 - \lambda)||\mathbf{x}^0|| + \lambda||\mathbf{x}|| = (1 - \lambda)f(\mathbf{x}^0) + \lambda f(\mathbf{x})$, so f is convex.

17.7

1. $f = u^2$, where $u = x + 2y + 3z$. So f is a convex function of a linear function, hence convex.

3. Because $\lambda(t) \geq 0$, $\lambda(t)f(x(t)) - \lambda(t)f(z) \leq f'(z)\lambda(t)x(t) - zf'(z)\lambda(t)$. Integrating each side w.r.t. t gives $\int_a^b \lambda(t)f(x(t))\,dt - f(z)\int_a^b \lambda(t)\,dt \leq f'(z)\int_a^b \lambda(t)x(t)\,dt - zf'(z)\int_a^b \lambda(t)\,dt$. But $\int_a^b \lambda(t)\,dt = 1$ and also $z = \int_a^b \lambda(t)x(t)\,dt$, so $\int_a^b \lambda(t)f(x(t))\,dt - f\left(\int_a^b \lambda(t)x(t)\,dt\right) \leq 0$.

17.8

1. (a) (i) $f''_{11} = -2 \leq 0$, $f''_{22} = 0 \leq 0$, and $f''_{11}f''_{22} - (f''_{12})^2 = 0 \geq 0$, so f is concave.
(ii) $f(x) = (x - y) + (-x^2)$ is a sum of two concave functions, hence concave.
(b) $F(u) = -e^{-u}$ is strictly increasing and concave ($F'(u) = e^{-u} > 0$ and $F''(u) = -e^{-u} < 0$). By Theorem 17.6, part (c), $z = -e^{-f(x,y)}$ is concave.

3. $f''_{11} = -12$, $f''_{22} = -2$, and $f''_{11}f''_{22} - (f''_{12})^2 = 24 - (2a + 4)^2 = -4a^2 - 16a + 8$. Because $f''_{11} < 0$, the function is never convex. It is concave iff $-4a^2 - 16a + 8 \geq 0$, that is, iff $-2 - \sqrt{6} \leq a \leq -2 + \sqrt{6}$.

5. Draw your own figure and use definition [17.14] of Section 17.6 to show that f is convex.

7. $(100, 300)$ is a stationary point for π. Moreover, $\pi''_{11} = -0.08 \leq 0$, $\pi''_{22} = -0.02 \leq 0$, and $\pi''_{11}\pi''_{22} - (\pi''_{12})^2 = (-0.08)(-0.02) - (0.01)^2 = 0.015 \geq 0$, so $(100, 300)$ is a (global) maximum point for π.

9. Direct verification of second-order conditions.

11. The Hessian matrix $\mathbf{H} = \begin{pmatrix} f_{11}'' & f_{12}'' \\ f_{21}'' & f_{22}'' \end{pmatrix}$ is

$$\begin{pmatrix} \dfrac{a}{x^2}(\ln x)^{a-2}(\ln y)^b(a-1-\ln x) & \dfrac{ab}{xy}(\ln x)^{a-1}(\ln y)^{b-1} \\[2ex] \dfrac{ab}{xy}(\ln x)^{a-1}(\ln y)^{b-1} & \dfrac{b}{y^2}(\ln y)^{b-2}(\ln x)^a(b-1-\ln y) \end{pmatrix}$$

Here $f_{11}'' < 0$ because $0 < a < 1$. Also $|\mathbf{H}|$ is equal to $f_{11}''f_{22}'' - (f_{12}'')^2$, or to

$$\dfrac{ab}{x^2 y^2}(\ln x)^{2a-2}(\ln y)^{2b-2} \cdot \big[\underbrace{1-(a+b)}_{>0} + \underbrace{(1-a)\ln y}_{>0} + \underbrace{(1-b)\ln x}_{>0} + \underbrace{\ln x \ln y}_{>0}\big]$$

This is positive, so f is strictly concave.

17.9

1. The only stationary point is $(0, 0, 0)$. The leading principal minors of the Hessian have the values $D_1 = 2$, $D_2 = 3$, and $D_3 = 4$, so $(0, 0, 0)$ is a local minimum point by Theorem 17.12, part (d).

3. When the Hessian is indefinite at $\mathbf{x}^0$, this point is neither a local maximum nor a local minimum, so it is a saddle point.

17.10

1. (a) f is linear, so quasi-concave.   (b) $\ln f(x, y) = x + \ln y$, which is the sum of concave functions. Because e^u is strictly increasing, f must be quasi-concave (Theorem 17.16 (b)).   (c) The set of points for which $f(x, y) \geq -1$ is $P_{-1} = \{(x, y) : y \leq x^{-2/3}\}$, which is not a convex set (see Fig. 46), so f is not quasi-concave. (It is quasi-convex in the first quadrant because of [17.32] (b).)

(d) The polynomial $x^3 + x^2 + 1$ is increasing in the interval $(-\infty, -2/3]$, and decreasing in $[-2/3, 0]$. So f is increasing in $(-\infty, -2/3]$ and decreasing

FIGURE 46

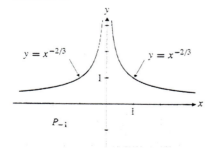

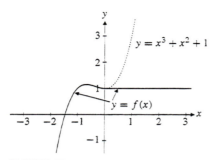

FIGURE 47

in $[-2/3, \infty)$. (See Fig. 47.) Then the level sets must be intervals, and it follows that f is quasi-concave.

3. Let $f_1(x) = 1 - x$ for $|x| \le 1$, 0 for $|x| > 1$; $f_2(x) = -x - 1$ for $|x + 2| \le 1$, 0 for $|x + 2| > 1$. Then f_1 and f_2 are quasi-concave, but $f_1 + f_2$ is not. (See Fig. 48.)

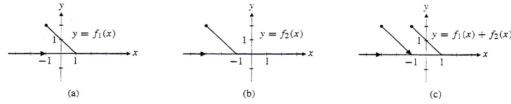

(a)   (b)   (c)

FIGURE 48

5. $f'(x) \ne 0$ for all x implies that f is quasi-concave. (In fact, $f'(x) \ne 0$ means that either f is (strictly) increasing or (strictly) decreasing. Then see Problem 2.)

7. From [16.13] in Section 16.3, $\phi''(x) = D_2(x, y)/(F_2')^3$ with $D_2(x, y)$ defined in Theorem 17.17. By part (a) of that theorem, $D_2(x, y) \ge 0$, so $\phi''(x) \ge 0$ and ϕ is convex.

Chapter 18

18.1

1. (a) $x = 1/2$ and $y = 3/4$ ($f_1'(x, y) = 1$, $f_2'(x, y) = 1$, $g_1'(x, y) = 2x$, $g_2'(x, y) = 1$, so [18.3] yields the equation $1/1 = 2x/1$. Then $x = 1/2$ and $y = 1 - (1/2)^2 = 3/4$.)
(b) $x = 4/5$ and $y = 8/5$

3. $x = 27/10$ and $y = 9/10$. ([18.3] yields $5x^{-1/2}y^{1/3}/(10/3)x^{1/2}y^{-2/3} = 2/4 = 1/2$, so $y = x/3$. Then $y = 9/10$, so $x = 27/10$.)

18.2

1. (a) $\mathcal{L}(x, y) = x + y - \lambda(x^2 + y - 1)$. The equations $\mathcal{L}_1' = 1 - 2\lambda x = 0$, $\mathcal{L}_2' = 1 - \lambda = 0$, and $x^2 + y = 1$ have the solution $x = 1/2$, $y = 3/4$, and $\lambda = 1$. (b) The solution is illustrated in Fig. 49. The minimization problem has no solution.

(c) $x = 0.5$ and $y = 0.85$. The change in the value function is $f^*(1.1) - f^*(1) = (0.5 + 0.85) - (0.5 + 0.75) = 0.1$. Because $\lambda = 1$, $\lambda \cdot dc = 1 \cdot 0.1 = 0.1$. So, in this case, [18.8] is satisfied with equality.

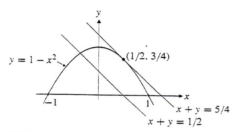

FIGURE 49

3. (a) Solution: $x = 50$ and $y = 50$, with $\lambda = 250$. To see that this solves the problem, let $x = 50 + h$ and $y = 50 + k$. Inserting these values of x and y into the constraint yields $50 + h + 50 + k = 100$, that is, $k = -h$. Then $x^2 + 3xy + y^2 = (50 + h)^2 + 3(50 + h)(50 + k) + (50 + k)^2 = 12,500 - h^2$, using $k = -h$ and simplifying. Now, $12,500 - h^2$ has a maximum for $h = 0$, that is, for $x = 50$, and then $y = 50$. (b) Solution: $x = 8/3$ and $y = 1$, with $\lambda = 4$. From the constraint equation, $y = 3 - 3x/4$. Because we must have $y \geq 0$, so $x \leq 4$. Now, if we let $h(x) = 12x\sqrt{3 - 3x/4}$, then $h'(x) = (72 - 27x)/2\sqrt{3 - 3x/4}$, and the sign variation of this derivative reveals that h is maximized at $x = 8/3$.

5. (a) $\mathcal{L}(x, y) = 10x^{1/2}y^{1/3} - \lambda(2x + 4y - m)$. The two first-order conditions $\mathcal{L}_1' = 5x^{-1/2}y^{1/3} - 2\lambda = 0$ and $\mathcal{L}_2' = (10/3)x^{1/2}y^{-2/3} - 4\lambda = 0$ imply that $(10/3)x^{1/2}y^{-2/3} = 10x^{-1/2}y^{1/3}$, so $x = 3y$. Substituting this into the constraint $2x + 4y = m$ gives $y = m/10$ and so $x = 3m/10$, with $\lambda = 2.5(10/27m)^{1/6}$.

(b) $f^*(m) = 10^{1/6}3^{1/2}m^{5/6}$ and $df^*(m)/dm = \lambda = 2.5 \cdot 10^{1/6}3^{-1/2}m^{-1/6}$.

7. (a) $(2, 1)$ (b) With $\mathcal{L}(x, y) = x + 2y - \lambda[p(x^2 + y^2) + x^2y^2 - 4]$, equating the first-order partials to 0 yields $\mathcal{L}_1' = 1 - 2\lambda px - 2\lambda xy^2 = 0$ and $\mathcal{L}_2' = 2 - 2\lambda py - 2\lambda x^2 y = 0$. Hence, $2\lambda x(p + y^2) = 1$ and $2\lambda y(p + x^2) = 2$. Eliminating λ yields the first equality in [**]. The second is just the constraint.

(c) Differentiating [**] w.r.t. p, with x and y as functions of p, yields
[1] $2x + 2px' - y - py' + 2x'y^2 + 4xyy' - 2xx'y - x^2y' = 0$ and
[2] $x^2 + 2pxx' + y^2 + 2pyy' + 2xx'y^2 + 2x^2yy' = 0$. Letting $p = 0$, recalling that $x(0) = 2$ and $y(0) = 1$, yields the equations $-2x'(0) + 4y'(0) = -3$ and

$4x'(0) + 8y'(0) = -5$, with the solution $x'(0) = 1/8$ and $y'(0) = -11/16$.

(d) $h(p) = x(p) + 2y(p)$, so $h'(0) = x'(0) + 2y'(0) = -5/4$.

18.3

1. The problem with systems of three equations and two unknowns is that they are usually inconsistent (have no solutions), not that they are difficult to solve. The equations $f_x'(x, y) = f_y'(x, y) = 0$ are *not* valid at the optimal point.

3. $x = -1$ and $y = 0$ solves the problem, with $f(-1, 0) = 1$. (Actually, this problem is quite tricky. The only stationary point of the Lagrangean is $(0, 0)$, with $\lambda = -4$, and with $f(0, 0) = 4$. The point is that at $(-1, 0)$ both $g_1'(-1, 0)$ and $g_2'(-1, 0)$ are 0, so the Lagrangean is not necessarily stationary at this point. The problem is to minimize the (square of the) distance from $(-2, 0)$ to a point on the graph of $g(x, y) = 0$. But the graph consists of the single point $(-1, 0)$ and a nice curve, as illustrated in Fig. 50.)

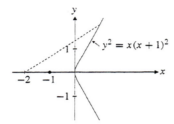

FIGURE 50

18.4

1. The Lagrangean $\mathcal{L}(x, y) = 10x^{1/2}y^{1/3} - \lambda(2x + 4y - m)$ is concave as a sum of two concave functions (see Example 17.18 in Section 17.8), so Theorem 18.2 applies.

18.5

1. (a) $\mathcal{L}(x, y, z) = x^2 + y^2 + z^2 - \lambda(x + y + z - 1)$. The only solution of the necessary conditions is $(1/3, 1/3, 1/3)$. (b) The problem is to find the shortest distance from the origin to a point in the plane $x + y + z = 1$. The corresponding maximization problem has no solution.

3. (a) $x = \alpha(wL + m)/p$, $y = \beta(wL + m)/q$, and $l = (\alpha + \beta)L - m(1 - \alpha - \beta)/w$. The condition given is equivalent to $l \geq 0$. (b) The solution is $l = 0$, with $x = \alpha m/(\alpha + \beta)p$ and $y = \beta m/(\alpha + \beta)q$. (In this case, unearned income is so high that it is optimal for the individual not to work at all.)

5. With linear equality constraints, we shall not resist the temptation to eliminate variables. In fact, adding the constraints gives $3x = 6$ and so $x = 2$. Thus $y = -(1 + z)$. Substituting for x and y in the objective function

reduces it to $2(1 + z)^2 + z^2 + z = 3z^2 + 5z + 2$. This quadratic polynomial has a minimum when $z = -5/6$. Then $y = -1/6$. The solution is $(x, y, z) = (2, -1/6, -5/6)$.

7. The Lagrangean is $\mathcal{L} = x + y - \lambda(x^2 + 2y^2 + z^2 - 1) - \mu(x + y + z - 1)$, which is stationary when [1] $\mathcal{L}'_x = 1 - 2\lambda x - \mu = 0$; [2] $\mathcal{L}'_y = 1 - 4\lambda y - \mu = 0$; [3] $\mathcal{L}'_z = -2\lambda z - \mu = 0$. From [1] and [2], $2\lambda(x - 2y) = 0$. If $\lambda = 0$, then [2] and [3] yield $\mu = 1$ and $\mu = 0$. Therefore $x = 2y$ instead. Substituting this value for x in the constraints gives $6y^2 + z^2 = 1$, $3y + z = 1$. Thus, $z = 1 - 3y$ and $1 = 6y^2 + (1 - 3y)^2 = 15y^2 - 6y + 1$. Hence $y = 0$ or $y = 2/5$, implying that $x = 0$ or $4/5$, and that $z = 1$ or $-1/5$. The only two solution candidates are $(x, y, z) = (0, 0, 1)$ with $\lambda = -1/2$, $\mu = 1$, and $(x, y, z) = (4/5, 2/5, -1/5)$ with $\lambda = 1/2$, $\mu = 1/5$. Because $x + y$ is 0 at $(0, 0, 1)$ and $6/5$ at $(4/5, 2/5, -1/5)$, these are respectively the minimum and the maximum. (The constraints determine geometrically the curve which is the intersection of an ellipsoid (see Fig. 15.12 in Section 15.2) and a plane. The continuous function $x + y$ does attain a maximum and a minimum over this closed bounded set.)

9. (a) Here $\mathcal{L} = (y + z - 3)^2 - \lambda(x^2 + y + z - 2) - \mu(x + y^2 + 2z - 2)$, which is stationary when [1] $\mathcal{L}'_x = -2\lambda x - \mu = 0$; [2] $\mathcal{L}'_y = 2(y + z - 3) - \lambda - 2\mu y = 0$; [3] $\mathcal{L}'_z = 2(y + z - 3) - \lambda - 2\mu = 0$. From (2) and (3), $\lambda + 2\mu y = \lambda + 2\mu$, so $\mu(y - 1) = 0$. If $\mu = 0$, then from [1] and [2], $\lambda x = 0$ and $2(y + z - 3) = \lambda$. Now $\lambda = 0$ would imply that $y + z = 3$ and so $x^2 = -1$ from the first constraint. Thus $\lambda \neq 0$ and so $\mu = 0 \Rightarrow x = 0$. Then the two constraints yield $y = 2 - z$ and $y^2 = 2(1 - z)$, so that $y^2 - 2y + 2 = 0$, which also has no real root. We conclude that $\mu \neq 0$ and so $y = 1$. The two constraints now imply that $x^2 + z = 1$ and $x + 2z = 1$. Hence $x^2 + \frac{1}{2}(1 - x) = 1$, which has roots $x = 1$ and $x = -1/2$. The only two solution candidates are $(x, y, z) = (1, 1, 0)$ and $(x, y, z) = (-1/2, 1, 3/4)$. The corresponding values of (λ, μ) are $(4/3, -8/3)$ and $(-5/6, -5/6)$ respectively. Because $(y + z - 3)^2$ is 4 at $(1, 1, 0)$ and $25/16$ at $(-1/2, 1, 3/4)$, the latter is the appropriate solution. (The method used in Problem 4 can be applied to show that this gives the minimum.) (b) The second solution, which is $(1, 1, 0)$, gives $f(1, 1, 0) = 4$. But $(-2, -2, 0)$, for example, satisfies both constraints, and gives $f(-2, -2, 0) = 25$.

11. Differentiating the constraint w.r.t. x_1 yields $g'_1 + g'_3(\partial x_3 / \partial x_1) = 0$, or (1) $\partial x_3 / \partial x_1 = -g'_1 / g'_3$. Similarly, (2) $\partial x_3 / \partial x_2 = -g'_2 / g'_3$. Now, the first-order conditions for the maximization of $z = f(x_1, x_2, x_3)$, where x_3 is a function of (x_1, x_2), are (3) $\partial z / \partial x_1 = f'_1 + f'_3(\partial x_3 / \partial x_1) = 0$ and (4) $\partial z / \partial x_2 = f'_2 + f'_3(\partial x_3 / \partial x_2) = 0$. Substitute from (1) and (2) into (3) and (4), letting $\lambda = f'_3 / g'_3$. This yields the equations $f'_1 - \lambda g'_1 = 0$ and $f'_2 - \lambda g'_2 = 0$, and by the definition of λ, $f'_3 - \lambda g'_3 = 0$. These are the conditions in (18.17) for $n = 3$.

18.6

1. $x = -\frac{1}{6}\sqrt{b}$, $y = -\frac{1}{3}\sqrt{b}$, $z = -\frac{3}{2}\sqrt{b}$, $\lambda = -3/\sqrt{b}$, $f^*(b) = -6\sqrt{b}$, $df^*/db = -3/\sqrt{b} = \lambda$.

3. (a) [4] $1 - \frac{1}{3}\lambda = \mu x_2 x_3 x_4$;   [5] $1 - \frac{1}{3}\lambda = \mu x_1 x_3 x_4$;   [6] $1 - \frac{1}{8}\lambda = \mu x_1 x_2 x_4$; [7] $1 - \frac{1}{8}\lambda = \mu x_1 x_2 x_3$, together with [1], [2], and [3].   (b) Note that $\mu = 0$ would give $1 - \frac{1}{3}\lambda = 1 - \frac{1}{8}\lambda = 0$, which is impossible. Because $x_1, \ldots, x_4$ are all nonzero, it follows from [4] and [5] that $x_1 = x_2$, and from [6] and [7] that $x_3 = x_4$. Then [4] and [5] imply that $1 - \frac{1}{3}\lambda = \mu x_1 x_3^2$, whereas [6] and [7] imply that $1 - \frac{1}{8}\lambda = \mu x_1^2 x_3$, and also $x_1^2 x_3^2 = 144$ by [2]. Hence, $x_1 x_3 = 12$ and also $\frac{2}{3}x_1 + \frac{1}{4}x_3 = 3$, from the first constraint. These last two equations have two solutions, which are $(x_1, x_3) = (3, 4)$ and $(3/2, 8)$. Maximizing $x_1 + x_2 + x_3 + x_4 = 2(x_1 + x_3)$ requires choosing the latter. Thus, $(x_1, x_2, x_3, x_4) = (3/2, 3/2, 8, 8)$ must solve the problem, with $\lambda = 13$ and $\mu = -5/144$.
(c) The change is approximately $\mu = -5/144$.

18.7

1. $x^* = m/2p$ and $y^* = m/2q$, with $\lambda = 5p^{-1/2}q^{-1/2}$, solves the problem. The optimal value function is $U^*(p, q, m) = 5p^{-1/2}q^{-1/2}m$, and [18.31] says that $\partial U^*/\partial p = -\lambda x^*$, $\partial U^*/\partial q = -\lambda y^*$ and $\partial U^*/\partial m = \lambda$. The correctness of these equalities is now easily checked.

3. (a) The first order conditions can be expressed as

$$\frac{au}{x_1} - \frac{bu}{x_1 + b - a} = \lambda p_1, \qquad \frac{(b - a)u}{x_2} = \lambda p_2$$

where $u = x_1^a x_2^{b-a}(x_1 + b - a)^{-b}$. Thus

$$\lambda p_1 x_1 = au - \frac{bux_1}{x_1 + b - a} = \frac{(b - a)(a - x_1)u}{x_1 + b - a}, \qquad \lambda p_2 x_2 = (b - a)u$$

From the first of these equations, $(b - a)u/\lambda = p_1 x_1 (x_1 + b - a)/(a - x_1)$, and hence from the second, $p_2 x_2 = (b - a)u/\lambda = p_1 x_1 (x_1 + b - a)/(a - x_1)$. Substituting in the budget constraint and solving for x_1 eventually yields $x_1 = am/(m + bp_1)$ and $x_2 = m(m + bp_1 - ap_1)/p_2(m + bp_1)$. These are the required demand functions. They are both positive.
(b) Use logarithmic differentiation to obtain $\partial x_1/\partial p_1 = -bx_1/(m + p_1 b) < 0$, $\partial x_1/\partial p_2 = 0$, $\partial x_1/\partial m = x_1/m - x_1/(m + p_1 b) > 0$, $\partial x_2/\partial p_1 = -amx_2/[m + p_1(b - a)](m + p_1 b) < 0$, $\partial x_2/\partial p_2 = -x_2/p_2 < 0$, and $\partial x_2/\partial m = x_2/m + p_1 ax_2/[m + p_1(b - a)](m + p_1 b) > 0$.   (c) Routine.

18.8

1. (a) $\mathcal{L}(x, y) = x^2 + 2y^2 - x - \lambda(x^2 + y^2 - 1)$, and [18.35] gives [1] $2x - 1 - 2\lambda x = 0$; [2] $4y - 2\lambda y = 0$. (b) $\lambda \geq 0$ ($= 0$ if $x^2 + y^2 < 1$)
   (c) Candidates: $(1/2, 0)$ with $\lambda = 0$; $(1, 0)$ with $\lambda = 1/2$; $(-1, 0)$ with $\lambda = 3/2$; and $(-1/2, \pm\sqrt{3}/2)$ with $\lambda = 2$. Maximum $9/4$ at $(-1/2, \sqrt{3}/2)$ and at $(-1/2, -\sqrt{3}/2)$.

3. (a) The Lagrangean is $\mathcal{L} = y - x^2 + \lambda y + \mu(y - x + 2) - \nu(y^2 - x)$, which is stationary when: [1] $-2x - \mu + \nu = 0$; [2] $1 + \lambda + \mu - 2\nu y = 0$. Also [3] $\lambda \geq 0$ ($= 0$ if $y > 0$); [4] $\mu \geq 0$ ($= 0$ if $y - x + 2 > 0$); [5] $\nu \geq 0$ ($= 0$ if $y^2 < x$).
   From [2], $2\nu y = 1 + \lambda + \mu > 0$, so $y > 0$. Then [3] implies $\lambda = 0$ and $2\nu y = 1 + \mu$. From [1], $x = \frac{1}{2}(\nu - \mu)$. But $x \geq y^2 > 0$, so $\nu > \mu \geq 0$. and from [5], $y^2 = x$.
   Suppose $\mu > 0$. Then $y - x + 2 = y - y^2 + 2 = 0$ with roots $y = -1$ and $y = 2$. Only $y = 2$ is a candidate. Then $x = y^2 = 4$. Because $\lambda = 0$, the first-order conditions become $-\mu + \nu = 8$ and $\mu - 4\nu = -1$, so $\nu = -7/3$, which contradicts $\nu \geq 0$, so $(x, y) = (4, 2)$ is not a candidate. Therefore $\mu = 0$ after all. Thus $x = \frac{1}{2}\nu = y^2$ and $1 = 2\nu y = 4y^3$. Hence $y = 4^{-1/3}$, $x = 4^{-2/3}$. This is the only candidate, with $\lambda = 0$, $\mu = 0$, and $\nu = 2 \cdot 4^{-2/3} = 4^{1/6}$. (b) $x = 1$ and $y = 0$ with $\lambda = 0$, $\mu = 2e - e^{-1}$, $\nu = 0$. ($\mathcal{L} = xe^{y-x} - 2ey + \lambda x + \mu y - \nu(y - 1 - x/z)$)

5. (a) With $\mathcal{L} = \ln x_1 + x_2 + x_3 - \lambda_1(x_1 + x_2 + x_3 - 1) - \lambda_2(-x_1 + 1) - \lambda_3(x_1^2 + x_2^2 - 2)$, the necessary conditions are [1] $1/x_1 - \lambda_1 + \lambda_2 - 2\lambda_3 x_1 = 0$; [2] $1 - \lambda_1 - 2\lambda_3 x_2 = 0$; [3] $1 - \lambda_1 = 0$; [4] $\lambda_1 \geq 0$ ($= 0$ if $x_1 + x_2 + x_3 < 1$); [5] $\lambda_2 \geq 0$ ($= 0$ if $x_1 > 1$); [6] $\lambda_3 \geq 0$ ($= 0$ if $x_1^2 + x_2^2 < 2$).
   (b) From [3] $\lambda_1 = 1$. Hence $x_1 + x_2 + x_3 = 1$, by [4]. Also $\lambda_3 x_2 = 0$, because of [2]. Suppose $\lambda_3 > 0$. Then $x_2 = 0$ and, by [6], $x_1 = \sqrt{2}$, so $\lambda_2 = 0$. But substituting in [1] gives $1/\sqrt{2} - 1 - 2\sqrt{2}\lambda_3 = 0$, which is impossible when $\lambda_3 > 0$. So $\lambda_3 = 0$ after all. With $\lambda_3 = 0$, condition [1] implies that $x_1 = 1/(1 - \lambda_2)$. This would imply $x_1 > 1$ if $\lambda_2 > 0$, contradicting [5]. Hence $x_1 = 1$ and $\lambda_2 = 0$. Also $x_2 + x_3 = 1 - x_1 = 0$. To summarize, all triples (x_1, x_2, x_3) with $x_1 = 1$, $x_2 + x_3 = 0$, and $x_2^2 \leq 2 - x_1^2 = 1$, and with $(\lambda_1, \lambda_2, \lambda_2) = (1, 0, 0)$, satisfy all the necessary conditions, and they all give the same value 0 to the objective function $\ln x_1 + x_2 + x_3$. So there are infinitely many solutions. (Using Theorem 18.4 in Section 18.10, one can show that all are optimal.)

18.9

1. (a) $1 - x^2 - y^2 \leq 1$ for all $x \geq 0$, $y \geq 0$, so the optimal solution must be $x = y = 0$. (b) With $\mathcal{L} = 1 - x^2 - y^2 - \lambda(-x) - \mu(-y)$, the Kuhn–Tucker conditions are [1] $\partial\mathcal{L}/\partial x = -2x + \lambda = 0$; [2] $\partial\mathcal{L}/\partial y = -2y + \mu = 0$;

[3] $\lambda \geq 0$ ($= 0$ if $x > 0$); and [4] $\mu \geq 0$ ($= 0$ if $y > 0$). From [1] and [2], $\lambda = 2x$ and $\mu = 2y$. If $\lambda > 0$, then [3] implies $x = 0$, which contradicts $\lambda = 2x$. Therefore, $\lambda = x = 0$. Similarly, $\mu = y = 0$.

3. A feasible triple (x_1^0, x_2^0, k^0) solves the problem iff there exist numbers λ and μ such that

$$1 - 2x_1^0 - \lambda \leq 0 \ (= 0 \text{ if } x_1^0 > 0)$$

$$3 - 2x_2^0 - \mu \leq 0 \ (= 0 \text{ if } x_2^0 > 0)$$

$$-2k^0 + \lambda + \mu \leq 0 \ (= 0 \text{ if } k^0 > 0)$$

$$\lambda \geq 0 \ (= 0 \text{ if } x_1^0 < k^0)$$

$$\mu \geq 0 \ (= 0 \text{ if } x_2^0 < k^0)$$

If $k^0 = 0$, then feasibility requires $x_1^0 = 0$ and $x_2^0 = 0$, and so the first and second statements in the display imply that $\lambda \geq 1$ and $\mu \geq 3$, which contradicts the third statement. Thus, $k^0 > 0$. Next, if $\mu = 0$, then $x_2^0 = 3/2$ and $\lambda = 2k^0 > 0$. So $x_1^0 = k^0 = 1/4$, contradicting $x_2^0 \leq k^0$. So $\mu > 0$, which implies that $x_2^0 = k^0$. Now, if $x_1^0 = 0 < k^0$, then $\lambda = 0$, which contradicts the first statement in the display. So $0 < x_1^0 = \frac{1}{2}(1 - \lambda)$. Next, if $\lambda > 0$, then $x_1^0 = k^0 = x_2^0 = \frac{1}{2}(1 - \lambda) = \frac{1}{2}(3 - \mu) = \frac{1}{2}(\lambda + \mu)$. But the last two equalities are only satisfied when $\lambda = -1/3$ and $\mu = 5/3$, which contradicts $\lambda \geq 0$. So $\lambda = 0$ after all, with $x_2^0 = k^0 > 0$, $\mu > 0$, $x_1^0 = \frac{1}{2}(1 - \lambda) = \frac{1}{2}$. Now, from the third equation in the display, it follows that $\mu = 2k^0$ and so, from the second equation, that $3 = 2x_2^0 + \mu = 4k^0$. The only possible solution is, therefore, $(x_1^0, x_2^0, k^0) = (1/2, 3/4, 3/4)$, with $\lambda = 0$ and $\mu = 3/2$.

5. The proof is quite similar to the proof of property 3.

18.10

1. (a) Use Theorem 17.9 in Section 17.8. (b) The Kuhn–Tucker conditions are: [1] $-2(x - 1) - 2\lambda x = 0$; [2] $-2ye^{y^2} - 2\lambda y = 0$; [3] $\lambda \geq 0$ ($= 0$ if $x^2 + y^2 < a$). So $x \doteq (1 + \lambda)^{-1}$ and $y = 0$. The constraint $x^2 + y^2 \leq a$ implies $(1 + \lambda)^{-2} \leq a$, or $1 + \lambda \geq a^{-1/2}$. For $0 < a < 1$, the solution is $x = \sqrt{a}$, $y = 0$, and $\lambda = a^{-1/2} - 1$; for $a \geq 1$, it is $x = 1$, $y = 0$, and $\lambda = 0$. Because $x^2 + y^2$ is convex, this is the optimum.

3. Consider the problem: max $U(x, y) = x^\alpha y^\beta$ s.t. $g(x, y) = px + y \leq m$. Here $(x_0, y_0) = \left(\alpha m/p(\alpha + \beta), \beta m/(\alpha + \beta)\right)$, with $\lambda = (\alpha/p)^\alpha \beta^\beta [m/(\alpha + \beta)]^{\alpha+\beta-1}$ is feasible and satisfies (a) and (b) in Theorem 18.4. Moreover, $U(x, y)$ is quasi-concave and $g(x, y)$ is linear, so condition (c) in Theorem 18.5 is satisfied. Also, $(U_1'(x_0, y_0), U_2'(x_0, y_0)) = \alpha^\alpha \beta^\beta [m/(\alpha + \beta)]^{\alpha+\beta-1}(p^{1-\alpha}, p^{-\alpha}) \neq (0, 0)$. Hence, (x_0, y_0) solves the problem. When

$\alpha = \beta = 1$ and $p = 2$, the pair $(x_0, y_0) = (m/4, m/2)$, with $\lambda = m/4$, solves the problem in Example 18.1 (see also Example 18.3 in Section 18.2).

5. (a) The solution is $x = 2$.   (b) Condition (b) is not satisfied. $x^0 = 1$ is not an optimum.

Chapter 19

19.1

1. (a) From Fig. 51, we see that the solution is at the intersection P of the two lines $3x_1 + 2x_2 = 6$ and $x_1 + 4x_2 = 4$. Solution: max $= 36/5$ for $(x_1, x_2) = (8/5, 3/5)$.   (b) From Fig. 52, we see that the solution is at the intersection P of the two lines $u_1 + 3u_2 = 11$ and $2u_1 + 5u_2 = 20$. Solution: min $= 104$ for $(u_1, u_2) = (5, 2)$.

(c) From a graph it can be seen that the solution is at the intersection of the lines $-2x_1 + 3x_2 = 6$ and $x_1 + x_2 = 5$. Hence max $= 98/5$ for $(x_1, x_2) = (9/5, 16/5)$.   (d) max $= 49$ for $(x_1, x_2) = (5, 1)$ (e) max $= -10/3$ for $(x_1, x_2) = (2, 2/3)$

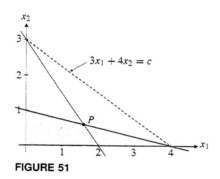

FIGURE 51

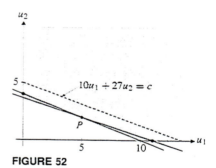

FIGURE 52

3. (a) max $= 18/5$ for $(x_1, x_2) = (4/5, 18/5)$.
   (b) max $= 8$ for $(x_1, x_2) = (8, 0)$.
   (c) max $= 24$ for $(x_1, x_2) = (8, 0)$.
   (d) min $= -28/5$ for $(x_1, x_2) = (4/5, 18/5)$.
   (e) max $= 16$ for all (x_1, x_2) of the form $(x_1, 4 - \frac{1}{2}x_1)$ where $x_1 \in [4/5, 8]$.
   (f) min $= -24$ for $(x_1, x_2) = (8, 0)$ (follows from the answer to (c)).

5. The slope of the line $20x_1 + tx_2 = c$ must lie between $-1/2$ (the slope of the flour border) and -1 (the slope of the butter border). For $t = 0$, the line is vertical and the solution is the point D in Fig. 19.2. For $t \neq 0$, the slope of the line is $-20/t$. Thus, $-1 \leq -20/t \leq -1/2$, which implies that $t \in [20, 40]$.

19.2

1. (a) $(x_1, x_2) = (2, 1/2)$ and $u_1^* = 4/5$ (b) $(x_1, x_2) = (7/5, 9/10)$ and $u_2^* = 3/5$ (c) Multiplying the two $\leq$ constraints by $4/5$ and $3/5$, respectively, and then adding yields $(4/5)(3x_1 + 2x_2) + (3/5)(x_1 + 4x_2) \leq 6 \cdot 4/5 + 4 \cdot 3/5$, which reduces to $3x_1 + 4x_2 \leq 36/5$.

3. $\min 8u_1 + 13u_2 + 6u_3$ subject to $\begin{cases} u_1 + 2u_2 + u_3 \geq 8 \\ 2u_1 + 3u_2 + u_3 \geq 9 \end{cases} u_1 \geq 0, u_2 \geq 0, u_3 \geq 0$

19.3

1. (a) $x = 0$ and $y = 3$ gives max $= 21$. See Fig. 53, where the optimum is P.

(b) $\min 20u_1 + 21u_2$ subject to $\begin{cases} 4u_1 + 3u_2 \geq 2 \\ 5u_1 + 7u_2 \geq 7 \end{cases} u_1 \geq 0, u_2 \geq 0$

has the solution $u_1 = 0$ and $u_2 = 1$, which gives min $= 21$. See Fig. 54.

(c) Yes.

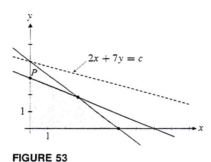

FIGURE 53   **FIGURE 54**

3. (a) The profit from selling x_1 small and x_2 medium television sets is $400x_1 + 500x_2$. The first constraint, $2x_1 + x_2 \leq 16$, says that we cannot use more hours in Division 1 than the hours available. The second constraint, $x_1 + 4x_2 \leq 16$, says that we cannot use more hours in Division 2 than the hours available. The third constraint, $x_1 + 2x_2 \leq 11$, says that we cannot use more hours in Division 3 than the hours available.   (b) The solution is max $= 3800$ for $x_1 = 7$ and $x_2 = 2$. (Supply your own graph.)   (c) Relaxing the first constraint to $2x_1 + x_2 \leq 17$ allows the new solution $x_1 = 23/3$, $x_2 = 5/3$, with an extra profit of 100. Relaxing the second constraint to $x_1 + 4x_2 \leq 17$ makes no difference, because some capacity in division 2 remanded unused anyway. Relaxing the third constraint to $x_1 + 2x_2 \leq 12$ allows the solution $x_1 = 20/3$, $x_2 = 8/3$, with an extra profit of 200. So division 3 should be the first to have its capacity increased.

19.4

1. According to formula [19.12], $\Delta z^* = u_1^* \Delta b_1 + u_2^* \Delta b_2 = 0 \cdot 0.1 + 1 \cdot (-0.2) = -0.2$.

19.5

1. $4u_1^* + 3u_2^* = 3 > 2$ and $x^* = 0$; $5u_1^* + 7u_2^* = 7$ and $y^* = 3 > 0$. Also $4x^* + 5y^* = 15 < 20$ and $u_1^* = 0$; $3x^* + 7y^* = 21$ and $u_2^* = 1 > 0$. So we see that [19.13] and [19.14] are satisfied.

3. (a) min $10,000y_1 + 8000y_2 + 11,000y_3$ s.t. $\begin{cases} 10y_1 + 20y_2 + 20y_3 \geq 300 \\ 20y_1 + 10y_2 + 20y_3 \geq 500 \end{cases}$
$y_1 \geq 0$, $y_2 \geq 0$, $y_3 \geq 0$.
(b) Solution of the dual: max $= 255,000$ for $x_1 = 100$ and $x_2 = 450$. Solution of the primal: min $= 255,000$ for $(y_1, y_2, y_3) = (20, 0, 5)$.
(c) The minimum cost will increase by 2000.

5. (a) For $x_3 = 0$, the solution is $x_1 = x_2 = 1/3$. For $x_3 = 3$, the solution is $x_1 = 1$ and $x_2 = 2$. (b) If $0 \leq x_3 \leq 7/3$, then $z_{max}(x_3) = 2x_3 + 5/3$ for $x_1 = 1/3$ and $x_2 = x_3 + 1/3$. If $7/3 < x_3 \leq 5$, then $z_{max}(x_3) = x_3 + 4$ for $x_1 = x_3 - 2$ and $x_2 = 5 - x_3$. If $x_3 > 5$, then $z_{max}(x_3) = 9$ for $x_1 = 3$ and $x_2 = 0$. (c) The solution to the original problem is $x_1 = 3$ and $x_2 = 0$, with x_3 as an arbitrary number ≥ 5.

Chapter 20

20.1

1. (a) According to [20.4], $x_t = 2^t[1 - 4/(1 - 2)] + 4/(1 - 2) = 5 \cdot 2^t - 4$
(b) $x_t = (1/3)^t + 1$ (c) $x_t = (-3/5)(-3/2)^t - 2/5$ (d) $x_t = -3t + 3$

3. (a) $x_1 = ax_0 + A_1$, $x_2 = ax_1 + A_2 = a(ax_0 + A_1) + A_2 = a^2x_0 + (aA_1 + A_2)$, and so on. Formally, an induction proof is required. (b) If $A_t = bc^t$, then
$$x_t = a^t x_0 + bc(a^{t-1} + a^{t-2}c + \cdots + c^{t-1}).$$ So $x_t = a^t x_0 + \dfrac{c^t - a^t}{c - a}b$ for $a \neq c$, whereas $x_t = a^t x_0 + ta^t b$ for $a = c$.

5. $x_1 = \sqrt{x_0 - 1} = \sqrt{5 - 1} = 2$, $x_2 = \sqrt{x_1 - 1} = \sqrt{2 - 1} = 1$, and $x_3 = \sqrt{1 - 1} = \sqrt{0} = 0$. Then $x_4 = \sqrt{0 - 1} = \sqrt{-1}$, which is not a real number.

20.2

1. $w_t = 1250(1.2)^t - 250$

3. (a) Let the remaining principal after January 1 of year n be L_n. Then $L_0 = L$. Because the principal repayment in year n is $L_{n-1} - L_n$ and the interest payment is rL_{n-1}, one has $L_{n-1} - L_n = \frac{1}{2}rL_{n-1}$, $n = 1, 2, \ldots$, whose solution is $L_n = (1 - \frac{1}{2}r)^n L$. (b) $(1 - r/2)^{10} L = (1/2)L$ implies that $r = 2 - 2 \cdot 2^{-1/10} \approx 0.133934$. (c) The payment in the nth year will be $I_{n-1} - I_n + rI_{n-1}(3/2)r(1 - \frac{1}{2}r)^{n-1}L$. The loan will never be totally repaid, even though $L_n \to 0$ as $n \to \infty$.

20.3

1. Using the notation defined by [3] and [5], the repayment each period is

$$z = \frac{\prod_{s=1}^{T}(1+r_s)B}{\sum_{k=1}^{T}\left(\prod_{s=k+1}^{T}(1+r_s)\right)}$$

which can also be written as

$$z = \frac{B}{\dfrac{1}{1+r_1} + \dfrac{1}{(1+r_1)(1+r_2)} + \cdots + \dfrac{1}{(1+r_1)(1+r_2)\cdots(1+r_T)}}$$

We see that z increases as any r_k increases. If interest rates rise enough without any increase in repayments, the debt will never be paid off, and could even go on increasing indefinitely. This happens when $z_t < r_t b_t$, where b_t denotes the outstanding balance at time t.

20.4

1. (a) If $x_t = A + 2t$, then $x_{t+1} = A + 2(t+1) = A + 2t + 2$ and $x_t + 2 = (A + 2t) + 2 = A + 2t + 2$, so $x_{t+1} = x_t + 2$. (b) If $x_t = A\,3^t + B\,4^t$, then $x_{t+2} - 7x_{t+1} + 12x_t = A\,3^{t+2} + B\,4^{t+2} - 7(A\,3^{t+1} + B\,4^{t+1}) + 12(A\,3^t + B\,4^t) = A\,3^t \cdot 3^2 + B\,4^t \cdot 4^2 - 7A\,3^t \cdot 3 - 7B\,4^t \cdot 4 + 12A\,3^t + 12B\,4^t = A\,3^t(9 - 21 + 12) + B\,4^t(16 - 28 + 12) = 0$

3. $x_t = A\,3^t + B\,4^t$ is a solution. Substituting $t = 0$ and $t = 1$ yields $A + B = x_0$ and $3A + 4B = x_1$, with solution $A = 4x_0 - x_1$ and $B = -3x_0 + x_1$. So $x_t = A\,3^t + B\,4^t$ is the general solution of the given equation.

5. (a) The homogeneous equation is $x_{t+1} = b^t x_t$, where $b = e^{-2a}$. Now, $x_1 = b^0 x_0 = x_0$, $x_2 = bx_1 = bx_0$, $x_3 = b^2 x_2 = b^2 bx_0 = b^{2+1} x_0$, $x_4 = b^3 x_3 = b^3 b^{2+1} x_0 = b^{3+2+1}$, and so on. In general, $x_t = b^{(t-1)+(t-2)+\cdots+3+2+1} x_0$. Now $(t-1) + (t-2) + \cdots + 3 + 2 + 1 = \frac{1}{2}(t-1)t$ (see Equation [B.5] in Section B.2), so $\tilde{x}_t = \tilde{x}_0 e^{-at(t-1)}$.
   (b) $u_{t+1}^* - e^{-2at}u_t^* = [e^{-at^2} - e^{-2at}e^{-a(t-1)^2}]/(1 - e^{-a}) = e^{-at^2}$. The general solution is $x_t = \tilde{x}_t + u_t^*$ for arbitrary $\tilde{x}_0$.

20.5

1. (a) $x_t = C_1 2^t + C_2 4^t$ (b) $x_t = C_1 4^t + C_2 t 4^t$ (c) $x_t = C_1 \sqrt{3}^t \cos\theta t + C_2 \sqrt{3}^t \sin\theta t$, where $\cos\theta = -\sqrt{3}/3$ and $\sin\theta = \sqrt{6}/3$.
   (d) $x_t = C_1 (2/3)^{t/2} \cos\pi t/2 + C_2 (2/3)^{t/2} \sin\pi t/2 + 4/5$

3. (a) $Y_t^* = b/(1-a)$ (b) $m^2 - a(1+c)m + ac = 0$. Two different real roots, a multiple real root, or two complex roots according as $a(1+c)^2 - 4c > 0$, $= 0$, or < 0.

5. If $a \neq -2$, then $D = c/(a+2)$. If $a = -2$, then $D = c/(a+4) = \frac{1}{2}c$.

7. (a) Stable.   (b) Not stable.   (c) Stable.   (d) Not stable.

9. (a) $Y_t^* = \dfrac{a(1+g)^t}{(1+g)^2 - b(1+g) - kg}$ (when the denominator is not $\neq 0$).

(b) $(b+k)^2 < 4k$ (c) $r = \sqrt{k}$. Damped oscillations when $k < 1$.

11. (a) $\sigma\beta < 4\alpha(1-\alpha)$ (b) $\sigma\beta < 4\alpha$ and $\alpha < 1$.

Chapter 21

21.1

1. If $x(t) = Ce^{-t} + \frac{1}{2}e^t$, then $\dot{x}(t) + x(t) = -Ce^{-t} + \frac{1}{2}e^t + Ce^{-t} + \frac{1}{2}e^t = \frac{1}{2}e^t + \frac{1}{2}e^t = e^t$.

3. Differentiate $xe^{tx} = C$ implicitly to obtain $\dot{x}e^{tx} + x[e^{tx}(x + t\dot{x})] = 0$. Canceling e^{tx} and rearranging gives $(1 + tx)\dot{x} = -x^2$.

5. If $x = Ct - C^2$, then $\dot{x} = C$, so $\dot{x}^2 = C^2$ and $t\dot{x} - x = tC - Ct + C^2 = C^2$. If $x = \frac{1}{4}t^2$, then $\dot{x} = \frac{1}{2}t$, so $\dot{x}^2 = \frac{1}{4}t^2$, and $t\dot{x} - x = \frac{1}{4}t^2$. We conclude that $x = Ct - C^2$ is not the general solution.

21.2

1. The solutions are $x = Ct$, for $t \neq 0$, with C an arbitrary constant. See Fig. 55.

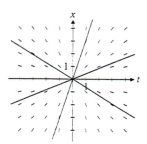

FIGURE 55

21.3

1. Separate: $x^2\, dx = (t+1)\, dt$. Integration yields $\frac{1}{3}x^3 = \frac{1}{2}t^2 + t + C$, or $x = \sqrt[3]{\frac{3}{2}t^2 + 3t + 3C}$. For $C = -7/6$, the integral curve passes through $(1, 1)$.

3. (a) $x = Ce^{t/2}$. For $C = 1$, the integral curve passes through $(0, 1)$.

(b) $x = Ce^{at}$. For $C = x_0 e^{-at_0}$, the integral curve passes through (t_0, x_0).

5. $x = Ce^{-\int a(t)\,dt}$. If $a(t) = a + bc^t$, then $\int a(t)\,dt = at + (b/\ln c)c^t$. This implies that $x = Ce^{-at}e^{(-b/\ln c)c^t} = C(e^{-a})^t(e^{-b/\ln c})^{c^t} = Cp^t q^{c^t}$, with $p = e^{-a}$ and $q = e^{-b/\ln c}$.

7. (a) $K = \left[\dfrac{An_0^{\alpha} a^b}{\alpha v + \varepsilon}(1 - b + c)e^{(\alpha v + \varepsilon)t} + C \right]^{1/(1-b+c)}$

(b) $|\alpha x - \beta|^{(\beta/\alpha)}|x - a|^{-a} = Ce^{(\alpha a - \beta)t}$

21.4

1. (a) $x = Cte^{-t}$; $C = 1$. (Separate: $dx/x = [(1/t) - 1]\,dt$. Integrate: $\ln|x| = \ln|t| - t + C_1$. Hence, $|x| = e^{\ln|t|-t+C_1} = e^{\ln|t|}e^{-t}e^{C_1} = C_2|t|e^{-t} = Cte^{-t}$, where $C = \pm C_2 = \pm e^{C_1}$.) (b) $x = C\sqrt[3]{1+t^3}$; $C = 2$.

3. The equation is equivalent to $f'(t) = (-r/K)(f(t) - 0)(f(t) - K)$, so formula [4] in Example 21.10 yields $f(t) = K/(1 - Ce^{-rt})$.

5. (a) $\dfrac{K}{L} = \left[\dfrac{K_0^{\alpha}}{L_0^{\alpha}e^{\alpha\lambda t}} + (sA/\lambda)(1 - e^{-\alpha\lambda t}) \right]^{1/\alpha} \to (sA/\lambda)^{1/\alpha}$ as $t \to \infty$. Also $X/L = A(K/L)^{1-\alpha} \to A(sA/\lambda)^{(1-\alpha)/\alpha}$.

(b) $\dot{K} = sAb^{\alpha}(t + a)^{p\alpha}K^{1-\alpha}$, so $K(t) = \{K_0^{\alpha} + s\alpha Ab^{\alpha}[(t + a)^{p\alpha+1} - a^{p\alpha+1}]/(p\alpha+1)\}^{1/\alpha}$. Hence, $\dfrac{K}{L} = \left[\dfrac{K_0^{\alpha} + s\alpha Ab^{\alpha}[(t + a)^{p\alpha+1} - a^{p\alpha+1}]}{(p\alpha + 1)b^{\alpha}(t + a)^{p\alpha}} \right]^{1/\alpha} \to \infty$ as $t \to \infty$.

21.5

1. Applying (21.7) with $a = -1$ and $b(t) = t$ yields $x = e^{-(-t)}[C + \int e^{-t}t\,dt] = e^t[C + \int t e^{-t}\,dt]$. Integrating by parts, $\int t e^{-t}\,dt = -te^{-t} + \int e^{-t}\,dt = -te^{-t} - e^{-t}$, and so the solution is $x = Ce^t - t - 1$.

3. (a) Since $C = aY + b$ and $I = k\dot{C} = ka\dot{Y}$, equation (1) implies that $Y = C + I = aY + b + ka\dot{Y}$. Solving for $\dot{Y}$ yields the specified equation.

(b) $Y(t) = [Y_0 - b/(1 - a)]e^{(1-a)t/ka} + b/(1 - a)$ and $I(t) = (1 - a)Y(t) - b$

(c) $1/(1 - a)$

5. (a) $x = Ce^{3t} - 5/3$. For $C = 8/3$, the integral curve passes through $(0, 1)$.

(b) $x = Ce^{-2t/3} - 8$. For $C = 9$, the integral curve passes through $(0, 1)$.

(c) $x = Ce^{-2t} + \frac{1}{2}t^2 - \frac{1}{2}t + \frac{1}{4}$. For $C = 3/4$, the integral curve passes through $(0, 1)$.

7. (a) $x(t) = X(t)/N(t)$ increases with t if $\alpha\sigma \geq \rho$. When $\sigma = 0.3$ and $\rho = 0.03$, this implies that $\alpha \geq 0.1 (= 10\%)$. (b) It is enough to note that $(1 - e^{-\xi t})/\xi > 0$ whenever $\xi \neq 0$, then apply this with $\xi = \alpha\sigma - \mu$. Faster growth per head is to be expected because, in this model, foreign aid contributes positively.

(c) Using Equation [6], note that

$$x(t) = \left[x(0) + \left(\frac{\sigma}{\alpha\sigma - \mu} \right) \frac{H_0}{N_0} \right] e^{-(\rho - \alpha\sigma)t} + \left(\frac{\sigma}{\mu - \alpha\sigma} \right) \frac{H_0}{N_0} e^{(\mu - \rho)t}$$

Even if $\alpha\sigma < \rho$, this is positive and growing for large t as long as $\mu > \rho$. So foreign aid must grow faster than the population.

21.6

1. (a) $\dot{x} + (2/t)x = -1$. Apply [21.11] with $a(t) = 2/t$ and $b = -1$. Then $\int a(t)\,dt = \int (2/t)\,dt = 2\ln|t| = \ln|t|^2 = \ln t^2$ and so $\exp(\int a(t)\,dt) = \exp(\ln t^2) = t^2$. Then, $x = (1/t^2)[C + \int t^2(-1)\,dt] = Ct^{-2} - \frac{1}{3}t$. (b) Here $\int a(t)\,dt = -\int (1/t)\,dt = -\ln t$, and [21.11] yields the solution $x = Ct + t^2$. (c) In this case, $\int a(t)\,dt = -\frac{1}{2}\ln(t^2 - 1)$, and [21.11] yields the solution $x = C\sqrt{t^2 - 1} + t^2 - 1$. (d) $x = Ct^2 + 2a^2/3t$

3. $p = Ce^{1/t} + e^{1/t} \int t^{-3} e^{-1/t}\,dt = Ce^{1/t} + 1/t + 1$, after integrating by parts. For $p(1) = 0$ one needs $C = -2/e$.

5. (a) Putting $z = x^{1-3} = x^{-2}$ gives the linear equation $\dot{z} = 2tz - 2t^3$ whose solution is $z = e^{t^2}(C - \int 2t^3 e^{-t^2}\,dt)$. After integrating by parts, this gives $x^{-2} = Ce^{t^2} + t^2 + 1$. (b) Putting $z = x^{-1}$ leads to $\dot{z} = 2(z/t) - 1$ whose solution implies that $x = 1/t(1 + Ct)$. (c) $x = (Ce^{2t} - e^t)^2$

7. If $x = u + 1/z$, then $\dot{x} = \dot{u} - \dot{z}/z^2$ and the Riccati equation is converted into the linear form $\dot{z} + [Q(t) + 2u(t)R(t)]z = -R(t)$ in case $u = u(t)$ is a special solution. For the equation $t\dot{x} = x - (x - t)^2$ and the special solution $u = t$, the transformation $x = t + 1/z$ creates the linear equation $t\dot{z} + z = 1$, whose solution is $tz = C + t$. Thus $x = t + t/(t + C)$ is the general solution.

21.7

1. (a) $x = 1$ is unstable. See Fig. 56.　(b) $x = 12$ is stable. See Fig. 57.
(c) $x = -3$ is stable; $x = 3$ is unstable. See Fig. 58.

FIGURE 56

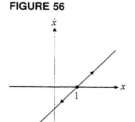

FIGURE 57

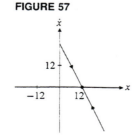

FIGURE 58

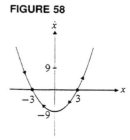

3. Note how $F(K, L) = AK^{1-\alpha}L^\alpha$ implies $f(k) = Ak^{1-\alpha}$. Then $sf(k) = \lambda k$ at $k^* = (sA/\lambda)^{1/\alpha}$, the same value as the limit of K/L in the cited problem.

5. (a) $\partial k^*/\partial s = f(k^*)/[\lambda - sf'(k^*)] > 0$ and $\partial k^*/\partial \lambda = -k^*/[\lambda - sf'(k^*)] < 0$ when $\lambda > sf'(k^*)$. At the equilibrium state, capital per worker increases as the savings rate increases, and decreases as the growth rate of the work force increases.

(b) From Equations [1] to [4], $c = (X - \dot{K})/L = (1-s)X/L = (1-s)f(k)$. But $sf(k^*) = \lambda k^*$, so when $k = k^*$ we have $c = f(k^*) - \lambda k^*$. The necessary first-order condition for this to be maximized w.r.t. k^* is that $f'(k^*) = \lambda$. But $F(K, L) = Lf(k)$ and so $F'_K = Lf'(k)dk/dK = f'(k)$ because $k = K/L$ with L fixed. Thus $\partial F/\partial K = \lambda$. (c) $0 = \dot{k}/k = \dot{K}/K - \dot{L}/L = \dot{K}/K - \lambda$ in the stationary state.

21.8

1. (a) $x = \frac{1}{6}t^3 + At + B$ (b) $x = -\sin t + At + B$ (c) $x = e^t + \frac{1}{12}t^4 + At + B$

3. (a) Direct verification. General solution: $x = Ae^{2t} + Be^{-3t}$
(b) $x = Ae^{2t} + Be^{-3t} - t - 1/6$

5. Substituting $x = (t + k)^{-1}$ eventually yields $k = a$ and $k = b$. General solution: $x = A(t + a)^{-1} + B(t + b)^{-1}$.

21.9

1. (a) $x = C_1 e^{\sqrt{3}t} + C_2 e^{-\sqrt{3}t}$; unstable. (b) $x = e^{-2t}(C_1 \cos 2t + C_2 \sin 2t)$; stable. (c) $x = C_1 + C_2 e^{-8t/3}$; stable. (d) $x = e^{-t/2}(C_1 + C_2 t)$; stable. (e) $x = C_1 e^{-3t} + C_2 e^{2t} - 4/3$; unstable. (f) $x = C_1 e^{-t} + C_2 e^{-2t} + (1/42)e^{5t}$; stable.

3. (a) $x = -(6 + t)e^{-t} + t^2 - 4t + 6$
(b) $x = \frac{1}{2} \sin 2t + (\pi/2 + 1/4)\cos 2t + t + 1/4$

5. $u^* = kt + L_0 + [\beta + \alpha(1 - \beta)]k/\delta^*$ is a particular solution. Oscillations occur iff $(\gamma^2/4)[\beta + \alpha(1 - \beta)]^2 + \gamma \delta^* < 0$.

7. By Problem 3 of Sec. C.1, setting $C = A \cos B$ and $D = -A \sin B$ gives $A \cos(\beta t + B) = A \cos \beta t \cos B - A \sin \beta t \sin B = C \cos \beta t + D \sin \beta t$.

9. $\ddot{p} + \lambda^2 p = a(d_0 - s_0)$. Solution: $p = C_1 \cos \lambda t + C_2 \sin \lambda t + (d_0 - s_0)/(s_1 - d_1)$, where $\lambda = [a(s_1 - d_1)]^{1/2}$.

Appendix A

Answers are given to all the problems in Appendix A.

A.1

1. (a) 216 (b) 4/9 (c) -1 (d) 0.09 (e) $(2.0)^4 = 16$ (f) $2^6 = 64$
(g) $(2 \cdot 3 \cdot 4)^2 = (24)^2 = 576$ (h) $6^6 = 46656$

2. (a) 15^3 (b) $(-1/3)^3$ (c) 10^{-1} (d) 10^{-7} (e) t^6 (f) $(a-b)^3$
   (g) a^2b^4 (h) $(-a)^3$

3. (a) a^6 (b) a^8 (c) x^3 (d) b^{-3} (e) x^6y^9
   (f) x^2 (g) z^{-2} (h) $3^{-6} = 1/729$

4. (a) $2^6 = 64$ (b) $64/27$ (c) $8/3$ (d) x^9 (e) y^{12} (f) $8x^3y^3$
   (g) $10^{-2} = 1/100$ (h) k^4 (i) $(x+1)^2$

5. (a) 0 (b) Undefined. (c) 0 (d) 0 (e) 1 (f) Undefined. (g) 1 (h) 1

6. (a) $x = 5$ (b) $x = 0$ (c) $x = 3$ (d) $x = 4$ (e) $x = 8$ (f) $x = 0$

7. (a) False. $3^5 = 243$, $5^3 = 125$ (b) False. $(5^2)^3 = 5^6$, whereas $5^{2^3} = 5^8$.
   (c) True. $(a^p)^q = (a^q)^p$ (d) True. $0^3 \cdot 4^0 = 0 \cdot 1 = 0$ (e) False. 0^{-2} is
   not defined. (f) False. $(5+7)^2 = (12)^2 = 144$, $5^2 + 7^2 = 25 + 49 = 74$
   (g) False. The correct value of the ratio is $(2x+4)/2 = x+2$. (h) True.
   Both equal $2x - 2y$. (i) True.

8. (a) False. $a^0 = 1$. (b) True. $c^{-n} = 1/c^n$ for all $c \neq 0$. (c) True. $a^m \cdot a^m =$
   $a^{m+m} = a^{2m}$. (d) False, unless $m = 0$. $a^m b^m = (ab)^m$. (e) False (unless
   $m = 1$). For example, $(a+b)^2$ is equal to $a^2 + 2ab + b^2$. (f) False (unless
   $a^m b^n = 1$). For example, $a^2 b^3$ is not equal to $(ab)^{2+3} = (ab)^6 = a^6 b^6$.

9. (a) $x^3 y^3 = (xy)^3 = 3^3 = 27$ (b) $(ab)^4 = (-2)^4 = 16$ (c) $(a^{20})^0 = 1$,
   for all $a \neq 0$. (d) $2n$ is $0, \pm 2, \pm 4, \ldots$, so $(-1)^{2n} = [(-1)^2]^n = 1^n = 1$
   (e) $x^3 y^3 = (x^{-1} y^{-1})^{-3} = 3^{-3} = 1/27$ (f) $(x^{-3})^6 (x^2)^2 = x^{-18} x^4 = x^{-14} =$
   $(x^7)^{-2} = 2^{-2} = 1/4$ (g) $(z/xy)^6 = (xy/z)^{-6} = [(xy/z)^{-2}]^3 = 3^3 = 27$
   (h) $(abc)^4 = (a^{-1}b^{-1}c^{-1})^{-4} = (1/4)^{-4} = 4^4 = 256$

10. (a) $16x^4$ (b) 4 (c) $6xyz$ (d) $a^{27}b^9$ (e) a^3 (f) x^{-15} (g) a^4 (h) 5^{-q}

11. (a) 19.5 (b) 144 (c) 11

12. 15%

13. (a) Given a constant interest rate of 11% per year, then in 8 years, an ini-
    tial investment of 50 francs will be worth $50 \cdot (1.11)^8 \approx 115.23$ francs.
    (b) Given a constant interest rate of 12% per year, then in 20 years, an initial
    investment of 10,000 rand will be worth $10,000 \cdot (1.12)^{20} \approx 96,462.93$ rand.
    (c) $5000 \cdot (1.07)^{-10} \approx 2541.75$ crowns is what you should have deposited
    10 years ago in order to have 5000 crowns today, given the constant interest
    rate of 7%.

14. $2^{10} = 1024$ and $10^3 = 1000$. So $2^{30} = (2^{10})^3$ is bigger than $(10^3)^3 = 10^9$.
    A calculator should say that $2^{30} = (1024)^3 = 1,073,741,824$.

A.2

1. (a) 3 (b) 40 (c) 10 (d) 5 (e) 1/6 (f) 0.7 (g) 1/10 (h) 1/5

2. (a) 81 (b) 4 (c) 623 (d) 15 (e) -1 (f) 3

3. (a) $\frac{6}{7}\sqrt{7}$ (b) 4 (c) $\frac{1}{8}\sqrt{6}$ (d) 1 (e) $\frac{1}{6}\sqrt{6}$ (f) $2\sqrt{2y}/y$ (g) $\sqrt{2x}/2$
   (h) $x + \sqrt{x}$

4. (a) $=$, by [A.6]. Also, both expressions $= 20$. (b) $\neq$. In fact, $\sqrt{25 + 16} =$
   $\sqrt{41} \neq 9 = \sqrt{25} + \sqrt{16}$ (c) $\neq$. In fact, $(a^{1/2} + b^{1/2})^2 = a + 2a^{1/2}b^{1/2} + b =$
   $a + b$ only when $ab = 0$. (d) $=$. In fact, $(\sqrt{a+b})^{-1} = [(a+b)^{1/2}]^{-1} =$
   $(a + b)^{-1/2}$

A.3

1. (a) 1 (b) 6 (c) -18 (d) -18 (e) $3x + 12$ (f) $45x - 27y$ (g) 3 (h) 0
   (i) -1

2. (a) $3a^2 - 5b$ (b) $-2x^2 + 3x + 4y$ (c) t (d) $2r^3 - 6r^2s + 3rs^2 + 2s^3$

3. (a) $-3n^2 + 6n - 9$ (b) $x^5 + x^2$ (c) $4n^2 - 11n + 6$ (d) $-18a^3b^3 + 30a^3b^2$
   (e) $a^3b - ab^3$ (f) $x^3 - 6x^2y + 11xy^2 - 6y^3$

4. (a) $a^2 - a$ (b) $x^2 + 4x - 21$ (c) $-3 + 3\sqrt{2}$ (d) $3 - 2\sqrt{2}$ (e) $x^3 - 3x^2 + 3x - 1$
   (f) $1 - b^4$ (g) $1 - x^4$ (h) $x^4 + 4x^3 + 6x^2 + 4x + 1$

5. (a) $2x$ (b) $a^2 - 4ab + 4b^2$ (c) $\frac{1}{4}x^2 - \frac{1}{9}y^2$ (d) $-x^2y - 3x - 2$
   (e) $x^2 + (a + b)x + ab$ (f) $x^3 - 6x^2y + 12xy^2 - 8y^3$

6. (a) $2t^3 - 5t^2 + 4t - 1$ (b) 4 (c) $x^2 + 2xy + 2xz + y^2 + 2yz + z^2$ (d) $4xy + 4xz$

7. (a) $9x^2 + 12xy + 4y^2$ (b) $5 + 2\sqrt{6}$ (c) $9u^2 - 48uv + 64v^2$ (d) $u^2 - 25v^2$

8. 500 (Note that $(252)^2 - (248)^2 = (252 + 248)(252 - 248) = 500 \cdot 4 = 2000$.)

9. (a) $x^4 - 2x^2y^2 + y^4$ (b) 1/2 (c) $a^2 - 2ab + b^2 + 2a - 2b + 1$ (d) $a - 2\sqrt{ab} + b$
   (e) 1 (f) $n^4 - 4n^3 + 6n^2 - 4n + 1$

10. (a) $acx^2 + (ad + bc)x + bd$ (b) $4 - t^2$ (c) $a^2 + b^2 + c^2 + 2ab + 2ac + 2bc$
    (d) $a^{10} - b^{10}$ (e) $2\sqrt{15} + 1$ (f) $u^4 - 2u^2v^2 + v^4$

11. In the first figure, the (big) square has sides of length $a + b$, so its area is
    $(a + b)^2$. The four rectangular parts have a combined area $a^2 + ab + ab + b^2 =$
    $a^2 + 2ab + b^2$. The two ways of computing the area must give the same
    result, so $(a + b)^2 = a^2 + 2ab + b^2$. The interpretation of the second figure
    is similar.

12. $(a^{10} - b^{10})/(a - b) = a^9 + a^8b + a^7b^2 + a^6b^3 + a^5b^4 + a^4b^5 + a^3b^6 + a^2b^7 +$
    $ab^8 + b^9$

A.4

1. (a) $2 \cdot 2 \cdot 7 \cdot a \cdot a \cdot b \cdot b \cdot b$ (b) $2 \cdot 2(x + 2y - 6z)$ (c) $2x(x - 3y)$ (d) $2a \cdot a \cdot b \cdot$
   $b(3a + 2b)$ (e) $7x(x - 7y)$ (f) $5x \cdot y \cdot y(1 - 3x)(1 + 3x)$ (g) $(4 + b)(4 - b)$
   (h) $3(x + 2)(x - 2)$

2. (a) $(x - 2)(x - 2)$ (b) $2 \cdot 2ts(t - 2s)$ (c) $2 \cdot 2(2a + b)(2a + b)$
   (d) $5xx(x + \sqrt{2}y)(x - \sqrt{2}y)$

3. (a) $K \cdot K(K - L)$ (b) $KL(L^2 + 1)$ (c) $(L + K)(L - K)$ (d) $(K - L)(K - L)$
   (e) $KL(K - 2L)(K - 2L)$ (f) $K^{-\rho}(1 - K^{-\rho})$

4. (a) $(x + 2)(x + 3)$ (b) $(x + 5)(x - 3)$ (c) $(p - 1)(p - 2)$ (d) $2(q - 3)(q + 11)$
   (e) $3(x + 1)(x - 5)$ (f) $-(p - 4)(p + 5)$

5. (a) $(5 + a)(x + 2y)$ (b) $(a + b)(c - d)$ (c) $(a + 2)(x + y)$ (d) $(2x - y)(x + 5z)$
   (e) $(p - q)(p + q + 1)$ (f) $(u - v)(u - v)(u + v)$

6. (a) $p(1 + rt)$ (b) $\pi r(r + 2h)$ (c) $\frac{1}{4}mn(r - 1)$ (d) $PR(R - Q)$
   (e) $(1 + r)(1 + r)(2 + r)$ (f) $\frac{1}{8}gh \cdot h(2h + g)(2h - g)$

7. (a) $(a^n - 5)(a^n + 5)$ (b) $(a + b + c)(a + b - c)$ (c) $(2a + 2b + c)c$
   (d) $(x^2 + y^2)(x + y)(x - y)$ (e) $(3 - c)(3 + c)(9 + c^2)$
   (f) $(x^3 - y^3)(x^3 + y^3) = (x - y)(x^2 + xy + y^2)(x + y)(x^2 - xy + y^2)$

A.5

1. (a) 2/7   (b) 13/12   (c) 5/24   (d) 2/25   (e) 9/5   (f) 1/2   (g) 1/2   (h) 11/27

2. (a) $3x/2$ (b) $3a/5$ (c) 1/5   (d) $\dfrac{-5x + 11}{12}$ (e) $-1/6b$ (f) $1/b$

3. (a) $\dfrac{4}{x^2 - 4}$ (b) $\dfrac{21}{2(2x + 1)}$ (c) $\dfrac{a}{a - 3b}$ (d) $\dfrac{5a - 2}{4ab(a^2 - 4)}$ (e) $\dfrac{-3t^2}{t + 2}$
   (f) $4(1 - a)$

4. (a) 1/2   (b) 6   (c) 5/7   (d) 9/2

5. (a) $\frac{1}{2}(\sqrt{7} - \sqrt{5})$ (b) $4 - \sqrt{15}$ (c) $-x(\sqrt{3} + 2)$ (d) $\dfrac{(\sqrt{x} - \sqrt{y})^2}{x - y}$
   (e) $\sqrt{x + h} + \sqrt{x}$ (f) $\dfrac{1}{x}(2\sqrt{x + 1} - x - 2)$

6. (a) $\dfrac{2 - 3x^2}{x(x + 1)}$ (b) $\dfrac{-2t}{4t^2 - 1}$ (c) $\dfrac{7x^2 + 1}{x^2 - 4}$ (d) $x + y$ (e) $\dfrac{-2x - h}{x^2(x + h)^2}$
   (f) $\dfrac{2x}{x - 1}$

7. $\dfrac{-8x}{x^2 + 2xy - 3y^2}$

8. (a) $\dfrac{-n}{n - 1}$ (b) $1/(x - 1)^2$

9. (a) 400   (b) 1   (c) $\dfrac{1}{a} + \dfrac{1}{b} = \dfrac{a + b}{ab}$

10. (a) $\frac{1}{5}a^2 b$ (b) $x - y$ (c) $\dfrac{2a - 3b}{2a + 3b}$ (d) $\dfrac{x(x + 2)}{2 - x}$

A.6

1. (a) $x = 5$ (b) $x = 3$ (c) $x = 6$ (d) Any x is a solution.   (e) $x = -12$
   (f) $x = 5/3$ (g) $x = -5$. (*Hint:* $x^2 + 10x + 25 = (x + 5)^2 = (x + 5^2)$)
   (h) $x = -1$

2. (a) $x = 3$ (b) $x = -7$ (c) $x = -28/11$ (d) $x = 5/11$ (e) $x = 1$
   (f) $x = 121$

3. (a) $x = 0$ (b) $x = -6$ (c) $x = 5$

4. (a) $2x + 5 = x - 3$. Solution: $x = -8$. (b) $x + (x + 1) + (x + 2) = 10 + 2x$.
   Solution: $x = 7$, so that the numbers are 7, 8, and 9. (c) If x is Ann's
   regular hourly wage, then $38x + (48 - 38)2x = 812$. Solution: $x = \$14$.
   (d) $15{,}000 \cdot 10\% + x \cdot 12\% = 2100$. Solution: $x = 5000$. (e) $\frac{2}{3}x + \frac{1}{4}x +$
   $1000 = x$. Solution: $x = 12{,}000$.

5. (a) $y = 17/23$ (b) $x = -4$ (c) $z = 4$ (d) $p = 15/16$

6. 10 minutes. (If x is the number of liters per minute from the first hosepipe,
   the two others give $2x/3$ and $x/3$ liters per minute. The number of minutes needed to fill the pool with all three hosepipes in use is given by the
   expression $20x/(x + 2x/3 + x/3)$, which is 10.)

A.7

1. (a), (b), (d), (f), and (h) are true; (c), (e), and (g) are false.

2. (a) $x < -9$ (b) Satisfied for all x. (c) $x \leq 25/2$ (d) $x \leq 19/7$
   (e) $t > -1/4$ (f) $x \leq -5$ or $x > -4$

3. (a) $-2 < x < 1$ (b) $x < -4$ or $x > 3$ (c) $-5 \leq a \leq 5$ (d) $-7 < x < -2$
   (e) $n \geq 160$ or $n < 0$ (f) $0 \leq g \leq 2$ (g) $p \geq -1$ and $p \neq 2$
   (h) $-4 < n < -10/3$ (i) $-1 < x < 0$ or $0 < x < 1$. (*Hint:* $x^4 - x^2 =$
   $x^2(x + 1)(x - 1)$.)

4. (a) $x > 1$ or $x < -4$ (b) $x > -4$ and $x \neq 1$ (c) $x \leq 1$ or $2 \leq x \leq 3$
   (d) $x < 1$ and $x \neq 1/5$ (e) $1/5 < x < 1$ (f) $x < 0$ (g) $-3 < x < -2$ or
   $x > 0$ (h) $-5 \leq x \leq 1$ (*Hint:* $x^2 + 4x - 5 = (x + 5)(x - 1)$.)
   (i) $-6 \leq x \leq 0$ or $x \geq 3$. (*Hint:* $-\frac{1}{3}x^3 - x^2 + 6x = -\frac{1}{3}x(x + 6)(x - 3)$.)

5. (a) $-41/6 < x \leq 2/3$ (b) $x < -1/5$ (c) $-1 < x < 0$

6. (a) Yes. (b) No, put $x = 1/2$, for example. (c) No, not for $x \leq 0$.
   (d) Yes, because the inequality is equivalent to $x^2 - 2xy + y^2 \geq 0$, or
   $(x - y)^2 \geq 0$, and this inequality *is* satisfied for all x and y.

7. (a) $\$120 + 0.167x$ (b) Smallest number of calls: 300. Largest number of
   calls: 400.

8. (a) Between $39.2°F$ and $42.8°F$ (b) Between $2.2°C$ and $4.4°C$, approximately.

A.8

1. (a) $x = 0$ and $x = 15$ (b) $p = \pm 4$ (c) $q = 3$ and $q = -4$
   (d) No solution. (e) $x = 0$ and $x = 3$ (f) $x = 2$

2. (a) $x^2 - 5x + 6 = (x - 2)(x - 3) = 0$ for $x = 2$ and $x = 3$
   (b) $y^2 - y - 12 = (y - 4)(y + 3) = 0$ for $y = 4$ and $y = -3$

(c) No solutions and no factorization.

(d) $-\frac{1}{4}x^2 + \frac{1}{2}x + \frac{1}{2} = -\frac{1}{4}[x - (1 + \sqrt{3})][x - (1 - \sqrt{3})] = 0$ for $x = 1 \pm \sqrt{3}$

(e) $m^2 - 5m - 3 = [m - \frac{1}{2}(5 + \sqrt{37})][m - \frac{1}{2}(5 - \sqrt{37})] = 0$ for $m = \frac{1}{2}(5 \pm \sqrt{37})$

(f) $0.1p^2 + p - 2.4 = 0.1(p - 2)(p + 12) = 0$ for $p = 2$ and $p = -12$

3. (a) $r = -13$, $r = 2$ (b) $p = -16$, $p = 1$ (c) $K = 100$, $K = 200$
   (d) $r = -\sqrt{3}$, $r = \sqrt{2}$ (e) $x = -0.5$, $x = 0.8$ (f) $p = -1/6$, $p = 1/4$

4. (a) $x = 1$, $x = 2$ (b) $t = \frac{1}{10}(1 \pm \sqrt{61})$ (c) $x = \frac{1}{4}(3 \pm \sqrt{13})$ (d) $x = \frac{1}{3}(-7 \pm \sqrt{5})$ (e) $x = -300$, $x = 100$ (f) $x = \frac{1}{6}(5 \pm \sqrt{13})$

5. (a) The rectangle has sides 5 cm and 15 cm. (If the sides have length x and y, then $2x + 2y = 40$, that is, $x + y = 20$, and $xy = 75$. So x and y are the roots of $r^2 - 20r + 75 = 0$, because the sum of the roots is 20 and the product is 75.)
   (b) $x^2 + (x + 1)^2 = 13 \Leftrightarrow x = -3$, $x = 2$. Thus, the two natural numbers must be 2 and 3. (c) $x^2 + (x + 14)^2 = (34)^2$. The shortest side is x and is 16 cm long. The longest side is 30 cm long. (d) 50 km/h. (If the usual driving speed is x km/h and the usual time spent is t hours, then $xt = 80$ and $(x + 10)(t - 16/60) = 80$. From the first equation, $t = 80/x$. Inserting this into the second equation, and then rearranging, we obtain $x^2 + 10x - 3000 = 0$, whose positive solution is $x = 50$.)

6. (a) $x = -2$, $x = 0$, $x = 2$ ($x(x^2 - 4) = 0$ or $x(x + 2)(x - 2) = 0$)
   (b) $x = -2$, $x = -1$, $x = 1$, $x = 2$ (Let $x^2 = u$.) (c) $x = -1/3$, $x = 1/5$ (Let $z^{-1} = u$.)

7. $4a^2x^2 + 4abx + b^2 = b^2 - 4ac$, that is, $(2ax + b)^2 = b^2 - 4ac$, and so on.

A.9

1. (a) $x = 8$, $y = 3$ (b) $x = 1/2$, $y = 1/3$ (c) $x = 1.1$, $y = -0.3$
2. (a) $K = 2.8$, $L = 5.75$ (b) $p = 2$, $q = 3$ (c) $r = 2.1$, $s = 0.1$
3. (a) 39 and 13 (b) \$120 for a table and \$60 for a chair. (c) 30 of quality A and 20 of quality B. (d) \$8000 at 7.2% and \$2000 at 5% interest.

Appendix B

B.1

1. (a) 55 (b) 585 (c) 36 (d) 22 (e) 20 (f) 73/12

3. (a) $\displaystyle\sum_{k=1}^{n} 4k$ (b) $\displaystyle\sum_{k=1}^{n} k^3$ (c) $\displaystyle\sum_{k=0}^{n} (-1)^k \frac{1}{2k + 1}$ (d) $\displaystyle\sum_{k=1}^{n} a_{ik}b_{kj}$

(e) $\sum_{n=1}^{6} 3^n x^n$ (f) $\sum_{j=3}^{p} a_i^j b_{i+j}$ (g) $\sum_{k=0}^{p} a_{i+k}^{k+3} b_{i+k+3}$

(h) $\sum_{k=0}^{3} (81,297 + 198k)$

5. (a) $\sum_{i=1}^{5} (x_i - \bar{x}) = \sum_{i=1}^{5} x_i - \sum_{i=1}^{5} \bar{x} = \sum_{i=1}^{5} x_i - 5\bar{x}$

(b) $\sum_{i=1}^{n} (x_i - \bar{x}) = \sum_{i=1}^{n} x_i - \sum_{i=1}^{n} \bar{x} = \sum_{i=1}^{n} x_i - n\bar{x}$

7. (a), (c), (d), and (e) are always true; (b) and (f) are generally not true.

B.2

1. $\sum_{k=1}^{n} (k^2 + 3k + 2) = \sum_{k=1}^{n} k^2 + 3 \sum_{k=1}^{n} k + \sum_{k=1}^{n} 2 =$
$\frac{1}{6}n(n + 1)(2n + 1) + 3[\frac{1}{2}n(n + 1)] + 2n = \frac{1}{3}n(n^2 + 6n + 11)$

3. (a) In both sums, all terms cancel pairwise, except $-a_1$, the last term within the first parentheses, and a_9 (or, generally, a_n), the first term within the last parentheses.   (b) (i) $1 - (1/51) = 50/51$ (ii) $3^{13} - 3$ (iii) $ar(r^n - 1)$

5. $\sum_{k=0}^{n-1} \frac{n}{x} \left(\frac{kx}{n}\right)^2 = \frac{x}{n} \sum_{k=0}^{n-1} k^2 = \frac{x}{n} \frac{1}{6}(n - 1)n[2(n - 1) + 1] =$
$\frac{1}{6}x(2n^2 - 3n + 1)$.

B.3

1. (a) $\sum_{i=1}^{3} \sum_{j=1}^{4} i \cdot 3^j = \sum_{i=1}^{3} (i \cdot 3 + i \cdot 9 + i \cdot 27 + i \cdot 81) = \sum_{i=1}^{3} 120i = 720$

(b) $\sum_{s=0}^{2} \sum_{r=2}^{4} \left(\frac{rs}{r + s}\right)^2 = \sum_{s=0}^{2} \left[\left(\frac{2s}{2 + s}\right)^2 + \left(\frac{3s}{3 + s}\right)^2 + \left(\frac{4s}{4 + s}\right)^2 \right]$

$= \left(\frac{2}{3}\right)^2 + \left(\frac{3}{4}\right)^2 + \left(\frac{4}{5}\right)^2 + \left(\frac{4}{4}\right)^2 + \left(\frac{6}{5}\right)^2 + \left(\frac{8}{6}\right)^2 = 5 + \frac{3113}{3600}$

(c) $\frac{1}{2}m(m + 1)k \frac{k^n - 1}{k - 1}$

3. (a) The total number of units of good i.
(b) The total number of units of all commodities owned by person j.
(c) The total number of units of goods owned by the group as a whole.

B.4

1. (a) $2^{-21} = 1/2^{21}$ (b) $(360)^3 = 46,656,000$ (c) 0
(d) $1/(1 + r_1)(1 + r_2)$

3. (a) $\prod_{i=1}^{n} ka_i = (ka_1)(ka_2) \cdots (ka_n) = k^n \prod_{i=1}^{n} a_i$, so the given equality is only satisfied for $n = 1$.

(b) True: $\prod_{i=1}^{n} y_i^3 = y_1^3 y_2^3 \cdots y_n^3 = (y_1 y_2 \cdots y_n)^3 = \left(\prod_{i=1}^{n} y_i \right)^3$

(c) True: $\prod_{i=1}^{n} x_i y_i \;=\; (x_1 y_1)(x_2 y_2)\cdots(x_n y_n) \;=\; (x_1 x_2 \cdots x_n)$
$(y_1 y_2 \cdots y_n) = \left(\prod_{i=1}^{n} x_i\right)\left(\prod_{i=1}^{n} y_i\right).$

(d) True: $\prod_{i=1}^{n}\left(\prod_{j=1}^{i} a_{ij}\right) = \left(\prod_{j=1}^{1} a_{1j}\right)\left(\prod_{j=1}^{2} a_{2j}\right)\cdots\left(\prod_{j=1}^{n} a_{nj}\right) =$
$(a_{11})(a_{21}a_{22})\cdots(a_{n1}a_{n2}\cdots a_{nn}) = (a_{11}a_{21}\cdots a_{n1})(a_{22}a_{32}\cdots a_{n2})\cdots a_{nn} =$
$\prod_{i=1}^{n} a_{i1} \prod_{i=2}^{n} a_{i2} \cdots \prod_{i=n}^{n} a_{in} = \prod_{j=1}^{n}\left(\prod_{i=j}^{n} a_{ij}\right)$

B.5

1. For $n = 1$, both sides are 1. Suppose [∗] is true for $n = k$. Then
$1+2+3+\cdots+k+(k+1) = \frac{1}{2}k(k+1)+(k+1) = \frac{1}{2}(k+1)(k+2)$, which
is [∗] for $n = k+1$. Thus, by induction, [∗] is true for all n.

3. (a) For $n = 1$, both sides are 1/2. Suppose (a) is true for $n = k$. Then
$$\frac{1}{1\cdot 2} + \frac{1}{2\cdot 3} + \frac{1}{3\cdot 4} + \cdots + \frac{1}{k(k+1)} + \frac{1}{(k+1)(k+2)}$$
$$= \frac{k}{k+1} + \frac{1}{(k+1)(k+2)} = \frac{k(k+2)+1}{(k+1)(k+2)} = \frac{(k+1)^2}{(k+1)(k+2)}$$
$$= \frac{k+1}{k+2}$$ which is [a] for $n = k+1$. Thus, by induction, [a] is true for all n.
(b) For $n = 1$, both sides are 3. Suppose [b] is true for $n = k$. Then
$3 + 3^2 + 3^3 + 3^4 + \cdots + 3^k + 3^{k+1} = \frac{1}{2}(3^{k+1} - 3) + 3^{k+1} = \frac{1}{2}(3^{k+2} - 3)$,
which is [b] for $n = k+1$. Thus, by induction, [b] is true for all n.

5. For $n = 1$, both sides are a. Suppose the formula is true for $n = m$. Then
$$a + ak + \cdots + ak^{m-1} + ak^m = a\frac{1-k^m}{1-k} + ak^m = (a)\frac{1-k^{m+1}}{1-k}$$ which is the
given formula for $n = k+1$. By induction, the formula is true for all n.

Appendix C

C.1

1. See Fig. 59. $OB = BP = \frac{1}{2}\sqrt{2}$, by Pythagoras's Theorem. Hence, $\sin 45° = BP/OP = \frac{1}{2}\sqrt{2} = \cos 45°$, whereas $\tan 45° = \sin 45°/\cos 45° = 1$.

FIGURE 59

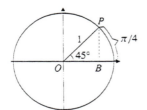

3. $\cos(x + y) = \cos[x - (-y)] = \cos x \cos(-y) + \sin x \sin(-y)$
$= \cos x \cos y - \sin x \sin y$

5. $\tan(x + \pi) = \dfrac{\sin(x + \pi)}{\cos(x + \pi)} = \dfrac{\sin x \cos \pi + \cos x \sin \pi}{\cos x \cos \pi - \sin x \sin \pi} = \dfrac{-\sin x}{-\cos x} = \tan x$

$\sin(x + \pi/2) = \sin x \cos \frac{1}{2}\pi + \cos x \sin \frac{1}{2}\pi = (\sin x) \cdot 0 + (\cos x) \cdot 1 = \cos x$

7. (a) $\sqrt{2} \sin(x + \pi/4) - \cos x = \sqrt{2}(\sin x \cos \pi/4 + \cos x \sin \pi/4) - \cos x$
$= \sqrt{2}(\sin x \cdot 1/\sqrt{2} + \cos x \cdot 1/\sqrt{2}) - \cos x = \sin x$
(b) $\tan(\alpha + \beta)$ $(\sin[\pi - (\alpha + \beta)] = \sin(\alpha + \beta), \cos[2\pi - (\alpha + \beta)] = \cos(\alpha + \beta).)$
(c) $-\cos a/\sin a$

9. $\sin(x + y) \sin(x - y) = (\sin x \cos y + \cos x \sin y)(\sin x \cos y - \cos x \sin y)$
$= \sin^2 x \cos^2 y - \cos^2 x \sin^2 y = \sin^2 x(1 - \sin^2 y) - (1 - \sin^2 x) \sin^2 y$
$= \sin^2 x - \sin^2 y$

11. (a) Because $|f(x)| = |(1/2)^x \sin x| \le (1/2)^x$ for all x, and $(1/2)^x \to 0$ as $x \to \infty$, the oscillations die out.   (b) Because $2^x \to \infty$ as $x \to \infty$, the oscillations explode.

13. Because $(AB)^2 = (b - a \cos x)^2 + (0 - a \sin x)^2 = c^2$, we have the identity $b^2 - 2ab \cos x + a^2 \cos^2 x + a^2 \sin^2 x = c^2$. Because $\sin^2 x + \cos^2 x = 1$, [C.10] follows immediately.

C.2

1. (a) $y' = \frac{1}{2} \cos \frac{1}{2}x$ (b) $y' = \cos x - x \sin x$ (c) $y' = \dfrac{2x}{\cos^2 x^2}$
(d) $y' = (-\sin x \sin x - \cos x \cos x)/\sin^2 x = -1/\sin^2 x$

3. (a) $\cos x - \sin x$ (b) $5x^4 \sin x + x^5 \cos x + (\frac{1}{2\sqrt{x}}) \cos x - \sqrt{x} \sin x$
(c) $\dfrac{1}{(x^2 + 1)^2} \left[\left(\dfrac{1}{2\sqrt{x}} - \dfrac{3x\sqrt{x}}{2} \right) \cos x - \sqrt{x}(1 + x^2) \sin x \right]$

5. (a) 2   (b) m/n (c) 1/2   (d) 0 (l'Hôpital's rule does not apply.)

7. $p'(t) = -\lambda C_1 \sin \lambda t + \lambda C_2 \cos \lambda t$ and $p''(t) = -\lambda^2 C_1 \cos \lambda t - \lambda^2 C_2 \sin \lambda t$, so $p''(t) + \lambda^2 p(t) = C_0 \lambda^2$. Thus, $K = C_0 \lambda^2$.

9. $f'(x) = 6 \cos 2x - 16 \sin 4x$

11. (a) $-\ln |\cos x| + C$ (b) $e^{\sin x} + C$ (c) $-\frac{1}{6} \cos^6 x + C$

13. (a) $\dfrac{2}{\sqrt{1 - 4x^2}}$ (b) $\dfrac{2x}{1 + (x^2 + 1)^2}$ (c) $-\dfrac{1}{2\sqrt{x}\sqrt{1 - x}}$

15. Let Q and R be the nearest points on the shoreline PP' to A and B. Let $a = AQ$, $b = BR$, $QR = l$, and $QC = x$. The time needed to reach the drowning swimmer is

$$T(x) = \dfrac{AC}{v_1} + \dfrac{BC}{v_2} = \dfrac{\sqrt{a^2 + x^2}}{v_1} + \dfrac{\sqrt{b^2 + (l - x)^2}}{v_2}, \qquad x \in [0, l]$$

The first-order condition for minimum w.r.t. x yields

$$\frac{x}{v_1\sqrt{a^2+x^2}} = \frac{l-x}{v_2\sqrt{b^2+(l-x)^2}}$$

which is equivalent to $\sin\alpha_1/v_1 = \sin\alpha_2/v_2$. This condition is also sufficient for a minimum because we find that $T''(x) > 0$ in $[0, l]$.

C.3

1. (a) $z + w = 5 - 2i$ (b) $zw = 21 - 9i$ (c) $z/w = (-3 - 7i)/6$
   (d) $|z| = \sqrt{2^2 + (-5)^2} = \sqrt{29}$
3. (a) $\frac{1}{2}(1 + 5i)$ (b) $-3 - 4i$ (c) $(1/26)(31 + 27i)$ (d) i

References

Bartle, R. G. *The Elements of Real Analysis*. 2d ed. New York: John Wiley & Sons, 1976.

Dixit, A. K. *Optimization in Economic Theory*. 2d ed. London: Oxford University Press, 1990.

Hadley, G. *Linear Algebra*. Reading, Mass.: Addison-Wesley, 1973.

Luenberger, D. G. *Introduction to Linear and Nonlinear Programming*. Reading, Mass.: Addison-Wesley, 1973.

Index